HISTORICAL ATLAS OF CANADA

HISTORICAL ATLAS OF CANADA

Volume I

From the Beginning to 1800

R. Cole Harris
EDITOR

Geoffrey J. Matthews
CARTOGRAPHER/DESIGNER

UNIVERSITY OF TORONTO PRESS
Toronto Buffalo London

In memory of Harold Adams Innis and Andrew Hill Clark

Toronto Buffalo London
Printed in Canada

ISBN 0-8020-2495-5

Cet ouvrage est également disponible en langue française
aux Presses de l'Université de Montréal.

Canadian Cataloguing in Publication Data

Main entry under title:

Historical atlas of Canada

V. 1. From the beginning to 1800 / R. Cole Harris, editor.
Includes bibliographical references and indexes.
ISBN 0-8020-2495-5 (v. 1).
1. Canada – Historical geography – Maps.
I. Matthews, Geoffrey J., 1932-
II. Harris, R. Cole.
G1116.S1H58 1987 911'.71 C87-094228-X

The research, cartography, and publication of
Volume I of the Historical Atlas of Canada
have been funded by the
Social Sciences and Humanities Research Council of Canada.

Contents

Prehistory

The Atlantic Realm

Inland Expansion

The St Lawrence Settlements

The Northwest

Foreword

I

For the past three decades there has been a vigorous and unprecedented production of national, regional, provincial, and thematic atlases in Canada. This activity parallels a worldwide proliferation of atlases (well over 8 500) in which a very wide range of topics has been mapped. The interest in the production of atlases, combined with the serial publication, beginning in the 1950s, of the Canadian Centenary Series, a nineteen-volume comprehensive history of the people and land of Canada, formed the environment in which the idea for the *Historical Atlas of Canada* was born.

In 1970 a group of geographers and historians met to explore the idea of publishing a major Canadian historical atlas focused on social and economic themes. This team of scholars, composed of Wm G. Dean, a geographer, W.J. Eccles, a historian, R. Cole Harris, a historical geographer, Jean-Pierre Wallot, a historian, and John Warkentin, a historical geographer, with the addition in 1973 of Thomas F. McIlwraith, a historical geographer, eventually generated the *Historical Atlas of Canada* project. In its earliest stages F.J. Thorpe, Chief of the History Division of the Canadian Museum of Civilization, also provided valuable advice and assistance. It was clear from our early discussions that a project of this magnitude would need public as well as private support. Thus we turned to Ottawa, first to the Canada Council, and later to the newly emerging Social Sciences and Humanities Research Council of Canada. Years of far-ranging discussions, draft proposals, revised budgets, and extensive consultation resulted in our proposal to the Social Sciences and Humanities Research Council of Canada in 1978.

Numerous meetings were held to refine our thinking and reduce our first proposals to realistic levels. The Canada Council and the University of Toronto supplied funds to bring together many scholars from a number of disciplines and institutions on several different occasions. Seed money generously granted by the University of Toronto funded our applications to the Social Sciences and Humanities Research Council. Members of the Council, through their sound advice, greatly improved our submissions. To all of these we express deep gratitude. The culmination of these efforts came in 1979 when the Council awarded a major editorial grant, payable over a period of nine years, to support the publication, in separate English and French editions, of a three-volume atlas: volume I, From the Beginning to 1800; volume II, The Nineteenth Century; and volume III, Addressing the Twentieth Century.

The atlas envisaged by the team was massive in scale, multidisciplinary in approach, and called upon the resources of individuals and institutions across Canada. Our aim was to use the latest research in historical geography, history, and related disciplines to present the social and economic evolution of Canada. The cartography was to be fresh and imaginative, with wide-ranging topical coverage, skilfully and elegantly displayed. Our research objectives were to be carried out by an Editor and an Editorial Board of up to eight scholars for each volume. (These scholars would also serve as the authors of one or more plates.) The whole operation was managed by an Executive Committee made up of the Director, two Co-Ordinating Editors, the Editors of the three volumes, the Cartographer, and a representative of the publisher.

The research has been undertaken by individual authors or teams of authors who have been invited to participate because they are at the forefront of research in their own fields. Most authors have been helped by research assistants, mainly graduate students. The material on the plates is compiled for cartography by 'core working groups' of one to three editorial assistants for each volume, who also assist the cartographers in the difficult and time-consuming task of preparing maps for final cartographic production. In all, nearly 250 authors and research assistants from 30 universities across Canada, literally from St John's to Victoria, from departments of the federal and several provincial public services, from private organizations, and from universities in the United States and Europe, have created this monumental endeavour. Without their specialized knowledge and talents, without their willing co-operation, dedication, and patience, the project would not exist.

The *Historical Atlas of Canada* offers a deliberately moulded visual approach to the Canadian past, with emphasis on the processes of social and economic change. Some maps reflect cultural or politial responses to change, while others illustrate the changes which result from political decisions. Through a detailed presentation of aspects of these various processes and responses in regions or parts of regions, in urban areas, sometimes in the whole country, historically significant changes or trends are made intelligible to the general reader. Maps on the nature and structure of past societies, their patterns of livelihood, and their transformation of the landscape present stimulating images of the lives of ordinary people. Through this approach these volumes communicate directly to the reader authoritative and original historical interpretation. The atlas also stands as a sound and lasting reference work, and as a quarry for specialized research by future generations of scholars.

No good atlas exists that did not cost more than was expected and take longer to produce than was projected. *The Historical Atlas of Canada* is no exception. The enormous costs in time and money required to complete this work are, however, part of the cost of being Canadian. Few of us realize how much distance permeates all our lives. Despite our virtually instantaneous electronic communications distance interferes. Countless decisions about details on maps require personal contact among author, editor, cartographer, translator, and copyeditor. Frustrating stresses and delays arise where participants are separated by transcontinental spaces. Scholarly maps are inexorably tyrannical taskmasters: specific, often idiosyncratic, data or clearcut explanations are needed at every turn. Thus the key to this complex enterprise has been communication. Canadians are, of necessity, communications specialists. From the beginnings of nationhood we have needed to bridge our spaces and to link our diverse regions together. The *Historical Atlas of Canada* is yet another illustration of Canadian strength and ingenuity in communications.

Many have participated in this pursuit of excellence in historical interpretation, in the never-ending process of finding out more about ourselves. Their names, those of the relentlessly overburdened Editors of the volumes, the Co-Ordinating Editors, the administrators of the project, and all the assistants, along with the fastidiously competent cartographers who mirrored the authors' and editors' ideas on maps, are all individually acknowledged on the pages that follow. The *Historical Atlas of Canada* would also like to record here its gratitude to the Social Sciences and Humanities Research Council, the generous patron of these volumes.

Wm G. Dean
University of Toronto, 1987

II

An organized society tries to understand itself and its past, yet no easy determinism can explain how and why a complex society like ours has evolved progressively and sometimes unpredictably on this continent over hundreds, even thousands, of years. The *Historical Atlas of Canada* has attempted to establish many of the relationships among the multitudinous factors (including demography, economy and society, government, and culture) that together, as in a musical score, have shaped our past. Has this objective been attained? Not completely, perhaps, but undoubtedly with more success than one could have dreamed of when the atlas began.

The Historical Atlas of Canada has aimed to make major facets of our past visible and eloquent, so to speak, through the use of maps and symbols that would establish direct links with readers, and also to create a coherent synthesis of old and new knowledge. As a matter of fact the lacunae in our knowledge and sources have been enormous. As a result, new research projects have had to be undertaken, and new dimensions added to projects already underway. Authors have delved into the most diverse sources, from archaeological remains, to old maps and manuscripts, to recent statistical sources and theses. It has not always been possible to grasp entirely the relationships between the people who came in numerous waves and the country they eventually created, its lands, its mountains, its forests, its waters, its icy wastes, and its apparently impenetrable interior.

It will be up to the reader to assess the value of the results. It is worthwhile, however, to highlight the important, unselfish commitment of a great many scholars who, like prospectors, attempted to discover the ore that would yield an understanding of our past. This intellectual venture could reward them only after a considerable time and then in the form of a collective work. Their common effort negates the mythology about selfish researchers; on the contrary, their generous efforts have yielded a rich gift to this country. Because of their work, Canadians will have a better understanding of themselves and, it is hoped, will be inspired to extend the frontiers of knowledge even further.

Jean-Pierre Wallot *Dominion Archivist*
Ottawa, April 1987

Preface

In 1979 the Social Sciences and Humanities Research Council of Canada provided funds for a historical atlas of Canada. There had been discussion of such an atlas for years, and the proposal accepted by the Council was for a three-volume work that was to provide both a scholarly reference tool and an accessible, up-to-date interpretation of the country. This is the first volume of that atlas. It begins during the late Wisconsinan glacial maximum (18 000-10 000 BC) when incontrovertible evidence of the presence of people in Canada is first available, and ends about AD 1800 when the export economy was still dominated by fish and furs, much of the border with the United States had just been settled, and the new technologies of industrial Britain had not yet crossed the Atlantic. The second volume deals with the 19th century, the third with the period to 1961. In sum the three volumes provide a broad, cartographically-based interpretation of the long development of Canada.

Volume I treats the radically different worlds of indigenous and European North America. The first section provides an outline of Canadian prehistory and a summary of the populations and economies of Canada early in the historic period. Thereafter the coverage becomes more regional, considering first the fishery and the larger development of Atlantic Canada, then the French commitment to the St Lawrence River and ensuing developments over some two centuries, and finally the ramifications in the West of the commercial conflict between fur traders from Hudson Bay and others from the St Lawrence River. These regions were not entirely separate and our coverage of them frequently overlaps, but this organization has seemed best to fit the nature of the data, the scale of the atlas, and the reality of early Canada. In the West the volume ends in 1821, when the Hudson's Bay Company and the North West Company merged, and in most of eastern Canada it ends between 1790 and 1810, depending on available data, although, following an early agreement with the Editor of volume II, the coming of the Loyalists to Québec and Ontario in the 1780s is treated in the second volume. No date carries equivalent meanings or connects with equivalent data across the varied territories of early Canada, and this is reflected in the irregular chronological boundary between volumes I and II.

We have taken similar liberties with spatial boundaries. As late as 1800 the present political territory of Canada did not exist, though much of it was well established. Then, as earlier, fur traders and native people moved back and forth across territory some of which would eventually become part of the United States. We have not imposed the current shape of Canada on northern North America before that shape existed, and therefore our treatment frequently extends well south of the present border between Canada and the United States.

Like any other work of humanistic scholarship, an atlas reflects its creators as well as its subject. At least some of our biases are intentional. We have sought to emphasize the economic and social circumstances of ordinary life rather than the more usual fare of historical atlases: geopolitical events and their territorial consequences. We have sought to give more attention to Atlantic Canada and to the West than is common in most general interpretations of early Canada. We have tried to accord full place to native peoples while knowing, in the end, that we have not succeeded in doing so. The archival record and the research based on it focus on people of European background. More than good will is required to penetrate an Indian realm glimpsed through white eyes. So it is, for example, that the native people of Atlantic Canada all but disappear from our treatment of that region in the historic period, not because they were not there, not because we were not interested in them, but because the data are woefully fragmented and unreliable. An atlas may lead research in some ways, but more commonly it must follow, reflecting the literature in which it is situated.

It also reflects the data that are available. For Canada before 1800 quantitative data can be obtained on some subjects for some places for some years, but hardly ever on the same subject in different places in different years. Often the most approximate locations are difficult to establish and there are no statistical series to allow maps of changing population densities, changing male-female ratios, or the changing percentage of land under given crops. The maps in volume I do the relatively simple things that the data allow: they show broad patterns of distribution, routes of movement, and, after the large-scale maps of the day, the layout of individual settlements. Yet, this limited opportunity is enough to allow volume I to describe the changing geographical pattern of early Canada much more comprehensively than heretofore. The volume has assembled an immense quantity of data, some commissioned for the volume, more offered by scholars who had the information at hand or were willing to dig it out, some previously published, more not; it presents the data clearly; and it lays out the geographical pattern of this early country so as to make accessible what was scattered, and tangible what was much more vaguely discerned.

The timing of the atlas coincided with the development of Canadian archaeology to the point that an empirically based synthesis of the distribution of cultures in prehistoric Canada had become possible. The synthesis presented here will be modified in many details, but perhaps not in general outline, as excavations continue and data accumulate. In the historic period the volume has tended to confirm Harold Innis's general insights, if rarely his more specific contentions. As Innis maintained, the pattern of Canada has been taking shape for almost 500 years and by New World standards is old. The early Canadian economy was dominated by staple trades in fish and furs that were dependent on long-distance transportation. From the beginning of the European encounter with North America, developments in the north, which led to Canada, were different from those farther south, which led to the United States. The country's southern boundary is not a geographical absurdity. The evolution of Canada cannot be understood in terms appropriate to Britain, France, or the United States. Innis was right about these matters. When he became more specific, he was often wrong, and he left out a good deal, but his great contribution was to bring elements of the pattern of Canada into focus. We have built on his foundation, clarifying, as we could, the structures of the early staple trades, treating the local economies (which Innis ignored) that became detached from staple trades and eventually supported far more people, exploring the insides of towns, and dealing wherever possible with demographic and social as well as economic data. The result is a considerably broader view of the pattern of early Canada than Innis was able to offer. The pattern that this volume identifies includes staple trades dependent on trans-Atlantic connections and isolated New World workplaces where the conditions of life were dominated by the terms of specialized, male work. It includes the towns that served these trades while also providing administrative and military functions. Urban employment was relatively diversified, and urban society was finely stratified. It includes the local agricultural economies, based on the family farm, that encouraged rapid population growth where farmland was available, but discouraged commercial expansion because markets were poor. Such agriculture tended to create relatively undifferentiated societies in which one farm family was much like the next and the socioeconomic gradient was not very steep. These components of early Canada, superimposed on the

Indians and scattered across much of a continent, were bounded by the configuration and the limitations of the land and, for years, by the bitter struggle between France and England for the control of the continent.

Volume I has drawn on many scholars across the country to deal with these matters. The work has been interdisciplinary – we have relied on archaeologists, geologists, botanists, historians, anthropologists, linguists, demographers, and a folklorist, as well as geographers – and could not have been otherwise. But in the main the volume has been done by historical geographers. Andrew H. Clark, himself a student of Innis, and more than anyone else the inspiration for historical geography in Canada, participated in early discussions about the atlas. If to Innis can be traced the interest in spatial economy that pervades this volume, to Clark should be attributed its equal interest in settlement and the local region. These are the geographical poles around which volume I has been built, Innis and Clark lie behind them, and the volume is dedicated to these two remarkable men.

For my part, as Editor, the volume has provided an opportunity to re-establish connections with an early period of Canadian development and with most of the scholars who know it. A Senior Killam Research Fellowship relieved me of teaching for two critical years. There has been a vast correspondence, an enormous amount of travel, flagrant impositions on friends, and the steady support of my family in Vancouver. In every corner of the country there has been co-operation, always the sense that the atlas was a unique opportunity and worth a lot of work to get right. Everyone who was asked to contribute did so, good manuscripts emerged, and authors tolerated the editing required to turn individual contributions into parts of a coherent book. Eventually a scholarly undertaking spread across the country had yielded as much as it could.

Every author has added to this volume, but none more than the archaeologist J.V. Wright, the geographer Conrad E. Heidenreich, and the historian Louise Dechêne. Dr Wright undertook the huge job of gathering the disparate findings of Canadian archaeology, creating preliminary maps, circulating them to colleagues across the country, and eventually producing the manuscript maps that became the basis for most of the prehistory plates. Professor Heidenreich brought his vast knowledge of exploration, of the Great Lakes basin, and of the Indians of the early historic period, as well as his love of maps and rare ability to create them, to plate after plate throughout the volume. Our most intractable problem, perhaps, was how to deal effectively with the French fur trade about which there has been much controversy and little agreement about basic data. Eventually Professor Heidenreich prepared an overwhelming series of manuscript maps showing the changing distributions during the French regime of Indian groups, trading posts, and missions, and of routes of trade, warfare, and migration. The problems associated with the French fur trade have not been solved, but they have been placed in context. Fittingly, the last plate in the volume is by Professor Heidenreich. Professor Dechêne is the author of two fastidiously prepared plates, one on seigneuries and the other on the occupational structure of the town of Québec in the 18th century, and she has also brought her critical judgment and uncompromising scholarly standards to bear on most of the volume. I have relied on her more than she knows, and her influence is pervasive. Without these three the volume could not have been completed in anything like its present form.

The Editorial Board – Louise Dechêne (McGill University), W.J. Eccles (University of Toronto), Conrad E. Heidenreich (York University), Alan G. Macpherson (Memorial University of Newfoundland), D. Wayne Moodie (University of Manitoba), Richard I. Ruggles (Queen's University), B.G. Trigger (McGill University), and J.V. Wright (Canadian Museum of Civilization) – met infrequently after the first discussions, but each member has commented on plates and texts at various editorial stages and has offered important advice. The essays that introduce the sections were written by the Editor and members of the Editorial Board in some combination; like the volume as a whole, they are intended to present a coherent general statement about the early development of Canada. The prehistory essay was largely written by Dr Wright; the essay on inland expansion was largely written by Professor Heidenreich and, where it touches the Seven Years' War, by Professor Eccles. Professor Moodie wrote much of the essay on the West, and Professors Arthur J. Ray (University of British Columbia) and James R. Gibson (York University) gave advice on it. Professor Graeme Wynn (University of British Columbia) wrote the portion of the Atlantic essay dealing with Nova Scotia after the Acadian deportations.

At an early stage in the preparation of manuscripts some authors sought advice from cartographers nearby. Professors C. Grant Head (Wilfrid Laurier University), Henry Castner (Queen's University), and Louise Marcotte (Université Laval) were particularly helpful in this regard. Most authors, however, submitted material that was not cartographically refined. This material was redrawn for clarity by a core working group in Toronto (at different times Ross Paterson, Pat Orr, Tanya Steinberg, and David Fletcher), and eventually a collection of clear undesigned manuscripts was prepared for each plate. I commented editorially, made suggestions about the layout of the plates, and eventually approved preliminary designs, but the task of transforming manuscripts into the well-designed maps and plates that comprise this volume fell to Geoffrey J. Matthews, Cartographer at the University of Toronto. In an atlas project editor and cartographer must understand their different roles, and after a time I did, relying on Geoff Matthews' consummate sense of design, his rigorous unwillingness to deal with manuscripts that are not clear, his disdain for sham, and his readiness to change a design that did not quite fit the author's and my intentions. The splendid cartography in this volume is his achievement. There were also times when the conceptual arrangement of the materials that would comprise a plate was more baffling to the author and to me than to him. Most important, perhaps, Geoff Matthews and I agreed about the intensity of data and the types of maps that were appropriate for this atlas. The staff of cartographers who scribed his designs were all wonderfully skilled; they are identified in the Acknowledgments, below. Here I must mention especially Byron Moldofsky, a superb craftsman and, as production co-ordinator, an absolutely accurate link between the cartographic laboratory and the editorial process.

That process led eventually to the University of Toronto Press whose Editor-in-Chief, Ian Montagnes, and Director, Harald Bohne, had long given the project much sound advice. Joan Bulger, exemplary copyeditor, gave all the English-language manuscripts her meticulous care. The manuscripts written in French were copyedited at Les Presses de l'Université de Montréal, under the direction of Pierre Filion, and then translated by the Editor of volume I. Translation from English into French was the responsibility of Les Presses de l'Université de Montréal. The varied subjects treated, the lists of specialized names, and the accuracy required in a work of this sort have made translation of atlas plates and essays particularly difficult. Translation became the responsibility of Marcel Paré (Université de Montréal); his sensitivity to nuances of meaning, commitment to exact translation, and hard work have enormously benefited the French edition of this work. Assisting M. Paré with the archaeological texts has been Dr Roger Marois (Canadian Museum of Civilization), and with the specialized vocabulary of the fishery Professor Laurier Turgeon (Université Laval). Professor Dechêne, who had already given so much to the atlas, advised M. Paré on translations dealing with the historic period. As a result of all this good work many translations are clearer and better than the originals.

Place names have posed particular problems, not just in translation, and we have worked out only approximate guidelines for them: except in special cases place names are given in the European language of the period and place in question, and again except in special cases spellings have been modernized. Very common place names, and names intended to provide background information, are translated in the French or English edition. Professor Maurice Saint-Yves (Université Laval) gave advice on the spelling of French place names, and checked the French spelling of place names on all typescripts and proofs, a huge service to the volume. The spelling of Indian names follows the Smithsonian *Handbooks.*

An overall administrative structure serves all three volumes. Professor William G. Dean (Univeristy of Toronto), Director of the

Historical Atlas of Canada, has managed the budget and the relationship of the atlas with the Social Sciences and Humanities Research Council and the University of Toronto Press. In the early 1970s he organized the original discussions that led to the atlas, and he has administered the whole project as it has moved from idea to reality. The Co-ordinating Editors, Professor John Warkentin (York University) and Dr Jean-Pierre Wallot (Dominion Archivist), both also involved with the project from the earliest discussions, have provided a background of solid advice to all four Editors. Many are the times I have relied on John Warkentin's understanding and wise counsel. His constant, helpful encouragement and availability underlie the entire project. The Editors of other volumes of the *Historical Atlas of Canada,* Professor R. Louis Gentilcore (McMaster University) of volume II and Professor Donald Kerr (University of Toronto) and Dr Deryck W. Holdsworth of volume III, generously assumed volume I's first access to the cartographers, a kindness not without implications for their own volumes. Donald Kerr and Deryck Holdsworth, whom for years I have seen in Toronto at short intervals, have been companions throughout this undertaking. At a final stage in the editorial process Deryck Holdsworth and Susan Laskin, a research associate for volume III, checked all the colour proofs against the original manuscripts.

Well before 1979 the Social Sciences and Humanities Research Council of Canada supported the idea of a historical atlas of Canada with enthusiasm and prudence. Inevitably an atlas of this scale is an expensive undertaking; yet, having committed itself to the atlas, the Council's support has been generous. In this sense volume I of the *Historical Atlas of Canada* is the Council's creation, and I would hope that the volume is tangible demonstration of the importance of the Council in Canadian life. People have worked so willingly and so hard on the atlas partly because it has been a public project, an opportunity, mediated by the Social Science and Humanities Research Council of Canada, for Canadian scholarship to report to the Canadian people about the nature of Canada.

R. Cole Harris
University of British Columbia, 1987

The production of an atlas of this complexity requires the skills, patience, and craft of a dedicated team of accomplished cartographers. The unique nature of this project developed inventiveness in each cartographer and honed their common skills. The list of technical specifications was not created for the atlas as a whole, but has developed one map at a time. Each map presented new problems and challenges and our list of specifications expanded. Technical decisions such as base-map line weights, colours for ethnic groups, type sizes and styles, and so on were established in the early stages, but beyond these there had to be great freedom to experiment in order to create attractive maps that would present the historical information accurately and clearly. Simplicity was always our key consideration. I should like to thank all the members of the cartographic team for their contributions to this project: Byron Moldofsky, Dan Poirier, Julienne Brown, Vince Corrigan, Rod McNeil, Julia Sandquist, Dorothy Woermke, and Diane Paquette.

Special thanks must go to Byron Moldofsky, who served as production co-ordinator. His technical maturity and ability to communicate with authors made the process of production function as smoothly as possible. I am most grateful to Dan Poirier who capably undertook production co-ordination for the last year of volume I, and to Vince Corrigan who co-ordinated all the translated and typeset material.

Much appreciation is also extended to the following cartographers from the Department of Geography, University of Toronto, who gave valuable assistance to the atlas project: Jane Davie, who transformed my pencil sketches into presentable design layouts; Chris Grounds, who drafted most of the research base maps and whose suggestions for cartographic improvement were always welcome; Hedy Later, who scribed the prototype atlas plate and advised on all perspective drawings; and Ada Cheung, for her meticulous proof corrections.

I am especially indebted to John Glover and Louisa Yick of the Faculty of Arts and Science Photographic Laboratory, University of Toronto, for the speed and precision with which they handled the constant requests for intermediate filmwork.

The photomechanical process, the science of transforming artwork to film, was entrusted to consultants Len Ugarenko and John Oosterloo at Northway Map Technology Limited, who produced exceptional filmwork throughout the project and have earned the gratitude of all the cartographic staff.

Geoffrey J. Matthews
University of Toronto, 1987

Acknowledgments

EXECUTIVE COMMITTEE

Wm G. Dean, Director
Jean-Pierre Wallot, Co-Ordinating Editor
John Warkentin, Co-Ordinating Editor
Geoffrey J. Matthews, Cartographer/Designer
R. Cole Harris, Editor, volume I
R.L. Gentilcore, Editor, volume II
Donald Kerr, Editor, volume III
Deryck W. Holdsworth, Editor, Volume III
Harald Bohne, Director, University of Toronto Press
Ian Montagnes, Editor-in-Chief, University of Toronto Press

ADMINISTRATION

Joanne Wainman, Administrative Assistant, 1983–7
James F. Walker, Administrative Assistant, 1979–83
Ludmilla Neiburgs, Accounting Supervisor, University of Toronto

SECRETARIES

Tina Bone
Andrew Chatwood
Judy Glucksman
Sandra Lapsky
Anne McMaster
Patricia Startin
Alixe M. Utgoff
Alison Ward
Sophia Wong

CORE WORKING GROUP

Ross H. Paterson, 1982
Patricia M. Orr, 1982–3
Tanya Steinberg, 1984
David Fletcher, 1984–5

RESEARCH ASSISTANTS AND ASSOCIATES

Michael Barkham
Kenneth Brean
R.M. Cruz
M.F. Da Conceicao
Blair Dwyer
Ronald Frye
Cécile Gallant
Robert M. Galois
Mark Hilton
Daphne Jamieson
Jean LaFleur
Mario Lalancette
Susan L. Laskin
Georges-Pierre Léonidoff
K.-B. Liu
Victor P. Lytwyn
D. Peter MacLeod
Christopher Moore
G.D. Morrissey
Françoise Noël
L. Nolan
Donna Porter
Normand Robert
Arthur Roberts
Sheila P. Robinson
J.G. Shields
E.H. Tomkins
Thomas Wien

CARTOGRAPHIC PRODUCTION

CARTOGRAPHER / DESIGNER
Geoffrey J. Matthews

PRODUCTION CO-ORDINATORS

Byron Moldofsky, 1980–6
Daniel E. Poirier, 1986–7

CARTOGRAPHERS

Julienne Patterson Brown
Vincent A. Corrigan
Roddie McNeil
Byron Moldofsky
Diane C. Paquette
Daniel E. Poirier
Julia Sandquist
Dorothy E. Woermke

Ada Cheung
Jane Davie
Christopher Grounds
Hedy Later

TOPONYMIC ADVISER

Maurice Saint-Yves

TRANSLATORS

English to French:
Marcel Paré,
with the assistance of Danielle Gratton,
Roger Marois, and Laurier Turgeon,
and in consultation with Louise Dechêne

French to English: R. Cole Harris

Prehistory

Slightly more than 50 years ago it was believed that human beings arrived in the New World about 2000 BC. Now there is clear evidence that there were people in much of North America by 10 000 BC, and disputed evidence of considerably earlier occupation. A cautious interpretation is that the first immigrants to the New World crossed into the unglaciated regions of Alaska and the Yukon some time before 12 000 BC on the land bridge connecting Asia and North America. These Asiatic hunters of big game possessed a stone-tool technology that included bifacially flaked knives and weapon tips and, less consistently, microblades - thin, razor-sharp flakes of stone struck from specially prepared cores - and were equipped to live in a rigorous steppe-tundra environment. Around 10 000 BC, as environmental conditions deteriorated in Alaska and the Yukon, descendants of these early North Americans spread south along a corridor between melting Laurentide and Cordilleran ice sheets into the heart of the New World. By this time they may have developed the distinctive projectile points and other traits that have permitted archaeologists to define a Fluted Point culture. Fluted Point culture spread rapidly across the habitable portion of the Western Hemisphere, and then changed in response to different environments and other factors. A later migration from Alaska and the Yukon of people using microblades led to the occupation of most of northern and coastal British Columbia about 8000 BC. Thousands of years later the last major migration from Asia brought the ancestors of the Eskimos and Aleuts.

After the occupation of Canada cultural continuity within regions became the rule, and major migrations and population replacements the exception. Diffusion and innovation rather than migration provided the common impetus for cultural change. Technologies were finely adapted to particular environments; in most places hunting and fishing, in some combination, dominated the economy until European contact.

The prehistoric cultures of Canada are identified by manufactured items (usually of stone) that have survived the passage of time, by subsistence practices, by the distribution and nature of archaeological sites, and by rock art and other indications (such as burial practices) of cultural beliefs. Based on this limited evidence, archaeologically identified cultures are only crude reflections of an unknown number of independent societies.

10 000–8000 BC

During these years the physical environment was changing rapidly (pl 4). Huge pro-glacial lakes fed by the melting glaciers formed and drained as the ice retreated and crustal uplift took place, sea levels rose rapidly, and the location of vegetation regions shifted dramatically. By 8000 BC the Cordilleran ice sheet had broken into many sections and the Laurentide sheet, although still a vast mass dominating the northeastern quarter of the continent, had retreated from the Gulf of St Lawrence.

FLUTED POINT By 9000 BC the carriers of Fluted Point culture (pls 2,3) had spread across most of North America and derivative forms of the culture were established in South America. Abundant game, including mammoth, mastodon, and other large Pleistocene mammals, apparently provided the impetus for this exceptionally rapid occupation. The Fluted Point peoples also consumed smaller animals and plants. It can be assumed that they wore hide and fur clothing and that their shelters protected them from the Late Pleistocene climate. The chipped-stone tools of Fluted Point people include the fluted projectile point and engraving, scraping, drilling, and cutting tools. Their bone and antler tools were few but sometimes striking, such as weapon foreshafts made of mammoth and mastodon bone.

Fluted Point sites are often found along the shorelines of former glacial lakes, suggesting that these people had watercraft. Many Fluted Point sites on the east coast have been destroyed by rising sea levels. A major site in Nova Scotia, believed to have been located where caribou could be intercepted in an open forest-tundra environment, provides evidence for special work areas and small family households. Some sites provide glimpses of the ceremonial life of these people. At a site in Montana the skeletons of two adolescents were accompanied by red ochre and many grave goods including bone weapon foreshafts, and at a site in Ontario a pit contained over a thousand fire-fractured implements and flakes.

Because the oldest dated Fluted Point sites are in the south-central United States, some archaeologists have suggested that the fluted projectile point, and possibly other diagnostic elements of Fluted Point culture, developed there and spread northward. However, as very few Fluted Point sites have been dated in northwestern Canada and Alaska, the origin of Fluted Point technology and the direction of its spread are still open questions awaiting more evidence.

EARLY MICROBLADE Sites producing microblades have been dated to at least 10 000 BC in the Yukon and to 9000 BC in Alaska. In Alaska other similarly dated sites have lacked microblades. Bifacially flaked tools, burins (engraving tools), and the bones of big-game animals are found with or without microblades at most of these sites. The erratic occurrence of microblades at early northern sites raises the possibility that Fluted Point culture and Early Microblade culture may have had the same ancestry.

8000–4000 BC

East of the continental divide there were two major developments from Fluted Point culture early in this period: Plano culture (pl 5) emerged on the plains and Early Archaic culture emerged in the eastern woodlands. Regional varieties of both Plano and Archaic cultures developed. After 6000 BC the term Plano is no longer used, giving way on the plains to Early Plains and in the Canadian Shield to Shield Archaic (pl 6). West of the continental divide Cordilleran culture, possibly derived from Fluted Point culture, spread north to southern British Columbia between 8000 and 7000 BC. After 8000 BC Microblade cultures were spreading south and southeast from Alaska and the Yukon. Before the end of the period Acasta culture, apparently derived primarily from Northern Interior Microblade, was established north of Great Slave Lake. The explosion of Mt Mazama in Oregon in 4800 BC deposited volcanic ash over an enormous area including much of southern British Columbia and the plains and provides a dated horizon marker in archaeological sites.

PLANO Like their Fluted Point ancestors these people were big-game hunters, and the two cultures are often found, stratigraphically separated, at the same site. A distinctive style of stone flaking, which appears to have developed late in the Fluted Point period, and a range of new projectile points that likely reflect improvements in the weapon system are the major diagnostic characteristics of Plano culture. New tools, such as ground-stone axes, appear in some sites, and cremation burial is recorded for the first time.

In Canada Plano sites are more abundant and, as the ice retreated, more widely distributed than Fluted Point sites. Some of these plainsmen penetrated the Interior Plateau and Peace River country of British Columbia, and small groups pushed north into the Keewatin District of the Northwest Territories. There they preyed upon caribou herds, lived in small family-size tents, and fashioned a number of varieties of tools found only in the north. Plano people also expanded eastward as glacial ice and lakes retreated, following a narrow band limited on the south by contemporaneous Early Archaic hunters and on the north by the shrinking continental glaciers. The environment favoured caribou, probably the major prey of these people. Their eastward advance continued down the St Lawrence valley, where there was a substantial remnant of the Champlain Sea, and into the Maritime provinces. Evidence of the transportation of Gaspé chert as much as 800 km up the St Lawrence suggests that these people had watercraft. At a number of sites in both eastern and western Canada and in the northern United States the distinctive stone tools of Plano and Early Archaic cultures have been found together, clear evidence of contact.

EARLY ARCHAIC Early Archaic culture developed out of Fluted Point culture in the woodlands of eastern North America. A number of sites provide evidence of a relatively rapid transition from the earlier stone-tool technology. A new method of side-notching points for hafting appears to be the most significant innovation and has been attributed to the introduction of the spear thrower. Subsistence and patterns of settlement changed little from the earlier period.

By 8000 BC Early Archaic bands from the south reached southern Ontario where they apparently encountered Plano hunters and an indigenous Early Archaic population derived from local Fluted Point people. In the Gulf of St Lawrence another indigenous Early Archaic people may have merged with people spreading north along the Atlantic Coast. These crucial, poorly known events laid the bases for the later native cultures of eastern Canada. Archaeological interpretation is complicated by the similarity of the simple Early Archaic tools to those of later cultures.

MIDDLE ARCHAIC Middle Archaic culture, dated between 6000 and 4000 BC, developed out of Early Archaic. New projectile-point styles appear, and in the south there is evidence of major changes in technology and way of life. However, Middle Archaic culture is little represented in Canada, appearing only along the north shore of Lake Erie and in the St Lawrence valley.

MARITIME ARCHAIC By 7000 BC the Gulf of St Lawrence was occupied by Maritime Archaic hunters of Early Archaic origin who had migrated north along the coast and mixed with local populations. These maritimers possessed the toggling harpoon, and must have used watercraft to capture large sea mammals such as walrus and whale. By 5500 BC they were constructing burial mounds of stone cobbles along the north shore of the Gulf of St Lawrence and the Labrador coast. The dead were provided with necessities for the afterlife: harpoons, spear heads, and woodworking tools. Throughout this period there is little information from the Atlantic coast, probably because coastal sites have been inundated by rising sea levels.

LAURENTIAN ARCHAIC Like Maritime Archaic, the Laurentian Archaic culture developed out of Early Archaic, but in the interior rather than along the coast. Laurentian Archaic people made broad, side-notched projectile points, and occupied an area from New England to the Ohio valley including the upper St Lawrence valley and much of southern Ontario. Evidence about Laurentian Archaic culture is very sparce until after 4000 BC.

EARLY PLAINS Plano culture prevailed on the plains until approximately 6000 BC when notched projectile points, reflecting new hunting methods, replaced earlier lanceolate and stemmed forms. By 5500 BC these notched points reached southeastern British Columbia. Usually the origin of the notched point on the plains is attributed to the migration of Early Archaic people or the diffusion of Early Archaic influence from the east and south.

The appearance of Early Plains culture correlates with the onset of the Altithermal, a long period (6000–2000 BC) of intermittent dry climate (pl 4). The Altithermal initiated a cycle of erosion and deposition that markedly modified the landscape and obscured or obliterated portions of the archaeological record. Like the tools of Early Archaic culture in the east, the simple stone tools of Early Plains culture, dominated by notched points, scrapers, and knives, are extremely difficult to distinguish from much later tools when removed from good archaeological contexts.

SHIELD ARCHAIC Unlike its southern and eastern Archaic neighbours, Shield Archaic is believed to have developed from Plano culture in southeastern Manitoba and the Keewatin District of the Northwest Territories. As plants and animals occupied the land being released from glaciers and glacial lakes, Shield Archaic hunters spread eastward to occupy nearly all the Canadian Shield. On the basis of site locations it is inferred that caribou and fish were the mainstays of these early hunters whose stone tools included chipped-stone scrapers, knives, and lanceolate and side-notched projectile points. Although there is no direct evidence, these people must have had tailored clothing, bark canoes, and snowshoes to survive in a subarctic land of rivers and lakes.

CORDILLERAN Cordilleran culture, probably of southern origin, occupied southern British Columbia after 8000 BC at approximately the same time that Coastal Microblade culture was beginning to spread south. The two cultures met and partially merged along the central coast. Coastal sites associated with the Cordilleran culture have been dated to 7000–6000 BC, and appear to have been near favourable locations for salmon fishing. The tools of Cordilleran culture – leaf-shaped projectile points and knives, simple scrapers, and cobble spall and core tools – persisted through much of the prehistory of British Columbia.

COASTAL MICROBLADE This southward-spreading culture appeared along the northern and central coast of British Columbia between 8000 and 7000 BC, and, presumably with the aid of substantial watercraft, reached the Queen Charlotte Islands by 5000 BC. Along the central coast Microblade and Cordilleran culture appear to have merged. Microblades are found at sites in the northern interior of British Columbia that are believed to date between 6000 and 5000 BC, but it is not clear whether they were introduced from the west or the north, or whether their presence reflects the migration of people or the diffusion of technology.

NORTHERN INTERIOR MICROBLADE Coastal and Northern Interior microblade cultures may be variants of a single culture, although the presence of burins and of bifacially flaked stone tools in the interior and their apparent absence along the coast suggest the taxonomic value of distinguishing between the two. Data, however, are limited and diagnostic tools are few. Mountainous terrain and a subarctic climate dispersed food resources; people lived at small, widely scattered campsites. Caribou and fish were major foods, and mountain sheep and goats were probably locally important.

ACASTA By 5000 BC the Acasta culture was established north of Great Slave Lake. Its western origin is suggested by the similarity of some Acasta projectile-point and burin styles to those found at Northern Interior Microblade sites west of the Mackenzie River. Acasta culture did not, however, include microblades. Bipointed knives, notched and stemmed points, scrapers, and burins characterized the Acasta stone tool kit. The descendants of these northern caribou hunters and fishermen are unidentified.

4000–1000 BC

By 4000 BC the pace of environmental change had slowed, and people lived in much more stable environments than had their predecessors. Only high-arctic and alpine glaciers remained, and sea levels were fairly stable near current levels. West of Hudson Bay vegetation provinces extended further north than they do now; when the climate became cooler and wetter after 2000 BC, the tree line retreated in places as much as 300 km south of its present location (pl 4), but this was a minor environmental change compared to those that had gone before. The archaeological record is less disrupted than previously, and in some areas both population growth and repeated seasonal occupation of favoured regions appear to account for the increasing density of sites. Populations were geographically stable; only in the Arctic were there major migrations of people (pl 7).

MARITIME ARCHAIC Early in this period Maritime Archaic hunters spread to Newfoundland and up the St Lawrence valley. The elaborate mortuary ritual of the preceding period continued. Along the Labrador coast longhouses more than 100 m long were constructed of cobbles and presumably covered with skin or bark. Ground-stone lances, projectile points, ulus, plummets (function unknown), and woodworking adzes and gouges became commonplace along with chipped-stone points and knives. Elaborate bone tools were used: toggling and fixed harpoons, harpoon foreshafts, projectile points, eyed needles, and many others. Among ornaments were the beaks of the extinct Giant Auk.

Around 1500 BC Maritime Archaic people moved down the Labrador coast, probably forced south by early Palaeo-Eskimos, who had first appeared along the Labrador coast several hundred years before. Shield Archaic hunters penetrated to the central Labrador coast and to the north shore of the Gulf of St Lawrence from the interior of Quebec around 1500 BC. Shortly after Maritime Archaic culture left the Labrador coast, it becomes difficult to trace in the archaeological record. The relationship between Maritime Archaic and the late prehistoric cultures in eastern Canada is still poorly understood.

LAURENTIAN ARCHAIC These people of the mixed hardwood forests combined a simple indigenous technology with borrowed traits to form a distinctive culture. Their mixed economy depended upon big game, particularly deer, and fish, plus a wide range of small game and plant foods such as nuts. Their stone tools comprised notched projectile points, knives, and many implements - ground-slate lances, projectile points, ulus, plummets, and gouges - adopted during thousands of years of contact with the Maritime Archaic culture to the east. Polished-stone spear-thrower weights were adopted from cultures to the south. Laurentian Archaic bone work produced eyed needles, unilaterally barbed harpoons, projectile points, awls, and other items. Around 3000 BC cemeteries containing graves richly provided with red ochre and grave goods, including objects made of native copper, appear at the larger campsites.

SHIELD ARCHAIC During this period Shield Archiac hunters were still expanding eastward into the enormous region of subarctic Quebec where scattered hunting bands sought meagre, periodically available food resources. Shield Archaic tools continued to include scrapers, knives, and projectile points, but around 1500 BC western Shield Archaic people began manufacturing tools from small nodular cherts. Throughout most of Quebec the traditional use of quartzite continued. By approximately 4000 BC native copper from Lake Superior was being exploited, and finished tools and raw nuggets were traded east and west (pl 14). Shield Archaic dwellings in the Keewatin District were of family size, with hearths and stone-lined pits. The floor, frequently semisubterranean, was outlined by weight stones that held the skin cover in place. There is little evidence of burial ritual, but it is known that stone and copper tools and ornaments such as bossed bracelets were sometimes placed with the dead.

MIDDLE PLAINS Plains culture continued to depend on the bison (pl 10). Herds were stampeded over cliffs or into pounds or ravines for killing, methods that depended on elaborate social organization. By 3000 BC there is evidence of increased or more concentrated population. People lived in tents, identified by circles of stone weights, called tipi rings, that appear in large numbers in some places. Extensive use was made of the parklands and the margins of the coniferous forest, and the influence of Plains culture extended north to the Mackenzie valley and east towards Lake Superior.

The most common stone tools were projectile points (particularly notched forms), scrapers, knives, and flaked cobbles. The use of the dog-drawn travois is inferred from slightly deformed dog skeletons. Ceremonial stone arrangements known as medicine wheels (pl 15) appear, and are thought to be associated with rites involving the bison. Some medicine wheels were added to over thousands of years, indicating a remarkable continuity of belief. Similarly, a cemetery in southwestern Saskatchewan containing some 500 skeletons was used by the same population for more than 2 000 years. Ordinary stone tools, eagle talons, copper from Lake Superior, and shell beads from the Atlantic were placed with the dead.

EARLY NESIKEP The relationship of this culture to Cordilleran culture and cultures of the Columbia drainage basin is uncertain; it appeared in the southern interior of British Columbia between 5500 and 4500 BC. These people possessed microblades (which ceased to be used after 2500 BC but may reappear, sporadically, after 1000 BC), large, corner-notched and side-notched projectile points, and a few other distinctive tools. By 2000 BC semisubterranean pit houses clustered in villages at favourable sites on salmon rivers had become common, beginning the historic pattern of semisedentary winter villages dependent on stored salmon.

EARLY NORTHWEST COAST Increasingly productive salmon, halibut, eulachon, and shellfish fisheries, along with red cedar, laid the foundation of Early Northwest Coast culture, which was established by the end of the period. Red cedar, which did not become abundant until 2000 BC, was used for everything from boxes to houses, and was fashioned with stone axes, adzes, chisels, knives, and wedges. Along the south coast ground-slate tools became abundant by 1500 BC. There is increasing evidence at the end of the period of trade, resource ownership, wealth, and social stratification (suggested by skull deformation, lip labrets, and other ornaments). A more sedentary way of life is suggested by large shell middens, although large plank houses are not identified before the end of the period. The first hints of the complex art of the historic period appear by 2000 BC, but the artistic rendering of artefacts was not yet widespread. By 2000 BC there is evidence for the regional culture differentiation of the south, central, and north coasts.

NORTHERN INTERIOR MICROBLADE Northern Interior Microblade culture continued until approximately 2500 BC, when the manufacture of microblades virtually ended and notched projectile points replaced lanceolate varieties. These developments introduced Northern Archaic culture.

NORTHERN ARCHAIC This tentative culture is identified by a single innovation, notched projectile points. Probably Northern Archaic developed out of Northern Interior Microblade culture, but some hold that it was introduced from the south at the beginning of this period by forest-dwellers who made notched points. At present the evidence is very unclear; microblades and notched projectile points are found together at some sites.

EARLY PALAEO-ESKIMO These people, the colonizers of the last major habitable region of the world, spread rapidly across the Arctic to Greenland around 2000 BC, and eventually southward into northern Saskatchewan, Manitoba, and Quebec, and to the Labrador coast, portions of the Gulf of St Lawrence, and Newfoundland (pl 11). Their origin is still obscure, although their technology, which was adapted to exploit the marine and land resources of the Arctic, clearly suggests that they came from Alaska and ultimately from Siberia. They manufactured tiny microblades with a consummate skill that is also expressed in their toggle harpoons, projectile points, knives, burins, and scrapers. Their dwellings consisted of single-family tents with central, stone-lined hearths. Seal, caribou, and muskoxen were their major prey.

1000 BC–AD 500

By 1000 BC environmental conditions in Canada were similar to those later encountered by Europeans (pl 4), and the basic cultural patterns of the historic period are generally discernible (pl 8). Populations were geographically stable; all the cultures considered in this period were rooted in the previous period. Diffusion and innovation were the major stimulants of cultural change. About 1000 BC pottery reached eastern Canada from the south, and the Yukon coast from the west. Slightly later the bow and arrow was widely accepted across Canada.

PROTO-MICMAC/MALISEET/PASSAMAQUODDY The sinking coastline of the Maritimes has left a very fragmented record of human occupation, and little is known about this tentatively identified culture. At the beginning of the period the area appears to have been occupied by people related to Maritime Archaic culture who added the bow and arrow to their weapons and adopted pottery from the St Lawrence valley and New England about 500 BC. About 2000 years ago the exploitation of shellfish became a major subsistence activity, and the westward trade in shell beads increased in importance.

PROTO-BEOTHUK This very hypthothetical culture is suggested by some recent evidence that there were contemporaneous Late Palaeo-Eskimo and proto-Beothuk cultures in Newfoundland. Additional data are required before the culture can be confirmed or rejected.

POINT PENINSULA/MEADOWOOD/SAUGEEN By 1000 BC the knowledge required to make pottery cooking vessels entered eastern Canada from the south and was adopted by most Archaic peoples, some of whom were already using soapstone vessels. For taxonomic purposes the adoption of pottery changes Laurentian Archaic culture to Point Peninsula/Meadowood/Saugeen culture. These names identify regional and, in part, temporal subcultures, each with somewhat different styles of pottery and classes of tools, but all derived from the preceding Laurentian Archaic. The bow and arrow was adopted, and there is also evidence of increased fishing. Cultural influences continued to emanate from the south: a cult practising earth-mound burial entered the region from the Ohio valley around 600 BC; and a later burial cult, also from the Ohio valley, appeared just over 2 000 years ago and was responsible for the 61-m-long Serpent Mound north of Lake Ontario. Pipes for smoking appeared near the beginning of the period. Some 2000 years ago the native silver deposits at Cobalt, Ontario, were exploited to produce beads, ear spools, and other ornaments.

SHIELD ARCHAIC Throughout most of Quebec north of the St Lawrence River traditional Shield Archaic technology was maintained during this period. The bow and arrow was adopted around 1000 BC but, for the most part, pottery was not.

LAUREL Laurel culture developed from the preceding Shield Archaic of western Quebec, northern Ontario, and much of Manitoba but is differentiated by the addition of pottery and other changes in the technology. Where campfire ash has neutralized normally acid soils, beaver-incisor knives, snowshoe needles, awls, detachable harpoons, pottery decorations, and other bone items have been recovered. Animal remains are primarily of caribou, moose, and beaver. Laurel populations along the Minnesota and Ontario borders practised burial-mound ceremonialism; the largest prehistoric earth mounds in Canada are found in this region. Elliptical multi-family dwellings have been uncovered in the same area. Native-copper implements are particularly common among the Laurel people in Ontario, and were used in trade that brought obsidian from Wyoming, chalcedony from North Dakota, pottery from southern Ontario, and many other items (pl 14). The expansion of Laurel culture into Saskatchewan appears to have been a late event.

MIDDLE PLAINS There was increasing technological variety on the northern plains within a way of life that remained dependent on the bison and on a basic set of tools (pl 10). Bison jumps and pounds continued to be used, as did dog travois, tipis, and medicine wheels. Pottery and the bow and arrow were introduced from the east about 2 000 years ago, and at approximately the same time a southern burial-mound cult appeared in southwestern Manitoba. Northern Plains people followed the bison beyond the peripheries of the plains proper and traded with peoples of adjacent cultures.

MIDDLE NESIKEP Archaeological sites in the interior plateau of British Columbia increased in size, number, and variety during this period. While the dependence on salmon continued, the gathering of bitterroot, mountain potato, wild onion, and balsam root became common after 500 BC. The tubers were roasted in large pits. New objects such as stone bowls appear, and microblades reappear in certain areas.

MIDDLE NORTHWEST COAST By this period all of the main features and regions of the historic culture of the northwest coast are apparent. There is evidence of large plank houses 2 000 years ago. The technique of pecking stone tools into shape became common, as did rock art. Microblades continued to be made in the south. Elaborate stone bowls and personal ornaments were made. Socially ranked burials and intricately worked objects give evidence of the concern for status, wealth, and display that typified historic Northwest Coast culture. The frequency of stone and bone clubs, fractured skulls and forearms, and trophy skulls suggests that warfare was common.

NORTHERN ARCHAIC In the interior of Alaska, the Yukon, and northern British Columbia the basic way of life and the stone technology of Northern Archaic culture was little changed.

TALTHEILEI By 500 BC Taltheilei culture, probably derived from Northern Archaic, occupied the barren grounds and forest boundaries of the eastern Mackenzie District and southern Keewatin District of the Northwest Territories, and spread subsequently into the northern prairie provinces. These people depended on caribou. Stemmed projectile points, scrapers, knives, and adzes dominated their stone tools.

LATE PALAEO-ESKIMO Late Palaeo-Eskimo (Dorset) culture coalesced in the region of Baffin Island (pl 11) between 1000 and 500 BC. Much of the Early Palaeo-Eskimo culture remained, reflected in microblades, harpoons, and other artefacts, but Late Palaeo-Eskimo people also made semisubterranean winter houses, stone lamps, ground-slate tools, and ground burins, innovations perhaps of Alaskan origin. At a few sites artefacts made from driftwood, ranging from burin and microblade handles to shaman masks, have been preserved by natural freeze-drying. No bow parts have been recovered; the Late Palaeo-Eskimos may have discarded the bow and arrow. Their remarkable carvings and engravings in bone, ivory, and wood often suggest shamanism (pl 15).

AD 500–European Contact

After AD 500 archaeogical data become much more abundant. Many populations were growing, and natural processes have had less time to destroy archaeological sites. Moreover, prehistoric and historic cultures can be associated, and the archaeological record complemented by historical data. In eastern Canada European contact begins in the 16th century whereas in parts of the Arctic it does not begin until the 20th century (pl 9).

MARITIME ALGONQUIAN Early in the 17th century Europeans identified two major populations who spoke dialects of Algonquian in the Maritime provinces.

The Maliseet and Passamaquoddy of southeastern New Brunswick and adjacent Maine lived in permanent villages comprising oval, semisubterranean family houses; within these houses, and in the large shell middens outside, fragmented pottery cooking vessels, bone and notched-stone arrowheads, barbed bone harpoons, fish gorges, knives, scrapers, bone awls, and polished stone axes for woodworking are commonly found. Shortly before the first historical records these coastal villages were abandoned: families scattered into the interior for the winter and gathered at coastal sites during the summer. The semisubterranean house was replaced by the conical wigwam; the manufacture of pottery vessels was discontinued. There is no environmental explanation for these dramatic changes, which may be a consequence of unrecorded native-European trade. Scattered settlements in the interior in winter would have facilitated the hunting of fur-bearing animals.

The Micmac of Nova Scotia, Prince Edward Island, and north-eastern New Brunswick, who used the same varieties of tools as the Maliseet and Passamaquoddy but made them slightly differently, exploited both coastal and interior resources in a finely tuned seasonal round and apparently never lived in permanent coastal villages. Like their southern neighbours they gave up the manufacture of pottery, which had spread to them from the St Lawrence, just before the historical record begins.

ST LAWRENCE IROQUOIS The people whom Jacques Cartier encountered along the St Lawrence River in the 1530s (pl 33) originated in the upper St Lawrence valley between Montréal and Cornwall. By the 13th century, if not earlier, corn, squash, sunflowers, followed by tobacco and beans, were introduced from Ontario and/or New York. Agriculture plus the rich fisheries of the St Lawrence, particularly for eels, apparently led to rapid population growth. Large palisaded villages, indicating warfare, and smaller summer fishing camps were established in the St Lawrence valley. Not long before Cartier arrived, this culture had expanded as far downriver as Québec while some of the villages above Montréal were abandoned. These people made pottery vessels and smoking pipes of outstanding quality; they used bone for arrowheads, awls, trophy-skull gorgets, pipes (from deer scapulae), beads, and hoes, and stone generally for metates and manos (corn-grinding tools), a few polished adzes, and soapstone beads.

ONTARIO IROQUOIS The adoption of agriculture marks the beginning of Ontario Iroquois culture (pl 12). Shortly after AD 500 corn was introduced to southern Ontario from the Ohio valley. Sunflowers appeared by the late 12th century. It is difficult to determine when squash was first adopted as it does not survive well in the archaeological record. Tobacco seeds have been recovered from 8th-century sites, but the sudden increase in pottery pipes in the mid-14th century is probably a more accurate indication of the extensive cultivation of this plant. With the introduction of protein-rich beans in the mid-14th century there appears to have been a rapid increase in population and a shift of village sites from sandy soils to richer loams.

By the 8th century Ontario Iroquois lived in multi-family houses in small, palisaded farming hamlets; by the 15th century there were palisaded villages over 3 ha in size occupied by nearly 2 000 people. Social change must have been dramatic; as the economy changed from hunting to farming, women became the main food producers. The Ontario Iroquois – Huron, Petun, and Neutral – likely numbered over 60 000 people at the beginning of the 17th century.

NORTHERN ALGONQUIAN (INCLUDING BEOTHUK) The Northern Algonquians – the historic Cree, Ojibwa, Algonquins, Montagnais, and, speculatively, the Beothuk – occupied an enormous area of subarctic coniferous forest. Their culture derived from Shield Archaic or from its western descendant, Laurel culture. Although the Algonquins and eastern Ojibwa, who were strongly influenced by the Ontario Iroquois, practised some agriculture and the western Ojibwa gathered wild rice, the Northern Algonquians were predominantly hunters and fishermen. They used pottery cooking vessels of several major styles and pottery and stone pipes; among the stone tools found at their campsites small scrapers, triangular arrowheads, and knives are particularly common. They painted or pecked abstract and naturalistic motifs on bedrock, and some of the western Ojibwa retained the burial-mound practices of their Laurel ancestors. The prehistoric Montagnais and Beothuk shared a somewhat distinctive Northern Algonquian technology. They created little or no pottery, smoking pipes, or rock art.

LATE PLAINS Ceramic evidence suggests that there were close relationships between the bison hunters of the northern plains and the farming villages in the Missouri valley. Throughout the period there were also close connections between the peoples of the forest edge and those of the plains proper, although the settlement of the eastern Canadian plains by the Siouan-speaking Assiniboine (from central Minnesota) and Algonquian speakers (from the Canadian Shield) apparently occurred early in the historic period. The Algonquian-speaking Blackfoot and Gros Ventre of the historic period can be traced to Late Plains culture. The origins of the Athapaskan-speaking Beaver, Sekani, and Sarcee are still obscure, but the ancestors of these people likely adopted a Plains way of life in northern Alberta sometime after AD 500. In southwestern Alberta Kootenai speakers also participated in Late Plains culture. The principal artefacts of the earlier period continue to be found, usually in increasing frequency. Horses reached the Canadian plains early in the 18th century (pl 57), well before there was a significant European presence in the area.

LATE NESIKEP Pit houses became more abundant after AD 750, suggesting population growth and a more sedentary way of life increasingly dependent on salmon. Polished stone tools and rock art became more common. Pit, cairn, and cist (wood-lined) burials were widespread. Within Late Nesikep culture, the precursor of Interior Salish, there was a great deal of regional variation, valley by valley, across southern British Columbia. Throughout the period strong influences from the coast reached the middle Fraser and Thompson Rivers.

LATE NORTHWEST COAST By the beginning of this period the historically documented ethnographic cultures of the northwest coast were clearly in place. On the north coast after AD 500 a culture that had been developing steadily over at least 5 000 years achieved its fullest expression. To the existing technology were added elaborate stone bowls, mauls, adzes, and slate mirrors. On the south coast, by contrast, the technology appears to have become less diverse after about AD 500. Many of the chipped-stone tools and carvings of the earlier period were no longer made. The evidence suggests that the prehistoric culture of the south coast had reached a technological climax by AD 500. Some new elements did appear, however, such as tubular stone pipes and toggling harpoons used to hunt large whales. Earthwork fortifications, which also appear during this time, may indicate that warfare had become more common. Throughout the Northwest coast population concentrations, based on abundant natural resources, remained large, ranked, and semisedentary.

NORTHERN ATHAPASKAN The bifacial chipped-stone tools of Northern Archaic culture decreased in importance and were replaced by bone arrowheads, scrapers, awls, and other bone tools. Northern Athapaskan culture derived from Northern Archaic and led to the Athapaskan-speaking Kutchin, Hare, Nahani, Slave, Dogrib, Tahltan, and Tsetsaut Indians of the historic period.

SOUTHERN ATHAPASKAN About AD 700 some Northern Athapaskans migrated southward following a massive fall of volcanic ash in the north. House-pits and a range of notched arrowheads, knives, and distinctive scrapers dominate the archaeological record of these people in British Columbia, the ancestors of the historic Chilcotin and Carrier.

EASTERN ATHAPASKAN About AD 800 the stemmed points of Taltheilei culture were replaced by smaller notched points associated, probably, with the introduction of the bow and arrow. Later these people, ancestors of the Athapaskan-speaking Yellowknife and Chipewyan, made use of native-copper deposits from the mouth of the Coppermine River on the Arctic Coast.

THULE Thule culture began to spread along the north coast of Alaska into Canada around AD 900 (pl 11) with maritime hunters who, using boats and sophisticated harpoon tackle, were able to capture bow-head whales. These people, the ancestors of the present-day Inuit, rapidly occupied most of the Canadian Arctic and Greenland by AD 1200, and eventually the Labrador coast nearly to the Gulf of St Lawrence, displacing the Late Palaeo-Eskimo. Able to amass large quantities of food, the Thule lived in winter villages comprising semisubterranean stone and sod houses with large whale-bone supports for the roofs. Their tools were usually made of bone, antler, or ivory. Stone cairns, used to channel caribou towards shooting pits, dot the Arctic landscape as do the stone weirs used to trap spawning char. Stone cairns also covered individual graves or acted as landmarks. Stone traps were made for fox and bear.

By the time of European contact most of Canada had been inhabited for thousands of years by many different peoples. At contact there were 12 language families in Canada and many more languages (pll 18, 66). Agriculture had been practised in southern Ontario for about 1 000 years, and had spread down the St Lawrence River as far as Québec. Elsewhere, as from the earliest times, people depended on hunting, fishing, and gathering.

The sudden spread of a relatively homogeneous Fluted Point culture across North America about 10 000 BC was a unique event, perhaps comparable only to the human occupation of Australia. After its initial occupation of most of the continent Fluted Point culture rapidly changed into regional cultures in different environments. The close association of culture and environment is particularly striking in Canadian prehistory. Distinct cultural traditions evolved in different environments: the northwest coast, the plains, the boreal forest around the eastern Great Lakes, the east coast, and the Arctic. Cultural continuities were marked within these regions, although innovations such as the spear thrower and the bow and arrow diffused rapidly and widely along networks of prehistoric trade that undoubtedly were conduits for human contact and communication. Other new elements, such as pottery, burial-mound ceremonialism, or agriculture, were much less widely accepted.

Such introductions could lead to abrupt changes in particular technologies but rarely to the replacement of one people by another. Occasionally a culture with a superior technology would push a people aside, as the Thule culture pushed aside the late Palaeo-Eskimo, although such events were exceptional. In the absence of pastoralists, and given the restricted areas of farming, the underlying causes of population replacement were markedly reduced. Generally hunters and gatherers had neither the resources to support campaigns of territorial acquisition nor the need to do so. Except along the northwest coast their population densities were low. People lived in small, mobile groups, dependent on their intimate knowledge of resources, on techniques of subsistence that were finely adapted to local environments, and on trading connections and alliances with neighbouring peoples. Usually their ancestors had lived in approximately the same way in approximately the same area for thousands of years. As Europeans began to penetrate these native worlds, they would frequently rely on the vast accumulation of native lore about the land and its resources and on many elements of native culture.

THE LAST ICE SHEETS, 18 000–10 000 BC

Authors: V. K. Prest, J.-S. Vincent (Glacial geology); J. H. McAndrews (Palaeobotany)

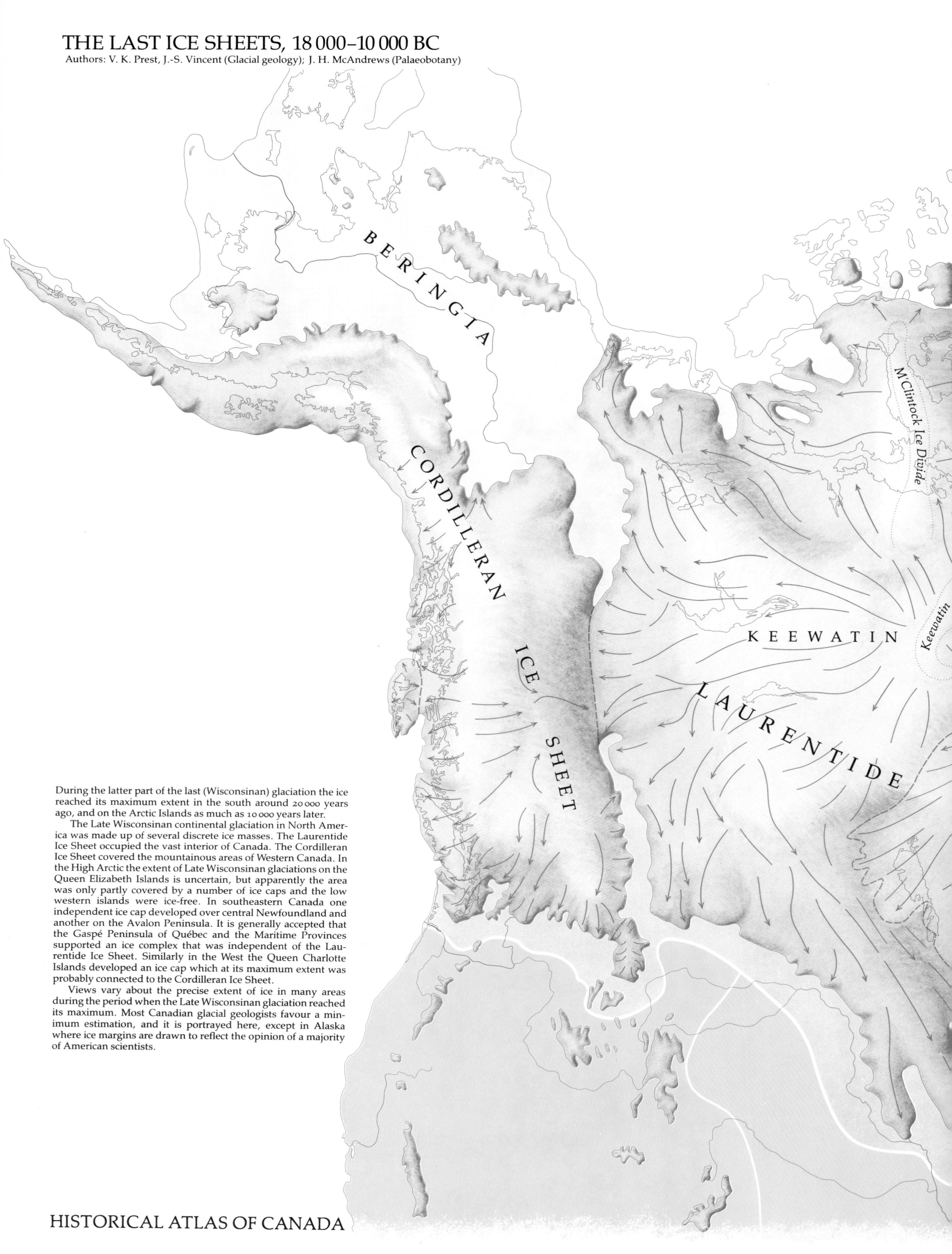
BERINGIA
CORDILLERAN
ICE
SHEET
KEEWATIN
LAURENTIDE
M'Clintock Ice Divide
Keewatin

During the latter part of the last (Wisconsinan) glaciation the ice reached its maximum extent in the south around 20 000 years ago, and on the Arctic Islands as much as 10 000 years later.

The Late Wisconsinan continental glaciation in North America was made up of several discrete ice masses. The Laurentide Ice Sheet occupied the vast interior of Canada. The Cordilleran Ice Sheet covered the mountainous areas of Western Canada. In the High Arctic the extent of Late Wisconsinan glaciations on the Queen Elizabeth Islands is uncertain, but apparently the area was only partly covered by a number of ice caps and the low western islands were ice-free. In southeastern Canada one independent ice cap developed over central Newfoundland and another on the Avalon Peninsula. It is generally accepted that the Gaspé Peninsula of Québec and the Maritime Provinces supported an ice complex that was independent of the Laurentide Ice Sheet. Similarly in the West the Queen Charlotte Islands developed an ice cap which at its maximum extent was probably connected to the Cordilleran Ice Sheet.

Views vary about the precise extent of ice in many areas during the period when the Late Wisconsinan glaciation reached its maximum. Most Canadian glacial geologists favour a minimum estimation, and it is portrayed here, except in Alaska where ice margins are drawn to reflect the opinion of a majority of American scientists.

PLATE 1

Although the Laurentide Ice Sheet was a single confluent ice sheet throughout much of Late Wisconsinan time, it was composed of three parts: the Labradorean, Keewatin, and Foxe-Baffin sectors. There were separate flow patterns and slightly different histories of development in each sector. Hudson Ice is the term used for a major mass of Late Wisconsinan ice within and south of Hudson Bay prior to a series of rapid ice advances into bordering glacial lakes (the Cochrane surges). New Québec Ice is the term for the retreating ice sheet in north-central Québec at the same time.

Ice-free areas served as refuges for plants and animals. In Late Wisconsinan time much of Alaska and the Yukon was covered by herb-dominated tundra and inhabited by mammoth, horse, bison, muskox, and caribou; it is controversial whether the tundra was productive enough to support large herds. South of the ice sheets a narrow, probably discontinuous zone of tundra separated the ice from a boreal woodland of well-spaced spruce and a denser boreal forest. In the West plant communities had no precise modern equivalents and large lowland forests were not yet established. Mammoth, caribou, and bison were widespread; mastodon were most abundant in the southeast.

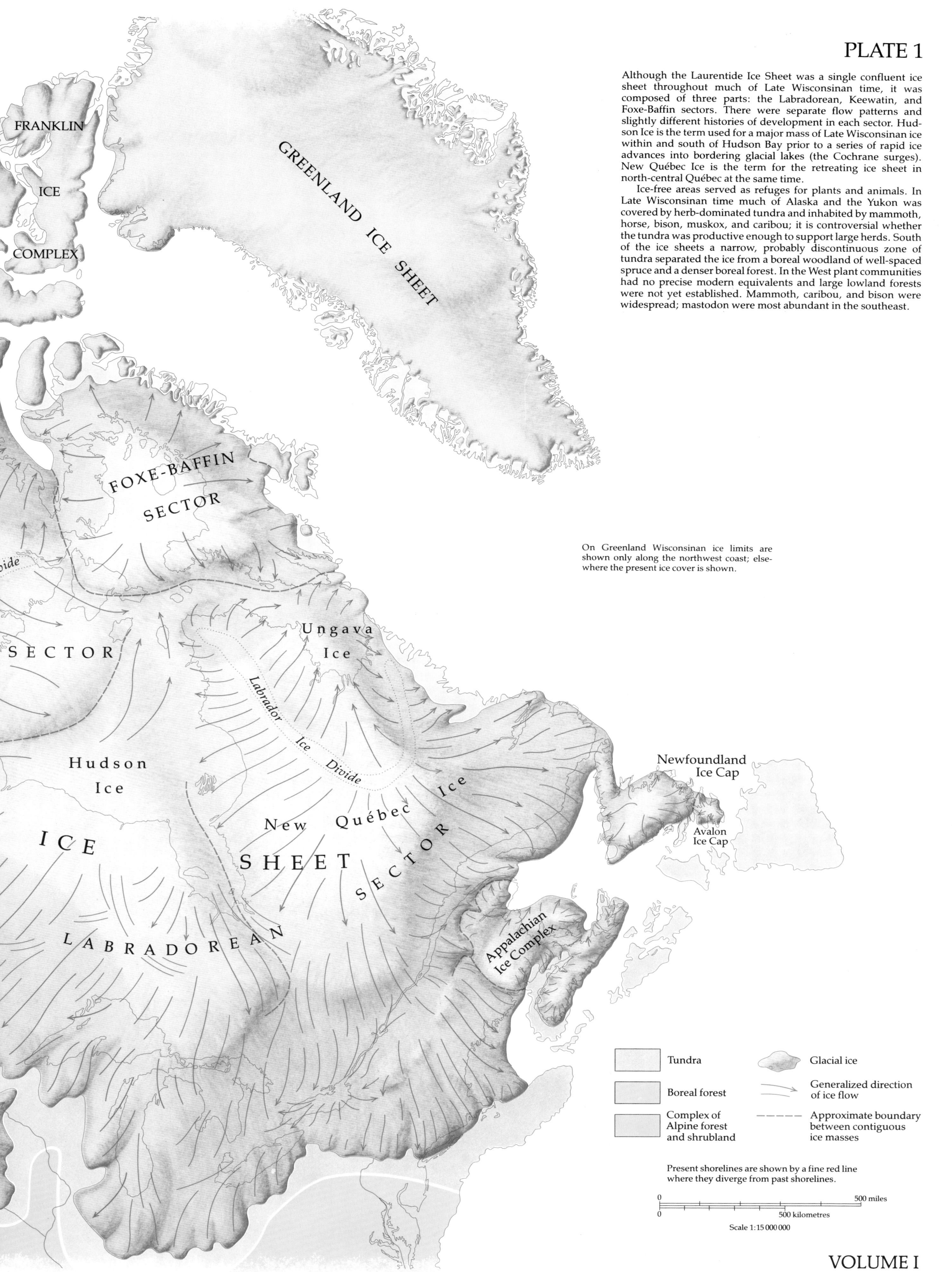

FRANKLIN
ICE
COMPLEX
GREENLAND ICE SHEET
FOXE-BAFFIN
SECTOR
SECTOR
Ungava
Ice
Labrador Ice Divide
Hudson
Ice
New Québec Ice
ICE
SHEET
SECTOR
LABRADOREAN
Newfoundland
Ice Cap
Avalon
Ice Cap
Appalachian
Ice Complex
On Greenland Wisconsinan ice limits are shown only along the northwest coast; elsewhere the present ice cover is shown.
Tundra
Boreal forest
Complex of
Alpine forest
and shrubland
Glacial ice
Generalized direction
of ice flow
Approximate boundary
between contiguous
ice masses
Present shorelines are shown by a fine red line where they diverge from past shorelines.
0
500 miles
0
500 kilometres
Scale 1:15 000 000

THE FLUTED POINT PEOPLE, 9500–8200 BC

Authors: Arthur Roberts (Archaeology); J.H. McAndrews (Palaeobotany); V.K. Prest, J.-S. Vincent (Glacial geology)

Fluted projectile points dating from 9500 to 8200 BC are the earliest indisputable evidence for the presence of people in North America. During these years the massive Laurentide and smaller Cordilleran ice sheets were melting as the climate warmed, rising sea levels closed the Bering Land Bridge, and tundra and lichen woodland occupied the land exposed by retreating ice. Palaeo-Indians, originally from Asia, hunted mammoth, mastodon, and bison along with smaller animals such as camel, horse, sloth, beaver, and caribou. Over a span of some 1 000 years these people occupied the central plains and eastern woodlands. Their fluted spear points were chipped from chert, chalcedony, jasper, quartz, quartzite, basalt, and obsidian, and thinned for hafting by the removal of long, channeled flakes or flutes extending from the base towards the tip on one or both sides. Such points are found from Alaska to the Gulf of Mexico.

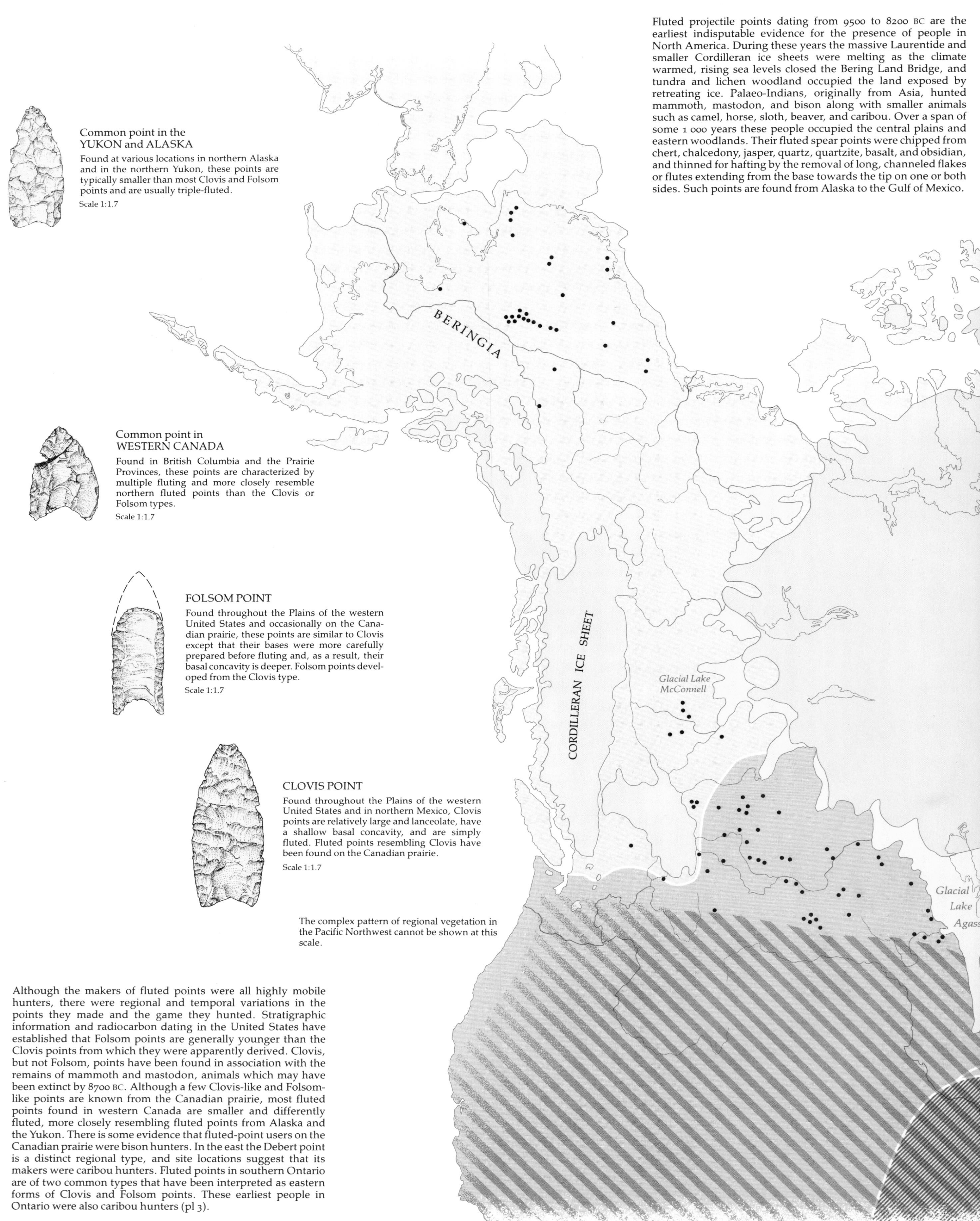
BERINGIA
CORDILLERAN ICE SHEET
Glacial Lake McConnell
Glacial Lake Agass

Common point in the YUKON and ALASKA

Found at various locations in northern Alaska and in the northern Yukon, these points are typically smaller than most Clovis and Folsom points and are usually triple-fluted.

Scale 1:1.7

Common point in WESTERN CANADA

Found in British Columbia and the Prairie Provinces, these points are characterized by multiple fluting and more closely resemble northern fluted points than the Clovis or Folsom types.

Scale 1:1.7

FOLSOM POINT

Found throughout the Plains of the western United States and occasionally on the Canadian prairie, these points are similar to Clovis except that their bases were more carefully prepared before fluting and, as a result, their basal concavity is deeper. Folsom points developed from the Clovis type.

Scale 1:1.7

CLOVIS POINT

Found throughout the Plains of the western United States and in northern Mexico, Clovis points are relatively large and lanceolate, have a shallow basal concavity, and are simply fluted. Fluted points resembling Clovis have been found on the Canadian prairie.

Scale 1:1.7

The complex pattern of regional vegetation in the Pacific Northwest cannot be shown at this scale.

Although the makers of fluted points were all highly mobile hunters, there were regional and temporal variations in the points they made and the game they hunted. Stratigraphic information and radiocarbon dating in the United States have established that Folsom points are generally younger than the Clovis points from which they were apparently derived. Clovis, but not Folsom, points have been found in association with the remains of mammoth and mastodon, animals which may have been extinct by 8700 BC. Although a few Clovis-like and Folsom-like points are known from the Canadian prairie, most fluted points found in western Canada are smaller and differently fluted, more closely resembling fluted points from Alaska and the Yukon. There is some evidence that fluted-point users on the Canadian prairie were bison hunters. In the east the Debert point is a distinct regional type, and site locations suggest that its makers were caribou hunters. Fluted points in southern Ontario are of two common types that have been interpreted as eastern forms of Clovis and Folsom points. These earliest people in Ontario were also caribou hunters (pl 3).

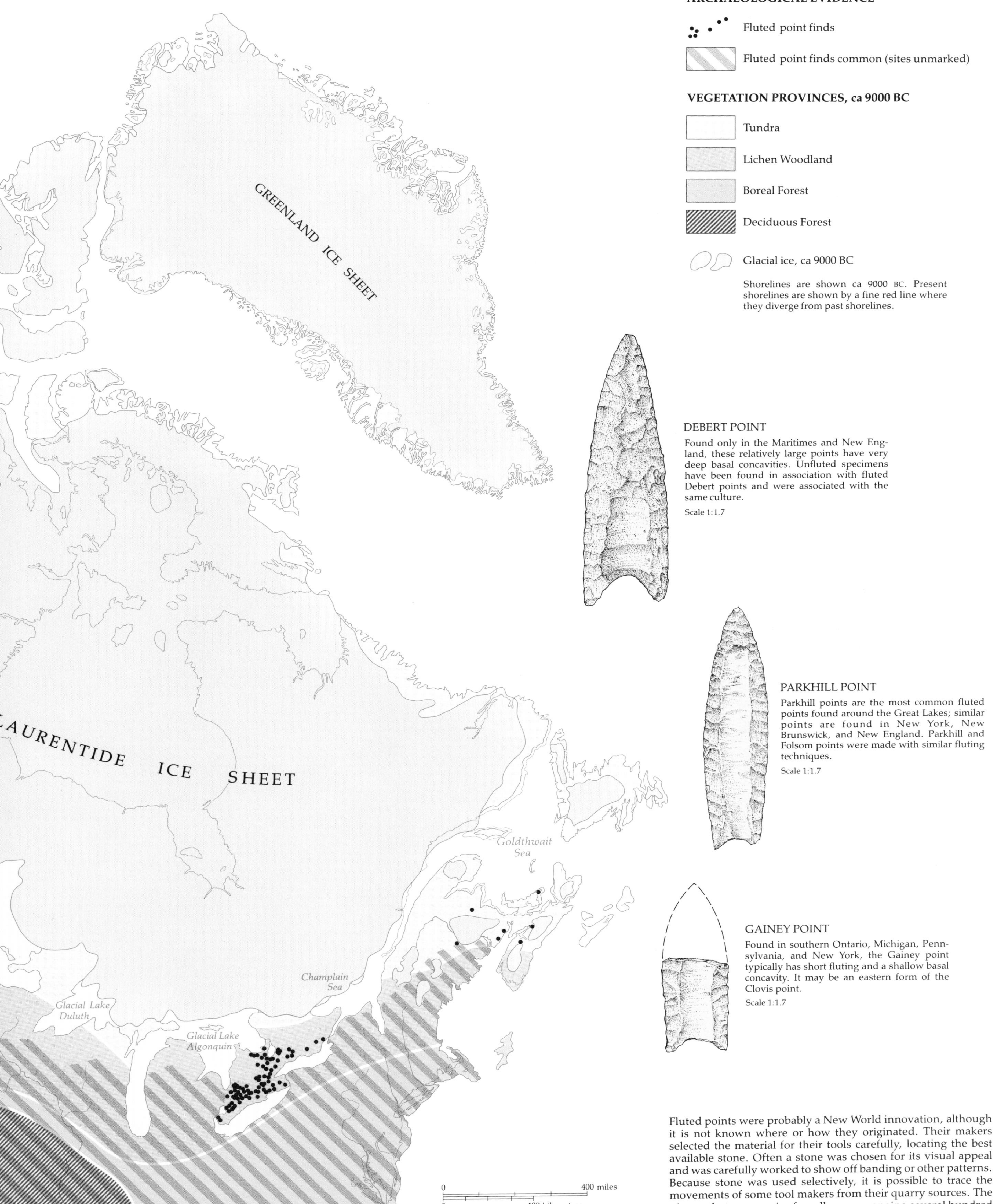
ARCHAEOLOGICAL EVIDENCE
Fluted point finds
Fluted point finds common (sites unmarked)
VEGETATION PROVINCES, ca 9000 BC
Tundra
Lichen Woodland
Boreal Forest
Deciduous Forest
Glacial ice, ca 9000 BC
Shorelines are shown ca 9000 BC. Present shorelines are shown by a fine red line where they diverge from past shorelines.
GREENLAND ICE SHEET
LAURENTIDE ICE SHEET
Goldthwait Sea
Champlain Sea
Glacial Lake Duluth
Glacial Lake Algonquin
0
400 miles
0
400 kilometres
Scale 1 : 18 000 000

DEBERT POINT

Found only in the Maritimes and New England, these relatively large points have very deep basal concavities. Unfluted specimens have been found in association with fluted Debert points and were associated with the same culture.

Scale 1:1.7

PARKHILL POINT

Parkhill points are the most common fluted points found around the Great Lakes; similar points are found in New York, New Brunswick, and New England. Parkhill and Folsom points were made with similar fluting techniques.

Scale 1:1.7

GAINEY POINT

Found in southern Ontario, Michigan, Pennsylvania, and New York, the Gainey point typically has short fluting and a shallow basal concavity. It may be an eastern form of the Clovis point.

Scale 1:1.7

Fluted points were probably a New World innovation, although it is not known where or how they originated. Their makers selected the material for their tools carefully, locating the best available stone. Often a stone was chosen for its visual appeal and was carefully worked to show off banding or other patterns. Because stone was used selectively, it is possible to trace the movements of some tool makers from their quarry sources. The picture that emerges is of small groups ranging several hundred kilometres annually and exchanging tools and raw materials with other groups of fluted point makers.

SOUTHERN ONTARIO, 8600 BC

Authors: Arthur Roberts; J.H. McAndrews (Palaeobotany)

The first people in southern Ontario, probably the makers of Gainey fluted points, arrived about 9000 BC. The limited archaeological evidence suggests that they hunted caribou and other Pleistocene animals, possibly including mastodon and mammoth.

By 8600 BC southwestern Ontario was covered by a boreal forest of spruce and pine, and the northeast by a more open lichen woodland. Herds of caribou wintered in the boreal forest and migrated in summer into the lichen woodland. Many Palaeo-Indian sites from this period have been found, often on relict shorelines of former glacial lakes. Whereas Lake Algonquin was well above present levels, Lake Erie and Lake Admiralty were well below them. Therefore the sites along Lake Algonquin are now some distance from the lakeshore, while most of those along Lake Erie and Lake Admiralty are probably under water.

The distribution of points made from different lithic (stone) sources and the remarkable similarity of these points across southern Ontario suggest that these people followed the caribou. There were at least two groups: one using Fossil Hill chert from the Fisher region and Detroit River chert from southwestern Ontario, and moving seasonally between the Parkhill and Fisher regions; and another using Detroit River chert and eastern Ontario quartz and quartzite and travelling from the Niagara peninsula along Lake Admiralty.

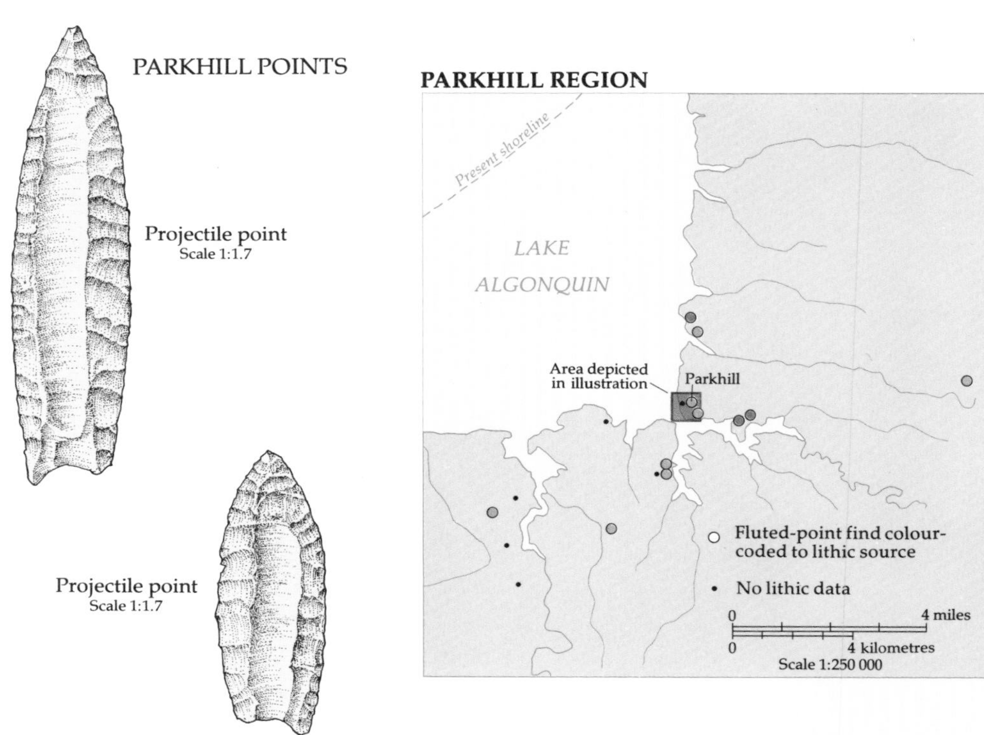
PARKHILL POINTS
Projectile point
Scale 1:1.7
Projectile point
Scale 1:1.7
PARKHILL REGION
Present shoreline
LAKE
ALGONQUIN
Area depicted in illustration
Parkhill
Fluted-point find colour-coded to lithic source
No lithic data
0
4 miles
0
4 kilometres
Scale 1:250 000

The Parkhill site produced over 90 fluted projectile points, all much like those at the Fisher site and probably made by the same people. Ten different activity areas have been identified at Parkhill. A channel flake from a fluted-point manufacturing area has been fitted to a broken fluted point discarded at a main camping area over 200 m away. Such 'cross-mends' clearly indicate that the activity areas were associated with each other. Other fluted-point sites, most with several activity areas, have been found near Parkhill.

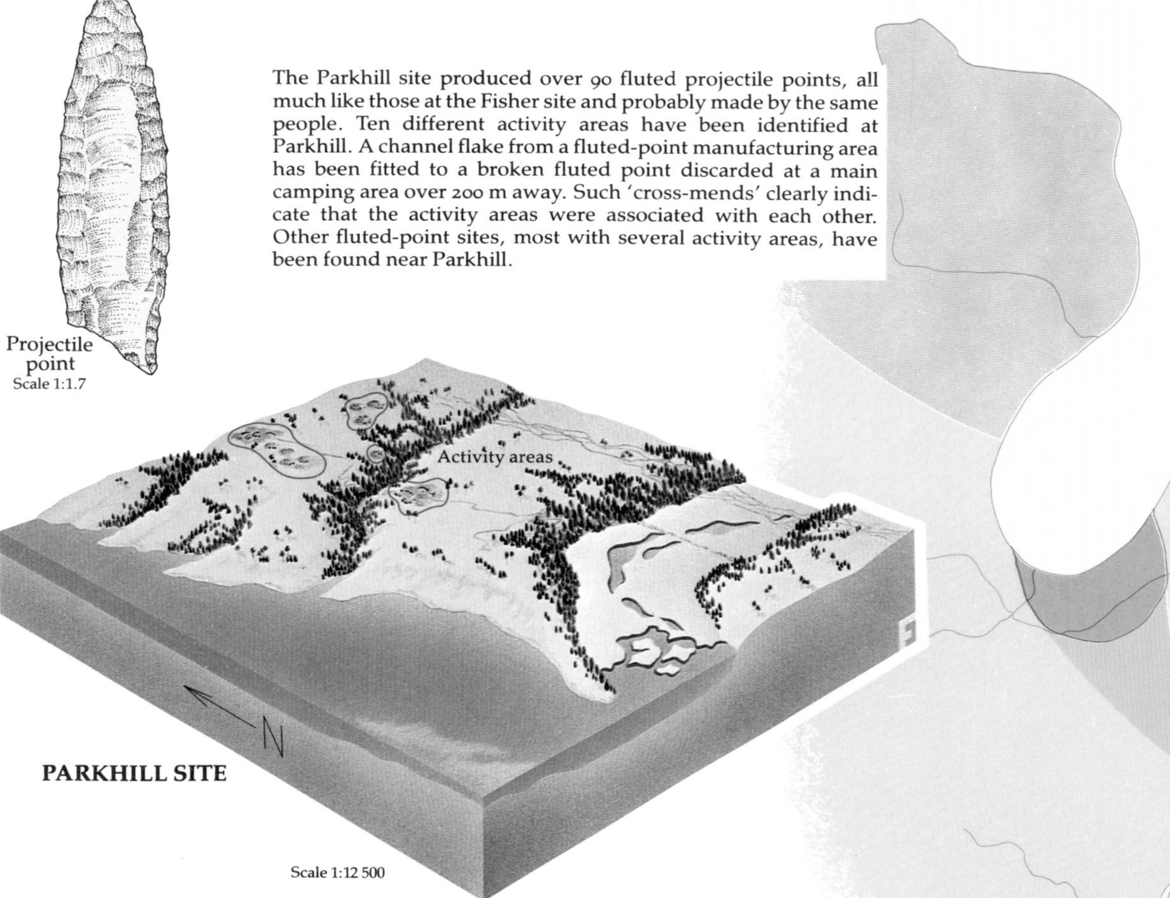
Projectile point
Scale 1:1.7
Activity areas
N
Catherine Farley
PARKHILL SITE
Scale 1:12 500

LAKE ALGONQUIN

FISHER SITE

PARKHILL REGION

Parkhill site

EARLY LAKE ERIE

Projectile points, usually used as spear points but sometimes as knives, are the principal diagnostic artefacts of Palaeo-Indian groups. Chert or quartzite, the usual tool-stone, could be fluted and worked to a sharp edge or point. Because of resharpening, the length of projectile points is not meaningful for cultural identification. However, variations in basal finishing and fluting are related to cultural groups.

Gainey points, the earliest in Ontario, have a relatively broad, shallow basal concavity with many short fluting flakes removed from one or both sides. Not found below Lake Algonquin levels, Gainey points are generally on higher terrain than the succeeding Parkhill points. Parkhill points, found in abundance in the excavations at the Parkhill and Fisher sites, fall into several subgroups, but all show careful basal preparation prior to fluting and a deep basal concavity. Crowfield points, found in concentration at one Ontario site and here and there throughout the region, are probably later. Their distinctive shape and manufacturing technique suggest that they may be transitional between Parkhill and Holcombe points. Holcombe points, the most recent shown on this plate, are not true fluted points although these thin, lanceolate points exhibit basal thinning.

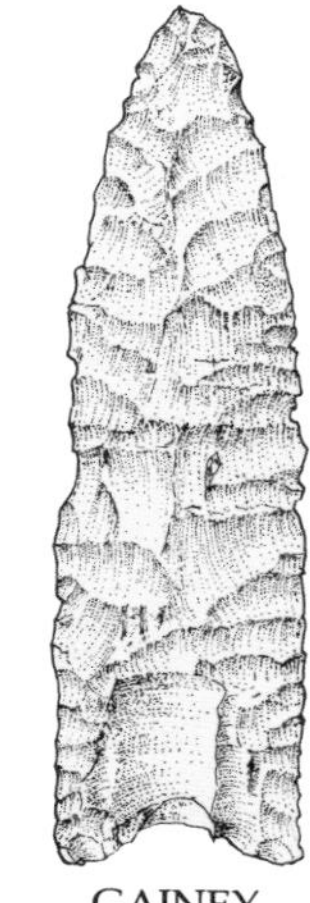
GAINEY projectile point
Scale 1:1.7

CROWFIELD projectile point

Scale 1:1.7

HOLCOMBE projectile point
Scale 1:1.7

VEGETATION PROVINCES

- Tundra
- Lichen Woodland
- Boreal Forest
- Glacial ice
- Lake
- Marine inundation

PLATE 3

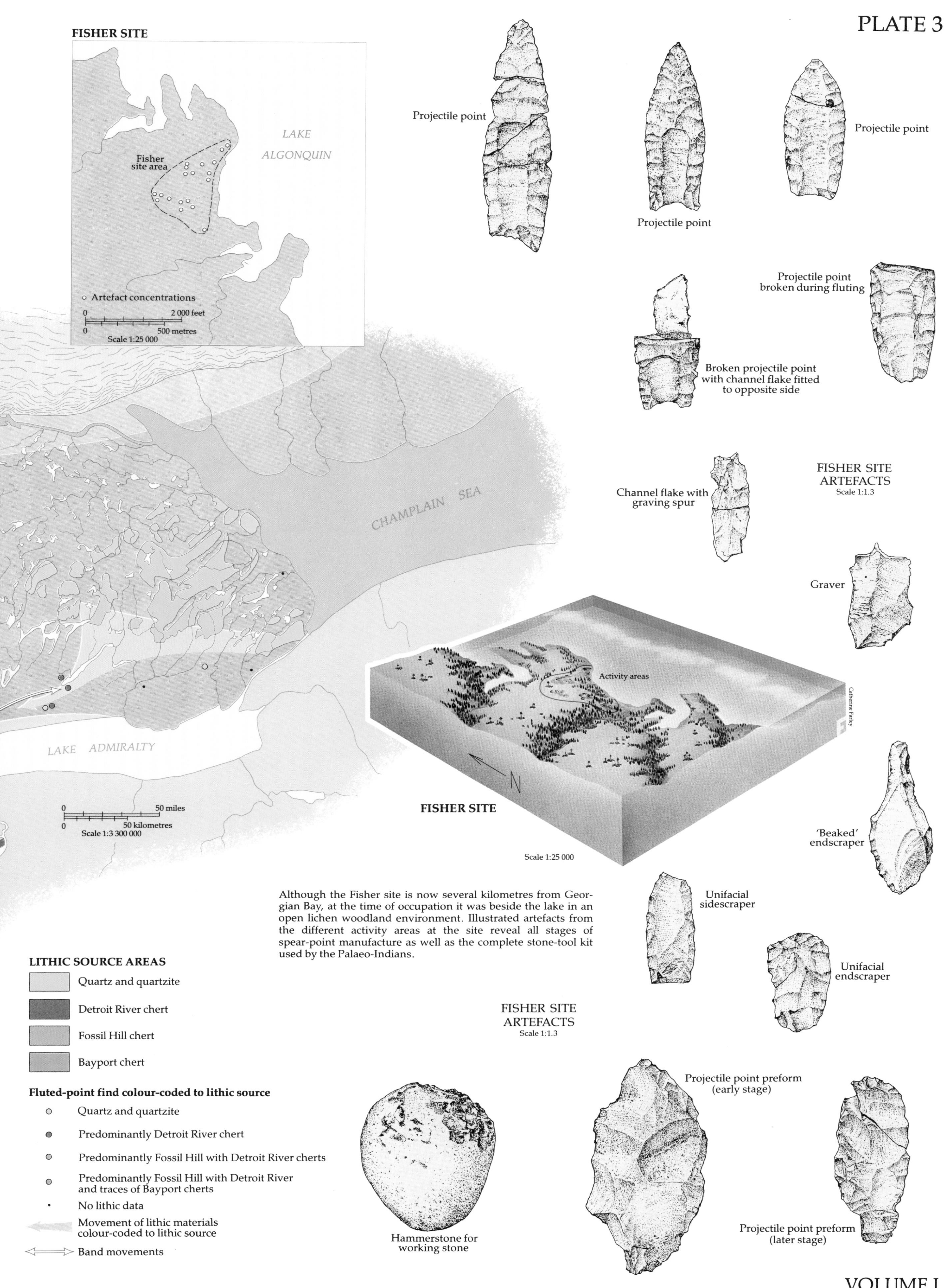

FISHER SITE
LAKE ALGONQUIN
Fisher site area
Artefact concentrations
0 2 000 feet
0 500 metres
Scale 1:25 000
CHAMPLAIN SEA
LAKE ADMIRALTY
0 50 miles
0 50 kilometres
Scale 1:3 300 000
Projectile point
Projectile point
Projectile point
Projectile point broken during fluting
Broken projectile point with channel flake fitted to opposite side
FISHER SITE ARTEFACTS
Scale 1:1.3
Channel flake with graving spur
Graver
Activity areas
Catherine Farley
N
FISHER SITE
Scale 1:25 000
'Beaked' endscraper
Unifacial sidescraper
Unifacial endscraper
FISHER SITE ARTEFACTS
Scale 1:1.3
Projectile point preform (early stage)
Projectile point preform (later stage)
Hammerstone for working stone
LITHIC SOURCE AREAS
Quartz and quartzite
Detroit River chert
Fossil Hill chert
Bayport chert
Fluted-point find colour-coded to lithic source
Quartz and quartzite
Predominantly Detroit River chert
Predominantly Fossil Hill with Detroit River cherts
Predominantly Fossil Hill with Detroit River and traces of Bayport cherts
No lithic data
Movement of lithic materials colour-coded to lithic source
Band movements

Although the Fisher site is now several kilometres from Georgian Bay, at the time of occupation it was beside the lake in an open lichen woodland environment. Illustrated artefacts from the different activity areas at the site reveal all stages of spear-point manufacture as well as the complete stone-tool kit used by the Palaeo-Indians.

ENVIRONMENTAL CHANGE AFTER 9000 BC

Authors: J.H. McAndrews, K.-B. Liu, G.C. Manville (Palaeobotany); V.K. Prest, J.-S. Vincent (Glacial geology)

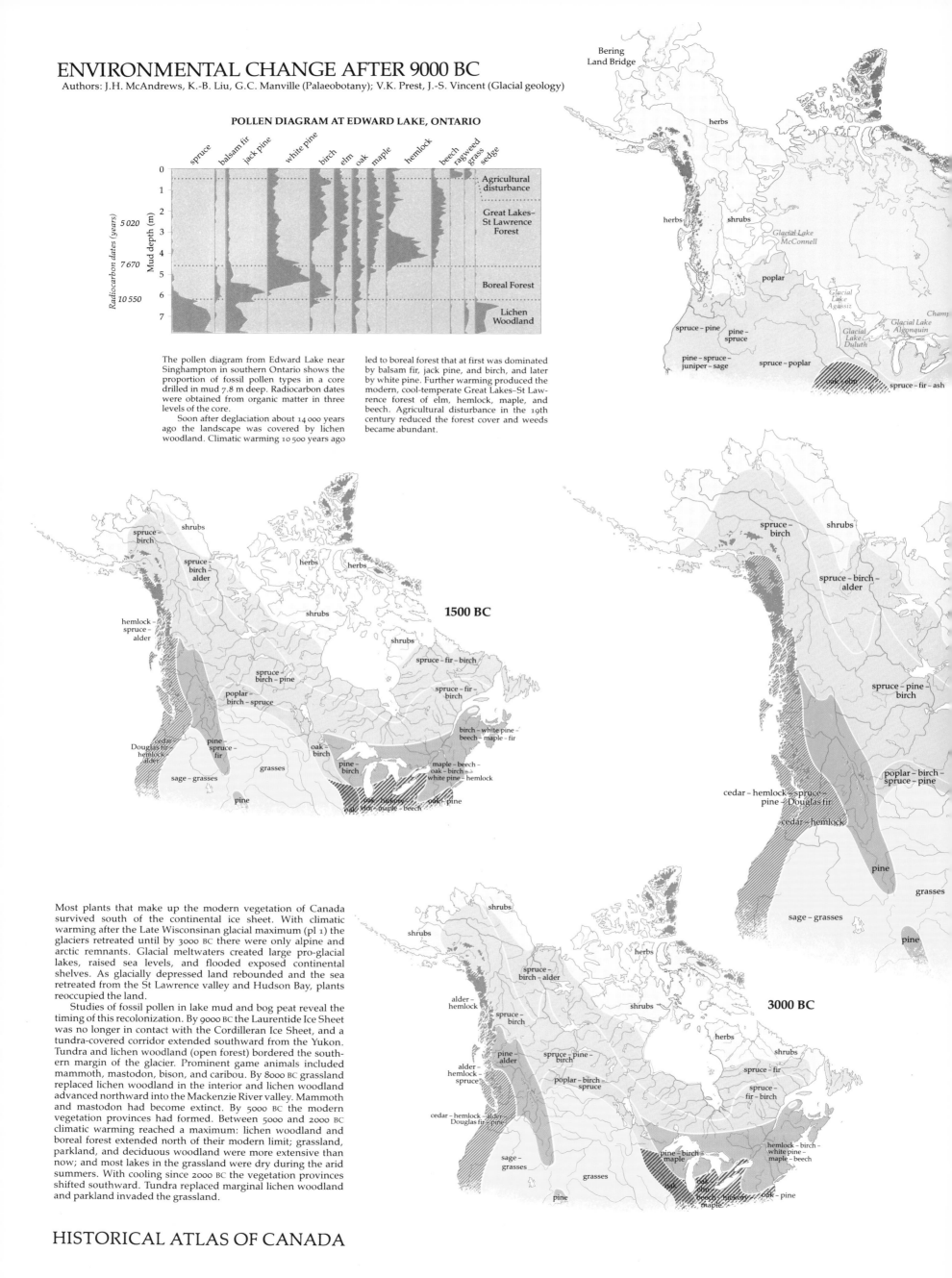

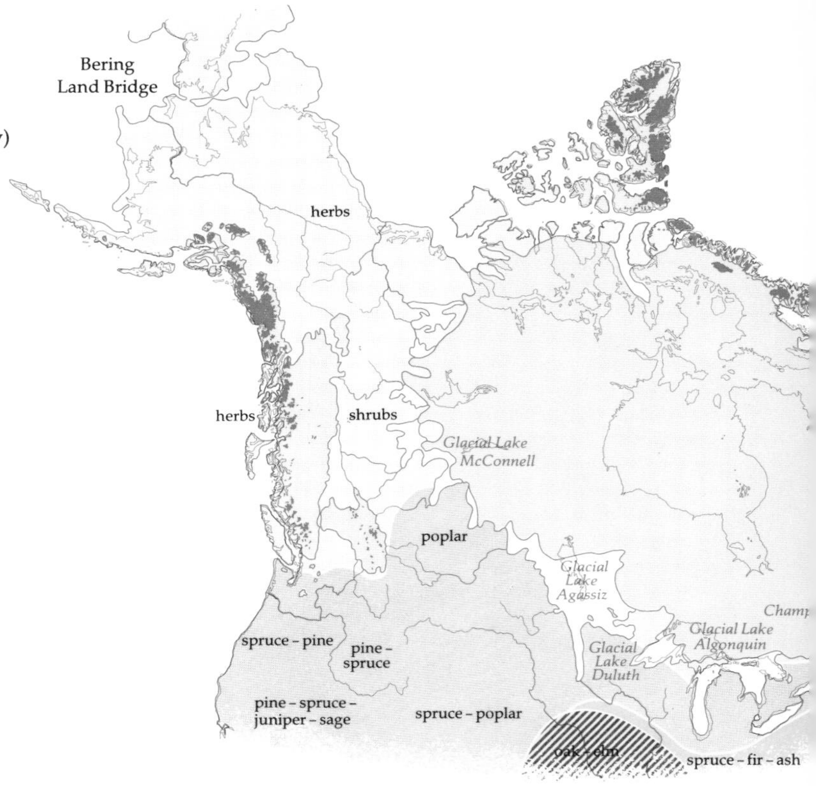

POLLEN DIAGRAM AT EDWARD LAKE, ONTARIO

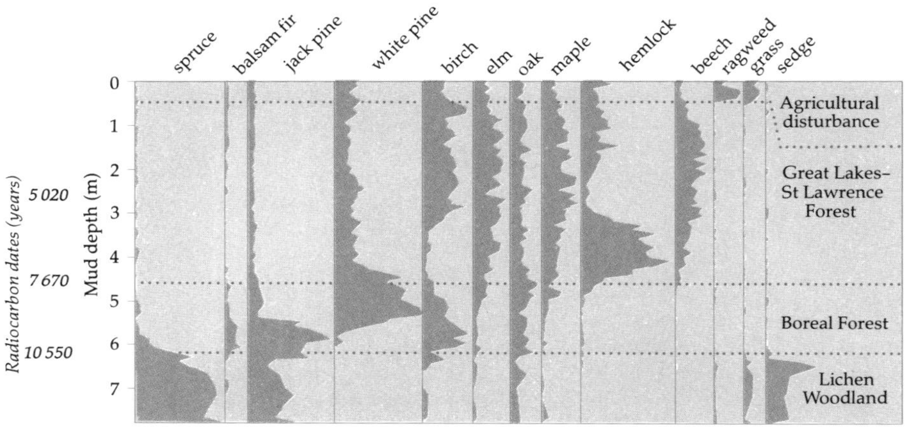

The pollen diagram from Edward Lake near Singhampton in southern Ontario shows the proportion of fossil pollen types in a core drilled in mud 7.8 m deep. Radiocarbon dates were obtained from organic matter in three levels of the core.

Soon after deglaciation about 14 000 years ago the landscape was covered by lichen woodland. Climatic warming 10 500 years ago led to boreal forest that at first was dominated by balsam fir, jack pine, and birch, and later by white pine. Further warming produced the modern, cool-temperate Great Lakes–St Lawrence forest of elm, hemlock, maple, and beech. Agricultural disturbance in the 19th century reduced the forest cover and weeds became abundant.

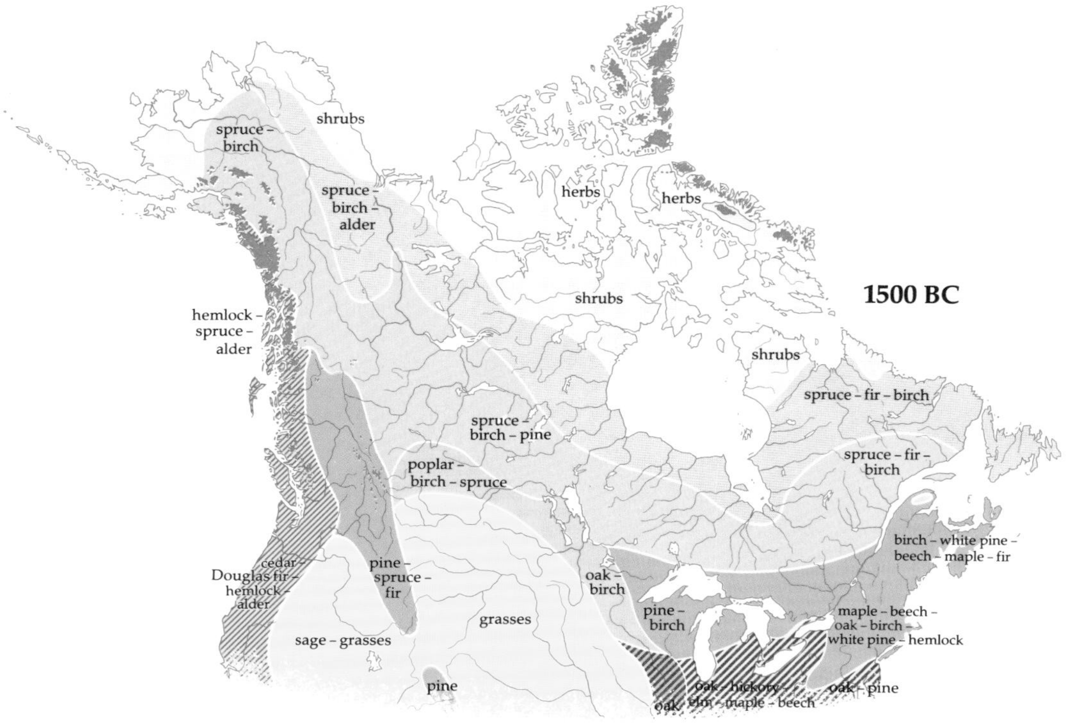

Most plants that make up the modern vegetation of Canada survived south of the continental ice sheet. With climatic warming after the Late Wisconsinan glacial maximum (pl 1) the glaciers retreated until by 3000 BC there were only alpine and arctic remnants. Glacial meltwaters created large pro-glacial lakes, raised sea levels, and flooded exposed continental shelves. As glacially depressed land rebounded and the sea retreated from the St Lawrence valley and Hudson Bay, plants reoccupied the land.

Studies of fossil pollen in lake mud and bog peat reveal the timing of this recolonization. By 9000 BC the Laurentide Ice Sheet was no longer in contact with the Cordilleran Ice Sheet, and a tundra-covered corridor extended southward from the Yukon. Tundra and lichen woodland (open forest) bordered the southern margin of the glacier. Prominent game animals included mammoth, mastodon, bison, and caribou. By 8000 BC grassland replaced lichen woodland in the interior and lichen woodland advanced northward into the Mackenzie River valley. Mammoth and mastodon had become extinct. By 5000 BC the modern vegetation provinces had formed. Between 5000 and 2000 BC climatic warming reached a maximum: lichen woodland and boreal forest extended north of their modern limit; grassland, parkland, and deciduous woodland were more extensive than now; and most lakes in the grassland were dry during the arid summers. With cooling since 2000 BC the vegetation provinces shifted southward. Tundra replaced marginal lichen woodland and parkland invaded the grassland.

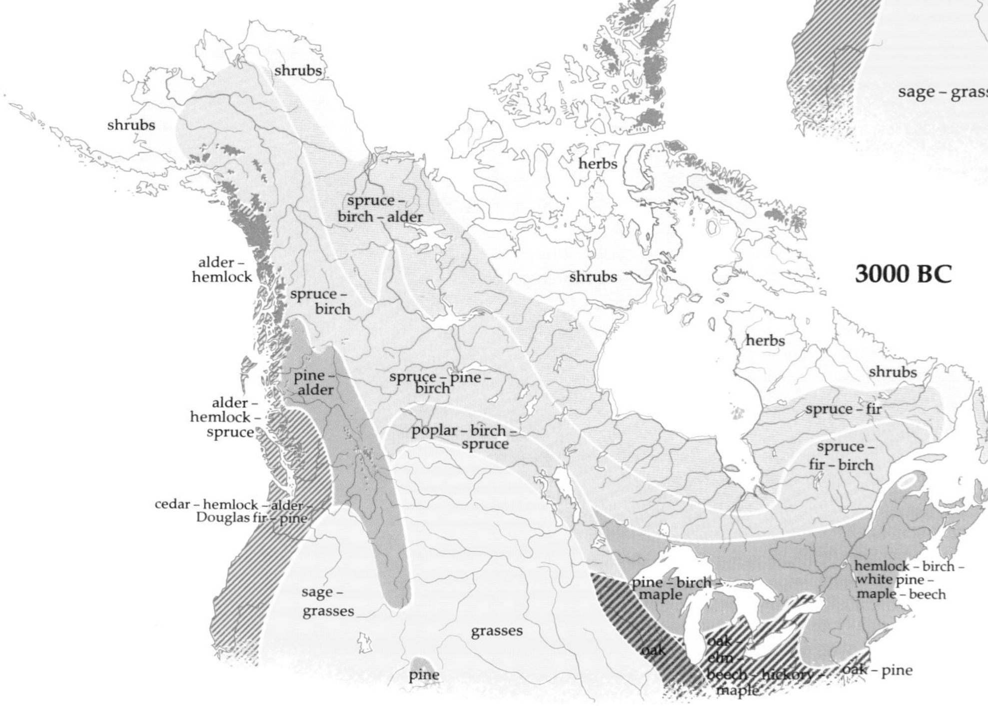

VEGETATION PROVINCES

- Tundra
- Lichen Woodland
- Boreal Forest
- Pacific Forest
- Columbia-Montane Forest
- Parkland
- Great Lakes–St Lawrence Forest
- Deciduous Woodland
- Deciduous Forest
- Grassland

9000 BC

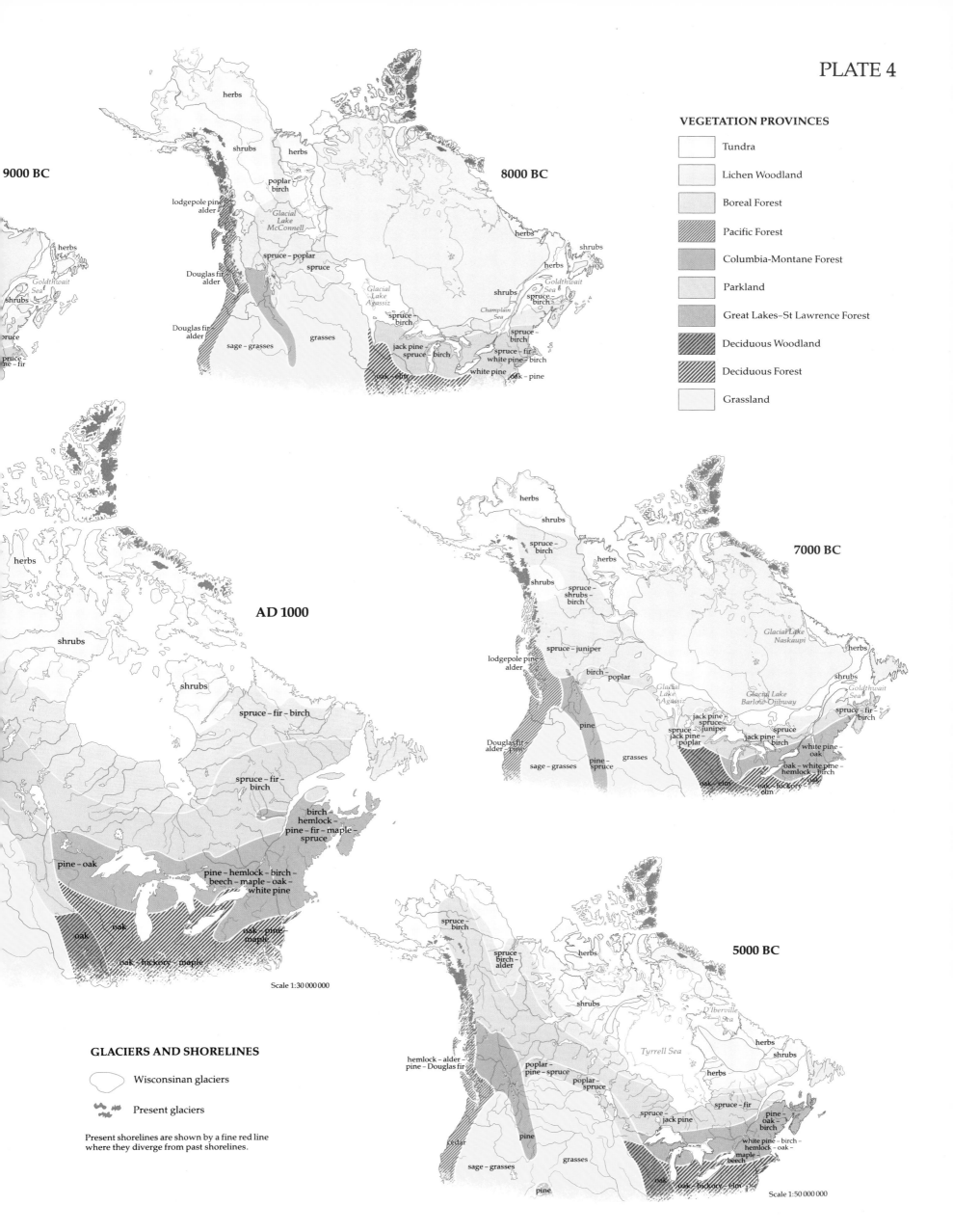

herbs
Goldthwait Sea
shrubs
spruce
spruce – pine – fir

8000 BC

herbs
shrubs
herbs
poplar – birch
lodgepole pine – alder
Glacial Lake McConnell
spruce – poplar
spruce
Douglas fir – alder
Douglas fir – alder
sage – grasses
grasses
Glacial Lake Agassiz
spruce – birch
jack pine – spruce – birch
oak – elm
herbs
shrubs
herbs
Goldthwait Sea
shrubs
spruce – birch
Champlain Sea
spruce – birch
spruce – fir
white pine – birch
white pine
oak – pine

7000 BC

herbs
shrubs
spruce – birch
herbs
shrubs
spruce – shrubs – birch
spruce – juniper
lodgepole pine – alder
birch – poplar
Glacial Lake Agassiz
Glacial Lake Naskaupi
Glacial Lake Barlow-Ojibway
herbs
shrubs
Goldthwait Sea
spruce – fir – birch
pine
Douglas fir – alder – pine
sage – grasses
pine – spruce
grasses
jack pine – spruce – juniper
spruce – jack pine – poplar
jack pine – birch
spruce
white pine – oak
oak – white pine – hemlock – birch
oak – elm
oak – hickory – elm
oak

AD 1000

herbs
shrubs
shrubs
spruce – fir – birch
spruce – fir – birch
birch – hemlock – pine – fir – maple – spruce
pine – oak
pine – hemlock – birch – beech – maple – oak – white pine
oak
oak
oak – pine – maple
oak – hickory – maple

Scale 1:30 000 000

5000 BC

spruce – birch
spruce – birch – alder
herbs
shrubs
D'Iberville Sea
Tyrrell Sea
herbs
shrubs
herbs
hemlock – alder – pine – Douglas fir
poplar – pine – spruce
poplar – spruce
spruce – fir
spruce – jack pine
pine – oak – birch
white pine – birch – hemlock – oak – maple – beech
cedar
pine
sage – grasses
grasses
pine
oak
oak – hickory – elm

Scale 1:50 000 000

GLACIERS AND SHORELINES

- Wisconsinan glaciers
- Present glaciers

Present shorelines are shown by a fine red line where they diverge from past shorelines.

THE PLANO PEOPLE, 8500–6000 BC

Authors: Arthur Roberts; J.V. Wright; V.K. Prest and J.-S. Vincent (Glacial geology)

The term 'Plano' embraces a number of hunting peoples, all descendents of the makers of fluted points (pl 2), who were first identified and probably originated on the great plains. Eventually small hunting bands moved off the plains. To the west of Hudson Bay they began hunting on land recently released by ice and glacial lakes. In the east they lived in contact with Early Archaic hunters (pl 6) who, in their turn, penetrated the plains. In different environments Plano technologies became more regional, but these people always used a distinctive collateral or ripple flaking technique to fashion their stone tools.

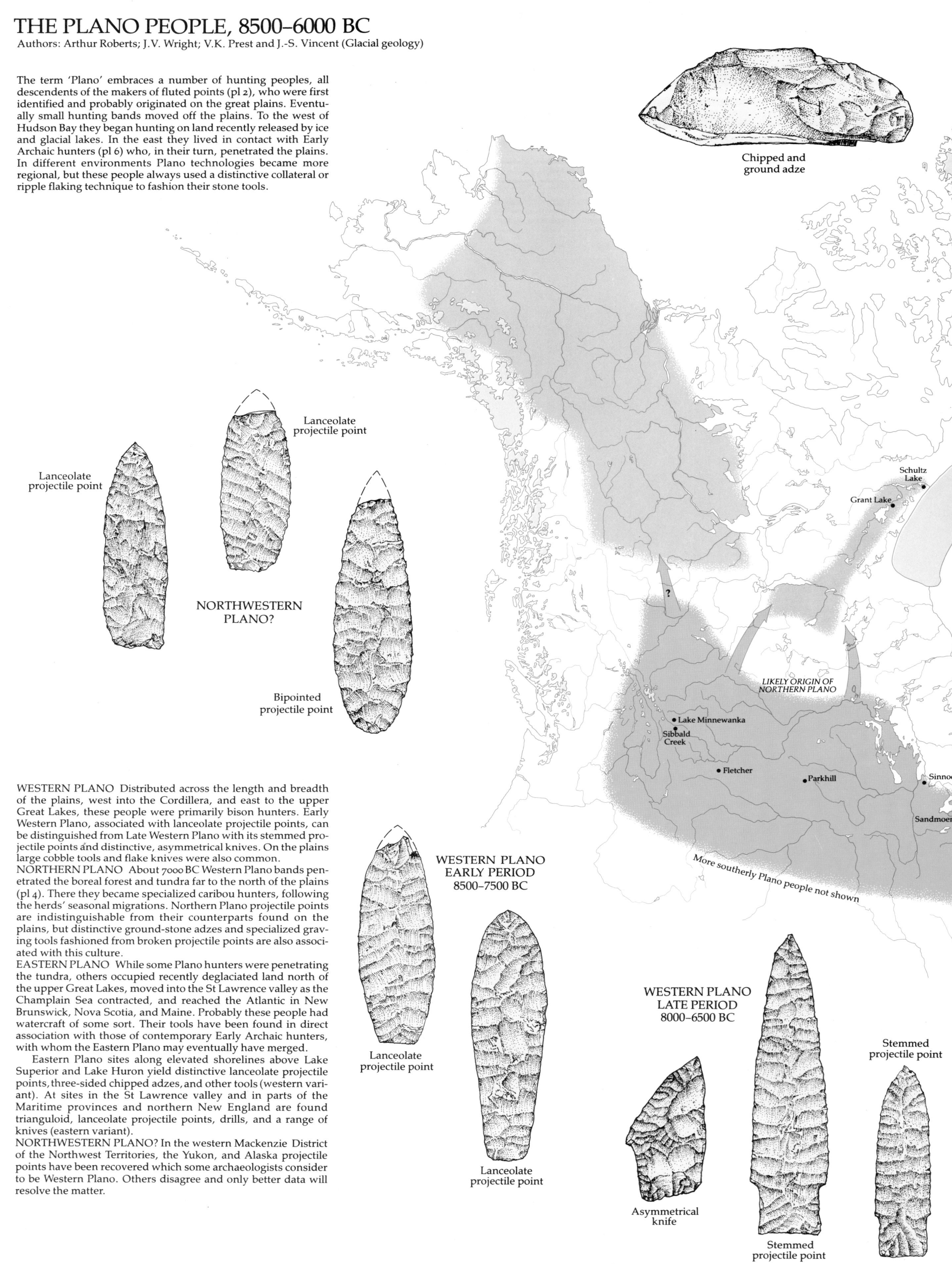
Chipped and ground adze
Lanceolate projectile point
Lanceolate projectile point
NORTHWESTERN PLANO?
Bipointed projectile point
Schultz Lake
Grant Lake
?
LIKELY ORIGIN OF NORTHERN PLANO
Lake Minnewanka
Sibbald Creek
Fletcher
Parkhill
Sinnock
Sandmoen
More southerly Plano people not shown
WESTERN PLANO EARLY PERIOD 8500–7500 BC
Lanceolate projectile point
Lanceolate projectile point
WESTERN PLANO LATE PERIOD 8000–6500 BC
Asymmetrical knife
Stemmed projectile point
Stemmed projectile point

WESTERN PLANO Distributed across the length and breadth of the plains, west into the Cordillera, and east to the upper Great Lakes, these people were primarily bison hunters. Early Western Plano, associated with lanceolate projectile points, can be distinguished from Late Western Plano with its stemmed projectile points and distinctive, asymmetrical knives. On the plains large cobble tools and flake knives were also common.

NORTHERN PLANO About 7000 BC Western Plano bands penetrated the boreal forest and tundra far to the north of the plains (pl 4). There they became specialized caribou hunters, following the herds' seasonal migrations. Northern Plano projectile points are indistinguishable from their counterparts found on the plains, but distinctive ground-stone adzes and specialized graving tools fashioned from broken projectile points are also associated with this culture.

EASTERN PLANO While some Plano hunters were penetrating the tundra, others occupied recently deglaciated land north of the upper Great Lakes, moved into the St Lawrence valley as the Champlain Sea contracted, and reached the Atlantic in New Brunswick, Nova Scotia, and Maine. Probably these people had watercraft of some sort. Their tools have been found in direct association with those of contemporary Early Archaic hunters, with whom the Eastern Plano may eventually have merged.

Eastern Plano sites along elevated shorelines above Lake Superior and Lake Huron yield distinctive lanceolate projectile points, three-sided chipped adzes, and other tools (western variant). At sites in the St Lawrence valley and in parts of the Maritime provinces and northern New England are found trianguloid, lanceolate projectile points, drills, and a range of knives (eastern variant).

NORTHWESTERN PLANO? In the western Mackenzie District of the Northwest Territories, the Yukon, and Alaska projectile points have been recovered which some archaeologists consider to be Western Plano. Others disagree and only better data will resolve the matter.

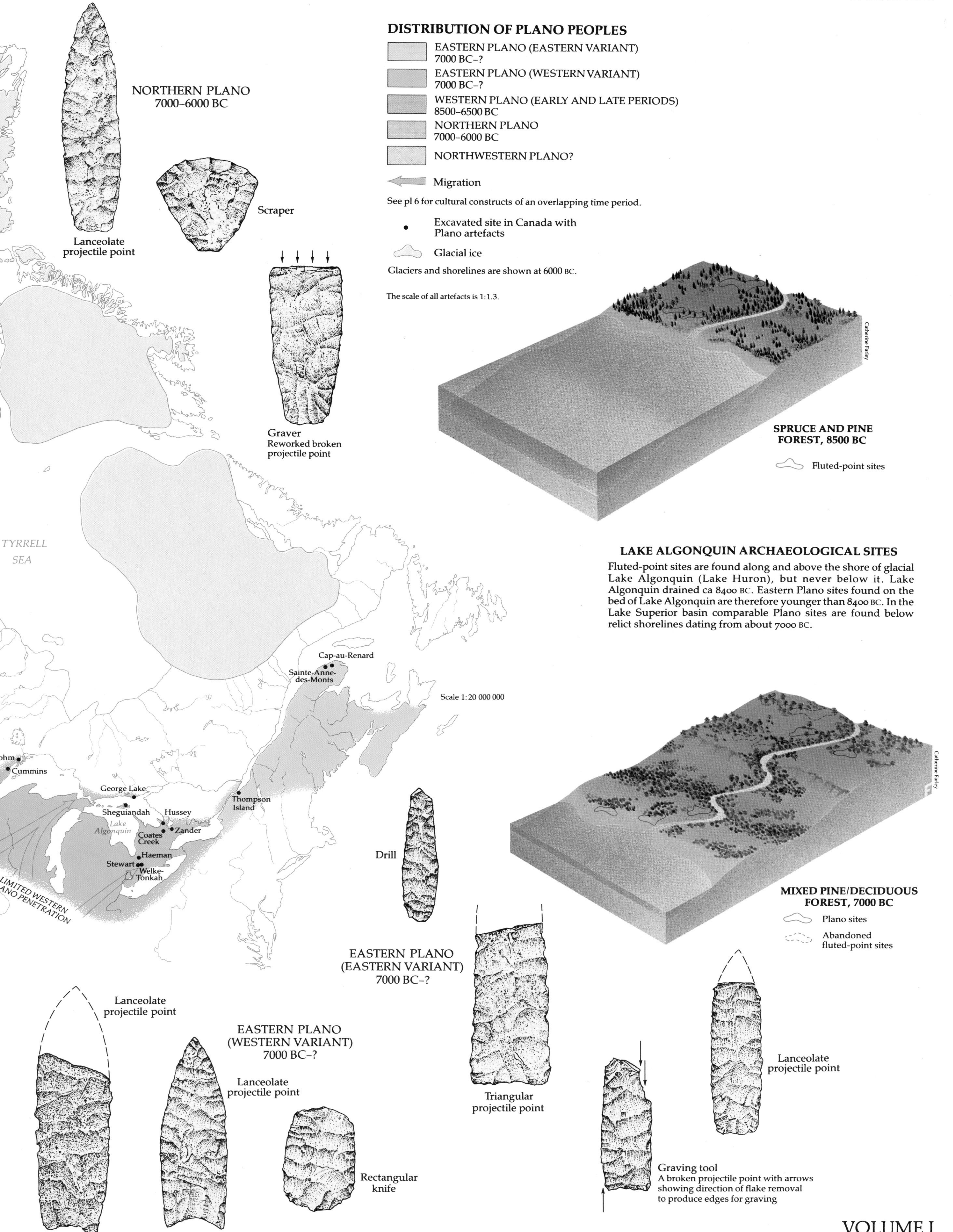
DISTRIBUTION OF PLANO PEOPLES
EASTERN PLANO (EASTERN VARIANT) 7000 BC–?
EASTERN PLANO (WESTERN VARIANT) 7000 BC–?
WESTERN PLANO (EARLY AND LATE PERIODS) 8500–6500 BC
NORTHERN PLANO 7000–6000 BC
NORTHWESTERN PLANO?
Migration
See pl 6 for cultural constructs of an overlapping time period.
Excavated site in Canada with Plano artefacts
Glacial ice
Glaciers and shorelines are shown at 6000 BC.
The scale of all artefacts is 1:1.3.
NORTHERN PLANO
7000–6000 BC
Lanceolate projectile point
Scraper
Graver
Reworked broken projectile point
SPRUCE AND PINE FOREST, 8500 BC
Fluted-point sites
TYRRELL SEA
Cap-au-Renard
Sainte-Anne-des-Monts
Scale 1:20 000 000
rohm
Cummins
George Lake
Sheguiandah
Hussey
Lake Algonquin
Coates Creek
Zander
Haeman
Stewart
Welke-Tonkah
Thompson Island
LIMITED WESTERN PLANO PENETRATION
Drill
MIXED PINE/DECIDUOUS FOREST, 7000 BC
Plano sites
Abandoned fluted-point sites
EASTERN PLANO
(EASTERN VARIANT)
7000 BC–?
Triangular projectile point
Lanceolate projectile point
Graving tool
A broken projectile point with arrows showing direction of flake removal to produce edges for graving
EASTERN PLANO
(WESTERN VARIANT)
7000 BC–?
Lanceolate projectile point
Lanceolate projectile point
Rectangular knife
Catherine Farley

LAKE ALGONQUIN ARCHAEOLOGICAL SITES

Fluted-point sites are found along and above the shore of glacial Lake Algonquin (Lake Huron), but never below it. Lake Algonquin drained ca 8400 BC. Eastern Plano sites found on the bed of Lake Algonquin are therefore younger than 8400 BC. In the Lake Superior basin comparable Plano sites are found below relict shorelines dating from about 7000 BC.

CULTURAL SEQUENCES, 8000–4000 BC

Authors: J.V. Wright (Archaeology); V.K. Prest, J.-S. Vincent (Glacial geology)

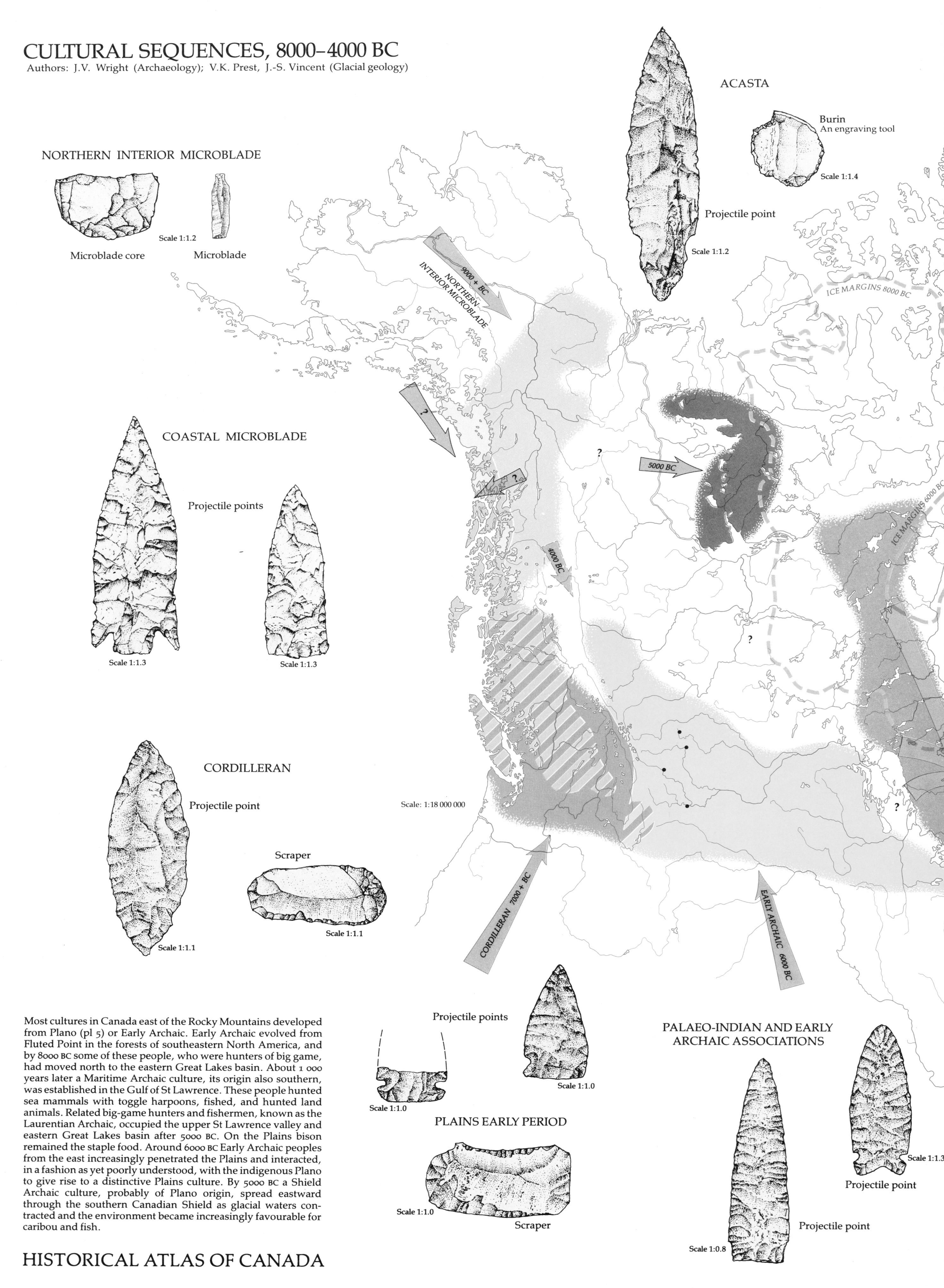
NORTHERN INTERIOR MICROBLADE
Scale 1:1.2
Microblade core
Microblade
ACASTA
Burin
An engraving tool
Scale 1:1.4
Projectile point
Scale 1:1.2
9000 + BC
NORTHERN INTERIOR MICROBLADE
ICE MARGINS 8000 BC
COASTAL MICROBLADE
Projectile points
Scale 1:1.3
Scale 1:1.3
5000 BC
4000 BC
ICE MARGINS 6000 BC
CORDILLERAN
Projectile point
Scraper
Scale 1:1.1
Scale 1:1.1
Scale: 1:18 000 000
CORDILLERAN 7000 + BC
EARLY ARCHAIC 6000 BC
Projectile points
Scale 1:1.0
Scale 1:1.0
PLAINS EARLY PERIOD
Scale 1:1.0
Scraper
PALAEO-INDIAN AND EARLY ARCHAIC ASSOCIATIONS
Scale 1:1.3
Projectile point
Projectile point
Scale 1:0.8

Most cultures in Canada east of the Rocky Mountains developed from Plano (pl 5) or Early Archaic. Early Archaic evolved from Fluted Point in the forests of southeastern North America, and by 8000 BC some of these people, who were hunters of big game, had moved north to the eastern Great Lakes basin. About 1 000 years later a Maritime Archaic culture, its origin also southern, was established in the Gulf of St Lawrence. These people hunted sea mammals with toggle harpoons, fished, and hunted land animals. Related big-game hunters and fishermen, known as the Laurentian Archaic, occupied the upper St Lawrence valley and eastern Great Lakes basin after 5000 BC. On the Plains bison remained the staple food. Around 6000 BC Early Archaic peoples from the east increasingly penetrated the Plains and interacted, in a fashion as yet poorly understood, with the indigenous Plano to give rise to a distinctive Plains culture. By 5000 BC a Shield Archaic culture, probably of Plano origin, spread eastward through the southern Canadian Shield as glacial waters contracted and the environment became increasingly favourable for caribou and fish.

PLATE 6

ARCHAEOLOGICAL CULTURAL CONSTRUCTS

Throughout this period of environmental change (pl 4) people adapted to changing conditions and cultures became more diversified. Between 7000 BC and 6000 BC quite different cultures such as Plano (pl 5) and Archaic came into direct contact with each other; by 4000 BC the outline of later regional cultures is discernible.

In the west people who made microblades (long, narrow flakes with a sharp cutting edge) lived in Alaska and the northern Yukon 15 000 or more years ago. Subsequently microblade technology, which is clearly of Asiatic origin, spread slowly east and south, and cultures emerged that are identified as Northern Interior Microblade and Coastal Microblade. Prior to 7000 BC a Cordilleran culture, possibly with Fluted Point antecedents (pl 2), developed in or spread northward into southern British Columbia. A caribou-hunting people known as Acasta were established north of the Great Slave Lake by 5000 BC; elements of their tools apparently were derived from both Cordilleran and Northern Interior Microblade cultures.

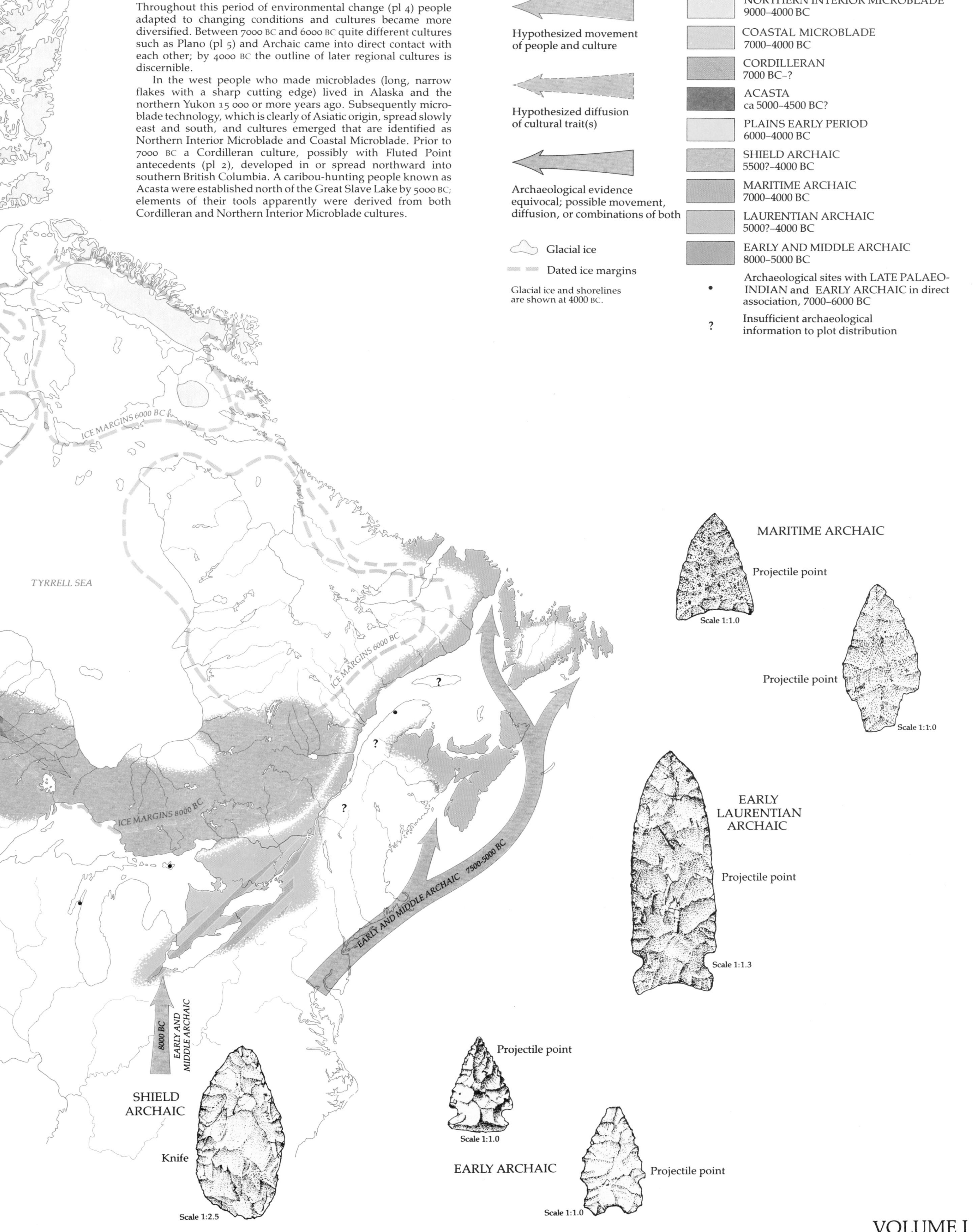

Hypothesized movement of people and culture
Hypothesized diffusion of cultural trait(s)
Archaeological evidence equivocal; possible movement, diffusion, or combinations of both
Glacial ice
Dated ice margins
Glacial ice and shorelines are shown at 4000 BC.
NORTHERN INTERIOR MICROBLADE 9000–4000 BC
COASTAL MICROBLADE 7000–4000 BC
CORDILLERAN 7000 BC–?
ACASTA ca 5000–4500 BC?
PLAINS EARLY PERIOD 6000–4000 BC
SHIELD ARCHAIC 5500?–4000 BC
MARITIME ARCHAIC 7000–4000 BC
LAURENTIAN ARCHAIC 5000?–4000 BC
EARLY AND MIDDLE ARCHAIC 8000–5000 BC
Archaeological sites with LATE PALAEO-INDIAN and EARLY ARCHAIC in direct association, 7000–6000 BC
?
Insufficient archaeological information to plot distribution
ICE MARGINS 6000 BC
TYRRELL SEA
ICE MARGINS 6000 BC
ICE MARGINS 8000 BC
EARLY AND MIDDLE ARCHAIC 7500–5000 BC
8000 BC
EARLY AND MIDDLE ARCHAIC
MARITIME ARCHAIC
Projectile point
Scale 1:1.0
Projectile point
Scale 1:1.0
EARLY LAURENTIAN ARCHAIC
Projectile point
Scale 1:1.3
SHIELD ARCHAIC
Knife
Scale 1:2.5
Projectile point
Scale 1:1.0
EARLY ARCHAIC
Projectile point
Scale 1:1.0

CULTURAL SEQUENCES, 4000–1000 BC

Author: J.V. Wright

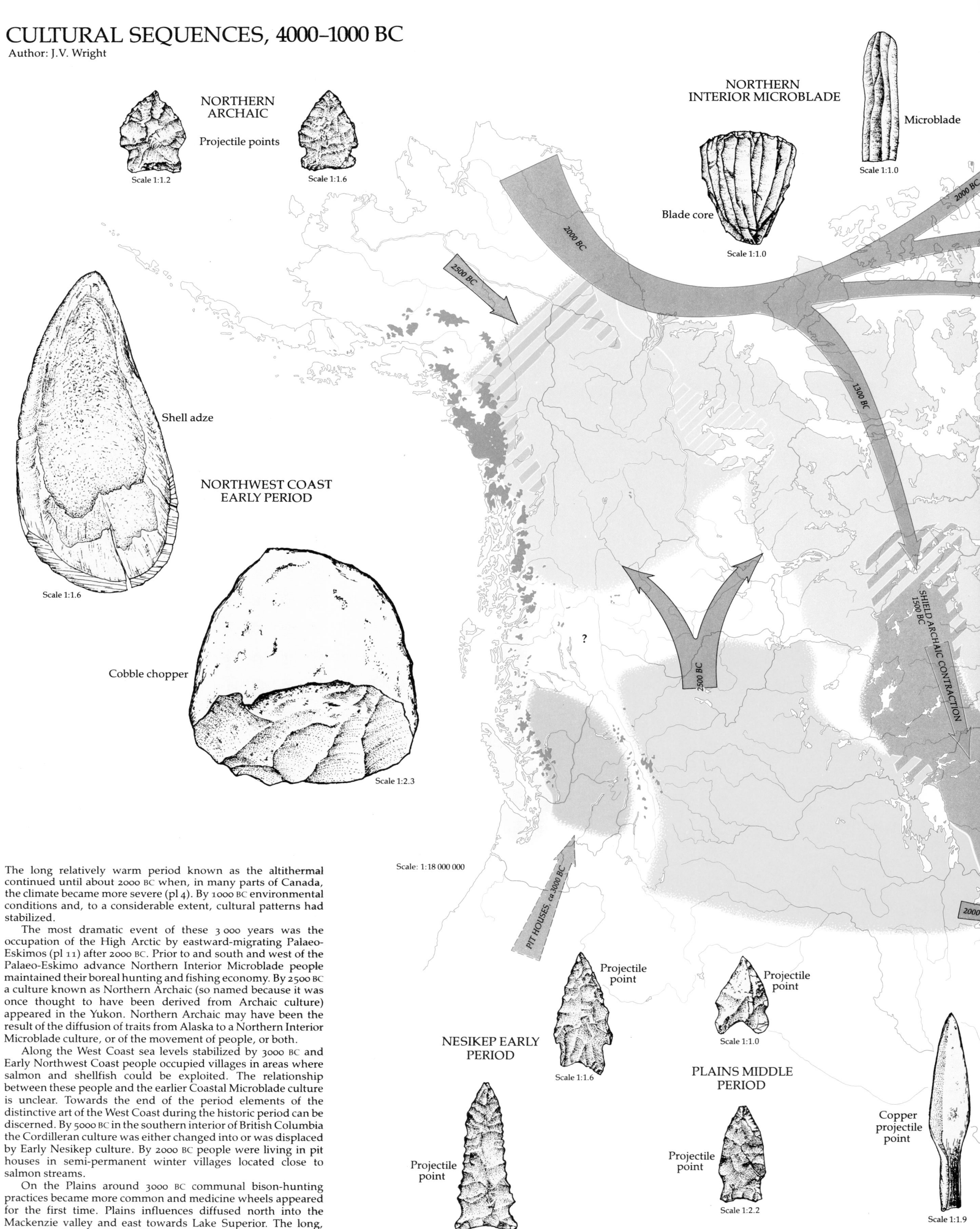

NORTHERN ARCHAIC
Projectile points
Scale 1:1.2
Scale 1:1.6
NORTHERN INTERIOR MICROBLADE
Microblade
Scale 1:1.0
Blade core
Scale 1:1.0
2000 BC
2000 BC
2500 BC
1300 BC
Shell adze
Scale 1:1.6
NORTHWEST COAST EARLY PERIOD
Cobble chopper
Scale 1:2.3
?
2500 BC
SHIELD ARCHAIC CONTRACTION 1500 BC
Scale: 1:18 000 000
PIT HOUSES, ca 3000 BC
2000
Projectile point
Scale 1:1.6
NESIKEP EARLY PERIOD
Projectile point
Scale 1:1.9
Projectile point
Scale 1:1.0
PLAINS MIDDLE PERIOD
Projectile point
Scale 1:2.2
Copper projectile point
Scale 1:1.9

The long relatively warm period known as the altithermal continued until about 2000 BC when, in many parts of Canada, the climate became more severe (pl 4). By 1000 BC environmental conditions and, to a considerable extent, cultural patterns had stabilized.

The most dramatic event of these 3 000 years was the occupation of the High Arctic by eastward-migrating Palaeo-Eskimos (pl 11) after 2000 BC. Prior to and south and west of the Palaeo-Eskimo advance Northern Interior Microblade people maintained their boreal hunting and fishing economy. By 2500 BC a culture known as Northern Archaic (so named because it was once thought to have been derived from Archaic culture) appeared in the Yukon. Northern Archaic may have been the result of the diffusion of traits from Alaska to a Northern Interior Microblade culture, or of the movement of people, or both.

Along the West Coast sea levels stabilized by 3000 BC and Early Northwest Coast people occupied villages in areas where salmon and shellfish could be exploited. The relationship between these people and the earlier Coastal Microblade culture is unclear. Towards the end of the period elements of the distinctive art of the West Coast during the historic period can be discerned. By 5000 BC in the southern interior of British Columbia the Cordilleran culture was either changed into or was displaced by Early Nesikep culture. By 2000 BC people were living in pit houses in semi-permanent winter villages located close to salmon streams.

On the Plains around 3000 BC communal bison-hunting practices became more common and medicine wheels appeared for the first time. Plains influences diffused north into the Mackenzie valley and east towards Lake Superior. The long, warm-dry altithermal, dated on the Plains between 6000 BC and 2000 BC, may have forced people out of portions of the Plains for considerable periods and may also have been responsible for cycles of erosion and deposition that have obscured the archaeological record.

PLATE 7

ARCHAEOLOGICAL CULTURAL CONSTRUCTS

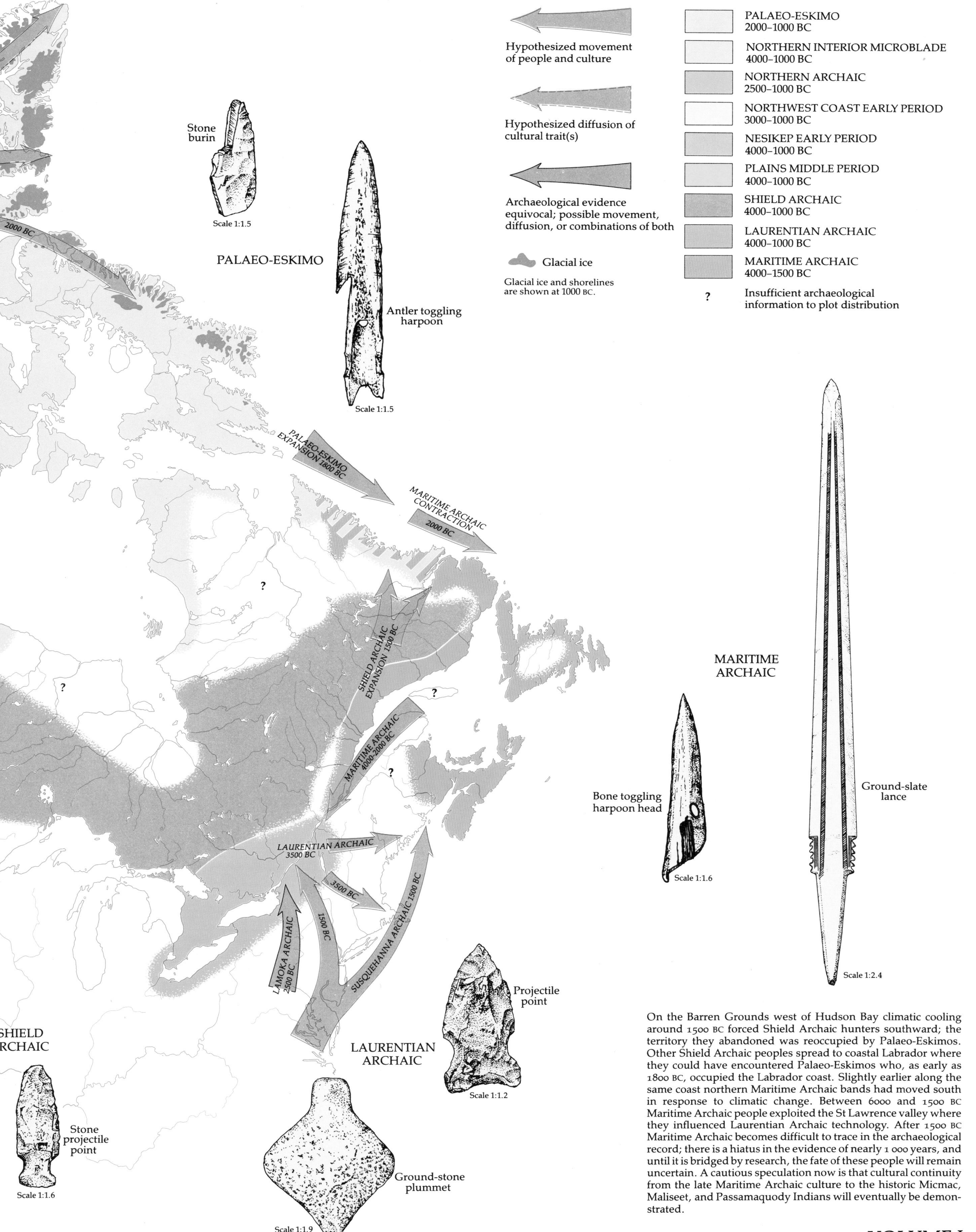

Hypothesized movement of people and culture
Hypothesized diffusion of cultural trait(s)
Archaeological evidence equivocal; possible movement, diffusion, or combinations of both
Glacial ice
Glacial ice and shorelines are shown at 1000 BC.
PALAEO-ESKIMO 2000–1000 BC
NORTHERN INTERIOR MICROBLADE 4000–1000 BC
NORTHERN ARCHAIC 2500–1000 BC
NORTHWEST COAST EARLY PERIOD 3000–1000 BC
NESIKEP EARLY PERIOD 4000–1000 BC
PLAINS MIDDLE PERIOD 4000–1000 BC
SHIELD ARCHAIC 4000–1000 BC
LAURENTIAN ARCHAIC 4000–1000 BC
MARITIME ARCHAIC 4000–1500 BC
? Insufficient archaeological information to plot distribution
Stone burin
Scale 1:1.5
PALAEO-ESKIMO
Antler toggling harpoon
Scale 1:1.5
2000 BC
PALAEO-ESKIMO EXPANSION 1800 BC
MARITIME ARCHAIC CONTRACTION 2000 BC
SHIELD ARCHAIC EXPANSION 1500 BC
MARITIME ARCHAIC 4000-2000 BC
LAURENTIAN ARCHAIC 3500 BC
3500 BC
1500 BC
LAMOKA ARCHAIC 2500 BC
SUSQUEHANNA ARCHAIC 1500 BC
MARITIME ARCHAIC
Bone toggling harpoon head
Scale 1:1.6
Ground-slate lance
Scale 1:2.4
Projectile point
Scale 1:1.2
LAURENTIAN ARCHAIC
Ground-stone plummet
Scale 1:1.9
SHIELD ARCHAIC
Stone projectile point
Scale 1:1.6

On the Barren Grounds west of Hudson Bay climatic cooling around 1500 BC forced Shield Archaic hunters southward; the territory they abandoned was reoccupied by Palaeo-Eskimos. Other Shield Archaic peoples spread to coastal Labrador where they could have encountered Palaeo-Eskimos who, as early as 1800 BC, occupied the Labrador coast. Slightly earlier along the same coast northern Maritime Archaic bands had moved south in response to climatic change. Between 6000 and 1500 BC Maritime Archaic people exploited the St Lawrence valley where they influenced Laurentian Archaic technology. After 1500 BC Maritime Archaic becomes difficult to trace in the archaeological record; there is a hiatus in the evidence of nearly 1 000 years, and until it is bridged by research, the fate of these people will remain uncertain. A cautious speculation now is that cultural continuity from the late Maritime Archaic culture to the historic Micmac, Maliseet, and Passamaquody Indians will eventually be demonstrated.

CULTURAL SEQUENCES, 1000 BC–AD 500

Author: J.V. Wright

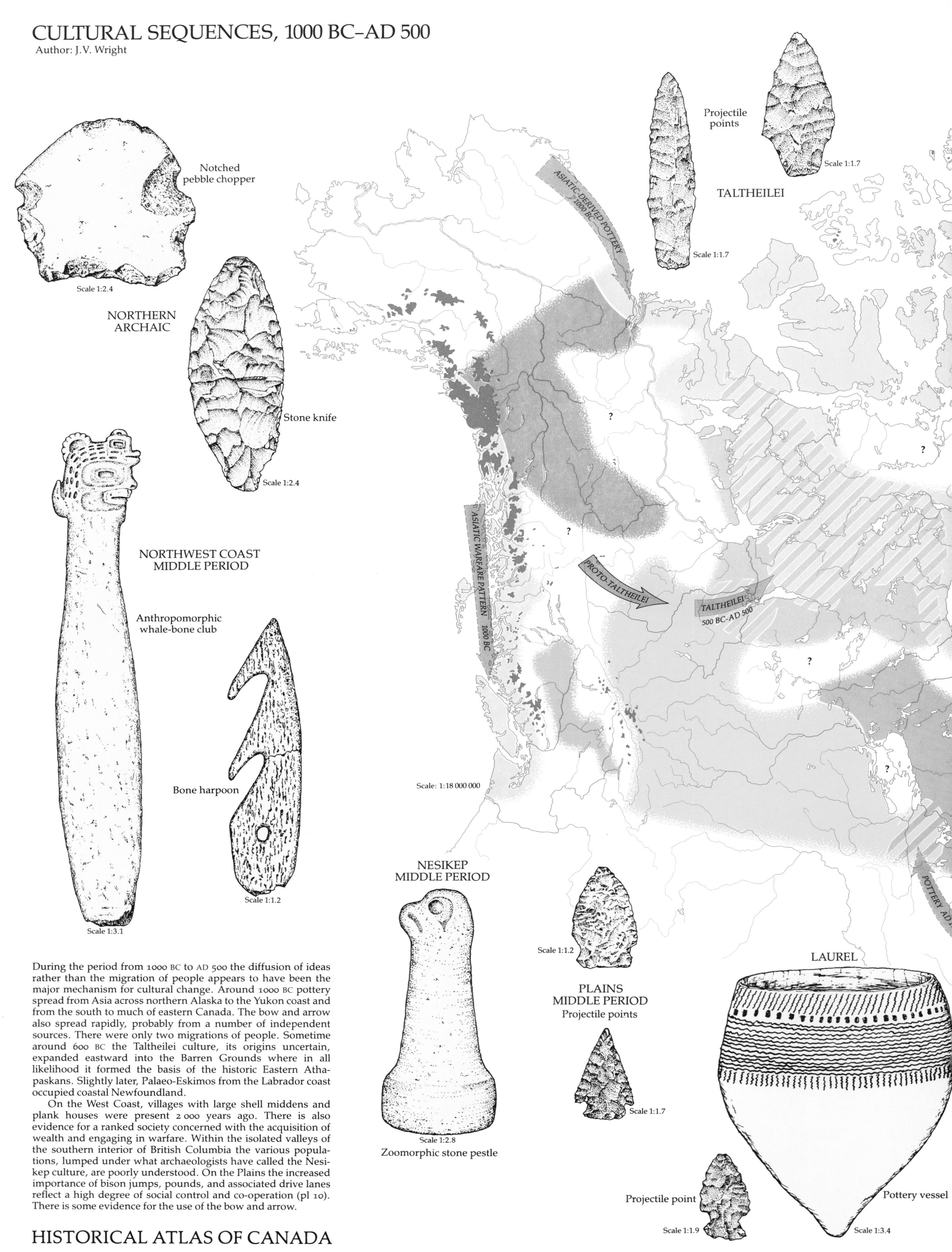
Notched
pebble chopper
Scale 1:2.4
NORTHERN
ARCHAIC
Stone knife
Scale 1:2.4
NORTHWEST COAST
MIDDLE PERIOD
Anthropomorphic
whale-bone club
Bone harpoon
Scale 1:1.2
Scale 1:3.1
Projectile
points
Scale 1:1.7
Scale 1:1.7
TALTHEILEI
ASIATIC-DERIVED POTTERY
1000 BC
ASIATIC WARFARE PATTERN
1000 BC
PROTO-TALTHEILEI
TALTHEILEI
500 BC–AD 500
POTTERY AD
?
Scale: 1:18 000 000
NESIKEP
MIDDLE PERIOD
Scale 1:2.8
Zoomorphic stone pestle
Scale 1:1.2
PLAINS
MIDDLE PERIOD
Projectile points
Scale 1:1.7
LAUREL
Projectile point
Scale 1:1.9
Pottery vessel
Scale 1:3.4

During the period from 1000 BC to AD 500 the diffusion of ideas rather than the migration of people appears to have been the major mechanism for cultural change. Around 1000 BC pottery spread from Asia across northern Alaska to the Yukon coast and from the south to much of eastern Canada. The bow and arrow also spread rapidly, probably from a number of independent sources. There were only two migrations of people. Sometime around 600 BC the Taltheilei culture, its origins uncertain, expanded eastward into the Barren Grounds where in all likelihood it formed the basis of the historic Eastern Athapaskans. Slightly later, Palaeo-Eskimos from the Labrador coast occupied coastal Newfoundland.

On the West Coast, villages with large shell middens and plank houses were present 2 000 years ago. There is also evidence for a ranked society concerned with the acquisition of wealth and engaging in warfare. Within the isolated valleys of the southern interior of British Columbia the various populations, lumped under what archaeologists have called the Nesikep culture, are poorly understood. On the Plains the increased importance of bison jumps, pounds, and associated drive lanes reflect a high degree of social control and co-operation (pl 10). There is some evidence for the use of the bow and arrow.

ARCHAEOLOGICAL CULTURAL CONSTRUCTS

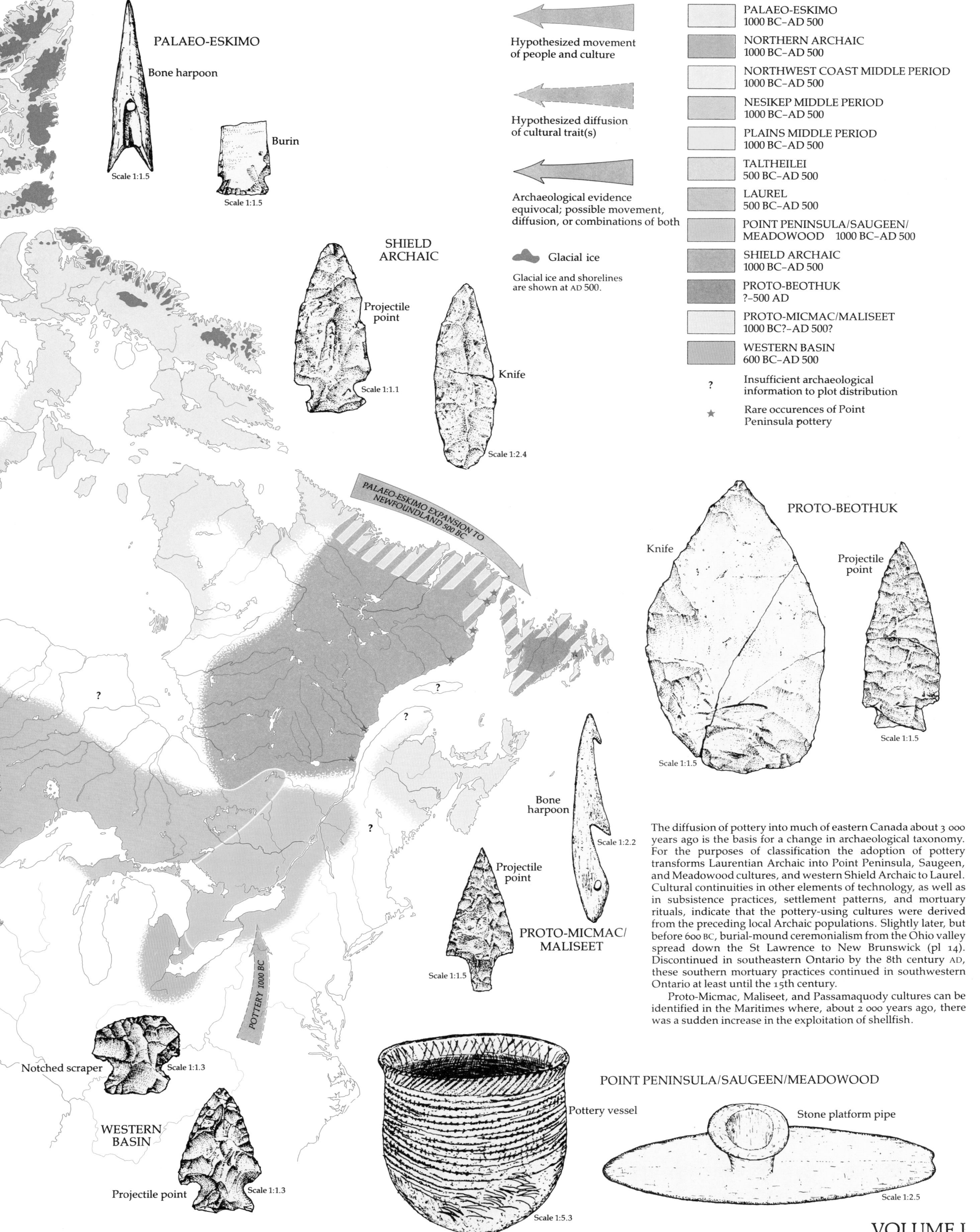

PALAEO-ESKIMO
1000 BC–AD 500
NORTHERN ARCHAIC
1000 BC–AD 500
NORTHWEST COAST MIDDLE PERIOD
1000 BC–AD 500
NESIKEP MIDDLE PERIOD
1000 BC–AD 500
PLAINS MIDDLE PERIOD
1000 BC–AD 500
TALTHEILEI
500 BC–AD 500
LAUREL
500 BC–AD 500
POINT PENINSULA/SAUGEEN/MEADOWOOD 1000 BC–AD 500
SHIELD ARCHAIC
1000 BC–AD 500
PROTO-BEOTHUK
?–500 AD
PROTO-MICMAC/MALISEET
1000 BC?–AD 500?
WESTERN BASIN
600 BC–AD 500
Hypothesized movement of people and culture
Hypothesized diffusion of cultural trait(s)
Archaeological evidence equivocal; possible movement, diffusion, or combinations of both
Glacial ice
Glacial ice and shorelines are shown at AD 500.
? Insufficient archaeological information to plot distribution
Rare occurences of Point Peninsula pottery
PALAEO-ESKIMO
Bone harpoon
Scale 1:1.5
Burin
Scale 1:1.5
SHIELD ARCHAIC
Projectile point
Scale 1:1.1
Knife
Scale 1:2.4
PALAEO-ESKIMO EXPANSION TO NEWFOUNDLAND 500 BC
PROTO-BEOTHUK
Knife
Scale 1:1.5
Projectile point
Scale 1:1.5
Bone harpoon
Scale 1:2.2
Projectile point
PROTO-MICMAC/MALISEET
Scale 1:1.5
POTTERY 1000 BC
Notched scraper
Scale 1:1.3
WESTERN BASIN
Projectile point
Scale 1:1.3
Pottery vessel
Scale 1:5.3
POINT PENINSULA/SAUGEEN/MEADOWOOD
Stone platform pipe
Scale 1:2.5

The diffusion of pottery into much of eastern Canada about 3 000 years ago is the basis for a change in archaeological taxonomy. For the purposes of classification the adoption of pottery transforms Laurentian Archaic into Point Peninsula, Saugeen, and Meadowood cultures, and western Shield Archaic to Laurel. Cultural continuities in other elements of technology, as well as in subsistence practices, settlement patterns, and mortuary rituals, indicate that the pottery-using cultures were derived from the preceding local Archaic populations. Slightly later, but before 600 BC, burial-mound ceremonialism from the Ohio valley spread down the St Lawrence to New Brunswick (pl 14). Discontinued in southeastern Ontario by the 8th century AD, these southern mortuary practices continued in southwestern Ontario at least until the 15th century.

Proto-Micmac, Maliseet, and Passamaquody cultures can be identified in the Maritimes where, about 2 000 years ago, there was a sudden increase in the exploitation of shellfish.

CULTURAL SEQUENCES, AD 500–EUROPEAN CONTACT

Author: J.V. Wright

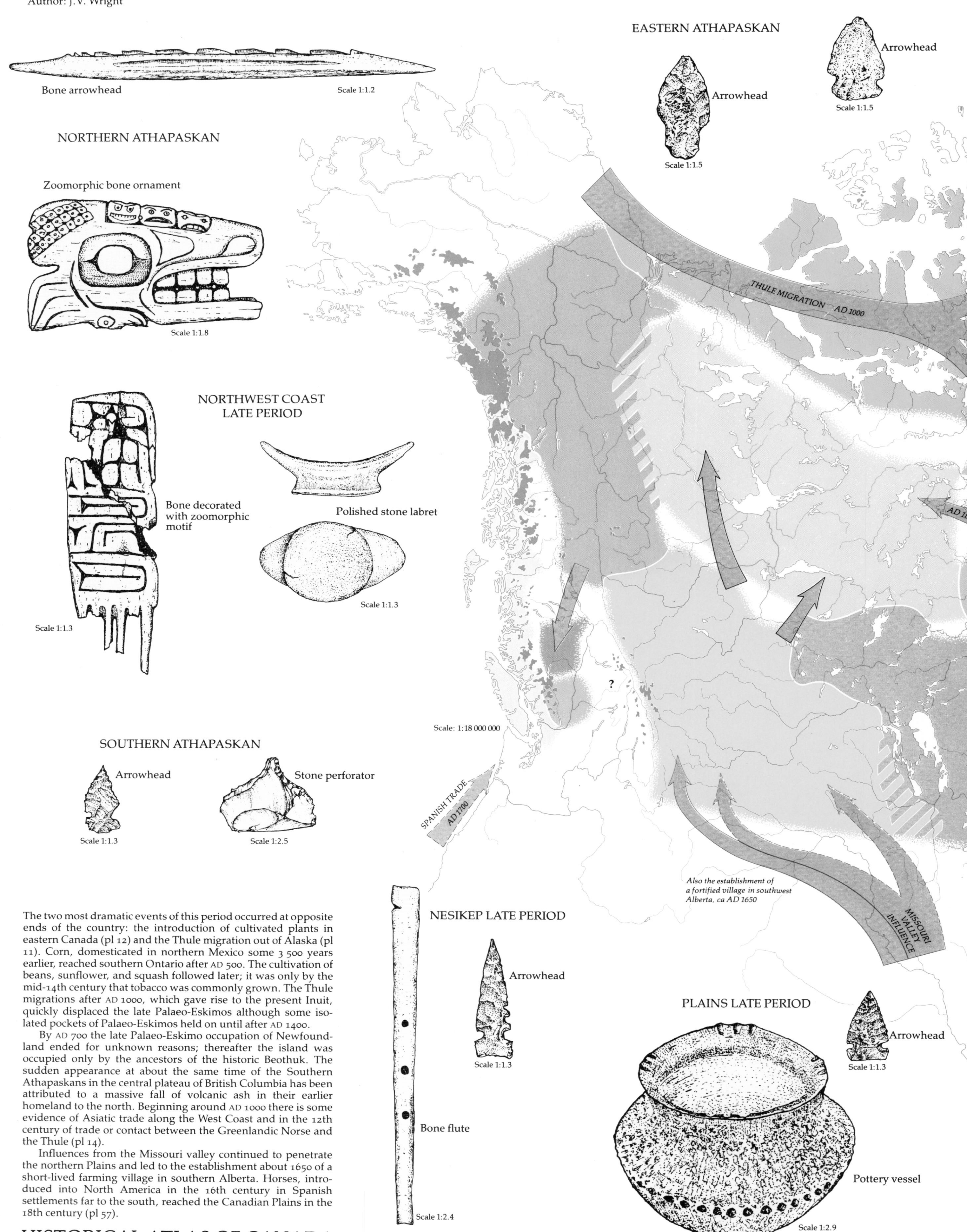

Bone arrowhead
Scale 1:1.2
NORTHERN ATHAPASKAN
Zoomorphic bone ornament
Scale 1:1.8
NORTHWEST COAST
LATE PERIOD
Bone decorated with zoomorphic motif
Scale 1:1.3
Polished stone labret
Scale 1:1.3
SOUTHERN ATHAPASKAN
Arrowhead
Scale 1:1.3
Stone perforator
Scale 1:2.5
EASTERN ATHAPASKAN
Arrowhead
Scale 1:1.5
Arrowhead
Scale 1:1.5
THULE MIGRATION AD 1000
AD 1800
Scale: 1:18 000 000
?
SPANISH TRADE
AD 1700
Also the establishment of a fortified village in southwest Alberta, ca AD 1650
MISSOURI VALLEY INFLUENCE
NESIKEP LATE PERIOD
Arrowhead
Scale 1:1.3
Bone flute
Scale 1:2.4
PLAINS LATE PERIOD
Arrowhead
Scale 1:1.3
Pottery vessel
Scale 1:2.9

The two most dramatic events of this period occurred at opposite ends of the country: the introduction of cultivated plants in eastern Canada (pl 12) and the Thule migration out of Alaska (pl 11). Corn, domesticated in northern Mexico some 3 500 years earlier, reached southern Ontario after AD 500. The cultivation of beans, sunflower, and squash followed later; it was only by the mid-14th century that tobacco was commonly grown. The Thule migrations after AD 1000, which gave rise to the present Inuit, quickly displaced the late Palaeo-Eskimos although some isolated pockets of Palaeo-Eskimos held on until after AD 1400.

By AD 700 the late Palaeo-Eskimo occupation of Newfoundland ended for unknown reasons; thereafter the island was occupied only by the ancestors of the historic Beothuk. The sudden appearance at about the same time of the Southern Athapaskans in the central plateau of British Columbia has been attributed to a massive fall of volcanic ash in their earlier homeland to the north. Beginning around AD 1000 there is some evidence of Asiatic trade along the West Coast and in the 12th century of trade or contact between the Greenlandic Norse and the Thule (pl 14).

Influences from the Missouri valley continued to penetrate the northern Plains and led to the establishment about 1650 of a short-lived farming village in southern Alberta. Horses, introduced into North America in the 16th century in Spanish settlements far to the south, reached the Canadian Plains in the 18th century (pl 57).

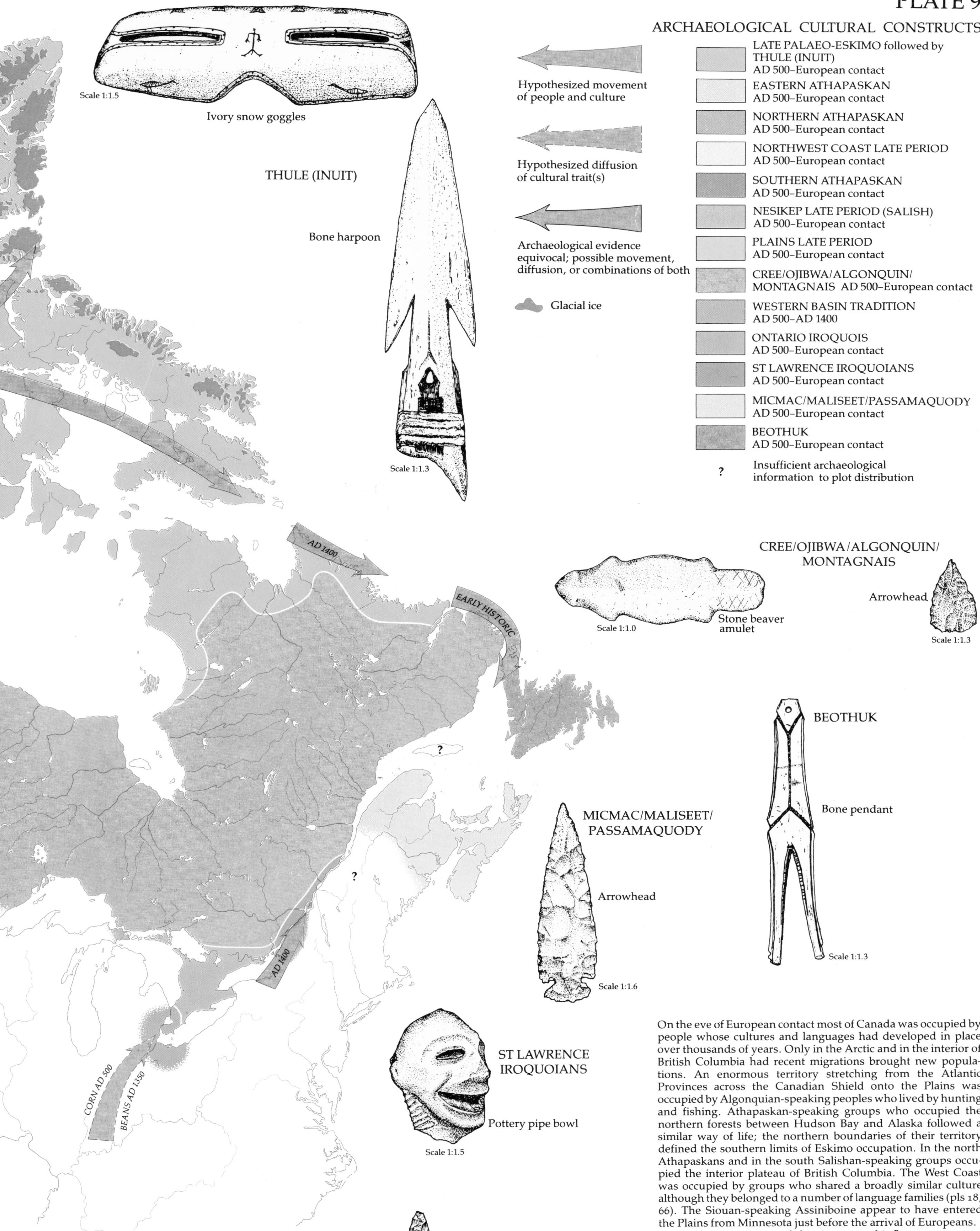
ARCHAEOLOGICAL CULTURAL CONSTRUCTS
LATE PALAEO-ESKIMO followed by THULE (INUIT) AD 500–European contact
EASTERN ATHAPASKAN AD 500–European contact
NORTHERN ATHAPASKAN AD 500–European contact
NORTHWEST COAST LATE PERIOD AD 500–European contact
SOUTHERN ATHAPASKAN AD 500–European contact
NESIKEP LATE PERIOD (SALISH) AD 500–European contact
PLAINS LATE PERIOD AD 500–European contact
CREE/OJIBWA/ALGONQUIN/ MONTAGNAIS AD 500–European contact
WESTERN BASIN TRADITION AD 500–AD 1400
ONTARIO IROQUOIS AD 500–European contact
ST LAWRENCE IROQUOIANS AD 500–European contact
MICMAC/MALISEET/PASSAMAQUODY AD 500–European contact
BEOTHUK AD 500–European contact
? Insufficient archaeological information to plot distribution
Hypothesized movement of people and culture
Hypothesized diffusion of cultural trait(s)
Archaeological evidence equivocal; possible movement, diffusion, or combinations of both
Glacial ice
Scale 1:1.5
Ivory snow goggles
THULE (INUIT)
Bone harpoon
Scale 1:1.3
AD 1400
EARLY HISTORIC
?
?
AD 1400
CORN AD 500
BEANS AD 1350
CREE/OJIBWA/ALGONQUIN/ MONTAGNAIS
Stone beaver amulet
Scale 1:1.0
Arrowhead
Scale 1:1.3
BEOTHUK
Bone pendant
Scale 1:1.3
MICMAC/MALISEET/ PASSAMAQUODY
Arrowhead
Scale 1:1.6
ST LAWRENCE IROQUOIANS
Pottery pipe bowl
Scale 1:1.5
ONTARIO IROQUOIS
Scale 1:1.3
Bone netting needle
Arrowhead
Scale 1:1.3

On the eve of European contact most of Canada was occupied by people whose cultures and languages had developed in place over thousands of years. Only in the Arctic and in the interior of British Columbia had recent migrations brought new populations. An enormous territory stretching from the Atlantic Provinces across the Canadian Shield onto the Plains was occupied by Algonquian-speaking peoples who lived by hunting and fishing. Athapaskan-speaking groups who occupied the northern forests between Hudson Bay and Alaska followed a similar way of life; the northern boundaries of their territory defined the southern limits of Eskimo occupation. In the north Athapaskans and in the south Salishan-speaking groups occupied the interior plateau of British Columbia. The West Coast was occupied by groups who shared a broadly similar culture although they belonged to a number of language families (pls 18, 66). The Siouan-speaking Assiniboine appear to have entered the Plains from Minnesota just before the arrival of Europeans.

For the most part, and despite external influences, ways of life changed only slowly. Among the Iroquoian-speaking peoples of the lower Great Lakes and the St Lawrence valley, however, the increasing reliance on agriculture was stimulating major, rapid cultural change.

BISON HUNTERS OF THE PLAINS

Authors: R.E. Morlan, M.C. Wilson

Although other foods were locally or seasonally important, bison dominated the subsistence economy of the Plains Indians. Bison kills provided fresh meat, a surplus that was dried for winter consumption or trade, and hides for clothing and shelters. Individuals hunted single animals; groups of people drove herds into traps or over cliffs. In bison drives the animals were driven out of grassy gathering basins and between lines of low cairns that rapidly converged on the jump or trap. People hiding by the cairns jumped up as the bison passed to startle the animals and sustain the stampede. Many jumps were associated with corral-like pounds into which the animals tumbled for the kill. Successful drive sites were used repeatedly long before and for some years after European contact. The maps show known locations of bison drives and of campsites associated with them.

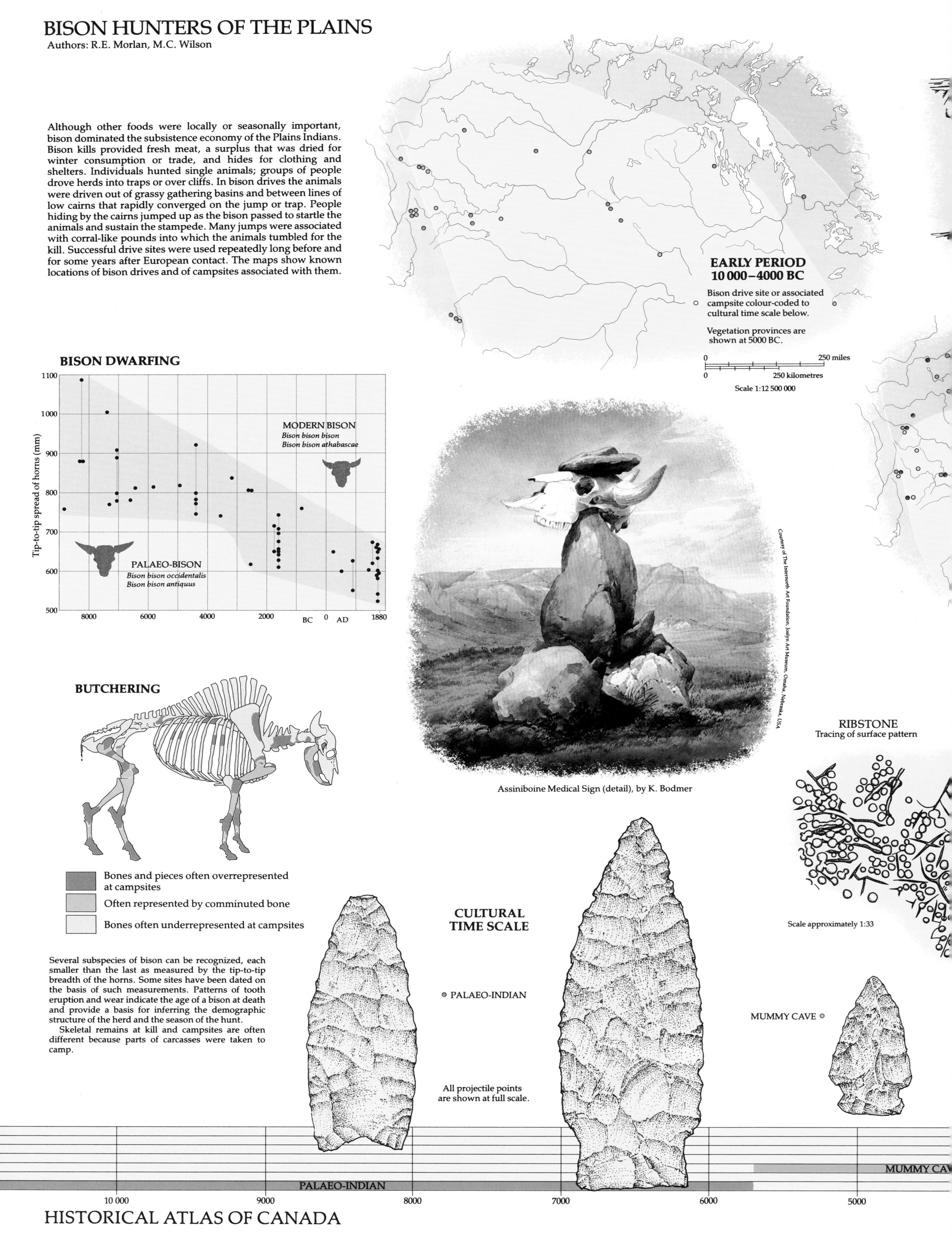
EARLY PERIOD
10 000–4000 BC
Bison drive site or associated campsite colour-coded to cultural time scale below.
Vegetation provinces are shown at 5000 BC.
0
250 miles
0
250 kilometres
Scale 1:12 500 000
BISON DWARFING
Tip-to-tip spread of horns (mm)
1100
1000
900
800
700
600
500
8000
6000
4000
2000
BC
0
AD
1880
MODERN BISON
Bison bison bison
Bison bison athabascae
PALAEO-BISON
Bison bison occidentalis
Bison bison antiquus
BUTCHERING
Bones and pieces often overrepresented at campsites
Often represented by comminuted bone
Bones often underrepresented at campsites
Courtesy of The Internorth Art Foundation, Joslyn Art Museum, Omaha, Nebraska, USA
RIBSTONE
Tracing of surface pattern
Scale approximately 1:33
CULTURAL TIME SCALE
PALAEO-INDIAN
MUMMY CAVE
All projectile points are shown at full scale.
PALAEO-INDIAN
MUMMY CAV
10 000
9000
8000
7000
6000
5000

Assiniboine Medical Sign (detail), by K. Bodmer

Several subspecies of bison can be recognized, each smaller than the last as measured by the tip-to-tip breadth of the horns. Some sites have been dated on the basis of such measurements. Patterns of tooth eruption and wear indicate the age of a bison at death and provide a basis for inferring the demographic structure of the herd and the season of the hunt.

Skeletal remains at kill and campsites are often different because parts of carcasses were taken to camp.

The bison came to be viewed as the provider, a link between creator and humans. A bison skull placed as an altar at the foot of the centre pole in a sun-dance lodge located the animal at the junction between the vertical axis of the creator and the horizontal plane of humankind. Large structures called medicine wheels (pl 15), widespread in the bison-hunting area of the northern Plains, were often located on prominent hill tops for easier communication with the spirits that brought rain, good forage, and large herds of bison. Several 'buffalo stones' or 'iniskim,' small pieces of fossil ammonite that resemble bison, were found during the excavations of a medicine wheel in Alberta. A bison skull placed on a large rock overlooking a valley was designed to invoke the herds. Ribstones, boulders about a metre long ornamented with carvings that suggest the bison, are also found in such settings. Medicine wheels, ribstones, and other objects associated with cosmology of the Indians of the northern Plains vary widely in size, form, and, doubtless, function, but their links with bison are strengthened as studies progress.

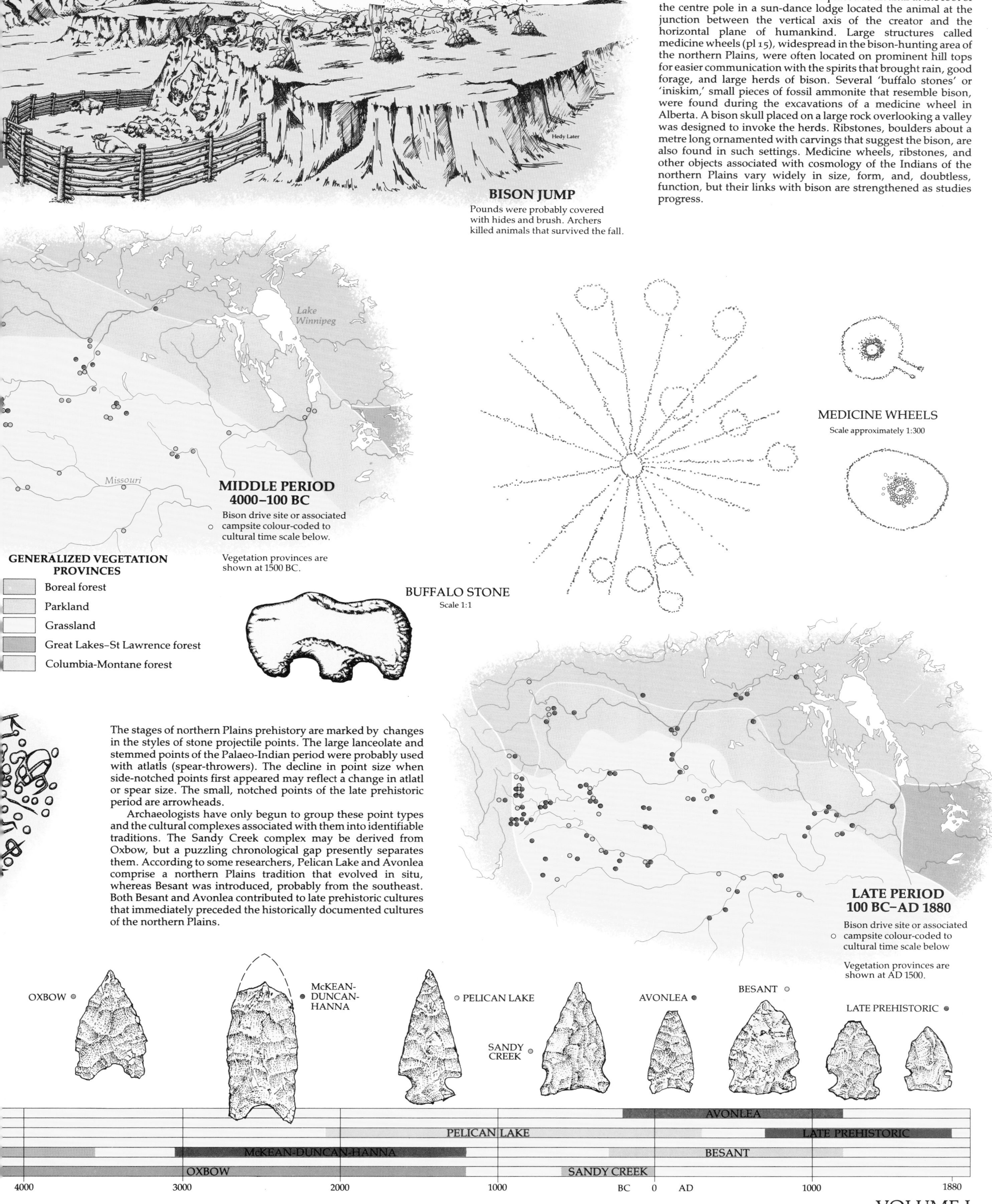
Hedy Later
BISON JUMP
Pounds were probably covered with hides and brush. Archers killed animals that survived the fall.
Lake Winnipeg
Missouri
MIDDLE PERIOD
4000–100 BC
Bison drive site or associated campsite colour-coded to cultural time scale below.
Vegetation provinces are shown at 1500 BC.
GENERALIZED VEGETATION PROVINCES
Boreal forest
Parkland
Grassland
Great Lakes–St Lawrence forest
Columbia-Montane forest
MEDICINE WHEELS
Scale approximately 1:300
BUFFALO STONE
Scale 1:1
LATE PERIOD
100 BC–AD 1880
Bison drive site or associated campsite colour-coded to cultural time scale below
Vegetation provinces are shown at AD 1500.
OXBOW
McKEAN-DUNCAN-HANNA
PELICAN LAKE
SANDY CREEK
AVONLEA
BESANT
LATE PREHISTORIC
AVONLEA
PELICAN LAKE
LATE PREHISTORIC
McKEAN-DUNCAN-HANNA
BESANT
OXBOW
SANDY CREEK
4000
3000
2000
1000
BC 0 AD
1000
1880

The stages of northern Plains prehistory are marked by changes in the styles of stone projectile points. The large lanceolate and stemmed points of the Palaeo-Indian period were probably used with atlatls (spear-throwers). The decline in point size when side-notched points first appeared may reflect a change in atlatl or spear size. The small, notched points of the late prehistoric period are arrowheads.

Archaeologists have only begun to group these point types and the cultural complexes associated with them into identifiable traditions. The Sandy Creek complex may be derived from Oxbow, but a puzzling chronological gap presently separates them. According to some researchers, Pelican Lake and Avonlea comprise a northern Plains tradition that evolved in situ, whereas Besant was introduced, probably from the southeast. Both Besant and Avonlea contributed to late prehistoric cultures that immediately preceded the historically documented cultures of the northern Plains.

PEOPLING THE ARCTIC

Author: Robert McGhee

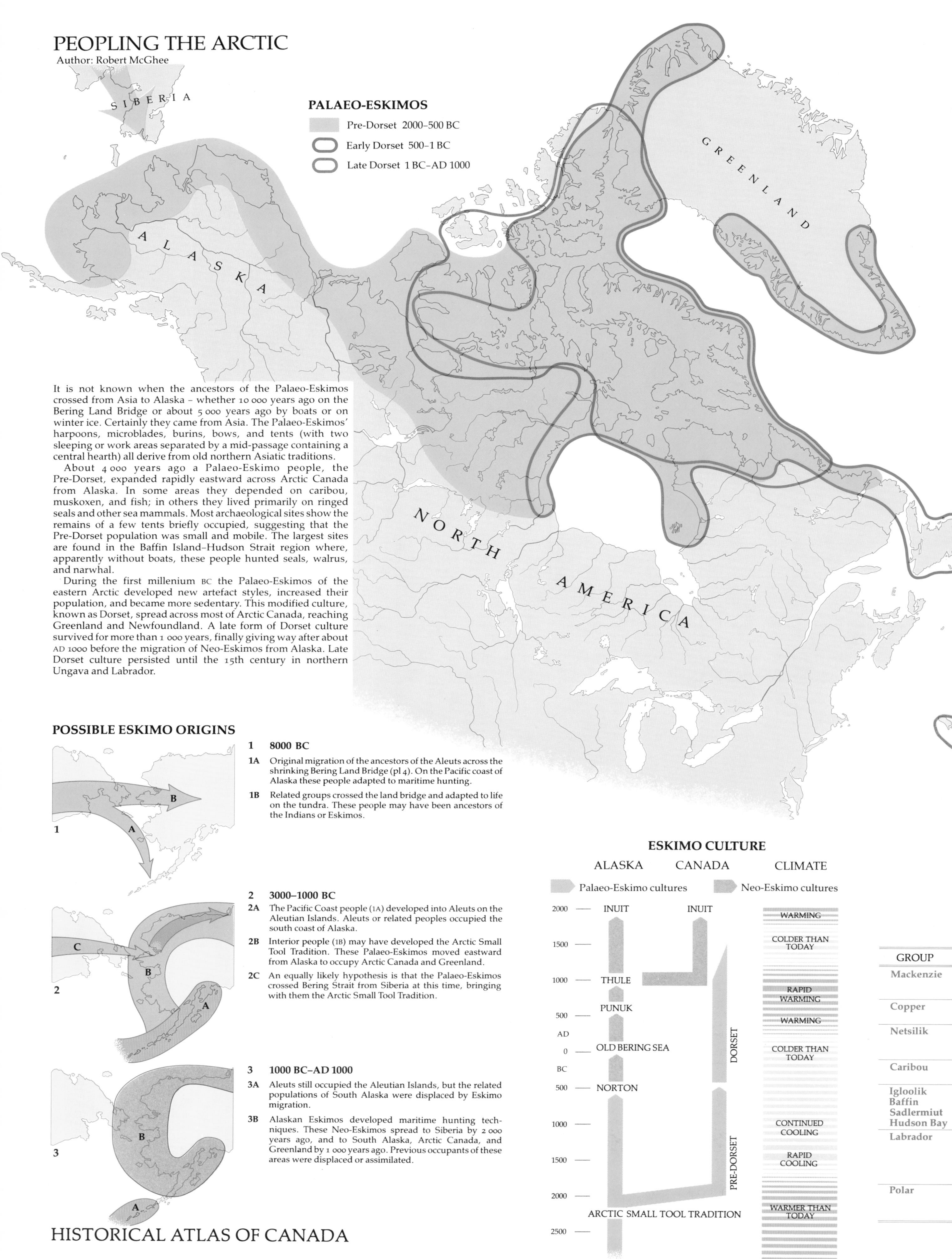

PALAEO-ESKIMOS
Pre-Dorset 2000–500 BC
Early Dorset 500–1 BC
Late Dorset 1 BC–AD 1000
SIBERIA
ALASKA
GREENLAND
NORTH AMERICA
A
B
C
1
2
3
ESKIMO CULTURE
ALASKA
CANADA
CLIMATE
Palaeo-Eskimo cultures
Neo-Eskimo cultures
2000
1500
1000
500
AD
0
BC
500
1000
1500
2000
2500
INUIT
INUIT
THULE
PUNUK
OLD BERING SEA
NORTON
ARCTIC SMALL TOOL TRADITION
DORSET
PRE-DORSET
WARMING
COLDER THAN TODAY
RAPID WARMING
WARMING
COLDER THAN TODAY
CONTINUED COOLING
RAPID COOLING
WARMER THAN TODAY
GROUP
Mackenzie
Copper
Netsilik
Caribou
Igloolik
Baffin
Sadlermiut
Hudson Bay
Labrador
Polar

It is not known when the ancestors of the Palaeo-Eskimos crossed from Asia to Alaska – whether 10 000 years ago on the Bering Land Bridge or about 5 000 years ago by boats or on winter ice. Certainly they came from Asia. The Palaeo-Eskimos' harpoons, microblades, burins, bows, and tents (with two sleeping or work areas separated by a mid-passage containing a central hearth) all derive from old northern Asiatic traditions.

About 4 000 years ago a Palaeo-Eskimo people, the Pre-Dorset, expanded rapidly eastward across Arctic Canada from Alaska. In some areas they depended on caribou, muskoxen, and fish; in others they lived primarily on ringed seals and other sea mammals. Most archaeological sites show the remains of a few tents briefly occupied, suggesting that the Pre-Dorset population was small and mobile. The largest sites are found in the Baffin Island–Hudson Strait region where, apparently without boats, these people hunted seals, walrus, and narwhal.

During the first millenium BC the Palaeo-Eskimos of the eastern Arctic developed new artefact styles, increased their population, and became more sedentary. This modified culture, known as Dorset, spread across most of Arctic Canada, reaching Greenland and Newfoundland. A late form of Dorset culture survived for more than 1 000 years, finally giving way after about AD 1000 before the migration of Neo-Eskimos from Alaska. Late Dorset culture persisted until the 15th century in northern Ungava and Labrador.

POSSIBLE ESKIMO ORIGINS

1 8000 BC

1A Original migration of the ancestors of the Aleuts across the shrinking Bering Land Bridge (pl 4). On the Pacific coast of Alaska these people adapted to maritime hunting.

1B Related groups crossed the land bridge and adapted to life on the tundra. These people may have been ancestors of the Indians or Eskimos.

2 3000–1000 BC

2A The Pacific Coast people (1A) developed into Aleuts on the Aleutian Islands. Aleuts or related peoples occupied the south coast of Alaska.

2B Interior people (1B) may have developed the Arctic Small Tool Tradition. These Palaeo-Eskimos moved eastward from Alaska to occupy Arctic Canada and Greenland.

2C An equally likely hypothesis is that the Palaeo-Eskimos crossed Bering Strait from Siberia at this time, bringing with them the Arctic Small Tool Tradition.

3 1000 BC–AD 1000

3A Aleuts still occupied the Aleutian Islands, but the related populations of South Alaska were displaced by Eskimo migration.

3B Alaskan Eskimos developed maritime hunting techniques. These Neo-Eskimos spread to Siberia by 2 000 years ago, and to South Alaska, Arctic Canada, and Greenland by 1 000 years ago. Previous occupants of these areas were displaced or assimilated.

HISTORICAL ATLAS OF CANADA

LINGUISTIC RELATIONSHIPS

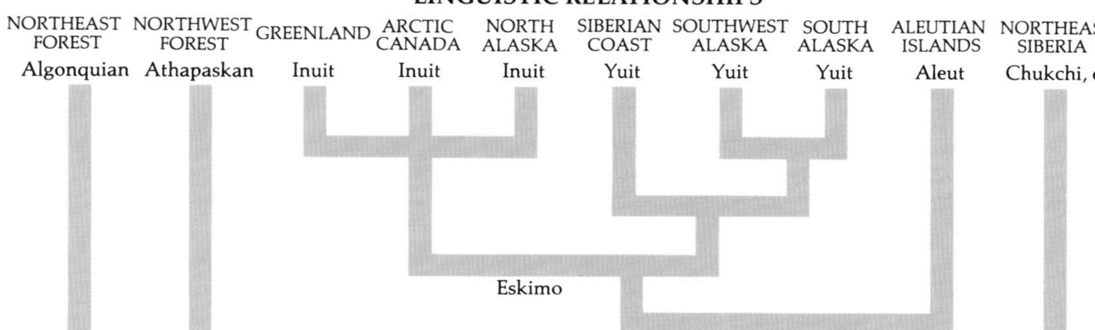
NORTHEAST FOREST
Algonquian
NORTHWEST FOREST
Athapaskan
GREENLAND
Inuit
ARCTIC CANADA
Inuit
NORTH ALASKA
Inuit
SIBERIAN COAST
Yuit
SOUTHWEST ALASKA
Yuit
SOUTH ALASKA
Yuit
ALEUTIAN ISLANDS
Aleut
NORTHEAST SIBERIA
Chukchi, etc.
Eskimo
Eskaleut
?
?

The Eskimos are more closely related, racially and linguistically, to peoples of northeastern Siberia than to North American Indians. These relationships provide further evidence that their ancestors arrived in North America relatively recently.

ETHNIC RELATIONSHIPS

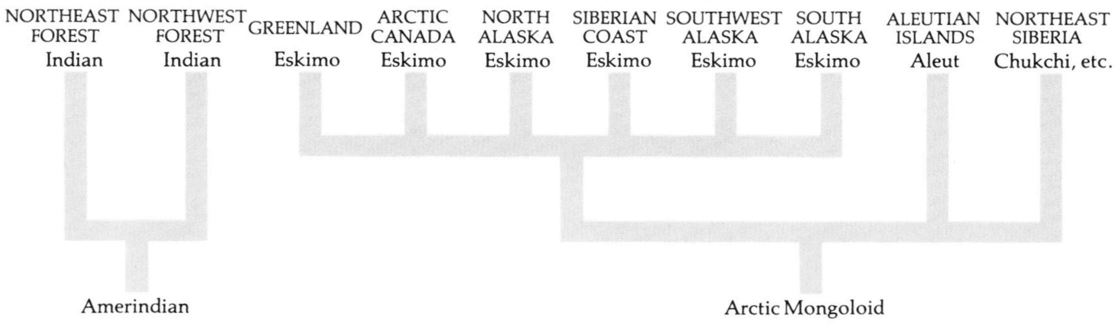

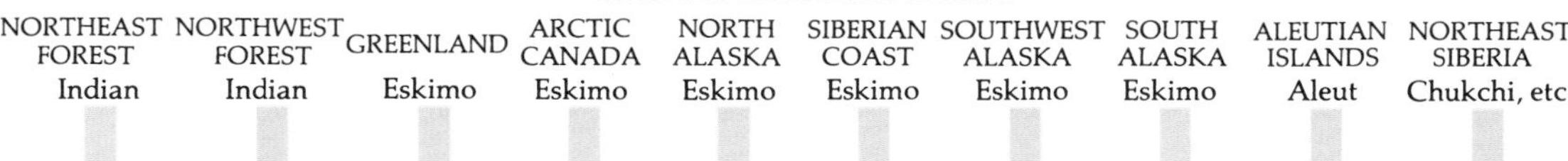
NORTHEAST FOREST
Indian
NORTHWEST FOREST
Indian
GREENLAND
Eskimo
ARCTIC CANADA
Eskimo
NORTH ALASKA
Eskimo
SIBERIAN COAST
Eskimo
SOUTHWEST ALASKA
Eskimo
SOUTH ALASKA
Eskimo
ALEUTIAN ISLANDS
Aleut
NORTHEAST SIBERIA
Chukchi, etc.

Amerindian

Arctic Mongoloid

During the first millennium BC Eskimos of western Alaska developed the tools, weapons, hunting techniques, and housing styles that culminated in the Old Bering Sea and Punuk Traditions of the Bering Strait region. These Neo-Eskimos used harpoons attached to floats to hunt from kayaks and umiaks and lived in permanent villages comprising semisubterranean wooden houses.

By about AD 1000 the Thule people of northern Alaska had adapted this maritime technology to the efficient hunting of bowhead whales. During a period of relatively moderate temperatures they began to follow the whales eastward. With boats, float harpoons, and sinew-backed bows the Thule were more efficient hunters than the Dorset. Dogsleds gave them greater mobility and, able to accumulate more food, they lived in larger villages. They built houses of stone and whalebone. Within a few generations the Thule Eskimos occupied most of Arctic Canada; their Dorset predecessors were killed, driven into untenable areas, or assimilated.

The Thule brought an Alaskan culture to Arctic Canada, and maintained it until climatic deterioration (pl 16) forced them to change. As the pack ice thickened in the central Arctic after about AD 1600 (during the Little Ice Age), permanent villages could not be maintained. In summer many people moved inland in search of caribou and fish; in winter they returned to the coast, where they lived in snow houses, often on the sea ice, and hunted ringed seals. Only in the eastern Arctic and Labrador did an essentially Thule way of life survive until European contact.

Contact brought further changes. Labrador Inuit moved south late in the 16th century to contact fishermen and trade baleen for European goods. Western Hudson Bay Inuit obtained guns from European whalers and moved inland to hunt caribou. The Inuit way of life as first described by explorers and anthropologists was not an ancient adaptation to Arctic Canada but a product of recent changes brought about by a deteriorating climate and by contact with Europeans.

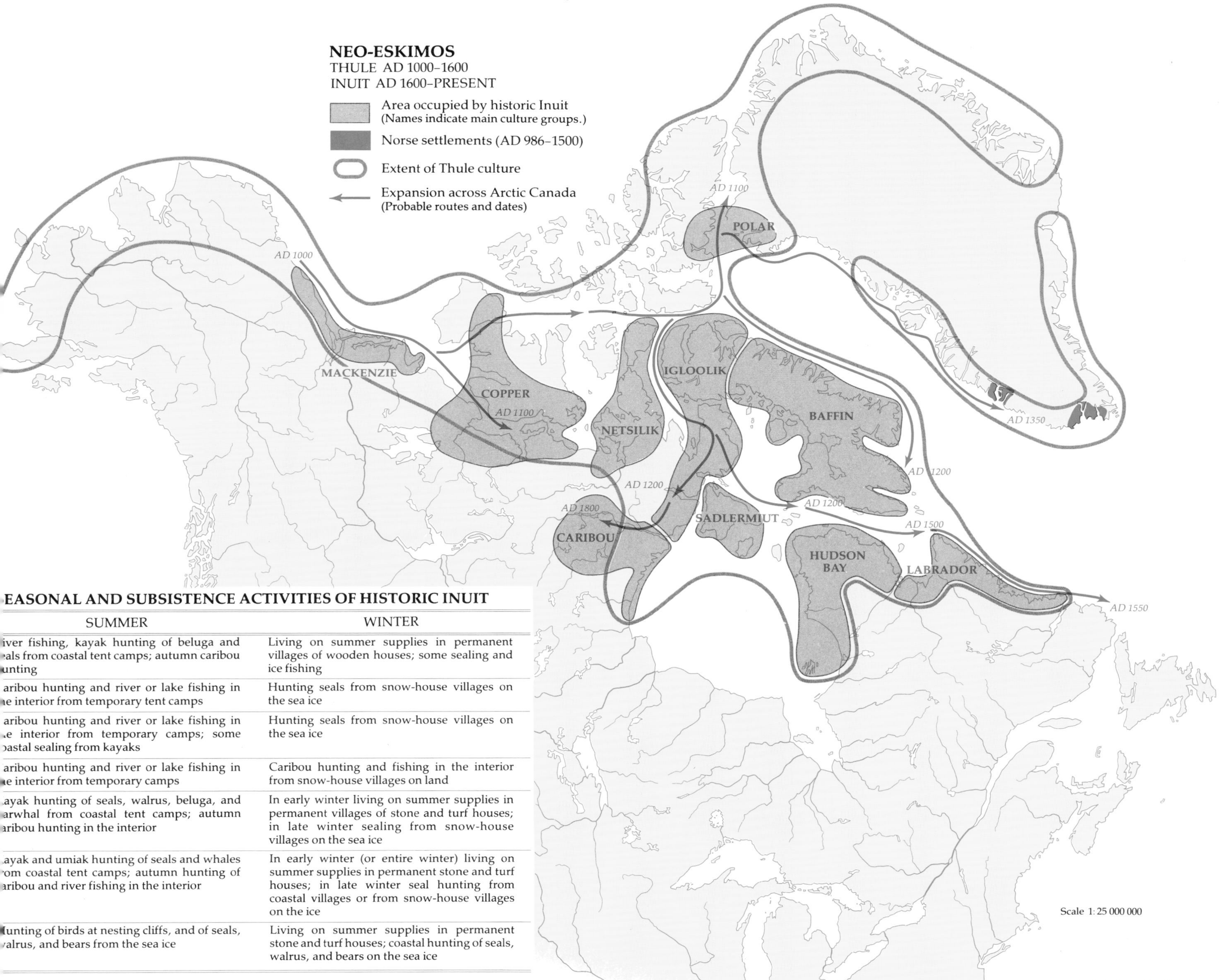

NEO-ESKIMOS

THULE AD 1000–1600
INUIT AD 1600–PRESENT

Area occupied by historic Inuit (Names indicate main culture groups.)
Norse settlements (AD 986–1500)
Extent of Thule culture
Expansion across Arctic Canada (Probable routes and dates)

AD 1000 · MACKENZIE · COPPER · AD 1100 · NETSILIK · IGLOOLIK · AD 1100 · POLAR · BAFFIN · AD 1350 · AD 1200 · AD 1200 · AD 1200 · AD 1800 · CARIBOU · SADLERMIUT · HUDSON BAY · AD 1500 · LABRADOR · AD 1550

Scale 1:25 000 000

EASONAL AND SUBSISTENCE ACTIVITIES OF HISTORIC INUIT

SUMMER	WINTER
iver fishing, kayak hunting of beluga and als from coastal tent camps; autumn caribou unting	Living on summer supplies in permanent villages of wooden houses; some sealing and ice fishing
aribou hunting and river or lake fishing in e interior from temporary tent camps	Hunting seals from snow-house villages on the sea ice
aribou hunting and river or lake fishing in e interior from temporary camps; some astal sealing from kayaks	Hunting seals from snow-house villages on the sea ice
aribou hunting and river or lake fishing in e interior from temporary camps	Caribou hunting and fishing in the interior from snow-house villages on land
ayak hunting of seals, walrus, beluga, and arwhal from coastal tent camps; autumn aribou hunting in the interior	In early winter living on summer supplies in permanent villages of stone and turf houses; in late winter sealing from snow-house villages on the sea ice
ayak and umiak hunting of seals and whales om coastal tent camps; autumn hunting of aribou and river fishing in the interior	In early winter (or entire winter) living on summer supplies in permanent stone and turf houses; in late winter seal hunting from coastal villages or from snow-house villages on the ice
unting of birds at nesting cliffs, and of seals, alrus, and bears from the sea ice	Living on summer supplies in permanent stone and turf houses; coastal hunting of seals, walrus, and bears on the sea ice

IROQUOIAN AGRICULTURAL SETTLEMENT

Authors: J.V. Wright; R. Fecteau (Graph)

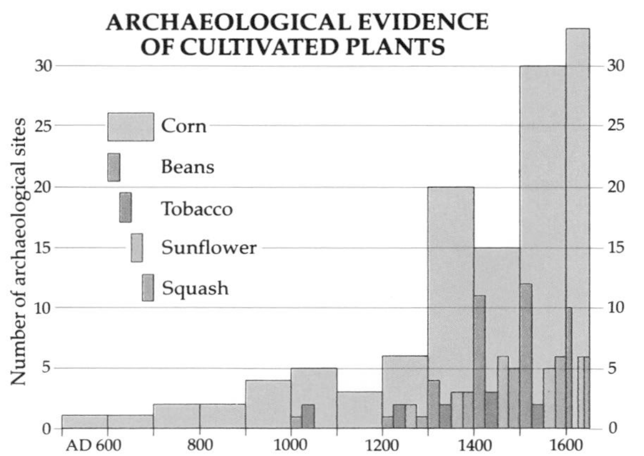

ARCHAEOLOGICAL EVIDENCE
OF CULTIVATED PLANTS
Corn
Beans
Tobacco
Sunflower
Squash
Number of archaeological sites
0
5
10
15
20
25
30
AD 600
800
1000
1200
1400
1600

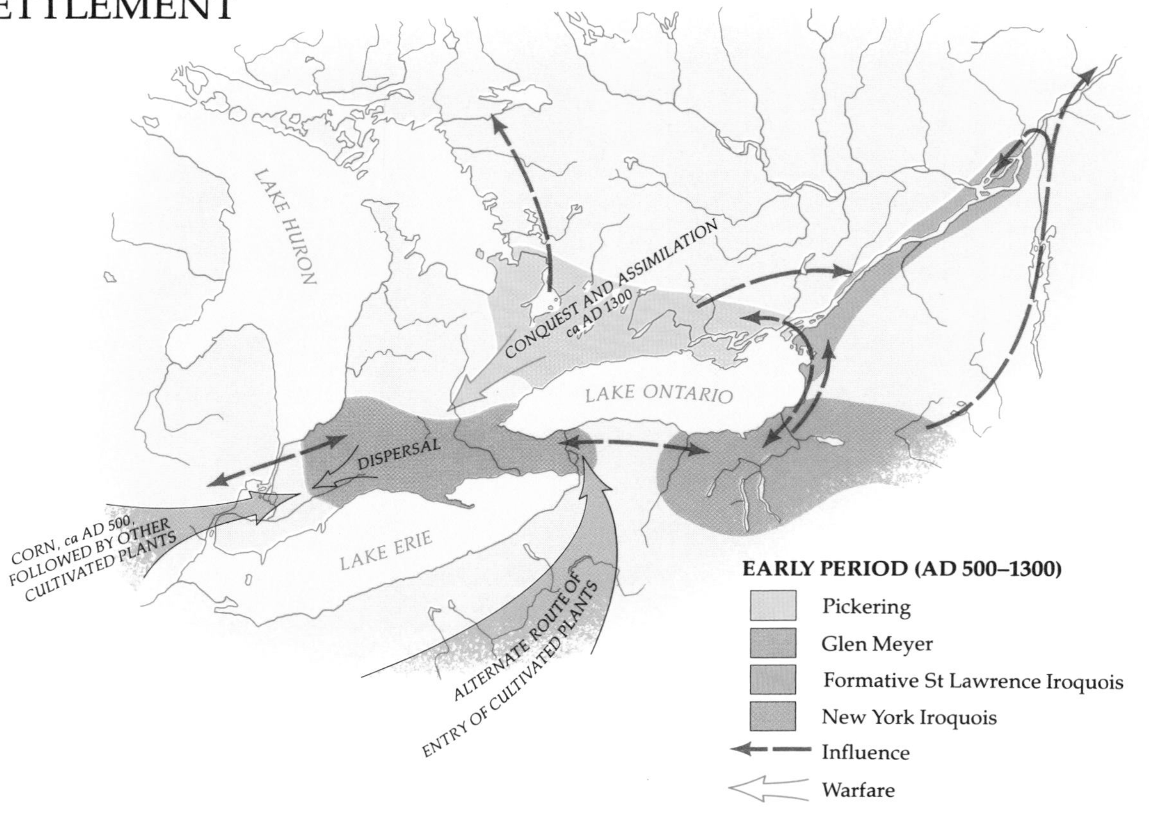

LAKE HURON
CONQUEST AND ASSIMILATION ca AD 1300
LAKE ONTARIO
DISPERSAL
CORN, ca AD 500, FOLLOWED BY OTHER CULTIVATED PLANTS
LAKE ERIE
ALTERNATE ROUTE OF ENTRY OF CULTIVATED PLANTS
EARLY PERIOD (AD 500–1300)
Pickering
Glen Meyer
Formative St Lawrence Iroquois
New York Iroquois
Influence
Warfare

Around AD 500 the people of southern Ontario adopted corn agriculture from their southern neighbours. The addition of cultivated crops to an earlier hunting and gathering economy resulted in a major population increase, changed settlement patterns, and probably modified social organization and beliefs. This plate emphasizes the changing pattern of settlement in southern Ontario after the introduction of agriculture.

The graph (above) suggests when each new agricultural species was introduced and indicates the growing importance of cultivated plants on Iroquoian sites in southern Ontario. Generally only plant materials that have been charred survive in archaeological sites. Because burning was accidental, and because some species carbonize better than others, there is little doubt that our quantitative and qualitative view of the relative importance and even of the presence of certain species is very imperfect.

MIDDLE PERIOD (AD 1300–1400)

The conquest (ca AD 1300) of the Glen Meyer people by the Pickering created a relatively homogeneous culture in Ontario, known as Uren-Middleport, that expanded into New York and influenced the St Lawrence Iroquois. Villages increased in number and size as the reliance on farming deepened and the population grew. In the largest 14th-century villages, more than two ha in size, there were more than 1 000 people.

The simplified plan (right) shows a 0.8 ha village of the mid-14th century. Double palisades were pinched together at a southern entrance which lined up with a house outside the defences. The western entrance led to a unique enclosure that probably was intended to prevent visitors from observing the village's internal defences. Inside the village, walls connected houses and interior palisades to create a series of defendable cul-de-sacs. Near the centre of the village a temporary house, perhaps for builders of the village, was torn down to make room for two permanent longhouses.

The longhouse floor plan (far right) is from this same village. Lines of posts from the north end of the house connect with the interior stockade to create a cul-de-sac between the stockade and the house wall. The other end of the house was torn down and extended. End cubicles in the enlarged house were used for the storage of wood and other items. The living area of the house comprised approximately 184 m² (1 980 ft²). Each of the five hearths was shared by two families.

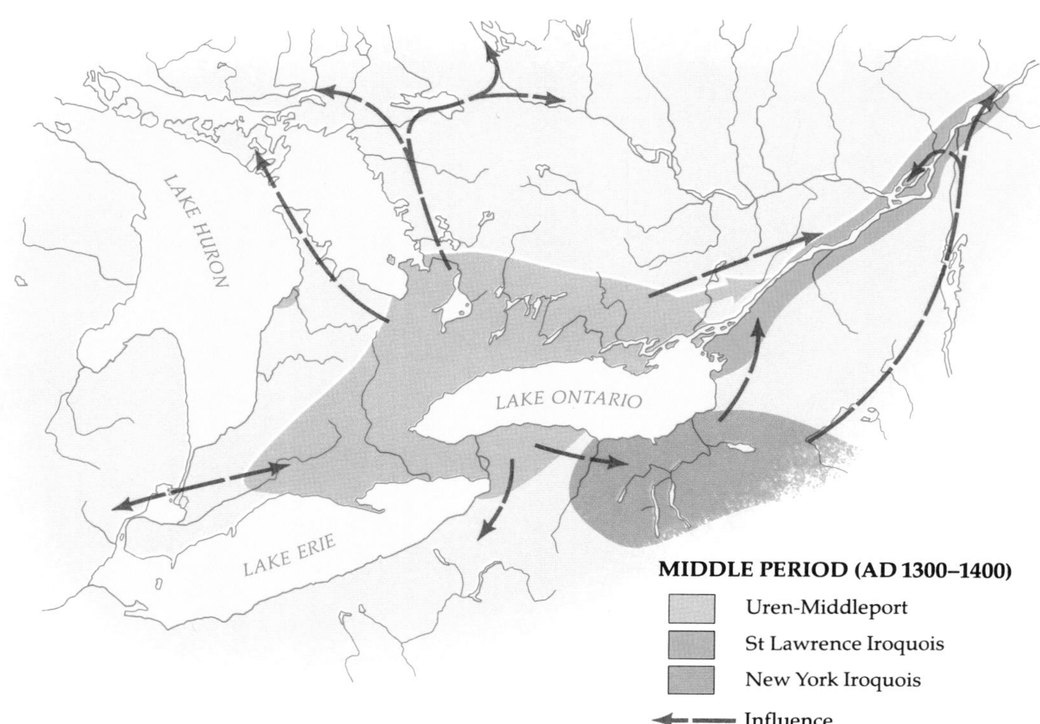

LAKE HURON
LAKE ONTARIO
LAKE ERIE
MIDDLE PERIOD (AD 1300–1400)
Uren-Middleport
St Lawrence Iroquois
New York Iroquois
Influence

LATE PERIOD (AD 1400–EUROPEAN CONTACT)

Around the beginning of the 15th century the St Lawrence Iroquois expanded downriver as far as the vicinity of Québec City where Jacques Cartier encountered them in 1535 (pl 33). By this time the St Lawrence Iroquois between Lake Ontario and Montréal had disappeared; archaeological evidence suggests that they had been conquered and partially absorbed by the Huron north of Lake Ontario. Before the end of the 16th century Huron villages became increasingly concentrated around the southern end of Georgian Bay. The Neutral shifted eastward to settle around the western end of Lake Ontario. Both movements were probably intended to create defensive buffer zones, one between the Huron and the League of Five Nations in New York State, and the other between the Neutral and the Fire Nation in the Michigan peninsula.

Villages continued to increase in size and complexity until the largest were more than 4 ha in size. Some houses were more than 90 m long. Calculations based on totally excavated villages suggest that some 600 people occupied each village hectare. When Champlain reached Huronia in 1615, there may have been as many as 25 Huron villages averaging some 2 ha in size; his estimate that there were 30 000 Hurons is archaeologically feasible.

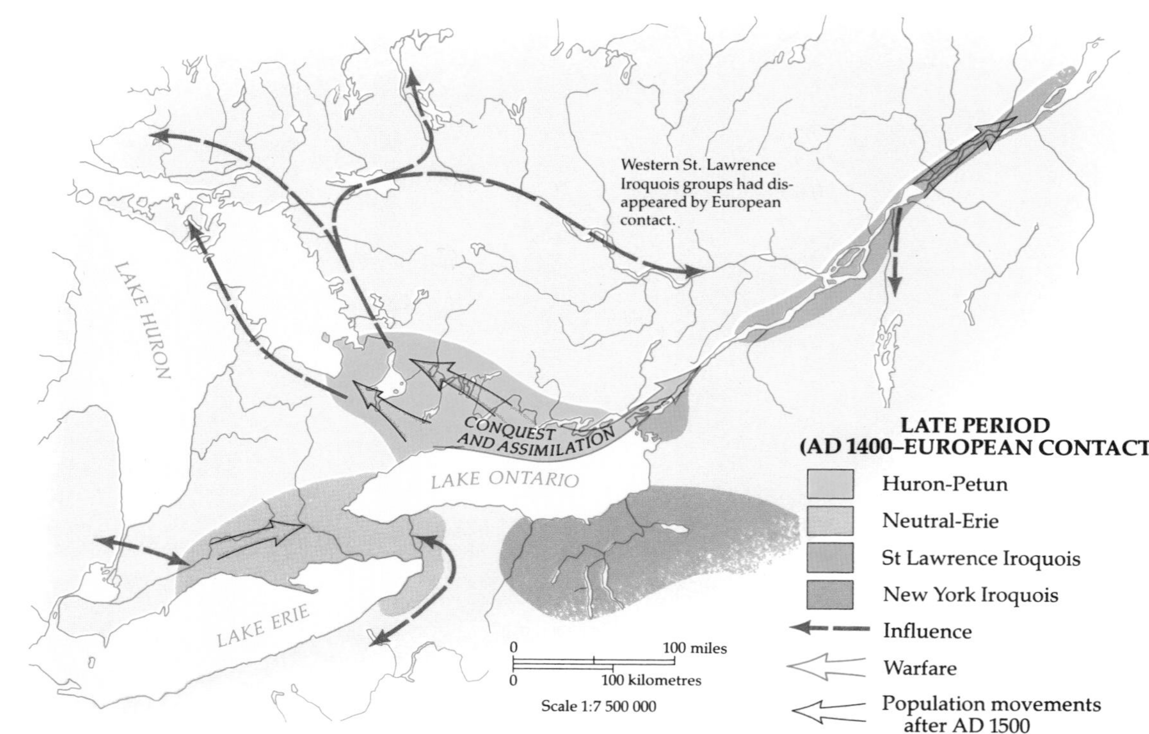

Western St. Lawrence Iroquois groups had disappeared by European contact.
LAKE HURON
CONQUEST AND ASSIMILATION
LAKE ONTARIO
LAKE ERIE
0
100 miles
0
100 kilometres
Scale 1:7 500 000
LATE PERIOD (AD 1400–EUROPEAN CONTACT)
Huron-Petun
Neutral-Erie
St Lawrence Iroquois
New York Iroquois
Influence
Warfare
Population movements after AD 1500

EARLY PERIOD (AD 500–1300)

The introduction of corn ca AD 500 was followed by beans, squash, sunflower, and tobacco. Three farming populations – Glen Meyer, Pickering, and Formative St Lawrence Iroquois – developed out of earlier non-agricultural cultures. There is evidence that about AD 1300 the Pickering people conquered and dispersed their Glen Meyer neighbours.

By AD 800 small palisaded villages up to one ha (hectare) in size were being constructed. The simplified plan (right) shows a Pickering village, built about AD 800, that probably had eight to nine longhouses and some 250 people. The floor plan (far right) of a longhouse from a Glen Meyer site over 80 km to the southwest shows two central hearths, suggesting occupation by four families. Later, villages and houses of the Glen Meyer and Pickering peoples increased in size and complexity; one 10th-century Glen Meyer village expanded from 0.5 to 1.2 ha in three different stages of construction.

EARLY PERIOD VILLAGE AND LONGHOUSE

VILLAGE

Insufficient excavation to determine house outlines

0 100 feet
0 30 metres

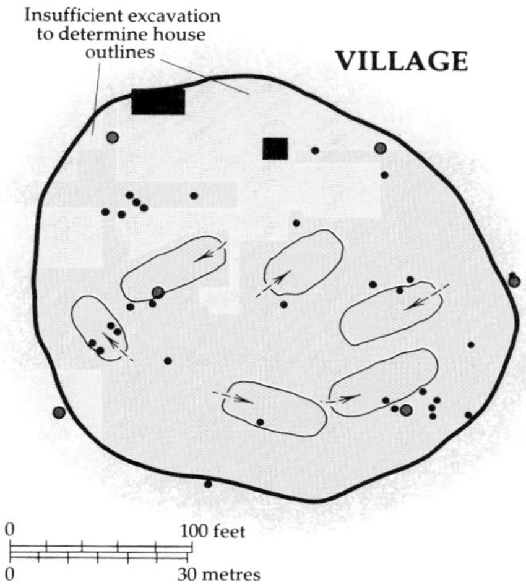

Palisade
Longhouse entrance
Burial site
Pit
Hearth
Modern structure
Posts
Longhouse
Excavated area

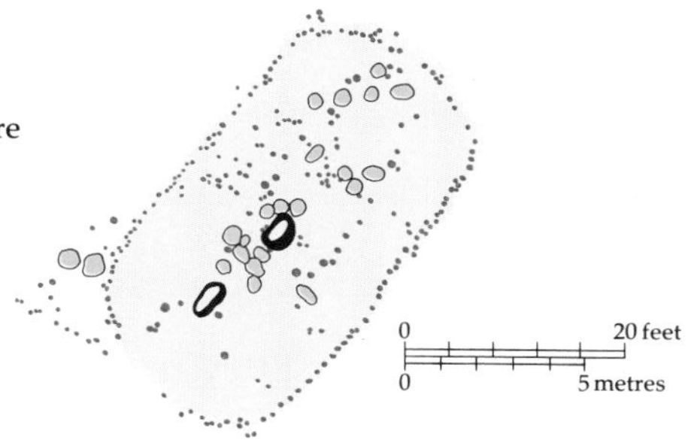

LONGHOUSE

0 20 feet
0 5 metres

MIDDLE PERIOD VILLAGE AND LONGHOUSE

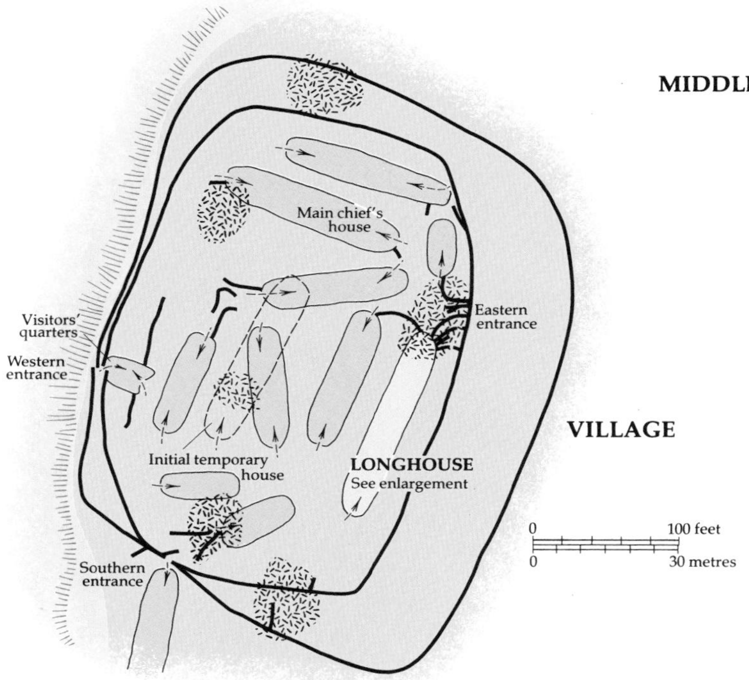

Palisade or interior defensive wall
Longhouse entrance
Pit
Hearth
Garbage dump
Partition
Bunkline
Original end of house
Posts
Longhouse

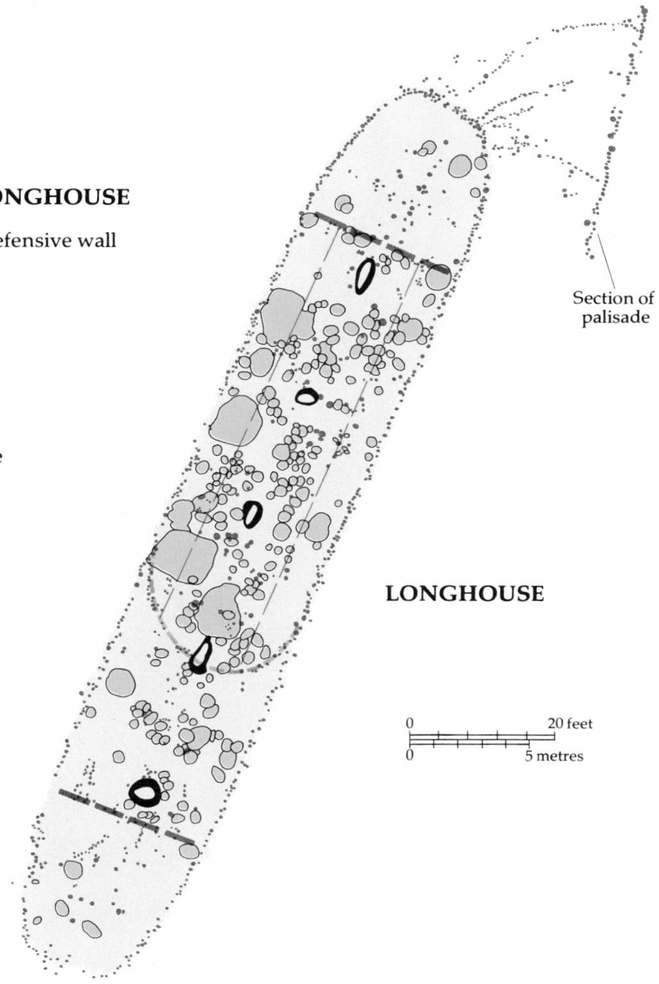

VILLAGE

Main chief's house
Visitors' quarters
Western entrance
Eastern entrance
Initial temporary house
LONGHOUSE See enlargement
Southern entrance

0 100 feet
0 30 metres

LONGHOUSE

Section of palisade

0 20 feet
0 5 metres

VILLAGE GROWTH

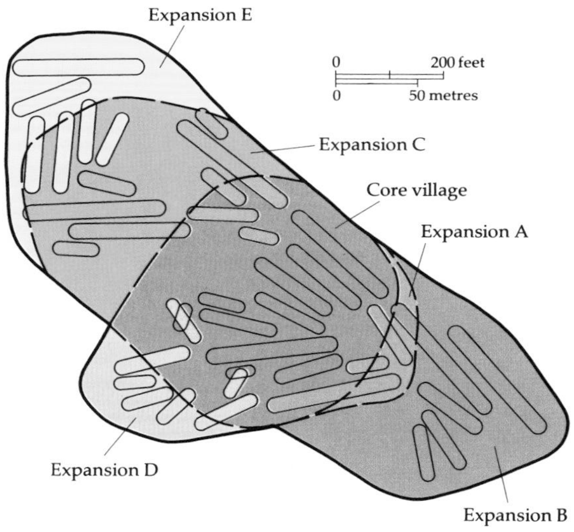

Expansion E
Expansion C
Core village
Expansion A
Expansion D
Expansion B

0 200 feet
0 50 metres

SITUATION OF A NEUTRAL VILLAGE

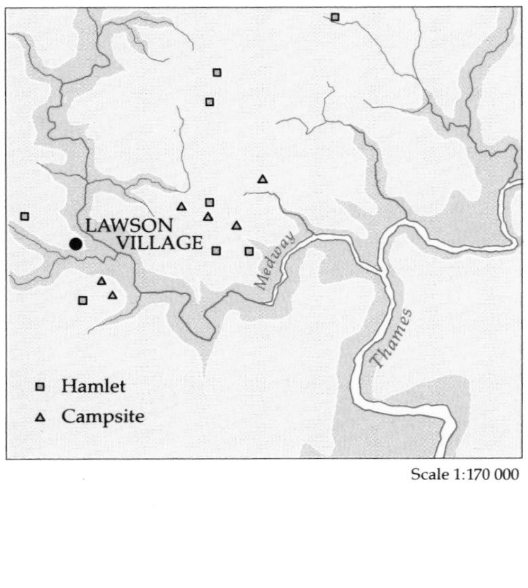

LAWSON VILLAGE
Medway
Thames
Hamlet
Campsite

Scale 1:170 000

LATE PERIOD VILLAGE

The Draper site (east of Toronto) shows the growth of a Huron village in the 16th century. The small original village comprised 11 houses and perhaps 600 people. Through a series of expansions it grew to 38 longhouses and more than 2 000 people on a site of almost 4 ha. The sketch, based on archaeological evidence, suggests the village's final appearance.

Most large villages were surrounded by satellite hamlets, as shown (left) around the Neutral village on the Lawson site, now within the city of London in southwestern Ontario.

THE COAST TSIMSHIAN, ca 1750

Authors: George F. MacDonald, Gary Coupland, David Archer

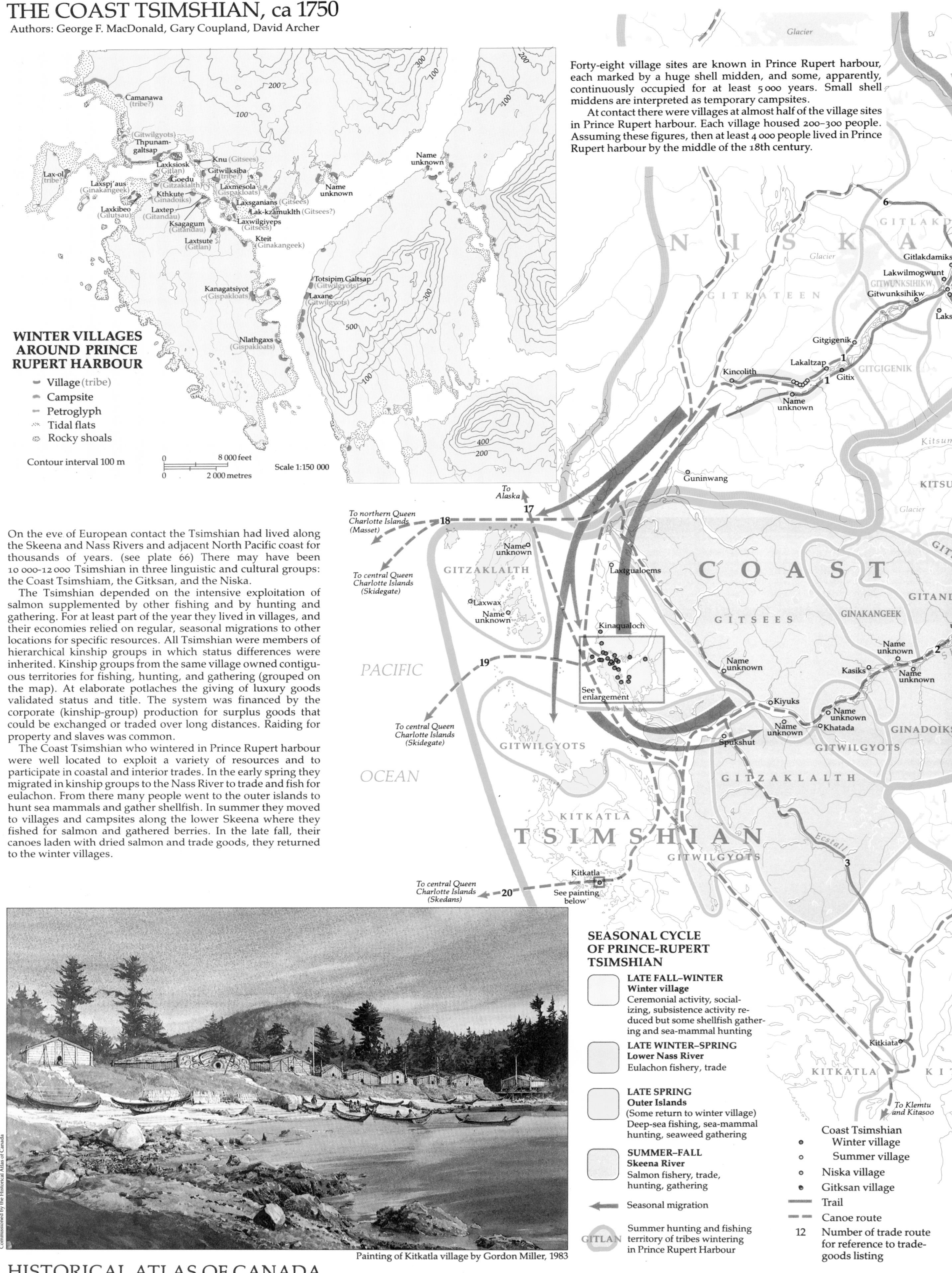

WINTER VILLAGES AROUND PRINCE RUPERT HARBOUR
Village (tribe)
Campsite
Petroglyph
Tidal flats
Rocky shoals
Contour interval 100 m
8 000 feet
2 000 metres
Scale 1:150 000
Camanawa (tribe?)
(Gitwilgyots)
Thpunam-galtsap
Knu (Gitsees)
Laxksiosk (Gitlan)
Gitwilksiba (tribe?)
Lax-ol (tribe?)
Laxspj'aus (Ginakangeek)
Goedu (Gitzaklalth)
Laxmesola (Gispakloats)
Kthkute (Ginadoiks)
Laxsganians (Gitsees)
Lak-kzamuklth (Gitsees?)
Laxkibeo (Gilutsau)
Laxtep (Gitandau)
Laxwilgiyeps (Gitsees)
Ksagagum (Gitandau)
Laxtsute (Gitlan)
Kteit (Ginakangeek)
Kanagatsiyot (Gispakloats)
Nlathgaxs (Gispakloats)
Totsipim Galtsap (Gitwilgyots)
Laxane (Gitwilgyots)
Name unknown
Forty-eight village sites are known in Prince Rupert harbour, each marked by a huge shell midden, and some, apparently, continuously occupied for at least 5 000 years. Small shell middens are interpreted as temporary campsites.
At contact there were villages at almost half of the village sites in Prince Rupert harbour. Each village housed 200–300 people. Assuming these figures, then at least 4 000 people lived in Prince Rupert harbour by the middle of the 18th century.
Glacier
N I S K A
GITLAKDAMIKS
GITKATEEN
Gitlakdamiks
Lakwilmogwunt
GITWUNKSIHIKW
Gitwunksihikw
Laksiluk
Gitgigenik
GITGIGENIK
Lakaltzap
Gitix
Kincolith
Name unknown
Kitsumkalum
KITSUMKALUM
Guninwang
To Alaska
To northern Queen Charlotte Islands (Masset)
To central Queen Charlotte Islands (Skidegate)
To central Queen Charlotte Islands (Skedans)
GITZAKLALTH
Laxtgualoems
Laxwax
C O A S T
GITLAN
GITANDAU
GINAKANGEEK
G I T S E E S
Kinaqualoch
See enlargement
PACIFIC
OCEAN
Kasiks
Kiyuks
Khatada
GINADOIKS
Spukshut
GITWILGYOTS
G I T Z A K L A L T H
KITKATLA
T S I M S H I A N
Ecstall
Kitkatla
See painting below
Kitkiata
To Klemtu and Kitasoo
SEASONAL CYCLE OF PRINCE-RUPERT TSIMSHIAN
LATE FALL–WINTER
Winter village
Ceremonial activity, socializing, subsistence activity reduced but some shellfish gathering and sea-mammal hunting
LATE WINTER–SPRING
Lower Nass River
Eulachon fishery, trade
LATE SPRING
Outer Islands
(Some return to winter village)
Deep-sea fishing, sea-mammal hunting, seaweed gathering
SUMMER–FALL
Skeena River
Salmon fishery, trade, hunting, gathering
Seasonal migration
GITLAN
Summer hunting and fishing territory of tribes wintering in Prince Rupert Harbour
Coast Tsimshian
Winter village
Summer village
Niska village
Gitksan village
Trail
Canoe route
12 Number of trade route for reference to trade-goods listing
Commissioned by the Historical Atlas of Canada

On the eve of European contact the Tsimshian had lived along the Skeena and Nass Rivers and adjacent North Pacific coast for thousands of years. (see plate 66) There may have been 10 000-12 000 Tsimshian in three linguistic and cultural groups: the Coast Tsimshiam, the Gitksan, and the Niska.

The Tsimshian depended on the intensive exploitation of salmon supplemented by other fishing and by hunting and gathering. For at least part of the year they lived in villages, and their economies relied on regular, seasonal migrations to other locations for specific resources. All Tsimshian were members of hierarchical kinship groups in which status differences were inherited. Kinship groups from the same village owned contiguous territories for fishing, hunting, and gathering (grouped on the map). At elaborate potlaches the giving of luxury goods validated status and title. The system was financed by the corporate (kinship-group) production for surplus goods that could be exchanged or traded over long distances. Raiding for property and slaves was common.

The Coast Tsimshian who wintered in Prince Rupert harbour were well located to exploit a variety of resources and to participate in coastal and interior trades. In the early spring they migrated in kinship groups to the Nass River to trade and fish for eulachon. From there many people went to the outer islands to hunt sea mammals and gather shellfish. In summer they moved to villages and campsites along the lower Skeena where they fished for salmon and gathered berries. In the late fall, their canoes laden with dried salmon and trade goods, they returned to the winter villages.

Painting of Kitkatla village by Gordon Miller, 1983

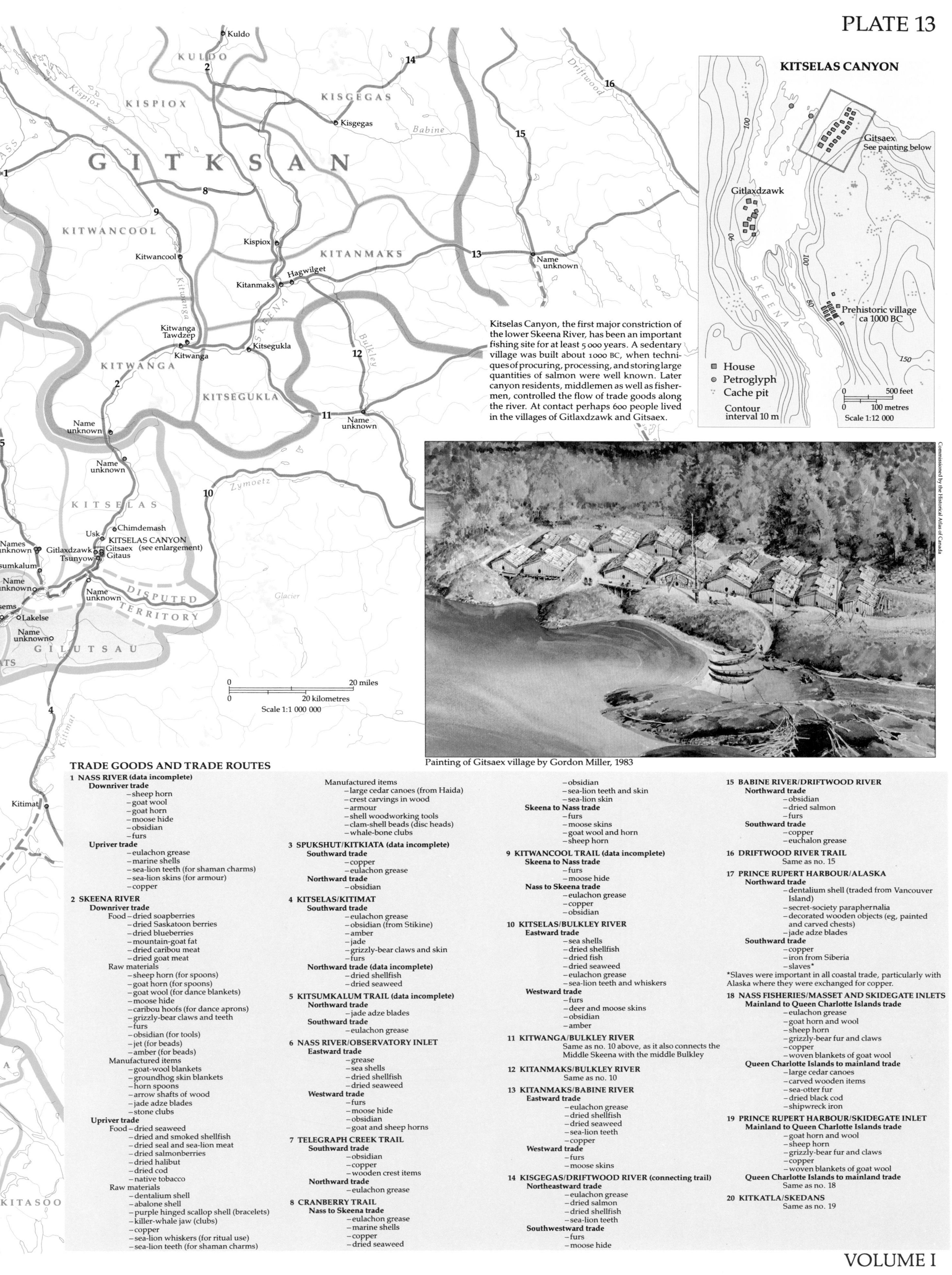
Kuldo
KULDO
KISPIOX
Kispiox
KISGEGAS
Kisgegas
Babine
Driftwood
GITKSAN
KITWANCOOL
Kitwancool
Kispiox
KITANMAKS
Hagwilget
Kitanmaks
Name unknown
Kitwanga
Kitwanga Tawdzep
Kitwanga
Kitsegukla
SKEENA
Bulkley
KITWANGA
KITSEGUKLA
Name unknown
Name unknown
Name unknown
Zymoetz
KITSELAS
Chimdemash
Usk
KITSELAS CANYON (see enlargement)
Gitlaxdzawk
Gitsaex
Gitaus
Tsunyow
Names unknown
Name unknown
Name unknown
DISPUTED TERRITORY
Glacier
Lakelse
Name unknown
GILUTSAU
Kitimat
Kitimat
KITASOO
0 20 miles
0 20 kilometres
Scale 1:1 000 000
KITSELAS CANYON
Gitsaex
See painting below
Gitlaxdzawk
SKEENA
Prehistoric village ca 1000 BC
House
Petroglyph
Cache pit
Contour interval 10 m
0 500 feet
0 100 metres
Scale 1:12 000

Kitselas Canyon, the first major constriction of the lower Skeena River, has been an important fishing site for at least 5 000 years. A sedentary village was built about 1000 BC, when techniques of procuring, processing, and storing large quantities of salmon were well known. Later canyon residents, middlemen as well as fishermen, controlled the flow of trade goods along the river. At contact perhaps 600 people lived in the villages of Gitlaxdzawk and Gitsaex.

Painting of Gitsaex village by Gordon Miller, 1983

Commissioned by the Historical Atlas of Canada

TRADE GOODS AND TRADE ROUTES

1 NASS RIVER (data incomplete)
Downriver trade
– sheep horn
– goat wool
– goat horn
– moose hide
– obsidian
– furs
Upriver trade
– eulachon grease
– marine shells
– sea-lion teeth (for shaman charms)
– sea-lion skins (for armour)
– copper

2 SKEENA RIVER
Downriver trade
Food – dried soapberries
– dried Saskatoon berries
– dried blueberries
– mountain-goat fat
– dried caribou meat
– dried goat meat
Raw materials
– sheep horn (for spoons)
– goat horn (for spoons)
– goat wool (for dance blankets)
– moose hide
– caribou hoofs (for dance aprons)
– grizzly-bear claws and teeth
– furs
– obsidian (for tools)
– jet (for beads)
– amber (for beads)
Manufactured items
– goat-wool blankets
– groundhog skin blankets
– horn spoons
– arrow shafts of wood
– jade adze blades
– stone clubs
Upriver trade
Food – dried seaweed
– dried and smoked shellfish
– dried seal and sea-lion meat
– dried salmonberries
– dried halibut
– dried cod
– native tobacco
Raw materials
– dentalium shell
– abalone shell
– purple hinged scallop shell (bracelets)
– killer-whale jaw (clubs)
– copper
– sea-lion whiskers (for ritual use)
– sea-lion teeth (for shaman charms)
Manufactured items
– large cedar canoes (from Haida)
– crest carvings in wood
– armour
– shell woodworking tools
– clam-shell beads (disc heads)
– whale-bone clubs

3 SPUKSHUT/KITKIATA (data incomplete)
Southward trade
– copper
– eulachon grease
Northward trade
– obsidian

4 KITSELAS/KITIMAT
Southward trade
– eulachon grease
– obsidian (from Stikine)
– amber
– jade
– grizzly-bear claws and skin
– furs
Northward trade (data incomplete)
– dried shellfish
– dried seaweed

5 KITSUMKALUM TRAIL (data incomplete)
Northward trade
– jade adze blades
Southward trade
– eulachon grease

6 NASS RIVER/OBSERVATORY INLET
Eastward trade
– grease
– sea shells
– dried shellfish
– dried seaweed
Westward trade
– furs
– moose hide
– obsidian
– goat and sheep horns

7 TELEGRAPH CREEK TRAIL
Southward trade
– obsidian
– copper
– wooden crest items
Northward trade
– eulachon grease

8 CRANBERRY TRAIL
Nass to Skeena trade
– eulachon grease
– marine shells
– copper
– dried seaweed
– obsidian
– sea-lion teeth and skin
– sea-lion skin
Skeena to Nass trade
– furs
– moose skins
– goat wool and horn
– sheep horn

9 KITWANCOOL TRAIL (data incomplete)
Skeena to Nass trade
– furs
– moose hide
Nass to Skeena trade
– eulachon grease
– copper
– obsidian

10 KITSELAS/BULKLEY RIVER
Eastward trade
– sea shells
– dried shellfish
– dried fish
– dried seaweed
– eulachon grease
– sea-lion teeth and whiskers
Westward trade
– furs
– deer and moose skins
– obsidian
– amber

11 KITWANGA/BULKLEY RIVER
Same as no. 10 above, as it also connects the Middle Skeena with the middle Bulkley

12 KITANMAKS/BULKLEY RIVER
Same as no. 10

13 KITANMAKS/BABINE RIVER
Eastward trade
– eulachon grease
– dried shellfish
– dried seaweed
– sea-lion teeth
– copper
Westward trade
– furs
– moose skins

14 KISGEGAS/DRIFTWOOD RIVER (connecting trail)
Northeastward trade
– eulachon grease
– dried salmon
– dried shellfish
– sea-lion teeth
Southwestward trade
– furs
– moose hide

15 BABINE RIVER/DRIFTWOOD RIVER
Northward trade
– obsidian
– dried salmon
– furs
Southward trade
– copper
– euchalon grease

16 DRIFTWOOD RIVER TRAIL
Same as no. 15

17 PRINCE RUPERT HARBOUR/ALASKA
Northward trade
– dentalium shell (traded from Vancouver Island)
– secret-society paraphernalia
– decorated wooden objects (eg, painted and carved chests)
– jade adze blades
Southward trade
– copper
– iron from Siberia
– slaves*

*Slaves were important in all coastal trade, particularly with Alaska where they were exchanged for copper.

18 NASS FISHERIES/MASSET AND SKIDEGATE INLETS
Mainland to Queen Charlotte Islands trade
– eulachon grease
– goat horn and wool
– sheep horn
– grizzly-bear fur and claws
– copper
– woven blankets of goat wool
Queen Charlotte Islands to mainland trade
– large cedar canoes
– carved wooden items
– sea-otter fur
– dried black cod
– shipwreck iron

19 PRINCE RUPERT HARBOUR/SKIDEGATE INLET
Mainland to Queen Charlotte Islands trade
– goat horn and wool
– sheep horn
– grizzly-bear fur and claws
– copper
– woven blankets of goat wool
Queen Charlotte Islands to mainland trade
Same as no. 18

20 KITKATLA/SKEDANS
Same as no. 19

PREHISTORIC TRADE

Authors: J.V. Wright; Roy L. Carlson (Obsidian)

Prehistoric people valued the volcanic glass obsidian for its cutting properties. Artefacts made from obsidian are widespread in the Cordillera and, when traced by X-ray fluorescence analysis to their quarries of origin, have been shown to come from six source areas. As early as 7000–6000 BC obsidian from Oregon was being used in southern British Columbia, and obsidian from Anahim Peak had reached the central coast. Later the use of obsidian, the number of quarries, and the average distance from quarry to consumer all appear to have increased gradually. Probably obsidian was traded; the distribution of artefacts made of obsidian certainly establishes that there was at least indirect contact among different Indian peoples of the Cordillera for thousands of years.

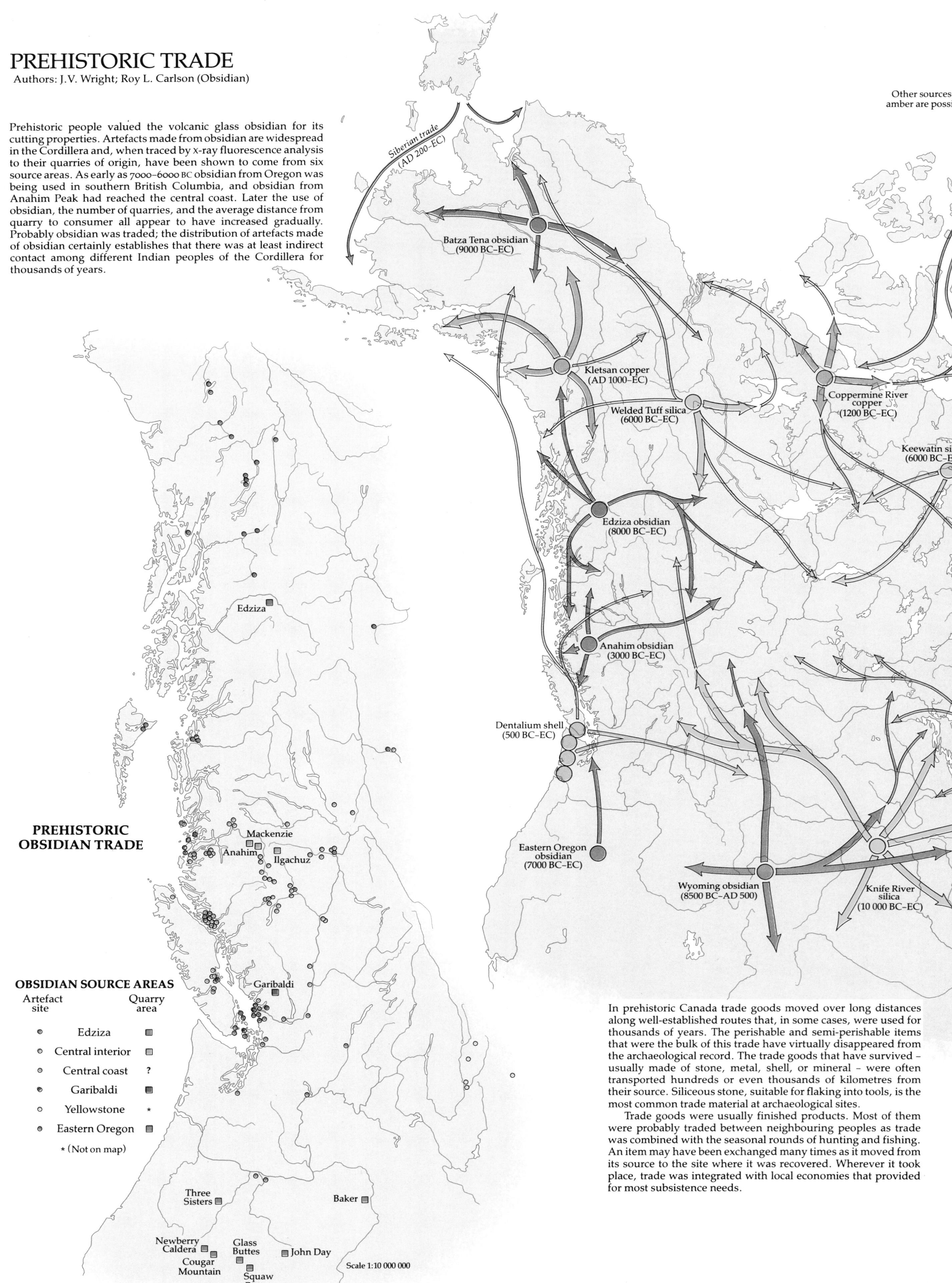

Other sources of amber are possible.
Siberian trade (AD 200–EC)
Batza Tena obsidian (9000 BC–EC)
Kletsan copper (AD 1000–EC)
Welded Tuff silica (6000 BC–EC)
Coppermine River copper (1200 BC–EC)
Keewatin silica (6000 BC–EC)
Edziza obsidian (8000 BC–EC)
Anahim obsidian (3000 BC–EC)
Dentalium shell (500 BC–EC)
Eastern Oregon obsidian (7000 BC–EC)
Wyoming obsidian (8500 BC–AD 500)
Knife River silica (10 000 BC–EC)
PREHISTORIC OBSIDIAN TRADE
Edziza
Mackenzie
Anahim
Ilgachuz
Garibaldi
Three Sisters
Baker
Newberry Caldera
Cougar Mountain
Glass Buttes
Squaw Butte
John Day
Scale 1:10 000 000
OBSIDIAN SOURCE AREAS
Artefact site
Quarry area
Edziza
Central interior
Central coast ?
Garibaldi
Yellowstone *
Eastern Oregon
* (Not on map)

In prehistoric Canada trade goods moved over long distances along well-established routes that, in some cases, were used for thousands of years. The perishable and semi-perishable items that were the bulk of this trade have virtually disappeared from the archaeological record. The trade goods that have survived – usually made of stone, metal, shell, or mineral – were often transported hundreds or even thousands of kilometres from their source. Siliceous stone, suitable for flaking into tools, is the most common trade material at archaeological sites.

Trade goods were usually finished products. Most of them were probably traded between neighbouring peoples as trade was combined with the seasonal rounds of hunting and fishing. An item may have been exchanged many times as it moved from its source to the site where it was recovered. Wherever it took place, trade was integrated with local economies that provided for most subsistence needs.

TRADE

Movement of trade goods

- Silver or galena
- Silica
- Obsidian
- Copper
- Amber
- Marine shell
- Meteoric iron
- External trade
- Source of trade material
- EC European contact

Frequency of trade

- Abundant
- Moderate
- Rare

Amber (AD 1000–EC)

Meteoric iron (AD 1000–EC)

Greenland Norse trade (AD 1000–1500)

Ramah silica (4000 BC–EC)

Norse settlement (ca AD 1000)

Albanel silica (3000 BC–EC)

Cobalt silver (200 BC–AD 200)

Lake Superior copper (4000 BC–EC)

Marine shell (2000 BC–EC)

Galena (1500–1000 BC)

Marine shell (2000 BC–EC)

larine shell
000 BC–EC)

Scale 1:19 000 000

Before 500 BC a burial cult associated with the Adena culture of the central Ohio valley spread in the St Lawrence valley and the Maritimes where it influenced several cultural groups. Prescribed, imported offerings were placed with the dead. The presence of such grave goods suggests that the cult required a wide network of trade involving, among other items, native copper from Lake Superior, marine shell from the east coast, fire-clay tubular pipes and flaked, two-faced blades from the Ohio valley and elsewhere, and polished slate gorgets of unknown origin.

SPREAD OF THE ADENA BURIAL CULT

- Burial mound
- Burial site
- Lake Superior copper
- Ohio fire-clay*
- Marine shell (conch)
- Ohio valley flint*

*Fire-clay and Ohio valley flint are probably under-represented because of the problem of identification.

- Major cult spread from the south
- Diffusion of cult into Canada
- Likely routes of copper imports to Adena heartland
- Copper-bearing formations of the Lake Superior basin

Evidence of cult not plotted south of this line

Source of Ohio valley flint

ADENA HEARTLAND

Source of Ohio fire-clay

Scale 1:15 000 000

COSMOLOGY

Author: J.V. Wright

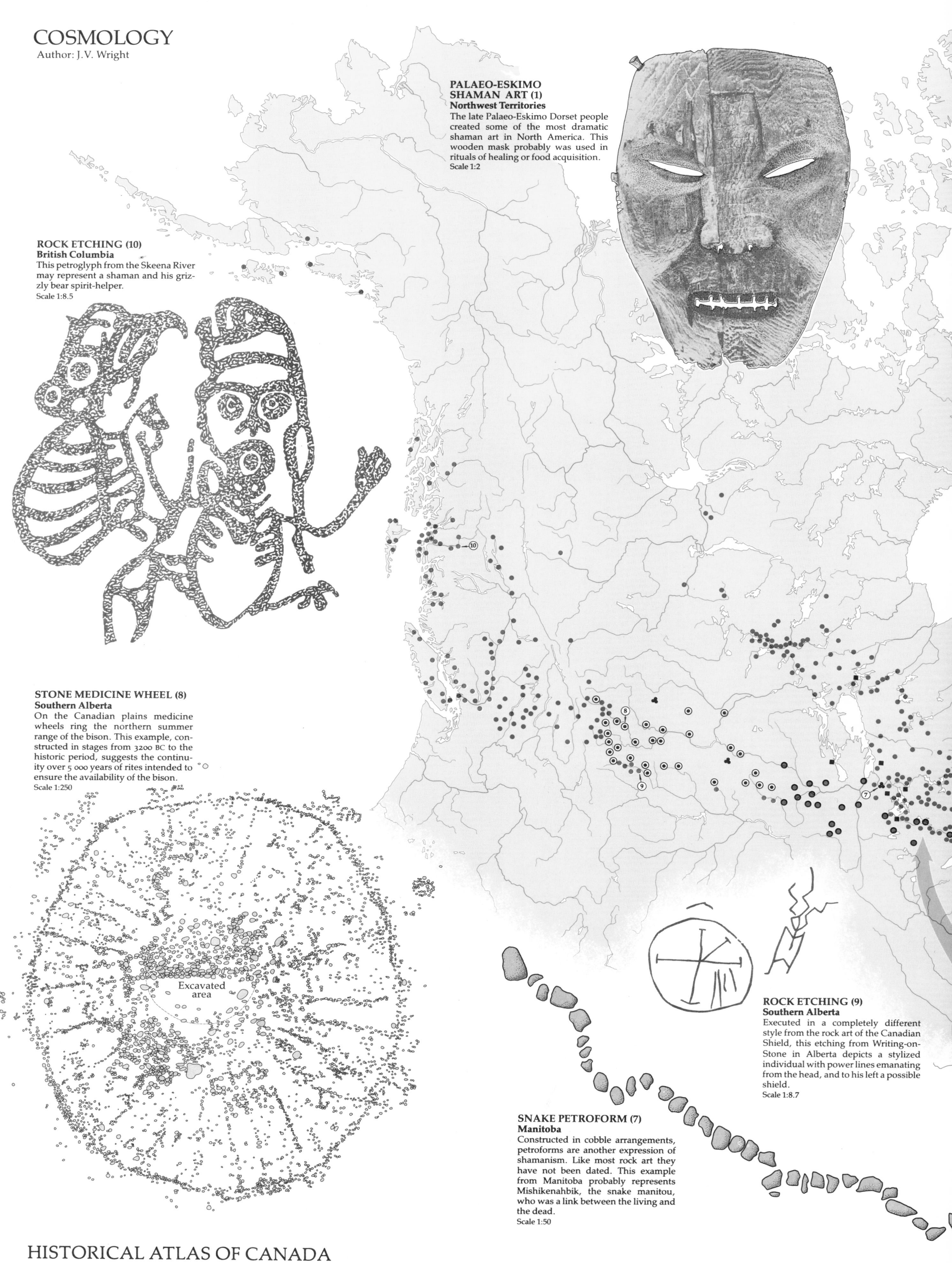

Excavated area

PALAEO-ESKIMO SHAMAN ART (1)
Northwest Territories
The late Palaeo-Eskimo Dorset people created some of the most dramatic shaman art in North America. This wooden mask probably was used in rituals of healing or food acquisition.
Scale 1:2

ROCK ETCHING (10)
British Columbia
This petroglyph from the Skeena River may represent a shaman and his grizzly bear spirit-helper.
Scale 1:8.5

STONE MEDICINE WHEEL (8)
Southern Alberta
On the Canadian plains medicine wheels ring the northern summer range of the bison. This example, constructed in stages from 3200 BC to the historic period, suggests the continuity over 5 000 years of rites intended to ensure the availability of the bison.
Scale 1:250

ROCK ETCHING (9)
Southern Alberta
Executed in a completely different style from the rock art of the Canadian Shield, this etching from Writing-on-Stone in Alberta depicts a stylized individual with power lines emanating from the head, and to his left a possible shield.
Scale 1:8.7

SNAKE PETROFORM (7)
Manitoba
Constructed in cobble arrangements, petroforms are another expression of shamanism. Like most rock art they have not been dated. This example from Manitoba probably represents Mishikenahbik, the snake manitou, who was a link between the living and the dead.
Scale 1:50

The objects mapped and illustrated on this plate are all associated with prehistoric native beliefs. While different regional styles and distributions are apparent – rock art in the Canadian Shield, for example, was very different from that in the Cordillera – the beliefs that underlay these dramatic archaeological objects are not apparent and can only be inferred.

Historical and ethnographic records suggest that the native people of Canada interpreted nature spiritually and assumed that all phenomena, including the dead, had spirit power. Such power was graded. Some of it could be ignored, but the spirits controlling food supply, warfare, health, and fertility required special attention as people sought to live in harmony with the mysterious surrounding world of dangerous and helpful spirits.

There were three major ways of placating and acquiring spirit power: by offering gifts and sacrifices to the appropriate spirit or spirits; by adhering to taboos in order to avoid giving offence to supernatural powers; and by prayer, often involving fasting and purification, which could lead to power-giving visions usually associated with a guardian spirit. Shamans, people with special abilities to communicate with the supernatural world, were the seers and healers of their societies or, if they used their powers for evil purposes, the sorcerers.

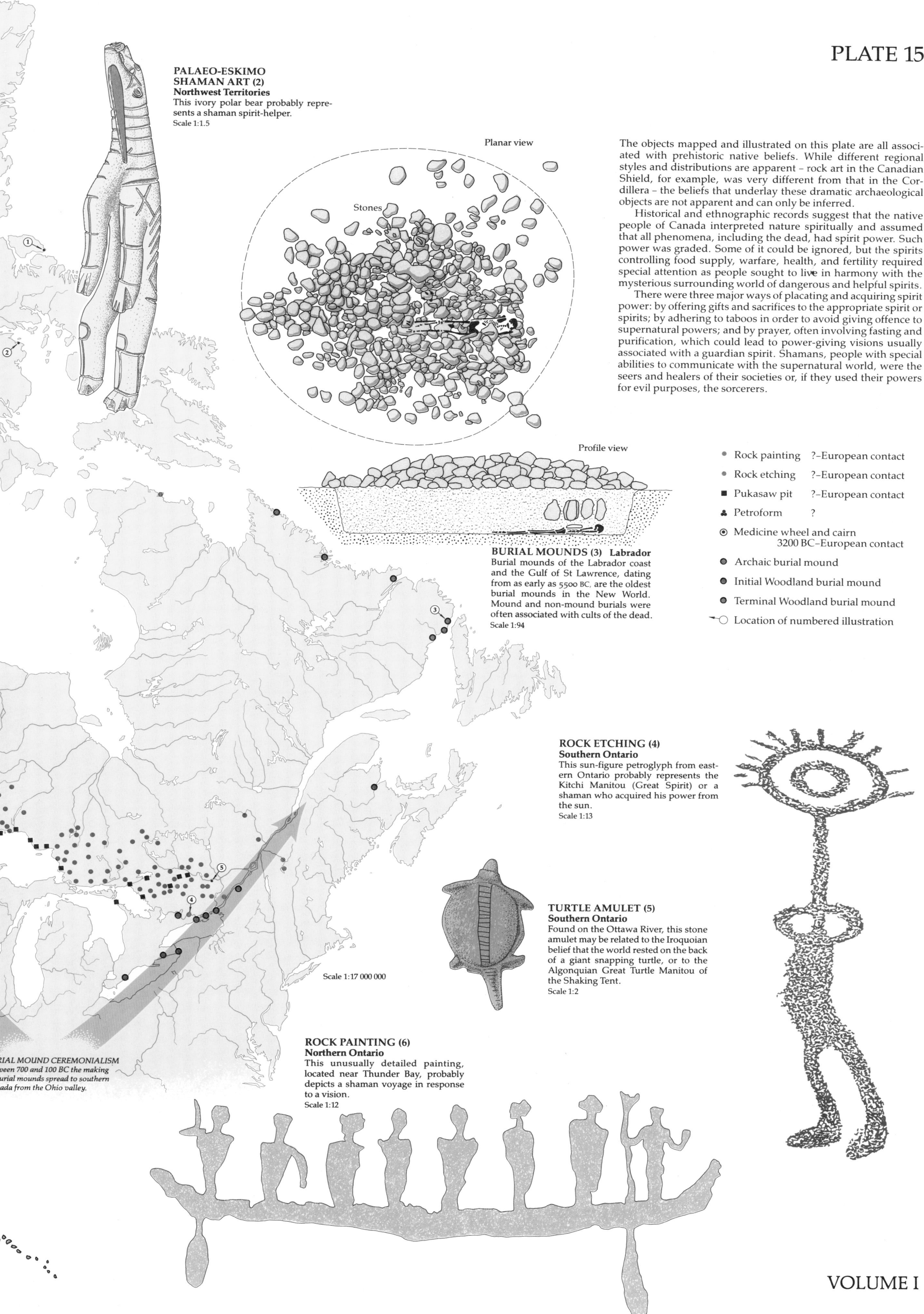

Planar view
Stones
Profile view
Rock painting ?–European contact
Rock etching ?–European contact
Pukasaw pit ?–European contact
Petroform ?
Medicine wheel and cairn 3200 BC–European contact
Archaic burial mound
Initial Woodland burial mound
Terminal Woodland burial mound
Location of numbered illustration
Scale 1:17 000 000

PALAEO-ESKIMO SHAMAN ART (2)
Northwest Territories
This ivory polar bear probably represents a shaman spirit-helper.
Scale 1:1.5

BURIAL MOUNDS (3) Labrador
Burial mounds of the Labrador coast and the Gulf of St Lawrence, dating from as early as 5500 BC, are the oldest burial mounds in the New World. Mound and non-mound burials were often associated with cults of the dead.
Scale 1:94

ROCK ETCHING (4)
Southern Ontario
This sun-figure petroglyph from eastern Ontario probably represents the Kitchi Manitou (Great Spirit) or a shaman who acquired his power from the sun.
Scale 1:13

TURTLE AMULET (5)
Southern Ontario
Found on the Ottawa River, this stone amulet may be related to the Iroquoian belief that the world rested on the back of a giant snapping turtle, or to the Algonquian Great Turtle Manitou of the Shaking Tent.
Scale 1:2

URIAL MOUND CEREMONIALISM
etween 700 and 100 BC the making f burial mounds spread to southern anada from the Ohio valley.

ROCK PAINTING (6)
Northern Ontario
This unusually detailed painting, located near Thunder Bay, probably depicts a shaman voyage in response to a vision.
Scale 1:12

NORSE VOYAGES AND SETTLEMENT

Authors: Alan Macpherson; Birgitta Wallace (L'Anse aux Meadows)

CLIMATIC CHANGE

This graph, prepared by W. Dansgaard and based on analyses of ice cores from central Greenland, depicts mean temperature change in the North Atlantic over the last 1 500 years. Warmer than average temperatures are to the right of the graph's central axis. In general, relatively warm periods before AD 1000 correspond to periods of early Irish and Norse navigation in the North Atlantic. A prolonged period of climatic cooling began about the middle of the 12th century, and continued through the rest of the Norse occupation of Greenland.

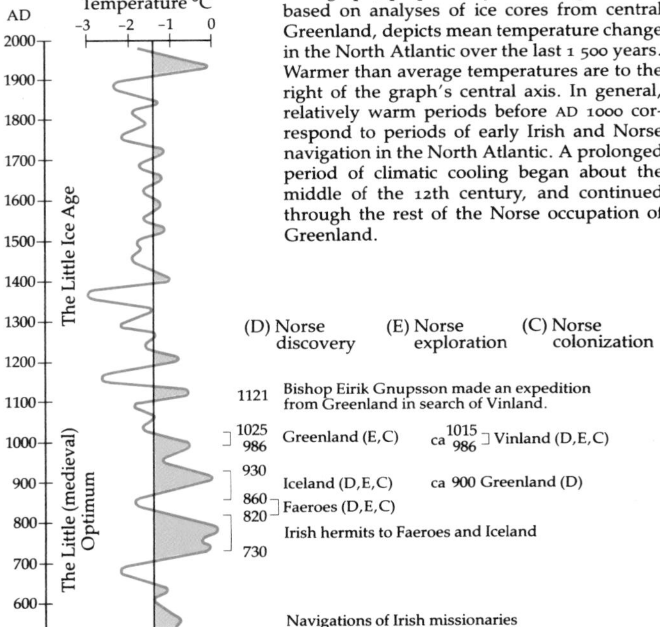
AD
Temperature °C
−3 −2 −1 0
2000
1900
1800
1700
1600
1500
1400
1300
1200
1100
1000
900
800
700
600
500
The Little Ice Age
The Little (medieval) Optimum
(D) Norse discovery
(E) Norse exploration
(C) Norse colonization
1121 Bishop Eirik Gnupsson made an expedition from Greenland in search of Vinland.
1025 986 Greenland (E,C)
ca 1015 986 Vinland (D,E,C)
930 860 Iceland (D,E,C)
ca 900 Greenland (D)
820 Faeroes (D,E,C)
730 Irish hermits to Faeroes and Iceland
Navigations of Irish missionaries

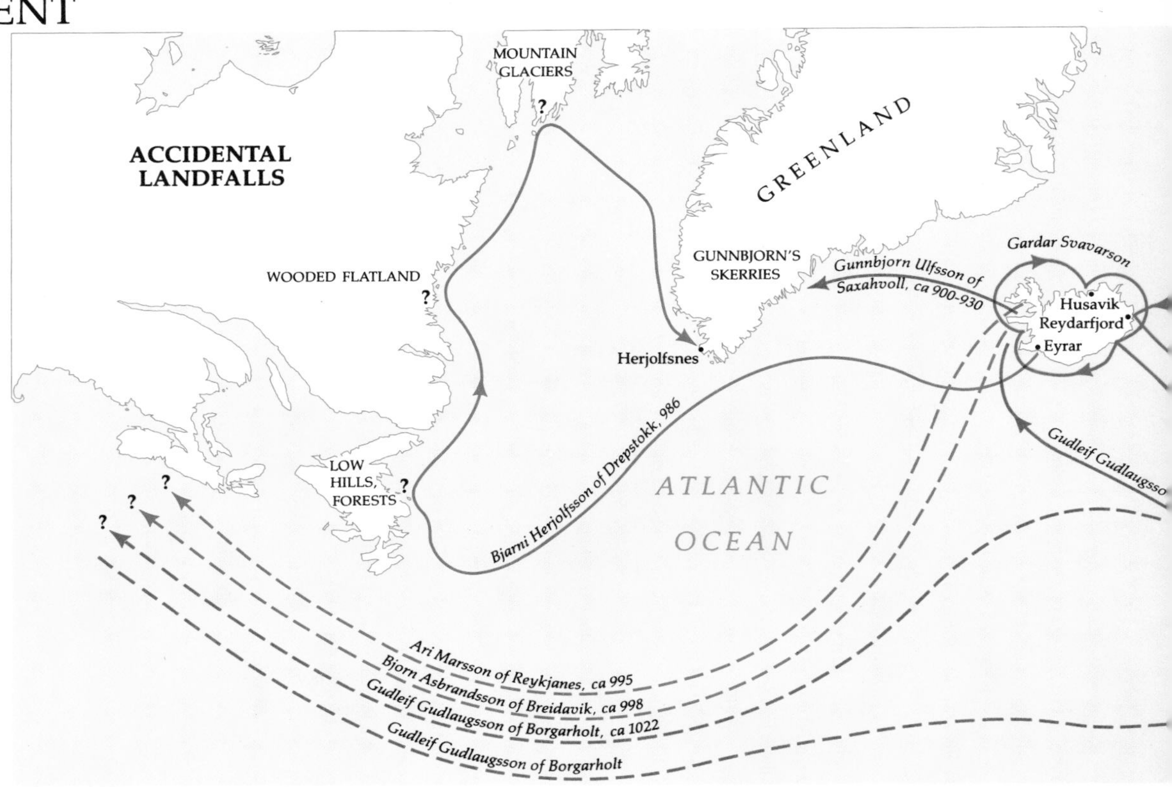
ACCIDENTAL LANDFALLS
MOUNTAIN GLACIERS
GREENLAND
WOODED FLATLAND
GUNNBJORN'S SKERRIES
Gunnbjorn Ulfsson of Saxahvoll, ca 900-930
Gardar Svavarson
Husavik
Reydarfjord
Eyrar
Herjolfsnes
LOW HILLS, FORESTS
Bjarni Herjolfsson of Drepstokk, 986
ATLANTIC
OCEAN
Gudleif Gudlaugsso
Ari Marsson of Reykjanes, ca 995
Bjorn Asbrandsson of Breidavik, ca 998
Gudleif Gudlaugsson of Borgarholt, ca 1022
Gudleif Gudlaugsson of Borgarholt

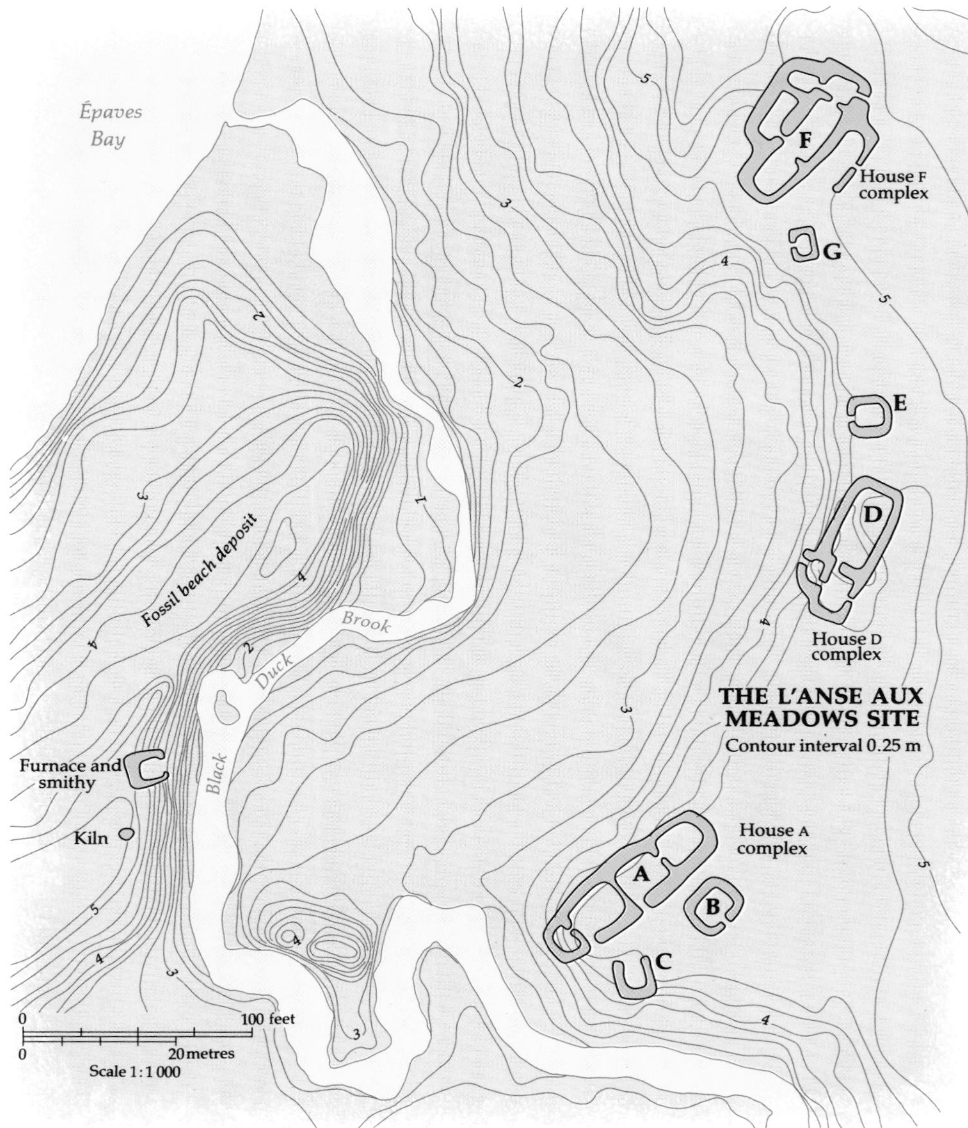
Épaves Bay
House F complex
F
G
E
D
House D complex
Fossil beach deposit
Brook
Duck
Black
THE L'ANSE AUX MEADOWS SITE
Contour interval 0.25 m
Furnace and smithy
Kiln
House A complex
A
B
C
0 100 feet
0 20 metres
Scale 1:1 000

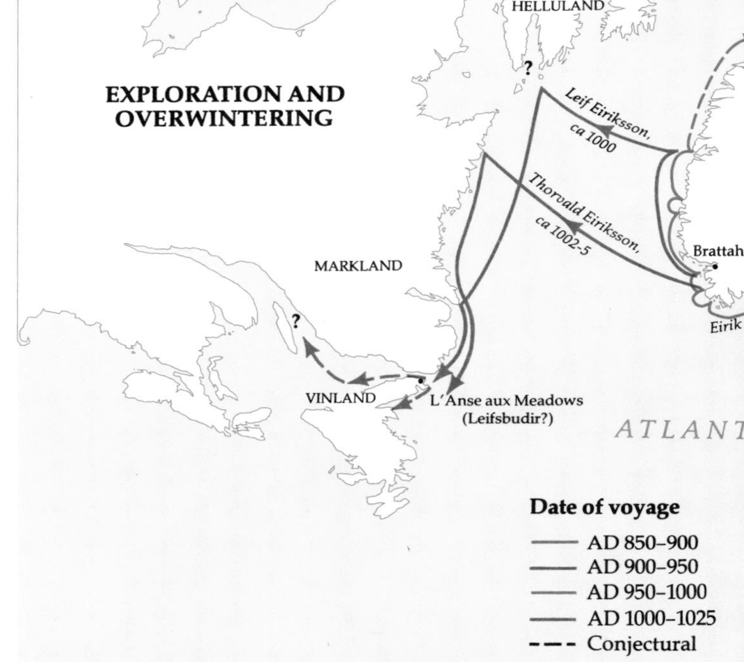
EXPLORATION AND OVERWINTERING
HELLULAND
Leif Eiriksson, ca 1000
Thorvald Eiriksson, ca 1002-5
MARKLAND
Brattahlid
Eirik the Re
VINLAND
L'Anse aux Meadows (Leifsbudir?)
ATLANTIC
Date of voyage
AD 850–900
AD 900–950
AD 950–1000
AD 1000–1025
Conjectural

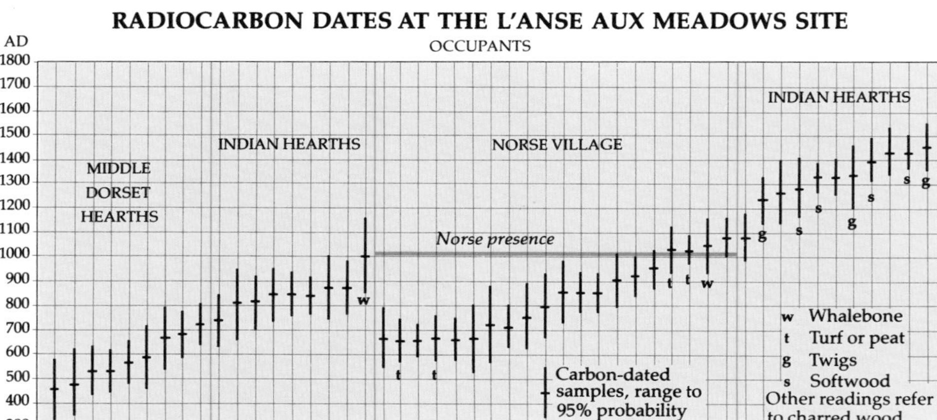
RADIOCARBON DATES AT THE L'ANSE AUX MEADOWS SITE
OCCUPANTS
AD
1800
1700
1600
1500
1400
1300
1200
1100
1000
900
800
700
600
500
400
300
MIDDLE DORSET HEARTHS
INDIAN HEARTHS
NORSE VILLAGE
INDIAN HEARTHS
Norse presence
Carbon-dated samples, range to 95% probability
w Whalebone
t Turf or peat
g Twigs
s Softwood
Other readings refer to charred wood.

An archaeological site near L'Anse aux Meadows at the northern tip of Newfoundland, located in 1960, has been established as a Norse settlement dating from about AD 1000. By virtue of its location, and in the absence of other confirmed Norse settlements in North America, it is a candidate for identification as Leifsbudir, Leif Eiriksson's settlement or *landnam* in the Vinland of the *Greenlanders' Saga*.

The settlement consisted of three dwelling complexes along a raised marine terrace, with a smithy and associated charcoal kiln across the brook. All the dwelling complexes were occupied at the same time and are of early 11th-century type. Like Icelandic homesteads of the period, each complex contained a large dwelling and workshops although, unlike Icelandic farms, there were no barns or byres. The number of iron boat rivets at the site suggests that boat repair was a principal activity. Rivets were made in the smithy. The smiths lived in house A, where one room was used for forging. Carpentry took place in the house D complex. In a workshop attached to house F old rusted boat rivets were replaced with those made on the site. The nature of the settlement is further suggested by the closeness of the buildings, uncommon for Norse farms but typical for places geared to crafts.

An unknown Indian group displaced earlier Dorset inhabitants of the L'Anse aux Meadows site around AD 800. For the brief Norse period radiocarbon dates are older than during the preceding Indian period, probably because the Norse cut and burned large, old trees. After the Norse left, the site was reoccupied by Indians.

COLONIZATION

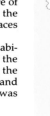

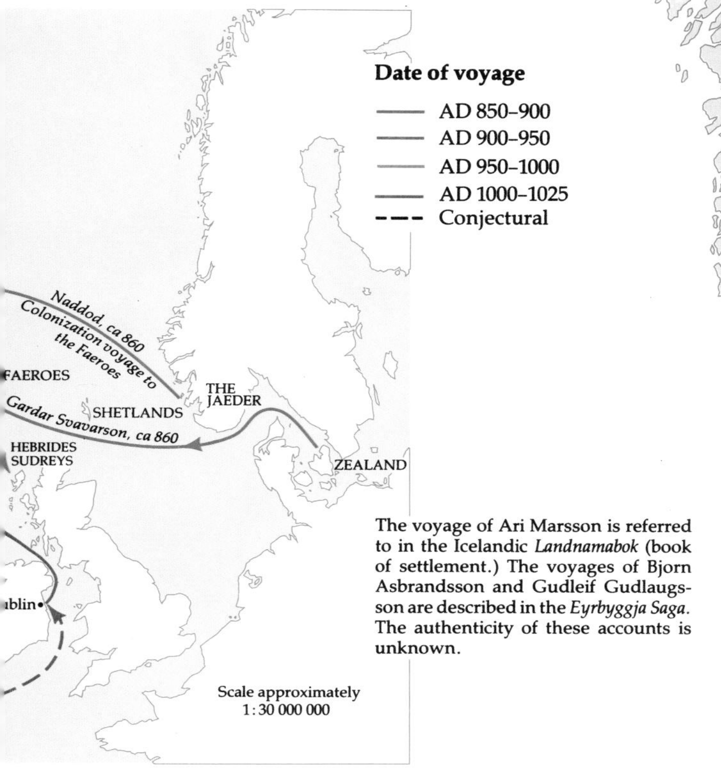

Date of voyage

- AD 850–900
- AD 900–950
- AD 950–1000
- AD 1000–1025
- Conjectural

Naddod, ca 860
Colonization voyage to the Faeroes
FAEROES
Gardar Svavarson, ca 860
SHETLANDS
THE JAEDER
HEBRIDES
SUDREYS
ZEALAND
ublin

The voyage of Ari Marsson is referred to in the Icelandic *Landnamabok* (book of settlement.) The voyages of Bjorn Asbrandsson and Gudleif Gudlaugsson are described in the *Eyrbyggja Saga.* The authenticity of these accounts is unknown.

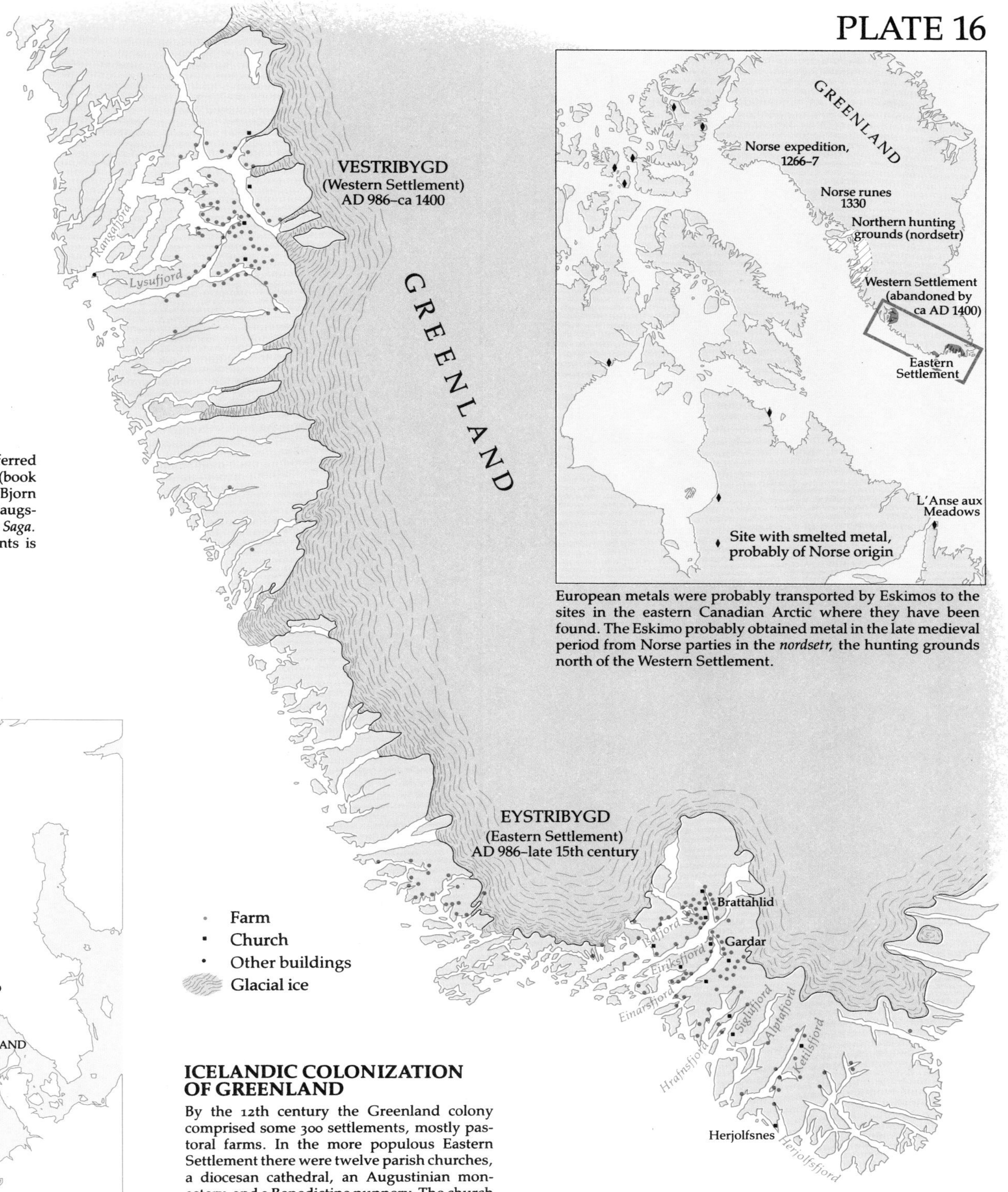

Scale approximately 1:30 000 000

VESTRIBYGD
(Western Settlement)
AD 986–ca 1400
Lysufjord
GREENLAND

GREENLAND
Norse expedition, 1266–7
Norse runes 1330
Northern hunting grounds (nordsetr)
Western Settlement (abandoned by ca AD 1400)
Eastern Settlement
L'Anse aux Meadows
Site with smelted metal, probably of Norse origin

European metals were probably transported by Eskimos to the sites in the eastern Canadian Arctic where they have been found. The Eskimo probably obtained metal in the late medieval period from Norse parties in the *nordsetr,* the hunting grounds north of the Western Settlement.

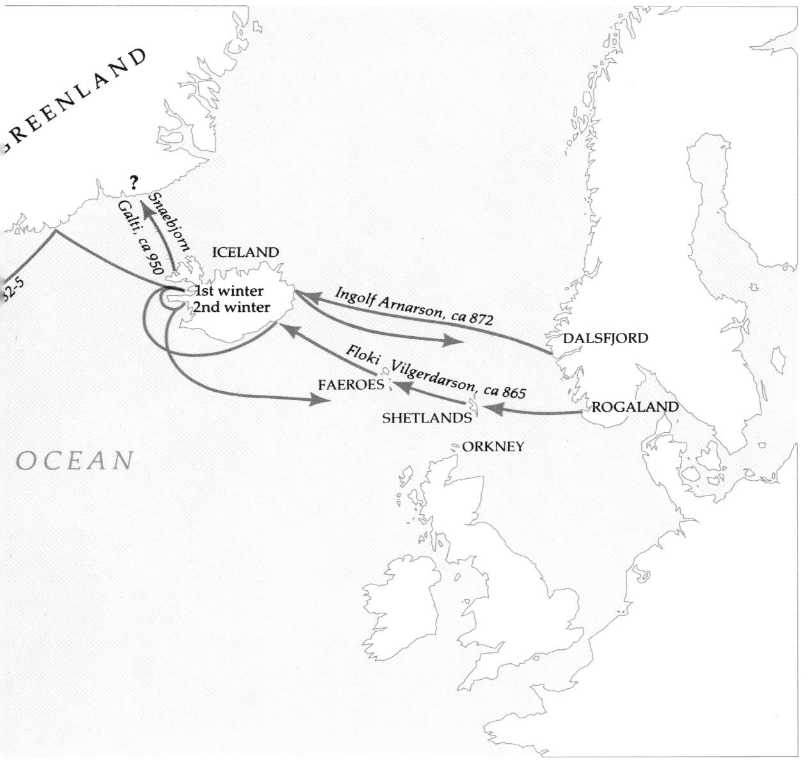

GREENLAND
?
Snaebjorn
Galti, ca 950
ICELAND
1st winter
2nd winter
Ingolf Arnarson, ca 872
Floki Vilgerdarson, ca 865
DALSFJORD
FAEROES
SHETLANDS
ROGALAND
ORKNEY
OCEAN

EYSTRIBYGD
(Eastern Settlement)
AD 986–late 15th century
Brattahlid
Gardar
Einarsfjord
Siglufjord
Hrafnsfjord
Ketilsfjord
Herjolfsnes
Herjolfsfjord

- Farm
- Church
- Other buildings
- Glacial ice

0 – 100 miles
0 – 100 kilometres
Scale 1:3 280 000

ICELANDIC COLONIZATION OF GREENLAND

By the 12th century the Greenland colony comprised some 300 settlements, mostly pastoral farms. In the more populous Eastern Settlement there were twelve parish churches, a diocesan cathedral, an Augustinian monastery, and a Benedictine nunnery. The church owned a third of all property and monopolized trade. By the early 15th century, as the climate deteriorated, ecclesiastical contact with Rome was lost. The Norse settlements declined and finally disappeared around 1500, probably as a result of environmental change, the weakness of the subsistence economy, and the collapse of trade with Europe.

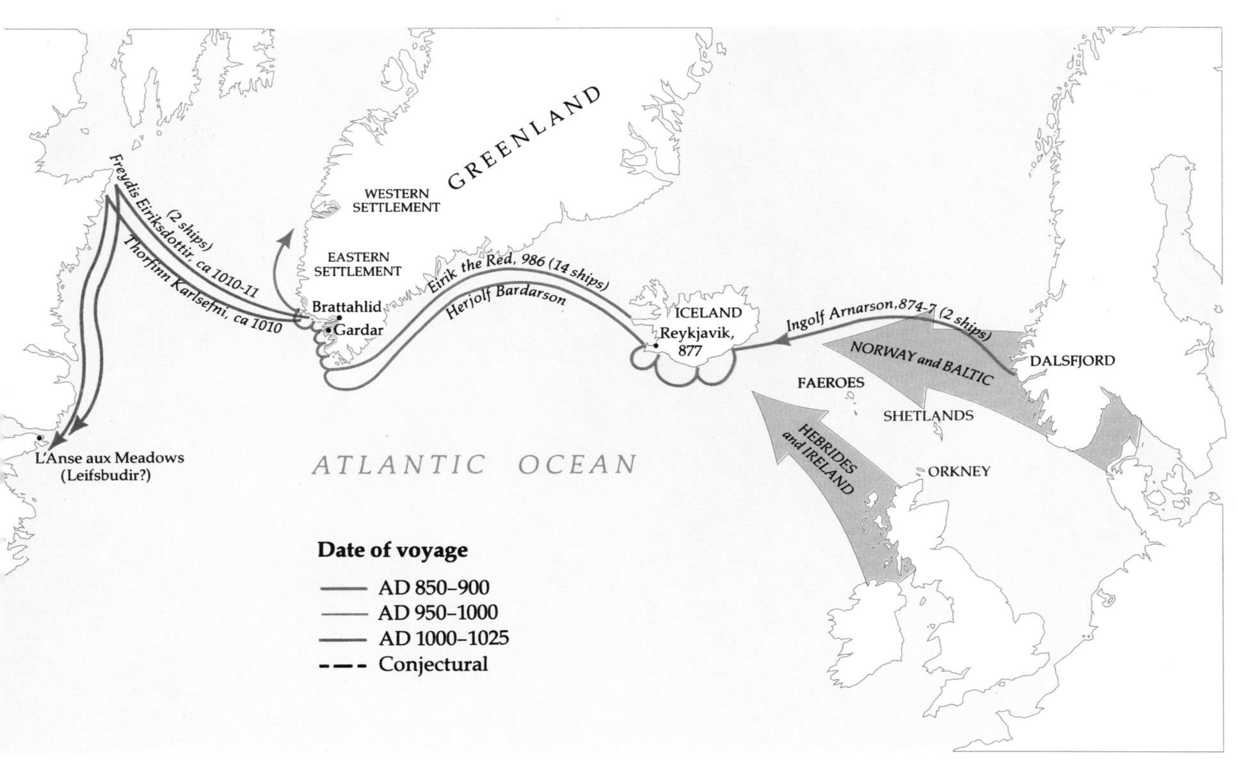
GREENLAND
WESTERN SETTLEMENT
EASTERN SETTLEMENT
Brattahlid
Gardar
Freydis Eiriksdottir, ca 1010-11
(2 ships)
Thorfinn Karlsefni, ca 1010
Eirik the Red, 986 (14 ships)
Herjolf Bardarson
ICELAND
Reykjavik, 877
Ingolf Arnarson, 874-7 (2 ships)
NORWAY and BALTIC
DALSFJORD
FAEROES
SHETLANDS
ORKNEY
HEBRIDES and IRELAND
L'Anse aux Meadows (Leifsbudir?)
ATLANTIC OCEAN
Date of voyage
AD 850–900
AD 950–1000
AD 1000–1025
Conjectural

During the 9th and 10th centuries the Norse extended a pastoral economy based on the *landnam,* or freehold estate, westward across the North Atlantic islands in a repeated pattern of accidental discovery, deliberate exploration, and colonization. Raids on the British Isles, beginning in AD 793, led the Norse to rediscover and colonize the Faeroes in the early 9th century. Norse interest in the Faeroes and in the Western Isles of Scotland led, in turn, to the accidental discovery of Iceland. Exploration and colonization followed between 865 and 930. Greenland, discovered accidentally about 900 during the colonization of Iceland, was most thoroughly explored by Eirik raude Thorvaldsson (Eirik the Red) from 982 to 985, and colonized by him and his son Leif over the next two or three decades. During the colonization of Greenland landfalls were made along the North American coast. Subsequent exploration and attempted colonization focused on a place known in the sagas as Leifsbudir (Leif's booths), now thought by some to be the Norse site near L'Anse aux Meadows.

According to the sagas, there were four expeditions to Leifsbudir, during each of which cut and dried timber was shipped to Greenland. Although two expeditions apparently brought settlers and cattle and stayed at least a year, the settlement was not sustained. After the early 11th century North America virtually disappears from the Norse records. The failure of the settlements probably had to do with the remoteness of the coast and the impossibility, in a forested environment and amid hostile natives, of establishing a Norse pastoral economy along the northeastern shores of Canada.

ECOLOGICAL REGIONS, ca AD 1500

Authors: J.H. McAndrews, G.C. Manville

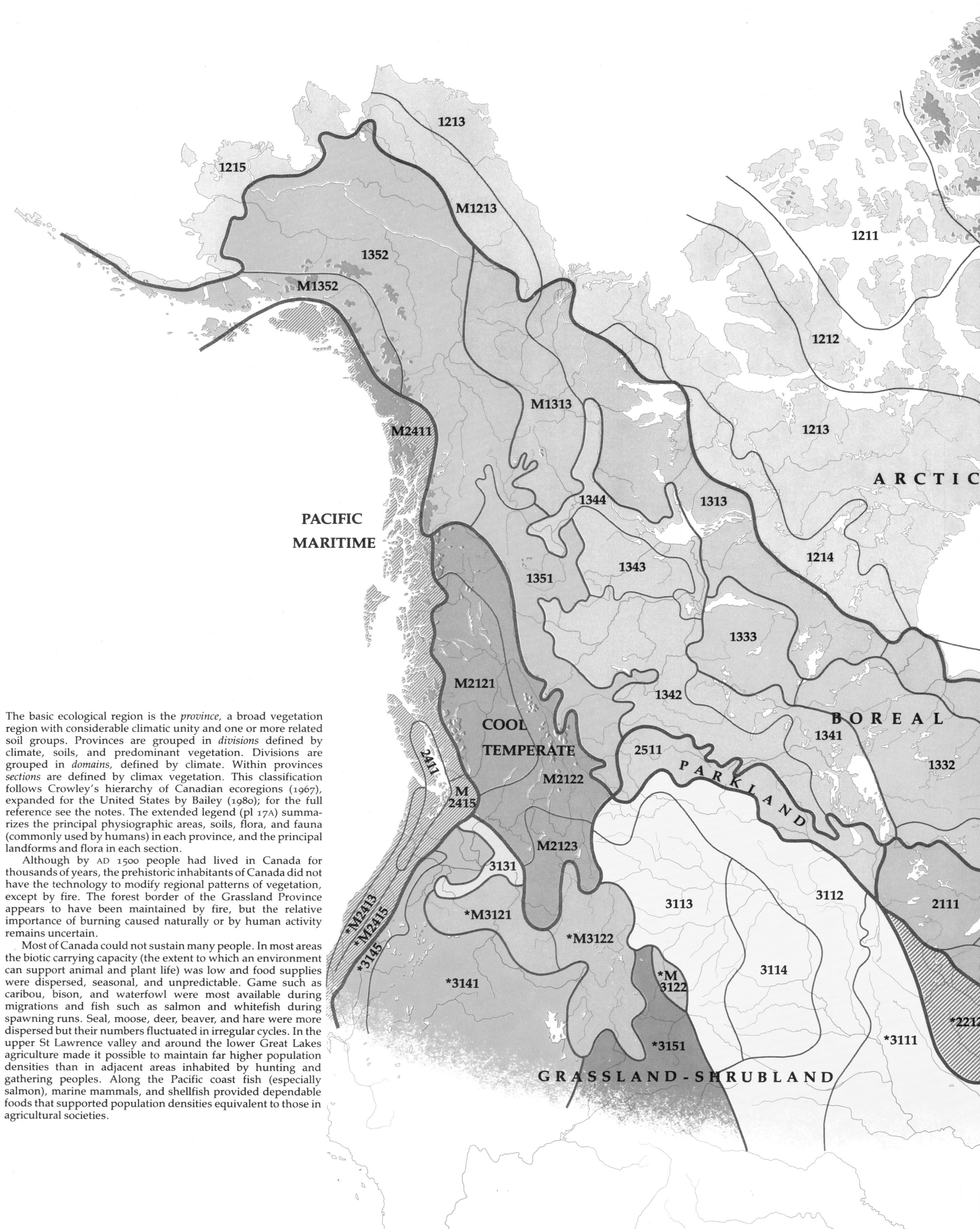

1213
1215
M1213
1352
M1352
1211
1212
M1313
M2411
1213
ARCTIC
1344
1313
PACIFIC
MARITIME
1343
1351
1214
1333
M2121
1342
BOREAL
COOL
TEMPERATE
1341
2511
PARKLAND
1332
2411
M
2415
M2122
M2123
3131
3113
3112
2111
*M3121
*M2413
*M2415
*3145
*M3122
*M
3122
3114
*3141
*3151
*3111
*2212
GRASSLAND-SHRUBLAND

The basic ecological region is the *province*, a broad vegetation region with considerable climatic unity and one or more related soil groups. Provinces are grouped in *divisions* defined by climate, soils, and predominant vegetation. Divisions are grouped in *domains*, defined by climate. Within provinces *sections* are defined by climax vegetation. This classification follows Crowley's hierarchy of Canadian ecoregions (1967), expanded for the United States by Bailey (1980); for the full reference see the notes. The extended legend (pl 17A) summarizes the principal physiographic areas, soils, flora, and fauna (commonly used by humans) in each province, and the principal landforms and flora in each section.

Although by AD 1500 people had lived in Canada for thousands of years, the prehistoric inhabitants of Canada did not have the technology to modify regional patterns of vegetation, except by fire. The forest border of the Grassland Province appears to have been maintained by fire, but the relative importance of burning caused naturally or by human activity remains uncertain.

Most of Canada could not sustain many people. In most areas the biotic carrying capacity (the extent to which an environment can support animal and plant life) was low and food supplies were dispersed, seasonal, and unpredictable. Game such as caribou, bison, and waterfowl were most available during migrations and fish such as salmon and whitefish during spawning runs. Seal, moose, deer, beaver, and hare were more dispersed but their numbers fluctuated in irregular cycles. In the upper St Lawrence valley and around the lower Great Lakes agriculture made it possible to maintain far higher population densities than in adjacent areas inhabited by hunting and gathering peoples. Along the Pacific coast fish (especially salmon), marine mammals, and shellfish provided dependable foods that supported population densities equivalent to those in agricultural societies.

RANGES OF CANADIAN CLIMATIC DATA

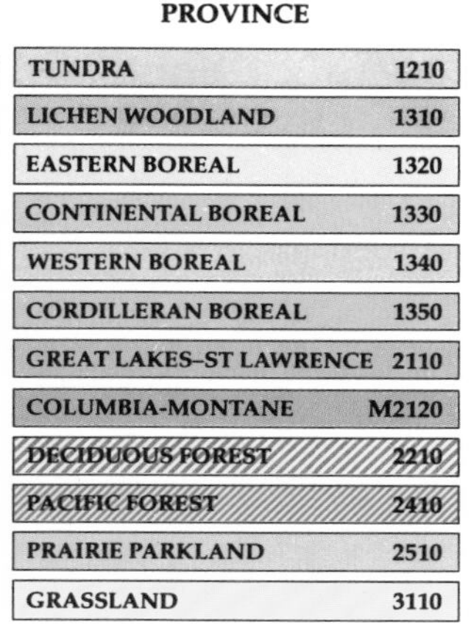
PROVINCE
TUNDRA 1210
LICHEN WOODLAND 1310
EASTERN BOREAL 1320
CONTINENTAL BOREAL 1330
WESTERN BOREAL 1340
CORDILLERAN BOREAL 1350
GREAT LAKES–ST LAWRENCE 2110
COLUMBIA-MONTANE M2120
DECIDUOUS FOREST 2210
PACIFIC FOREST 2410
PRAIRIE PARKLAND 2510
GRASSLAND 3110

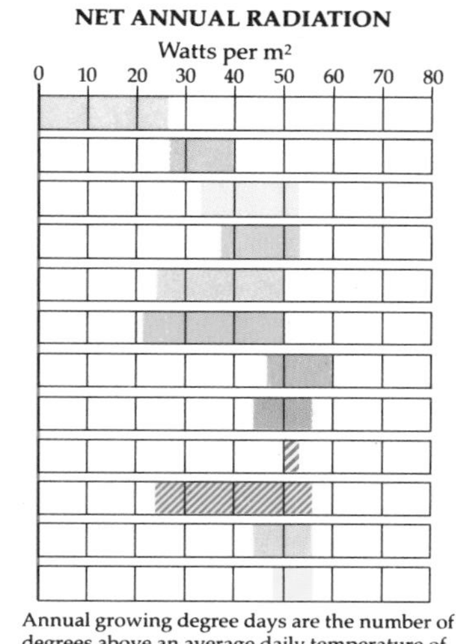
NET ANNUAL RADIATION
Watts per m²
0 10 20 30 40 50 60 70 80

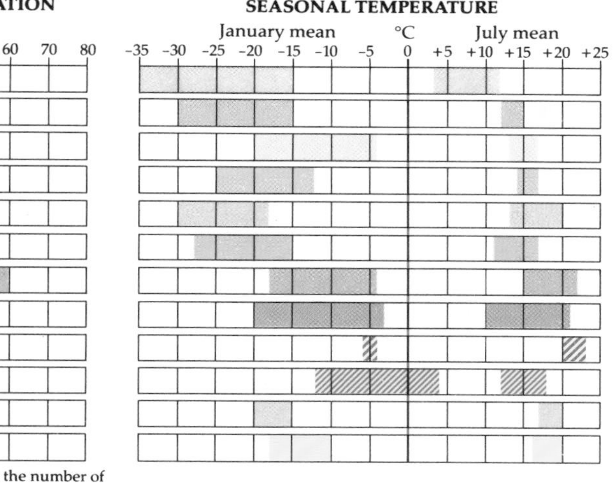
SEASONAL TEMPERATURE
January mean °C July mean
−35 −30 −25 −20 −15 −10 −5 0 +5 +10 +15 +20 +25

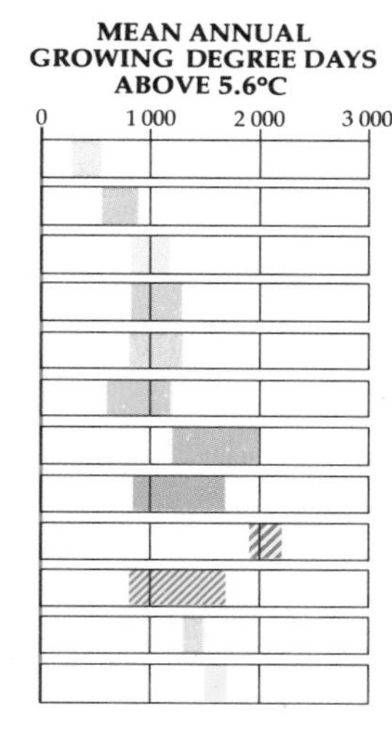
MEAN ANNUAL GROWING DEGREE DAYS ABOVE 5.6°C
0 1 000 2 000 3 000

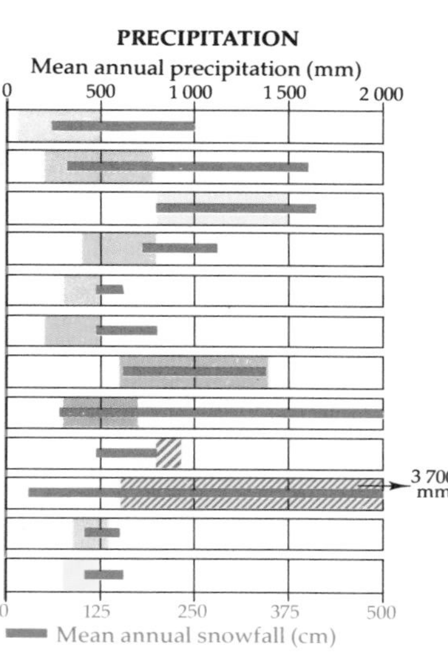
PRECIPITATION
Mean annual precipitation (mm)
0 500 1 000 1 500 2 000
3 700 mm
0 125 250 375 500
Mean annual snowfall (cm)

Annual growing degree days are the number of degrees above an average daily temperature of 5.6°C, totalled for a year.

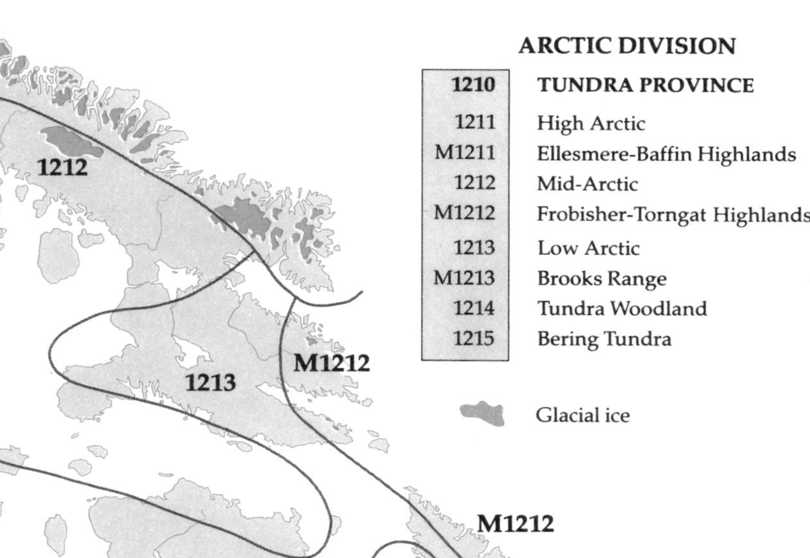
1211
1212
1213
M1212
M1212
1213

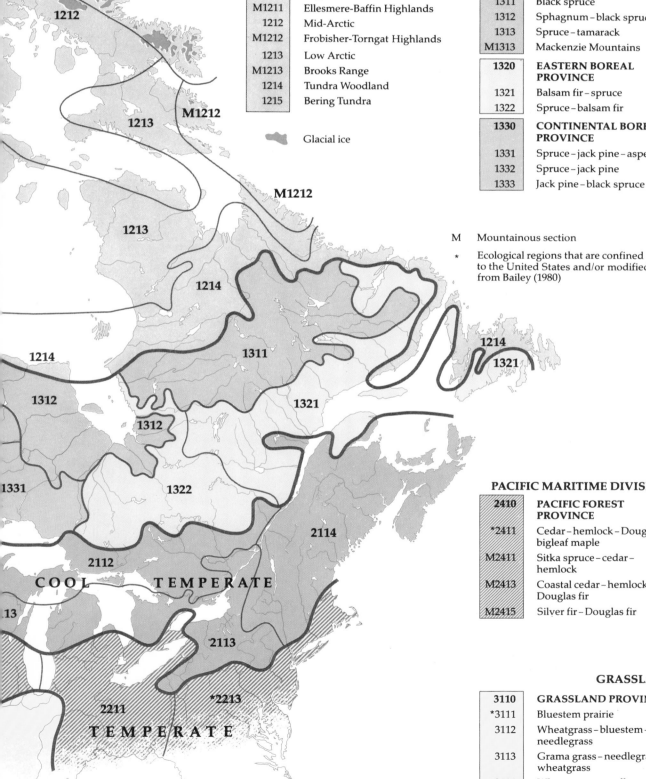

CIRCUMPOLAR DOMAIN

ARCTIC DIVISION

1210	**TUNDRA PROVINCE**
1211	High Arctic
M1211	Ellesmere-Baffin Highlands
1212	Mid-Arctic
M1212	Frobisher-Torngat Highlands
1213	Low Arctic
M1213	Brooks Range
1214	Tundra Woodland
1215	Bering Tundra

Glacial ice

BOREAL DIVISION

1310	**LICHEN WOODLAND PROVINCE**
1311	Black spruce
1312	Sphagnum – black spruce
1313	Spruce – tamarack
M1313	Mackenzie Mountains
1320	**EASTERN BOREAL PROVINCE**
1321	Balsam fir – spruce
1322	Spruce – balsam fir
1330	**CONTINENTAL BOREAL PROVINCE**
1331	Spruce – jack pine – aspen
1332	Spruce – jack pine
1333	Jack pine – black spruce
1340	**WESTERN BOREAL PROVINCE**
1341	Black spruce – tamarack – jack pine – poplar
1342	Aspen – spruce
1343	Black spruce – aspen
1344	Spruce – poplar
1350	**CORDILLERAN BOREAL PROVINCE**
1351	Spruce – lodgepole pine
1352	White spruce – birch
M1352	Alaska Range

M Mountainous section

* Ecological regions that are confined to the United States and/or modified from Bailey (1980)

HUMID TEMPERATE DOMAIN

COOL TEMPERATE DIVISION

2110	**GREAT LAKES – ST LAWRENCE FOREST PROVINCE**
2111	Pine – spruce – birch
2112	Maple – birch – pine
2113	Maple – hemlock
2114	Spruce – fir – maple
M2120	**COLUMBIA-MONTANE FOREST PROVINCE**
M2121	Spruce – aspen lodgepole pine
M2122	Cedar – hemlock – Douglas fir
M2123	Douglas fir

TEMPERATE DIVISION

2210	**DECIDUOUS FOREST PROVINCE**
2211	Beech – maple
*2212	Maple – basswood forest/ oak savannah
*2213	Appalachian oak

PACIFIC MARITIME DIVISION

2410	**PACIFIC FOREST PROVINCE**
*2411	Cedar – hemlock – Douglas fir bigleaf maple
M2411	Sitka spruce – cedar – hemlock
M2413	Coastal cedar – hemlock – Douglas fir
M2415	Silver fir – Douglas fir

PARKLAND DIVISION

2510	**PRAIRIE PARKLAND PROVINCE**
2511	Aspen

DRY DOMAIN

GRASSLAND-SHRUBLAND DIVISION

3110	**GRASSLAND PROVINCE**
*3111	Bluestem prairie
3112	Wheatgrass – bluestem – needlegrass
3113	Grama grass – needlegrass – wheatgrass
3114	Wheatgrass – needlegrass
M3120	**ROCKY MOUNTAIN FOREST PROVINCE**
*M3121	Grand fir – Douglas fir
*M3122	Douglas fir
3130	**PALOUSE PROVINCE**
3131	Wheatgrass – fescue – bluegrass
***3140**	**INTERMONTANE SHRUBLAND PROVINCE**
*3141	Sagebrush – wheatgrass
*3145	Ponderosa pine woodland
***3150**	**WYOMING BASIN PROVINCE**
3151	Wheatgrass – needlegrass – sagebrush

1214 1311 1214 1321 1312 1321 1312 1331 1322 2114 2112 COOL TEMPERATE 13 2113 2211 *2213 TEMPERATE

0 500 miles
0 500 kilometres
Scale 1:17 000 000

DESCRIPTIONS OF ECOLOGICAL REGIONS

Authors: J.H. McAndrews, G.C. Manville

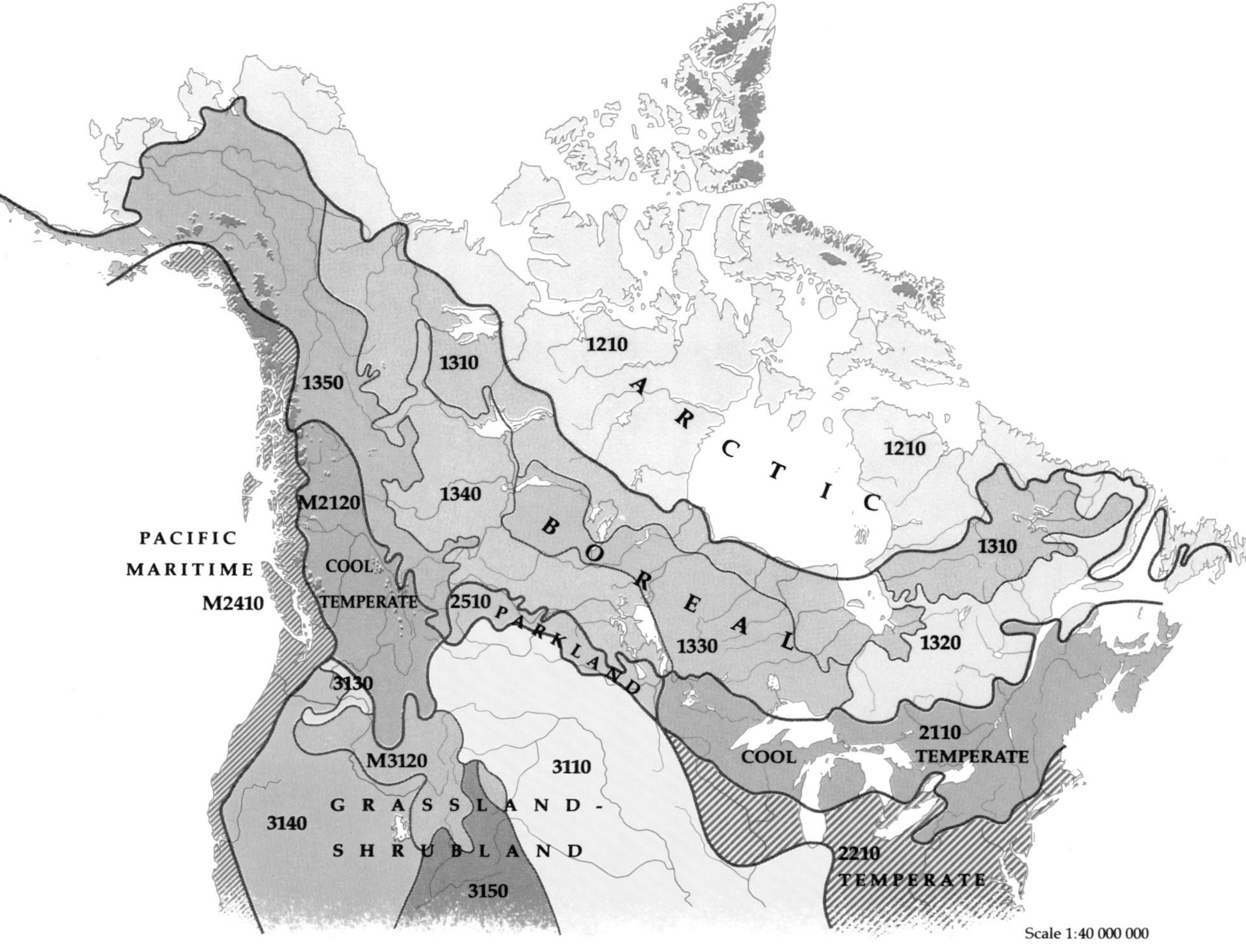

1210
A R C T I C
1210
1350
1310
1340
M2120
B O R E A L
1310
PACIFIC
MARITIME
M2410
COOL
TEMPERATE
2510
PARKLAND
1330
1320
3130
M3120
3110
COOL
2110
TEMPERATE
G R A S S L A N D -
S H R U B L A N D
3140
3150
2210
TEMPERATE
Scale 1:40 000 000

DOMAIN A subcontinental area of broadly similar climate. The three Canadian domains are distinguished by air-mass frequency, mean July temperature, degree days (accumulated number of degrees each day's temperature is above 5.6° C) in the growing season (number of days with an average temperature over 5.6° C), mean annual precipitation, season of maximum precipitation, and mean annual evaporation from small lakes.

DIVISION A subdivision of a domain, defined by regional climate, soil order, extent of permafrost, and dominant vegetation

PROVINCE A subdivision of a division, defined by soil groups, flora, and fauna. The mammals and birds listed are mainly those important for human subsistence. Fish are described by importance to native users (most important staple, staple, unimportant), by productivity in kg/km^2 (kilograms per square kilometre), and by occurrence in fresh water or in the sea (marine).

SECTION A subdivision of a province, defined by landforms, relief, elevation range and average, glacial and water deposits, percentage of fresh water and wetlands, and flora

1000 CIRCUMPOLAR DOMAIN

Dominated by Arctic air in winter and spring; mean July temperature 3–20° C; less than 1 300 degree-days in growing season; mean annual precipitation 100–1 500 mm with summer maximum; evaporation from small lakes less than 200 mm per year

1200 ARCTIC DIVISION

Mean July temperatures under 12° C; net annual radiation 0–28 W/m^2 (watts per square metre). Dominated by Arctic air throughout the year. Regosols, brunisols, and rockland; permafrost continuous. Tundra

1210 TUNDRA PROVINCE

SOILS Cryic regosol with melanic brunisol in south
VEGETATION Tundra (graminoids, forbs, cushion plants, mosses, lichens), with shrubs in valleys and wetlands; trees in sheltered habitats in south
FAUNA Mammals *Upland* Barren-ground caribou, arctic hare, and muskox (except Quebec and Baffin Island). *Marine* Widespread: ringed seal, bearded seal, and beluga whale; Atlantic coast: walrus and seasonally harp seal, hooded seal, and bowhead whale; Beaufort Sea coast: walrus and bowhead whale
Birds *Seasonal* Snow goose, Canada goose, brant goose, eider duck, puffin, great auk. *Resident* Ptarmigan, grouse
Fish Staple (productivity less than 10). *Freshwater* Arctic char, whitefish, lake trout, arctic cisco, grayling, inconnu, sucker, pike, burbot. *Marine* Herring, cod, halibut, smelt, saury, chub, perch (eel in Newfoundland)

1211 HIGH ARCTIC SECTION
LANDFORMS Plateaus, lowlands; elevation 0–600 m, average 100 m. Marine and till deposits. Fresh water 1%, wetlands less than 1%
VEGETATION Rock desert with cover less than 5% (mosses, lichens, avens, saxifrages, bell heather)

M1211 ELLESMERE-BAFFIN HIGHLANDS SECTION
LANDFORMS Mountains, plateaus, uplands; elevation 0–2 500 m, average 800 m. Extensive glaciers. Till deposits. Fresh water 1%, wetlands less than 1%
VEGETATION Rock desert (mosses, lichens, avens, saxifages, bell heather)

1212 MID-ARCTIC SECTION
LANDFORMS Lowlands, uplands, plateaus; elevation 0–400 m, average 100 m. Marine deposits in lowlands, till on eastern plateaus and uplands (Banks Island unglaciated). Fresh water 6%, wetlands less than 1%
VEGETATION Stony lichen-heath (lichens with scattered blueberry, crowberry, Labrador tea, grasses, and sedges)

M1212 FROBISHER-TORNGAT HIGHLANDS SECTION
LANDFORMS Mountains, uplands; elevation 0–700 m, average 500 m. Till on highlands, marine and lake deposits in lowlands. Fresh water 1%, wetlands less than 1%
VEGETATION Rock desert (lichens with woodrushes, sedges, avens, and saxifrages)

1213 LOW ARCTIC SECTION
LANDFORMS Uplands, plateaus, plains; flat; elevation 0–600 m, average 300 m. Till, marine, and lake deposits. Fresh water 9%, wetlands 3%
VEGETATION Shrub tundra (dwarf birch, alder, willow, Labrador tea, blueberry, lingonberry, crowberry, bluejoint, sedges, lichens, and mosses)

M1213 BROOKS RANGE SECTION
LANDFORMS Mountains, highlands, hills; rugged; elevation 900–3 000 m, average 1 500 m. Till. Fresh water 2%, wetlands 4%
VEGETATION Shrub tundra and wet tundra (dwarf birch, alder, willow, crowberry, Arctic blueberry, cranberry, cottongrass, bluejoint, bistort, mosses, lichens)

1214 TUNDRA WOODLAND SECTION
LANDFORMS Plains, uplands; flat; elevation 300–600 m, average 500 m. Till, marine, and lake deposits. Fresh water 10%, wetlands 12%
VEGETATION Tundra (dwarf birch, alder, willow, crowberry, Arctic blueberry, cranberry, cottongrass, lichens, mosses) interspersed with forest patches (black spruce, tamarack)

***1215 BERING TUNDRA SECTION**
LANDFORMS Coastal plain rising eastward, locally rugged; elevation 0–1 500 m, average 300 m. Fresh water over 10%
VEGETATION Wet tundra (sedges, cottongrass, dwarf birch, willow, alder). Valley woodland (white spruce, cottonwood, balsam poplar, alder)

1300 BOREAL DIVISION

Short, cool summers; mean July temperatures 11–20° C; net radiation 21–53 W/m^2 per year. Dominated by Arctic air in winter, non-Arctic air in summer. Podzols, organic soils, and brunisols. Permafrost widespread in north. Spruce dominant

1310 LICHEN WOODLAND PROVINCE

SOILS Ferric-humic podzol, dystric brunisol, cryic fibrisol
VEGETATION Spruce forest in valleys, scattered spruce on exposed sites (black spruce prominent). Willow, dwarf birch, lichens, mosses on uplands
FAUNA Mammals Woodland caribou, moose (except 1311), snowshoe hare, porcupine, beaver, Dall sheep (in M1313)
Birds *Resident* Spruce grouse, ruffed grouse. *Transient* Geese and ducks
Fish Staple (productivity 10–20). *Freshwater* Lake trout, whitefish, pike, sucker, burbot, salmon, grayling, cisco

1311 BLACK SPRUCE SECTION
LANDFORMS Plateaus, lowlands; flat to rolling, locally rugged; elevation 0–900 m, average 500 m. Till with marine clay in lowlands. Fresh water 9%, wetlands 4%
VEGETATION Woodland (black and white spruce, shrub birch, alder), and lowland bog (mosses, lichens, black spruce, Labrador tea)

1312 SPHAGNUM–BLACK SPRUCE SECTION
LANDFORMS Lowlands; flat; elevation 0–300 m, average 100 m. Marine and till deposits overlain by cryic fibrisols. Fresh water 3%, wetlands (fen, bog, salt marsh) 78%
VEGETATION Fens (sedges, peat mosses, hypnaceous mosses); bog (black spruce, shrub birch, alder, peat and hair-cap mosses); and salt marsh (glasswort, grasses). Forest along rivers (white spruce, balsam fir, aspen, balsam poplar, white birch)

1313 SPRUCE–TAMARACK SECTION
LANDFORMS Uplands, plains; flat; elevation 150–600 m, average 400 m. Shallow till. Fresh water 13%, wetlands (bog, muskeg) 12%
VEGETATION Black spruce, tamarack, alder, willow, shrub birch, reindeer lichens

M1313 MACKENZIE MOUNTAINS SECTION
LANDFORMS Mountains, highlands; rugged; elevation 600–2400 m, average 1 200 m. Local till. Fresh water less than 1%, wetlands 1%
VEGETATION Alpine (bell heather, sedge, bluegrass, avens, willow); conifer and shrub patches (white spruce, shrub birch, willow) in grassland (fescue)

1320 EASTERN BOREAL PROVINCE

SOILS Ferric-humic podzol and rockland
VEGETATION Forest (balsam fir, spruce)
FAUNA Mammals Moose, woodland caribou, white-tailed deer, snowshoe hare, beaver, porcupine
Birds *Seasonal* Common goldeneye, black duck. *Resident* Spruce grouse, ruffed grouse. *Transient* Canada goose
Fish Staple (productivity 20–30). *Freshwater* Lake trout, cisco, whitefish, pike, sucker, walleye, burbot, salmon, brook trout, sturgeon, perch, sauger, eel. *Marine* Herring, cod, smelt, haddock, silver hake, mackerel, flounder, halibut, tom cod

1321 BALSAM FIR–SPRUCE SECTION
LANDFORMS Plains, highlands, hills, mountains; flat and rolling to rugged; elevation 0–900 m, average 400 m. Till, marine, lake deposits. Fresh water 5%, wetlands 4%
VEGETATION Balsam fir, red spruce, black spruce, white birch

1322 SPRUCE–BALSAM FIR SECTION
LANDFORMS Lowlands, uplands; flat, rolling; elevation 0–900 m, average 400 m. Till, lake deposits, outwash. Fresh water 8%, wetlands (fen, bog, muskeg, marsh) 12%
VEGETATION Black and white spruce, balsam fir, white birch

1330 CONTINENTAL BOREAL PROVINCE

SOILS Ferric-humic podzol, gray luvisol, and fibrisol
VEGETATION Forest (spruce, jack pine)
FAUNA Mammals Woodland caribou, moose, snowshoe hare, beaver, porcupine.
Birds *Resident* Spruce grouse, sharp-tailed grouse, ruffed grouse. *Transient* Ducks
Fish Staple (productivity 10–36). *Freshwater* Cisco, whitefish, pike, sturgeon, sucker, perch, walleye, burbot, brook trout, goldeye, smallmouth bass, sauger

1331 SPRUCE–JACK PINE–ASPEN SECTION
LANDFORMS Uplands; elevation 300–600 m, average 450 m. Till, lake deposits, outwash. Fresh water 8%, wetlands 8%
VEGETATION Black spruce, white birch, jack pine, aspen, white spruce, tamarack

1332 SPRUCE–JACK PINE SECTION
LANDFORMS Plains, uplands; rolling to rugged; elevation 150–610 m, average 200 m. Till. Fibrisols and luvisols in central part, podzols elsewhere. Fresh water 17%, wetlands (muskeg, marsh) 15%
VEGETATION Spruce, jack pine, tamarack

1333 JACK PINE–BLACK SPRUCE SECTION
LANDFORMS Plains; elevation 300–600 m, average 450 m. Till, local lake deposits. Fresh water 12%, wetlands 4%
VEGETATION Jack pine, black spruce

1340 WESTERN BOREAL PROVINCE

SOILS Grey luvisol, gleysol, fibrisol, and cryic fibrisol
VEGETATION Mixed-wood forest with prominent aspen or balsam poplar. Shrubs frequent
FAUNA Mammals *Widespread* Moose, snowshoe hare, beaver, porcupine. *In north* Woodland caribou. *In south* Bison, wapiti, white-tailed and mule deer
Birds *Resident* Spruce, sharp-tailed, and ruffed grouse
Fish Staple (productivity 10–20). *Freshwater* Lake trout, cisco, whitefish, grayling, goldeye, pike, sucker, yellow perch, walleye, burbot, inconnu

1341 BLACK SPRUCE–TAMARACK–JACK PINE–POPLAR SECTION
LANDFORMS Plains; flat; elevation 150–300 m, average 200 m. Lake deposits. Fresh water 20%, wetlands (marsh, fen, muskeg) 22%
VEGETATION Black spruce, tamarack, jack pine, balsam poplar, willow, alder, blueberry, Labrador tea, sedge, peat moss

1342 ASPEN–SPRUCE SECTION
LANDFORMS Plains; flat except in east along Shield; elevation 150–900 m, average 600 m. Till, lake deposits, disintegration moraines. Fresh water 4%, wetlands (muskeg) 24%
VEGETATION Aspen, spruce, jack pine, balsam poplar, willow, alder, sedge, peat moss

1343 BLACK SPRUCE–ASPEN SECTION
LANDFORMS Plateaus, lowlands, plains; flat; elevation 150–900 m, average 300 m. Till, lake deposits. Fresh water 7%, wetlands (muskeg) 19%
VEGETATION Black spruce, aspen, white spruce, willow, alder, sedge, peat moss

1344 SPRUCE–POPLAR SECTION
LANDFORMS Plains; flat; elevation 0–310 m, average 150 m. Lake deposits, alluvium. Fresh water 7%, wetlands (muskeg) 19%
VEGETATION White spruce, balsam poplar, jack pine, willow, alder, peat moss

1350 CORDILLERAN BOREAL PROVINCE
SOILS Eutric brunisol, grey luvisol, and rockland
VEGETATION Spruce, lodgepole pine, birch forest
FAUNA Mammals *Widespread* Moose, snowshoe hare, beaver, porcupine. *In south* Woodland caribou, goat. *In north* Barren-ground caribou, Dall sheep
Birds *Resident* Spruce, blue, and ruffed grouse
Fish Unimportant (productivity less than 10); a staple along Yukon River in section 1352, with fauna as in 1210
1351 SPRUCE–LODGEPOLE PINE SECTION
LANDFORMS Mountains, plateaus, plains, trenches; rugged; elevation 900–3 000 m, average 1 000 m. Till, lake deposits. Fresh water 1%, wetlands 9%
VEGETATION Spruce, lodgepole pine
1352 WHITE SPRUCE–BIRCH SECTION
LANDFORMS Mountains, plateaus; rugged; elevation 900–3 000 m, average 1 000 m. Mountain glaciers, till. Fresh water 4%, wetlands 1%
VEGETATION Plateaus and mountains (white spruce, white birch, alpine fir); alpine tundra (bell heather, willow, sedges, bluegrass, avens)
M1352 ALASKA RANGE SECTION
LANDFORMS Mountains, trenches, lowlands; rugged; elevation 0–6 800 m, average 2 500 m. Fresh water 1%, wetland less than 1%
VEGETATION Valley forests (white spruce, cottonwood, black spruce bogs); upland forests (white spruce, birch, aspen, poplar); alpine tundra (avens, grasses, sedges); coastal fens (sedges, cottongrass, alder, willow)

2000 HUMID TEMPERATE DOMAIN

Dominated by maritime Pacific or tropical air masses at least in summer; mean July temperature 10–24° C; 900–2 000 degree-days in growing season; mean annual precipitation 300 to over 2 000 mm with maxima at various seasons; evaporation from small lakes 200–800 mm per year

2100 COOL TEMPERATE DIVISION

Mountainous west dominated by maritime Pacific air with winter precipitation maximum. From the Great Lakes eastward southern boundary approximates the mean winter position of Pacific air mass; net annual radiation 24–56 W/m². Podzols and luvisols. Glaciers and permafrost local in western mountains. Conifers dominate western forests; conifers and hardwoods form eastern mixed forest.

2110 GREAT LAKES–ST. LAWRENCE FOREST PROVINCE
SOILS Humic-ferric podzol, grey-brown and grey luvisols
VEGETATION Mixed deciduous and coniferous forest
FAUNA Mammals *In north* Moose and snowshoe hare. *In 2113* White-tailed deer, wapiti, and woodchuck. *Widespread* Black bear, beaver, porcupine
Birds *Seasonal* Passenger pigeon, black duck, sandhill crane, Canada goose. *Resident* Spruce and ruffed grouse. *Transient* Waterfowl
Fish Staple (productivity 70–175). *Freshwater* Trout, whitefish, sucker, sauger, walleye, eel, burbot, catfish, salmon, cisco, sturgeon, rainbow smelt, pike, muskellunge, perch, bass, drum. *Marine* Herring, cod, smelt, haddock, silver hake, mackerel, flounder, halibut, capelin
2111 PINE–SPRUCE–BIRCH SECTION
LANDFORMS Uplands; flat to undulating; elevation 300–600 m, average 450 m. Till, lake deposits. Fresh water 18%, wetlands (marsh, bog) 15%
VEGETATION White, red, and jack pine, spruce, birch, fir
2112 MAPLE–BIRCH–PINE SECTION
LANDFORMS Lowlands, uplands, highlands, hills; flat to undulating, locally rugged; elevation 0–600 m, average 300 m. Till, lake deposits, local outwash. Fresh water 11%, wetlands 1%
VEGETATION Sugar maple, yellow birch, white pine, red pine, spruce, fir, hemlock
2113 MAPLE–HEMLOCK SECTION
LANDFORMS Lowlands, plains; flat, locally rugged; elevation 100–600 m, average 300 m. Till, moraines, marine and lake deposits. Fresh water 19%, wetlands 1%
VEGETATION Sugar maple, beech, oak, hemlock, white pine
2114 SPRUCE–FIR–MAPLE SECTION
LANDFORMS Uplands, lowlands, mountains, highlands, hills; broad, rolling, locally rugged; elevation 0–900 m, average 400 m. Till, lake deposits. Fresh water 3%, wetlands 2%
VEGETATION Sugar maple, yellow birch, red spruce, balsam fir, hemlock, white pine

M2120 COLUMBIA-MONTANE FOREST PROVINCE
SOILS Grey luvisol, ferric-humic podzol, dystric brunisol, rockland
VEGETATION Forests, tundra, and grassland cover determined by local climates. Pine savannah (ponderosa pine, Douglas fir, lodgepole pine, aspen) at low elevation; subalpine forest (spruce, fir, lodgepole pine) and interior wet forest (western hemlock, western red cedar) at higher elevations; alpine tundra above tree line
FAUNA Mammals *Widespread* Moose, caribou, goat, mountain sheep, snowshoe hare, marmot, beaver, porcupine. *In south* White-tailed deer and wapiti
Birds *Resident* Willow ptarmigan, spruce, blue, and ruffed grouse. *Transient* Waterfowl
Fish Staple (productivity 140–175). *Freshwater* Salmon, trout, whitefish, sturgeon, chiselmouth, peamouth, squawfish, sucker, burbot
M2121 SPRUCE–ASPEN–LODGEPOLE PINE SECTION
LANDFORMS Plateaus, uplands; rolling to rugged with wide valleys; elevation 900–2 400 m, average 1 800 m. Till, lake deposits. Fresh water 1%, wetlands 1%
VEGETATION Subalpine forest (lodgepole pine, Douglas fir, aspen, white spruce); pine savannah (ponderosa pine, Douglas fir, wheatgrass, fescue); grassland (wheatgrass, needlegrass, bluegrass)
M2122 CEDAR–HEMLOCK–DOUGLAS FIR SECTION
LANDFORMS Mountains, highlands, foothills, plateaus, trenches; wide river valleys with broad plains; elevation 1 200–3 050 m, average 2 500 m. Till, alluvium. Fresh water 3%, wetlands 1%
VEGETATION Interior wet forest (western hemlock, western red cedar, Douglas fir); subalpine forest (Engelmann spruce, alpine fir, lodgepole pine); alpine tundra (sedges, grasses, willow, bell heather, avens)
***M2123 DOUGLAS FIR SECTION**

2200 TEMPERATE DIVISION

Mean July temperature over 20° C; net annual radiation more than 53 W/m². Northern boundary at mean summer convergence of Pacific and tropical air masses. Hardwoods dominant

2210 DECIDUOUS FOREST PROVINCE
SOILS Grey-brown luvisol, humic gleysol
VEGETATION Hardwood forest
FAUNA Mammals White-tailed deer, wapiti, black bear, cottontail rabbit, woodchuck, beaver, porcupine
Birds *Seasonal* Passenger pigeon, black duck, mallard *Resident* Turkey, ruffed grouse. *Transient* Waterfowl
Fish Staple (productivity 35–105). *Freshwater* Lake trout, cisco, whitefish, sturgeon, mooneye, pumpkinseed, bass, pike, muskellunge, sucker, redhorse, perch, sauger, walleye, drum, eel, burbot, catfish, salmon, brook trout, goldeye
2211 BEECH – MAPLE SECTION
LANDFORMS Lowlands, plains; flat, rolling; elevation 0–600 m, average 350 m. Till, lake deposits. Fresh water 10%, wetlands 1%
VEGETATION Broadleaf forest (sugar maple, beech, hickory, oak, butternut, walnut, elm, ash)
2212 MAPLE–BASSWOOD FOREST–OAK SAVANNAH SECTION
LANDFORMS Lowlands, plains; flat to hilly; elevation 300–500 m, average 300 m. Till, outwash
VEGETATION Broadleaf forest (sugar maple, basswood, oaks, and elm); on dry or fire-prone sites, grassland that contains bur oak or white oak, scattered singly or in groves
2213 APPALACHIAN OAK SECTION
LANDFORMS Mountains, plateaus; rolling to rugged; elevation 0–1 000 m, average 500 m
VEGETATION Broadleaf forest (white oak, red oak, red maple, sweet birch, hickory, chestnut, beech)

2400 PACIFIC MARITIME DIVISION

Freezing temperatures rare; Pacific air mass dominant; net annual radiation 26–53 W/m². Precipitation usually over 1 500 mm per year. Podzols, rockland. Conifers dominant

M2410 PACIFIC FOREST PROVINCE
SOILS Ferric-humic podzol
VEGETATION Forests of large conifers with undergrowth of heaths and ferns. Wet alpine tundra. Shoreline salt marshes and bogs
FAUNA Mammals Mule deer, mountain goat, whales, sea otter, sea-lion, fur seal
Birds *Seasonal* Summer: cormorants, puffins, murrelets, guillemots; winter: waterfowl. *Resident* Blue grouse. *Transient* Ducks, geese, swans
Fish Most important staple (productivity 140–175). *Freshwater* Salmon, trout, sturgeon, squawfish, sucker, eulachon. *Marine* Halibut, herring, surf smelt, capelin, cod, tom cod, saury, chub, mackerel, tuna, perch, rockfish, flounder, sole. Mussels, urchins, clams
2411 CEDAR–HEMLOCK–DOUGLAS FIR–BIGLEAF MAPLE SECTION
LANDFORMS Lowland, plains with hills; elevation 0–460 m, average 100 m. Till, outwash, alluvium and lacustrine deposits
VEGETATION Coniferous forest (western and red cedar, Douglas fir, western hemlock, grand fir, and bigleaf maple) that includes areas of grassland and open stands of Douglas fir and Oregon white oak
M2411 SITKA SPRUCE–CEDAR–HEMLOCK SECTION
LANDFORMS Mountains, highlands, foothills; rugged, dissected by fjords and inlets; elevation 0–3 000 m, average 1 800 m. Till. Local glaciers and permafrost
VEGETATION Pacific Coast forest (Douglas fir, western hemlock, western red cedar, yellow cedar); subalpine forest (mountain hemlock, amabalis fir, alpine fir); alpine tundra (blueberries, grasses, sedges, mosses, liverworts); salt marshes (glasswort, grasses)
M2413 COASTAL CEDAR–HEMLOCK–DOUGLAS FIR SECTION
LANDFORMS Mountains; rugged; elevation 150–2 500 m, average 1 500 m
VEGETATION Coniferous forest (western red cedar, western hemlock, Douglas fir, grand fir, Sitka spruce)
***M2415 SILVER FIR–DOUGLAS FIR SECTION**

2500 PARKLAND DIVISION

Mean July temperature 17–20° C; net annual radiation 42–56 W/m². Chernozem. Aspen parkland

2510 PRAIRIE PARKLAND PROVINCE
SOILS Black chernozem
VEGETATION Forest groves in grassland matrix
FAUNA Mammals Bison, white-tailed deer, mule deer, wapiti, beaver, porcupine
Birds *Seasonal* Mallard, redhead, shoveller, gadwall, American widgeon, double-crested cormorant, white pelican. *Resident* Sharp-tailed grouse. *Transient* Waterfowl, shorebirds
Fish Unimportant (productivity less than 10)
2513 ASPEN SECTION
LANDFORMS Plains; flat with gradual rise in elevation westward; elevation 300–600 m, average 450 m. Hummocky moraines, lake deposits. Fresh water 5%, wetlands 2%
VEGETATION Aspen at least 75% of forest cover; birch, spruce, balsam poplar present. Forest interspersed with prairie. Shrubs (saskatoons, chokecherry, rose, wolfberry) prominent. In west: aspen, white birch, needlegrass, fescue. In east: aspen, bur oak, hazel, wheatgrass, needlegrass

3000 DRY DOMAIN

Dominated by modified Pacific air mass for at least half the year; mean July temperature over 18° C; over 2 000 degree days in growing season; mean annual precipitation 200–500 mm with maximum in summer; annual evaporation from small lakes 800–1 000 mm

3100 GRASSLAND – SHRUBLAND DIVISION

Mean January temperature –18 to –10° C; net annual radiation 48–50 W/m². Chernozems. Grassland

3110 GRASSLAND PROVINCE
SOILS Brown and dark brown chernozems, brown solonetz
VEGETATION Grasses, forbs, shrubs; trees along rivers
FAUNA Mammals Bison, white-tailed deer, mule deer, wapiti, antelope
Birds *Seasonal* Mallard, redhead, American widgeon, canvasback, gadwall. *Resident* Greater prairie chicken, sharp-tailed grouse. *Transient* Waterfowl
Fish Unimportant (productivity less than 10)
3111 BLUESTEM PRAIRIE SECTION
LANDFORMS Lowlands, plains; flat to rolling; elevation 400–600 m, average 450 m
VEGETATION Tall grasses (big bluestem, little bluestem, switch grass, Indian grass), mid-grasses (needle grass), and forbs (composites and legumes)
3112 WHEATGRASS–BLUESTEM–NEEDLEGRASS SECTION
LANDFORMS Plains; flat; elevation 150–900 m, average 600 m. Hummocky moraines and lake deposits
VEGETATION Mid-grasses (wheatgrass, grama grass, needlegrass), tall grasses (bluestem), composites, sedges. Along rivers: elm, ash, birch, cottonwood. In east: scattered oak
3113 GRAMA GRASS–NEEDLEGRASS–WHEATGRASS SECTION
LANDFORMS Plains; flat, rise in elevation westward; elevation 610–1 800 m, average 1 000 m. Hummocky disintegration moraine, till; unglaciated in south
VEGETATION Short grass prairie (grama grass, wheatgrass, needlegrass); ash, cottonwood, and shrubs along rivers
3114 WHEATGRASS–NEEDLEGRASS SECTION
LANDFORMS Plateaus, foothills, low mountains; rolling to locally rugged; elevation 450–2 000 m, average 500 m
VEGETATION Mid-grasses (needle grass, western wheatgrass), short grasses (blue grama), and composites

M3120 ROCKY MOUNTAIN FOREST PROVINCE
SOILS Grey-brown and grey luvisols, dark brown chernozems
VEGETATION Forests with grassland in some valleys
FAUNA Mammals Mule deer, elk, bighorn sheep, moose, beaver
Birds *Resident* Blue grouse, ruffed grouse, quail. *Transient* Waterfowl
Fish Staple (productivity 140–170). *Freshwater* Salmon, trout, whitefish, sturgeon, squawfish, suckers
M3121 GRAND FIR–DOUGLAS FIR SECTION
LANDFORMS Plateaus and mountains; rolling to rugged; elevation 500–3 000 m, average 1 800 m
VEGETATION Coniferous forest (grand fir, Douglas fir, western larch, western white pine, trembling aspen)
***M3122 DOUGLAS FIR SECTION**
LANDFORMS Mountains; rugged; elevation 1 800–3 600 m, average 2 600 m
VEGETATION Coniferous forest (Douglas fir, white fir, white spruce, lodgepole pine, ponderosa pine, trembling aspen)

3130 PALOUSE PROVINCE
SOILS Dark brown chernozem on loess
VEGETATION Grasses with few shrubs
FAUNA Mammals Mule deer, antelope, wapiti, jack rabbit
Birds *Resident* Sharp-tailed grouse, quail
Fish Most important staple (productivity 140–170). *Freshwater* Salmon, trout, whitefish, sturgeon, squawfish, suckers
3131 WHEATGRASS–FESCUE–BLUEGRASS SECTION
LANDFORMS Plateaus; hilly; elevation 200–1 200 m, average 1 000 m
VEGETATION Low to medium-tall grassland (bluebunch wheatgrass, Idaho fescue, Bandberg blue grass)

3140 INTERMONTANE SHRUBLAND PROVINCE
SOILS Desert soils, alluvium, dry lake beds
VEGETATION Shrubs with sparse grasses
FAUNA Mammals Antelope, bighorn sheep, mule deer, wapiti, jack rabbit
Birds *Resident* Sage grouse, quail. *Transient* Sandhill crane, waterfowl
Fish Local staple along large rivers (productivity up to 170). *Freshwater* Salmon, sturgeon, whitefish, trout, squawfish, suckers
3141 SAGEBRUSH–WHEATGRASS SECTION
LANDFORMS Plains with low to high mountain ranges; flat to locally rugged; elevation 500–2 800 m, average 1 500 m
VEGETATION Dense to open shrubland and grassland (sagebrush, bluebunch wheatgrass, Idaho fescue); sparse coniferous forest of juniper on mountains
3145 PONDEROSA PINE WOODLAND SECTION
LANDFORMS Mountains and foothills, locally rugged; elevation 1 000–1 8000 m, average 1 500 m
VEGETATION Open coniferous forest with shrubs (ponderosa pine, Douglas fir, manzanitas, mountain mahogany, ninebark, bitterbrush, snowberries)

3150 WYOMING BASIN PROVINCE
SOILS Desert soils, alluvium, dry lake beds, dune sand, loess
VEGETATION Shrubland with grasses
FAUNA Mammals Bison, antelope, mule deer, jack rabbit
Birds *Resident* Sage grouse. *Transient* Waterfowl
Fish Unimportant (productivity less than 10). *Freshwater* Suckers
3151 WHEATGRASS–NEEDLEGRASS–SAGEBRUSH SECTION
LANDFORMS Plains with hills and low mountains; rolling; elevation 1 000–1 800 m, average 1 200 m
VEGETATION Grassland with scattered dwarf shrubs (western wheatgrass, plains bluegrass, needle-and-thread grass, sagebrushes, greasewood)

M Mountainous section
* Ecological regions that are confined to the United States and/or modified from Bailey (1980)

POPULATION AND SUBSISTENCE

Authors: Conrad E. Heidenreich; J.V. Wright (Prehistoric subsistence)

LINGUISTIC FAMILIES AND IDENTIFIABLE GROUPS

ALGONQUIAN LINGUISTIC FAMILY

Eastern Algonquian Groups

Mc **Micmac** Mc1 Gaspegeoag, 2 Sigentigteog, 3 Epigoitnag, 4 Pigtogeoag, 5 Onamag, 6 Esgigeoag, 7 Segepenegatig, 8 Gespogoitnag

Ma **Maliseet-Passamaquoddy** Ma1 Maliseet, 2 Passamaquoddy

Ae **Eastern Abenaki** Ae1 Penobscot, 2 Kennebec, 3 Arosaguntacook, 4 Pigwaket

Aw **Western Abenaki** Aw1 Sokoki, 2 Cowasuk, 3 Winnepesaukee, 4 Penacook, 5 Amoskeag

M **Mahican**

Ar **Southern New England groups** Ar1 Pawtucket, 2 Massachusett, 3 Pokanokett, 4 Naragansett, 5 Pequot-Mohegan

De **Delaware** De1 Munsee, 2 Northern Umami, 3 Southern Umami

Northern Algonquian Groups

O **Ojibwa** O1 Outchibous, 2 Marameg, 3 Mantouek, 4 Noquet, 5 Saulteaux, 6 Mississauga, 7 Nikikouet, 8 Amikwa, 9 Achiligouan (**N**, **Ot**), 10 Ouchougai (**N**, **Ot**), 11 Ouasouarini, 12 Sagahanirini

Ot **Ottawa**

Me **Menominee**

Pt **Potawatomi**

N **Nipissing**

S **Sauk-Fox-Kikapoo-Mascouten** S1 Sauk, 2 Fox, 3 Kikapoo, 4 Mascouten

M **Miami-Illinois** M1 Miami, 2 Illinois

Al **Algonquin** Al1 Onontchataronon, 2 Weskarini, 3 Matouweskarini, 4 Keinouche, 5 Kichesipirini, 6 Ottagoutouemin, 7 Sagnitaouigama, 8 Outimagami (N)

Cr **Cree-Gens de Terre** Cr1 Alimbegouek, 2 Monsoni, 3 Ataouabouskatouek, 4 Nisibourounik, 5 Pitchibourounik, 6 Gesseirinioueteh, 7 Opinagauirinioueteh, 8 Grand Mistassirini, 9 Petit Mistassirini, 10 Attikirinioueteh, 11 Nitchikirinioueteh, 12 Outchichagamioueteh, 13 Escurieux, 14 Nopeming-dach-irinioucek, 15 Outoulibi, 16 Timiscimi, 17 Abitibi, 18 Piscoutagami

Mt **Montagnais-Naskapi** Mt1 Tadoussacien, 2 Kakouchaki, 3 Chicoutimi, 4 Attikamek, 5 Nekoubaniste, 6 Chomonchouaniste, 7 Oumatachirini, 8 Papinachois, 9 Oukesestigouek, 10 Chisedech, 11 Bersiamites, 12 Oueneskapi, 13 Oumamiouek, 14 Outakouamiouek, 15 Outabitibec

Western Algonquian Groups

Ch **Cheyenne**

BEOTHUK LINGUISTIC FAMILY

Be **Beothuk**

IROQUOIAN LINGUISTIC FAMILY

Ir **Iroquoian** Ir1 Huron, 2 Petun (Tionontate), 3 Neutral, 4 Wenro, 5 Erie, 6 Seneca, 7 Cayuga, 8 Onondaga, 9 Oneida, 10 Mohawk, 11 Susquehannock

SIOUAN LINGUISTIC FAMILY

Da **Dakota**

W **Winnebago**

A **Assiniboine**

In the east, where the French compiled much ethnographic information before European diseases spread through the Great Lakes basin in the 1630s (pl 35), the distribution of early 17th-century populations is approximately known. Most of the St Lawrence valley was uninhabited (pl 33), population densities were low wherever the economy depended on hunting, fishing, and gathering, and sharply higher where agriculture was practised. Non-agricultural peoples were highly mobile; although territories were extensive, contact between neighbouring groups was frequent.

Linguistic groups

- Algonquian
- Beothuk
- Iroquoian
- Siouan

Scale 1:12 500 000

The analysis of discarded bones and shells from an archaeological site can indicate when the site was occupied, what animals were eaten, and the relative importance of different foods. Where soils are acidic, as in the Canadian Shield, such remains are rarely preserved, however, and very little prehistoric hunting and fishing equipment survives: stone, bone, and copper tips for spears and arrows are most common, whereas objects such as sinew or rope snares, nets, and traps usually have disappeared. Some stone structures used to channel caribou and trap fish, as well as portions of wooden fishing weirs buried under water in mud, have survived. Over all, archaeological data permit only a partial picture of patterns of subsistence in late prehistoric Canada.

SUBSISTENCE
Archaeological Data

- Corn, deer, fish
- Fish, sea mammals, caribou
- Fish, shellfish, moose, sea mammals
- Deer, fish
- Caribou, fish
- Caribou, fish, moose
- Bison
- Shellfish, fish, sea mamm

- Wooden caribou surroun
- Stone caribou drive-lanes
- Bison entrapment
- Stone fish weir
- Wooden fish weir

Scale 1:35 000 000

At the beginning of the 17th-century there were 12 linguistic families in native Canada. Within most of these linguistic families there were a number of languages and many dialects. Linguistic variety was greatest in the Cordillera (pl 66), whereas Algonquian speakers occupied a vast territory from the foothills of the Rockies to Labrador and the Maritimes. Europeans observed that it was not uncommon for natives to speak more than one language as trade and diplomacy required.

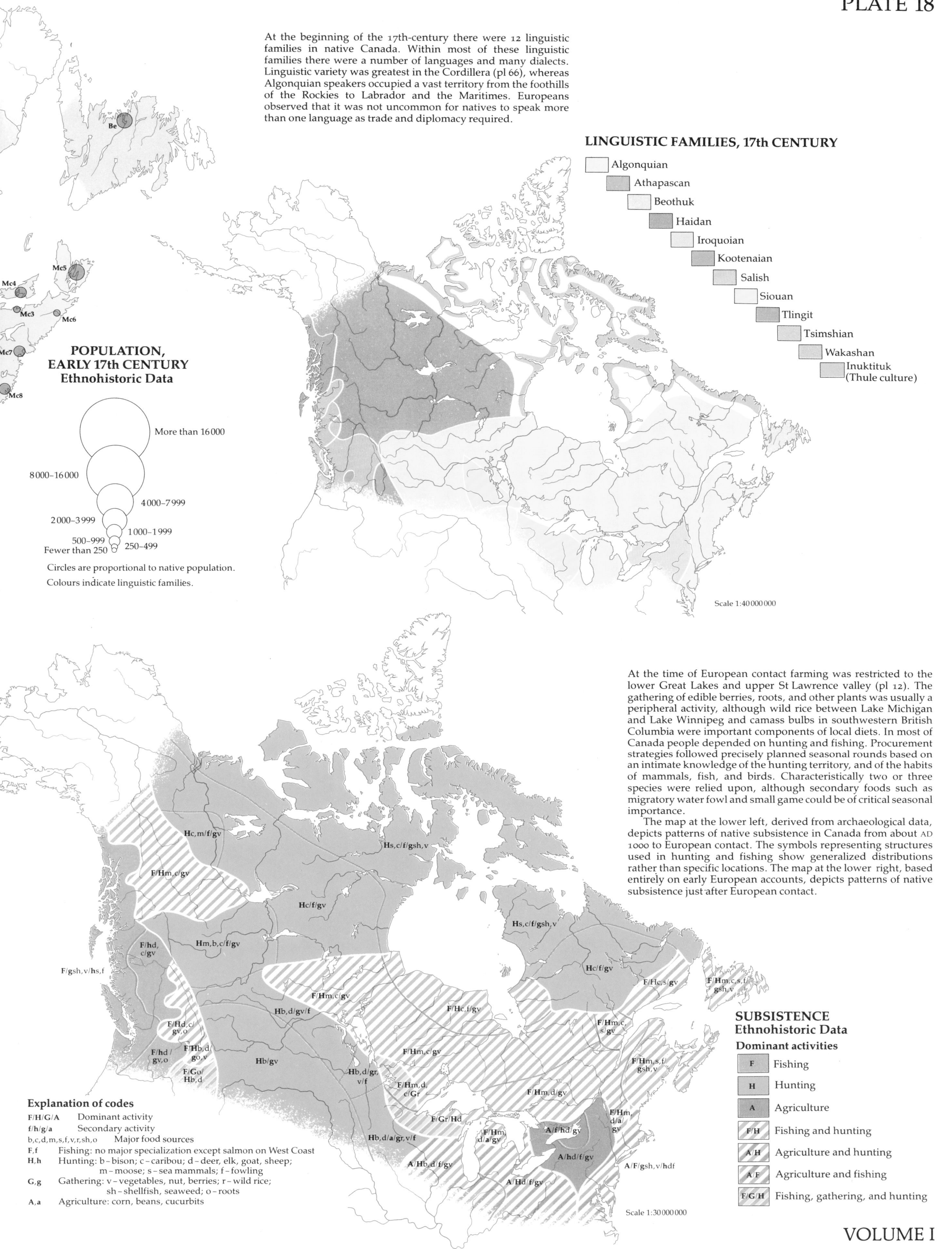
LINGUISTIC FAMILIES, 17th CENTURY
Algonquian
Athapascan
Beothuk
Haidan
Iroquoian
Kootenaian
Salish
Siouan
Tlingit
Tsimshian
Wakashan
Inuktituk (Thule culture)
Be
Mc4
Mc5
Mc3
Mc6
Mc7
Mc8
POPULATION, EARLY 17th CENTURY
Ethnohistoric Data
More than 16000
8000–16000
4000–7999
2000–3999
1000–1999
500–999
250–499
Fewer than 250
Circles are proportional to native population.
Colours indicate linguistic families.
Scale 1:40000000
Hc,m/f/gv
Hs,c/f/gsh,v
F/Hm,c/gv
Hc/f/gv
Hs,c/f/gsh,v
F/hd,
c/gv
Hm,b,c/f/gv
Hc/f/gv
F/gsh,v/hs,f
F/Hc,s/gv
F/Hm,c,s,f/
gsh,v
F/Hm,c/gv
F/Hc,f/gv
Hb,d/gv/f
F/Hd,c/
gv,o
F/Hm,c,
s/gv
F/hd /
gv,o
F/Hb,d/
go,v
Hb/gv
F/Hm,c/gv
F/Go/
Hb,d
Hb,d/gr,
v/f
F/Hm,s,f/
gsh,v
F/Hm,d,
c/Gr
F/Hm,d/gv
F/Gr/Hd
F/Hm,
d/a/
gv
Hb,d/a/gr,v/f
F/Hm,
d/a/gv
A/f/hd/gv
A/hd/f/gv
A/Hb,d/f/gv
A/F/gsh,v/hdf
A/Hd/f/gv
Scale 1:30000000
Explanation of codes
F/H/G/A Dominant activity
f/h/g/a Secondary activity
b,c,d,m,s,f,v,r,sh,o Major food sources
F,f Fishing: no major specialization except salmon on West Coast
H,h Hunting: b – bison; c – caribou; d – deer, elk, goat, sheep; m – moose; s – sea mammals; f – fowling
G,g Gathering: v – vegetables, nut, berries; r – wild rice; sh – shellfish, seaweed; o – roots
A,a Agriculture: corn, beans, cucurbits
SUBSISTENCE
Ethnohistoric Data
Dominant activities
F Fishing
H Hunting
A Agriculture
F/H Fishing and hunting
A/H Agriculture and hunting
A/F Agriculture and fishing
F/G/H Fishing, gathering, and hunting

At the time of European contact farming was restricted to the lower Great Lakes and upper St Lawrence valley (pl 12). The gathering of edible berries, roots, and other plants was usually a peripheral activity, although wild rice between Lake Michigan and Lake Winnipeg and camass bulbs in southwestern British Columbia were important components of local diets. In most of Canada people depended on hunting and fishing. Procurement strategies followed precisely planned seasonal rounds based on an intimate knowledge of the hunting territory, and of the habits of mammals, fish, and birds. Characteristically two or three species were relied upon, although secondary foods such as migratory water fowl and small game could be of critical seasonal importance.

The map at the lower left, derived from archaeological data, depicts patterns of native subsistence in Canada from about AD 1000 to European contact. The symbols representing structures used in hunting and fishing show generalized distributions rather than specific locations. The map at the lower right, based entirely on early European accounts, depicts patterns of native subsistence just after European contact.

The Atlantic Realm

During the 16th century the Atlantic rim of what is now Canada was incorporated in the European economy as fishermen from many European ports came to catch and process cod. With them came fishing techniques worked out in the northeastern Atlantic during the middle ages, ships and navigational principles developed principally by Portuguese and Basques in the 15th century, and the organization of early-modern mercantile capitalism. Throughout the 16th century Europeans were in Canada only seasonally, but they came in their summer numbers year after year, and their iron, cloth, and arms were far beyond the capacity of native manufacture. The maritime edge of northeastern North America began to participate in quite different economic realms: cod and a few furs were shipped to Europe while European trade goods entered native economies. Local natives suddenly faced European competition for summer fishing sites, while other natives – the Thule (Inuit) from northern Labrador, and perhaps the St Lawrence Iroquoians from the lower St Lawrence – made summer trading or raiding trips to obtain European goods from fishermen at the Strait of Belle Isle.

The European fishery had reached rocky, coniferous land with almost no agricultural potential (pl 20). In spring and summer the Labrador current brought floe ice and icebergs offshore, new to European experience. But there were good and numerous harbours and cod in abundance in coastal waters and on the continental shelf. Possibly the European fishery in these waters preceded John Cabot's voyage of 1497 (pl 19); certainly it was in existence soon thereafter. As it developed, it scattered knowledge of the configuration and resources of the northeastern North American coast through the fishing ports of western Europe, knowledge that often far surpassed the more official records of exploration.

For more than a century the prospect of a sea route to Asia and of New World treasure encouraged most official exploration of northeastern North America. When the Italian Giovanni de Verrazzano (sailing for France) and the Spaniard Esteban Gomez sailed along the coast between Newfoundland and Florida in the 1520s (pl 19), the conceptual discovery of North America had certainly been made, and Europeans began their attempts to explore or, more often, to get around or through this unknown, unpromising land. The expeditions led by Jacques Cartier and Jean-Francois La Rocque de Roberval into the Gulf of St Lawrence in 1534, 1535–6, and 1541–3 (pls 19, 33) were French attempts, authorized by the king, to break Spanish and Portuguese monopolies in the New World, to repeat glittering Spanish discoveries, and to open a route to Asia. Later in the 16th century Elizabethan gentlemen-adventurers, representing Protestant England against Catholic Spain and drawn by the lure of Spanish treasure and oriental trade, sought honour in the North Atlantic as their ancestors had sought it on the soil of France. A few of them – particularly Martin Frobisher and John Davis – penetrated the strait between Greenland and Baffin Island looking for a westward passage (pl 19). Henry Hudson, Thomas Button, Luke Foxe, Thomas James, and the Dane Jens Munk continued this search into Hudson Bay until, by the 1630s, it was judged to be fruitless.

All the while the fishery drew thousands of men across the Atlantic each year. A well-tried technology, established channels of financing and marketing, and a growing demand for fish in the rapidly increasing European population underlay a trans-Atlantic rush to new resources. Late in the 15th century voyages to distant fishing grounds were common in Europe (pl 22). Fishermen from Germany, Holland, and eastern England sailed to Iceland and the Lofoten Islands (off northern Norway) for cod. Basque whalers operated along the coasts of Cantabria and Galicia. Portuguese fished for tuna and sardines along the Atlantic Coast of the Sahara. Waters south of Ireland attracted Portuguese, French, Basque, and English fishermen, and it was some of these fishermen who, as soon as New World cod stocks were known, began to cross the Atlantic to fish along the coast of Newfoundland. The Portuguese and French were there first, followed by Basques by the 1520s, but not by English fishermen in numbers until after 1570 when the Danes reasserted control of the Icelandic fishery. By the end of the 16th century most European ports from Cadiz to Bristol had participated in the New World fisheries (pl 22). The number of men and ships and the tonnages involved are still unknown. In 1578 Anthony Parkhurst, an English merchant who had made several voyages to Newfoundland, thought there were nearly 400 ships – 150 French, 100 Spanish (Basque), 50 Portuguese, 30–50 English, plus 20–30 Basque whalers – and current research in the relevant European archives should soon tell us whether he was approximately right. Most of the cod ships were small (40–100 tons) and unspecialized, for this fishery did not require specialized ships. The Basque galleons that visited the summer whaling stations in the Strait of Belle Isle were much larger, commonly 400–600 tons. Together the whale and cod fisheries involved an annual trans-Atlantic migration of hundreds of ships and thousands of men. Less spectacular than Spanish activities in the Caribbean, Mexico, and Peru, the fisheries in the northwestern Atlantic involved more ships and men. The Spanish Basque fleet for Newfoundland in 1571 was about 15,000 tons, half as large again as the Spanish fleet that year for the West Indies and Central America.

The New World cod fishery probably began in the inshore waters of the Avalon Peninsula; its early concentrations appear to have been there and along the Strait of Belle Isle. As the English pushed other fishermen off the eastern Avalon Peninsula after 1570, the fishery expanded around much of coastal Newfoundland, into the Gulf of St Lawrence, and south along the Atlantic coast of what is now Nova Scotia (pl 22). The practice of sending some ships early in the year to fish the offshore banks, salt the cod in their holds, and return to Europe without landing in the New World (the banks fishery, producing wet or green cod, pl 21) was probably established by 1550. But throughout the 16th century many more ships made for harbours along the coast; there they were anchored or beached, and fishing took place from small boats close to shore (the inshore fishery, producing primarily dried cod, pl 21). Boats of many different type were used; but the shallop, a keel boat, pointed at both ends, that could be rowed or sailed, that could be transported overseas in sections, and that was large, seaworthy, and manoeuvrable enough (length 25–30 ft, capacity 4–6 tons) to work troubled inshore waters and carry a day's catch, quickly became the common boat of the inshore fishery. Fish were lightly salted and dried ashore, at first, probably, on beach cobbles and eventually, in many places, on drying platforms (flakes). The cod fishery produced three products: oil from cod livers; wet (or green or salted) cod for markets in northern Europe; and dried cod, a more thoroughly processed and more easily preserved food, for markets in southern Europe and, eventually, in the West Indies.

The shore drying of cod by migratory fishermen required the building of cabins, wharves (stages), drying platforms (flakes), washing cages, and oil vats – activities that occupied a crew for two or three weeks after a ship arrived in a fishing harbour. At the end of the season the crew either dismantled its earlier constructions, or left them, hoping that something would be useful the following season. Between these activities men fished from shallops, processed cod ashore, and then loaded the ship. The men and boys who performed these tasks usually came from the ship's port of embarkation or its immediate hinterland, and were bound to a rigid, specialized work discipline in what were virtually unmechanized seasonal factories overseas. The fishery was hard, dangerous work, but less dangerous than voyages to the West Indies. It was entered into by farmers without enough land to support their families, by tradesmen with insufficient trade, by orphaned lads – by a considerable cross-section of the poor near the fishing ports – for all of whom it offered indentured wages that were usually a little above those for agricultural workers and some prospect of advancement. Most of these men would return to Europe, their participation in the fishery a particularly specialized form of the seasonal migrations that were part of the survival strategy of many of the European poor.

This migration was managed by merchants and watched over by governments. Merchants imposed as much control as possible upon a trade subject to the inevitable uncertainties of supply and price and the additional risks of shipwreck, piracy, and war. For governments the fishery was a nursery for seamen, a basis for territorial claims, and a sizable component of international trade.

Although labour-intensive, the cod fishery made little use of native labour. The Beothuk Indians of Newfoundland were too few to be of much service to fishermen, who easily pre-empted summer fishing sites and increased the dependence of the Beothuk on the meagre resources of the interior where, archaeological evidence suggests, their camps were increasingly located. Attempts by the Beothuk to steal goods they could rarely afford to purchase only heightened European animosity towards them. Along the coast of Labrador after 1550 Inuit hunters drove off European fishermen and attacked Basque whaling stations; later the French faced recurrent Inuit harassment of their seasonal fishery along the Northern Peninsula of Newfoundland (Le Petit Nord). In the Gulf of St Lawrence a few Indians were occasionally employed to dry cod or to work in the seasonal whaling stations. More commonly fishermen and Indians met to trade furs. As the Indians sought more European durable goods, they spent more of the year trapping in the interior. The depletion of fur-bearing animals may have increased native warfare as bands sought to expand their hunting territories. By the 1530s the Micmac may have been at war with the St Lawrence Iroquoians and seem eventually to have driven them from their summer fishing grounds around the Gaspé Peninsula. The Maliseet and Passamoquoddy abandoned their coastal villages to hunt in winter in small bands in the interior. Warfare, as well as the limited number of places where trade could be carried on regularly with Europeans, apparently encouraged the amalgamation of neighbouring bands and enhanced the position of chiefs who traded directly with Europeans. All the while European diseases must have taken their toll. In 1616 the Jesuit Pierre Biard estimated that there were about 3 000 Micmac. Although we do not know, their numbers were probably much higher when the fishery began.

In 1600 there was still no permanent white settlement in northeastern North America. Seasonal French fisheries operated from the south and northeast coasts of Newfoundland and from points in the Gulf of St Lawrence (pl 22). Normans, Bretons, and fishermen from the Loire to the Garonne fished the offshore banks. In summer migrant English fishermen, still much less numerous than the French, controlled the east coast of the Avalon Peninsula and Trinity Bay as far north as Cape Bonavista. Portuguese and Spanish-Basque fisheries were in rapid decline. They had lost men and ships to the Spanish Armada and faced rapidly rising prices for supplies and labour in the Iberian peninsula following the import of bullion from the New World, heavy government taxation, and the effects of English privateering. By 1600 English dried cod undersold the Basque product in Spain. Most of the Basque whaling stations along the Strait of Belle Isle had been abandoned; whaling moved to bases in Spitzbergen where, increasingly, the Basques were outmatched by the Dutch.

Early in the 17th century the governments of England and France authorized the establishment of permanent settlements in North America. In 1604 Pierre du Gua, Sieur de Monts, brought 79 men to the mouth of the St Croix River, the first attempted settlement in Acadia, and the next year he relocated the settlement at Port Royal on the opposite side of the Bay of Fundy. In 1608 his associate, Samuel de Champlain, established a trading post at Quebec. In 1610 the Newfoundland Company, an English joint-stock company, planted a settlement in Conception Bay. Thereafter several proprietors obtained land from the Newfoundland Company and tried to settle elsewhere on the Avalon Peninsula: the Welsh visionary Sir William Vaughan in 1617 at Renews; Bristol merchants at Harbour Grace the same year; Henry Cary (Viscount Falkland) at Renews in 1623; John Slany and William Payne at St John's by 1624; George Calvert (later Lord Baltimore) at Ferryland in 1632; and David Kirke at Ferryland in 1638. All these Newfoundland proprietors gave up. Calvert, who had come to 'build, and settle and sowe' where agriculture was as difficult as anywhere in the middle latitudes, left 'this wofull country' where 'from the middest of October to the middest of May there is a sadd face of wynter upon all this land' with the intention of settling in Virginia. Another titled Englishman advised his father: 'if ever you look for money again in this country, you must send fishermen.' In Acadia, where the physical limitations on agriculture were less severe, there was a succession of starts, raids, and abandonments until the Treaty of Saint-Germain-en-Laye (1632) gave France some security of title.

The chartered colonization schemes were financial disasters for their investors, but they demonstrated that overwintering and extended residence were possible, and they left behind a few men who began prosecuting the fishery on their own accounts, encouraging settlement to develop out of the migratory fishery. In Acadia descendants of a few colonists sent after 1632 began to farm the tidal marshes around the Bay of Fundy.

The advantages and disadvantages of settlement in Newfoundland were argued throughout the 17th century in both England and France. On the one side were arguments (usually advanced by merchants who were successful in the migratory fishery) that Newfoundland was uninhabitable. Were it to be settled, residents would pre-empt the best fishing sites, destroy equipment left by migratory fishermen, debauch seamen, and by reducing the labour pool drive up wages at home. The mother country would lose a crucial supply of seamen, and her merchants and tradesmen would lose business to foreigners. On the other side were these views: Newfoundland was habitable, settlement would encourage a more efficient fishery by reducing the expense of annual building and by lengthening the effective fishing season, and its settlement would forestall the French (or the English). Throughout the 17th century neither side could prevail. An English regulation of 1671 requiring captains to bring back seamen and encouraging settlers to move to Jamaica was not enforced. The decision late in the 1650s to establish a permanent French Settlement at Plaisance faced the immediate, vociferous opposition of the French Basques and obstruction for the next 50 years. Nevertheless, the practical advantages of settlement were becoming increasingly apparent as the century wore on. The English shore between Trepassy and Bonavista, effectively British territory but not a colony, had no customs officials and was largely exempt from the Navigation Acts (which required that enumerated goods be carried in British ships); its ports became centres of free trade in the northwestern Atlantic. Although Plaisance was more regulated, it too was beginning to serve as an international port. Moreover French and English merchants could protect valuable trading locations and shore constructions by leaving men there, reduce the cost of the homeward passage, and, if the men survived and did not get away to New England, ensure a labour supply for the following season. Some merchants themselves began to spend the winters in Newfoundland. These resident boat masters (planters, habitants-pêcheurs) owned a few shallops, hired crews each season, and sold dried cod to ships from England, France, or New England.

Almost all these 'overwinterers' expected to return home and, if they survived, most of them did. 'Soe longe as their comes noe women,' wrote an English commander, 'they are not fixed.' Coves that came to be occupied each winter were rarely occupied for many years by the same people. Overwintering lengthened the period of residence but did not change the migratory character of the fishing community. Yet some women did come, usually wives or servants of planters. By the 1670s there was at least one family in

30 different English settlements along the east coast of Newfoundland. St John's had almost 30 planter families, Plaisance about a dozen (pl 23).

Demographically these early English and French settlements in Newfoundland were characterized by the overwhelming predominance of men, most of whom were overwintering servants, the scarcity of families, and the mobility of almost everyone – servants more than planters, single planters more than those with Newfoundland families, men more than women, but almost everyone part of the ebb and flow of a trans-Atlantic fishery. Newfoundland was a temporary workplace where kitchen gardens, livestock, fish, and seabirds were supplemented by imported food; and where rum was a principal comfort for many a lonely man by an isolated shore. We do not know how many of these temporary settlers and migrant workers left with more than they came. Undoubtedly many accumulated only debt, and a good many of these debtors, especially in the English fishery, seized any opportunity to slip away to New England and another New World start.

By 1690, at the beginning of some 20 years of war between France and England, the English fishery in eastern Newfoundland was well established from Bonavista to Trepassy (pl 23). It was still primarily a migratory fishery, increasingly from southern England rather than the West Country, but with a growing residential component. The French controlled the rest of coastal Newfoundland and the Gulf of St Lawrence (pl 23). Fishermen from Saint Malo and Granville conducted an entirely migratory fishery to the Northern Peninsula of Newfoundland (Le Petit Nord). French Basques from Bayonne and Saint-Jean-du-Luz were the most common fishermen in the Gulf. There were both resident and migratory French fisheries in southern Newfoundland where Plaisance was a seat of colonial administration. With a governor, troops, a few settlers sent by the crown, a fortification, church, and regularly surveyed lots (pl 23) Plaisance probably had a more ordered existence and a more stable resident population than any other fishing settlement north of New England. By 1698 its 29 families included a few men and more women who had been born and raised there. It was a tiny settlement precariously balanced between the rival interests of residential and migratory fisheries, but undoubtedly some of its own planters, operating between fishermen and outside merchants, no longer planned to return to France.

A very different economy and society developed around the Bay of Fundy (pl 29). Beginning with de Monts' settlements at Sainte-Croix and Port Royal, a succession of merchant colonizers attempted to establish settlements in the Bay of Fundy for the primary purpose of fur trading, but as the limited Acadian fur trade required little white labour, most colonists turned to agriculture. As early as the 1630s the few families at Port Royal were dyking and cultivating tidal marshes on which they planted cereals and raised cattle. By 1670 the population at Port Royal had grown by natural increase and immigration to about 350 people, and soon after, as marshland near Port Royal became scarce, some young people migrated to the larger marshes at the head of the bay. In 1700 there were some 1400 Acadians around the Bay of Fundy, almost all of them members of farm families.

Demographically balanced and detached from trans-Atlantic migration, Acadian society soon became a dense web of blood relationships. The founding stock comprised about 40 families and a few men who married daughters of the Acadian families. Descendants from the early families intermarried and spread to all the major Fundy marshlands. Their farms produced a rough sufficiency, and sometimes a little surplus that entered a coastal trade with New England. We have little documentary evidence about Acadian society, but it cannot have been sharply stratified. Seigneurial institutions all but disappeared, and the parish lost the official administrative functions with which it was associated in France. Colonial government, intermittently established at Port Royal, exerted little influence on the settlements at the head of the bay. Even the militia, called up at Port Royal when the English attacked, must have been a makeshift force. In effect, the marshlands provided a niche for the French peasant family and an amalgam (from different French regions) of French peasant ways, but little of the dense social and economic hierarchy of rural France. Houses and farm buildings reflected the local availability of wood, building techniques widely known in peasant Europe, and the limitations of the local economy. Only at Port Royal, where there was usually a fort, a garrison, and a governor, were there traces of French elegance, but even they, as Jean-Baptiste Louis Franquelin's map of 1686 shows (pl 29), were faint enough. By 1710 Port Royal supported a considerable temporary population of soldiers and artisans, but most Acadian life turned around the marshland farms of which French military engineer Delabat's remarkable map (pl 29) is the best surviving glimpse.

From 1689 to 1713 the colonies and fisheries in the northwestern Atlantic were caught in more than two decades of almost continuous warfare between France and England (The War of the League of Augsburg, 1689–97; The War of Spanish Succession, 1701–13). In 1696–7 and again in 1705 and 1709 the French devastated the English settlements on the Avalon, but, as they did not establish permanent garrisons, English fishermen returned as the French left. In 1709 two English attacks on Port Royal were beaten off, but in 1710 the tiny garrison surrendered to a force more than ten times its size. The Treaty of Utrecht (1713) confirmed this conquest. Much of Acadia was ceded to Britain; henceforth most of the rapidly growing Acadian population lived under nominal English control. The French retained fishing rights in western and northern Newfoundland and controlled Île Royale (Cape Breton Island) and the Gulf of St Lawrence.

After the Treaty of Utrecht the planter families at Plaisance moved to Louisbourg on Île Royale where, in 1717, the French government began a major fortification intended as a naval base to protect French interests in the Gulf of St Lawrence. The resident population of Île Royale, dependent on the fishery, international trade, and French military spending, grew rapidly to more than 5 000 in the early 1750s. Louisbourg quickly became one of the busier ports in North America (pl 24).

The fishery on Île Royale was controlled primarily by residents, most of them planters who had a shore room and two or three shallops, hired 10–15 men a season, and operated on credit from buyers and suppliers. So organized, the shallop fishery produced a scattering of tiny coastal settlements. At the same time some planters on Île Royale began to buy schooners from New Englanders and fish the banks. The schooner, a manoeuvrable, relatively inexpensive ship of 30–70 tons that could be sailed by three or four men and fished by six to ten, could stay on the banks for days or weeks, salting cod as in the green fishery and then bringing it ashore for drying. Schooners tended to be associated with the larger settlements where there were usually better harbours and more capital and labour. On Île Royale they operated principally from Louisbourg (pl 24).

At Louisbourg, where France superimposed a garrison town on a fishing port, trade soon flourished. The town traded in French manufactures: West Indian sugar, molasses, and rum; New England, Canadian, and Acadian grain, meat, and timber; and local fish. Merchants based in France or New England sent ships to Louisbourg, and some of its own merchants amassed sizable fortunes and lived in comfort. Social life was dominated by merchant power and wage relationships, and by rank in the French military or colonial service. Louisbourg was a cultural melting pot: fishermen and merchant families from Plaisance, Acadian girls who had married in Louisbourg, people from many regions and walks of life in France, and the flux associated with a port and the fishery.

France and England were again at war during most of the 1740s and 1750s (the War of Austrian Succession, 1742–8; the Seven Years' War, 1756–63), and the North American consequences were catastrophic for France. Louisbourg fell to a force of New Englanders in 1745, was returned by the British three years later, and retaken after a massive assault by British regulars in 1758 (pl 42). This time the fortress town was blown up. A decision to deport the Acadians was of even more drastic long-term consequence. For British officials in Acadia, who had long suspected Acadian claims of neutrality, deportation seemed a permanent solution to the problem of ruling people of doubtful loyalty. For the Acadians it was a tragedy. The decision to deport them, taken in 1755 without approval from London, was carried out with determination over several years (pl 30). Some of the almost 13 000 Acadians in 1755 escaped to Canada, others, temporarily, to Île Royale. Sooner or later most were caught. Those rounded up in 1755 were sent to the British colonies along the Atlantic seaboard; many captured later were sent to France or England. These deportations transformed the linguistic and religious future of Atlantic Canada. At the end of the Seven Years' War Louisbourg was a ruin, the French fisheries on Île Royale and in Gaspé were gone, and the Acadians no longer farmed around the Bay of Fundy. Other people were beginning to move onto the marshes (pl 31). France retained tiny islands in the Gulf of St Lawrence, and held concurrent fishing rights in western and northern Newfoundland.

In the last decades of the 18th century the French migratory fishery continued to the northern peninsula and west coast of Newfoundland where it still supported large seasonal settlements (pls 21, 25). The English fishery in Newfoundland, still substantially migratory, expanded west from Placentia Bay and northwest from Trinity Bay, reaching Labrador by 1770 (pl 25). By 1790 Newfoundland had only about 10 000 long-term residents in a winter population of 20 000 and a summer population of perhaps 25 000. Resident men outnumbered women by five to one. Women married at an average age of 19, compared to an age of 26 for men, and were more likely than men to remain in Newfoundland. A growing percentage of the population was Irish. As early as the 1720s Irish labour was being recruited by English fishing captains; some of these men remained in Newfoundland, and before the end of the 18th century the Irish were beginning to dominate the resident population in St John's, south along the southern shore to Cape Race, and in most of the southern Avalon Peninsula. Whether settlements were Irish or English, the demographic imbalance was much the same, drunkenness rampant, mobs not infrequent, and poverty the common lot. Where populations were unstable, people struggled to live, the institutions of community not yet in place, the merchants the only, indispensable connection to the outside world. In 1765 the governor, Sir Hugh Palliser, thought that the inhabitants were 'no better than the property or Slaves of the Merchant Supplyers to whom by Exorbitant high Prices on their Goods they are all largely in Debt, more than they can work out during life.'

Yet the resident population increased during the 18th century, and as it did, the organization of the fishery and the pattern of settlement gradually changed. Increasingly shallop crews and shore workers were made up of kin living together in tiny settlements. Such producers were scattered and dependent on merchants who provided goods on credit and took the catch – the European putting-out system adapted to the fishery. Merchant headquarters became dominant regional centres where imports and immigrant workers were redistributed through the merchants' territories and from which, often, schooners and other vessels sailed to the banks. This system could be run by agents for firms in England or by firms based in Newfoundland. It could be combined with the migratory fishery, as it was by the Lesters in Trinity (pl 26).

Like their predecessors, all these late-18th-century merchants participated in intricate networks of international trade that were endlessly varied in detail but that reveal common patterns (pl 28). Men, salt, and some foodstuffs came from Britain or France, and rum and molasses from the West Indies. New Englanders carried much of the West Indian rum and molasses, supplementing such cargoes with grain from the Middle Colonies; in Newfoundland they sought bills of exchange that would be used to purchase British manufactures. Most of the fish taken in the French fishery was consumed in France: green cod in the north, particularly in Paris and the Channel towns, dried cod in the south. The market for either variety was principally urban and among the relatively well off because good cod was more expensive than beef. Cod taken in the English fishery, always dried, was marketed in Iberian and Mediterranean ports to which English ships took New World cod, and procured wines, fruits and nuts, cork, salt, and olive oil for the voyage to England. Whatever the details, this far-flung trade was dependent on credit and mercantile contacts and vulnerable to war.

After a life of more than 200 years the English migratory fishery finally collapsed during the Napoleonic Wars. The principal merchants and most of the work force became Newfoundland residents. As this happened, local centres emerged to dominate the Newfoundland fishery. With its centrally located harbour and largest resident population in late-18th-century Newfoundland, St John's quickly became the island's principal city (pl 27). Commercial links that once extended directly from many Newfoundland harbours to English ports increasingly focused on St John's, which in turn was connected to Liverpool, Glasgow, and London, rather than to the older English ports of the Newfoundland fishery. By 1810 St John's had about 7 000 people, more than half of them long-term residents. Larger than Poole or Dartmouth, it replaced their commercial facilities. Even more than Louisbourg, St John's was the creation of mercantile capital in a setting where there was neither the buffer of tradition nor the significant alternative of agriculture. Merchants controlled most of the city's life.

To the south the political territory 'Acadia' disappeared after the Seven Years' War and the area that is now the three Maritime Provinces became the British colony of Nova Scotia. Halifax was the seat of government. Founded in 1749 as a counterpoise to Louisbourg, Halifax had grown suddenly (with an influx of British and Protestant German and Swiss settlers sent by the British government) to 5 000–6 000 people by 1752, then declined as the Germans and Swiss were relocated in Lunenburg and others left. After the Acadian deportations, Halifax, Lunenburg, and the small garrisons at Annapolis, Chignecto, and Minas were European enclaves in an almost empty peninsula. In 1759 there were almost 7 000 white civilians in all Nova Scotia: perhaps 1 500 Acadians still hiding in the forests, 1 500 Germans and Swiss at Lunenburg, about 2 000 people, mostly British, in Halifax, and perhaps another thousand along the south coast, at Canso, and near the Fundy garrisons. Perhaps there were 2 000 Micmac Indians.

In these circumstances colonial officials set about attracting settlers. A proclamation of 1759 announced that land was to be laid out in townships approximately 12 miles square, that heads of households would receive 100 acres and each family member 50 additional acres. Newcomers were offered 'full liberty of Conscience.' Dissenters were excused tithes in support of the Church of England, and New Englanders were assured that 'the Government of Nova Scotia is constituted like those of neighbouring colonies.' Such terms soon interested land-hungry New Englanders. By the fall of 1759 arrangements had been made for the settlement of eight agricultural townships. By 1765 there were perhaps 7 000 New Englanders in Nova Scotia (pl 31). Distributed between the Bay of Fundy and the Atlantic Coast, they comprised two broad groups: farmers and craftsmen from increasingly crowded agricultural townships occupied the former Acadian lands; and fishermen, drawn from eastern Massachusetts by the promise of better access to the fishery, settled the south shore. In both groups migrants were often kin.

In Nova Scotia these newcomers confronted the economic imperatives that had long dominated Acadia. Those around the Bay of Fundy soon cultivated former Acadia and newly reclaimed marshland and, bypassing the newly surveyed town plots, lived in dispersed farmsteads on upland lots around the edge of the marshes (pl 31). Markets for agricultural products remained meagre and unreliable, and the New Englanders' farms, like the Acadians', were largely self-sufficient. Families produced their own maple sugar, tallow and soap, as well as much of their woolen and linen cloth, and mixed farming yielded a variety of grains, meat, milk, and garden produce. On the south shore fishermen divided beach room among themselves, erected the sheds, stagings, and flakes necessary for their livelihoods, and built small frame houses at the back of them. Agriculture was unimportant, but crude sawmills often appeared on suitable streams to provide local needs and to supplement export cargoes of fish. Few prospered in these isolated settings. On-shore fish runs were less reliable than around Cape Breton and cured fish were often of poor or intermediate quality. Hardship and struggle were common and, as so often in the resident fishery, debts to merchants were part of fishermen's lives.

At the end of the 1760s the economy was stagnant, emigration probably exceeded immigration, and exports of fish from Nova Scotia were lower than those from Île Royale in the 1730s. The colony was a net importer of agricultural produce. Furs were a locally important export in the Saint John valley, and small coastal sawmills produced two or three million feet of boards. Overall there was no considerable economic motor. Settlements were scattered and depressed. A framework of government was in place, county boundaries appeared on maps, and there were new land surveys in local settlements, but settlers were wanting and the economies to draw them. The two groups that came in the early 1770s were pushed rather than pulled: Highland Scots emigrating for cultural and religious as well as economic reasons, who came to Pictou and the Island of St John (later Prince Edward Island), and a few Yorkshiremen, substantial tenant farmers angered by rent increases, who came to Chignecto (pl 31).

These economic doldrums gave way to war. During the American Revolution privateers raided almost every settlement in the colony except Halifax, and sporadically as far north as the sealing stations on the Labrador coast. Bloodshed was rare, but spoils were considerable. Ships, provisions, and valuables were carried away, 'neutral Yankees' were taunted, and some were drawn to the American side. Commerce in Halifax was revitalized by the presence of wealthy exiles, military officers, and troops with money to spend. By 1782, it was clear that large numbers of loyal refugees were to be settled in Nova Scotia. Enormous quantities of land, previously granted but unoccupied, were reclaimed by the crown and dispensed to the Loyalists in free grants. In all, more than 30 000 people came and stayed: about 19 000 in what is now peninsular Nova Scotia, 11 000 in New Brunswick (divided from Nova Scotia in 1784 to become a separate, largely Loyalist colony), perhaps 300 on the Island of St John, and somewhat more on Cape Breton Island (pl 32).

The Loyalist influx transformed the human geography of the region. The population of the Nova Scotian peninsula was approximately doubled. Unsettled areas were occupied and the density of older settlements was increased. Shelburne, the most spectacular achievement and greatest failure in this period of flux, briefly had 10 000 residents. Its fine harbour could not compensate for its rocky hinterland and by 1789 most of the town was uninhabited. On Cape Breton Island Sydney became the principal settlement, and in New Brunswick Parrtown became the administrative centre of the Saint John valley. By 1787 a thin, broken ribbon of civilian and disbanded military settlement extended up the Saint John River as far as Pine Island (near present Woodstock), but most newcomers were concentrated along the intervale lands of the lower valley. With increased demand roads were improved; the Bay of Fundy became a busy commercial waterway as its butter, livestock, and cheese moved to market in unprecedented quantity. In 1783 the closure of British West Indian ports to American vessels created Caribbean opportunities for Nova Scotian and New Brunswick merchants even if the cargoes in their vessels were largely American. Sawmilling for local consumption developed and shipbuilding soon became important; by 1793 some 160 sloops, schooners, and square-rigged vessels had been built in New Brunswick alone. New Brunswick replaced the New England colonies as a supplier of masts and spars for the British navy.

Much of this prosperity was gone by 1800 (pl 32). Privateering after the outbreak of war with France in 1793 and Jay's Treaty in 1794 – which opened British Caribbean ports to American shipping – had undermined the region's West Indian trade. But for the exports of masts and spars, New Brunswick had become a commercial backwater, its economy based on nearly subsistence farmers and on small merchants who continued a contraband trade with the Americans in fish and gypsum. From Prince Edward Island, as the Island of St John was known after 1798, a little salt herring was being shipped to the West Indies and a few cattle to Newfoundland and Halifax. The Scots, perhaps 2 000 of them, who in the 1790s had settled on Prince Edward Island, Cape Breton Island, and the Nova Scotian north shore were not yet noticeably better off than they had been on West Highland farms. Halifax, on the other hand, was prospering. War increased its garrison and navy, and privateers bringing prizes into port put cash into circulation. Like St John's in Newfoundland, Halifax was emerging as the mercantile centre for a sizeable region, organizing the fishery and other trades, and redistributing imports. Without its own agricultural hinterland, Halifax's growth created markets for farmers on the Bay of Fundy where, in 1800, there were pockets of commercial farming. Overall, the region presented many contrasts and incongruities: a few large, well-established farms pointed up how little cleared land most settlers had; hard-scrabble fishing settlements bore little resemblance to the well-cultivated marshland fringes of the Bay of Fundy; the social world of the Halifax élite was a vast remove from the humble settings of most lives. Yet the basic ethnic divisions that were to characterize the region throughout the nineteenth century – an English south and west strongly influenced by New England, a Scottish Gulf, and a cluster of Acadian enclaves in Madawaska, northeastern New Brunswick, eastern Prince Edward Island, southeastern Cape Breton and St Mary's Bay – were already coming into focus. And the essential and persistent pattern of settlement in the region was clear: most people occupied modest farms or coastal villages; their distribution was basically peripheral, with fingers of population following the region's major valleys inland.

In 1800 most of these settlements were recent, but the European presence in the northwestern Atlantic was three centuries old. Throughout this long time an international fishery dominated the regional economy, while control of the shores along which it was practised had become increasingly British. Of almost 100 000 people in Atlantic Canada in 1800 most were English-speaking. More than 40 years after the deportations there were only 7 000 Acadians, few of them living near their ancestral lands (pl 30). Native people were a residual presence. Not numerous to begin with, ravaged by malnutrition and disease and lacking guns, their summer fishing stations pre-empted by fishermen and their winter villages subject to the depredations of furriers, the Beothuk of Newfoundland became extinct early in the 19th century. Elsewhere the Indians survived in small numbers, their participation in the white economy limited by a declining fur trade. The fishery did not require them, and even subsistence farming depended on European techniques and assumptions.

EXPLORING THE ATLANTIC COAST

Author: Richard I. Ruggles

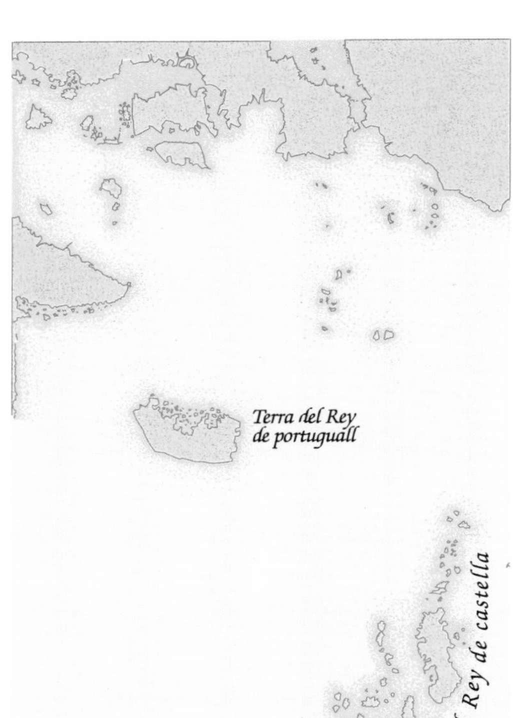

Terra del Rey
de portuguall
Las antillas del Rey de castella
Oceanus
occidētalis

CANTINO MAP, 1502 (portion)

An anonymous Portuguese map of the world, obtained by Alberto Cantino, agent for the Duke of Ferrara, depicts the land discovered by Cabot and the Corte Real brothers as an island far south and west of Greenland. Most of the Caribbean islands were fairly well known.

RIBEIRO MAP, 1529 (portion)

Diogo Ribeiro, a Portuguese, recorded new discoveries on the official Spanish map of the world. By 1529 Esteban Gomez and Giovanni da Verrazano had established that there was a continuous coastline between Florida and the Gulf of St Lawrence. Between C. del breton and C. rasso (Cape Race) Ribeiro located a broad bay, an indication, perhaps, that the existence of the Gulf of St Lawrence was known. To the north Ribeiro named Labrador and Greenland.

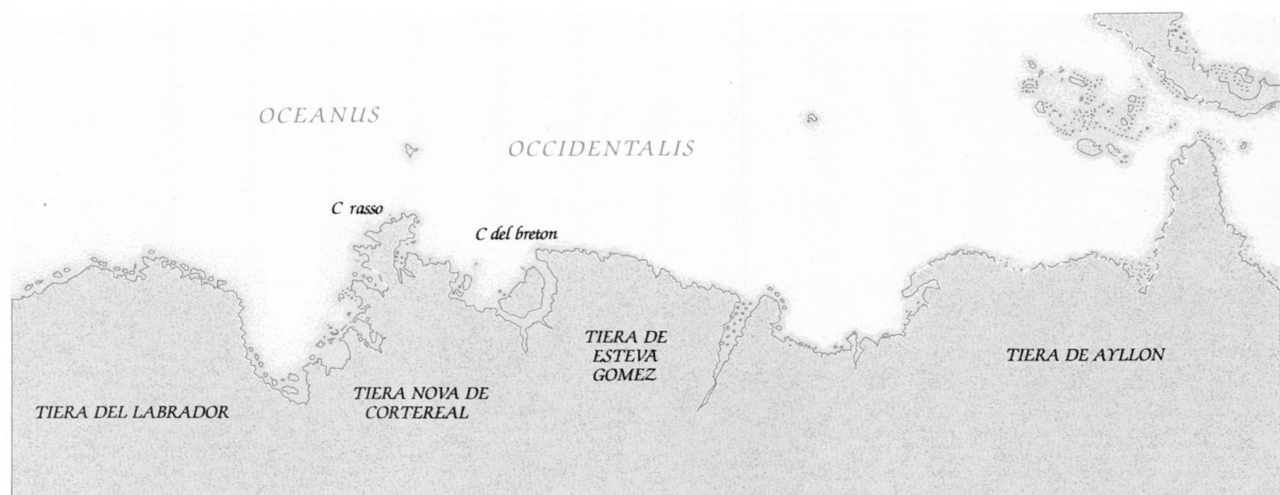

OCEANUS
OCCIDENTALIS
C rasso
C del breton
TIERA DEL LABRADOR
TIERA NOVA DE
CORTEREAL
TIERA DE
ESTEVA
GOMEZ
TIERA DE AYLLON

JAMES MAP, 1632 (portion)

By 1616 William Baffin had established the general outline of Baffin Bay; by 1632 Luke Foxe and Thomas James had explored the western shores of Hudson Bay and James Bay. A northwest passage had not been found, although there were still reports, not to be followed up until much later, of openings to the west.

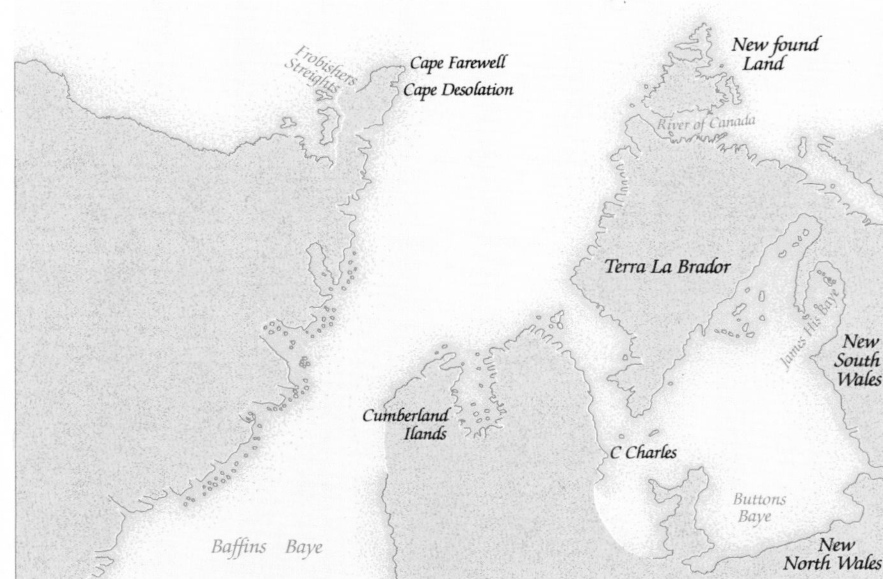

Frobishers
Streights
Cape Farewell
Cape Desolation
New found
Land
River of Canada
Terra La Brador
James his Baye
New
South
Wales
Cumberland
Ilands
C Charles
Buttons
Baye
Baffins Baye
New
North Wales

Shoreline known to explorers

Davis Strait

Ungava Bay

Baffin Bay

Hudson Bay

PRINCIPAL EXPLORATIONS

English

- Cabot (after Morison), 1497
- Frobisher, 1576, 1577, 1578
- Davis, 1585, 1586, 1587
- Hudson, 1610–11
- Button, 1612–13
- Baffin and Bylot, 1615, 1616
- Foxe, 1631
- James, 1631–2

Portuguese

- Corte Real (after Morison), 1500, 1501
- Fagundes, 1520 ?, 1521–5 ?

French

- Verrazano, 1524
- Cartier, 1534, 1535–6
- Bellenger, 1583

Spanish

- Gomez, 1524–5

Danish

- Munk, 1619–20

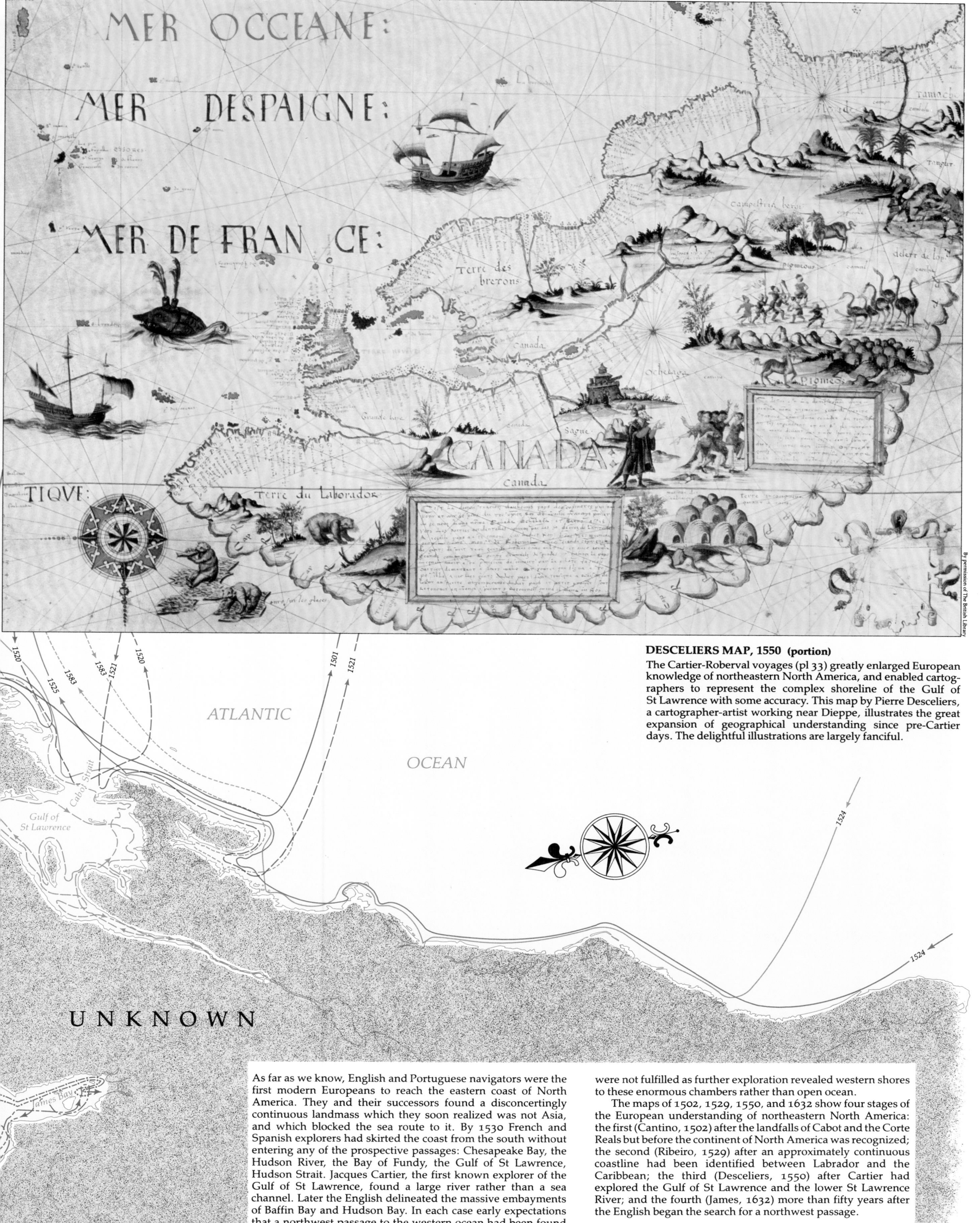
MER OCCEANE:
MER DESPAIGNE:
MER DE FRAN CE:
TIQVE:
Terre des bretons
Canada
Grande baye
Sague
CANADA
Terre du Laborador
ATLANTIC
OCEAN
Gulf of St Lawrence
Cabot Strait
James Bay
UNKNOWN
1520
1525
1583
1521
1501
1524

DESCELIERS MAP, 1550 (portion)

The Cartier-Roberval voyages (pl 33) greatly enlarged European knowledge of northeastern North America, and enabled cartographers to represent the complex shoreline of the Gulf of St Lawrence with some accuracy. This map by Pierre Desceliers, a cartographer-artist working near Dieppe, illustrates the great expansion of geographical understanding since pre-Cartier days. The delightful illustrations are largely fanciful.

As far as we know, English and Portuguese navigators were the first modern Europeans to reach the eastern coast of North America. They and their successors found a disconcertingly continuous landmass which they soon realized was not Asia, and which blocked the sea route to it. By 1530 French and Spanish explorers had skirted the coast from the south without entering any of the prospective passages: Chesapeake Bay, the Hudson River, the Bay of Fundy, the Gulf of St Lawrence, Hudson Strait. Jacques Cartier, the first known explorer of the Gulf of St Lawrence, found a large river rather than a sea channel. Later the English delineated the massive embayments of Baffin Bay and Hudson Bay. In each case early expectations that a northwest passage to the western ocean had been found were not fulfilled as further exploration revealed western shores to these enormous chambers rather than open ocean.

The maps of 1502, 1529, 1550, and 1632 show four stages of the European understanding of northeastern North America: the first (Cantino, 1502) after the landfalls of Cabot and the Corte Reals but before the continent of North America was recognized; the second (Ribeiro, 1529) after an approximately continuous coastline had been identified between Labrador and the Caribbean; the third (Desceliers, 1550) after Cartier had explored the Gulf of St Lawrence and the lower St Lawrence River; and the fourth (James, 1632) more than fifty years after the English began the search for a northwest passage.

THE ATLANTIC REALM

Authors: Graeme Wynn; Ralph Pastore (Beothuk);
Bernard G. Hoffman (Micmac)

Once Europeans had reconnoitred the land behind the Atlantic coast of northeastern North America, they largely ignored it. Cold by comparison with equivalent latitudes in western Europe, wet, heavily forested, with generally thin and acidic soils, and rimmed in many places by highlands, the land held few attractions for them. There was neither obvious mineral wealth nor the prospect of successful agriculture in territory that was as bleak as any in the middle latitudes. Yet the waters off-shore contained one of the world's largest stocks of edible fish, and as Europeans began to exploit this resource they named the coastline, occupied harbours in summer, and used beaches to dry fish (pls 21 and 22). Their activity faced the sea and backed into the land as, in much of the Atlantic region, it would continue to do for centuries.

The fishery brought natives and Europeans into contact. Well before the end of the 16th century Micmac and European traders met at established summer trading places to barter furs. Nicolas Denys, who has left the fullest account of this trade, reported that the natives were being destroyed by drink. Certainly European goods and diseases were introduced and native numbers were declining. Yet there are very few precise data. Although the distribution of major groups at the end of the 16th century is generally known (below), the details cannot be filled in. This plate does show the parts of the Micmac coast that were frequented by French traders in the 16th century, as well as the distribution of archaeological sites, none of them from the 16th century, associated with the prehistoric and historic Beothuk natives of Newfoundland.

NATIVE PEOPLES, AD 1600

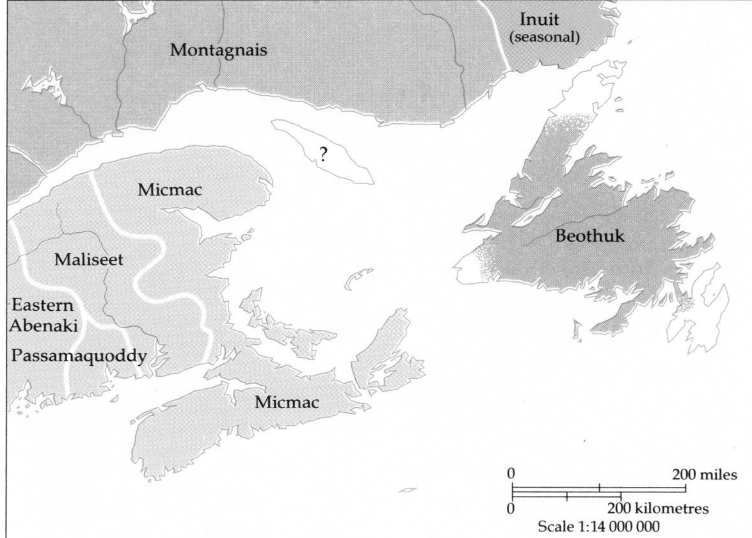
Inuit
(seasonal)
Montagnais
?
Micmac
Beothuk
Maliseet
Eastern
Abenaki
Passamaquoddy
Micmac
0
200 miles
0
200 kilometres
Scale 1:14 000 000

By 1600 the St Lawrence Iroquoian had disappeared from the St Lawrence valley (pl 33) and Thule eskimos (Inuit) had advanced along the coast of Labrador and into the Gulf of St Lawrence (pl 11). In 1611 the Jesuit Father Biard estimated that there were 3 000–3 500 Micmac. 'They are astonished,' he reported, 'and often complain that since the French mingle with and carry on trade with them they are dying fast and the population is thinning out. They assert that … all their countries were very populous, and they tell how one by one different coasts, according as they have begun to traffic with us, have been more reduced by disease.' We may suspect a drastic 16th-century decline in Micmac population.

Agricultural capability
(for the mixed agriculture practised by northwestern Europeans)

- Fair or better
- Very limited
- None

Surface currents and depth

- Persistent current
- Variable current
- 200 Bathymetric contours (in metres)

Sea ice

- Direction of movement
- Coast usually icebound more than one month

Cod migration

- Usual seaward limit of Atlantic cod
- *winter* Direction and season of cod migration

The Beothuk site at Boyd's Cove in eastern Notre Dame Bay probably dates from the period between 1670 and 1720. Boyd's Cove lies within a maze of islands and treacherous shallows – fit for canoes but dangerous for European ships. Such a location would have permitted pilfering and trading while minimizing the danger of European intrusion.

Stone tools of the Little Passage type, tools made from European iron objects (usually nails), and trade beads have been found at Boyd's Cove. People lived in wigwams erected in shallow excavations some 10–15 cm deep. The excavated earth was piled around the walls, and poles to support the roof were set into the earthen walls. No evidence for such structures has been found at Little Passage sites.

- Beothuk burial sites
- Cache of Beothuk carved bone pieces
- Beothuk habitation sites
- Little Passage (Prehistoric Beothuk) habitation sites
- Beothuk and Little Passage sites
- Micmac coast frequented by French traders, 16th century

GULF OF
GRAND MANAN BANK
JEFFREY BANK
PLATT BANK
ROSEWAY BANK
LE HAVE BANK
EMERALD BANK
BROWNS BANK
GEORGES BANKS
winter
100
200
1 000

0 100 miles
0 100 kilometres
Scale 1:3 850 000

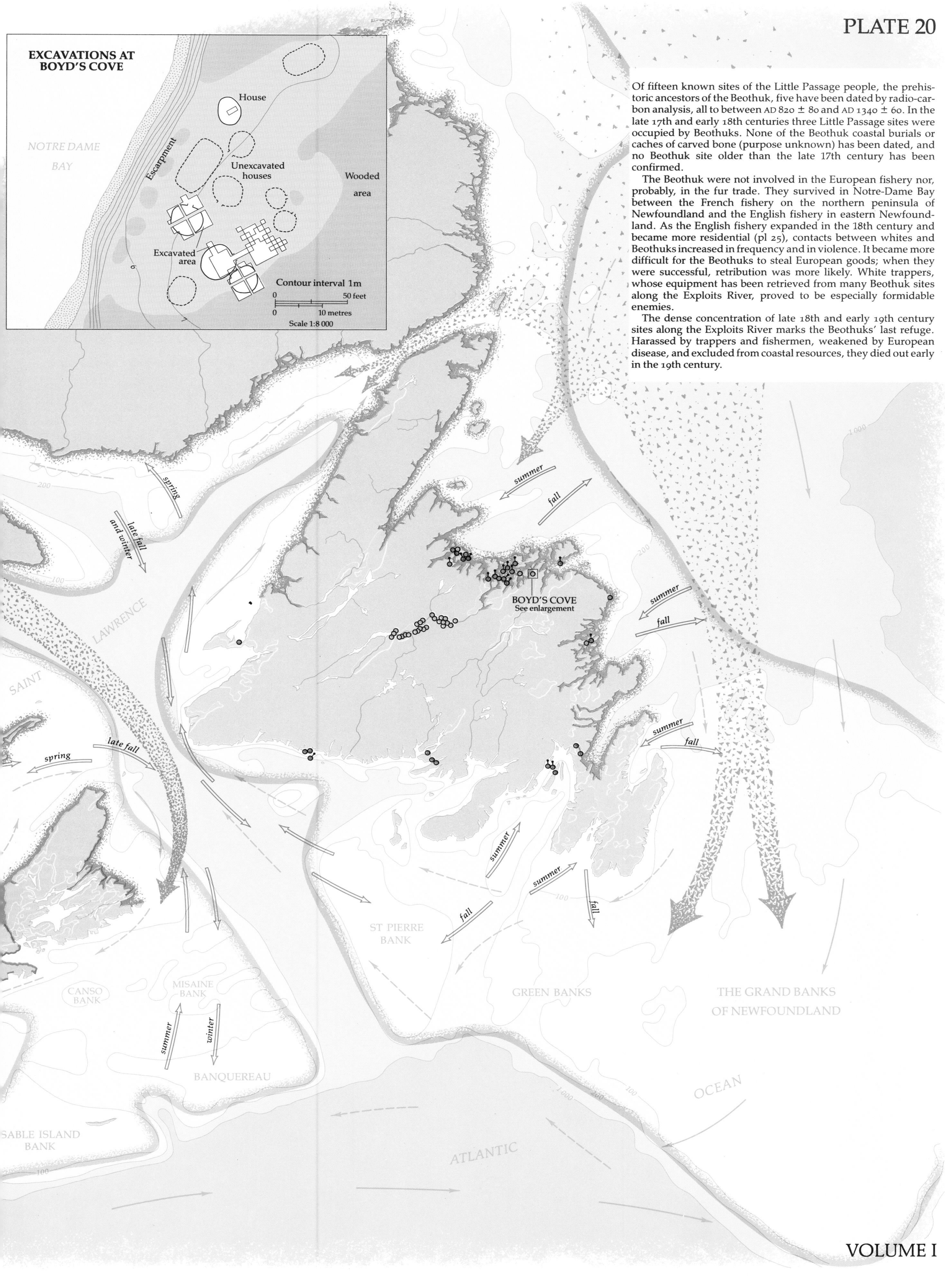

Of fifteen known sites of the Little Passage people, the prehistoric ancestors of the Beothuk, five have been dated by radio-carbon analysis, all to between AD 820 ± 80 and AD 1340 ± 60. In the late 17th and early 18th centuries three Little Passage sites were occupied by Beothuks. None of the Beothuk coastal burials or caches of carved bone (purpose unknown) has been dated, and no Beothuk site older than the late 17th century has been confirmed.

The Beothuk were not involved in the European fishery nor, probably, in the fur trade. They survived in Notre-Dame Bay between the French fishery on the northern peninsula of Newfoundland and the English fishery in eastern Newfoundland. As the English fishery expanded in the 18th century and became more residential (pl 25), contacts between whites and Beothuks increased in frequency and in violence. It became more difficult for the Beothuks to steal European goods; when they were successful, retribution was more likely. White trappers, whose equipment has been retrieved from many Beothuk sites along the Exploits River, proved to be especially formidable enemies.

The dense concentration of late 18th and early 19th century sites along the Exploits River marks the Beothuks' last refuge. Harassed by trappers and fishermen, weakened by European disease, and excluded from coastal resources, they died out early in the 19th century.

EXCAVATIONS AT BOYD'S COVE
House
NOTRE DAME BAY
Escarpment
Unexcavated houses
Wooded area
Excavated area
Contour interval 1m
50 feet
10 metres
Scale 1:8 000
BOYD'S COVE
See enlargement
summer
fall
spring
late fall and winter
late fall
SAINT LAWRENCE
ST PIERRE BANK
GREEN BANKS
THE GRAND BANKS OF NEWFOUNDLAND
CANSO BANK
MISAINE BANK
winter
BANQUEREAU
SABLE ISLAND BANK
ATLANTIC
OCEAN

THE MIGRATORY FISHERIES

Authors: John Mannion, C. Grant Head

MIGRATORY INSHORE DRY FISHERY

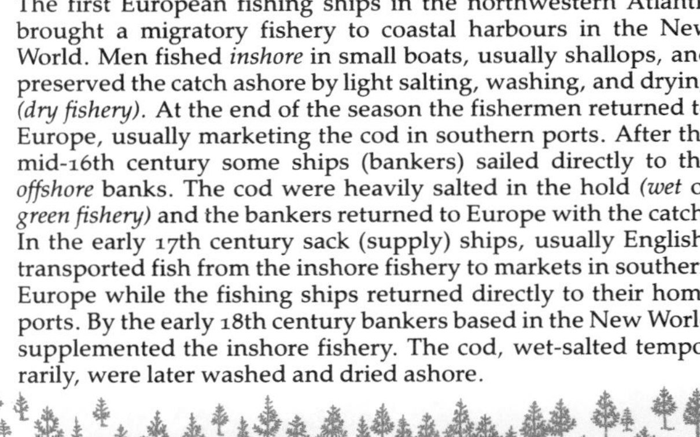
Fishing ships (usually laid up
in harbour during season)
Boats, usually
shallops
Banks

The first European fishing ships in the northwestern Atlantic brought a migratory fishery to coastal harbours in the New World. Men fished *inshore* in small boats, usually shallops, and preserved the catch ashore by light salting, washing, and drying *(dry fishery)*. At the end of the season the fishermen returned to Europe, usually marketing the cod in southern ports. After the mid-16th century some ships (bankers) sailed directly to the *offshore* banks. The cod were heavily salted in the hold *(wet* or *green fishery)* and the bankers returned to Europe with the catch. In the early 17th century sack (supply) ships, usually English, transported fish from the inshore fishery to markets in southern Europe while the fishing ships returned directly to their home ports. By the early 18th century bankers based in the New World supplemented the inshore fishery. The cod, wet-salted temporarily, were later washed and dried ashore.

MIGRATORY BANKS FISHERY

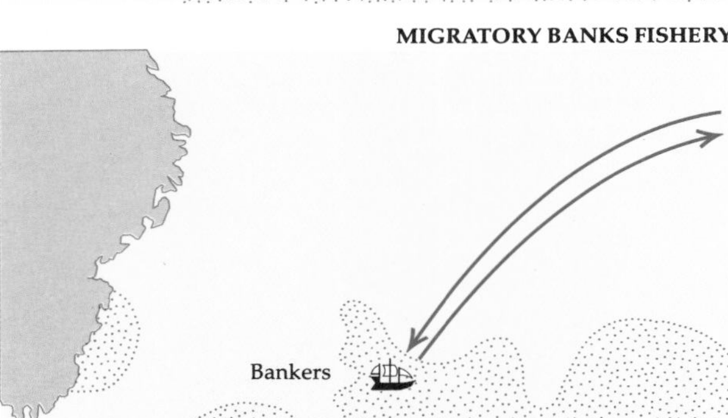
Bankers

ENGLISH VARIANT, INTRODUCED 17th CENTURY

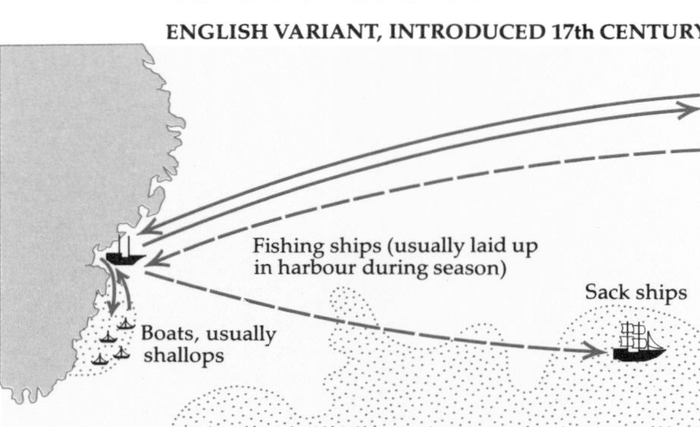
Fishing ships (usually laid up
in harbour during season)
Sack ships
Boats, usually
shallops

RESIDENT BANKS FISHERY, 18th CENTURY

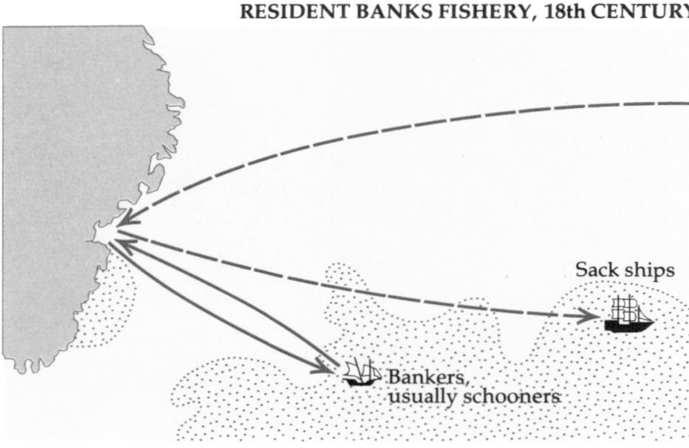
Sack ships
Bankers,
usually schooners

'PLAN OF THE STAGES AND BEACHES AT TROIS ISLES, NEWFOUNDLAND, 1785'

after Gontier Descartets

The roofs are colour-coded by building function.

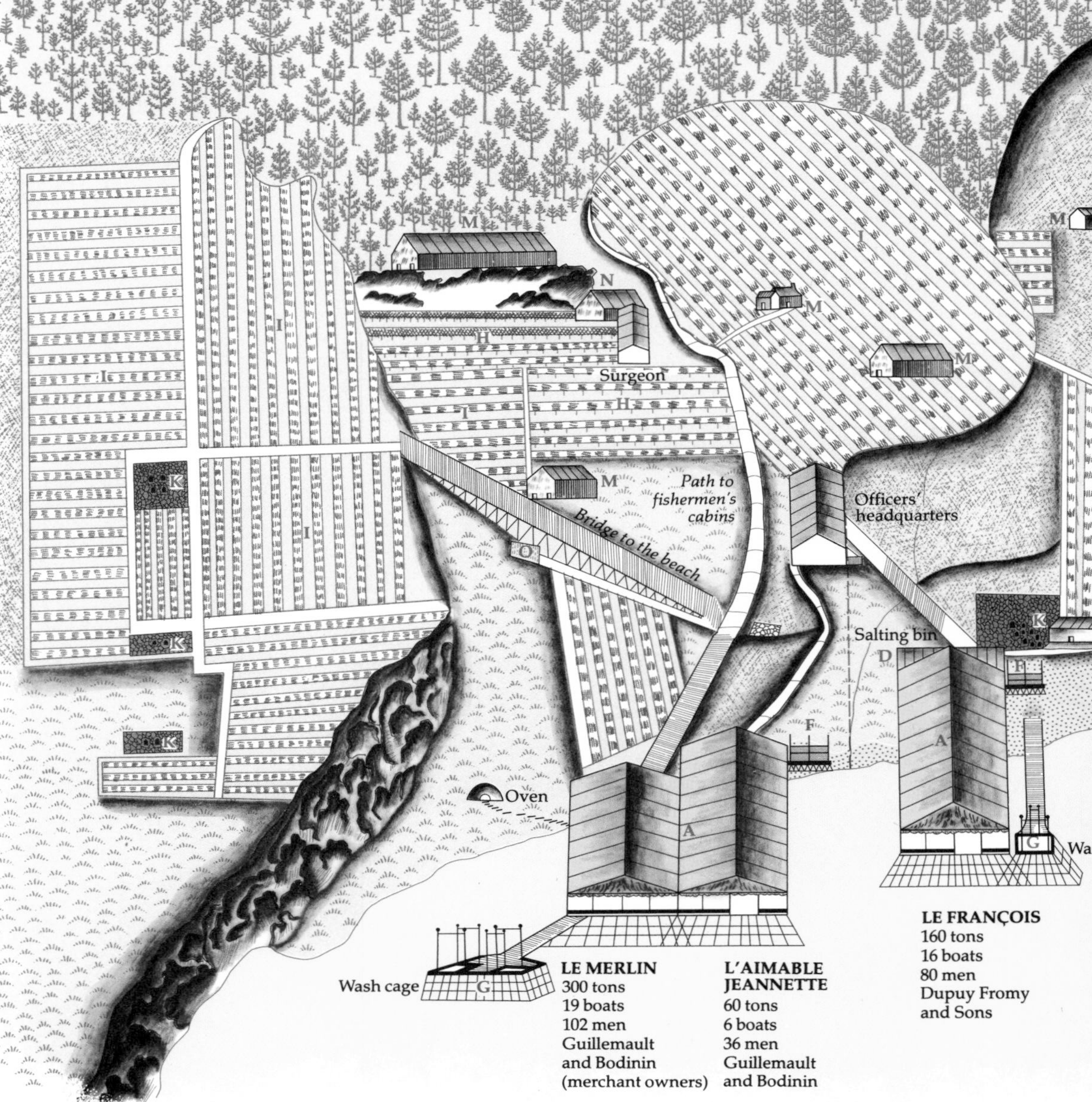
A Stage (A)
M Fishermen's or shore-workers' cabin (M)
N Officers' cabin (N)
F Oil vat (F)
H Flakes (H)
I Rances (I)
K Bed of cobbles with piles of cod (K)
O Garden (O)
Probable boundary between properties or 'rooms'
Surgeon
Path to fishermen's cabins
Bridge to the beach
Officers' headquarters
Salting bin
Oven
Wash cage
Wash c
LE MERLIN
300 tons
19 boats
102 men
Guillemault and Bodinin
(merchant owners)
L'AIMABLE JEANNETTE
60 tons
6 boats
36 men
Guillemault and Bodinin
LE FRANÇOIS
160 tons
16 boats
80 men
Dupuy Fromy and Sons

The map depicts a seasonally occupied harbour in the Bay of Islands in western Newfoundland in 1785. That spring seven ships averaging 157 tons arrived from Saint-Malo with 470 men. Using 84 shallops they caught and cured over 12 000 quintals (1 quintal = 112 English pounds or about 50 kilograms) of dried cod and processed 180 barrels of oil – a small, probably unprofitable production for the number of men involved.

Ships of 30–150 tons participated in the banks fishery. They came from many ports and brought many different techniques and customs to the banks, but all bankers preserved their catch by the wet process, which produced a more perishable product than the dry fishery but with much less labour.

Fishermen on the bankers stood in barrels (1) and were further protected by heavy leather aprons and by shields (2) rigged in front of them. Their hempen lines, carrying 5-lb (2.3-kg) weights and one or two baited hooks, were variously deployed. The fishermen hauled the cod on deck and cut out their tongues (as a measure of the number caught). Boys carried the cod to the header (3), who stood in a barrel beside the table on which he beheaded and gutted the cod. On the other side of the table the splitter (4) removed backbones and dropped the split cod into the hold, where the salters (5) packed them between layers of salt. A boy (6) put the livers in a barrel on deck.

BANKER

Side elevation of a 100-ton banker from Sables-d'Olonne, 18th century

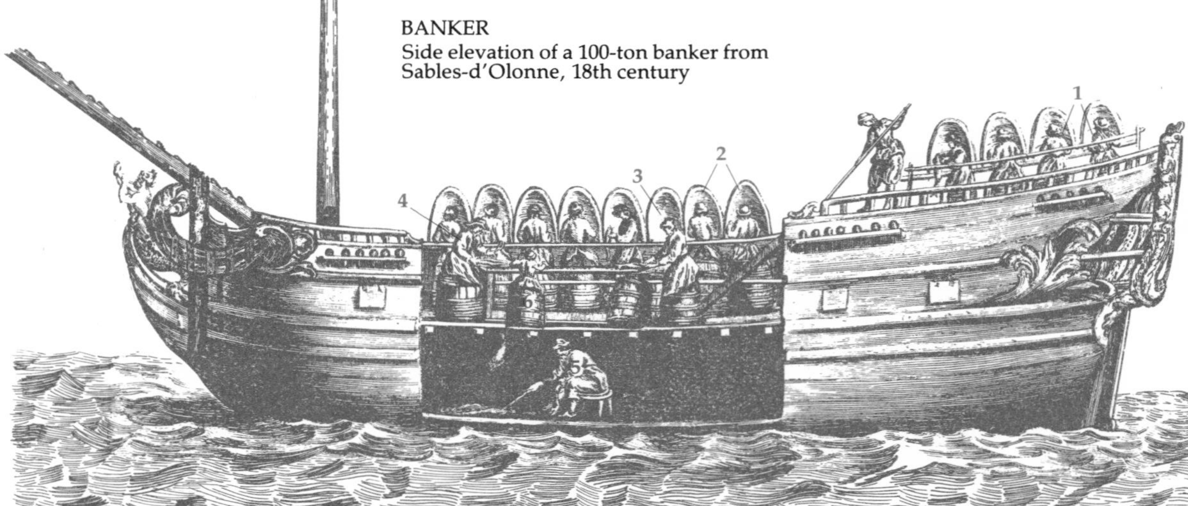
1
2
3
4

Duhamel du Monceau, 1772

PLATE 21

PROCESSING COD AT THE STAGE

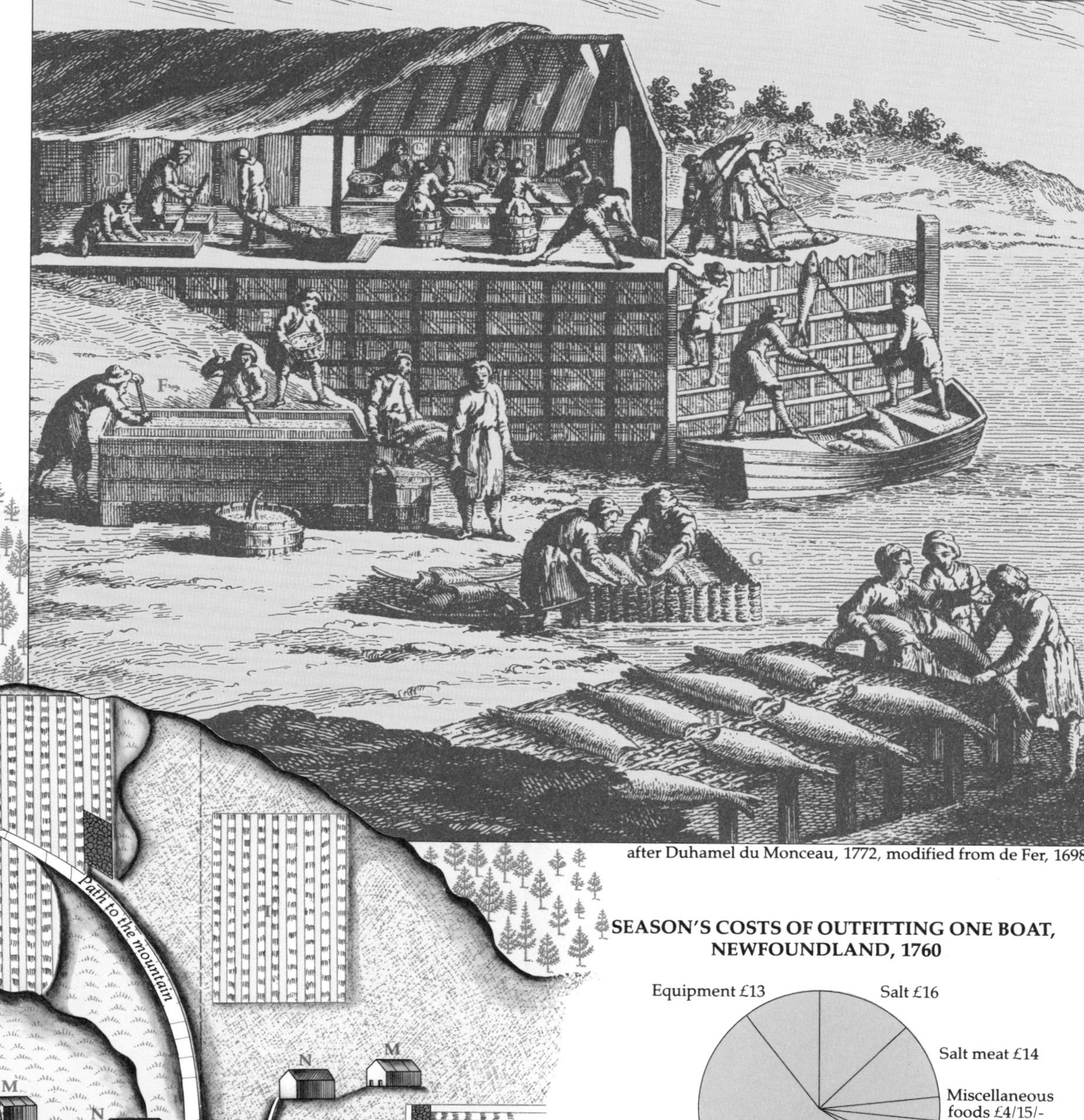

after Duhamel du Monceau, 1772, modified from de Fer, 1698

The dry fishery was capital- and labour-intensive. It required many ships, boats, and men, and created large, seasonal workplaces.

The cod, usually caught from shallops with three-man crews, were landed at the end of a stage (A), where boys passed them indoors to headers (B) and splitters (C). The split cod were carried to salters (D), who piled them between layers of salt; livers were collected in baskets and taken by boys (E) to the oil vat (F). After some days the salted cod were carried to the wash cage (G), washed, and piled again to drain. Then they were spread out to dry: on flakes (long, narrow platforms around 50 cm high and made of poles and spruce boughs) (H); on labour-saving rances, (rows of boughs placed on the beach) (I); or directly on the beach cobbles (J). The cod, turned at mid-day and piled (K) at night, were sufficiently dry after 10 days of good drying.

The shoremen usually slept in lofts (L) on the stages (A) or in cabins (M) nearby. Fishermen slept in similar cabins and officers had slightly more ample quarters (N). There might be a brewery for spruce beer, an outdoor oven, and tiny gardens (O).

Brewery

Path to the mountain

Cross

Bridge

Wash cage

'AIMABLE JULIE
60 tons
2 boats
37 men
Duguen Quenet
and Company

L'ANPHYTRIE
150 tons
11 boats
63 men
Duguen Quenet
and Company

M. Pelé's stage

M. Morvan's stage

All statistics are from French records of cod fishery from Saint-Malo at Trois-Isles, Bay of Islands (western Newfoundland), spring, summer, and fall 1785.

SEASON'S COSTS OF OUTFITTING ONE BOAT, NEWFOUNDLAND, 1760

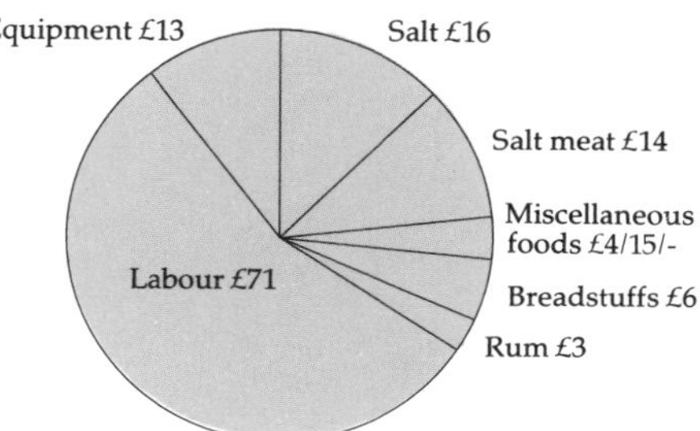
Equipment £13
Salt £16
Salt meat £14
Miscellaneous foods £4/15/-
Breadstuffs £6
Rum £3
Labour £71

DRYING COD ASHORE

after Duhamel du Monceau, 1772

FISHERMAN, HEADER, AND SPLITTER AT WORK ON A BANKER

4
3
2
1

Duhamel du Monceau, 1772

THE 16th CENTURY FISHERY

Authors: John Mannion, Selma Barkham

The earliest trans-Atlantic fishery was conducted by French and Portuguese fishermen, soon joined by Basques, who took cod in coastal waters and dried them ashore (the dry fishery, pl 21). Early in the 16th century fishermen appear to have frequented primarily the south and east coasts of Newfoundland and the Strait of Belle Isle. Later fishermen from northern France began to exploit the banks (the wet fishery, pl 21). Around 1540 Spanish and French Basques, sending out large ships (up to 600 tons) with crews of as many as 130 men, established seasonal whaling stations along the Labrador shore.

English fishermen were relative latecomers: they arrived in numbers only by the 1570s, but by 1600 they controlled most of the eastern Avalon Peninsula of Newfoundland. At the end of the century Portuguese and Spanish Basque fisheries were in decline, suffering from royal exactions of men and capital for military ventures (including the Spanish Armada of 1588) and from piracy. French and French Basque fishermen operated in the Gulf of St Lawrence and around much of Newfoundland.

Fishermen and explorers (pl 20) gave European names to a new coastline. Capes, headlands, offshore islands, and large harbours were most frequently named, and these names, often transferred from fishermen's maps, were recorded by cartographers in Europe. Shown here are 16th-century names, most of them taken from French or Portuguese sources, that can be located precisely on modern maps. They are spelled as first recorded, and frequently jumble languages.

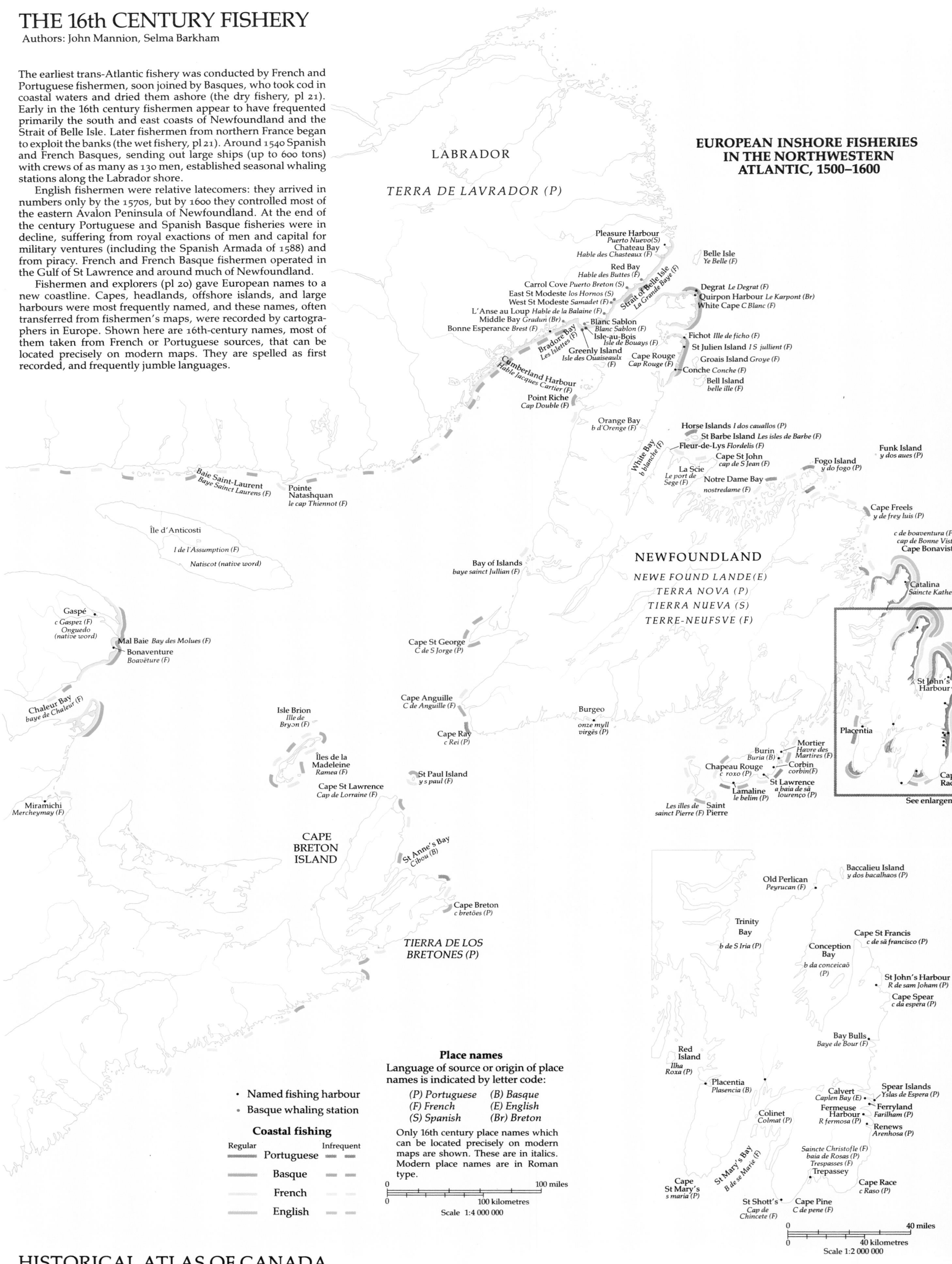
EUROPEAN INSHORE FISHERIES IN THE NORTHWESTERN ATLANTIC, 1500–1600
LABRADOR
TERRA DE LAVRADOR (P)
Pleasure Harbour Puerto Nuevo(S)
Chateau Bay Hable des Chasteaux (F)
Belle Isle Ye Belle (F)
Red Bay Hable des Buttes (F)
Strait of Belle Isle La Grande Baye (F)
Carrol Cove Puerto Breton (S)
East St Modeste los Hornos (S)
West St Modeste Samadet (F)
L'Anse au Loup Hable de la Balaine (F)
Middle Bay Gradun (Br)
Bonne Esperance Brest (F)
Blanc Sablon Blanc Sablon (F)
Isle-au-Bois Isle de Bouays (F)
Bradore Bay Les Islettes (F)
Greenly Island Isle des Ouaiseaulx (F)
Degrat Le Degrat (F)
Quirpon Harbour Le Karpont (Br)
White Cape C Blanc (F)
Fichot Ille de ficho (F)
St Julien Island I S jullient (F)
Groais Island Groye (F)
Cape Rouge Cap Rouge (F)
Conche Conche (F)
Bell Island belle ille (F)
Cumberland Harbour Hable Jacques Cartier (F)
Point Riche Cap Double (F)
Orange Bay b d'Orenge (F)
Horse Islands I dos cauallos (P)
St Barbe Island Les isles de Barbe (F)
Fleur-de-Lys Flordelis (F)
White Bay b blanche (F)
Cape St John cap de S Jean (F)
La Scie Le port de Sege (F)
Notre Dame Bay nostredame (F)
Fogo Island y do fogo (P)
Funk Island y dos aues (P)
Cape Freels y de frey luis (P)
c de boaventura (P) cap de Bonne Viste (F) Cape Bonavista
Catalina Saincte Katherine
Baie Saint-Laurent Baye Sainct Laurens (F)
Pointe Natashquan le cap Thiennot (F)
Île d'Anticosti
I de l'Assumption (F)
Natiscot (native word)
NEWFOUNDLAND
NEWE FOUND LANDE (E)
TERRA NOVA (P)
TIERRA NUEVA (S)
TERRE-NEUFSVE (F)
Bay of Islands baye sainct Jullian (F)
Gaspé c Gaspez (F) Onguedo (native word)
Mal Baie Bay des Molues (F)
Bonaventure Boavêture (F)
Cape St George C de S Jorge (P)
St John's Harbour
Chaleur Bay baye de Chaleur (F)
Cape Anguille C de Anguille (F)
Burgeo onze myll virgês (P)
Isle Brion Ille de Bryon (F)
Cape Ray c Rei (P)
Placentia
Îles de la Madeleine Ramea (F)
St Paul Island y s paul (F)
Mortier Havre des Martires (F)
Burin Buria (B)
Corbin corbin(F)
Chapeau Rouge c roxo (P)
St Lawrence a baia de sã lourenço (P)
Cape Race
Cape St Lawrence Cap de Lorraine (F)
Lamaline le belim (P)
Les illes de saint Pierre (F) Saint Pierre
See enlargement
Miramichi Mercheymay (F)
CAPE BRETON ISLAND
St Anne's Bay Cibou (B)
Cape Breton c bretões (P)
TIERRA DE LOS BRETONES (P)
Baccalieu Island y dos bacalhaos (P)
Old Perlican Peyrucan (F)
Trinity Bay b de S Iria (P)
Cape St Francis c de sã francisco (P)
Conception Bay b da conceicaõ (P)
St John's Harbour R de sam Joham (P)
Cape Spear c da espera (P)
Bay Bulls Baye de Bour (F)
Red Island Ilha Roxa (P)
Placentia Plasencia (B)
Calvert Caplen Bay (E)
Spear Islands Yslas de Espera (P)
Ferryland Farilham (P)
Fermeuse Harbour R fermosa (P)
Renews Arenhosa (P)
Colinet Colmat (P)
Saincte Christofle (F) baia de Rosas (P) Trespasses (F) Trepassey
St Mary's Bay B de se Marie (F)
Cape St Mary's s maria (P)
Cape Race c Raso (P)
St Shott's Cap de Chincete (F)
Cape Pine C de pene (F)
0 40 miles
0 40 kilometres
Scale 1:2 000 000
• Named fishing harbour
• Basque whaling station
Coastal fishing
Regular Infrequent
Portuguese
Basque
French
English
Place names
Language of source or origin of place names is indicated by letter code:
(P) Portuguese (B) Basque
(F) French (E) English
(S) Spanish (Br) Breton
Only 16th century place names which can be located precisely on modern maps are shown. These are in italics. Modern place names are in Roman type.
0 100 miles
0 100 kilometres
Scale 1:4 000 000

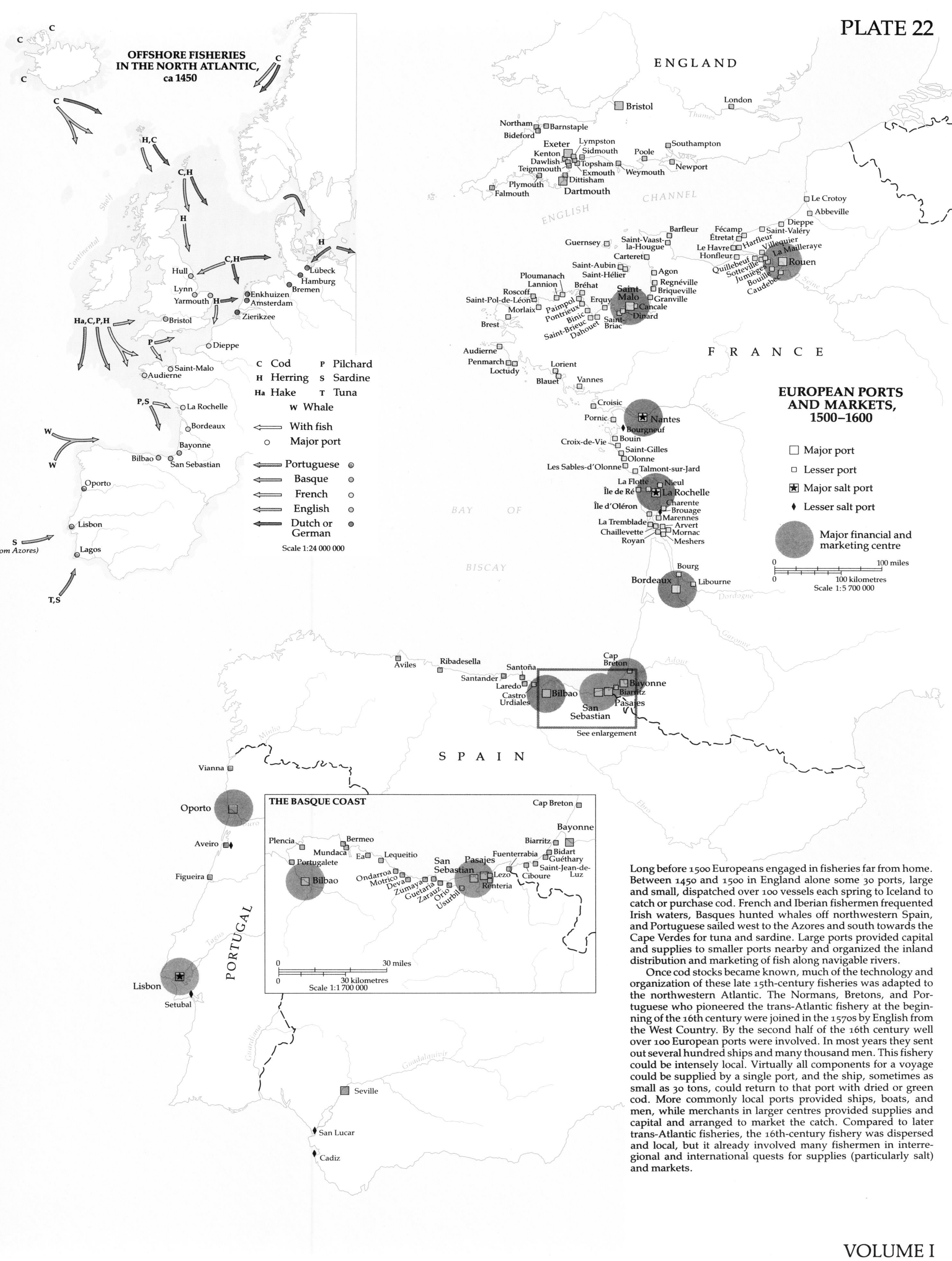
OFFSHORE FISHERIES IN THE NORTH ATLANTIC, ca 1450
C Cod
H Herring
Ha Hake
P Pilchard
S Sardine
T Tuna
W Whale
With fish
Major port
Portuguese
Basque
French
English
Dutch or German
Scale 1:24 000 000
Continental Shelf
Hull
Lynn
Yarmouth
Lübeck
Hamburg
Bremen
Enkhuizen
Amsterdam
Zierikzee
Bristol
Dieppe
Saint-Malo
Audierne
La Rochelle
Bordeaux
Bayonne
Bilbao
San Sebastian
Oporto
Lisbon
Lagos
(from Azores)
EUROPEAN PORTS AND MARKETS, 1500–1600
Major port
Lesser port
Major salt port
Lesser salt port
Major financial and marketing centre
100 miles
100 kilometres
Scale 1:5 700 000
ENGLAND
FRANCE
SPAIN
PORTUGAL
ENGLISH CHANNEL
BAY OF BISCAY
Bristol
London
Thames
Northam
Barnstaple
Bideford
Exeter
Lympston
Kenton
Sidmouth
Dawlish
Topsham
Teignmouth
Exmouth
Dittisham
Plymouth
Falmouth
Dartmouth
Poole
Weymouth
Southampton
Newport
Le Crotoy
Abbeville
Dieppe
Saint-Valéry
Fécamp
Étretat
Harfleur
Le Havre
Honfleur
Villequier
La Mailleraye
Quillebeuf
Sotteville
Jumièges
Bouille
Caudebec
Rouen
Seine
Barfleur
Guernsey
Saint-Vaast-la-Hougue
Carteret
Saint-Aubin
Saint-Hélier
Agon
Regnéville
Briqueville
Granville
Cancale
Saint-Malo
Dinard
Saint-Briac
Ploumanach
Lannion
Bréhat
Roscoff
Saint-Pol-de-Léon
Morlaix
Paimpol
Pontrieux
Erquy
Binic
Saint-Brieuc
Dahouet
Brest
Audierne
Penmarch
Loctudy
Lorient
Blauet
Vannes
Croisic
Pornic
Nantes
Bourgneuf
Loire
Croix-de-Vie
Bouin
Saint-Gilles
Olonne
Les Sables-d'Olonne
Talmont-sur-Jard
La Flotte
Nieul
Île de Ré
La Rochelle
Île d'Oléron
Charente
Brouage
Marennes
La Tremblade
Arvert
Chaillevette
Mornac
Royan
Meshers
Bourg
Bordeaux
Libourne
Dordogne
Garonne
Adour
Cap Breton
Bayonne
Biarritz
Pasajes
San Sebastian
Bilbao
Castro Urdiales
Laredo
Santoña
Santander
Ribadesella
Aviles
See enlargement
Minho
Douro
Tagus
Guadiana
Guadalquivir
Ebro
Vianna
Oporto
Aveiro
Figueira
Lisbon
Setubal
Seville
San Lucar
Cadiz
THE BASQUE COAST
Cap Breton
Bayonne
Biarritz
Bidart
Guéthary
Saint-Jean-de-Luz
Ciboure
Fuenterrabia
Lezo
Renteria
Pasajes
San Sebastian
Usurbil
Orio
Zarauz
Guetaria
Zumaya
Deva
Motrico
Ondarroa
Lequeitio
Ea
Bermeo
Mundaca
Plencia
Portugalete
Bilbao
30 miles
30 kilometres
Scale 1:1 700 000

Long before 1500 Europeans engaged in fisheries far from home. Between 1450 and 1500 in England alone some 30 ports, large and small, dispatched over 100 vessels each spring to Iceland to catch or purchase cod. French and Iberian fishermen frequented Irish waters, Basques hunted whales off northwestern Spain, and Portuguese sailed west to the Azores and south towards the Cape Verdes for tuna and sardine. Large ports provided capital and supplies to smaller ports nearby and organized the inland distribution and marketing of fish along navigable rivers.

Once cod stocks became known, much of the technology and organization of these late 15th-century fisheries was adapted to the northwestern Atlantic. The Normans, Bretons, and Portuguese who pioneered the trans-Atlantic fishery at the beginning of the 16th century were joined in the 1570s by English from the West Country. By the second half of the 16th century well over 100 European ports were involved. In most years they sent out several hundred ships and many thousand men. This fishery could be intensely local. Virtually all components for a voyage could be supplied by a single port, and the ship, sometimes as small as 30 tons, could return to that port with dried or green cod. More commonly local ports provided ships, boats, and men, while merchants in larger centres provided supplies and capital and arranged to market the catch. Compared to later trans-Atlantic fisheries, the 16th-century fishery was dispersed and local, but it already involved many fishermen in interregional and international quests for supplies (particularly salt) and markets.

THE 17th CENTURY FISHERY

Authors: John Mannion, Gordon Handcock

In 1675 the English fishery remained relatively concentrated in the numerous harbours along the east coast of Newfoundland. The French fishery was more scattered. Fishermen from Saint-Malo and their neighbours controlled the North Arm of Newfoundland (le Petit Nord). French Basques dominated the fishery along the South Shore where Plaisance was a regional centre. Ships from Norman ports and from Les Sables-d'Olonne, close to a third of the French fleet, fished the banks. To the north the Inuit restricted French access to the Labrador shore. To the south New Englanders, using much smaller ships and operating closer to their home ports, quickly dominated the waters off Nova Scotia. In the Gulf of St Lawrence Gaspé was the mainland base of the French migratory fishery.

In the 17th century caretakers were left in some harbours over the winter; eventually family residence began. In Newfoundland French settlement was confined to the South Shore where, in 1687, there were some forty families in a French overwintering population of perhaps 1 000. In 1675 about 1 700 English overwinterers, a third of them members of families and the rest single men, were scattered in 30 harbours and coves. Whether French or English, the resident population was unstable. Few families residing in Newfoundland during the 1670s or 1680s became part of the 18th-century population.

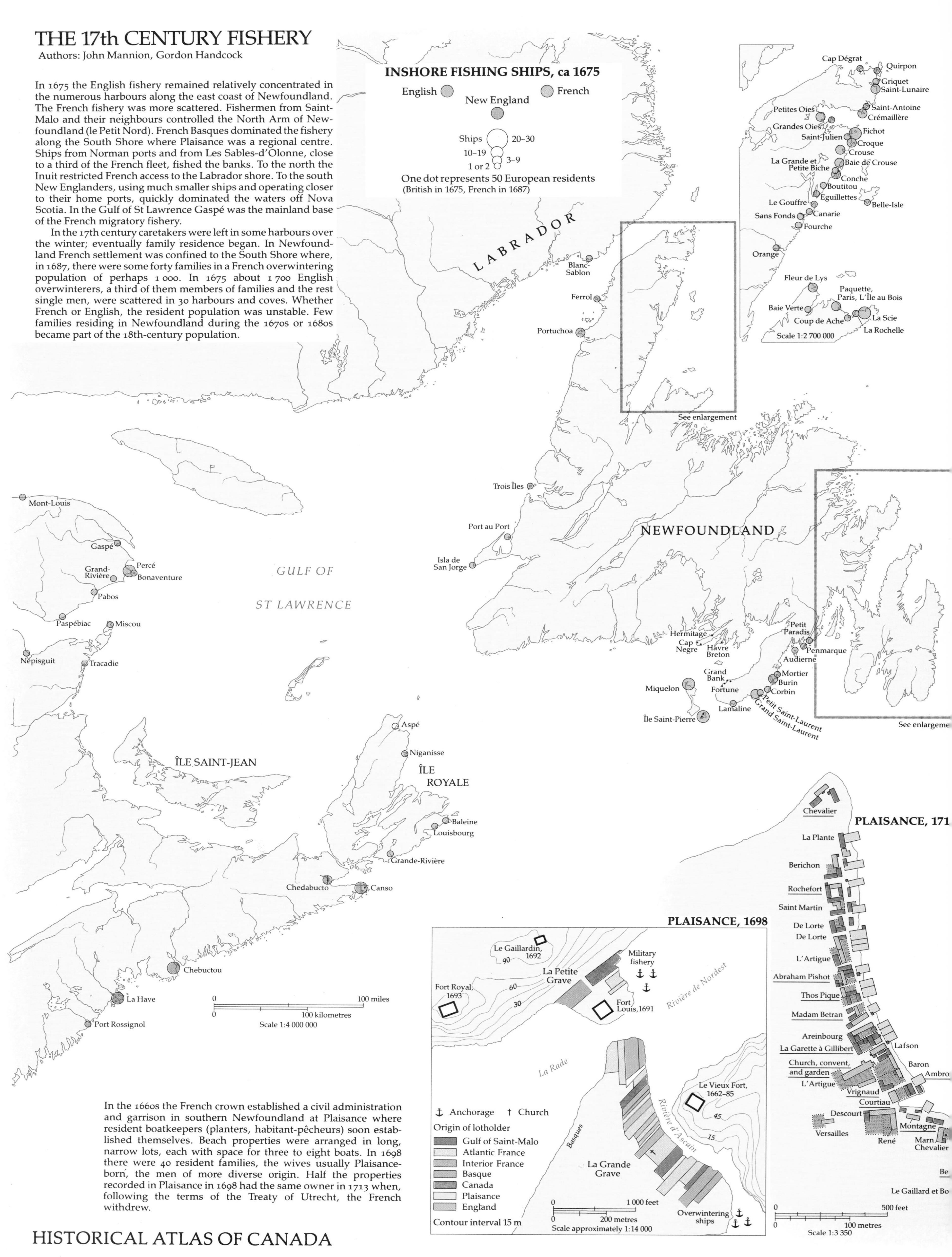
INSHORE FISHING SHIPS, ca 1675
English
New England
French
Ships
20–30
10–19
3–9
1 or 2
One dot represents 50 European residents
(British in 1675, French in 1687)
LABRADOR
Blanc-Sablon
Ferrol
Portuchoa
See enlargement
NEWFOUNDLAND
Trois Îles
Port au Port
Isla de San Jorge
GULF OF ST LAWRENCE
Mont-Louis
Gaspé
Percé
Grand-Rivière
Bonaventure
Pabos
Paspébiac
Miscou
Népisguit
Tracadie
Hermitage
Cap Negre
Havre Breton
Grand Bank
Fortune
Lamaline
Petit Paradis
Penmarque
Audierne
Mortier
Burin
Corbin
Petit Saint-Laurent
Grand Saint-Laurent
Miquelon
Île Saint-Pierre
Cap Dégrat
Quirpon
Griquet
Saint-Lunaire
Saint-Antoine
Crémaillère
Petites Oies
Grandes Oies
Fichot
Saint-Julien
Croque
Crouse
La Grande et Petite Biche
Baie de Crouse
Conche
Boutitou
Eguillettes
Belle-Isle
Le Gouffre
Canarie
Sans Fonds
Fourche
Orange
Fleur de Lys
Paquette, Paris, L'Île au Bois
Baie Verte
Coup de Ache
La Scie
La Rochelle
Scale 1:2 700 000
ÎLE SAINT-JEAN
ÎLE ROYALE
Aspé
Niganisse
Baleine
Louisbourg
Grande-Rivière
Chedabucto
Canso
Chebuctou
La Have
Port Rossignol
100 miles
100 kilometres
Scale 1:4 000 000
PLAISANCE, 1698
Le Gaillardin, 1692
La Petite Grave
Military fishery
Fort Royal, 1693
Fort Louis, 1691
Rivière de Nordest
La Rade
Le Vieux Fort, 1662–85
Rivière d'Ascain
Basques
La Grande Grave
Anchorage
Church
Origin of lotholder
Gulf of Saint-Malo
Atlantic France
Interior France
Basque
Canada
Plaisance
England
Contour interval 15 m
1 000 feet
200 metres
Scale approximately 1:14 000
Overwintering ships
PLAISANCE, 171
Chevalier
La Plante
Berichon
Rochefort
Saint Martin
De Lorte
De Lorte
L'Artigue
Abraham Pishot
Thos Pique
Madam Betran
Areinbourg
La Garette à Gillibert
Lafson
Church, convent, and garden
Baron
Ambro
L'Artigue
Vrignaud
Courtiau
Descourt
Versailles
René
Montagne
Marn. Chevalier
Le Gaillard et Bo
500 feet
100 metres
Scale 1:3 350

In the 1660s the French crown established a civil administration and garrison in southern Newfoundland at Plaisance where resident boatkeepers (planters, habitant-pêcheurs) soon established themselves. Beach properties were arranged in long, narrow lots, each with space for three to eight boats. In 1698 there were 40 resident families, the wives usually Plaisance-born, the men of more diverse origin. Half the properties recorded in Plaisance in 1698 had the same owner in 1713 when, following the terms of the Treaty of Utrecht, the French withdrew.

Many of the small French and English ports that had engaged in the trans-Atlantic cod fishery ceased to do so in the 17th century, victims of the growing centralization of commerce along the European shore. Fishing ships were generally larger than those of the 16th century; increasingly they were based in a few major ports where manpower, capital, and supplies were available.

In 1664 the banks fishery accounted for roughly a third of the French cod fleet. Based in Le Havre, Honfleur, and Les Sables-d'Olonne, it supplied green fish to a huge market along the Seine and Loire Rivers to Paris and Orléans. Ships from the other major fishing ports in France produced dried cod and competed with the English for markets in southern France, Iberia, and Italy. The English fishery grew rapidly in the early decades of the 17th century and became more concentrated than the French. It soon employed well over 200 ships but never exceeded the French cod fleet, which in the mid-17th century comprised over 400 ships, large and small, and almost 10 000 men.

ENGLAND

Bristol
London
Barnstaple
Bideford
Southampton
Topsham
Poole
Teignmouth
Weymouth
Plymouth
Dartmouth
Abbeville
Dieppe
Le Havre (97)
Saint-Valéry
Rouen
Honfleur
Channel Islands
Bréhat
Paimpol
Portrieux
Binic
Leguée
Granville
Saint-Malo (61)

FRANCE

Le Croisic
Saint-Nazaire
Le Pellerin
Le Pouliguen
Nantes
Pornic
Bourgneuf
Saint-Gilles
Les Sables-d'Olonne (73)
Île de Ré
La Rochelle
Île d'Oléron
Brouage
Marennes
La Tremblade
Mornac
Royan
Bordeaux
Bayonne
Saint-Jean-de-Luz

0 – 100 miles
0 – 100 kilometres
Scale 1:5 850 000

FISHING SHIPS BOUND FOR NEWFOUNDLAND

English 1675
French 1664
Ships
60–100
26–60
11–25
6–10
1–5

Circles are proportional to number of fishing ships.

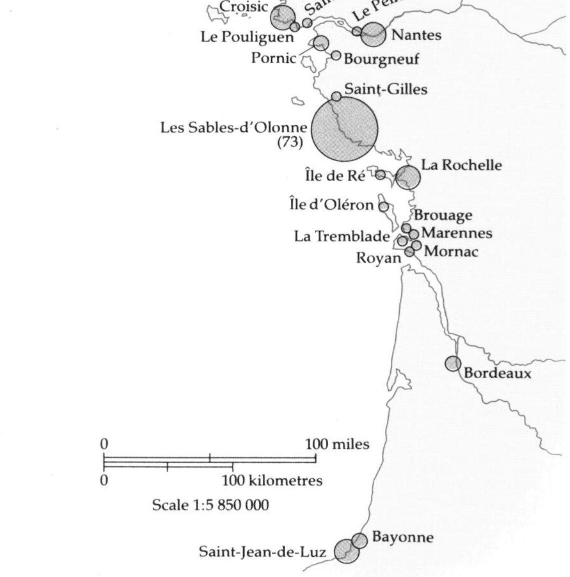

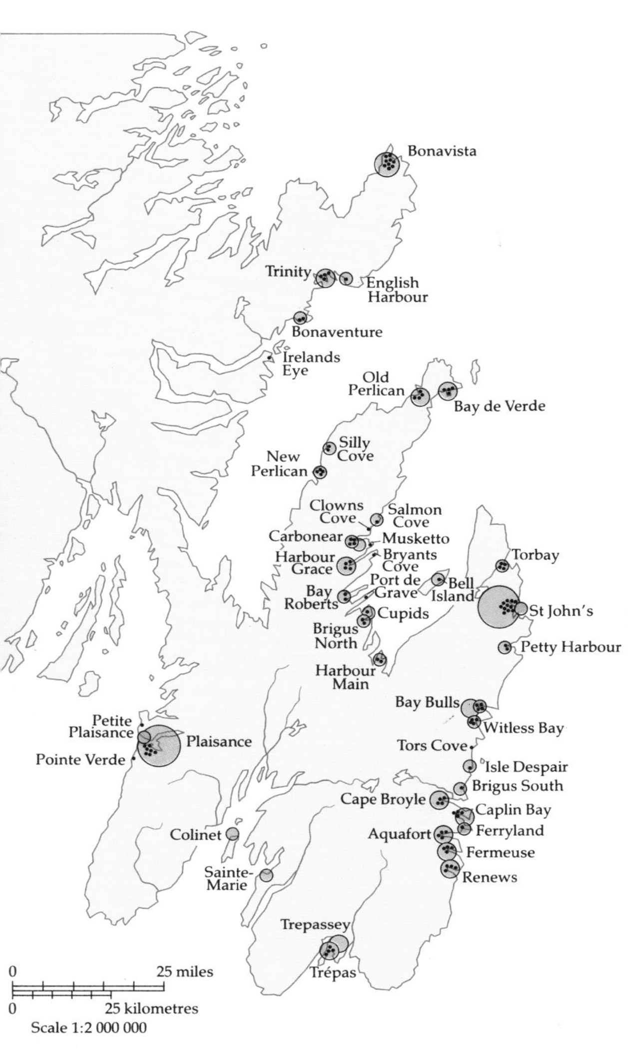

Bonavista
Trinity
English Harbour
Bonaventure
Irelands Eye
Old Perlican
Bay de Verde
Silly Cove
New Perlican
Clowns Cove
Salmon Cove
Carbonear
Musketto
Harbour Grace
Bryants Cove
Port de Grave
Bay Roberts
Bell Island
Torbay
St John's
Cupids
Brigus North
Petty Harbour
Harbour Main
Bay Bulls
Witless Bay
Petite Plaisance
Plaisance
Pointe Verde
Tors Cove
Isle Despair
Brigus South
Cape Broyle
Caplin Bay
Ferryland
Aquafort
Fermeuse
Renews
Colinet
Sainte-Marie
Trepassey
Trépas
0 – 25 miles
0 – 25 kilometres
Scale 1:2 000 000

ORIGIN OF ENGLISH FISHERMEN IN NEWFOUNDLAND, 1675–1681

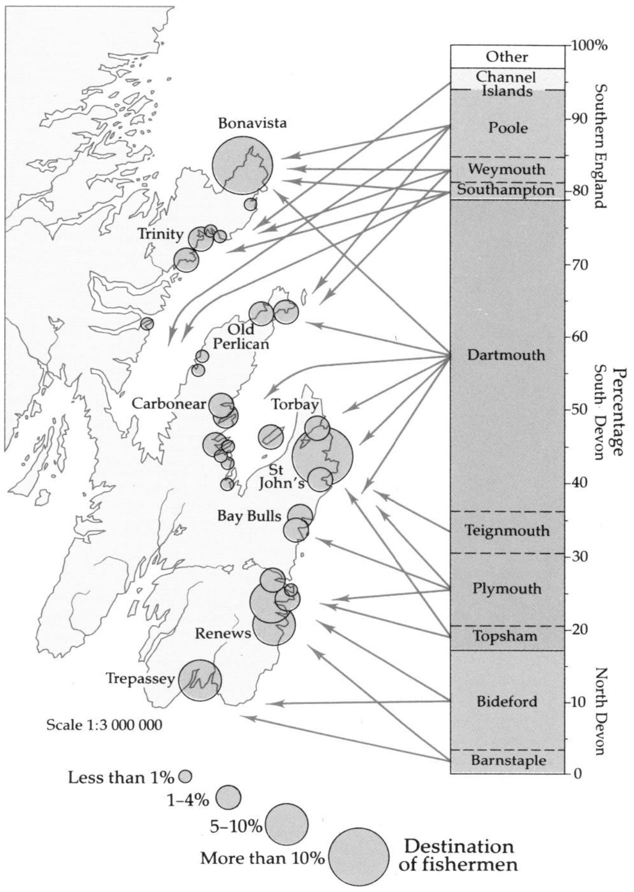

Bonavista
Trinity
Old Perlican
Carbonear
Torbay
St John's
Bay Bulls
Renews
Trepassey
Scale 1:3 000 000

Other
Channel Islands
Poole
Weymouth
Southampton
Dartmouth
Teignmouth
Plymouth
Topsham
Bideford
Barnstaple

Southern England
South Devon
North Devon
Percentage
100% – 90 – 80 – 70 – 60 – 50 – 40 – 30 – 20 – 10 – 0

Less than 1%
1–4%
5–10%
More than 10%
Destination of fishermen

English trade with Newfoundland at the end of the 17th century depended on ships, manpower, manufactured goods, and foodstuffs from southern England; brandy and above all salt from France and the Iberian Peninsula; foodstuffs (bread, beef, pork, and butter) from Ireland; and, in small quantities, rum, molasses, and sugar from the West Indies (perhaps via New England). Almost all the cod went to Spain, Portugal, and Italy, and cod oil to home ports in England.

PLAISANCE, 1713

after British Board of Ordinance, 1714

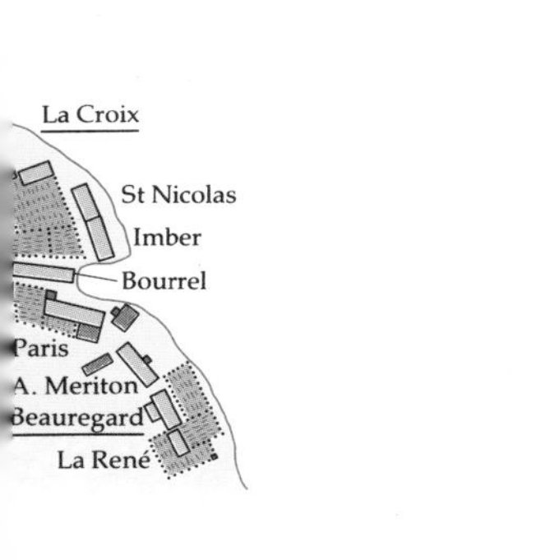

- Building
- Wharf
- Oil vat
- Fish store
- Garden

La Croix — Plots occupied by the same owner in 1698 and 1713 are underlined.

La Croix
St Nicolas
Imber
Bourrel
Paris
A. Meriton
Beauregard
La René

ENGLISH COD TRADE, 1697

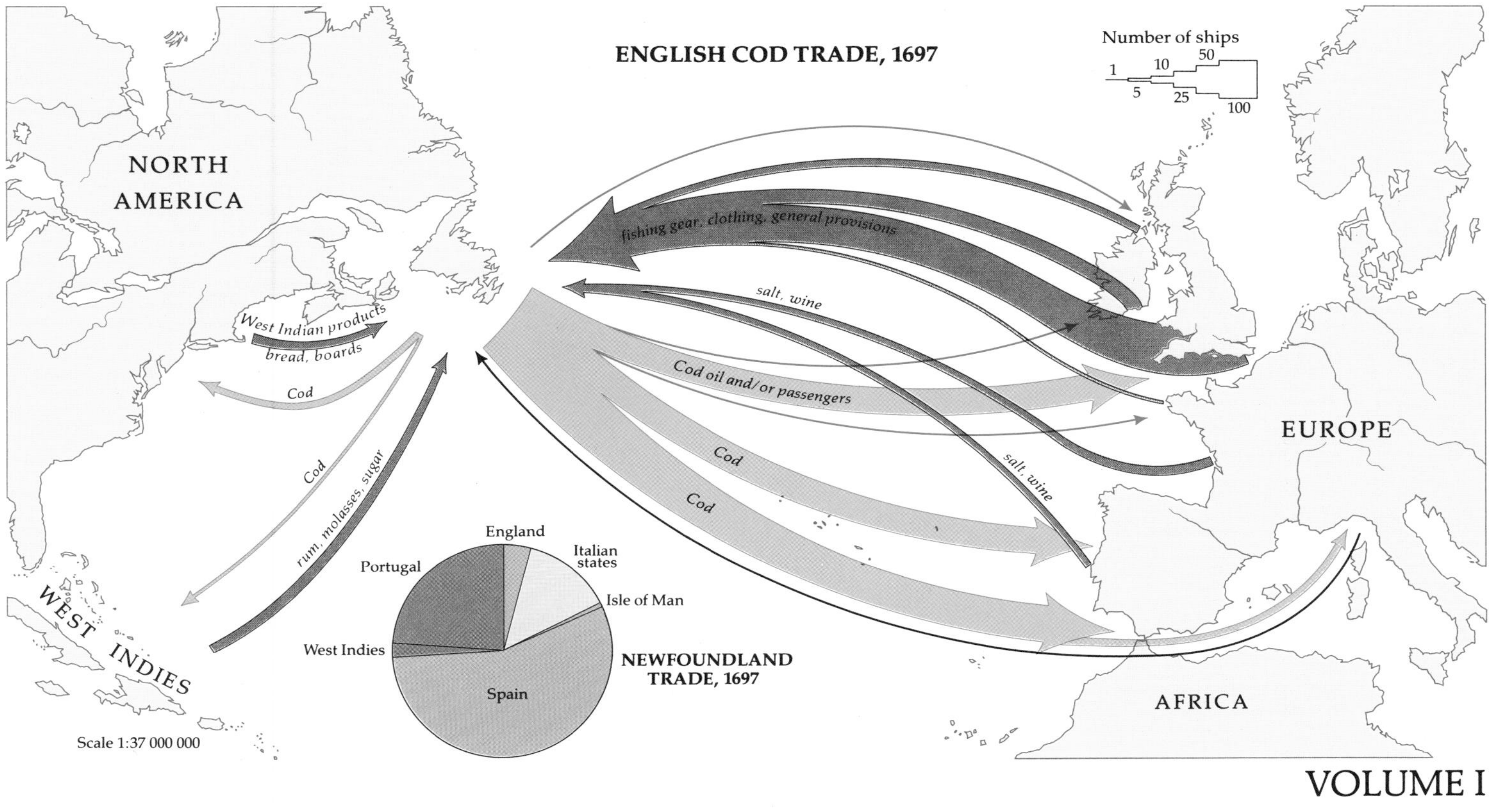

Number of ships
1, 5, 10, 25, 50, 100

NORTH AMERICA
EUROPE
AFRICA
WEST INDIES
fishing gear, clothing, general provisions
salt, wine
West Indian products
bread, boards
Cod
Cod oil and/or passengers
Cod
Cod
salt, wine
Cod
rum, molasses, sugar
Scale 1:37 000 000

NEWFOUNDLAND TRADE, 1697
England
Italian states
Isle of Man
Portugal
West Indies
Spain

ÎLE ROYALE, 18th CENTURY

Author: Kenneth Donovan

When the Treaty of Utrecht (1713) confirmed British possession of mainland Nova Scotia and extended British title to all of Newfoundland, French attention shifted to Île Royale (Cape Breton Island). The resident and migratory French fisheries in southern Newfoundland (pl 23) moved to Île Royale in 1713; four years later the French government began a major fortification at Louisbourg, the largest of its kind in North America.

The Île Royale fisheries were soon substantial; by 1720 they produced about 150 000 quintals (1 quintal = about 50 kg) of dried cod a year, almost half the output of the English fisheries at Newfoundland. Migrants and residents, fishing from many ports in eastern Île Royale, practised an inshore boat fishery. Schooners, most of them based in Louisbourg, made voyages of 20–30 days to the fishing banks. Fish and fish oil were Île Royale's only locally generated exports.

At the same time Louisbourg became a major entrepôt. From France came manufactured goods, fishing supplies, and foodstuffs; from the French West Indies molasses, sugar, and some rum. New Englanders, who in some years sent almost as many ships to Louisbourg as to the Caribbean, brought foodstuffs and building supplies and took specie, molasses, French manufactures, and cod. In the 1730s foodstuffs from Canada were imported in considerable quantity. Thereafter Canadian trade dwindled; supplies that French officials hoped would come from Canada came, increasingly, from New England.

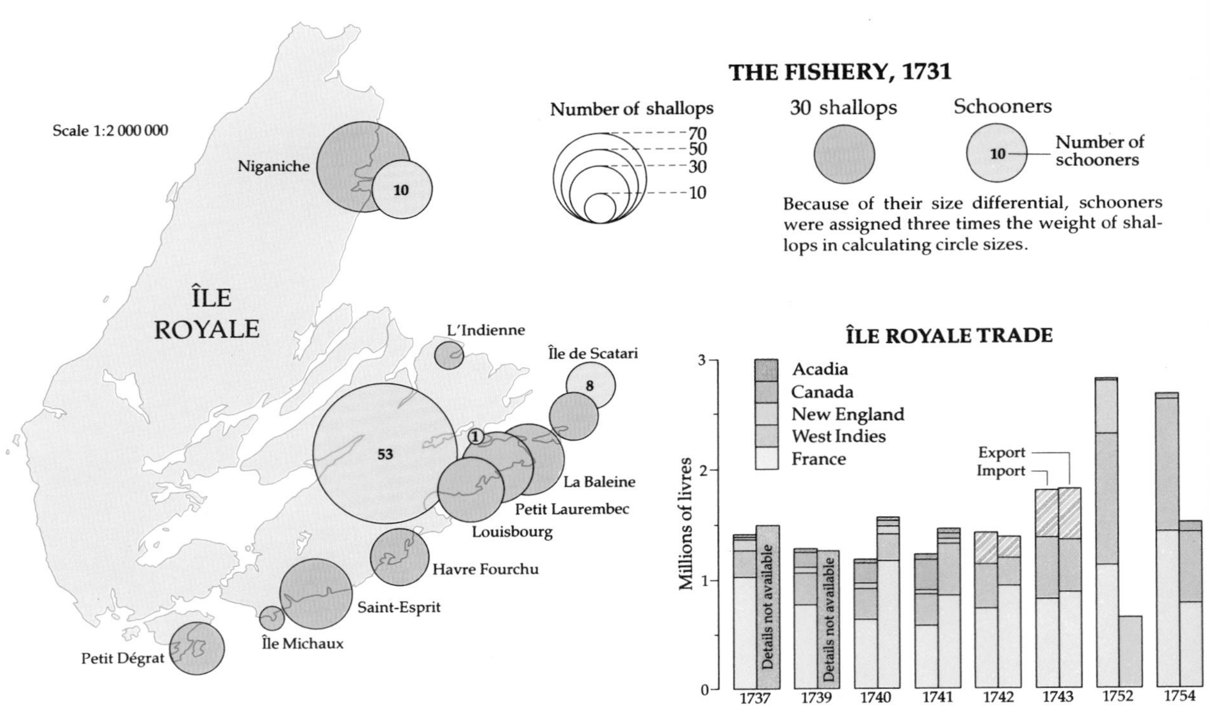
Scale 1:2 000 000
Niganiche
10
ÎLE ROYALE
L'Indienne
Île de Scatari
8
53
1
La Baleine
Petit Laurembec
Louisbourg
Havre Fourchu
Saint-Esprit
Île Michaux
Petit Dégrat
THE FISHERY, 1731
Number of shallops
70
50
30
10
30 shallops
Schooners
10
Number of schooners
Because of their size differential, schooners were assigned three times the weight of shallops in calculating circle sizes.
ÎLE ROYALE TRADE
Acadia
Canada
New England
West Indies
France
Export
Import
Millions of livres
Details not available
Details not available
1737
1739
1740
1741
1742
1743
1752
1754

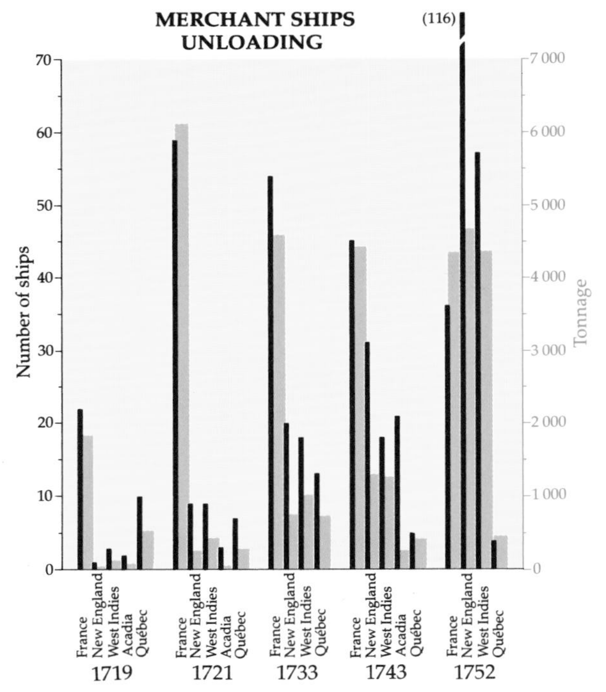
MERCHANT SHIPS UNLOADING
(116)
Number of ships
Tonnage
France
New England
West Indies
Acadia
Québec
1719
1721
1733
1743
1752

Painting of Louisbourg viewed from the harbour, by Verrier fils

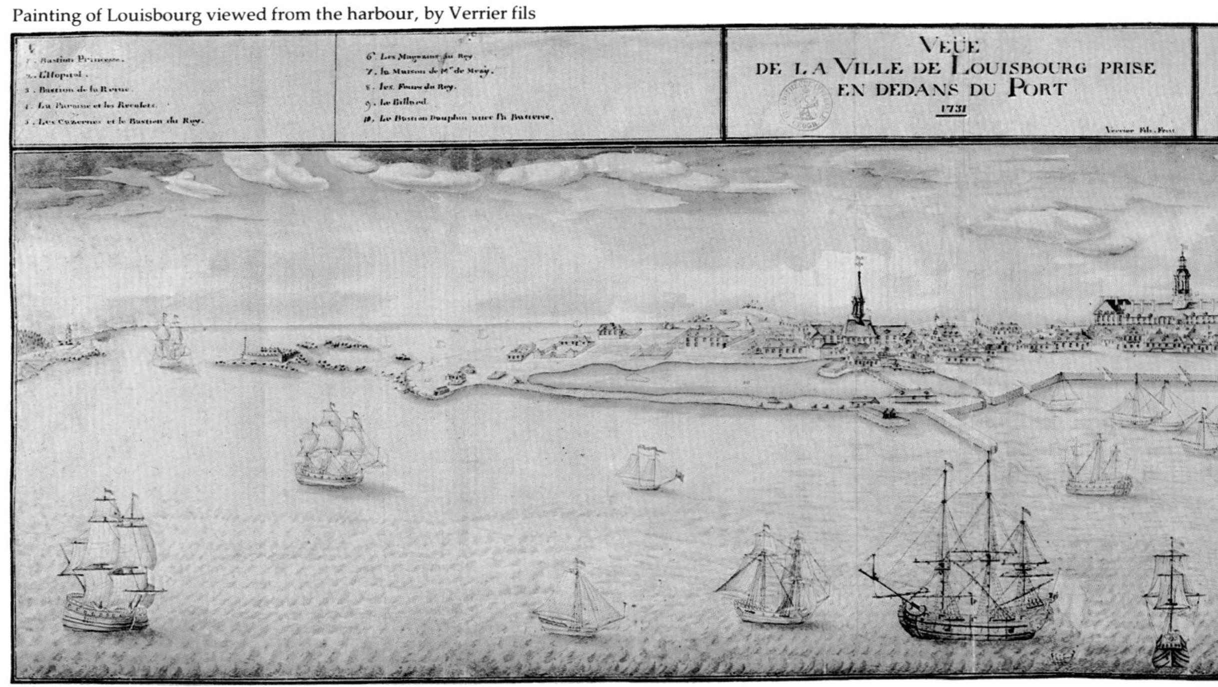
VEUE DE LA VILLE DE LOUISBOURG PRISE EN DEDANS DU PORT
1731

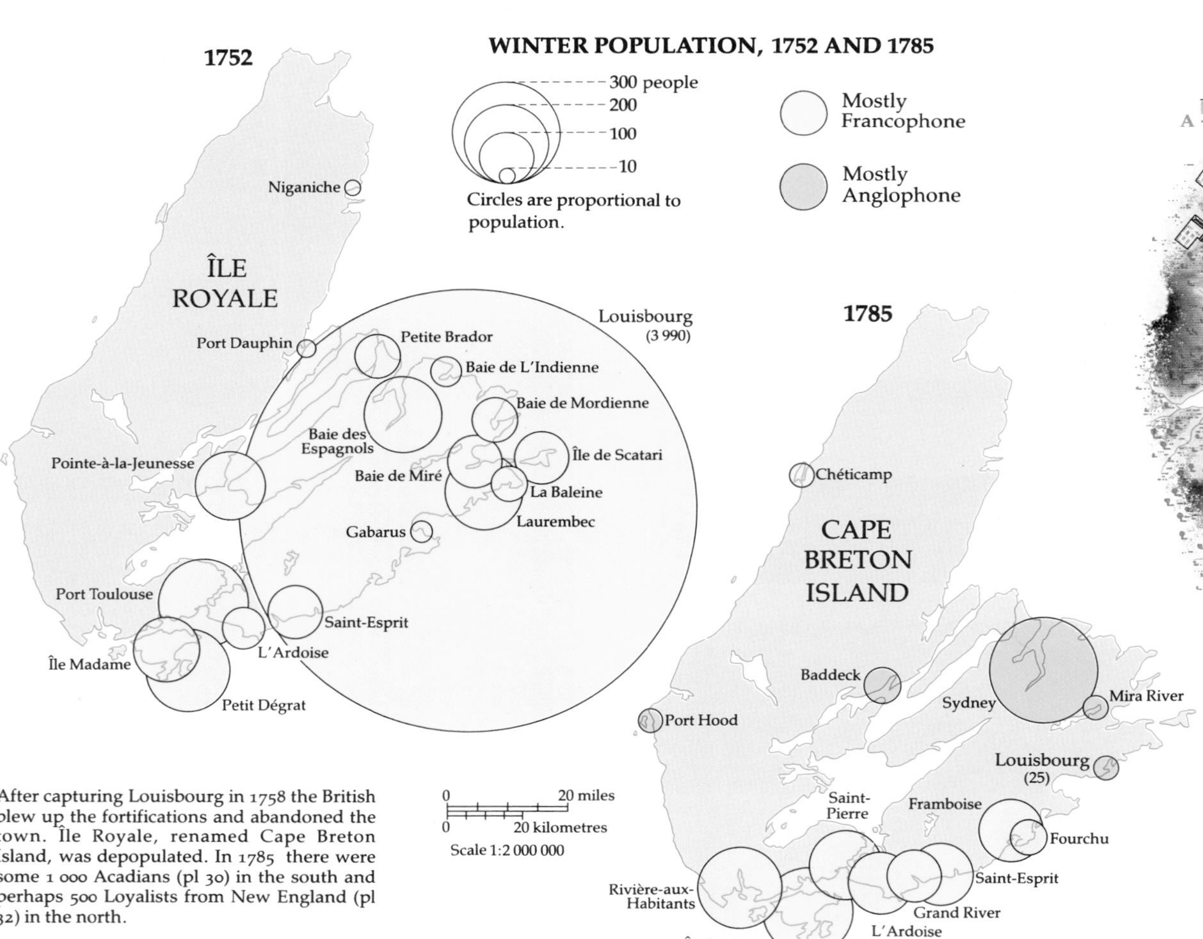
WINTER POPULATION, 1752 AND 1785
300 people
200
100
10
Circles are proportional to population.
Mostly Francophone
Mostly Anglophone
1752
Niganiche
ÎLE ROYALE
Port Dauphin
Petite Brador
Louisbourg (3 990)
Baie de L'Indienne
Baie de Mordienne
Baie des Espagnols
Île de Scatari
Pointe-à-la-Jeunesse
Baie de Miré
La Baleine
Laurembec
Gabarus
Port Toulouse
Saint-Esprit
L'Ardoise
Île Madame
Petit Dégrat
0 20 miles
0 20 kilometres
Scale 1:2 000 000
1785
Chéticamp
CAPE BRETON ISLAND
Baddeck
Sydney
Mira River
Port Hood
Louisbourg (25)
Saint-Pierre
Framboise
Fourchu
Saint-Esprit
Rivière-aux-Habitants
Grand River
L'Ardoise
Île Madame

After capturing Louisbourg in 1758 the British blew up the fortifications and abandoned the town. Île Royale, renamed Cape Breton Island, was depopulated. In 1785 there were some 1 000 Acadians (pl 30) in the south and perhaps 500 Loyalists from New England (pl 32) in the north.

PROFILE OF MAUREPAS' BASTION, 1741

After 'Les Différents Profils de la Nouvelle Enceinte de Louisbourg,' by Verrier fils

LOUISBOURG FORTIFICATIONS, 1745

After 'Plan de Louisbourg dans l'Île Royale,' by Verrier fils

Éperon; Petit Étang; Rue du Quai; Rue Royale; Rue d'Orléans; Rue Dauphine; Rue Toulouse; Rue Louis; Rue Saint-; Rue de l'Étang; Rue de l'Hôpital; Rue d'Estrées; Rue France; Rue de Scatari; Rue des Remparts; Rue du Petit Étang; Plaine de Gabarus

- I Dauphin's bastion
- II Royal bastion
- III Queen's bastion
- IV Princess' bastion
- V Brouillan's bastion
- VI Maurepas' bastion
- VII The quay
- VIII Parade ground
- IX Dauphin's gate
- X Queen's gate
- XI Maurepas' gate
- XII Barracks and governor's residence
- XIII Guardhouse
- XIV Powder magazine
- XV New barracks (proposed)
- XVI Powder magazine (proposed)

0 800 feet / 0 200 metres

Scale approximately 1:9 250

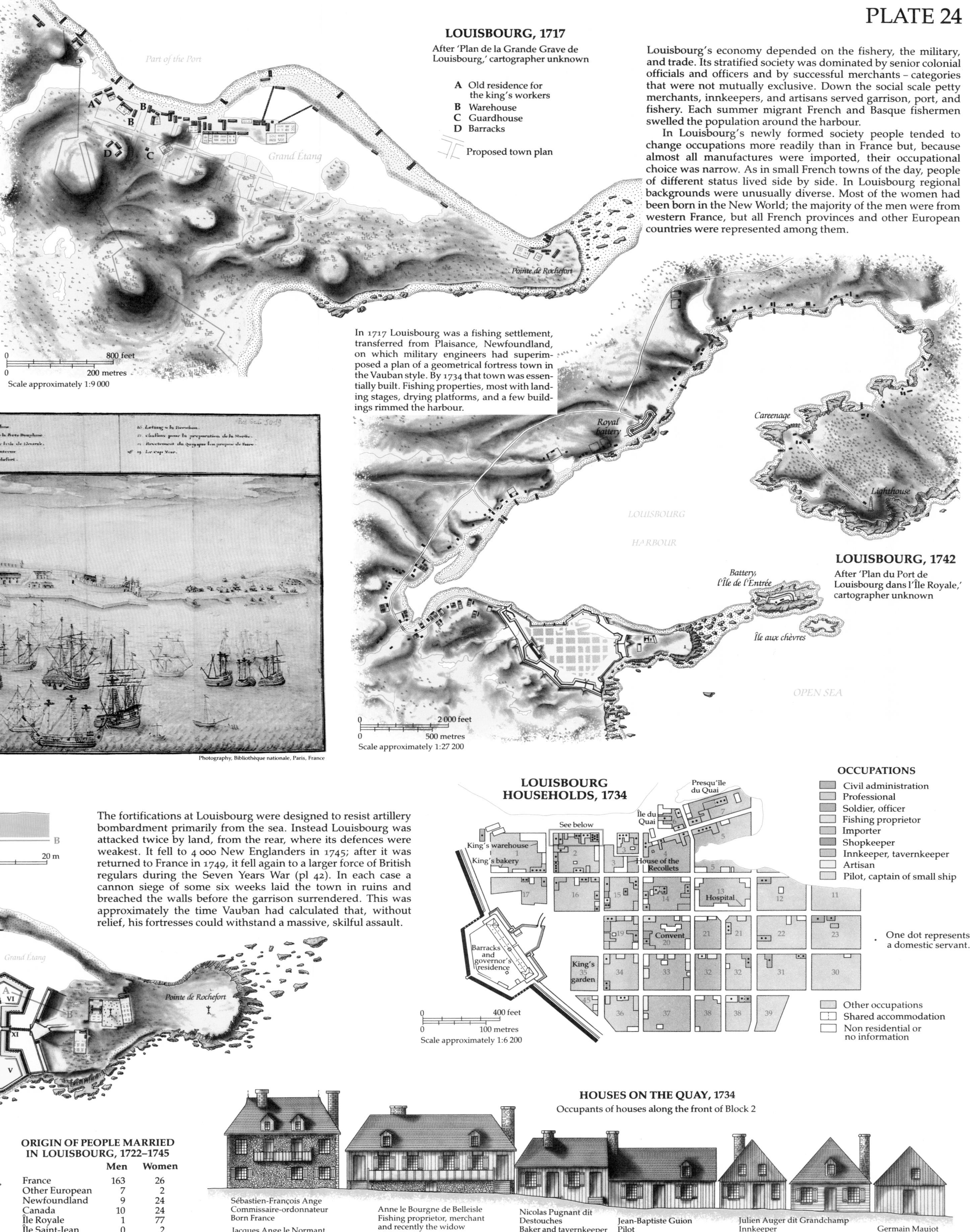
LOUISBOURG, 1717
After 'Plan de la Grande Grave de Louisbourg,' cartographer unknown
A Old residence for the king's workers
B Warehouse
C Guardhouse
D Barracks
Proposed town plan
Part of the Port
Grand Étang
Pointe de Rochefort
0 800 feet
0 200 metres
Scale approximately 1:9 000
Royal battery
Careenage
Lighthouse
LOUISBOURG HARBOUR
Battery, l'Île de l'Entrée
Île aux chèvres
OPEN SEA
LOUISBOURG, 1742
After 'Plan du Port de Louisbourg dans l'Île Royale,' cartographer unknown
0 2 000 feet
0 500 metres
Scale approximately 1:27 200
Photography, Bibliothèque nationale, Paris, France
B
20 m
Grand Étang
Pointe de Rochefort
LOUISBOURG HOUSEHOLDS, 1734
Presqu'île du Quai
Île du Quai
See below
King's warehouse
King's bakery
House of the Recollets
Hospital
Convent
Barracks and governor's residence
King's garden
OCCUPATIONS
Civil administration
Professional
Soldier, officer
Fishing proprietor
Importer
Shopkeeper
Innkeeper, tavernkeeper
Artisan
Pilot, captain of small ship
One dot represents a domestic servant.
Other occupations
Shared accommodation
Non residential or no information
0 400 feet
0 100 metres
Scale approximately 1:6 200
HOUSES ON THE QUAY, 1734
Occupants of houses along the front of Block 2

Louisbourg's economy depended on the fishery, the military, and trade. Its stratified society was dominated by senior colonial officials and officers and by successful merchants – categories that were not mutually exclusive. Down the social scale petty merchants, innkeepers, and artisans served garrison, port, and fishery. Each summer migrant French and Basque fishermen swelled the population around the harbour.

In Louisbourg's newly formed society people tended to change occupations more readily than in France but, because almost all manufactures were imported, their occupational choice was narrow. As in small French towns of the day, people of different status lived side by side. In Louisbourg regional backgrounds were unusually diverse. Most of the women had been born in the New World; the majority of the men were from western France, but all French provinces and other European countries were represented among them.

In 1717 Louisbourg was a fishing settlement, transferred from Plaisance, Newfoundland, on which military engineers had superimposed a plan of a geometrical fortress town in the Vauban style. By 1734 that town was essentially built. Fishing properties, most with landing stages, drying platforms, and a few buildings rimmed the harbour.

The fortifications at Louisbourg were designed to resist artillery bombardment primarily from the sea. Instead Louisbourg was attacked twice by land, from the rear, where its defences were weakest. It fell to 4 000 New Englanders in 1745; after it was returned to France in 1749, it fell again to a larger force of British regulars during the Seven Years War (pl 42). In each case a cannon siege of some six weeks laid the town in ruins and breached the walls before the garrison surrendered. This was approximately the time Vauban had calculated that, without relief, his fortresses could withstand a massive, skilful assault.

ORIGIN OF PEOPLE MARRIED IN LOUISBOURG, 1722–1745

	Men	Women
France	163	26
Other European	7	2
Newfoundland	9	24
Canada	10	24
Île Royale	1	77
Île Saint-Jean	0	2
Acadia	13	15
Unknown	27	59
Total	**230**	**229**

Sébastien-François Ange
Commissaire-ordonnateur
Born France

Jacques Ange le Normant De Mézy
Retired Commissaire and father of Sébastien-François
Born France
8 servants (estimated)

Anne le Bourgne de Belleisle
Fishing proprietor, merchant and recently the widow of the Portuguese, Jean-Baptiste Rodrigue
Born Acadia
7 children
2 servants

Nicolas Pugnant dit Destouches
Baker and tavernkeeper
Born France
Wife Marie Brunet
Born France
3 children
2 servants

Jean-Baptiste Guion
Pilot
Born Acadia
Wife Anne-Magdelaine La Chaume
Born France
5 children

Julien Auger dit Grandchamp
Innkeeper
Born France
Wife Louise-Thérèse Petit
Born Canada
1 child
1 servant

Germain Maujot
Innkeeper
Born Flanders
1 servant

THE NEWFOUNDLAND FISHERY, 18th CENTURY

Authors: John Mannion, Gordon Handcock, Alan Macpherson

The treaty of Utrecht (1713) established British title to Newfoundland. During the following century the British fishery expanded well beyond the old English shore in southeastern Newfoundland; it quickly occupied the south coast when the French fishermen moved to Île Royale (pl 24), reached the west coast by the 1760s, and established resident fisheries on the Petit-Nord (the northern peninsula of Newfoundland) and the Labrador coast before 1800. The small French residential fishery was confined to the islands of Saint-Pierre and Miquelon. About a quarter of the French migratory fishery went directly to the banks. Most of the rest crowded into the harbours of the Petit-Nord where France retained fishing rights and practised an inshore fishery (pl 21).

The British fishery was even more varied. Planters (resident fishing proprietors) hired shallop crews for the inshore fishery. The migratory fishery, operating out of English ports, sent ships to the inshore fishery and bankers to the Grand Bank where cod were salted aboard and dry-cured ashore (as in the schooner fishery, pl 21). Some migrants–masters and men known collectively as by-boatmen–came out as passengers on English fishing vessels and operated independently in the inshore fishery. As late as 1790 planters and migratory men divided production almost equally between them, but the Napoleonic Wars eliminated the by-boatmen and drastically reduced the migratory ship-fishery. By 1805 planters accounted for over 90% of the catch.

BRITISH COD PRODUCTION
Total and percentage by sector

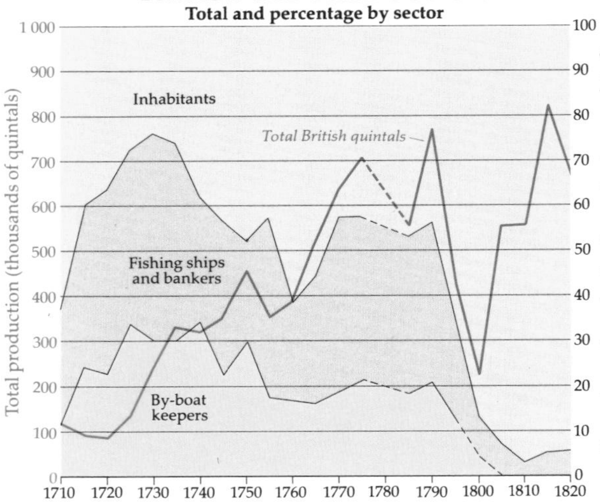

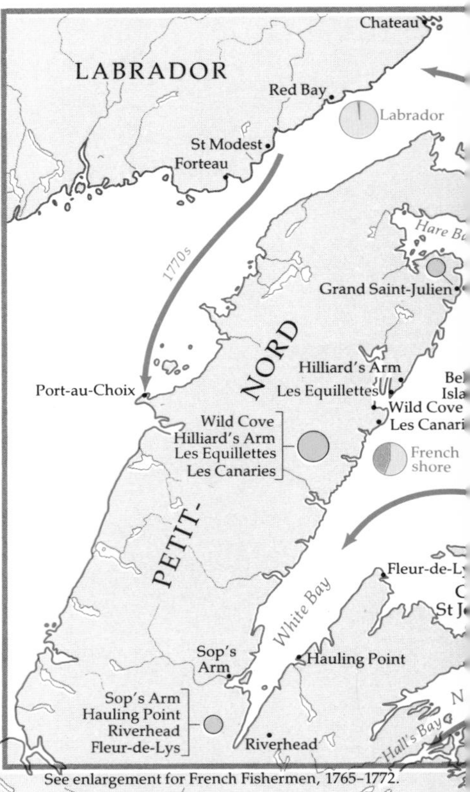

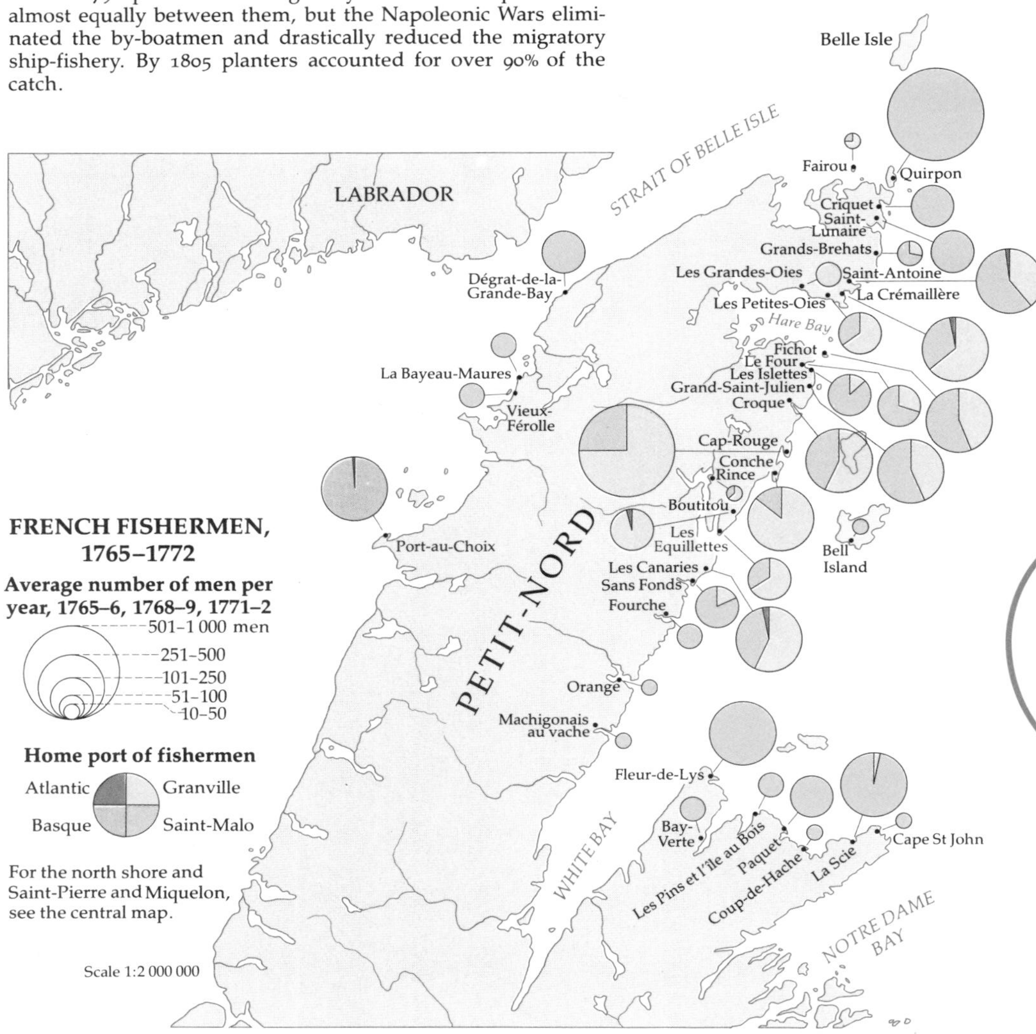

Total production (thousands of quintals) · Percentage of production by sector (accumulated)

Inhabitants · Total British quintals · Fishing ships and bankers · By-boat keepers

FRENCH FISHERMEN, 1765–1772

Average number of men per year, 1765–6, 1768–9, 1771–2

501–1 000 men · 251–500 · 101–250 · 51–100 · 10–50

Home port of fishermen: Atlantic Basque · Granville · Saint-Malo

For the north shore and Saint-Pierre and Miquelon, see the central map.

Scale 1:2 000 000

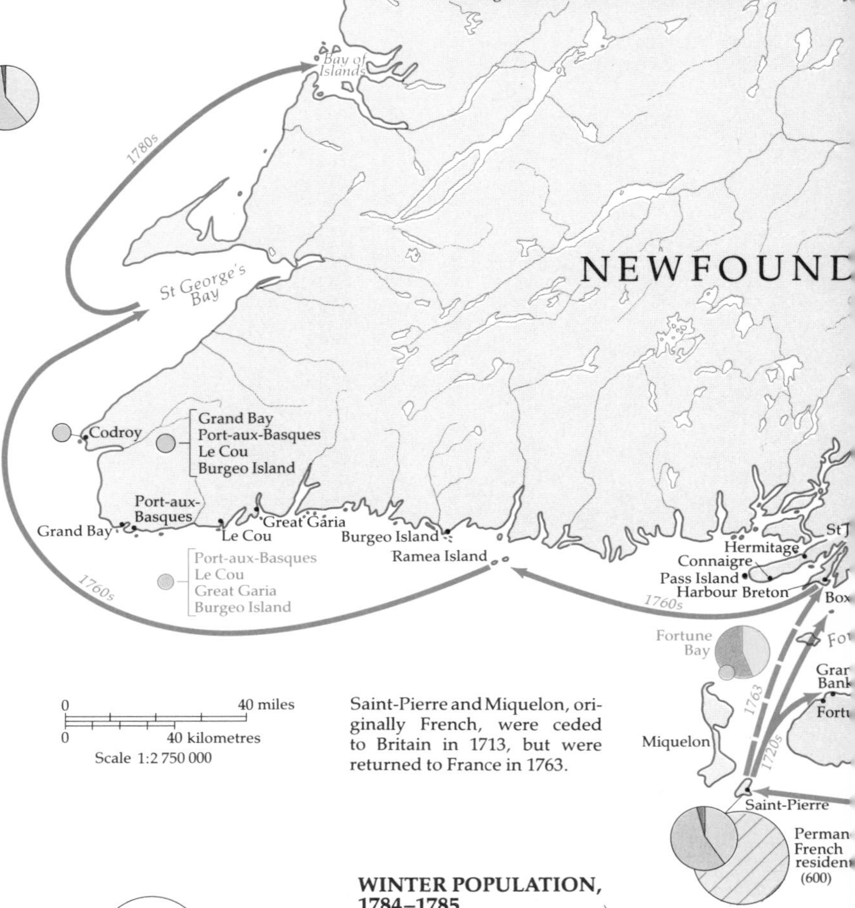

See enlargement for French Fishermen, 1765–1772.

Saint-Pierre and Miquelon, originally French, were ceded to Britain in 1713, but were returned to France in 1763.

Scale 1:2 750 000

BRITISH POPULATION, NEWFOUNDLAND

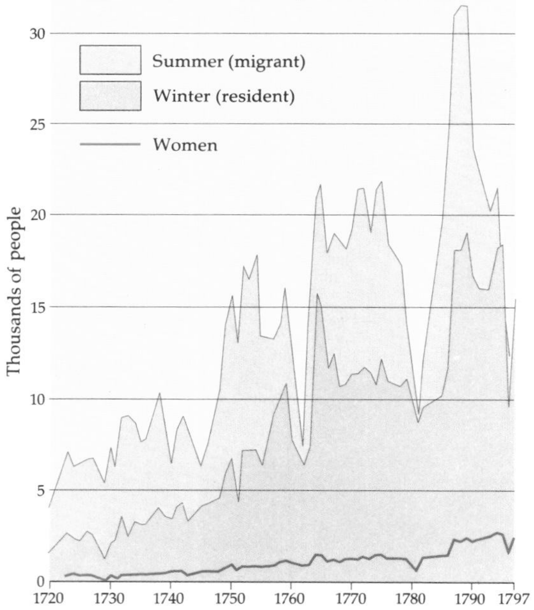

Summer (migrant) · Winter (resident) · Women

Thousands of people

WINTER POPULATION, 1737–1738

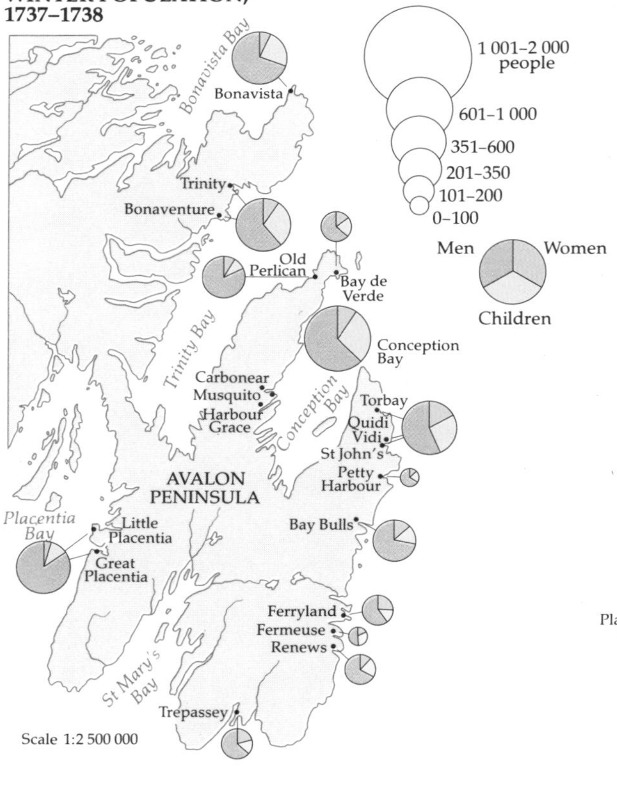

1 001–2 000 people · 601–1 000 · 351–600 · 201–350 · 101–200 · 0–100

Men · Women · Children

Scale 1:2 500 000

WINTER POPULATION, 1784–1785

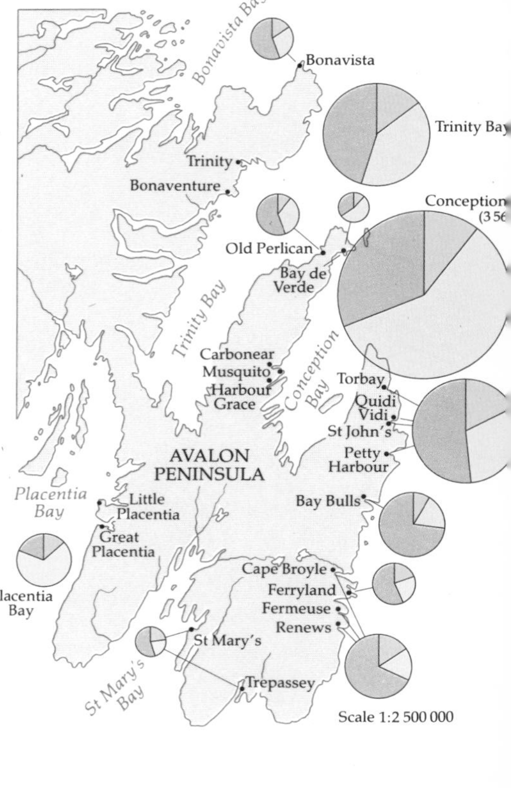

Scale 1:2 500 000

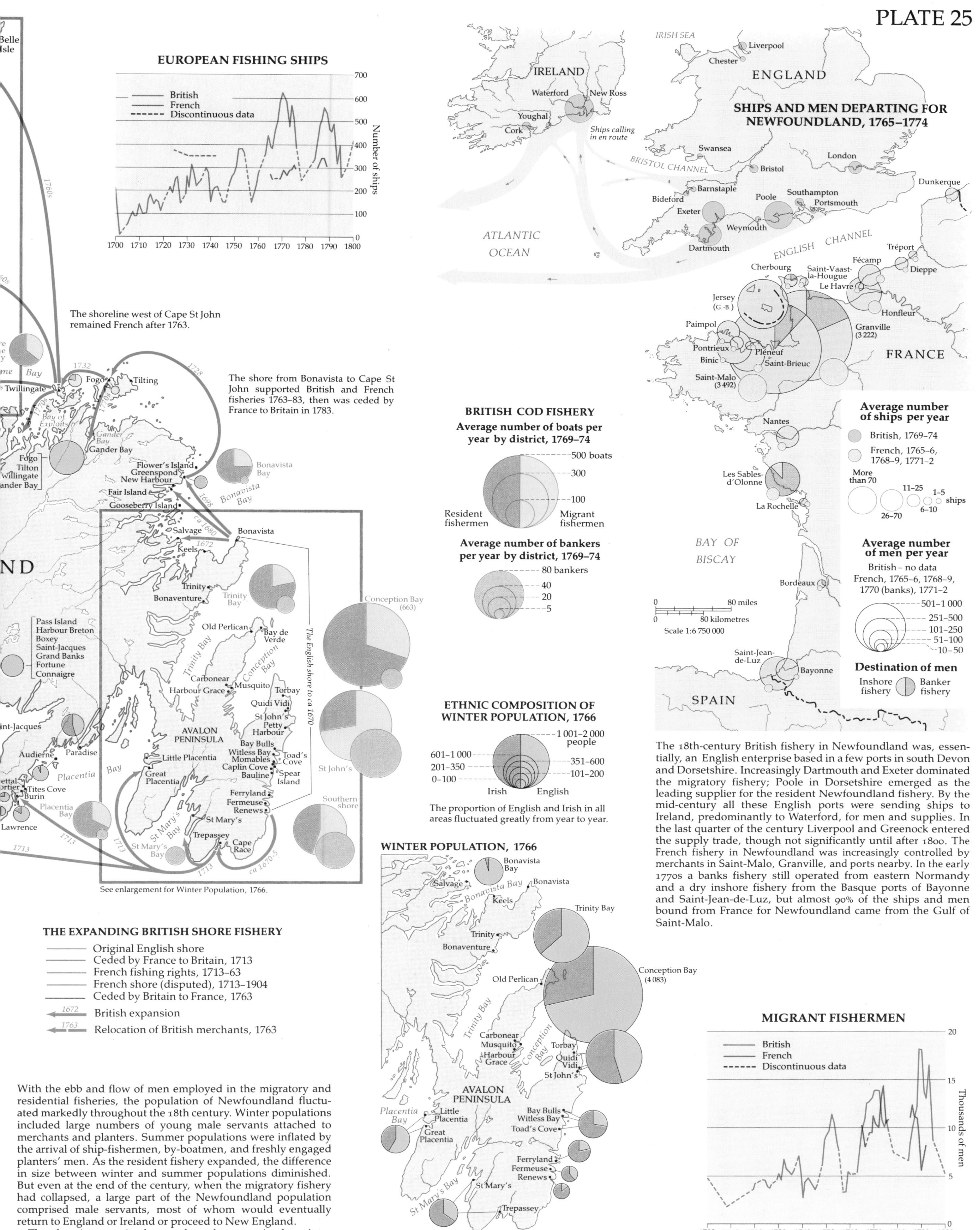
EUROPEAN FISHING SHIPS
British
French
Discontinuous data
Number of ships
0
100
200
300
400
500
600
700
1700 1710 1720 1730 1740 1750 1760 1770 1780 1790 1800
SHIPS AND MEN DEPARTING FOR NEWFOUNDLAND, 1765–1774
IRISH SEA
Liverpool
Chester
ENGLAND
IRELAND
Waterford
New Ross
Youghal
Cork
Ships calling in en route
Swansea
BRISTOL CHANNEL
Bristol
London
Dunkerque
Barnstaple
Bideford
Poole
Southampton
Portsmouth
Exeter
Weymouth
Dartmouth
ATLANTIC OCEAN
ENGLISH CHANNEL
Tréport
Fécamp
Dieppe
Cherbourg
Saint-Vaast-la-Hougue
Le Havre
Jersey (G.-B.)
Honfleur
Paimpol
Granville (3 222)
Pontrieux
Pléneuf
Binic
Saint-Brieuc
FRANCE
Saint-Malo (3 492)
Nantes
Les Sables-d'Olonne
La Rochelle
BAY OF BISCAY
Bordeaux
0 80 miles
0 80 kilometres
Scale 1:6 750 000
Saint-Jean-de-Luz
Bayonne
SPAIN
Average number of ships per year
British, 1769–74
French, 1765–6, 1768–9, 1771–2
More than 70
26–70
11–25
6–10
1–5 ships
Average number of men per year
British – no data
French, 1765–6, 1768–9, 1770 (banks), 1771–2
501–1 000
251–500
101–250
51–100
10–50
Destination of men
Inshore fishery
Banker fishery
BRITISH COD FISHERY
Average number of boats per year by district, 1769–74
500 boats
300
100
Resident fishermen
Migrant fishermen
Average number of bankers per year by district, 1769–74
80 bankers
40
20
5
ETHNIC COMPOSITION OF WINTER POPULATION, 1766
1 001–2 000 people
601–1 000
201–350
0–100
351–600
101–200
Irish
English
The proportion of English and Irish in all areas fluctuated greatly from year to year.
WINTER POPULATION, 1766
Bonavista Bay
Salvage
Bonavista
Keels
Trinity Bay
Trinity
Bonaventure
Old Perlican
Conception Bay (4 083)
Carbonear
Musquito
Harbour Grace
Torbay
Quidi Vidi
St John's
AVALON PENINSULA
Placentia Bay
Little Placentia
Great Placentia
Bay Bulls
Witless Bay
Toad's Cove
Ferryland
Fermeuse
Renews
St Mary's Bay
St Mary's
Trepassey
Scale 1:2 500 000
MIGRANT FISHERMEN
British
French
Discontinuous data
Thousands of men
0
5
10
15
20
1700 1710 1720 1730 1740 1750 1760 1770 1780 1790 1800
Belle Isle
The shoreline west of Cape St John remained French after 1763.
The shore from Bonavista to Cape St John supported British and French fisheries 1763–83, then was ceded by France to Britain in 1783.
1760s
1732
1728
1698
ca 1680
1672
1713
ca 1670–5
Fogo
Tilting
Twillingate
Bay of Exploits
Gander Bay
Fogo
Tilton
Twillingate
Gander Bay
Flower's Island
Greenspond
New Harbour
Fair Island
Gooseberry Island
Bonavista Bay
Salvage
Bonavista
Keels
Trinity
Bonaventure
Trinity Bay
Old Perlican
Bay de Verde
Conception Bay
Conception Bay (663)
The English shore to ca 1670
Carbonear
Harbour Grace
Musquito
Torbay
Quidi Vidi
St John's
Petty Harbour
AVALON PENINSULA
Bay Bulls
Witless Bay
Momables
Caplin Cove
Bauline
Toad's Cove
Spear Island
St John's
Little Placentia
Great Placentia
Ferryland
Fermeuse
Renews
St Mary's
Southern shore
St Mary's Bay
Trepassey
Cape Race
Pass Island
Harbour Breton
Boxey
Saint-Jacques
Grand Banks
Fortune
Connaigre
Saint-Jacques
Audierne
Paradise
Placentia Bay
Tites Cove
Burin
Lawrence
See enlargement for Winter Population, 1766.
THE EXPANDING BRITISH SHORE FISHERY
Original English shore
Ceded by France to Britain, 1713
French fishing rights, 1713–63
French shore (disputed), 1713–1904
Ceded by Britain to France, 1763
British expansion
Relocation of British merchants, 1763

The 18th-century British fishery in Newfoundland was, essentially, an English enterprise based in a few ports in south Devon and Dorsetshire. Increasingly Dartmouth and Exeter dominated the migratory fishery; Poole in Dorsetshire emerged as the leading supplier for the resident Newfoundland fishery. By the mid-century all these English ports were sending ships to Ireland, predominantly to Waterford, for men and supplies. In the last quarter of the century Liverpool and Greenock entered the supply trade, though not significantly until after 1800. The French fishery in Newfoundland was increasingly controlled by merchants in Saint-Malo, Granville, and ports nearby. In the early 1770s a banks fishery still operated from eastern Normandy and a dry inshore fishery from the Basque ports of Bayonne and Saint-Jean-de-Luz, but almost 90% of the ships and men bound from France for Newfoundland came from the Gulf of Saint-Malo.

With the ebb and flow of men employed in the migratory and residential fisheries, the population of Newfoundland fluctuated markedly throughout the 18th century. Winter populations included large numbers of young male servants attached to merchants and planters. Summer populations were inflated by the arrival of ship-fishermen, by-boatmen, and freshly engaged planters' men. As the resident fishery expanded, the difference in size between winter and summer populations diminished. But even at the end of the century, when the migratory fishery had collapsed, a large part of the Newfoundland population comprised male servants, most of whom would eventually return to England or Ireland or proceed to New England.

The slow increase in the number of women in the winter populations is the best measure of long-term population growth, heralding the demise of the servant system and its replacement by the family fishing system characteristic of outport Newfoundland in the 19th century.

TRINITY, 18th CENTURY

Authors: Gordon Handcock, Alan Macpherson

Between 1713 and 1760 merchants from Poole, England, developed Trinity as the focus of their trade in northeastern Newfoundland. They built warehouses, stores, and wharves, most of them on a small peninsula in the centre of Trinity harbour. By the end of the century the largest of these establishments resembled the Lester property shown below. Such firms employed agents, clerks, bookkeepers, tradesmen, seamen, and fishermen; dealt with resident boat masters (planters) in sundry smaller settlements; and established an intricate network of trade, dependence, and debt along the coast of northeastern Newfoundland.

Early in the century migratory, seasonal fishermen and shoreworkers sent out by the fishing firms caught and processed much of the catch in Trinity Bay. By the end of the century most workers were overwinterers; fishing firms purchased fish from planters who, in turn, employed local or indentured labour. A planter operated at least one boat, and to do so required five men (three to fish, two to process the fish ashore) and a shore property that included a dwelling, stage, wharf, flakes (drying platforms), outbuildings, and, usually, a small vegetable garden. Such properties were scattered in outharbours along the coast. Within Trinity harbour, Pease Cove and Maggotty Cove resembled characteristic outharbours. The trade of the outharbours was controlled by merchant firms in Trinity such as Benjamin Lester and Co., J. Jeffrey and Co., and F. Street and Sons.

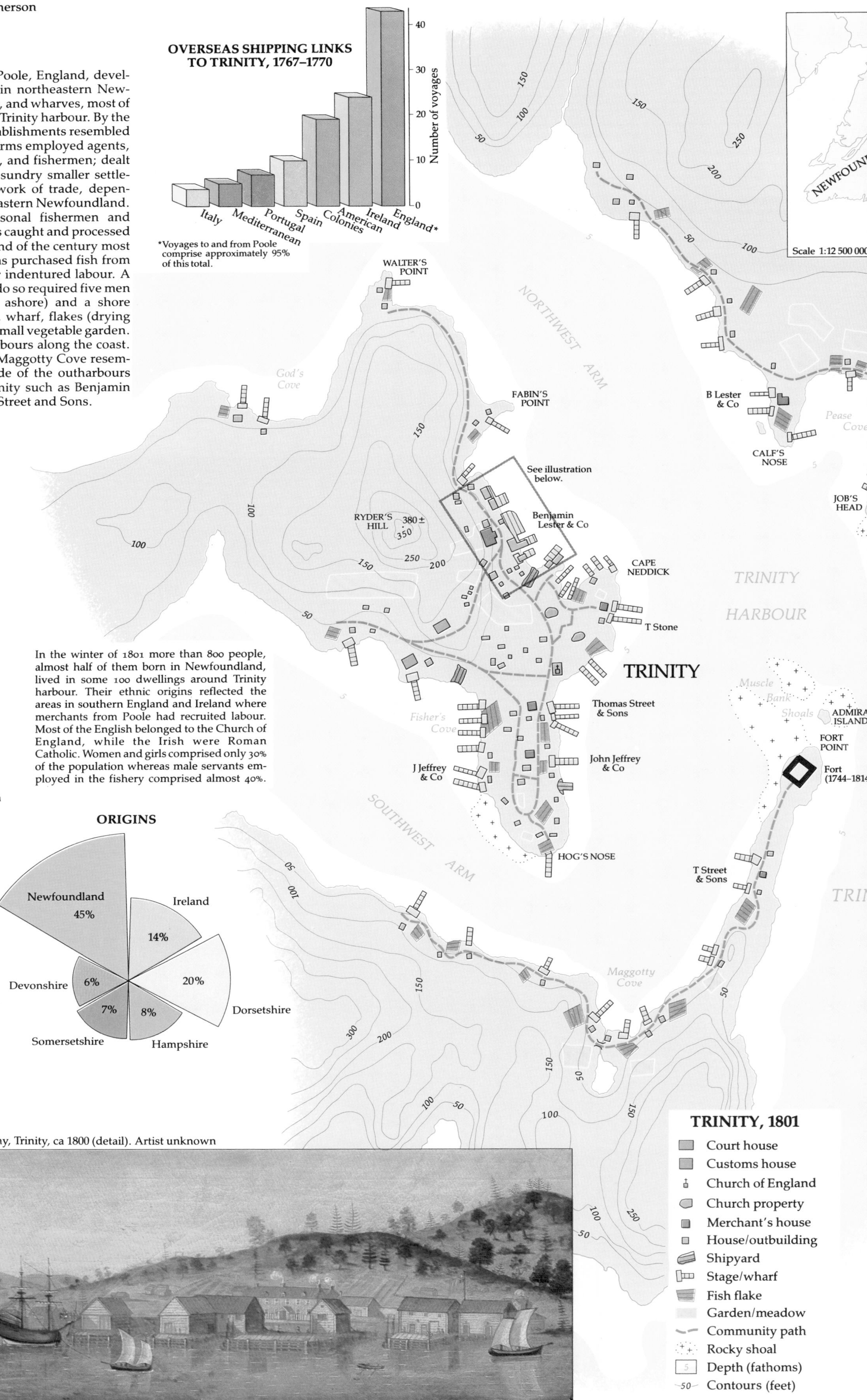
OVERSEAS SHIPPING LINKS TO TRINITY, 1767–1770
Number of voyages
0
10
20
30
40
Italy
Mediterranean
Portugal
Spain
Colonies
American
Ireland
England*
*Voyages to and from Poole comprise approximately 95% of this total.
WALTER'S POINT
NORTHWEST ARM
God's Cove
FABIN'S POINT
See illustration below.
RYDER'S HILL
380±
350
250
200
150
100
50
Benjamin Lester & Co
CAPE NEDDICK
T Stone
TRINITY
Thomas Street & Sons
Fisher's Cove
J Jeffrey & Co
John Jeffrey & Co
SOUTHWEST ARM
HOG'S NOSE
Muscle Bank
Shoals
ADMIRAL'S ISLAND
FORT POINT
Fort (1744–1814)
T Street & Sons
Maggotty Cove
B Lester & Co
Pease Cove
CALF'S NOSE
JOB'S HEAD
TRINITY HARBOUR
TRINIT
NEWFOUNDLAND
Scale 1:12 500 000
TRINITY, 1801
Court house
Customs house
Church of England
Church property
Merchant's house
House/outbuilding
Shipyard
Stage/wharf
Fish flake
Garden/meadow
Community path
Rocky shoal
Depth (fathoms)
Contours (feet)
0
1 000 feet
0
300 metres
Scale 1:15 000
POPULATION TRINITY HARBOUR, 1801
COMPOSITION
Servants 39%
Masters 15%
Women 17%
Boys 16%
Girls 13%
RELIGION
Protestant 82%
Roman Catholic 18%
ORIGINS
Newfoundland 45%
Ireland 14%
Dorsetshire 20%
Hampshire 8%
Somersetshire 7%
Devonshire 6%

In the winter of 1801 more than 800 people, almost half of them born in Newfoundland, lived in some 100 dwellings around Trinity harbour. Their ethnic origins reflected the areas in southern England and Ireland where merchants from Poole had recruited labour. Most of the English belonged to the Church of England, while the Irish were Roman Catholic. Women and girls comprised only 30% of the population whereas male servants employed in the fishery comprised almost 40%.

The properties of Benjamin Lester and Company, Trinity, ca 1800 (detail). Artist unknown

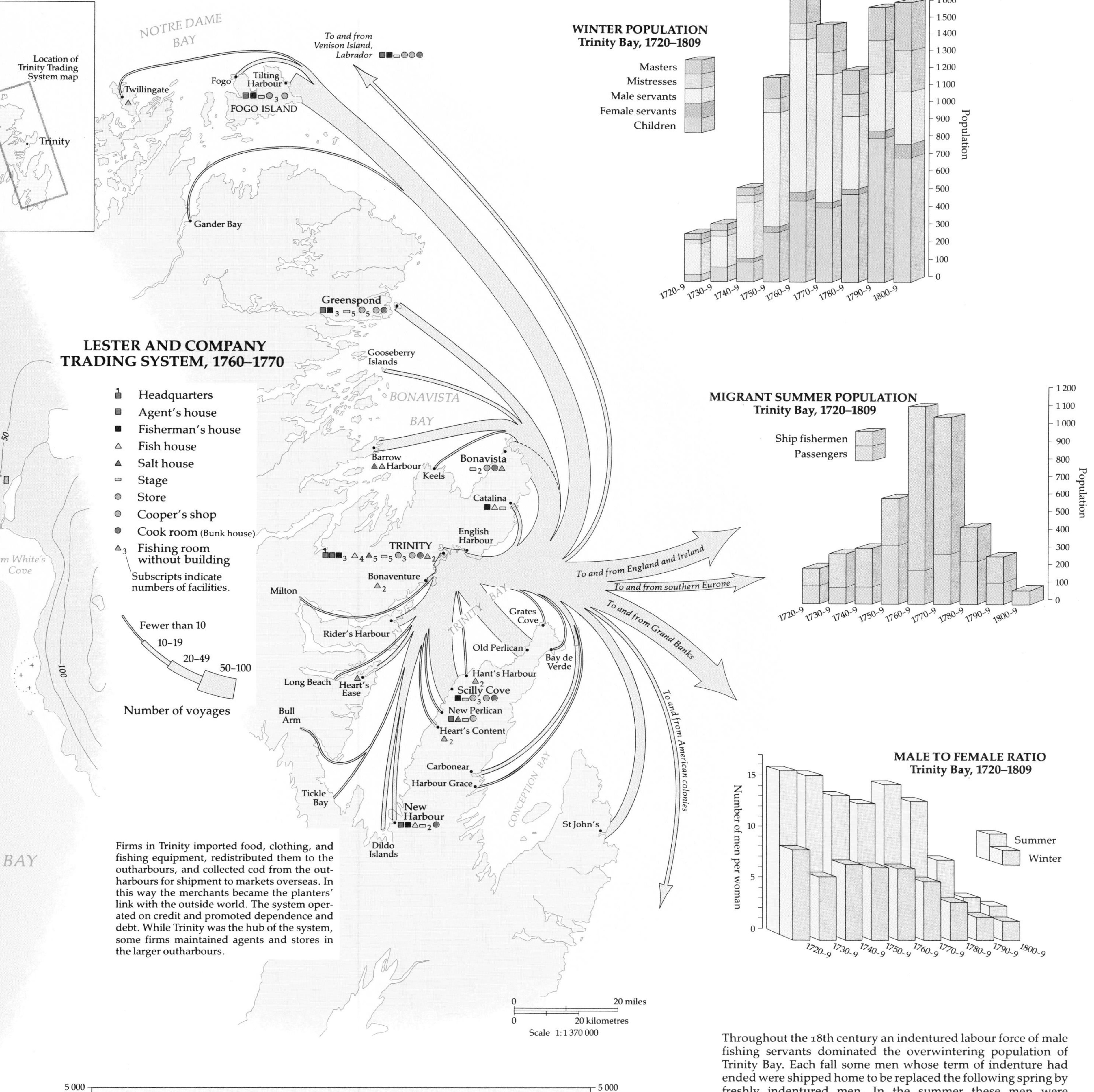
LESTER AND COMPANY TRADING SYSTEM, 1760–1770
Headquarters
Agent's house
Fisherman's house
Fish house
Salt house
Stage
Store
Cooper's shop
Cook room (Bunk house)
Fishing room without building
Subscripts indicate numbers of facilities.
Number of voyages
Fewer than 10
10–19
20–49
50–100
Location of Trinity Trading System map
Trinity
NOTRE DAME BAY
BONAVISTA BAY
TRINITY BAY
CONCEPTION BAY
To and from Venison Island, Labrador
Twillingate
Fogo
Tilting Harbour
FOGO ISLAND
Gander Bay
Greenspond
Gooseberry Islands
Barrow Harbour
Keels
Bonavista
Catalina
English Harbour
TRINITY
Bonaventure
Milton
Rider's Harbour
Long Beach
Heart's Ease
Bull Arm
Tickle Bay
Dildo Islands
New Harbour
Grates Cove
Old Perlican
Bay de Verde
Hant's Harbour
Scilly Cove
New Perlican
Heart's Content
Carbonear
Harbour Grace
St John's
To and from England and Ireland
To and from southern Europe
To and from Grand Banks
To and from American colonies
Scale 1:1 370 000
0 20 miles
0 20 kilometres
WINTER POPULATION
Trinity Bay, 1720–1809
Masters
Mistresses
Male servants
Female servants
Children
Population
1720–9
1730–9
1740–9
1750–9
1760–9
1770–9
1780–9
1790–9
1800–9
MIGRANT SUMMER POPULATION
Trinity Bay, 1720–1809
Ship fishermen
Passengers
Population
MALE TO FEMALE RATIO
Trinity Bay, 1720–1809
Number of men per woman
Summer
Winter

Firms in Trinity imported food, clothing, and fishing equipment, redistributed them to the outharbours, and collected cod from the outharbours for shipment to markets overseas. In this way the merchants became the planters' link with the outside world. The system operated on credit and promoted dependence and debt. While Trinity was the hub of the system, some firms maintained agents and stores in the larger outharbours.

TRINITY BAY POPULATION, 1720–1810

Population: 0, 1 000, 2 000, 3 000, 4 000, 5 000

Summer

Winter

1720 1730 1740 1750 1760 1770 1780 1790 1800 1810

Throughout the 18th century an indentured labour force of male fishing servants dominated the overwintering population of Trinity Bay. Each fall some men whose term of indenture had ended were shipped home to be replaced the following spring by freshly indentured men. In the summer these men were employed in the cod fishery; in winter they went sealing, built boats and ships, and maintained shore facilities.

The harbours around Trinity Bay were also frequented each summer by a migratory inshore fishery (pl 21) based in southern England. Ship fishermen worked to the account of the ship that had brought them across the Atlantic; passengers (masters and fishermen) were not tied to that ship and made other arrangements in Newfoundland. Until about 1780 these summer migrants nearly doubled the population; thereafter the migratory fishery declined rapidly and it disappeared entirely early in the 19th century.

As long as the fishery was supplied by indentured or migratory male labourers, most of whom returned to England or Ireland, women were heavily outnumbered. In the 1720s the adult male/female ratio in summer was 16:1, and even in winter about 8:1, an imbalance that did not decline substantially until the 1770s. As late as the first decade of the 19th century there were still almost three times as many men as women around Trinity Bay.

ST JOHN'S

Author: John Mannion

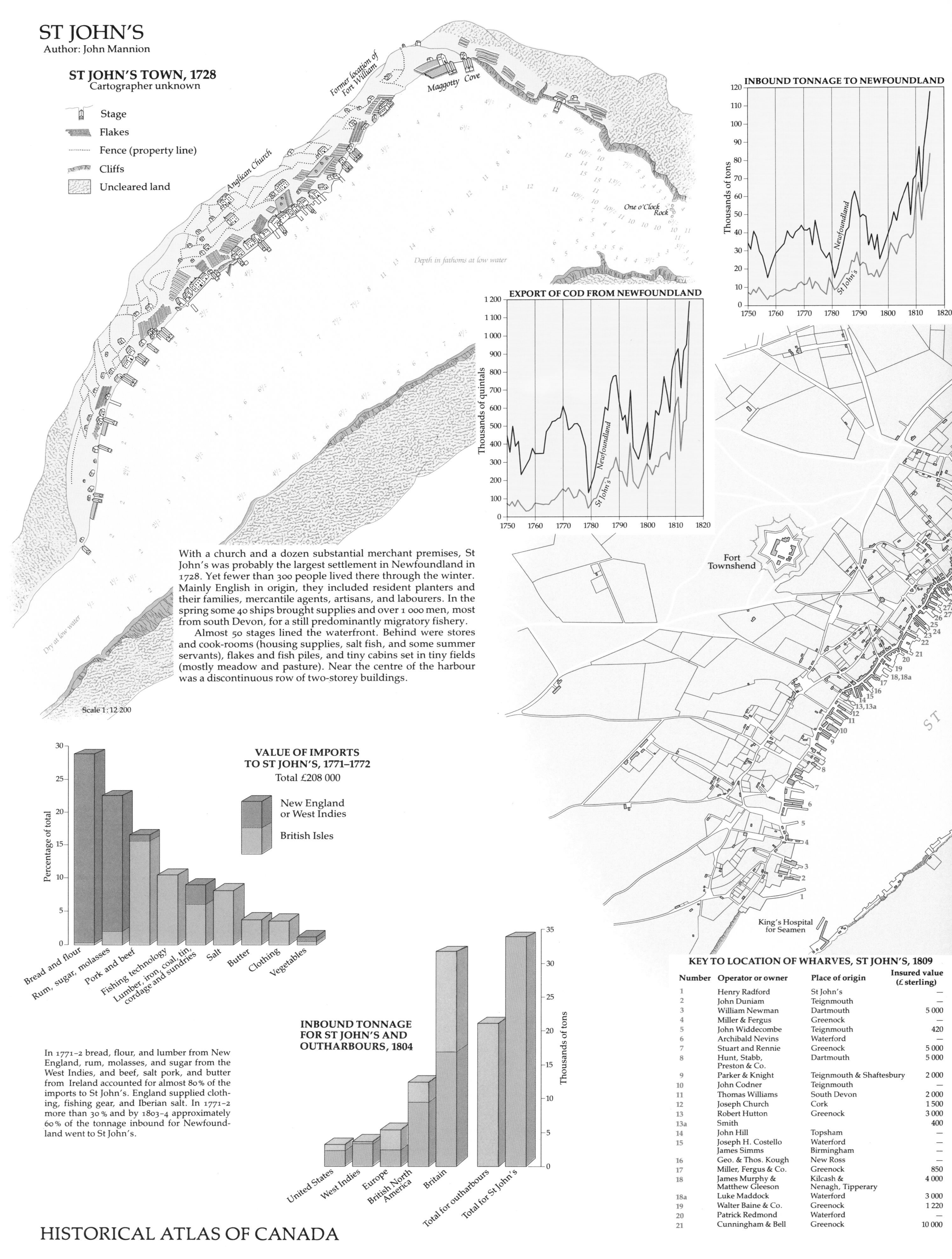

ST JOHN'S TOWN, 1728
Cartographer unknown
Stage
Flakes
Fence (property line)
Cliffs
Uncleared land
Former location of Fort William
Maggotty Cove
Anglican Church
One o'Clock Rock
Depth in fathoms at low water
Dry at low water
Scale 1:12 200
INBOUND TONNAGE TO NEWFOUNDLAND
Thousands of tons
Newfoundland
St John's
EXPORT OF COD FROM NEWFOUNDLAND
Thousands of quintals
Fort Townshend
King's Hospital for Seamen
ST
VALUE OF IMPORTS TO ST JOHN'S, 1771–1772
Total £208 000
New England or West Indies
British Isles
Percentage of total
Bread and flour
Rum, sugar, molasses
Pork and beef
Fishing technology
Lumber, iron, coal, tin, cordage and sundries
Salt
Butter
Clothing
Vegetables
INBOUND TONNAGE FOR ST JOHN'S AND OUTHARBOURS, 1804
Thousands of tons
United States
West Indies
Europe
British North America
Britain
Total for outharbours
Total for St John's

With a church and a dozen substantial merchant premises, St John's was probably the largest settlement in Newfoundland in 1728. Yet fewer than 300 people lived there through the winter. Mainly English in origin, they included resident planters and their families, mercantile agents, artisans, and labourers. In the spring some 40 ships brought supplies and over 1 000 men, most from south Devon, for a still predominantly migratory fishery.

Almost 50 stages lined the waterfront. Behind were stores and cook-rooms (housing supplies, salt fish, and some summer servants), flakes and fish piles, and tiny cabins set in tiny fields (mostly meadow and pasture). Near the centre of the harbour was a discontinuous row of two-storey buildings.

In 1771–2 bread, flour, and lumber from New England, rum, molasses, and sugar from the West Indies, and beef, salt pork, and butter from Ireland accounted for almost 80% of the imports to St John's. England supplied clothing, fishing gear, and Iberian salt. In 1771–2 more than 30% and by 1803–4 approximately 60% of the tonnage inbound for Newfoundland went to St John's.

KEY TO LOCATION OF WHARVES, ST JOHN'S, 1809

Number	Operator or owner	Place of origin	Insured value (£ sterling)
1	Henry Radford	St John's	—
2	John Duniam	Teignmouth	—
3	William Newman	Dartmouth	5 000
4	Miller & Fergus	Greenock	—
5	John Widdecombe	Teignmouth	420
6	Archibald Nevins	Waterford	—
7	Stuart and Rennie	Greenock	5 000
8	Hunt, Stabb, Preston & Co.	Dartmouth	5 000
9	Parker & Knight	Teignmouth & Shaftesbury	2 000
10	John Codner	Teignmouth	—
11	Thomas Williams	South Devon	2 000
12	Joseph Church	Cork	1 500
13	Robert Hutton	Greenock	3 000
13a	Smith		400
14	John Hill	Topsham	—
15	Joseph H. Costello	Waterford	—
	James Simms	Birmingham	—
16	Geo. & Thos. Kough	New Ross	—
17	Miller, Fergus & Co.	Greenock	850
18	James Murphy & Matthew Gleeson	Kilcash & Nenagh, Tipperary	4 000
18a	Luke Maddock	Waterford	3 000
19	Walter Baine & Co.	Greenock	1 220
20	Patrick Redmond	Waterford	—
21	Cunningham & Bell	Greenock	10 000

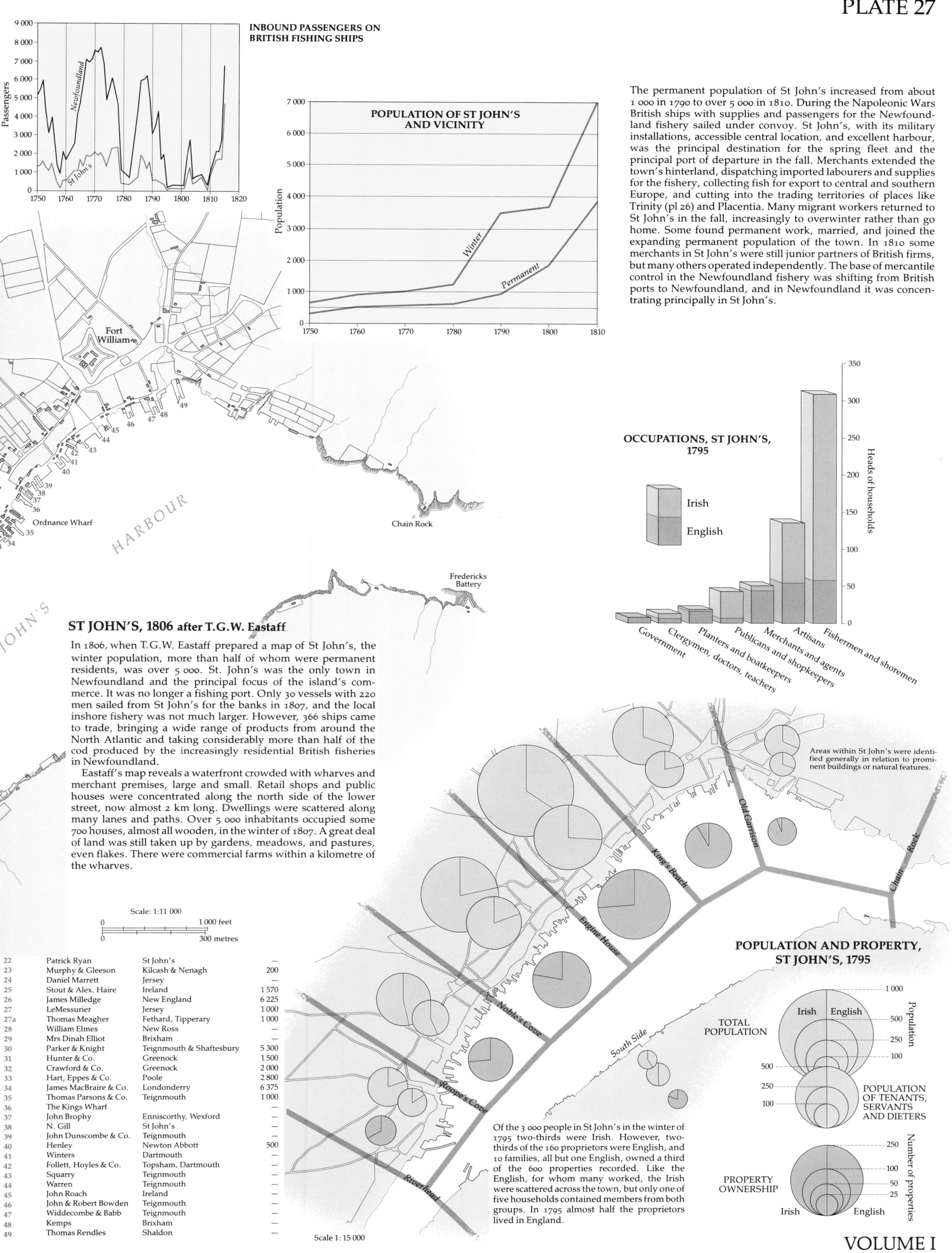

INBOUND PASSENGERS ON BRITISH FISHING SHIPS
Passengers
Newfoundland
St John's
POPULATION OF ST JOHN'S AND VICINITY
Population
Winter
Permanent
Fort William
Ordnance Wharf
HARBOUR
JOHN'S
Chain Rock
Fredericks Battery
Scale: 1:11 000
0
1 000 feet
0
300 metres
OCCUPATIONS, ST JOHN'S, 1795
Irish
English
Heads of households
Government
Clergymen, doctors, teachers
Planters and boatkeepers
Publicans and shopkeepers
Merchants and agents
Artisans
Fishermen and shoremen
Areas within St John's were identified generally in relation to prominent buildings or natural features.
Old Garrison
King's Beach
Engine House
Noble's Cove
Hoope's Cove
Riverhead
Chain Rock
South Side
POPULATION AND PROPERTY, ST JOHN'S, 1795
TOTAL POPULATION
Irish
English
Population
POPULATION OF TENANTS, SERVANTS AND DIETERS
PROPERTY OWNERSHIP
Number of properties
Scale 1 : 15 000

The permanent population of St John's increased from about 1 000 in 1790 to over 5 000 in 1810. During the Napoleonic Wars British ships with supplies and passengers for the Newfoundland fishery sailed under convoy. St John's, with its military installations, accessible central location, and excellent harbour, was the principal destination for the spring fleet and the principal port of departure in the fall. Merchants extended the town's hinterland, dispatching imported labourers and supplies for the fishery, collecting fish for export to central and southern Europe, and cutting into the trading territories of places like Trinity (pl 26) and Placentia. Many migrant workers returned to St John's in the fall, increasingly to overwinter rather than go home. Some found permanent work, married, and joined the expanding permanent population of the town. In 1810 some merchants in St John's were still junior partners of British firms, but many others operated independently. The base of mercantile control in the Newfoundland fishery was shifting from British ports to Newfoundland, and in Newfoundland it was concentrating principally in St John's.

ST JOHN'S, 1806 after T.G.W. Eastaff

In 1806, when T.G.W. Eastaff prepared a map of St John's, the winter population, more than half of whom were permanent residents, was over 5 000. St. John's was the only town in Newfoundland and the principal focus of the island's commerce. It was no longer a fishing port. Only 30 vessels with 220 men sailed from St John's for the banks in 1807, and the local inshore fishery was not much larger. However, 366 ships came to trade, bringing a wide range of products from around the North Atlantic and taking considerably more than half of the cod produced by the increasingly residential British fisheries in Newfoundland.

Eastaff's map reveals a waterfront crowded with wharves and merchant premises, large and small. Retail shops and public houses were concentrated along the north side of the lower street, now almost 2 km long. Dwellings were scattered along many lanes and paths. Over 5 000 inhabitants occupied some 700 houses, almost all wooden, in the winter of 1807. A great deal of land was still taken up by gardens, meadows, and pastures, even flakes. There were commercial farms within a kilometre of the wharves.

22	Patrick Ryan	St John's	—
23	Murphy & Gleeson	Kilcash & Nenagh	200
24	Daniel Marrett	Jersey	—
25	Stout & Alex. Haire	Ireland	1 570
26	James Milledge	New England	6 225
27	LeMessurier	Jersey	1 000
27a	Thomas Meagher	Fethard, Tipperary	1 000
28	William Elmes	New Ross	—
29	Mrs Dinah Elliot	Brixham	—
30	Parker & Knight	Teignmouth & Shaftesbury	5 300
31	Hunter & Co.	Greenock	1 500
32	Crawford & Co.	Greenock	2 000
33	Hart, Eppes & Co.	Poole	2 800
34	James MacBraire & Co.	Londonderry	6 375
35	Thomas Parsons & Co.	Teignmouth	1 000
36	The Kings Wharf		—
37	John Brophy	Enniscorthy, Wexford	—
38	N. Gill	St John's	—
39	John Dunscombe & Co.	Teignmouth	—
40	Henley	Newton Abbott	500
41	Winters	Dartmouth	—
42	Follett, Hoyles & Co.	Topsham, Dartmouth	—
43	Squarry	Teignmouth	—
44	Warren	Teignmouth	—
45	John Roach	Ireland	—
46	John & Robert Bowden	Teignmouth	—
47	Widdecombe & Babb	Teignmouth	—
48	Kemps	Brixham	—
49	Thomas Rendles	Shaldon	—

Of the 3 000 people in St John's in the winter of 1795 two-thirds were Irish. However, two-thirds of the 160 proprietors were English, and 10 families, all but one English, owned a third of the 600 properties recorded. Like the English, for whom many worked, the Irish were scattered across the town, but only one of five households contained members from both groups. In 1795 almost half the proprietors lived in England.

THE FISHERY IN ATLANTIC COMMERCE

Authors: C. Grant Head, Christopher Moore, Michael Barkham

In the 18th century the Newfoundland fishery remained principally a trans-Atlantic enterprise weakly connected to Canada and only slightly more to New England and the West Indies. Most men and supplies came from France or England. Green cod (pl 21) was returned to ports in northern France, and dried cod to southern France, the Iberian peninsula, or Italy. From there wines, cork, and nuts were shipped to northern ports, completing a triangle of trade that linked the two sides of the Atlantic and southern and northern Europe. The French fishery was more self-contained than the English, which relied on salt and markets in southern Europe. Each employed a large volume of North Atlantic shipping.

FISHING AND TRADING VOYAGES

LE CANTABRE, 1750

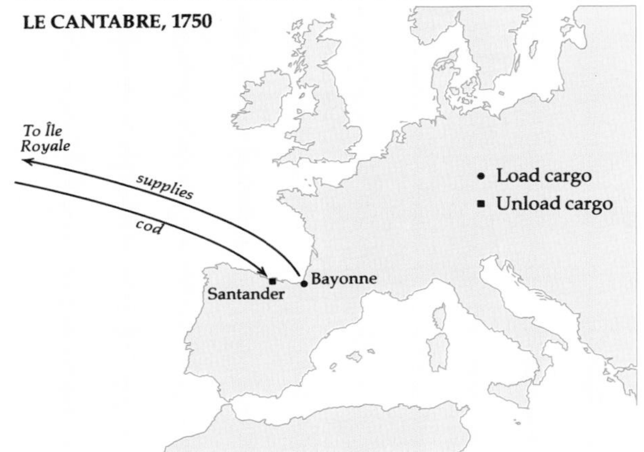
To Île Royale
supplies
cod
• Load cargo
▪ Unload cargo
Santander
Bayonne

L'ASTRÉE, 1735–1736

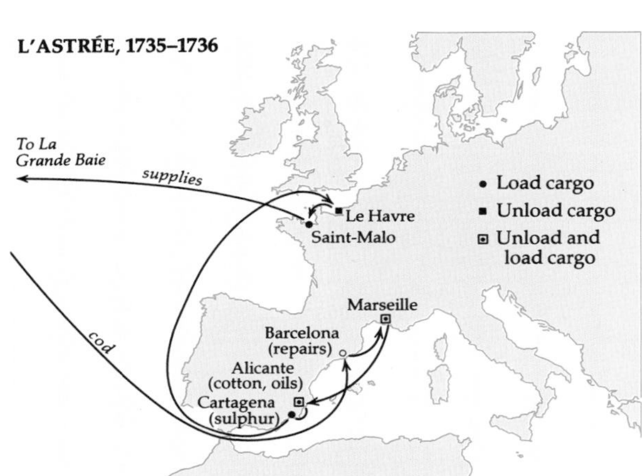
To La Grande Baie
supplies
cod
• Load cargo
▪ Unload cargo
⊡ Unload and load cargo
Le Havre
Saint-Malo
Marseille
Barcelona (repairs)
Alicante (cotton, oils)
Cartagena (sulphur)

SALLY, 1770–1771

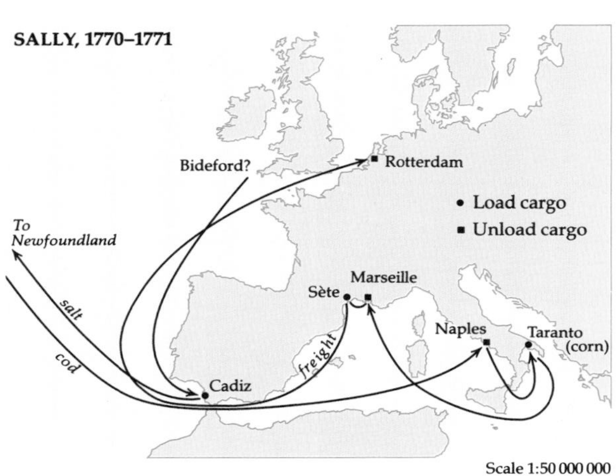
Bideford?
Rotterdam
To Newfoundland
salt
cod
• Load cargo
▪ Unload cargo
Sète
Marseille
freight
Naples
Taranto (corn)
Cadiz
Scale 1:50 000 000

When in 1750 *Le Cantabre* took supplies from Bayonne to Île Royale (Cape Breton Island), loaded cod, and returned to market at Santander, close to home, she followed the simplest and probably oldest marketing strategy of the trans-Atlantic cod fishery. The voyage of *L'Astrée* in 1735 illustrates the trading triangle that had already become common in the 17th century. As the trek of the *Sally* in 1770–1 shows, selling and back-loading often required several stops. French vessels had access to domestic salt, but British ships often made a voyage in ballast to purchase Iberian salt before sailing on to Newfoundland. Different as the individual voyages were, cod imports to principal ports such as Oporto and Marseille (right) continued year after year except when interrupted by war.

THE NEWFOUNDLAND TRADING SYSTEM, ca 1771

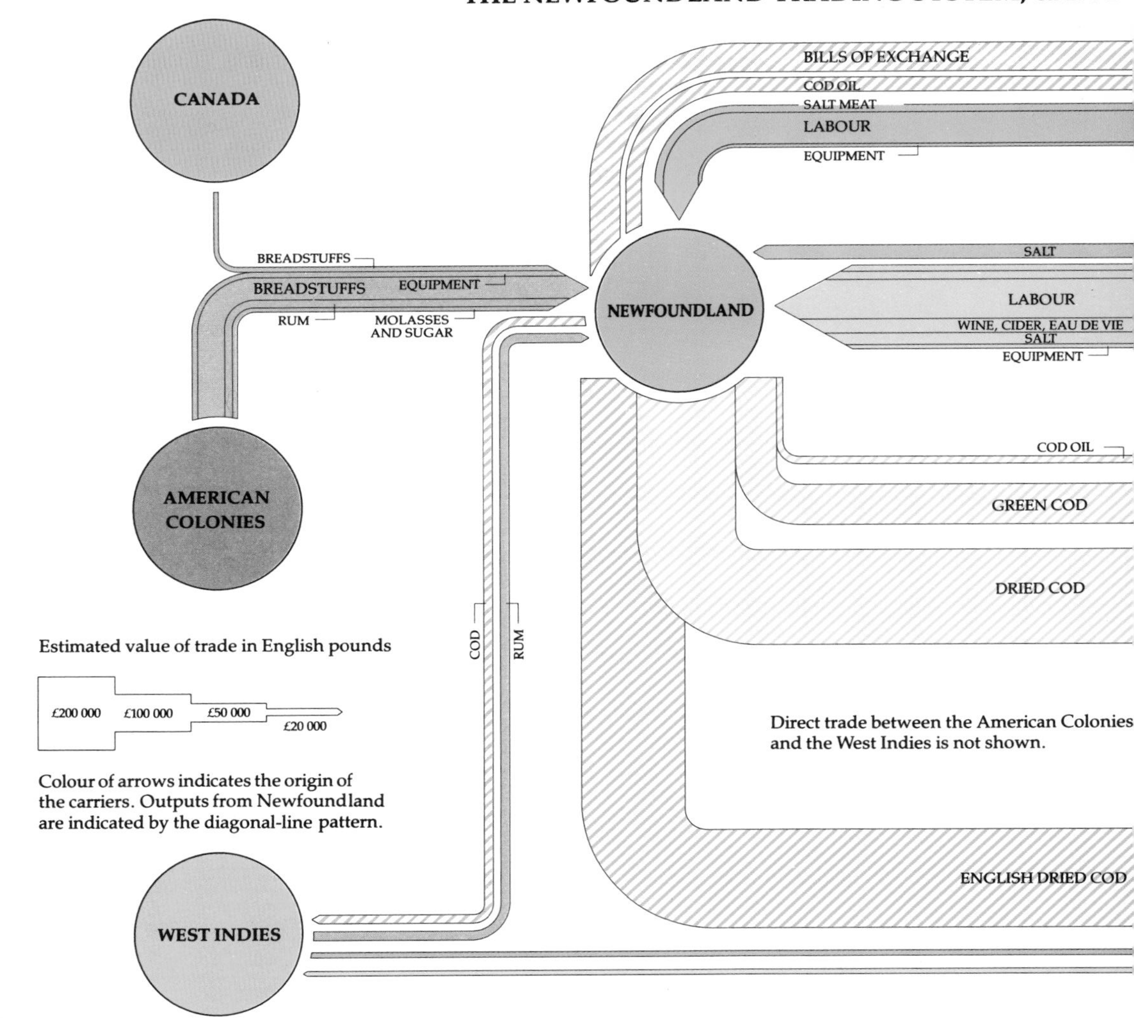
CANADA
AMERICAN COLONIES
WEST INDIES
NEWFOUNDLAND
BILLS OF EXCHANGE
COD OIL
SALT MEAT
LABOUR
EQUIPMENT
BREADSTUFFS
BREADSTUFFS
EQUIPMENT
RUM
MOLASSES AND SUGAR
SALT
LABOUR
WINE, CIDER, EAU DE VIE
SALT
EQUIPMENT
COD OIL
GREEN COD
DRIED COD
COD
RUM
ENGLISH DRIED COD
Estimated value of trade in English pounds
£200 000
£100 000
£50 000
£20 000
Colour of arrows indicates the origin of the carriers. Outputs from Newfoundland are indicated by the diagonal-line pattern.
Direct trade between the American Colonies and the West Indies is not shown.

Political and military considerations dramatically influenced the marketing of cod. The cartogram, left, shows the collapse of cod imports from Newfoundland at Bilbao, Spain, during the American Revolution (1780) and the Napoleonic Wars (1800). The graph immediately below shows the sudden growth of cod exports from Marseille to Spain when Britain and Spain went to war in 1739, and the collapse of this trade five years later when France joined the war.

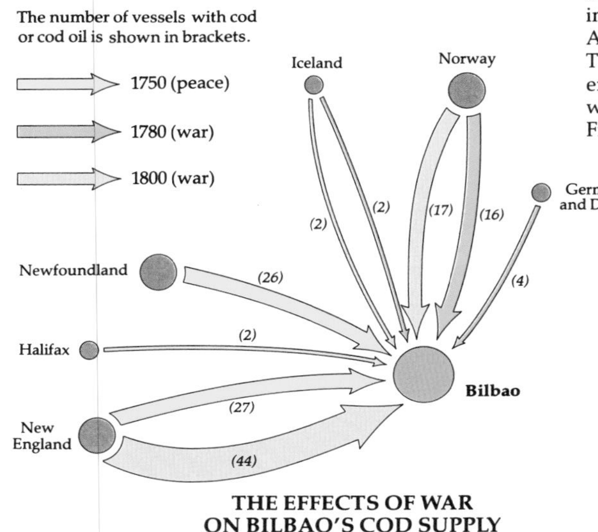
The number of vessels with cod or cod oil is shown in brackets.
1750 (peace)
1780 (war)
1800 (war)
Iceland
Norway
Germany and Denmark
Newfoundland
Halifax
New England
Bilbao
(2)
(2)
(17)
(16)
(4)
(26)
(2)
(27)
(44)

THE EFFECTS OF WAR ON BILBAO'S COD SUPPLY

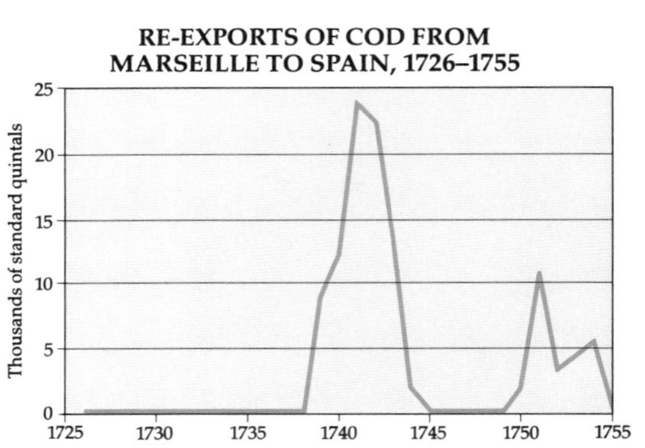
RE-EXPORTS OF COD FROM MARSEILLE TO SPAIN, 1726–1755
Thousands of standard quintals
0
5
10
15
20
25
1725
1730
1735
1740
1745
1750
1755

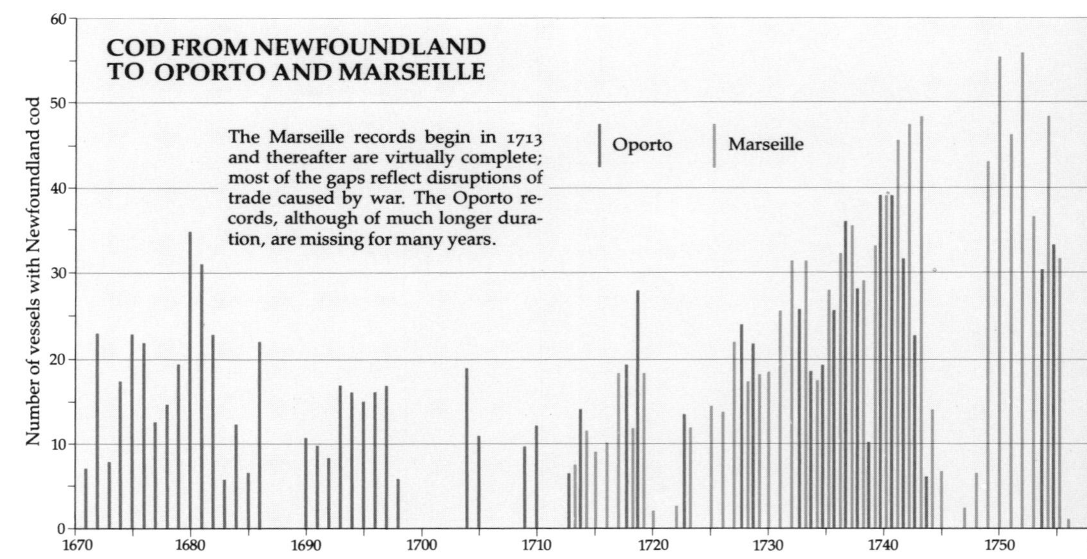
COD FROM NEWFOUNDLAND TO OPORTO AND MARSEILLE
The Marseille records begin in 1713 and thereafter are virtually complete; most of the gaps reflect disruptions of trade caused by war. The Oporto records, although of much longer duration, are missing for many years.
Oporto
Marseille
Number of vessels with Newfoundland cod
0
10
20
30
40
50
60
1670
1680
1690
1700
1710
1720
1730
1740
1750

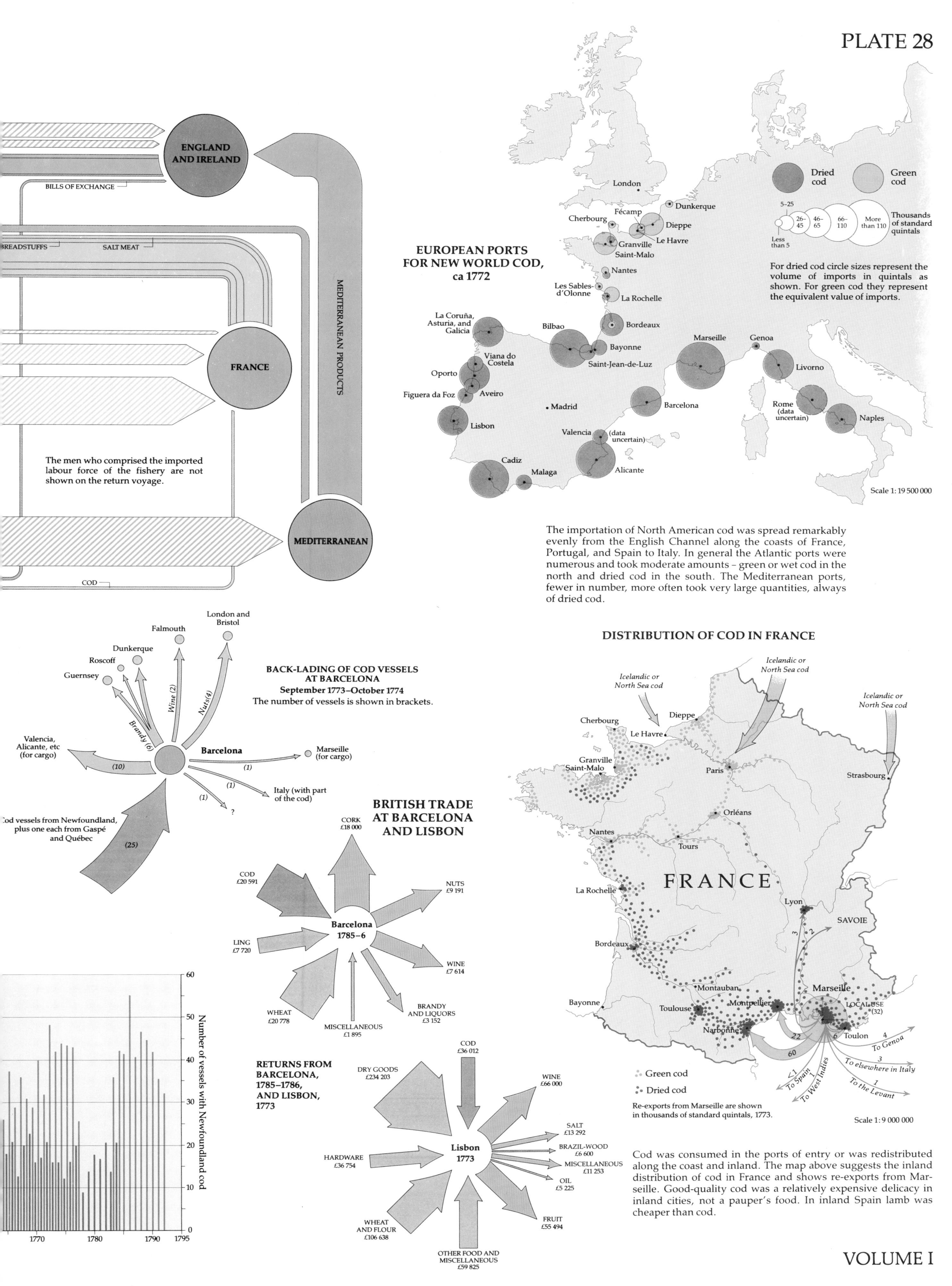
ENGLAND AND IRELAND
BILLS OF EXCHANGE
BREADSTUFFS
SALT MEAT
MEDITERRANEAN PRODUCTS
FRANCE
MEDITERRANEAN
COD
The men who comprised the imported labour force of the fishery are not shown on the return voyage.
EUROPEAN PORTS FOR NEW WORLD COD, ca 1772
Dried cod
Green cod
Less than 5
5–25
26–45
46–65
66–110
More than 110
Thousands of standard quintals
For dried cod circle sizes represent the volume of imports in quintals as shown. For green cod they represent the equivalent value of imports.
London
Dunkerque
Fécamp
Cherbourg
Dieppe
Granville
Le Havre
Saint-Malo
Nantes
Les Sables-d'Olonne
La Rochelle
Bordeaux
La Coruña, Asturia, and Galicia
Bilbao
Bayonne
Saint-Jean-de-Luz
Marseille
Genoa
Livorno
Viana do Costela
Oporto
Figuera da Foz
Aveiro
Madrid
Lisbon
Barcelona
Rome (data uncertain)
Naples
Valencia (data uncertain)
Cadiz
Malaga
Alicante
Scale 1: 19 500 000
BACK-LADING OF COD VESSELS AT BARCELONA
September 1773–October 1774
The number of vessels is shown in brackets.
London and Bristol
Falmouth
Dunkerque
Roscoff
Guernsey
Brandy (6)
Wine (2)
Nuts(4)
Valencia, Alicante, etc (for cargo)
(10)
Barcelona
(1)
Marseille (for cargo)
(1)
Italy (with part of the cod)
(1)
?
Cod vessels from Newfoundland, plus one each from Gaspé and Québec
(25)
BRITISH TRADE AT BARCELONA AND LISBON
CORK £18 000
COD £20 591
NUTS £9 191
Barcelona 1785–6
LING £7 720
WINE £7 614
WHEAT £20 778
MISCELLANEOUS £1 895
BRANDY AND LIQUORS £3 152
RETURNS FROM BARCELONA, 1785–1786, AND LISBON, 1773
COD £36 012
DRY GOODS £234 203
WINE £66 000
SALT £13 292
BRAZIL-WOOD £6 600
HARDWARE £36 754
Lisbon 1773
MISCELLANEOUS £11 253
OIL £5 225
FRUIT £55 494
WHEAT AND FLOUR £106 638
OTHER FOOD AND MISCELLANEOUS £59 825
Number of vessels with Newfoundland cod
0
10
20
30
40
50
60
1770
1780
1790
1795
DISTRIBUTION OF COD IN FRANCE
Icelandic or North Sea cod
Icelandic or North Sea cod
Icelandic or North Sea cod
Dieppe
Cherbourg
Le Havre
Granville
Saint-Malo
Paris
Strasbourg
Orléans
Nantes
Tours
FRANCE
La Rochelle
Lyon
SAVOIE
Bordeaux
Marseille
Montauban
Bayonne
Toulouse
Montpellier
LOCAL USE (32)
Narbonne
Toulon
22
60
6
4 To Genoa
3 To elsewhere in Italy
1 To the Levant
<1 To Spain
1 To West Indies
Green cod
Dried cod
Re-exports from Marseille are shown in thousands of standard quintals, 1773.
Scale 1: 9 000 000

The importation of North American cod was spread remarkably evenly from the English Channel along the coasts of France, Portugal, and Spain to Italy. In general the Atlantic ports were numerous and took moderate amounts – green or wet cod in the north and dried cod in the south. The Mediterranean ports, fewer in number, more often took very large quantities, always of dried cod.

Cod was consumed in the ports of entry or was redistributed along the coast and inland. The map above suggests the inland distribution of cod in France and shows re-exports from Marseille. Good-quality cod was a relatively expensive delicacy in inland cities, not a pauper's food. In inland Spain lamb was cheaper than cod.

ACADIAN MARSHLAND SETTLEMENT

Author: Jean Daigle

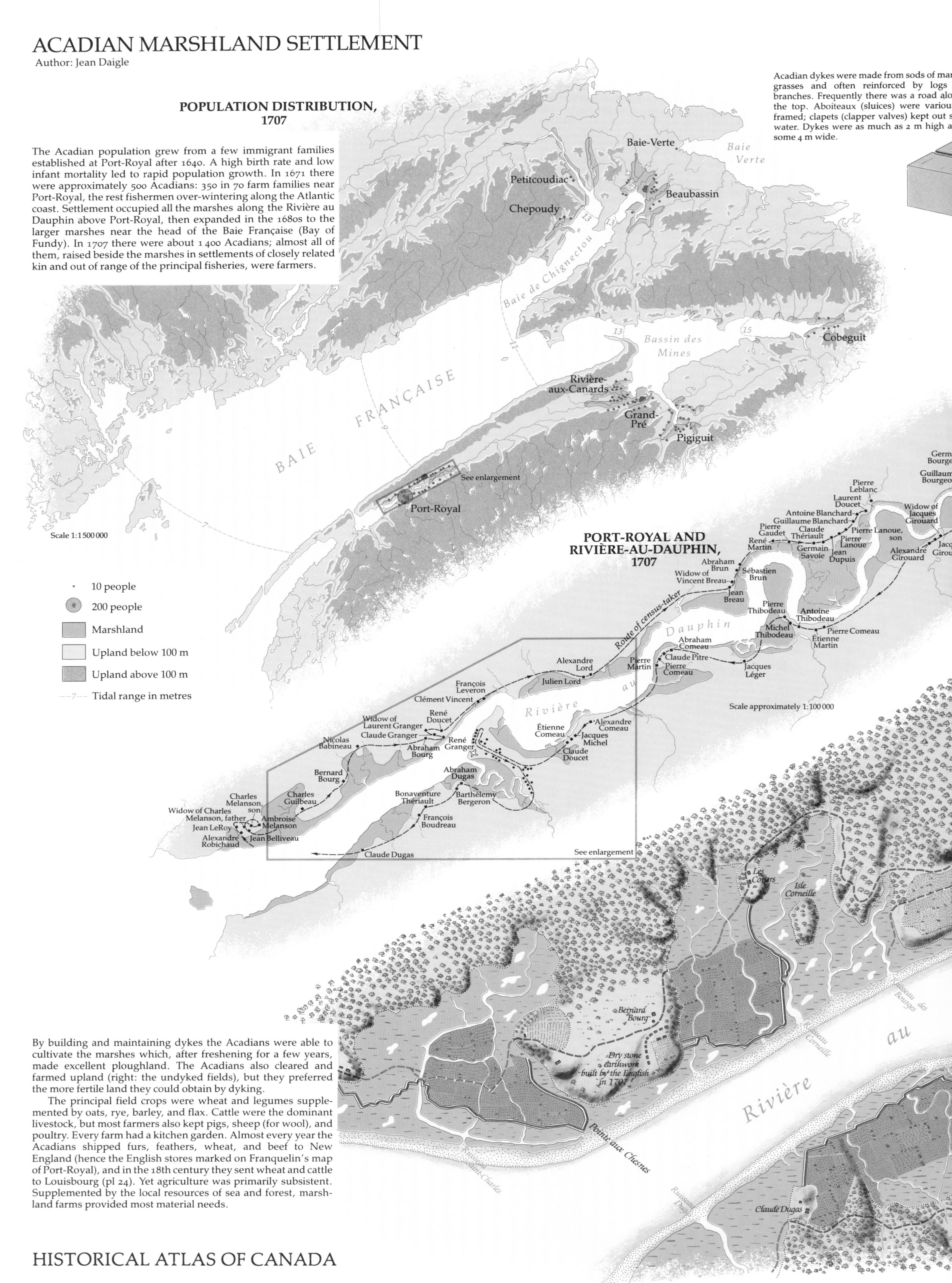
POPULATION DISTRIBUTION, 1707
Baie-Verte
Baie Verte
Petitcoudiac
Beaubassin
Chepoudy
Baie de Chignectou
Bassin des Mines
Cobeguit
BAIE FRANÇAISE
Rivière-aux-Canards
Grand-Pré
Pigiguit
See enlargement
Port-Royal
Scale 1:1500000
10 people
200 people
Marshland
Upland below 100 m
Upland above 100 m
Tidal range in metres
PORT-ROYAL AND RIVIÈRE-AU-DAUPHIN, 1707
Route of census-taker
Rivière au Dauphin
Scale approximately 1:100 000
See enlargement
Pierre Leblanc
Laurent Doucet
Antoine Blanchard
Guillaume Blanchard
Pierre Gaudet
Claude Thériault
René Martin
Germain Savoie
Jean Dupuis
Pierre Lanoue
Pierre Lanoue, son
Widow of Jacques Girouard
Alexandre Girouard
Abraham Brun
Sébastien Brun
Widow of Vincent Breau
Jean Breau
Pierre Thibodeau
Antoine Thibodeau
Michel Thibodeau
Pierre Comeau
Étienne Martin
Abraham Comeau
Pierre Martin
Claude Pitre
Pierre Comeau
Jacques Léger
Alexandre Lord
Julien Lord
François Leveron
Clément Vincent
René Doucet
Widow of Laurent Granger
Claude Granger
René Granger
Nicolas Babineau
Abraham Bourg
Étienne Comeau
Alexandre Comeau
Jacques Michel
Claude Doucet
Bernard Bourg
Abraham Dugas
Charles Guilbeau
Bonaventure Thériault
Barthélemy Bergeron
François Boudreau
Charles Melanson, son
Widow of Charles Melanson, father
Ambroise Melanson
Jean LeRoy
Alexandre Robichaud
Jean Belliveau
Claude Dugas
Les Cotiers
Isle Corneille
Bernard Bourg
Dry stone earthwork built by the English in 1707
Rivière au
Pointe aux Chesnes
Ruisseau Corneille
Ruisseau des Bourges
Ruisseau Saint-Charles
Claude Dugas

POPULATION DISTRIBUTION, 1707

The Acadian population grew from a few immigrant families established at Port-Royal after 1640. A high birth rate and low infant mortality led to rapid population growth. In 1671 there were approximately 500 Acadians: 350 in 70 farm families near Port-Royal, the rest fishermen over-wintering along the Atlantic coast. Settlement occupied all the marshes along the Rivière au Dauphin above Port-Royal, then expanded in the 1680s to the larger marshes near the head of the Baie Française (Bay of Fundy). In 1707 there were about 1 400 Acadians; almost all of them, raised beside the marshes in settlements of closely related kin and out of range of the principal fisheries, were farmers.

Acadian dykes were made from sods of mars grasses and often reinforced by logs branches. Frequently there was a road alo the top. Aboiteaux (sluices) were various framed; clapets (clapper valves) kept out sa water. Dykes were as much as 2 m high ar some 4 m wide.

PORT-ROYAL AND RIVIÈRE-AU-DAUPHIN, 1707

By building and maintaining dykes the Acadians were able to cultivate the marshes which, after freshening for a few years, made excellent ploughland. The Acadians also cleared and farmed upland (right: the undyked fields), but they preferred the more fertile land they could obtain by dyking.

The principal field crops were wheat and legumes supplemented by oats, rye, barley, and flax. Cattle were the dominant livestock, but most farmers also kept pigs, sheep (for wool), and poultry. Every farm had a kitchen garden. Almost every year the Acadians shipped furs, feathers, wheat, and beef to New England (hence the English stores marked on Franquelin's map of Port-Royal), and in the 18th century they sent wheat and cattle to Louisbourg (pl 24). Yet agriculture was primarily subsistent. Supplemented by the local resources of sea and forest, marshland farms provided most material needs.

Franquelin's and Delabat's maps show traces of French Baroque style at Port-Royal (the layout of the gardens, the church steeple, the small fort in the Vauban style), but French visitors had few kind words for the Acadian settlements. Small and simple houses reflected peasant techniques of construction, local materials (principally wood, clay, and thatch), and a largely subsistence economy. Nevertheless, with the construction of a new fort and the establishment of a garrison of some 150 men, by 1710 Port-Royal was a considerable village, housing merchants, tradesmen, and officials associated with the fort and the colonial administration.

According to Delabat, a French engineer and cartographer, the fort was badly located. Its garrison and local militia repulsed two English attacks in 1707 but surrendered in 1710 before an overwhelming force of 36 ships and 3 500 men. Delabat's map shows the siege positions.

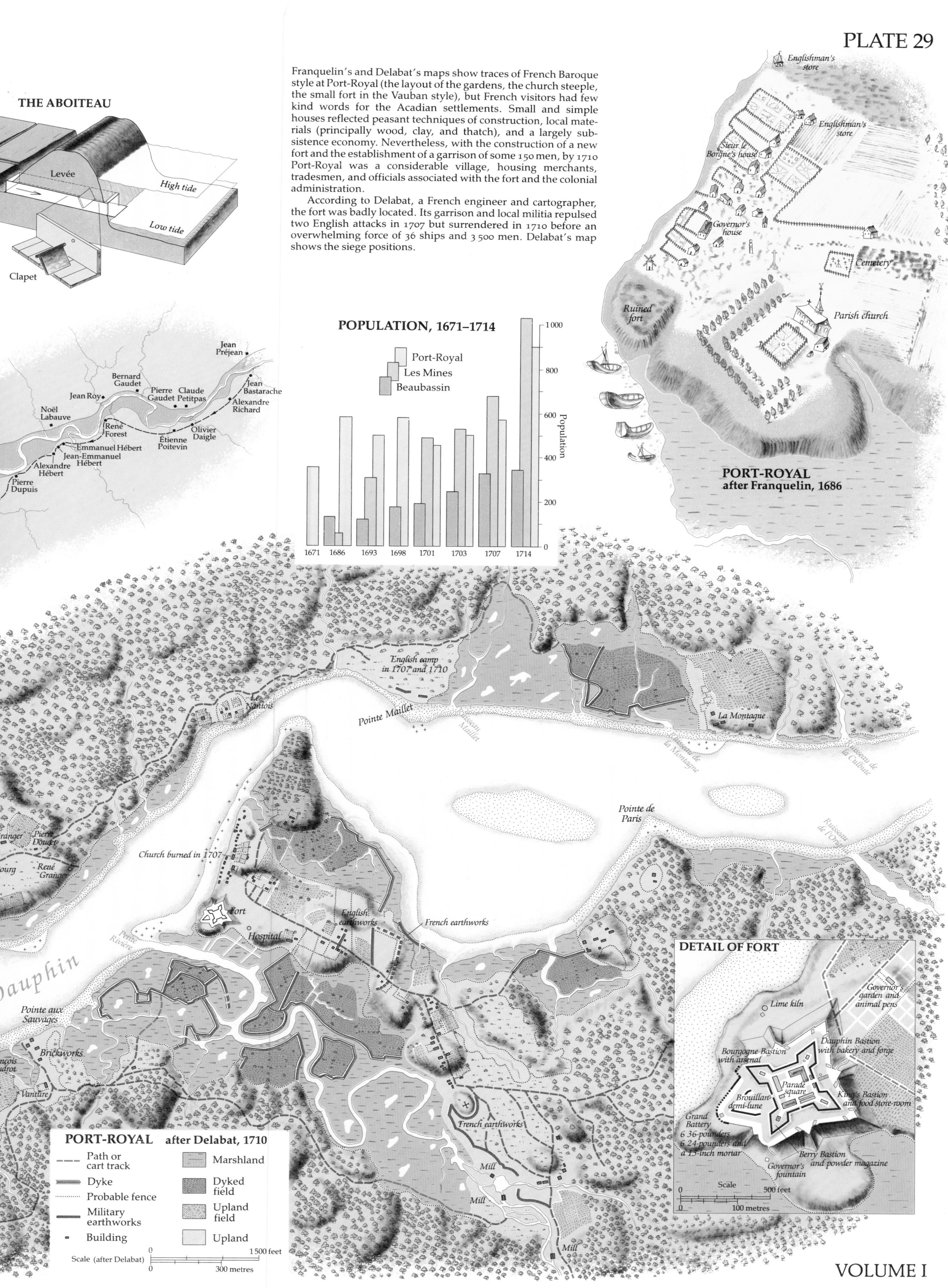
THE ABOITEAU
Levée
High tide
Low tide
Clapet
Jean Préjean
Bernard Gaudet
Jean Roy
Pierre Gaudet
Claude Petitpas
Jean Bastarache
Alexandre Richard
Noël Labauve
René Forest
Olivier Daigle
Étienne Poitevin
Emmanuel Hébert
Jean-Emmanuel Hébert
Alexandre Hébert
Pierre Dupuis
POPULATION, 1671–1714
Port-Royal
Les Mines
Beaubassin
Population
0
200
400
600
800
1 000
1671
1686
1693
1698
1701
1703
1707
1714
Englishman's store
Englishman's store
Sieur le Borgne's house
Governor's house
Cemetery
Ruined fort
Parish church
PORT-ROYAL
after Franquelin, 1686
English camp in 1707 and 1710
Le Nantois
Pointe Maillet
Ruisseau Maillet
La Montagne
Ruisseau de la Montagne
Ruisseau de la Culbute
Pointe de Paris
Ruisseau de l'Orignal
Church burned in 1707
Fort
English earthworks
French earthworks
Hospital
Petite Rivière
Dauphin
Pointe aux Sauvages
Brickworks
Vanture
Pierre Doucet
René Granger
Bourg
French earthworks
Mill
Mill
Mill
DETAIL OF FORT
Governor's garden and animal pens
Lime kiln
Bourgogne Bastion with arsenal
Dauphin Bastion with bakery and forge
Parade square
Brouillan demi-lune
King's Bastion and food store-room
Grand Battery 6 36-pounders 6 24-pounders and a 13-inch mortar
Berry Bastion and powder magazine
Governor's fountain
Scale
0
500 feet
0
100 metres
PORT-ROYAL after Delabat, 1710
Path or cart track
Dyke
Probable fence
Military earthworks
Building
Marshland
Dyked field
Upland field
Upland
Scale (after Delabat)
0
1 500 feet
0
300 metres

ACADIAN DEPORTATION AND RETURN

Authors: Jean Daigle, Robert LeBlanc

POPULATION DISTRIBUTION 1750

French control — British control

French fort — British fort

4 000 / 2 000 / 1 000 / 500

Circles are proportional to population of major settlements.

Acadians — Other French — British

· One dot represents 25 people.

Scale 1:2 900 000

The British captured Port-Royal in 1710. In 1713, when the Treaty of Utrecht confirmed British control of peninsular Nova Scotia, most Acadians found themselves in British territory.

For more than thirty years they were left alone; their settlements filled the Fundy marshes. Then, during most of the 1740s, Britain and France were again at war. Louisbourg fell to New England militiamen in 1745, and when the British returned it after the Treaty of Aix-la-Chapelle in 1748, they embarked on a rival fortification at Halifax. The French strengthened Louisbourg. In 1755, at the start of the Seven Years War (pl 42), nervous British officials in Nova Scotia, suspecting Acadian claims of neutrality, decided to deport the Acadians, who by then numbered almost 13 000 people.

1758 –1762

Scale 1:19 000 000

1 000

500

250 or less

Number unknown

Arrows are proportional to Acadian population movements.

1755 –1757

Acadian deportation

Acadian flight

Acadian migration

Origin of deported Acadians

Deportation began without consultation with the British government or notification of officials in the colonies to which the Acadians were being sent. Before the end of 1755 more than half of the Acadians had been sent to British colonies south of Acadia. Authorities in Virginia, fearing that the Acadians would be a public expense, rerouted them to England. Refugees from the deportation of 1755 escaped to the south shore of the Gulf of St Lawrence, Île Saint-Jean (Prince Edward Island), or the French settlements along the St Lawrence River. In 1758, when Louisbourg was captured for the second time and the French could no longer protect the Gulf, the British rounded up another 2 500 Acadians, sending them to England or France. Others fled to the Miramichi River or to the islands of Saint-Pierre and Miquelon where, before 1763, most were caught and deported. Finally, during the American Revolution the remaining Acadian refugees on Saint-Pierre and Miquelon were sent to France.

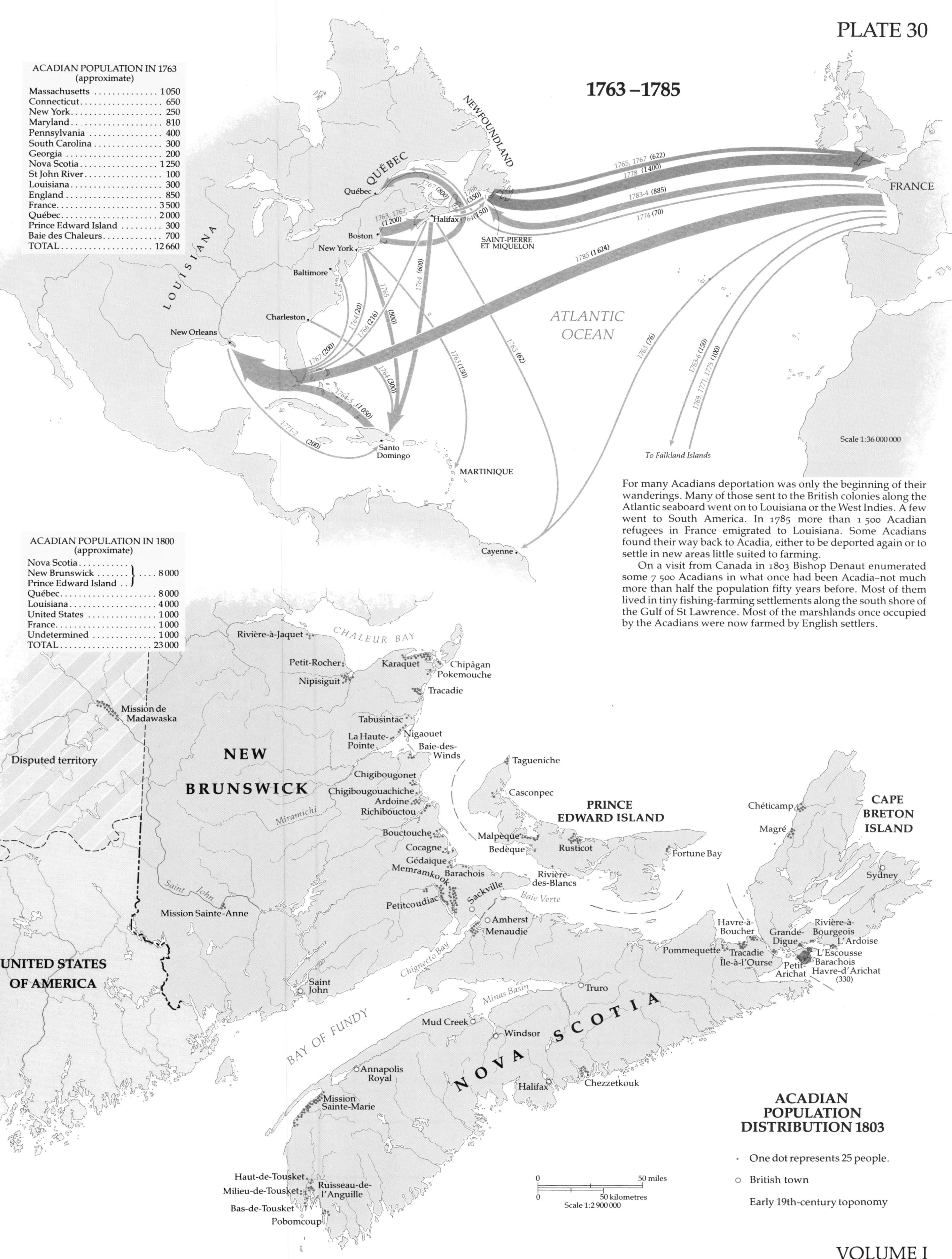
1763 –1785
NEWFOUNDLAND
QUÉBEC
Québec
LOUISIANA
Boston
New York
Halifax
Baltimore
Charleston
New Orleans
Santo Domingo
MARTINIQUE
Cayenne
SAINT-PIERRE ET MIQUELON
FRANCE
ATLANTIC OCEAN
To Falkland Islands
1765, 1767 (622)
1778 (1400)
1783-4 (885)
1774 (70)
1785 (1624)
1767 (800)
1766 (350)
1763, 1767 (1200)
1764 (150)
1764 (20)
1766 (216)
1765 (500)
1764 (600)
1767 (200)
1764 (300)
1763 (150)
1763 (62)
1763 (76)
1763-6 (150)
1769, 1771, 1775 (100)
1764-5 (1050)
1771-2 (200)
Scale 1:36 000 000
CHALEUR BAY
Rivière-à-Jaquet
Petit-Rocher
Nipisiguit
Karaquet
Chipâgan
Pokemouche
Tracadie
Mission de Madawaska
Disputed territory
NEW BRUNSWICK
Tabusintac
La Haute-Pointe
Nigaouet
Baie-des-Winds
Chigibougonet
Chigibougouachiche
Ardoine
Richibouctou
Miramichi
Bouctouche
Cocagne
Gédaïque
Memramkook
Barachois
Petitcoudiac
Sackville
Saint John
Mission Sainte-Anne
UNITED STATES OF AMERICA
Tagueniche
Casconpec
PRINCE EDWARD ISLAND
Malpèque
Bedèque
Rusticot
Fortune Bay
Rivière-des-Blancs
Baie Verte
Amherst
Menaudie
Chignecto Bay
Saint John
BAY OF FUNDY
Minas Basin
Mud Creek
Windsor
Truro
NOVA SCOTIA
Annapolis Royal
Mission Sainte-Marie
Halifax
Chezzetkook
Haut-de-Tousket
Milieu-de-Tousket
Ruisseau-de-l'Anguille
Bas-de-Tousket
Pobomcoup
Pommequette
Havre-à-Boucher
Tracadie
Île-à-l'Ourse
Grande-Digue
Petit-Arichat
Rivière-à-Bourgeois
L'Ardoise
L'Escousse
Barachois
Havre-d'Arichat (330)
Chéticamp
Magré
CAPE BRETON ISLAND
Sydney
0 50 miles
0 50 kilometres
Scale 1:2 900 000
ACADIAN POPULATION DISTRIBUTION 1803
One dot represents 25 people.
British town
Early 19th-century toponomy

ACADIAN POPULATION IN 1763 (approximate)

Massachusetts	1050
Connecticut	650
New York	250
Maryland	810
Pennsylvania	400
South Carolina	300
Georgia	200
Nova Scotia	1250
St John River	100
Louisiana	300
England	850
France	3500
Québec	2000
Prince Edward Island	300
Baie des Chaleurs	700
TOTAL	12660

ACADIAN POPULATION IN 1800 (approximate)

Nova Scotia, New Brunswick, Prince Edward Island	8000
Québec	8000
Louisiana	4000
United States	1000
France	1000
Undetermined	1000
TOTAL	23000

For many Acadians deportation was only the beginning of their wanderings. Many of those sent to the British colonies along the Atlantic seaboard went on to Louisiana or the West Indies. A few went to South America. In 1785 more than 1 500 Acadian refugees in France emigrated to Louisiana. Some Acadians found their way back to Acadia, either to be deported again or to settle in new areas little suited to farming.

On a visit from Canada in 1803 Bishop Denaut enumerated some 7 500 Acadians in what once had been Acadia–not much more than half the population fifty years before. Most of them lived in tiny fishing-farming settlements along the south shore of the Gulf of St Lawrence. Most of the marshlands once occupied by the Acadians were now farmed by English settlers.

PRE-LOYALIST NOVA SCOTIA

Authors: Graeme Wynn; Debra McNabb (Horton Township)

In 1761 when the surveyor-general enumerated families, marshland, and cleared upland in Nova Scotia, New Englanders already occupied some former Acadian lands. Farmers and craftsmen from crowded agricultural townships in New England had been encouraged by Nova Scotian officials to move to the Fundy marshes. Fishermen from eastern Massachusetts had settled on the rocky south shore. These migrations continued in the early 1760s, and by 1767 there were some 7 000 New Englanders in rural Nova Scotia. Then, with renewed New England interest in settlement to the west and the transfer of the Halifax military establishment to Boston in 1768, expansion slowed. Immigration in the 1770s came from Britain: approximately 1 000 Yorkshiremen went to Chignecto and several hundred Highland Scots to the southeastern shore of the Gulf of St Lawrence. By 1775 there were about 20 000 people in Nova Scotia.

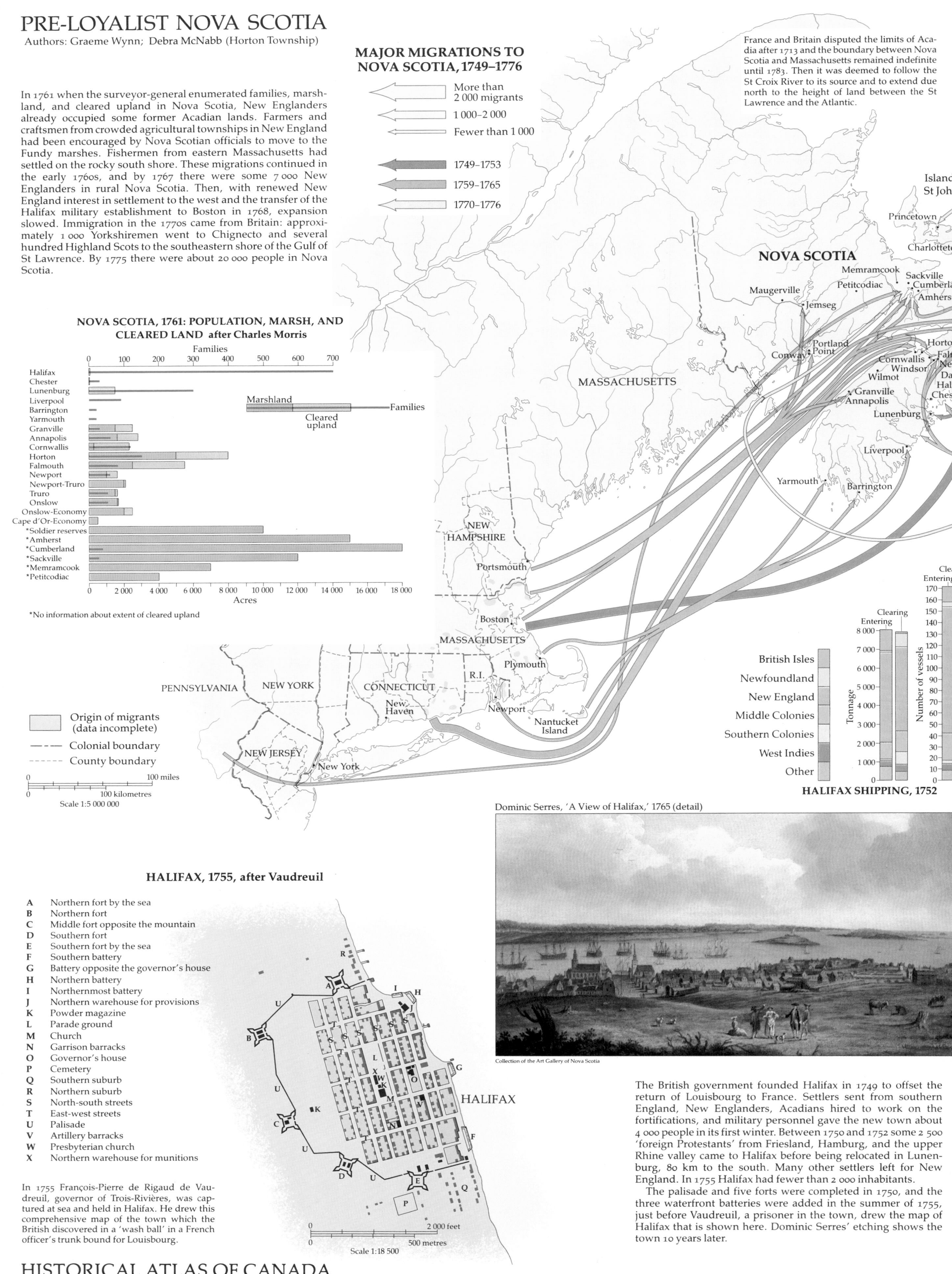
MAJOR MIGRATIONS TO NOVA SCOTIA, 1749–1776
More than 2 000 migrants
1 000–2 000
Fewer than 1 000
1749–1753
1759–1765
1770–1776
France and Britain disputed the limits of Acadia after 1713 and the boundary between Nova Scotia and Massachusetts remained indefinite until 1783. Then it was deemed to follow the St Croix River to its source and to extend due north to the height of land between the St Lawrence and the Atlantic.
Island of St John's
Princetown
Charlottetown
NOVA SCOTIA
Memramcook
Petitcodiac
Sackville
Cumberland
Amherst
Maugerville
Jemseg
Portland Point
Conway
Horton
Cornwallis
Windsor
Wilmot
Falmouth
Newport
Dartmouth
Halifax
Chester
Granville
Annapolis
Lunenburg
Liverpool
Yarmouth
Barrington
MASSACHUSETTS
NEW HAMPSHIRE
Portsmouth
Boston
MASSACHUSETTS
Plymouth
R.I.
Newport
Nantucket Island
PENNSYLVANIA
NEW YORK
CONNECTICUT
New Haven
NEW JERSEY
New York
Origin of migrants (data incomplete)
Colonial boundary
County boundary
100 miles
100 kilometres
Scale 1:5 000 000
NOVA SCOTIA, 1761: POPULATION, MARSH, AND CLEARED LAND after Charles Morris
Families
0 100 200 300 400 500 600 700
Halifax
Chester
Lunenburg
Liverpool
Barrington
Yarmouth
Granville
Annapolis
Cornwallis
Horton
Falmouth
Newport
Newport-Truro
Truro
Onslow
Onslow-Economy
Cape d'Or-Economy
*Soldier reserves
*Amherst
*Cumberland
*Sackville
*Memramcook
*Petitcodiac
Marshland
Cleared upland
Families
0 2 000 4 000 6 000 8 000 10 000 12 000 14 000 16 000 18 000
Acres
*No information about extent of cleared upland
HALIFAX SHIPPING, 1752
British Isles
Newfoundland
New England
Middle Colonies
Southern Colonies
West Indies
Other
Tonnage
Entering
Clearing
Number of vessels
HALIFAX, 1755, after Vaudreuil
A Northern fort by the sea
B Northern fort
C Middle fort opposite the mountain
D Southern fort
E Southern fort by the sea
F Southern battery
G Battery opposite the governor's house
H Northern battery
I Northernmost battery
J Northern warehouse for provisions
K Powder magazine
L Parade ground
M Church
N Garrison barracks
O Governor's house
P Cemetery
Q Southern suburb
R Northern suburb
S North-south streets
T East-west streets
U Palisade
V Artillery barracks
W Presbyterian church
X Northern warehouse for munitions
HALIFAX
2 000 feet
500 metres
Scale 1:18 500

In 1755 François-Pierre de Rigaud de Vaudreuil, governor of Trois-Rivières, was captured at sea and held in Halifax. He drew this comprehensive map of the town which the British discovered in a 'wash ball' in a French officer's trunk bound for Louisbourg.

Dominic Serres, 'A View of Halifax,' 1765 (detail)

Collection of the Art Gallery of Nova Scotia

The British government founded Halifax in 1749 to offset the return of Louisbourg to France. Settlers sent from southern England, New Englanders, Acadians hired to work on the fortifications, and military personnel gave the new town about 4 000 people in its first winter. Between 1750 and 1752 some 2 500 'foreign Protestants' from Friesland, Hamburg, and the upper Rhine valley came to Halifax before being relocated in Lunenburg, 80 km to the south. Many other settlers left for New England. In 1755 Halifax had fewer than 2 000 inhabitants.

The palisade and five forts were completed in 1750, and the three waterfront batteries were added in the summer of 1755, just before Vaudreuil, a prisoner in the town, drew the map of Halifax that is shown here. Dominic Serres' etching shows the town 10 years later.

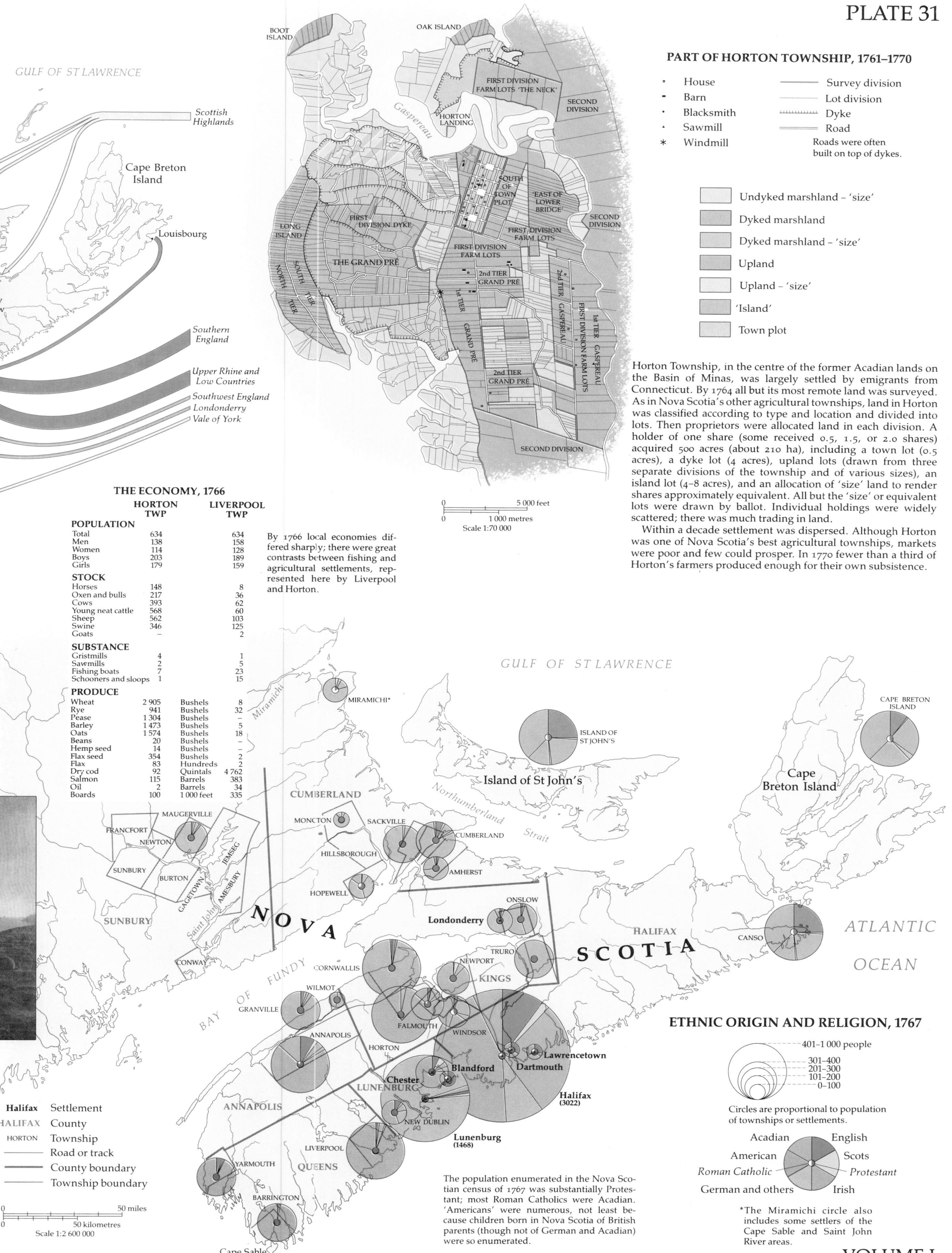

GULF OF ST LAWRENCE
Scottish Highlands
Cape Breton Island
Louisbourg
Southern England
Upper Rhine and Low Countries
Southwest England
Londonderry
Vale of York
PART OF HORTON TOWNSHIP, 1761–1770
House
Barn
Blacksmith
Sawmill
Windmill
Survey division
Lot division
Dyke
Road
Roads were often built on top of dykes.
Undyked marshland – 'size'
Dyked marshland
Dyked marshland – 'size'
Upland
Upland – 'size'
'Island'
Town plot
BOOT ISLAND
OAK ISLAND
FIRST DIVISION FARM LOTS 'THE NECK'
SECOND DIVISION
Gaspereau
HORTON LANDING
SOUTH OF TOWN PLOT
'EAST OF LOWER BRIDGE'
FIRST DIVISION DYKE
LONG ISLAND
THE GRAND PRÉ
FIRST DIVISION FARM LOTS
2nd TIER GRAND PRÉ
NORTH TIER
SOUTH TIER
1st TIER GRAND PRÉ
2nd TIER GASPEREAU
FIRST DIVISION FARM LOTS
1st TIER GASPEREAU
SECOND DIVISION
0 5 000 feet
0 1 000 metres
Scale 1:70 000
GULF OF ST LAWRENCE
MIRAMICHI*
Miramichi
ISLAND OF ST JOHN'S
Island of St John's
CAPE BRETON ISLAND
Cape Breton Island
Northumberland Strait
CUMBERLAND
MAUGERVILLE
FRANCFORT
NEWTON
SUNBURY
BURTON
GAGETOWN
JEMSEG
AMESBURY
MONCTON
SACKVILLE
CUMBERLAND
HILLSBOROUGH
AMHERST
HOPEWELL
SUNBURY
Saint John
CONWAY
NOVA SCOTIA
ONSLOW
Londonderry
TRURO
HALIFAX
CANSO
ATLANTIC OCEAN
BAY OF FUNDY
CORNWALLIS
NEWPORT
KINGS
WILMOT
GRANVILLE
FALMOUTH
WINDSOR
ANNAPOLIS
HORTON
Lawrencetown
Dartmouth
Chester
Blandford
LUNENBURG
Halifax (3022)
NEW DUBLIN
Lunenburg (1468)
ANNAPOLIS
LIVERPOOL
QUEENS
YARMOUTH
BARRINGTON
Cape Sable
Halifax Settlement
HALIFAX County
HORTON Township
Road or track
County boundary
Township boundary
0 50 miles
0 50 kilometres
Scale 1:2 600 000
ETHNIC ORIGIN AND RELIGION, 1767
401–1 000 people
301–400
201–300
101–200
0–100
Circles are proportional to population of townships or settlements.
Acadian
English
American
Scots
Roman Catholic
Protestant
German and others
Irish
*The Miramichi circle also includes some settlers of the Cape Sable and Saint John River areas.

Horton Township, in the centre of the former Acadian lands on the Basin of Minas, was largely settled by emigrants from Connecticut. By 1764 all but its most remote land was surveyed. As in Nova Scotia's other agricultural townships, land in Horton was classified according to type and location and divided into lots. Then proprietors were allocated land in each division. A holder of one share (some received 0.5, 1.5, or 2.0 shares) acquired 500 acres (about 210 ha), including a town lot (0.5 acres), a dyke lot (4 acres), upland lots (drawn from three separate divisions of the township and of various sizes), an island lot (4–8 acres), and an allocation of 'size' land to render shares approximately equivalent. All but the 'size' or equivalent lots were drawn by ballot. Individual holdings were widely scattered; there was much trading in land.

Within a decade settlement was dispersed. Although Horton was one of Nova Scotia's best agricultural townships, markets were poor and few could prosper. In 1770 fewer than a third of Horton's farmers produced enough for their own subsistence.

THE ECONOMY, 1766

	HORTON TWP		LIVERPOOL TWP
POPULATION			
Total	634		634
Men	138		158
Women	114		128
Boys	203		189
Girls	179		159
STOCK			
Horses	148		8
Oxen and bulls	217		36
Cows	393		62
Young neat cattle	568		60
Sheep	562		103
Swine	346		125
Goats	–		2
SUBSTANCE			
Gristmills	4		1
Sawmills	2		5
Fishing boats	7		23
Schooners and sloops	1		15
PRODUCE			
Wheat	2 905	Bushels	8
Rye	941	Bushels	32
Pease	1 304	Bushels	–
Barley	1 473	Bushels	5
Oats	1 574	Bushels	18
Beans	20	Bushels	–
Hemp seed	14	Bushels	–
Flax seed	354	Bushels	2
Flax	83	Hundreds	2
Dry cod	92	Quintals	4 762
Salmon	115	Barrels	383
Oil	2	Barrels	34
Boards	100	1 000 feet	335

By 1766 local economies differed sharply; there were great contrasts between fishing and agricultural settlements, represented here by Liverpool and Horton.

The population enumerated in the Nova Scotian census of 1767 was substantially Protestant; most Roman Catholics were Acadian. 'Americans' were numerous, not least because children born in Nova Scotia of British parents (though not of German and Acadian) were so enumerated.

MARITIME CANADA, LATE 18th CENTURY

Authors: Graeme Wynn; L.D. McCann (Halifax)

ORIGINS OF NEW BRUNSWICK LOYALISTS*

Other
Carolinas
Massachusetts
Pennsylvania
Connecticut
New York
New Jersey

DISTRIBUTION OF LOYALISTS, ca 1785

(3000) Major centre and population
One dot represents 50 people.
Colonial boundary
County boundary

NEW BRUNSWICK
YORK
NORTHUMBERLAND
SUNBURY
QUEENS
WESTMORLAND
KINGS
SAINT JOHN
CHARLOTTE
CUMBERLAND
U.S.
Saint John (2 000)

ISLAND OF ST JOHN
PRINCE
QUEENS
KINGS

CAPE BRETON ISLAND
Sydney

NOVA SCOTIA
KINGS
HANTS
HALIFAX
SYDNEY
Halifax
ANNAPOLIS
LUNENBURG
QUEENS
SHELBURNE
Shelburne (5 000)

Scale 1:3 500 000

ORIGINS OF SHELBURNE LOYALISTS**

Other
Virginia
Carolinas
Massachusetts
New Jersey
Pennsylvania
New York

*Based on 1870 family heads and single adult males
**Approximately 700 Loyalists

POPULATION AND LOYALISTS' GRANTS IN NOVA SCOTIA, 1780s

Escheats for non-improvement
Permanent grants
Departed Loyalists
Black Loyalists
Military Loyalists
Civilian Loyalists

Grants/population

ANNAPOLIS
CUMBERLAND
HALIFAX
HANTS
KINGS
LUNENBURG
QUEENS
SYDNEY
SHELBURNE

Almost 40 000 Loyalists came to the British colony of Nova Scotia in the early 1780s. Of these, perhaps a fifth left almost immediately, 13 500 settled in what is now New Brunswick, and some 19 000 settled in peninsular Nova Scotia. These settlers, most of whom came from the Middle Colonies, were largely American-born (90%), civilian (60%), and from the middle or lower ranks of the societies they left. With their coming instant towns sprang up on rocky shores. Shelburne soon declined, but Parrtown grew into Saint John, the largest city in the new colony of New Brunswick. Records of land grants allow the number of Loyalists per county and the distribution of Loyalists in 1785 to be established approximately. Clearly this sudden influx of new settlers was an enormous boost to local development; vacant lands were occupied, domestic markets created, and enterprise encouraged.

HALIFAX SHIPPING

Number of vessels
Tonnage of vessels (000)
Entering 1779 Clearing
Entering 1790 Clearing
Entering 1790 Clearing

United Kingdom
Canada
Newfoundland
New England
Mid-Atlantic States
South Atlantic States
West Indies
Other

In 1783 Halifax was a provincial capital, garrison outpost, and mercantile town of some 5 000 people. Substantial wharves and warehouses lined the waterfront, but manufacturing was limited. In the densely built-up core people of different social, economic, and ethnic backgrounds lived close together. There was more segregation on the periphery, with labourers and German Protestants concentrated in the northern suburbs and government officials and some merchants in the south. Sydney, founded with some pretension in 1783, was a garrisoned village in 1800.

HALIFAX, 1784

After Charles Blaskowitz, 'Plan of the Town of Halifax 1784,' and others

Scale 1:40 000

Major public buildings

1 Naval hospital
2 Dutch Church (Anglican)
3 Grenadier barracks
4 Red barracks
5 Court-house
6 Public stores
7 Parade grounds
8 Market house
9 St Paul's Anglican Church
10 Governor's house
11 Powder magazine
12 Assembly house
13 St Mather's Dissenters Church
14 Provost
15 General hospital
16 Prison
17 Cemetery
18 Engineer's yard

Densely developed

SYDNEY, 1795

After James Miller, 'Map of the Town of Sydney, 1795'

Scale 1:14 000

Major public buildings

1 Military cemetery
2 Four-gun sod battery
3 Prison
4 Store
5 Infirmary
6 Barracks
7 Governor's house
8 Court-house
9 Church
10 Cemetery
11 Court-house
12 Ruined King's store

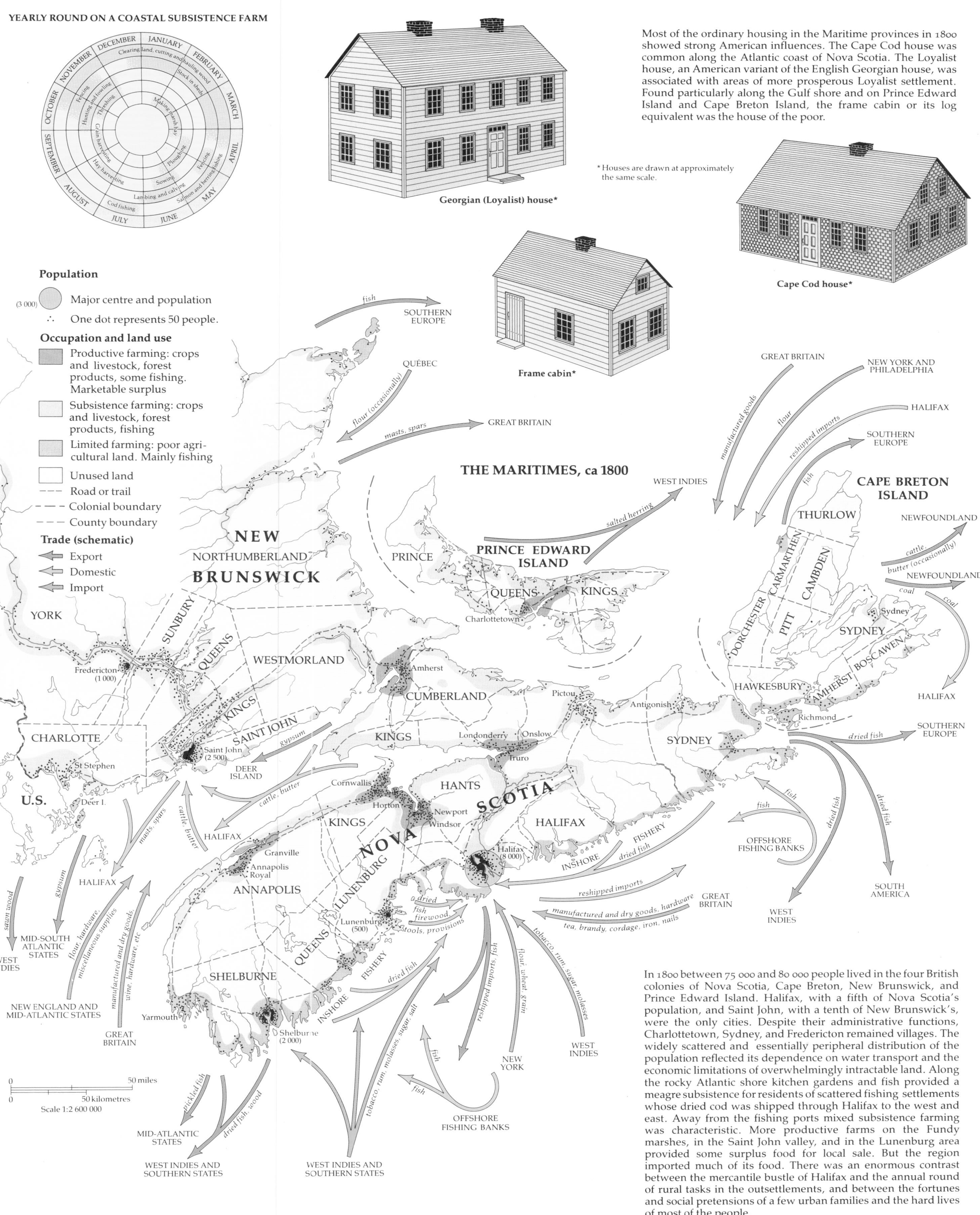
YEARLY ROUND ON A COASTAL SUBSISTENCE FARM
JANUARY
FEBRUARY
MARCH
APRIL
MAY
JUNE
JULY
AUGUST
SEPTEMBER
OCTOBER
NOVEMBER
DECEMBER
Clearing land, cutting and hauling wood
Stock in sheds
Making marsh hay
Ploughing
Fencing
Salmon and herring fishing
Sowing
Lambing and calving
Cod fishing
Hay harvesting
Grain harvesting
Threshing
Hunting and fowling
Fencing
Georgian (Loyalist) house*
Frame cabin*
Cape Cod house*
* Houses are drawn at approximately the same scale.
Population
(3 000) Major centre and population
One dot represents 50 people.
Occupation and land use
Productive farming: crops and livestock, forest products, some fishing. Marketable surplus
Subsistence farming: crops and livestock, forest products, fishing
Limited farming: poor agricultural land. Mainly fishing
Unused land
Road or trail
Colonial boundary
County boundary
Trade (schematic)
Export
Domestic
Import
THE MARITIMES, ca 1800
NEW BRUNSWICK
NOVA SCOTIA
PRINCE EDWARD ISLAND
CAPE BRETON ISLAND
NORTHUMBERLAND
YORK
SUNBURY
QUEENS
KINGS
WESTMORLAND
SAINT JOHN
CHARLOTTE
PRINCE
KINGS
QUEENS
CUMBERLAND
HANTS
HALIFAX
LUNENBURG
ANNAPOLIS
SHELBURNE
SYDNEY
THURLOW
CARMARTHEN
CAMBDEN
DORCHESTER
PITT
SYDNEY
BOSCAWEN
AMHERST
HAWKESBURY
U.S.
Fredericton (1 000)
Saint John (2 500)
St Stephen
Deer I.
DEER ISLAND
Charlottetown
Amherst
Pictou
Antigonish
Londonderry
Onslow
Truro
Cornwallis
Horton
Newport
Windsor
Granville
Annapolis Royal
Halifax (8 000)
Lunenburg (500)
Yarmouth
Shelburne (2 000)
Sydney
Richmond
INSHORE FISHERY
OFFSHORE FISHING BANKS
SOUTHERN EUROPE
QUÉBEC
GREAT BRITAIN
WEST INDIES
NEW YORK AND PHILADELPHIA
HALIFAX
NEWFOUNDLAND
SOUTH AMERICA
NEW YORK
MID-SOUTH ATLANTIC STATES
NEW ENGLAND AND MID-ATLANTIC STATES
MID-ATLANTIC STATES
WEST INDIES AND SOUTHERN STATES
fish
flour (occasionally)
masts, spars
salted herring
manufactured goods
flour
reshipped imports
cattle, butter (occasionally)
coal
dried fish
gypsum
cattle, butter
sawn wood
flour, hardware, miscellaneous supplies
manufactured and dry goods, wine, hardware, etc
pickled fish
dried fish, wood
tobacco, rum, molasses, sugar, salt
reshipped imports, fish
flour, wheat, grain
tobacco, rum, sugar, molasses
manufactured and dry goods, hardware
tea, brandy, cordage, iron, nails
fish firewood tools, provisions
0 50 miles
0 50 kilometres
Scale 1:2 600 000

Most of the ordinary housing in the Maritime provinces in 1800 showed strong American influences. The Cape Cod house was common along the Atlantic coast of Nova Scotia. The Loyalist house, an American variant of the English Georgian house, was associated with areas of more prosperous Loyalist settlement. Found particularly along the Gulf shore and on Prince Edward Island and Cape Breton Island, the frame cabin or its log equivalent was the house of the poor.

In 1800 between 75 000 and 80 000 people lived in the four British colonies of Nova Scotia, Cape Breton, New Brunswick, and Prince Edward Island. Halifax, with a fifth of Nova Scotia's population, and Saint John, with a tenth of New Brunswick's, were the only cities. Despite their administrative functions, Charlottetown, Sydney, and Fredericton remained villages. The widely scattered and essentially peripheral distribution of the population reflected its dependence on water transport and the economic limitations of overwhelmingly intractable land. Along the rocky Atlantic shore kitchen gardens and fish provided a meagre subsistence for residents of scattered fishing settlements whose dried cod was shipped through Halifax to the west and east. Away from the fishing ports mixed subsistence farming was characteristic. More productive farms on the Fundy marshes, in the Saint John valley, and in the Lunenburg area provided some surplus food for local sale. But the region imported much of its food. There was an enormous contrast between the mercantile bustle of Halifax and the annual round of rural tasks in the outsettlements, and between the fortunes and social pretensions of a few urban families and the hard lives of most of the people.

Inland Expansion

The 16th Century

Early in the 16th century the St Lawrence valley was occupied by two agricultural Iroquoian-speaking groups collectively known as the St Lawrence Iroquoians (pl 33). On the Island of Montréal the heavily fortified village of Hochelaga, with about 50 longhouses and perhaps 1500 people, controlled the resources of the St Lawrence from the mouth of the Ottawa River to the entrance of Lac Saint-Pierre. Downstream from Hochelaga, on the north side of the river between Portneuf and Cap Tourmente, were seven small, apparently unfortified villages, with a total population of about 3 000 people. Jacques Cartier called this area 'the province of Canada' after the local Iroquoian word for 'village.' The inhabitants of Canada, termed Stadaconans by modern writers after their best-known village, ranged from Lac Saint-Pierre to the mouth of the Saguenay River and made fishing expeditions to the Gaspé and along the north shore of the lower St Lawrence. Politically these villages seem to have been independent, although Cartier implied that the headman of Stadacona, Donnacona, exercised some influence in the four villages downstream from his, and that all the St Lawrence villagers were 'subjects' of the Hochelagans.

When Cartier arrived in the 1530s the Hochelagans and Stadaconans were at peace with each other. Both groups, however, were at war with other neighbours, the Hochelagans with the Agojuda *(mauvaise gens)*, whose warriors came from the west, and the Stadaconans with the Toudaman who lived to the south of Stadacona. The Stadaconans also indicated that warring groups lived in the interior, up the Richelieu River.

South of the Canadian Shield in south-central Ontario lived the Huron-Petun. Southwest of them were the Neutral, and south of Lake Ontario the five Iroquois tribes (pl 33). All were primarily agriculturalists living in substantial villages , the largest of which were fortified (pl 12). All spoke Iroquoian dialects. The Ontario groups may have comprised some 60 000 people and those south of the lake 25 000. Well before Cartier's arrival the Huron-Petun were engaged in wars with the St Lawrence Iroquoians and probably also with the New York Iroquois, while the Neutral were warring with agricultural Algonquian groups in southwestern Ontario and Michigan. Through the 15th and 16th centuries these warring groups were moving further from each other; clusters of villages separated by vast no-man's-lands used as hunting territories were making their appearance.

In the Canadian Shield north of the Iroquoian groups were Algonquian bands that depended on fishing (spring to autumn) and hunting (winter) and traded with the Ontario Iroquoians. Along the north shore of the Gulf of St Lawrence from the mouth of the Saguenay River to the Strait of Belle Isle small Montagnais bands fished and hunted for sea mammals in summer and fall, and hunted caribou in the interior in winter. On the south shore, from Chaleur Bay eastward to the Atlantic coast of Nova Scotia, Micmac bands depended on fish and seals from spring to fall and on moose and caribou in winter.

Recorded European contact with the natives around the Gulf of St Lawrence began in 1534 with the first voyage of Jacques Cartier. As elsewhere the natives greeted the newcomers enthusiastically and attempted to barter what they had for whatever the Europeans were willing to give. Cartier and his men, frightened by the number of Micmac they saw, were more apprehensive. They had come to find a route to the Orient, not to trade, and eventually gave gifts and traded to establish friendly relations. Later Cartier kidnapped two Stadaconans, the sons of the headman Donnacona, at the Gaspé, hoping they would eventually act as guides.

On his second voyage a year later Cartier was obsessed with the search for precious metals and a route to the Orient. The Stadaconans, among whom he landed, wanted to establish a formal alliance, including an exchange of people. In return they offered to guide Cartier to Hochelaga. Undoubtedly the Stadaconans were impressed by French arms, and probably thought an alliance would bring prestige among the local villages and some measure of pre-eminence over the Hochelagans. Cartier showed no interest in an alliance, however, and his visit to the Hochelagans, without Stadaconan guides, created distrust between him and the Stadaconans that no amount of gift giving could overcome. He and his men overwintered near the Stadaconans (pl 33), and suffered terribly; 25 men died of scurvy before natives told Cartier of a cure. In the spring the Stadaconans began to fuel Cartier's obsession with precious minerals with stories of a wealthy kingdom of Saguenay – stories probably designed to rid the Stadaconans of a heavily armed menace in their midst that could not be bound by an alliance. If so, their plan miscarried; Cartier kidnapped Donnacona, his two sons, and seven others so they could repeat their stories to King François I. None of these captives returned to the St Lawrence but their tales took root at the French court and circulated as far as Spain and Portugal.

War between France and Spain (1536–8) delayed another expedition until 1541. This time Cartier was to found a colony, find a way through the Lachine rapids, and make contact with the Kingdom of Saguenay. Cartier established a fortified base upstream from the troublesome Stadaconans, but by winter met organized resistance from all the neighbouring villages. By spring prospects seemed hopeless, and Cartier departed with a load of gold and diamonds that turned out to be pyrites and quartz. His vice-regal superior in the colonization venture, Jean-François de La Rocque de Roberval, arrived later that year but had no more success. Canada acquired a dismal image in France. Its climate was hard, its impoverished, hostile natives had nothing worthwhile to trade. If there were a sea to the west, there was no easy way to get there. French colonizing efforts turned to Brazil (1555) and Florida (1562 and 1564). All Huguenot ventures, these colonies were soon destroyed by Portugal and Spain. In France Catholic-Huguenot rivalry prevented further colonizing ventures until the last quarter of the century.

Truce with the Huguenots in 1577 and the first profitable trickle of fur from the Gulf of St Lawrence seem to have revived royal interest in Canada. In that year Henry III gave Troilus de La Roche de Mesgouez, a Breton, a comprehensive grant to establish a colony and exploit new lands. La Roche's grant and his connections with shipowners of St Malo probably led to the first voyages specifically for fur trading. In 1581 and 1582 a small Breton ship made a profitable voyage to the Gulf. In 1583 three ships from St Malo traded at the Lachine rapids, while a ship from Le Havre, financed by merchants from Rouen, traded between Cape Breton and the Penobscot River. The attraction of Canada as a source of furs was increased fortuitously in 1583 when the Swedes captured Narva, the Baltic port through which the Russians had exported furs. Five ships were outfitted from St Malo in 1584, ten in 1585. In 1588 Jacques Noël, a nephew of Cartier, obtained a monopoly of the Canadian trade in return for a promise to renew the colony, but pressures from other merchants forced the king to rescind the monopoly and Noël to shelve plans for the colony.

By the end of the 16th century the French court had come to realize that a successful fur trade required a permanent base in Canada. In 1599 Henry IV awarded Pierre de Chauvin de Tonnetuit, a Huguenot, a trading monopoly, ordering him to 'live in the country and build a stronghold.' Already familiar with the Canadian cod and fur trades, Chauvin maintained a trading post at Tadoussac at the mouth of the Saguenay River over the winter of 1600–1. After two years of successful trading Chauvin died and was briefly succeeded by Aymar de Chaste who, ordered by Henry IV to determine whether the St Lawrence valley was suitable for settlement, organized the first geographical survey of the St Lawrence since Cartier. In 1603 this survey was carried out by Samuel de Champlain.

Champlain's survey disclosed an attractive, uninhabited valley. At various places along the river he was shown grassy areas where the villages of the St Lawrence Iroquoians had stood. Later, during a visit to the Island of Montréal, Champlain observed 60 arpents (about 20 ha) of grassland along the St Pierre River that were 'formerly cultivated fields.' Contemporary writers were certain this was the site of Hochelaga. Of the Hochelagans, Stadaconans, and the other St Lawrence Iroquoians there was no trace. Early 17th century opinion was that they were destroyed by warfare late in the 16th century. Algonquian informants blamed the Huron for the destruction of Hochelaga. Marc Lescarbot writing in 1610 and the Récollet Denis Jamet writing in 1615 both blamed the Iroquois (pl 33).

Trade and Settlement along the St Lawrence, 1600–1630

In 1603 Pierre Du Gua de Monts took over de Chaste's monopoly. Discouraged by the winters at Tadoussac, he decided to begin a colony in Acadia while continuing to trade on the St Lawrence. In 1607 his monopoly was rescinded, and on the urging of Champlain Du Gua switched his colonizing efforts to the St Lawrence in 1608 (pl 35). Champlain was to build a post and explore, while pursuing the fur trade. Québec, the site Champlain chose for a post, commanded the river, was near fertile land for an agricultural colony, and was within range of friendly natives accustomed to trading. Champlain was made to understand by the natives that security at Québec, trade, and inland exploration required French participation in native wars. When a *habitation* was erected at Québec, he accompanied a Montagnais-Algonquin-Huron war party up the Richelieu valley to Lake Champlain to make a raid on the Mohawk. For Champlain the raid was an opportunity to explore and to cement an alliance, promised by Henry IV to the Montagnais in 1602, and for his native companions it was proof of French good will. For the Mohawk it marked the beginning of French interference in their affairs. In 1610 Champlain participated in a second battle and acquired a special status with his native allies; they regarded other traders as 'women, who wish to make war only on our beavers.' The Algonquin and Huron were willing to receive a French boy (probably Étienne Brûlé) in exchange for a Huron boy (Savignon), that each learn the other's customs and languages, a gesture that furthered the alliance.

Champlain had proved himself to his allies, but the trade promised by the Huron had not developed. In 1613 he tried to explore the Ottawa River route to the Huron without native support and was turned back by the Kichesipirini, a group of Ottawa-valley Algonquins, who probably sought to protect their own trade with the French. Only the promise of aid on yet another raid against the Iroquois finally enabled Champlain, Brûlé, 13 soldiers, and the Récollet priest Joseph Le Caron, to travel to the Huron country in 1615 (pl 36). From there Champlain, his soldiers, and 500 Huron set out to attack the Oneida (or Onondaga) while Brulé was sent to bring warriors from the Susquehannock, Huron allies in Virginia. A major village was attacked but not taken and Champlain was wounded, but he had achieved his main objectives: consolidating the French-Huron alliance, bringing the Huron into the fur trade, establishing contact with the Nipissing, Ottawa, and Petun, and obtaining an impression of the natives and the geography of the eastern Great Lakes.

Champlain's supposition that the Huron would play an increasing role in the fur trade proved to be correct. Their well-developed trade connections with the Neutral and Petun and with Algonquian bands to the north provided a framework for the collection of furs and the distribution of French trade goods throughout the eastern Great Lakes. By the early 1620s the Huron displaced the Ottawa Algonquins as major suppliers of French goods to the interior groups. The Algonquin responded by imposing higher tolls on Huron or Nipissing traders who passed down the Ottawa (pl 35). As Huron trade with their neighbours grew, so did Huron control of it. Although the French tried to contact other groups, no Neutral, Petun, Ottawa, or Ojibwa ever travelled to the St Lawrence and by the late 1620s no French traders operated west of the Lachine rapids.

To the south on the upper Hudson River regular Dutch trade began in 1614 with the local Algonquian Mahican and expanded to the Mohawk. By the early 1620s the Dutch were trying to reach Algonquian groups north of the St Lawrence through the Mahican, a dangerous relationship in Mohawk eyes. In order to cover their northern frontier the Mohawk made peace with the French and their Algonquian allies in 1624, and then attacked the Mahican, defeating a Dutch-Mahican force in 1626 and driving the Mahican from Fort Orange in 1628. With access to the Dutch secured, the Mohawk turned against their traditional northern enemies.

By the mid 1620s the annual French fur trade in the St Lawrence valley amounted to 12 000–15 000 beaver, but there were only about 20 permanent settlers at Québec. Few natives had been converted to Christianity. The Jesuits, better manned, organized, and financed than the Récollets, entered the missionary enterprise in 1625, and the two orders joined in complaints about the lamentable state of the colony. In 1627 Cardinal Richelieu, now responsible for the colonies and commerce of France, created the large, well-financed Compagnie des Cent-Associés which, in return for a trading monopoly, was charged to bring 4 000 settlers to Canada in 15 years and promote native missions. The next year the company's first expedition – 4 ships and 400 colonists – was captured by a British force commissioned by Charles I and financed by a London merchant company that also intended to trade in and colonize the St Lawrence valley. Starved into submission, Champlain capitulated the following year. For three years, until the Treaty of Saint-Germain-en-Laye (1632) restored Canada to France, an Anglo-Scottish trading company maintained some 200 men at Québec and operated the St Lawrence trade at considerable profit.

The Iroquois Wars and the Depopulation of Southern Ontario, 1630–1653

After France regained Canada, agricultural settlement spread slowly along the river near Québec and new posts were established at Trois-Rivières in 1634 and at Montréal and Fort Richelieu (at the mouth of the Richelieu) in 1642. Although the Mohawk had not bothered Québec, they attacked these new settlements, which they regarded as within their sphere of influence, and increased attacks on anyone travelling along the upper St Lawrence. As a result Fort Richelieu had to be abandoned in 1645.

The missionary enterprise, relaunched with the full zeal of the Counter-Reformation, was now in the hands of the Jesuits. Richelieu had prohibited the return of the Récollets. Only the Jesuits, their servants, and occasionally soldiers sent to protect them would be allowed in the interior. The Compagnie des Cent-Associés would concentrate on colonization and trade at the St Lawrence posts, Jesuit missions in the interior would function without secular interference, while native traders would control the interior trade. Such was official French policy, and it would not change appreciably until 1681.

The Jesuits' first permanent mission was established in 1634 among the western Huron (Attignawantan). In 1639, under the guidance of Father Jérôme Lalemant, Sainte-Marie-among-the-Hurons was built as a central mission (pl 34). From it missionaries were assigned as parish priests to the principal Huron villages, in some of which churches were eventually built to serve fledgling Christian communities. As the number of Jesuits increased, other missions were opened to non-Huron groups. Unlike the Récollets, the Jesuits sought to replace only those customs they judged to be incompatible with Christianity.

Between 1634 and 1640 epidemic diseases devastated the Huron and neighbouring groups (pl 35). The French, and particularly the Jesuits, were blamed as carriers or accused of deliberately spreading the diseases. Some Huron wanted to kill the priests and sever relations with the French; others argued that French trade and the French alliance were necessary to keep off the Iroquois. The latter faction increasingly drew their strength from their relations with the Jesuits who began to make real progress in native conversions in the early 1640s.

In the 1630s there were sporadic Iroquois raids (usually by the Onondaga and Seneca) into Huronia, while the Mohawk and Oneida raided along the route between the lower Ottawa River and Trois-Rivières. The main aims of these raids seem to have been to provide an opportunity for a warrior to prove himself or to avenge an earlier raid. Usually a few people were killed, some were captured, and occasionally furs and trade goods were taken, but the Huron-French fur trade continued through the 1630s. The Huron also made raids on the Iroquois but apparently less frequently.

By the late 1630s the Mohawk were obtaining muskets from illegal Dutch traders and also from English traders on the Connecticut River. In 1639 the Dutch West India Company, which had obeyed Dutch strictures against the sale of arms, lost its monopoly. The illegal sale of muskets escalated, and in 1641 the Dutch, alarmed over the arming of the Mohawk, reissued an ordinance prohibiting such sales. As soon as the Mohawk saw their supply of arms dry up, they sought to negotiate a peace with the French, a peace they made contingent on obtaining muskets and excluding native allies of the French from the negotiations. As the French did not trade arms even to their allies, they could not agree to these demands; however, when Governor Charles Huault de Montmagny realized that some of the Mohawk were armed, he decided to sell muskets to baptized native allies. The collapse of the peace talks and the founding of Montréal and Fort Richelieu resulted in a flurry of Mohawk attacks that closed the trade routes to the St Lawrence and began the dispersal of the Onontchataronon and the Ottawa-valley Algonquins. Meanwhile the Dutch, fearing problems with the Esopus tribe on the Hudson River and realizing that they were unlikely to trade with any native groups beyond the Mohawk, concluded a treaty with the Mohawk in 1643. For a time the Mohawk traded freely for Dutch muskets, of which they had at least 400 by 1644.

For the French and their allies the early 1640s were difficult years. Virtually every summer the western Iroquois raided Huronia and carried off captives. Mohawk harassment of native traders along the Ottawa River and upper St Lawrence effectively closed this route in some years. Few furs got to the St Lawrence from 1642 to 1644, and in 1645 the Compagnie des Cent-Associés faltered and turned over its monopoly to a company led by the prominent merchants of New France, the Communauté des Habitants. Huron response to Iroquois raids weakened; clearly the Iroquois were growing in power.

Faced with these developments Governor Montmagny resumed peace negotiations with the Mohawk, who were prepared to deal with the French because the Dutch had again officially prohibited the sale of muskets. The Mohawk considered a treaty with the French to be an opportunity to play off the two European powers against each other and to regain Mohawk captives taken by the French and their allies. They insisted on gaining or regaining hunting rights in the St Lawrence–Ottawa River area and on the right to make separate treaties with the native allies of the French. For their part the French thought they could retain their native alliance, stop the wars that were destroying trade, and draw the Mohawk into their orbit. A peace treaty between the French and Mohawk was concluded in 1645.

This treaty expanded the Ottawa–St Lawrence trade to a record 30 000 pounds of fur in 1645 and to more the following year. However, Algonquin resistance to Mohawk hunting parties north of the St Lawrence and opposition to the peace by the other Iroquois tribes were leading to renewed hostilities. Late in 1646 Father Isaac Jogues, the Jesuit priest who had come to open a mission to the Mohawk, was murdered. The peace was shattered.

In 1646–7 the Mohawk dispersed the remaining Ottawa River Algonquin, and the Seneca defeated the Aondironnon, a Neutral group. In 1647 the Huron did not come to trade, but they came in 1648, led by five chiefs with many warriors. Along the way they defeated an Iroquois war party. In their absence another Iroquois force struck eastern Huronia, destroying two villages and taking 700 captives. The same year the Dutch lifted their official ban on the sale of arms and sold 400 muskets to the Mohawk, apparently with the understanding that they would be used against the native allies of the French. In 1649 a well-armed force of 1 000 Iroquois attacked and dispersed the Huron and then the Petun. Following these successes the Iroquois dispersed the Nipissing and the Neutral. Most of the Iroquian-speaking survivors of these attacks settled among, and were adopted by, their conquerors. About 600 Huron settled near Québec and another 500 to 1 000 Huron and Petun, joined by the Algonquian bands around Lake Huron, fled westward to settle around Green Bay and later along the south shore of Lake Superior (pls 35, 37). By 1653 southern Ontario was deserted.

The causes of the Iroquois wars have been much debated. Clearly the French and Dutch had settled among natives who belonged to opposing alliances. In order to secure their colony and their trade, the French supported their northern trading partners. The Dutch, who initially sided with the Mahican, were forced by the Mohawk into the southern alliance. Through the 1620s and 1630s both the Huron and Mohawk, the most powerful groups in their respective alliances, tried to consolidate their special positions, whereas the Europeans would have preferred to deal with all natives. In the late 1630s and through the 1640s the wars intensified as the Iroquois became increasingly aggressive. Some scholars have interpreted these events as an escalating war by the Iroquois to gain control over the hunting territories of their enemies to the north as their own lands were running short of beaver. Witnesses to these events, however, pointed out that native warfare was not for economic or territorial gain and that there was no decline of beaver in the Iroquois areas before the 1660s. They reported rather that the balance of traditional warfare had been upset by the Dutch trade in muskets, of which the Iroquois had at least 800 by 1648, and that the Iroquois seized this new technology to destroy their old enemies. Their ideal to unite all Iroquoian speakers into one people and only one land, reported by Father Jogues in 1643 and Father Paul Le Jeune in 1656, as well as their need to replace their depleted population seem to have been additional motives.

The weakness of the Huron and their allies is partly attributable to their inability to respond collectively to the rapidly escalating crisis of the late 1640s. The Neutral and Petun did not participate in the wars until it was too late. The Huron were badly divided between Christians and traditionalists, the latter having some Iroquois sympathies. The Huron almost always fought village by village rather than on a tribal or confederacy level as did the Iroquois in the late 1640s, and a considerable body of men were away trading each summer. Unable to act together, and lacking firearms and French military support, the Huron and their native allies were destroyed piecemeal and absorbed by the better armed and better organized Iroquois.

It is doubtful, as some have argued, that the Huron maintained their relations with the French because they had become economically dependent on European trade goods. Such goods made life easier and were desired, but in their absence the Huron economy would function. Knowledge of traditional ways had not been lost in less than a generation. Huron trade with the French continued because the Huron's only hope of survival as a distinct people lay within the French alliance. To kill or eject the Jesuits and sever the French trade would end the French alliance and leave the Huron exposed to the growing, Dutch-backed power of the Iroquois. The Huron hope for survival lay in obtaining firearms and military support from the French. Neither was forthcoming; in the end the French alliance proved to be militarily ineffectual.

The Re-Establishment of Trade, 1654–1666

The dispersal of native groups allied to the French was disastrous for the St Lawrence fur trade and for the tiny colony that depended on it. By 1651–2 even the trade of the St Maurice and Saguenay valleys had been reduced to a trickle. In 1653, with the colony and the debt-ridden Communauté des Habitants in despair, the western Iroquois, led by the Onondaga, arrived at Montréal and the Mohawk at Trois-Rivières to negotiate peace and the transfer of the Huron refugees near Québec. The Iroquois as a whole favoured peace in the hope they could play off the Dutch and French against each other, but the Onondaga wanted trade with the French to offset growing Mohawk domination of the confederacy, an aim resented and opposed by the Mohawk.

Desperate for peace, the French agreed to open a mission and trading post among the Onondaga and tried to convince the reluctant Huron to join their former enemies. Without Huron agreement a shaky peace was concluded. The western Iroquois, their northern flank secured, now attacked and, after a bitter war, defeated, dispersed, and later (1680s) assimilated the Erie. In 1656, as this war wound down, the Jesuits began a mission that also served as a trading post and had a small garrison at Sainte-Marie-de-Gannentaha among the Onondaga. At the same time the struggle continued for the remnant Huron, whom the Iroquois wanted to assimilate and the French were now prepared to abandon, an obstacle to the Iroquois peace. While the Onondaga and Oneida pressured the Huron to join them, the Mohawk lost patience and attacked, killing some Huron and capturing others. Eventually about 400 Huron were persuaded to go, the Attignawantan to the Mohawk and the Arendahronon to the Onondaga. Along the way some of the Arendahronon men were murdered. The Huron who stayed behind, most of them Attigneenongnahac, became the ancestors of the contemporary Huron at Lorette. Peace between the Iroquois and the French was collapsing as anti-French factions strengthened among the Iroquois and as the French decided against further appeasement. In March 1658 the complement of 53 Frenchmen at Sainte-Marie-de-Gannentaha fled to Québec after warnings by converts that an attack was imminent. The Iroquois wars resumed, spreading rapidly to the northwest and into the Ohio and St Lawrence valleys. In 1660 Dollard des Ormeaux, commander of the garrison at Montréal, and 16 men were killed at the Long Sault rapids on the Ottawa River; the Mohawk boasted that the French 'were not able to goe over a door to pisse' without being shot.

The fur trade resumed during the brief interlude of peace with the Iroquois. In 1654 about 120 Ottawa and Wyandot (Huron-Petun) arrived with a large supply of beaver for which they wanted muskets, shot, and powder (pl 37). Governor Jean de Lauson granted permission to Chouart des Groseilliers to return to the west with them. In 1656 Groseilliers was back on the St Lawrence with 50 fur-laden canoes, and a favourable assessment of the western Great Lakes for trade and missions (pl 36). In 1657 about 90 canoes arrived, but with the renewal of the Iroquois wars only nine canoes came to Montréal from the west in 1658 and only six in 1659. The Mississauga, who came in 1659, made it clear that they wanted French escorts. Although forbidden to do so, Pierre Esprit Radisson and Groseilliers departed with the Mississauga, returning the following year (1660) with 60 canoes and 300 native traders. Their voyage brought needed capital to the colony, but their furs were confiscated and Groseilliers was briefly imprisoned. For the next two years the Iroquois again blocked the St Lawrence from the interior.

Radisson and Groseilliers had returned with detailed knowledge of the western Great Lakes and the upper Mississippi valley. From the Cree they also learned about the rich fur country between Lake Superior and Hudson Bay. Smarting from their treatment in 1660 and unable to attract support in New France for a maritime trading venture into Hudson Bay to bypass the Iroquois blockade, they took their knowledge to Boston in 1662 and eventually to England, where they found willing backers for the voyages that would lead to the founding of the Hudson's Bay Company. The Jesuits also recognized the importance of Radisson and Groseillier's discoveries, seeing an opportunity to rebuild their interior missions. In 1660 Father René Ménard departed with eight other Frenchmen and a load of trade goods to begin a mission at Chagouamigon (Saint-Esprit) among the refugee Wyandot, Ottawa, and Ojibwa (pl 37). Although Father Ménard died on the journey and the men who returned in 1663 traded at a loss, the Jesuits were convinced that Chagouamigon could be a successful mission. When 400 Ottawa came to Montréal in 1665, Father Claude Allouez and six Frenchmen departed with them to continue Father Ménard's mission. Their success led to three other missions in the upper Great Lakes by 1668 (pl 38). Unlike the massive Huron and Onondaga missions that experience had shown to be costly and vulnerable, each of these was operated by a single priest with servants.

In 1663 Louis XIV assumed direct control of the administration of New France; its economic affairs became the responsibilityof Jean-Baptiste Colbert, Louis XIV's minister of finance. In 1665 Alexandre de Prouville de Tracy was dispatched from France with 600 soldiers of the Carignan-Salières regiment to 'exterminate' the Iroquois. Upon arrival the regiment built five forts from the mouth of the Richelieu River to Lake Champlain. Reeling from a smallpox epidemic in 1662 and defeats at the hands of the Saulteaux (1662) and Susquehannock (1661, 1662, 1663), the four western Iroquois tribes were not ready for war and negotiated a peace in December 1665. The Mohawk, now isolated, also treated for peace, but too late. In October 1666 de Tracy marched an army of 600 regular troops, 600 militiamen, and 100 Huron-Algonquin allies to the Mohawk country and devastated villages and crops. The five Iroquois tribes were opened to Jesuit missionaries.

French Inland Expansion, 1667–1696

Colbert planned to increase agricultural settlement and establish industries along the lower St Lawrence while relying on natives to bring furs there. Edicts were again issued prohibiting Frenchmen from travelling in the interior without permission and, with the Iroquois at peace, natives again arrived at Montréal. When they departed, however, French traders went with them, and servants accompanied the Jesuits (pl 38). An illegal French trade developed in the *pays d'en haut* encouraged by merchants in Montréal and beyond official power to stop. These illegal traders became known as coureurs de bois (those who later travelled legally were known as voyageurs). By the late 1660s perhaps 100 to 200 of them operated throughout the upper Great Lakes, trading out of temporary huts.

At this time the Great Lakes basin seethed with the tensions of recent warfare and population displacement. Some of the Nipissing and most of the Ojibwa returned to their homelands around Lake Huron at the conclusion of the Iroquois peace. In 1668 some Iroquois groups (Seneca, Cayuga, and Mohawk), faced with declining furs and game and pressed by the Susquehannock, began to settle the north shore of Lake Ontario; other Mohawk settled on the St Lawrence opposite Montréal. From these villages they hunted over most of southern Ontario and southern Québec, traded with the Ottawa and Ojibwa on Lake Huron and with various groups farther west, and took many of their furs to Albany, which the English had taken from the Dutch in 1664. West of Lake Michigan there were frequent hostilities between different refugee groups, between refugees and the resident Winnebago, and, as overcrowding pushed hunting territories westward, between these peoples and the Siouan-speaking Dakota. In 1670 war with the Dakota broke out along a broad front from Lake Superior to the Illinois River. In response, the Miami and Illinois moved towards the south end of Lake Michigan while some Ottawa and Wyandot, unsuccessful in their aggressions against the Dakota, fled to the mission of Saint-Ignace at the Strait of Mackinac, and other Ottawa reoccupied their original home on Manitoulin Island. Beyond all this, news reached New France in 1670 that the English had established trading posts on James Bay.

Forbidden by Colbert to establish posts and engage directly in the interior trade, the Intendant Jean Talon ordered instead a series of 'exploring' expeditions to claim new lands for France, discover minerals, and develop trading and military alliances with native groups. Between 1670 and 1673 these expeditions vastly expanded French knowledge of the interior (pl 36) but, because the English paid more for beaver, did not stop the erosion of trade or the illegal activities of the coureurs de bois. Most of the Cree traded with the English at James Bay and, increasingly, the Ottawa and Ojibwa traded with the Iroquois, who traded with the English on the Hudson River. In New France the price of beaver was controlled and taxed (25%), and the one company allowed to export furs paid dearly for its monopoly. French trade goods were frequently more costly than the English; merchants in Montréal could hope to compete only by carrying trade directly to natives in the interior.

Even the governor, Louis de Buade de Frontenac, tried to circumvent Colbert's orders, building Fort Frontenac (1673) and Fort Niagara (1676) on Lake Ontario, both as bulwarks against Iroquois expansion as well as to gain personal control of the fur trade on the lower Great Lakes. Frontenac's favourite, René-Robert, Cavelier de La Salle, who was given permission to explore a route to the Gulf of Mexico, established a series of posts on the Illinois River and became an active fur trader. The Montréal merchants opposed to Frontenac increased their penetration of the upper Great Lakes, establishing major posts at the Strait of Mackinac and on Green Bay, trade relations with the Cree and Monsoni around Lake Superior, and posts as far north as Lakes Abitibi and Mistassini. In 1679 French officials estimated that some 200 and 300 coureurs de bois were trading in the *pays d'en haut*.

In 1681 Colbert finally reversed his policy of keeping French traders out of the west, legalizing the interior trade through a permit *(congé)* system, and pardoning the coureurs de bois. Up to 25 *congés* would be granted each year, but no one was to receive a *congé* for more than two years running. Each *congé* was a permit for one canoe-load of trade goods with three men per canoe. A *congé* could be sold by its holder, and it could be issued by the governor or the intendant to non-traders to raise money for charitable causes. A canoe-load of trade goods could be expected to produce two canoe-loads of beaver at 40 packs per canoe and, in favourable circumstances, a profit of 40–60%. In addition to the *congés* both the governor and the intendant issued private licences. Because licences were issued for canoe-loads, they stimulated the building of larger canoes. By the late 1680s freight canoe lengths had increased from 7 m to 8.5 m and cargo capacities from 700 kg to 1 000 kg. By the end of the French regime canoes of 10 m with cargo capacities of 3 000 kg were common. Manned by eight men these canoes could cover 110–160 km a day in good conditions.

The legalization of the interior fur trade led to a rapid increase in the number of fur posts. Such posts made it unnecessary for native traders to come to Montréal, and counteracted to some extent the competitive advantage of English prices. Fort Buade at Mackinac, Fort Saint-Louis on the Illinois River, and Fort La Baie on Green Bay became entrepôts where furs were assembled for shipment to Montréal. Entirely in native hands until the late 1660s, the carrying trade to the St Lawrence valley had become French.

The Iroquois peace on which the French fur trade depended came to an end in the early 1680s. Following English successes against the Abenaki in 1675 and the Susquehannock in 1677 (pl 44), the governor of New York, Edmond Andros, openly solicited the Iroquois to drive the French out of the lower Great Lakes. Cautious about renewing war with the French, the Iroquois expanded their hunting and trapping westward towards their old foes the Illinois, Miami, and Ottawa, who were allied with the French. Fighting soon broke out and the French, unprepared for war with the Iroquois, attempted to appease them with presents, while the Iroquois, sensing French weakness, attacked French traders, and, in 1682, pillaged the stores at Fort Frontenac. A small army assembled by Governor Joseph Antoine Le Febvre de La Barre reached Fort Frontenac in 1684 but was struck by influenza. Seizing the opportunity, the Iroquois forced La Barre to accept a humiliating agreement to withdraw French protection from the Illinois and Miami.

With its native alliances crumbling and its trade threatened in the north by the English on Hudson Bay and in the south by the Iroquois-English alliance, New France was in a perilous position. La Barre was replaced, and the new governor, Jacques-René de Brisay de Denonville, arrived in 1685 with 500 Troupes de la Marine, about half of what he thought he needed to subdue the Iroquois. Of the threats to New France, Denonville decided to tackle first the English posts on James Bay which, in the French view, were on lands claimed by France. In 1686 an overland expedition of 105 men led by Pierre de Troyes captured Moose Factory, Fort Rupert, and Fort Albany, and with them 50 000 prime beaver. The English recaptured Fort Albany in 1693, but would not regain their former position on Hudson Bay and James Bay until the Treaty of Utrecht in 1713. In the south Denonville with a French-native force of about 1 000 men burned the Seneca villages and their corn supplies in 1687. His men too ill and exhausted to proceed further, Denonville was forced to retreat. The Iroquois retaliated in 1689 with devastating raids by some 1 500 men on Lachine and other settlements near Montréal. The French, who lacked the forces to attack the Iroquois directly, responded in 1690 with mid-winter attacks on Schenectady and three frontier villages in New England. English retaliatory expeditions by land and sea were beaten back in 1690 and 1691. When a daring midwinter raid destroyed the Mohawk villages in 1693, New France was beginning to gain the upper hand. The following year long-awaited troops arrived from France, and in 1696 French troops and native allies destroyed the villages of the Onondaga and Oneida. In 1697 England concluded a separate peace with France. Reduced in strength from 2 600 to 1 200 men, abandoned by the English, and then attacked and pushed out of southern Ontario by the Ottawa and Ojibwa, the Iroquois finally came to Montréal in 1701 to ratify a treaty with the French and some 30 native groups; it guaranteed their neutrality in any future French-English conflict.

Retrenchment and Expansion, 1697–1739

The legalization of the French trade in the interior in 1681 and the elimination of English competition from James Bay in 1686 created a glut of beaver in Montréal. By 1696, with the Iroquois war effectively over and the interior relatively secure from Iroquois-English influence, French officials decided that the time had come to reduce military expenses and curtail the fur trade. A royal edict ordered all interior posts closed except Michilimackinac, Saint-Joseph, Fort Frontenac, and Fort Saint-Louis (pl 39), ended the *congé* system, and banned the trade in beaver. Native traders were again expected to travel to Montréal. Endorsed by the Jesuits, who had always condemned the effects of native contact with French traders, this policy was bitterly opposed by the merchants. About 200 coureurs de bois remained in the interior and, banned from the St Lawrence, many of them took their fur to the English.

By 1701 the French had established bases east of the mouth of the Mississippi (Mobile and Biloxi), founded Détroit, and garrisoned the remaining interior posts, the beginnings of a continental strategy to contain the English east of the Appalachians. Fur traders were allowed to operate out of Louisiana, missions were established on the upper Mississippi (Cahokia, 1699; Kaskaskia, 1703), and forts were built from the Gulf of Mexico to the Great Lakes. As it turned out the founding of Détroit was probably a mistake, as it encouraged the repopulation of the southern Great Lakes, territory easily influenced by the Iroquois and the English. The Wyandot and Ottawa moved to Détroit from Michilimackinac; a number of Ojibwa groups settled in southern Ontario, and by 1710 the Sauk, Fox, Kikapoo, Potawatomie, and Mascouten had returned to their original homeland in southeastern Michigan. Further west, the Miami moved to the Wabash River and the Illinois to the missions on the Mississippi. It did not take long for some of these groups to establish trading relations with the Iroquois and occasional contacts with English traders on the Ohio.

Between 1702 and 1713, with England and France again at war, the French tried to hold the Iroquois to their treaty of neutrality, distributed lavish yearly presents to native allies, and turned a blind eye to a good deal of illegal trade. The Détroit area was a tinder box, and in 1712 fighting broke out there between traditional enemies, the Fox-Mascouten and the Ottawa-Potawatomie. Fearing a plot by the Fox and Iroquois to drive them from Détroit, the French supported the Ottawa and Potawatomie and attacked the Fox. Suffering heavy losses, the Fox fled to the Green Bay area where they retaliated against native allies of the French such as the Illinois. A second French campaign against the Fox in 1716 brought a temporary peace.

The Treaty of Utrecht in 1713 ended more than a decade of war between France and Britain and introduced 30 years of peace between them. In the interior of North America France was forced to recognize British claims to the shores of Hudson Bay (pl 40). Northern and southern boundaries between New France and the British possessions were to be established by a joint commision. France was to recognize British 'dominion' over the Iroquois. In the interior the natives were to be free to trade with either nation. With the signing of this treaty, the French moved swiftly to restore trade along the vulnerable southern frontier and to garrison all posts there (pl 39). At the same time Michilimackinac was officially reopened. Aiding these endeavours was the recovery of the market for beaver; by 1714 the huge surplus was gone, consumed by vermin. With the Fox at peace and the southern frontier secure, the *congé* system was restored in 1716, and when the Lake Superior posts were reopened in 1717, New France had essentially returned to her pre-1697 position in the interior.

Most of the interior posts focused on Montréal, a few on New Orleans. Michilimackinac, a transshipment point by the 1670s, became a major entrepôt in the upper Great Lakes, and Détroit assumed this position in the lower Great Lakes (pl 41). Approximately equidistant from Montréal, both were strategically located about halfway to the western extremities of the Great Lakes. They served as interior headquarters for the Montréal traders, as transshipment points for trade goods and furs, and as major Jesuit missions. Détroit was also an important military base and was intended to supply agricultural products to the garrisons of the lower Great Lakes. Kaskaskia on the upper Mississippi was the equivalent entrepôt for the posts and trade dependent on New Orleans. Below the level of the entrepôt were district posts, all of them fortified and those on the southern frontier garrisoned. Dependent on the district posts were smaller posts that were opened and closed depending on native relations and market demands. Trade at all posts was authorized by the crown. In some cases monopolies were given to the highest bidder or to military commanders; in others trade operated through the *congé* system. Whatever the arrangement, holders of monopolies were expected to help bear the cost of constructing, operating, and defending posts, and to maintain native good will with costly presents. The fur trade was to pay for much of the French inland empire. The only exceptions were the king's posts around Lake Ontario and later in the Ohio valley, which were maintained for strategic reasons.

By the early 1720s native middlemen had all but disappeared from the French fur trade as native hunters took their furs to posts nearby. The middleman system, involving native collectors of fur and distributors of trade goods, still operated from the British posts on Hudson Bay. In the Ohio valley British traders came overland with pack-horses to prearranged meeting places where they would trade for a few days and then depart.

Although the French operated a considerable network of posts in the interior, their control of the fur trade was far from secure. Increasingly, itinerant British traders in the Ohio valley were in contact with the Delaware, Shawnee, Miami, and groups near Détroit. In 1725 the Iroquois allowed the British to build a fort at Oswego, their first on the Great Lakes. From Oswego the British traded directly with the Mississauga in southern Ontario. The Chickasaw, instigated, the French were sure, by British merchants in Carolina, raided the French and their native allies in the Wabash-Illinois area. The Fox again disrupted trade and exploration west of Lake Michigan.

These problems awaited the new governor of New France, Charles Beauharnois de La Boische, in 1726. Under Beauharnois goods at the posts on Lake Ontario were sold at a loss if necessary and a limited brandy trade was permitted in an effort to deter the Mississauga and others from trading at Oswego, where rum was cheaply available. In 1728 an army of 1 600 French troops, Canadian militia, and native allies burned the Fox villages. Other expeditions had to be sent in 1730, 1731, and 1734 before the Fox ceased raiding. In the northwest Beauharnois encouraged Pierre-Gaultier de La Vérendrye's efforts, begun in 1731, to find a route to the western sea, thought to be somewhere in the western interior of Canada (pl 36). By 1739 La Vérendrye had built posts on the Assiniboine River, visited the Mandan on the Missouri, and established Fort Bourbon on the northwest shore of Lake Winnipeg. The Montréal fur trade had penetrated the hinterland of York Factory, the principal Hudson's Bay Company post in the western corner of Hudson Bay. It also penetrated Cree-Assiniboine territory west of Lake Superior and involved the French in warfare between these peoples and their traditional enemies, the Ojibwa and the Dakota. La Vérendrye managed to secure a peace between the Cree and Ojibwa in 1736, but not with the Dakota. Just as the Fox wars ended, the Dakota wars began, and in 1737 the interior posts dependent on Green Bay had to be abandoned. The Chickasaw raids were regarded as a problem for Louisiana, but after an ineffective attempt to deal with the Chickasaw from Louisiana Beauharnois was forced to send troops in 1739. This venture, the first major French expedition down the Ohio River, led to a uneasy truce with the Chickasaw in 1740.

France Secures the Interior, 1740–1755

In 1743 the long peace between France and Britain came to an end in the War of the Austrian Succession (King George's War). New France did not have the troops for extensive campaigns; instead native groups settled along the St Lawrence, especially the Abenaki, occasionally aided by Canadian militia, raided English settlements from Albany to Boston (pl 40). In 1744 British warships began to blockade the Gulf of St Lawrence; few supplies reached New France, trade goods were scarce and expensive, and the lavish presents to native allies had to be stopped. By 1747 the French feared a general uprising in the west. The Mohawk had broken the peace the previous year. Some Huron, who had moved from Détroit to Sandusky, were beginning to attack French traders. The Miami and other groups in the lower Great Lakes were incited by British traders to attack French posts, and destroyed Fort des Miamis in 1747.

When the war between Britain and France ended in 1748, French trade and French-native alliances were quickly restored except in the Ohio country. In 1749 the commandant of the rebuilt Fort des Miamis estimated that 300 English traders were in the area, flooding the lower Great Lakes with cheap trade goods. Moreover, in 1748 the British crown had given title to half a million acres in the Ohio valley to the Ohio Company, a group of London merchants and prominent Virginian plantation owners. France had to respond to these initiatives, and in 1749 Roland-Michel Barrin de La Galissonière sent a force of 230 men to stake claim to the Ohio valley, re-establish French-native alliances there, and eject British traders. The effect of the expedition was slight; in 1751 the Miami, declaring open support for the English, destroyed Fort Vincennes.

In 1752 La Galissonière was succeeded by Ange de Menneville, marquis de Duquesne, whose instructions were to let the natives trade with the British if they wished, but to drive British traders from the Ohio valley. Charles-Michel Mouet de Langlande, an officer–fur trader with broad influence among the Indians, was sent with 300 Ottawa, Saulteaux, and French to raid the Miami village of Pickawillany. The English post there was destroyed, the Miami chief La Demoiselle (Memeskia) killed, and the British traders ejected. British influence in the area declined. Duquesne followed the attack on Pickawillany by sending 2 000 troops into the Ohio country where, over the remonstrances of the Iroquois, Shawnee, and Delaware, four forts were built between Lake Erie and the junction of the Ohio and Monongahela Rivers in 1753 and 1754. British objections, delivered by George Washington in 1753, were politely rejected. The following year Washington returned and, although France and Britain were at peace, attacked a small French detachment. The French struck back, forcing his surrender at Fort Necessity and ending for the time being the British presence in the Ohio valley. Farther west, French traders negotiated a peace between the Ojibwa and eastern Dakota in 1750, and between the

Cree and eastern Dakota in 1752. Now under peaceful conditions the French fur trade expanded vigorously into the headwaters of the Mississippi. In the northwest posts were built at least as far west as the forks of the Saskatchewan River. French claims to the lands north of Lake Superior were enforced with the construction of Fort-à-la-Carpe (1751) on the Albany River and the destruction by natives allied to the French of Henley House (1755), a Hudson's Bay Company outpost, also on the Albany.

By 1755 France had virtually succeeded in excluding British traders from the continental interior west of Montréal. The southern frontier was secured by garrisoned forts from Montréal through Lake Ontario to Fort Duquesne on the Ohio (pl 40). The southwestern area was anchored by a string of forts between growing agricultural colonies at Détroit and Kaskaskia. Native relations along the entire southern frontier were stabilized by troops, gift giving, and trade. Although the area produced mainly hides, which were often traded at a loss, its strategic value warranted the cost of securing it. The central Great Lakes basin was anchored by the entrepôt at Michilimackinac (pl 41) and the loyalty of the Ottawa and Ojibwa. Along the northern frontier French posts were established on or near the headwaters of all the major rivers flowing into Hudson Bay. There, where most of the valuable fur was obtained, competition with the Hudson's Bay Company was keen. As in the south the French relaxed strictures against the sale of brandy to meet British competition.

Native Territory and the Seven Years' War

None of the meetings of the joint commission struck after the Treaty of Utrecht to settle the boundaries between New France and the British possessions in North America had produced any results, and neither side recognized the claims of the other. In fact, as late as 1755 the central interior of the continent was still native territory. Perhaps 3 000 French people lived there among some 50 000 natives. Of the two European powers that laid claim to the area, France was more ready than Britain to accept this reality. With a small French-speaking population along the lower St Lawrence, France made no attempt to displace natives by settlement; the French claim to land outside the St Lawrence colony was a claim against British interference in the fur trade. Official French involvement in native affairs was generally limited to securing native alliances, protecting trade (by force of arms, if necessary), and, at times, fomenting intertribal warfare. Except perhaps in the missions near Montréal and Québec, the French no longer tried to remake native cultures in French moulds; converts to Christianity were sought far more passively than in the years of the Huron and Onondaga missions. Native groups were regarded as independent; they were neither French subjects nor bound by French law.

Native cultures had changed, but not primarily because natives had been drawn to European values (to which, the evidence suggests, there was general native aversion) or because they had become reliant on European goods. Such goods often made life easier but did not soon destroy the skills required to make their traditional equivalents. Of the European goods offered for trade, natives quickly became dependent only on muskets, powder, and shot - to ward off native enemies so armed. Natives acquired European goods by expanding their production of furs within traditional strategies of resource procurement. The mixing of different native peoples as a result of warfare probably induced more cultural change than did contact with Europeans and European goods. War displaced populations, reduced numbers, forced people to adjust to different environments, and mingled cultures. At the root of most of the native wars were pre-European rivalries that were aggravated as the two European powers joined different alliances and, sooner or later, supplied them with firearms.

Native control of the land around the southern Great Lakes was finally relinquished after the Seven Years' War (pl 42). During the early years of this war the initiative lay with the French and their native allies, but in 1758 the fortunes of war began to turn. Under their new prime minister, William Pitt, the British resolved to end once and for all French rule in North America with a force of unprecedented magnitude. In a surprise attack British troops burned Fort Frontenac, and with it ships and supplies destined for the Ohio forts. At the same time a British army invaded the Ohio country. The key to the French hold on the Lake Ontario–Ohio frontier lay with their native allies. At a conference held at Easton, Pennsylvania, in October 1758 Pennsylvania authorities promised the Ohio natives that they would renounce all claims on Indian land west of the Appalachians. Their major war aim achieved, these groups stopped fighting, forcing the French to relinquish the Ohio country.

British plans for 1759 involved a three-pronged attack: a naval assault on Québec up the St Lawrence, an army to advance up the Lake Champlain corridor, and a second army to Lake Ontario and down the St Lawrence to Montréal (pl 42). Vastly outnumbered, and without significant native support, the Lake Ontario garrisons fell to the British. In the Lake Champlain area French forces abandoned Crown Point and Ticonderoga and retired to Fort Île aux Noix. When Québec fell to General James Wolfe's army in September 1759 (pl 43), the end was in sight. Caught between Jeffery Amherst's army coming from Lake Ontario, James Murray moving up from Québec, and William Haviland by way of the Richelieu, Governor Pierre de Rigaud de Vaudreuil was forced to surrender at Montréal in September 1760.

In the terms of capitulation Vaudreuil inserted a clause, agreed to by General Amherst, that France's native allies would not suffer for having borne arms and would maintain their lands unmolested. These terms were ignored, and English-speaking settlers flooded into the Ohio valley. In 1763 native groups led by Pontiac, an Ottawa war chief, and others launched a series of attacks (pl 44) to safeguard their remaining lands. Lacking the logistical support and the direction previously given by the French, they were crushed by the British army after a few campaigns. The Ohio valley was now open for European settlement.

THE ST LAWRENCE VALLEY, 16th CENTURY

Author: B.G. Trigger

European penetration of the St Lawrence valley during the 16th century affected native peoples as far west as the lower Great Lakes. Early in the century groups of St Lawrence Iroquoians were settled along the St Lawrence River: the Stadaconans around Québec and the Hochelagans at Montréal. The Iroquoian-speaking Huron, Neutral, and Iroquois lived near Lake Ontario.

In 1535 Cartier explored the St Lawrence River to Hochelaga while searching for gold and a route to the Pacific Ocean. He and his crew spent the following winter near Stadacona. Lured by tales of precious minerals and gems in the interior (perhaps references to native copper around Lake Superior), in 1541 Cartier and his vice-regal superior, La Rocque de Roberval, founded a substantial French settlement at Cap Rouge, a few miles west of Stadacona. They faced severe winters and hostile natives (in 1536 Cartier had kidnapped several Stadaconans including their chief, Donnacona), but found no precious metals, and abandoned the settlement in 1543. For almost forty years thereafter the Stadaconans prevented Europeans from travelling upriver beyond Tadoussac.

Nevertheless, increasing numbers of European whalers and fishermen traded for furs with the Indians around the Gulf of St Lawrence. Some annual trade apparently began at Tadoussac as early as 1550, and after 1580 ships came to the St Lawrence River especially to trade for furs. In particular, the Indians sought iron axes, knives, arrowheads, and other cutting tools. European goods travelled up the St Lawrence as far as Hochelaga, but, as long as the Hochelagans were there, apparently not farther inland by this route.

STADACONAN VILLAGES AND FRENCH SETTLEMENTS

ROYAUME DE CANADA

Starnatam

Ajoaste

Tailla

Sitadin

Cartier, Winter 1535–6

Stadacona

Tequenonday

Achelacy/ Hagouchonda

ST LAWRENCE

Charlesbourg-Royal, 1541–2 France-Roy, 1542–3

● Indian village

● French settlement

0 20 miles

0 20 kilometres

Scale 1:1 000 000

TRADE PATTERNS AND WARFARE, ca 1530

MONTAGNAIS

TOUDAMAN (MICMAC)

STADACONANS

See enlargement.

ALGONQUIN

ST LAWRENCE IROQUOIAN

HOCHELAGANS

See enlargement

HURON

NEUTRAL

NEUTRAL

ERIE

ERIE

WENRO

ONEIDA

MOHAWK

ONONDAGA

CAYUGA

SENECA

IROQUOIS

Iroquoian peoples, 1530–1600

- St Lawrence Iroquoian group
- Huron group
- Neutral group
- Erie group
- Iroquois group

Flow of goods

- Stadaconan fishing/ trading expeditions
- Native copper from Lake Superior
- Marine shells
- Huron-Algonquian trade
- Algonquin trade/travel routes
- Regular penetration of European goods
- Sporadic penetration of European goods

Warfare

- Inferred from archaeological sources
- Inferred from historical sources
- Forced population movement

European settlements

- ○ Summer trading station
- ● Trading post
- □ Basque whaling station

0 200 miles

0 200 kilometres

Scale 1:7 500 000

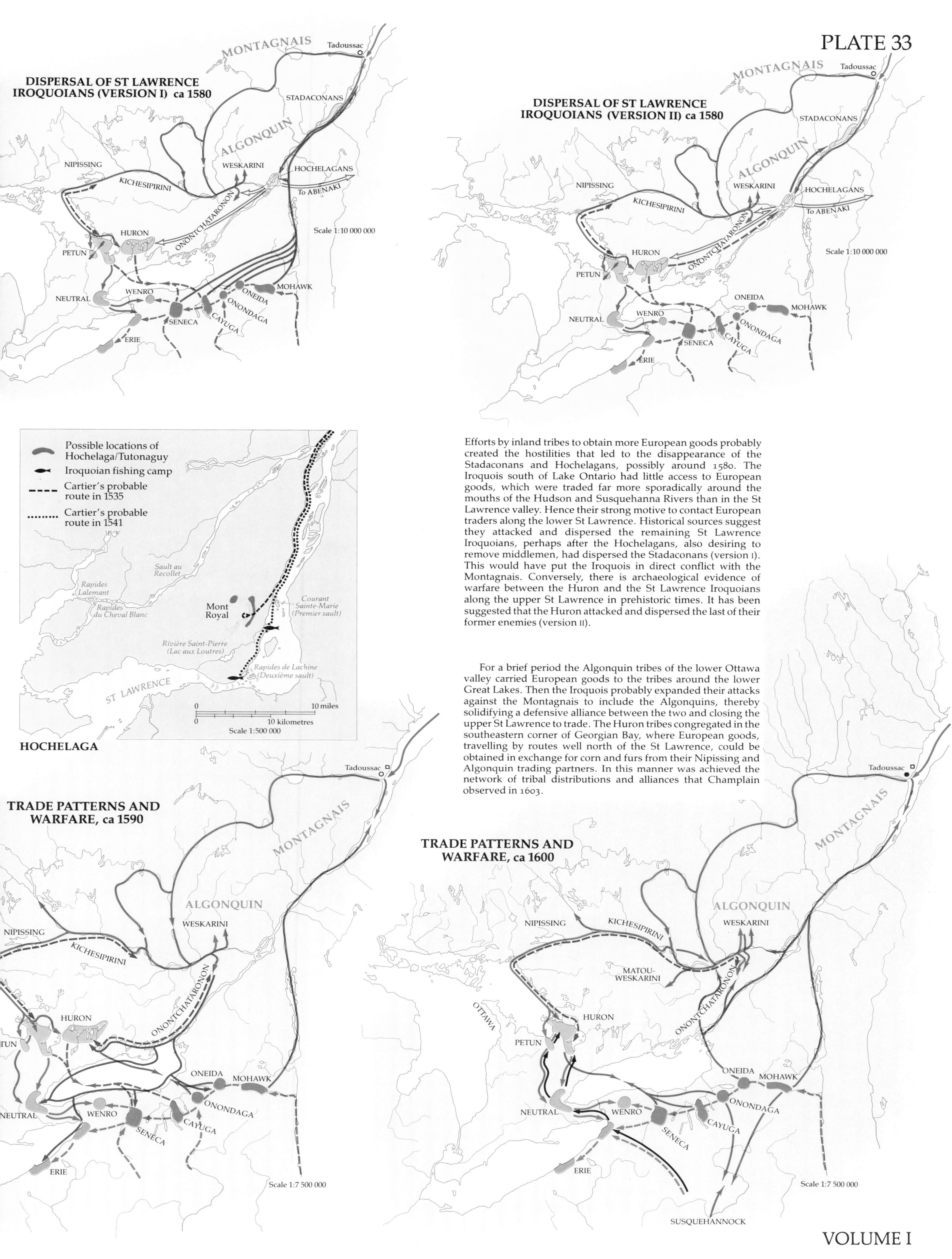
DISPERSAL OF ST LAWRENCE IROQUOIANS (VERSION I) ca 1580
MONTAGNAIS
Tadoussac
STADACONANS
ALGONQUIN
NIPISSING
WESKARINI
HOCHELAGANS
KICHESIPIRINI
To ABENAKI
ONONTCHATARONON
HURON
PETUN
Scale 1:10 000 000
NEUTRAL
WENRO
MOHAWK
ONEIDA
ONONDAGA
SENECA
CAYUGA
ERIE
DISPERSAL OF ST LAWRENCE IROQUOIANS (VERSION II) ca 1580
Possible locations of Hochelaga/Tutonaguy
Iroquoian fishing camp
Cartier's probable route in 1535
Cartier's probable route in 1541
Sault au Recollet
Rapides Lalemant
Rapides du Cheval Blanc
Mont Royal
Courant Sainte-Marie (Premier sault)
Rivière Saint-Pierre (Lac aux Loutres)
Rapides de Lachine (Deuxième sault)
ST LAWRENCE
0
10 miles
0
10 kilometres
Scale 1:500 000
HOCHELAGA
TRADE PATTERNS AND WARFARE, ca 1590
Scale 1:7 500 000
TRADE PATTERNS AND WARFARE, ca 1600
MATOU-WESKARINI
OTTAWA
SUSQUEHANNOCK

Efforts by inland tribes to obtain more European goods probably created the hostilities that led to the disappearance of the Stadaconans and Hochelagans, possibly around 1580. The Iroquois south of Lake Ontario had little access to European goods, which were traded far more sporadically around the mouths of the Hudson and Susquehanna Rivers than in the St Lawrence valley. Hence their strong motive to contact European traders along the lower St Lawrence. Historical sources suggest they attacked and dispersed the remaining St Lawrence Iroquoians, perhaps after the Hochelagans, also desiring to remove middlemen, had dispersed the Stadaconans (version I). This would have put the Iroquois in direct conflict with the Montagnais. Conversely, there is archaeological evidence of warfare between the Huron and the St Lawrence Iroquoians along the upper St Lawrence in prehistoric times. It has been suggested that the Huron attacked and dispersed the last of their former enemies (version II).

For a brief period the Algonquin tribes of the lower Ottawa valley carried European goods to the tribes around the lower Great Lakes. Then the Iroquois probably expanded their attacks against the Montagnais to include the Algonquins, thereby solidifying a defensive alliance between the two and closing the upper St Lawrence to trade. The Huron tribes congregated in the southeastern corner of Georgian Bay, where European goods, travelling by routes well north of the St Lawrence, could be obtained in exchange for corn and furs from their Nipissing and Algonquin trading partners. In this manner was achieved the network of tribal distributions and alliances that Champlain observed in 1603.

SETTLEMENTS AND MISSIONARIES, 1615–1650

Author: Conrad E. Heidenreich

Of the Iroquoian-speaking agricultural peoples in southern Ontario at the beginning of the 17th century (pl 33), the Huron became most involved with contemporary Europeans and are best known to us today. Before the epidemics (pl 35) there were perhaps 20 000 Huron. They lived in 18–25 villages scattered across about 900 km^2 between Lake Simcoe and the southeastern corner of Georgian Bay, an average population density of 23 people per square kilometre. Their villages, located close to springs and to light soils suitable for corn, were connected by trails. The larger villages were surrounded by strong, wide palisades composed of rows of posts up to 30 cm in diameter and sheathed with heavy bark. The other Iroquoian speakers in southern Ontario – the Petun just west of the Huron and the Neutral at the western end of Lake Ontario – lived in similar settlements.

Cahiagué was the principal village of the Arendaronon, one of the Huron tribes, during Champlain's time. It was made up of two parts which, according to Champlain, had 200 longhouses. Houses were occupied by maternal extended families and varied in length with the number of nuclear families. Some were almost 60 m long. Each house had a series of central hearths, one for every two nuclear families.

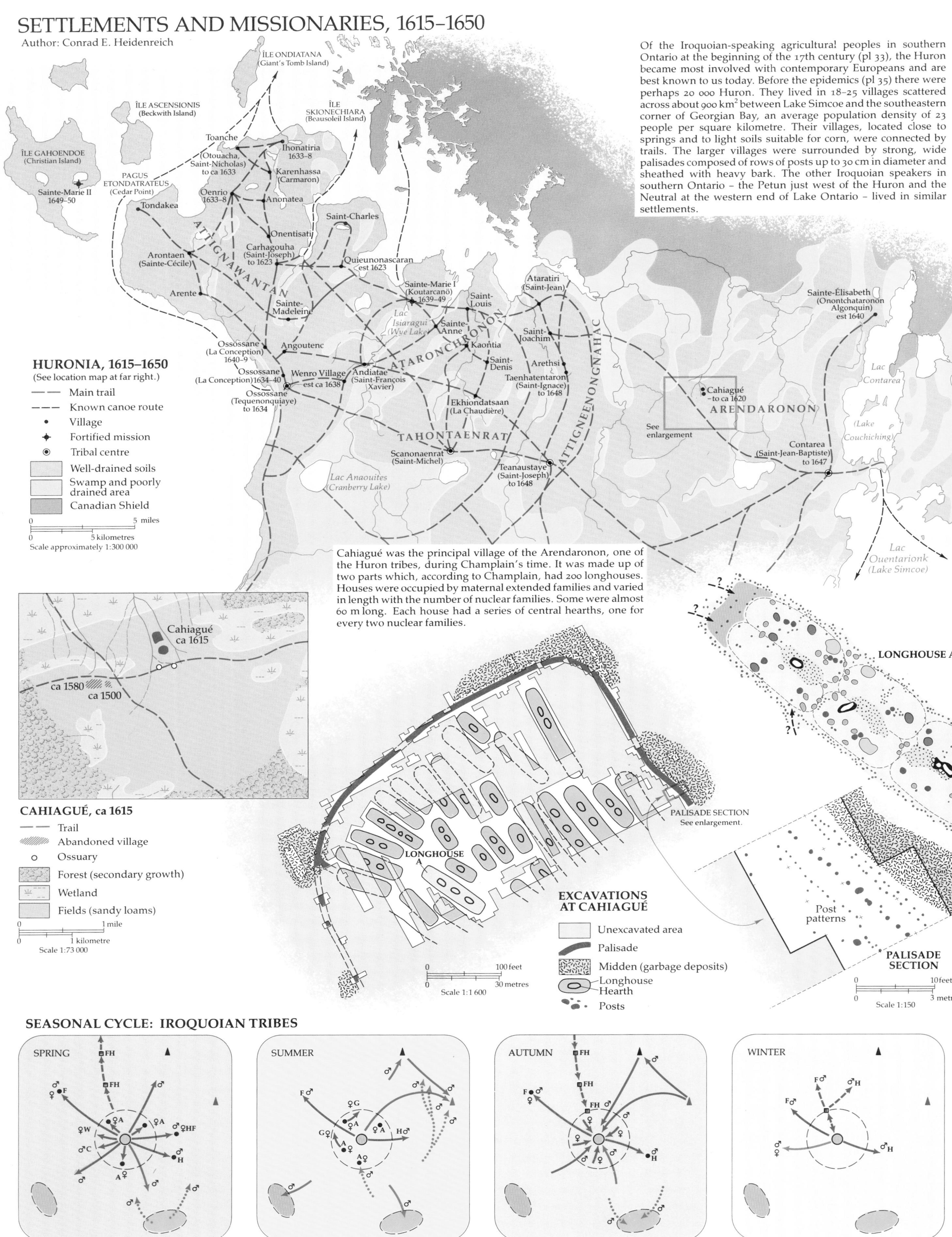

HURONIA, 1615–1650
(See location map at far right.)
Main trail
Known canoe route
Village
Fortified mission
Tribal centre
Well-drained soils
Swamp and poorly drained area
Canadian Shield
0 5 miles
0 5 kilometres
Scale approximately 1:300 000
ÎLE ONDIATANA (Giant's Tomb Island)
ÎLE ASCENSIONIS (Beckwith Island)
ÎLE SKIONECHIARA (Beausoleil Island)
ÎLE GAHOENDOE (Christian Island)
Sainte-Marie II 1649–50
PAGUS ETONDATRATEUS (Cedar Point)
Toanche (Otouacha, Saint-Nicholas) to ca 1633
Ihonatiria 1633–8
Karenhassa (Carmaron)
Oenrio 1633–8
Anonatea
Tondakea
ATTIGNAWANTAN
Saint-Charles
Onentisati
Carhagouha (Saint-Joseph) to 1623
Quieunonascaran est 1623
Arontaen (Sainte-Cécile)
Arente
Sainte-Madeleine
Sainte-Marie I (Koutarcanó) 1639–49
Lac Isiaragui (Wye Lake)
Saint-Louis
Ataratiri (Saint-Jean)
Sainte-Anne
ATARONCHRONON
Saint-Joachim
Kaontia
Ossossane (La Conception) 1640–9
Angoutenc
Saint-Denis
Arethsi
Ossossane (La Conception) 1634–40
Wenro Village est ca 1638
Andiatae (Saint-François Xavier)
Taenhatentaron (Saint-Ignace) to 1648
Ossossane (Tequenonquiaye) to 1634
Ekhiondatsaan (La Chaudière)
ATTIGNEENONGNAHAC
TAHONTAENRAT
Scanonaenrat (Saint-Michel)
Teanaustaye (Saint-Joseph) to 1648
Lac Anaouites (Cranberry Lake)
Sainte-Élisabeth (Onontchataronon Algonquin) est 1640
Cahiagué – to ca 1620
ARENDARONON
See enlargement
Lac Contarea
(Lake Couchiching)
Contarea (Saint-Jean-Baptiste) to 1647
Lac Ouentarionk (Lake Simcoe)
Cahiagué ca 1615
ca 1580
ca 1500
CAHIAGUÉ, ca 1615
Trail
Abandoned village
Ossuary
Forest (secondary growth)
Wetland
Fields (sandy loams)
0 1 mile
0 1 kilometre
Scale 1:73 000
LONGHOUSE A
PALISADE SECTION See enlargement.
EXCAVATIONS AT CAHIAGUÉ
Unexcavated area
Palisade
Midden (garbage deposits)
Longhouse
Hearth
Posts
0 100 feet
0 30 metres
Scale 1:1 600
Post patterns
PALISADE SECTION
0 10 feet
0 3 metres
Scale 1:150
SEASONAL CYCLE: IROQUOIAN TRIBES
SPRING
SUMMER
AUTUMN
WINTER

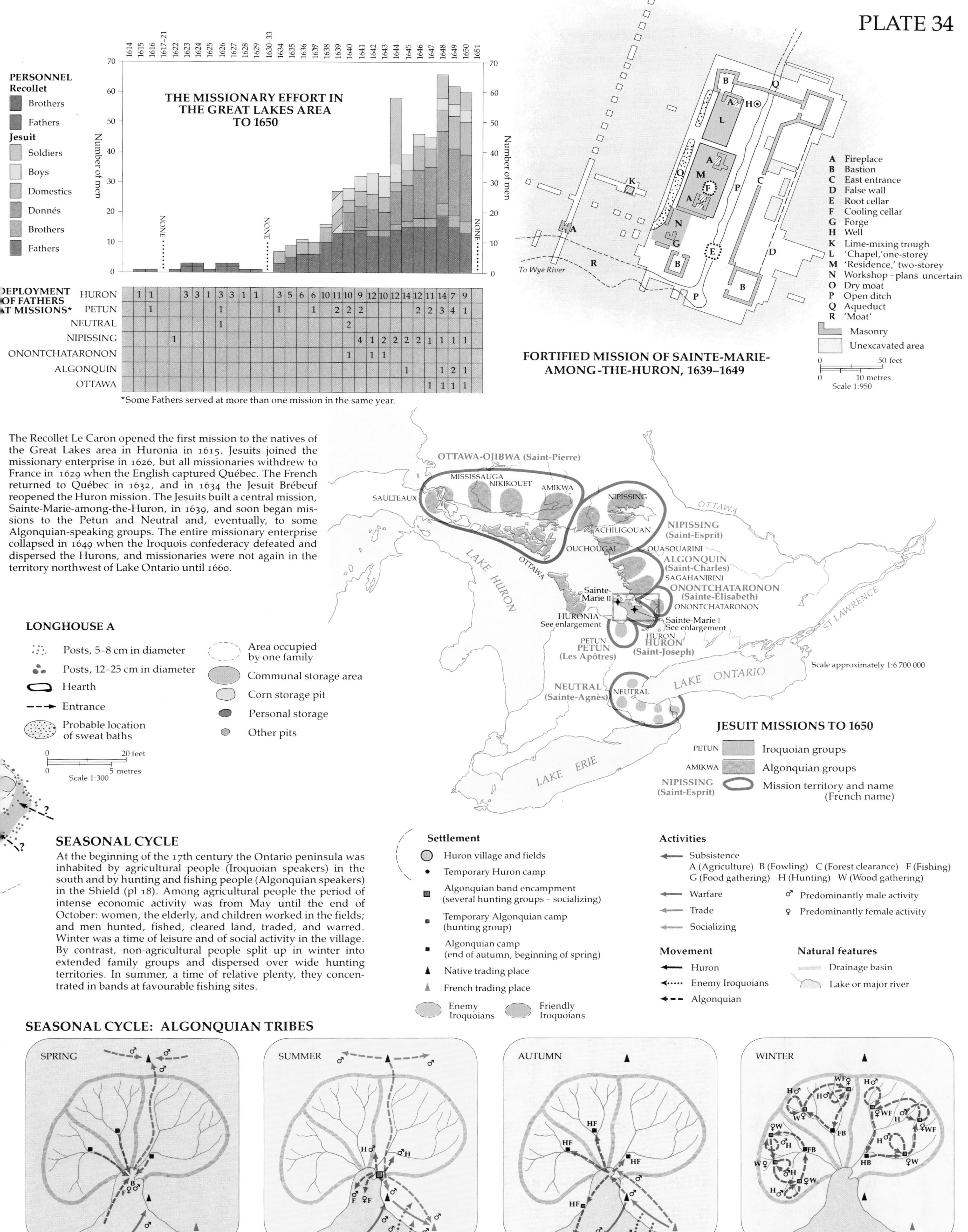
THE MISSIONARY EFFORT IN THE GREAT LAKES AREA TO 1650
PERSONNEL
Recollet
Brothers
Fathers
Jesuit
Soldiers
Boys
Domestics
Donnés
Brothers
Fathers
Number of men
NONE
FORTIFIED MISSION OF SAINTE-MARIE-AMONG-THE-HURON, 1639–1649
A Fireplace
B Bastion
C East entrance
D False wall
E Root cellar
F Cooling cellar
G Forge
H Well
K Lime-mixing trough
L 'Chapel,' one-storey
M 'Residence,' two-storey
N Workshop - plans uncertain
O Dry moat
P Open ditch
Q Aqueduct
R 'Moat'
Masonry
Unexcavated area
To Wye River
Scale 1:950
OTTAWA-OJIBWA (Saint-Pierre)
MISSISSAUGA
NIKIKOUET
AMIKWA
SAULTEAUX
NIPISSING
ACHILIGOUAN
OUCHOUGAI
NIPISSING (Saint-Esprit)
OUASOUARINI
ALGONQUIN (Saint-Charles)
SAGAHANIRINI
ONONTCHATARONON (Sainte-Élisabeth)
ONONTCHATARONON
Sainte-Marie II
HURONIA See enlargement
Sainte-Marie I See enlargement
PETUN
PETUN (Les Apôtres)
HURON
HURON (Saint-Joseph)
NEUTRAL (Sainte-Agnès)
NEUTRAL
LAKE HURON
LAKE ONTARIO
LAKE ERIE
OTTAWA
ST LAWRENCE
Scale approximately 1:6 700 000
JESUIT MISSIONS TO 1650
Iroquoian groups
Algonquian groups
Mission territory and name (French name)
LONGHOUSE A
Posts, 5–8 cm in diameter
Posts, 12–25 cm in diameter
Hearth
Entrance
Probable location of sweat baths
Area occupied by one family
Communal storage area
Corn storage pit
Personal storage
Other pits
Scale 1:300
Settlement
Huron village and fields
Temporary Huron camp
Algonquian band encampment (several hunting groups - socializing)
Temporary Algonquian camp (hunting group)
Algonquian camp (end of autumn, beginning of spring)
Native trading place
French trading place
Enemy Iroquoians
Friendly Iroquoians
Activities
Subsistence
A (Agriculture) B (Fowling) C (Forest clearance) F (Fishing) G (Food gathering) H (Hunting) W (Wood gathering)
Warfare
Trade
Socializing
Predominantly male activity
Predominantly female activity
Movement
Huron
Enemy Iroquoians
Algonquian
Natural features
Drainage basin
Lake or major river
SEASONAL CYCLE: ALGONQUIAN TRIBES
SPRING
SUMMER
AUTUMN
WINTER
From Huron
To Huron

DEPLOYMENT OF FATHERS AT MISSIONS*

	1614	1615	1616	1617–21	1622	1623	1624	1625	1626	1627	1628	1629	1630–33	1634	1635	1636	1637	1638	1639	1640	1641	1642	1643	1644	1645	1646	1647	1648	1649	1650	1651
HURON		1	1			3	3	1	3	3	1	1		3	5	6	6	10	11	10	9	12	10	12	14	12	11	14	7	9	
PETUN			1						1					1			1		2	2	2					2	2	3	4	1	
NEUTRAL									1											2											
NIPISSING					1																4	1	2	2	2	2	1	1	1	1	
ONONTCHATARONON																				1		1	1								
ALGONQUIN																									1			1	2	1	
OTTAWA																											1	1	1	1	

*Some Fathers served at more than one mission in the same year.

The Recollet Le Caron opened the first mission to the natives of the Great Lakes area in Huronia in 1615. Jesuits joined the missionary enterprise in 1626, but all missionaries withdrew to France in 1629 when the English captured Québec. The French returned to Québec in 1632, and in 1634 the Jesuit Brébeuf reopened the Huron mission. The Jesuits built a central mission, Sainte-Marie-among-the-Huron, in 1639, and soon began missions to the Petun and Neutral and, eventually, to some Algonquian-speaking groups. The entire missionary enterprise collapsed in 1649 when the Iroquois confederacy defeated and dispersed the Hurons, and missionaries were not again in the territory northwest of Lake Ontario until 1660.

SEASONAL CYCLE

At the beginning of the 17th century the Ontario peninsula was inhabited by agricultural people (Iroquoian speakers) in the south and by hunting and fishing people (Algonquian speakers) in the Shield (pl 18). Among agricultural people the period of intense economic activity was from May until the end of October: women, the elderly, and children worked in the fields; and men hunted, fished, cleared land, traded, and warred. Winter was a time of leisure and of social activity in the village. By contrast, non-agricultural people split up in winter into extended family groups and dispersed over wide hunting territories. In summer, a time of relative plenty, they concentrated in bands at favourable fishing sites.

THE GREAT LAKES BASIN, 1600–1653

Author: Conrad E. Heidenreich

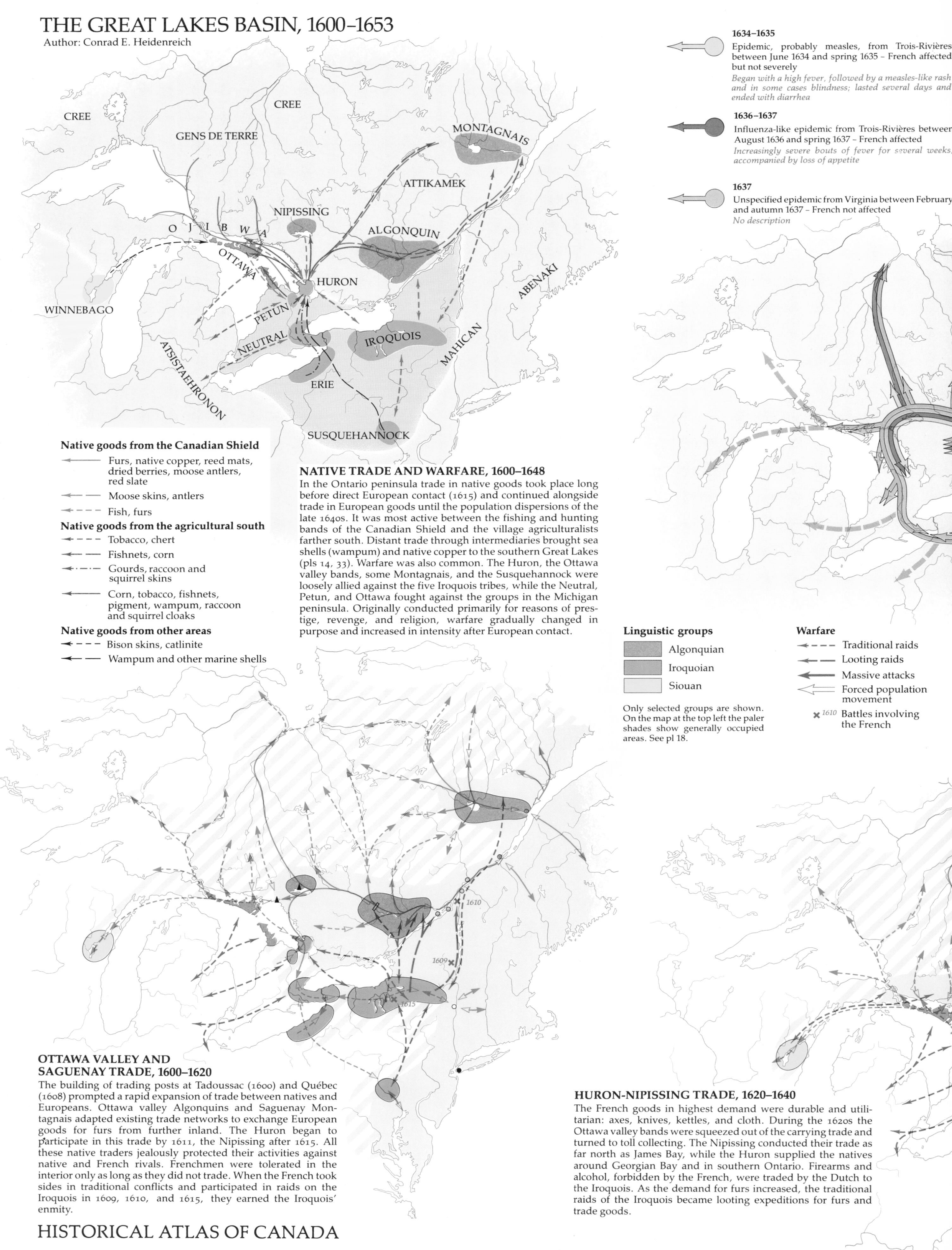
CREE
CREE
GENS DE TERRE
MONTAGNAIS
ATTIKAMEK
NIPISSING
OJIBWA
ALGONQUIN
OTTAWA
HURON
ABENAKI
WINNEBAGO
PETUN
NEUTRAL
IROQUOIS
MAHICAN
ATSISTAEHRONON
ERIE
SUSQUEHANNOCK
Native goods from the Canadian Shield
Furs, native copper, reed mats, dried berries, moose antlers, red slate
Moose skins, antlers
Fish, furs
Native goods from the agricultural south
Tobacco, chert
Fishnets, corn
Gourds, raccoon and squirrel skins
Corn, tobacco, fishnets, pigment, wampum, raccoon and squirrel cloaks
Native goods from other areas
Bison skins, catlinite
Wampum and other marine shells
1634–1635
Epidemic, probably measles, from Trois-Rivières between June 1634 and spring 1635 – French affected but not severely
Began with a high fever, followed by a measles-like rash and in some cases blindness; lasted several days and ended with diarrhea
1636–1637
Influenza-like epidemic from Trois-Rivières between August 1636 and spring 1637 – French affected
Increasingly severe bouts of fever for several weeks, accompanied by loss of appetite
1637
Unspecified epidemic from Virginia between February and autumn 1637 – French not affected
No description
Linguistic groups
Algonquian
Iroquoian
Siouan
Only selected groups are shown. On the map at the top left the paler shades show generally occupied areas. See pl 18.
Warfare
Traditional raids
Looting raids
Massive attacks
Forced population movement
1610 Battles involving the French
1610
1609
1615

NATIVE TRADE AND WARFARE, 1600–1648

In the Ontario peninsula trade in native goods took place long before direct European contact (1615) and continued alongside trade in European goods until the population dispersions of the late 1640s. It was most active between the fishing and hunting bands of the Canadian Shield and the village agriculturalists farther south. Distant trade through intermediaries brought sea shells (wampum) and native copper to the southern Great Lakes (pls 14, 33). Warfare was also common. The Huron, the Ottawa valley bands, some Montagnais, and the Susquehannock were loosely allied against the five Iroquois tribes, while the Neutral, Petun, and Ottawa fought against the groups in the Michigan peninsula. Originally conducted primarily for reasons of prestige, revenge, and religion, warfare gradually changed in purpose and increased in intensity after European contact.

OTTAWA VALLEY AND SAGUENAY TRADE, 1600–1620

The building of trading posts at Tadoussac (1600) and Québec (1608) prompted a rapid expansion of trade between natives and Europeans. Ottawa valley Algonquins and Saguenay Montagnais adapted existing trade networks to exchange European goods for furs from further inland. The Huron began to participate in this trade by 1611, the Nipissing after 1615. All these native traders jealously protected their activities against native and French rivals. Frenchmen were tolerated in the interior only as long as they did not trade. When the French took sides in traditional conflicts and participated in raids on the Iroquois in 1609, 1610, and 1615, they earned the Iroquois' enmity.

HURON-NIPISSING TRADE, 1620–1640

The French goods in highest demand were durable and utilitarian: axes, knives, kettles, and cloth. During the 1620s the Ottawa valley bands were squeezed out of the carrying trade and turned to toll collecting. The Nipissing conducted their trade as far north as James Bay, while the Huron supplied the natives around Georgian Bay and in southern Ontario. Firearms and alcohol, forbidden by the French, were traded by the Dutch to the Iroquois. As the demand for furs increased, the traditional raids of the Iroquois became looting expeditions for furs and trade goods.

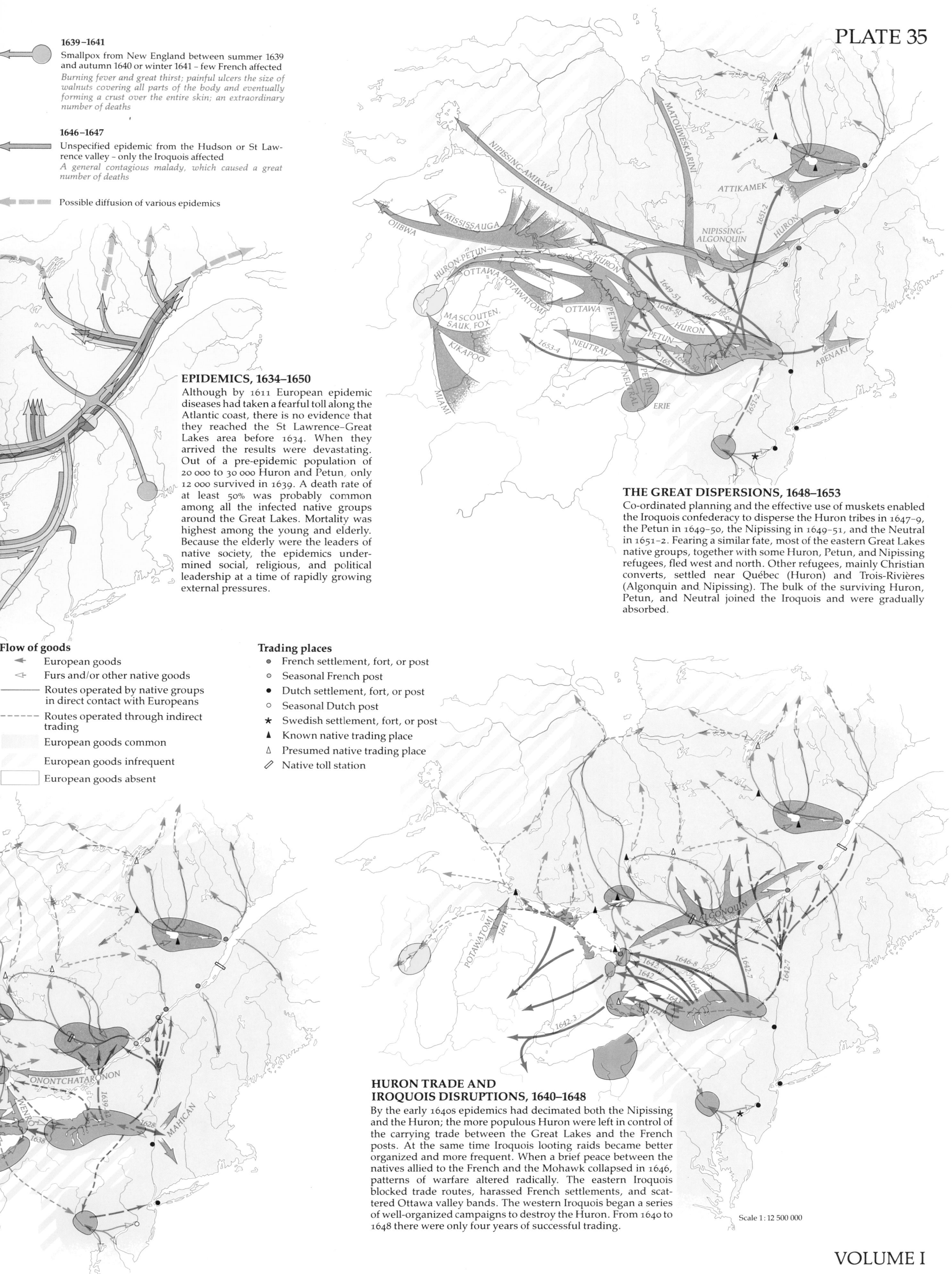
1639–1641
Smallpox from New England between summer 1639 and autumn 1640 or winter 1641 – few French affected
Burning fever and great thirst; painful ulcers the size of walnuts covering all parts of the body and eventually forming a crust over the entire skin; an extraordinary number of deaths
1646–1647
Unspecified epidemic from the Hudson or St Lawrence valley – only the Iroquois affected
A general contagious malady, which caused a great number of deaths
Possible diffusion of various epidemics
MATOUWESKARINI
NIPISSING-AMIKWA
ATTIKAMEK
MISSISSAUGA
OJIBWA
NIPISSING-ALGONQUIN
HURON
HURON-PETUN
OTTAWA
POTAWATOMI
MASCOUTEN, SAUK, FOX
KIKAPOO
MIAMI
NEUTRAL
PETUN
ERIE
ABENAKI
1651-2
1649-51
1648-50
1649
1653-4
1651
Flow of goods
European goods
Furs and/or other native goods
Routes operated by native groups in direct contact with Europeans
Routes operated through indirect trading
European goods common
European goods infrequent
European goods absent
Trading places
French settlement, fort, or post
Seasonal French post
Dutch settlement, fort, or post
Seasonal Dutch post
Swedish settlement, fort, or post
Known native trading place
Presumed native trading place
Native toll station
ONONTCHATARONON
WENRO
MAHICAN
1639-42
1628
1638
ALGONQUIN
POTAWATOMI
1641
1646-8
1642
1645
1643
1647
1642-3
1642-7
Scale 1 : 12 500 000

EPIDEMICS, 1634–1650

Although by 1611 European epidemic diseases had taken a fearful toll along the Atlantic coast, there is no evidence that they reached the St Lawrence–Great Lakes area before 1634. When they arrived the results were devastating. Out of a pre-epidemic population of 20 000 to 30 000 Huron and Petun, only 12 000 survived in 1639. A death rate of at least 50% was probably common among all the infected native groups around the Great Lakes. Mortality was highest among the young and elderly. Because the elderly were the leaders of native society, the epidemics undermined social, religious, and political leadership at a time of rapidly growing external pressures.

THE GREAT DISPERSIONS, 1648–1653

Co-ordinated planning and the effective use of muskets enabled the Iroquois confederacy to disperse the Huron tribes in 1647–9, the Petun in 1649–50, the Nipissing in 1649–51, and the Neutral in 1651–2. Fearing a similar fate, most of the eastern Great Lakes native groups, together with some Huron, Petun, and Nipissing refugees, fled west and north. Other refugees, mainly Christian converts, settled near Québec (Huron) and Trois-Rivières (Algonquin and Nipissing). The bulk of the surviving Huron, Petun, and Neutral joined the Iroquois and were gradually absorbed.

HURON TRADE AND IROQUOIS DISRUPTIONS, 1640–1648

By the early 1640s epidemics had decimated both the Nipissing and the Huron; the more populous Huron were left in control of the carrying trade between the Great Lakes and the French posts. At the same time Iroquois looting raids became better organized and more frequent. When a brief peace between the natives allied to the French and the Mohawk collapsed in 1646, patterns of warfare altered radically. The eastern Iroquois blocked trade routes, harassed French settlements, and scattered Ottawa valley bands. The western Iroquois began a series of well-organized campaigns to destroy the Huron. From 1640 to 1648 there were only four years of successful trading.

FRENCH EXPLORATION

Authors: Richard I. Ruggles, Conrad E. Heidenreich

Early in the 17th century the French began to explore the rivers draining into the St Lawrence valley. Usually they gathered geographical information from natives, set objectives for exploration based on these accounts, and, when opportunity arose, travelled with native guides. Verbal accounts, maps, and journals transmitted the French discoveries. By the early 1680s officials in Québec were responsible for compiling and sending maps to the *Ministère de la Marine* in Paris where authorized personnel had access to them.

The search for a route across the continent was a continuing motive for exploration throughout the French regime, but usually was set within more limited objectives. Fur traders sought Indian suppliers; missionaries sought Indian converts. Territorial claims and the search for minerals were sometimes important motives for exploration. Occasionally military expeditions yielded new geographical knowledge.

The direction and speed of exploration varied with motives and opportunities. By helping natives in their wars Champlain was able to explore much of the eastern Great Lakes basin; by expanding their missions Recollet, Jesuit, and Sulpician priests obtained new geographical information (pl 34). After 1681, when the interior trade was legalized, French traders explored well beyond the Great Lakes (pl 38). In the 18th century westward exploration accelerated under the pressure of British competition from Hudson Bay and the Ohio valley.

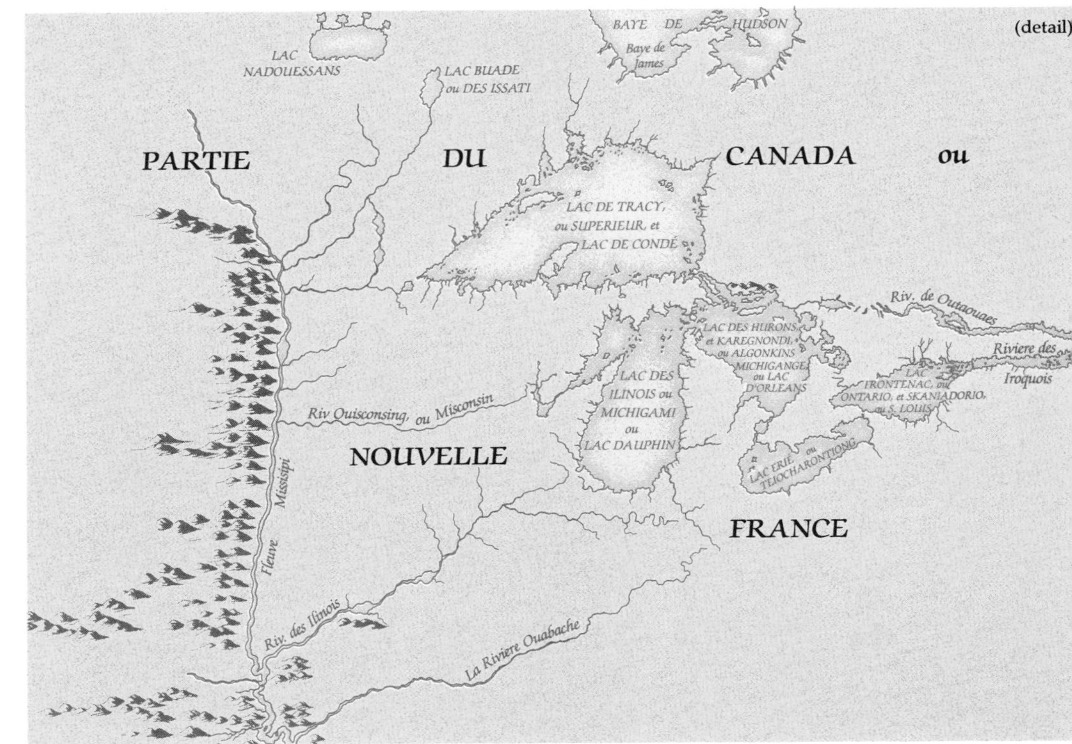
(detail)
LAC NADOUESSANS
LAC BUADE ou DES ISSATI
BAYE DE HUDSON
Baye de James
PARTIE
DU
CANADA
ou
LAC DE TRACY, ou SUPERIEUR, et LAC DE CONDÉ
Riv. de Outaouaes
Riviere des Iroquois
LAC DES HURONS et KAREGNONDI, ALGONKINS
MICHIGANGE ou LAC D'ORLEANS
LAC DES ILINOIS ou MICHIGAMI ou LAC DAUPHIN
LAC FRONTENAC, ou ONTARIO, et SKANIADORIO, ou S. LOUIS
LAC ERIE ou TEIOCHARONTIONG
Riv. Ouisconsing, ou Misconsin
NOUVELLE
FRANCE
Fleuve Missisipi
Riv. des Ilinois
La Riviere Ouabache

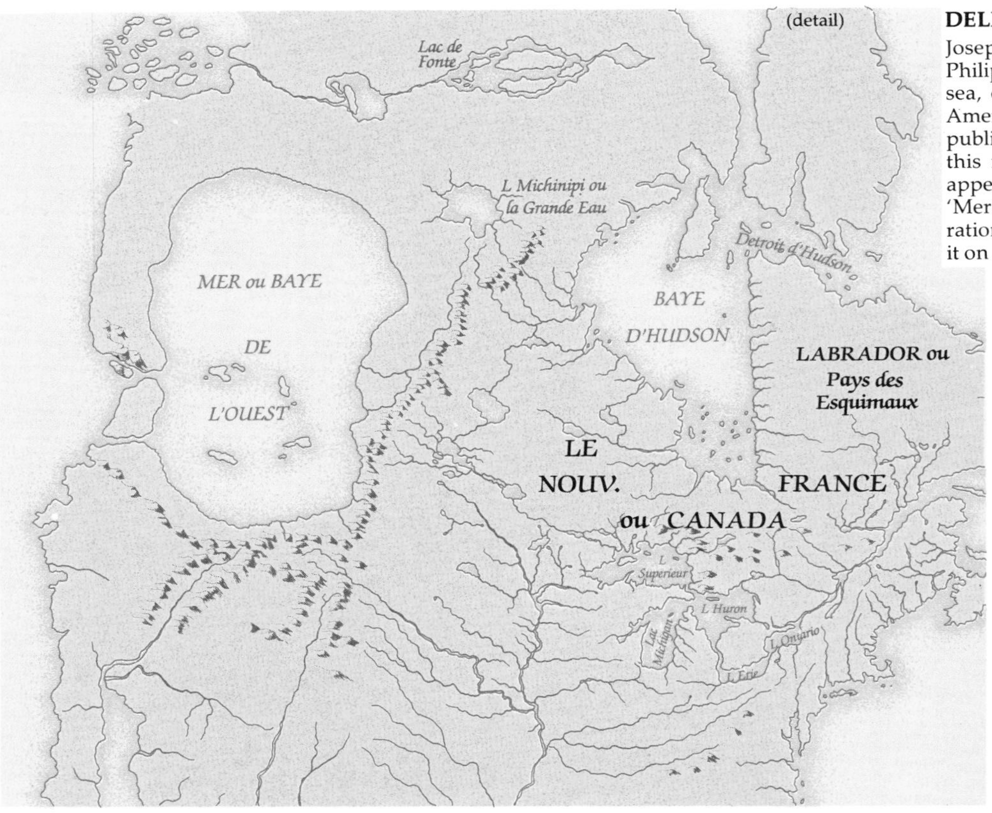

(detail)

Lac de Fonte
L. Michinipi ou la Grande Eau
Detroit d'Hudson
MER ou BAYE DE L'OUEST
BAYE D'HUDSON
LABRADOR ou Pays des Esquimaux
LE NOUV. FRANCE ou CANADA
L. Superieur
L. Huron
Lac Michigan
L. Ontario
L. Erie

DELISLE MAP, 1752

Joseph-Nicholas Delisle and his nephew by marriage, Philippe Buache, were obsessed by the idea of a vast sea, connected to the Pacific in northwestern North America. Beginning in 1752, Delisle and Buache published a series of maps and memoirs describing this mythical 'Mer de l'ouest'; some of their maps appeared as late as 1779 in Diderot's *Encyclopédie*. The 'Mer de l'ouest' had been a strong motive for exploration but as early as the 1740s few others dared place it on a map.

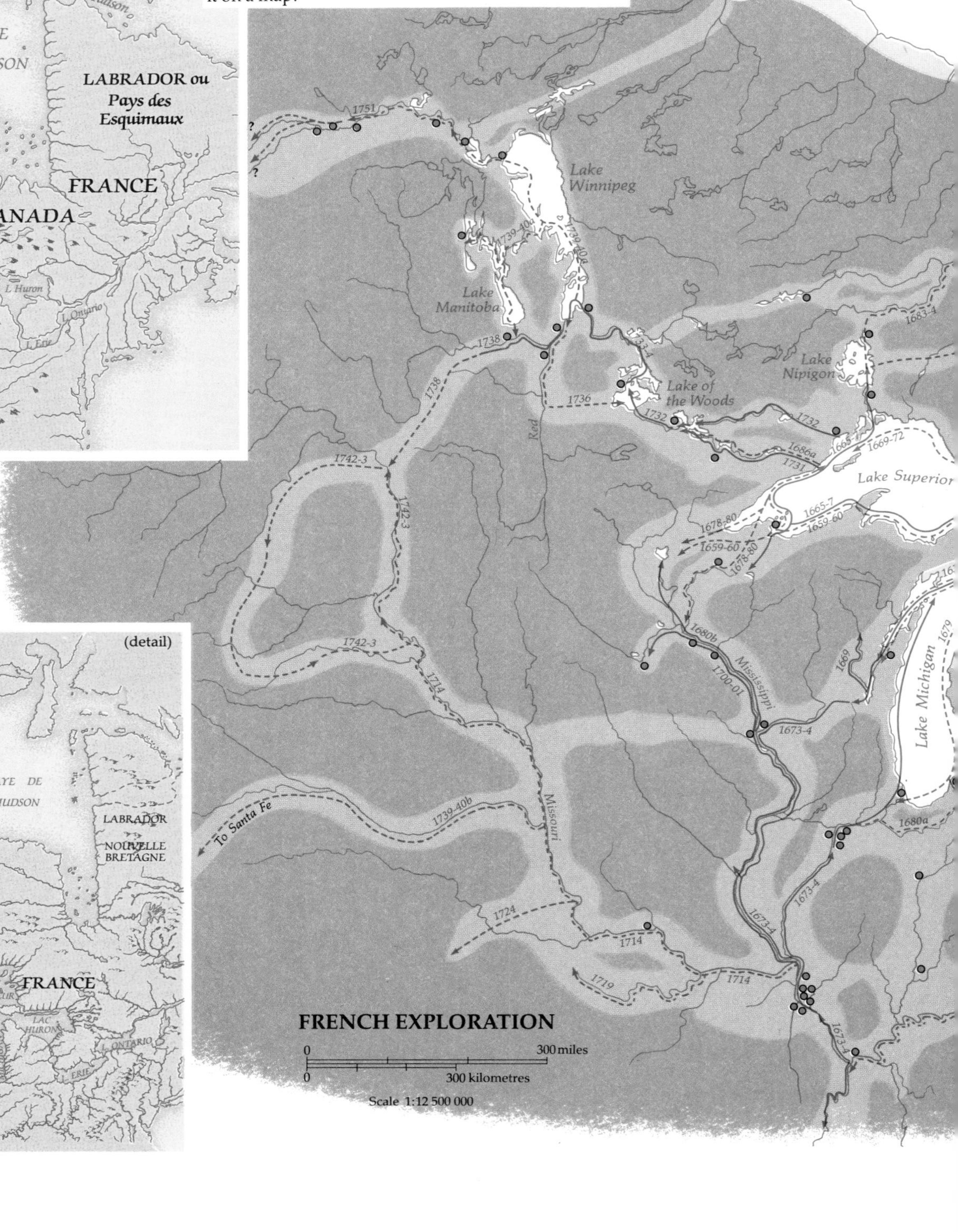

BELLIN MAP, 1755

When he made this map, Jacques-Nicolas Bellin was chief engineer of the cartographic section of the *Ministère de la Marine*, the depository for journals and maps from New France. Bellin used this material to good advantage and, beginning in 1743, produced a series of maps of New France that incorporated the latest available information about the North American interior. His map of 1755, the last original map in this set, includes data from La Vérendrye (1750), Bonnécamps (1749), Chaussegros de Léry and La Ronde (1735), and Father Laure (1731–3).

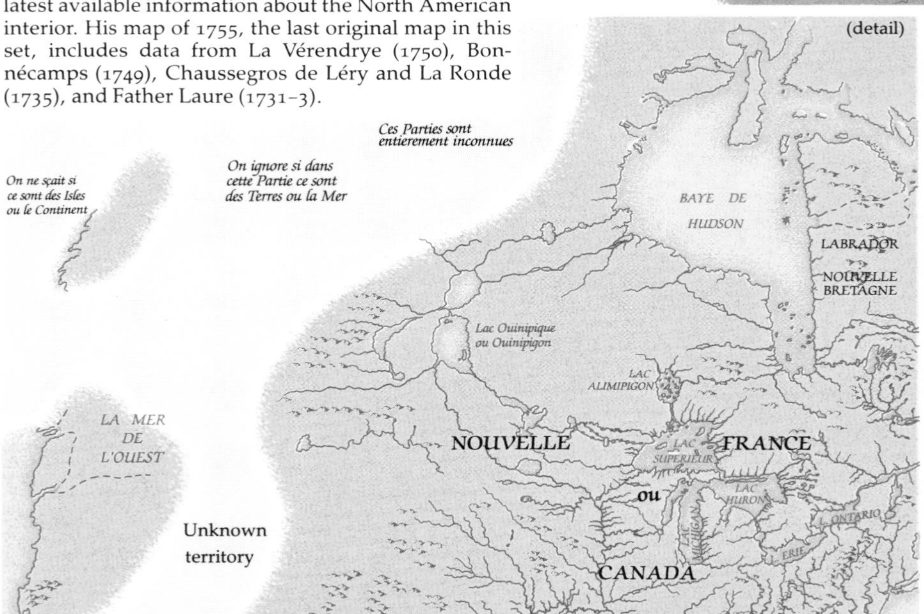

(detail)

Ces Parties sont entierement inconnues
On ignore si dans cette Partie ce sont des Terres ou la Mer
On ne sçait si ce sont des Isles ou le Continent
BAYE DE HUDSON
LABRADOR
NOUVELLE BRETAGNE
Lac Ouinipique ou Ouinipigon
LAC ALIMIPIGON
LA MER DE L'OUEST
NOUVELLE FRANCE ou CANADA
LAC SUPERIEUR
LAC HURONS
ONTARIO
ERIE
Unknown territory

FRENCH EXPLORATION

HUDSON BAY
Lake Winnipeg
Lake Manitoba
Lake of the Woods
Lake Nipigon
Lake Superior
Lake Michigan
Red
Missouri
Mississippi
To Santa Fe

0 — 300 miles
0 — 300 kilometres
Scale 1:12 500 000

CORONELLI MAP, 1688

Vincenzo Coronelli, an Italian friar in the Minorite Order of Franciscans, was commissioned to construct a huge globe for Louis XIV. His sojourn in Paris 1681–3 brought him into contact with cartographic material from New France, in particular the manuscripts of J.-B. Franquelin, then chief hydrographer at Québec, and La Salle. Coronelli's map of the Great Lakes, probably compiled in 1684–5 and published in 1688, was the first printed map of Canada to incorporate information from the explorations of Allouez, La Salle, Hennepin, and Jolliet.

SANSON MAP, 1656

Nicolas Sanson, founder of the great French school of cartography, was appointed *Géographe ordinaire du Roi* in 1630 and had access to the latest geographical information from New France. His maps of 1650 and 1656 are the first to show portions of all the Great Lakes more or less in their true positions. Sanson relied on the Jesuits, whose understanding of the Great Lakes basin derived from their own observations, native accounts, and informants such as Brûlé and Nicollet.

DATE	EXPLORERS	Search for route to Orient and northern sea	Missionary activities	Military expeditions	Territorial claims	Expansion of fur trade	Search for minerals	Diplomatic missions
		MOTIVATION						
1603	Samuel de Champlain	*						
1604–7	Samuel de Champlain	*			*		*	
1609	Samuel de Champlain			*				
1613	Samuel de Champlain	*				*		
1615	Samuel de Champlain	*		*		*		*
1615–18	Étienne Brûlé			*				*
1621–3	Étienne Brûlé					*		
1626	Joseph de La Roche Daillon		*					
1634	Jean Nicollet	*				*		*
1640–1	Jean de Brébeuf and Pierre Chaumonot		*					
1641	Isaac Jogues and Charles Raymbault		*					
1646	Isaac Jogues and Jean Bourdon		*					*
1647	Jean de Quen		*					
1651	Jacques Buteux		*					
1654	Simon Le Moyne		*					
1654–6	Médard Chouart Des Groseilliers		*			*		
1655	Pierre Chaumonot and Claude Dablon		*					
1656	Pierre Chaumonot		*					
1659–60	M. Chouart Des Groseilliers and P. Radisson	*				*		
1661	Claude Dablon and Gabriel Druillettes	*	*					
1663	G.Couture, P.D. de La Chesnaye, J. Langlois	*				*		
1665–7	Claude Allouez		*					
1669	Claude Allouez		*					
1669–70	F. Dollier, R. de Bréhant de Galinée, A. Jolliet	*	*		*			
1669–72	Jean Peré					*	*	
1671	Charles Albanel and Paul Denys de Saint-Simon	*	*		*	*		
1673–4	Louis Jolliet and Jacques Marquette	*	*		*	*		
1675	Henri Nouvel		*					
1678–80	Daniel de Greysolon Dulhut	*			*	*		*
1678	Robert Cavelier de La Salle				*	*		
1679	Henri de Tonty				*	*		
1680a	Robert Cavelier de La Salle				*	*		
1680b	M. Accault, A. Auguel, and L. Hennepin				*	*		
1683–4	Daniel de Greysolon Dulhut					*		*
1684	Jean Peré	*			*	*		
1686a	Jacques de Noyon	*				*		
1686b	Pierre de Troyes	*		*				
1700–1	Pierre Charles Le Sueur					*	*	
1714	Étienne de Véniard de Bourgmond	*				*		*
1719	Claude Charles Dutisné	*				*		*
1724	Étienne de Véniard de Bourgmond	*				*		
1731	C.D. de La Jemerais and J.-B. G. de LaVérendrye	*				*		
1732	Pierre Gaultier de La Vérendrye	*				*		
1733–4	C.D. de La Jemerais and J.-B.G. de LaVérendrye	*			*	*		
1736	J.-B. and P. G. de La Vérendrye	*			*	*		
1738	Louis-Joseph, François, and P.G. de La Vérendrye	*			*	*		
1739	C. Le Moyne de Longueuil, P.-J. Céloron de Blainville, and G. Chaussegros de Léry (fils)			*	*			
1739–40a	Louis-Joseph Gaultier de La Vérendrye	*				*		
1739–40b	Pierre Antoine and Paul Mallet					*		*
1742–3	L.-J. and F. Gaultier de La Vérendrye	*			*			*
1749	P.J. C. de Blainville and J. P. de Bonnécamps			*	*			*
1751	Boucher de Niverville	*				*		

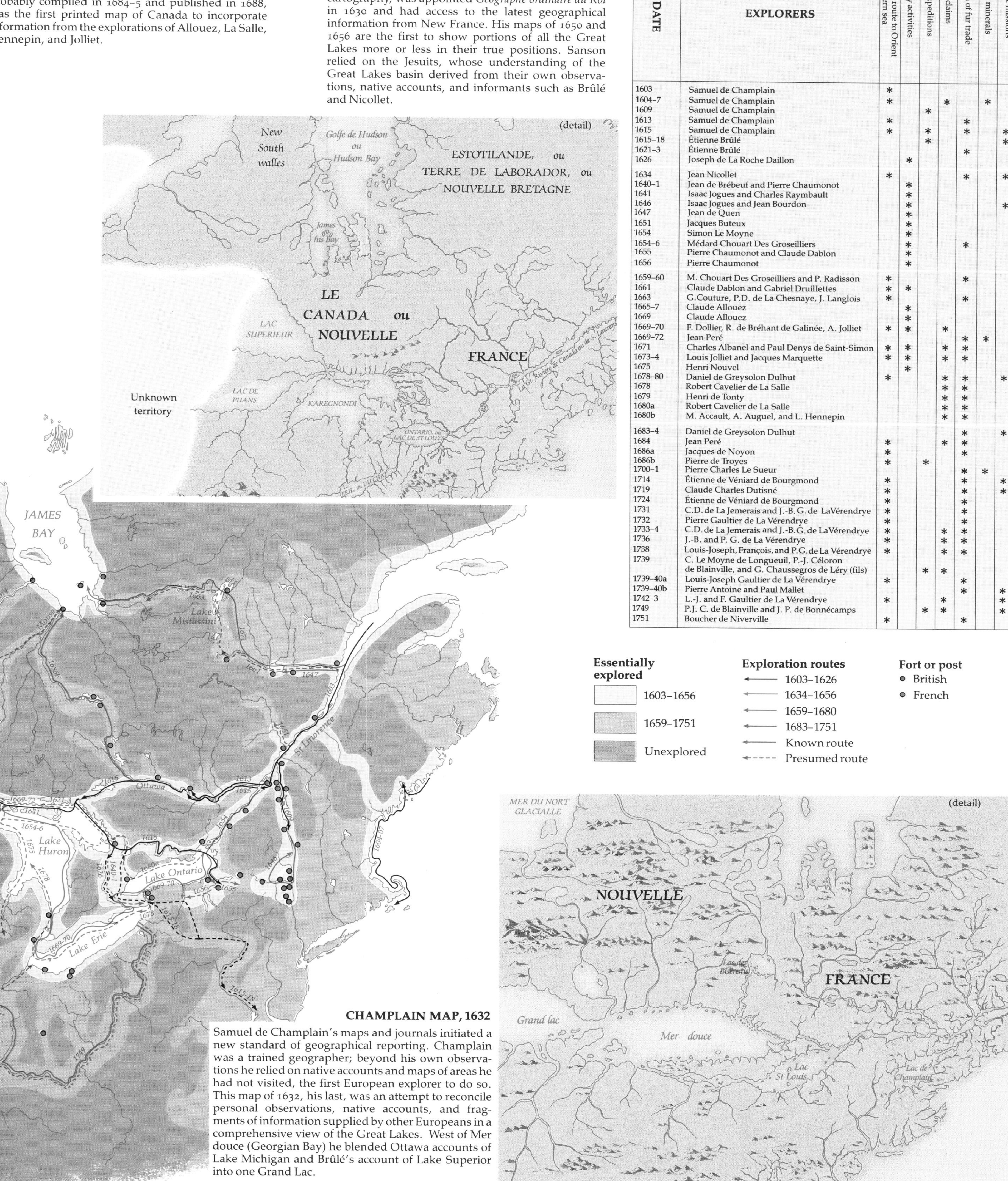
(detail)
New South walles
Golfe de Hudson ou Hudson Bay
ESTOTILANDE, ou TERRE DE LABORADOR, ou NOUVELLE BRETAGNE
James his Bay
LE CANADA ou NOUVELLE FRANCE
LAC SUPERIEUR
LAC DE PUANS
KAREGNONDI
ONTARIO, ou LAC DE ST LOUIS
Unknown territory
JAMES BAY
Lake Mistassini
Albany
Moose
Ottawa
St Lawrence
Lake Huron
Lake Ontario
Lake Erie
Essentially explored
1603–1656
1659–1751
Unexplored
Exploration routes
1603–1626
1634–1656
1659–1680
1683–1751
Known route
Presumed route
Fort or post
British
French
(detail)
MER DU NORT GLACIALLE
NOUVELLE
FRANCE
Grand lac
Mer douce
Lac St Louis
Lac de Champlain

CHAMPLAIN MAP, 1632

Samuel de Champlain's maps and journals initiated a new standard of geographical reporting. Champlain was a trained geographer; beyond his own observations he relied on native accounts and maps of areas he had not visited, the first European explorer to do so. This map of 1632, his last, was an attempt to reconcile personal observations, native accounts, and fragments of information supplied by other Europeans in a comprehensive view of the Great Lakes. West of Mer douce (Georgian Bay) he blended Ottawa accounts of Lake Michigan and Brûlé's account of Lake Superior into one Grand Lac.

RE-ESTABLISHMENT OF TRADE, 1654–1666

Author: Conrad E. Heidenreich

TRADE RESUMES, 1654–1660

Between 1634 and 1651 epidemics and warfare depopulated most of the eastern Great Lakes region (pl 33). After 1649 the St Lawrence valley was cut off from the west until 1654 when a group of Ottawa and Wyandot (Huron-Petun), now relocated west of Lake Michigan, came to Montréal to re-establish trade. Coureurs de bois and missionaries who followed them back to Green Bay and Lake Superior noted that these groups, as well as the Saulteaux and Potawatomi, had begun a carrying trade between their native neighbours and the French. Meanwhile, Montagnais bands along the Saint-Maurice and Saguenay Rivers continued as middlemen between the French and more northerly bands.

From 1654 to 1658 peace between the French and all the Iroquois except the Mohawk gave the Seneca, Cayuga, and Onondaga the opportunity to disperse the Erie and the refugee Petun and Neutral and to carry the war south to the Shawnee. In the upper Mississippi a group of westward-migrating Ottawa and Wyandot initiated a protracted conflict when they tried to take hunting territory from the Dakota.

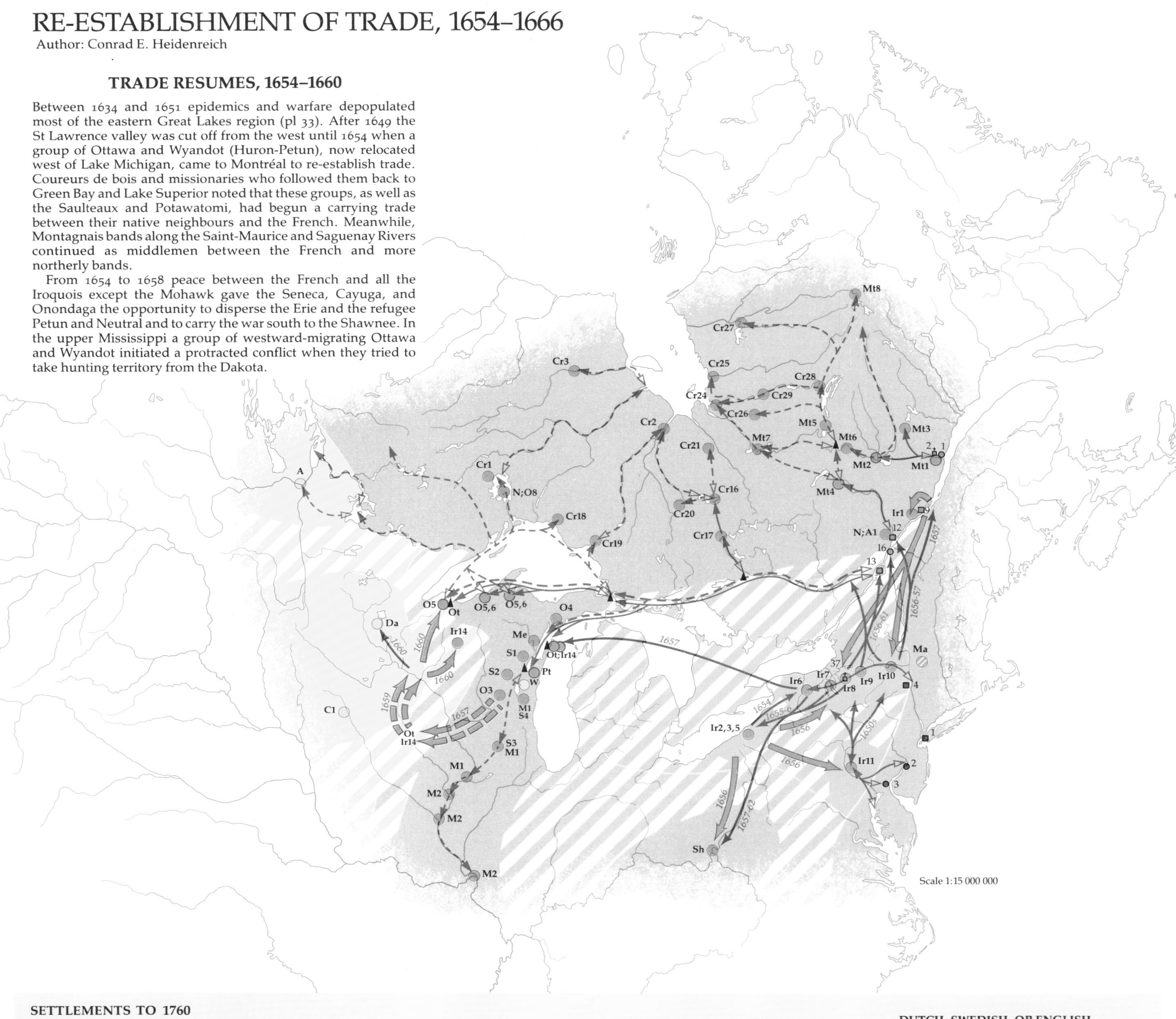

Mt8
Cr27
Cr25
Cr28
Cr24
Cr29
Cr26
Cr3
Cr2
Mt5
Mt6
Mt3
Mt7
Cr21
Mt2
Mt1
Cr1
N;O8
A
Cr16
Mt4
Cr18
Cr20
Ir1
Cr19
Cr17
N;A1
O5
Ot
O5,6
O5,6
O4
Da
Ir14
Me
Ot;Ir14
S1
S2
Pt
W
O3
M1
S4
Ma
Ir6
Ir7
Ir8
Ir9
Ir10
C1
Ot
Ir14
Ir2,3,5
S3
M1
Ir11
M1
M2
M2
Sh
M2
1654
1655–6
1656
1656–57
1657
1659
1660
Scale 1:15 000 000

SETTLEMENTS TO 1760

FRENCH SETTLEMENT

1 Tadoussac: 1600–*
2 Sainte-Croix: 1641–70; 1720–*
3 Chicoutimi: ca 1660–*
4 Mission de Chicoutimi: 1670–99; 1720–*
5 Métabetchouan (Notre-Dame-du Lac): 1665–*
6 Mistassini: ca 1674–*
7 Chomonchouane (Chomoukchouan): ca 1690
8 Nemiscou: 1681–?
9 Québec: 1608–*
10 Lorette: (a) 1673–97; (b) 1697–*
11 Sainte-Marie-aux-Hurons: (a) 1639–49; (b) 1649–50
12 Trois-Rivières: 1634–*
13 Montréal: 1642–*
14 La Prairie (Saint-Xavier-des-Prés): 1667–*
15 Lac-des-Deux-Montagnes: 1721–*
16 Fort Richelieu (Sorel): 1641–*
17 Fort Saint-Louis (Chambly): 1665–1702; 1711–*
18 Fort Saint-Jean: 1666–?; 1748–*
19 Fort Sainte-Thérèse: 1665–1730
20 Fort Sainte-Anne (La Mothe): 1666–*
21 Fort Pointe-à-la-Chevelure (Saint-Frédéric): 1731–*
22 Fort Coulonge: 1695–*
23 Fort Dumoine: ca 1730–?
24 Témiscamingue: (a) ca 1677–86; (b) 1686–8; 1720–*
25 Fort des Abitibis: 1686–ca 1688; 1720–*
26 Piscoutagami (Saint-Germain): ca 1673–?
27 Saint-Régis: ca 1750–*
28 Fort La Présentation: 1748–*
29 Fort Frontenac: 1673–89; 1694–*
30 Saint-Francis: 1700–*
31 Fort Rouillé (Toronto): 1720–30; 1750–*
32 Fort Niagara: 1668–75; 1679–89; 1720–*
33 Portage Niagara (Magasin): 1720–*
34 Mission de Kenté: 1668–79
35 Mohawk (Sainte-Marie; Saint-Pierre; Holy Trinity): 1667–87; 1702–8
36 Oneida (Saint-François-Xavier): 1667–87; 1702–8
37 Onondaga (Sainte-Marie-de-Gannentaha; Saint-Jean-Baptiste): 1654–8; 1667–87; 1702–8
38 Cayuga (Saint-Joseph): 1668–87; 1702–8
39 Seneca (Saint-Michel; La Conception; Saint-Jacques): 1668–84; 1702–8
40 Irondequoit: ca 1680–ca 1685; ca 1733–ca 1745
41 Fort Presqu'isle : 1753–*
42 Fort Le Boeuf: 1753–*
43 Fort Machault: 1753–*
44 Fort Duquesne: 1754–*
45 Fort Sandusky: 1751–3
46 Saguin Post (Cayahoga): 1742–?
47 Fort Pontchartrain (Détroit): 1701–*
48 Fort Saint-Joseph (Détroit du Lac Érié): 1686–9
49 Fort des Miamis: (a) 1719–47; (b) 1750–*
50 Fort Saint-Joseph: (a) 1679–91; (b) 1691–8; 1701–*
51 Ouiatanon: 1717–*
52 Fort Vincennes (Sainte-Anne): 1731–*
53 Tannerie de Juchereau de Saint-Denis: 1702–4
54 Fort Chicagou: 1680–1706
55 La Conception (Kaskaskia): 1675–91
56 Fort Saint-Louis (Starved Rock): 1682–92; 1716–?
57 Fort Crèvecoeur: 1680
58 Fort Saint-Louis (Pimiteoui; Peoria): 1692–1724; ca 1750–*
59 Cahokia: 1699–*
60 Saint-Philippe: 1723–*
61 Fort de Chartres: 1718
62 Prairie-du-Rocher: 1733–*
63 Kaskaskia: 1703–*
64 Sainte-Geneviève: 1735–*
65 Fort d'Orléans: 1723–6
66 Fort Cavagnolle (Kansés): ca 1740–*
67 Fort de la Baie-des-Puants (Saint-Antoine): 1670–98; 1717–28; 1731–*
68 Saint-François-Xavier (De père): 1668–1705; 1717–28; 1731–*
69 Fort Saint-Nicolas (Prairie du Chien): 1686–98
70 Fort Marin (Vaudreuil): 1752–4
71 (Trempaleau): 1685–6; 1731–6
72 Fort Pépin (Bonsecours): 1695–1702
73 Fort Saint-Antoine (Perrot): 1686–9
74 Fort Beauharnois: 1727–30; 1732–7
75 Fort Le Sueur: 1695–8
76 Fort L'Huillier (Vert): 1700–1703; 1739–*
77 Fort Sainte-Croix: 1683–ca 1700
78 Sainte-Marie-du-Sault: 1668–98; ca 1715–*
79 Fort Sauvage (Repentigny): 1689–98; ca 1730–*
80 Saint-Ignace : 1668–1711
81 Fort Buade: 1683–1706
82 Michilimackinac: 1712–*
83 Saint-François-de-Borgia: 1677–1706
84 Saint-Simon: 1670–4
85 Saint-Ignace (L'Arbre Croche): 1741–*
86 Saint-Esprit (Chagouamigon): 1660–70
87 La Pointe (Chagouamigon): 1693–8; 1718–*
88 Michipicoton: 1726–*
89 Népigon: 1679–98; 1717–*
90 Fort La Tourette (La Maune): 1684–98
91 Fort des Français: 1685–ca 1687
92 Fort Kaministiquia: 1678–98; 1717–*
93 Lac-à-la-Carpe: 1751–*
94 Petit Fort Vermillion: 1736–?
95 Fort Saint-Pierre: 1731–*
96 Fort Saint-Charles: 1732–*
97 Fort Maurepas: (a) 1734–8; (b) 1739–*
98 Fort La Reine: 1738–*
99 Fort Rouge (La Fourche): 1738–ca 1748
100 Fort Bourbon: (a) ca 1739–ca 1750; (b) 1743–*
101 Fort Dauphin: 1741–*
102 Fort Paskoya: ca 1750–* (1748?)
103 Fort Des Prairies (Saint-Louis; La Corne): 1753–*
104 Fort La Jonquière (Saint-Pierre): 1751–2
105 Fort La Jonquière (Marin): 1750–6
106 Fort Duquesne (Marin): 1753–*

DUTCH, SWEDISH, OR ENGLISH SETTLEMENT

1 New York: 1664–*. New Amsterdam (Dutch): 1626–64
2 Fort Nassau: 1664–*. Fort Nassau (Dutch): 1622–64
3 Wilmington: 1664–*. Fort Christina (Swedish): 1638–55; (Dutch): 1655–64
4 Albany: 1664–*. Fort Orange (Dutch): 1624–64
5 Schenectady: 1664–* Corlaer (Dutch): 1661–64
6 Saratoga: 1703–*
7 Fort Ann: 1703–*
8 Fort Hunter: 1712–*
9 Fort Bull: ca 1720–*
10 Fort Williams: ?–*
11 Fort Hendrick: 1740–*
12 Fort Oswego (Chouagouen): 1726–*
13 Fort Necessity: 1754–*
14 Fort Cumberland: 1754–*
15 Redstone Station and Gist's Post: ?–1754
16 Shamokin: 1740s–*
17 Logstown (Chiningué): ca 1743–53
18 Pickawillany: 1748–52
19 Croghan's Post (Canahogue): 1744–50
20 Croghan's Post (Conchake): 1750–3
21 Venango: ca 1751–3
22 Sandusky Post: ca 1745–8
23 Rupert House (Eng.): 1668–86. Fort Saint-Jacques (Fr.): 1686–93
24 Moose Factory (Eng.): 1673–86; 1730–* Fort Saint-Louis (Fr.): 1686–93
25 Fort Albany (Eng.): 1679–86; 1693–* Fort Sainte-Anne (Fr.): 1686–93
26 Eastmain:1684–1719; 1723–*
27 Fort Severn (Eng.): 1685–90. Fort Sainte-Thérèse (Fr.): 1691–1713
28 Richmond Post: 1750–*
29 Henley House: 1743–55
30 York Factory (Eng.): 1684–94; 1713–* Fort Bourbon (Fr.): 1682–4; 1694–1713
31 Churchill: 1717–*

*To 1760

The series of maps (pls 37–40) begun on this plate treats, period by period, the inland development of New France. The maps present an integrated view of French, English, and Indian trade, warfare, and settlement in the central interior of North America.

NATIVE GROUPS

IROQUOIAN LINGUISTIC FAMILY

Ir Iroquoian
- **Ir1** Huron
- **2** Petun (Tionontate)
- **3** Neutral
- **4** Wenro
- **5** Erie
- **6** Seneca
- **7** Cayuga
- **8** Onondaga
- **9** Oneida
- **10** Mohawk
- **11** Susquehannock
- **12** Tuscarora
- **13** Mingo (Seneca/Cayuga)
- **14** Wyandot (Huron/Petun)

SIOUAN LINGUISTIC FAMILY

Da Dakota
- **Da1** Santee
- **2** Yankton
- **3** Teton

W Winnebago
A Assiniboine
M Mandan
H Hidatsa-Crow
De Dhegiha
- **De1** Omaha
- **2** Ponca
- **3** Osage
- **4** Kansa

C Chiwere
- **C1** Iowa
- **2** Oto
- **3** Missouri

CADDOAN LINGUISTIC FAMILY

A Arikara
P Pawnee

ALGONQUIAN LINGUISTIC FAMILY

Western Language Group

A Arapaho
- **A1** Arapaho
- **2** Atsina

B Blackfoot
- **B1** Siksika
- **2** Blood
- **3** Piegan

C Cheyenne

Central Language Group

O Ojibwa
- **O1** Outchibous
- **2** Marameg
- **3** Mantouek
- **4** Noquet
- **5** Saulteaux
- **6** Mississauga
- **7** Nikikouet
- **8** Amikwa
- **9** Achiligouan (**N**) (**Ot**)
- **10** Ouchougai (**N**) (**Ot**)
- **11** Ouasouarini
- **12** Sagahanirini
- **13** Graisse Ours
- **14** Not specified

Ot Ottawa
Me Menominee
Pt Potawatomi
N Nipissing
S Sauk-Fox-Kikapoo-Mascouten
- **S1** Sauk
- **2** Fox
- **3** Kikapoo
- **4** Mascouten

M Miami-Illinois
- **M1** Miami
- **2** Illinois

Al Algonquin
Sh Shawnee
Mt Montagnais-Naskapi
- **Mt1** Tadoussacien
- **2** Kakouchaki
- **3** Chicoutimi
- **4** Attikamek
- **5** Nekoubaniste
- **6** Chomonchouaniste
- **7** Oumatachirini (**Cr**)
- **8** Nitchikirinouetch (**Cr**)

Central Language Group

Cr Cree–Gens de Terre

West Main Cree
- **Cr1** Alimbegouek
- **2** Monsoni
- **3** Ataouabouskatouek
- **4** Washahoe
- **5** Weenusk
- **6** Penneswagewan
- **7** Maskegon
- **8** Michinipi
- **9** Nameoulini
- **10** Christinaux du bois fort
- **11** Christinaux du Puant
- **12** Christinaux l'eau troublé
- **13** Kinougeoulini
- **14** Qeunebigonhelini
- **15** Non-specified

Gens de Terre
- **Cr16** Abitibi
- **17** Timiscimi (**A1**)
- **18** Outoulibi
- **19** Nopeming
- **20** Piscoutagami
- **21** Outchichagamiouetch
- **22** Non-specified

East Main Cree
- **Cr24** Nisibourounik
- **25** Pitchibourounik
- **26** Gesseirinioueth
- **27** Opinaguairiniouetch
- **28** Grands Mistassirini (**Mt**)
- **29** Escurieux

Eastern Language Group

Ma Mahican
De Delaware
Aw Western Abenaki
Ae Eastern Abenaki

Goods and traders

- European goods
- Native goods
- Natives trading with Europeans
- Natives trading with natives
- Annual French traders
- Occasional French traders

Settlements and trading places
(see numbered list below)

- French village or town
- French mission
- French fort or post
- Dutch village, English after 1664
- Dutch fort or post, English after 1664
- Known native trading place

Warfare

- Native warfare
- French warfare
- Forced native migration
- Peaceful native migration

Native population

- Language and native group, eg Ir6 Iroquoian (Seneca) (see comprehensive list at right)
- Principal native traders
- Area generally occupied
- Area seasonally occupied

Native languages

- Central Algonquian
- Eastern Algonquian
- Iroquoian
- Siouan

IROQUOIS DISRUPTIONS, 1660–1666

The Ottawa, Wyandot, and Saulteaux of Lake Superior and the Potawatomi at Green Bay, although harassed by the Dakota, consolidated their positons as principal native traders. The Nipissing and Amikwa who had fled to Lake Nipigon in 1650–3 began a new carrying trade between Montréal and interior Cree groups.

The Iroquois war resumed in 1658. Despite a smallpox epidemic in 1662 and defeats suffered at the hands of the Saulteaux, Susquehannock, and Huron, the Iroquois managed to disperse the Attikamek by 1665 and to disrupt the Montagnais trade. In 1664 the French court sent troops to New France to destroy the Iroquois. Late in 1666 this force of 1 200 soldiers, led by Prouville de Tracy, burned the four principal villages of their most implacable foe, the Mohawk, and forced a peace on the Iroquois confederacy.

Scale 1:15 000 000

EXPANSION OF FRENCH TRADE, 1667–1696

Author: Conrad E. Heidenreich

With the Iroquois peace some Ojibwa and Ottawa bands reoccupied their former homeland while French coureurs de bois, now free from the Iroquois threat, accelerated their penetration of the interior. It is estimated that 200 men were involved in this illegal trade. Their temporary posts, erected near the Jesuit missions and major concentrations of native population, reduced the number of native traders travelling to Montréal.

In the east the Iroquois received missionaries and took advantage of the peace with the French to disperse the Shawnee from the rich Ohio valley. In part to escape Susquehannock attacks, as well as to trap furs, some Iroquois established settlements on the north shore of Lake Ontario. There they initiated trade with the Ottawa and Ojibwa of Georgian Bay and began to redirect some furs from the Great Lakes to the English at Albany where, because the French crown taxed beaver heavily, fur prices were higher. At this time English traders built a post on James Bay (1668); its success led to the founding of the Hudson's Bay Company in 1670.

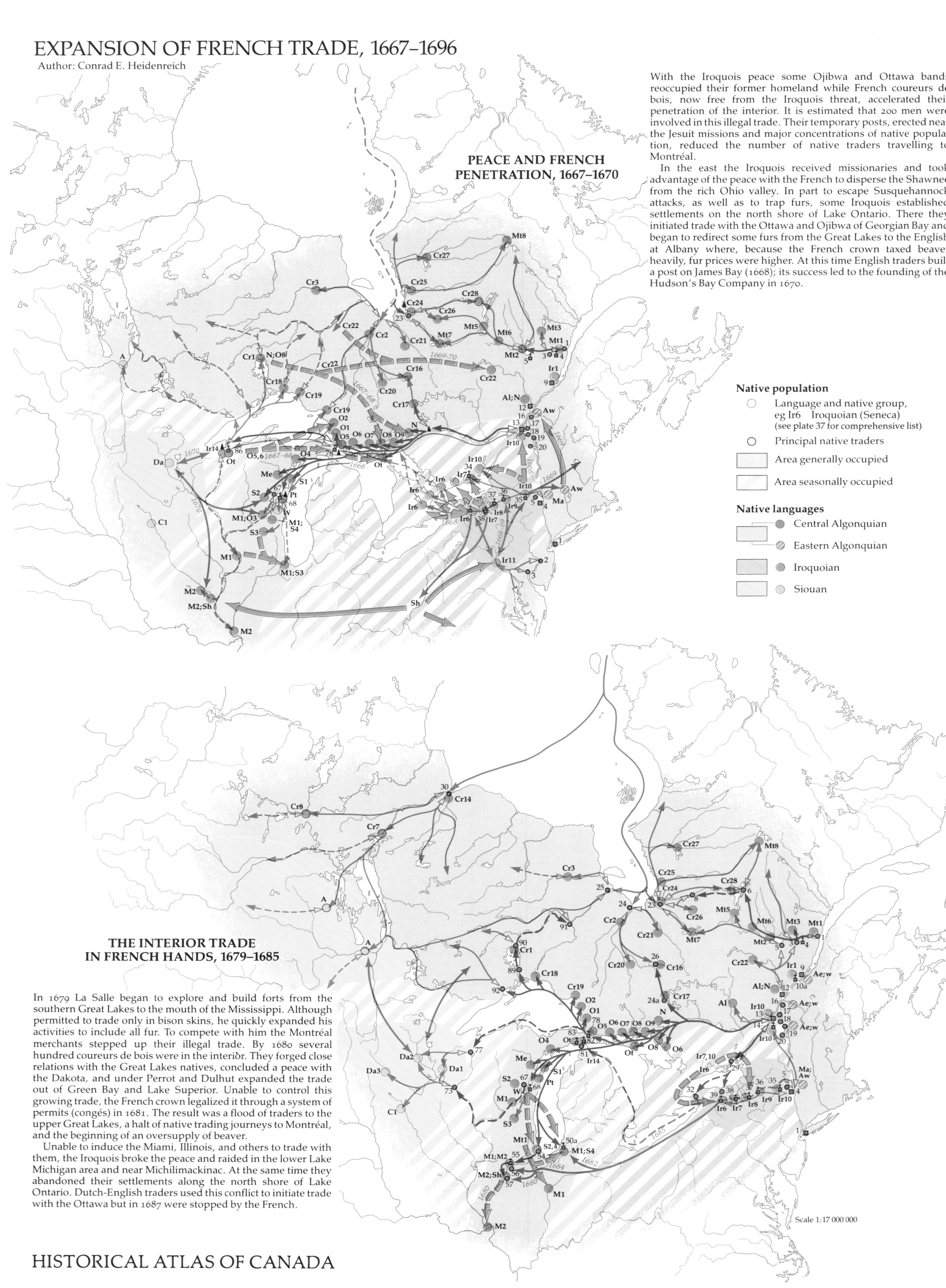
PEACE AND FRENCH PENETRATION, 1667–1670
Native population
Language and native group, eg Ir6 Iroquoian (Seneca) (see plate 37 for comprehensive list)
Principal native traders
Area generally occupied
Area seasonally occupied
Native languages
Central Algonquian
Eastern Algonquian
Iroquoian
Siouan
THE INTERIOR TRADE IN FRENCH HANDS, 1679–1685
Scale 1:17 000 000

In 1679 La Salle began to explore and build forts from the southern Great Lakes to the mouth of the Mississippi. Although permitted to trade only in bison skins, he quickly expanded his activities to include all fur. To compete with him the Montréal merchants stepped up their illegal trade. By 1680 several hundred coureurs de bois were in the interior. They forged close relations with the Great Lakes natives, concluded a peace with the Dakota, and under Perrot and Dulhut expanded the trade out of Green Bay and Lake Superior. Unable to control this growing trade, the French crown legalized it through a system of permits (congés) in 1681. The result was a flood of traders to the upper Great Lakes, a halt of native trading journeys to Montréal, and the beginning of an oversupply of beaver.

Unable to induce the Miami, Illinois, and others to trade with them, the Iroquois broke the peace and raided in the lower Lake Michigan area and near Michilimackinac. At the same time they abandoned their settlements along the north shore of Lake Ontario. Dutch-English traders used this conflict to initiate trade with the Ottawa but in 1687 were stopped by the French.

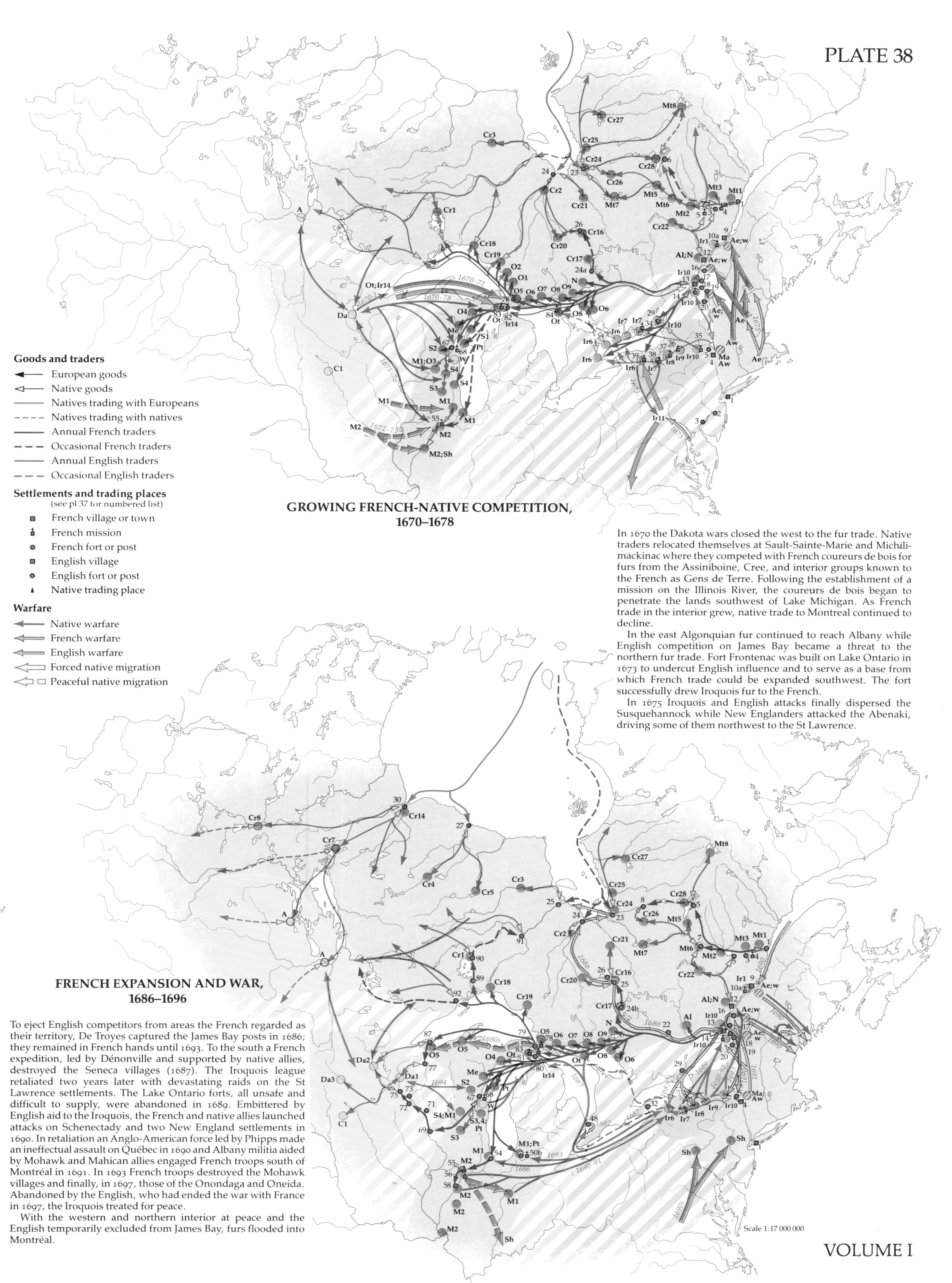
Goods and traders
European goods
Native goods
Natives trading with Europeans
Natives trading with natives
Annual French traders
Occasional French traders
Annual English traders
Occasional English traders
Settlements and trading places
(see pl 37 for numbered list)
French village or town
French mission
French fort or post
English village
English fort or post
Native trading place
Warfare
Native warfare
French warfare
English warfare
Forced native migration
Peaceful native migration
Scale 1:17 000 000

GROWING FRENCH-NATIVE COMPETITION, 1670–1678

In 1670 the Dakota wars closed the west to the fur trade. Native traders relocated themselves at Sault-Sainte-Marie and Michilimackinac where they competed with French coureurs de bois for furs from the Assiniboine, Cree, and interior groups known to the French as Gens de Terre. Following the establishment of a mission on the Illinois River, the coureurs de bois began to penetrate the lands southwest of Lake Michigan. As French trade in the interior grew, native trade to Montreal continued to decline.

In the east Algonquian fur continued to reach Albany while English competition on James Bay became a threat to the northern fur trade. Fort Frontenac was built on Lake Ontario in 1673 to undercut English influence and to serve as a base from which French trade could be expanded southwest. The fort successfully drew Iroquois fur to the French.

In 1675 Iroquois and English attacks finally dispersed the Susquehannock while New Englanders attacked the Abenaki, driving some of them northwest to the St Lawrence.

FRENCH EXPANSION AND WAR, 1686–1696

To eject English competitors from areas the French regarded as their territory, De Troyes captured the James Bay posts in 1686; they remained in French hands until 1693. To the south a French expedition, led by Dénonville and supported by native allies, destroyed the Seneca villages (1687). The Iroquois league retaliated two years later with devastating raids on the St Lawrence settlements. The Lake Ontario forts, all unsafe and difficult to supply, were abandoned in 1689. Embittered by English aid to the Iroquois, the French and native allies launched attacks on Schenectady and two New England settlements in 1690. In retaliation an Anglo-American force led by Phipps made an ineffectual assault on Québec in 1690 and Albany militia aided by Mohawk and Mahican allies engaged French troops south of Montréal in 1691. In 1693 French troops destroyed the Mohawk villages and finally, in 1697, those of the Onondaga and Oneida. Abandoned by the English, who had ended the war with France in 1697, the Iroquois treated for peace.

With the western and northern interior at peace and the English temporarily excluded from James Bay, furs flooded into Montréal.

TRADE AND EMPIRE, 1697–1739

Authors: Conrad E. Heidenreich, Françoise Noël

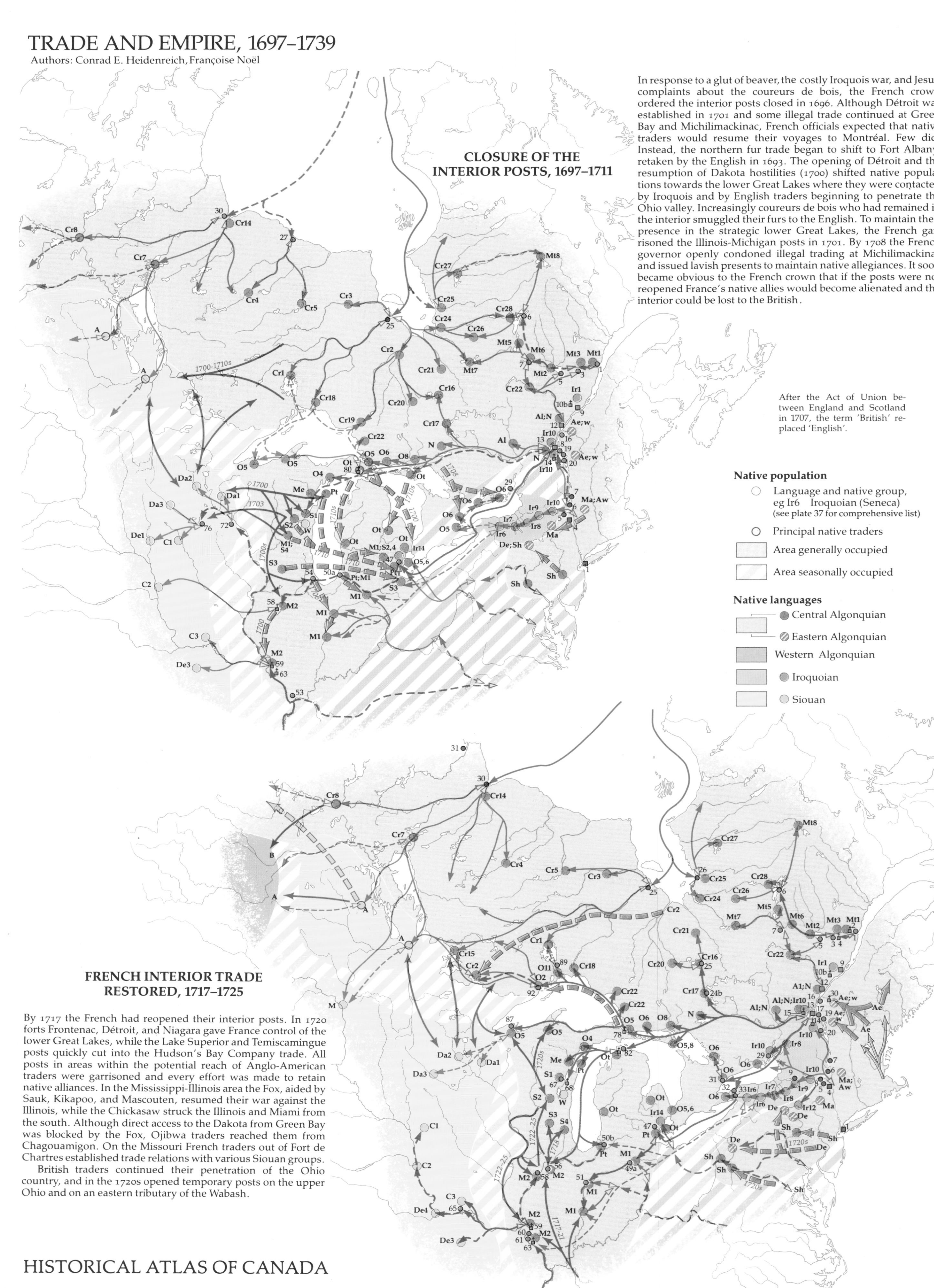
Native population
Language and native group, eg Ir6 Iroquoian (Seneca)
(see plate 37 for comprehensive list)
Principal native traders
Area generally occupied
Area seasonally occupied
Native languages
Central Algonquian
Eastern Algonquian
Western Algonquian
Iroquoian
Siouan

CLOSURE OF THE INTERIOR POSTS, 1697–1711

In response to a glut of beaver, the costly Iroquois war, and Jesuit complaints about the coureurs de bois, the French crown ordered the interior posts closed in 1696. Although Détroit was established in 1701 and some illegal trade continued at Green Bay and Michilimackinac, French officials expected that native traders would resume their voyages to Montréal. Few did. Instead, the northern fur trade began to shift to Fort Albany, retaken by the English in 1693. The opening of Détroit and the resumption of Dakota hostilities (1700) shifted native populations towards the lower Great Lakes where they were contacted by Iroquois and by English traders beginning to penetrate the Ohio valley. Increasingly coureurs de bois who had remained in the interior smuggled their furs to the English. To maintain their presence in the strategic lower Great Lakes, the French garrisoned the Illinois-Michigan posts in 1701. By 1708 the French governor openly condoned illegal trading at Michilimackinac and issued lavish presents to maintain native allegiances. It soon became obvious to the French crown that if the posts were not reopened France's native allies would become alienated and the interior could be lost to the British.

After the Act of Union between England and Scotland in 1707, the term 'British' replaced 'English'.

FRENCH INTERIOR TRADE RESTORED, 1717–1725

By 1717 the French had reopened their interior posts. In 1720 forts Frontenac, Détroit, and Niagara gave France control of the lower Great Lakes, while the Lake Superior and Temiscamingue posts quickly cut into the Hudson's Bay Company trade. All posts in areas within the potential reach of Anglo-American traders were garrisoned and every effort was made to retain native alliances. In the Mississippi-Illinois area the Fox, aided by Sauk, Kikapoo, and Mascouten, resumed their war against the Illinois, while the Chickasaw struck the Illinois and Miami from the south. Although direct access to the Dakota from Green Bay was blocked by the Fox, Ojibwa traders reached them from Chagouamigon. On the Missouri French traders out of Fort de Chartres established trade relations with various Siouan groups.

British traders continued their penetration of the Ohio country, and in the 1720s opened temporary posts on the upper Ohio and on an eastern tributary of the Wabash.

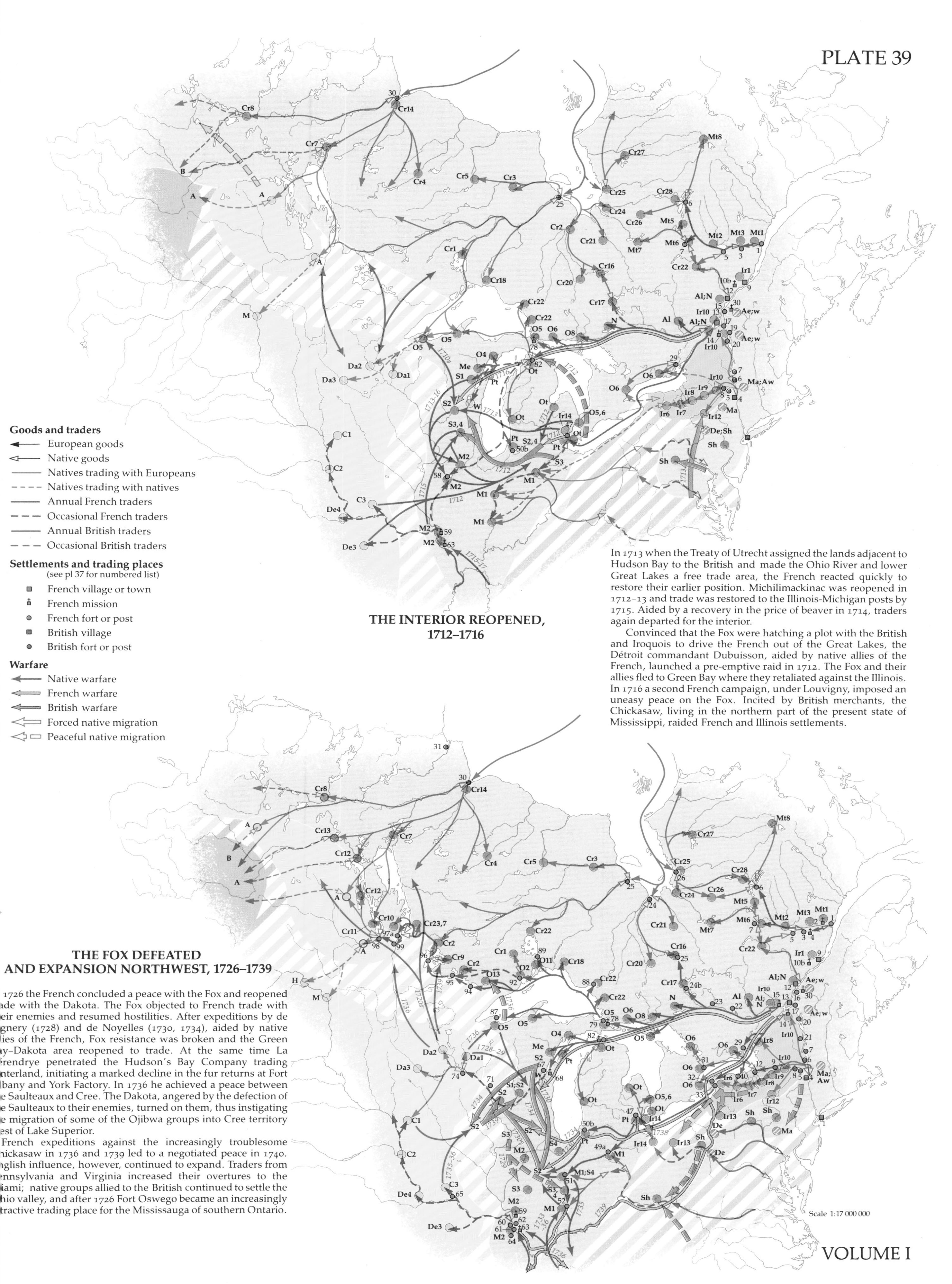
Goods and traders
European goods
Native goods
Natives trading with Europeans
Natives trading with natives
Annual French traders
Occasional French traders
Annual British traders
Occasional British traders
Settlements and trading places
(see pl 37 for numbered list)
French village or town
French mission
French fort or post
British village
British fort or post
Warfare
Native warfare
French warfare
British warfare
Forced native migration
Peaceful native migration
Scale 1:17 000 000

THE INTERIOR REOPENED, 1712–1716

In 1713 when the Treaty of Utrecht assigned the lands adjacent to Hudson Bay to the British and made the Ohio River and lower Great Lakes a free trade area, the French reacted quickly to restore their earlier position. Michilimackinac was reopened in 1712–13 and trade was restored to the Illinois-Michigan posts by 1715. Aided by a recovery in the price of beaver in 1714, traders again departed for the interior.

Convinced that the Fox were hatching a plot with the British and Iroquois to drive the French out of the Great Lakes, the Détroit commandant Dubuisson, aided by native allies of the French, launched a pre-emptive raid in 1712. The Fox and their allies fled to Green Bay where they retaliated against the Illinois. In 1716 a second French campaign, under Louvigny, imposed an uneasy peace on the Fox. Incited by British merchants, the Chickasaw, living in the northern part of the present state of Mississippi, raided French and Illinois settlements.

THE FOX DEFEATED AND EXPANSION NORTHWEST, 1726–1739

1726 the French concluded a peace with the Fox and reopened ade with the Dakota. The Fox objected to French trade with eir enemies and resumed hostilities. After expeditions by de gnery (1728) and de Noyelles (1730, 1734), aided by native ies of the French, Fox resistance was broken and the Green ay–Dakota area reopened to trade. At the same time La rendrye penetrated the Hudson's Bay Company trading nterland, initiating a marked decline in the fur returns at Fort bany and York Factory. In 1736 he achieved a peace between e Saulteaux and Cree. The Dakota, angered by the defection of e Saulteaux to their enemies, turned on them, thus instigating e migration of some of the Ojibwa groups into Cree territory est of Lake Superior.

French expeditions against the increasingly troublesome ickasaw in 1736 and 1739 led to a negotiated peace in 1740. glish influence, however, continued to expand. Traders from nnsylvania and Virginia increased their overtures to the iami; native groups allied to the British continued to settle the hio valley, and after 1726 Fort Oswego became an increasingly tractive trading place for the Mississauga of southern Ontario.

FRANCE SECURES THE INTERIOR, 1740–1755

Authors: Conrad E. Heidenreich, Françoise Noël

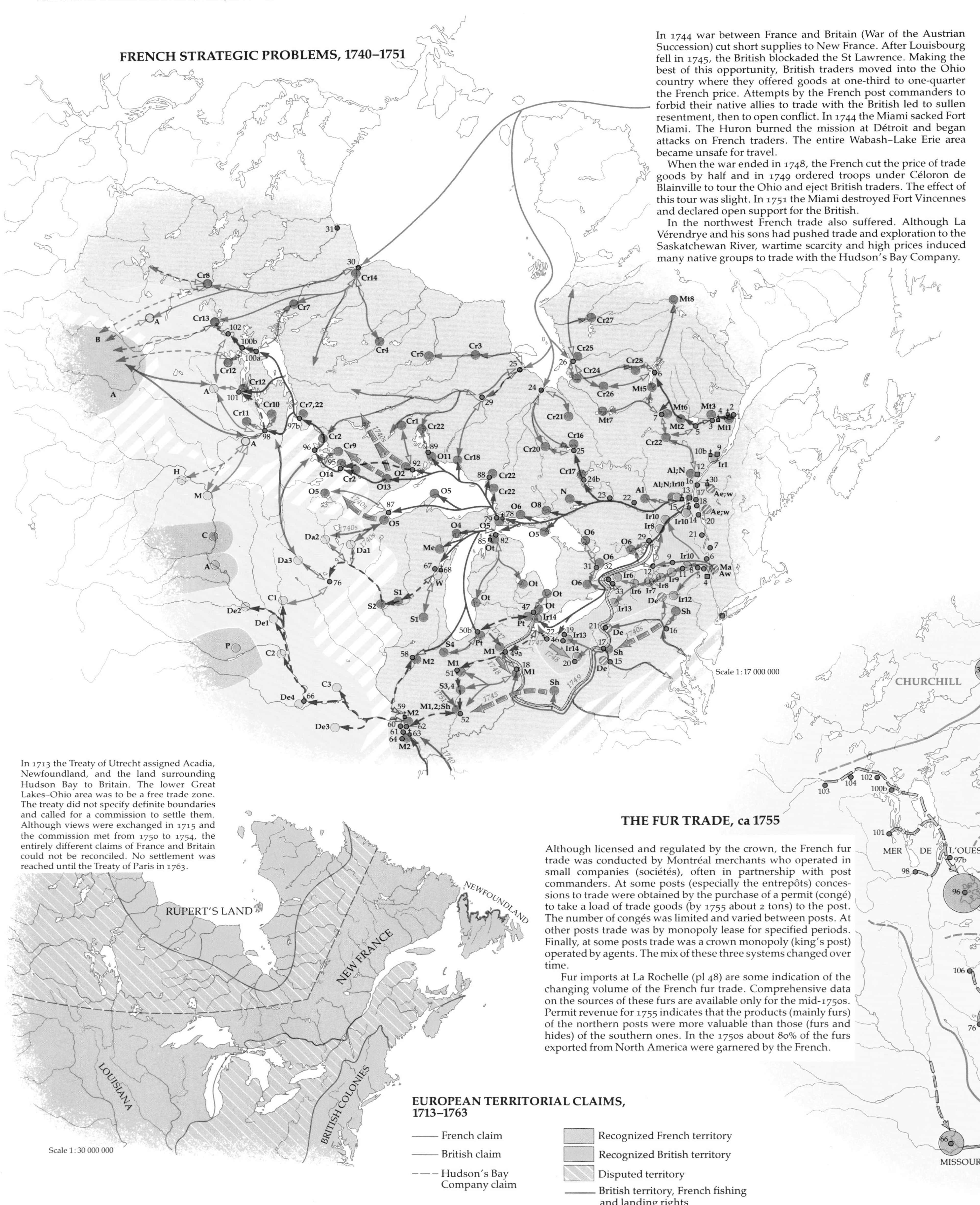
FRENCH STRATEGIC PROBLEMS, 1740–1751
Scale 1:17 000 000
CHURCHILL
MER DE L'OUEST
MISSOURI
THE FUR TRADE, ca 1755
RUPERT'S LAND
NEWFOUNDLAND
NEW FRANCE
LOUISIANA
BRITISH COLONIES
Scale 1:30 000 000
EUROPEAN TERRITORIAL CLAIMS, 1713–1763
French claim
British claim
Hudson's Bay Company claim
Recognized French territory
Recognized British territory
Disputed territory
British territory, French fishing and landing rights

FRENCH STRATEGIC PROBLEMS, 1740–1751

In 1744 war between France and Britain (War of the Austrian Succession) cut short supplies to New France. After Louisbourg fell in 1745, the British blockaded the St Lawrence. Making the best of this opportunity, British traders moved into the Ohio country where they offered goods at one-third to one-quarter the French price. Attempts by the French post commanders to forbid their native allies to trade with the British led to sullen resentment, then to open conflict. In 1744 the Miami sacked Fort Miami. The Huron burned the mission at Détroit and began attacks on French traders. The entire Wabash–Lake Erie area became unsafe for travel.

When the war ended in 1748, the French cut the price of trade goods by half and in 1749 ordered troops under Céloron de Blainville to tour the Ohio and eject British traders. The effect of this tour was slight. In 1751 the Miami destroyed Fort Vincennes and declared open support for the British.

In the northwest French trade also suffered. Although La Vérendrye and his sons had pushed trade and exploration to the Saskatchewan River, wartime scarcity and high prices induced many native groups to trade with the Hudson's Bay Company.

EUROPEAN TERRITORIAL CLAIMS, 1713–1763

In 1713 the Treaty of Utrecht assigned Acadia, Newfoundland, and the land surrounding Hudson Bay to Britain. The lower Great Lakes–Ohio area was to be a free trade zone. The treaty did not specify definite boundaries and called for a commission to settle them. Although views were exchanged in 1715 and the commission met from 1750 to 1754, the entirely different claims of France and Britain could not be reconciled. No settlement was reached until the Treaty of Paris in 1763.

THE FUR TRADE, ca 1755

Although licensed and regulated by the crown, the French fur trade was conducted by Montréal merchants who operated in small companies (sociétés), often in partnership with post commanders. At some posts (especially the entrepôts) concessions to trade were obtained by the purchase of a permit (congé) to take a load of trade goods (by 1755 about 2 tons) to the post. The number of congés was limited and varied between posts. At other posts trade was by monopoly lease for specified periods. Finally, at some posts trade was a crown monopoly (king's post) operated by agents. The mix of these three systems changed over time.

Fur imports at La Rochelle (pl 48) are some indication of the changing volume of the French fur trade. Comprehensive data on the sources of these furs are available only for the mid-1750s. Permit revenue for 1755 indicates that the products (mainly furs) of the northern posts were more valuable than those (furs and hides) of the southern ones. In the 1750s about 80% of the furs exported from North America were garnered by the French.

The lessons of the previous ten years were not lost on the French. The Ohio-Wabash country was of little economic value for the fur trade but was strategically of the highest importance. The French recognized that, if the lower Great Lakes natives were alienated, the Mississippi colonies would be cut off from Canada, and in time the upper Great Lakes Indians would drift to the British. Without native support, affirmed through treaties, competitive prices, and a show of strength, the interior would be lost.

In 1752 treaties with the eastern Dakota permitted the vigorous expansion of trade along the upper Mississippi. In the same year the French coerced the Miami back into the French alliance when an Indian party assisted by French soldiers destroyed the Miami's main village, built around a British post at Pickawillany. In 1753–4 French troops occupied four new posts in the upper Ohio, an area always claimed by France. Henley House, a Hudson's Bay outpost on the Albany River, was destroyed in 1755 by natives. For a time the French had secured the interior of North America.

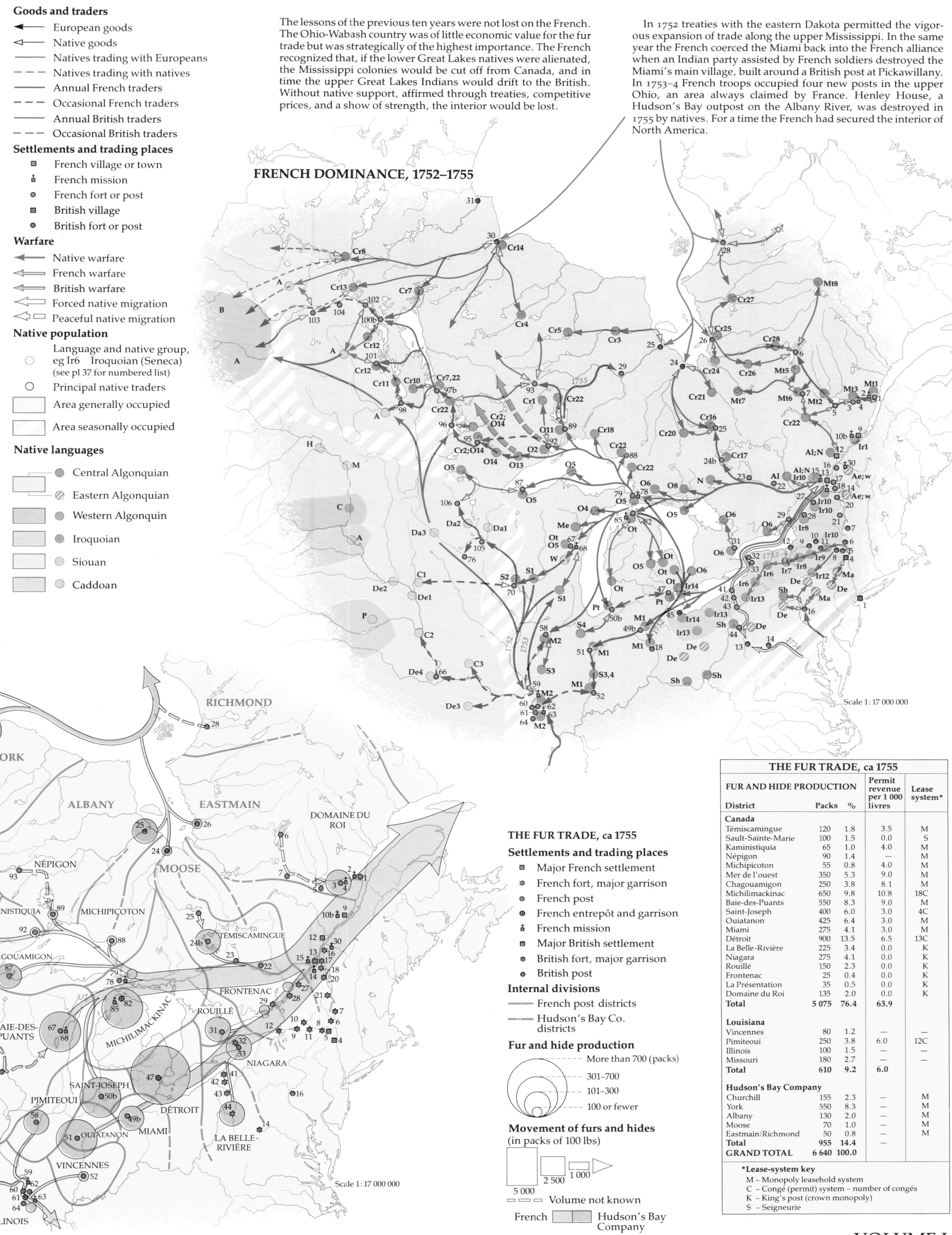
FRENCH DOMINANCE, 1752–1755
Goods and traders
European goods
Native goods
Natives trading with Europeans
Natives trading with natives
Annual French traders
Occasional French traders
Annual British traders
Occasional British traders
Settlements and trading places
French village or town
French mission
French fort or post
British village
British fort or post
Warfare
Native warfare
French warfare
British warfare
Forced native migration
Peaceful native migration
Native population
Language and native group, eg Ir6 Iroquoian (Seneca)
(see pl 37 for numbered list)
Principal native traders
Area generally occupied
Area seasonally occupied
Native languages
Central Algonquian
Eastern Algonquian
Western Algonquin
Iroquoian
Siouan
Caddoan
Scale 1: 17 000 000
THE FUR TRADE, ca 1755
Settlements and trading places
Major French settlement
French fort, major garrison
French post
French entrepôt and garrison
French mission
Major British settlement
British fort, major garrison
British post
Internal divisions
French post districts
Hudson's Bay Co. districts
Fur and hide production
More than 700 (packs)
301–700
101–300
100 or fewer
Movement of furs and hides
(in packs of 100 lbs)
5 000
2 500
1 000
Volume not known
French
Hudson's Bay Company
RICHMOND
YORK
ALBANY
EASTMAIN
DOMAINE DU ROI
MOOSE
NÉPIGON
MINISTIQUIA
MICHIPICOTON
TÉMISCAMINGUE
HAGOUAMIGON
FRONTENAC
ROUILLÉ
BAIE-DES-PUANTS
MICHILIMACKINAC
NIAGARA
SAINT-JOSEPH
PIMITEOUI
DÉTROIT
MIAMI
OUIATANON
LA BELLE-RIVIÈRE
VINCENNES
ILLINOIS
Scale 1: 17 000 000

THE FUR TRADE, ca 1755

FUR AND HIDE PRODUCTION District	Packs	%	Permit revenue per 1 000 livres	Lease system*
Canada				
Témiscamingue	120	1.8	3.5	M
Sault-Sainte-Marie	100	1.5	0.0	S
Kaministiquia	65	1.0	4.0	M
Népigon	90	1.4	—	M
Michipicoton	55	0.8	4.0	M
Mer de l'ouest	350	5.3	9.0	M
Chagouamigon	250	3.8	8.1	M
Michilimackinac	650	9.8	10.8	18C
Baie-des-Puants	550	8.3	9.0	M
Saint-Joseph	400	6.0	3.0	4C
Ouiatanon	425	6.4	3.0	M
Miami	275	4.1	3.0	M
Détroit	900	13.5	6.5	13C
La Belle-Rivière	225	3.4	0.0	K
Niagara	275	4.1	0.0	K
Rouillé	150	2.3	0.0	K
Frontenac	25	0.4	0.0	K
La Présentation	35	0.5	0.0	K
Domaine du Roi	135	2.0	0.0	K
Total	**5 075**	**76.4**	**63.9**	
Louisiana				
Vincennes	80	1.2	—	—
Pimiteoui	250	3.8	6.0	12C
Illinois	100	1.5	—	—
Missouri	180	2.7	—	—
Total	**610**	**9.2**	**6.0**	
Hudson's Bay Company				
Churchill	155	2.3	—	M
York	550	8.3	—	M
Albany	130	2.0	—	M
Moose	70	1.0	—	M
Eastmain/Richmond	50	0.8	—	M
Total	**955**	**14.4**	—	
GRAND TOTAL	**6 640**	**100.0**		

***Lease-system key**
M – Monopoly leasehold system
C – Congé (permit) system – number of congés
K – King's post (crown monopoly)
S – Seigneurie

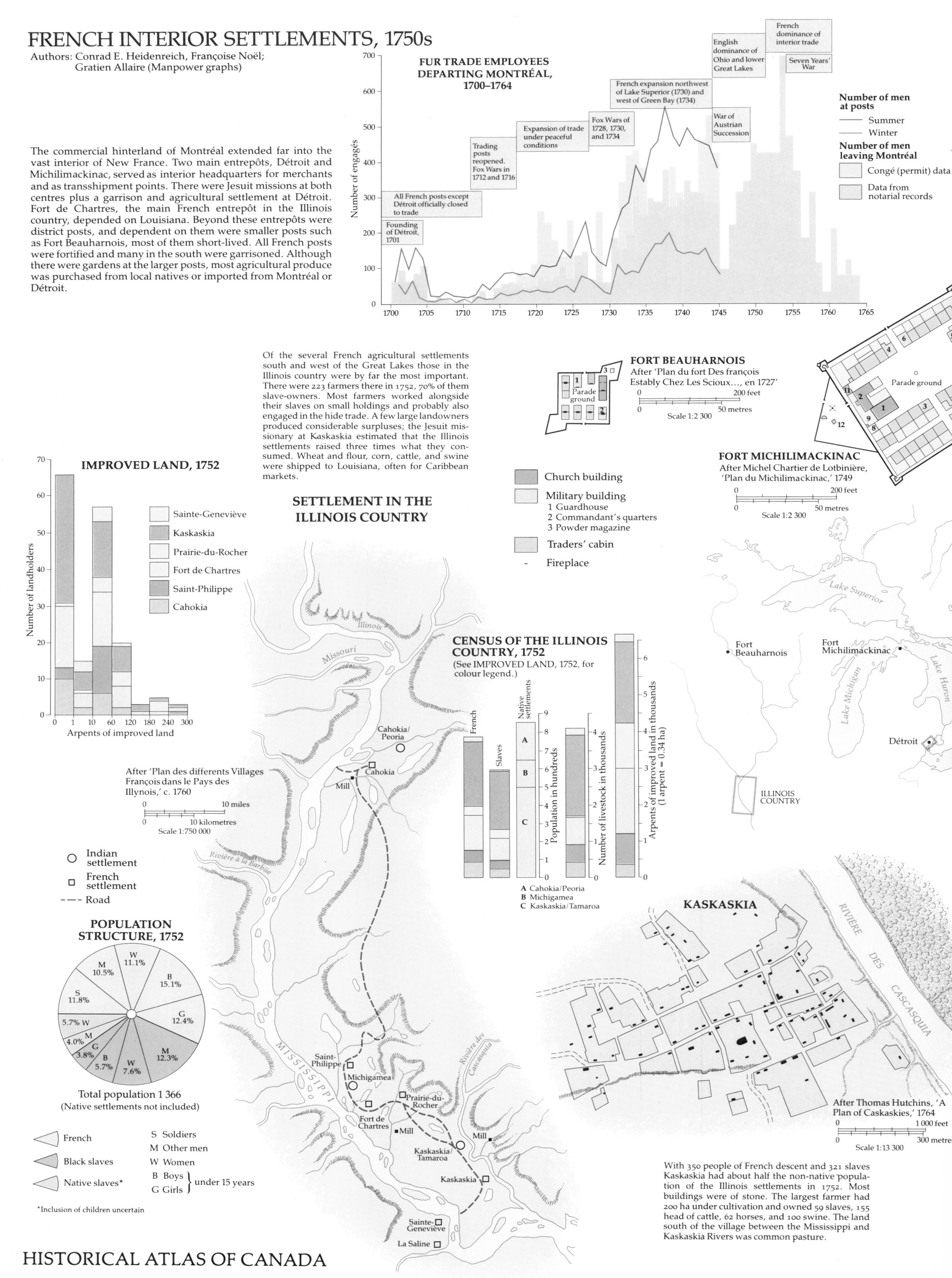
FRENCH INTERIOR SETTLEMENTS, 1750s
Authors: Conrad E. Heidenreich, Françoise Noël; Gratien Allaire (Manpower graphs)
The commercial hinterland of Montréal extended far into the vast interior of New France. Two main entrepôts, Détroit and Michilimackinac, served as interior headquarters for merchants and as transshipment points. There were Jesuit missions at both centres plus a garrison and agricultural settlement at Détroit. Fort de Chartres, the main French entrepôt in the Illinois country, depended on Louisiana. Beyond these entrepôts were district posts, and dependent on them were smaller posts such as Fort Beauharnois, most of them short-lived. All French posts were fortified and many in the south were garrisoned. Although there were gardens at the larger posts, most agricultural produce was purchased from local natives or imported from Montréal or Détroit.
FUR TRADE EMPLOYEES DEPARTING MONTRÉAL, 1700–1764
Number of engagés
Founding of Détroit, 1701
All French posts except Détroit officially closed to trade
Trading posts reopened. Fox Wars in 1712 and 1716
Expansion of trade under peaceful conditions
Fox Wars of 1728, 1730, and 1734
French expansion northwest of Lake Superior (1730) and west of Green Bay (1734)
War of Austrian Succession
English dominance of Ohio and lower Great Lakes
French dominance of interior trade
Seven Years' War
Number of men at posts
Summer
Winter
Number of men leaving Montréal
Congé (permit) data
Data from notarial records
Of the several French agricultural settlements south and west of the Great Lakes those in the Illinois country were by far the most important. There were 223 farmers there in 1752, 70% of them slave-owners. Most farmers worked alongside their slaves on small holdings and probably also engaged in the hide trade. A few large landowners produced considerable surpluses; the Jesuit missionary at Kaskaskia estimated that the Illinois settlements raised three times what they consumed. Wheat and flour, corn, cattle, and swine were shipped to Louisiana, often for Caribbean markets.
FORT BEAUHARNOIS
After 'Plan du fort Des françois Estably Chez Les Scioux..., en 1727'
Parade ground
Scale 1:2 300
FORT MICHILIMACKINAC
After Michel Chartier de Lotbinière, 'Plan du Michilimackinac,' 1749
Parade ground
Scale 1:2 300
Church building
Military building
1 Guardhouse
2 Commandant's quarters
3 Powder magazine
Traders' cabin
Fireplace
IMPROVED LAND, 1752
Number of landholders
Arpents of improved land
Sainte-Geneviève
Kaskaskia
Prairie-du-Rocher
Fort de Chartres
Saint-Philippe
Cahokia
SETTLEMENT IN THE ILLINOIS COUNTRY
After 'Plan des differents Villages François dans le Pays des Illynois,' c. 1760
Scale 1:750 000
Indian settlement
French settlement
Road
Illinois
Missouri
Rivière à la Barbüe
MISSISSIPPI
Rivière des Cascasquia
Cahokia/Peoria
Cahokia
Mill
Saint-Philippe
Michigamea
Prairie-du-Rocher
Fort de Chartres
Kaskaskia/Tamaroa
Kaskaskia
Sainte-Geneviève
La Saline
CENSUS OF THE ILLINOIS COUNTRY, 1752
(See IMPROVED LAND, 1752, for colour legend.)
French
Slaves
Native settlements
Population in hundreds
Number of livestock in thousands
Arpents of improved land in thousands (1 arpent = 0.34 ha)
A Cahokia/Peoria
B Michigamea
C Kaskaskia/Tamaroa
POPULATION STRUCTURE, 1752
Total population 1 366
(Native settlements not included)
French
Black slaves
Native slaves*
S Soldiers
M Other men
W Women
B Boys
G Girls
under 15 years
*Inclusion of children uncertain
Lake Superior
Lake Michigan
Lake Huron
Fort Beauharnois
Fort Michilimackinac
Détroit
ILLINOIS COUNTRY
KASKASKIA
RIVIÈRE DES CASCASQUIA
After Thomas Hutchins, 'A Plan of Caskaskies,' 1764
Scale 1:13 300
With 350 people of French descent and 321 slaves Kaskaskia had about half the non-native population of the Illinois settlements in 1752. Most buildings were of stone. The largest farmer had 200 ha under cultivation and owned 59 slaves, 155 head of cattle, 62 horses, and 100 swine. The land south of the village between the Mississippi and Kaskaskia Rivers was common pasture.
HISTORICAL ATLAS OF CANADA

FORT MICHILIMACKINAC, 1749–1750, AND FORT BEAUHARNOIS, 1727

Michilimackinac was the major entrepôt of the upper Great Lakes. In 1750 28 traders had establishments within the post and 10 families lived there; the summer population of traders and voyageurs was about 200.

Typical of small interior posts, Fort Beauharnois was built in 1727 for the Compagnie des Sioux. The ramparts were constructed of 4-m uprights in four days; buildings and furnishings took one month to complete. The post was open 1727–30 and 1732–7.

Three series of notarial documents – congés (permits), permissions, and contrats d'engagement – give some statistical information about the personnel of the fur trade. Established in 1681, abolished in 1696, and re-established in 1716, the permit system soon became almost indistinguishable from the permissions the governor granted to officers, merchants, and missionaries to send trade canoes and merchandise to particular posts. The holder of a permit or permission hired canoemen and frequently spelled out the terms of such work in a contrat d'engagement.

Judging by these sources, the men employed by the fur trade came, increasingly, from rural Montréal Island and from seigneuries nearby. There is record of 15 canoes leaving Montréal in 1715 and 77 in 1750. Between 1716 and 1730 the number of men per canoe doubled from three to six. By the 1730s the documents record some 400–500 men involved in most years, almost a third of them overwintering in the interior. In 1754, at the height of the French fur trade, there is record of almost 700 men employed seasonally. By this date the voyageur recorded in the contrats d'engagement was usually a canoeman hired to transport merchandise from Montréal to Détroit or Michilimackinac and return with a consignment of furs.

DESTINATION	1705	1715	1725		1735		1745		1755
	A	A	A	B	A	B	A	B	A
Unspecified*		1	33		2				
Témiscamingue				9		18		24	
Nipissing		1							
Michilimackinac		27	27	35	89	38	108	65	187
Michipicoton/Nipigon					5	23	5	36	20
Chagouamigon				16	6	24	2	30	10
Kamanistiquia				20	1	60	3	18	55
Mer l'Ouest					34	6	21	80	
La Baie				34	2	11	18	54	36
Les Sioux					23	22			
Saint Joseph			2	17	10	32	16	31	9
Illinois				13	17	18		7	13
Fort Chartres					1				
Lac Ontario		3					4		2
Détroit	111	16	8	45	57	102	102	55	130
Miami/Rivière Wabash			3	47	7	33	7	30	15
Ohio					2	5			1
TOTAL	111	48	73	236	256	392	286	430	478

*Pays d'en haut
A Individual contracts (engagés)
B Licenses issued to traders (congés)

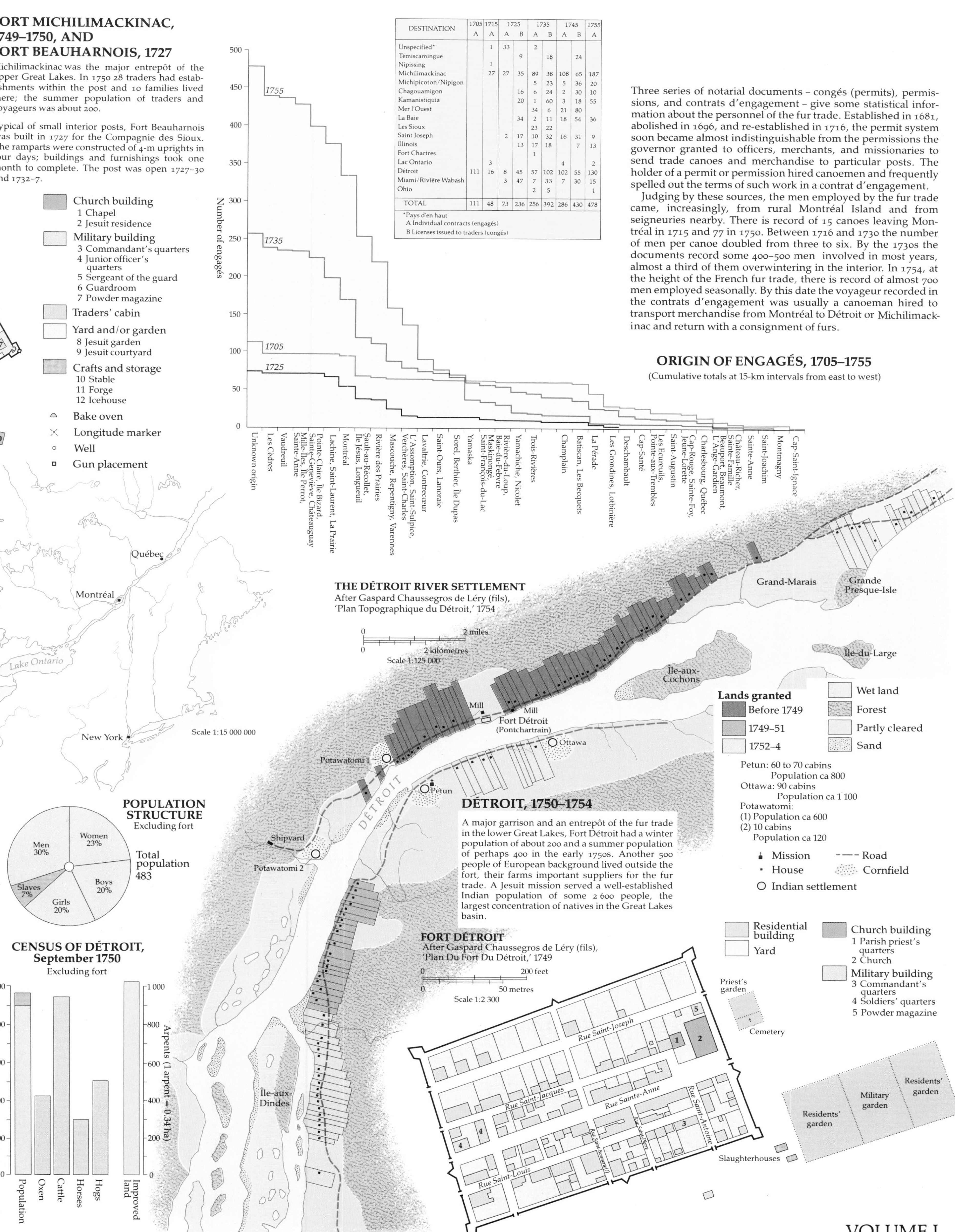

Church building
1 Chapel
2 Jesuit residence
Military building
3 Commandant's quarters
4 Junior officer's quarters
5 Sergeant of the guard
6 Guardroom
7 Powder magazine
Traders' cabin
Yard and/or garden
8 Jesuit garden
9 Jesuit courtyard
Crafts and storage
10 Stable
11 Forge
12 Icehouse
Bake oven
Longitude marker
Well
Gun placement
Québec
Montréal
Lake Ontario
New York
Scale 1:15 000 000
Number of engagés
1755
1735
1705
1725
Unknown origin
Les Cèdres
Vaudreuil
Mille-Îles, Île Perrot, Sainte-Anne
Pointe-Claire, Île Bizard, Sainte-Geneviève, Châteauguay
Lachine, Saint-Laurent, La Prairie
Montréal
Île Jésus, Longueuil
Sault-au-Récollet, Rivière des Prairies
Mascouche, Repentigny, Varennes
L'Assomption, Saint-Sulpice, Verchères, Saint-Charles
Lavaltrie, Contrecoeur
Saint-Ours, Lanoraie
Sorel, Berthier, Île Dupas
Yamaska
Maskinongé, Saint-François-du-Lac
Rivière-du-Loup, Baie-du-Febvre
Yamachiche, Nicolet
Trois-Rivières
Champlain
Batiscan, Les Becquets
La Pérade
Les Grondines, Lotbinière
Deschambault
Cap-Santé
Les Écureuils, Pointe-aux-Trembles
Saint-Augustin
Cap-Rouge, Sainte-Foy, Jeune-Lorette
Charlesbourg, Québec
Beauport, Beaumont, L'Ange-Gardien
Château-Richer, Sainte-Famille
Sainte-Anne
Saint-Joachim
Montmagny
Cap-Saint-Ignace
ORIGIN OF ENGAGÉS, 1705–1755
(Cumulative totals at 15-km intervals from east to west)
THE DÉTROIT RIVER SETTLEMENT
After Gaspard Chaussegros de Léry (fils), 'Plan Topographique du Détroit,' 1754
2 miles
2 kilometres
Scale 1:125 000
Grand-Marais
Grande Presque-Isle
Île-du-Large
Île-aux-Cochons
Mill
Fort Détroit (Pontchartrain)
Ottawa
Potawatomi 1
Petun
DÉTROIT
Shipyard
Potawatomi 2
Île-aux-Dindes
Lands granted
Before 1749
1749–51
1752–4
Wet land
Forest
Partly cleared
Sand
Petun: 60 to 70 cabins
Population ca 800
Ottawa: 90 cabins
Population ca 1 100
Potawatomi:
(1) Population ca 600
(2) 10 cabins
Population ca 120
Mission
House
Road
Cornfield
Indian settlement
POPULATION STRUCTURE
Excluding fort
Women 23%
Men 30%
Boys 20%
Girls 20%
Slaves 7%
Total population 483
CENSUS OF DÉTROIT, September 1750
Excluding fort
Population
Oxen
Cattle
Horses
Hogs
Improved land
Arpents (1 arpent = 0.34 ha)
FORT DÉTROIT
After Gaspard Chaussegros de Léry (fils), 'Plan Du Fort Du Détroit,' 1749
200 feet
50 metres
Scale 1:2 300
Residential building
Yard
Church building
1 Parish priest's quarters
2 Church
Military building
3 Commandant's quarters
4 Soldiers' quarters
5 Powder magazine
Priest's garden
Cemetery
Rue Saint-Joseph
Rue Saint-Jacques
Rue Sainte-Anne
Rue Saint-Antoine
Rue Saint-Louis
Residents' garden
Military garden
Slaughterhouses

DÉTROIT, 1750–1754

A major garrison and an entrepôt of the fur trade in the lower Great Lakes, Fort Détroit had a winter population of about 200 and a summer population of perhaps 400 in the early 1750s. Another 500 people of European background lived outside the fort, their farms important suppliers for the fur trade. A Jesuit mission served a well-established Indian population of some 2 600 people, the largest concentration of natives in the Great Lakes basin.

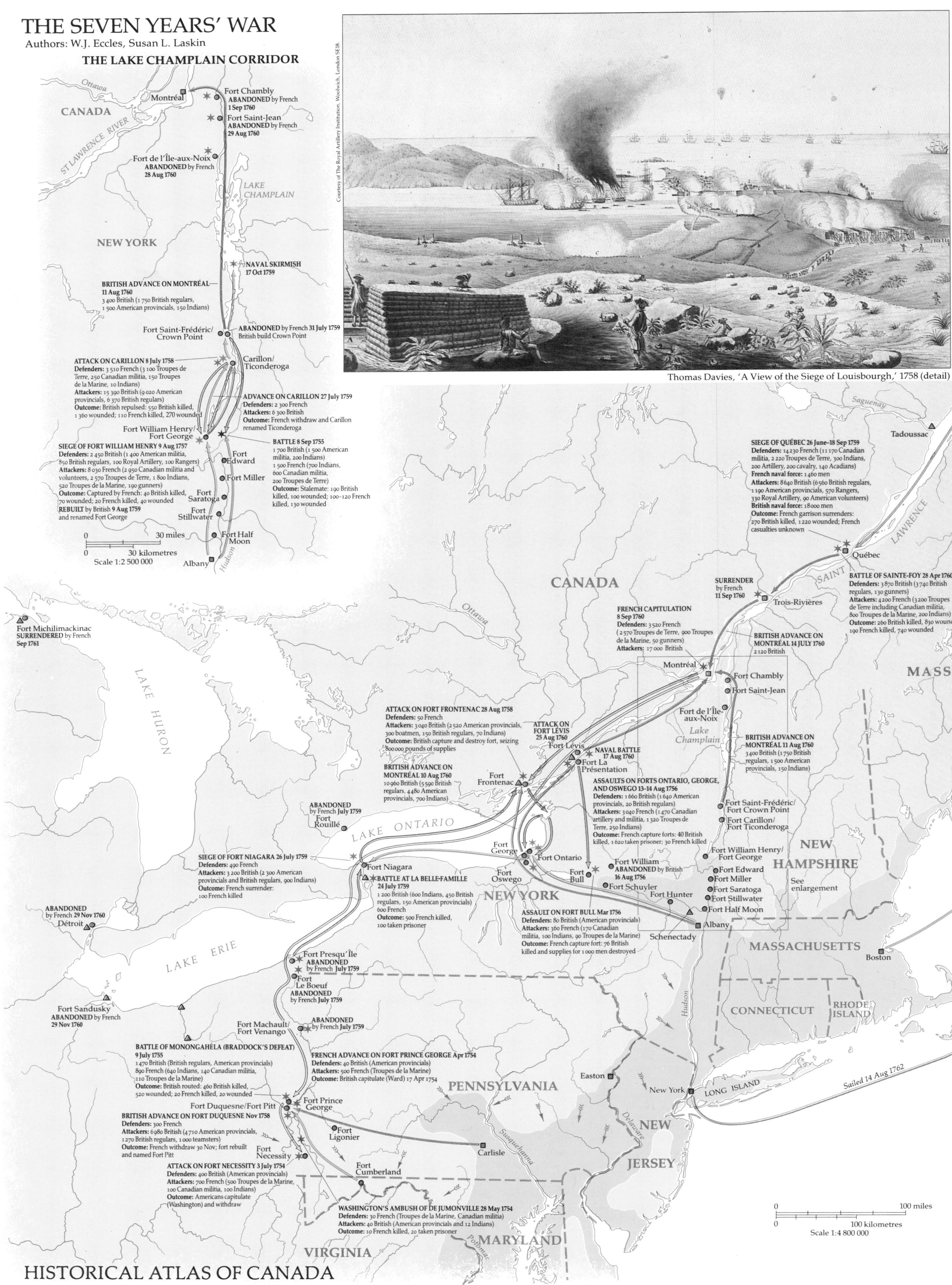

THE SEVEN YEARS' WAR
Authors: W.J. Eccles, Susan L. Laskin
THE LAKE CHAMPLAIN CORRIDOR
Ottawa
Montréal
CANADA
ST LAWRENCE RIVER
Fort Chambly
ABANDONED by French
1 Sep 1760
Fort Saint-Jean
ABANDONED by French
29 Aug 1760
Fort de l'Île-aux-Noix
ABANDONED by French
28 Aug 1760
LAKE CHAMPLAIN
NEW YORK
NAVAL SKIRMISH
17 Oct 1759
BRITISH ADVANCE ON MONTRÉAL
11 Aug 1760
3 400 British (1 750 British regulars, 1 500 American provincials, 150 Indians)
Fort Saint-Frédéric/ Crown Point
ABANDONED by French 31 July 1759
British build Crown Point
ATTACK ON CARILLON 8 July 1758
Defenders: 3 510 French (3 100 Troupes de Terre, 250 Canadian militia, 150 Troupes de la Marine, 10 Indians)
Attackers: 15 390 British (9 020 American provincials, 6 370 British regulars)
Outcome: British repulsed: 550 British killed, 1 360 wounded; 110 French killed, 270 wounded
Carillon/ Ticonderoga
ADVANCE ON CARILLON 27 July 1759
Defenders: 2 300 French
Attackers: 6 300 British
Outcome: French withdraw and Carillon renamed Ticonderoga
Fort William Henry/ Fort George
SIEGE OF FORT WILLIAM HENRY 9 Aug 1757
Defenders: 2 450 British (1 400 American militia, 850 British regulars, 100 Royal Artillery, 100 Rangers)
Attackers: 8 030 French (2 950 Canadian militia and volunteers, 2 570 Troupes de Terre, 1 800 Indians, 520 Troupes de la Marine, 190 gunners)
Outcome: Captured by French: 40 British killed, 70 wounded; 20 French killed, 40 wounded
REBUILT by British 9 Aug 1759 and renamed Fort George
BATTLE 8 Sep 1755
1 700 British (1 500 American militia, 200 Indians)
1 500 French (700 Indians, 600 Canadian militia, 200 Troupes de Terre)
Outcome: Stalemate: 190 British killed, 100 wounded; 100–120 French killed, 130 wounded
Fort Edward
Fort Miller
Fort Saratoga
Fort Stillwater
Fort Half Moon
Albany
Hudson
0 30 miles
0 30 kilometres
Scale 1:2 500 000
Courtesy of The Royal Artillery Institution, Woolwich, London SE18.
Saguenay
Tadoussac
SIEGE OF QUÉBEC 26 June–18 Sep 1759
Defenders: 14 230 French (11 170 Canadian militia, 2 220 Troupes de Terre, 300 Indians, 200 Artillery, 200 cavalry, 140 Acadians)
French naval force: 1 460 men
Attackers: 8 640 British (6 560 British regulars, 1 190 American provincials, 570 Rangers, 330 Royal Artillery, 90 American volunteers)
British naval force: 18 000 men
Outcome: French garrison surrenders: 270 British killed, 1 220 wounded; French casualties unknown
LAWRENCE
SAINT
Québec
BATTLE OF SAINTE-FOY 28 Apr 1760
Defenders: 3 870 British (3 740 British regulars, 130 gunners)
Attackers: 4 200 French (3 200 Troupes de Terre including Canadian militia, 800 Troupes de la Marine, 200 Indians)
Outcome: 260 British killed, 830 wounded; 190 French killed, 740 wounded
CANADA
SURRENDER by French 11 Sep 1760
Trois-Rivières
FRENCH CAPITULATION 8 Sep 1760
Defenders: 3 520 French (2 570 Troupes de Terre, 900 Troupes de la Marine, 50 gunners)
Attackers: 17 000 British
BRITISH ADVANCE ON MONTRÉAL 14 JULY 1760
2 120 British
MASSAC
Ottawa
Fort Michilimackinac
SURRENDERED by French
Sep 1761
LAKE HURON
Montréal
Fort Chambly
Fort Saint-Jean
Fort de l'Île-aux-Noix
Lake Champlain
BRITISH ADVANCE ON MONTRÉAL 11 Aug 1760
3400 British (1 750 British regulars, 1 500 American provincials, 150 Indians)
ATTACK ON FORT FRONTENAC 28 Aug 1758
Defenders: 50 French
Attackers: 3 040 British (2 520 American provincials, 300 boatmen, 150 British regulars, 70 Indians)
Outcome: British capture and destroy fort, seizing 800 000 pounds of supplies
ATTACK ON FORT LEVIS 25 Aug 1760
Fort Lévis
NAVAL BATTLE 17 Aug 1760
Fort La Présentation
BRITISH ADVANCE ON MONTRÉAL 10 Aug 1760
10 960 British (5 590 British regulars, 4 480 American provincials, 700 Indians)
Fort Frontenac
ASSAULTS ON FORTS ONTARIO, GEORGE, AND OSWEGO 13–14 Aug 1756
Defenders: 1 660 British (1 640 American provincials, 20 British regulars)
Attackers: 3 040 French (1 470 Canadian artillery and militia, 1 320 Troupes de Terre, 250 Indians)
Outcome: French capture forts: 40 British killed, 1 620 taken prisoner; 30 French killed
Fort Saint-Frédéric/ Fort Crown Point
Fort Carillon/ Fort Ticonderoga
ABANDONED by French July 1759
Fort Rouillé
LAKE ONTARIO
Fort George
Fort Ontario
Fort Oswego
Fort Bull
Fort William ABANDONED by British 16 Aug 1756
Fort Schuyler
Fort William Henry/ Fort George
Fort Edward
Fort Miller
Fort Saratoga
Fort Stillwater
Fort Half Moon
NEW HAMPSHIRE
See enlargement
SIEGE OF FORT NIAGARA 26 July 1759
Defenders: 490 French
Attackers: 3 200 British (2 300 American provincials and British regulars, 900 Indians)
Outcome: French surrender: 100 French killed
Fort Niagara
BATTLE AT LA BELLE-FAMILLE 24 July 1759
1 200 British (600 Indians, 450 British regulars, 150 American provincials)
600 French
Outcome: 500 French killed, 100 taken prisoner
NEW YORK
Fort Hunter
ASSAULT ON FORT BULL Mar 1756
Defenders: 80 British (American provincials)
Attackers: 360 French (170 Canadian militia, 100 Indians, 90 Troupes de la Marine)
Outcome: French capture fort: 76 British killed and supplies for 1 000 men destroyed
Albany
Schenectady
ABANDONED by French 29 Nov 1760
Détroit
LAKE ERIE
Fort Presqu'Île ABANDONED by French July 1759
Fort Le Boeuf ABANDONED by French July 1759
MASSACHUSETTS
Boston
Hudson
Fort Sandusky
ABANDONED by French
29 Nov 1760
Fort Machault/ Fort Venango
ABANDONED by French July 1759
CONNECTICUT
RHODE ISLAND
BATTLE OF MONONGAHELA (BRADDOCK'S DEFEAT)
9 July 1755
1 470 British (British regulars, American provincials)
890 French (640 Indians, 140 Canadian militia, 110 Troupes de la Marine)
Outcome: British routed: 460 British killed, 520 wounded; 20 French killed, 20 wounded
FRENCH ADVANCE ON FORT PRINCE GEORGE Apr 1754
Defenders: 40 British (American provincials)
Attackers: 500 French (Troupes de la Marine)
Outcome: British capitulate (Ward) 17 Apr 1754
PENNSYLVANIA
Easton
New York
LONG ISLAND
Sailed 14 Aug 1762
Fort Duquesne/Fort Pitt
Fort Prince George
BRITISH ADVANCE ON FORT DUQUESNE Nov 1758
Defenders: 300 French
Attackers: 6 980 British (4 710 American provincials, 1 270 British regulars, 1 000 teamsters)
Outcome: French withdraw 30 Nov; fort rebuilt and named Fort Pitt
Fort Ligonier
Fort Necessity
Carlisle
Susquehanna
Delaware
NEW JERSEY
ATTACK ON FORT NECESSITY 3 July 1754
Defenders: 400 British (American provincials)
Attackers: 700 French (500 Troupes de la Marine, 100 Canadian militia, 100 Indians)
Outcome: Americans capitulate (Washington) and withdraw
Fort Cumberland
WASHINGTON'S AMBUSH OF DE JUMONVILLE 28 May 1754
Defenders: 30 French (Troupes de la Marine, Canadian militia)
Attackers: 40 British (American provincials and 12 Indians)
Outcome: 10 French killed, 20 taken prisoner
MARYLAND
Potomac
VIRGINIA
0 100 miles
0 100 kilometres
Scale 1:4 800 000

Thomas Davies, 'A View of the Siege of Louisbourgh,' 1758 (detail)

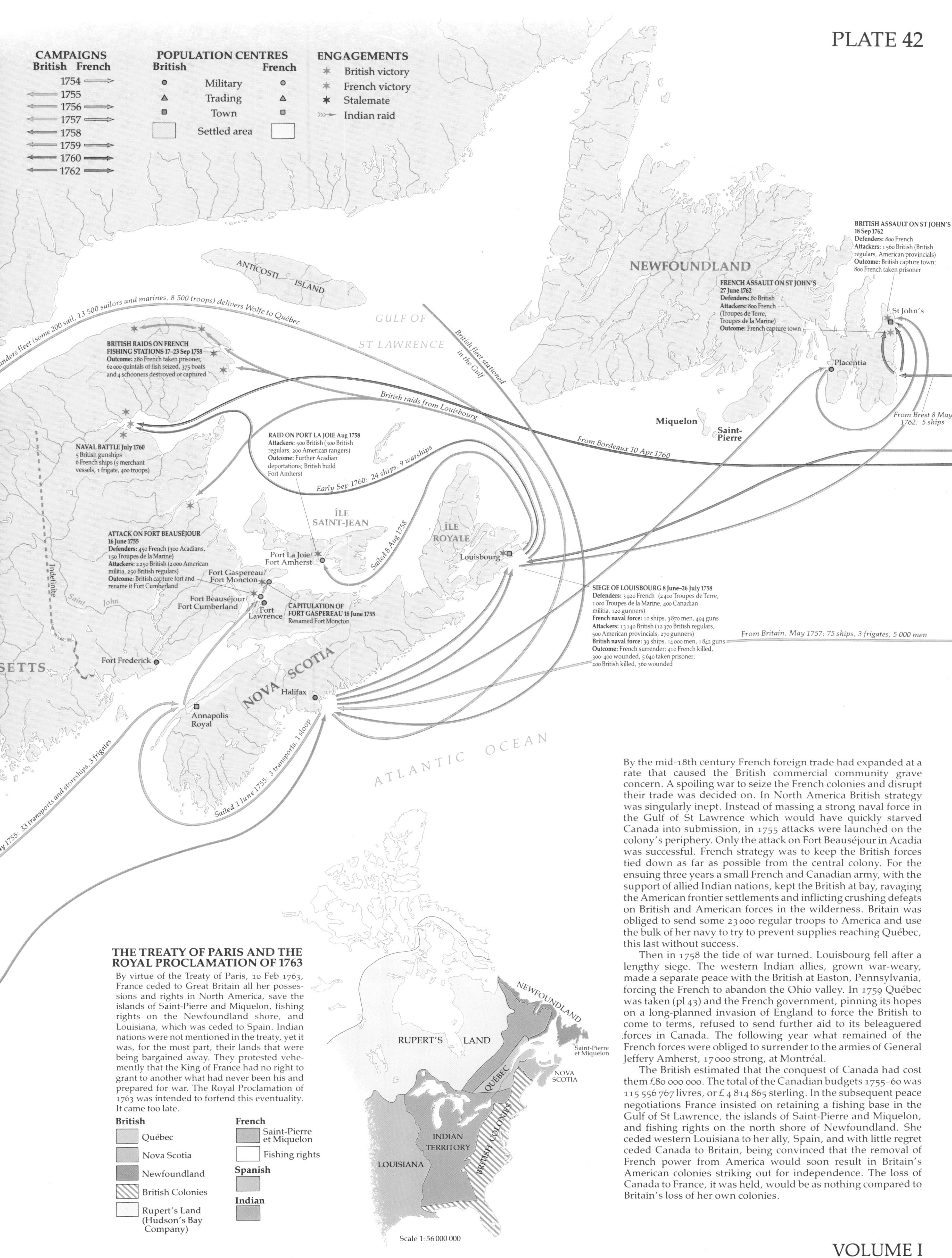
CAMPAIGNS
British French
1754
1755
1756
1757
1758
1759
1760
1762
POPULATION CENTRES
British French
Military
Trading
Town
Settled area
ENGAGEMENTS
British victory
French victory
Stalemate
Indian raid
ANTICOSTI ISLAND
NEWFOUNDLAND
GULF OF ST LAWRENCE
aunders' fleet (some 200 sail, 13 500 sailors and marines, 8 500 troops) delivers Wolfe to Québec
British fleet stationed in the Gulf
BRITISH RAIDS ON FRENCH FISHING STATIONS 17–23 Sep 1758
Outcome: 280 French taken prisoner, 62 000 quintals of fish seized, 375 boats and 4 schooners destroyed or captured
British raids from Louisbourg
NAVAL BATTLE July 1760
5 British gunships
6 French ships (5 merchant vessels, 1 frigate, 400 troops)
RAID ON PORT LA JOIE Aug 1758
Attackers: 500 British (300 British regulars, 200 American rangers)
Outcome: Further Acadian deportations; British build Fort Amherst
Early Sep 1760: 24 ships, 9 warships
From Bordeaux 10 Apr 1760
BRITISH ASSAULT ON ST JOHN'S 18 Sep 1762
Defenders: 800 French
Attackers: 1 560 British (British regulars, American provincials)
Outcome: British capture town: 800 French taken prisoner
FRENCH ASSAULT ON ST JOHN'S 27 June 1762
Defenders: 80 British
Attackers: 800 French (Troupes de Terre, Troupes de la Marine)
Outcome: French capture town
St John's
Placentia
Miquelon
Saint-Pierre
From Brest 8 May 1762: 5 ships
ÎLE SAINT-JEAN
Sailed 8 Aug 1758
ÎLE ROYALE
Louisbourg
Port La Joie/ Fort Amherst
ATTACK ON FORT BEAUSÉJOUR 16 June 1755
Defenders: 450 French (300 Acadians, 150 Troupes de la Marine)
Attackers: 2 250 British (2 000 American militia, 250 British regulars)
Outcome: British capture fort and rename it Fort Cumberland
Fort Gaspereau/ Fort Moncton
Fort Beauséjour/ Fort Cumberland
Fort Lawrence
CAPITULATION OF FORT GASPEREAU 18 June 1755
Renamed Fort Moncton
Indefinite
Saint John
Fort Frederick
SETTS
SIEGE OF LOUISBOURG 8 June–26 July 1758
Defenders: 3 920 French (2 400 Troupes de Terre, 1 000 Troupes de la Marine, 400 Canadian militia, 120 gunners)
French naval force: 10 ships, 3 870 men, 494 guns
Attackers: 13 140 British (12 370 British regulars, 500 American provincials, 270 gunners)
British naval force: 39 ships, 14 000 men, 1 842 guns
Outcome: French surrender: 410 French killed, 300-400 wounded, 5 640 taken prisoner; 200 British killed, 360 wounded
From Britain, May 1757: 75 ships, 3 frigates, 5 000 men
NOVA SCOTIA
Halifax
Annapolis Royal
ATLANTIC OCEAN
Sailed 1 June 1755: 3 transports, 1 sloop
ay 1755: 33 transports and storeships, 3 frigates
NEWFOUNDLAND
RUPERT'S LAND
QUÉBEC
Saint-Pierre et Miquelon
NOVA SCOTIA
INDIAN TERRITORY
LOUISIANA
BRITISH COLONIES
British
Québec
Nova Scotia
Newfoundland
British Colonies
Rupert's Land (Hudson's Bay Company)
French
Saint-Pierre et Miquelon
Fishing rights
Spanish
Indian
Scale 1:56 000 000

THE TREATY OF PARIS AND THE ROYAL PROCLAMATION OF 1763

By virtue of the Treaty of Paris, 10 Feb 1763, France ceded to Great Britain all her possessions and rights in North America, save the islands of Saint-Pierre and Miquelon, fishing rights on the Newfoundland shore, and Louisiana, which was ceded to Spain. Indian nations were not mentioned in the treaty, yet it was, for the most part, their lands that were being bargained away. They protested vehemently that the King of France had no right to grant to another what had never been his and prepared for war. The Royal Proclamation of 1763 was intended to forfend this eventuality. It came too late.

By the mid-18th century French foreign trade had expanded at a rate that caused the British commercial community grave concern. A spoiling war to seize the French colonies and disrupt their trade was decided on. In North America British strategy was singularly inept. Instead of massing a strong naval force in the Gulf of St Lawrence which would have quickly starved Canada into submission, in 1755 attacks were launched on the colony's periphery. Only the attack on Fort Beauséjour in Acadia was successful. French strategy was to keep the British forces tied down as far as possible from the central colony. For the ensuing three years a small French and Canadian army, with the support of allied Indian nations, kept the British at bay, ravaging the American frontier settlements and inflicting crushing defeats on British and American forces in the wilderness. Britain was obliged to send some 23 000 regular troops to America and use the bulk of her navy to try to prevent supplies reaching Québec, this last without success.

Then in 1758 the tide of war turned. Louisbourg fell after a lengthy siege. The western Indian allies, grown war-weary, made a separate peace with the British at Easton, Pennsylvania, forcing the French to abandon the Ohio valley. In 1759 Québec was taken (pl 43) and the French government, pinning its hopes on a long-planned invasion of England to force the British to come to terms, refused to send further aid to its beleaguered forces in Canada. The following year what remained of the French forces were obliged to surrender to the armies of General Jeffery Amherst, 17 000 strong, at Montréal.

The British estimated that the conquest of Canada had cost them £80 000 000. The total of the Canadian budgets 1755–60 was 115 556 767 livres, or £4 814 865 sterling. In the subsequent peace negotiations France insisted on retaining a fishing base in the Gulf of St Lawrence, the islands of Saint-Pierre and Miquelon, and fishing rights on the north shore of Newfoundland. She ceded western Louisiana to her ally, Spain, and with little regret ceded Canada to Britain, being convinced that the removal of French power from America would soon result in Britain's American colonies striking out for independence. The loss of Canada to France, it was held, would be as nothing compared to Britain's loss of her own colonies.

THE BATTLES FOR QUÉBEC, 1759 AND 1760

Authors: W.J. Eccles, Susan L. Laskin

THE BATTLE OF QUÉBEC, 13 SEPTEMBER 1759

After fruitless manoeuvering along the Beauport shore during the summer of 1759 Major-General Wolfe decided on one final attempt to take Québec. His brigadiers recommended landing the army upriver to cut the road to the French supply base at Batiscan. Wolfe chose instead to land at Anse-au-Foulon, leaving the French supply route open. Landing in three waves, with a force less than 4 500 strong, the British army assembled on a slope with high ground between it and Québec. On that high ground Montcalm mustered his main force, some 4 500 regulars and militia. In Wolfe's rear, two hours' march away, was Bougainville's 3 000-man élite force. On Wolfe's flanks were the Canadian militia and Indians. Montcalm, who had some 13 000 men at his disposal, merely had to bring up his cannon and then wait for Bougainville to arrive. Wolfe's men could not remain where they were. To attack Montcalm's position in the face of cannon fire while it was being attacked in the rear and on both flanks by vastly superior numbers would assuredly have resulted in the destruction of Wolfe's army, for whom retreat was impossible. Wolfe had dug a grave for his army but Montcalm marched his own army into it. Instead of waiting to gather his forces he rushed his hastily assembled main force of 4 500 in a headlong attack on Wolfe. Holding their fire until the French columns were at close range, the British volleys sent the French reeling back. Only the Canadian militia on the flanks prevented the British from pursuing the French into the city. At a council of war the French officers refused to give battle again; they insisted on retiring upriver to regroup. Attempts to get supplies and reinforcements into Québec were baulked by Commandant de Ramezay's precipitate surrender of the city on 18 September.

THE BATTLE, 13 SEPTEMBER 1759

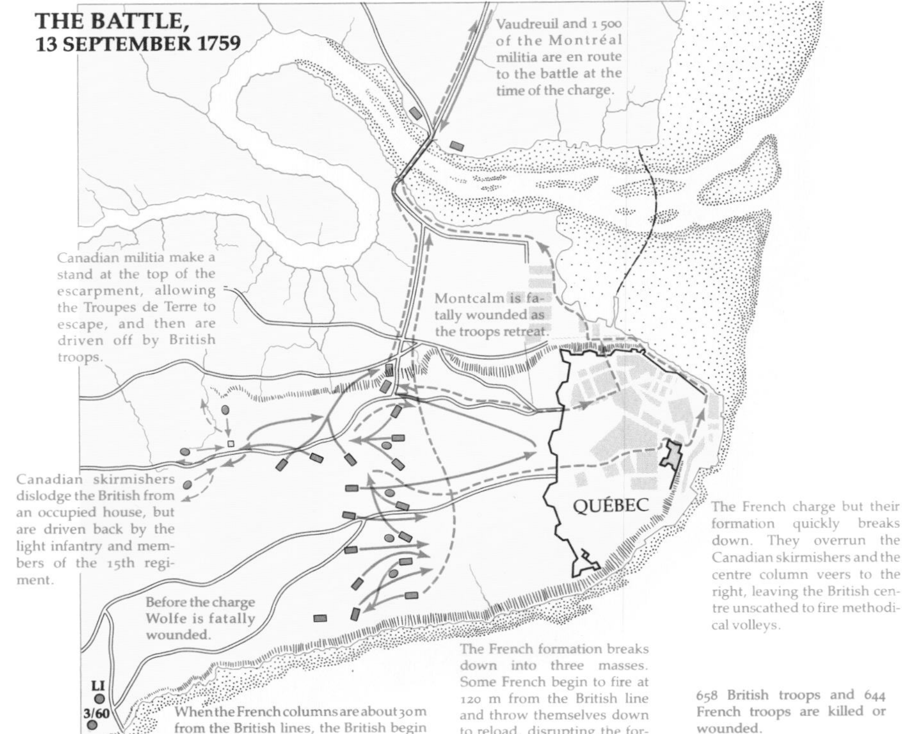

Vaudreuil and 1 500 of the Montréal militia are en route to the battle at the time of the charge.
Canadian militia make a stand at the top of the escarpment, allowing the Troupes de Terre to escape, and then are driven off by British troops.
Montcalm is fatally wounded as the troops retreat.
Canadian skirmishers dislodge the British from an occupied house, but are driven back by the light infantry and members of the 15th regiment.
QUÉBEC
The French charge but their formation quickly breaks down. They overrun the Canadian skirmishers and the centre column veers to the right, leaving the British centre unscathed to fire methodical volleys.
Before the charge Wolfe is fatally wounded.
LI
3/60
The French formation breaks down into three masses. Some French begin to fire at 120 m from the British line and throw themselves down to reload, disrupting the formation.
658 British troops and 644 French troops are killed or wounded.
When the French columns are about 30 m from the British lines, the British begin to fire by platoons. They then advance a few metres and fire in a general volley. The French columns crumble and retreat, pursued by the British.

AFTERMATH, 13 SEPTEMBER 175…

Bougainville had not been informed of the British landing until 9:00 am and arrives on the battlefield with about 2 000 men after the battle is over.

Bougainville s… some troops … capture the S… battery, but the… driven back b… light infantry… the 3/60 regim…

LI
3/60

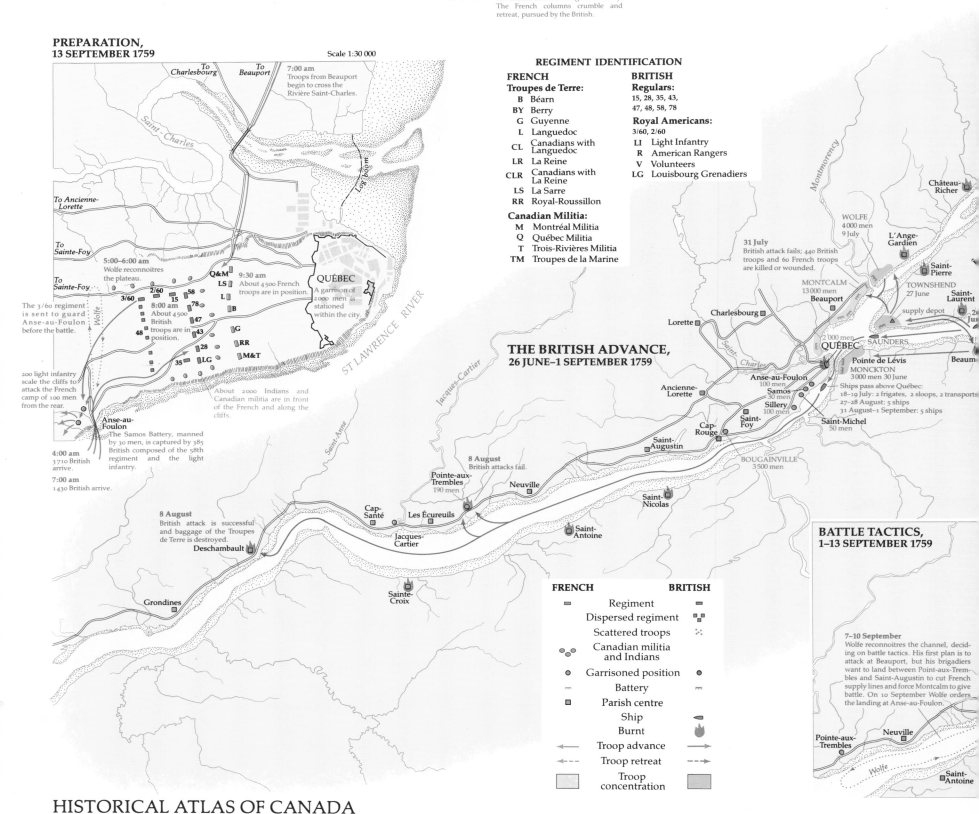

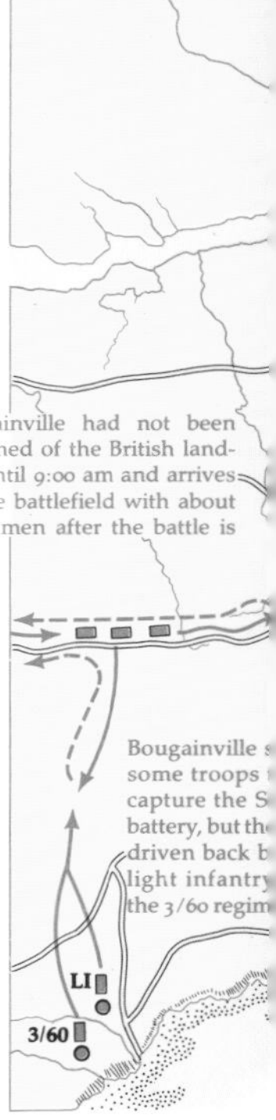

PREPARATION, 13 SEPTEMBER 1759

Scale 1:30 000

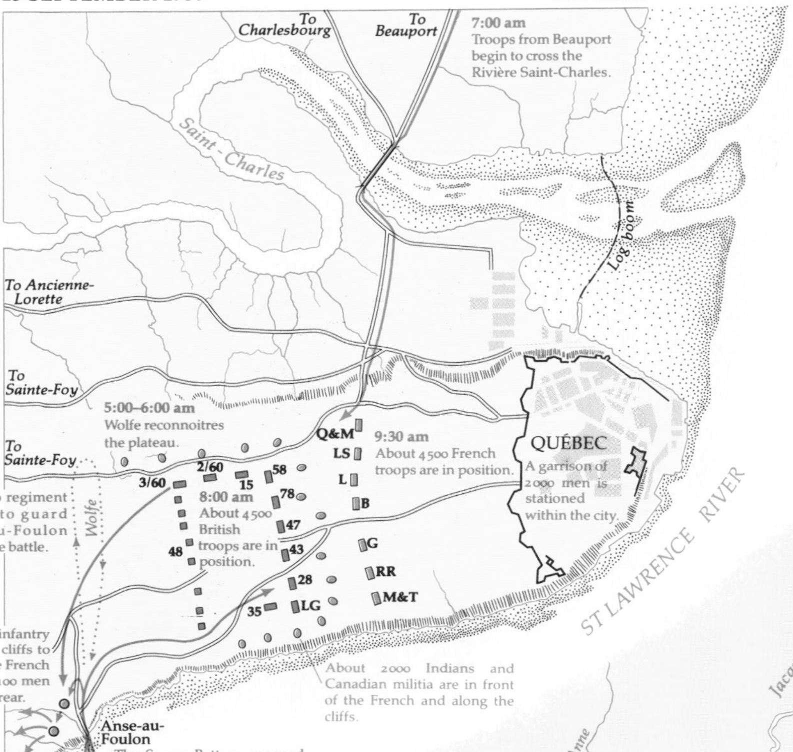

To Charlesbourg
To Beauport
7:00 am Troops from Beauport begin to cross the Rivière Saint-Charles.
Saint-Charles
Log boom
To Ancienne-Lorette
To Sainte-Foy
To Sainte-Foy
5:00–6:00 am Wolfe reconnoitres the plateau.
Q&M
LS
L
B
G
RR
M&T
9:30 am About 4 500 French troops are in position.
QUÉBEC
A garrison of 2 000 men is stationed within the city.
3/60
2/60
15
58
78
47
43
48
28
35
LG
8:00 am About 4 500 British troops are in position.
ST LAWRENCE RIVER
Wolfe
The 3/60 regiment is sent to guard Anse-au-Foulon before the battle.
200 light infantry scale the cliffs to attack the French camp of 100 men from the rear.
Anse-au-Foulon
The Samos Battery, manned by 30 men, is captured by 385 British composed of the 58th regiment and the light infantry.
About 2000 Indians and Canadian militia are in front of the French and along the cliffs.
4:00 am 3 710 British arrive.
7:00 am 1 430 British arrive.

REGIMENT IDENTIFICATION

FRENCH

Troupes de Terre:

B	Béarn
BY	Berry
G	Guyenne
L	Languedoc
CL	Canadians with Languedoc
LR	La Reine
CLR	Canadians with La Reine
LS	La Sarre
RR	Royal-Roussillon

Canadian Militia:

M	Montréal Militia
Q	Québec Militia
T	Trois-Rivières Militia
TM	Troupes de la Marine

BRITISH

Regulars:
15, 28, 35, 43, 47, 48, 58, 78

Royal Americans:
3/60, 2/60

LI	Light Infantry
R	American Rangers
V	Volunteers
LG	Louisbourg Grenadiers

THE BRITISH ADVANCE, 26 JUNE–1 SEPTEMBER 1759

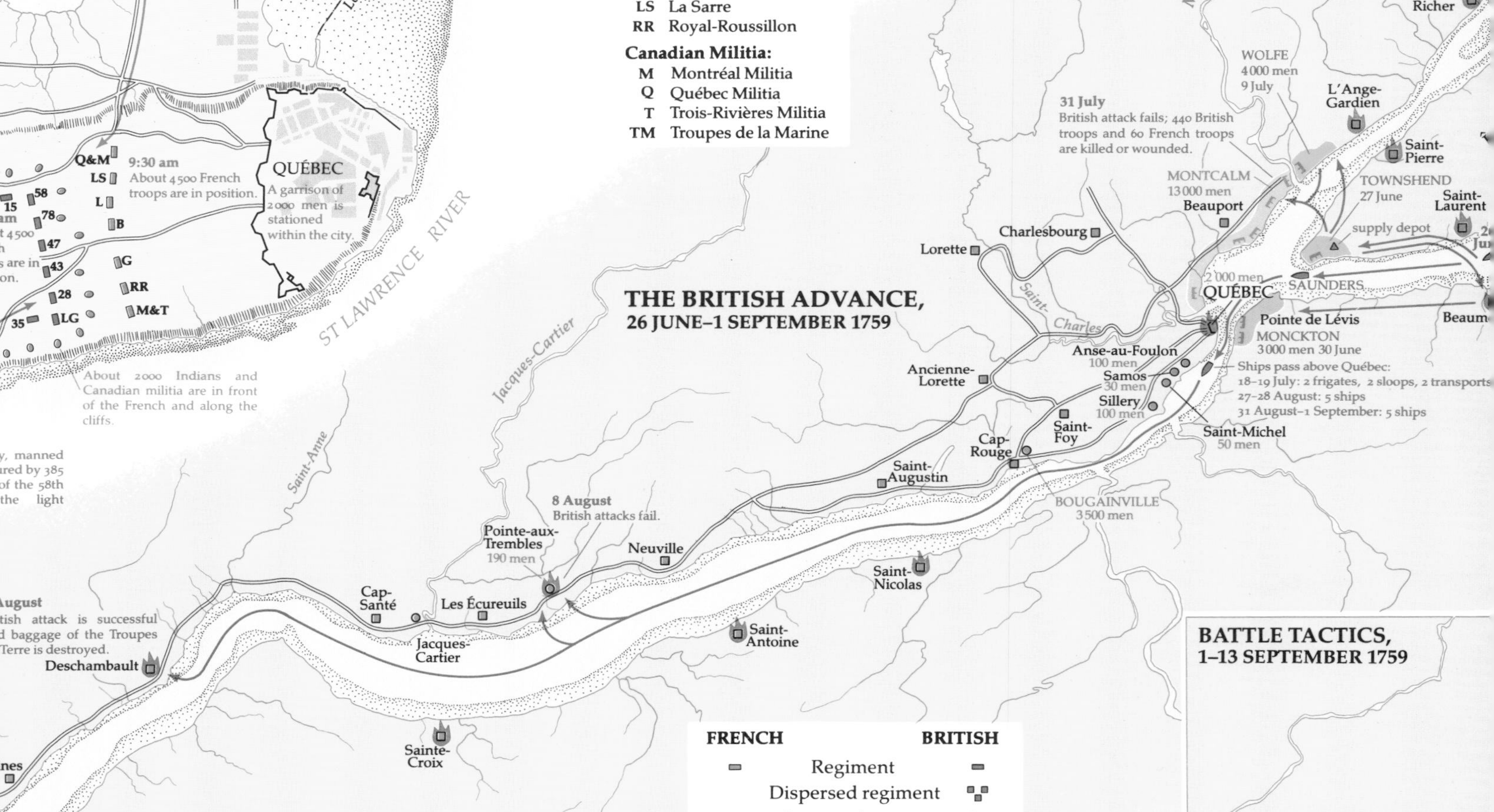

Montmorency
Château-Richer
WOLFE 4 000 men 9 July
L'Ange-Gardien
31 July British attack fails; 440 British troops and 60 French troops are killed or wounded.
Saint-Pierre
TOWNSHEND 27 June
Saint-Laurent
MONTCALM 13 000 men
Beauport
supply depot
Charlesbourg
Lorette
2 000 men
QUÉBEC
SAUNDERS
Beaum…
Saint-Charles
Pointe de Lévis
MONCKTON 3 000 men 30 June
Anse-au-Foulon 100 men
Samos 30 men
Sillery 100 men
Ships pass above Québec: 18–19 July: 2 frigates, 2 sloops, 2 transports; 27–28 August: 5 ships; 31 August–1 September: 5 ships
Saint-Michel 50 men
Ancienne-Lorette
Sainte-Foy
Cap-Rouge
Saint-Augustin
BOUGAINVILLE 3 500 men
Jacques-Cartier
Saint-Anne
8 August British attacks fail.
Pointe-aux-Trembles 190 men
Neuville
Saint-Nicolas
Cap-Santé
Les Écureuils
Jacques-Cartier
Saint-Antoine
8 August British attack is successful and baggage of the Troupes de Terre is destroyed.
Deschambault
Sainte-Croix
Grondines

FRENCH		BRITISH
▭	Regiment	▭
	Dispersed regiment	▫
	Scattered troops	⁘
◦◦	Canadian militia and Indians	
●	Garrisoned position	●
	Battery	
▪	Parish centre	
	Ship	▬
	Burnt	♨
←	Troop advance	→
←--	Troop retreat	--→
▭	Troop concentration	▭

BATTLE TACTICS, 1–13 SEPTEMBER 1759

7–10 September Wolfe reconnoitres the channel, deciding on battle tactics. His first plan is to attack at Beauport, but his brigadiers want to land between Point-aux-Trembles and Saint-Augustin to cut French supply lines and force Montcalm to give battle. On 10 September Wolfe orders the landing at Anse-au-Foulon.

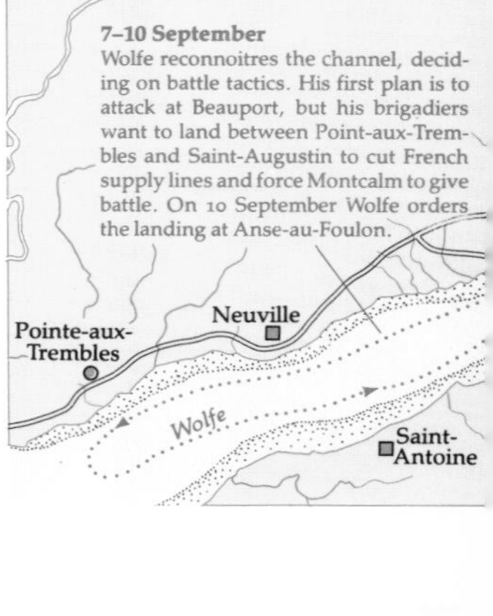

Pointe-aux-Trembles
Neuville
Wolfe
Saint-Antoine

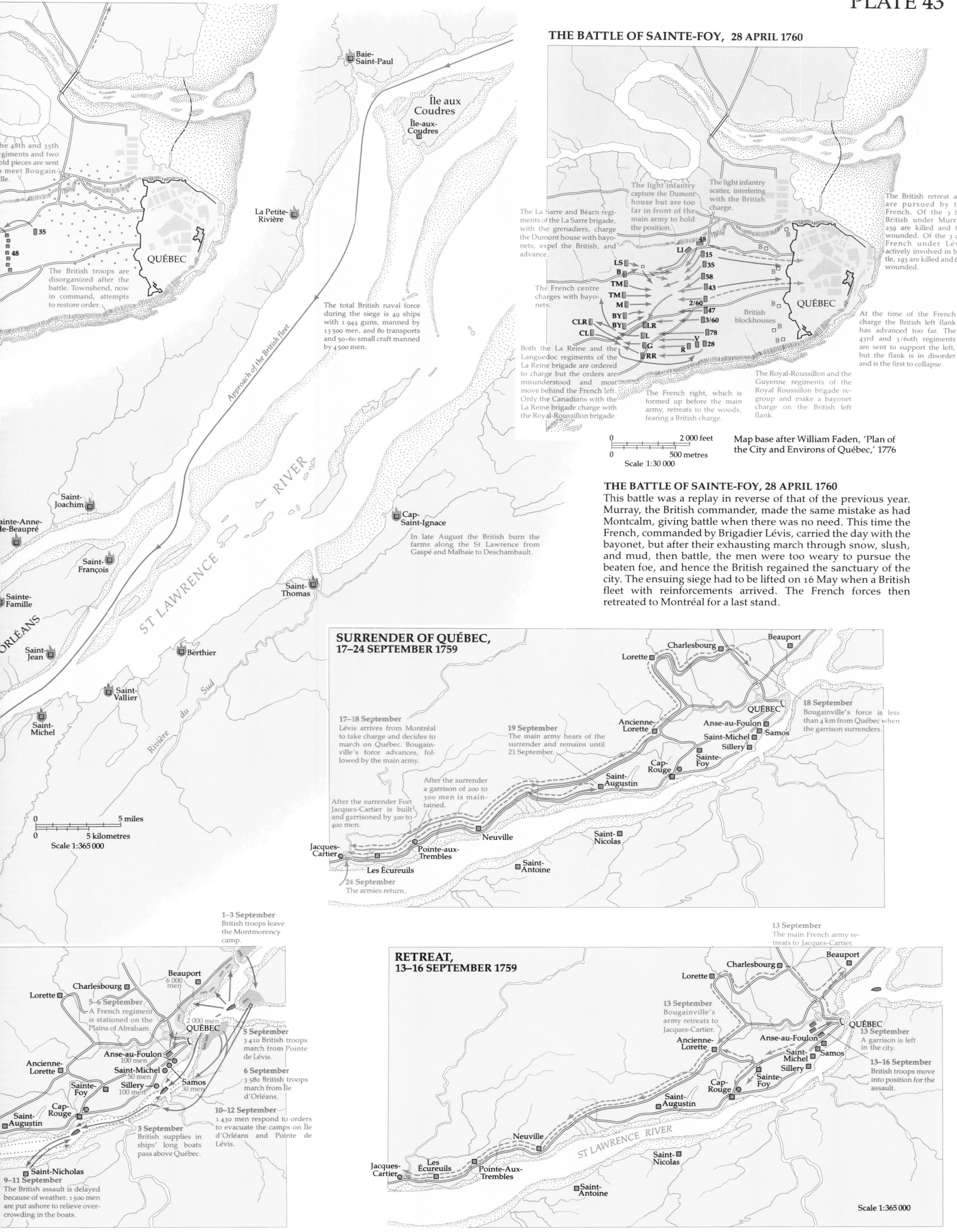
THE BATTLE OF SAINTE-FOY, 28 APRIL 1760
The light infantry capture the Dumont house but are too far in front of the main army to hold the position.
The light infantry scatter, interfering with the British charge.
The La Sarre and Béarn regiments of the La Sarre brigade, with the grenadiers, charge the Dumont house with bayonets, expel the British, and advance.
The British retreat and are pursued by the French. Of the 3 866 British under Murray, 259 are killed and 829 wounded. Of the 3 928 French under Lévis actively involved in battle, 193 are killed and 640 wounded.
The French centre charges with bayonets.
British blockhouses
QUÉBEC
At the time of the French charge the British left flank has advanced too far. The 43rd and 3/60th regiments are sent to support the left, but the flank is in disorder and is the first to collapse.
Both the La Reine and the Languedoc regiments of the La Reine brigade are ordered to charge but the orders are misunderstood and most move behind the French left. Only the Canadians with the La Reine brigade charge with the Royal-Roussillon brigade.
The French right, which is formed up before the main army, retreats to the woods, fearing a British charge.
The Royal-Roussillon and the Guyenne regiments of the Royal Roussillon brigade regroup and make a bayonet charge on the British left flank.
LI
48
15
35
58
43
2/60
47
3/60
78
28
LS
B
TM
TM
M
BY
BY
CLR
CL
LR
L
G
RR
R
Y
2 000 feet
500 metres
Scale 1:30 000
Map base after William Faden, 'Plan of the City and Environs of Québec,' 1776
Baie-Saint-Paul
Île aux Coudres
Île-aux-Coudres
La Petite-Rivière
The 48th and 35th regiments and two field pieces are sent to meet Bougainville.
35
48
QUÉBEC
The British troops are disorganized after the battle. Townshend, now in command, attempts to restore order.
The total British naval force during the siege is 49 ships with 1 944 guns, manned by 13 500 men, and 80 transports and 50–60 small craft manned by 4 500 men.
Approach of the British fleet
Saint-Joachim
Sainte-Anne-de-Beaupré
Saint-François
Sainte-Famille
ORLÉANS
Saint-Jean
Cap-Saint-Ignace
In late August the British burn the farms along the St Lawrence from Gaspé and Malbaie to Deschambault.
Saint-Thomas
ST LAWRENCE RIVER
Berthier
Saint-Vallier
Saint-Michel
Rivière du Sud
5 miles
5 kilometres
Scale 1:365 000
SURRENDER OF QUÉBEC, 17–24 SEPTEMBER 1759
Charlesbourg
Beauport
Lorette
QUÉBEC
18 September
Bougainville's force is less than 4 km from Québec when the garrison surrenders.
Ancienne-Lorette
Anse-au-Foulon
Saint-Michel
Samos
Sillery
Sainte-Foy
Cap-Rouge
Saint-Augustin
17–18 September
Lévis arrives from Montréal to take charge and decides to march on Québec. Bougainville's force advances, followed by the main army.
19 September
The main army hears of the surrender and remains until 21 September.
After the surrender a garrison of 200 to 300 men is maintained.
After the surrender Fort Jacques-Cartier is built and garrisoned by 300 to 400 men.
Jacques-Cartier
Pointe-aux-Trembles
Neuville
Les Écureuils
Saint-Nicolas
Saint-Antoine
24 September
The armies return.
1–3 September
British troops leave the Montmorency camp.
Beauport
6 000 men
Charlesbourg
Lorette
5–6 September
A French regiment is stationed on the Plains of Abraham.
2 000 men
QUÉBEC
5 September
3 410 British troops march from Pointe de Lévis.
Anse-au-Foulon
100 men
Saint-Michel
50 men
6 September
3 580 British troops march from Île d'Orléans.
Ancienne-Lorette
Sainte-Foy
Sillery
100 men
Samos
30 men
Cap-Rouge
Saint-Augustin
10–12 September
1 430 men respond to orders to evacuate the camps on Île d'Orléans and Pointe de Lévis.
3 September
British supplies in ships' long boats pass above Québec.
Saint-Nicholas
9–11 September
The British assault is delayed because of weather. 1 500 men are put ashore to relieve overcrowding in the boats.
13 September
The main French army retreats to Jacques-Cartier.
RETREAT, 13–16 SEPTEMBER 1759
Beauport
Charlesbourg
Lorette
13 September
Bougainville's army retreats to Jacques-Cartier.
QUÉBEC
13 September
A garrison is left in the city.
Ancienne-Lorette
Anse-au-Foulon
Saint-Michel
Samos
Sillery
13–16 September
British troops move into position for the assault.
Sainte-Foy
Cap-Rouge
Saint-Augustin
Neuville
ST LAWRENCE RIVER
Jacques-Cartier
Les Écureuils
Pointe-Aux-Trembles
Saint-Nicolas
Saint-Antoine
Scale 1:365 000

THE BATTLE OF SAINTE-FOY, 28 APRIL 1760

This battle was a replay in reverse of that of the previous year. Murray, the British commander, made the same mistake as had Montcalm, giving battle when there was no need. This time the French, commanded by Brigadier Lévis, carried the day with the bayonet, but after their exhausting march through snow, slush, and mud, then battle, the men were too weary to pursue the beaten foe, and hence the British regained the sanctuary of the city. The ensuing siege had to be lifted on 16 May when a British fleet with reinforcements arrived. The French forces then retreated to Montréal for a last stand.

INDIAN WAR AND AMERICAN INVASION

Authors: W.J. Eccles, M.N. McConnell, Susan L. Laskin

After the capitulation of the French forces at Montréal in September 1760 (pl 42) British and American provincial troops occupied the French posts around and south of the Great Lakes. American traders moved in but their abusive attitudes and dishonest trade practices, in marked contrast to the well-regulated French trade, antagonized the Indians. At the same time General Jeffery Amherst terminated the customary 'presents,' which the Indians regarded as compensation for the right to trade in and travel through their lands. Despite the assurances given the Indian nations by the British, American settlers flooded into their country. Realizing what the future held, the Indians, in a loose federation, struck back. They attacked the British-held forts and the American encroachers who fled back over the mountains. It remained to the undermanned British army to counterattack. The Indians were unable, despite early victories, to sustain a long campaign. They had no supply of munitions other than those that they could seize from the enemy. They were also weakened by an epidemic of smallpox when, on Amherst's orders, clothing from the victims of the disease was distributed among them. By the autumn of 1764 they were forced to submit.

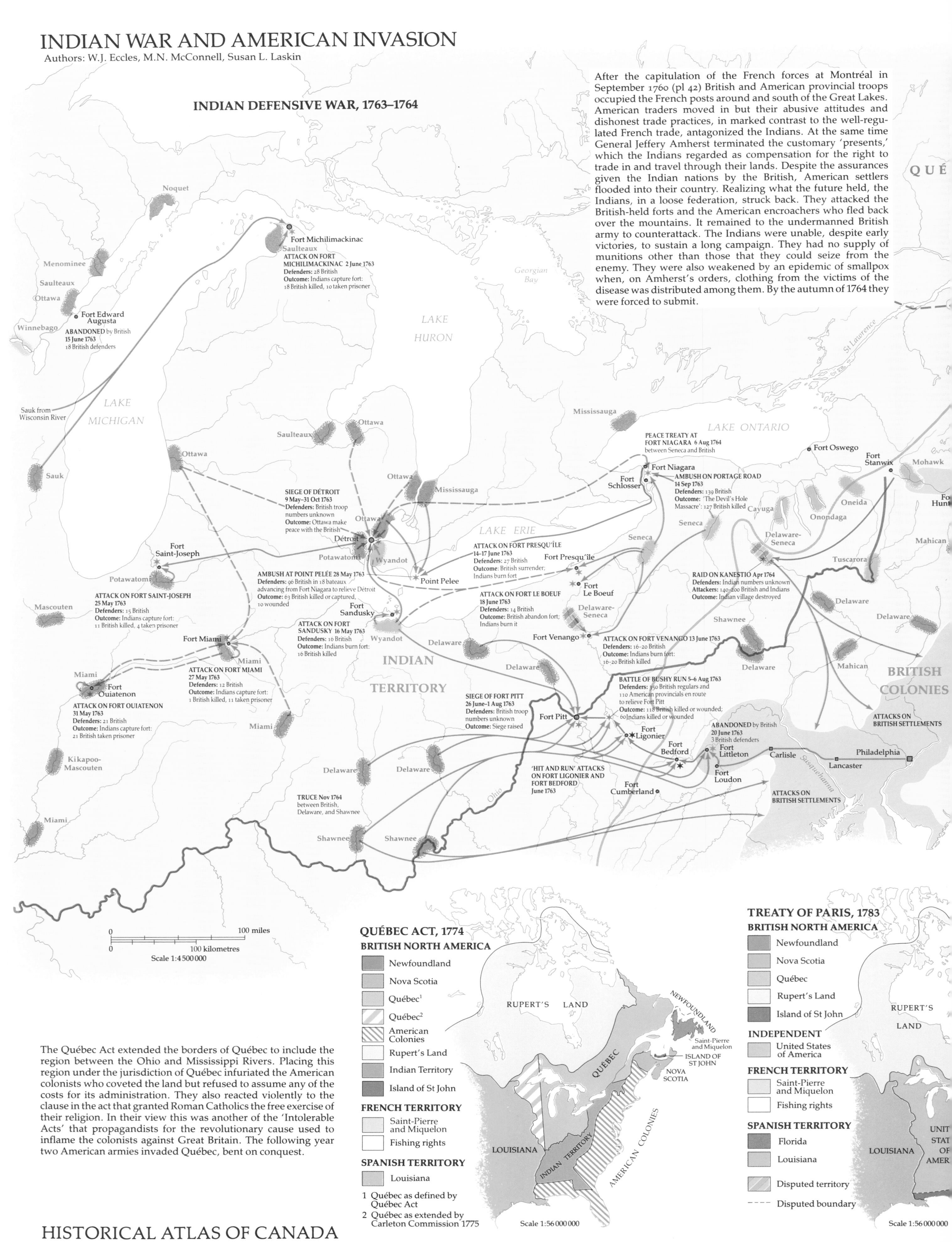
INDIAN DEFENSIVE WAR, 1763–1764
Noquet
Fort Michilimackinac
Saulteaux
ATTACK ON FORT MICHILIMACKINAC 2 June 1763
Defenders: 28 British
Outcome: Indians capture fort: 18 British killed, 10 taken prisoner
Menominee
Saulteaux
Ottawa
Fort Edward Augusta
Winnebago
ABANDONED by British 15 June 1763
18 British defenders
Georgian Bay
LAKE HURON
LAKE MICHIGAN
Sauk from Wisconsin River
Sauk
Ottawa
Saulteaux
Ottawa
Ottawa
Mississauga
SIEGE OF DÉTROIT
9 May–31 Oct 1763
Defenders: British troop numbers unknown
Outcome: Ottawa make peace with the British
Ottawa
Détroit
Potawatomi
Wyandot
Fort Saint-Joseph
Potawatomi
AMBUSH AT POINT PELÉE 28 May 1763
Defenders: 96 British in 18 bateaux advancing from Fort Niagara to relieve Détroit
Outcome: 63 British killed or captured, 10 wounded
Point Pelee
ATTACK ON FORT SAINT-JOSEPH
25 May 1763
Defenders: 15 British
Outcome: Indians capture fort: 11 British killed, 4 taken prisoner
Mascouten
Fort Sandusky
ATTACK ON FORT SANDUSKY 16 May 1763
Defenders: 16 British
Outcome: Indians burn fort: 16 British killed
Wyandot
Fort Miami
Miami
ATTACK ON FORT MIAMI
27 May 1763
Defenders: 12 British
Outcome: Indians capture fort: 1 British killed, 11 taken prisoner
Miami
Fort Ouiatenon
ATTACK ON FORT OUIATENON
31 May 1763
Defenders: 21 British
Outcome: Indians capture fort: 21 British taken prisoner
Miami
Kikapoo-Mascouten
Miami
INDIAN TERRITORY
Mississauga
LAKE ERIE
LAKE ONTARIO
St Lawrence
QUÉ
PEACE TREATY AT FORT NIAGARA 6 Aug 1764
between Seneca and British
Fort Niagara
Fort Schlosser
AMBUSH ON PORTAGE ROAD
14 Sep 1763
Defenders: 139 British
Outcome: 'The Devil's Hole Massacre': 127 British killed
Fort Oswego
Fort Stanwix
Mohawk
Fo Hunt
Cayuga
Oneida
Onondaga
Seneca
Seneca
Delaware-Seneca
Mahican
Tuscarora
ATTACK ON FORT PRESQU'ÎLE
14–17 June 1763
Defenders: 27 British
Outcome: British surrender; Indians burn fort
Fort Presqu'île
Fort Le Boeuf
ATTACK ON FORT LE BOEUF
18 June 1763
Defenders: 14 British
Outcome: British abandon fort; Indians burn it
Delaware-Seneca
RAID ON KANESTIO Apr 1764
Defenders: Indian numbers unknown
Attackers: 140–200 British and Indians
Outcome: Indian village destroyed
Delaware
Delaware
Shawnee
Fort Venango
ATTACK ON FORT VENANGO 13 June 1763
Defenders: 16–20 British
Outcome: Indians burn fort: 16–20 British killed
Delaware
Delaware
Delaware
Mahican
BRITISH COLONIES
BATTLE OF BUSHY RUN 5–6 Aug 1763
Defenders: 350 British regulars and 110 American provincials en route to relieve Fort Pitt
Outcome: 118 British killed or wounded; 60 Indians killed or wounded
SIEGE OF FORT PITT
26 June–1 Aug 1763
Defenders: British troop numbers unknown
Outcome: Siege raised
Fort Pitt
Fort Ligonier
Fort Bedford
ABANDONED by British
20 June 1763
3 British defenders
Fort Littleton
Carlisle
Fort Loudon
Lancaster
Philadelphia
Susquehanna
ATTACKS ON BRITISH SETTLEMENTS
ATTACKS ON BRITISH SETTLEMENTS
Delaware
Delaware
'HIT AND RUN' ATTACKS ON FORT LIGONIER AND FORT BEDFORD June 1763
Fort Cumberland
TRUCE Nov 1764
between British, Delaware, and Shawnee
Ohio
Shawnee
Shawnee
0 100 miles
0 100 kilometres
Scale 1:4 500 000
QUÉBEC ACT, 1774
BRITISH NORTH AMERICA
Newfoundland
Nova Scotia
Québec[1]
Québec[2]
American Colonies
Rupert's Land
Indian Territory
Island of St John
FRENCH TERRITORY
Saint-Pierre and Miquelon
Fishing rights
SPANISH TERRITORY
Louisiana
1 Québec as defined by Québec Act
2 Québec as extended by Carleton Commission 1775
RUPERT'S LAND
NEWFOUNDLAND
Saint-Pierre and Miquelon
ISLAND OF ST JOHN
NOVA SCOTIA
QUÉBEC
LOUISIANA
INDIAN TERRITORY
AMERICAN COLONIES
Scale 1:56 000 000
TREATY OF PARIS, 1783
BRITISH NORTH AMERICA
Newfoundland
Nova Scotia
Québec
Rupert's Land
Island of St John
INDEPENDENT
United States of America
FRENCH TERRITORY
Saint-Pierre and Miquelon
Fishing rights
SPANISH TERRITORY
Florida
Louisiana
Disputed territory
Disputed boundary
RUPERT'S LAND
LOUISIANA
UNIT STAT OF AMER
Scale 1:56 000 000

The Québec Act extended the borders of Québec to include the region between the Ohio and Mississippi Rivers. Placing this region under the jurisdiction of Québec infuriated the American colonists who coveted the land but refused to assume any of the costs for its administration. They also reacted violently to the clause in the act that granted Roman Catholics the free exercise of their religion. In their view this was another of the 'Intolerable Acts' that propagandists for the revolutionary cause used to inflame the colonists against Great Britain. The following year two American armies invaded Québec, bent on conquest.

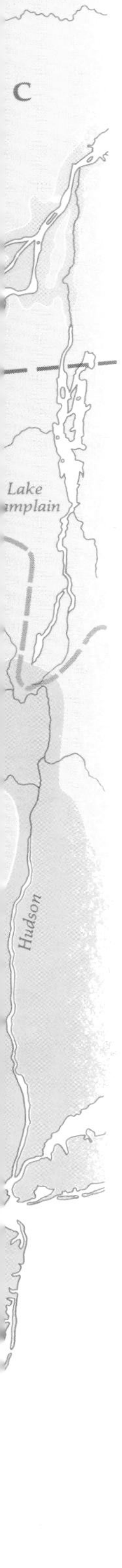

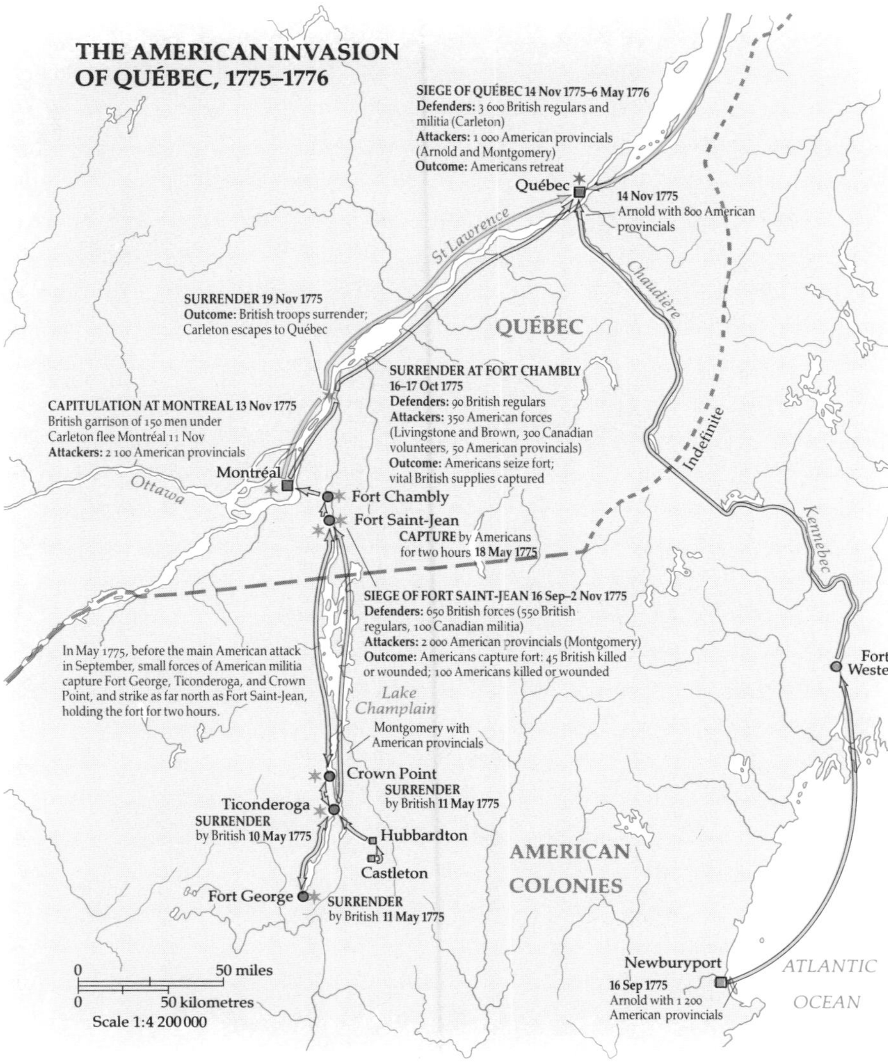

THE AMERICAN INVASION OF QUÉBEC, 1775–1776

SIEGE OF QUÉBEC 14 Nov 1775–6 May 1776
Defenders: 3 600 British regulars and militia (Carleton)
Attackers: 1 000 American provincials (Arnold and Montgomery)
Outcome: Americans retreat

Québec

14 Nov 1775
Arnold with 800 American provincials

St Lawrence

Chaudière

SURRENDER 19 Nov 1775
Outcome: British troops surrender; Carleton escapes to Québec

QUÉBEC

SURRENDER AT FORT CHAMBLY 16–17 Oct 1775
Defenders: 90 British regulars
Attackers: 350 American forces (Livingstone and Brown, 300 Canadian volunteers, 50 American provincials)
Outcome: Americans seize fort; vital British supplies captured

CAPITULATION AT MONTREAL 13 Nov 1775
British garrison of 150 men under Carleton flee Montréal 11 Nov
Attackers: 2 100 American provincials

Montréal

Ottawa

Fort Chambly

Fort Saint-Jean

CAPTURE by Americans for two hours 18 May 1775

Indefinite

Kennebec

SIEGE OF FORT SAINT-JEAN 16 Sep–2 Nov 1775
Defenders: 650 British forces (550 British regulars, 100 Canadian militia)
Attackers: 2 000 American provincials (Montgomery)
Outcome: Americans capture fort: 45 British killed or wounded; 100 Americans killed or wounded

In May 1775, before the main American attack in September, small forces of American militia capture Fort George, Ticonderoga, and Crown Point, and strike as far north as Fort Saint-Jean, holding the fort for two hours.

Lake Champlain

Montgomery with American provincials

Fort Western

Crown Point

SURRENDER by British 11 May 1775

Ticonderoga

SURRENDER by British 10 May 1775

Hubbardton

Castleton

AMERICAN COLONIES

Fort George

SURRENDER by British 11 May 1775

Newburyport

16 Sep 1775
Arnold with 1 200 American provincials

ATLANTIC OCEAN

0 50 miles
0 50 kilometres
Scale 1:4 200 000

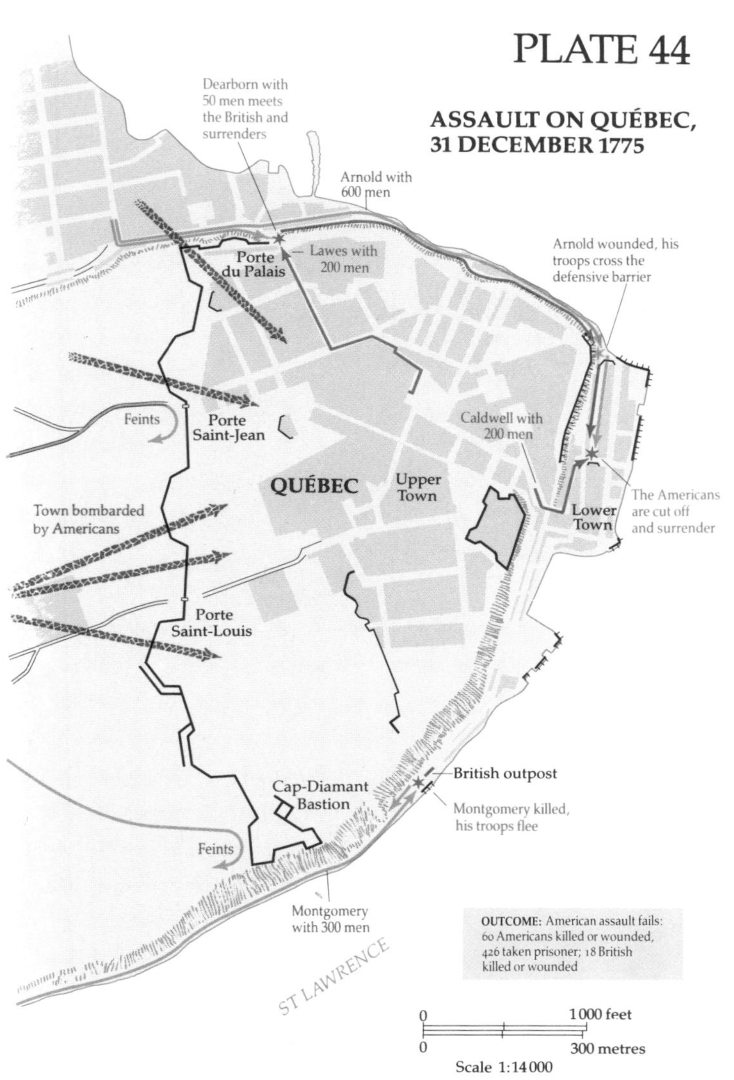

ASSAULT ON QUÉBEC, 31 DECEMBER 1775

Dearborn with 50 men meets the British and surrenders

Arnold with 600 men

Porte du Palais

Lawes with 200 men

Arnold wounded, his troops cross the defensive barrier

Feints

Porte Saint-Jean

Caldwell with 200 men

QUÉBEC

Upper Town

Town bombarded by Americans

Lower Town

The Americans are cut off and surrender

Porte Saint-Louis

British outpost

Cap-Diamant Bastion

Montgomery killed, his troops flee

Feints

Montgomery with 300 men

ST LAWRENCE

OUTCOME: American assault fails: 60 Americans killed or wounded, 426 taken prisoner; 18 British killed or wounded

0 1 000 feet
0 300 metres
Scale 1:14 000

Lake Champlain

Hudson

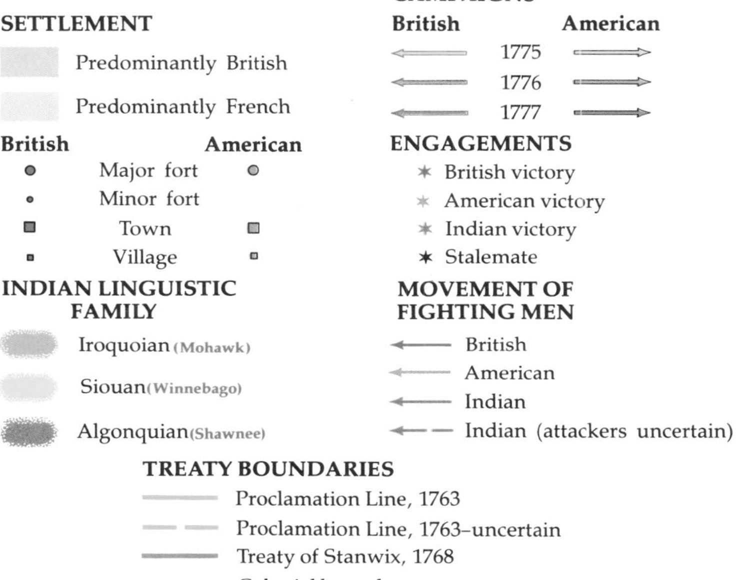
SETTLEMENT
Predominantly British
Predominantly French
British
American
Major fort
Minor fort
Town
Village
INDIAN LINGUISTIC FAMILY
Iroquoian (Mohawk)
Siouan (Winnebago)
Algonquian (Shawnee)
CAMPAIGNS
British
American
1775
1776
1777
ENGAGEMENTS
British victory
American victory
Indian victory
Stalemate
MOVEMENT OF FIGHTING MEN
British
American
Indian
Indian (attackers uncertain)
TREATY BOUNDARIES
Proclamation Line, 1763
Proclamation Line, 1763–uncertain
Treaty of Stanwix, 1768
Colonial boundary

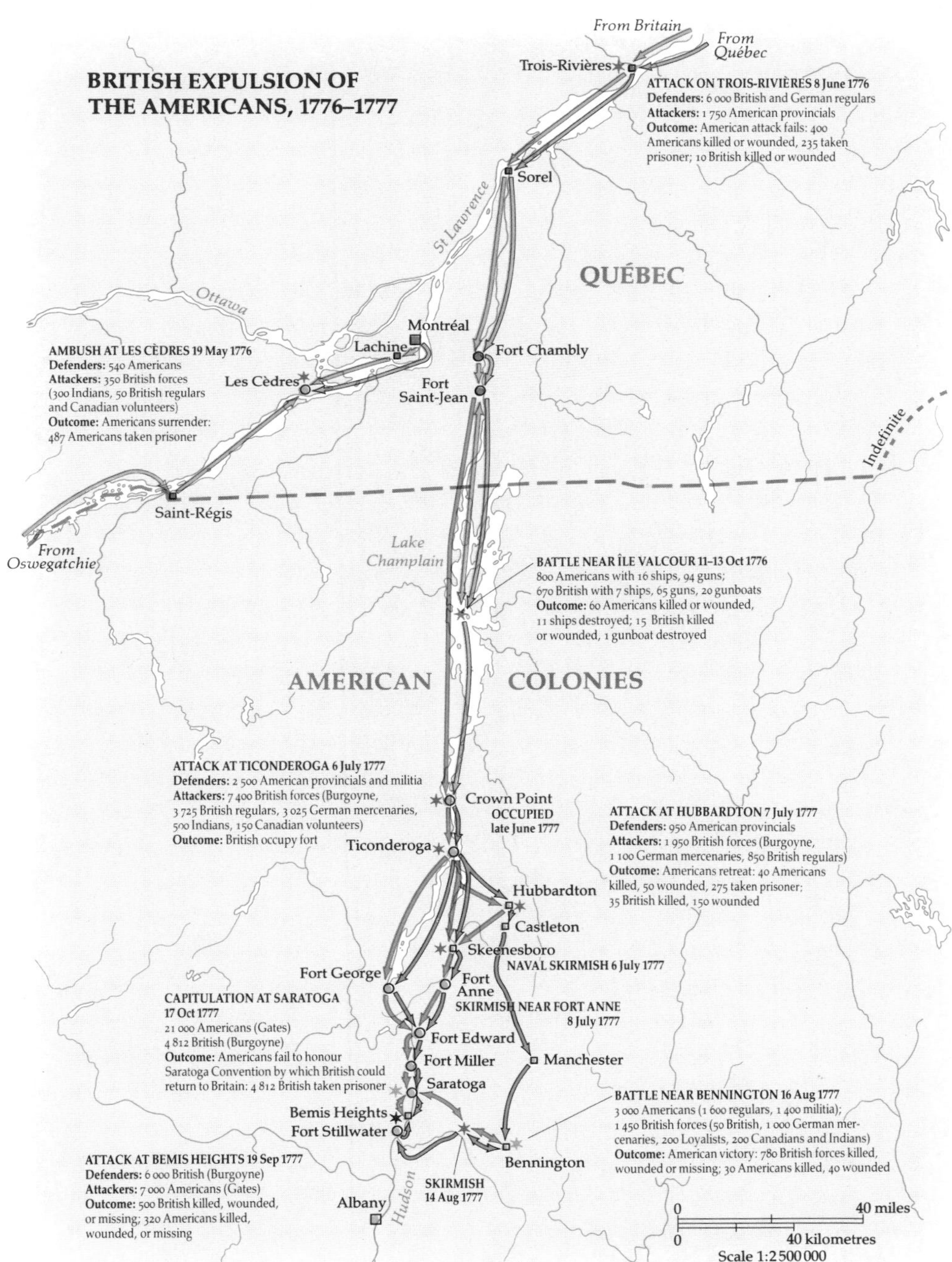
BRITISH EXPULSION OF THE AMERICANS, 1776–1777
From Britain
From Québec
Trois-Rivières
ATTACK ON TROIS-RIVIÈRES 8 June 1776
Defenders: 6 000 British and German regulars
Attackers: 1 750 American provincials
Outcome: American attack fails: 400 Americans killed or wounded, 235 taken prisoner; 10 British killed or wounded
Sorel
St Lawrence
QUÉBEC
Ottawa
Montréal
Lachine
Fort Chambly
AMBUSH AT LES CÈDRES 19 May 1776
Defenders: 540 Americans
Attackers: 350 British forces (300 Indians, 50 British regulars and Canadian volunteers)
Outcome: Americans surrender: 487 Americans taken prisoner
Les Cèdres
Fort Saint-Jean
Indefinite
Saint-Régis
From Oswegatchie
Lake Champlain
BATTLE NEAR ÎLE VALCOUR 11–13 Oct 1776
800 Americans with 16 ships, 94 guns;
670 British with 7 ships, 65 guns, 20 gunboats
Outcome: 60 Americans killed or wounded, 11 ships destroyed; 15 British killed or wounded, 1 gunboat destroyed
AMERICAN COLONIES
ATTACK AT TICONDEROGA 6 July 1777
Defenders: 2 500 Americans provincials and militia
Attackers: 7 400 British forces (Burgoyne, 3 725 British regulars, 3 025 German mercenaries, 500 Indians, 150 Canadian volunteers)
Outcome: British occupy fort
Crown Point
OCCUPIED late June 1777
Ticonderoga
ATTACK AT HUBBARDTON 7 July 1777
Defenders: 950 American provincials
Attackers: 1 950 British forces (Burgoyne, 1 100 German mercenaries, 850 British regulars)
Outcome: Americans retreat: 40 Americans killed, 50 wounded, 275 taken prisoner; 35 British killed, 150 wounded
Hubbardton
Castleton
Skeenesboro
NAVAL SKIRMISH 6 July 1777
Fort George
Fort Anne
SKIRMISH NEAR FORT ANNE 8 July 1777
CAPITULATION AT SARATOGA 17 Oct 1777
21 000 Americans (Gates)
4 812 British (Burgoyne)
Outcome: Americans fail to honour Saratoga Convention by which British could return to Britain: 4 812 British taken prisoner
Fort Edward
Fort Miller
Manchester
Saratoga
BATTLE NEAR BENNINGTON 16 Aug 1777
3 000 Americans (1 600 regulars, 1 400 militia);
1 450 British forces (50 British, 1 000 German mercenaries, 200 Loyalists, 200 Canadians and Indians)
Outcome: American victory: 780 British forces killed, wounded or missing; 30 Americans killed, 40 wounded
Bemis Heights
Fort Stillwater
Bennington
ATTACK AT BEMIS HEIGHTS 19 Sep 1777
Defenders: 6 000 British (Burgoyne)
Attackers: 7 000 Americans (Gates)
Outcome: 500 British killed, wounded, or missing; 320 Americans killed, wounded, or missing
SKIRMISH 14 Aug 1777
Albany
Hudson
0 40 miles
0 40 kilometres
Scale 1:2 500 000

NEWFOUNDLAND

Saint-Pierre and Miquelon

ISLAND OF ST JOHN

QUÉBEC

NOVA SCOTIA

FLORIDA

In June 1775 the Continental Congress voted for the invasion of Canada to forestall a British drive up Lake Champlain to the Hudson River, which would have isolated New England from the other rebelling colonies. An American army, 3 000 strong, commanded by Richard Montgomery advanced on Montréal in August, forcing Governor-General Guy Carleton to flee to Québec. In September another American army of some 1 200 men, led by Benedict Arnold, began its ascent up the Kennebec River towards Québec. On 8 November Arnold's army, reduced by disease and desertion to some 800 men, reached the St Lawrence opposite Québec. Montgomery joined it with the bulk of his forces and the combined American army laid siege to the city. An assault on Lower Town on the night of 30/31 December was beaten back with heavy American losses. Montgomery was killed. The siege continued until 6 May when the vanguard of the British relief fleet appeared. The Americans then fled. There was some skirmishing near Montréal but the invasion had been crushed.

In 1777 a British army led by General John Burgoyne retook Ticonderoga and marched for the Hudson River, headed for New York. Eventually, his army reduced and surrounded by more than 30 000 American militia, Burgoyne negotiated the Convention of Saratoga whereby his men would lay down their arms, be granted the honours of war, and return to Great Britain. Once disarmed, his troops were imprisoned.

The St Lawrence Settlements

Jacques Cartier, the European explorer of much of the Gulf of St Lawrence in 1534 and of the St Lawrence River in 1535, was sent by Francis I, king of France, 'to discover certain islands and lands where it is said that a great quantity of gold and other precious things are to be found.' Equally enticing was the prospect of a direct sea-route to China (pls 20, 33). Native tales of gold in the Kingdom of Saguenay drew Cartier back in 1541 with five ships and a large number of colonists. Within two years Cartier and his successors in the colonization venture withdrew from the St Lawrence valley, discouraged by repeated Indian attacks, the rigours of winter in a northern continental climate, and the failure to gain any additional information about the Kingdom of Saguenay or a sea route to Asia. Forty years later, when the French returned, their motives were different. By this time the fur trade was separating from the cod fishery and moving westward towards the great river and the natives who could bring out the furs of the continental interior. French fur traders reached the Island of Montréal in the early 1580s and began to trade each summer at Tadoussac at the mouth of the Saguenay River (pl 33). In 1600 Chauvin de Tonnetuit built a post there and some of his men overwintered. In 1608 Samuel de Champlain established a post at Québec, an easily fortified site farther up the St Lawrence River at the head of navigation for large ships. This time the French were on the St Lawrence to stay, although for years Champlain's *habitation* was simply an outpost of the fur trade.

The French establishment on the St Lawrence River, one of the principal entrances (along with Hudson Bay, the Hudson-Mohawk River system, and the Mississippi River) to the continental interior, was some 1500 km from the open Atlantic. Closely bounding the St Lawrence River to the north lay the Canadian Shield, a rocky upland of acid soils and lingering winters, unsuited for agriculture. To the south, a little farther from the St Lawrence River and less daunting, lay the Appalachian Highlands. Between was a narrow valley covered by a dense forest of conifers and deciduous trees and near the northern climatic limit for the cereal crops of northwestern Europe (pl 46). When Champlain arrived, the St Lawrence valley was uninhabited, although after the dispersion of the St Lawrence Iroquoians in about 1580 Algonquian-speaking Montagnais bands from the Canadian Shield and Iroquoian-speaking Mohawk from southeast of Lake Ontario fished and hunted there in summer (pl 33). Champlain had slipped into a contested, unsettled no-man's-land.

Champlain was soon involved with natives, principally Algonquian-speaking peoples from the Ottawa valley and Iroquoian-speaking Huron from Georgian Bay on Lake Huron. They insisted on an alliance and Champlain's participation in raids against their enemies, the Mohawk and other Iroquois tribes living south and southwest of Lake Ontario. These developments, which would eventually involve almost all the peoples of the continental interior and Britain and France in a protracted struggle for the control of North America, are described by pls 33–44. Pls 45–56 consider the settlements along the lower St Lawrence River, the heart of the vast, vaguely delimited colony approached through the Gulf of St Lawrence and known during the French regime as New France or Canada.

For 26 years Québec was the only French settlement on the St Lawrence. Trois-Rivières at the mouth of the Saint-Maurice River was not founded until 1634, and Montréal, at the head of navigation for small ships and boats on the St Lawrence and near the abandoned St Lawrence Iroquoian village of Hochelaga, not until 1642. During these years Canada was held by the Compagnie des Cent-Associés, a proprietary company created out of rival trading interests by Cardinal Richelieu in 1627 and, in return for its trading monopoly, required to colonize. Before 1660 the company and some of the seigneurs it had created did bring several thousand settlers to Canada, a considerable achievement in the face of the English capture of the company's first shiploads of colonists in 1628, the English occupation of Québec in 1629, and, soon after France regained Canada in 1632, the beginning of the Iroquois wars. Although most of these immigrants returned to France, agricultural settlement began to spread along the river, first near Québec, then near Trois-Rivières and Montréal. In 1663, when the French crown revoked the charter of the Compagnie des Cent-Associés and assumed the administration of Canada, some 2 500 people of French background lived along the lower St Lawrence, 500 of them at Québec. Thereafter the population grew more rapidly. During the first decade of royal government the crown sent regular contingents of settlers, including about 1 000 women, and encouraged soldiers to settle in Canada. Later, female immigration virtually stopped, male immigration was reduced to a trickle, and the population grew largely through natural increases (pl 45). With an annual birth rate near 55 per 1 000 and a death rate that averaged about 30 per 1 000 the population doubled in less than 30 years (pl 46). Québec and Montréal grew into small towns. Settlement spread along the river. By the end of the French regime some 70 000 people of European origin lived in the St Lawrence valley. The banks of the river were occupied from a few miles above Montréal to well downriver below Québec.

At the same time the lower St Lawrence was being settled by native peoples (pl 47). Montagnais groups from the Canadian Shield, their beaver supplies exhausted, settled near Québec in 1638. Ottawa-valley Algonquins, under Iroquois attack in the 1640s, settled near Montréal and Trois-Rivières. Refugees from Huronia reached Québec in 1650 and 1651. Abenaki from New England, defeated in King Philip's War, moved north into the St Lawrence valley in the late 1670s, by which time some Mohawk and Oneida, following the treaty of peace between the French and Iroquois in 1667, had settled near Montréal to be better placed for the fur trade. Other native groups arrived later. Almost all these people lived somewhat apart from the French settlements in missions directed by Jesuit or Sulpician priests. Over the years the numbers at these missions tended to decline as native people were decimated by European diseases and by the wars in which they participated as French allies. At the end of the French regime only 3 000–4 000 natives lived along the lower St Lawrence.

As time went on, the great majority of the people in the towns and countryside of early Canada were descendants of immigrants from France. Few immigrants had come in families. Most of them were single, young, and had been sent as soldiers or indentured servants or, in the case of the women recruited by the crown in the 1660s and early 1670s, as potential brides. From a French perspective Canada was remote and unappealing; even the crown soon lost interest in colonization. From the founding of Québec to its capture by the British in 1759 fewer than 10 000 immigrants from France settled and left descendants along the lower St Lawrence (pl 45). Many others, mostly indentured servants, soldiers, or sailors, came and left.

These emigrants from France had left an age-old, densely populated, overwhelmingly rural country of more than 20 million people. Agriculture employed far more French people than any other activity; land remained the principal source of wealth and status. A large population pressed against known, finite resources, raising the value of land, depressing the value of labour. The rural poor scrounged for food and fuel in forest, marsh, moor, hedgerow, or field after harvest. Title to land was tenaciously defended, carefully inherited, craved because land could provide economic security and social position. Like the rest of western Europe, France was still intensely regional. Many people did not speak French, and many French regional dialects were barely comprehensible to other French speakers. Local cultures no more than a day's walk apart were often very different; people from outside the local region were strangers, not to be trusted. Yet everywhere French society was sharply stratified, the social gradations steep, nuanced, and understood. Different peasant occupations carried different social meanings. In most villages a few peasants held large farms, while many others did not have enough land to support their families, and others were landless. Status affected a peasant's seat in church, his position in a parade on a saint's day. Above the peasantry were the intricate hierarchies of the church, the older nobility (*noblesse d'épée* or *de sang*), and the newer nobility associated with public office (*noblesse de robe*). Apart from and somewhat disparaged by these élites, but growing in wealth and power, were the merchants. The countryside was dotted with estates and châteaux, but the towns, where little more than 10% of the population of France lived, were the focal points of commerce, civil and clerical administration, and the military. Because of the concentration of disposable income, the towns drew labourers and a wide range of artisans.

When emigrants made the two- or three-month crossing of the Atlantic to Canada, this old, known, densely populated France was suddenly far behind them. They had come to a forested, New World valley. Land was abundant, but labour was scarce and expensive. The climate was unsuitable for plantation crops, but the crops of northwestern France could be grown. At one end of the valley canoe routes led to the continental interior and the fur trade; at the other end shipping led to France or, nearer at hand, to fishing stations in the Gulf of St Lawrence. Local markets were small and external markets thousands of kilometres away. For years only fish and furs could be exported profitably. Yet some members of all the main French social classes came to this isolated pocket of the New World. Merchants, drawn by the fur trade, created the first settlements, and were always active in the colony. Missionaries came and many of the formal institutions of the church were soon established. The Compagnie des Cent-Associés granted many of its seigneuries to people of noble birth, and intendants continued to do so after Canada became a crown colony in 1663 (pl 51). At that time some institutions and officials of a French province were put in place. Most of the soldiers demobilized along the lower St Lawrence had been recruited among the poorer of the French peasantry, as had most indentured servants. All in all, the 9 000–10 000 French immigrants who settled in Canada during the French regime were a fairly representative cross-section of French society, minus the *grande noblesse*.

The Towns

Merchants engaged in the fur trade built permanent trading posts along the St Lawrence River to facilitate contacts with native traders, protect monopoly privileges, store trade goods, and reduce the costs of trans-Atlantic shipping. For the crown, which chartered the trading companies and encouraged permanent settlement, such posts consolidated French territorial claims. For the religious orders that became involved with Canada permanent settlements served as bases for missionary operations. To the commercial activities that created Québec and Trois-Rivières administrative and military functions were soon added. Founded as a mission, Montréal became a centre of trade. Over the years these tiny settlements grew as their commercial, administrative, and military functions expanded.

Québec, a deep-sea port, was the Canadian point of contact with North Atlantic trade. It required only two or three ships a year to supply its needs during the proprietary period before 1663, and about 10 a year during the 1720s and 1730s. In the last two, war-torn decades of the French regime shipping increased immeasurably (pl 48). Furs and hides were carried to La Rochelle in one or two ships each year. In the eighteenth century exports of foodstuffs to fishing stations in the Gulf of St Lawrence, Louisbourg, or the West Indies required more but smaller ships; and the import trade from France, in which Québec's merchants were increasingly active, drew many ships that would leave Québec in ballast to look for cargoes at Louisbourg (fish) or in the West Indies (sugar, molasses, rum). Several small private shipyards built ships in the town. In 1663 Québec became the capital of a royal colony, receiving a new governor, an intendant, their staffs, and a small garrison. Fortifications were improved; eventually the upper town was enclosed by a massive stone wall with over 200 cannon and mortars. Québec was the seat of colonial administration and a bulwark, in the struggle against the British, of the French defence of Canada. Several religious orders – Jesuits, Récollets, Ursulines, and Hospitalières – established their Canadian headquarters there. Tradesmen, labourers, and small merchants were drawn by the port trade, by the requirements for goods and services of civil and clerical administrations and the military, and, from 1739, by employment in royal shipyards equipped to make large warships. By 1744 almost 5 000 people lived in Québec (pl 51).

Montréal was the point of transshipment from small ships or river boats to canoes that could be portaged around the rapids of the upper St Lawrence and the Ottawa Rivers. In the late 1650s, after the collapse of Huronia, merchants began to outfit canoe brigades for the interior (pl 37), although native traders continued to come to Montréal each year until 1681, when the crown finally legalized French trade in the interior. Montréal's merchant community dealt in furs, French goods shipped upriver from Québec, and, eventually, grain from farms on the Montréal plain. The Sulpicians (seigneurs of the Island of Montréal), the Récollets, and the Jesuits maintained establishments there. The town was a seat of regional administration and of a large garrison. Montréal was enclosed by a wooden palisade in 1688 for protection against the Iroquois, and by stone bastions and walls in the 18th century. In the 1740s it was about half as populous as Québec. Trois-Rivières, which drew furs from the relatively restricted Saint-Maurice valley and had little good agricultural land nearby, commanded much less trade than either Québec or Montréal. Not an important military site, it housed small civil and clercial administrations and a small garrison, and was little more than a village of some 800 inhabitants at the end of the French regime.

The physical growth of Québec and Montréal during the French regime is described on pl 49. Well before the end of the 17th century land use in Québec was sharply differentiated, with a congested lower town, on a narrow strip of land between cliff and river, dominated by the commercial activities of a port, and a much more spacious upper town dominated by royal and clercial officials and the garrison. The large institutional buildings of the upper town were handsome French baroque structures; much of the land around them was laid out in garden plots arranged geometrically and walled. In the lower town, where land was scarce, buildings were contiguous along a street and, by the 18th century, many were three storeys high. Streetscapes were dominated by spare, symmetrical stone facades, large, well-proportioned, shuttered windows, steeply-pitched roofs, narrow dormers, and massive chimneys – as in the towns of northwestern France. Outside the wall to the north in the mid-18th-century suburb of Saint-Roch houses were much smaller, detached, and usually of timber-frame or log construction. Labourers and artisans, many of whom worked in the royal shipyard nearby, lived there. Overall, 18th-century visitors were impressed by Québec, often likening it to a French provincial capital. Land use in Montréal was much less differentiated, although commerce dominated the riverbank, and institutional buildings were set back towards the town's interior wall. People of different social and economic positions were scattered through a small, walled, approximately rectangular space in which, even at the end of the French regime, much of the land was cultivated.

These first Canadian towns, Québec especially, were remarkably comprehensive transplantations of French urban life. They performed the same general functions as French towns, housed much the same social classes, and looked like small towns from northwestern France – minus the medieval buildings. Their populations were sharply stratified by occupation and income, and by fine social distinctions. They were centres of authority and power where government officials, military officers, the most important clerics, and the most prosperous merchants lived; where instructions arrived from France; where laws were made and judgments passed; and where offenders were gaoled, tried, pardonned, or punished. Occupationally they were diverse, as were French towns, far more diverse than any other populations in early Canada. Some 40% of heads of households were artisans representing all the basic trades associated with a port, construction, and the provision of common consumer goods. Ordinary boots and shoes were made in Québec and Montréal whereas fancy shoes were usually imported. Steel and copperware came from France, and a major new enterprise, such as the royal shipyards, would require skills that had to be imported. However, there were silversmiths, wigmakers, cabinetmakers, stocking makers, and tailors and seamstresses making fashionable clothing for gentlemen and ladies. The variety of craftmanship was greater in Québec than Montréal, but apprenticeship was carefully regulated in both towns. The Canadian urban population was of unusually diverse origin, a reflection of the many parts of France from which immigrants had come to Canada. The range between the very rich and the very poor was not as great as in most French towns because available land in the countryside provided an outlet for the poor, and recent settlement and a limited economy had not yet allowed great landed or commercial fortunes to emerge. Overall the towns in the St Lawrence valley closely reflected those in northwestern France, from whence they had sprung.

The Countryside

Land along the lower St Lawrence was conceded in seigneuries within which all rural settlement took place. The Compagnie des Cent-Associés made its first seigneurial grants near Québec in 1634. Over the next 30 years the company granted several dozen seigneuries, some to people of noble birth, others to religious orders or merchants, a few to very ordinary people, usually with the hopeful clause in the seigneurial title that settlers brought to Canada by the seigneur would be credited to the company's charter obligation to colonize. After the crown assumed the administration of Canada in 1663, Jean Talon and the intendants who succeeded him made many new seigneurial grants, filling in the areas between the company's earlier concessions, conceding seigneuries along tributaries of the St Lawrence where agriculture was feasible, and granting extensions (*augmentations*) to some seigneuries (pl 51). The seigneurs thus created could grant sub-seigneuries (*arrière-fiefs*) within their seigneuries, or grant small concessions to people who were expected to live on them. The holders of such concessions would pay annual rents, and also pay for services (such as milling) provided by the seigneur. They would make a token payment, the *cens,* to indicate that their land could not be sub-granted. Notaries in Canada called such lots '*concessions*' or '*habitations,*' and the people who lived on them were known as *habitants.* The habitants' rights were considerable. As long as they paid the seigneurial charges, their tenures were secure; their land could be inherited, deeded, or sold, but not detached from the seigneurial obligations specified in the title deed.

The first farm lots conceded in Canada were long, narrow trapezoids fronting on the river. Although other surveys were attempted, the long lot, with a common but never standardized ratio of width to length of about 1:10 and an area of some 60–120 arpents (1 arpent = 5/6 of an acre or about 1/3 of a hectare), became the characteristic concession in Canada (pl 52). Farm lots of this shape were frequently conceded along colonization roads in medieval Europe, and were well known in Normandy, source of many of the earliest immigrants to Canada. Along the St Lawrence the shape suited new settlements of farmers who lived on their own land. Long lots were easily and cheaply surveyed, gave all farmers frontage on the river or, eventually, a public road, and allowed them to live on their own farms yet close to neighbours. Further, because survey lines were approximately at right angles to ecological boundaries that tended to run parallel to the river, long lots gave most farmers access to several soil and vegetation types. The disadvantage of the shape for some farm activities was balanced by its advantages for ploughing. A group of long-lot farms was known as a *côte* (pl 52).

The work of establishing a farm was sometimes assisted by indentured servants recently arrived from France, or by locally available wage labourers, but labour usually came almost entirely from the farm family, the basic unit of rural settlement. A young man arriving penniless from France could not move directly onto his own concession. The cost of simple tools, a few animals, seed, and provisions for at least a year and a half before a farm lot could begin to provide for its occupants was prohibitive. He would work for some years, perhaps to pay off his contract of indenture; eventually he would have a little money and a concession of land, enough to start a farm and marry. Quite possibly the attempt to farm would fail, defeated by sickness, accident, or work that was too unfamiliar and too hard. Sometimes the family would move after a few years, selling a lot that clearing had given some value, and starting again somewhere else. At best two arpents could be cleared and planted each year, then less as farm work demanded more time. For the children of established farmers the process was a little easier. They had grown up with the work involved, and if a father had acquired additional concessions near the family farm for his sons, as was often done, a young man could live at home while starting a new farm. In either case the work was unremitting; a farm of 30–40 cleared arpents was the product of a lifetime of clearing, working the land, and building.

The establishment of a farm along the lower St Lawrence embodied the transplantation of a European sentiment of the family and French peasant techniques to a forested valley near the climatic margin for agriculture. Eventually the fur trade did not require more white labour (pl 41), and the towns offered little new work. As the population grew, people turned to agriculture to live, in a setting where land was available, the local market for farm products was small, and the export market was non-existent until the 18th century. Canadian prices for agricultural products were not linked to French prices. They declined sharply in the latter half of the 17th century, stabilized in the first third of the 18th century, and then turned upward (pl 53) as local markets expanded and Canadian wheat and flour, peas, and meat began to find markets in the Gulf of St Lawrence, at Louisbourg, and in the French Antilles (pl 48).

In these circumstances farming developed primarily in response to the needs of farm families. A farm was an unspecialized, mixed operation that provided as much as possible for domestic consumption, and some surplus for sale. Its basic components were a kitchen garden, in which a wide variety of vegetables, tobacco, and perhaps a few fruit trees were grown; ploughed fields, which were planted primarily in wheat but also in legumes (a field crop in Canada), barley, and oats (usually in a two-course rotation, that is, crops one year followed by fallow the next); some meadow and pasture; and, depending on the age of the farm, more or less forest. Pigs, sturdy animals that could fend for themselves most of the year, were kept for meat. Cattle were kept for meat and milk, and oxen as draft animals. Sheep were raised for their wool. By the 18th century there were horses on most farms, used for hauling. Every farm had poultry. Such were the elements of almost all established farms from one end of the colony to the other. Wheat and some fruits did better towards Montréal, where the growing season was longer than near Québec, but the census of 1739, the most comprehensive survey of agriculture in Canada before the 19th century, reveals little market specialization (pl 53). Larger farms produced more of the same things than smaller ones. With 20 arpents cleared there was hardly a surplus for sale; with 40 cleared there usually was: some wheat, a cow or two, perhaps a pig or some piglets, perhaps a few tubs of butter. No farm family could be, or wanted to be, self-sufficient. There were rents and tithes to pay; religious, notarial, and medical services to buy; perhaps livestock to buy or land to purchase for a son; perhaps a pension to pay to elderly parents in return for the use of their farm, or payments to siblings for their part of an inheritance. Some manufactured goods had to be purchased: iron tools, some kitchenware, some items of clothing, and, if it could be afforded, an iron stove made in the ironworks near Trois-Rivières. Most of these payments were made in kind.

Serving the rural population were a few artisans, sometimes part-time farmers themselves, who were scattered along the côtes. A water- or wind-powered gristmill was needed for every 40 or 50 families. Sawmills, cutting for the local market, were almost as common. Blacksmiths, carpenters, wheelwrights, harness makers, and masons (near Québec and Montréal) provided services that were beyond the capacity of most households. Pedlars and merchants visited the countryside, selling goods from the towns, buying wheat and other farm produce. In the 18th century most of the older parishes had resident merchants. Despite government plans for them, the village was not a form of rural settlement in the 17th century, and only slowly emerged in the 18th. The residential open-field village of northern France was not reproduced in Canada as people settled on their own land, bypassing most of the collective practices of open-field agriculture and a daily walk to their fields. As long as the rural population density was low and the market economy was weak, there was no need for a market village or a rural service centre. Towards the end of the French regime such villages were appearing near Montréal (pl 53). Even then the overwhelming majority of rural families lived on their own farms, overlooking the river or on a road, their nearest neighbours some 100–200 m away. Visitors travelling along the St Lawrence River likened Canadian rural settlement to a continuous, straggling village.

Habitant society was much less stratified than the French peasantry. In a weak commercial economy there were no really wealthy habitants, no counterparts of the few peasants who often rented most of the land of a French village. As long as new farmland was available, there were few landless families or beggars in the Canadian countryside. Farms of equivalent age were usually fairly similar; recently established farms were small, older farms were larger. Once established, the Canadian farm provided the basics; enough to eat, rough clothing, shelter, fuel in winter, some surplus for sale. As long as there was opportunity to establish such farms, ordinary Canadian habitants were better off than their French peasant counterparts. On average they married younger, had more children, and lived longer. The Canadian farm served its essential purpose.

Seigneurs, priests, merchants, and the militia were also part of rural life. Many seigneurs were absentee landlords who lived in the towns, depended on royal appointments or on the fur trade, and paid little attention to their sparsely settled seigneuries, knowing they would collect the rents sooner or later. Yet some of them did live on their seigneuries, and a few were active colonizers. The seigneurial domain, land that seigneurs set aside for their own use, was usually the size of several concessions, and the domainal farm was the largest farm in most seigneuries. Sometimes the seigneur and his family worked this farm themselves; more commonly it was worked by tenants, sharecroppers, or hired hands. The seigneurial manor, small by European standards, was usually considerably larger than the habitant house. When a seigneurie had 40 or 50 families it was profitable, and by the 1730s a good many seigneuries had at least this many families. Although seigneurial charges for land were only a few bushels of wheat per farm per year, there were also charges for milling (a seigneurial monopoly), a seigneurial tax on land sales (the *lods et ventes*, 1/12 of the sale price), and seigneurial reserves of timber and fishing sites. Such charges and reserves were a considerable burden to people who depended largely on subsistence farming. Habitants paid reluctantly, prevaricating as they could. The parish was quite separate from the seigneurie, and was usually founded soon after the settlement of a given côte began. Eventually a church would be built and a parish priest, or curé, maintained in residence. Inevitably the curé was a major figure in local society, the parish an important rural institution, and the tithe, 1/26 of the grain harvest, another charge to be paid. Merchants from the towns also were active in the countryside, particularly from the 1720s when the colony began to export flour, beef, pork, and dried peas to Louisbourg and the French islands in the Antilles (pl 48). The merchants bartered and extended credit; many habitants were in debt to them. There were no royal taxes, but habitants were required to perform road work and, in wartime, to serve in the militia. In these ways traditional sources of power in rural France penetrated the relatively undifferentiated Canadian countryside.

Most immigrants to Canada were young and single; eventually they would marry someone who, in all probability, had come – or whose people had come – from another part of France, and would settle along a côte whose inhabitants could be traced to different regions of France. In these circumstances no particular French regional culture could be reproduced along the lower St Lawrence. Common peasant assumptions – for example, about the importance of land, the primacy of the family, and the need for frugality – were transferred. For the rest an unconscious selection of remembered ways reinforced common immigrant memories or memories that were particularly relevant to the demands of settlement along the lower St Lawrence. Languages other than French, and many dialects of French, quickly disappeared. The wooden habitant house was not associated with any of the major regions from which emigrants came to Canada. Rather it drew on building techniques that had been common in early medieval Europe when the forest was at hand, had largely lapsed when it was cleared, and had re-emerged, never entirely forgotten, when migration suddenly returned some French people to the forest (pl 56). In effect, some memories were reinforced by migration and resettlement and others were lost. A few introductions from the Indians aside, habitant life in Canada was French in most details, but was not of any particular French composition. A distinctive Canadian culture was emerging. Because agriculture developed within broadly similar environmental and economic constraints from one end of the lower St Lawrence to the other, and because part of the habitant population was remixed, generation after generation, as young adults moved from areas where all agricultural land was occupied to others where it was still available (commonly they moved westward, towards the Montréal plain), the emerging rural culture of early Canada was expansive and probably fairly uniform. Towards Montréal, in the parishes where young men were recruited for the canoe brigades (pl 41), the fur trade considerably penetrated the rural culture, as did the fishery below Québec where the St Lawrence River began to open into the Gulf (pl 54).

At the end of the French regime about 60 000 people, some 85% of the Canadian population, lived in the countryside of the lower St Lawrence. Almost all of these people were farmers on their own long-lot farms. Settlement lined the St Lawrence, several concessions deep in some places, for hundreds of kilometres, and extended up the few tributaries of the lower St Lawrence where there was arable land (pl 46 shows the pattern in 1739). Near Québec land for agricultural expansion was no longer available. Everywhere the forest has been pushed back, replaced by tended countryside. Parish churches dotted the lines of settlement, more conspicuous than the grist and sawmills. Here and there a manor stood out from the houses around it, a reflection of a seigneur's growing revenue as a seigneurial population rose. The predominant building in the countryside was the small habitant house, usually built of squared logs dovetailed at the corners and mortised to vertical posts around windows, chimney, and doors; usually whitewashed to preserve the logs; usually roofed with thatch (which could last for 50 years) or cedar planks. The ground floor of these houses was divided into two or three small rooms with an attic above (pls 55, 56). Averaging about 8 m long by 6 m wide, such houses and the farms surrounding them were the setting of rural family life as it developed in the remarkable circumstances of the lower St Lawrence valley in the 17th and 18th centuries. There, as forest gave way to farmland, there was opportunity to establish family farms, local communities, and a vibrant, distinctive peasant culture.

Changes, 1760–1800

During the massive British assault on Québec in the summer of 1759 British cannon at Pointe de Lévis, firing across the river, reduced most of Québec to rubble, while British soldiers burned farms along the river (pl 43). When Québec fell in September, the French defence of North America rested on Montréal where, a year later, surrounded and hopelessly outnumbered, the remainder of the French army in North America surrendered. In 1763 the Treaty of Paris confirmed the British conquest of Canada (pl 42).

With the conquest civil and military power passed to the victors, and many of the Canadian élite returned to France. The new governor and his staff, the new officers and their men, were British. The church remained, although its political position was fragile. Canadian merchants found it difficult to compete with British merchants who were supported by the new government and connected to suppliers and agents in London, now the focus of Canadian external trade. As the fur trade resumed after the conquest, it was increasingly controlled by British merchants based in Québec, as were the former Canadian fisheries in the Gulf of St Lawrence (pl 54). Many seigneuries passed into British hands, some confiscated by the military governor, some purchased at bargain prices from seigneurs who had returned to France, some acquired by the marriage of a merchant or an army officer to the daughter of a seigneurial family, her father perhaps killed in the war.

The towns were dominated by the new, British élite. In Québec the army took over much of the upper town, repairing and expanding the fortifications and deflecting urban growth to a new suburb, Saint-Jean, outside the wall. The British colonial officials and military officers who governed the colony lived in the upper town, close to the citadel that was built in the 1780s on Cap-aux-Diamants. The suburbs remained Canadian, as did much of the lower town, although most of the importers, wholesalers, and small traders who operated there were British. English had become the language of authority, and British civic architecture began to appear. In many basic ways, however, the towns had not changed. They were still administrative, commercial, and military centres served by a wide variety of artisans. They were not growing rapidly: in 1800 the civil population of Québec was barely 8 000, of Montréal perhaps 6 000. At the end of the century no more ships were calling each year at Québec than in the 1750s. Agricultural products were a larger percentage of total exports than during the French regime, finding markets for a time in the British Isles and in southern Europe (pl 48), but British merchants had not been notably more successful than their predecessors in diversifying Canadian exports.

In 1800 some 7% of the population of Lower Canada was urban, half the percentage 40 years before. The rural population had grown to almost 200 000. Of these perhaps 15 000–20 000 were English-speakers, most of whom came from New England or New York. Some arrived before the American Revolution, some later as Loyalists in 1783–4, a few at the end of the century as land-seekers. They settled principally along the Richelieu River, the route by which most had come, near the towns (particularly Montréal) where they tended to buy well-established farms, or in the townships newly laid out between the seigneurial lands of the St Lawrence valley and the American border. There, at the end of the century, the northern edge of the American settlement frontier began to spill into British North America (pl 68). Most of the expansion of rural settlement was not associated with these English-speaking newcomers. Canadian birth and death rates remained approximately at pre-conquest levels, and Acadian refugees at the end of the French regime added to the rural, Canadian stock, as did people who moved away from the towns, now dominated by the British. The countryside loomed larger in Canadian life. By 1800 some 180 000 French-speaking people, almost 95% of the total in Lower Canada, lived there.

As the rural population grew, settlement expanded rapidly inland, away from the river, occupying all arable land in many seigneuries, and spreading rapidly across the Montréal plain, the last large reservoir of unconceded farmland in the lower St Lawrence valley. As land became scarce, its value rose. In some areas family land was held as tenaciously as in France, and there was no agricultural niche for outsiders unless it were created by marriage. Seigneurial revenues increased as the population rose, and the local market economy expanded. The export economy may have slightly exceeded the level, per capita, of the 1730s and early 1740s, the best years for agricultural exports during the French regime. Villages became more common, small service centres for farmers nearby. Artisans, small merchants, and professionals, as well as the curé and a few farm families, usually lived there (pl 53). Seigneurial manors became a little larger, and the architecture of some of them began to reflect the origins of a new group of seigneurs. Here and there a few habitant farms were much larger and more specialized than the rest. Overall, the agricultural economy remained unspecialized, still oriented much more to the immediate needs of farm families than to the market. The domestic economy and the distinctive rural society that had evolved along the lower St Lawrence when farmland was widely available and agricultural prices were low were still viable, still expanding, still supporting a people within the St Lawrence valley. The day was not far off, however, when all the arable lowland would be occupied. Then the young would not be able to establish new farms, at least not in the St Lawrence lowlands, and many new decisions would face a people who had lived for generations with a distinctive, but limited, and, in the end, temporary opportunity.

THE FRENCH ORIGINS OF THE CANADIAN POPULATION, 1608–1759

Authors: Hubert Charbonneau, Normand Robert

Of some 9 000 Europeans who settled in the St Lawrence valley before 1760, only about 350 were not French. Marriage certificates usually indicate the parish of origin of couples married in Canada. Other sources–marriage contracts, confirmation lists, indenture contracts, and death certificates–provide additional information, so that in the great majority of cases the origin of an immigrant, whether married in Canada or not, can be established.

Four times as many men as women and nearly as many urban as rural people emigrated to Canada, about half of them in the 17th century. Two periods of heavy immigration, almost a hundred years apart, can be identified. The first, under Jean Talon's administration, coincided with the arrival in Canada of the 'Filles du roi' and the Carignan regiment, the second with the arrival of troops during the Seven Years' War. These two waves of immigration contributed 40% of male immigrants and the majority of female immigrants. In the 17th century women accounted for a third of all immigrants. However, after 1673 their number dropped to an average of three per year, a level maintained until the end of the French regime. Nearly all immigrants were single: one man in twenty and one woman in five were married or widowed. Couples married in France accounted for only 250 families.

Over all, the rate of emigration from the towns was nearly five times as high as from the countryside. One woman in three came from Rouen, La Rochelle, or Paris. Paris alone contributed 10% of all immigrants, and one woman in five. Indeed, two-thirds of the female immigrants were of urban origin.

IMMIGRANTS BY SEX AND DECADE, 1608–1759

Period	Men	Women	Total
Before 1630	15	6	21
1630-1639	88	51	139
1640-1649	141	86	227
1650-1659	403	239	642
1660-1669	1075	623	1698
1670-1679	429	369	798
1680-1689	486	56	542
1690-1699	490	32	522
1700-1709	283	24	307
1710-1719	293	18	311
1720-1729	420	14	434
1730-1739	483	16	499
1740-1749	576	16	592
1750-1759	1699	52	1751
Unknown	27	17	44
TOTAL	**6908**	**1619**	**8527**

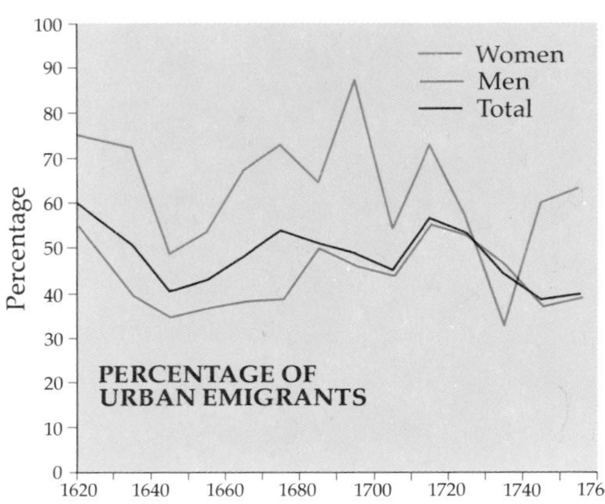
PERCENTAGE OF URBAN EMIGRANTS
Women
Men
Total
Percentage
100
90
80
70
60
50
40
30
20
10
0
1620
1640
1660
1680
1700
1720
1740
1760

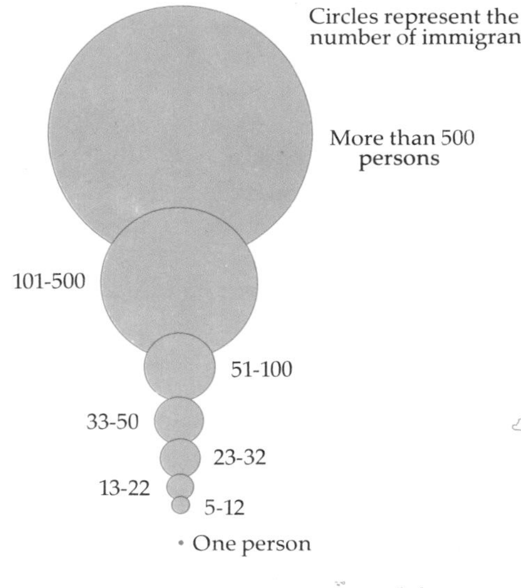
Circles represent the number of immigrants.
More than 500 persons
101-500
51-100
33-50
23-32
13-22
5-12
One person

Brest
BRETAGNE
Quimper

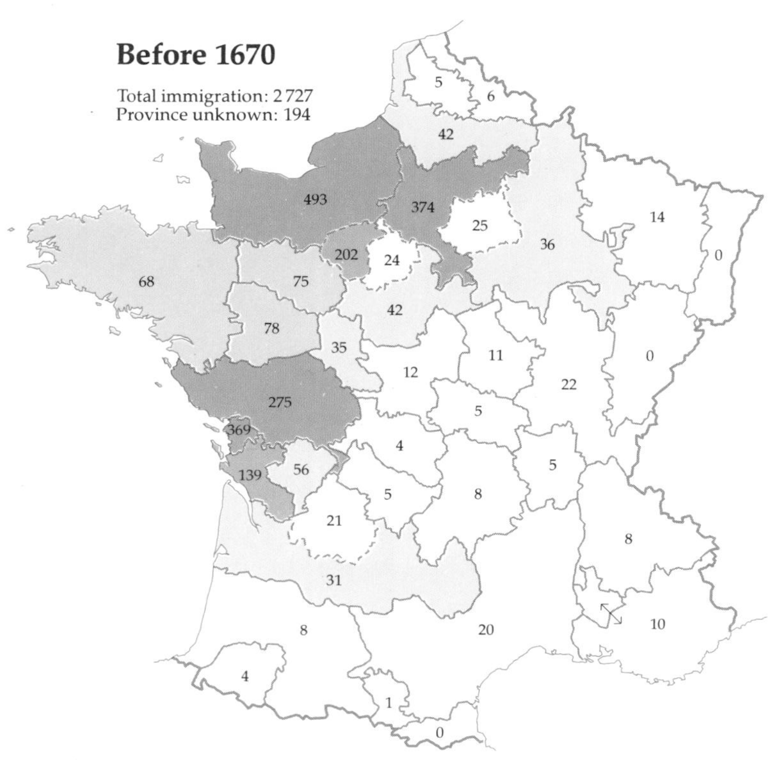
Before 1670
Total immigration: 2 727
Province unknown: 194

1670–1699

Total immigration: 1 862
Province unknown: 162

IMMIGRATION BY PROVINCE OF ORIGIN

- More than 10%
- 5.1-10%
- 2.1-5%
- 1.1-2%
- Less than 1%
- No immigration

The numbers show immigrants from each province.

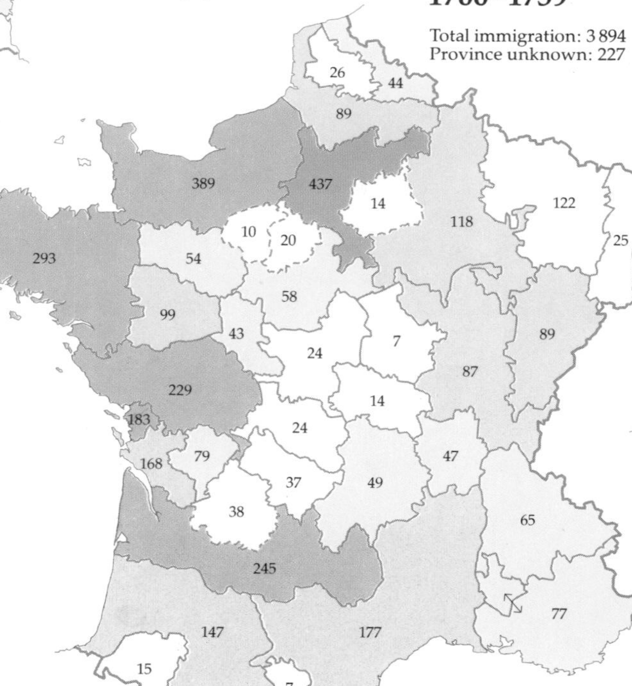
1700–1759
Total immigration: 3 894
Province unknown: 227
Scale 1:10 000 000

Settlers came from all the provinces of France, but about three-quarters were from west of a line between Bordeaux and Soissons. Besides Paris, the main regions of emigration lay in the hinterlands of the major ports of embarkation: La Rochelle, Bordeaux, Rouen, Dieppe, Saint-Malo, Granville. The foremost provinces were Normandy and Île-de-France, followed by Poitou, Aunis, Brittany, and Saintonge. Prior to 1670 Normandy ranked first, but it was later superseded by the Île-de-France. Along with Poitou-Charentes, these three areas contributed two-thirds of all the 17th century immigrants. After 1700 the Midi also contributed immigrants; soldiers from the southwest and east tended to succeed the indentured servants of the central west and northwest.

ORIGIN OF IMMIGRANTS

Sub-province
Provincial boundary
Boundary of France
Liège
Lille
ARTOIS
Arras
FLANDRE
Cambrai
Dieppe (88)
Amiens
PICARDIE
Saint-Quentin
Le Havre
Rouen (194)
Caen
Soissons
ÎLE-DE-FRANCE
Metz
Saint-Malo (55)
Granville
NORMANDIE
Châlons-sur-Marne
LORRAINE
Nancy
BRIE
Mortagne (51)
Paris (789)
CHAMPAGNE
Strasbourg
ALSACE
PERCHE
Chartres
Rennes
MAINE
BEAUCE
Troyes
Sens
Le Mans
Orléans (48)
ANJOU
ORLÉANAIS
Blois
Tours (45)
Nantes (49)
Angers (45)
Dijon
Besançon
TOURAINE
NIVERNAIS
FRANCHE-COMTÉ
Bourges
Nevers
BERRY
BOURGOGNE
POITOU
Poitiers (98)
Fontenay-le-Comte (45)
Moulins
BOURBONNAIS
Saint-Martin-de-Ré (42)
Niort (45)
AUNIS
Guéret
La Rochelle (351)
MARCHE
Clermont-Ferrand
LYONNAIS
Lyon
ANGOUMOIS
Saintes (40)
Limoges
Angoulême
LIMOUSIN
AUVERGNE
SAINTONGE
Grenoble
PÉRIGORD
DAUPHINÉ
Bordeaux (98)
GUYENNE
Agen
COMTAT VENAISSIN
Nîmes
GASCOGNE
LANGUEDOC
PROVENCE
Auch
Montpellier
Bayonne
Toulouse
Marseille
Pau
BÉARN
Toulon
Carcassonne
COMTÉ DE FOIX
Perpignan
ROUSSILLON
0
100 miles
0
100 kilometres
Scale 1:3 000 000

RESETTLING THE ST LAWRENCE VALLEY

Authors: Hubert Charbonneau; R. Cole Harris (Population distribution)

After the dispersal of the St Lawrence Iroquoians most of the St Lawrence valley was virtually uninhabited. French fur traders came each summer to Tadoussac at the mouth of the Saguenay River, but Iroquois raiders blocked the St Lawrence River. European trade goods, carried by Montagnais and Algonquins, reached the Great Lakes by a roundabout, northern route (pl 33).

Early in the 17th century the French established permanent settlements at Québec (1608), Trois-Rivières (1634), and Montréal (1642). Initially they were tiny outposts of European-Indian trade, but as the population increased, farming became the common way of life. Settlements spread along the St Lawrence River, a progression marked by the establishment of parishes. By 1739 (date of the last general census taken during the French regime) the land along the banks of the St Lawrence was occupied for almost 500 km. To the north lay the fringe of the Canadian Shield and to the south the Appalachian Highlands. The St Lawrence valley was bounded agricultural space close to the climatic limit for cereal crops.

After the early years when men far outnumbered women and the period of rapid immigration during the 1660s and early 1670s the population grew largely from natural increase at an average annual rate of 2.5%. Immigration raised the marriage rate before 1675 and the end of immigration depressed this rate until, by the late 1680s, a generation of Canadian-born had reached marriage age. The marriage rate remained relatively constant thereafter. In the early years low birth rates reflected the shortage of women, and in the 1680s the declining rate of marriage. The death rate fluctuated sharply, its peaks caused by major epidemics. Overall, the death rate in the 18th century was approximately 30 per 1 000 and the birth rate almost 55 per 1 000. Without immigration such a population would double in just under thirty years. By 1760 the 9 000 French settlers over the previous 150 years (pl 45) had become a population of more than 70 000 people. If this rate of natural increase continued through the last decades of the 18th century, then in 1800 some 190 000 people of French descent lived along the lower St Lawrence. At this date there were also some 25 000 to 30 000 people of British background in Lower Canada, making a total population of about 220 000.

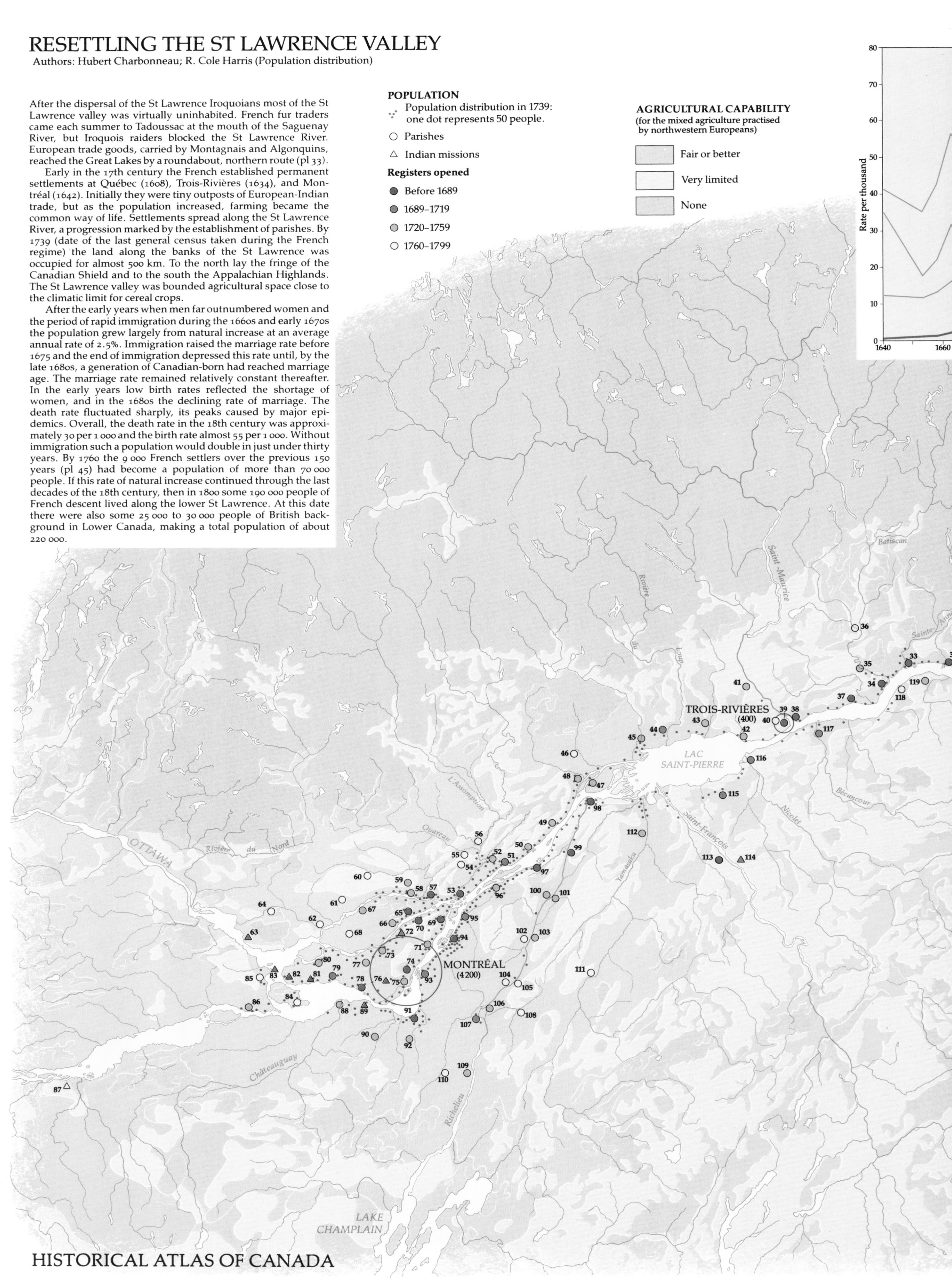

POPULATION
Population distribution in 1739: one dot represents 50 people.
Parishes
Indian missions
Registers opened
Before 1689
1689–1719
1720–1759
1760–1799
AGRICULTURAL CAPABILITY
(for the mixed agriculture practised by northwestern Europeans)
Fair or better
Very limited
None
Rate per thousand
80
70
60
50
40
30
20
10
0
1640
1660
TROIS-RIVIÈRES
(400)
MONTRÉAL
(4 200)
LAC SAINT-PIERRE
LAKE CHAMPLAIN
OTTAWA
Rivière du Nord
Ouareau
L'Assomption
Rivière du Loup
Saint-Maurice
Batiscan
Sainte-Anne
Bécancour
Nicolet
Saint-François
Yamaska
Richelieu
Châteauguay

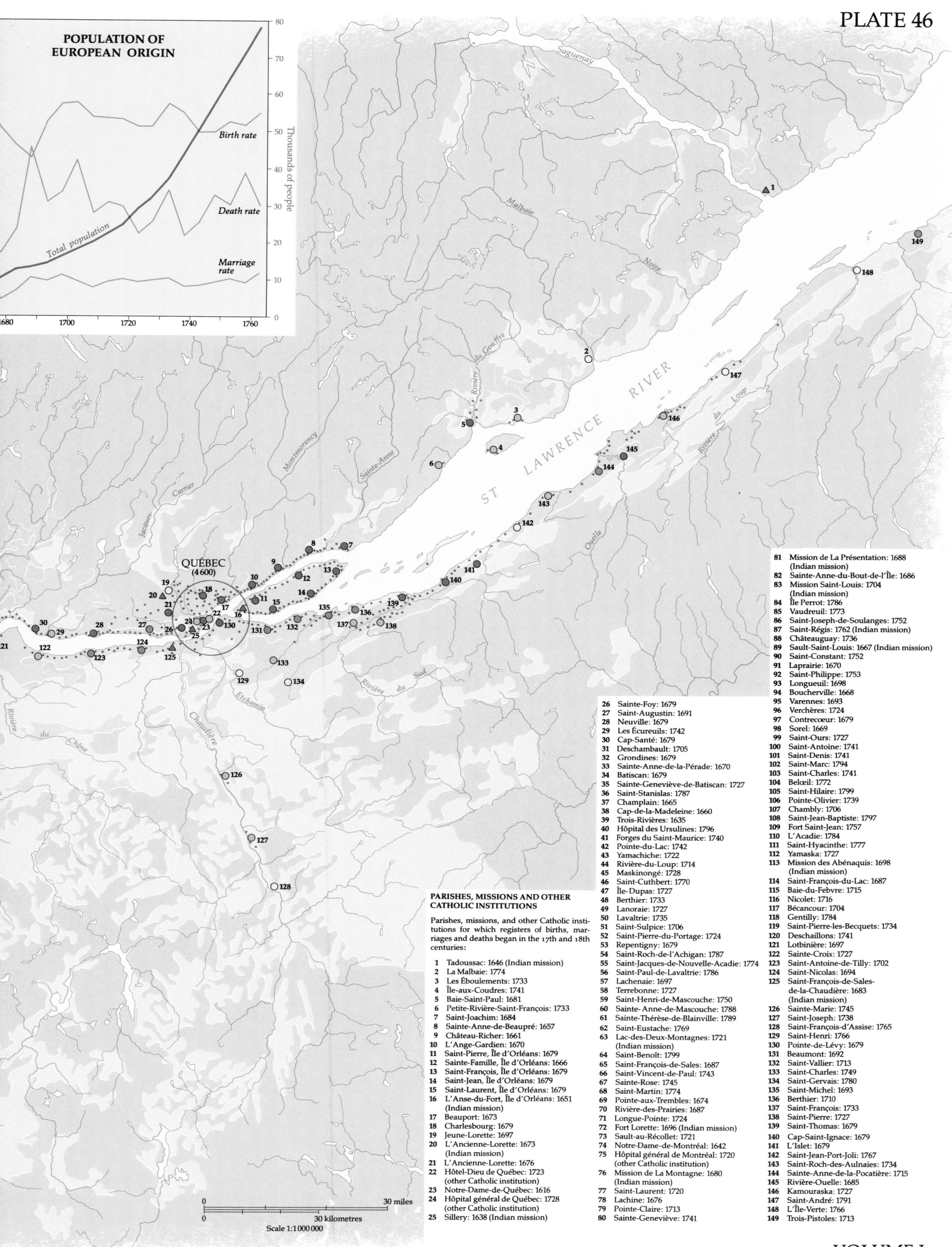
POPULATION OF EUROPEAN ORIGIN
Birth rate
Death rate
Total population
Marriage rate
Thousands of people
0
10
20
30
40
50
60
70
80
1680
1700
1720
1740
1760
Saguenay
Malbaie
Notre
Rivière du Gouffre
Montmorency
Sainte-Anne
Cartier
Jacques
ST LAWRENCE RIVER
QUÉBEC
(4600)
Rivière du Loup
Ouelle
Rivière du Sud
Etchemin
Chaudière
Rivière du Chêne
0
30 miles
0
30 kilometres
Scale 1:1 000 000
PARISHES, MISSIONS AND OTHER CATHOLIC INSTITUTIONS
Parishes, missions, and other Catholic institutions for which registers of births, marriages and deaths began in the 17th and 18th centuries:
1 Tadoussac: 1646 (Indian mission)
2 La Malbaie: 1774
3 Les Éboulements: 1733
4 Île-aux-Coudres: 1741
5 Baie-Saint-Paul: 1681
6 Petite-Rivière-Saint-François: 1733
7 Saint-Joachim: 1684
8 Sainte-Anne-de-Beaupré: 1657
9 Château-Richer: 1661
10 L'Ange-Gardien: 1670
11 Saint-Pierre, Île d'Orléans: 1679
12 Sainte-Famille, Île d'Orléans: 1666
13 Saint-François, Île d'Orléans: 1679
14 Saint-Jean, Île d'Orléans: 1679
15 Saint-Laurent, Île d'Orléans: 1679
16 L'Anse-du-Fort, Île d'Orléans: 1651 (Indian mission)
17 Beauport: 1673
18 Charlesbourg: 1679
19 Jeune-Lorette: 1697
20 L'Ancienne-Lorette: 1673 (Indian mission)
21 L'Ancienne-Lorette: 1676
22 Hôtel-Dieu de Québec: 1723 (other Catholic institution)
23 Notre-Dame-de-Québec: 1616
24 Hôpital général de Québec: 1728 (other Catholic institution)
25 Sillery: 1638 (Indian mission)
26 Sainte-Foy: 1679
27 Saint-Augustin: 1691
28 Neuville: 1679
29 Les Écureuils: 1742
30 Cap-Santé: 1679
31 Deschambault: 1705
32 Grondines: 1679
33 Sainte-Anne-de-la-Pérade: 1670
34 Batiscan: 1679
35 Sainte-Geneviève-de-Batiscan: 1727
36 Saint-Stanislas: 1787
37 Champlain: 1665
38 Cap-de-la-Madeleine: 1660
39 Trois-Rivières: 1635
40 Hôpital des Ursulines: 1796
41 Forges du Saint-Maurice: 1740
42 Pointe-du-Lac: 1742
43 Yamachiche: 1722
44 Rivière-du-Loup: 1714
45 Maskinongé: 1728
46 Saint-Cuthbert: 1770
47 Île-Dupas: 1727
48 Berthier: 1733
49 Lanoraie: 1727
50 Lavaltrie: 1735
51 Saint-Sulpice: 1706
52 Saint-Pierre-du-Portage: 1724
53 Repentigny: 1679
54 Saint-Roch-de-l'Achigan: 1787
55 Saint-Jacques-de-Nouvelle-Acadie: 1774
56 Saint-Paul-de-Lavaltrie: 1786
57 Lachenaie: 1697
58 Terrebonne: 1727
59 Saint-Henri-de-Mascouche: 1750
60 Sainte-Anne-de-Mascouche: 1788
61 Sainte-Thérèse-de-Blainville: 1789
62 Saint-Eustache: 1769
63 Lac-des-Deux-Montagnes: 1721 (Indian mission)
64 Saint-Benoît: 1799
65 Saint-François-de-Sales: 1687
66 Saint-Vincent-de-Paul: 1743
67 Sainte-Rose: 1745
68 Saint-Martin: 1774
69 Pointe-aux-Trembles: 1674
70 Rivière-des-Prairies: 1687
71 Longue-Pointe: 1724
72 Fort Lorette: 1696 (Indian mission)
73 Sault-au-Récollet: 1721
74 Notre-Dame-de-Montréal: 1642
75 Hôpital général de Montréal: 1720 (other Catholic institution)
76 Mission de La Montagne: 1680 (Indian mission)
77 Saint-Laurent: 1720
78 Lachine: 1676
79 Pointe-Claire: 1713
80 Sainte-Geneviève: 1741
81 Mission de La Présentation: 1688 (Indian mission)
82 Sainte-Anne-du-Bout-de-l'Île: 1686
83 Mission Saint-Louis: 1704 (Indian mission)
84 Île Perrot: 1786
85 Vaudreuil: 1773
86 Saint-Joseph-de-Soulanges: 1752
87 Saint-Régis: 1762 (Indian mission)
88 Châteauguay: 1736
89 Sault-Saint-Louis: 1667 (Indian mission)
90 Saint-Constant: 1752
91 Laprairie: 1670
92 Saint-Philippe: 1753
93 Longueuil: 1698
94 Boucherville: 1668
95 Varennes: 1693
96 Verchères: 1724
97 Contrecoeur: 1679
98 Sorel: 1669
99 Saint-Ours: 1727
100 Saint-Antoine: 1741
101 Saint-Denis: 1741
102 Saint-Marc: 1794
103 Saint-Charles: 1741
104 Belœil: 1772
105 Saint-Hilaire: 1799
106 Pointe-Olivier: 1739
107 Chambly: 1706
108 Saint-Jean-Baptiste: 1797
109 Fort Saint-Jean: 1757
110 L'Acadie: 1784
111 Saint-Hyacinthe: 1777
112 Yamaska: 1727
113 Mission des Abénaquis: 1698 (Indian mission)
114 Saint-François-du-Lac: 1687
115 Baie-du-Febvre: 1715
116 Nicolet: 1716
117 Bécancour: 1704
118 Gentilly: 1784
119 Saint-Pierre-les-Becquets: 1734
120 Deschaillons: 1741
121 Lotbinière: 1697
122 Sainte-Croix: 1727
123 Saint-Antoine-de-Tilly: 1702
124 Saint-Nicolas: 1694
125 Saint-François-de-Sales-de-la-Chaudière: 1683 (Indian mission)
126 Sainte-Marie: 1745
127 Saint-Joseph: 1738
128 Saint-François-d'Assise: 1765
129 Saint-Henri: 1766
130 Pointe-de-Lévy: 1679
131 Beaumont: 1692
132 Saint-Vallier: 1713
133 Saint-Charles: 1749
134 Saint-Gervais: 1780
135 Saint-Michel: 1693
136 Berthier: 1710
137 Saint-François: 1733
138 Saint-Pierre: 1727
139 Saint-Thomas: 1679
140 Cap-Saint-Ignace: 1679
141 L'Islet: 1679
142 Saint-Jean-Port-Joli: 1767
143 Saint-Roch-des-Aulnaies: 1734
144 Sainte-Anne-de-la-Pocatière: 1715
145 Rivière-Ouelle: 1685
146 Kamouraska: 1727
147 Saint-André: 1791
148 L'Île-Verte: 1766
149 Trois-Pistoles: 1713

NATIVE RESETTLEMENT, 1635–1800

Author: B.G. Trigger

After the dispersal of the St Lawrence Iroquoians (pl 33) French settlements in the no-man's-land between the Montagnais and Algonquin to the north and Iroquois to the south attracted various native groups to settle along the St Lawrence River. Fur traders and government officials welcomed this settlement for economic, political, and military reasons. As French officials required at least nominal adherence to Christianity, most Indian settlements were organized as Jesuit or Sulpician missions. This policy met with varying degrees of covert resistance; much native culture was preserved despite periodic efforts to make Indians 'live like Frenchmen.'

It is impossible to trace the movement and settlement history of all native groups in the St Lawrence valley during almost 200 years of major dislocation and shifting ethnic identity. This plate summarizes the available data.

A Jesuit residential mission for Montagnais groups that had exhausted local supplies of beaver and lacked access to northern trade routes was established at Sillery in 1638; it was, *de facto*, the first reserve in Canada. In 1650 and 1651, following their defeat by the Iroquois, 600 Huron Christians came as refugees to Québec, where their descendants still live. As Algonquins from the Ottawa valley came under increasing Iroquois attack in the 1640s, they, too, sought protection near the French settlements. One group lived near Trois-Rivières until 1830. The Algonquin and Nipissing in the Montréal area were drawn together at Lac-des-Deux-Montagnes after 1721, but they continued to hunt in their former Ottawa valley territories.

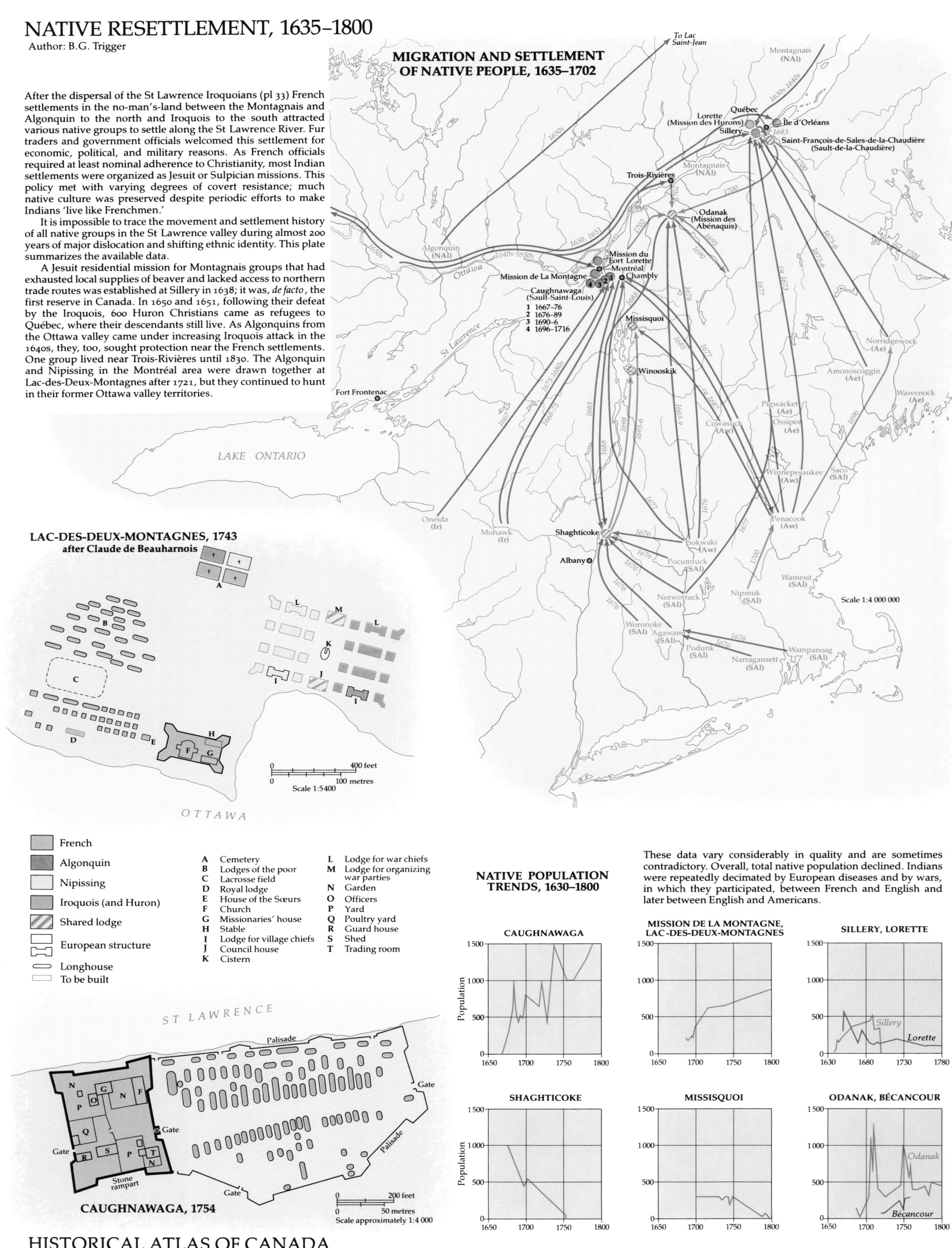

MIGRATION AND SETTLEMENT OF NATIVE PEOPLE, 1635–1702
To Lac Saint-Jean
Montagnais (NAI)
Québec
Lorette (Mission des Hurons)
Sillery
Île d'Orléans
Saint-François-de-Sales-de-la-Chaudière (Sault-de-la-Chaudière)
Trois-Rivières
Odanak (Mission des Abénaquis)
Algonquin (NAI)
Mission du Fort Lorette
Montréal
Mission de La Montagne
Chambly
Caughnawaga (Sault-Saint-Louis)
1 1667–76
2 1676–89
3 1690–6
4 1696–1716
Missisquoi
Winooskik
Fort Frontenac
LAKE ONTARIO
Ottawa
St Lawrence
Norridgewock (Ae)
Amonoscoggin (Ae)
Wawenock (Ae)
Pigwacket (Ae)
Ossipee (Ae)
Cowasuck (Aw)
Winnepesaukee (Aw)
Saco (SAI)
Oneida (Ir)
Mohawk (Ir)
Shaghticoke
Albany
Penacook (Aw)
Sokwaki (Aw)
Pocumtuck (SAI)
Wamesit (SAI)
Norwottuck (SAI)
Nipmuk (SAI)
Woronoke (SAI)
Agawam (SAI)
Podunk (SAI)
Narragansett (SAI)
Wampanoag (SAI)
Scale 1:4 000 000
LAC-DES-DEUX-MONTAGNES, 1743
after Claude de Beauharnois
Scale 1:5400
OTTAWA
French
Algonquin
Nipissing
Iroquois (and Huron)
Shared lodge
European structure
Longhouse
To be built
A Cemetery
B Lodges of the poor
C Lacrosse field
D Royal lodge
E House of the Sœurs
F Church
G Missionaries' house
H Stable
I Lodge for village chiefs
J Council house
K Cistern
L Lodge for war chiefs
M Lodge for organizing war parties
N Garden
O Officers
P Yard
Q Poultry yard
R Guard house
S Shed
T Trading room
ST LAWRENCE
Palisade
Gate
Stone rampart
CAUGHNAWAGA, 1754
Scale approximately 1:4 000
NATIVE POPULATION TRENDS, 1630–1800
CAUGHNAWAGA
MISSION DE LA MONTAGNE, LAC-DES-DEUX-MONTAGNES
SILLERY, LORETTE
Sillery
Lorette
SHAGHTICOKE
MISSISQUOI
ODANAK, BÉCANCOUR
Odanak
Bécancour
Population

These data vary considerably in quality and are sometimes contradictory. Overall, total native population declined. Indians were repeatedly decimated by European diseases and by wars, in which they participated, between French and English and later between English and Americans.

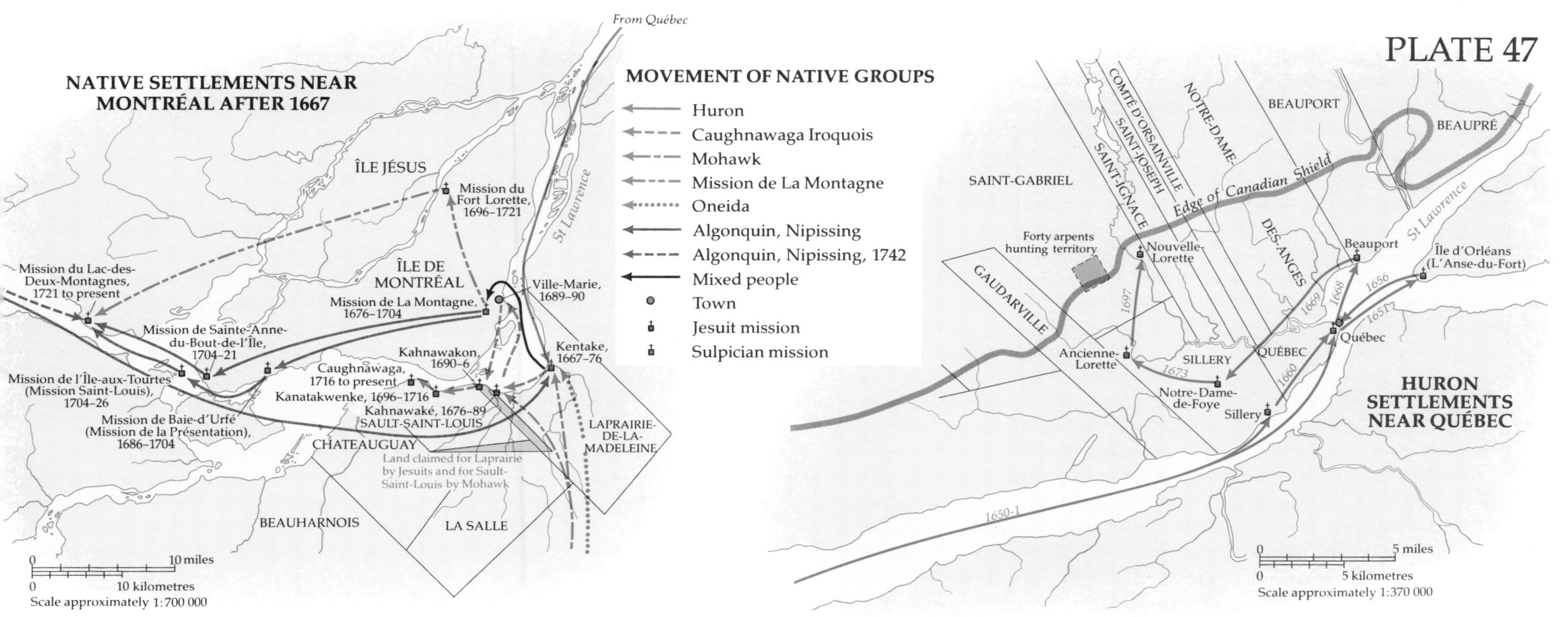
From Québec
NATIVE SETTLEMENTS NEAR MONTRÉAL AFTER 1667
MOVEMENT OF NATIVE GROUPS
Huron
Caughnawaga Iroquois
Mohawk
Mission de La Montagne
Oneida
Algonquin, Nipissing
Algonquin, Nipissing, 1742
Mixed people
Town
Jesuit mission
Sulpician mission
ÎLE JÉSUS
Mission du Fort Lorette, 1696–1721
St Lawrence
ÎLE DE MONTRÉAL
Mission du Lac-des-Deux-Montagnes, 1721 to present
Mission de La Montagne, 1676–1704
Ville-Marie, 1689–90
Mission de Sainte-Anne-du-Bout-de-l'Île, 1704–21
Kentake, 1667–76
Kahnawakon, 1690–6
Mission de l'Île-aux-Tourtes (Mission Saint-Louis), 1704–26
Caughnawaga, 1716 to present
Kanatakwenke, 1696–1716
Kahnawaké, 1676–89
SAULT-SAINT-LOUIS
Mission de Baie-d'Urfé (Mission de la Présentation), 1686–1704
CHATEAUGUAY
LAPRAIRIE-DE-LA-MADELEINE
Land claimed for Laprairie by Jesuits and for Sault-Saint-Louis by Mohawk
BEAUHARNOIS
LA SALLE
10 miles
10 kilometres
Scale approximately 1:700 000
BEAUPORT
BEAUPRÉ
COMTE D'ORSAINVILLE
SAINT-JOSEPH
SAINT-IGNACE
NOTRE-DAME-DES-ANGES
Edge of Canadian Shield
SAINT-GABRIEL
Forty arpents hunting territory
Nouvelle-Lorette
Beauport
Île d'Orléans (L'Anse-du-Fort)
GAUDARVILLE
Ancienne-Lorette
SILLERY
QUÉBEC
Québec
Notre-Dame-de-Foye
Sillery
HURON SETTLEMENTS NEAR QUÉBEC
5 miles
5 kilometres
Scale approximately 1:370 000

MIGRATION AND SETTLEMENT OF NATIVE PEOPLE, 1635–1800

Movement of people, 1635–1702

- Prior to King Philip's War, 1675
- Until the War of the League of Augsburg, 1689
- Until the War of the Spanish Succession, 1702

Movement of people, 1703–1800

- Until the Seven Years' War
- During the Seven Years' War, 1755–63
- During the British Occupation, 1763–1800

European settlement

- French
- British

Ethnic identity of tribes*

- (Ir) Iroquois
- (Ae) Eastern Abenaki
- (Aw) Western Abenaki
- (SAI) Southern New England Algonquians
- (NAI) Northern Algonquians

Resettlement communities*

- Huron
- Mohawk
- Nipissing
- Montagnais, Algonquin
- New England Algonquian
- Mohawk Indian reserve

Hunting limits

- Southern limit of Western Abenaki hunting parties of 1763
- Southern limit of Western Abenaki hunting parties after 1800

*The ethnic identity is derived from the predominant group in the settlement.

MIGRATION AND SETTLEMENT OF NATIVE PEOPLE, 1703–1800

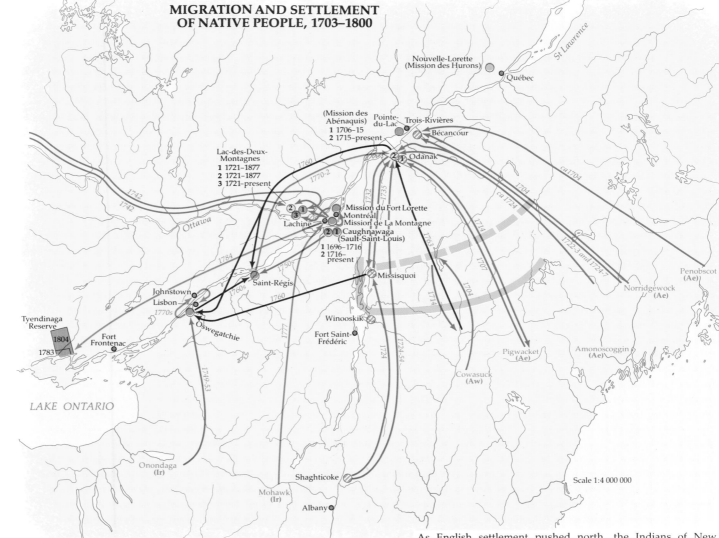

Scale 1:4 000 000

As English settlement pushed north, the Indians of New England allied themselves with the French. In wartime they sought refuge around Québec, Bécancour, and along the Saint-François River; in peacetime they attempted to re-establish themselves in what remained of their tribal lands. By 1800 American settlement had reached the Canadian border, and Odanak emerged as the main centre for the Abenaki and other New England peoples who had retreated to Canada. During the 18th century the Abenaki and Algonquin recognized all land south of the St Lawrence as Abenaki hunting territory.

NATIVE AGE AND SEX PROFILES

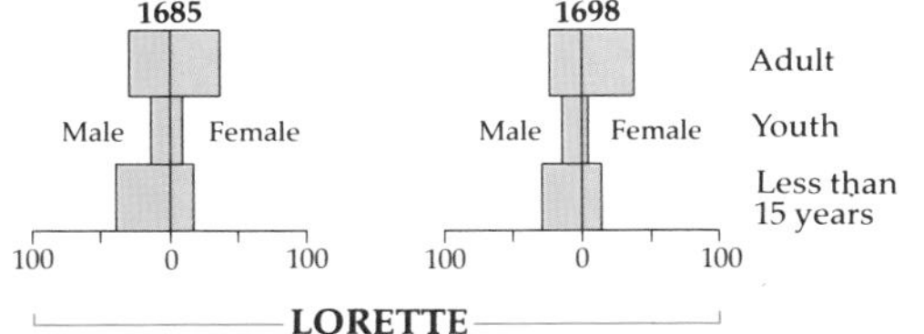
1685
1698
Adult
Youth
Less than 15 years
Male
Female
100
0
100
LORETTE

After they made peace with the French in 1667, Iroquois (mainly Mohawk) began to settle along the St Lawrence, in so doing realizing their long-standing ambition to ally themselves and trade with both the French and the Dutch (later the English). Their settlement south of the St Lawrence became modern Caughnawaga (Kahnawaké); the other, on Montréal Island, later moved to Lac-des-Deux-Montagnes. In the 18th century these native groups, like others living near French settlements, were heavily involved in illicit trading between New France and Albany. In the mid-18th century some Mohawk from Caughnawaga established a new settlement at Saint-Régis, while other Iroquois (mainly Onondaga) joined another mission settlement at Oswegatchie, well located for trade on the St Lawrence River. Loyalist Mohawk from Fort Hunter were the final groups to move north. They lived near Lachine from 1777 to 1784 when they moved to the Tyendinaga Reserve on the Bay of Quinte.

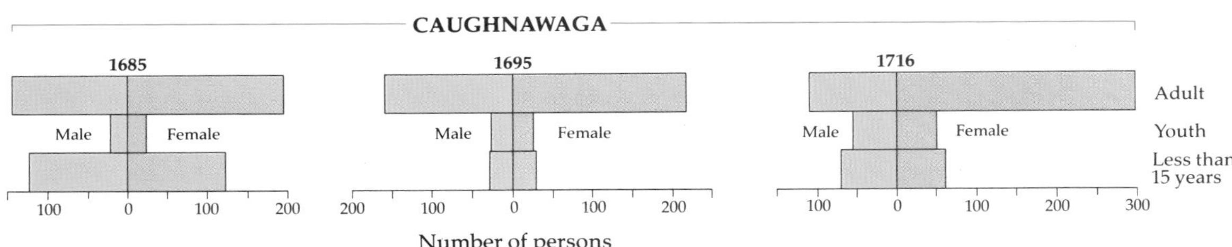
CAUGHNAWAGA
1685
1695
1716
Adult
Youth
Less than 15 years
Male
Female
Number of persons

CANADIAN NORTH ATLANTIC TRADE

Authors: Thomas Wien, James Pritchard

Two export trades, united by a common demand for European goods, dominated Canadian commerce in the later 17th and 18th centuries. Although it required few ships, the fur trade was the colony's *grand commerce*, accounting for almost all exports in the 17th century and for some 60% towards the end of the 18th century. A very different trade, involving more and usually smaller ships, dealt in products of the St Lawrence valley: chiefly wheat, timber, and fish. At various times there were markets for these goods at fishing stations in the Gulf of St Lawrence, at Louisbourg, on the slave plantations in the French and British West Indies, in neighbouring British colonies, and in southern Europe. But Québec, icebound for part of the year and remote, was not an ideal Atlantic port. Its exports apart from furs were usually available at more advantageous locations. Canada's commerce remained relatively small, accounting for less than 10% of the value of French colonial trade in the 1730s and for less than 5% of British trade with North America in the 1770s.

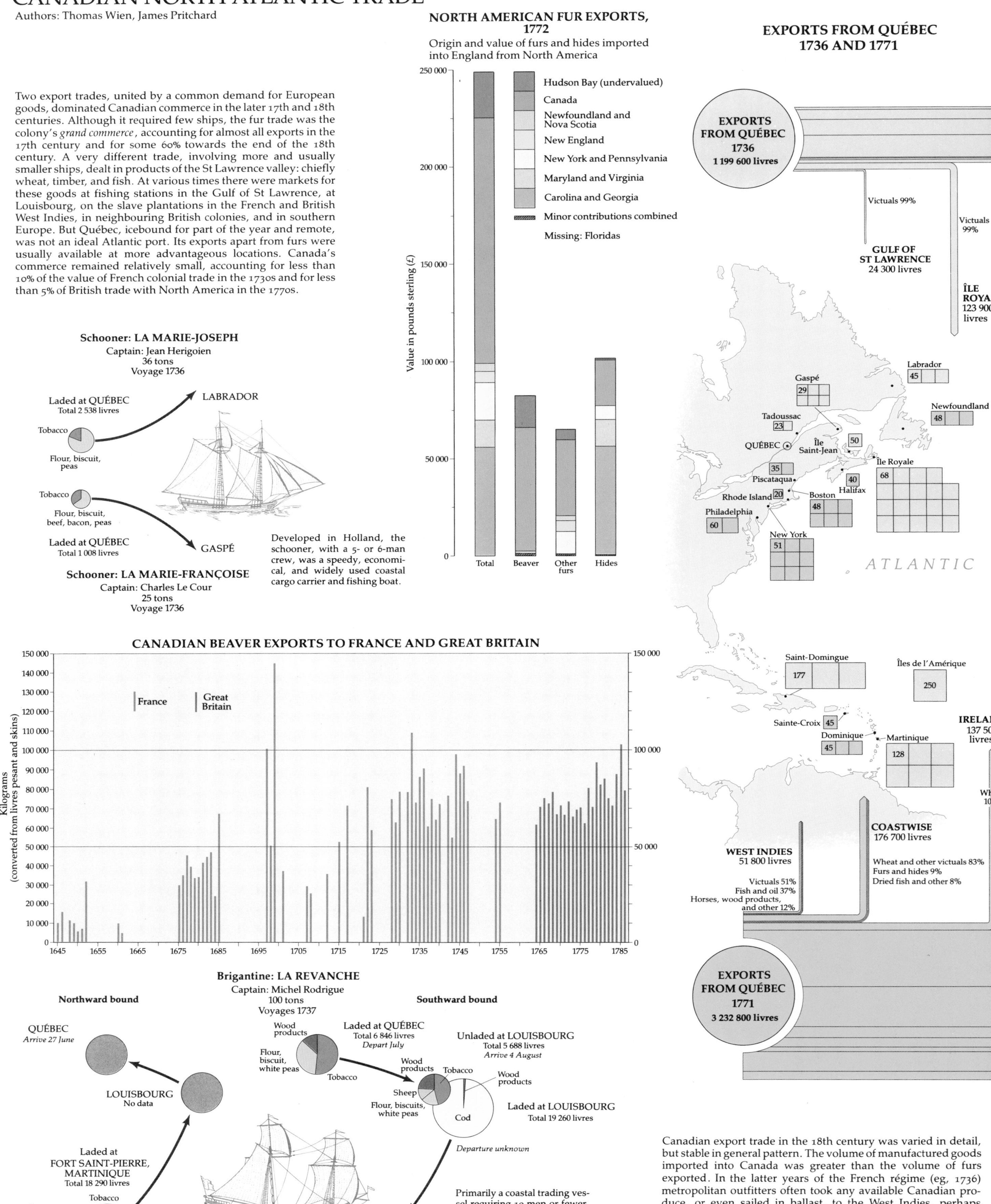

Schooner: LA MARIE-JOSEPH
Captain: Jean Herigoien
36 tons
Voyage 1736
Laded at QUÉBEC
Total 2 538 livres
LABRADOR
Tobacco
Flour, biscuit, peas
Tobacco
Flour, biscuit, beef, bacon, peas
Laded at QUÉBEC
Total 1 008 livres
GASPÉ
Schooner: LA MARIE-FRANÇOISE
Captain: Charles Le Cour
25 tons
Voyage 1736
Developed in Holland, the schooner, with a 5- or 6-man crew, was a speedy, economical, and widely used coastal cargo carrier and fishing boat.
NORTH AMERICAN FUR EXPORTS, 1772
Origin and value of furs and hides imported into England from North America
Value in pounds sterling (£)
250 000
200 000
150 000
100 000
50 000
0
Hudson Bay (undervalued)
Canada
Newfoundland and Nova Scotia
New England
New York and Pennsylvania
Maryland and Virginia
Carolina and Georgia
Minor contributions combined
Missing: Floridas
Total
Beaver
Other furs
Hides
EXPORTS FROM QUÉBEC 1736 AND 1771
EXPORTS FROM QUÉBEC 1736
1 199 600 livres
Victuals 99%
Victuals 99%
GULF OF ST LAWRENCE
24 300 livres
ÎLE ROYALE
123 900 livres
Labrador
45
Gaspé
29
Newfoundland
48
Tadoussac
23
QUÉBEC
Île Saint-Jean
50
Île Royale
35
Piscataqua
40
Halifax
68
Rhode Island
20
Boston
48
Philadelphia
60
New York
51
ATLANTIC
Saint-Domingue
177
Îles de l'Amérique
250
Sainte-Croix
45
Dominique
45
Martinique
128
IRELAND
137 500 livres
COASTWISE
176 700 livres
WEST INDIES
51 800 livres
Wheat and other victuals 83%
Furs and hides 9%
Dried fish and other 8%
Victuals 51%
Fish and oil 37%
Horses, wood products, and other 12%
EXPORTS FROM QUÉBEC 1771
3 232 800 livres
CANADIAN BEAVER EXPORTS TO FRANCE AND GREAT BRITAIN
Kilograms (converted from livres pesant and skins)
150 000
140 000
130 000
120 000
110 000
100 000
90 000
80 000
70 000
60 000
50 000
40 000
30 000
20 000
10 000
0
France
Great Britain
1645
1655
1665
1675
1685
1695
1705
1715
1725
1735
1745
1755
1765
1775
1785
Brigantine: LA REVANCHE
Captain: Michel Rodrigue
100 tons
Voyages 1737
Northward bound
Southward bound
QUÉBEC
Arrive 27 June
LOUISBOURG
No data
Wood products
Laded at QUÉBEC
Total 6 846 livres
Depart July
Flour, biscuit, white peas
Tobacco
Unladed at LOUISBOURG
Total 5 688 livres
Arrive 4 August
Wood products
Tobacco
Wood products
Sheep
Flour, biscuits, white peas
Cod
Laded at LOUISBOURG
Total 19 260 livres
Departure unknown
Laded at FORT SAINT-PIERRE, MARTINIQUE
Total 18 290 livres
Tobacco
Common sugar
Sugar syrup
Rum
Depart 29 April
WEST INDIES
No data
Primarily a coastal trading vessel requiring 10 men or fewer, the brigantine, variously rigged, was developed from the swift, manoeuvrable vessels used by Mediterranean pirates.

Canadian export trade in the 18th century was varied in detail, but stable in general pattern. The volume of manufactured goods imported into Canada was greater than the volume of furs exported. In the latter years of the French régime (eg, 1736) metropolitan outfitters often took any available Canadian produce, or even sailed in ballast, to the West Indies, perhaps stopping at Louisbourg in search of additional ladings, before returning to France with sugar. Usually operating at a smaller scale, colonial merchants supplied foodstuffs and lumber to the Gulf, Louisbourg, and the slave colonies. Later (eg, 1771) Canadian grain and flour were increasingly marketed in southern Europe, but many vessels returned lightly loaded to Britain.

The number of ships sailing to Québec increased in the mid-1660s when the crown assumed direct control of Canada, and again in the 1680s and 1690s when the colony was at war with the English colonies and the Iroquois. The growth of shipping after 1740, and particularly after 1755, also reflected French military support. British shipping to Québec in the 1760s fell well below the French wartime level, then grew in the 1770s in response to expanding trade and the American Revolution. The perennial Canadian problem of establishing an export other than furs is reflected in the decline of trade in the 1780s.

In response to changes in European demand, merchants altered the composition of their fur shipments over the long term. In general, beaver dominated 17th-century exports, while other furs and hides accounted for much of the growth of 18th-century exports. The relative importance of particular furs and hides and of different regional trades in these commodities is shown for 1772.

The graphs of exports and imports of furs and hides should be used cautiously. Data are lacking on the volume of shipments to Albany during the first half of the 18th century, and to Le Havre in the 1730s. The proportion of La Rochelle's fur imports that came from Louisiana is unclear. While the La Rochelle records underestimate the value of imports, the London records probably err in the opposite direction.

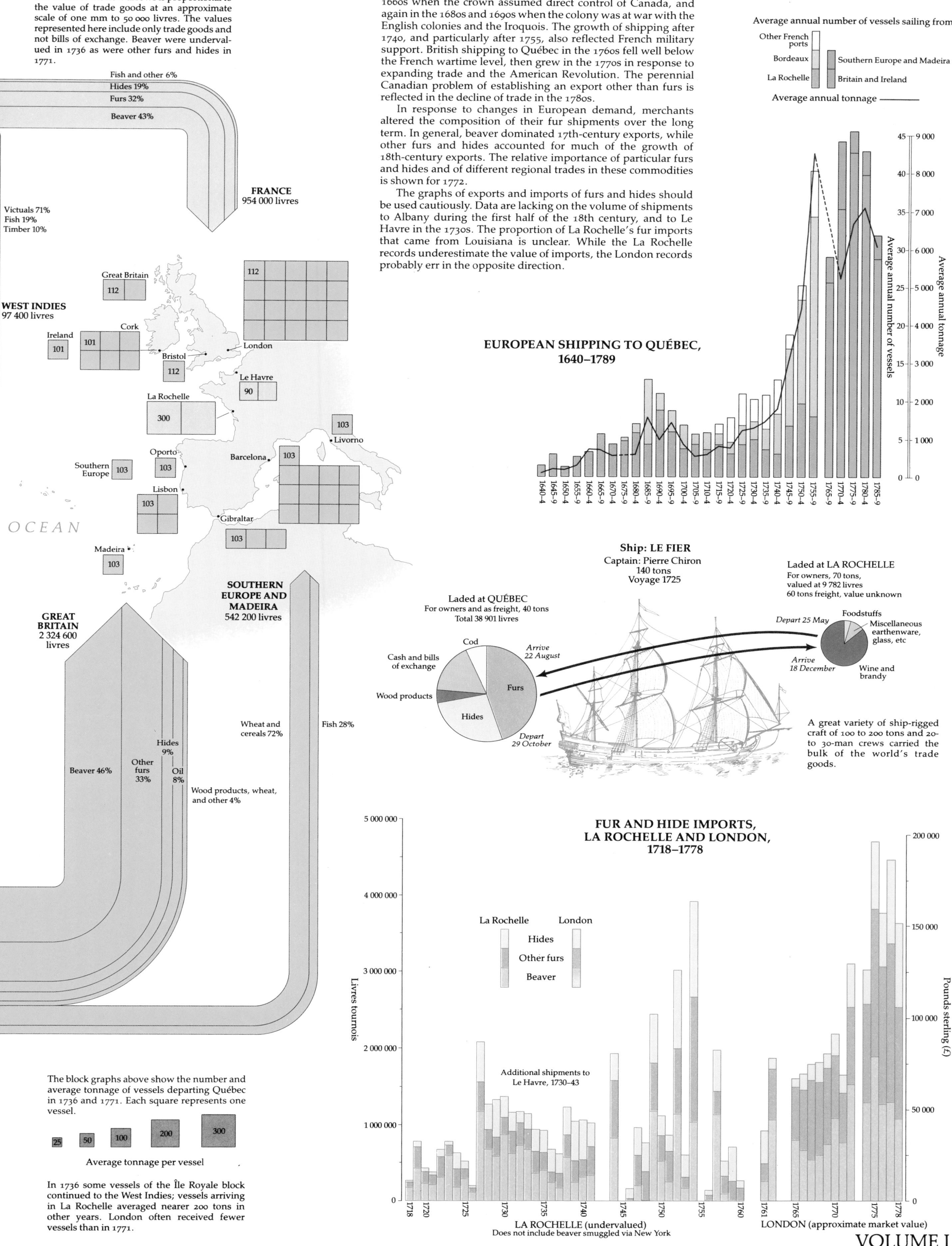

The width of the flow arrows is proportional to the value of trade goods at an approximate scale of one mm to 50 000 livres. The values represented here include only trade goods and not bills of exchange. Beaver were undervalued in 1736 as were other furs and hides in 1771.
Fish and other 6%
Hides 19%
Furs 32%
Beaver 43%
FRANCE
954 000 livres
Victuals 71%
Fish 19%
Timber 10%
WEST INDIES
97 400 livres
Great Britain
Ireland
Cork
Bristol
London
Le Havre
La Rochelle
Oporto
Southern Europe
Lisbon
Barcelona
Livorno
Gibraltar
Madeira
OCEAN
112
101
90
300
103
GREAT BRITAIN
2 324 600 livres
SOUTHERN EUROPE AND MADEIRA
542 200 livres
Beaver 46%
Other furs 33%
Hides 9%
Oil 8%
Wood products, wheat, and other 4%
Wheat and cereals 72%
Fish 28%
The block graphs above show the number and average tonnage of vessels departing Québec in 1736 and 1771. Each square represents one vessel.
25
50
100
200
300
Average tonnage per vessel
In 1736 some vessels of the Île Royale block continued to the West Indies; vessels arriving in La Rochelle averaged nearer 200 tons in other years. London often received fewer vessels than in 1771.
Average annual number of vessels sailing from
Other French ports
Bordeaux
La Rochelle
Southern Europe and Madeira
Britain and Ireland
Average annual tonnage
EUROPEAN SHIPPING TO QUÉBEC, 1640–1789
Average annual number of vessels
Average annual tonnage
1640–4
1645–9
1650–4
1655–9
1660–4
1665–9
1670–4
1675–9
1680–4
1685–9
1690–4
1695–9
1700–4
1705–9
1710–4
1715–9
1720–4
1725–9
1730–4
1735–9
1740–4
1745–9
1750–4
1755–9
1765–9
1770–4
1775–9
1780–4
1785–9
Ship: LE FIER
Captain: Pierre Chiron
140 tons
Voyage 1725
Laded at QUÉBEC
For owners and as freight, 40 tons
Total 38 901 livres
Cod
Cash and bills of exchange
Wood products
Furs
Hides
Arrive 22 August
Depart 29 October
Laded at LA ROCHELLE
For owners, 70 tons, valued at 9 782 livres
60 tons freight, value unknown
Depart 25 May
Arrive 18 December
Foodstuffs
Miscellaneous earthenware, glass, etc
Wine and brandy
A great variety of ship-rigged craft of 100 to 200 tons and 20- to 30-man crews carried the bulk of the world's trade goods.
FUR AND HIDE IMPORTS, LA ROCHELLE AND LONDON, 1718–1778
La Rochelle
London
Hides
Other furs
Beaver
Livres tournois
Pounds sterling (£)
Additional shipments to Le Havre, 1730–43
LA ROCHELLE (undervalued)
Does not include beaver smuggled via New York
LONDON (approximate market value)

THE TOWNS

Authors: Marc Lafrance, André Charbonneau

Québec (1608) and Trois-Rivières (1634) began as trading posts, and Montréal (1642) as a religious mission. For years they were tiny European outposts on the banks of the St Lawrence River; eventually local authorities drew up town plans, organized the distribution of lots, and oversaw the development of small towns.

These earliest Canadian towns were commercial, military, and administrative centres. The European dichotomy between upper and lower town emerged very early, with the ecclesiastical *cité* and fortifications on higher ground and the commercial centre along the river. Gardens and orchards gave the upper towns a somewhat rural appearance, whereas the lower towns were densely built up urban areas. As the towns grew, official interest in ordered, symmetrical development was challenged by the spontaneous creation of suburbs.

Merchants and their families, colonial officials, men and women of the church, soldiers, artisans and tradespeople, domestic servants and day labourers all lived in the towns and, especially in Québec, there was also a considerable migratory population associated with the port. In 1757 Montcalm considered Québec the equal of any French town, excluding the first ten.

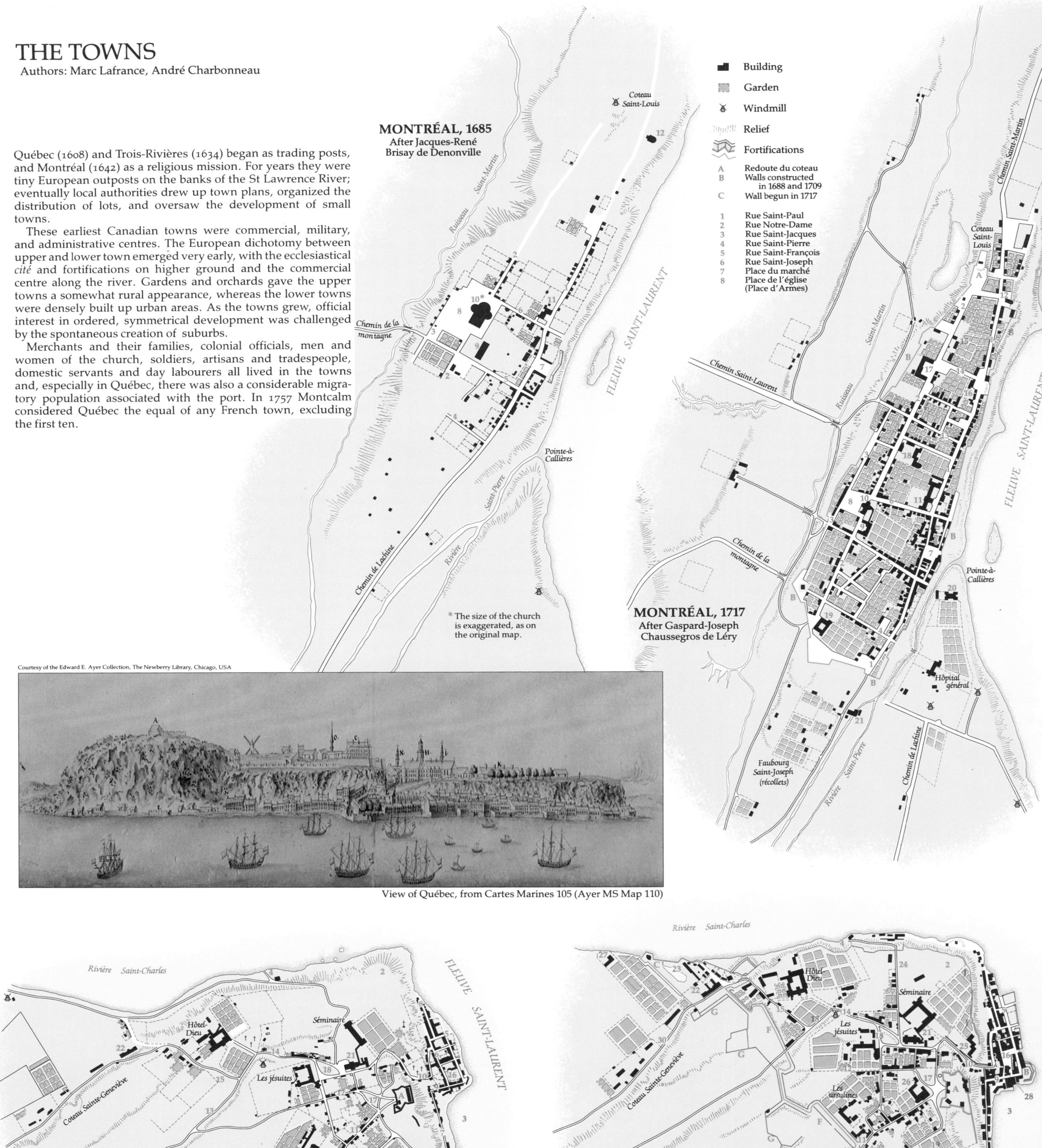
MONTRÉAL, 1685
After Jacques-René Brisay de Denonville
Coteau Saint-Louis
Ruisseau Saint-Martin
Chemin de la montagne
Chemin de Lachine
Rivière Saint-Pierre
Pointe-à-Callières
FLEUVE SAINT-LAURENT
* The size of the church is exaggerated, as on the original map.
Building
Garden
Windmill
Relief
Fortifications
A Redoute du coteau
B Walls constructed in 1688 and 1709
C Wall begun in 1717
1 Rue Saint-Paul
2 Rue Notre-Dame
3 Rue Saint-Jacques
4 Rue Saint-Pierre
5 Rue Saint-François
6 Rue Saint-Joseph
7 Place du marché
8 Place de l'église (Place d'Armes)
MONTRÉAL, 1717
After Gaspard-Joseph Chaussegros de Léry
Chemin Saint-Martin
Chemin Saint-Laurent
Coteau Saint-Louis
Hôpital général
Faubourg Saint-Joseph (récollets)
Courtesy of the Edward E. Ayer Collection, The Newberry Library, Chicago, USA
Rivière Saint-Charles
FLEUVE SAINT-LAURENT
Hôtel-Dieu
Séminaire
Les jésuites
Les ursulines
Coteau Sainte-Geneviève
Cap-Diamant
QUÉBEC, 1685
After Robert de Villeneuve
QUÉBEC, 1709
After Jacques Levasseur de Neré

View of Québec, from Cartes Marines 105 (Ayer MS Map 110)

Québec, the port and capital of Canada, had some 500 inhabitants in 1660 and almost 5 000 by 1744 (pl 50). The common European dichotomy between an administrative and military upper town and a commercial lower town emerged there very early. Bounded by river and cliff, the lower town was congested by the end of the 17th century. The upper town, more open and with its streets converging on the Château Saint-Louis, was separated from the countryside by a succession of walls, on the last of which construction began in 1745. At this time Québec's population was growing rapidly; a substantial suburb, Saint-Roch, developed beyond the walls.

Building — Relief
Garden — Cemetery
Windmill — Fortifications

Québec maps: scale approximately 1:15 000

Founded as a mission, Montréal rapidly became and long remained a centre of the fur trade. By the end of the 17th century a town had developed on a narrow band of low land along the river, its approximate grid plan created by the Sulpicians, seigneurs of the Island of Montréal. A refuge for the surrounding population during the Iroquois wars, Montréal was walled and bastioned in 1688, and so remained throughout the French regime, despite important changes to its fortifications during the 18th century.

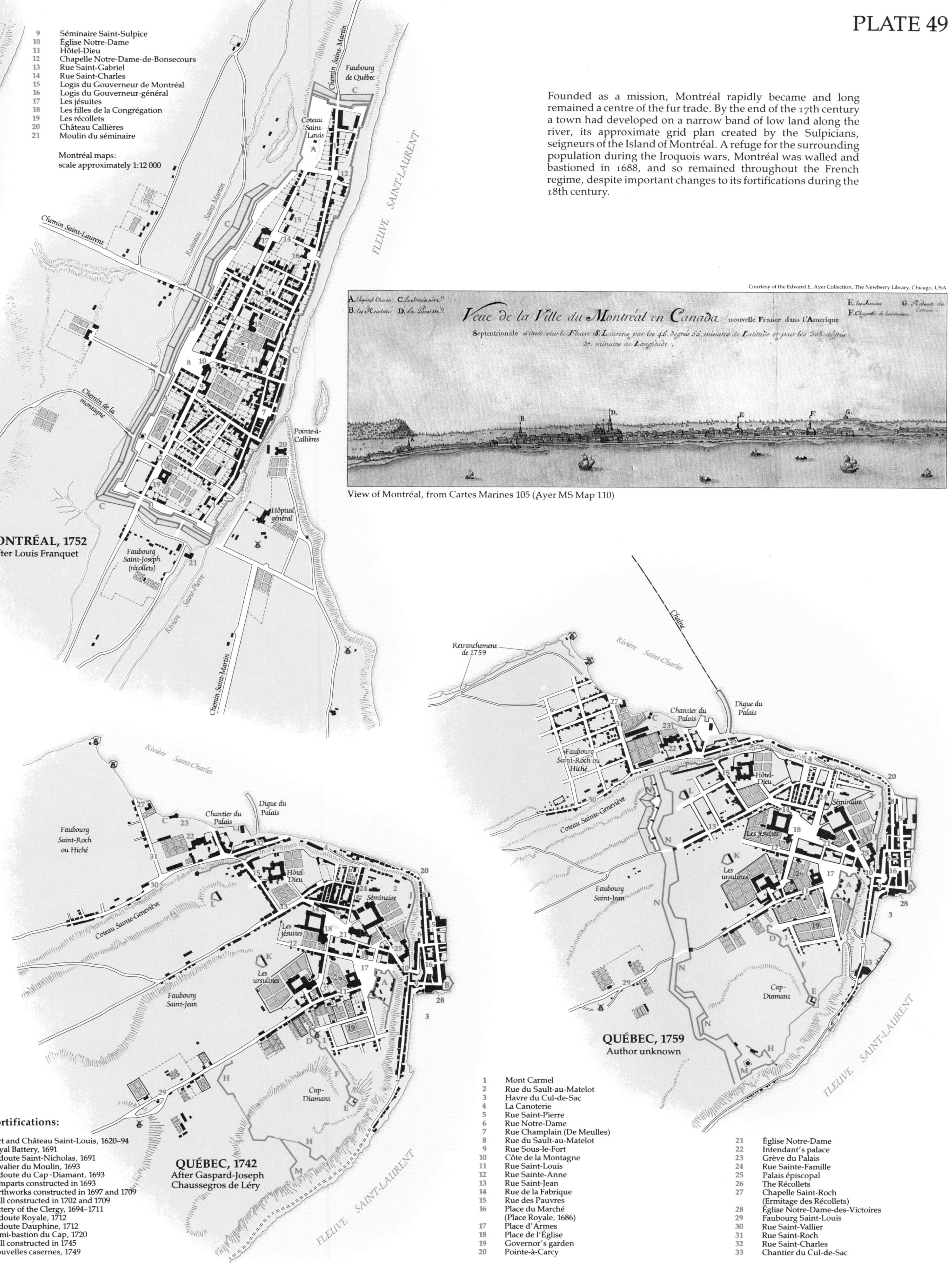
9 Séminaire Saint-Sulpice
10 Église Notre-Dame
11 Hôtel-Dieu
12 Chapelle Notre-Dame-de-Bonsecours
13 Rue Saint-Gabriel
14 Rue Saint-Charles
15 Logis du Gouverneur de Montréal
16 Logis du Gouverneur-général
17 Les jésuites
18 Les filles de la Congrégation
19 Les récollets
20 Château Callières
21 Moulin du séminaire
Montréal maps:
scale approximately 1:12 000
Chemin Saint-Martin
Faubourg de Québec
Coteau Saint-Louis
Chemin Saint-Laurent
Ruisseau Saint-Martin
FLEUVE SAINT-LAURENT
Chemin de la montagne
Pointe-à-Callières
Hôpital général
Faubourg Saint-Joseph (récollets)
Rivière Saint-Pierre
Chemin Saint-Martin
MONTRÉAL, 1752
After Louis Franquet
Courtesy of the Edward E. Ayer Collection, The Newberry Library, Chicago, USA
Veue de la Ville du Montréal en Canada nouvelle France dans l'Amerique Septentrionale
Retranchement de 1759
Rivière Saint-Charles
Chaîne
Chantier du Palais
Digue du Palais
Faubourg Saint-Roch ou Hiché
Hôtel-Dieu
Séminaire
Coteau Sainte-Geneviève
Les jésuites
Les ursulines
Faubourg Saint-Jean
Cap-Diamant
QUÉBEC, 1759
Author unknown
FLEUVE SAINT-LAURENT
Rivière Saint-Charles
Faubourg Saint-Roch ou Hiché
Chantier du Palais
Digue du Palais
Hôtel-Dieu
Séminaire
Coteau Sainte-Geneviève
Les jésuites
Les ursulines
Faubourg Saint-Jean
Cap-Diamant
FLEUVE SAINT-LAURENT
QUÉBEC, 1742
After Gaspard-Joseph Chaussegros de Léry

View of Montréal, from Cartes Marines 105 (Ayer MS Map 110)

Fortifications:

Fort and Château Saint-Louis, 1620–94
Royal Battery, 1691
Redoute Saint-Nicholas, 1691
Cavalier du Moulin, 1693
Redoute du Cap-Diamant, 1693
Ramparts constructed in 1693
Earthworks constructed in 1697 and 1709
Wall constructed in 1702 and 1709
Battery of the Clergy, 1694–1711
Redoute Royale, 1712
Redoute Dauphine, 1712
Demi-bastion du Cap, 1720
Wall constructed in 1745
Nouvelles casernes, 1749

1 Mont Carmel
2 Rue du Sault-au-Matelot
3 Havre du Cul-de-Sac
4 La Canoterie
5 Rue Saint-Pierre
6 Rue Notre-Dame
7 Rue Champlain (De Meulles)
8 Rue du Sault-au-Matelot
9 Rue Sous-le-Fort
10 Côte de la Montagne
11 Rue Saint-Louis
12 Rue Sainte-Anne
13 Rue Saint-Jean
14 Rue de la Fabrique
15 Rue des Pauvres
16 Place du Marché (Place Royale, 1686)
17 Place d'Armes
18 Place de l'Église
19 Governor's garden
20 Pointe-à-Carcy
21 Église Notre-Dame
22 Intendant's palace
23 Grève du Palais
24 Rue Sainte-Famille
25 Palais épiscopal
26 The Récollets
27 Chapelle Saint-Roch (Ermitage des Récollets)
28 Église Notre-Dame-des-Victoires
29 Faubourg Saint-Louis
30 Rue Saint-Vallier
31 Rue Saint-Roch
32 Rue Saint-Charles
33 Chantier du Cul-de-Sac

THE TOWN OF QUÉBEC, 18th CENTURY

Author: Louise Dechêne

The small maps and graphs on this plate are based on three censuses of the parish of Notre-Dame-de-Québec. To standardize the data only the number of households and the occupations of heads of households are used for the analysis of three *quartiers* in the Lower Town, three in the Upper Town, and the two suburbs.

The Lower Town, where Québec began, and its extension along Champlain Road accounted for 64% of households in 1716; only 20% were in the Quartier Saint-Louis, around the governor's mansion and the parish church. Thereafter, the relative importance of the Lower Town declined despite development near the Intendant's Palace and the shipyards. Two new *quartiers*, created from land belonging to the Séminaire de Québec and the Hôtel-Dieu (hospital), absorbed nearly all population growth before the conquest. Later, the suburbs performed this function as religious and, above all, military landholding blocked domestic construction within the walls.

The graph showing the number of households is an accurate reflection of the urban population which, with an average of 4.7 individuals per household, was 2 265 in 1716, 4 750 in 1744, and 7 160 in 1795. An annual growth rate of 2.8% between 1716 and 1744 probably continued to 1759, but slowed considerably after the conquest despite the arrival of immigrants from Britain and elsewhere. These newcomers and their descendents, one-quarter of the heads of households in 1795, were concentrated in Quartier Saint-Louis and Quartier Saint-Jean, near the administrative functions which they monopolized.

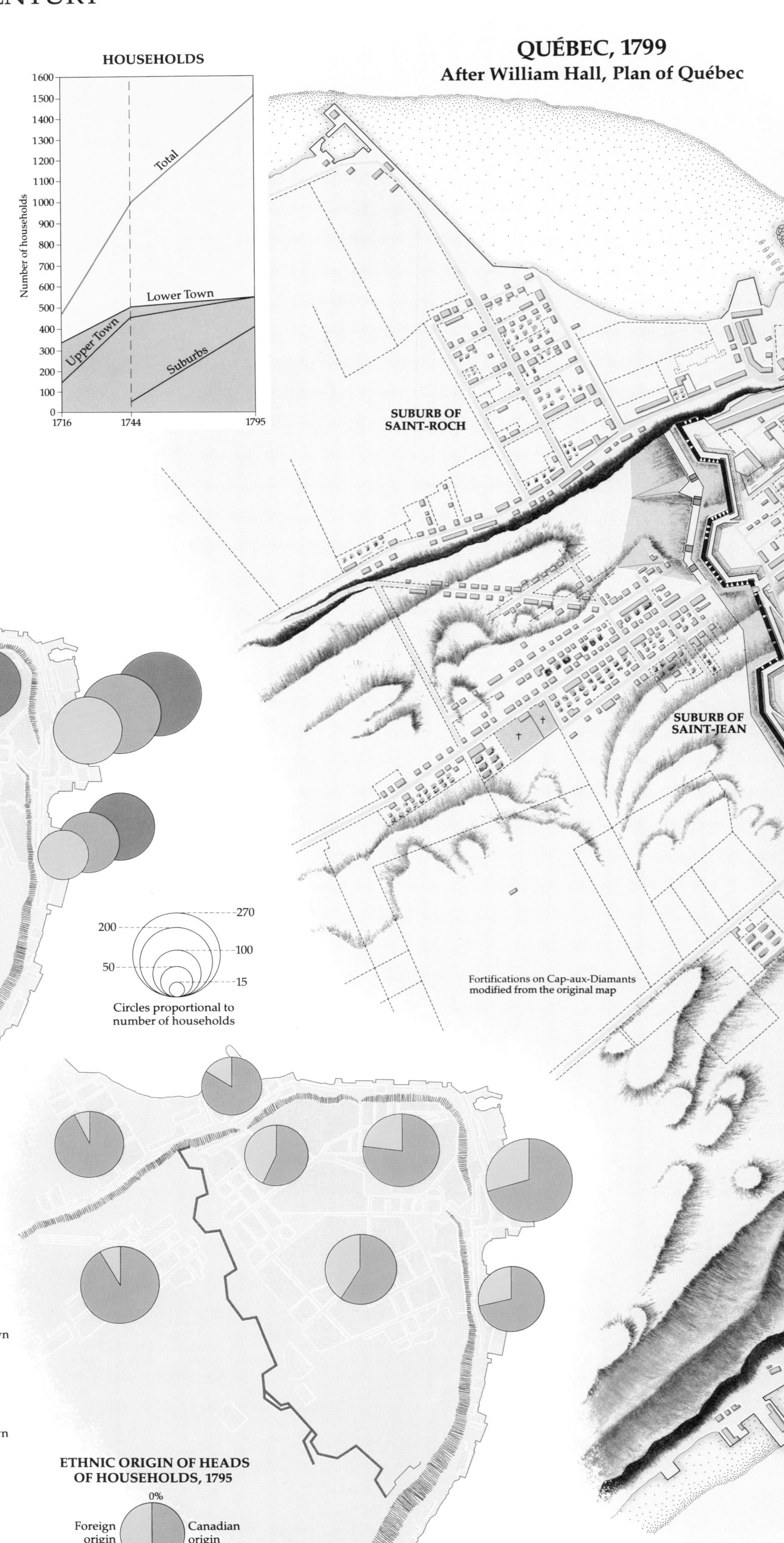

HOUSEHOLDS
Number of households
1600
1500
1400
1300
1200
1100
1000
900
800
700
600
500
400
300
200
100
0
1716
1744
1795
Total
Lower Town
Upper Town
Suburbs
QUÉBEC, 1799
After William Hall, Plan of Québec
SUBURB OF SAINT-ROCH
SUBURB OF SAINT-JEAN
Fortifications on Cap-aux-Diamants modified from the original map
200
270
100
50
15
Circles proportional to number of households
ETHNIC ORIGIN OF HEADS OF HOUSEHOLDS, 1795
0%
Foreign origin
Canadian origin
50%
Scale 1:14 000

DISTRIBUTION OF HOUSEHOLDS BY QUARTIERS AND SUBURBS

1795
1744
1716

CHANGING RELATIVE POPULATION

1716
1744
1795
Percentage
100
90
80
70
60
50
40
30
20
10
0
Suburbs
Upper Town
Lower Town
458
1007
1536
Number of households

During the second half of the century Québec underwent considerable physical upheaval. The siege in 1759 had left the town in ruins and levelled the suburb of Saint-Roch. They were rapidly rebuilt, but Québec suffered again in 1775 when the suburb of Saint-Jean was demolished to prevent American soldiers from approaching the walls. It, too, was soon rebuilt. New quays were constructed along the waterfront. Above all, after 1760 Québec was shaped by its increasingly military character.

By appropriating some 40% of the land within the walls the British army reduced the residential and commercial area, contributed to crowding, and accelerated the expansion of the suburbs. The ramparts were repaired, extended, and reinforced. The Jesuit College, the Intendant's Palace, and several other buildings were transformed into barracks and military stores. A temporary citadel, completed in 1783, dominated Cape Diamond. By the end of the century military personnel were about one-fifth of the civil population.

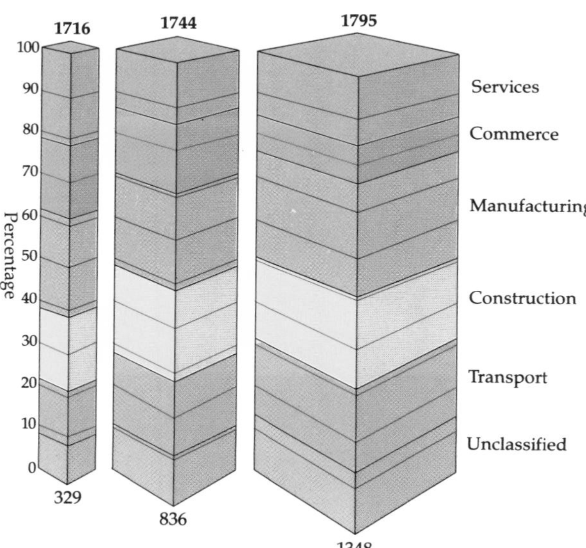
CHANGE IN RELATIVE IMPORTANCE OF ECONOMIC SECTORS
1716
1744
1795
Percentage
100
90
80
70
60
50
40
30
20
10
0
Services
Commerce
Manufacturing
Construction
Transport
Unclassified
329
836
1348

Numbers of heads of households with occupation known

QUARTIER DU PALAIS ET DE LA CANOTERIE

QUARTIER DU SÉMINAIRE

QUARTIER SAINT-JEAN

QUARTIER DE LA BASSE-VILLE

QUARTIER SAINT-LOUIS

QUARTIER CHAMPLAIN

SAINT LAWRENCE

0 1 000 feet

0 250 metres

Scale 1:7 250

ECONOMIC ACTIVITIES BY QUARTIERS AND SUBURBS

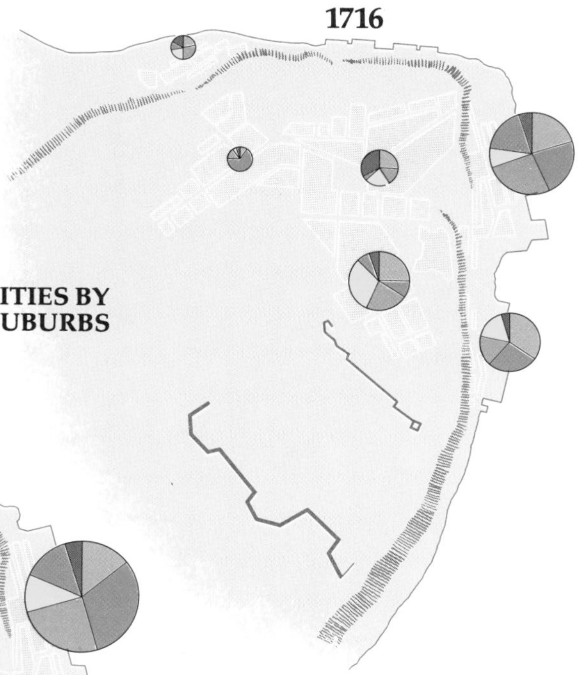

1716

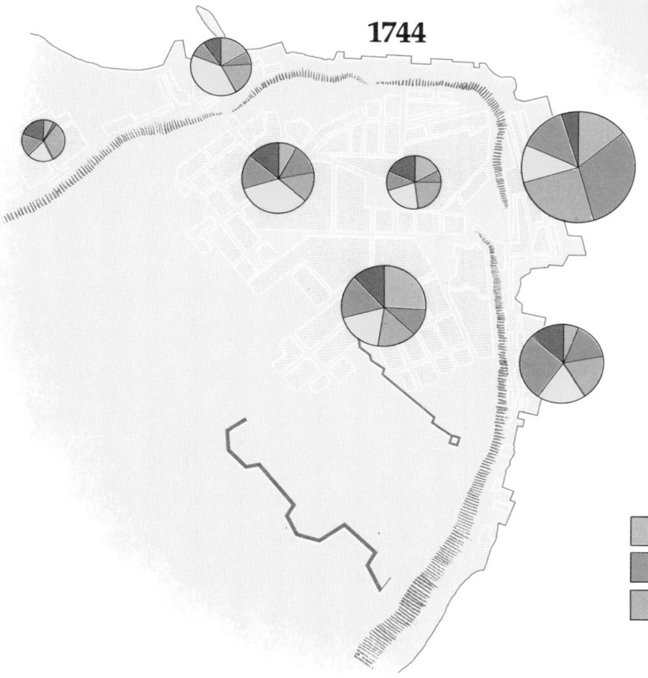

1744

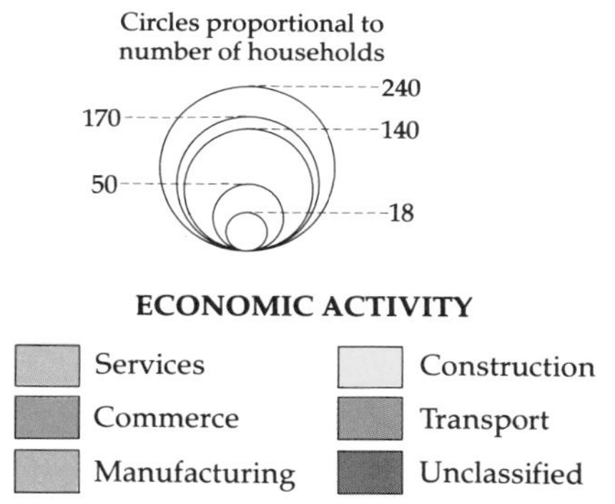

Circles proportional to number of households

240
170
140
50
18

ECONOMIC ACTIVITY

Services
Commerce
Manufacturing
Construction
Transport
Unclassified

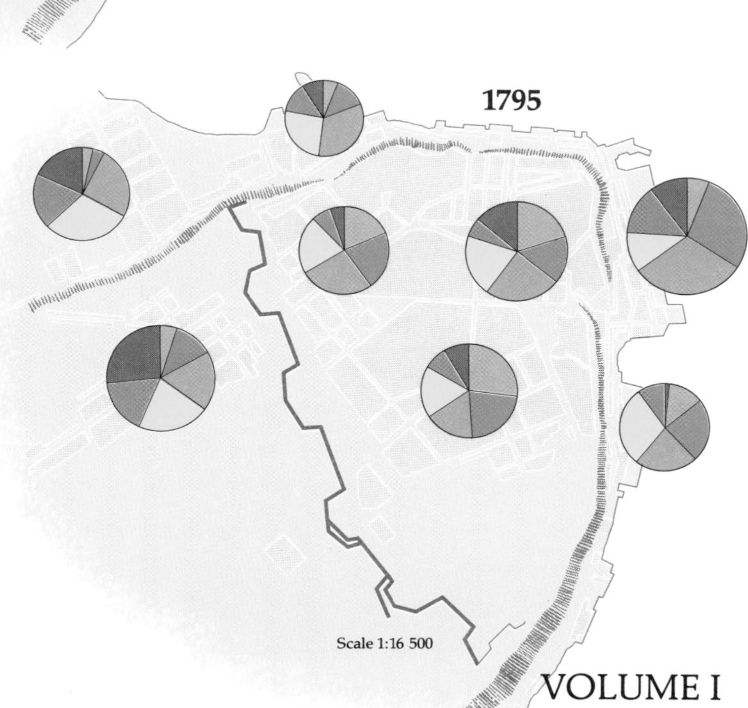
1795
Scale 1:16 500

Three maps and a graph (above right) illustrate the evolving structure of the urban economy as revealed by the occupations of heads of households, which are classified in six economic sectors. For Québec as a whole variations in the relative importance of the sectors are partly due to gaps in the census data for 1716 and 1744. For example, the apparent increase of day labourers (unclassified sector) reflects the fact that day labourers were better enumerated in 1795. The increase in services, usually tied to administration, became increasingly the norm for the period. The relative importance of the commercial sector, and of the transportation sector (carters and seamen), did not vary. Artisans, working in the manufacturing and construction sectors, were a large part of the work force (40-45%). There was little occupational segregation. Importers and artisans mixed in the Lower Town. There was a preponderance of individuals in service occupations in the Upper Town, although shopkeepers were settling there at the end of the century and labourers and tradesmen were being displaced to the suburbs. Seamen and shipbuilders were concentrated along the river, near their work.

Sluggish population growth and economic stability: these were the dominant traits of this small colonial capital in the 18th century.

THE SEIGNEURIES

Author: Louise Dechêne

GOVERNMENT OF MONTRÉAL

1 **Petite-Nation**
1674 François de Laval
1791 Seminary of Québec
2 **Argenteuil**
1680 Charles J. d'Ailleboust des Muceaux
1791 Pierre Louis Panet
3 **Lac-des-Deux-Montagnes**
1717 Seminary of Saint-Sulpice de Montréal
1791 Seminary of Saint-Sulpice de Montréal
3a **augmentation**
1733 Seminary of Saint-Sulpice de Montréal
1791 Seminary of Saint-Sulpice de Montréal
4 **Mille-Îles or Du-Chêne**
1683 Michel-Sidrac Dugué de Boisbriand
1791 Eustache Louis Lambert Dumont
4a **augmentation**
1752 Eustache Lambert Dumont
1791 Eustache Louis Lambert Dumont
5 **Blainville (part of Mille-Îles)**
1683 Michel-Sidrac Dugué de Boisbriand
1791 Heirs of J.-B. Céloron de Blainville
6 **Terrebonne**
1673 André Daulier Des Landes
1791 Jacob Jordan
7 **Des Plaines**
1731 Louis Lepage
1791 Jacob Jordan
7a **augmentation**
1753 Louis de La Corne de Chaptes
1791 Jacob Jordan
8 **Lachenaie (part of Repentigny)**
1647 Pierre Le Gardeur de Repentigny
1791 Gabriel Christie
9 **L'Assomption or Repentigny**
1647 Pierre Le Gardeur de Repentigny
1791 P.R. de Saint-Ours, Christie, M. Martel, etc
10 **Saint-Sulpice**
1640 La Société Notre-Dame de Montréal
1791 Seminary of Saint-Sulpice de Montréal
11 **Lavaltrie**
1672 Séraphin Margane de Lavaltrie
1791 Pierre-Paul Margane de Lavaltrie
11a **augmentation**
1734 Pierre Margane de Lavaltrie
1791 Pierre-Paul Margane de Lavaltrie
12 **Lanoraie**
1688 Heirs of Charles Sevestre
1791 James Cuthbert
12a **augmentation**
1739 Jean-Baptiste Neveu
1791 James Cuthbert
13 **Dautré**
1637 Jean Bourdon
1791 James Cuthbert
13a **augmentation**
1647 Jean Bourdon
1791 James Cuthbert
14 **D'Ailleboust**
1736 Jean d'Ailleboust d'Argenteuil
1791 Heirs of Joseph and Louis Gauthier
15 **De Ramezay**
1736 Geneviève de Ramezay
1791 Heirs of Joseph and Louis Gauthier
16 **Antaya or Dorvilliers**
1672 Philippe Gaultier de Comporté
1791 J. Janton dit Dauphiné
17 **Berthier**
1672 Hugues Randin
1791 James Cuthbert
17a **augmentation**
1674 Alexandre Berthier
1791 James Cuthbert
17b **augmentation**
1732 Pierre de Lestage
1791 James Cuthbert
18 **Chicot and Île Dupas**
1672 Pierre Dupas
1791 François Hénault and Brisset family
19 **Pointe-à-L'Orignal**
1674 François Provost
1791 J. Dominique Le Moyne de Longueuil
20 **Rigaud**
1732 P. and F.P. de Rigaud de Vaudreuil
1791 M.E.G. Alain Chartier de Lotbinière
21 **Vaudreuil**
1702 Philippe de Rigaud de Vaudreuil
1791 M.E.G. Alain Chartier de Lotbinière
22 **Nouvelle-Longueuil**
1734 Joseph Le Moyne de Longueuil
1791 J.D. Emmanuel Le Moyne de Longueuil
23 **Soulanges**
1702 Pierre Jacques de Joybert de Soulanges
1791 J.D. Emmanuel Le Moyne de Longueuil
24 **Île Perrot**
1672 François-Marie Perrot
1791 Thomas Dennis
25 **Île Bizard**
1678 Jacques Bizard
1791 Pierre Fortier
26 **Île Jésus**
1636 The Jesuits
1791 Seminary of Québec
27 **Île de Montréal**
1640-59 La Société Notre-Dame de Montréal
1791 Seminary of Saint-Sulpice de Montréal
28 **Île Saint-Paul**
1664 Jacques Leber, Claude Robutel, Jean Tessier
1791 The Congregation of Notre-Dame
29 **Beauharnois or Villechauve**
1729 Charles and Claude de Beauharnois
1791 Michel Chartier de Lotbinière
30 **Châteauguay**
1673 Charles Le Moyne de Longueuil
1791 L'Hôpital général de Montréal
31 **Sault-Saint-Louis**
1680 The Iroquois/The Jesuits
1791 Crown land (Jesuit Estates)
32 **La Salle**
1750 Jean-Baptiste Leber de Senneville
1791 Estate of Simon Sanguinet
33 **Laprairie-de-la-Madeleine**
1647 The Jesuits
1791 Crown land (Jesuit Estates)
34 **De Léry**
1733 Gaspard Chaussegros de Léry
1791 Gabriel Christie
35 **Lacolle or Beaujeu**
1743 Daniel Liénard de Beaujeu
1791 Gabriel Christie
35a **augmentation**
1752 Daniel Liénard de Beaujeu
1791 In American territory
36 **Bedout**
1752 Jean Antoine Bedout
1791 In American territory
37 **Estèbe**
1744 Guillaume Estèbe
1791 In American territory
38 **Ramezay-la-Gesse**
1749 Louise de Ramezay
1791 In American territory
39 **Hocquart**
1743 Gilles Hocquart
1791 In American territory
40 **Daneau**
1752 Jacques Pierre Daneau de Muy
1791 In American territory
41 **La Moinaudière**
1736 Pierre Raimbault
1791 In American territory
42 **Grande-Île or Pancalon**
1749 François Daine
1791 In American territory
43 **Saint-Armand**
1748 Nicolas René Levasseur
1791 Thomas Dunn
44 **Foucault or Caldwell Manor**
1733 François Foucault
1791 James Murray
44a **augmentation**
1743-44 François Foucault
1791 In American territory
45 **Noyan or Île-aux-Noix**
1733 Pierre Jacques Payen de Noyan
1791 Gabriel Christie
46 **Sabrevois**
1733 Charles Sabrevois de Bleury
1791 Gabriel Christie
47 **Bleury**
1733 Clément Sabrevois de Bleury
1791 Gabriel Christie
48 **Longueuil**
1657 Charles Le Moyne
1791 David Alexander Grant
48a **augmentation**
1672 Charles Le Moyne
1791 David Alexander Grant
48b **augmentation**
1698 Charles Le Moyne de Longueuil
1791 David Alexander Grant
48c **augmentation**
1710 Charles Le Moyne de Longueuil
1791 David Alexander Grant
49 **Du Tremblay (part of Varennes)**
1672 René Gaultier de Varennes
1791 J. Boucher-La Broquerie, J.-P. Dubuc, J. Lemoine
50 **Boucherville**
1672 Pierre Boucher
1791 René A. Boucher de Boucherville and family
51 **Varennes**
1672 René Gaultier de Varennes
1791 Christophe Sanguinet, Gaspard Massue, etc.
52 **Île Sainte-Thérèse**
1672 Michel-Sidrac Dugué de Boisbriand
1791 Joseph Bernard dit Ainse
53 **Montarville**
1710 Pierre Boucher de Boucherville
1791 René Boucher de La Bruère
54 **Chambly**
1672 Jacques de Chambly
1791 Hertel and Boucher-Niverville, Grant, Jennison
55 **Monnoir**
1708 Claude de Ramezay
1791 Ramezay family
55a **augmentation**
1739 Children of the late Claude de Ramezay
1791 Ramezay family
56 **Cap-Saint-Michel and Cap-de-La-Trinité**
1668 Michel Messier and Jacques Le Moyne
1791 Messier family, Amable Le Moyne de Martigny
57 **La Guillaudière**
1672 Laurent Borry
1791 Heirs of Joseph Hertel de Saint-François
58 **Belœil**
1694 Joseph-François Hertel
1791 David Alexander Grant
58a **augmentation**
1713 Charles Le Moyne de Longueuil
1791 David Alexander Grant
59 **Rouville**
1694 Jean-Baptiste Hertel de Rouville
1791 René-Ovide Hertel de Rouville
60 **Verchères (and Simblin)**
1672 François Jarret de Verchères
1791 J.-B. Hertel-R. and family, R.A. Boucher-Boucherville
60a **augmentation**
1678 François Jarret de Verchères
1791 J.-B. Hertel-R. and family, R.A. Boucher-Boucherville
61 **Îles Bouchard**
1677 René Robineau de Bécancour
1791 C.F. Lemaire dit Saint-Germain
62 **Bellevue**
1672 Charles Denys de Vitré
1791 M. Boisseau and Pierre Chicoine
63 **Cournoyer**
1695 Jacques Hertel de Cournoyer
1791 Antoine Lefebvre de Bellefeuille and family
64 **Saint-Charles or Île-aux-Cerfs**
1695 Zacharie François Hertel de La Fresnière
1791 Heirs of John Jennison
65 **Contrecœur**
1672 Antoine Pécaudy de Contrecœur
1791 F. Boucher-La Perrière, J. Boucher-Montarville
66 **Saint-Denis**
1694 Louis de Gannes de Falaise
1791 Joseph Boucher de Montarville
67 **Saint-Hyacinthe**
1748 François Pierre Rigaud de Vaudreuil
1791 Heirs of J. Hyacinthe, Simon dit Delorme
68 **Saint-Ours**
1672 Pierre de Saint-Ours
1791 Paul Roch de Saint-Ours and family
69 **Sorel**
1672 Pierre de Saurel
1791 Crown land
69a **augmentation**
1739 The daughters of Claude de Ramezay
1791 Crown land
70 **Bourgchemin**
1695 Jacques François Hamelin de Bourgchemin
1791 Seminary of Saint-Sulpice de Montréal
70a **augmentation**
1731 Pierre Herman Dosquet
1791 Thomas Barrow
71 **Bourgmarie (west and east)**
1708 Marie-Josèphe Fèzeret
1791 Thomas Barrow
72 **Bonsecours**
1702 Les Frères hospitaliers
1791 Thomas Barrow
73 **Saint-Charles-d'Yamaska**
1701 René Fèzeret
1791 Thomas Barrow
74 **Ramezay**
1710 Claude de Ramezay
1791 Joseph Howard

GOVERNMENT OF TROIS-RIVIÈRES

1 **Maskinongé**
1672 P. Noël and J.B. Le Gardeur
1791 J. Cuthbert, P. Baril Duchesny family, L. Bélair
2 **Du Sablé**
1739 Louis Adrien Dandonneau Du Sablé
1791 James Cuthbert
3 **Carufel**
1705 Jean Sicard de Carufel
1791 Pierre Baril Duchesny and family
4 **Lac Maskinongé or de Lanaudière**
1750 C.F.-Xavier Tarieu de Lanaudière
1791 Charles Louis Tarieu de Lanaudière
5 **Saint-Jean**
1701 The Ursulines of Trois-Rivières
1791 The Ursulines of Trois-Rivières
5a **augmentation**
1727 The Ursulines of Trois-Rivières
1791 The Ursulines of Trois-Rivières
6 **Rivière-du-Loup**
1683 Jean Lechasseur
1791 The Ursulines of Trois-Rivières
7 **Grandpré**
1695 Louis Boucher de Grandpré
1791 Heirs of Conrad Gugy
8 **Grosbois or Machiche**
1653 Pierre Boucher
1791 Heirs of Conrad Gugy and the Lesieur family
9 **Dumontier**
1708 François Dumontier
1791 Heirs of Conrad Gugy and the Lesieur family
10 **Gastineau**
1672 Pierre Boucher de Boucherville
1791 Thomas Coffin, J.-M. Godefroy de Tonnancour
10a **augmentation**
1750 M.-Josèphe Gastineau Duplessis
1791 Alexander Davidson and John Lee
11 **Tonnancour or Pointe-du-Lac**
1670 Louis Godefroy de Normanville
1791 Thomas Coffin
11a **augmentation**
1734 René Godefroy de Tonnancour
1791 Thomas Coffin
12 **Tonnancour or Pointe-du-Lac**
1656 Jean Sauvaget and Étienne Seigneuret
1791 Thomas Coffin
13 **Vieuxpont**
1649 Michel Leneuf Du Hérisson
1791 J. Godefroy de Normanville
14 **Sainte-Marguerite**
1691 Jacques Dubois
1791 J.-Claude Boucher de Niverville
15 **Fiefs in the town of Trois-Rivières and suburbs**
16 **Saint-Maurice**
1676 J. Jallot widow of Maurice Poulin
1791 Crown land
16a **augmentation (Saint-Étienne)**
1737 La compagnie des Forges
1791 Crown land
17 **Cap-de-la-Madeleine**
1636 Jacques de La Ferté, abbé de La Madeleine
1791 Crown land (Jesuit Estates)
18 **Champlain**
1664 Étienne Pézard de La Touche
1791 Joseph Drapeau
18a **augmentation**
1697 Madeleine Mullois, widow of E. Pézard
1791 Joseph Drapeau
19 **Batiscan**
1636 Jacques de La Ferté, abbé de La Madeleine
1791 Crown land (Jesuit Estates)
20 **Sainte-Marie**
1672 Jean Lemoine
1791 Augustin Jobin dit Boisvert
20a **augmentation**
1711 M.-Madeleine de Chavigny, widow of Lemoine
1791 Augustin Jobin dit Boisvert
21 **Sainte-Anne (de La Pérade)**
1672 T. Tarieu de Lanouguère and E. de Suève
1791 C. Tarieu-Lanaudière, P.F. Chorel-Dorvilliers
21a **augmentation**
1700 Pierre Thomas Tarieu de La Pérade
1791 Charles Tarieu de Lanaudière
21b **augmentation**
1735 Pierre Thomas Tarieu de La Pérade
1791 Charles Tarieu de Lanaudière
22 **Yamaska**
1683 Michel Leneuf de La Vallière
1791 Heirs of L.-J. Godefroy de Tonnancour
23 **Saint-François**
1662 Pierre Boucher
1791 Joseph Crevier and family
23a **augmentation**
1678 Jean Crevier
1791 Crevier family and the Abenaki Indians
24 **Lussodière**
1683 Dominique La Motte de Lucière
1791 J.-Marie Delorme, wife of D. Debartzch
25 **Pierreville**
1683 Laurent Philippe
1791 F.J. Lemaître Duaime, the Abenaki Indians
26 **Deguire or Rivière-David**
1751 Joseph Deguire
1791 Jonathan Ekhart

GOVERNMENT OF TROIS-RIVIÈRES
GOVERNMENT OF MONTRÉAL

ORIGINAL SEIGNEURS

SEIGNEURS IN 1791

Church
Colonial nobility and descendants
Other seigneurs of French origin
Seigneurs of British origin
Seigneuries held by the crown
Urban area

Ottawa
LAKE CHAMPLAIN
CANADA
UNITED STATES

0 10 leagues
0 40 kilometres
Scale 1:1 250 000

Scale 1:2 250 000

Based on a map by William Vondenvelden and Louis Charland (London, 1803). One league equals 4 km or 2.5 miles.

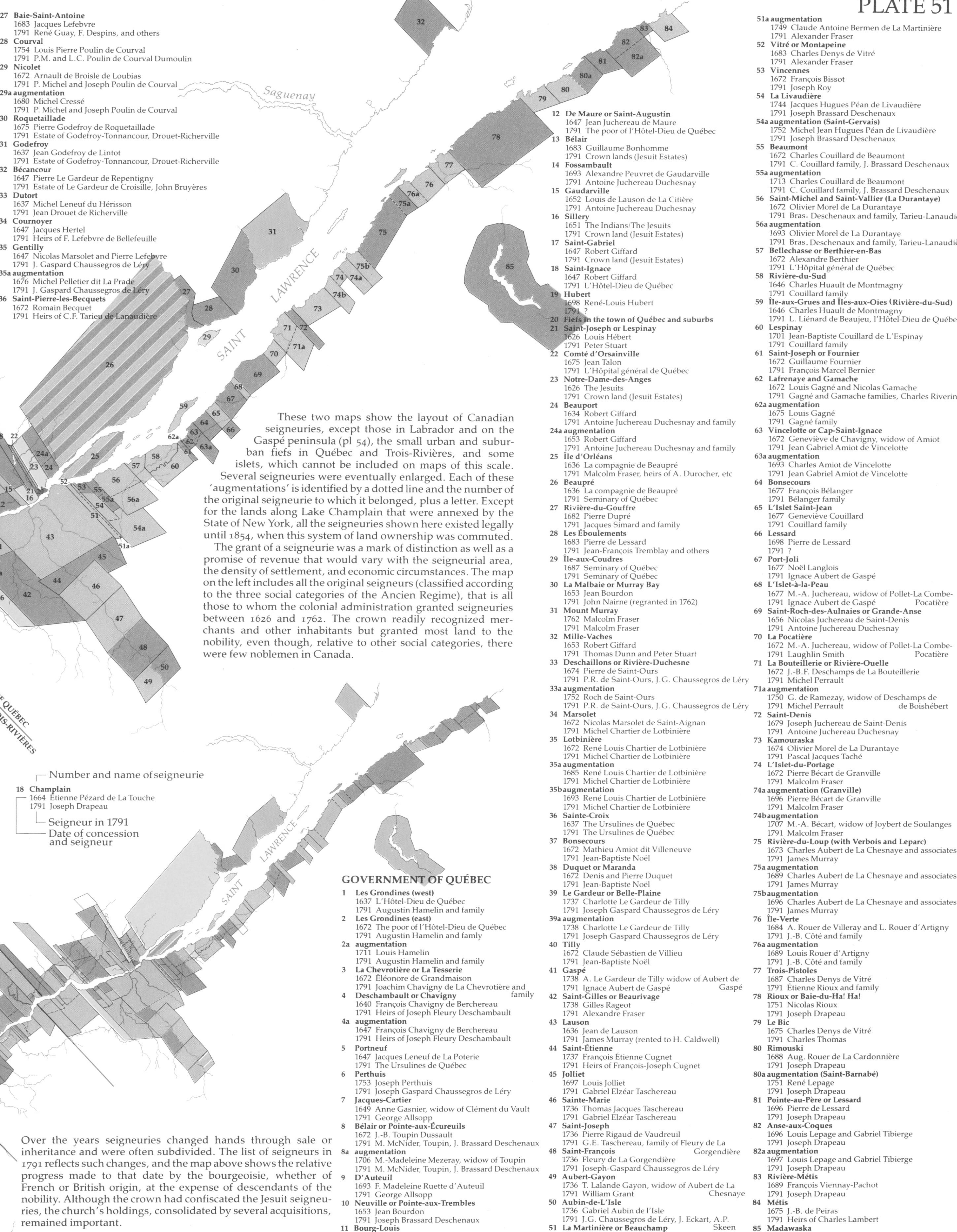

Saguenay
SAINT LAWRENCE
OF QUÉBEC
TROIS-RIVIÈRES
SAINT LAWRENCE

27 Baie-Saint-Antoine
1683 Jacques Lefebvre
1791 René Guay, F. Despins, and others

28 Courval
1754 Louis Pierre Poulin de Courval
1791 P.M. and L.C. Poulin de Courval Dumoulin

29 Nicolet
1672 Arnault de Broisle de Loubias
1791 P. Michel and Joseph Poulin de Courval

29a augmentation
1680 Michel Cressé
1791 P. Michel and Joseph Poulin de Courval

30 Roquetaillade
1675 Pierre Godefroy de Roquetaillade
1791 Estate of Godefroy-Tonnancour, Drouet-Richerville

31 Godefroy
1637 Jean Godefroy de Lintot
1791 Estate of Godefroy-Tonnancour, Drouet-Richerville

32 Bécancour
1647 Pierre Le Gardeur de Repentigny
1791 Estate of Le Gardeur de Croisille, John Bruyères

33 Dutort
1637 Michel Leneuf du Hérisson
1791 Jean Drouet de Richerville

34 Cournoyer
1647 Jacques Hertel
1791 Heirs of F. Lefebvre de Bellefeuille

35 Gentilly
1647 Nicolas Marsolet and Pierre Lefebvre
1791 J. Gaspard Chaussegros de Léry

35a augmentation
1676 Michel Pelletier dit La Prade
1791 J. Gaspard Chaussegros de Léry

36 Saint-Pierre-les-Becquets
1672 Romain Becquet
1791 Heirs of C.F. Tarieu de Lanaudière

These two maps show the layout of Canadian seigneuries, except those in Labrador and on the Gaspé peninsula (pl 54), the small urban and suburban fiefs in Québec and Trois-Rivières, and some islets, which cannot be included on maps of this scale. Several seigneuries were eventually enlarged. Each of these 'augmentations' is identified by a dotted line and the number of the original seigneurie to which it belonged, plus a letter. Except for the lands along Lake Champlain that were annexed by the State of New York, all the seigneuries shown here existed legally until 1854, when this system of land ownership was commuted.

The grant of a seigneurie was a mark of distinction as well as a promise of revenue that would vary with the seigneurial area, the density of settlement, and economic circumstances. The map on the left includes all the original seigneurs (classified according to the three social categories of the Ancien Regime), that is all those to whom the colonial administration granted seigneuries between 1626 and 1762. The crown readily recognized merchants and other inhabitants but granted most land to the nobility, even though, relative to other social categories, there were few noblemen in Canada.

Number and name of seigneurie

18 Champlain
1664 Étienne Pézard de La Touche
1791 Joseph Drapeau

Seigneur in 1791
Date of concession and seigneur

Over the years seigneuries changed hands through sale or inheritance and were often subdivided. The list of seigneurs in 1791 reflects such changes, and the map above shows the relative progress made to that date by the bourgeoisie, whether of French or British origin, at the expense of descendants of the nobility. Although the crown had confiscated the Jesuit seigneuries, the church's holdings, consolidated by several acquisitions, remained important.

GOVERNMENT OF QUÉBEC

1 Les Grondines (west)
1637 L'Hôtel-Dieu de Québec
1791 Augustin Hamelin and family

2 Les Grondines (east)
1672 The poor of l'Hôtel-Dieu de Québec
1791 Augustin Hamelin and family

2a augmentation
1711 Louis Hamelin
1791 Augustin Hamelin and family

3 La Chevrotière or La Tesserie
1672 Éléonore de Grandmaison
1791 Joachim Chavigny de La Chevrotière and family

4 Deschambault or Chavigny
1640 François Chavigny de Berchereau
1791 Heirs of Joseph Fleury Deschambault

4a augmentation
1647 François Chavigny de Berchereau
1791 Heirs of Joseph Fleury Deschambault

5 Portneuf
1647 Jacques Leneuf de La Poterie
1791 The Ursulines de Québec

6 Perthuis
1753 Joseph Perthuis
1791 Joseph Gaspard Chaussegros de Léry

7 Jacques-Cartier
1649 Anne Gasnier, widow of Clément du Vault
1791 George Allsopp

8 Bélair or Pointe-aux-Écureuils
1672 J.-B. Toupin Dussault
1791 M. McNider, Toupin, J. Brassard Deschenaux

8a augmentation
1706 M.-Madeleine Mezeray, widow of Toupin
1791 M. McNider, Toupin, J. Brassard Deschenaux

9 D'Auteuil
1693 F. Madeleine Ruette d'Auteuil
1791 George Allsopp

10 Neuville or Pointe-aux-Trembles
1653 Jean Bourdon
1791 Joseph Brassard Deschenaux

11 Bourg-Louis
1741 Louis Fornel
1791 Antoine Panet

12 De Maure or Saint-Augustin
1647 Jean Juchereau de Maure
1791 The poor of l'Hôtel-Dieu de Québec

13 Bélair
1683 Guillaume Bonhomme
1791 Crown lands (Jesuit Estates)

14 Fossambault
1693 Alexandre Peuvret de Gaudarville
1791 Antoine Juchereau Duchesnay

15 Gaudarville
1652 Louis de Lauson de La Citière
1791 Antoine Juchereau Duchesnay

16 Sillery
1651 The Indians/The Jesuits
1791 Crown land (Jesuit Estates)

17 Saint-Gabriel
1647 Robert Giffard
1791 Crown land (Jesuit Estates)

18 Saint-Ignace
1647 Robert Giffard
1791 L'Hôtel-Dieu de Québec

19 Hubert
1698 René-Louis Hubert
1791 ?

20 Fiefs in the town of Québec and suburbs

21 Saint-Joseph or Lespinay
1626 Louis Hébert
1791 Peter Stuart

22 Comté d'Orsainville
1675 Jean Talon
1791 L'Hôpital général de Québec

23 Notre-Dame-des-Anges
1626 The Jesuits
1791 Crown land (Jesuit Estates)

24 Beauport
1634 Robert Giffard
1791 Antoine Juchereau Duchesnay and family

24a augmentation
1653 Robert Giffard
1791 Antoine Juchereau Duchesnay and family

25 Île d'Orléans
1636 La compagnie de Beaupré
1791 Malcolm Fraser, heirs of A. Durocher, etc

26 Beaupré
1636 La compagnie de Beaupré
1791 Seminary of Québec

27 Rivière-du-Gouffre
1682 Pierre Dupré
1791 Jacques Simard and family

28 Les Éboulements
1683 Pierre de Lessard
1791 Jean-François Tremblay and others

29 Île-aux-Coudres
1687 Seminary of Québec
1791 Seminary of Québec

30 La Malbaie or Murray Bay
1653 Jean Bourdon
1791 John Nairne (regranted in 1762)

31 Mount Murray
1762 Malcolm Fraser
1791 Malcolm Fraser

32 Mille-Vaches
1653 Robert Giffard
1791 Thomas Dunn and Peter Stuart

33 Deschaillons or Rivière-Duchesne
1674 Pierre de Saint-Ours
1791 P.R. de Saint-Ours, J.G. Chaussegros de Léry

33a augmentation
1752 Roch de Saint-Ours
1791 P.R. de Saint-Ours, J.G. Chaussegros de Léry

34 Marsolet
1672 Nicolas Marsolet de Saint-Aignan
1791 Michel Chartier de Lotbinière

35 Lotbinière
1672 René Louis Chartier de Lotbinière
1791 Michel Chartier de Lotbinière

35a augmentation
1685 René Louis Chartier de Lotbinière
1791 Michel Chartier de Lotbinière

35b augmentation
1693 René Louis Chartier de Lotbinière
1791 Michel Chartier de Lotbinière

36 Sainte-Croix
1637 The Ursulines de Québec
1791 The Ursulines de Québec

37 Bonsecours
1672 Mathieu Amiot dit Villeneuve
1791 Jean-Baptiste Noël

38 Duquet or Maranda
1672 Denis and Pierre Duquet
1791 Jean-Baptiste Noël

39 Le Gardeur or Belle-Plaine
1737 Charlotte Le Gardeur de Tilly
1791 Joseph Gaspard Chaussegros de Léry

39a augmentation
1738 Charlotte Le Gardeur de Tilly
1791 Joseph Gaspard Chaussegros de Léry

40 Tilly
1672 Claude Sébastien de Villieu
1791 Jean-Baptiste Noël

41 Gaspé
1738 A. Le Gardeur de Tilly widow of Aubert de Gaspé
1791 Ignace Aubert de Gaspé

42 Saint-Gilles or Beaurivage
1738 Gilles Rageot
1791 Alexandre Fraser

43 Lauson
1636 Jean de Lauson
1791 James Murray (rented to H. Caldwell)

44 Saint-Étienne
1737 François Étienne Cugnet
1791 Heirs of François-Joseph Cugnet

45 Jolliet
1697 Louis Jolliet
1791 Gabriel Elzéar Taschereau

46 Sainte-Marie
1736 Thomas Jacques Taschereau
1791 Gabriel Elzéar Taschereau

47 Saint-Joseph
1736 Pierre Rigaud de Vaudreuil
1791 G.E. Taschereau, family of Fleury de La Gorgendière

48 Saint-François
1736 Fleury de La Gorgendière
1791 Joseph-Gaspard Chaussegros de Léry

49 Aubert-Gayon
1736 T. Lalande Gayon, widow of Aubert de La Chesnaye
1791 William Grant

50 Aubin-de-L'Isle
1736 Gabriel Aubin de l'Isle
1791 J.G. Chaussegros de Léry, J. Eckart, A.P. Skeen

51 La Martinière or Beauchamp
1692 Louis Claude Bermen de La Martinière
1791 Alexander Fraser

51a augmentation
1749 Claude Antoine Bermen de La Martinière
1791 Alexander Fraser

52 Vitré or Montapeine
1683 Charles Denys de Vitré
1791 Alexander Fraser

53 Vincennes
1672 François Bissot
1791 Joseph Roy

54 La Livaudière
1744 Jacques Hugues Péan de Livaudière
1791 Joseph Brassard Deschenaux

54a augmentation (Saint-Gervais)
1752 Michel Jean Hugues Péan de Livaudière
1791 Joseph Brassard Deschenaux

55 Beaumont
1672 Charles Couillard de Beaumont
1791 C. Couillard family, J. Brassard Deschenaux

55a augmentation
1713 Charles Couillard de Beaumont
1791 C. Couillard family, J. Brassard Deschenaux

56 Saint-Michel and Saint-Vallier (La Durantaye)
1672 Olivier Morel de La Durantaye
1791 Bras. Deschenaux and family, Tarieu-Lanaudière

56a augmentation
1693 Olivier Morel de La Durantaye
1791 Bras. Deschenaux and family, Tarieu-Lanaudière

57 Bellechasse or Berthier-en-Bas
1672 Alexandre Berthier
1791 L'Hôpital général de Québec

58 Rivière-du-Sud
1646 Charles Huault de Montmagny
1791 Couillard family

59 Île-aux-Grues and Îles-aux-Oies (Rivière-du-Sud)
1646 Charles Huault de Montmagny
1791 L. Liénard de Beaujeu, l'Hôtel-Dieu de Québec

60 Lespinay
1701 Jean-Baptiste Couillard de L'Espinay
1791 Couillard family

61 Saint-Joseph or Fournier
1672 Guillaume Fournier
1791 François Marcel Bernier

62 Lafrenaye and Gamache
1672 Louis Gagné and Nicolas Gamache
1791 Gagné and Gamache families, Charles Riverin

62a augmentation
1675 Louis Gagné
1791 Gagné family

63 Vincelotte or Cap-Saint-Ignace
1672 Geneviève de Chavigny, widow of Amiot
1791 Jean Gabriel Amiot de Vincelotte

63a augmentation
1693 Charles Amiot de Vincelotte
1791 Jean Gabriel Amiot de Vincelotte

64 Bonsecours
1677 François Bélanger
1791 Bélanger family

65 L'Islet Saint-Jean
1677 Geneviève Couillard
1791 Couillard family

66 Lessard
1698 Pierre de Lessard
1791 ?

67 Port-Joli
1677 Noël Langlois
1791 Ignace Aubert de Gaspé

68 L'Islet-à-la-Peau
1677 M.-A. Juchereau, widow of Pollet-La Combe-Pocatière
1791 Ignace Aubert de Gaspé

69 Saint-Roch-des-Aulnaies or Grande-Anse
1656 Nicolas Juchereau de Saint-Denis
1791 Antoine Juchereau Duchesnay

70 La Pocatière
1672 M.-A. Juchereau, widow of Pollet-La Combe-Pocatière
1791 Laughlin Smith

71 La Bouteillerie or Rivière-Ouelle
1672 J.-B.F. Deschamps de La Bouteillerie
1791 Michel Perrault

71a augmentation
1750 G. de Ramezay, widow of Deschamps de Boishébert
1791 Michel Perrault

72 Saint-Denis
1679 Joseph Juchereau de Saint-Denis
1791 Antoine Juchereau Duchesnay

73 Kamouraska
1674 Olivier Morel de La Durantaye
1791 Pascal Jacques Taché

74 L'Islet-du-Portage
1672 Pierre Bécart de Granville
1791 Malcolm Fraser

74a augmentation (Granville)
1696 Pierre Bécart de Granville
1791 Malcolm Fraser

74b augmentation
1707 M.-A. Bécart, widow of Joybert de Soulanges
1791 Malcolm Fraser

75 Rivière-du-Loup (with Verbois and Leparc)
1673 Charles Aubert de La Chesnaye and associates
1791 James Murray

75a augmentation
1689 Charles Aubert de La Chesnaye and associates
1791 James Murray

75b augmentation
1696 Charles Aubert de La Chesnaye and associates
1791 James Murray

76 Île-Verte
1684 A. Rouer de Villeray and L. Rouer d'Artigny
1791 J.-B. Côté and family

76a augmentation
1689 Louis Rouer d'Artigny
1791 J.-B. Côté and family

77 Trois-Pistoles
1687 Charles Denys de Vitré
1791 Étienne Rioux and family

78 Rioux or Baie-du-Ha! Ha!
1751 Nicolas Rioux
1791 Joseph Drapeau

79 Le Bic
1675 Charles Denys de Vitré
1791 Charles Thomas

80 Rimouski
1688 Aug. Rouer de La Cardonnière
1791 Joseph Drapeau

80a augmentation (Saint-Barnabé)
1751 René Lepage
1791 Joseph Drapeau

81 Pointe-au-Père or Lessard
1696 Pierre de Lessard
1791 Joseph Drapeau

82 Anse-aux-Coques
1696 Louis Lepage and Gabriel Tibierge
1791 Joseph Drapeau

82a augmentation
1697 Louis Lepage and Gabriel Tibierge
1791 Joseph Drapeau

83 Rivière-Métis
1689 François Viennay-Pachot
1791 Joseph Drapeau

84 Métis
1675 J.-B. de Peiras
1791 Heirs of Charles Lambert

85 Madawaska
1683 Charles Aubert de La Chesnaye
1791 James Murray

THE COUNTRYSIDE

Author: R. Cole Harris

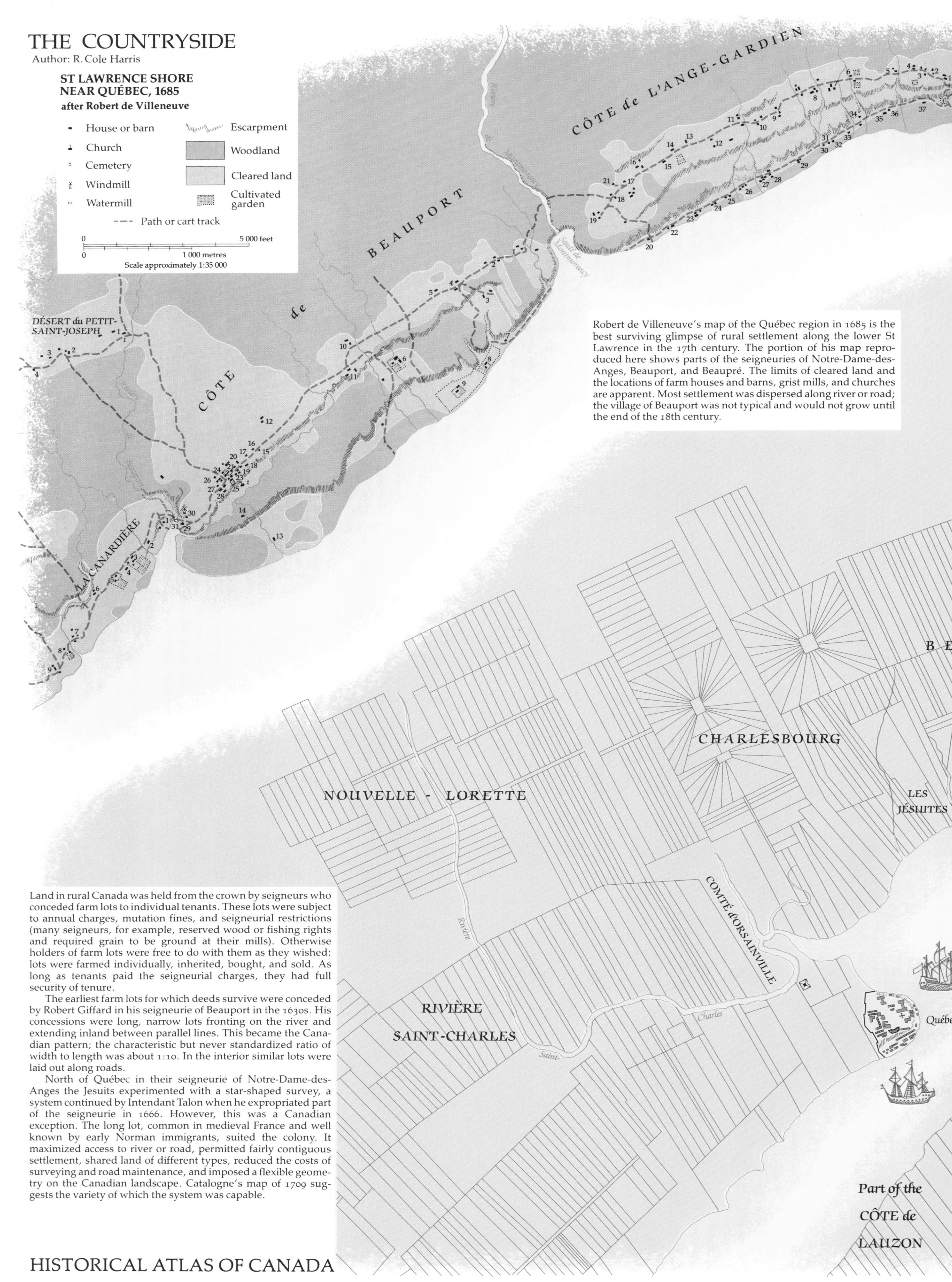

ST LAWRENCE SHORE
NEAR QUÉBEC, 1685
after Robert de Villeneuve
House or barn
Church
Cemetery
Windmill
Watermill
Escarpment
Woodland
Cleared land
Cultivated garden
Path or cart track
5 000 feet
1 000 metres
Scale approximately 1:35 000
CÔTE de L'ANGE-GARDIEN
CÔTE de BEAUPORT
DÉSERT du PETIT-SAINT-JOSEPH
LA CANARDIÈRE
Rivière de Montmorency
Sault de Montmorency
Rivière Beauport
CHARLESBOURG
NOUVELLE - LORETTE
LES JÉSUITES
COMTÉ d'ORSAINVILLE
RIVIÈRE SAINT-CHARLES
Rivière Saint-Charles
Québec
Part of the CÔTE de LAUZON

Robert de Villeneuve's map of the Québec region in 1685 is the best surviving glimpse of rural settlement along the lower St Lawrence in the 17th century. The portion of his map reproduced here shows parts of the seigneuries of Notre-Dame-des-Anges, Beauport, and Beaupré. The limits of cleared land and the locations of farm houses and barns, grist mills, and churches are apparent. Most settlement was dispersed along river or road; the village of Beauport was not typical and would not grow until the end of the 18th century.

Land in rural Canada was held from the crown by seigneurs who conceded farm lots to individual tenants. These lots were subject to annual charges, mutation fines, and seigneurial restrictions (many seigneurs, for example, reserved wood or fishing rights and required grain to be ground at their mills). Otherwise holders of farm lots were free to do with them as they wished: lots were farmed individually, inherited, bought, and sold. As long as tenants paid the seigneurial charges, they had full security of tenure.

The earliest farm lots for which deeds survive were conceded by Robert Giffard in his seigneurie of Beauport in the 1630s. His concessions were long, narrow lots fronting on the river and extending inland between parallel lines. This became the Canadian pattern; the characteristic but never standardized ratio of width to length was about 1:10. In the interior similar lots were laid out along roads.

North of Québec in their seigneurie of Notre-Dame-des-Anges the Jesuits experimented with a star-shaped survey, a system continued by Intendant Talon when he expropriated part of the seigneurie in 1666. However, this was a Canadian exception. The long lot, common in medieval France and well known by early Norman immigrants, suited the colony. It maximized access to river or road, permitted fairly contiguous settlement, shared land of different types, reduced the costs of surveying and road maintenance, and imposed a flexible geometry on the Canadian landscape. Catalogne's map of 1709 suggests the variety of which the system was capable.

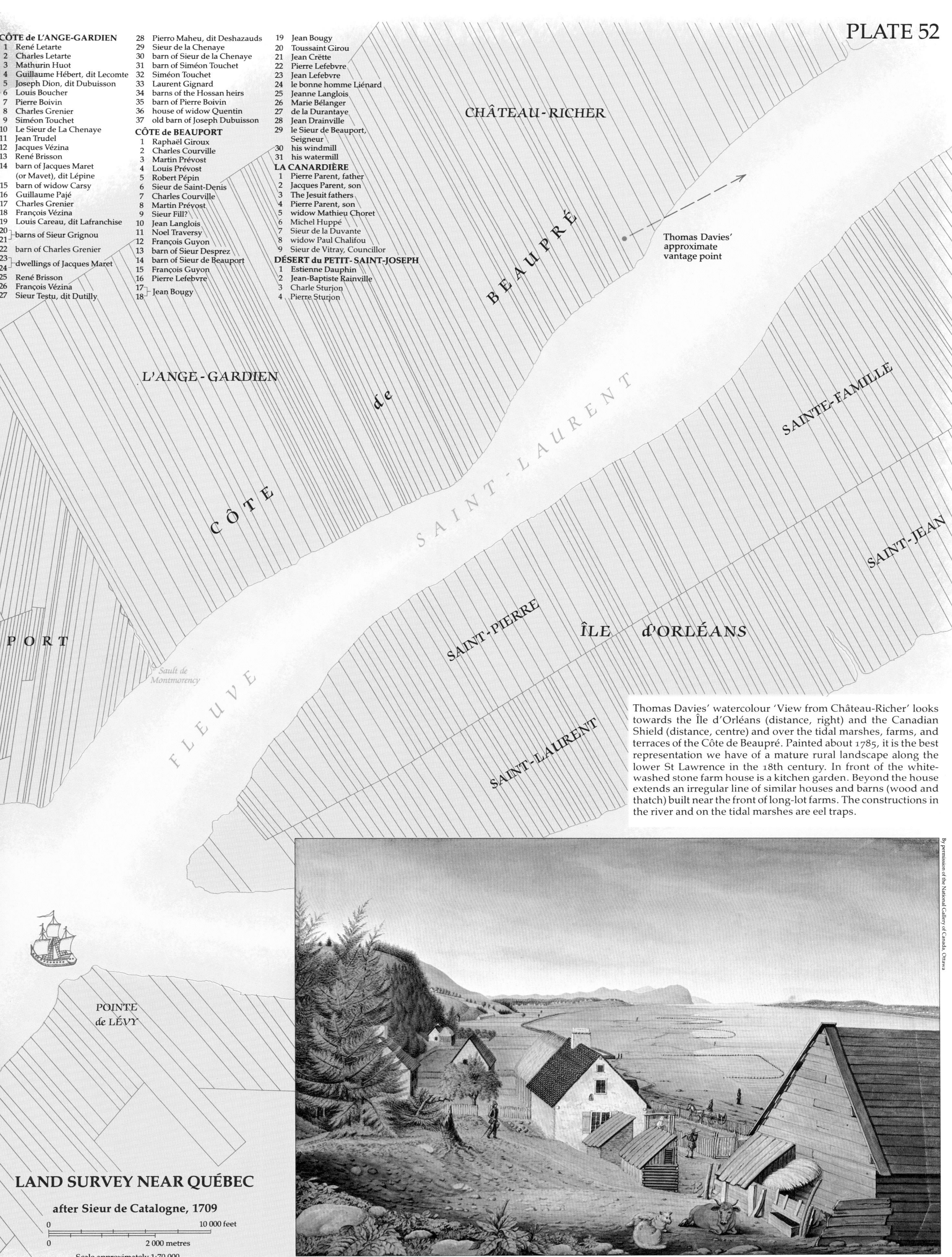
CÔTE de L'ANGE-GARDIEN
1 René Letarte
2 Charles Letarte
3 Mathurin Huot
4 Guillaume Hébert, dit Lecomte
5 Joseph Dion, dit Dubuisson
6 Louis Boucher
7 Pierre Boivin
8 Charles Grenier
9 Siméon Touchet
10 Le Sieur de La Chenaye
11 Jean Trudel
12 Jacques Vézina
13 René Brisson
14 barn of Jacques Maret (or Mavet), dit Lépine
15 barn of widow Carsy
16 Guillaume Pajé
17 Charles Grenier
18 François Vézina
19 Louis Careau, dit Lafranchise
20–21 barns of Sieur Grignou
22 barn of Charles Grenier
23–24 dwellings of Jacques Maret
25 René Brisson
26 François Vézina
27 Sieur Testu, dit Dutilly
28 Pierro Maheu, dit Deshazauds
29 Sieur de la Chenaye
30 barn of Sieur de la Chenaye
31 barn of Siméon Touchet
32 Siméon Touchet
33 Laurent Gignard
34 barns of the Hossan heirs
35 barn of Pierre Boivin
36 house of widow Quentin
37 old barn of Joseph Dubuisson
CÔTE de BEAUPORT
1 Raphaël Giroux
2 Charles Courville
3 Martin Prévost
4 Louis Prévost
5 Robert Pépin
6 Sieur de Saint-Denis
7 Charles Courville
8 Martin Prévost
9 Sieur Fill?
10 Jean Langlois
11 Noel Traversy
12 François Guyon
13 barn of Sieur Desprez
14 barn of Sieur de Beauport
15 François Guyon
16 Pierre Lefebvre
17–18 Jean Bougy
19 Jean Bougy
20 Toussaint Girou
21 Jean Crëtte
22 Pierre Lefebvre
23 Jean Lefebvre
24 le bonne homme Liénard
25 Jeanne Langlois
26 Marie Bélanger
27 de la Durantaye
28 Jean Drainville
29 le Sieur de Beauport, Seigneur
30 his windmill
31 his watermill
LA CANARDIÈRE
1 Pierre Parent, father
2 Jacques Parent, son
3 The Jesuit fathers
4 Pierre Parent, son
5 widow Mathieu Choret
6 Michel Huppé
7 Sieur de la Duvante
8 widow Paul Chalifou
9 Sieur de Vitray, Councillor
DÉSERT du PETIT-SAINT-JOSEPH
1 Estienne Dauphin
2 Jean-Baptiste Rainville
3 Charle Sturjon
4 Pierre Sturjon
CHÂTEAU-RICHER
CÔTE de BEAUPRÉ
L'ANGE-GARDIEN
Thomas Davies' approximate vantage point
FLEUVE SAINT-LAURENT
SAINTE-FAMILLE
SAINT-JEAN
SAINT-PIERRE
ÎLE d'ORLÉANS
SAINT-LAURENT
PORT
Sault de Montmorency
POINTE de LÉVY
LAND SURVEY NEAR QUÉBEC
after Sieur de Catalogne, 1709
0 10 000 feet
0 2 000 metres
Scale approximately 1:70 000

Thomas Davies' watercolour 'View from Château-Richer' looks towards the Île d'Orléans (distance, right) and the Canadian Shield (distance, centre) and over the tidal marshes, farms, and terraces of the Côte de Beaupré. Painted about 1785, it is the best representation we have of a mature rural landscape along the lower St Lawrence in the 18th century. In front of the white-washed stone farm house is a kitchen garden. Beyond the house extends an irregular line of similar houses and barns (wood and thatch) built near the front of long-lot farms. The constructions in the river and on the tidal marshes are eel traps.

By permission of the National Gallery of Canada, Ottawa

Thomas Davies, 'View from Château-Richer,' ca 1785

THE AGRICULTURAL ECONOMY

Author: R.Cole Harris

PRICE OF WHEAT, 1660–1795

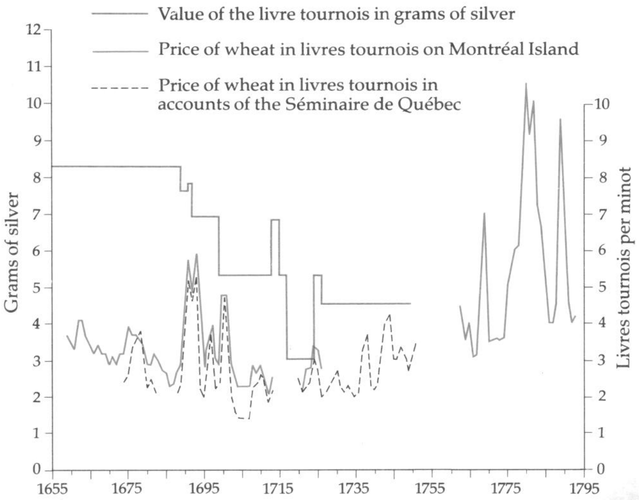

The mixed crop–livestock farming of northwestern Europe could be practised in the St Lawrence valley. Farm lots were readily available (pl 52) to immigrants and their offspring (pls 45 and 46), although markets were remote. There were no Canadian agricultural exports in the 17th century, and in the 18th century they developed fitfully (pl 48). In these circumstances agricultural prices, unlike those in France, declined precipitously in the latter half of the 17th century (especially considering the declining real value of the livre tournois), tended to stabilize between 1700 and 1735, and to increase thereafter.

WHEAT PRODUCTION, 1739

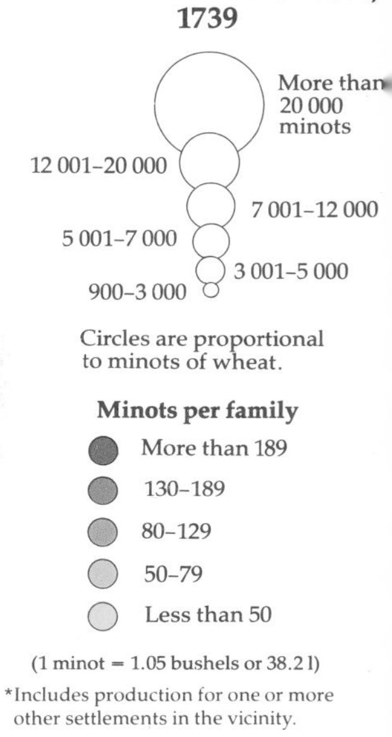

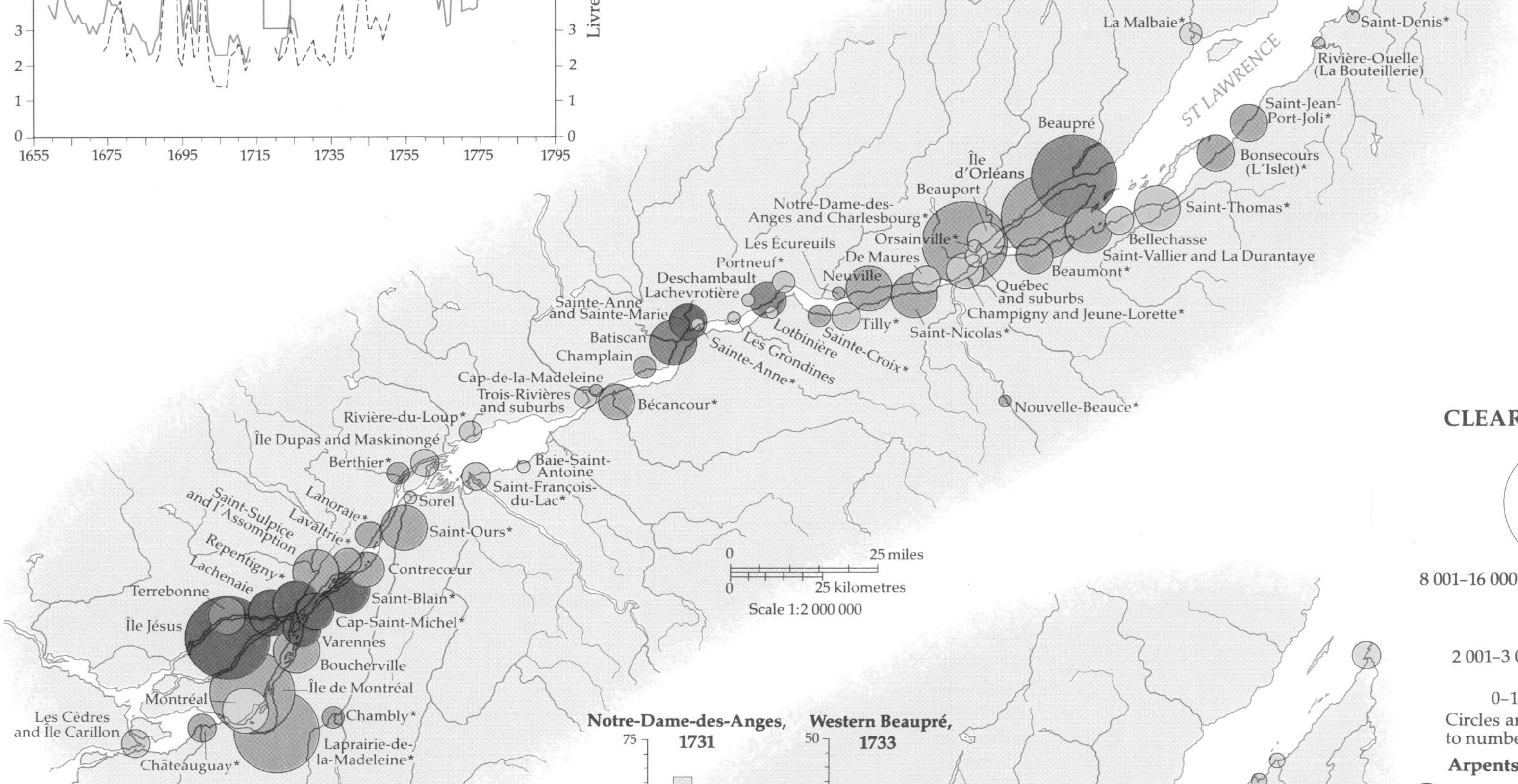

CLEARED LAND, 1739

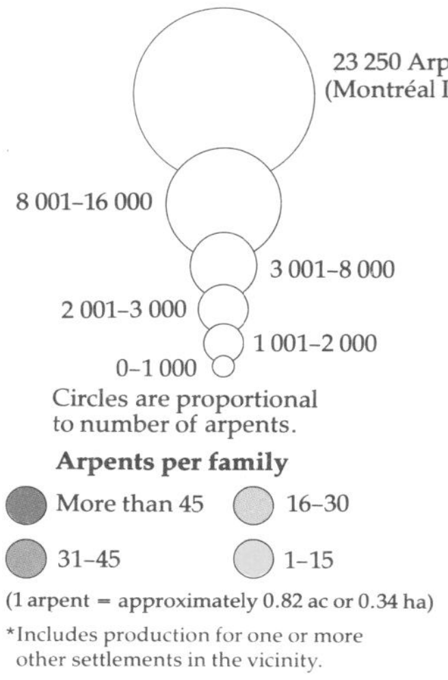

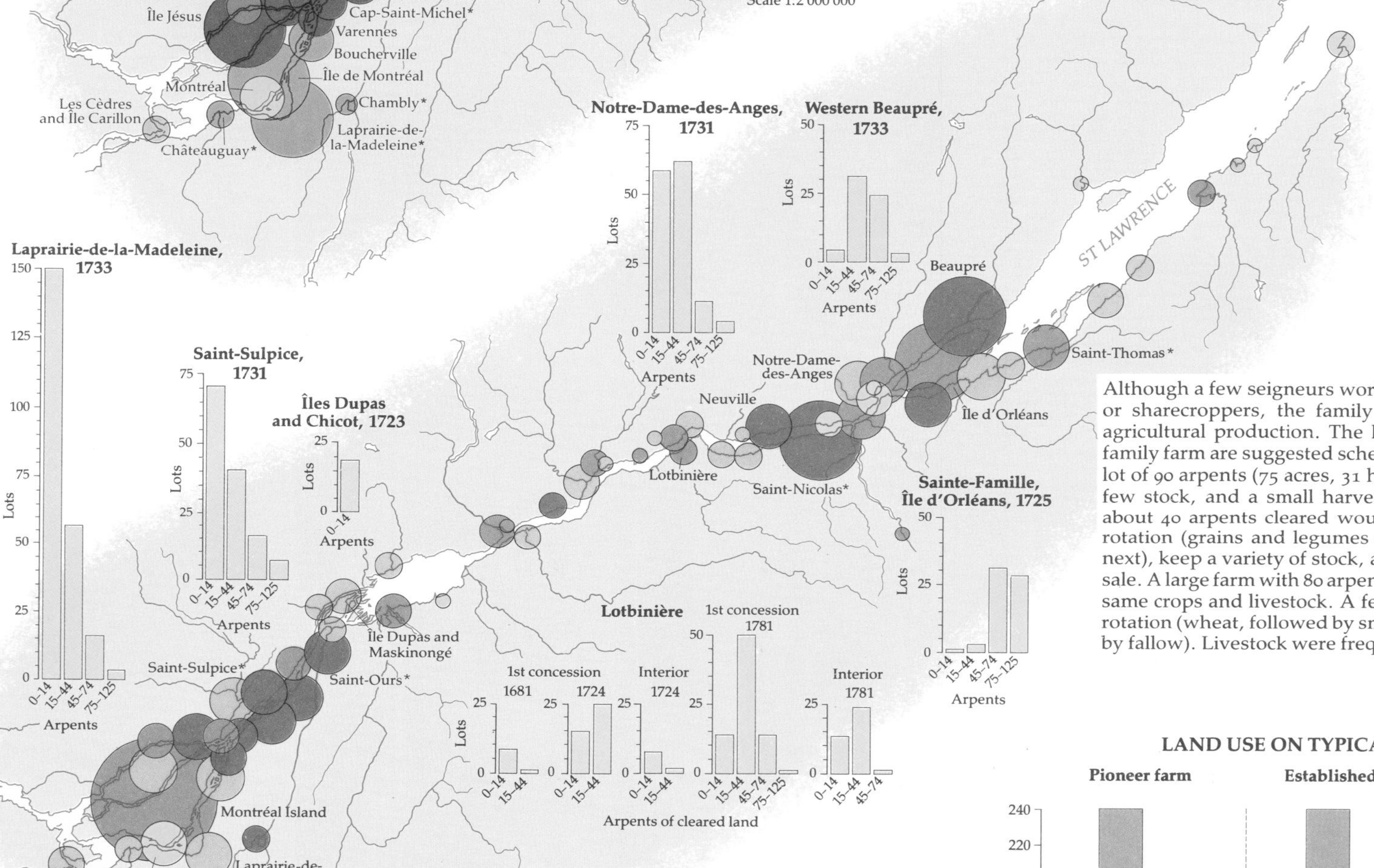

Although a few seigneurs worked large farms with hired labour or sharecroppers, the family farm was the common unit of agricultural production. The land use and productivity of the family farm are suggested schematically below. A new farm on a lot of 90 arpents (75 acres, 31 ha) would have little cleared land, few stock, and a small harvest. A well-established farm with about 40 arpents cleared would probably follow a two-course rotation (grains and legumes one year followed by fallow the next), keep a variety of stock, and produce a modest surplus for sale. A large farm with 80 arpents cleared would raise more of the same crops and livestock. A few farms practised a three-course rotation (wheat, followed by small grains and legumes, followed by fallow). Livestock were frequently pastured on commons.

LAND USE ON TYPICAL FARMS (Schematic)

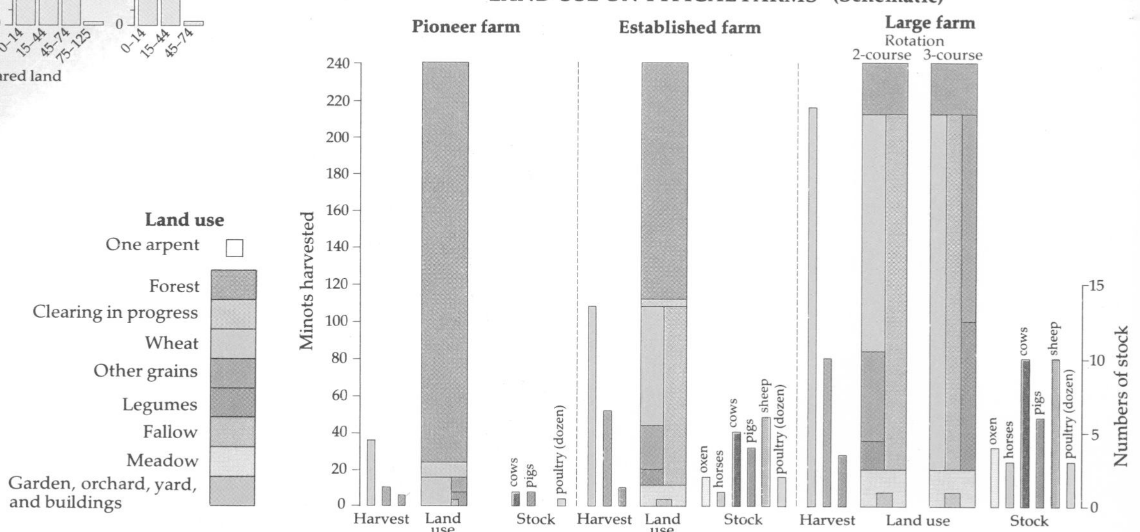

The bar graphs on the map above show the amount of cleared land per farm in particular places and times. Much of the variation reflects the length of settlement: in 1725 all the land on the Île d'Orléans had been settled for years whereas on Îles Dupas and Chicot settlement was just beginning. In Lotbinière clearings on farms in the 1st concession (along the river) were larger than on more recently conceded land in the interior, although in 1781, after more than 100 years of settlement, there were still almost no large farms anywhere in Lotbinière.

The census of 1739 is the last in the 18th century to provide comprehensive data about Canadian agriculture. In that year most farms were still within 50 km of Québec or Montréal. The amount of cultivated land per family was generally greater in the older settlements near the towns; wheat production per family was relatively high near Montréal; and the number of cattle and sheep per family were high in some areas near Québec. Overall, however, Canadian agriculture was not very specialized. Most production was for domestic consumption; the market itself was unspecialized.

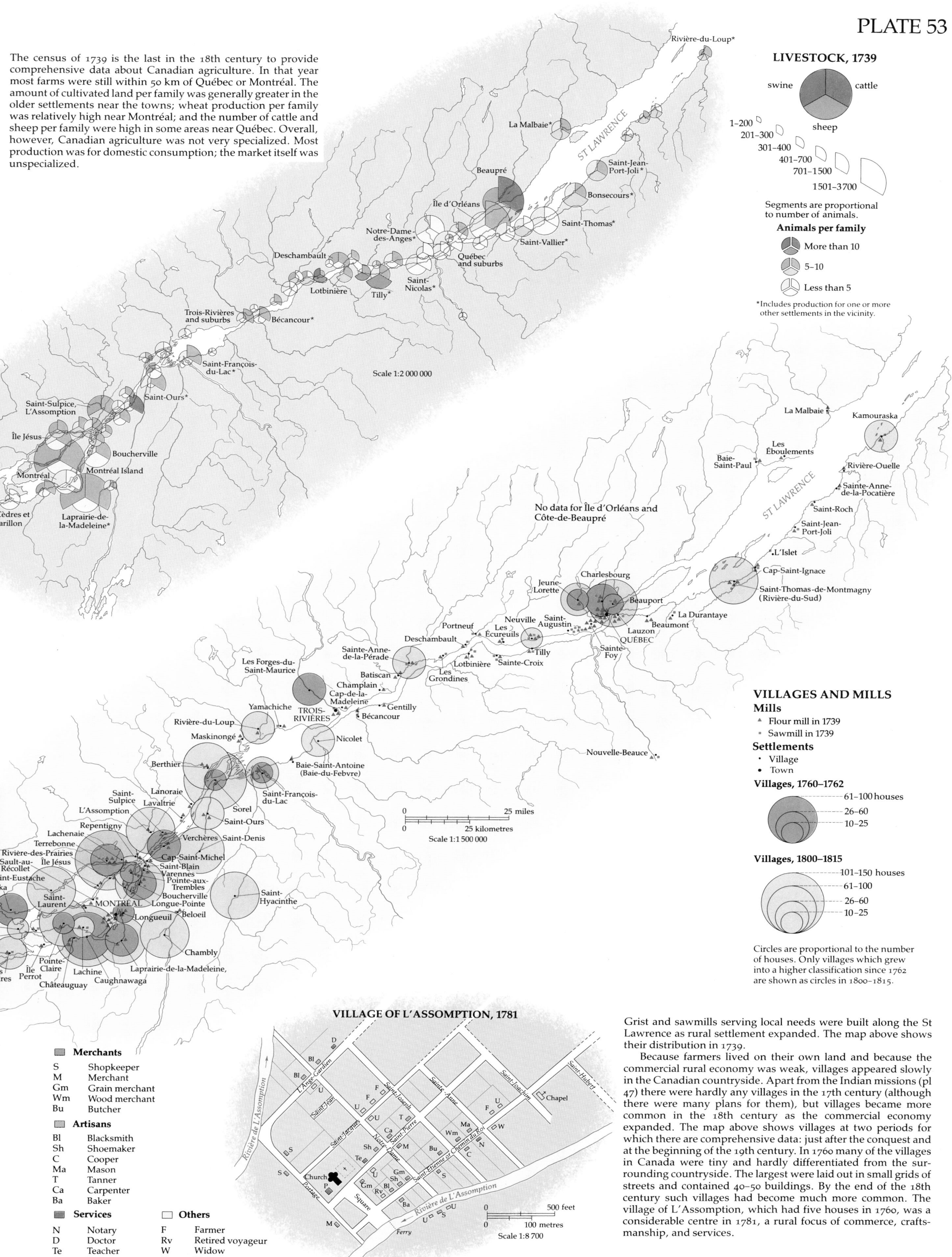

LIVESTOCK, 1739
swine
cattle
sheep
1–200
201–300
301–400
401–700
701–1500
1501–3700
Segments are proportional to number of animals.
Animals per family
More than 10
5–10
Less than 5
*Includes production for one or more other settlements in the vicinity.
Scale 1:2 000 000
ST LAWRENCE
No data for Île d'Orléans and Côte-de-Beaupré
VILLAGES AND MILLS
Mills
Flour mill in 1739
Sawmill in 1739
Settlements
Village
Town
Villages, 1760–1762
61–100 houses
26–60
10–25
Villages, 1800–1815
101–150 houses
61–100
26–60
10–25
Circles are proportional to the number of houses. Only villages which grew into a higher classification since 1762 are shown as circles in 1800–1815.
25 miles
25 kilometres
Scale 1:1 500 000
VILLAGE OF L'ASSOMPTION, 1781
Merchants
S Shopkeeper
M Merchant
Gm Grain merchant
Wm Wood merchant
Bu Butcher
Artisans
Bl Blacksmith
Sh Shoemaker
C Cooper
Ma Mason
T Tanner
Ca Carpenter
Ba Baker
Services
N Notary
D Doctor
Te Teacher
P Priest
Others
F Farmer
Rv Retired voyageur
W Widow
U Unknown
Rivière de L'Assomption
Church
Chapel
Square
Ferry
500 feet
100 metres
Scale 1:8 700

Grist and sawmills serving local needs were built along the St Lawrence as rural settlement expanded. The map above shows their distribution in 1739.

Because farmers lived on their own land and because the commercial rural economy was weak, villages appeared slowly in the Canadian countryside. Apart from the Indian missions (pl 47) there were hardly any villages in the 17th century (although there were many plans for them), but villages became more common in the 18th century as the commercial economy expanded. The map above shows villages at two periods for which there are comprehensive data: just after the conquest and at the beginning of the 19th century. In 1760 many of the villages in Canada were tiny and hardly differentiated from the surrounding countryside. The largest were laid out in small grids of streets and contained 40–50 buildings. By the end of the 18th century such villages had become much more common. The village of L'Assomption, which had five houses in 1760, was a considerable centre in 1781, a rural focus of commerce, craftsmanship, and services.

EXPLOITATION OF THE GULF OF ST LAWRENCE

Author: Mario Lalancette

From the 16th century most European settlement in the Gulf of St Lawrence was dominated by the cod fishery. An analysis of Canadian fisheries in the Gulf in the 17th and 18th centuries reveals their importance in the early Canadian economy and the intensity of competition between metropolitan and colonial interests. Competition focused on a stable resource and on well-known fishing and curing sites in a region disrupted by war until the end of the 18th century.

The Labrador shore was administered from Newfoundland after 1763; its French and Canadian fisheries were replaced by others from Britain, Newfoundland, and New England. British merchants in Québec, acquiring Canadian fishing properties, managed to avoid expropriation. In 1774 Labrador was reattached to Québec. Its fisheries, devastated by the Americans in 1778, quickly resumed after 1783. The Labrador seigneuries were exploited from Québec by British merchants using French Canadian labour. Merchants from Newfoundland and Britain operated along the Strait of Belle-Isle and the Atlantic coast of Labrador. Whalers and cod fishermen from New England were a presence almost everywhere.

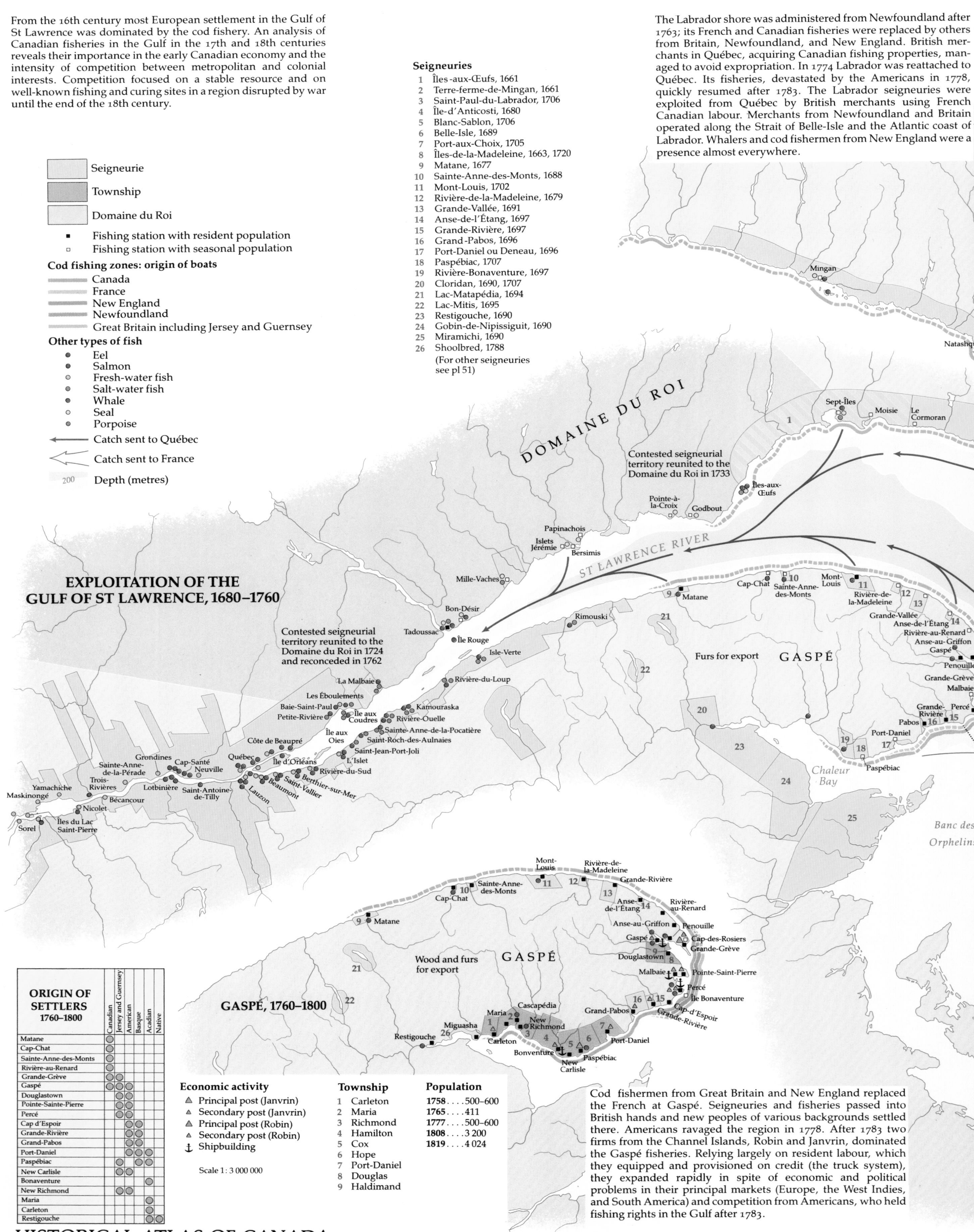
Seigneurie
Township
Domaine du Roi
Fishing station with resident population
Fishing station with seasonal population
Cod fishing zones: origin of boats
Canada
France
New England
Newfoundland
Great Britain including Jersey and Guernsey
Other types of fish
Eel
Salmon
Fresh-water fish
Salt-water fish
Whale
Seal
Porpoise
Catch sent to Québec
Catch sent to France
200 Depth (metres)
Seigneuries
1 Îles-aux-Œufs, 1661
2 Terre-ferme-de-Mingan, 1661
3 Saint-Paul-du-Labrador, 1706
4 Île-d'Anticosti, 1680
5 Blanc-Sablon, 1706
6 Belle-Isle, 1689
7 Port-aux-Choix, 1705
8 Îles-de-la-Madeleine, 1663, 1720
9 Matane, 1677
10 Sainte-Anne-des-Monts, 1688
11 Mont-Louis, 1702
12 Rivière-de-la-Madeleine, 1679
13 Grande-Vallée, 1691
14 Anse-de-l'Étang, 1697
15 Grande-Rivière, 1697
16 Grand-Pabos, 1696
17 Port-Daniel ou Deneau, 1696
18 Paspébiac, 1707
19 Rivière-Bonaventure, 1697
20 Cloridan, 1690, 1707
21 Lac-Matapédia, 1694
22 Lac-Mitis, 1695
23 Restigouche, 1690
24 Gobin-de-Nipissiguit, 1690
25 Miramichi, 1690
26 Shoolbred, 1788
(For other seigneuries see pl 51)
EXPLOITATION OF THE GULF OF ST LAWRENCE, 1680–1760
DOMAINE DU ROI
ST LAWRENCE RIVER
GASPÉ
Contested seigneurial territory reunited to the Domaine du Roi in 1733
Contested seigneurial territory reunited to the Domaine du Roi in 1724 and reconceded in 1762
Furs for export
Mingan
Natashquan
Sept-Îles
Moisie
Le Cormoran
Îles-aux-Œufs
Pointe-à-la-Croix
Godbout
Papinachois
Islets Jérémie
Bersimis
Mille-Vaches
Bon-Désir
Tadoussac
Île Rouge
Isle-Verte
Rivière-du-Loup
La Malbaie
Les Éboulements
Baie-Saint-Paul
Petite-Rivière
Île aux Coudres
Kamouraska
Rivière-Ouelle
Sainte-Anne-de-la-Pocatière
Saint-Roch-des-Aulnaies
Saint-Jean-Port-Joli
L'Islet
Île aux Oies
Côte de Beaupré
Québec
Île d'Orléans
Rivière-du-Sud
Berthier-sur-Mer
Saint-Vallier
Beaumont
Lauzon
Grondines
Cap-Santé
Neuville
Sainte-Anne-de-la-Pérade
Trois-Rivières
Lotbinière
Saint-Antoine-de-Tilly
Bécancour
Yamachiche
Maskinongé
Nicolet
Sorel
Îles du Lac Saint-Pierre
Rimouski
Matane
Cap-Chat
Sainte-Anne-des-Monts
Mont-Louis
Rivière-de-la-Madeleine
Grande-Vallée
Anse-de-l'Étang
Rivière-au-Renard
Anse-au-Griffon
Gaspé
Penouille
Grande-Grève
Malbaie
Grande-Rivière
Percé
Pabos
Port-Daniel
Paspébiac
Chaleur Bay
Banc des Orphelins
GASPÉ, 1760–1800
Wood and furs for export
Grande-Rivière
Rivière-au-Renard
Cap-des-Rosiers
Douglastown
Pointe-Saint-Pierre
Île Bonaventure
Cap-d'Espoir
Grand-Pabos
Cascapédia
New Richmond
Maria
Miguasha
Restigouche
Carleton
Bonventure
New Carlisle
Economic activity
Principal post (Janvrin)
Secondary post (Janvrin)
Principal post (Robin)
Secondary post (Robin)
Shipbuilding
Scale 1 : 3 000 000
Township
1 Carleton
2 Maria
3 Richmond
4 Hamilton
5 Cox
6 Hope
7 Port-Daniel
8 Douglas
9 Haldimand
Population
1758....500–600
1765....411
1777....500–600
1808....3 200
1819....4 024

ORIGIN OF SETTLERS 1760–1800

	Canadian	Jersey and Guernsey	American	Basque	Acadian	Native
Matane	●					
Cap-Chat	●					
Sainte-Anne-des-Monts	●					
Rivière-au-Renard	●					
Grande-Grève	●	●				
Gaspé	●	●	●			
Douglastown		●	●			
Pointe-Sainte-Pierre		●	●			
Percé		●	●			
Cap d'Espoir			●	●		
Grande-Rivière			●	●		
Grand-Pabos			●	●		
Port-Daniel			●	●	●	
Paspébiac		●		●	●	
New Carlisle		●	●			
Bonaventure					●	
New Richmond		●	●			
Maria					●	
Carleton					●	
Restigouche					●	●

Cod fishermen from Great Britain and New England replaced the French at Gaspé. Seigneuries and fisheries passed into British hands and new peoples of various backgrounds settled there. Americans ravaged the region in 1778. After 1783 two firms from the Channel Islands, Robin and Janvrin, dominated the Gaspé fisheries. Relying largely on resident labour, which they equipped and provisioned on credit (the truck system), they expanded rapidly in spite of economic and political problems in their principal markets (Europe, the West Indies, and South America) and competition from Americans, who held fishing rights in the Gulf after 1783.

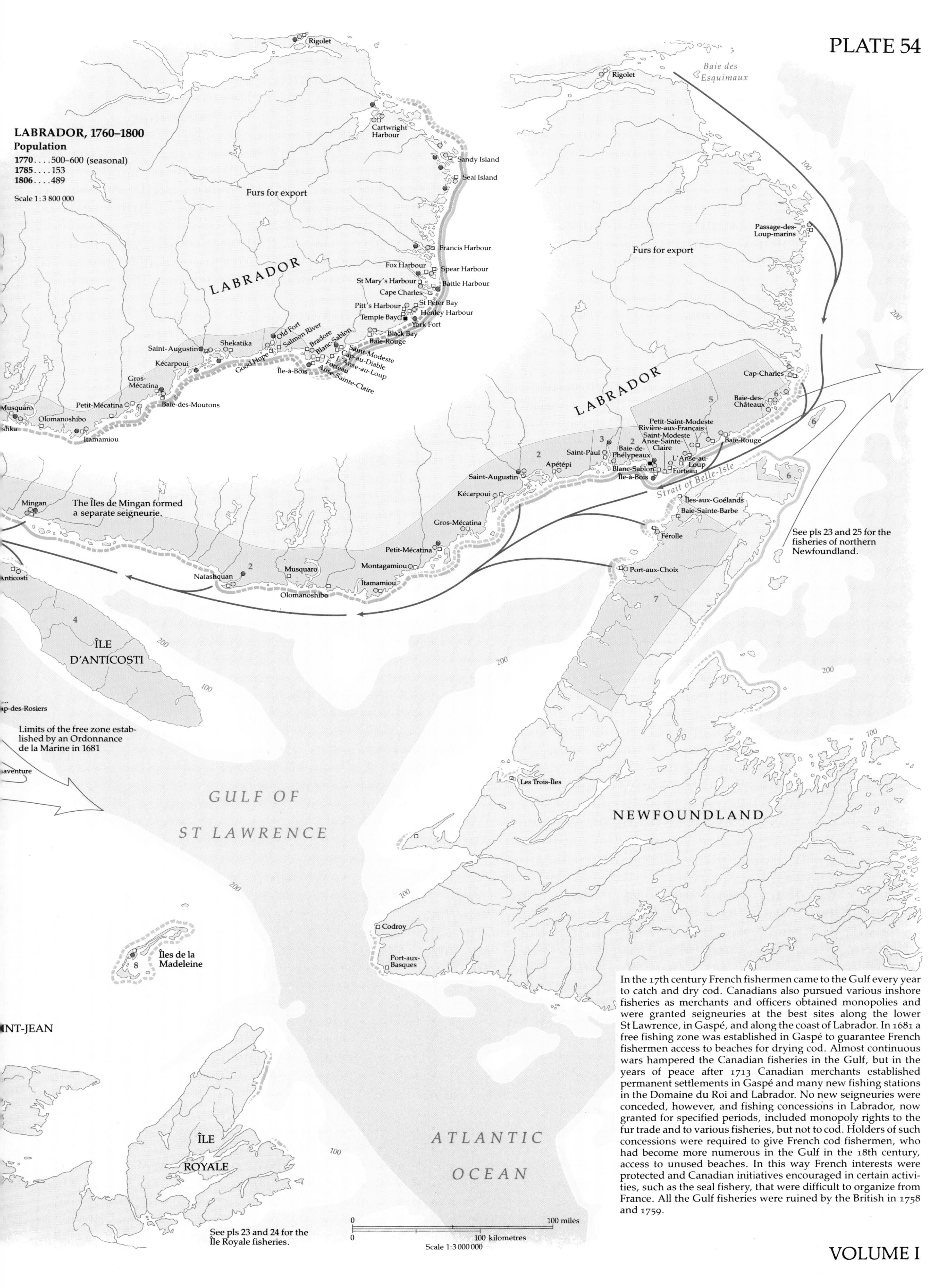

LABRADOR, 1760–1800
Population
1770....500–600 (seasonal)
1785....153
1806....489
Scale 1:3 800 000
Furs for export
LABRADOR
Rigolet
Cartwright Harbour
Sandy Island
Seal Island
Francis Harbour
Fox Harbour
Spear Harbour
St Mary's Harbour
Battle Harbour
Cape Charles
Pitt's Harbour
St Peter Bay
Temple Bay
Henley Harbour
York Fort
Black Bay
Baie-Rouge
Saint-Augustin
Shekatika
Old Fort
Salmon River
Bradore
Blanc-Sablon
Saint-Modeste
Cap-au-Diable
L'Anse-au-Loup
Forteau
Anse-Sainte-Claire
Île-à-Bois
Good Hope
Kécarpoui
Gros-Mécatina
Petit-Mécatina
Baie-des-Moutons
Musquaro
Olomanoshibo
Itamamiou
Baie des Esquimaux
Passage-des-Loup-marins
Cap-Charles
Baie-des-Châteaux
Petit-Saint-Modeste
Rivière-aux-Français
Saint-Modeste
Anse-Sainte-Claire
Baie-de-Phélypeaux
Saint-Paul
Apétépi
L'Anse-au-Loup
Forteau
Baie-Rouge
Blanc-Sablon
Île-à-Bois
Strait of Belle-Isle
Îles-aux-Goélands
Baie-Sainte-Barbe
Férolle
Port-aux-Choix
See pls 23 and 25 for the fisheries of northern Newfoundland.
Mingan
The Îles de Mingan formed a separate seigneurie.
Natashquan
Montagamiou
Anticosti
ÎLE D'ANTICOSTI
Limits of the free zone established by an Ordonnance de la Marine in 1681
GULF OF ST LAWRENCE
Les Trois-Îles
NEWFOUNDLAND
Codroy
Port-aux-Basques
Îles de la Madeleine
ÎLE ROYALE
ATLANTIC OCEAN
See pls 23 and 24 for the Île Royale fisheries.
100 miles
100 kilometres
Scale 1:3 000 000

In the 17th century French fishermen came to the Gulf every year to catch and dry cod. Canadians also pursued various inshore fisheries as merchants and officers obtained monopolies and were granted seigneuries at the best sites along the lower St Lawrence, in Gaspé, and along the coast of Labrador. In 1681 a free fishing zone was established in Gaspé to guarantee French fishermen access to beaches for drying cod. Almost continuous wars hampered the Canadian fisheries in the Gulf, but in the years of peace after 1713 Canadian merchants established permanent settlements in Gaspé and many new fishing stations in the Domaine du Roi and Labrador. No new seigneuries were conceded, however, and fishing concessions in Labrador, now granted for specified periods, included monopoly rights to the fur trade and to various fisheries, but not to cod. Holders of such concessions were required to give French cod fishermen, who had become more numerous in the Gulf in the 18th century, access to unused beaches. In this way French interests were protected and Canadian initiatives encouraged in certain activities, such as the seal fishery, that were difficult to organize from France. All the Gulf fisheries were ruined by the British in 1758 and 1759.

THE HOUSE, 1660–1800

Author: Georges-Pierre Léonidoff

Before 1800 the common rural house along the lower St Lawrence was a one-storey wooden building roofed with thatch, planks, or shingles and built by its first occupants. Techniques of construction differed (pl 56), but the average dimensions of these small houses, usually of two rooms, changed relatively little through the years. Stone houses, characteristically larger than the wooden houses, first became common in Québec, then in Montréal, and then in the countryside near these towns.

The graphs on this plate show the frequency with which various materials were used for the construction of walls, roofs, and chimneys. Average ground-floor dimensions of houses are also indicated. The circles on the maps show the distribution of stone houses, and the illustrations provide some examples of them. The endnotes explain how the data were derived.

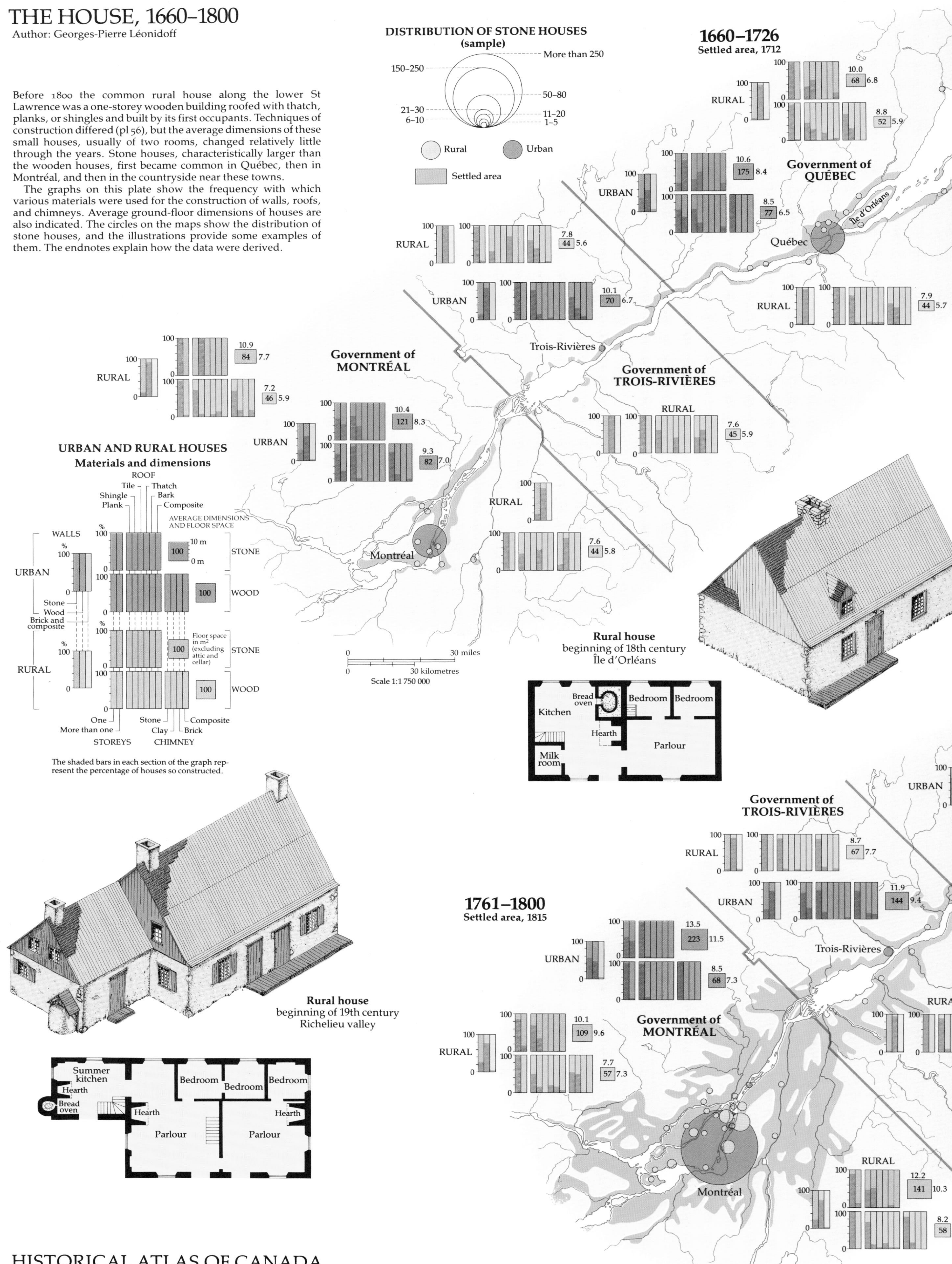

DISTRIBUTION OF STONE HOUSES (sample)
More than 250
150–250
50–80
21–30
11–20
6–10
1–5
Rural
Urban
Settled area
1660–1726
Settled area, 1712
Government of QUÉBEC
Québec
Île d'Orléans
Trois-Rivières
Government of TROIS-RIVIÈRES
Government of MONTRÉAL
Montréal
RURAL
URBAN
URBAN AND RURAL HOUSES
Materials and dimensions
ROOF
Tile
Thatch
Shingle
Bark
Plank
Composite
AVERAGE DIMENSIONS AND FLOOR SPACE
WALLS
STONE
WOOD
Stone
Wood
Brick and composite
Floor space in m² (excluding attic and cellar)
One
More than one
STOREYS
Stone
Clay
Composite
Brick
CHIMNEY
The shaded bars in each section of the graph represent the percentage of houses so constructed.
0
30 miles
30 kilometres
Scale 1:1 750 000
Rural house
beginning of 18th century
Île d'Orléans
Kitchen
Bread oven
Bedroom
Bedroom
Hearth
Parlour
Milk room
Rural house
beginning of 19th century
Richelieu valley
Summer kitchen
Hearth
Bread oven
Bedroom
Bedroom
Bedroom
Hearth
Hearth
Parlour
Parlour
1761–1800
Settled area, 1815

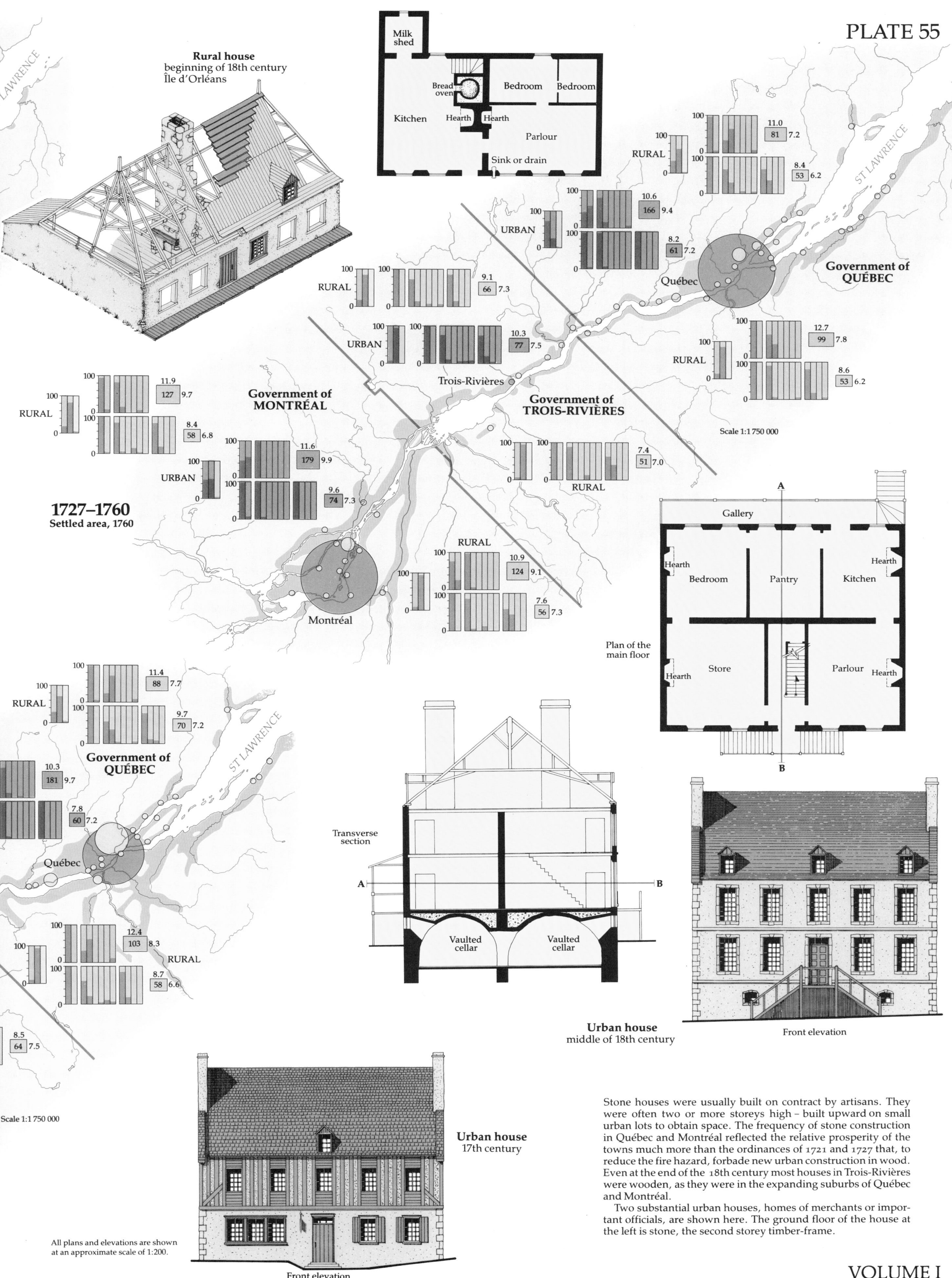
Rural house
beginning of 18th century
Île d'Orléans
Milk shed
Bread oven
Bedroom
Bedroom
Kitchen
Hearth
Hearth
Parlour
Sink or drain
ST LAWRENCE
RURAL
URBAN
Québec
Government of QUÉBEC
Trois-Rivières
Government of TROIS-RIVIÈRES
Government of MONTRÉAL
Montréal
1727–1760
Settled area, 1760
Scale 1:1 750 000
Gallery
Hearth
Bedroom
Pantry
Kitchen
Plan of the main floor
Store
Parlour
Transverse section
Vaulted cellar
Vaulted cellar
Urban house
middle of 18th century
Front elevation
Urban house
17th century
All plans and elevations are shown at an approximate scale of 1:200.

Stone houses were usually built on contract by artisans. They were often two or more storeys high – built upward on small urban lots to obtain space. The frequency of stone construction in Québec and Montréal reflected the relative prosperity of the towns much more than the ordinances of 1721 and 1727 that, to reduce the fire hazard, forbade new urban construction in wood. Even at the end of the 18th century most houses in Trois-Rivières were wooden, as they were in the expanding suburbs of Québec and Montréal.

Two substantial urban houses, homes of merchants or important officials, are shown here. The ground floor of the house at the left is stone, the second storey timber-frame.

THE WOODEN HOUSE

Author: Georges-Pierre Léonidoff

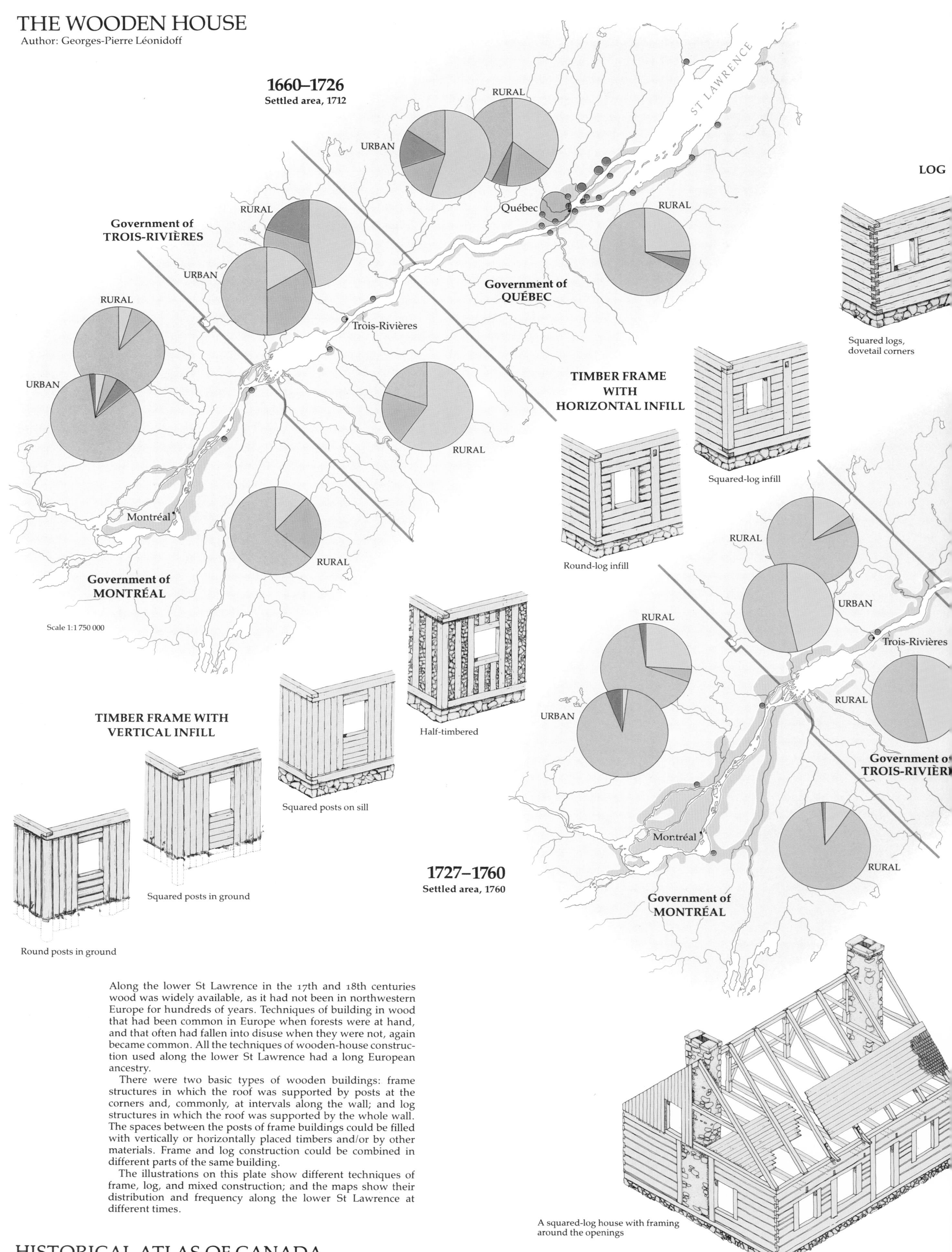
1660–1726
Settled area, 1712
RURAL
URBAN
ST LAWRENCE
Québec
RURAL
Government of QUÉBEC
Government of TROIS-RIVIÈRES
RURAL
URBAN
RURAL
URBAN
Trois-Rivières
RURAL
Montréal
RURAL
Government of MONTRÉAL
Scale 1:1 750 000
LOG
TIMBER FRAME WITH HORIZONTAL INFILL
TIMBER FRAME WITH VERTICAL INFILL
1727–1760
Settled area, 1760
RURAL
URBAN
Trois-Rivières
RURAL
URBAN
RURAL
Government of TROIS-RIVIÈRES
Montréal
RURAL
Government of MONTRÉAL

Squared logs, dovetail corners

Squared-log infill

Round-log infill

Half-timbered

Squared posts on sill

Squared posts in ground

Round posts in ground

A squared-log house with framing around the openings

Along the lower St Lawrence in the 17th and 18th centuries wood was widely available, as it had not been in northwestern Europe for hundreds of years. Techniques of building in wood that had been common in Europe when forests were at hand, and that often had fallen into disuse when they were not, again became common. All the techniques of wooden-house construction used along the lower St Lawrence had a long European ancestry.

There were two basic types of wooden buildings: frame structures in which the roof was supported by posts at the corners and, commonly, at intervals along the wall; and log structures in which the roof was supported by the whole wall. The spaces between the posts of frame buildings could be filled with vertically or horizontally placed timbers and/or by other materials. Frame and log construction could be combined in different parts of the same building.

The illustrations on this plate show different techniques of frame, log, and mixed construction; and the maps show their distribution and frequency along the lower St Lawrence at different times.

For reasons yet unexplained, the log house was always the characteristic wooden house in Montréal and the surrounding countryside, whereas during the French regime frame construction predominated in and near Québec. The relatively square dimensions of houses in the Montréal region (pl 55) stem from this difference.

The walls of frame houses were characteristically infilled with lengths of log, left round or squared. When placed horizontally these lengths were slotted into the vertical posts. Stone rubble and clay and straw infill were used near Québec, and occasionally elsewhere, but by the late 18th century such half-timbered house were rarely built. Frame construction of any type had become infrequent. The squared-log house, often with posts framing doors, windows, and chimney, had become the typical wooden house throughout the St Lawrence lowland.

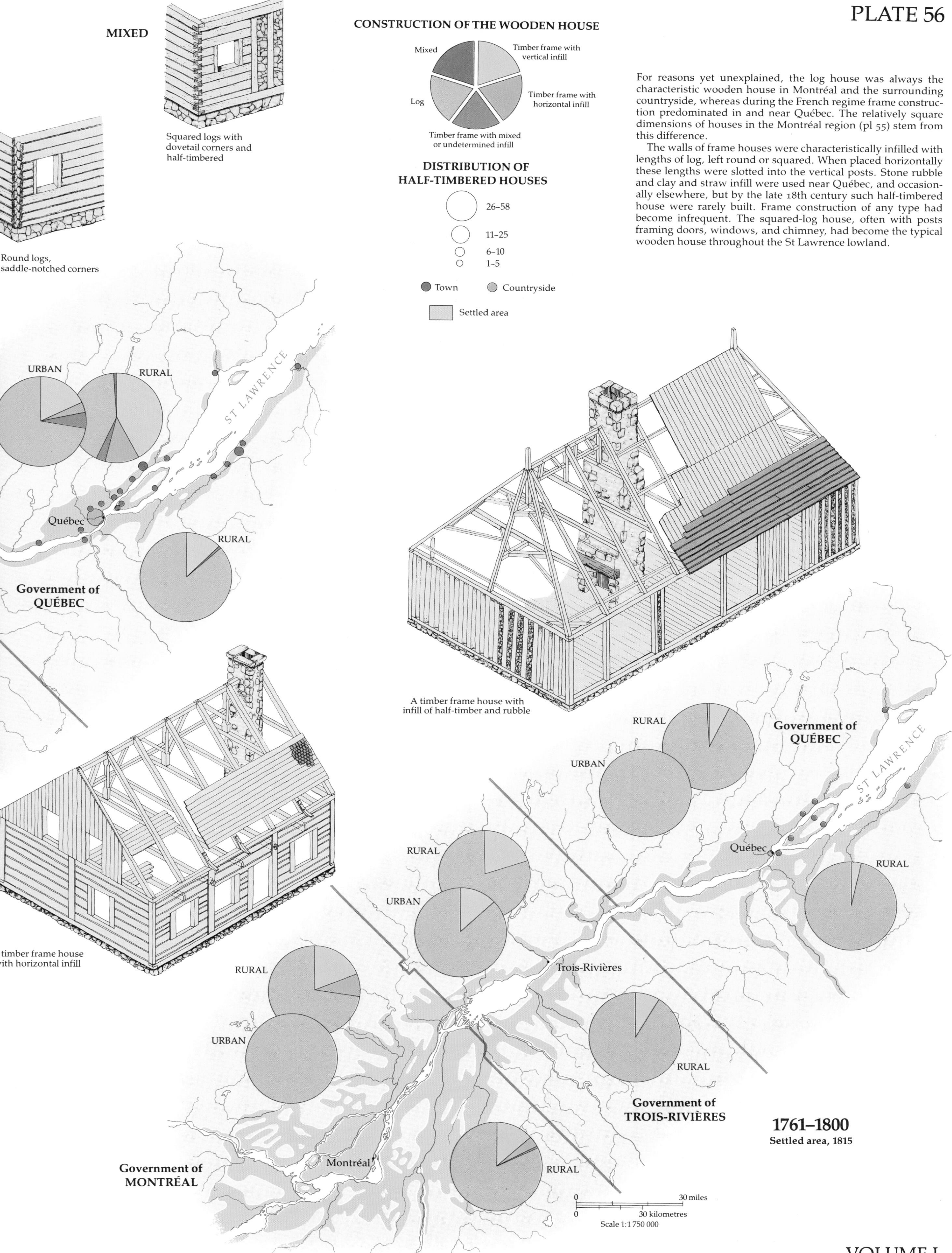
MIXED
Squared logs with dovetail corners and half-timbered
Round logs, saddle-notched corners
CONSTRUCTION OF THE WOODEN HOUSE
Mixed
Timber frame with vertical infill
Timber frame with horizontal infill
Timber frame with mixed or undetermined infill
Log
DISTRIBUTION OF HALF-TIMBERED HOUSES
26–58
11–25
6–10
1–5
Town
Countryside
Settled area
URBAN
RURAL
ST LAWRENCE
Québec
RURAL
Government of QUÉBEC
A timber frame house with infill of half-timber and rubble
A timber frame house with horizontal infill
RURAL
URBAN
Government of QUÉBEC
ST LAWRENCE
Québec
RURAL
RURAL
URBAN
Trois-Rivières
RURAL
URBAN
RURAL
Government of TROIS-RIVIÈRES
Government of MONTRÉAL
Montréal
RURAL
1761–1800
Settled area, 1815
0
30 miles
0
30 kilometres
Scale 1:1 750 000

The Northwest

In the 17th century European influences began to reach beyond Hudson Bay and the Great Lakes well into the northwestern interior of North America. Before mid-century networks of native trade carried French goods obtained along the lower St Lawrence River as far as the Assiniboine and Cree west of Lake Superior. By 1670, when Charles II granted the Hudson's Bay Company a charter for the lands and trade around Hudson Bay, French traders were active around Lake Michigan and Lake Superior and the English were trading at the southern end of James Bay. By 1685 French traders operated posts around the Great Lakes, in the upper Mississippi valley, and in the Canadian Shield north of Lake Superior; and the Hudson's Bay Company maintained six posts around Hudson Bay and James Bay. Horses, which were brought to North America by the Spanish, were being traded and mastered by successive groups of Indians, but had not yet reached the northern plains (pl 57). The northwest coast of North America, the northern Cordillera, and the western Arctic remained well beyond any European influence.

The northern continental interior is a vast, harsh land that at the time of European contact was thinly inhabited by peoples of different languages, economies, and cultures. The rock-bound, ice-scoured Canadian Shield, its surface covered with interconnected lakes, swamps, and rivers, lay in a huge crescent around Hudson Bay. Southwest of the Canadian Shield were the plains, forested along their northern and eastern margins, then more open parkland, then grassland (pl 17). Between the Canadian Shield and the southwestern shores of Hudson Bay and James Bay was marshy lowland, territory that had been inundated by the Tyrrell Sea (pl 4) as the Late Wisconsinan glaciers melted. In the north the predominantly coniferous boreal forest thinned out, giving way to lichen woodland then to tundra. The peoples who lived in these different environments all depended on hunting, fishing, and some gathering, but often overwhelmingly on a particular game animal. In the boreal forest they usually gathered in summer at favourable fishing sites, then dispersed in small, extended-family groups for winter hunting. Along the parkland-grassland margin they followed the bison into the parkland in winter and onto the plains in summer. Along the forest-parkland margin they hunted and fished in the forest in summer and wintered in the parkland with the bison. Farther north, along the lichen-woodland–tundra margin, they moved into the tundra with the caribou in summer and back into the forest with the caribou in winter. Territories overlapped somewhat, but peoples considered themselves to be distinct (pl 57). In 1670 bands of Cree, Algonquian-speakers, occupied much of the territory between Hudson Bay and Lake Superior, part of the northern plains, and the adjacent parkland and boreal forest. By this time some Ojibwa, also Algonquian-speakers, had returned to the north shore of Lake Huron (pl 38). The Assiniboine, Siouan-speakers, occupied the forest-grassland margin of the northeastern plains from the Red River to the Saskatchewan (pl 18). To their west lived the bison hunters of the northern plains, among them the Algonquian-speaking Blackfoot. North of the Cree along the lichen-woodland–tundra margin, lived the Chipewyans, Athapaskan-speaking caribou hunters. There were Inuit along the northwest coast of Hudson Bay, Inuktituk-speakers whose Thule ancestors had arrived in the region after AD 1200 (pl 11).

The Early Fur Trades

The French and English fur trades expanded in this territory, among these peoples. Soon the two European nations fought for control of Hudson Bay, the most convenient route of entry to the northern continental interior. In 1686 a French force from the St Lawrence captured Fort Albany and two other English posts on James Bay, and a few years later French ships took York Factory and Fort Severn (pl 38). For several years the northern fur trade was almost entirely in French hands and furs glutted the warehouses in Montréal. In 1696 French officials closed most of the interior posts (pl 39), and did not reopen most of them until after the Treaty of Utrecht (1713) established English control of the shores of Hudson Bay and relegated the French to the St Lawrence–Great Lakes route to the northwest. Then began the commercial struggle between the St Lawrence River and Hudson Bay that would dominate the fur trade of the northern continental interior for the next hundred years. The Hudson's Bay Company consolidated its trade at two river-mouth posts, Fort Albany on James Bay and York Factory at the southwestern corner of Hudson Bay, later adding Fort Churchill, Moose Factory, and Eastmain (pl 39). Two largely independent systems of Hudson's Bay Company–Indian trade evolved, one focused on the posts at the south end of James Bay and the other on York Factory and Fort Churchill on the west coast of Hudson Bay. Plate 60 shows the goods moving through these posts. The French expanded westward, first challenging the Hudson's Bay Company in the hinterland of Fort Albany and other posts on James Bay and then, when Pierre Gaultier de La Vérendrye reached Lake Winnipeg in 1733, breaking the Hudson's Bay Company's monopoly of Indian trade in the vast hinterland of York Factory. In the 1740s French traders established several posts on the Saskatchewan River (pl 40), and took much of the trade that once had gone to York Factory (pl 60).

To some extent the two trades were complementary, as the French (with higher transportation costs) took many of the more valuable furs and would not take muskrat. Rising fur prices in Europe offset the declining volume of Hudson's Bay Company trade; although the company occasionally sent servants to live with the Indians and persuade them to trade at the Bay, it was not forced to establish trading posts in the interior. Competition increased the prices European traders paid for furs, but higher prices did not increase the supply. Native demand for durable goods was inelastic. If the price of furs rose, fewer furs were traded and Indian traders and trappers had more time for other activities. Faced with such a market, both French and English traders relied on alcohol and tobacco to draw native trade. In 1755, at the height of the French fur trade in North America, French and Hudson's Bay Company traders divided the trade of the drainage basin of Hudson Bay approximately equally, although, as most furs and hides garnered by the French came from farther south, the total volume of the furs shipped from Montréal was several times that shipped from the Bay (pl 41).

The native people who became involved in the fur trade neither quickly lost traditional techniques of tool manufacture and subsistence nor soon became dependent on European goods (except muskets for defence against other Indians so armed). Yet they desired such goods, and the introduction of them began to change native patterns of settlement and warfare. Some Cree families settled permanently near the Bayside posts (Home Guard Cree), supplying provisions and trading locally obtained furs. Eventually a population of mixed bloods emerged, some to become part of trading-post society. Other Cree and some Assiniboine began to expand their trapping territories into the lands of others. The early French trade on the St Lawrence may have drawn some Assiniboine and Cree traders eastward, but the establishment of York Factory (1684) and other English posts on Hudson Bay and of French posts in the interior stimulated far larger and generally more westerly movements. Cree and Assiniboine traders consolidated their position on the Nelson River and, initially better supplied with firearms than their neighbours, forcibly expanded their trapping and trading areas. Fighting raged along the Cree-Chipewyan border. The Assiniboine, who had expanded into the territories of the Blackfoot and several other groups on the Plains, were slaughtered when they could not obtain powder and shot from the Hudson's Bay Company. 'The wars,' wrote the chief trader at York Factory, 'has almost ruined this Country it being so thinly Peopled at the best.' Although motivated somewhat differently, on a smaller scale, and less final, these wars were the counterpart in the northwest of the devastating Iroquois wars in southern Ontario (pl 35). In the East the Ojibwa began moving into territory west of Lake Superior vacated by the Cree (pls 39, 40, 60).

After 1720 conditions appear to have become more peaceful. The Chipewyans, as well armed as the Cree after the establishment of Fort Churchill (1717), checked the northward expansion of the Cree. As the Indians of the northern Plains adopted the horse (pl 57), their dependence on bison probably increased, and they were more ready to rely on Cree and Assiniboine traders to make the long trip to York Factory. These increasingly specialized traders returned to the parkland in winter to live off bison, and in spring traded used European goods for furs before making another trip to the Bay. As the French began to intersect this trading system in the 1730s, they diverted some Cree and Assiniboine from their annual trip to the Bay (pls 39, 40). In the south war continued between the Assiniboine Cree and the Dakota Sioux. The Assiniboine withdrew from southeastern Manitoba, and were replaced by the Ojibwa (pl 60). By 1760 much of the Red River valley above the Assiniboine River had become a no-man's-land.

Competition and Consolidation, 1760–1821

During the Seven Years' War the French closed most of their interior posts before Québec and Montréal capitulated (pls 42, 43). In the scramble to renew the western fur trade after the conquest, traders from New York and New England preceded British troops to Fort Michilimackinac in 1761. By 1765 Montréal traders were again operating on the Saskatchewan River. Although many French Canadian merchants participated in the restored western trade and some continued to operate in the Great Lakes basin until the 1790s, most were soon displaced by British merchants, frequently New Englanders or Scots. The skilled labour of voyageur, guide, and interpreter, on which the extended Montréal trade depended, remained French Canadian.

Sustained by an experienced labour force and ready financial backing, the St Lawrence fur trade soon expanded beyond its old limits. In 1776 Montréal traders reached the upper Churchill River, and traded profitably with Chipewyans at Portage du Traite and on Lake Ile-à-la-Crosse. Two years later Peter Pond crossed the Methye Portage, the divide between the Saskatchewan River (Hudson Bay drainage) and the Athabaska River (Arctic drainage), and established a trading post on Lake Athabaska (pl 58). The Athabaska-Mackenzie region was opened up by traders from Montréal who soon tapped the main fur-producing areas along the Athabaska, Peace, and Mackenzie Rivers. In 1789, when Alexander Mackenzie reached the Arctic Ocean (pl 67), the outer limits of the fur trade east of the Cordillera were defined.

In the years immediately after the conquest the St Lawrence fur trade was carried on by a miscellany of individuals, partnerships, and companies who vied with each other, with the Hudson's Bay Company, and with traders from the British colonies along the Atlantic seaboard for the Indian trade of the interior. The weaker traders were soon eliminated or absorbed and more powerful organizations emerged, conspicuous among them the North West Company. Organized into a general co-partnership in 1779, by 1787 it had absorbed many of its competitors in a loosely organized company. Traders dissatisfied with their lot in the company and with the growing power of its Montréal financiers left the company from time to time to resume independent trading, but a much greater threat to the North West Company came after Jay's Treaty (1794) forced British traders to evacuate posts south of the international border drawn through the Great Lakes in 1783. The Forsyth and Ogilvy Companies, two of the Montréal-based firms that had been active in the southwest, redirected their resources and soon penetrated the northwest as far as the Athabaska country, previously the preserve of the North West Company. These companies united in 1800, creating the XY Company, and were joined by disaffected Nor'Westers, the most prominent of whom was Alexander Mackenzie. The ensuing bitter rivalry between two trading companies based in Montréal proved ruinous to the smaller company and, as in the past, the North West Company absorbed its opposition. From this union in 1804 until 1821 a monopoly based on the St Lawrence River faced another on Hudson Bay.

By the beginning of the 19th century the St Lawrence trade required an investment in posts and personnel and a system of supply that were well beyond the capacity of small companies. An elaborate network of strategically located entrepôts shuttled trade goods, furs, and men between Montréal and the outer limits of the St Lawrence trade in a single season. As the system evolved, agricultural produce from the lower St Lawrence, Detroit, and Michilimackinac provisioned the canoe brigades between Montréal and Grand Portage (after 1803 Fort William) at the head of Lake Superior. From this main depot corn and wild rice provisioned the western brigades to the prairie margins. Beyond Lake Winnipeg pemmican from provisioning posts in the parkland supplied the brigades that fanned out into the boreal forest. The system depended on the tight consignment of goods, the improved carrying capacities of the *canots du maitre* on the Great Lakes and of the *canots du nord* on the rivers beyond (pl 63), and the skill and stamina of the voyageurs who manned them.

Throughout its first century the Hudson's Bay Company traded only at Bayside, and had only a vague knowledge of the vast territories inland from its river-mouth posts. Few of its personnel knew how to live in the interior or wanted to go there, but by 1774 the intensity of competition from St Lawrence traders forced the Hudson's Bay Company to abandon its 'sleep by a frozen sea.' Cumberland House was built on the Saskatchewan River some 800 km from the Bay. Thereafter the company strove to catch up to its competitors throughout most of the northwestern interior, building posts and emulating many of the Montréalers' practices. Short of material with which to build canoes, the Hudson's Bay Company developed shallow-draft bateaux and boats (pl 63) for use on the main rivers flowing into Hudson Bay. Although slow and cumbersome, these craft were safer than canoes, required fewer men, and had a far greater carrying capacity. They extended low-cost transportation well inland, but did not allow the Hudson's Bay Company to compete effectively in the Athabasca country, which remained the preserve of the Nor'Westers until 1815 when the Hudson's Bay Company, recruiting voyageurs in Montréal and using canoes, was finally able to compete in this fur-rich region.

The vast territory west of Lake Winnipeg, known by the traders from Montréal as the Grand Nord, was tied by navigable waterways to York Factory on Hudson Bay or to Grand Portage on Lake Superior. From York Factory the route led to Lake Winnipeg via the Hayes River and was channelled through the depot of Jack River House, later called Norway House, at the northern outflow of Lake Winnipeg. From Grand Portage the route led to Lake Winnipeg via the French canoe route along the border lakes and the Winnipeg River to the depot of Bas-de-la-Rivière Ouinipique, later called Fort Alexander. Lake Winnipeg was the platform from which both Hudson's Bay Company and St Lawrence traders expanded into the Grand Nord. The routes to Lake Winnipeg on the south and west flanked what the Montréal traders called the Petit Nord, the wide isthmus east of Lake Winnipeg between Lake Superior and Hudson Bay, but neither provided easy access to it. The Hudson's Bay Company entered the Petit Nord from Moose Factory, Fort Severn, and Fort Albany on James Bay, while the St Lawrence traders entered mainly from Lake Nipigon. Rather than expanding steadily west, the fur trade developed separately in these two regions. As late as 1815 an officer of the Hudson's Bay Company thought that 'Perhaps there is no extensive district in this part of America so little known as the tract of country to the East of Lake Winipic.'

In most of the Grand Nord and the Petit Nord the pioneer

European settlement was the trading post. There French or British traders lived in direct, prolonged contact with the Canadian environment and its native inhabitants. A sustained commerce bound natives and Europeans together in a distinctive frontier of European expansion that aimed neither to transform the wilderness nor to displace its native people, yet exploited both.

Competition led to the proliferation of posts, most of them short-lived, and monopoly led to fewer, more lasting posts. In the spring of 1774 there were 17 posts in the northwest, 7 belonging to the Hudson's Bay Company and 10 to St Lawrence traders. By 1789 some 90 new posts had been built, at least 65 of them by St Lawrence traders. As a rule they built the most forward posts and took the windfall profits. By 1789 they had posts well supported by strategic depots and transfer points in all the major fur regions east of the Cordillera. The Hudson's Bay Company had managed to build half as many posts as its St Lawrence competitors in the Petit Nord, but in the Grand Nord it lagged much farther behind, building 14 posts as against 47, and almost matching its competitors only along the Saskatchewan River. During the next 15 years of intense competition (1790–1804) at least 323 new posts were built, 194 by St Lawrence traders, 129 by the Hudson's Bay Company. Montréal traders established posts along the Mackenzie River, but elsewhere the fur trade turned inward, infilling rather than expanding. Rivals of the North West Company, competing with the Nor'Wester even in the Athabasca country, built many of the St Lawrence posts. In the Petit Nord the Hudson's Bay Company built on Lake Nipigon and Lake Superior; in the Grand Nord it also matched the Montréalers, often post for post, except in Athabasca. This was ruinous competition: expenses soared, profits fell, beaver were depleted in some areas, and no company commanded the majority of the trade. In 1804, when the North West Company absorbed the XY Company, St Lawrence traders operated 108 posts in the West and the Hudson's Bay Company 57.

When it gained monopoly control of the St Lawrence trade, the North West Company closed most of the XY Company's posts and some of its own; and the Hudson's Bay Company rationalized its operations. In 1814 the North West Company operated 59 posts, the Hudson's Bay Company 42. Although the two companies opened at least 171 new posts in the northwestern interior from 1805 to 1821, as they sought out and depleted the remaining pockets of fur-bearing animals, most were quickly closed. In 1815 the Hudson's Bay Company finally penetrated the Athabasca country, building many unprofitable posts but destroying the Nor'Westers' monopoly in the region.

By this time the rivalry between the Hudson's Bay and North West Companies verged on open warfare. The Nor'Westers considered Lord Selkirk's settlement of evicted farmers from the Scottish Highlands on the Red River in 1812 to be a threat to their pemmican supplies, correctly as it turned out. In 1815 they harassed the settlement, burning crops and buildings. The next year the governor and 21 settlers were ambushed and killed. Selkirk retaliated by taking Fort William with a private force of Swiss and German mercenaries which, in 1817, reached and restored the Red River colony. In Athabasca the Nor'Westers captured the Hudson's Bay Company's district headquarters and several other posts. Two years later, in 1819, mercenaries hired by the Hudson's Bay Company ambushed the Nor'Westers' main brigade on the Grand Rapids of the Saskatchewan. At this point the British government intervened, the evidence in a published collection of *Papers relating to the Red River Settlement, 1815–1819* supporting its conclusion that competition was ruining the fur trade. The two companies were pressed to amalgamate. In March 1821 an agreement between equals created a new partnership and gave it the charter rights and monopoly privileges of the Hudson's Bay Company, plus a monopoly of the Indian trade over the rest of British North America, save the colonies in the east. That partnership soon became a company, retaining the name of the Hudson's Bay Company. The sea route to Hudson Bay that the French had fought for and the Nor'Westers had coveted became the maritime conduit of the fur trade of the northwestern interior of North America (pl 61). The former headquarters of the North West Company at Fort William was reduced to a trading post from which a few furs were sent to Montreal. The number of active posts east of the Rockies declined from 109 in 1821 to 45 four years later (pl 62).

Trading Post Society and Native Life

The main types of posts in the northwestern interior at the beginning of the 19th century are shown on plate 64. The smallest, flying posts (log tents or 'hog styes'), were built in a few days and provided minimal winter accommodation for a trader in an Indian encampment. The largest, palisaded compounds containing many buildings, were the main depots on Hudson Bay or Lake Superior. All were strictly utilitarian settlements, built to facilitate trade and, where possible, to accommodate gardens and livestock. Trading-post society was hierarchical, multiracial, and predominantly male. Seasonal labourers, almost always Indians or mixed bloods, were at the bottom of the social order. Above them were permanent labourers – usually French Canadian or Indian (usually of Iroquois descent) in the St Lawrence posts; and (until the company began employing French Canadians after 1815) Orkneymen, Englishmen, Scots, and mixed bloods in Hudson's Bay Company posts. Clerks and skilled tradesmen were usually French Canadians, Orkneymen, English, or Scots, less commonly mixed bloods. The St Lawrence posts were managed by profit-sharing partners, most of whom were of Scottish, and some of English, descent. Officers in charge of Hudson's Bay Company posts usually were English. In the earlier years women at the posts were Indian, later commonly mixed bloods as men at the posts took country wives from growing populations of mixed bloods nearby. At some posts several languages, European and native, were spoken.

During the first two decades of the 19th century the North West Company maintained about 900 permanent employees in the northwestern interior, the great majority of whom were French Canadians. They lived in posts in the boreal forest and parkland along the axis of the St Lawrence fur trade from Lake Superior to the Athabaska country (pl 65). The Hudson's Bay Company had 435 permanent employees in the northwestern interior in 1805-6, three-quarters of them from Orkney, and virtually all living within the drainage basin of Hudson Bay. By 1819 the Hudson's Bay Company's permanent employees had doubled in number and become more diversified in origin. A third were from Orkney, the rest were French Canadians, Scots, mixed bloods, English, or Irish. There were perhaps a thousand mixed bloods scattered through the northwest, and roughly another thousand people at Red River: Highland Scots, French Canadians, and Swiss.

Indian populations are much more difficult to estimate. In 1781 smallpox contracted from the natives along the Missouri River spread to the Assiniboine, Ojibwa, Cree, and Blackfoot. Apparently almost half of the affected populations died, a mortality rate comparable to that among the Ontario Iroquois in the 1630s (pl 35). After this disaster the Assiniboine populations increased rapidly, the Cree and Ojibwa more slowly. Then in 1818–19 measles and whooping cough struck, again apparently killing a third to a half of affected populations. After the epidemics of 1818–19 there may have been 15 000–20 000 Indians in the northwestern interior, excluding the Blackfoot and other Indians of the grasslands with whom fur traders had little contact. Within the boreal forest and parkland Indians outnumbered whites by perhaps no more than six to one.

The proliferation of trading posts in the western interior after 1774 eliminated the Cree and Assiniboine traders who previously had transported furs hundreds of kilometres to posts at the Bay. By the end of the 18th century few Indians in the boreal forest or parkland lived more than 200 km from a trading post, and in hotly contested areas both the North West Company and the Hudson's Bay Company built flying posts or sent traders on regular winter visits to Indian bands, completely undermining the native carrying trade. At the same time the rapid proliferation of trading posts created a large market for provisions: fried bison meat, grease, and pemmican from the parkland and grassland; fish, venison, and fowl from the boreal forest. Many Cree and Assiniboine, who had long been accustomed to trading and held trapping in disdain, became provisioners for the trading companies. After years of moving northwest to be more favourably situated for trapping and trading, the Assiniboine turned southward, establishing themselves in the parkland and on the grassland margin (pls 65, 69), and in summer striking out across the grasslands as far as the Missouri. The Cree abandoned the territory between the Lake of the Woods and Lake Winnipeg, as well as most of the interlake region of Manitoba, and by 1820 some of them, the Plains Cree, lived with the Assiniboine in the parkland belt. The territory vacated by the Cree west, south, and east of Lake Winnipeg was occupied by Ojibwa, who continued to trap there. Along the southern margin of Assiniboine-Cree-Ojibwa territory war continued with the Dakota Sioux, and increased with the Blackfoot and with the Mandan along the Missouri with whom the Assiniboine, and to a lesser extent the Plains Cree, now competed for the same resources. In the north the decline in Cree population following the smallpox epidemic of 1781 and the southward drift of Cree bands to participate in the provisioning trade opened territory for their enemies, the Chipewyans (pls 60, 65), whose former territory was occupied by the Caribou Inuit (pl 11).

An intensely competitive fur trade soon began to deplete the fur-bearing animals and game of the boreal forest. With posts in abundance the time that Indians previously used for travel became available for trapping and hunting. Furthermore, Indians were no longer limited by the carrying capacities of their canoes - about 300 beaver pelts per canoe, 150 per man - a technological constraint that had limited the consumption of trade goods and moderated the environmental impact of the fur trade. As posts stocked with trade goods proliferated among the Indians and long canoe trips became unnecessary, the per capita consumption of trade goods, especially liquor, probably increased, and with it hunting pressure on species in strong demand. By 1820 beaver and the big game animals hunted for the provisioning trade were scarce in most of the boreal forest south and east of the Churchill River (pl 63). In the Rainy River region of northern Ontario deer and moose had become so scarce by the 1820s that the Hudson's Bay Company had to import bison hides so local Indians could make moccasins and clothing. The Indians' food supply was also in jeopardy, especially during cyclical downturns in populations of small game. Company traders responded by importing food from the parklands, Europe, and eastern North America (by sea). Food and other trade goods were paid for with furs, provisions, or, increasingly, with seasonal labour at the posts or in the brigades. Overall, traditional Indian economies were becoming less viable. Periodic dependence on employment and foodstuffs at the posts was becoming a fact of Indian life. When the Hudson's Bay Company and North West Company merged in 1821, years of unregulated competition had overextended fur companies, depleted fur-bearing animals, and undermined the ecological basis of Indian economies. Earlier in the fur trade Indians had become dependent on supplies of muskets, powder, and shot to ward off enemies who possessed these articles; in the early 19th century they were also becoming dependent on clothing and food provided by Europeans. They were not losing traditional techniques of subsistence, rather the natural resources on which their lives depended.

The Maritime and Cordilleran Fur Trades

Along the northwest coast of North America and in the northern Cordillera Indians and Europeans met later than they had east of the Rockies and in considerably different circumstances. European explorers reached the coast of British Columbia only in the 1770s: Spaniards, who sailed north from Mexico in tiny ships after word came from Madrid that Russians were encroaching on territory the Spanish did not know but considered theirs; Captain James Cook, who was sent by the British Admiralty to look for the western entrance, thought to lie about 60° N latitude, of the Northwest Passage (pl 66). Apart from Alexander Mackenzie's overland expedition to the Pacific (1793), no one of European background ventured into the northern Cordillera until the first decade of the 19th century. The area was exceedingly remote. By sea the northwest coast was as far from Europe as Australia; by land the northern Cordillera was at the logistical limit of canoe travel from Montréal.

The Russians, the first Europeans to reach the northwest coast of North America, quietly conducted a trade in sea-otter pelts with the Chinese for years before some of Cook's men, trading sea-otter pelts at Nootka on Vancouver Island and selling them in Canton, inadvertently discovered this profitable connection. By 1785 a competitive international trade for sea otter was beginning along the outer coast of British Columbia. The trade in land furs, an extension of the North West Company's operation in Athabasca, began in 1805 after the Nor'Westers absorbed the XY Company, releasing manpower, energy, and capital; and Simon McTavish, the powerful financial partner in Montréal who had long opposed Alexander Mackenzie's plans for expansion to the Pacific, had died. Simon Fraser crossed from the Peace River to the upper Fraser (pl 67 and established several posts in north central British Columbia some 5 000 km from Montréal, in an area the Nor'Westers called New Caledonia. The Indians whom the maritime fur traders contacted on the coast and the Nor'Westers met in the interior along the salmon rivers were primarily fishermen, not hunters. Culturally and linguistically they were exceedingly diverse (pl 66), and they were far more numerous than the Indians of the Canadian Shield or even those of the plains (pl 69).

By 1820 there had been almost 650 sailings to the northwest coast, most by Russian or American traders (pl 66). British traders were hampered in the China trade by the monopoly of the British East Indian Company, while Spaniards, who maintained a garrison at Nootka for several years, never tried to develop the sea-otter trade with China. At Nootka Spain attempted to assert control of the northwest coast of North America, but as the maritime fur trade gained in momentum, it became apparent that one small garrison could not defend the indented northwest coast of a continent. In 1795 the Spaniards withdrew to more congenial outposts in California, leaving in their eyes a dismal, rain-bound coast without resources. After Nootka there would be no European settlement in coastal British Columbia for more than 30 years, although there were Russian posts to the north and south - Sitka (1799) on the Alaskan panhandle and Fort Ross (1812) near San Francisco - and an American post, Astoria, at the mouth of the Columbia (1811). Maritime fur traders and Indians met at the trading places shown on plate 66, at first on the outer coast, later, as sea-otter pelts became scarce, in the intricate waterways off the inner coast. The maritime fur trade was a competitive scramble for a scarce resource. Both furs and the goods traded for them moved through well-developed pre-contact networks of native trade. Prices rose rapidly, the relative weath of some native groups increased, and overall much new wealth was introduced to the coast. So were European diseases and alcohol, although it is extremely difficult to assess their influence before 1820. Native life incorporated iron, firearms, and textiles and may otherwise have continued much as before. The northwest coast came into European focus - it had been magnificently chartered by Captain George Vancouver in 1792 and visited by hundreds of ships - but in the early 1820s, almost 50 years after the first Spanish voyages, no one of European background lived along it between Fort George at the mouth of the Columbia River and the Russian settlement at Sitka.

The land-based fur trade, in contrast, generated trading posts and limited but fairly permanent European settlement as soon as it crossed the continental divide. In 1808, when Simon Fraser descended the river named after him to its mouth, there were four posts in New Caledonia. Fraser, who thought he was on the Columbia River until he reached tidewater, had negotiated an intimidating canyon that could not become a regular canoe route; the posts of New Caledonia continued to depend on the canoe brigades that relayed supplies from Montréal. In 1811–12 John Jacob Astor's Pacific Fur Company, an American trading company more accustomed to the horse than the canoe, moved quickly to secure the trade of the Columbia basin. The Astorians sent a ship around the Horn and a party overland from the Missouri (by horse), built several posts in the Columbia basin (pl 66), established packhorse trails, and supplied their Columbian operations by sea.

They were well established on the Columbia in 1813 when, with Britain and the United States at war (the War of 1812) and news that a British warship was expected at the mouth of the Columbia, they withdrew. For the next eight years the land-based fur trades of the Columbia basin and of New Caledonia were monopolized by the North West Company. Facing no competition, the Nor'Westers operated only nine posts in the Cordillera in 1821 (pl 66). Their problems were otherwise: the vast distance from Montréal; an environment little suited to a transportation system that had developed around the edge of the Canadian Shield; Indians who were not reliable trappers or hunters (partly because Indian traders supplied them with goods from the coast). The company began to supply its Columbian operation by sea, began using pack horses and dugout canoes, and imported labour (Iroquois Indians, Hawaiian Islanders, and others) to form large trapping brigades. An overland connection the Astorians had discovered between the Columbia District and New Caledonia became a packhorse trail, and carried dispatches and some furs and supplies, making New Caledonia less dependent on its eastward connections. For the Nor'Westers these were bold innovations, but they did not make the Columbian trade profitable, and it remained a heavy financial drain on the company until the merger in 1821.

In 1755 the chief cartographer of the Ministère de la Marine in Paris, with access to the latest information from New France, left most of the area west of Lake Winnipeg blank on his map of North America (pl 36). 'We do not know,' noted Jacques-Nicolas Bellin cautiously in this space, 'whether there is land or sea in these parts.' But soon the matter was settled. The explorations of Samuel Hearne and Mackenzie to the Arctic Ocean and of Cook along the northwest coast established the outline of this quarter of the continent (pll 58, 67). Assisted by Indian guides and, frequently, by Indian maps (pl 59), Pond, Phillip Turnor, Peter Fidler, Fraser, David Thompson, and many others filled in details of the river systems. In 1795 the cartographer Aaron Arrowsmith in London, incorporating data from Vancouver's survey of the northwest coast and Mackenzie's journey to the Pacific, drew the first map that showed Hudson Bay, the Pacific Coast, the Rocky Mountains, and the main lakes and rivers of the northwestern interior in approximately their correct relative locations (pl 67). Arrowsmith tentatively connected the upper Fraser explored by Mackenzie with the mouth of the Columbia River, known by this time, and he had no data for many areas. In subsequent editions surmise gave way to fact and the blanks contracted, although when the Hudson's Bay Company and the North West Company merged in 1821 Europeans still had little knowledge of the area north of the Peace River and west of the Mackenzie River, of the High Arctic, of the lichen woodlands and tundra northwest of Hudson Bay, and even, away from the principal rivers of the Plains, of the northern grassland (pl 67).

But the broad axis of the western fur trade through the boreal forest and the parkland belt and on into the Cordillera was well known, as was most of the river-and-lake-strewn land east of Lake Winnipeg. Fur traders had travelled in these areas for years, building posts, dealing with natives, and shipping furs to Hudson Bay or Montréal. The northern edge of the French fur trade had been extended after New France fell, competing and eventually merging with the expanding trade from Hudson Bay. The spatial economy of the fur trade created a British presence in the West, and in 1818 when a convention between Great Britain and the United States established the 49th parallel from the Lake of the Woods to the Rocky Mountains as a northern boundary of the United States, that boundary marked, as much as any parallel of latitude could, the effective southern limit of the British fur trade in the northwestern interior of North America.

RUPERT'S LAND

Authors: Arthur J. Ray, D. Wayne Moodie, Conrad E. Heidenreich

In 1670 Charles II granted the Hudson's Bay Company exclusive trading privileges in the territory called Rupert's Land, the area drained by rivers flowing into Hudson Bay. At this time the English had no idea of the size of Rupert's Land and knew little about its geography.

Rupert's Land comprised several broadly different physiographic regions. The extensive marshy lowlands and slow-moving rivers around Hudson Bay and James Bay are rimmed by the rugged, ice-scoured, lake-filled mass of the Canadian Shield. Beyond the Shield lie the Great Lakes to the south and the northern plains to the west. This vast area was thinly populated by hunting and fishing peoples, principally Assiniboine, Cree, and Chipewyan in the interior, and Inuit around the northern margins of Hudson Bay. Biogeographic diversity encouraged regional economic specialization. People followed migratory game animals such as caribou and bison across ecological boundaries; in so doing they came in contact with other groups and engaged in trade.

With the establishment of the French on the St Lawrence and the English on Hudson Bay, two trading systems competed for the furs of Rupert's Land. By the 1750s the French operated a network of posts that extended as far west as the forks of the Saskatchewan River (pls 37–40), but they could not prevent some natives from trading at the English posts on Hudson Bay. For the Indians competition raised fur prices and provided alternative suppliers of European goods.

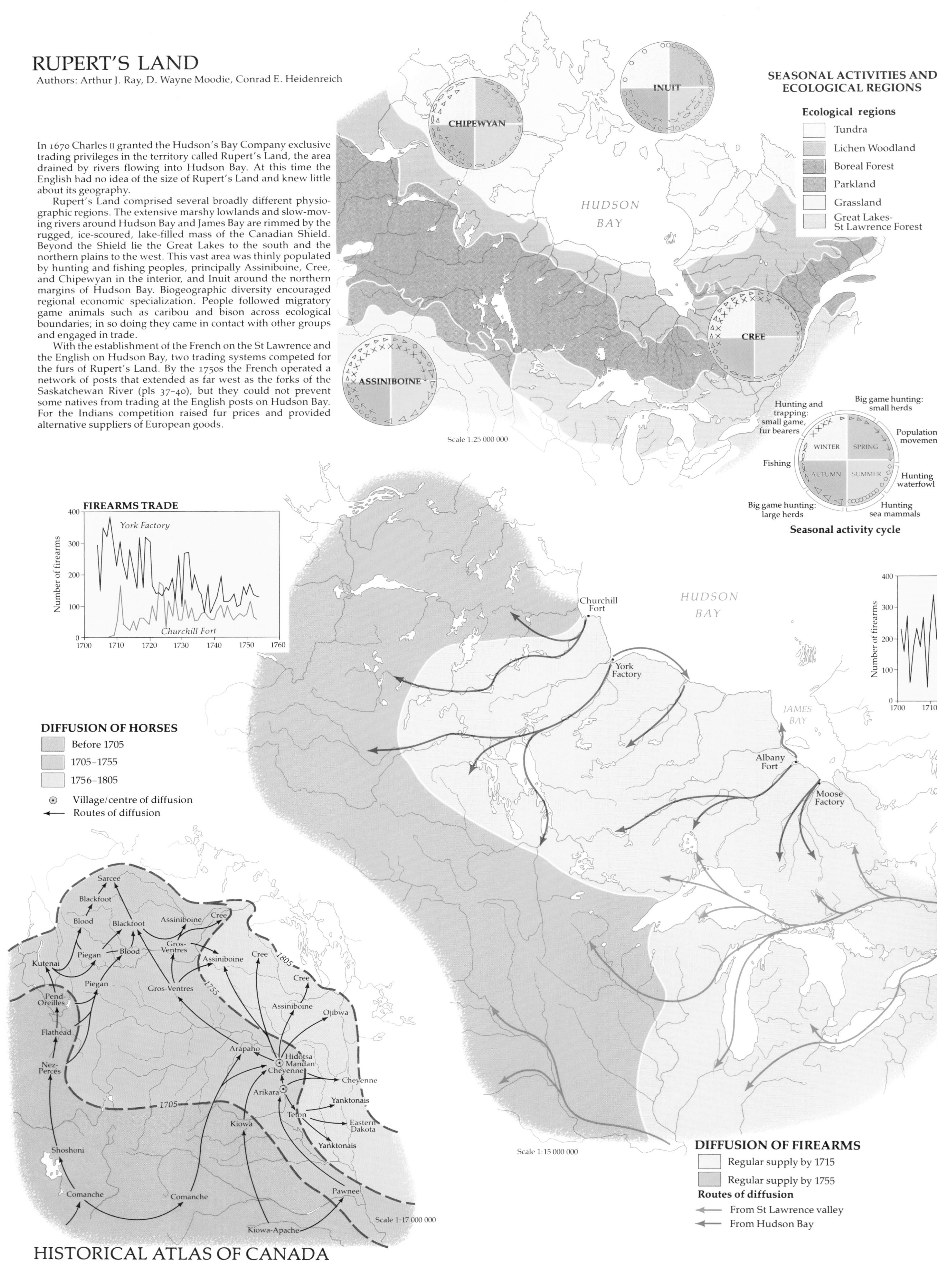
SEASONAL ACTIVITIES AND ECOLOGICAL REGIONS
Ecological regions
Tundra
Lichen Woodland
Boreal Forest
Parkland
Grassland
Great Lakes-St Lawrence Forest
CHIPEWYAN
INUIT
CREE
ASSINIBOINE
HUDSON BAY
Scale 1:25 000 000
Hunting and trapping: small game, fur bearers
Big game hunting: small herds
Population movement
WINTER
SPRING
AUTUMN
SUMMER
Fishing
Hunting waterfowl
Big game hunting: large herds
Hunting sea mammals
Seasonal activity cycle
FIREARMS TRADE
Number of firearms
400
300
200
100
0
1700
1710
1720
1730
1740
1750
1760
York Factory
Churchill Fort
DIFFUSION OF HORSES
Before 1705
1705–1755
1756–1805
Village/centre of diffusion
Routes of diffusion
Sarcee
Blackfoot
Blood
Blackfoot
Assiniboine
Cree
Gros-Ventres
Kutenai
Piegan
Blood
Assiniboine
Cree
1805
Piegan
Gros-Ventres
1755
Cree
Pend-Oreilles
Assiniboine
Ojibwa
Flathead
Arapaho
Hidotsa
Mandan
Nez-Percés
Cheyenne
Cheyenne
Arikara
1705
Yanktonais
Teton
Kiowa
Eastern Dakota
Yanktonais
Shoshoni
Comanche
Comanche
Pawnee
Kiowa-Apache
Scale 1:17 000 000
Churchill Fort
HUDSON BAY
York Factory
JAMES BAY
Albany Fort
Moose Factory
Scale 1:15 000 000
DIFFUSION OF FIREARMS
Regular supply by 1715
Regular supply by 1755
Routes of diffusion
From St Lawrence valley
From Hudson Bay

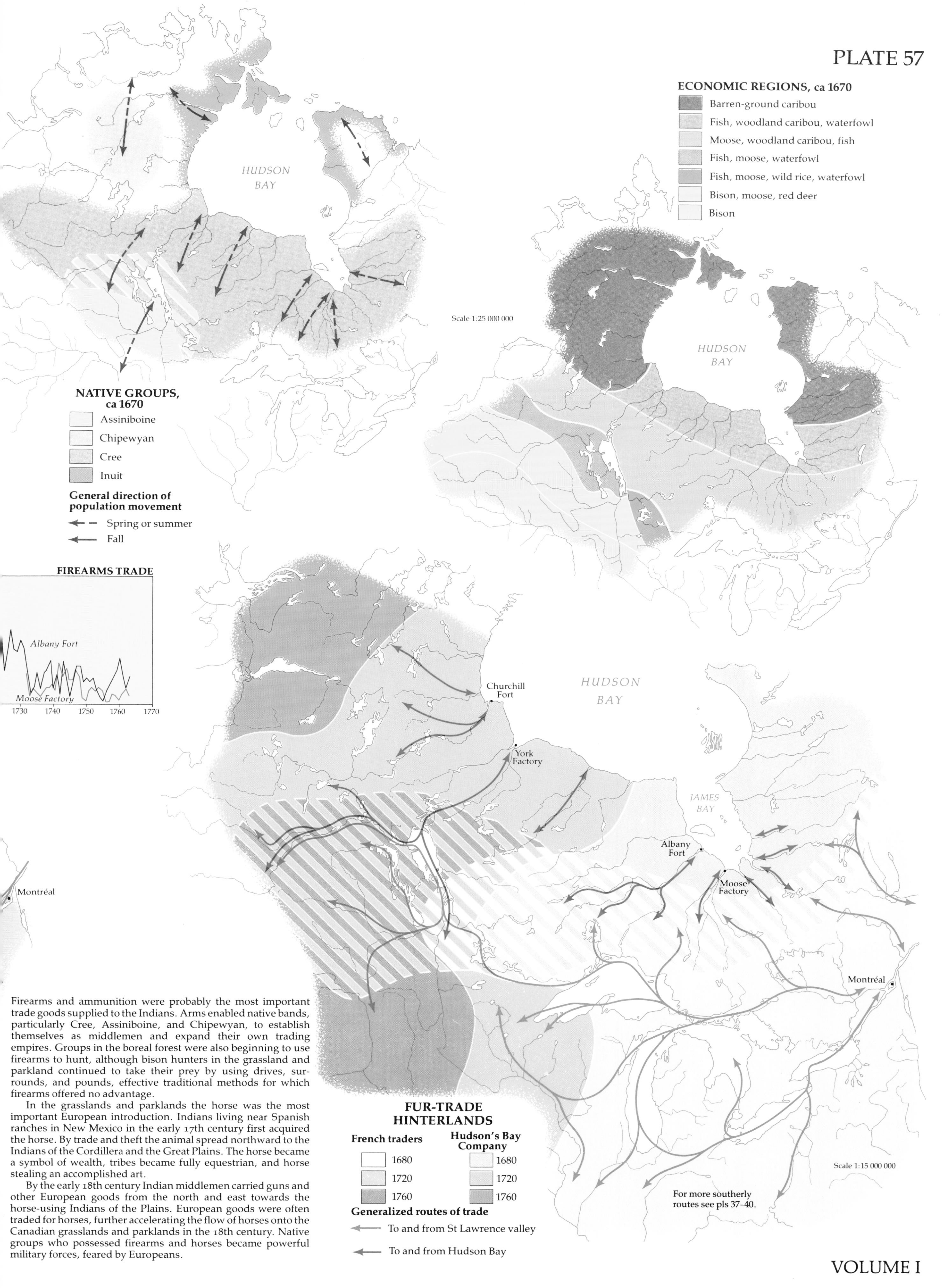
ECONOMIC REGIONS, ca 1670
Barren-ground caribou
Fish, woodland caribou, waterfowl
Moose, woodland caribou, fish
Fish, moose, waterfowl
Fish, moose, wild rice, waterfowl
Bison, moose, red deer
Bison
HUDSON BAY
Scale 1:25 000 000
NATIVE GROUPS, ca 1670
Assiniboine
Chipewyan
Cree
Inuit
General direction of population movement
Spring or summer
Fall
FIREARMS TRADE
Albany Fort
Moose Factory
1730
1740
1750
1760
1770
Montréal
Churchill Fort
York Factory
JAMES BAY
Albany Fort
Moose Factory
FUR-TRADE HINTERLANDS
French traders
Hudson's Bay Company
1680
1720
1760
Generalized routes of trade
To and from St Lawrence valley
To and from Hudson Bay
Scale 1:15 000 000
For more southerly routes see pls 37–40.

Firearms and ammunition were probably the most important trade goods supplied to the Indians. Arms enabled native bands, particularly Cree, Assiniboine, and Chipewyan, to establish themselves as middlemen and expand their own trading empires. Groups in the boreal forest were also beginning to use firearms to hunt, although bison hunters in the grassland and parkland continued to take their prey by using drives, surrounds, and pounds, effective traditional methods for which firearms offered no advantage.

In the grasslands and parklands the horse was the most important European introduction. Indians living near Spanish ranches in New Mexico in the early 17th century first acquired the horse. By trade and theft the animal spread northward to the Indians of the Cordillera and the Great Plains. The horse became a symbol of wealth, tribes became fully equestrian, and horse stealing an accomplished art.

By the early 18th century Indian middlemen carried guns and other European goods from the north and east towards the horse-using Indians of the Plains. European goods were often traded for horses, further accelerating the flow of horses onto the Canadian grasslands and parklands in the 18th century. Native groups who possessed firearms and horses became powerful military forces, feared by Europeans.

EXPLORATION FROM HUDSON BAY

Author: Richard I. Ruggles

Exploration of the interior was an intended by-product of the fur trades conducted out of Montréal and Hudson Bay. Traders from Montréal frequented Lake Winnipeg by the 1730s (pl 36), and established posts on the Saskatchewan River by the 1750s (pl 40). Although the Hudson's Bay Company did not open an interior trading post until 1774 (pl 62), as early as 1691 one of its young traders, Henry Kelsey, crossed the boreal forest and the parkland belt to reach the edge of the grasslands (pl 17), and then wintered with Indian bands on their trapping grounds. After 1754 HBC traders visited the parkland and grasslands annually; one of them, Anthony Henday, may have been the first European to see the Rocky Mountains from the Canadian plains.

In 1772 another HBC employee, Samuel Hearne, finally succeeded in crossing the barren ground to reach the Arctic Ocean at the mouth of the Coppermine River. He found native reports of rich deposits of copper to be greatly exaggerated, and demonstrated that there was not a water passage to the Pacific from Hudson Bay. Navigators had long probed the inlets of the northwestern bay, looking for such a passage (pl 19).

NORTON MAP, 1760

Moses Norton, a HBC trader at Fort Churchill, questioned Indians about their homelands when they came to trade. On the basis of their accounts and sketch maps he drafted a remarkably comprehensive map of northern Canada. The map shown here, a re-oriented and amended version of the original, suggests the identity of many geographical features.

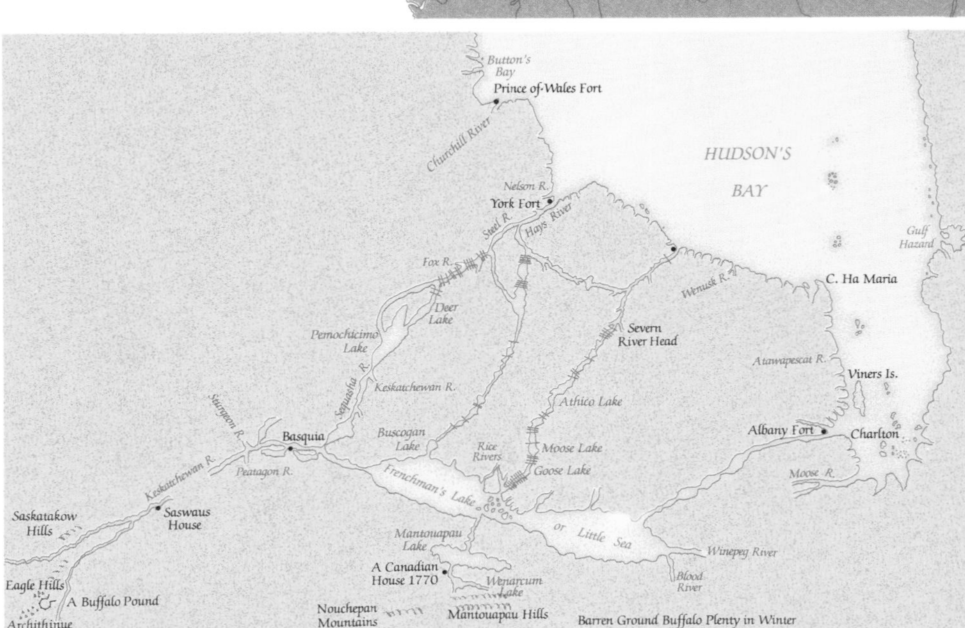
Button's Bay
Prince of-Wales Fort
Churchill River
HUDSON'S BAY
Nelson R.
York Fort
Steel R.
Hays River
Gulf Hazard
Fox R.
Deer Lake
Wenusk R.
C. Ha Maria
Pemochicimo Lake
Severn River Head
Keskatchewan R.
Atawapescat R.
Viners Is.
Athico Lake
Basquia
Buscogan Lake
Rice Rivers
Moose Lake
Goose Lake
Albany Fort
Charlton
Peatagon R.
Frenchman's Lake
Moose R.
Saskatakow Hills
Saswaus House
or Little Sea
Winepeg River
Mantouapau Lake
A Canadian House 1770
Weniacum Lake
Blood River
Eagle Hills
A Buffalo Pound
Nouchepan Mountains
Mantouapau Hills
Barren Ground Buffalo Plenty in Winter
Archithinue Tents

GRAHAM MAP, 1772–1774

Andrew Graham, a HBC trader at Fort York, collected geographical information from Indians and from company traders who wintered inland. This map, a composite of two of Graham's, draws particularly on William Tomison, who journeyed up the Severn River and across Lakes Winnipeg (Frenchman's Lake or Little Sea) to reach the grasslands in the Assiniboine valley; and on Matthew Cocking, who explored upstream from the forks of the Saskatchewan River and south through Eagle Hills.

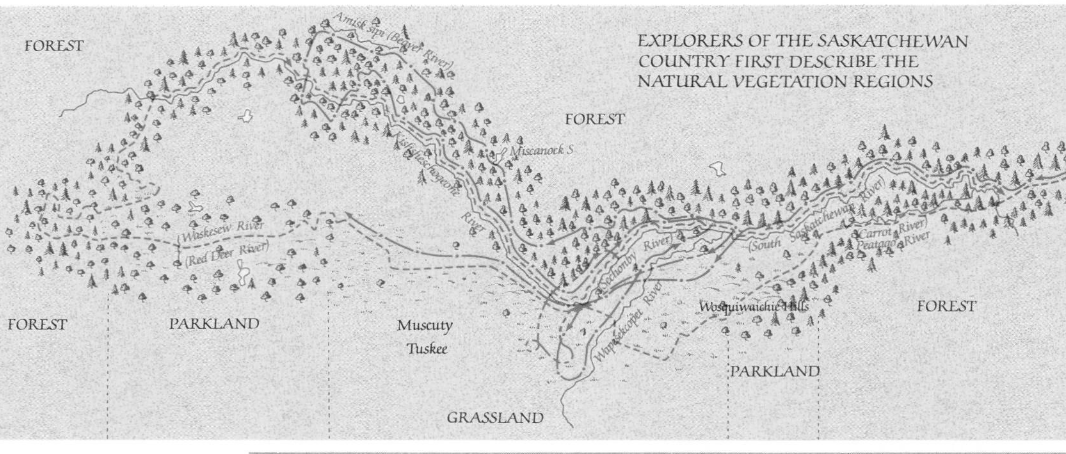
EXPLORERS OF THE SASKATCHEWAN COUNTRY FIRST DESCRIBE THE NATURAL VEGETATION REGIONS
FOREST
FOREST
FOREST
FOREST
PARKLAND
PARKLAND
GRASSLAND
Muscuty Tuskee
Waskesew River (Red Deer River)
Wisquiwatchie Hills
Carrot River
Amisk sepe (Beaver River)

Interpreted from Hudson's Bay Company explorers' journals

This map shows how HBC traders understood the Saskatchewan country in the early 1770s, by which time many of them had penetrated the region by canoe or on foot. Some (notably Kelsey, Henday, Pink, and Cocking) kept daily journals and made regular environmental notations. Henday, who in 1754–5 was perhaps the first European trader to traverse the regions between northern Manitoba and the foothills of the Rocky Mountains, lived with Indians and relied on Indian guides; he left the most comprehensive survey.

Scale 1:12 500 000

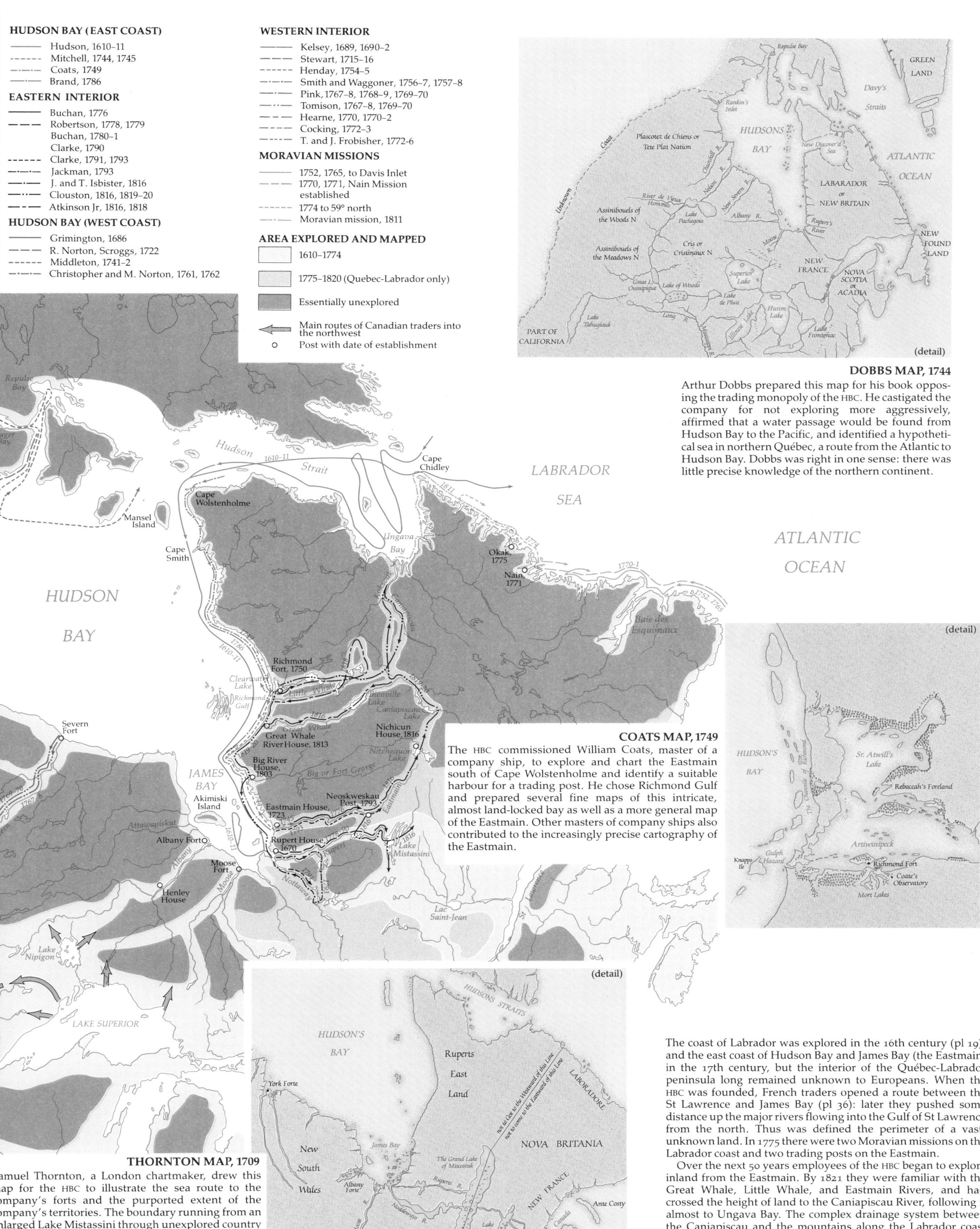
HUDSON BAY (EAST COAST)
Hudson, 1610-11
Mitchell, 1744, 1745
Coats, 1749
Brand, 1786
EASTERN INTERIOR
Buchan, 1776
Robertson, 1778, 1779
Buchan, 1780-1
Clarke, 1790
Clarke, 1791, 1793
Jackman, 1793
J. and T. Isbister, 1816
Clouston, 1816, 1819-20
Atkinson Jr, 1816, 1818
HUDSON BAY (WEST COAST)
Grimington, 1686
R. Norton, Scroggs, 1722
Middleton, 1741-2
Christopher and M. Norton, 1761, 1762
WESTERN INTERIOR
Kelsey, 1689, 1690-2
Stewart, 1715-16
Henday, 1754-5
Smith and Waggoner, 1756-7, 1757-8
Pink, 1767-8, 1768-9, 1769-70
Tomison, 1767-8, 1769-70
Hearne, 1770, 1770-2
Cocking, 1772-3
T. and J. Frobisher, 1772-6
MORAVIAN MISSIONS
1752, 1765, to Davis Inlet
1770, 1771, Nain Mission established
1774 to 59° north
Moravian mission, 1811
AREA EXPLORED AND MAPPED
1610-1774
1775-1820 (Quebec-Labrador only)
Essentially unexplored
Main routes of Canadian traders into the northwest
Post with date of establishment
Hudson Strait
Cape Chidley
LABRADOR SEA
ATLANTIC OCEAN
Cape Wolstenholme
Mansel Island
Cape Smith
Ungava Bay
Okak, 1775
Nain, 1771
HUDSON BAY
Baie des Esquimaux
Richmond Fort, 1750
Clearwater Lake
Richmond Gulf
Bienville Lake
Caniapiscau Lake
Severn Fort
Great Whale River House, 1813
Nichicun House, 1816
Big River House, 1803
JAMES BAY
Akimiski Island
Eastmain House, 1723
Neoskweskau Post, 1793
Albany Fort
Rupert House, 1670
Lake Mistassini
Moose Fort
Henley House
Lac Saint-Jean
Lake Nipigon
LAKE SUPERIOR
(detail)

DOBBS MAP, 1744

Arthur Dobbs prepared this map for his book opposing the trading monopoly of the HBC. He castigated the company for not exploring more aggressively, affirmed that a water passage would be found from Hudson Bay to the Pacific, and identified a hypothetical sea in northern Québec, a route from the Atlantic to Hudson Bay. Dobbs was right in one sense: there was little precise knowledge of the northern continent.

COATS MAP, 1749

The HBC commissioned William Coats, master of a company ship, to explore and chart the Eastmain south of Cape Wolstenholme and identify a suitable harbour for a trading post. He chose Richmond Gulf and prepared several fine maps of this intricate, almost land-locked bay as well as a more general map of the Eastmain. Other masters of company ships also contributed to the increasingly precise cartography of the Eastmain.

THORNTON MAP, 1709

Samuel Thornton, a London chartmaker, drew this map for the HBC to illustrate the sea route to the company's forts and the purported extent of the company's territories. The boundary running from an enlarged Lake Mistassini through unexplored country was proposed by the company but resolutely rejected by the French. In 1709 there had been no detailed exploration of the Eastmain north of the Big River.

The coast of Labrador was explored in the 16th century (pl 19), and the east coast of Hudson Bay and James Bay (the Eastmain) in the 17th century, but the interior of the Québec-Labrador peninsula long remained unknown to Europeans. When the HBC was founded, French traders opened a route between the St Lawrence and James Bay (pl 36): later they pushed some distance up the major rivers flowing into the Gulf of St Lawrence from the north. Thus was defined the perimeter of a vast, unknown land. In 1775 there were two Moravian missions on the Labrador coast and two trading posts on the Eastmain.

Over the next 50 years employees of the HBC began to explore inland from the Eastmain. By 1821 they were familiar with the Great Whale, Little Whale, and Eastmain Rivers, and had crossed the height of land to the Caniapiscau River, following it almost to Ungava Bay. The complex drainage system between the Caniapiscau and the mountains along the Labrador coast was not entered until later.

INDIAN MAPS

Author: D. Wayne Moodie

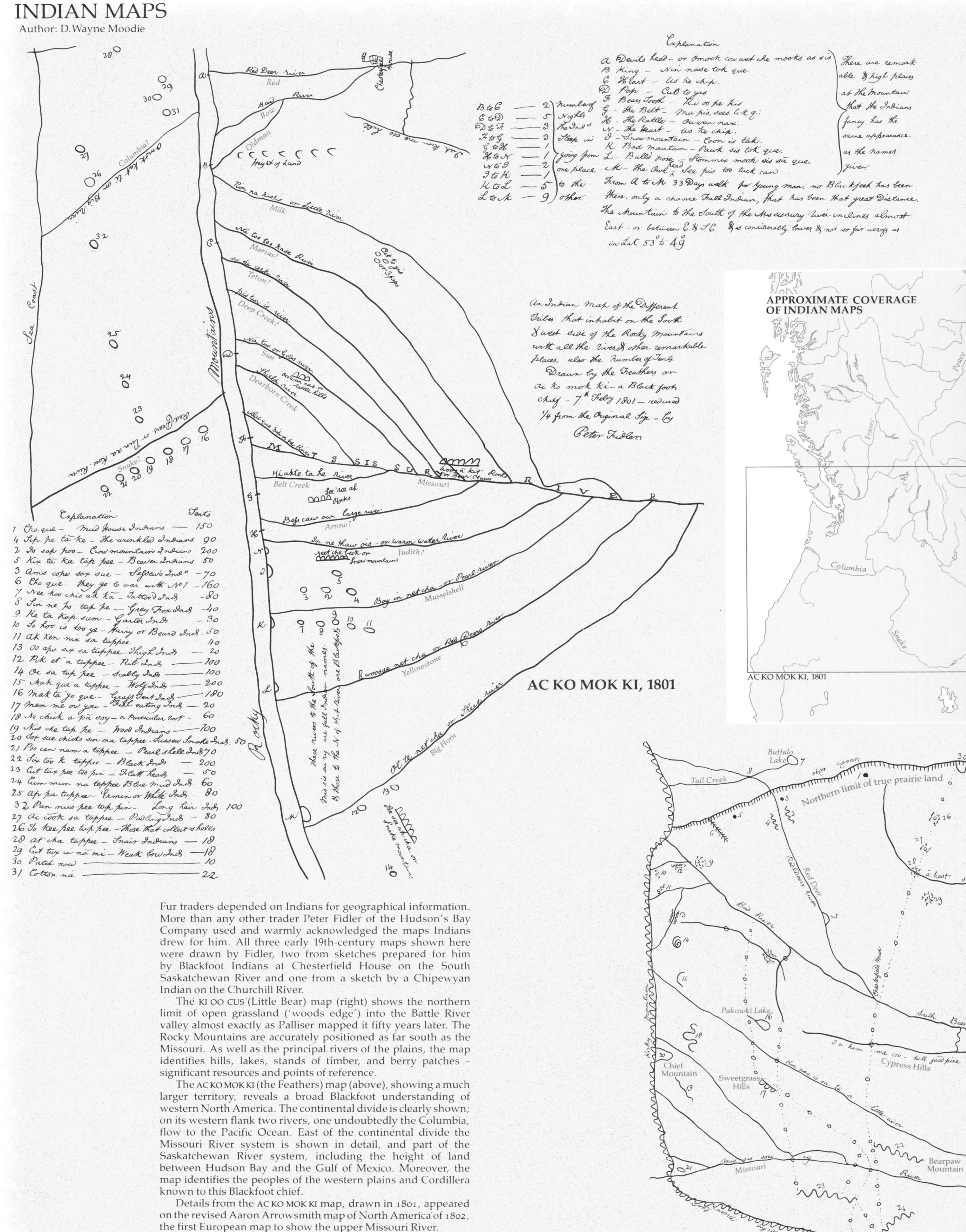
Red
Bow
Oldman
Milk
Marias?
Teton?
Deep Creek?
Sun
Dearborn Creek
Belt Creek
Missouri
Arrow?
Judith?
Musselshell
Yellowstone
Big Horn
Columbia?
Snake?
APPROXIMATE COVERAGE OF INDIAN MAPS
Peace
Fraser
Columbia
Snake
AC KO MOK KI, 1801
Buffalo Lake
Tail Creek
Northern limit of true prairie land
Red Deer
Pakowki Lake
Chief Mountain
Sweetgrass Hills
Cypress Hills
Bearpaw Mountain
Missouri

AC KO MOK KI, 1801

Fur traders depended on Indians for geographical information. More than any other trader Peter Fidler of the Hudson's Bay Company used and warmly acknowledged the maps Indians drew for him. All three early 19th-century maps shown here were drawn by Fidler, two from sketches prepared for him by Blackfoot Indians at Chesterfield House on the South Saskatchewan River and one from a sketch by a Chipewyan Indian on the Churchill River.

The KI OO CUS (Little Bear) map (right) shows the northern limit of open grassland ('woods edge') into the Battle River valley almost exactly as Palliser mapped it fifty years later. The Rocky Mountains are accurately positioned as far south as the Missouri. As well as the principal rivers of the plains, the map identifies hills, lakes, stands of timber, and berry patches – significant resources and points of reference.

The AC KO MOK KI (the Feathers) map (above), showing a much larger territory, reveals a broad Blackfoot understanding of western North America. The continental divide is clearly shown; on its western flank two rivers, one undoubtedly the Columbia, flow to the Pacific Ocean. East of the continental divide the Missouri River system is shown in detail, and part of the Saskatchewan River system, including the height of land between Hudson Bay and the Gulf of Mexico. Moreover, the map identifies the peoples of the western plains and Cordillera known to this Blackfoot chief.

Details from the AC KO MOK KI map, drawn in 1801, appeared on the revised Aaron Arrowsmith map of North America of 1802, the first European map to show the upper Missouri River.

The COT AW NEY YAZ ZAH map, drawn by a Chipewyan Indian in 1810, provides essential information for canoe travel between the Churchill River and Lake Athabasca. As is typical of Indian route maps, scale is exaggerated to clarify important connections, such as the major portage from Deers River (Mudjatik River) across the height of land between Hudson Bay and the Arctic Ocean. The recommended route to Black Lake from Indian Lake (Cree Lake) is down the swiftly flowing Indian River (Cree River). The return route avoids this strong current and follows a double backway to Trout Lake (Weitzel Lake) and thence to Indian Lake. Woodland Indians frequently used such indirect backways to avoid dangers or to reduce travel time and toil.

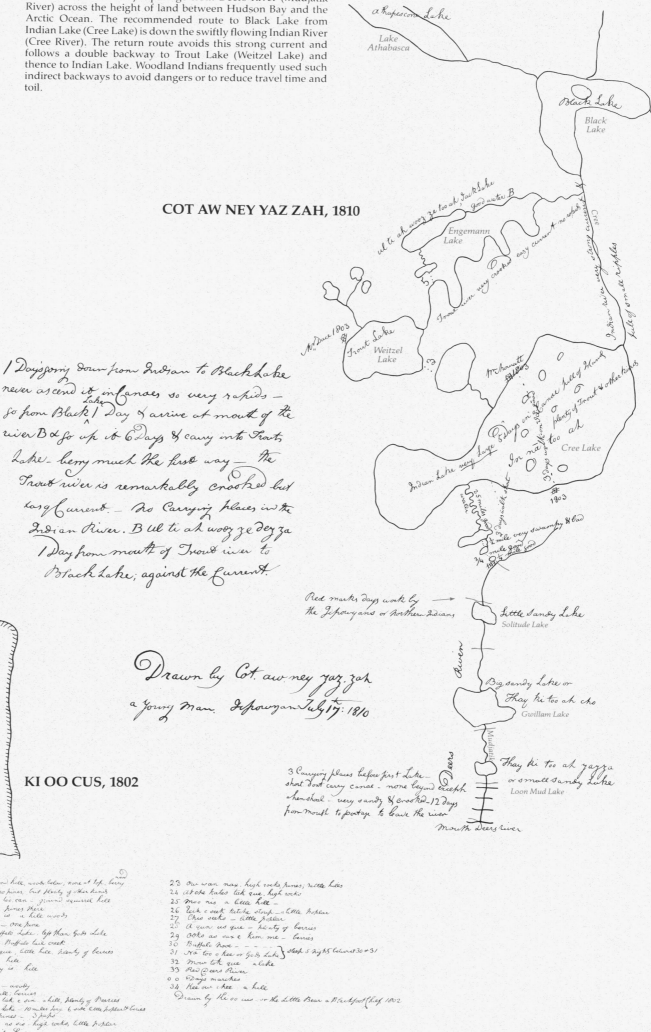

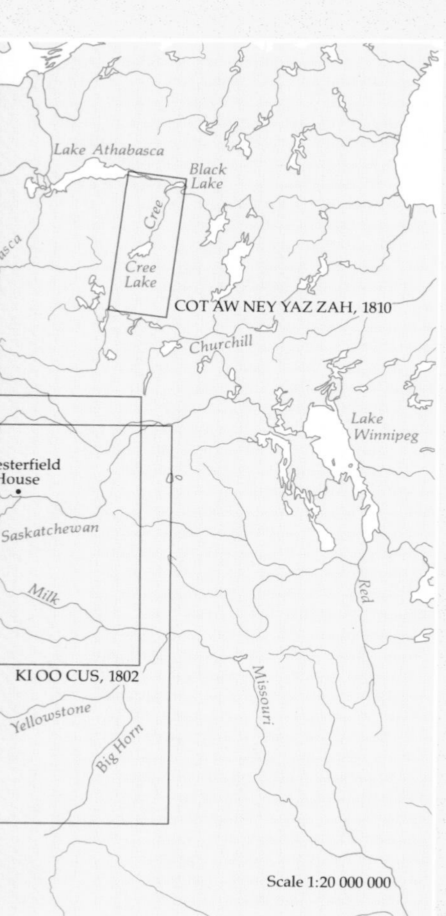
Lake Athabasca
Black Lake
Cree
Cree Lake
COT AW NEY YAZ ZAH, 1810
Churchill
Lake Winnipeg
Saskatchewan
Milk
Red
Missouri
KI OO CUS, 1802
Yellowstone
Big Horn
Scale 1:20 000 000

COT AW NEY YAZ ZAH, 1810

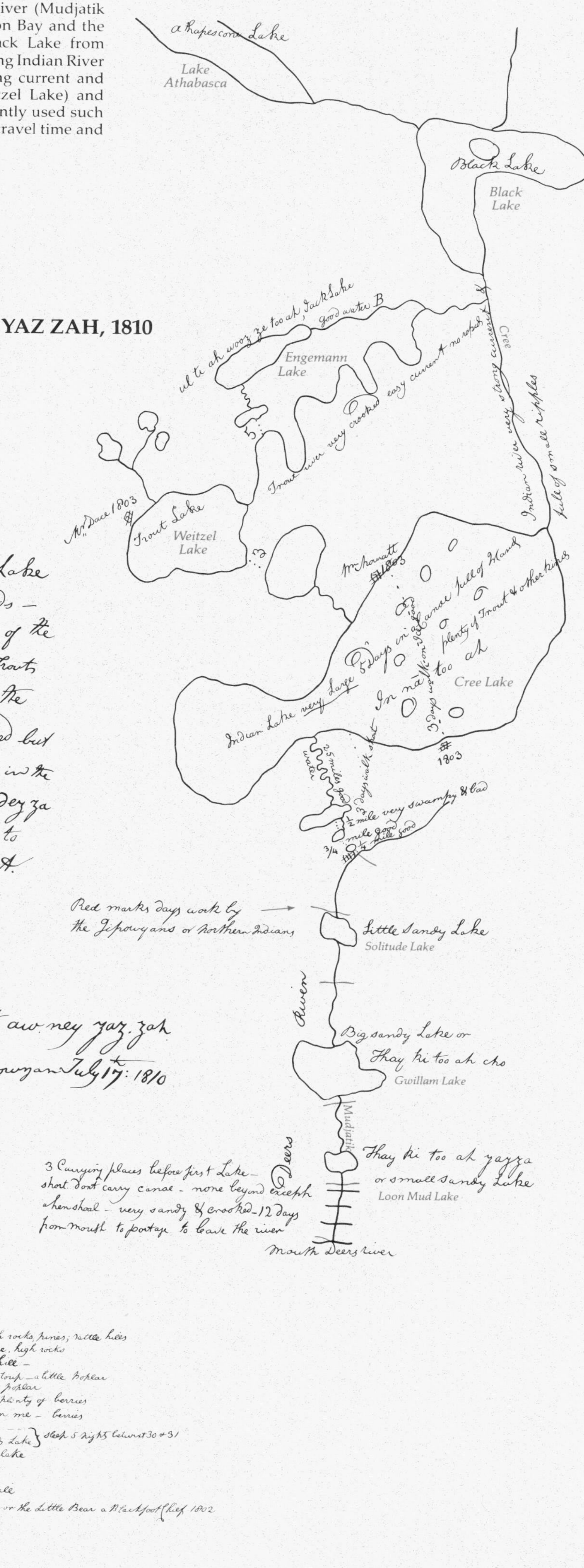
a Rapescon Lake
Lake Athabasca
Black Lake
Black Lake
ul ti ah wooz ze too ah, Sack Lake
good water B
Engemann Lake
Cree
Trout river very crooked easy current no rapids
Indian river very strong current
full of small rapples
Mr. Dace 1803
Trout Lake
Weitzel Lake
Mr. Harratt 1803
5 Days in a Canoe full of Island
plenty of Trout & other fishes
In na thee too ah
Cree Lake
Indian Lake very large
1803
1/2 mile very swampy & bad
Red marks days work by the Jepowyans or Northern Indians
Little Sandy Lake
Solitude Lake
River
Big sandy Lake or Thay ki too ah cho
Gwillam Lake
Mudjatik
Deers
Thay ki too ah yazza or small Sandy Lake
Loon Mud Lake
3 Carrying places before first Lake – short dont carry canoe – none beyond except shenshoal – very sandy & crooked – 12 days from mouth to portage to leave the river
Mouth Deers river

1 Days going down from Indian to Black Lake never ascend it in Canoes so very rapids – go from Black Lake 1 Day & arrive at mouth of the river B & go up it 6 Days & carry into Trout Lake – berry much the first way – the Trout river is remarkably crooked but easy Current. – No Carrying places in the Indian River. B ul ti ah wooz ze dez za 1 Day from mouth of Trout river to Black Lake; against the Current.

Drawn by Cot. aw ney yaz. zah a Young Man. Jepowyan July 17: 1810

KI OO CUS, 1802

Manito Lake

Sounding Lake

on Snake river

Gods Lake

Manito Lake enlargement

South Saskatchewan

1 Can ne wa see, around hill, woods below, none at top, berry wood
2 OO chis chis hill no pines, but plenty of other kinds
3 O mock wa ut tow too can – ground squirrel hill
4 Kee keep a hill, pines there
5 Hay now too can is a hill woods
6 Nee too luck keps – one pine
7 E new o kee, Buffalo Lake, less than Gods Lake
8 E new oo suy yis Buffalo tail creek
9 Caw sapis spatche que, little hill, plenty of berries
10 nee coo lux que – hill
11 Koos, caw pus. suy is hill
12 Spitcheyie
13 A kane us que – woody
14 Moo coo wans – hill; berries
15 ak ken ne kin ne tak e sin a hill, plenty of Berries
16 Pock a kee – stinking Lake – 10 miles long. 6 side little poplar & berries
17 Coch to yis – good pines – 3 paps
18 Pit chicks in ooks as sis high rocks, little poplar
19 OO saks. Rocks high, Pines
20 Nin nase tok que the King
21 Is se cut to yis
22 Ki oochis – Bears Paw. high rocks, Pines
23 Ow wan nax, high rocks, pines; rattle hills
24 At che kates tak que, high rocks
25 Moo nis a little hill –
26 Eech e seek kitche stoup – a little poplar
27 Chis seeks – little poplar
28 A qun us que – plenty of berries
29 Ooks as sax e kim me – berries
30 Buffalo Nose – – – – –
31 Na too o kee or Gods Lake } sleep 5 nights betwixt 30 & 31
32 Mow tok que a lake
33 Red Deers River
o o Days marches
34 Kee ow chee a hill

Drawn by Ki oo cus or the Little Bear a Blackfoot Chief 1802

BAYSIDE TRADE, 1720–1780

Author: Arthur J. Ray

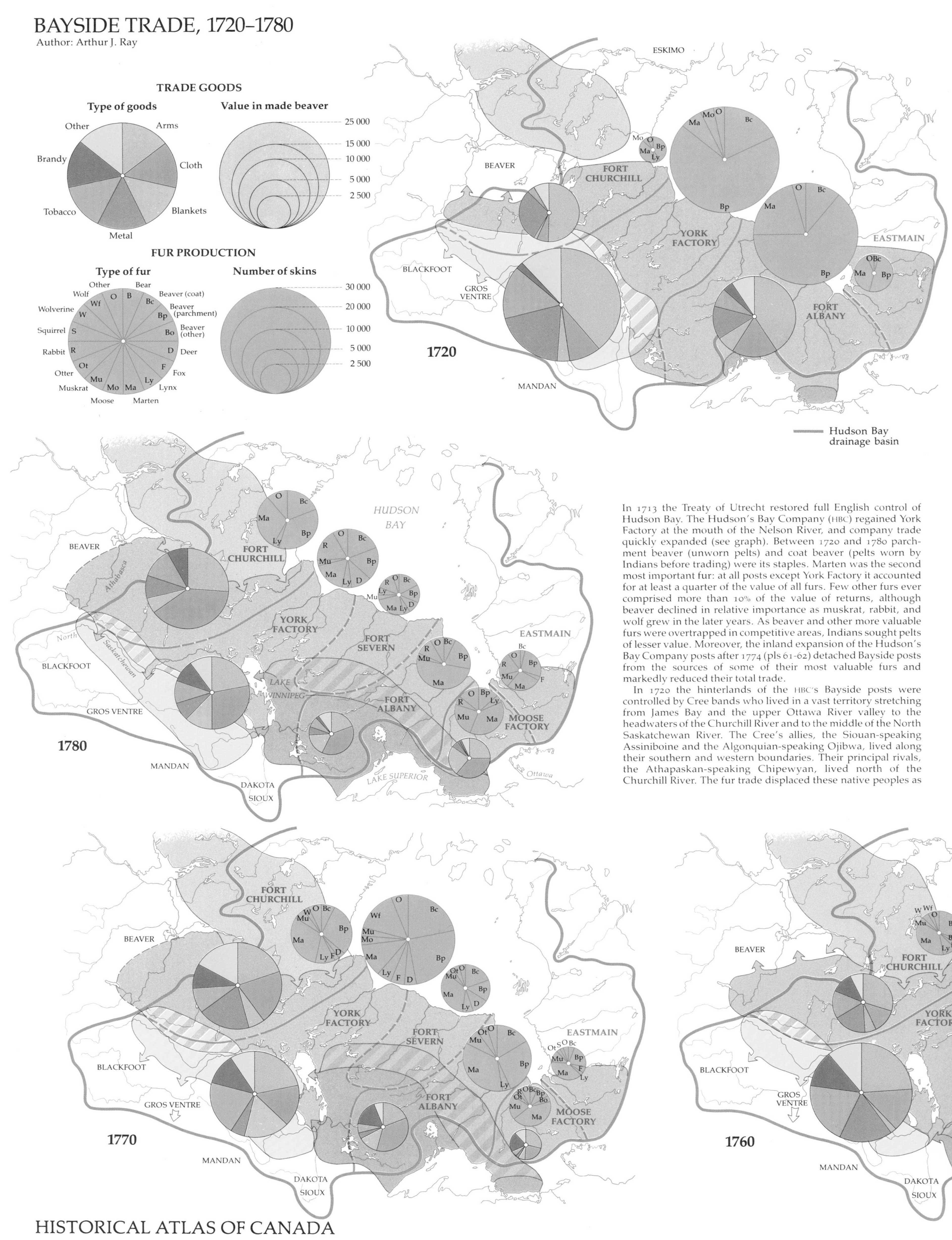
TRADE GOODS
Type of goods
Other
Arms
Brandy
Cloth
Tobacco
Blankets
Metal
Value in made beaver
25 000
15 000
10 000
5 000
2 500
FUR PRODUCTION
Type of fur
Other
Bear
Wolf
Beaver (coat)
Beaver (parchment)
Wolverine
Squirrel
Beaver (other)
Rabbit
Deer
Otter
Fox
Muskrat
Lynx
Moose
Marten
Number of skins
30 000
20 000
10 000
5 000
2 500
ESKIMO
BEAVER
FORT CHURCHILL
YORK FACTORY
EASTMAIN
BLACKFOOT
GROS VENTRE
FORT ALBANY
MANDAN
1720
Hudson Bay drainage basin
HUDSON BAY
Athabasca
North Saskatchewan
FORT SEVERN
LAKE WINNIPEG
MOOSE FACTORY
LAKE SUPERIOR
Ottawa
DAKOTA SIOUX
1780
1770
1760

In 1713 the Treaty of Utrecht restored full English control of Hudson Bay. The Hudson's Bay Company (HBC) regained York Factory at the mouth of the Nelson River, and company trade quickly expanded (see graph). Between 1720 and 1780 parchment beaver (unworn pelts) and coat beaver (pelts worn by Indians before trading) were its staples. Marten was the second most important fur: at all posts except York Factory it accounted for at least a quarter of the value of all furs. Few other furs ever comprised more than 10% of the value of returns, although beaver declined in relative importance as muskrat, rabbit, and wolf grew in the later years. As beaver and other more valuable furs were overtrapped in competitive areas, Indians sought pelts of lesser value. Moreover, the inland expansion of the Hudson's Bay Company posts after 1774 (pls 61-62) detached Bayside posts from the sources of some of their most valuable furs and markedly reduced their total trade.

In 1720 the hinterlands of the HBC's Bayside posts were controlled by Cree bands who lived in a vast territory stretching from James Bay and the upper Ottawa River valley to the headwaters of the Churchill River and to the middle of the North Saskatchewan River. The Cree's allies, the Siouan-speaking Assiniboine and the Algonquian-speaking Ojibwa, lived along their southern and western boundaries. Their principal rivals, the Athapaskan-speaking Chipewyan, lived north of the Churchill River. The fur trade displaced these native peoples as

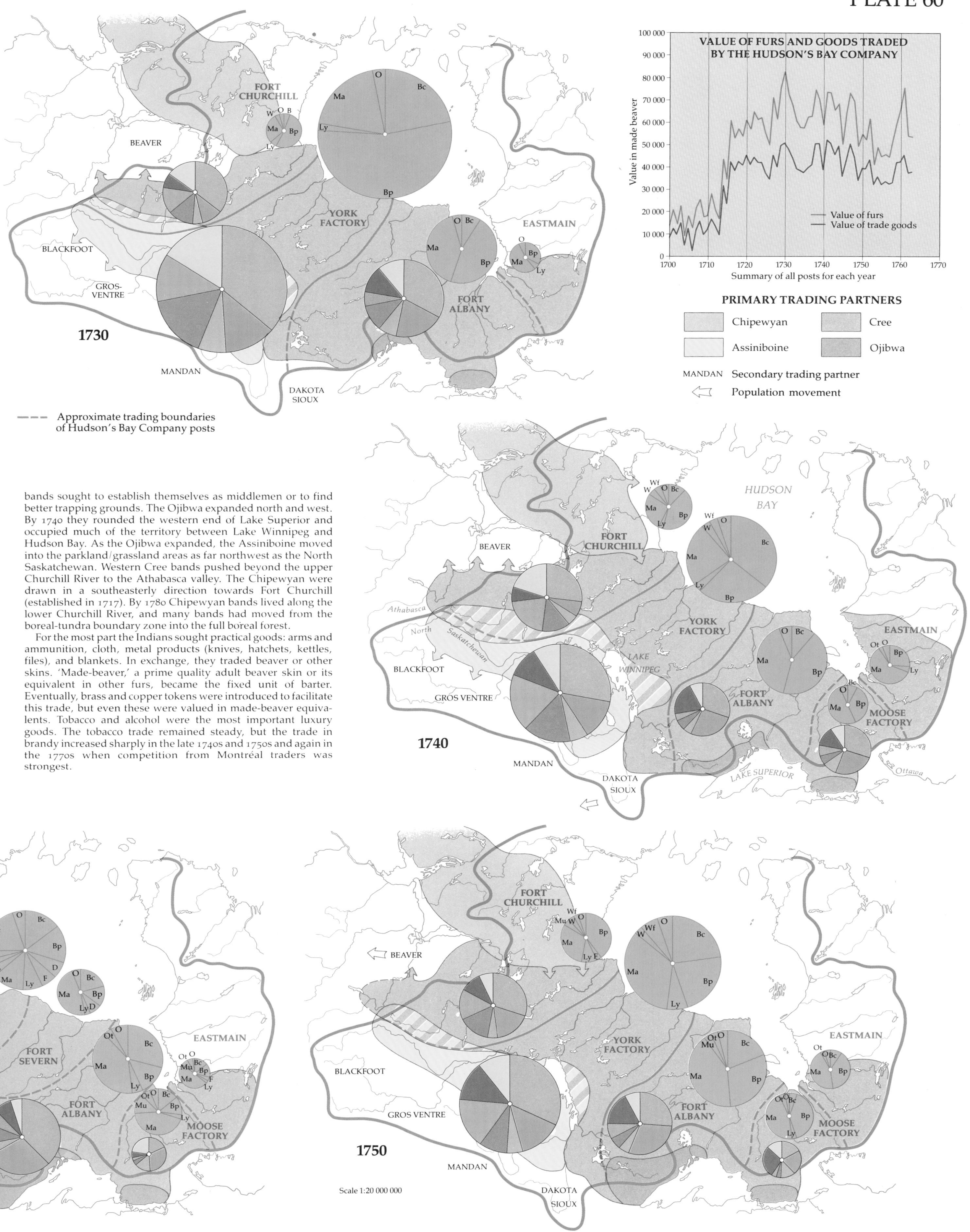
VALUE OF FURS AND GOODS TRADED BY THE HUDSON'S BAY COMPANY
Value in made beaver
Value of furs
Value of trade goods
Summary of all posts for each year
PRIMARY TRADING PARTNERS
Chipewyan
Cree
Assiniboine
Ojibwa
MANDAN Secondary trading partner
Population movement
Approximate trading boundaries of Hudson's Bay Company posts
1730
1740
1750
FORT CHURCHILL
YORK FACTORY
FORT ALBANY
EASTMAIN
MOOSE FACTORY
FORT SEVERN
BEAVER
BLACKFOOT
GROS VENTRE
MANDAN
DAKOTA SIOUX
HUDSON BAY
LAKE WINNIPEG
LAKE SUPERIOR
Athabasca
North Saskatchewan
Ottawa
Scale 1:20 000 000

bands sought to establish themselves as middlemen or to find better trapping grounds. The Ojibwa expanded north and west. By 1740 they rounded the western end of Lake Superior and occupied much of the territory between Lake Winnipeg and Hudson Bay. As the Ojibwa expanded, the Assiniboine moved into the parkland/grassland areas as far northwest as the North Saskatchewan. Western Cree bands pushed beyond the upper Churchill River to the Athabasca valley. The Chipewyan were drawn in a southeasterly direction towards Fort Churchill (established in 1717). By 1780 Chipewyan bands lived along the lower Churchill River, and many bands had moved from the boreal-tundra boundary zone into the full boreal forest.

For the most part the Indians sought practical goods: arms and ammunition, cloth, metal products (knives, hatchets, kettles, files), and blankets. In exchange, they traded beaver or other skins. 'Made-beaver,' a prime quality adult beaver skin or its equivalent in other furs, became the fixed unit of barter. Eventually, brass and copper tokens were introduced to facilitate this trade, but even these were valued in made-beaver equivalents. Tobacco and alcohol were the most important luxury goods. The tobacco trade remained steady, but the trade in brandy increased sharply in the late 1740s and 1750s and again in the 1770s when competition from Montréal traders was strongest.

COMPETITION AND CONSOLIDATION, 1760–1825

Authors: D. Wayne Moodie, Victor P. Lytwyn, Barry Kaye, Arthur J. Ray

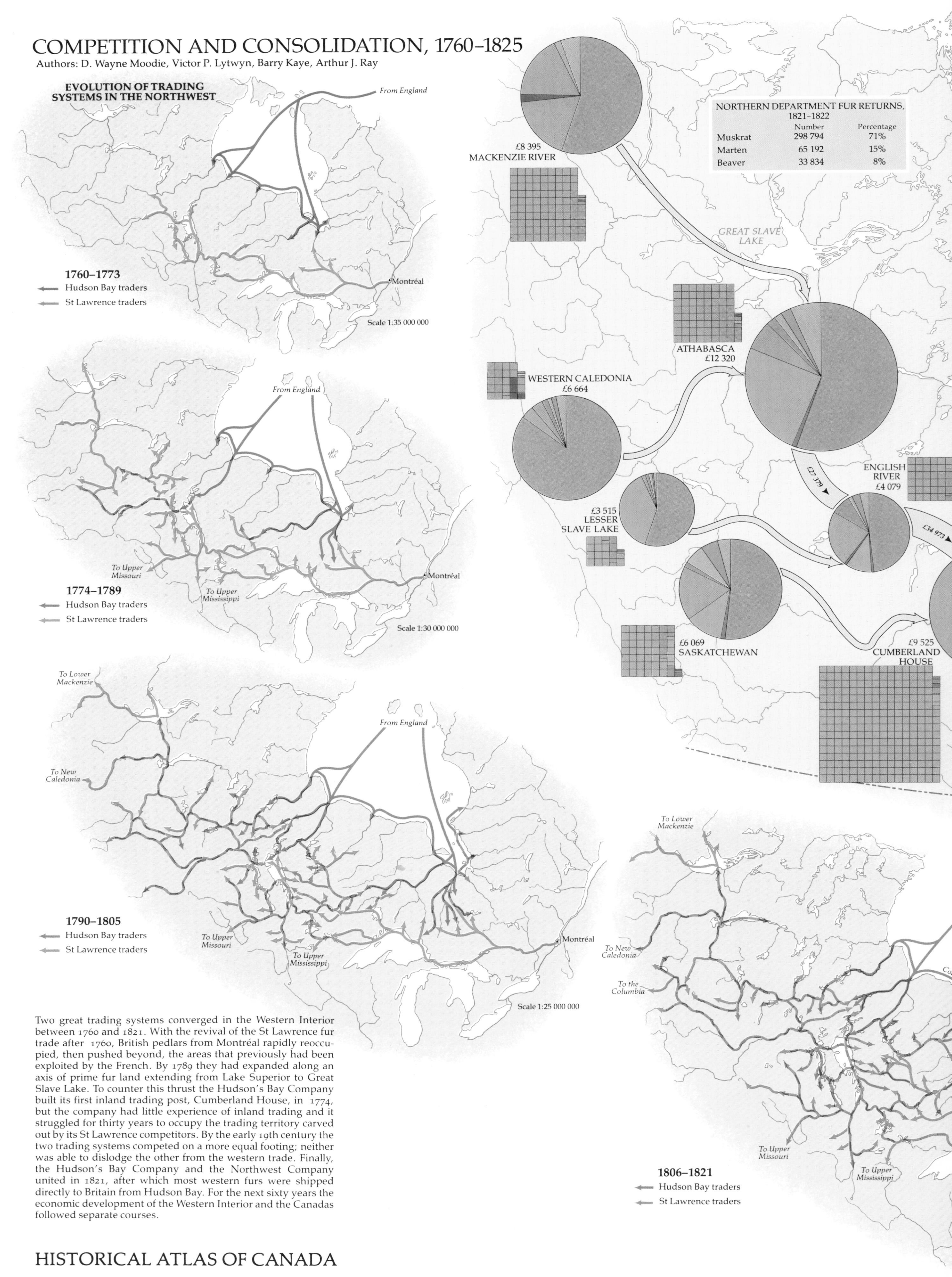

EVOLUTION OF TRADING SYSTEMS IN THE NORTHWEST
From England
1760–1773
Hudson Bay traders
St Lawrence traders
Montréal
Scale 1:35 000 000
From England
To Upper Missouri
To Upper Mississippi
1774–1789
Hudson Bay traders
St Lawrence traders
Montréal
Scale 1:30 000 000
To Lower Mackenzie
To New Caledonia
From England
To Upper Missouri
To Upper Mississippi
1790–1805
Hudson Bay traders
St Lawrence traders
Montréal
Scale 1:25 000 000
To Lower Mackenzie
To New Caledonia
To the Columbia
To Upper Missouri
To Upper Mississippi
1806–1821
Hudson Bay traders
St Lawrence traders
NORTHERN DEPARTMENT FUR RETURNS, 1821–1822
Number
Percentage
Muskrat 298 794 71%
Marten 65 192 15%
Beaver 33 834 8%
£8 395
MACKENZIE RIVER
GREAT SLAVE LAKE
ATHABASCA
£12 320
WESTERN CALEDONIA
£6 664
ENGLISH RIVER
£4 079
£27 379
£34 973
£3 515
LESSER SLAVE LAKE
£6 069
SASKATCHEWAN
£9 525
CUMBERLAND HOUSE

Two great trading systems converged in the Western Interior between 1760 and 1821. With the revival of the St Lawrence fur trade after 1760, British pedlars from Montréal rapidly reoccupied, then pushed beyond, the areas that previously had been exploited by the French. By 1789 they had expanded along an axis of prime fur land extending from Lake Superior to Great Slave Lake. To counter this thrust the Hudson's Bay Company built its first inland trading post, Cumberland House, in 1774, but the company had little experience of inland trading and it struggled for thirty years to occupy the trading territory carved out by its St Lawrence competitors. By the early 19th century the two trading systems competed on a more equal footing; neither was able to dislodge the other from the western trade. Finally, the Hudson's Bay Company and the Northwest Company united in 1821, after which most western furs were shipped directly to Britain from Hudson Bay. For the next sixty years the economic development of the Western Interior and the Canadas followed separate courses.

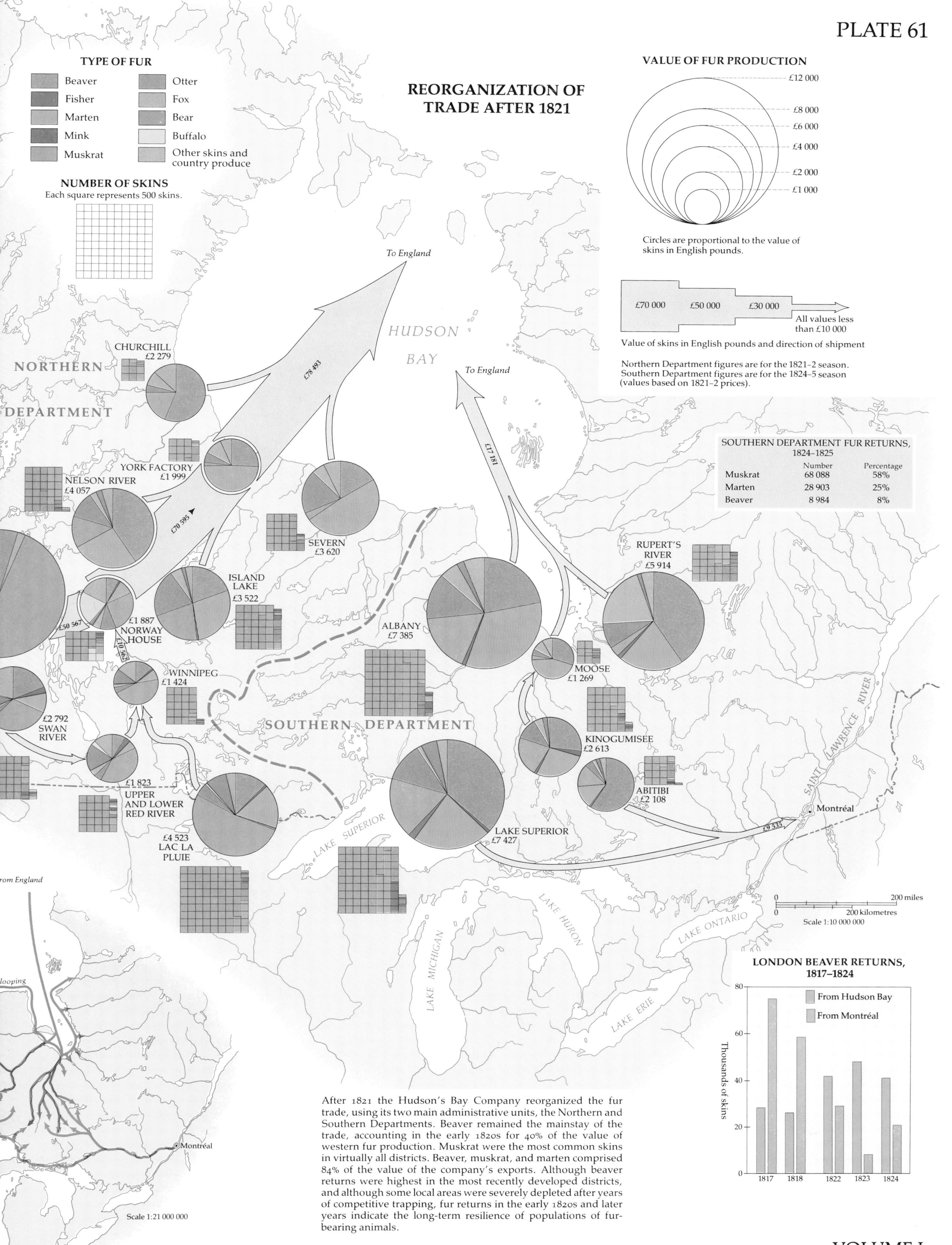
REORGANIZATION OF TRADE AFTER 1821
TYPE OF FUR
Beaver
Fisher
Marten
Mink
Muskrat
Otter
Fox
Bear
Buffalo
Other skins and country produce
NUMBER OF SKINS
Each square represents 500 skins.
VALUE OF FUR PRODUCTION
£12 000
£8 000
£6 000
£4 000
£2 000
£1 000
Circles are proportional to the value of skins in English pounds.
£70 000
£50 000
£30 000
All values less than £10 000
Value of skins in English pounds and direction of shipment
Northern Department figures are for the 1821–2 season. Southern Department figures are for the 1824–5 season (values based on 1821–2 prices).
SOUTHERN DEPARTMENT FUR RETURNS, 1824–1825
Number
Percentage
Muskrat 68 088 58%
Marten 28 903 25%
Beaver 8 984 8%
To England
To England
HUDSON BAY
NORTHERN DEPARTMENT
SOUTHERN DEPARTMENT
CHURCHILL £2 279
£78 493
YORK FACTORY £1 999
NELSON RIVER £4 057
£70 595
SEVERN £3 620
ISLAND LAKE £3 522
£1 887 NORWAY HOUSE
£50 567
£10 562
WINNIPEG £1 424
£2 792 SWAN RIVER
£1 823 UPPER AND LOWER RED RIVER
£4 523 LAC LA PLUIE
ALBANY £7 385
£17 181
RUPERT'S RIVER £5 914
MOOSE £1 269
KINOGUMISEE £2 613
ABITIBI £2 108
LAKE SUPERIOR £7 427
£9 535
Montréal
SAINT LAWRENCE RIVER
LAKE SUPERIOR
LAKE MICHIGAN
LAKE HURON
LAKE ERIE
LAKE ONTARIO
0 200 miles
0 200 kilometres
Scale 1:10 000 000
From England
Slooping
Montréal
Scale 1:21 000 000
LONDON BEAVER RETURNS, 1817–1824
From Hudson Bay
From Montréal
Thousands of skins
80
60
40
20
0
1817
1818
1822
1823
1824

After 1821 the Hudson's Bay Company reorganized the fur trade, using its two main administrative units, the Northern and Southern Departments. Beaver remained the mainstay of the trade, accounting in the early 1820s for 40% of the value of western fur production. Muskrat were the most common skins in virtually all districts. Beaver, muskrat, and marten comprised 84% of the value of the company's exports. Although beaver returns were highest in the most recently developed districts, and although some local areas were severely depleted after years of competitive trapping, fur returns in the early 1820s and later years indicate the long-term resilience of populations of fur-bearing animals.

TRADING POSTS, 1774–1821

Authors: D. Wayne Moodie, Victor P. Lytwyn, Barry Kaye

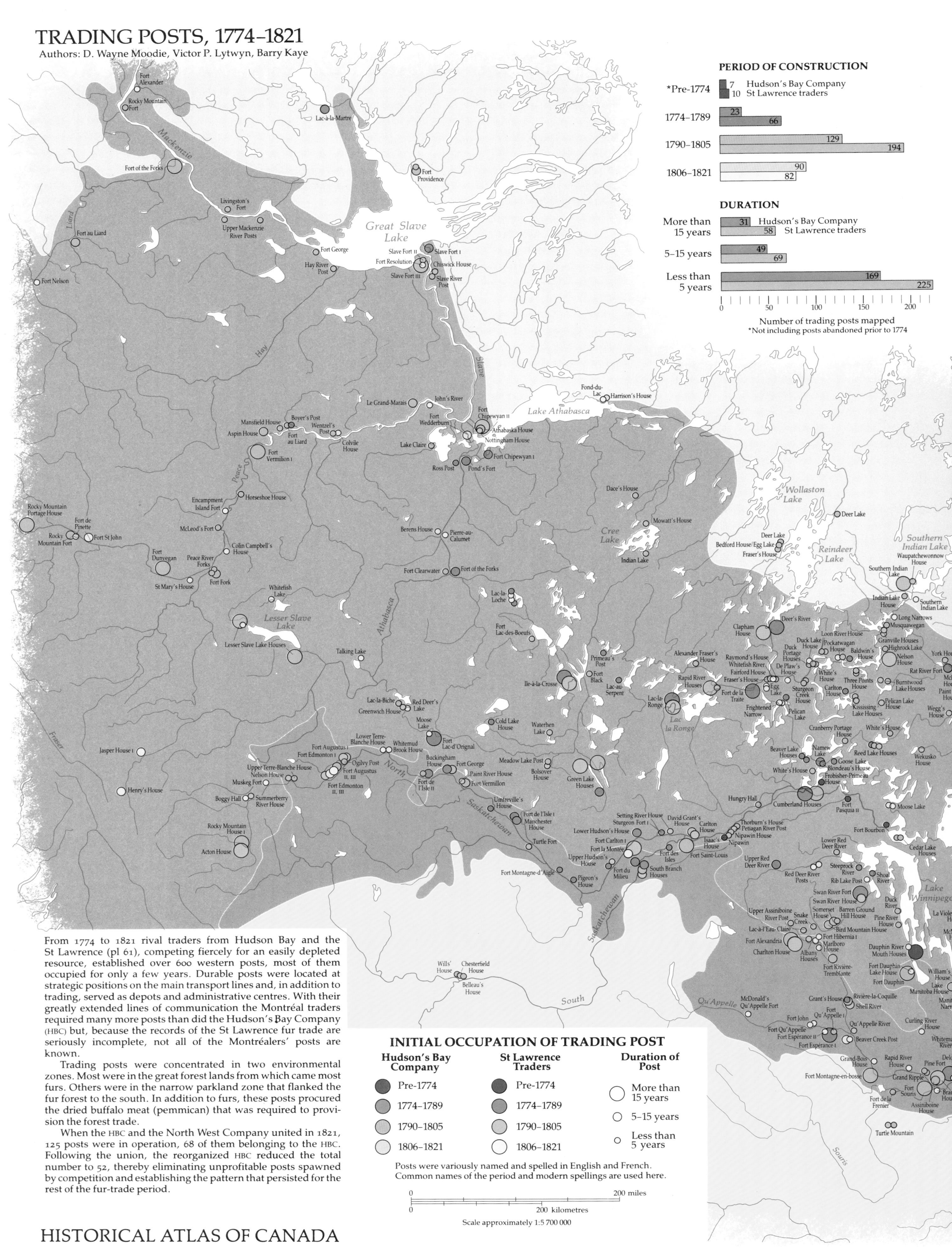
PERIOD OF CONSTRUCTION
*Pre-1774 7 Hudson's Bay Company 10 St Lawrence traders
1774–1789 23 66
1790–1805 129 194
1806–1821 90 82
DURATION
More than 15 years 31 Hudson's Bay Company 58 St Lawrence traders
5–15 years 49 69
Less than 5 years 169 225
0 50 100 150 200
Number of trading posts mapped
*Not including posts abandoned prior to 1774
INITIAL OCCUPATION OF TRADING POST
Hudson's Bay Company
St Lawrence Traders
Duration of Post
Pre-1774
1774–1789
1790–1805
1806–1821
More than 15 years
5–15 years
Less than 5 years
Posts were variously named and spelled in English and French. Common names of the period and modern spellings are used here.
0 200 miles
0 200 kilometres
Scale approximately 1:5 700 000
Fort Alexander
Rocky Mountain Fort
Lac-à-la-Martre
Mackenzie
Fort of the Forks
Fort Providence
Livingston's Fort
Upper Mackenzie River Posts
Great Slave Lake
Liard
Fort au Liard
Fort George
Hay River Post
Slave Fort II
Slave Fort I
Fort Resolution
Chiswick House
Slave Fort III
Slave River Post
Fort Nelson
Hay
Slave
Fond-du-Lac
Harrison's House
Lake Athabasca
Le Grand-Marais
John's River
Fort Chipewyan II
Fort Wedderburn
Athabaska House
Nottingham House
Mansfield House
Boyer's Post
Wentzel's Post
Aspin House
Fort au Liard
Colvile House
Lake Claire
Fort Vermilion I
Fort Chipewyan I
Ross Post
Pond's Fort
Peace
Dace's House
Wollaston Lake
Deer Lake
Encampment Island Fort
Horseshoe House
Rocky Mountain Portage House
Fort de Pinette
Rocky Mountain Fort
Fort St John
McLeod's Fort
Berens House
Pierre-au-Calumet
Mowatt's House
Cree Lake
Indian Lake
Deer Lake
Bedford House/Egg Lake
Fraser's House
Reindeer Lake
Southern Indian Lake
Waupatchewonnow House
Colin Campbell's House
Fort Dunvegan
Peace River Forks
Fort Fork
St Mary's House
Fort Clearwater
Fort of the Forks
Southern Indian Lake
Indian Lake House
Southern Indian Lake
Whitefish Lake
Lac-la-Loche
Athabasca
Lesser Slave Lake
Lesser Slave Lake Houses
Fort Lac-des-Boeufs
Talking Lake
Long Narrows
Musquawegan
Clapham House
Deer's River
Loon River House
Duck Lake House
Pockatwagan House
Granville Houses
Highrock Lake
Duck Portage Houses
Baldwin's House
York House
Nelson House
Alexander Fraser's House
Primeau's Post
Raymond's House
Whitefish River
Fairford House
Fraser's House
De Plaw's House
White's House
Three Points House
Rat River Fort
Burntwood Lake Houses
Ile-à-la-Crosse
Fort Black
Lac-au-Serpent
Rapid River Houses
Fort de la Traite
Egg Lake
Sturgeon Creek House
Carlton House
Pelican Lake House
Lac-la-Ronge
Frightened Narrow
Pelican Lake
Kississing Lake Houses
Wegg's House
Lac-la-Biche
Greenwich House
Red Deer's Lake
Moose Lake
Fort Lac-d'Orignal
Cold Lake House
Waterhen Lake
Lac la Ronge
Cranberry Portage House
White's House
Fraser
Jasper House I
Lower Terre-Blanche House
Whitemud Brook House
Fort Augustus I
Fort Edmonton I
Ogilvy Post
Fort Augustus II, III
Upper Terre-Blanche House
Nelson House
Fort Edmonton II, III
Muskeg Fort
Buckingham House
Fort George
Paint River House
Fort Vermillon
Fort de l'Isle II
North
Meadow Lake Post
Bolsover House
Green Lake Houses
Beaver Lake Houses
Namew Lake
Reed Lake Houses
Goose Lake
Blondeau's House
Wekusko House
White's House
Frobisher-Primeau House
Henry's House
Boggy Hall
Summerberry River House
Saskatchewan
Umfreville's House
Fort de l'Isle I
Manchester House
Hungry Hall
Cumberland Houses
Fort Pasquia II
Moose Lake
Rocky Mountain House I
Acton House
Turtle Fort
Setting River House
Sturgeon Fort I
David Grant's House
Carlton House
Thorburn's House
Petiagan River Post
Nipawin House
Nipawin
Lower Hudson's House
Fort Carlton I
Fort la Montée
Isaac's House
Fort Saint-Louis
Fort des Isles
Fort Bourbon
Lower Red Deer River
Cedar Lake Houses
Upper Hudson's House
Fort du Milieu
South Branch Houses
Upper Red Deer River
Steeprock River
Fort Montagne-d'Aigle
Pigeon's House
Red Deer River Posts
Rib Lake Post
Shoal River
Lake Winnipeg
Swan River Fort
Swan River House
Duck River
Upper Assiniboine River Post
Snake Creek
Somerset House
Barren Ground Hill House
La Violette
Pine River House
Lac-à-l'Eau-Claire
Bird Mountain House
Fort Alexandria
Fort Hibernia I
Marlboro House
Charlton House
Albany Houses
Dauphin River Mouth Houses
Saskatchewan
Wills' House
Chesterfield House
Belleau's House
Fort Rivière-Tremblante
Fort Dauphin Lake House
Fort Dauphin
William's House
Lake Manitoba House
South
Qu'Appelle
McDonald's Qu'Appelle Fort
Grant's House
Rivière-la-Coquille
Shell River
Fort Qu'Appelle I
Fort John
Fort Qu'Appelle
Fort Espérance II
Qu'Appelle River
Curling River House
Fort Espérance I
Beaver Creek Post
Grand-Bois House
Rapid River House
Pine Fort
Fort Montagne-en-bosse
Grand Ripple
Fort de la Frenier
Fort Souris
Assiniboine House
Turtle Mountain
Souris

From 1774 to 1821 rival traders from Hudson Bay and the St Lawrence (pl 61), competing fiercely for an easily depleted resource, established over 600 western posts, most of them occupied for only a few years. Durable posts were located at strategic positions on the main transport lines and, in addition to trading, served as depots and administrative centres. With their greatly extended lines of communication the Montréal traders required many more posts than did the Hudson's Bay Company (HBC) but, because the records of the St Lawrence fur trade are seriously incomplete, not all of the Montréalers' posts are known.

Trading posts were concentrated in two environmental zones. Most were in the great forest lands from which came most furs. Others were in the narrow parkland zone that flanked the fur forest to the south. In addition to furs, these posts procured the dried buffalo meat (pemmican) that was required to provision the forest trade.

When the HBC and the North West Company united in 1821, 125 posts were in operation, 68 of them belonging to the HBC. Following the union, the reorganized HBC reduced the total number to 52, thereby eliminating unprofitable posts spawned by competition and establishing the pattern that persisted for the rest of the fur-trade period.

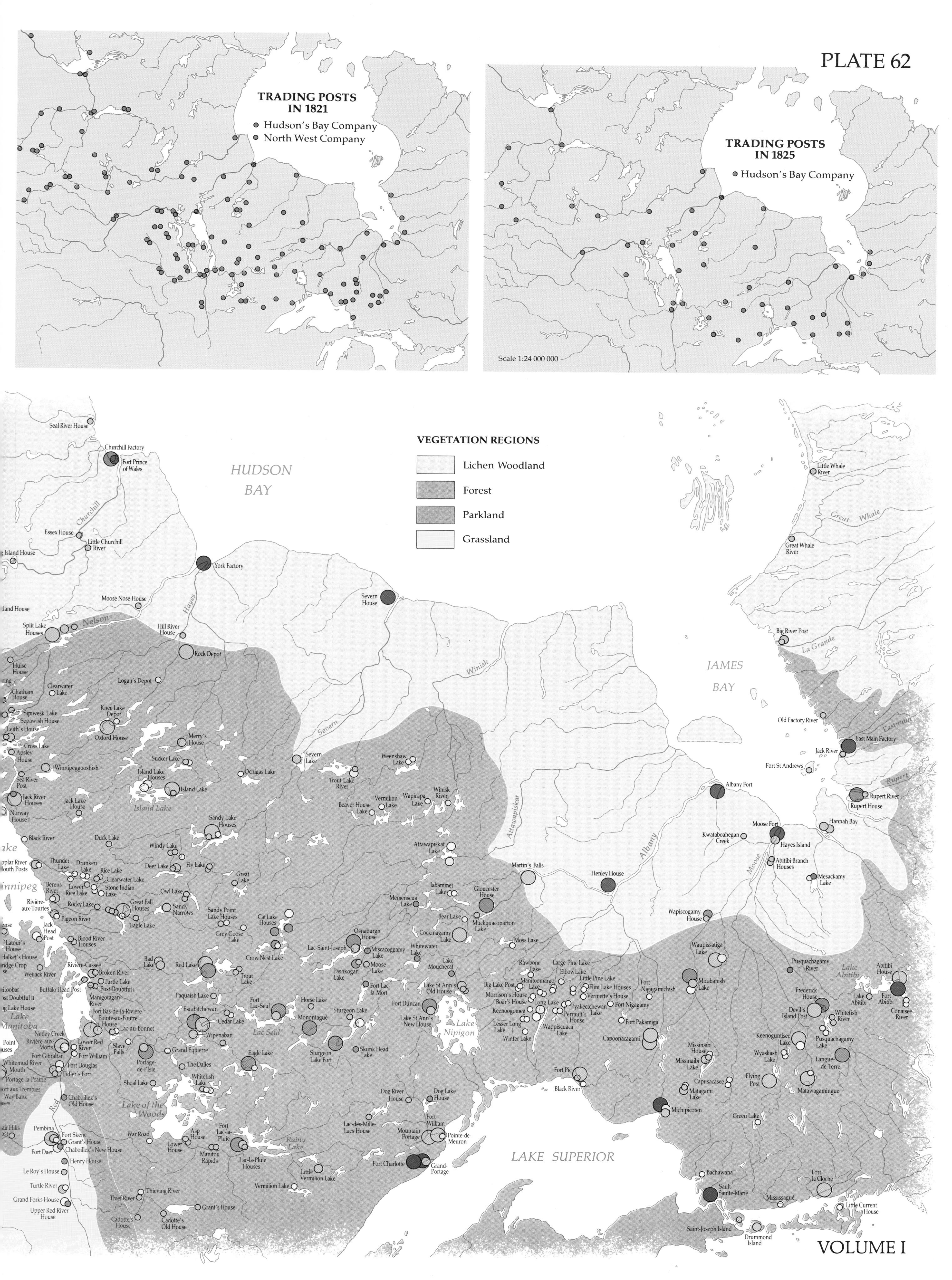
TRADING POSTS IN 1821
Hudson's Bay Company
North West Company
TRADING POSTS IN 1825
Hudson's Bay Company
Scale 1:24 000 000
VEGETATION REGIONS
Lichen Woodland
Forest
Parkland
Grassland
HUDSON BAY
JAMES BAY
LAKE SUPERIOR
Lake Winnipeg
Lake Manitoba
Lake Nipigon
Lake Abitibi
Island Lake
Lac Seul
Lake of the Woods
Rainy Lake
Churchill
Nelson
Hayes
Severn
Winisk
Attawapiskat
Albany
Moose
Red
La Grande
Great Whale
Eastmain
Rupert
Seal River House
Churchill Factory
Fort Prince of Wales
Essex House
Little Churchill River
York Factory
Moose Nose House
Split Lake Houses
Hill River House
Rock Depot
Hulse House
Clearwater Lake
Chatham House
Logan's Depot
Sipiwesk Lake
Sepawish House
Knee Lake Depot
Oxford House
Leith's House
Cross Lake
Apsley House
Merry's House
Sucker Lake
Winnipeggooshish
Ochigas Lake
Island Lake Houses
Island Lake
Sea River Post
Jack River Houses
Jack Lake House
Norway House
Black River
Duck Lake
Sandy Lake Houses
Windy Lake
Deer Lake
Fly Lake
Thunder Lake
Drunken Lake
Rice Lake
Clearwater Lake
Berens River
Lower Rice Lake
Stone Indian Lake
Great Lake
Owl Lake
Rivière-aux-Tourtes
Rocky Lake
Great Fall Houses
Eagle Lake
Sandy Narrows
Pigeon River
Sandy Point Lake Houses
Jack Head Post
Blood River Houses
Grey Goose Lake
Cat Lake Houses
Latour's House
Halket's House
Weijack River
Rivière-Cassée
Broken River
Turtle Lake
Post Doubtful I
Buffalo Head Post
Bad Lake
Red Lake
Trout Lake
Crow Nest Lake
Manigotagan River
Fort Bas-de-la-Rivière
Pointe-au-Foutre House
Lac-du-Bonnet
Paquaish Lake
Escabitchewan
Cedar Lake
Fort Lac-Seul
Wipenaban
Netley Creek
Rivière-aux-Morts
Lower Red River
Fort Gibraltar
Fort William
Fort Douglas
Fidler's Fort
Whitemud River Mouth
Portage-la-Prairie
Slave Falls
Portage-de-l'Isle
Grand Equierre
The Dalles
Eagle Lake
Shoal Lake
Whitefish Lake
Chaboillez's Old House
Pembina
Fort Skene
Grant's House
Chaboillez's New House
Fort Daer
Henry House
Le Roy's House
Turtle River
Grand Forks House
Upper Red River House
War Road
Asp House
Lower House
Fort Lac-la-Pluie
Manitou Rapids
Lac-la-Pluie Houses
Thieving River
Thiel River
Grant's House
Cadotte's House
Cadotte's Old House
Severn House
Severn Lake
Weenshaw Lake
Trout Lake River
Beaver House Lake
Vermilion Lake
Wapicapa Lake
Winisk River
Attawapiskat Lake
Iabammet Lake
Gloucester House
Memenscua Lake
Bear Lake
Muckquacoparton Lake
Cockinagamy Lake
Osnaburgh House
Lac-Saint-Joseph
Miscacoggamy Lake
Whitewater Lake
Pashkogan Lake
Moose Lake
Lake Mouchecat
Fort Lac-la-Mort
Lake St Ann's Old House
Horse Lake
Fort Duncan
Monontagué
Sturgeon Lake
Lake St Ann's New House
Sturgeon Lake Fort
Skunk Head Lake
Dog River House
Dog Lake House
Lac-des-Mille-Lacs House
Fort William
Mountain Portage
Pointe-de-Meuron
Fort Charlotte
Grand-Portage
Little Vermilion Lake
Vermilion Lake
Martin's Falls
Henley House
Moss Lake
Rawbone Lake
Large Pine Lake
Elbow Lake
Little Pine Lake
Big Lake Post
Manitoomargo Lake
Flint Lake Houses
Morrison's House
Boar's House
Vermette's House
Fort Nigagamichish
Keenoogomeg
Long Lake
Pyakectchewan Lake
Fort Nigagamy
Perrault's House
Lesser Long Lake
Wappiscuaca Lake
Fort Pakamiga
Winter Lake
Capoonacagami
Fort Pic
Black River
Michipicoten
Albany Fort
Kwataboahegan Creek
Moose Fort
Hayes Island
Abitibi Branch Houses
Mesackamy Lake
Wapiscogamy House
Waupissatiga Lake
Micabanish Lake
Missinaibi House
Missinaibi Lake
Capusacasee
Matagami Lake
Flying Post
Green Lake
Bachawana
Sault-Sainte-Marie
Mississagué
Saint-Joseph Island
Drummond Island
Fort la Cloche
Little Current House
Little Whale River
Great Whale River
Big River Post
Old Factory River
East Main Factory
Jack River
Fort St Andrews
Rupert River
Rupert House
Hannah Bay
Pusquachagamy River
Abitibi House
Frederick House
Lake Abitibi
Fort Abitibi
Conaisee River
Devil's Island Post
Whitefish River
Keenogumisee Lake
Pusquachagamy Lake
Wyaskash Lake
Langue-de-Terre
Matawagamingue

TRANSPORTATION IN THE PETIT NORD

Author: Victor P. Lytwyn

Like the rest of the Northwest the Petit Nord presented a major transportation problem for a trade that depended on the long-distance movement of furs and supplies. Bounding the area are, in the northeast, the flat marshy lowlands along Hudson Bay and James Bay and, in the south, the mountainous edge of the Canadian Shield along the north shore of Lake Superior. The interior is a maze of lakes, swamps, rivers, and ice-scoured rock that made overland travel impossible in summer. Traders had to travel by water, hauling or carrying equipment and trade goods over portages, and engage in an annual race against winter freeze-up, which could leave them stranded hundreds of kilometres from their destinations.

Successful trade required vessels that moved cargoes quickly. By using experienced French Canadian voyageurs and birchbark canoes that Indians built to trade specifications the Montréal traders were able to extend a familiar transportation system into the Petit Nord. The HBC, however, had to develop a transportation system almost from scratch. At first it relied on boat and bateaux brigades on the principal rivers, but eventually it hired voyageurs and purchased Indian-built canoes for use where neither boats nor bateaux could penetrate.

In the Petit Nord (the area bounded by Hudson Bay, James Bay, Lake Superior, and Lake Winnipeg) French-Canadian fur traders from Montréal had pushed deeply into the Albany River basin and also established a transport corridor from Lake Superior to Lake Winnipeg well before 1760. After 1760 the Montréal trade was expanded by a variety of entrepreneurs, among whom a Jewish trader, Ezekiel Solomon, soon became the most important. When Solomon retired in 1784, his 'Little Empire' was quickly taken over by the Northwest Company, which then competed directly with the Hudson's Bay Company (HBC) in most of the Petit Nord (pls 61, 62).

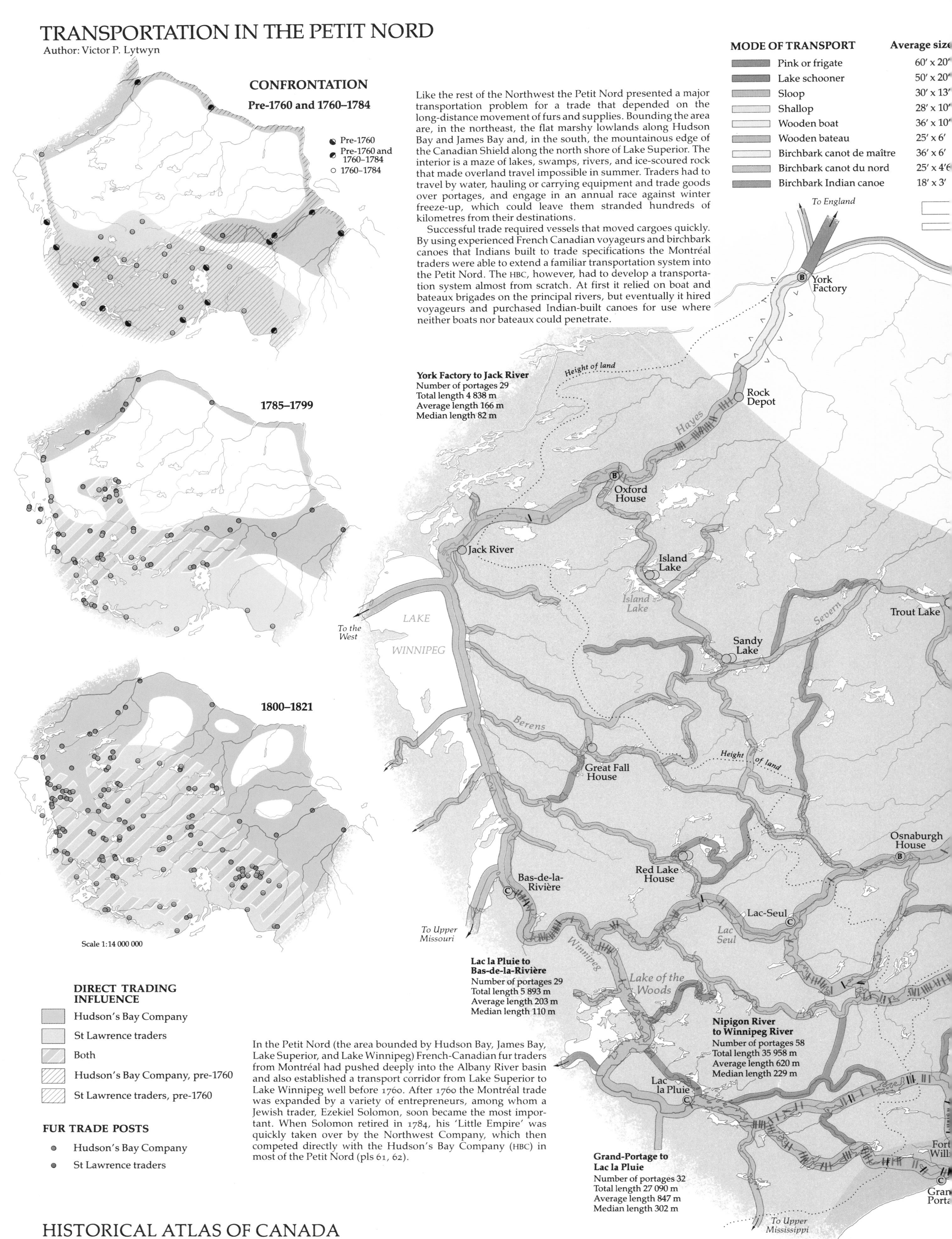

CONFRONTATION
Pre-1760 and 1760–1784
Pre-1760
Pre-1760 and 1760–1784
1760–1784
1785–1799
1800–1821
Scale 1:14 000 000
DIRECT TRADING INFLUENCE
Hudson's Bay Company
St Lawrence traders
Both
Hudson's Bay Company, pre-1760
St Lawrence traders, pre-1760
FUR TRADE POSTS
Hudson's Bay Company
St Lawrence traders
MODE OF TRANSPORT
Average size
Pink or frigate 60′ x 20′
Lake schooner 50′ x 20′
Sloop 30′ x 13′
Shallop 28′ x 10′
Wooden boat 36′ x 10′
Wooden bateau 25′ x 6′
Birchbark canot de maître 36′ x 6′
Birchbark canot du nord 25′ x 4′6
Birchbark Indian canoe 18′ x 3′
To England
York Factory
Rock Depot
Hayes
Height of land
York Factory to Jack River
Number of portages 29
Total length 4 838 m
Average length 166 m
Median length 82 m
Oxford House
Jack River
Island Lake
Island Lake
To the West
LAKE WINNIPEG
Severn
Trout Lake
Sandy Lake
Berens
Great Fall House
Height of land
Osnaburgh House
Red Lake House
Bas-de-la-Rivière
Lac-Seul
Lac Seul
To Upper Missouri
Winnipeg
Lac la Pluie to Bas-de-la-Rivière
Number of portages 29
Total length 5 893 m
Average length 203 m
Median length 110 m
Lake of the Woods
Nipigon River to Winnipeg River
Number of portages 58
Total length 35 958 m
Average length 620 m
Median length 229 m
Lac la Pluie
Grand-Portage to Lac la Pluie
Number of portages 32
Total length 27 090 m
Average length 847 m
Median length 302 m
To Upper Mississippi

Cargo capacity
200 tons
75 tons
40 tons
10 tons
12 tons
2 tons
3 tons
1.5 tons
0.75 tons

lajor route
linor route

Portages (major routes only)
More than 1 000 m
200 to 1 000 m
Less than 200 m
Tracking with lines

Depots and/or break-of-bulk points
Hudson's Bay Company
St Lawrence traders
Major boat-building centre
Major canoe-building centre

Physiographic regions
Hudson Bay lowland
Shield upland
Shield highland

FUR-TRADE WATERWAYS

Albany Fort to Lac-Seul
Number of portages 22
Total length 4 402 m
Average length 200 m
Median length 128 m

Fort William to Lac la Pluie
Number of portages 35
Total length 20 284 m
Average length 596 m
Median length 183 m

Scale 1:4 000 000

OUTBOUND BRIGADES IN SPRING

AVERAGE TRAVEL TIMES BETWEEN SELECTED POSTS
(in days)

Hudson's Bay Company
St Lawrence traders

Based mainly on Hudson's Bay Company post journals, ca 1774–1821

Fall journeys inland fought currents with heavy loads of trade goods; spring journeys outbound with furs were accomplished far more quickly. The travel times shown here are averages based on HBC records and on several well-documented accounts by travellers along the major routes from Lake Superior to Lake Winnipeg.

INBOUND BRIGADES IN FALL

The local depletion of beaver spurred the fur trade's territorial expansion. Beaver were never abundant in the Hudson Bay lowlands and were quickly trapped out around Lake Superior and along the transportation axis to Lake Winnipeg. By 1800, when competition had driven rival traders into much of the rugged land between Lake Superior and Hudson Bay, beaver returns from the Petit Nord reached about 50 000 pelts per year. Thereafter, interior districts reported, one by one, that beaver were scarce. Shortly after the union of the HBC and the Northwest Company in 1821 the annual beaver return from the Petit Nord was below 7 000 pelts.

DEPLETION OF BEAVER

Isolines delimit areas where beaver were still reported to be plentiful in the years shown.

Scale 1:12 500 000

FUR-TRADE SETTLEMENTS

Authors: D. Wayne Moodie, Victor P. Lytwyn

The economic functions of fur-trading posts in the northwest were reflected in their size and layout. Bayside settlements such as York Factory and Fort Albany and the North West Company's main depot on Lake Superior (located first at Grand Portage and later at Fort William) commanded the entrances to the fur lands and were the most elaborate settlements of the fur trade. In later years fur trading was incidental at these establishments; located at points of transshipment, they were entrepôts with service and administrative functions.

Within the fur-bearing regions smaller entrepôts developed at strategic sites. Frequently these sites were occupied jointly by competing companies (eg, Cumberland House). The plans of these settlements (eg, Naosquiscaw, Cumberland House, Edmonton House, and Lesser Slave Lake House) illustrate the variety of economic functions performed within their well-fortified stockades. Fortifications were a measure of the value of these sites to the fur traders and of the threat of attack from rival traders and from natives who in the parkland belt were numerous, warlike, and equestrian.

Most trading posts built in the forested lands of the Northwest were manned only in winter and only for a few years. From these posts men dispersed to trade directly with natives on their winter hunts. Usually one building served for living, trading, and storage (as Red Lake House). Such buildings were simple log structures designed to meet the minimal requirements of trade and survival.

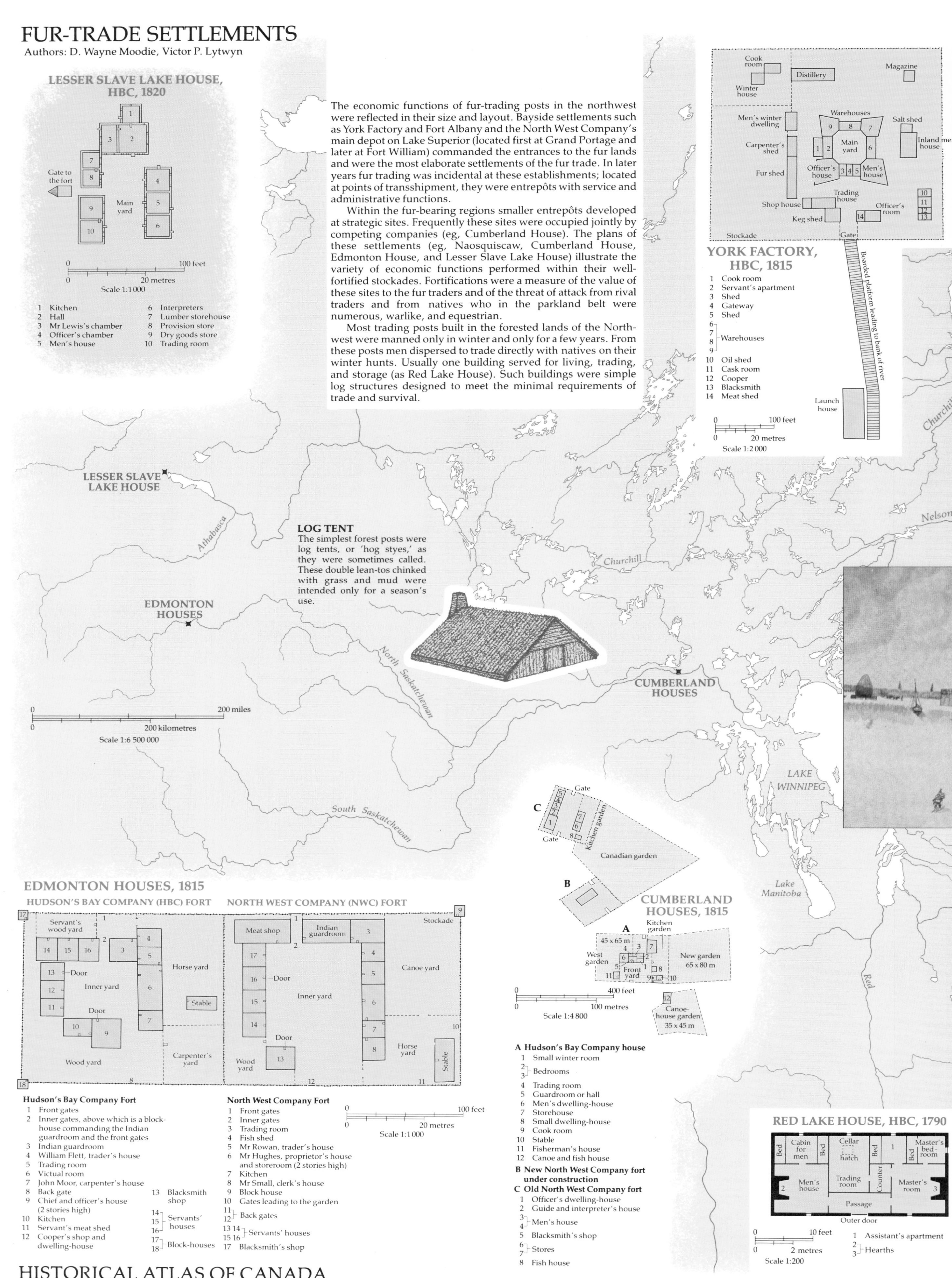
LESSER SLAVE LAKE HOUSE, HBC, 1820
Gate to the fort
Main yard
0 100 feet
0 20 metres
Scale 1:1 000
1 Kitchen
2 Hall
3 Mr Lewis's chamber
4 Officer's chamber
5 Men's house
6 Interpreters
7 Lumber storehouse
8 Provision store
9 Dry goods store
10 Trading room
YORK FACTORY, HBC, 1815
Cook room
Winter house
Distillery
Magazine
Men's winter dwelling
Warehouses
Salt shed
Inland men's house
Carpenter's shed
Main yard
Fur shed
Officer's house
Men's house
Trading house
Shop house
Officer's room
Keg shed
Stockade
Gate
Boarded platform leading to bank of river
Launch house
1 Cook room
2 Servant's apartment
3 Shed
4 Gateway
5 Shed
6–9 Warehouses
10 Oil shed
11 Cask room
12 Cooper
13 Blacksmith
14 Meat shed
0 100 feet
0 20 metres
Scale 1:2 000
LESSER SLAVE LAKE HOUSE
Athabasca
LOG TENT
The simplest forest posts were log tents, or 'hog styes,' as they were sometimes called. These double lean-tos chinked with grass and mud were intended only for a season's use.
Churchill
Nelson
EDMONTON HOUSES
North Saskatchewan
CUMBERLAND HOUSES
0 200 miles
0 200 kilometres
Scale 1:6 500 000
South Saskatchewan
LAKE WINNIPEG
Lake Manitoba
Red
EDMONTON HOUSES, 1815
HUDSON'S BAY COMPANY (HBC) FORT
NORTH WEST COMPANY (NWC) FORT
Servant's wood yard
Door
Inner yard
Horse yard
Stable
Wood yard
Carpenter's yard
Meat shop
Indian guardroom
Stockade
Canoe yard
Inner yard
Wood yard
Horse yard
Stable
Hudson's Bay Company Fort
1 Front gates
2 Inner gates, above which is a block-house commanding the Indian guardroom and the front gates
3 Indian guardroom
4 William Flett, trader's house
5 Trading room
6 Victual room
7 John Moor, carpenter's house
8 Back gate
9 Chief and officer's house (2 stories high)
10 Kitchen
11 Servant's meat shed
12 Cooper's shop and dwelling-house
13 Blacksmith shop
14–16 Servants' houses
17–18 Block-houses
North West Company Fort
1 Front gates
2 Inner gates
3 Trading room
4 Fish shed
5 Mr Rowan, trader's house
6 Mr Hughes, proprietor's house and storeroom (2 stories high)
7 Kitchen
8 Mr Small, clerk's house
9 Block house
10 Gates leading to the garden
11–12 Back gates
13 14 15 16 Servants' houses
17 Blacksmith's shop
0 100 feet
0 20 metres
Scale 1:1 000
Gate
C
Kitchen garden
Canadian garden
B
CUMBERLAND HOUSES, 1815
A
Kitchen garden
45 x 65 m
West garden
Front yard
New garden 65 x 80 m
Canoe-house garden 35 x 45 m
0 400 feet
0 100 metres
Scale 1:4 800
A Hudson's Bay Company house
1 Small winter room
2–3 Bedrooms
4 Trading room
5 Guardroom or hall
6 Men's dwelling-house
7 Storehouse
8 Small dwelling-house
9 Cook room
10 Stable
11 Fisherman's house
12 Canoe and fish house
B New North West Company fort under construction
C Old North West Company fort
1 Officer's dwelling-house
2 Guide and interpreter's house
3–4 Men's house
5 Blacksmith's shop
6–7 Stores
8 Fish house
RED LAKE HOUSE, HBC, 1790
Cabin for men
Bed
Cellar hatch
Master's bed-room
Men's house
Trading room
Counter
Master's room
Passage
Outer door
0 10 feet
0 2 metres
Scale 1:200
1 Assistant's apartment
2–3 Hearths

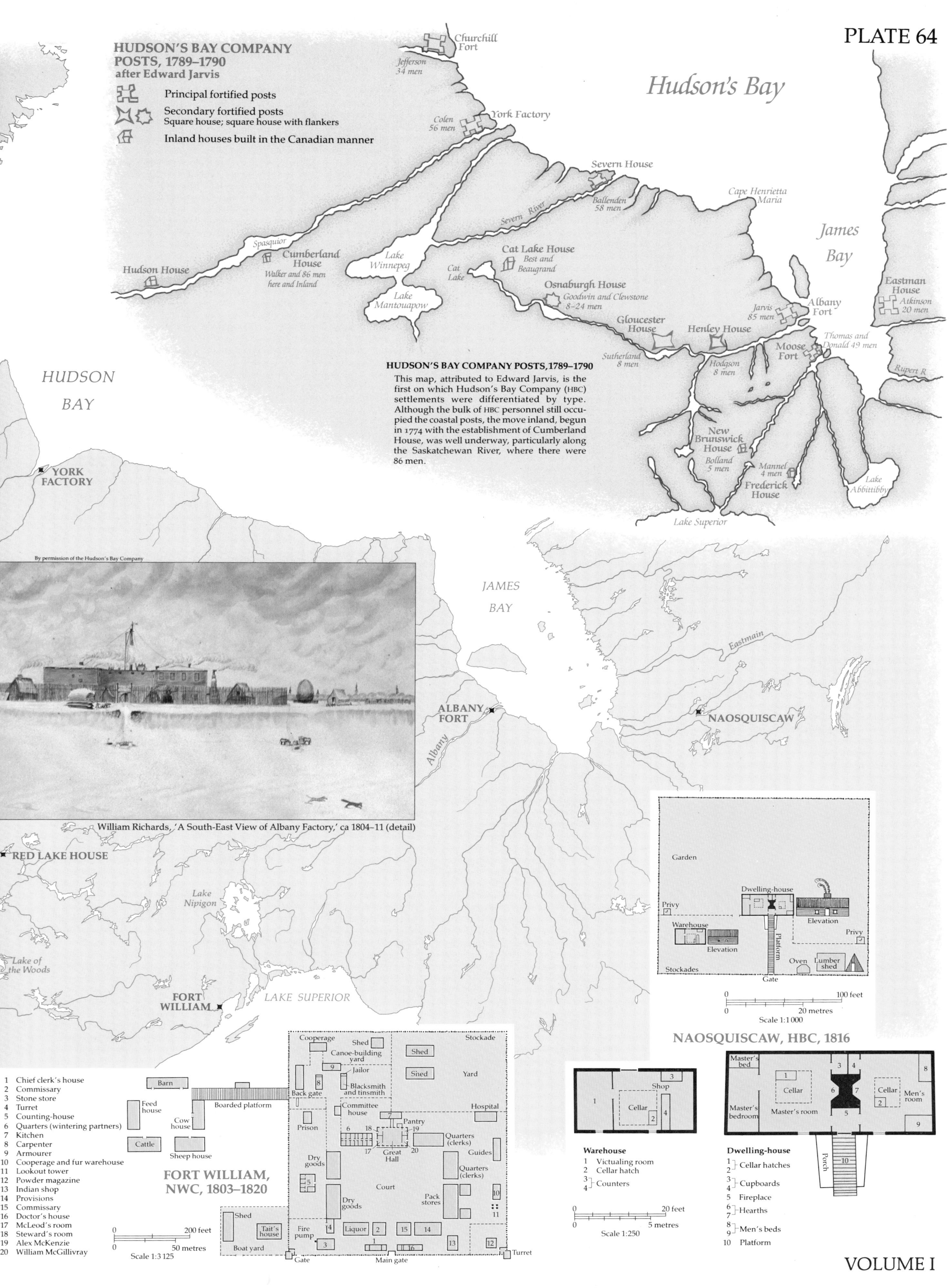
HUDSON'S BAY COMPANY POSTS, 1789–1790
after Edward Jarvis
Principal fortified posts
Secondary fortified posts
Square house; square house with flankers
Inland houses built in the Canadian manner
Hudson's Bay
Churchill Fort
Jefferson 34 men
York Factory
Colen 56 men
Severn House
Ballenden 58 men
Severn River
Cape Henrietta Maria
James Bay
Spasquior
Cumberland House
Walker and 86 men here and Inland
Hudson House
Lake Winnepeg
Lake Mantouapow
Cat Lake
Cat Lake House
Best and Beaugrand
Osnaburgh House
Goodwin and Clewstone 8–24 men
Gloucester House
Henley House
Sutherland 8 men
Jarvis 85 men
Albany Fort
Eastman House
Atkinson 20 men
Thomas and Donald 49 men
Moose Fort
Hodgson 8 men
Rupert R
New Brunswick House
Bolland 5 men
Mannel 4 men
Frederick House
Lake Abbittibby
Lake Superior
HUDSON BAY
YORK FACTORY
JAMES BAY
Eastmain
ALBANY FORT
Albany
NAOSQUISCAW
RED LAKE HOUSE
Lake Nipigon
Lake of the Woods
FORT WILLIAM
LAKE SUPERIOR
By permission of the Hudson's Bay Company
Garden
Dwelling-house
Privy
Elevation
Warehouse
Elevation
Platform
Privy
Oven
Lumber shed
Stockades
Gate
0 100 feet
0 20 metres
Scale 1:1 000
NAOSQUISCAW, HBC, 1816
Shop
Cellar
Warehouse
1 Victualing room
2 Cellar hatch
3, 4 Counters
0 20 feet
0 5 metres
Scale 1:250
Master's bed
Cellar
Master's bedroom
Master's room
Men's room
Porch
Dwelling-house
1, 2 Cellar hatches
3, 4 Cupboards
5 Fireplace
6, 7 Hearths
8, 9 Men's beds
10 Platform
Cooperage
Shed
Canoe-building yard
Stockade
Jailor
Blacksmith and tinsmith
Yard
Barn
Back gate
Boarded platform
Feed house
Cow house
Committee house
Hospital
Prison
Pantry
Cattle
Sheep house
Quarters (clerks)
Great Hall
Guides
Dry goods
Court
Pack stores
Fire pump
Liquor
Boat yard
Tait's house
Gate
Main gate
Turret
FORT WILLIAM, NWC, 1803–1820
1 Chief clerk's house
2 Commissary
3 Stone store
4 Turret
5 Counting-house
6 Quarters (wintering partners)
7 Kitchen
8 Carpenter
9 Armourer
10 Cooperage and fur warehouse
11 Lookout tower
12 Powder magazine
13 Indian shop
14 Provisions
15 Commissary
16 Doctor's house
17 McLeod's room
18 Steward's room
19 Alex McKenzie
20 William McGillivray
0 200 feet
0 50 metres
Scale 1:3 125

HUDSON'S BAY COMPANY POSTS, 1789–1790

This map, attributed to Edward Jarvis, is the first on which Hudson's Bay Company (HBC) settlements were differentiated by type. Although the bulk of HBC personnel still occupied the coastal posts, the move inland, begun in 1774 with the establishment of Cumberland House, was well underway, particularly along the Saskatchewan River, where there were 86 men.

William Richards, 'A South-East View of Albany Factory,' ca 1804–11 (detail)

PEOPLES OF THE BOREAL FOREST AND PARKLAND

Authors: D. Wayne Moodie, Barry Kaye, Victor P. Lytwyn; Arthur J. Ray (Indians)

The proliferation of trading posts tended to stabilize Indian populations near the posts (post bands), to increase the number of people of mixed blood, and to eliminate Indian middlemen south and east of Lake Athabasca. Even in the Mackenzie valley Cree and Chipewyan people no longer controlled the supply of arms and lost their military advantage. Almost everywhere former Assiniboine, Cree, and Chipewyan middlemen sought alternative ways of obtaining the furs or country produce they exchanged for European goods. Cree migration to the northwest stopped, and by 1820 many Cree were moving south to the parkland belt, there to become buffalo hunters. Similarly some of the Ojibwa, who had also been moving northwestward, tended to settle in the parkland/grassland regions of the lower Saskatchewan, Assiniboine, and Red River valleys. North of the Churchill River the Chipewyan continued to push south and southwest into the better fur lands of the boreal forest. In all regions Indians greatly outnumbered whites.

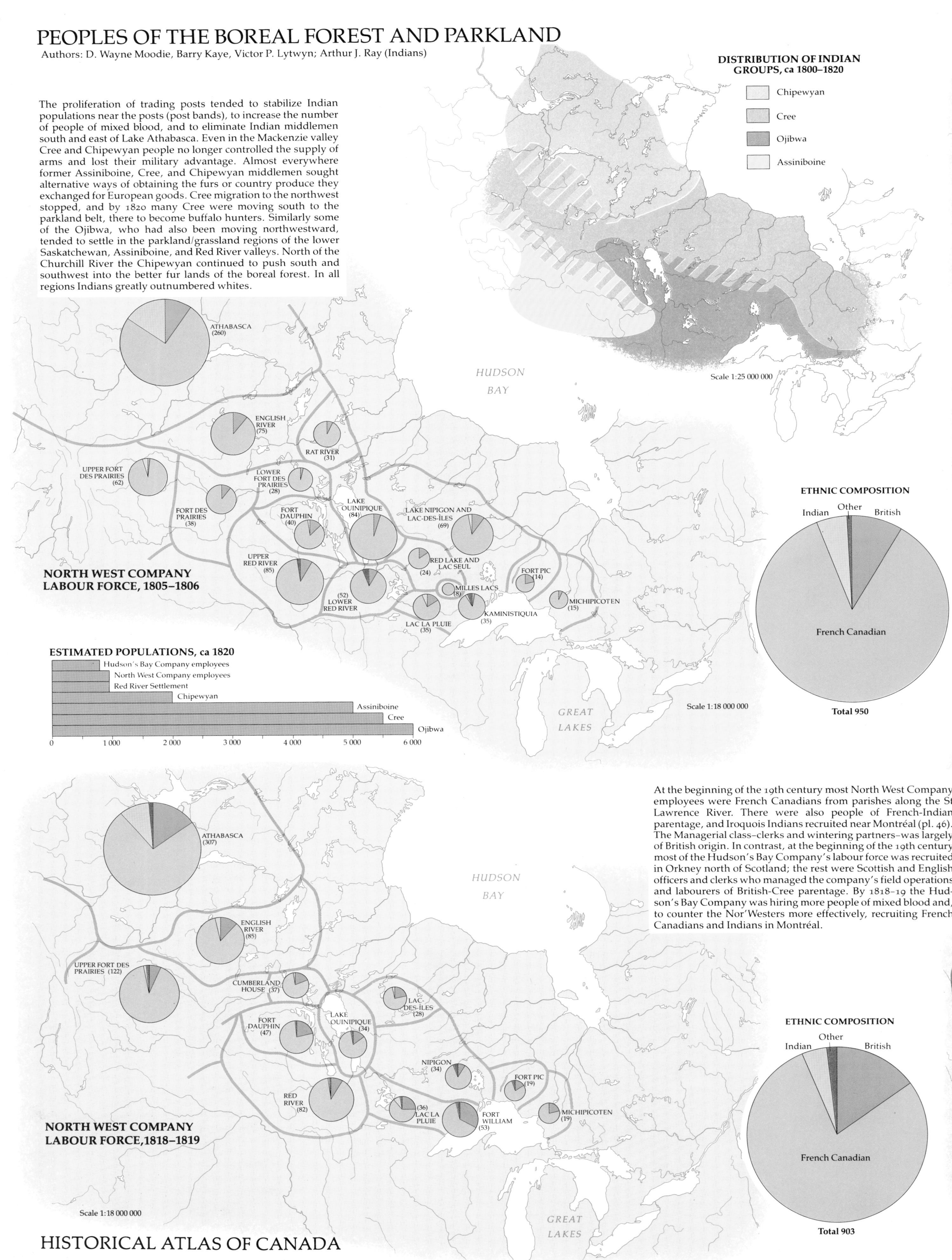

DISTRIBUTION OF INDIAN GROUPS, ca 1800–1820
Chipewyan
Cree
Ojibwa
Assiniboine
Scale 1:25 000 000
HUDSON BAY
NORTH WEST COMPANY LABOUR FORCE, 1805–1806
ATHABASCA (260)
ENGLISH RIVER (75)
RAT RIVER (31)
UPPER FORT DES PRAIRIES (62)
LOWER FORT DES PRAIRIES (28)
FORT DES PRAIRIES (38)
FORT DAUPHIN (40)
LAKE OUINIPIQUE (84)
LAKE NIPIGON AND LAC-DES-ÎLES (69)
UPPER RED RIVER (85)
(52) LOWER RED RIVER
RED LAKE AND LAC SEUL (24)
MILLES LACS (8)
FORT PIC (14)
MICHIPICOTEN (15)
KAMINISTIQUIA (35)
LAC LA PLUIE (35)
ETHNIC COMPOSITION
Indian
Other
British
French Canadian
Total 950
ESTIMATED POPULATIONS, ca 1820
Hudson's Bay Company employees
North West Company employees
Red River Settlement
Chipewyan
Assiniboine
Cree
Ojibwa
0
1 000
2 000
3 000
4 000
5 000
6 000
GREAT LAKES
Scale 1:18 000 000
HUDSON BAY
NORTH WEST COMPANY LABOUR FORCE,1818–1819
ATHABASCA (307)
ENGLISH RIVER (85)
UPPER FORT DES PRAIRIES (122)
CUMBERLAND HOUSE (37)
LAC-DES-ÎLES (28)
FORT DAUPHIN (47)
LAKE OUINIPIQUE (34)
NIPIGON (34)
FORT PIC (19)
RED RIVER (82)
(36) LAC LA PLUIE
FORT WILLIAM (53)
MICHIPICOTEN (19)
ETHNIC COMPOSITION
Indian
Other
British
French Canadian
Total 903
Scale 1:18 000 000
GREAT LAKES

At the beginning of the 19th century most North West Company employees were French Canadians from parishes along the St Lawrence River. There were also people of French-Indian parentage, and Iroquois Indians recruited near Montréal (pl. 46). The Managerial class–clerks and wintering partners–was largely of British origin. In contrast, at the beginning of the 19th century most of the Hudson's Bay Company's labour force was recruited in Orkney north of Scotland; the rest were Scottish and English officers and clerks who managed the company's field operations and labourers of British-Cree parentage. By 1818–19 the Hudson's Bay Company was hiring more people of mixed blood and, to counter the Nor'Westers more effectively, recruiting French Canadians and Indians in Montréal.

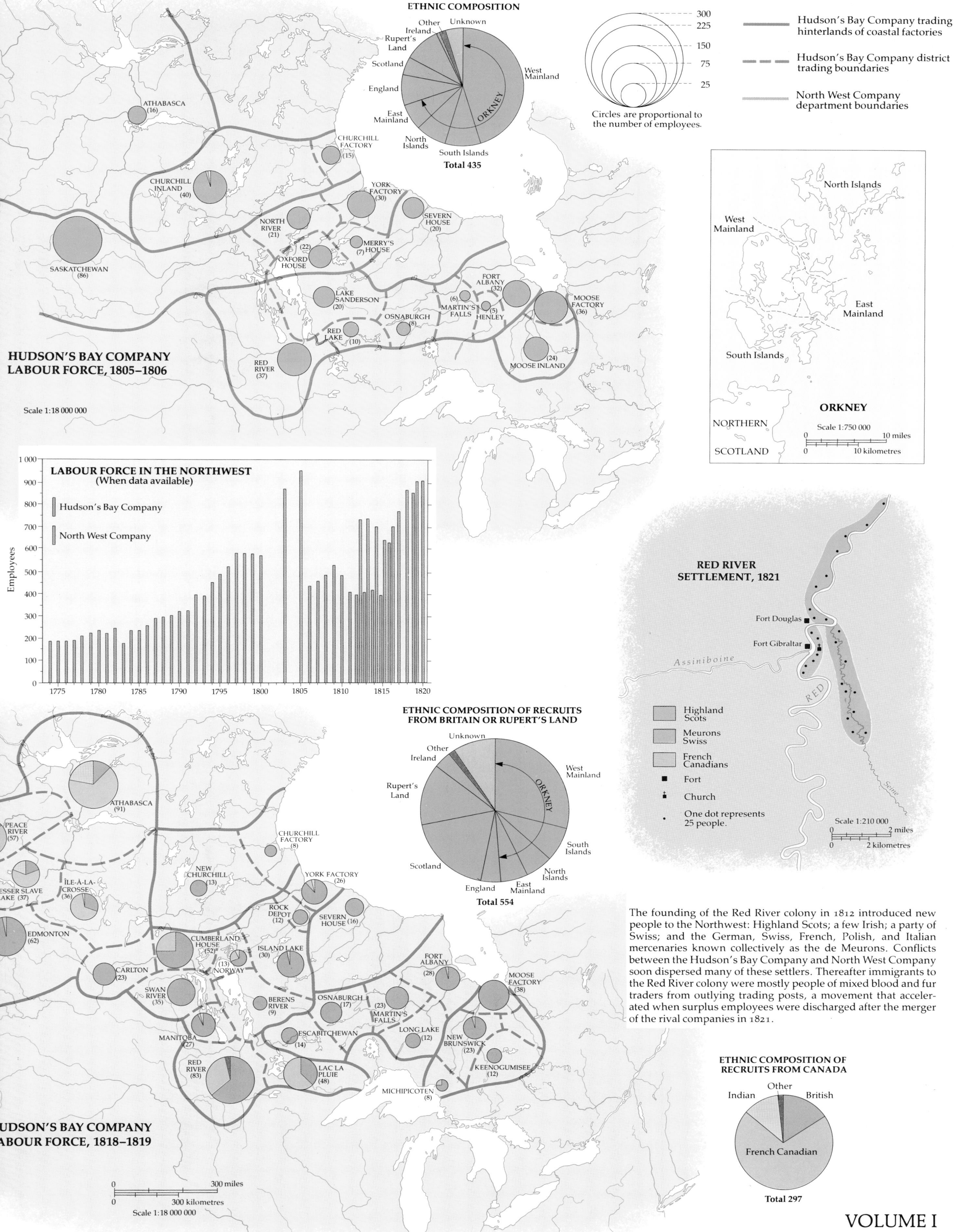

ETHNIC COMPOSITION
Other
Unknown
Ireland
Rupert's Land
Scotland
England
East Mainland
North Islands
South Islands
West Mainland
ORKNEY
Total 435
300
225
150
75
25
Circles are proportional to the number of employees.
Hudson's Bay Company trading hinterlands of coastal factories
Hudson's Bay Company district trading boundaries
North West Company department boundaries
ATHABASCA (16)
CHURCHILL FACTORY (15)
CHURCHILL INLAND (40)
YORK FACTORY (30)
SEVERN HOUSE (20)
NORTH RIVER (21)
(22) OXFORD HOUSE
(7) MERRY'S HOUSE
SASKATCHEWAN (86)
LAKE SANDERSON (20)
FORT ALBANY (32)
(6) MARTIN'S FALLS
(5) HENLEY
MOOSE FACTORY (36)
OSNABURGH (8)
RED LAKE (10)
RED RIVER (37)
(24) MOOSE INLAND
HUDSON'S BAY COMPANY LABOUR FORCE, 1805–1806
Scale 1:18 000 000
North Islands
West Mainland
East Mainland
South Islands
ORKNEY
NORTHERN SCOTLAND
Scale 1:750 000
10 miles
10 kilometres
LABOUR FORCE IN THE NORTHWEST
(When data available)
Hudson's Bay Company
North West Company
Employees
1 000
900
800
700
600
500
400
300
200
100
0
1775
1780
1785
1790
1795
1800
1805
1810
1815
1820
RED RIVER SETTLEMENT, 1821
Fort Douglas
Fort Gibraltar
Assiniboine
RED
Seine
Highland Scots
Meurons Swiss
French Canadians
Fort
Church
One dot represents 25 people.
Scale 1:210 000
2 miles
2 kilometres
ETHNIC COMPOSITION OF RECRUITS FROM BRITAIN OR RUPERT'S LAND
Unknown
Other
Ireland
Rupert's Land
Scotland
England
East Mainland
North Islands
South Islands
West Mainland
ORKNEY
Total 554
ATHABASCA (91)
PEACE RIVER (57)
CHURCHILL FACTORY (8)
LESSER SLAVE LAKE (37)
ILE-A-LA-CROSSE (36)
NEW CHURCHILL HOUSE (13)
YORK FACTORY (26)
ROCK DEPOT (12)
SEVERN HOUSE (16)
EDMONTON (62)
CUMBERLAND HOUSE (52)
(13) NORWAY
ISLAND LAKE (30)
CARLTON (23)
FORT ALBANY (28)
MOOSE FACTORY (38)
SWAN RIVER (35)
BERENS RIVER (9)
OSNABURGH (17)
(23) MARTIN'S FALLS
MANITOBA (27)
ESCABITCHEWAN (14)
LONG LAKE (12)
NEW BRUNSWICK (23)
RED RIVER (83)
LAC LA PLUIE (48)
KEENOGUMISEE (12)
MICHIPICOTEN (8)
HUDSON'S BAY COMPANY LABOUR FORCE, 1818–1819
300 miles
300 kilometres
Scale 1:18 000 000
ETHNIC COMPOSITION OF RECRUITS FROM CANADA
Other
Indian
British
French Canadian
Total 297

The founding of the Red River colony in 1812 introduced new people to the Northwest: Highland Scots; a few Irish; a party of Swiss; and the German, Swiss, French, Polish, and Italian mercenaries known collectively as the de Meurons. Conflicts between the Hudson's Bay Company and North West Company soon dispersed many of these settlers. Thereafter immigrants to the Red River colony were mostly people of mixed blood and fur traders from outlying trading posts, a movement that accelerated when surplus employees were discharged after the merger of the rival companies in 1821.

NEW CALEDONIA AND COLUMBIA

Authors: M.D. Kinkade, Wayne Suttles (Linguistics);
Robert M. Galois, Sheila P. Robinson (Fur trades)

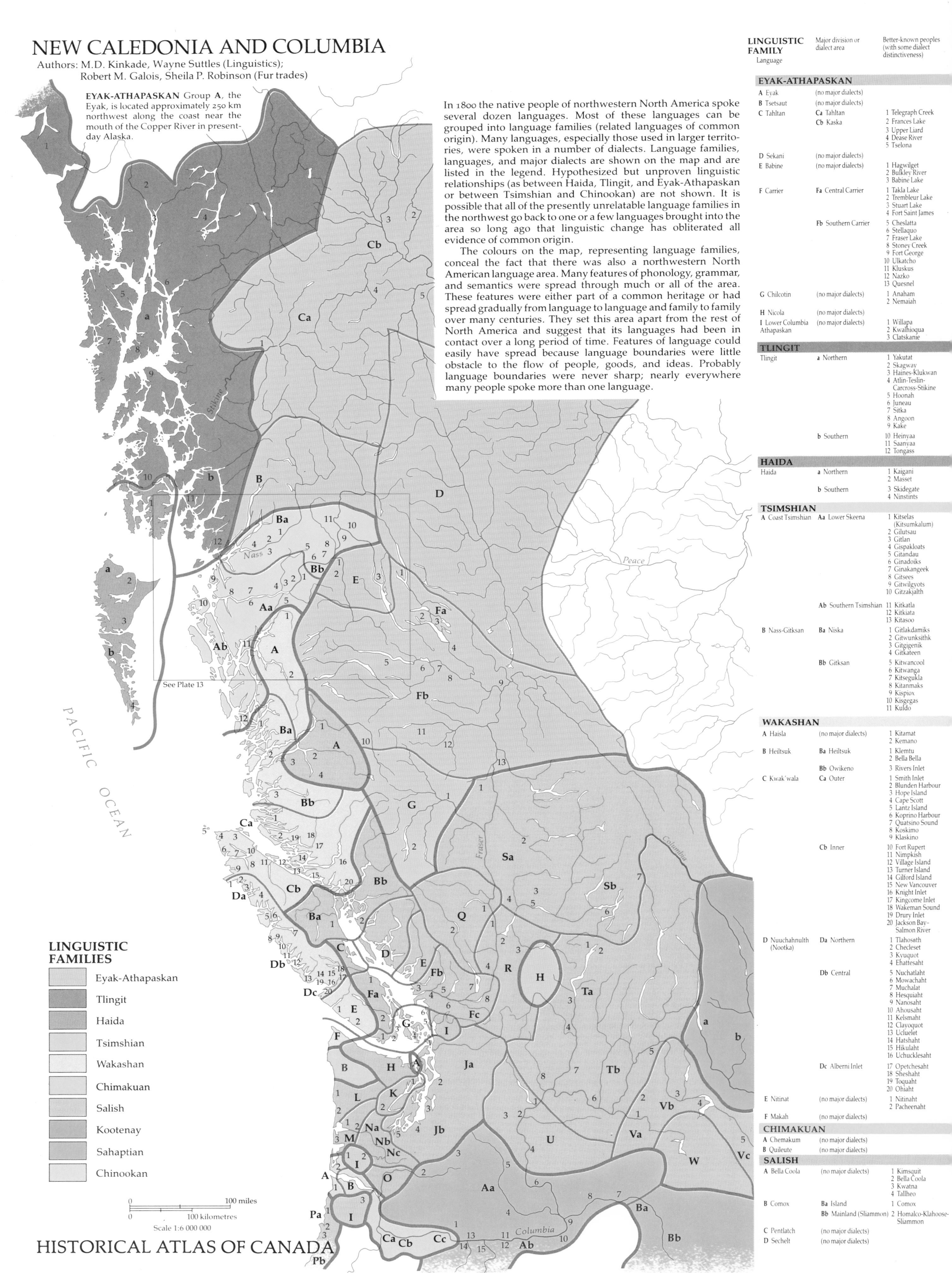
EYAK-ATHAPASKAN Group **A**, the Eyak, is located approximately 250 km northwest along the coast near the mouth of the Copper River in present-day Alaska.
Stikine
Nass
Peace
Fraser
Columbia
PACIFIC OCEAN
See Plate 13
LINGUISTIC FAMILIES
Eyak-Athapaskan
Tlingit
Haida
Tsimshian
Wakashan
Chimakuan
Salish
Kootenay
Sahaptian
Chinookan
100 miles
100 kilometres
Scale 1:6 000 000

In 1800 the native people of northwestern North America spoke several dozen languages. Most of these languages can be grouped into language families (related languages of common origin). Many languages, especially those used in larger territories, were spoken in a number of dialects. Language families, languages, and major dialects are shown on the map and are listed in the legend. Hypothesized but unproven linguistic relationships (as between Haida, Tlingit, and Eyak-Athapaskan or between Tsimshian and Chinookan) are not shown. It is possible that all of the presently unrelatable language families in the northwest go back to one or a few languages brought into the area so long ago that linguistic change has obliterated all evidence of common origin.

The colours on the map, representing language families, conceal the fact that there was also a northwestern North American language area. Many features of phonology, grammar, and semantics were spread through much or all of the area. These features were either part of a common heritage or had spread gradually from language to language and family to family over many centuries. They set this area apart from the rest of North America and suggest that its languages had been in contact over a long period of time. Features of language could easily have spread because language boundaries were little obstacle to the flow of people, goods, and ideas. Probably language boundaries were never sharp; nearly everywhere many people spoke more than one language.

LINGUISTIC FAMILY Language	Major division or dialect area	Better-known peoples (with some dialect distinctiveness)
EYAK-ATHAPASKAN		
A Eyak	(no major dialects)	
B Tsetsaut	(no major dialects)	
C Tahltan	**Ca** Tahltan	1 Telegraph Creek
	Cb Kaska	2 Frances Lake 3 Upper Liard 4 Dease River 5 Tselona
D Sekani	(no major dialects)	
E Babine	(no major dialects)	1 Hagwilget 2 Bulkley River 3 Babine Lake
F Carrier	**Fa** Central Carrier	1 Takla Lake 2 Trembleur Lake 3 Stuart Lake 4 Fort Saint James
	Fb Southern Carrier	5 Cheslatta 6 Stellaquo 7 Fraser Lake 8 Stoney Creek 9 Fort George 10 Ulkatcho 11 Kluskus 12 Nazko 13 Quesnel
G Chilcotin	(no major dialects)	1 Anaham 2 Nemaiah
H Nicola	(no major dialects)	
I Lower Columbia Athapaskan	(no major dialects)	1 Willapa 2 Kwalhioqua 3 Clatskanie
TLINGIT		
Tlingit	**a** Northern	1 Yakutat 2 Skagway 3 Haines-Klukwan 4 Atlin-Teslin-Carcross-Stikine 5 Hoonah 6 Juneau 7 Sitka 8 Angoon 9 Kake
	b Southern	10 Heinyaa 11 Saanyaa 12 Tongass
HAIDA		
Haida	**a** Northern	1 Kaigani 2 Masset
	b Southern	3 Skidegate 4 Ninstints
TSIMSHIAN		
A Coast Tsimshian	**Aa** Lower Skeena	1 Kitselas (Kitsumkalum) 2 Gilutsau 3 Gitlan 4 Gispakloats 5 Gitandau 6 Ginadoiks 7 Ginakangeek 8 Gitsees 9 Gitwilgyots 10 Gitzakjalth
	Ab Southern Tsimshian	11 Kitkatla 12 Kitkiata 13 Kitasoo
B Nass-Gitksan	**Ba** Niska	1 Gitlakdamiks 2 Gitwunksithk 3 Gitgigenik 4 Gitkateen
	Bb Gitksan	5 Kitwancool 6 Kitwanga 7 Kitsegukla 8 Kitanmaks 9 Kispiox 10 Kisgegas 11 Kuldo
WAKASHAN		
A Haisla	(no major dialects)	1 Kitamat 2 Kemano
B Heiltsuk	**Ba** Heiltsuk	1 Klemtu 2 Bella Bella
	Bb Owikeno	3 Rivers Inlet
C Kwak'wala	**Ca** Outer	1 Smith Inlet 2 Blunden Harbour 3 Hope Island 4 Cape Scott 5 Lantz Island 6 Koprino Harbour 7 Quatsino Sound 8 Koskimo 9 Klaskino
	Cb Inner	10 Fort Rupert 11 Nimpkish 12 Village Island 13 Turner Island 14 Gilford Island 15 New Vancouver 16 Knight Inlet 17 Kingcome Inlet 18 Wakeman Sound 19 Drury Inlet 20 Jackson Bay-Salmon River
D Nuuchahnulth (Nootka)	**Da** Northern	1 Tlahosath 2 Checleset 3 Kyuquot 4 Ehattesaht
	Db Central	5 Nuchatlaht 6 Mowachaht 7 Muchalat 8 Hesquiaht 9 Nanosaht 10 Ahousaht 11 Kelsmaht 12 Clayoquot 13 Ucluelet 14 Hatshaht 15 Hikulaht 16 Uchucklesaht
	Dc Alberni Inlet	17 Opetchesaht 18 Sheshaht 19 Toquaht 20 Ohiaht
E Nitinat	(no major dialects)	1 Nitinaht 2 Pacheenaht
F Makah	(no major dialects)	
CHIMAKUAN		
A Chemakum	(no major dialects)	
B Quileute	(no major dialects)	
SALISH		
A Bella Coola	(no major dialects)	1 Kimsquit 2 Bella Coola 3 Kwatna 4 Tallheo
B Comox	**Ba** Island	1 Comox
	Bb Mainland (Sliammon)	2 Homalco-Klahoose-Sliammon
C Pentlatch	(no major dialects)	
D Sechelt	(no major dialects)	

PLATE 66

SALISH (continued)		
E Squamish	(no major dialects)	
F Halkomelem	Fa Island	1 Nanaimo 2 Cowichan
	Fb Downriver	3 Musqueam 4 Kwantlen 5 Katzie
	Fc Upriver (Upper Stalo)	6 Chilliwack 7 Chehalis 8 Tait
G Northern Straits	(no major dialects)	1 Sooke 2 Songhees 3 Saanich 4 Samish 5 Lummi 6 Semiahmoo
H Clallam	(no major dialects)	
I Nooksack	(no major dialects)	
J Lushootseed	Ja Northern	1 Skagit 2 Snohomish
	Jb Southern	3 Duwamish-Suquamish 4 Puyallup 5 Nisqually
K Twana	(no major dialects)	1 Quilcene 2 Skokomish
L Quinault	(no major dialects)	1 Queets 2 Quinault
M Lower Chehalis	(no major dialects)	1 Humptulips 2 Wynoochee 3 Westport-Shoalwater
N Upper Chehalis	Na Satsop	
	Nb Oakville Chehalis	
	Nc Tenino Chehalis	
O Cowlitz	(no major dialects)	
P Tillamook	Pa Tillamook	1 Nehalem 2 Garibaldi-Nestucca
	Pb Siletz	3 Siletz
Q Lillooet	(no major dialects)	1 Lillooet-Fountain 2 Mount Currie-Douglas
R Thompson	(no major dialects)	1 Lytton 2 Thompson Canyon 3 Nicola Valley 4 Spuzzum-Boston Bar
S Shuswap	Sa Western	1 Fraser River 2 Canim Lake 3 Chu Chua 4 Pavillion-Bonaparte 5 Deadman's Creek-Kamloops
	Sb Eastern	6 Shuswap Lake 7 Kinbasket
T Okanagan	Ta Northern	1 Head of the Lakes 2 Vernon 3 Penticton 4 Similkameen
	Tb Southern	5 Lakes-Colville-Inchelium 6 San Poil-Nespelem 7 Southern Okanogan 8 Methow
U Columbian	(no major dialects)	1 Chelan 2 Entiat 3 Wenatchee (Pesquous) 4 Moses Columbia
V Kalispel	Va Spokane	1 Spokane
	Vb Kalispel	2 Chewelah 3 Kalispel 4 Pend Oreille
	Vc Flathead	5 Flathead
W Coeur d'Alene	(no major dialects)	
KOOTENAY		
Kootenay	a Lower Kootenay	
	b Upper Kootenay	
SAHAPTIAN		
A Sahaptin	Aa Northern	1 Klickitat 2 Taitnapam 3 Upper Nisqually 4 Yakima 5 Pshwanwapam 6 Wanapam 7 Palouse 8 Lower Snake 9 Walla Walla
	Ab Southern	10 Umatilla 11 Rock Creek 12 John Day 13 Celilo 14 Tenino 15 Tygh Valley
B Nez perce	Ba Lower (Western)	
	Bb Upper Eastern	
CHINOOKAN		
A Lower Chinook	(no major dialects)	1 Clatsop 2 Chinook (Shoalwater)
B Cathlamet	(no major dialects)	
C Kiksht	Ca Clackamas	
	Cb Cascades	
	Cc Wasco-Wishram	

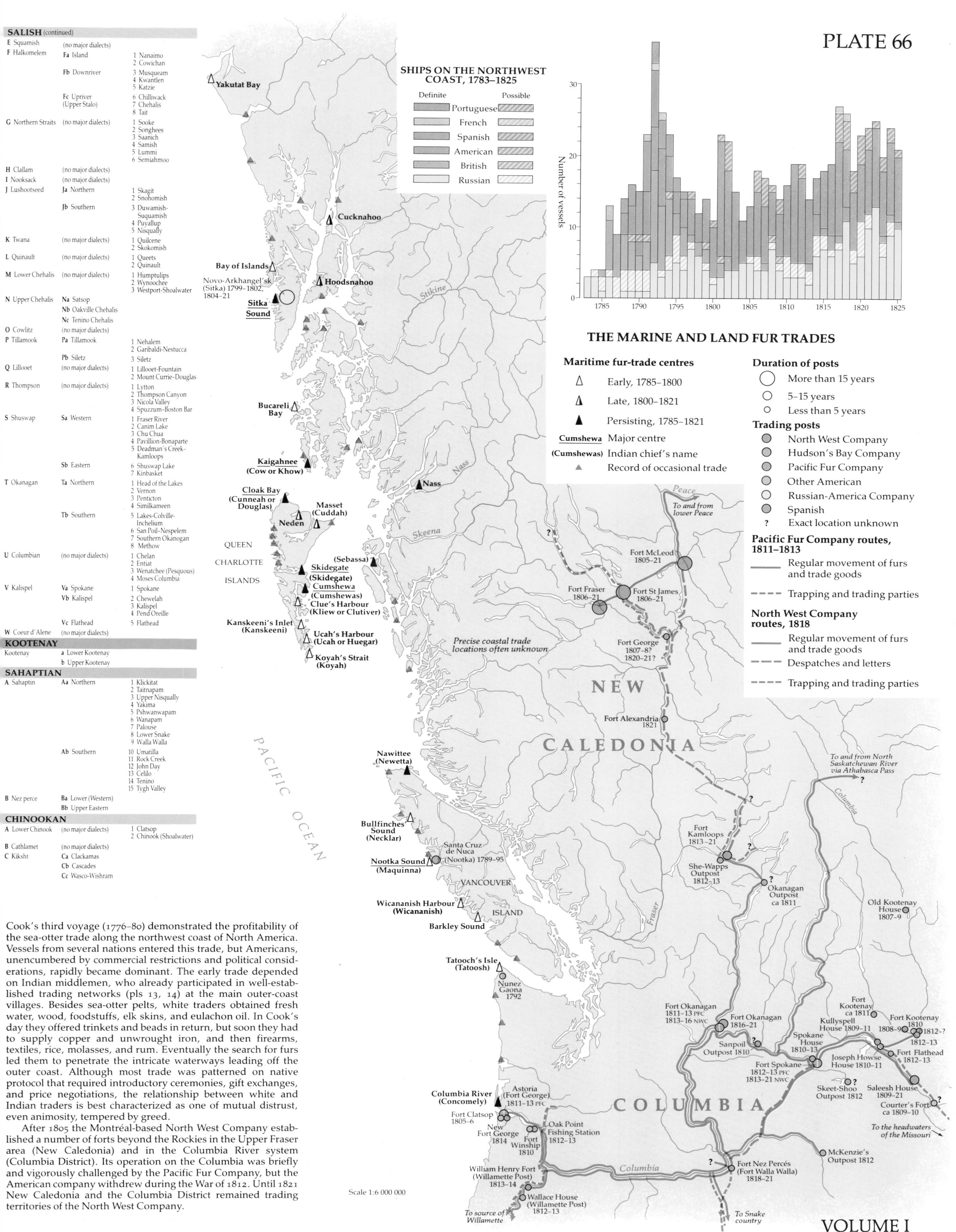

SHIPS ON THE NORTHWEST COAST, 1783–1825
Definite
Possible
Portuguese
French
Spanish
American
British
Russian
Number of vessels
THE MARINE AND LAND FUR TRADES
Maritime fur-trade centres
Early, 1785–1800
Late, 1800–1821
Persisting, 1785–1821
Cumshewa Major centre
(Cumshewas) Indian chief's name
Record of occasional trade
Duration of posts
More than 15 years
5–15 years
Less than 5 years
Trading posts
North West Company
Hudson's Bay Company
Pacific Fur Company
Other American
Russian-America Company
Spanish
? Exact location unknown
Pacific Fur Company routes, 1811–1813
Regular movement of furs and trade goods
Trapping and trading parties
North West Company routes, 1818
Regular movement of furs and trade goods
Despatches and letters
Trapping and trading parties
Yakutat Bay
Cucknahoo
Bay of Islands
Hoodsnahoo
Novo-Arkhangel'sk (Sitka) 1799–1802, 1804–21
Sitka Sound
Stikine
Bucareli Bay
Kaigahnee (Cow or Khow)
Nass
Cloak Bay (Cunneah or Douglas)
Masset (Cuddah)
Neden
Skeena
QUEEN CHARLOTTE ISLANDS
(Sebassa)
Skidegate (Skidegate)
Cumshewa (Cumshewas)
Clue's Harbour (Kliew or Clutiver)
Kanskeeni's Inlet (Kanskeeni)
Ucah's Harbour (Ucah or Huegar)
Koyah's Strait (Koyah)
Precise coastal trade locations often unknown
Peace
To and from lower Peace
Fort McLeod 1805–21
Fort Fraser 1806–21
Fort St James 1806–21
Fort George 1807–8? 1820–21?
NEW CALEDONIA
Fort Alexandria 1821
PACIFIC OCEAN
Nawittee (Newetta)
Bullfinches' Sound (Necklar)
Santa Cruz de Nuca (Nootka) 1789–95
Nootka Sound (Maquinna)
VANCOUVER ISLAND
Wicananish Harbour (Wicananish)
Barkley Sound
Fort Kamloops 1813–21
She-Wapps Outpost 1812–13
Okanagan Outpost ca 1811
Fraser
To and from North Saskatchewan River via Athabasca Pass
Columbia
Old Kootenay House 1807–9
Tatooch's Isle (Tatoosh)
Nunez Gaona 1792
Fort Okanagan 1811–13 PFC 1813–16 NWC
Fort Okanagan 1816–21
Sanpoil Outpost 1810
Spokane House 1810–13
Fort Kootenay ca 1811
Kullyspell House 1809–11
Fort Kootenay 1810
1808–9
1812–?
1812–13
Fort Flathead 1812–13
Fort Spokane 1812–13 PFC 1813–21 NWC
Joseph Howse House 1810–11
Skeet-Shoo Outpost 1812
Saleesh House 1809–21
Courter's Fort ca 1809–10
To the headwaters of the Missouri
COLUMBIA
Columbia River (Concomely)
Astoria (Fort George) 1811–13 PFC
Fort Clatsop 1805–6
New Fort George 1814
Fort Winship 1810
Oak Point Fishing Station 1812–13
William Henry Fort (Willamette Post) 1813–14
Wallace House (Willamette Post) 1812–13
To source of Willamette
Fort Nez Percés (Fort Walla Walla) 1818–21
McKenzie's Outpost 1812
To Snake country
Scale 1:6 000 000

Cook's third voyage (1776–80) demonstrated the profitability of the sea-otter trade along the northwest coast of North America. Vessels from several nations entered this trade, but Americans, unencumbered by commercial restrictions and political considerations, rapidly became dominant. The early trade depended on Indian middlemen, who already participated in well-established trading networks (pls 13, 14) at the main outer-coast villages. Besides sea-otter pelts, white traders obtained fresh water, wood, foodstuffs, elk skins, and eulachon oil. In Cook's day they offered trinkets and beads in return, but soon they had to supply copper and unwrought iron, and then firearms, textiles, rice, molasses, and rum. Eventually the search for furs led them to penetrate the intricate waterways leading off the outer coast. Although most trade was patterned on native protocol that required introductory ceremonies, gift exchanges, and price negotiations, the relationship between white and Indian traders is best characterized as one of mutual distrust, even animosity, tempered by greed.

After 1805 the Montréal-based North West Company established a number of forts beyond the Rockies in the Upper Fraser area (New Caledonia) and in the Columbia River system (Columbia District). Its operation on the Columbia was briefly and vigorously challenged by the Pacific Fur Company, but the American company withdrew during the War of 1812. Until 1821 New Caledonia and the Columbia District remained trading territories of the North West Company.

EXPLORATION IN THE FAR NORTHWEST

Author: Richard I. Ruggles

Except for the few Russian traders who obtained sea-otter pelts in western Alaska and sold them in Mongolia, the northwestern corner of North America remained outside the range of European knowledge until the last quarter of the 18th century. In 1770 trade in land furs had not reached the Mackenzie drainage basin and barely touched the Rocky Mountains (pls 58, 61, 62), while the Spanish (who claimed the entire West Coast of the New World) had just begun to establish outposts in southern California. On world maps of the day northwestern North America was blank.

This was soon changed. In the mid 1770s the Spaniards Pérez and Quadra sailed north along the West Coast in search of Russian interlopers. Finding none, they quickly left. In 1778 a British expedition under Cook spent a month at Nootka on Vancouver Island, then sailed northward to search for the passage that the admiralty thought might lie about 60°N. After Cook the broad outline of the Northwest Coast was known. In the early 1790s British and Spanish surveys, the most extensive by Vancouver, filled in many details.

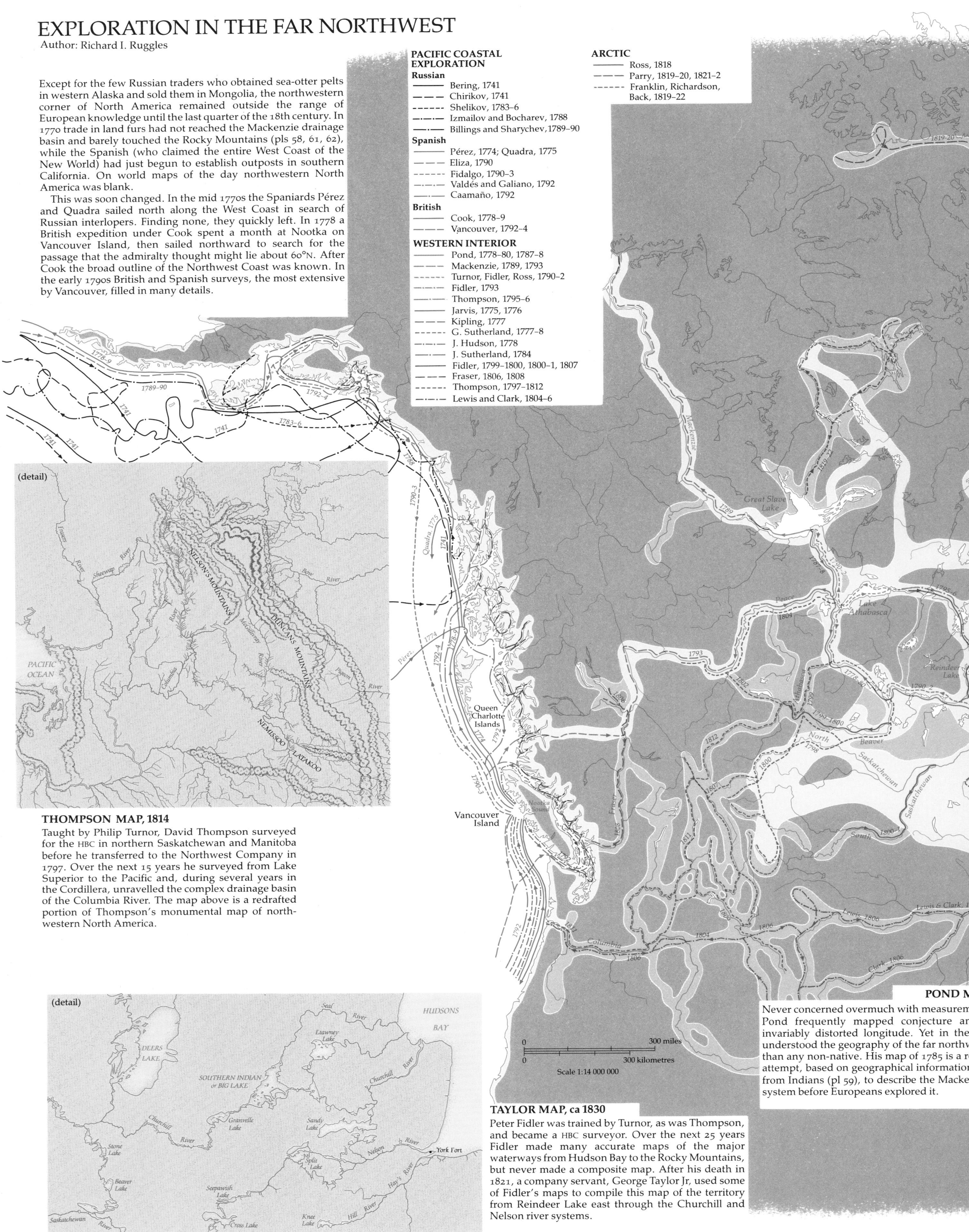
PACIFIC COASTAL EXPLORATION
Russian
Bering, 1741
Chirikov, 1741
Shelikov, 1783–6
Izmailov and Bocharev, 1788
Billings and Sharychev, 1789–90
Spanish
Pérez, 1774; Quadra, 1775
Eliza, 1790
Fidalgo, 1790–3
Valdés and Galiano, 1792
Caamaño, 1792
British
Cook, 1778–9
Vancouver, 1792–4
WESTERN INTERIOR
Pond, 1778–80, 1787–8
Mackenzie, 1789, 1793
Turnor, Fidler, Ross, 1790–2
Fidler, 1793
Thompson, 1795–6
Jarvis, 1775, 1776
Kipling, 1777
G. Sutherland, 1777–8
J. Hudson, 1778
J. Sutherland, 1784
Fidler, 1799–1800, 1800–1, 1807
Fraser, 1806, 1808
Thompson, 1797–1812
Lewis and Clark, 1804–6
ARCTIC
Ross, 1818
Parry, 1819–20, 1821–2
Franklin, Richardson, Back, 1819–22
Mackenzie
Great Slave Lake
Lake Athabasca
Peace
Reindeer Lake
North
Beaver
Saskatchewan
South
Queen Charlotte Islands
Vancouver Island
Nootka Sound
Columbia
Lewis
Clark
(detail)
PACIFIC OCEAN
NELSON'S MOUNTAINS
DUNCAN'S MOUNTAINS
NEMISSOO
LATAKOO
Bow River
Sheewap River
(detail)
HUDSONS BAY
DEERS LAKE
SOUTHERN INDIAN or BIG LAKE
Churchill River
Granville Lake
Sandy Lake
Nelson River
York Fort
Split Lake
Stone Lake
Beaver Lake
Seepawish Lake
Knee Lake
Cross Lake
Hill River
Hay's River
Seal River
Etawney Lake
Saskatchewan River
0 300 miles
0 300 kilometres
Scale 1:14 000 000

THOMPSON MAP, 1814
Taught by Philip Turnor, David Thompson surveyed for the HBC in northern Saskatchewan and Manitoba before he transferred to the Northwest Company in 1797. Over the next 15 years he surveyed from Lake Superior to the Pacific and, during several years in the Cordillera, unravelled the complex drainage basin of the Columbia River. The map above is a redrafted portion of Thompson's monumental map of northwestern North America.

TAYLOR MAP, ca 1830
Peter Fidler was trained by Turnor, as was Thompson, and became a HBC surveyor. Over the next 25 years Fidler made many accurate maps of the major waterways from Hudson Bay to the Rocky Mountains, but never made a composite map. After his death in 1821, a company servant, George Taylor Jr, used some of Fidler's maps to compile this map of the territory from Reindeer Lake east through the Churchill and Nelson river systems.

POND M
Never concerned overmuch with measurem Pond frequently mapped conjecture an invariably distorted longitude. Yet in the understood the geography of the far northw than any non-native. His map of 1785 is a re attempt, based on geographical information from Indians (pl 59), to describe the Macker system before Europeans explored it.

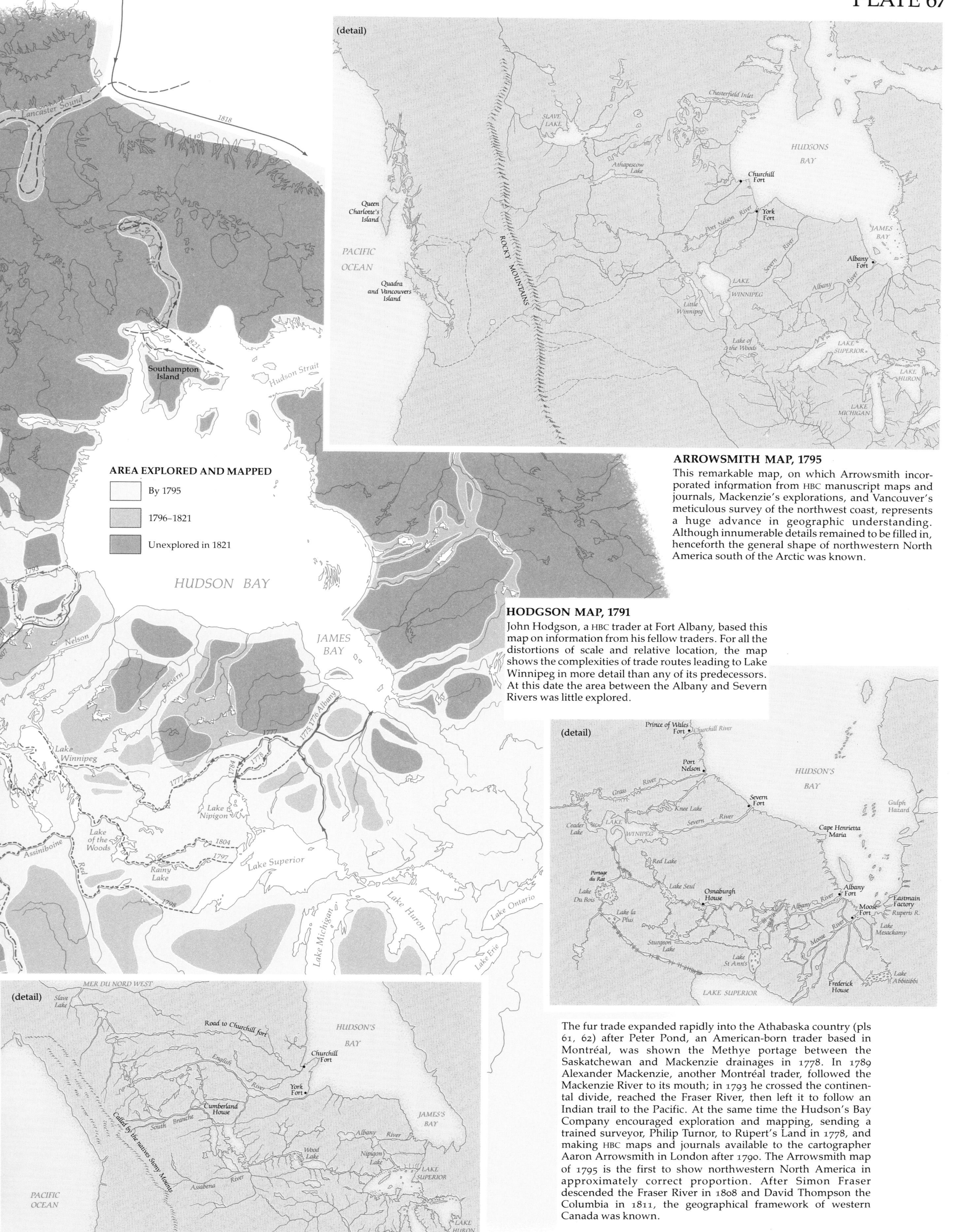
AREA EXPLORED AND MAPPED
By 1795
1796–1821
Unexplored in 1821
Lancaster Sound
1818
Southampton Island
1821-2
Hudson Strait
HUDSON BAY
JAMES BAY
Nelson
Severn
Albany
1807
1793
1777
1775,1776
1778
1777-8
1784
1797
1804
1798
Lake Winnipeg
Lake Nipigon
Lake of the Woods
Rainy Lake
Assiniboine
Red
Lake Superior
Lake Michigan
Lake Huron
Lake Ontario
Lake Erie
(detail)
Chesterfield Inlet
SLAVE LAKE
HUDSONS BAY
Athapescow Lake
Churchill Fort
York Fort
Port Nelson River
Queen Charlotte's Island
PACIFIC OCEAN
Quadra and Vancouvers Island
ROCKY MOUNTAINS
JAMES BAY
Albany Fort
Severn River
LAKE WINNIPEG
Little Winnipeg
Albany River
Lake of the Woods
LAKE SUPERIOR
LAKE HURON
LAKE MICHIGAN
(detail)
Prince of Wales Fort
Churchill River
Port Nelson
HUDSON'S BAY
Grass River
Knee Lake
Severn Fort
Severn River
Ceader Lake
LAKE WINIPEG
Gulph Hazard
Cape Henrietta Maria
Red Lake
Portage du Rat
Lake Seul
Osnaburgh House
Lake Du Bois
Lake la Plus
Albany River
Albany Fort
Moose Fort
Eastmain Factory
Ruperts R.
Lake Mesackamy
Moose River
Sturgeon Lake
Lake St Ann's
Lake Abbitibbi
Frederick House
LAKE SUPERIOR
(detail)
MER DU NORD WEST
Slave Lake
Road to Churchill fort
HUDSON'S BAY
Churchill Fort
English River
York Fort
Cumberland House
South Branche
Called by the natives Stony Mounts
JAMES'S BAY
Albany River
Wood Lake
Nipigon Lake
LAKE SUPERIOR
Assabena River
PACIFIC OCEAN
LAKE HURON

ARROWSMITH MAP, 1795

This remarkable map, on which Arrowsmith incorporated information from HBC manuscript maps and journals, Mackenzie's explorations, and Vancouver's meticulous survey of the northwest coast, represents a huge advance in geographic understanding. Although innumerable details remained to be filled in, henceforth the general shape of northwestern North America south of the Arctic was known.

HODGSON MAP, 1791

John Hodgson, a HBC trader at Fort Albany, based this map on information from his fellow traders. For all the distortions of scale and relative location, the map shows the complexities of trade routes leading to Lake Winnipeg in more detail than any of its predecessors. At this date the area between the Albany and Severn Rivers was little explored.

The fur trade expanded rapidly into the Athabaska country (pls 61, 62) after Peter Pond, an American-born trader based in Montréal, was shown the Methye portage between the Saskatchewan and Mackenzie drainages in 1778. In 1789 Alexander Mackenzie, another Montréal trader, followed the Mackenzie River to its mouth; in 1793 he crossed the continental divide, reached the Fraser River, then left it to follow an Indian trail to the Pacific. At the same time the Hudson's Bay Company encouraged exploration and mapping, sending a trained surveyor, Philip Turnor, to Rupert's Land in 1778, and making HBC maps and journals available to the cartographer Aaron Arrowsmith in London after 1790. The Arrowsmith map of 1795 is the first to show northwestern North America in approximately correct proportion. After Simon Fraser descended the Fraser River in 1808 and David Thompson the Columbia in 1811, the geographical framework of western Canada was known.

Canada in 1800

Early in the American Revolution American armies attacked Québec, as the British but largely French-speaking colony centred on the St Lawrence River was then called, capturing Montréal and laying midwinter siege to the town of Québec. The siege failed and the fleeing Americans were chased south of Lake Champlain (pl 44). Later the American delegation at the peace negotiations in Paris sensed that Britain, wishing to contain the influence of France, would seek a speedy settlement and the good will of her former colonies, and demanded the whole of Québec for the United States. By such terms Britain would retain in North America only Newfoundland, Nova Scotia, and Rupert's Land (pl 57). These terms were unacceptable to the British, but they were prepared to cede the continental heartland south and west of the Great Lakes, abandoning the Ohio valley, the upper Mississippi valley, and trading posts and Indian allies there. Territory that the French had explored and that the St Lawrence fur trade had dominated for years passed to the United States.

Yet the boundary drawn in 1783 – with minor adjustments the present southern boundary of eastern Canada – reflected a long-established European position in North America. In 1783 British North America included the main fisheries in the northwestern Atlantic, begun by French and Portuguese fishermen at the beginning of the 16th century, and principally English and French at the end of the 18th century. It included Acadia, the French colony centred on the Bay of Fundy, although in 1783 the Acadians were largely gone, other settlers had come, and the area was known as Nova Scotia. It included the Gulf of St Lawrence, explored by Jacques Cartier in the 1530s, and the entrance to the colony of Canada (New France) throughout the French regime. It included the St Lawrence River where Cartier tried to plant a settlement and Samuel de Champlain eventually succeeded in doing so; the towns of Québec, Trois-Rivières, and Montréal; and the farming population that spread from them along the river. It included the fur trade connection with the West, not all of it, but its productive northern edge, a well-established canoe route to the northwest. A relationship with the continental interior had been preserved. After 1783 Montréal remained a gateway to the interior fur trade, with the difference that, after the border settlement and the eventual closure of British posts in American territory, almost all the fur brigades went to Lake Superior to rendezvous with others coming from the Petit Nord (north of Lake Superior) or the Grand Nord (northwest of Lake Winnipeg).

What had been lost was the largely unrealized agricultural potential of the area that would become the Middle West of the United States. Late in the French regime, at Kaskaskia and other settlements on the upper Mississippi and at Vincennes on the Wabash (pl 41), the agricultural bounty of this region was recognized. Father Louis Vivier, a Jesuit who served the Illinois settlements, reported the yield of corn there in amazement: the most successful landholder at Kaskaskia worked some 200 ha of arable land, owned 60 slaves (including women and children), and grazed many hundred cattle, swine, and horses on the common south of the village. With good land, a moderate climate, and a market (in the French sugar islands) a type and scale of agriculture unknown along the lower St Lawrence was emerging. After the conquest British policy, although increasingly difficult to enforce as settlers from the seaboard colonies began to spill across the Appalachians, was to preserve the interior for native groups, at least for the time being, to avoid another costly war. In 1783 Britain ceded to the United States territory in which the fur trade was doomed, and which, given the numbers to the south, the small population along the lower St Lawrence would not be able to colonize. The border settlement closed off an unexploited agricultural possibility and, in the long run, a different, more abundant direction of North American development. The surviving British position in North America was conservative and ironic. It comprised the heart of the 17th-century French position in North America plus Rupert's Land and all of Newfoundland. In this area were two well-established staple trades, the towns associated with them, several small, rockbound patches of agricultural settlement, and a vast area of rock and forest in which Indians were still the principal or, in many places, the only population.

At the end of the Seven Years' War (1763) there had been three British colonies in the area that would remain as British North America after the American Revolution: Québec, the core of the truncated French colony of Canada (pl 42); Nova Scotia; and Newfoundland. A few years later the crown surveyed the Island of St John in the colony of Nova Scotia into 66 lots (townships) of some 20 000 acres each, and disposed of most of the lots by lottery to absentee proprietors in Britain. The new landlords petitioned for the political separation of their island from mainland Nova Scotia, and in 1769 the colony of the Island of St John (renamed Prince Edward Island in 1798) came into being with barely 300 settlers. In the early 1780s Loyalist migrations led to the further fragmentation of Nova Scotia, from which the colonies of New Brunswick and Cape Breton Island were created in 1784. In the colony of Québec Loyalist migration to land along the upper St Lawrence River and the eastern Great Lakes introduced a sizeable English-speaking population to a colony with French civil laws and land tenure. In 1791, following the Constitutional Act, Québec was divided into Upper and Lower Canada, each with different provisions for law, language, and religion. The ill-defined northern boundary of these colonies was the southern boundary of Rupert's Land, the territory around Hudson Bay granted to the Hudson's Bay Company in 1670 (pl 57). In these ways were established the colonial boundaries within British North America that are shown on plate 68.

In Newfoundland, along much of the Atlantic coast of Cape Breton Island and Nova Scotia, and around the northern and western Gulf of St Lawrence, the pattern of settlement at the end of the 18th century was the creation of the cod fishery. Except for two small islands south of Newfoundland, Saint-Pierre and Miquelon, France had lost her territorial base for a resident fishery, but her migratory fishery continued year after year until interrupted by the Napoleonic Wars, creating seasonal fishing stations in northern and western Newfoundland (pls 21, 25, and 68) to supplement the residential fishery on Saint-Pierre and Miquelon, and sending many ships directly to the banks. The English fishery had become largely residential, relying on local rather than immigrant labour and, increasingly at the end of the century, on merchant houses based in the New World. In 1800 some 16 000 people, virtually all of them dependent on the fishery, lived around the coast of Newfoundland. Fish merchants dominated St John's, Harbour Grace, Carbonear, and Trinity, sending supply ships and agents along the coast and collecting fish. The tiny, ramshackle fishing settlements perched above the sea were connected to the outside world by these merchants who bought their catch, sold supplies, and extended credit. Debt was the fisherman's common lot. The lines of power were simple and direct: the economy was dominated by merchants, the outports by the towns where the merchants lived, and daily life by the routine of the fishery. In Cape Breton and along the Atlantic coast of Nova Scotia the pattern was much the same, although the merchant firms that controlled these fisheries operated from Halifax, Jersey, or New England. In Gaspé the principal merchants were from Jersey or the town of Québec. Merchants from Québec operated migratory fisheries along the forbidding north shore of the Gulf of St Lawrence, while merchants from Newfoundland or from Devon, Bristol, and Jersey dominated the northeastern corner of the Gulf and the Strait of Belle Isle. At only a few harbours along the Strait of Belle Isle were there any winter residents, although much of this coast had been fished continually for 300 years.

In 1800, as from the beginning, the cod fishery did not use native labour. Labour was supplied seasonally by migrants from Europe or by residents of European stock. In 1800 the resident fishermen in Newfoundland all spoke English, in accents from the West Country, southern England, or Ireland; almost half of them were Irish. On Cape Breton Island most fishermen were Acadians. In Nova Scotia most had come from fishing villages in New England, although many Lunenburgers, who spoke a German dialect, were fishermen. On the Gaspé the fishery was more diverse ethnically than anywhere else: French-speaking Canadians and Acadians, some New Englanders, some Channel Islanders, some English and Irish. Although the techniqes of catching and processing cod, the merchant system, and the poverty of the fishermen were everywhere much the same, the fishery supported inbred and ethnically distinctive communities in tiny, isolated settlements dependent on a resource that could sustain the local young for several generations. In some outports one or two surnames accounted for all families; throughout the fishing settlements the symbols of ethnicity were full of meaning.

The fur trade, which had drawn French settlement to the St Lawrence valley and the Bay of Fundy and for a time was conducted there, had long since expanded inland. In 1800 its most profitable territory was more than 4 000 km by canoe from Montréal in the drainage basin of the Mackenzie River (pls 61, 62). Plate 68 shows two of the main routes to the interior fur trade; from Montréal to the upper Great Lakes, and from Fort Albany to the fur country north of Lake Superior. Supplies and trade goods passed along them inbound for dozens of posts scattered across huge territories, and furs and some hides passed outbound for London, England. These high-value, low-bulk exports, which could be carried by a couple of ships a year sailing from the town of Québec or from the posts along Hudson Bay, were the sole export from Hudson Bay in 1800 and easily the principal export (by value) from the lower St Lawrence. Unlike the cod fishery the fur trade spread across a continent and brought Indians and Europeans together, but it too drew capital and labour from Europe, and created isolated settlements dominated by the work routines of a staple trade and the transportation connection to distant supplies and markets. In the 16th century the fur trade had grown slowly out of the cod fishery, and at the end of the 18th century fish merchants operating along the Labrador shore still traded for a few furs. Otherwise the two activities were completely separate: differently owned, organized, and supplied with labour, and with nothing to trade to the other.

The towns along the St Lawrence had grown very slowly since the end of the French regime. Québec, the largest town in British North America in 1800, had not many more than 8 000 civil inhabitants, Montréal not more than 6 000. As merchant control of the fishery shifted across the Atlantic, several small towns emerged in Newfoundland, the largest of them, St John's, with some 3 000 inhabitants in 1800. Halifax, laid out as a garrison town in 1749 and by 1800 a busy Atlantic port, was a little larger; Saint John, created by Loyalist settlement along the Saint John River in New Brunswick, somewhat smaller. Located on navigable water, these small, preindustrial towns depended on commerce, administration, and the military in some combination. Supporting these functions was an array of services and the trades associated with a port, construction, and the manufacture of relatively inexpensive and often bulky consumer goods. Occupationally the towns were fairly diverse, and socially they were sharply stratified, their élites made up of colonial officials, military officers, and merchants – more of one than another in different places. The conquest, which had little impact on the functions of Québec, Montréal, and Trois-Rivières, had largely replaced their élites. Ethnically the towns were differently composed – those in Newfoundland primarily English and Irish; those in Lower Canada predominantly Canadian but with additions from Britain, New York, and New England; Saint John made up primarily of Loyalists from several former colonies plus various elements directly from Britain; Halifax, a mix of New Englanders, English, and a few Scots, Irish, Acadians, Germans, and blacks – but all these towns tended to be more diverse ethnically than their counterparts in western Europe. They were not part of a simple system or hierarchy of British North American towns; the towns of the different British North American colonies commanded local trades and were connected to the outside world but were little connected to each other.

Taken together the towns accounted for less than 10% of the some 350 000 people who lived in the seven British North American colonies in 1800. Virtually everyone in Newfoundland and the majority along the Atlantic coasts of Nova Scotia and Cape Breton Island and around the Gaspé peninsula depended on the fishery. Elsewhere most rural people were farmers. Farming and the local agricultural economy directly supported some three-quarters of the non-native population of British North America in 1800.

Farming took place fairly close to the climatic margin on land that was bounded, rarely far away, by rock and soils that could not be cultivated. Usually there was neither a sizeable local market for agricultural products nor much opportunity to sell abroad. Although coasting vessels, local merchants, and town markets provided commercial outlets and although flour, biscuits, dried peas, and meat were exported, agriculture was at least as much a subsistence as a commercial activity in the British North American colonies. The Atlantic colonies were substantial net importers of agricultural goods. In all colonies almost all farms were small, mixed operations providing most of the subsistence needs of the families that worked them, plus an erratic surplus for sale – a livelihood, rarely much more, in return for hard work with simple tools on indifferent land far from markets.

Where the population was small, the pace of immigration slow, and land that could be worked available, sons and daughters would establish their own farms close to their parents'. Communities of interrelated people would soon emerge. When such land was no longer to be had, land prices would rise, some farms would be divided, and many of the young would have to leave the circumscribed local worlds of their upbringing. Stability and movement, cultural continuity within familiar local communities and change when people left them, were being built into the structure of rural life. The availability, however limited, of agricultural land tended to provide opportunities for the poor, while the weakness of markets made prosperity elusive for everyone. In many rural areas the social range was not very great. Where there were locational advantages (eg near a town), or where accessible land was particularly good (eg much of the Montréal plain or some of the former Acadian land around the Bay of Fundy), agriculture was more commercial, land values higher, and the social gradient steeper. In the new settlements of Upper Canada British military spending, capital brought by settlers, and the availability of good land created a vigorous agricultural start; by 1800 the export-oriented wheat economy of the region in the early 19th century was beginning to emerge. In Lower Canada where the countryside near the towns had been settled for six or more generations and the rural population was far larger than anywhere else in British North America, the agricultural economy was sluggish. Yet in 1800 almost 400 000 bushels of wheat, flour, and biscuits were exported. Some merchants amassed modest fortunes from rural dealings, and the weight of numbers in well-settled seigneuries produced sizeable revenues for their seigneurs. Some of the British merchants who gained control of the import and export trades of the St Lawrence soon after the conquest invested in seigneuries (pl 51).

Considered overall, however, the scattered patches of agricultural land in British North America in 1800 were not very attractive for investment. The commercial economy focused elsewhere. Agriculture tended to draw people of limited means to land of modest value where, with inordinate work, a family farm might be achieved. Because of the weakness of the rural economy, town and countryside were not very well connected. In only a few places – for example, the parishes near Montréal that supplied most of the voyageurs for the Montréal fur trade or the farms near Québec that supplied foodstuffs for the seasonal fisheries in the Gulf – did agriculture and the staple trades intersect.

The introverted pockets of agricultural settlement scattered across the British North American colonies had been created at different times by different people who knew little or nothing of each other. In 1800 by far the largest population was along the lower St Lawrence River where there were some 215 000 people, roughly 190 000 of whom were descendants of immigrants to Canada from France during the French regime (pl 45). Of the latter, at least 95% lived in the countryside; their farms filled the closely rimmed lowlands near Québec and were rapidly expanding across the Montréal plain, drawing settlers from all the parishes along the river where there was no unclaimed agricultural land. English-speaking people in Lower Canada, perhaps 25 000 of them, controlled the towns and somewhat penetrated the countryside. They bought farms and traded along the Richelieu River, the route of entry from the south; lived near Montréal and Québec with an eye to the urban markets nearby; and, here and there, acquired seigneuries, farms, or set up trades in an overwhelmingly French-speaking rural world. In Upper Canada, where settlement spread discontinuously along the upper St Lawrence River and the north shores of Lake Ontario and Lake Erie, there were perhaps 35 000 people: 2 400 French-speakers along the St Clair River opposite Detroit whose ancestors had settled the area during the French regime; 3 000 Gaelic-speaking Highlanders just established 800 km away at the other end of the colony, near the border with Lower Canada; some 2 000 Indians who had settled in the 1780s on reserves in the Grand River valley, and perhaps 23 000 Loyalists, late Loyalists, and their descendants, most of whom had come from upstate New York. In the Atlantic colonies the farm population, principally Loyalist, was largely from New England and the Middle Colonies, but there were also Acadians tucked away in tiny settlements along the south shore of the Gulf of St Lawrence and around parts of the Bay of Fundy, communities of Gaelic-speakers from the Highlands along the north shore of Nova Scotia, a few Yorkshiremen at the head of the Bay of Fundy, and Lunenburgers south of Halifax. Characteristically these different peoples were separated by rock and distance. Overland transportation was rudimentary. Nothing like a continuous, expanding agricultural frontier mixed peoples of different backgrounds.

In the seven British colonies there were perhaps 18 000 Indians, a small fraction of the population of these areas at the time of European contact. The Beothuk of Newfoundland, pushed off their summer fishing grounds and harassed by white trappers in the interior, were almost extinct. The remnant Micmac in Nova Scotia and New Brunswick lived on reserves. No longer able to rely on game animals and fur bearers, which had been decimated by overhunting, and usually unable to farm because they lacked the land or the skills for this unfamiliar, confining way of life, they were a destitute, starving people. The once-populous Montagnais along the north shore of the Gulf of St Lawrence had been involved with the fur trade and European diseases for almost 300 years. Although their numbers were small and declining, they still occupied their former territory, gathering in bands of up to 100 people along the coast in summer and dispersing far inland in winter to trap and hunt caribou. The Indian groups on reservations in the St Lawrence lowlands and in Upper Canada were mostly refugees, the former from the Iroquois Wars and King Philip's War in the 17th century (pls 35 and 47), the latter from the American Revolution. Economic life was a little easier for these people, many of whom were traditionally agriculturalists. Although increasingly curtailed by white settlement and the depletion of game, some hunting and fishing continued, and some men found seasonal employment, often in the fur trade. Remnants of different peoples lived on the reserves in Upper Canada. Some 2 000 people of nine ethnic backgrounds from three language families lived on the Six Nations Reserve along the Grand River. To the north and northwest some Algonquian groups practised a little agriculture, but most still followed a migratory round of hunting and fishing that was threatened by declining resources. In some areas moose, deer, and woodland caribou were nearly extinct. People depended on fish and small game such as the snowshoe hare, and starved when the hare was at the bottom of its population cycle.

However difficult native life had frequently become, natives were still the predominant and in many areas the only population in most of British North America. Whites were concentrated in a few eastern patches of settlement while some 175 000 native people occupied the rest of British North America (pl 69). In parts of the east 300 years of white contact had spread disease, intensified native warfare, disrupted native economies, and, at worst, left native people with little means of support. In the great crescent of boreal forest, rock, and lake stretching from the Mackenzie valley to central Québec, where the fur trade had long held sway, Indians still hunted and fished in small migratory groups, and many elements of traditional native economies and ways of life survived. Whites were not challenging natives for land. But after years of competitive fur trading, which alcohol sustained when native demands for material goods were satisfied, fur-bearing and game animals were disappearing. As their resource base diminished natives eked out an increasingly precarious existence, or starved, or came to depend on whites for seasonal employment and supplies. Beyond the fur trade, or where it had recently penetrated, native ways held. The Plains Indians, equestrian bison hunters, were only marginally involved with the fur trade and barely tolerated traders. As late as the 1820s the Hudson's Bay Company had only a precarious toehold on the edge of Blackfoot lands, and after several attempts American fur companies had achieved even less. In most of the High Arctic and the vast interior west of the Mackenzie River, Europeans had never been seen. In the Cordillera and along the Pacific Coast newly established fur trades had increased native wealth but had not yet transformed native cultures.

This, in outline, was British North America, approximately the territory that was to become the country of Canada, at the beginning of the 19th century. It was not a premeditated creation, and it was not cohesive, culturally or economically. Different peoples going about different, unconnected activities lived far apart, quite oblivious, for the most part, of each other. For a third of these people the abstract assumption that they were British subjects was an absurdity, and for the majority of the rest, who also did not speak English, British rule was acknowledged ruefully. Yet, British North America in 1800 was the product of some 300 years of European activity in northern North America that began with the cod fishery in eastern Newfoundland, penetrated the Gulf of St Lawrence and the St Lawrence valley, and, dependent on native cultures, spread across much of a continent. This European penetration of North America created the workplaces of staple trades, the towns that eventually supported them, and the pockets of agricultural settlement that developed somewhat inadvertently in their train. In these settings, confined by the land and the limitations of the economy, Europeans worked out their North American lives, in so doing shaping the early story and the emerging pattern of modern Canada.

EASTERN CANADA IN 1800

Authors: R. Cole Harris, David Wood (Upper Canada)

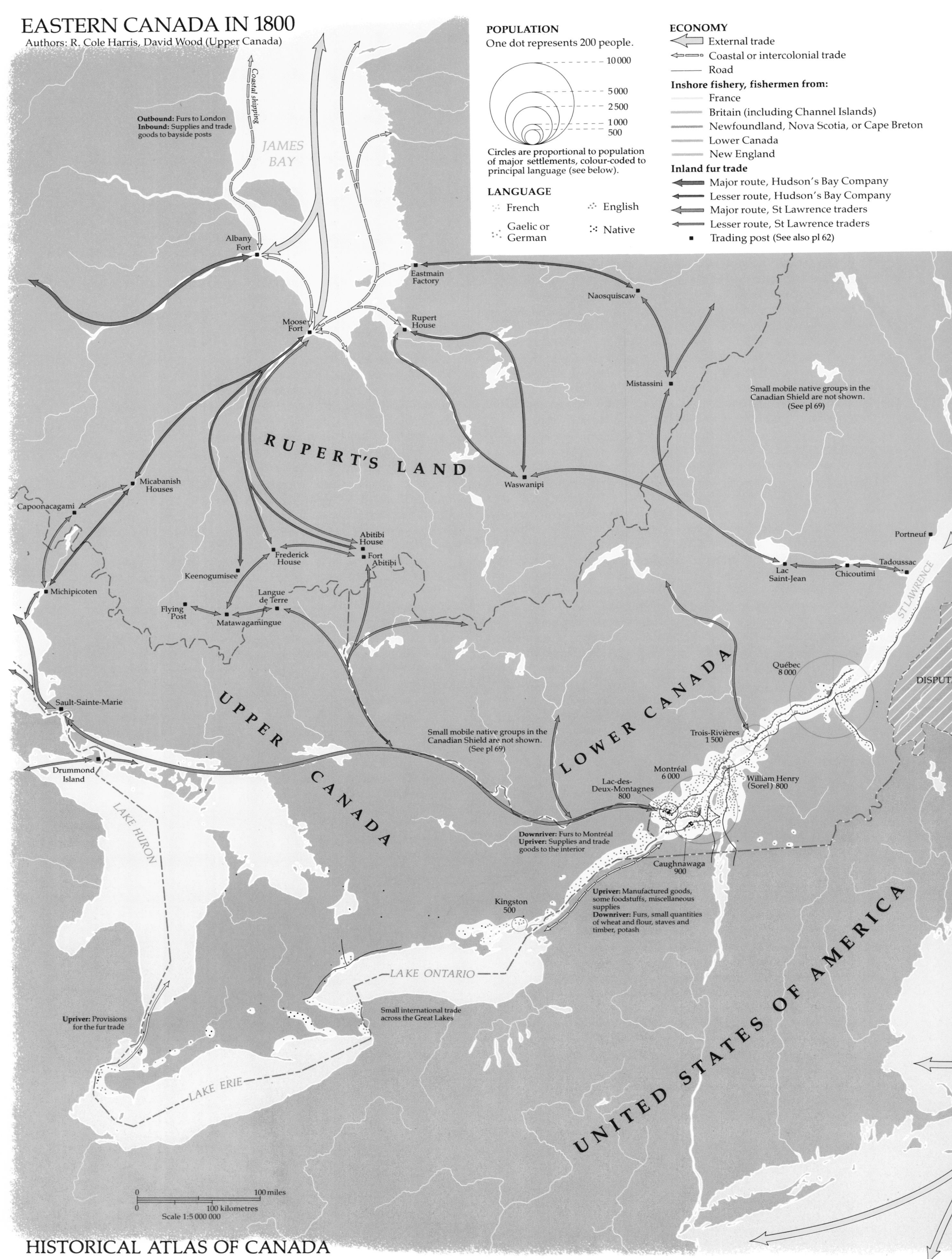
POPULATION
One dot represents 200 people.
10 000
5 000
2 500
1 000
500
Circles are proportional to population of major settlements, colour-coded to principal language (see below).
LANGUAGE
French
English
Gaelic or German
Native
ECONOMY
External trade
Coastal or intercolonial trade
Road
Inshore fishery, fishermen from:
France
Britain (including Channel Islands)
Newfoundland, Nova Scotia, or Cape Breton
Lower Canada
New England
Inland fur trade
Major route, Hudson's Bay Company
Lesser route, Hudson's Bay Company
Major route, St Lawrence traders
Lesser route, St Lawrence traders
Trading post (See also pl 62)
Outbound: Furs to London
Inbound: Supplies and trade goods to bayside posts
Coastal shipping
JAMES BAY
Albany Fort
Eastmain Factory
Moose Fort
Rupert House
Naosquiscaw
Mistassini
Small mobile native groups in the Canadian Shield are not shown. (See pl 69)
RUPERT'S LAND
Waswanipi
Micabanish Houses
Capoonacagami
Abitibi House
Frederick House
Fort Abitibi
Keenogumisee
Langue de Terre
Flying Post
Matawagamingue
Michipicoten
Portneuf
Tadoussac
Lac Saint-Jean
Chicoutimi
ST LAWRENCE
Québec 8 000
DISPUTE
LOWER CANADA
UPPER CANADA
Sault-Sainte-Marie
Small mobile native groups in the Canadian Shield are not shown. (See pl 69)
Trois-Rivières 1 500
Montréal 6 000
William Henry (Sorel) 800
Lac-des-Deux-Montagnes 800
Drummond Island
Downriver: Furs to Montréal
Upriver: Supplies and trade goods to the interior
Caughnawaga 900
LAKE HURON
Upriver: Manufactured goods, some foodstuffs, miscellaneous supplies
Downriver: Furs, small quantities of wheat and flour, staves and timber, potash
Kingston 500
LAKE ONTARIO
Small international trade across the Great Lakes
Upriver: Provisions for the fur trade
LAKE ERIE
UNITED STATES OF AMERICA
0 100 miles
0 100 kilometres
Scale 1:5 000 000

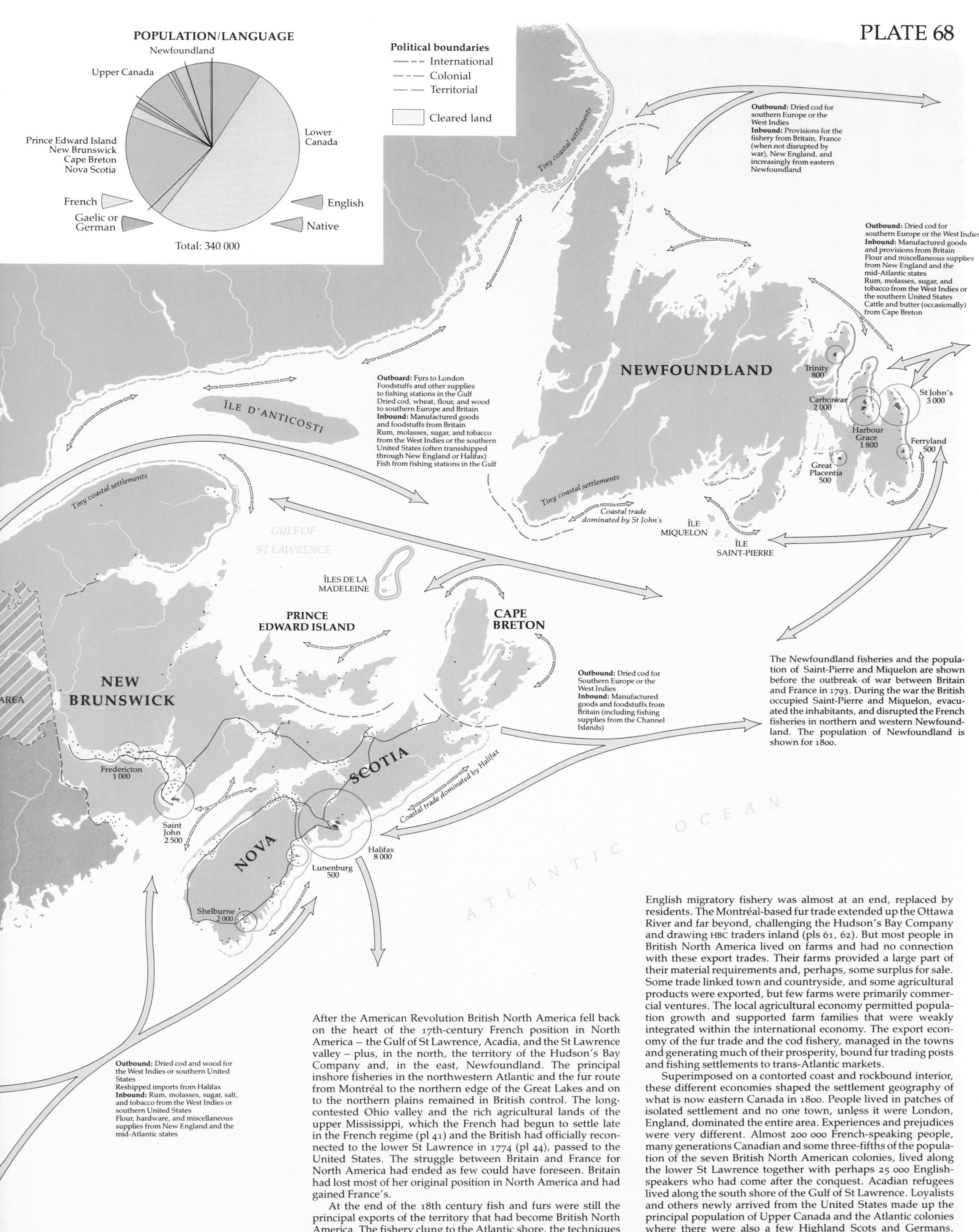
POPULATION/LANGUAGE
Newfoundland
Upper Canada
Lower Canada
Prince Edward Island
New Brunswick
Cape Breton
Nova Scotia
French
English
Gaelic or German
Native
Total: 340 000
Political boundaries
International
Colonial
Territorial
Cleared land
Outbound: Dried cod for southern Europe or the West Indies
Inbound: Provisions for the fishery from Britain, France (when not disrupted by war), New England, and increasingly from eastern Newfoundland
Tiny coastal settlements
Outbound: Dried cod for southern Europe or the West Indies
Inbound: Manufactured goods and provisions from Britain
Flour and miscellaneous supplies from New England and the mid-Atlantic states
Rum, molasses, sugar, and tobacco from the West Indies or the southern United States
Cattle and butter (occasionally) from Cape Breton
NEWFOUNDLAND
Trinity 800
Carbonear 2 000
Harbour Grace 1 800
St John's 3 000
Ferryland 500
Great Placentia 500
Outboard: Furs to London
Foodstuffs and other supplies to fishing stations in the Gulf
Dried cod, wheat, flour, and wood to southern Europe and Britain
Inbound: Manufactured goods and foodstuffs from Britain
Rum, molasses, sugar, and tobacco from the West Indies or the southern United States (often transshipped through New England or Halifax)
Fish from fishing stations in the Gulf
ÎLE D'ANTICOSTI
Tiny coastal settlements
Tiny coastal settlements
Coastal trade dominated by St John's
ÎLE MIQUELON
ÎLE SAINT-PIERRE
GULF OF ST LAWRENCE
ÎLES DE LA MADELEINE
PRINCE EDWARD ISLAND
CAPE BRETON
NEW BRUNSWICK
AREA
Outbound: Dried cod for Southern Europe or the West Indies
Inbound: Manufactured goods and foodstuffs from Britain (including fishing supplies from the Channel Islands)
Fredericton 1 000
Saint John 2 500
SCOTIA
NOVA
Coastal trade dominated by Halifax
Halifax 8 000
Lunenburg 500
Shelburne 2 000
ATLANTIC OCEAN
Outbound: Dried cod and wood for the West Indies or southern United States
Reshipped imports from Halifax
Inbound: Rum, molasses, sugar, salt, and tobacco from the West Indies or southern United States
Flour, hardware, and miscellaneous supplies from New England and the mid-Atlantic states

The Newfoundland fisheries and the population of Saint-Pierre and Miquelon are shown before the outbreak of war between Britain and France in 1793. During the war the British occupied Saint-Pierre and Miquelon, evacuated the inhabitants, and disrupted the French fisheries in northern and western Newfoundland. The population of Newfoundland is shown for 1800.

After the American Revolution British North America fell back on the heart of the 17th-century French position in North America – the Gulf of St Lawrence, Acadia, and the St Lawrence valley – plus, in the north, the territory of the Hudson's Bay Company and, in the east, Newfoundland. The principal inshore fisheries in the northwestern Atlantic and the fur route from Montréal to the northern edge of the Great Lakes and on to the northern plains remained in British control. The long-contested Ohio valley and the rich agricultural lands of the upper Mississippi, which the French had begun to settle late in the French regime (pl 41) and the British had officially reconnected to the lower St Lawrence in 1774 (pl 44), passed to the United States. The struggle between Britain and France for North America had ended as few could have foreseen. Britain had lost most of her original position in North America and had gained France's.

At the end of the 18th century fish and furs were still the principal exports of the territory that had become British North America. The fishery clung to the Atlantic shore, the techniques of catching and processing cod little changed from the 16th century. The French migratory inshore fishery was now largely confined to northern and western Newfoundland, and the English migratory fishery was almost at an end, replaced by residents. The Montréal-based fur trade extended up the Ottawa River and far beyond, challenging the Hudson's Bay Company and drawing HBC traders inland (pls 61, 62). But most people in British North America lived on farms and had no connection with these export trades. Their farms provided a large part of their material requirements and, perhaps, some surplus for sale. Some trade linked town and countryside, and some agricultural products were exported, but few farms were primarily commercial ventures. The local agricultural economy permitted population growth and supported farm families that were weakly integrated within the international economy. The export economy of the fur trade and the cod fishery, managed in the towns and generating much of their prosperity, bound fur trading posts and fishing settlements to trans-Atlantic markets.

Superimposed on a contorted coast and rockbound interior, these different economies shaped the settlement geography of what is now eastern Canada in 1800. People lived in patches of isolated settlement and no one town, unless it were London, England, dominated the entire area. Experiences and prejudices were very different. Almost 200 000 French-speaking people, many generations Canadian and some three-fifths of the population of the seven British North American colonies, lived along the lower St Lawrence together with perhaps 25 000 English-speakers who had come after the conquest. Acadian refugees lived along the south shore of the Gulf of St Lawrence. Loyalists and others newly arrived from the United States made up the principal population of Upper Canada and the Atlantic colonies where there were also a few Highland Scots and Germans. English and Irish fishermen, many of them temporary residents, lived in Newfoundland. There were native people in each colony (pl 69).

NATIVE CANADA, ca 1820

Authors: Conrad E. Heidenreich; Robert M. Galois (New Caledonia)

In the early 1820s the native population of what is now Canada was about 175 000, a significant drop from the 250 000 estimated for the early 17th century (pl 18). Until the late 18th century epidemic disease and, to a degree, warfare were the principal causes of population decline. As the 19th century progressed, starvation took an increasing toll as some areas were over-hunted, and as European settlement increasingly restricted the seasonal mobility of native peoples. The search for provisions and furs precipitated gradual movements of population, particularly towards the foods of the grasslands and tundra and the furs and foods of the northwest. In some areas where the population was expanding bitter warfare ensued as traditional enemies came into closer contact. Seasonal movement was extensive where native groups had access to migratory game.

BEAUFORT SEA
RUSSIAN AMERICA (1825)
Great Bear Lake
Great Slave Lake
Lake Athabasca
PACIFIC OCEAN
NEW CALEDONIA
Lake Winnipeg
COLUMBIA DISTRICT
SPANISH AMERICA
UNITED STATES OF AMERICA

On the east coast native hunting was destroyed, seasonal movements disrupted, and the transition to agriculture made difficult as natives were confined to small parcels of poor land. Harassed and barred from coastal resources, the Beothuk were nearing extinction. Along the upper St Lawrence and lower Great Lakes traditionally agricultural peoples, mostly ethnically and linguistically diverse refugees from the United States, practised a viable mixed farming. The groups of the eastern boreal forest, still masters of their land, were deeply involved in the fur trade and fishing, but faced seasonal food shortages as big game became scarce. Throughout the west and northwest traditional economies based on hunting and fishing persisted, immeshed in fur or pemmican trades. The sea-otter trade had all but disappeared from the northwest coast, but other marine resources remained plentiful and supported large populations. Throughout the intermontane area and the eastern Arctic European-native contact was infrequent, and it had not yet taken place in the High Arctic.

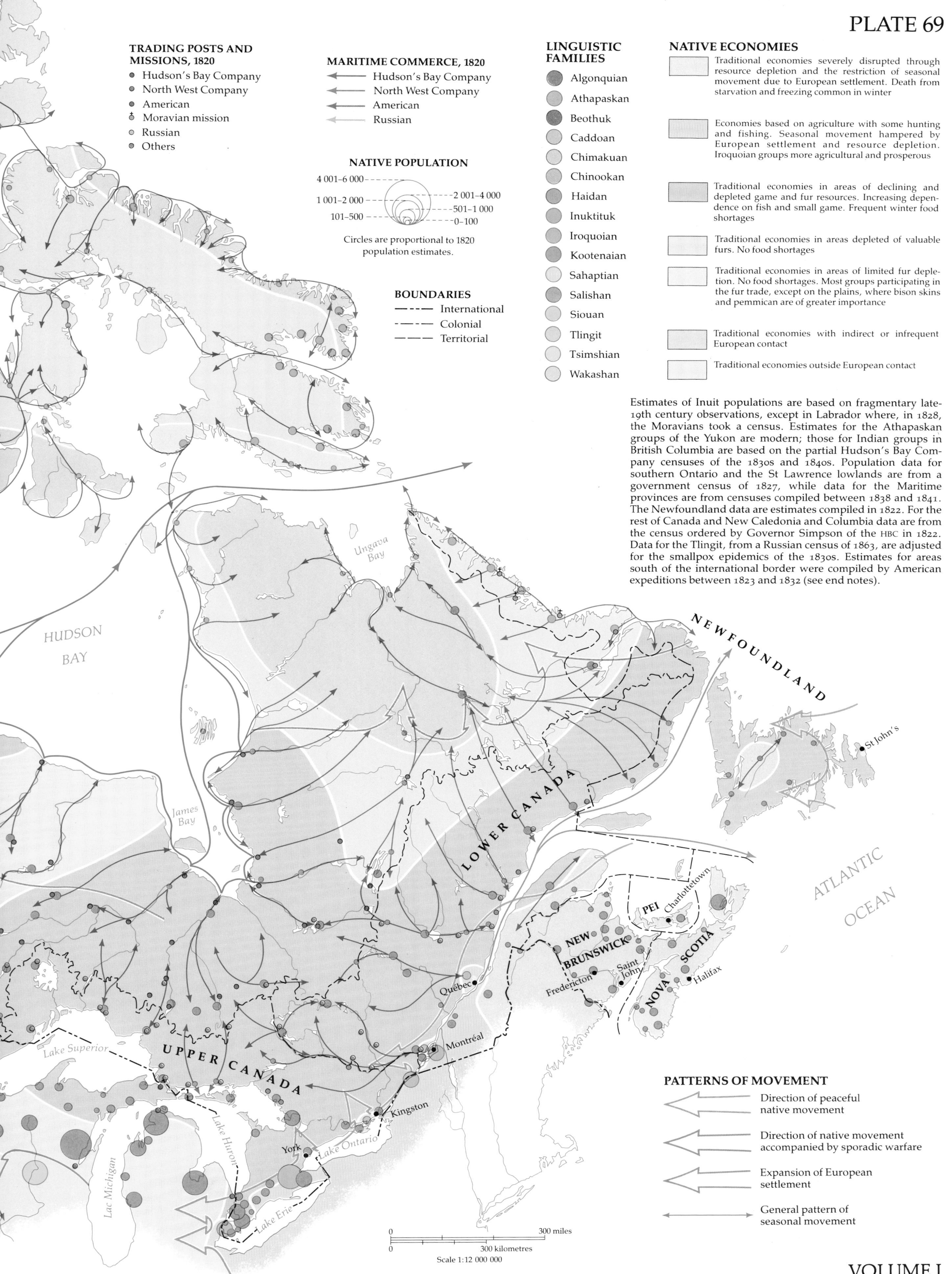
TRADING POSTS AND MISSIONS, 1820
Hudson's Bay Company
North West Company
American
Moravian mission
Russian
Others
MARITIME COMMERCE, 1820
Hudson's Bay Company
North West Company
American
Russian
NATIVE POPULATION
4 001–6 000
1 001–2 000
101–500
2 001–4 000
501–1 000
0–100
Circles are proportional to 1820 population estimates.
BOUNDARIES
International
Colonial
Territorial
LINGUISTIC FAMILIES
Algonquian
Athapaskan
Beothuk
Caddoan
Chimakuan
Chinookan
Haidan
Inuktituk
Iroquoian
Kootenaian
Sahaptian
Salishan
Siouan
Tlingit
Tsimshian
Wakashan
NATIVE ECONOMIES
Traditional economies severely disrupted through resource depletion and the restriction of seasonal movement due to European settlement. Death from starvation and freezing common in winter
Economies based on agriculture with some hunting and fishing. Seasonal movement hampered by European settlement and resource depletion. Iroquoian groups more agricultural and prosperous
Traditional economies in areas of declining and depleted game and fur resources. Increasing dependence on fish and small game. Frequent winter food shortages
Traditional economies in areas depleted of valuable furs. No food shortages
Traditional economies in areas of limited fur depletion. No food shortages. Most groups participating in the fur trade, except on the plains, where bison skins and pemmican are of greater importance
Traditional economies with indirect or infrequent European contact
Traditional economies outside European contact
HUDSON BAY
Ungava Bay
James Bay
NEWFOUNDLAND
St John's
LOWER CANADA
UPPER CANADA
ATLANTIC OCEAN
PEI
Charlottetown
NEW BRUNSWICK
NOVA SCOTIA
Fredericton
Saint John
Halifax
Québec
Montréal
Kingston
York
Lake Superior
Lake Huron
Lac Michigan
Lake Ontario
Lake Erie
PATTERNS OF MOVEMENT
Direction of peaceful native movement
Direction of native movement accompanied by sporadic warfare
Expansion of European settlement
General pattern of seasonal movement
0
300 miles
0
300 kilometres
Scale 1:12 000 000

Estimates of Inuit populations are based on fragmentary late-19th century observations, except in Labrador where, in 1828, the Moravians took a census. Estimates for the Athapaskan groups of the Yukon are modern; those for Indian groups in British Columbia are based on the partial Hudson's Bay Company censuses of the 1830s and 1840s. Population data for southern Ontario and the St Lawrence lowlands are from a government census of 1827, while data for the Maritime provinces are from censuses compiled between 1838 and 1841. The Newfoundland data are estimates compiled in 1822. For the rest of Canada and New Caledonia and Columbia data are from the census ordered by Governor Simpson of the HBC in 1822. Data for the Tlingit, from a Russian census of 1863, are adjusted for the smallpox epidemics of the 1830s. Estimates for areas south of the international border were compiled by American expeditions between 1823 and 1832 (see end notes).

Notes

ANQ	Archives nationales du Québec
CHR	*Canadian Historical Review*
CMC	Canadian Museum of Civilization (formerly National Museum of Man)
CO	Colonial Office (London)
DCB	*Dictionary of Canadian Biography*
DU	Dalhousie University
ECHP	Environment Canada, National Historic Parks (formerly Parks Canada)
GSC	Geological Survey of Canada
HBC	Hudson's Bay Company
Hist Soc	*Histoire sociale / Social History*
MAU	Mount Allison University
MCGU	McGill University
MUN	Memorial University of Newfoundland
NMC	National Map Collection, Public Archives of Canada
NMM	National Museum of Man (see also CMC)
PAC	Public Archives of Canada
PAM	Provincial Archives of Manitoba
PANL	Provincial Archives of Newfoundland and Labrador
PANS	Public Archives of Nova Scotia
PRO	Public Record Office (London)
QU	Queen's University
ROM	Royal Ontario Museum
SFU	Simon Fraser University
UA	University of Alberta
UBC	University of British Columbia
UC	University of Calgary
UL	Université Laval
UMan	University of Manitoba
UMonc	Université de Moncton
UMont	Université de Montréal
UO	University of Ottawa
UT	University of Toronto
WLU	Wilfrid Laurier University
YU	York University

PLATE 1

The Last Ice Sheet, 18 000–10 000 BC

V.K. PREST (Glacial Geology, Geological Survey of Canada)
J.-S. VINCENT (Glacial Geology, Geological Survey of Canada)
J.H. McANDREWS (Department of Botany, Royal Ontario Museum and University of Toronto)

Ice sheet A large-scale ice mass, more than 50 000 km^2, mainly confined by the underlying topography and free to move outward in all directions; a continental-scale glacier such as that now present on Greenland

Primary sources

Prest, V.K. *Retreat of Wisconsin and Recent Ice in North America.* GSC, Map 1257A. 1969
Prest, V.K., D.R. Grant, and V.N. Rampton. *Glacial Map of Canada.* GSC, Map 1253A. 1968

Secondary sources

Dyke, A.S., L.A. Dredge, and J.-S. Vincent. 'Configuration and Dynamics of the Laurentide Ice Sheet during the Late Wisconsinan Maximum.' *Géographie physique et quaternaire* 36 (1982): 5–14
Prest, V.K. 'The Late Wisconsin Glacier Complex.' In R.J. Fulton, ed. *A Canadian Contribution to IGCP Project 24.* 21–36. GSC, Paper 84-10. 1984

The directions of ice flow have been determined by measuring the orientation of ice-flow features recorded on rock surfaces (glacial striae and the upstream ends of glacially smoothed outcrops) and by major drift forms (drumlins and end moraines).

PLATE 2

The Fluted Point People, 9500–8200 BC

ARTHUR ROBERTS (Department of Geography, Simon Fraser University)
J.H. McANDREWS (Department of Botany, Royal Ontario Museum and University of Toronto)
V.K. PREST (Glacial Geology, Geological Survey of Canada)
J.-S. VINCENT (Glacial Geology, Geological Survey of Canada)

Primary sources

The site locations have been established by personal correspondence with Palaeo-Indian archaeologists in Canada. The artefacts illustrated are from the ROM, the CMC, and university collections.

Secondary sources

Clarke, D.W., and A.M. Clark. 'Fluted Points at the Batza Tena Obsidian Source, Northwestern Interior Alaska.' In D.L. Browman, ed. *Early Native Americans.* 142–59. New York: Mouton, 1980
Dumond, D.E. 'The Archaeology of Alaska and the Peopling of America.'' *Science* 209 (1980): 984–91
Fladmark, K.R. 'Routes: Alternate Migration Corridors for Early Man in North America.' *American Antiquity* 44, no. 1 (1979): 55–69
– 'Paleo-Indian Artifacts from the Peace River District.' *B.C. Studies* 48 (Winter 1980–1): 124–36
Gryba, E.M. 'Archaeological Field Work in the Sibbald Flat Area, Alaska.' *Archaeology in Alberta, 1980.* Occasional Paper 17 (1981): 139–51
Haynes, C.V. 'Were Clovis Progenitors in Beringia?' In *Paleoecology of Beringia.* Ed D.M. Hopkins, J.V. Matthews, Jr, C.E. Schweger, and S.B. Young. 383–98. New York: Academic Press, 1982
Kehoe, T.F. 'The Distribution and Implications of Fluted Points in Saskatchewan.' *American Antiquity* 31 (1966): 530–9
MacDonald, G.F. 'Debert, a Paleo-Indian Site in Central Nova Scotia.' *Anthropology Papers,* no. 16. Ottawa: National Museums of Canada, 1968
Morlan, R.E., and J. Cinq-Mars. 'Ancient Beringians: Human Occupation in the Late Pleistocene of Alaska and the Yukon Territory.' In *Paleoecology of Beringia.* Ed D.M. Hopkins, J.V. Matthews, Jr, C.E. Schweger, and S.B. Young. 353–81. New York: Academic Press, 1982
Pettipas, L. 'A Further Contribution to the Paleo-Indian Prehistory of Manitoba.' *Manitoba Archaeological Quarterly* 5, no. 2 (1981): 38–54
Prest, V.K. *Retreat of Wisconsin and Recent Ice in North America.* GSC, Map 1257A. 1969
Prest, V.K., D.R. Grant, and V.N. Rampton. *Glacial Map of Canada.* GSC, Map 1253A. 1968
Storck, P.L. 'Early Man Research in Northeastern North America.' *Early Man News.* vol 314, Newsletter for Human Paleoecology. Ed D.W. Clark, H. Laville, H. Muller-Beck, and M. Valishko. 83–91. Tübingen: Commission for the Paleoecology of Early Man of International Union for Quaternary Research, 1979
Wilson, M. 'Once upon a River: Archaeology and Geology of the Bow River at Calgary, Alberta, Canada.' PH D thesis, UC, 1981

All known Canadian and Alaskan Fluted Point finds are shown as accurately as the scale permits. The environment is described at ca 9500 BC. The position of the ice margin has been determined by the systematic mapping of ice-marginal features. The age control of the margin is based on radiocarbon dating of organic deposits (shells, wood, peat, lake deposits, etc).

Critical comments and data from the following have made this plate possible: D. Clark, J. Cinq-Mars, M. Doll, K. Fladmark, E. Gryba, D. Keenleyside, G. Lowther, G. MacDonald, R. Morlan, L. Pettipas, B. Reeves, W. Roosa, P. Storck, M. Wilson, J. Wright.

PLATE 3

Southern Ontario, 8600 BC

ARTHUR ROBERTS (Department of Geography, Simon Fraser University)
J.H. McANDREWS (Department of Botany, Royal Ontario Museum and University of Toronto)

Primary sources

The site locations come from personal correspondence with all the active Palaeo-Indian archaeologists in Ontario, extensive personal field work, and the publications listed below. The artefacts illustrated are from the ROM or from university research collections.

Secondary sources

Deller, D.B. 'Paleo-Indian Locations on Late Pleistocene Shorelines, Middlesex County, Ontario.' *Ontario Archaeology* 26 (1976): 3–19
– 'Paleo-Indian Reconnaissance in the Counties of Lambton and Middlesex, Ontario.' *Ontario Archaeology* 32 (1979): 3–20
Deller, D.B., and C. Ellis. 'Crowfield: A Preliminary Report on a Probable Paleo-Indian Cremation in Southwestern Ontario.' *Archaeology of Eastern North America* 12 (1984): 41–71
Garrad, C. 'Ontario Fluted Point Survey.' *Ontario Archaeology* 16 (1971): 3–18
Kidd, E.E. 'Fluted Points in Ontario.' *American Antiquity* 16, no. 3 (1951): 260
Roberts, A. 'Paleo-Indian on the North Shore of Lake Ontario.' *Archaeology of Eastern North America* 12 (1984): 248–65
Roosa, W.B., and D.B. Deller. 'The Parkhill Complex and Eastern Great Lakes Paleo Indian.' *Ontario Archaeology* 37 (1982): 3–15
Storck, P.L. 'Paleo-Indian Settlement Patterns.' *Canadian Journal of Archaeology* 6, no. 1 (1982): 1–32
– 'Research into the Paleo-Indian Occupations of Ontario: A Review.' *Ontario Archaeology* 41 (1984): 3–28
For vegetation patterns see pl 4.

The block diagrams of the Fisher and Parkhill sites were produced at SFU from aerial photographs of these sites and using analytical photogrammetric and computer-mapping procedures. These results were used by Catherine Farley as sources for her drawings.

The following have contributed invaluable advice and data: D.B. Deller, G. Dibb, C. Ellis, C. Garrad, L. Jackson, W. Roosa, P. Storck, P. Von Bitter.

PLATE 4

Environmental Change After 9000 BC

J.H. McANDREWS (Department of Botany, Royal Ontario Museum and University of Toronto)
K.-B. LIU (Department of Geography and Anthropology, Louisiana State University)
G.C. MANVILLE (Department of Botany, Academy of Natural Sciences, Philadelphia)
V.K. PREST (Glacial Geology, Geological Survey of Canada)
J.-S. VINCENT (Glacial Geology, Geological Survey of Canada)

Secondary sources

Bernabo, J.C., and T. Webb. 'Changing Patterns in the Holocene Pollen Record of Northeastern North America: A Mapped Summary.' *Quaternary Research* 8 (1977): 64–97
Delcourt, P.A., and H.A. Delcourt. 'Vegetation Maps for Eastern North America: 40,000 yr BP to the Present.' In R.C. Romans, ed. *Geobotany II.* New York: Plenum, 1981
Denton, G.H., and T.J. Hughes, eds. *The Last Great Ice Sheets.* New York: Wiley, 1981
Hopkins, D.M., J.V. Matthews, Jr, C.E. Schweger, and S.B. Young, eds. *Paleoecology of Beringia.* New York: Academic Press, 1982
Liu, K.-B. 'Pollen Evidence of Late-Quaternary Climatic Changes in Canada: A Review. Part I: Western Canada.' *Ontario Geography* 15 (1980): 83–101
– 'Pollen Evidence of Late-Quaternary Climatic Changes in Canada: A Review. Part II: Eastern Arctic and Sub-Arctic Canada.' *Ontario Geography* 17 (1981): 61–82
Matthews, J.V., Jr. 'Tertiary and Quaternary Environments: Historical Background for an Analysis of the Canadian Insect Fauna'. In *Canada and Its Insects.* Ed. H.V. Danks. *Memoirs of the Entomological Society of Canada* 108 (1979): 31–86
Prest, V.K. 'Quaternary Geology of Canada.' In R.J.W. Douglas, ed. *The Geology and Economic Minerals of Canada.* 677–763. GSC, Economic Report No. 1. Ottawa, 1970
Ritchie, J.C. *Past and Present Vegetation of the Far Northwest of Canada.* Toronto: University of Toronto Press, 1984
Wright, H.E., Jr, ed. *Late-Quaternary Environments of the United States.* 2 vols. Minneapolis: University of Minnesota Press, 1983

PLATE 5

The Plano People, 8500–6000 BC

ARTHUR ROBERTS (Department of Geography, Simon Fraser University)
J.V. WRIGHT (Archaeological Survey of Canada, Canadian Museum of Civilization)
V.K. PREST (Glacial Geology, Geological Survey of Canada)
J.-S. VINCENT (Glacial Geology, Geological Survey of Canada)

Primary sources

The distributions of Plano groups are based on correspondence and discussions with most of the Palaeo archaeologists in Canada. Although the general picture is fairly clear, data are limited, and there is considerable ambiguity and much debate about details. The artefacts illustrated are from the ROM or the CMC. The block diagrams were drafted by Catherine Farley from illustrations prepared from aerial photographs of relict shores of Lake Algonquin. The position of the ice margin has been determined by the systematic mapping of ice-marginal features. The age control of the margin is based on radiocarbon dating of organic deposits (shells, wood, peat, lake deposits, etc).

Secondary sources

Clark, D.W. 'Is There a Northern Cordilleran Tradition?' *Canadian Journal of Archaeology* 7, no. 1 (1983): 23–48
Ellis, C.J., and D.B. Deller. 'Hi-Lo Materials from Southwestern Ontario.' *Ontario Archaeology* 38 (1982): 3–22
Noble, W.C. 'Prehistory of the Great Slave Lake and Great Bear Lake Region.' In *Subarctic.* Vol 6 of *Handbook of North American Indians.'* Ed J. Helm. 97–106. Washington: Smithsonian Institution, 1981
Pettipas, L. 'A Further Contribution to the Prehistory of Manitoba.' *Manitoba Archaeological Quarterly* 5, no. 2 (1981): 38–54
Prest, V.K. *Retreat of Wisconsin and Recent Ice in North America.* GSC, Map 1257A. 1969
Prest, V.K., D.R. Grant, and V.N. Rampton. *Glacial Map of Canada.* GSC, Map 1253A. 1968
Roberts, A. *Preceramic Occupations along the North Shore of Lake Ontario.* Mercury Series, Archaeological Survey of Canada, Paper 132. Ottawa: NMM, 1985
Stewart, A. 'Hell Gap: A Possible Occurrence in South Central Ontario.' *Canadian Journal of Archaeology* 7, no. 1 (1983): 87–92
Storck, P.L. *A Report on the Banting and Hussey Sites: Two Paleo-Indian Campsites in Simcoe County, Southern Ontario.'* Mercury Series, Archaeological Survey of Canada, Paper 93. Ottawa: NMM, 1979
Wright, J.V. 'Prehistory of the Canadian Shield.' In *Subarctic.* Vol 6 of *Handbook of North American Indians.* Ed J. Helm. 86–96. Washington: Smithsonian Institution, 1981

The following have contributed invaluable advice and data: J. Beymoual, D.B. Deller, G. Dibb, C. Ellis, K. Fladmark, E. Gryba, P. Julig, D. Keenleyside, L. Pettipas, W. Ross, A. Stewart, P. Storck, C. Turnbull, J. Wright.

PLATE 6

Cultural Sequences, 8000–4000 BC

J.V. WRIGHT (Archaeological Survey of Canada, Canadian Museum of Civilization)
V.K. PREST (Glacial Geology, Geological Survey of Canada)
J.-S. VINCENT (Glacial Geology, Geological Survey of Canada)

Primary sources

Plates 6–9, 12, 14, and 15 are based on technical published reports, unpublished manuscripts, consultation with colleagues in the Archaeological Survey of Canada, CMC, the responses of 20 archaeologists across the country to initial plate drafts, and information provided on request by colleagues throughout Canada.

Prest, V.K. *Retreat of Wisconsin and Recent Ice in North America.* GSC, Map 1257A. 1969
Prest, V.K., D.R. Grant, and V.N. Rampton. *Glacial Map of Canada.* GSC, Map 1253A. 1968

Secondary sources

'Development in Canadian Prehistory since 1970 – A Symposium held at the Annual CAA Convention, Hamilton, 1982.' *Canadian Journal of Archaeology* 6 (1982): 47–218
Epp, Henry T., and Ian Dyck, eds. *Tracking Ancient Hunters, Prehistoric Archaeology in Saskatchewan.* Regina: Saskatchewan Archaeological Society, 1983
Fladmark, K.R. *Prehistory of British Columbia.* Ottawa: NMM, 1986
McGhee, Robert. *Canadian Arctic Prehistory.* Toronto: Van Nostrand Reinhold, 1978

Tuck, James A. *Newfoundland and Labrador Prehistory.* Ottawa: NMM, 1976
– *Maritime Provinces Prehistory.* Ottawa: NMM, 1984
Wright, J.V. *Ontario Prehistory: An Eleven-Thousand-Year Archaeological Outline.* Ottawa: NMM, 1972
– *Quebec Prehistory.* Toronto: Van Nostrand Reinhold, 1979
– 'The Development of Prehistory in Canada, 1935–1985.' *American Antiquity* 50, no. 4 (1985): 421–33

These are the first comprehensive maps of the prehistory of Canada. Draft maps were prepared by staff of the Archaeological Survey of Canada, CMC, under the direction of J.V. Wright. The drafts were then sent to archaeologists across Canada for review. This process was repeated a number of times for each plate. A substantial amount of the information on which the plates were based is either unpublished or in publications that are not easily obtained.

The position of the ice margins through time has been determined by the systematic mapping of ice-marginal features. The time control of the margins is based on radiocarbon dating of organic deposits (shells, wood, peat, lake deposits, etc.).

PLATE 7

Cultural Sequences, 4000–1000 BC

J.V. WRIGHT (Archaeological Survey of Canada, Canadian Museum of Civilization)

See pl 6.

PLATE 8

Cultural Sequences, 1000 BC–AD 500

J.V. WRIGHT (Archaeological Survey of Canada, Canadian Museum of Civilization)

See pl 6.

PLATE 9

Cultural Sequences, AD 500–European Contact

J.V. WRIGHT (Archaeological Survey of Canada, Canadian Museum of Civilization)

See pl 6.

PLATE 10

Bison Hunters of the Plains

R.E. MORLAN (Archaeological Survey of Canada, Canadian Museum of Civilization)
M.C. WILSON (Department of Geology, University of Calgary)

Secondary sources

Buchner, A.P., et al. *Introducing Manitoba Prehistory.* Papers in Manitoba Archaelogy, Popular Series No. 4. Winnipeg: Manitoba Department of Cultural Affairs and Historical Resources, 1983
Burley, David, ed. *Contributions to Plains Prehistory.* Occasional Paper No. 26, Archaeological Survey of Alberta. Edmonton: Alberta Culture, 1985
Epp, Henry T., and Ian Dyck, eds. *Tracking Ancient Hunters: Prehistoric Archaeology in Saskatchewan.* Regina: Saskatchewan Archaeological Society, 1983
Frison, George C. *Prehistoric Hunters of the High Plains.* New York: Academic Press, 1978
Moore, T.A., ed. *Alberta Archaeology: Prospect and Retrospect.* Lethbridge: The Archaeological Society of Alberta, 1981

The temporal scale on this plate was constructed after calibrating all relevant radiocarbon dates according to tables in:

Klein, J., J.C. Lerman, P.E. Damon, and E.K. Ralph. 'Calibration of Radiocarbon Dates: Tables Based on the Consensus Data of the Workshop on Calibrating the Radiocarbon Time Scale.' *Radiocarbon* 24, no. 2 (1982): 103–50

PLATE 11

Peopling the Arctic

ROBERT McGHEE (Archaeological Survey of Canada, Canadian Museum of Civilization)

Sources

Dumond, D.E. *The Eskimos and Aleuts.* London: Thames and Hudson, 1977
McGhee, Robert. *Canadian Arctic Prehistory.* Toronto: Van Nostrand Reinhold, 1978
Maxwell, Moreau S. *Prehistory of the Eastern Arctic.* Orlando: Academic Press, 1985

PLATE 12

Iroquoian Agricultural Settlement

J.V. WRIGHT (Archeological Survey of Canada, Canadian Museum of Civilization)
R.D. FECTEAU (Department of Botany, Royal Ontario Museum)

Primary sources

See pl 6.

Secondary sources

See pl 6 and the following:
Clermont, Norman, Claude Chapdelaine, and Georges Barré. 'Le site iroquoien de Lanoraie: Témoignage d'une maison-longue.' *Recherches amérindiennes au Québec.* Montréal, 1983
Finlayson, William D. *The 1975 and 1978 Rescue Excavations at the Draper Site: Introduction and Settlement Patterns.* Mercury Series, Archaeological Survey of Canada, Paper 130. Ottawa, NMM, 1985
Fitzgerald, William. *Lest the Beaver Run Loose: The Early 17th Century Christianson Site and Trends in Historic Neutral Archaeology.* Mercury Series, Archaeological Survey of Canada, Paper 111. Ottawa: NMM, 1982
Lennox, Paul A. *The Hood Site: A Historic Neutral Town of 1640 A.D.; The Bogle I and Bogle II Sites: Historic Neutral Hamlets of the Northern Tier.* Mercury Series, Archaeological Survey of Canada, Paper 121. Ottawa: NMM 1984
Noble, William C. 'Van Besien (AfHd-2): A Study in Glen Meyer Development.' *Ontario Archaeology* 24 (1975): 3–95
Warrick, Gary A. *Reconstructing Ontario Iroquoian Village Organization.* Christine F. Dodd. *Ontario Iroquois Tradition Longhouses.* Mercury Series, Archaeological Survey of Canada, Paper 124. Ottawa: NMM, 1984
Wright, J.V. *The Nodwell Site.* Mercury Series, Archaeological Survey of Canada, Paper 22. Ottawa: NMM, 1974
– *The Ontario Iroquois Tradition.* National Museums of Canada, Bulletin 210. Ottawa, 1966
Wright, Milton J. *The Walker Site.* Paul Anthony Lennox. *The Hamilton Site: A Late Historic Neutral Town.* Mercury Series, Archaeological Survey of Canada, Paper 103. Ottawa: NMM, 1981

PLATE 13

The Coast Tsimshian, ca 1750

GEORGE F. MacDONALD (Archaeological Survey of Canada, Canadian Museum of Civilization)
GARY COUPLAND (Department of Anthropology and Sociology, University of British Columbia)
DAVID ARCHER (Department of Anthropology, University of Calgary)

Petroglyph   A carving or inscription on rock
Cache pit   A small pit dug into the ground, often used for food storage
Eulachon grease   The oil rendered from the eulachon (*Thaleichthys pacificus*), a small anadromous fish of the Pacific Northwest

Primary sources

Canadian Centre for Folk Culture Studies, National Museums of Canada. Marius Barbeau. Unpublished field notes
– Marius Barbeau and William Beynon. Tsimshian notes

Secondary sources

Allaire, Louis. 'The Cultural Sequence at Gitaus: A Case of Prehistoric Acculturation.' In Richard Inglis and George F. MacDonald, eds. *Skeena River Prehistory.* 18–52. Mercury Series, Archaeological Survey of Canada, Paper 87. Ottawa: NMM, 1979
Archer, David. 'Prince Rupert Harbour Project: Heritage Site Evaluation and Impact Assessment'. Mimeographed. Ottawa: NMM, 1984
Coupland, Gary. 'Prehistoric Cultural Change at Kitselas Canyon'. PHD thesis, UBC, 1986

Inglis, Richard, and George F. MacDonald, eds. *Skeena River Prehistory.* Mercury Series, Archaeological Survey of Canada, Paper 87. Ottawa: NMM, 1979
MacDonald, George F., and Richard Inglis. *The Dig.* Ottawa: NMM, 1975

Trade lists and historic population estimates are based on the two primary sources cited.

Thanks are due to Marjorie Halpin and Moira Irvine, UBC.

PLATE 14

Prehistoric Trade

J.V. WRIGHT (Archaeological Survey of Canada, Canadian Museum of Civilization)
ROY L. CARLSON (Department of Archaeology, Simon Fraser University)

Sources

See pl 6 and the following:
Carlson, R.L. 'Prehistory of the Northwest Coast.' In R.L. Carlson, ed. *Indian Art Trade Traditions of the Northwest Coast.* 13–32. Burnaby: Archaeology Press, SFU, 1983
Nelson, D. Erle, J.M. D'Auria, and R.B. Bennett. 'Characterization of Pacific Northwest Obsidian by X-ray Fluorescence Analysis.' *Archaeometry* 16, no. 1 (1975): 112–15

The obsidian-trade map is based on research undertaken by Roy L. Carlson under Canada Council grant S74-0739. Technical analysis of most obsidian samples was made by D.E. Nelson. Additional identifications were made by A. Cormie and D. Godfrey-Smith. The data are stored at the Department of Archaeology, SFU. X-ray fluorescence is described in the journal *Archaeometry* 16, no. 1 (1975): 112–15.

PLATE 15

Cosmology

J.V. WRIGHT (Archaeological Survey of Canada, Canadian Museum of Civilization)

See pl 6.

PLATE 16

Norse Voyages and Settlement

ALAN G. MACPHERSON (Department of Geography, Memorial University of Newfoundland)
BIRGITTA WALLACE (Environment Canada, National Historic Parks, Halifax)

Secondary sources

Bruun, Daniel. 'The Icelandic Colonization of Greenland and the Finding of Vineland.' *Meddelelser om Grønland.* Bd. 57. Copenhagen, 1918
Dansgaard, W., et al. 'Climatic Changes, Norsemen and Modern Man.' *Nature* 255 (1975): 24–8
Gad, Finn. *The History of Greenland.* Vol 1. Montréal: McGill-Queen's University Press, 1971
Ingstad, Anne Stine. 'The Norse Settlements at l'Anse aux Meadows, Newfoundland: A Preliminary Report from the Excavations, 1961–68.' *Acta Archaeologica* 41 (1970)
– *The Discovery of a Norse Settlement in America: Excavations at l'Anse aux Meadows, Newfoundland, 1961–1968.* Vol 1. Oslo: Universitetsforlaget, 1977
Ingstad, Anne Stine, and Helge Marcus Ingstad. *The Norse Discovery of America.* 2 vols. Oslo: Universitetsforlaget, 1986
Ingstad, Helge Marcus. *Westward to Vinland: the Discovery of Pre-Columbian Norse House-Sites in North America.* Toronto: Macmillan, 1969
Jones, Gwyn. *The Norse Atlantic Saga, being the Norse Voyages of Discovery and Settlement to Iceland, Greenland, and North America.* Oxford: Oxford University Press, 1964
Magnusson, Magnus, and Hermann Pálsson. *The Vinland Sagas: The Norse Discovery of America.* London: Penguin Books, 1965
McGhee, Robert. 'Contact between Native North Americans and the Medieval Norse: A Review of the Evidence.' *American Antiquity* 49, no. 1 (1984): 4–26
Pálsson, Hermann, and Paul Edwards. *The Book of Settlements: Landnámabók.* Winnipeg: University of Manitoba Press, 1972
Roussell, Aage. *Farms and Churches in the Mediaeval Norse Settlements of Greenland.* Copenhagen: I Kommission hos C.A. Reitzels Forlag, 1941
Vigfusson, Gudbrand, and F. York Powell. *Origines Islandicae: A Collection of the More Important Sagas and Other Native Writings Relating to the Settlement and Early History of Iceland.* Oxford: Clarendon Press, 1905
Wallace, Birgitta Linderoth. 'The L'Anse aux Meadows Site.' In Gwyn Jones. *The Norse Atlantic Saga, being the Norse Voyages of Discovery and Settlement to Iceland, Greenland, and North America.* 285–304. Oxford: Oxford University Press, 1964
– 'Further Development in Research on the Native and Norse Occupations at L'Anse aux Meadows, Newfoundland.' Paper presented at the annual meeting of the Canadian Archaeological Association, 1 May 1982. Typescript on file with ECHP, Halifax

The radiocarbon graph is based on a list on file with ECHP, Halifax, of the L'Anse aux Meadows radiocarbon dates in order of occupation.

Original map of the L'Anse aux Meadows site is by ECHP, Halifax.

PLATE 17

Ecological Regions, ca AD 1500

J.H. McANDREWS (Department of Botany, Royal Ontario Museum and University of Toronto)
G.C. MANVILLE (Department of Botany, Academy of Natural Sciences, Philadelphia)

Secondary sources

Banfield, A.W.F. *The Mammals of Canada.* Toronto: University of Toronto Press, 1974
Bailey, R.G. *Descriptions of the Ecoregions of the United States.* 1–77. United States Department of Agriculture, Miscellaneous Publication 139. 1980
Bryson, R.A., and F.K. Hare. 'The Climates of North America.' In R.A. Bryson and F.K. Hare, eds. *World Survey of Climatology.* Vol. 2: *Climates of North America.* 1–48. Amsterdam: Elsevier, 1974
Canada, Energy, Mines and Resources. *The National Atlas of Canada.* 4th ed, rev. Toronto: Macmillan, 1974
Crowley, J.M. 'Biogeography.' *Canadian Geographer* 9 (1967): 312–26
Godfrey, W.E. *The Birds of Canada.* Ottawa: National Museum of Natural Sciences, 1979
Handbook of North American Indians. Vol 6: *Subarctic.* Ed J. Helm. Washington: Smithsonian Institution, 1981
Handbook of North American Indians. Vol 15: *Northeast.* Ed B.G. Trigger. Washington: Smithsonian Institution, 1978
Hare, F.K., and J.E. Hay. 'The Climate of Canada and Alaska.' In *World Survey of Climatology.* Vol 2: *Climates of North America.* 49–192. Amsterdam: Elsevier, 1974
Hare, F.K., and M.K. Thomas. *Climate Canada.* 2nd ed. Toronto: Wiley, 1979
Rostlund, E. 'Freshwater Fish and Fishing in Native North America.' *University of California Publications in Geography* 9 (1952): 1–313
Rowe, J.S. *Forest Regions of Canada.* Canadian Forestry Service Publication 1300. Ottawa: Department of Fisheries and Environment, 1972
Scott, W. B., and E.J. Crossman. *Freshwater Fishes of Canada.* Fisheries Research Board of Canada Bulletin 184. Ottawa: Department of Fisheries and Environment, 1973

We thank the following for their advice and criticism: Christine L. Caroppo, Edwin J. Crossman, Judith L. Eger, Ross D. James, and Deborah A. Metsger of the ROM; and William G. Dean, F. Kenneth Hare, James C. Ritchie, and Howard G. Savage of UT.

PLATE 17A

Descriptions of Ecological Regions

J.H. McANDREWS (Department of Botany, Royal Ontario Museum and University of Toronto)
G.C. MANVILLE (Department of Botany, Academy of Natural Sciences, Philadelphia)

See pl 17.

PLATE 18

Population and Subsistence

CONRAD E. HEIDENREICH (Department of Geography, York University)
J.V. WRIGHT (Archaeological Survey of Canada, Canadian Museum of Civilization)

Primary sources

See pll 35–40.

Secondary sources

Banfield, A.W.F. *The Mammals of Canada.* Toronto: University of Toronto Press, 1981
Handbook of North American Indians. Vol 6: *Subarctic.* Ed J. Helm. Washington: Smithsonian Institution, 1981
Handbook of North American Indians. Vol 15: *Northeast.* Ed B.G. Trigger. Washington: Smithsonian Institution, 1978
Jenness, D. *The Indians of Canada.* 7th ed. Toronto: University of Toronto Press, 1977

Ethnohistoric population Early population data are meagre. The populations given here are estimates based on a few references to pre-epidemic populations. These references were transferred to other groups in similar environments with similar socioeconomic conditions.
Linguistic families Based on secondary sources with some adjustments in distribution indicated by primary sources
Subsistence (ethnohistoric data) Based on secondary sources with extensive adjustments according to earliest European observations

PLATE 19

Exploring the Atlantic Coast

RICHARD I. RUGGLES (Department of Geography, Queen's University)

Baffin, William (1584–1622) DCB 1: 74–5
Bellenger, Étienne (fl 1580–4) DCB 1: 87–9
Button, Sir Thomas (ca 1577–1634) DCB 1: 144–5
Bylot, Robert (fl 1610–16) DCB 1: 145
Cabot, John (fl 1497–8) DCB 1: 146–52
Cartier, Jacques (1491–1557) DCB 1: 165–72
Corte-Real, Gaspar (ca 1450–1501) DCB 1: 234–6
Corte-Real, Miguel (ca 1450–1502) DCB 1: 236
Davis, John (ca 1550–1605) DCB 1: 251–2
Fagundes, João Alvares (fl 1521) DCB 1: 303–4
Foxe (Fox), Luke (1586–1635) DCB 1: 311–12
Frobisher, Sir Martin (ca 1535–94) DCB 1: 316–19
Gómez, Esteban (in Portuguese Estevão Gomes) (1484–1538) DCB 1: 342–3
Hudson, Henry (fl 1607–11) DCB 1: 374–9
James, Thomas (ca 1593–1635) DCB 1: 384–5
La Rocque de Roberval, Jean-François de (1500–60) DCB 1: 422–5
Munk, Jens (1579–1628) DCB 1: 514–15
Ribero, Diogo (d 1533) Portuguese royal cartographer in Spanish service
Verrazzano, Giovanni da (ca 1485–1528) DCB 1: 657–60

Secondary sources

Brebner, J.B. *The Explorers of North America, 1492–1806*. London: A. & C. Black, 1933
Canada, Energy, Mines and Resources. *The National Atlas of Canada.* 4th ed, rev. Toronto: Macmillan, 1974
Cooke, Alan, and Clive Holland. *The Exploration of Northern Canada.* Toronto: Arctic History Press, 1978
Crone, Gerald. *The Discovery of America.* London: Hamilton, 1969
Cumming, W.P., R.A. Skelton, and D.B. Quinn. *The Discovery of North America.* London: Elek, 1971
Klemp, Egon. *America in Maps, Dating from 1500 to 1856.* London: Holmes & Meier, 1976
Morison, Samuel E. *The European Discovery of America.* New York: Oxford University Press, 1971–4
Quinn, D.B. *England and the Discovery of America 1481–1620.* New York: Knopf, 1974
Tooley, R.V., and Charles Bricker. *Landmarks of Mapping, An Illustrated Survey of Maps and Mapmakers.* New York: Crowell, 1968

PLATE 20

The Atlantic Realm

GRAEME WYNN (Department of Geography, University of British Columbia)
RALPH PASTORE (Department of History, Memorial University of Newfoundland)
BERNARD G. HOFFMAN (Vienna, Virginia)

Little Passage complex An archaeological culture defined by its stone tools. These diagnostic tools are small-stemmed and corner-notched projectile points with triangular bifaces made from fine-grained grey-green to blue-green cherts. Linear cutting tools and thumbnail scrapers were made from random flakes. The makers of this tool complex were ancestors of the Beothuk.

Primary sources

British Library, London. Additional Mss 38352
Cell, Gillian T., ed. *Newfoundland Discovered.* Hakluyt Society, Second Series, vol 160. London: Hakluyt Society, 1982
Howley, James P. *The Beothucks or Red Indians: The Aboriginal Inhabitants of Newfoundland.* Cambridge: University of Cambridge Press, 1915. Repr Toronto: Coles, 1974
Lescarbot, Marc. *The History of New France.* 3 vols. English translation, notes, and appendices by W.L. Grant. Toronto: Champlain Society, 1907–14
Thwaites, R.G., ed. *The Jesuit Relations and Allied Documents.* Cleveland: Burrows, 1896–1901

Secondary sources

Black, W.A. 'Gulf of St Lawrence Ice Survey.' *Geographical Branch Papers* 19 (1958); 23 (1959); 25 (1960); 32 (1961); 36 (1962)
Brookes, Ian, 'The Physical Geography of the Atlantic Provinces.' In A.G. Macpherson, ed. *The Atlantic Provinces.* Toronto: University of Toronto Press, 1972
Carignan, Paul C. *Beothuk Archaeology in Bonavista Bay.* Mercury Series, Archaeological Survey Of Canada, Paper 69. Ottawa: NMM, 1977
Forward, C.M. 'Ice Distribution in the Gulf of St Lawrence during the Break-Up Season.' *Geographical Bulletin* 6 (1954): 45–84
Hachey, H.B. 'Oceanography and Canadian Atlantic Waters.' *Fisheries Resources Board Bulletin* no. 134 (1961)
Head, C. Grant. *Eighteenth Century Newfoundland.* Toronto: McClelland and Stewart, 1976
Hoffman, B.G. 'Historical Ethnography of the Micmac of the 16th and 17th Centuries.' PHD thesis, University of California, Berkeley, 1955
– *Cabot to Cartier: Sources for a Historical Ethnography of Northeastern North America, 1491–1550.* Toronto: University of Toronto Press, 1961
Kohler, A.C. 'Fish Stocks of the Nova Scotia Banks and Gulf of St Lawrence.' Technical Report No. 80. St Andrews, NB: Fisheries Research Board, 1968
Leim, A.H., and W.B. Scott. 'Fishes of the Atlantic Coast of Canada.' *Fisheries Resources Board Bulletin* no. 155 (1966)
McGuire,B.E. *Environmental Atlas of the Bay of Fundy.* Environmental Protection Service, Atlantic Region. 1977
Marshall, Ingeborg. 'A New Collection of Beothuk Indian Decorated Bone Pieces.' *Man in the Northeast* 8 (1974): 41–55
Rowe, Frederick. *Extinction.* Toronto: McGraw-Hill Ryerson, 1977
Scarratt, D.J., ed. *Canadian Atlantic Offshore Fishery Atlas.* Canadian Special Publication of Fisheries and Aquatic Sciences 4–7 rev. Ottawa: Department of Fisheries and Oceans, 1982
Snow, D.R. 'The Ethnohistoric Base Line of the Eastern Abenaki.' *Ethnohistory* 23 (1976) 291–306
– 'Late Prehistory of the East Coast.' In *Handbook of NorthAmerican Indians,* Vol 15: *Northeast.* Ed. B.G. Trigger. 58–69. Washington: Smithsonian Institution, 1978
Tuck, James A. *Newfoundland and Labrador Prehistory.* Ottawa: NMM, 1976
Upton, L.F.S. 'The Extermination of the Beothuks of Newfoundland,' CHR 58 (1977): 133–53

The majority of Newfoundland sites shown on this plate were derived from site-record forms on file in the Newfoundland Museum, St John's.
Agricultural capacity is based on the map series, 'Soil Capability for Agriculture' (Ottawa: Surveys and Mapping Branch, Department of Energy, Mines, and Resources, various dates). Classes 1–3 are considered fair or better, classes 4–6 very limited.

Thanks are due to H.F. McGee, St Mary's University; V. Miller, DU; B.G. Trigger, MCGU; Ruth Whitehead, Nova Scotia Museum; James A. Tuck, MUN; and Jane Sproull-Thomson, Newfoundland Museum.

PLATE 21

The Migratory Fisheries

JOHN J. MANNION (Department of Geography, Memorial University of Newfoundland)
C. GRANT HEAD (Department of Geography, Wilfrid Laurier University)

Primary sources

Archives nationales, Paris, France. Fonds des Colonies, C12A, vol 10. Also in PAC, NMC 19196
Duhamel Du Monceau, Henri-Louis. *Traité général des pêches.* Paris: Saillant et Nyon, 1769–82
PRO. CO 194/15, folios 22–3; CO 194/21, folio 39

Secondary sources

Bosher, J.F. 'A Fishing Company of Louisbourg, Les Sables d'Olonne and Paris: La Société du Baron d'Huart, 1750–1775.' *French Historical Studies* 9, no. 2 (1975): 263–77
Brière, Jean-François. 'Le Trafic terre-neuvier malouin dans la première moitié du XVIIIe siècle, 1713–1755.' *Hist Soc* 11, no. 2 (1978): 356–74
Cell, Gillian T. *English Enterprise in Newfoundland, 1577–1660.* Toronto: University of Toronto Press, 1969
Head, C. Grant. *Eighteenth Century Newfoundland: A Geographer's Perspective.* Toronto: McClelland and Stewart, 1976
Innis, Harold A. *The Cod Fisheries: The History of an International Economy.* Rev ed. Toronto: University of Toronto Press, 1954
La Morandière, Charles de. *Histoire de la pêche française de la morue dans l'Amérique septentrionale ...* 3 vols. Paris: Maisonneuve et Larose, 1962–6
Quinn, D.B. *New American World: A Documentary History of North America to 1612.* New York: Arno Press, 1979

The labour costs given on the graph are calculated on the assumption of one boat's master at £23 per season and four other men at £12 each; see CO 194/15, folios 22–3.

Thanks are due to Sandy Balcomb, ECHP, Halifax; and to Edward Tompkins, PANL, St John's.

PLATE 22

The 16th Century Fishery

JOHN J. MANNION (Department of Geography, Memorial University of Newfoundland)
SELMA BARKHAM (Department of Geography, Memorial University of Newfoundland)

Secondary sources

Cell, Gillian T. *English Enterprise in Newfoundland, 1577–1660.* Toronto: University of Toronto Press, 1969
Cortesão, A., and A.T. Da Mota. *Portugaliae Monumenta Cartographica,* vol 5. Lisbon: Comissão Executiva, Comemoraçoes do V Centenário da Morte do Infante D. Henrique, 1960
Davis, Ralph. *The Rise of the Atlantic Economies.* Ithaca: Cornell University Press, 1973
Dollinger, Philippe. *The German Hansa.* London: Macmillan, 1970
Ganong. W.F. *Crucial Maps in the Early Cartography of the Atlantic Coast of Canada.* Toronto: University of Toronto Press, 1964
Godinho, V.M. *L'économie de l'empire portugais aux XVe et XVIe siècles.* Paris: S.E.V.P.E.N., 1969
Harrisse, H. *Découverte et évolution cartographique de Terre-Neuve.* Paris: Welter, 1900
Hoffman, Bernard G. *Cabot to Cartier: Sources for a Historical Ethnography of Northeastern North America, 1497–1550.* Toronto: University of Toronto Press, 1961
Innis, Harold A. *The Cod Fisheries: The History of an International Economy.* Rev ed. Toronto: University of Toronto Press, 1954
La Morandière, Charles de. *Histoire de la pêche française de la morue dans l'Amérique septentrionale ...* 3 vols. Paris: Maisonneuve et Larose, 1962–6
Marcus, G.J. *The Conquest of the North Atlantic.* Woodbridge, Suffolk: Boydell Press, 1980
Mauro, Frédéric. *Le Portugal et l'Atlantique au XVIIe siècle.* Paris: CNRS, 1960
Michell, A.R. 'The European Fisheries in Early Modern History.' In *Cambridge Economic History of Europe.* Vol 5: 133–84. Cambridge: Cambridge University Press, 1977
Quinn, David B., ed. *Newfoundland from Fishery to Colony.* New York: Arno Press, 1979
Seary, E.R. *Place Names of the Avalon Peninsula.* Toronto: University of Toronto Press, 1971
Story, G.M., ed. *Early European Settlement and Exploitation in Atlantic Canada: Selected Papers.* St John's: MUN, 1952

Apart from the Basque coast, the locations of European ports are based on national, regional, and port histories of the fisheries and overseas trade in the sixteenth century.

Thanks are due to Professeur J. Bernard, Université Bordeaux III; W. Gordon Handcock and E.R. Seary (deceased), MUN; Maura Mannion; and E.A. Tompkins, PANL.

PLATE 23

The 17th Century Fishery

JOHN J. MANNION (Department of Geography, Memorial University of Newfoundland)
W. GORDON HANDCOCK (Department of Geography, Memorial University of Newfoundland)

Primary sources

Canada. PAC. NMC 52, [1714]. 'A Plan of the Settlement and Fishing Room Belonging to the French Inhabitants of the Beach of Placentia.' PAC photo reproduction
France. Archives nationales, Paris. Section Outre-mer, G1, vol. 467, Recensement, 1687, and Recensement général des habitants de Plaisence en l'Isle de Terre-Neuve en 1698. PAC transcripts
– Bibliothèque nationale, Paris. Colbert, Cinq-cents, vol 199, Recensement des navires, 1664
– Bibliothèque nationale, Paris. Cartes et plans, SHM, Archives no. 23 (Catalogue Foncin, 157), [Sr. de Courcelles, Royal Navy, Census of French Fishing Ships at Newfoundland, 1675]. PAC, NMC 225

Secondary sources

Humphreys, John. *Plaisance: Problems of Settlement at this Newfoundland Outpost of New France, 1660–1690.* National Museums of Canada, Publications in History No. 3. Ottawa, 1970
Innis, Harold A. *The Cod Fisheries: The History of an International Economy.* Rev ed. Toronto: University of Toronto Press, 1954
La Morandière, Charles de. *Histoire de la pêche française de la morue dans l'Amérique septentrionale ...* 3 vols. Paris: Maisonneuve et Larose, 1962–6
Proulx, Jean-Pierre. *The Military History of Placentia: A Study of French Fortifications*. Parks Canada, History and Archaeology, no. 26. Ottawa, 1979
Richard, Robert. 'Comptes et profits de navires terreneuviers du Havre au XVIIe siècle.' *Revue d'histoire économique et sociale* 54, no. 4 (1976): 476–524
Turgeon, Laurier. 'Pour une histoire de la pêche: le marché de la morue à Marseille au XVIIIe siècle.' *Hist Soc* 14, no. 28 (1981): 295–322
– 'Colbert et la pêche française à Terre Neuve.' In Roland Mousnier, ed. *Un nouveau Colbert.* 255–68. Actes du Colloque pour le tricentenaire de la mort de Colbert tenu à Paris du 4 au 6 octobre, 1983. Paris: CDU Sedes, 1984

Thanks are due to Selma Barkham (MUN), Maura Mannion, and Laurier Turgeon (UL).

PLATE 24

Île Royale, 18th Century

KENNETH DONOVAN (Environment Canada, National Historic Parks, Louisbourg)

Primary sources

LOUISBOURG 1717
Archives nationales, Paris, France. Section Outre-mer, Dépôt des fortifications des colonies, carton 3, pièce 145

LOUISBOURG 1742
Archives du ministère des Armées, Paris, France. Bibliothèque du Génie, Génie-14-Louisbourg, tablette, 5

LOUISBOURG HOUSEHOLDS, 1734
Court records, official correspondence, and numerous rental agreements. See particularly:
Archives nationales. Section Outre-mer, G1, vol 466, pièce 69, 1734, 'Recensement de l'Isle Royale, 1734'; pièce 85, fols 2–41, 'Etat des terrains concedes dans la ville de Louisbourg sous le bon plaisir du Roy par Mm. Les Gouverneur et Commissaire-Ordonnateur de l'Isle Royale jusqu'au 15 octobre 1734'

RESIDENTS ON THE QUAY, 1734

Archives du ministère des Armées. Archives du Génie (Vincennes, France), article 14, Louisbourg, tablette, 22, 'Plan pour servir au projet representé en jaune du revetement du quay du port de la ville de Louisbourg à L'Isle Royale 1731,' by Verrier fils

Archives nationales. Section Outre-mer, G^1, vol 466, pièce 69, 'Recensement de l'Isle Royale, 1734'

LOUISBOURG FORTIFICATIONS, 1745, AND MAUREPAS' BASTION, 1741

Archives nationales. Section Outre-mer, Dépôt des fortifications des colonies, IV-219, 'Plan de Louisbourg dans l'Île Royale,' by Verrier fils; IV-194, 'Les différents profils de la nouvelle enceinte de Louisbourg,' by Verrier fils

WINTER POPULATION, 1752 AND 1785

Archives nationales. Section Outre-mer, G^1, vol 466, pièce 81, 'Recensement fait par le Sieur de la Roque, arpenteur du Roi, des habitants de tous les ports, havres, anses, rivières de l'Ile Royale et de l'Île St. Jean, commencé le 5 fevrier 1752 par ordre de M. le Comte de Raymond.' For a published version see *Report Concerning Canadian Archives for the Year 1905.* Vol II: *Tour of Inspection Made by the Sieur de La Roque.* 3-172

For 1785 see pl 30.

MERCHANT SHIPS UNLOADING

Archives nationales. Section Outre-mer, G^1, vol 466, 59, 1719; Fonds des Colonies, C^{11C}, vol 9, fols 10-20, 1721; C^{11C}, vol 16, n.p., 1752 (New England data); C^{11B}, vol 14, fols 276-92^V, 1733; F^{2B}, vol 11, fols 20-3. Archives départementales, Charente-Maritime, B, registre 272,1743

THE FISHERY, 1731

Archives nationales. Section Outre-mer, C^{11B}, vol 12, fol 64, Île Royale, 1731, 'Récapitulation de la pêche de 1731'

ÎLE ROYALE TRADE

Archives nationales. Fonds des Colonies, F^{2B}, vol 11, Tableaux de commerce, 1752-4; C^{11C}, vol 9, fols 50-95, 1737; B, vol 70, fol 400, 1739; B, vol 72, fol 442, 1740; B, vol 74, fol 581, 1741; B, vol 76, fol 510, 1742; B, vol 78, fol 405, 1743

LOUISBOURG VIEWED FROM THE HARBOUR

Bibliothèque nationale, Paris, France. Sections des Cartes et Collections géographiques, c.18830, 'Vue de la Ville de Louisbourg prise en dedans du port 1731,' by Verrier fils

Secondary sources

Balcom, B.A. *The Cod Fishery of Isle Royale, 1713-1758.* Ottawa: Parks Canada, Department of the Environment, 1984

Donovan, Kenneth. 'Communities and Families: Family Life and Living Conditions in Eighteenth-Century Louisbourg.' *Material History Bulletin* no. 15 (1982): 33-47

– ed. *Cape Breton at 200. Historical Essays in Honour of the Island's Bicentennial, 1785-1985.* Sydney: University College of Cape Breton Press, 1985

Fry, Bruce. 'An Appearance of Strength: The Fortifications of Louisbourg.' Studies in Archaeology, Architecture, and History, 2 vols. Ottawa: Parks Canada, Department of the Environment, 1984

Greer, Alan. *The Soldiers of Isle Royale, 1720-45.* History and Archaeology, no. 28. Ottawa: Parks Canada, 1979

Johnston, A.J.B. *Religion in Life at Louisbourg, 1713-1758.* Montréal: McGill-Queen's University Press, 1984

Moore, Christopher. 'Commodity Imports of Louisbourg.' *Manuscript Report No.317.* 1-115. Ottawa: Parks Canada, 1975

– 'The Other Louisbourg: Merchant Trade and Enterprise in Île Royale.' *Hist Soc* 12 (1979): 79-96

– *Louisbourg Portraits: Life in an Eighteenth-Century Garrison Town.* Toronto: Macmillan, 1982

Schmeisser, Barbara. 'The Population of Louisbourg, 1713-1758.' *Manuscript Report No.303.* 1-123. Ottawa: Parks Canada, 1976

I am indebted to ECHP, Fortress of Louisbourg National Historic Park. Special thanks are due William O'Shea, A.J.B. Johnston, Eric Krause, and Blair Dwyer.

PLATE 25

The Newfoundland Fishery, 18th Century

JOHN J. MANNION (Department of Geography, Memorial University of Newfoundland)

W. GORDON HANDCOCK (Department of Geography, Memorial University of Newfoundland)

ALAN G. MACPHERSON (Department of Geography, Memorial University of Newfoundland)

Primary sources

FRANCE

Ships and men departing France, 1765-72, and distribution of French fisheries in Newfoundland: Archives nationales, Paris. Fonds des Colonies, C^{11F}, vols 3, 4: État des pêches françaises sur les bancs et à Saint-Pierre, 1770-4. Archives nationales. Fonds des Colonies, C^{12}, vol 19

French fishing vessels, totals: Archives nationales, Paris. Fonds de la Marine. CC 598, C^5, vol 52 (1787). Bibliothèque nationale, Nouvelles acquisitions françaises 2550 (1725)

GREAT BRITAIN

Ships departing England, 1765-74: PANL. GB/5, Second Report, State of Trade to Newfoundland, 24 April 1793. Appendix 6^B, 425-6

Maritime History Archives, MUN. Lloyd's List and Registers of Shipping, London, 1765-74

British cod fishery: PRO. CO/194, Governors' returns on the inhabitants and fisheries at Newfoundland, 1700-1820

Secondary sources

Brière, Jean-François. 'Le trafic terre-neuvier malouin dans la première moitié du XVIIIe siècle, 1713-1755.' *Hist Soc* 11, no. 2 (1978): 356-74

– 'Le reflux des Terre-Neuviers malouins sur les côtes du Canada dans la première moitié du XVIIIe siècle: réponse à un changement de climat?' *Hist Soc*, 12, no. 23 (1979): 166-9

Handcock, W. Gordon. 'English Migration to Newfoundland.' In John J. Mannion, ed. *The Peopling of Newfoundland: Essays in Historical Geography*, 15-48. St John's: Iser Press, 1977

– 'The West Country Migrations to Newfoundland.' *Bulletin of Canadian Studies* 5, no. 1 (1981): 5-24

Head, C. Grant. *Eighteenth-Century Newfoundland: A Geographer's Perspective.* Toronto: McClelland and Stewart, 1976

Innis, Harold A. *The Cod Fisheries: The History of an International Economy.* Rev ed. Toronto: Univerity of Toronto Press, 1954

Lounsbury, R.G. *British Fishery at Newfoundland, 1634-1763.* New Haven: Yale University Press, 1934

La Morandière, Charles de. *Histoire de la pêche française de la morue dans l'Amérique septentrionale ...* 3 vols. Paris: Maisonneuve et Larose, 1962-6

Macpherson, Alan G. 'A Modal Sequence in the Peopling of Central Bonavista Bay, 1676-1857.' In John J. Mannion, ed. *The Peopling of Newfoundland: Essays in Historical Geography.* St John's: Iser Press, 1977

Mannion, John J. 'The Waterford Merchants and the Irish-Newfoundland Provisions Trade, 1770-1820.' In D.H. Akenson, ed. *Canadian Papers in Rural History III.* 178-203. Gananoque: Langdale Press, 1982

Ommer, Rosemary E. ' "A Peculiar and Immediate Dependence of the Crown": The Basis of the Jersey Merchant Triangle.' *Business History* 25, no. 2 (1983): 107-24

Turgeon, Laurier. 'La crise de l'armement morutier basco-bayonnais dans la première moitié du XVIIIe siècle.' *Société des Sciences, Lettres et Arts de Bayonne* 139 (1983): 75-91

Whiteley, W.H. 'Governor Hugh Palliser and the Newfoundland and Labrador Fishery, 1764-1768.' CHR 50, no. 2 (1969): 141-63

– 'James Cook, Hugh Palliser and the Newfoundland Fishery.' *The Newfoundland Historical Society* 5, no. 1 (1972): 17-22

– 'Newfoundland, Quebec and the Administration of the Coast of Labrador, 1774-1783.' *Acadiensis* 6, no. 1 (1976): 92-111

Thanks are due to R.H. Mackinnon (UBC), Maura Mannion, and E.S. Tompkins (PANL).

PLATE 26

Trinity, 18th Century

W. GORDON HANDCOCK (Department of Geography, Memorial University of Newfoundland)
ALAN G. MACPHERSON (Department of Geography, Memorial University of Newfoundland)

Boatmaster   A captain of an inshore fishing craft
Flake   A platform for drying fish
Outharbour   A small inhabited harbour or cove related to a larger harbour where mercantile establishments were located: a small primary-producing fishing community
Planter   A settler, normally a fisherman and owner of fishing premises and boats who engaged a crew to work in the fishery
Servant   A general term for a labourer engaged in the fishery
Ship fisherman   A migratory fisherman who came each summer to fish as a member of a ship's company
Stage   A fishing wharf

Primary sources

Dorset Record Office, Dorchester, Eng. D365, Diary of Benjamin Lester
PAC. NMC, Partie de la baye de la Trinite, 1762 (map)
PANL. GN5/4/B[1], Northern District Court Records, vol 1, 1753–74; vol 2, 1775–1811
– Pole Papers, Census of 1800–1
– Trinity Parish Records, St Paul's
PRO. CO194, Governors' returns on the inhabitants and fisheries at Newfoundland. A partial finding aid is in C. Grant Head. *Eighteenth Century Newfoundland: A Geographer's Perspective.* Toronto: McClelland and Stewart, 1976

Secondary sources

Handcock, W. Gordon. 'English Migration to Newfoundland.' In John J. Mannion, ed. *The Peopling of Newfoundland,* 15–48. Institute of Social and Economic Research, MUN. St John's, 1977
– 'The Origin and Development of Trinity in 1800.' Manuscript, MUN. 1981
– 'The Poole Mercantile Community and the Growth of Trinity, 1700–1839.' *Newfoundland Quarterly* 80, no. 3 (1985)
Head, C. Grant. *Eighteenth Century Newfoundland: A Geographer's Perspective.* Toronto: McClelland and Stewart, 1976

The data for the graph on overseas shipping links and the maps on the trading system of Trinity were compiled from references to shipping in the diaries of Benjamin Lester. The map of Trinity in 1801 combines data from the census of 1800–1 and from several contemporary maps and charts. The graphs of population structure for Trinity in 1801 are drawn from the census of 1800–1, parish registers, court records, and wills. The four graphs dealing with the population of Trinity Bay are drawn from the Governors' returns.

Thanks are due to Heather Wareham, Maritime History Archives, MUN; Phillip Hollett; Albert Jones, Government of Newfoundland.

PLATE 27

St John's

JOHN J. MANNION (Department of Geography, Memorial University of Newfoundland)

Primary sources

PANL. Board of Ordinance, St John's Town, 1728
– GN1/13, Nominal census of St John's (1795)
– T.G.W. Eastaff, Plan of the Town and Harbour of St John's, 12 September 1806
– P7/8, Jenkin Jones, Report on St John's to Phoenix Fire Insurance Co., London, 6 June 1804
PRO. CO194, Governors' returns on the inhabitants and fisheries at Newfoundland, 1750–1820
– CO194/32, 3, List of Imports, St John's, 1772

Secondary sources

O'Neill, Paul. *The Oldest City: The Story of St. John's, Newfoundland.* 2 vols. Erin: Porcépic Press, 1975, 1976

Thanks are due to W. Gordon Handcock, MUN; R.A. MacKinnon, UBC; Maura Mannion; and E.A. Tompkins, PANL.

PLATE 28

The Fishery in Atlantic Commerce

C. GRANT HEAD (Department of Geography, Wilfrid Laurier University)
CHRISTOPHER MOORE (Toronto)
MICHAEL BARKHAM (Department of Geography, Cambridge University)

Quintal   The standard quintal, used as a measure of dried cod, is 112 lbs. The Marseille quintal of 92 lbs is converted here to standard.

Primary sources

Bideford Public Library, Bideford, England. Robert Wren's Account Book, 1767–1812
Brière, J.-F. 'L'armement français pour la pêche de Terre-Neuve au XVIIIe siècle.' PH D thesis, YU, 1980
Cocula, Anne Marie. 'Gens de la rivière de la Dordogne.' Doctoral thesis, Université de Bordeaux, 1978
Ferreira, J.A. Pinto. 'Visitas de Saúde às Embarçacoes Entradas na Barra do Douro Nos Séculos XVIe XVII.' Câmara Municipal do Porto, Gabinete de História da Cidade, 1977
France. Archives municipales. Archives de la Chambre de commerce de Marseille. Commerce, I
Rau, Virginia. *O Movimento da Barra do Doura durante o Século XVIII: uma interpretação.* Oporto, 1958

Secondary sources

Carrière, C. 'La pêche de Terre-Neuve.' *Revue d'histoire économique et sociale* 42, no. 2 (1964): 255–65
Dardel, Pierre. *Navires et marchandises dans les ports de Rouen et du Havre au XVIIIe siècle.* Paris: SEVPEN, 1963
Fisher, H.E.S. *The Portugal Trade: A Study of Anglo-Portuguese Commerce, 1700–1770.* London: Methuen, 1971
Head, C. Grant. *Eighteenth Century Newfoundland: A Geographer's Perspective.* Toronto: McClelland and Stewart, 1976
Huetz de Lemps, C. *Géographie du commerce de Bordeaux à la fin du règne de Louis XIV.* Paris, 1975
La Morandière, Charles de. *Histoire de la pêche française de la morue dans l'Amérique septentrionale ...* 3 vols. Paris: Maisonneuve et Larose, 1962–6
Larra'uga, R. Basurto. *Comercio y Burguesia Mercantil de Bilbao en la segunda unitad del siglo XVII.* Bilbao, 1983
Turgeon, Laurier. 'Pour une histoire de la pêche: la marché de la morue à Marseille au XVIIIe siècle.' *Hist Soc* 14, no. 28 (1981), 299–322
– 'Consommation de morue et sensibilité alimentaire en France au XVIIIe siècle.' In Canadian Historical Association, *Historical Papers,* 1984. Ottawa, 1985

The material on this plate should be considered generally typical. It is the result of careful and extensive enquiry by the three plate authors, each most familiar with the English, French, and Spanish trade areas respectively. Extrapolation from known statistical data has been necessary to create the complete view that graphic presentation requires. For example, we have calculated volumes of cod at a few market ports using *numbers* of cod-laden vessels and a sample of volumes of cod per vessel. The map symbols representing carefully chosen 'ranges' generalize the data.

We wish to thank the academics, librarians, and archivists in Canada, the United States, England, France, Portugal, Spain, and Italy who helped us during our research. Laurier Turgeon shared early research on cod imports into France, and Fátima de Conceição and Rosa Cruz of Toronto extracted data in Portugal. WLU assisted through Short-Term Research Grants at two stages in this work.

PLATE 29

Acadian Marshland Settlement

JEAN DAIGLE (Département d'histoire, Université de Moncton)

Primary sources

Acadian censuses: Archives nationales, Paris, France. Section Outre-mer, G[1], vol 466
Dièreville. 'Voyage à l'Acadie, 1699–1700.' La Société historique acadienne, *Les cahiers* 16, nos. 3–4 (1985): 9–173
Maps of explorers, travellers, and cartographers of the seventeenth and eighteenth centuries: Bibliothèque nationale, Paris, France. Service hydrographique de la Marine, Cartes et plans

Secondary sources

Arseneault, Samuel, et al. *Atlas de l'Acadie. Petit atlas des francophones des Maritimes*. Moncton: Éditions d'Acadie, 1976
Christianson, David J. *Belleisle 1983: Excavations at a Pre-Expulsion Acadian Site*. Nova Scotia Museum, Curatorial Report no. 48. Halifax, 1984
Clark, Andrew H. *Acadia: The Geography of Early Nova Scotia to 1760*. Madison: University of Wisconsin Press, 1968
Daigle, Jean, ed. *Les Acadiens des Maritimes: études thématiques*. Moncton: Centre d'études acadiennes, 1980
– ed. *The Acadians of the Maritimes: Thematic Studies*. Moncton: Centre d'études acadiennes, 1982
De Grâce, Eloi. *Noms géographiques de l'Acadie*. Moncton: Société historique acadienne, 1974
Lapierre, J.-W., and M. Roy. *Les Acadiens*. Paris: Presses universitaires de France, 1983

PLATE 30

Acadian Deportation and Return

JEAN DAIGLE (Département d'histoire, Université de Moncton)
ROBERT LeBLANC (Department of Geography, University of New Hampshire)

Primary sources

Akins, Thomas B., ed. *Selections from the Public Documents of the Province of Nova Scotia*. Halifax: Annand, 1869
'Le journal des visites pastorales de Mgr Joseph-Octave Plessis en Acadie, 1811, 1812, 1815.' La Société historique acadienne, *Les cahiers* 11, nos. 1, 2, 3 (1980): 10–311
'Visite pastorale de Mgr Denaut en Acadie en 1803.' *Le bulletin des recherches historiques* 10, no. 10 (1904): 289–300

Secondary sources

Clark, Andrew H. *Acadia: The Geography of Early Nova Scotia to 1760*. Madison: University of Wisconsin Press, 1968
Daigle, Jean, ed. *Les Acadiens des Maritimes: études thématiques*. Moncton: Centre d'études acadiennes, 1980
– ed. *The Acadians of the Maritimes: Thematic Studies*. Moncton: Centre d'études acadiennes, 1982
Fergusson, Charles Bruce. *Place-Names and Places of Nova Scotia*. Halifax: PANS, 1967
Griffiths, Naomi E.S. *The Acadian Deportation: Deliberate Perfidy or Cruel Necessity?* Toronto: Copp Clark, 1969
Lapierre, J.-W., and M. Roy. *Les Acadiens*. Paris: Presses universitaires de France, 1983
Lauvrière, Émile. *La tragédie d'un peuple: histoire du peuple acadien, de ses origines à nos jours*. 2 vols. Paris: Goulet, 1922
LeBlanc, Robert. 'The Acadian Migrations.' *Cahiers de Géographie de Québec* 24 (1967): 523–41. Also in *Canadian Geographical Journal* 81, no. 1 (1970): 10–19
Rayburn, Alan. *Geographical Names of Prince Edward Island*. Ottawa: Department of Energy, Mines and Resources, 1973
– *Geographical Names of New Brunswick*. Ottawa: Department of Energy, Mines and Resources, 1975
Winzerling, Oscar. *Acadian Odyssey*. Baton Rouge: Louisiana State University Press, 1955

PLATE 31

Pre-Loyalist Nova Scotia

GRAEME WYNN (Department of Geography, University of British Columbia)
DEBRA McNABB (Halifax)

Primary sources

Migrant origins in New England, derived from local histories and township records, including: Cornwallis, PANS, MG4, vol 18a–19; Horton, PANS, MG4, vol 74; Liverpool, PANS, MG4, vol 180; Sackville, PAC, MG9 A 12, 6, vol 1
Morris, C. 'Description and state of the new settlements in Nova Scotia 1761, by the Chief Surveyor.' PAC *Report* (1904): 289–300
Nova Scotia Department of Lands and Forests, Research and Registry Division, map 13-5, 'Horton Township' [Plan of Lower Horton]
PANS. MG 1, vol 181, nos 12, 53, 81, 83, 210, 211, 270, 278, 280, Survey Bills
– RG 1, vol 362, Horton Township Partition Book
– RG 1, vol 443, doc 1, A general return of the several townships in the province of Nova Scotia, the first of January, 1767
– RG 3, vol 188, Minutes of the Executive Council
– RG 20, Series 'C', vol 89, Land Papers, Kings County, NS, 1760–1842
– RG 47, reel 1273, Kings County, NS, Deeds
– RG 48, reels 712, 744, Kings County, NS, Probate Records, Wills
– Micro: Places: Nova Scotia: Land Grants, 3–35
PRO. State Papers Domestic Naval 1711 and 1755, vol 38, folio 224, Vaudreuil. Plan of Halifax showing line of forts, batteries and all buildings in the town [1755]. Copy in Map Division, PANS

Secondary sources

Bell, Winthrop Pickard. *The 'Foreign Protestants' and the Settlement of Nova Scotia*. Toronto: University of Toronto Press, 1961
Brebner, John Bartlett. *The Neutral Yankees of Nova Scotia*. New York: Columbia University Press, 1937
Bumsted, J.M. *The People's Clearance. Highland Emigration to British North America, 1770–1815*. Edinburgh: University of Edinburgh Press, 1982
Eagles, Douglas E. *A History of Horton Township*. Sarnia, 1970
Eaton, A.W.H. *History of Kings County*. Salem, 1910. Repr Belleville: Mika Studio, 1972
McNabb, Debra Ann. 'Land and Families in Horton Township, Nova Scotia, 1760–1830.' MA thesis, UBC, 1986
MacNutt, William Stewart. *The Atlantic Provinces. The Formation of a Colonial Society, 1712–1857*. Toronto: McClelland and Stewart, 1965
Martell, J.S. 'Pre-Loyalist Settlements around the Minas Basin.' MA thesis, DU, 1933
Wynn, Graeme. 'Late Eighteenth-Century Agriculture on the Bay of Fundy Marshlands.' *Acadiensis* 8 (1979): 80–9

Thanks are due to L.D. McCann (MAU), for assistance on the Halifax shipping data, 1752.

PLATE 32

Maritime Canada, Late 18th Century

GRAEME WYNN (Department of Geography, University of British Columbia)
L.D. McCANN (Department of Geography, Mount Allison University)

Primary sources

Campbell, Patrick. *Travels in the Interior Inhabited Parts of North America in the Years 1791 and 1792*. New ed. Ed H.H. Langton and W. Francis. Toronto: Champlain Society, 1937
PAC. MG23 D1 (1), vol 24, General Returns of Loyalists
PANS. RG1, vol 443, 444, 444½, Poll Tax Returns
[Perkins, Simeon]. *The Diary of Simeon Perkins*. Ed H.A. Innis, D.C. Harvey, and C.B. Fergusson. 5 vols. Toronto: Champlain Society, 1948–78
'Report on Nova Scotia by Col. Robert Morse, R.E., 1784.' PAC, *Report, 1884*, note C, xxvii–lix. Ottawa, 1885
Raymond, W.O., ed. *Winslow Papers, A.D. 1776–1826*. St John: Sun Printing Co., 1901

Secondary sources

Condon, A.G. *The Envy of the American States. The Loyalist Dream for New Brunswick*. Fredericton: New Ireland Press, 1984
Ells, M. 'Clearing the Decks for the Loyalists.' Canadian Historical Association. *Report* (1933): 56–8
– 'Settling the Loyalists in Nova Scotia.' Canadian Historical Association. *Report* (1935): 105–9
Temperley, H. 'Frontierism, Capital and the American Loyalists in Canada.' *Journal of American Studies* 13 (1979): 5–27
Walker, J.W.St.G. *The Black Loyalists. The Search for a Promised Land in Nova Scotia and Sierra Leone, 1783–1870*. New York: Africana Publishing Co., 1976
Wright, E.C. *The Loyalists of New Brunswick*. Moncton: Moncton Publishing Co., [1972]

Thanks are due to Peter M, Ennals (MAU) for comment on building types and Stephen Hornsby for alerting me to the map of Sydney.

PLATE 33

The St Lawrence Valley, 16th Century

B.G. TRIGGER (Department of Anthropology, McGill University)

St Lawrence Iroquoian refers to the many Iroquoian tribes that inhabited the St Lawrence Valley between the east end of Lake Ontario and the area around the present city of Québec in late prehistoric times. The groups living west of Montreal disappeared in the late prehistoric period leaving only Stadaconans and Hochelagans in place at the time of Cartier's visits.

Tutonaguy as a place name appears only in the record of Cartier's 1541 visit to Montreal. It may be: an alternative name for Hochelaga; the real name for Hochelaga, while Hochelaga was the name of its inhabitants; a new village founded by a periodic relocation of the Hochelagan community; or the name of another Iroquoian community on the Island of Montréal.

Primary sources

Biggar, Henry P. *The Voyages of Jacques Cartier: Published from the Originals with Translations, Notes, and Appendices.* Publications of the PAC, no. 11. Ottawa, 1924

– *A Collection of Documents Relating to Jacques Cartier and the Sieur de Roberval.* Publications of the PAC, no 14. Ottawa 1930

Pendergast, James F., and Bruce G. Trigger. *Cartier's Hochelaga and the Dawson Site.* Montréal: McGill-Queen's University Press, 1972

Quinn, David B., ed. *New American World: A Documentary History of North America to 1612.* 5 vols. New York: Arno and Bye, 1979

Secondary sources

Chapdelaine, Claude. 'L'ascendance culturelle des Iroquoiens du Saint-Laurent.' *Recherches Amérindiennes au Québec* 10 (1980): 145–52

Bailey, Alfred G. 'Vanished Iroquoians.' In *Culture and Personality: Essays by A.G. Bailey.* 14–28. Toronto: McClelland and Stewart, 1972

Biggar, Henry P. *The Early Trading Companies of New France.* Toronto: UT Studies in History, 1901

Ganong, W.F. *Crucial Maps in the Early Cartography and Place-Nomenclature of the Atlantic Coast of Canada.* Toronto: University of Toronto Press, 1964

Hoffman, Bernard G. *Cabot to Cartier: Sources for a Historical Ethnography of Northeastern North America, 1497–1550.* Toronto: University of Toronto Press, 1961

Pendergast, James F. 'An in-situ Hypothesis to Explain the Origin of the St. Lawrence Iroquoians.' *Ontario Archaeology* 25 (1975): 47–55

Trigger, Bruce G. *The Children of Aataentsic: A History of the Huron People to 1660.* 2 vols. Montréal: McGill-Queen's University Press, 1976

– *Natives and Newcomers: Canada's 'Heroic Age' Reconsidered.* Montréal: McGill-Queen's University Press, 1985

Trigger, Bruce G., and James F. Pendergast. 'Saint Lawrence Iroquoians.' In *Handbook of North American Indians.* Vol 15: *Northeast.* Ed Bruce G. Trigger. Washington: Smithsonian Institution, 1978

Trudel, Marcel. *Histoire de la Nouvelle-France.* Vol 1: *Les vaines tentatives.* Montréal: Fides, 1963

Wright, J.V. *Quebec Prehistory.* Toronto: Van Nostrand Reinhold, 1979

PLATE 34

Settlements and Missionaries, 1615–1650

CONRAD E. HEIDENREICH (Department of Geography, York University)

Donné A man who gives himself in service to a religious establishment, without wages and for life, in return for care and security in old age

Brébeuf, Jean de, 1593–1649 DCB 1: 121–6
Champlain, Samuel de, 1570–1635 DCB 1: 186–200
Le Caron, Joseph, 1586–1632 DCB 1: 436–8

Primary sources

Biggar, Henry P., ed. *The Works of Samuel de Champlain*. 6 vols. Toronto: Champlain Society, 1922–36

Kidd, Kenneth E. *The Excavation of Ste. Marie I.* Toronto: University of Toronto Press, 1949

Sagard, Gabriel. *The Long Journey to the Country of the Hurons.* Ed. G.M. Wrong; transl. H.H. Langton. Toronto: Champlain Society, 1939

Thwaites, R.G., ed. *The Jesuit Relations and Allied Documents.* 73 vols. Cleveland: Burrows Bros, 1896–1901

Secondary sources

Heidenreich, Conrad E. *Huronia: A History and Geography of the Huron Indians, 1600–1650.* Toronto: McClelland and Stewart, 1971

Jones, Arthur E. *'8endake Ehen' or Old Huronia.* Fifth Report of the Bureau of Archives for the Province of Ontario. Toronto: L.K. Cameron, 1909

Thanks are due to Kenneth E. Kidd, Trent University, for updating the plan of Sainte-Marie, and Alan E. Tyyksa, Ontario Ministry of Culture and Recreation, for providing supplemental data on Cahiagué. The original archaeological work there was conducted by the late J. Norman Emerson, UT.

PLATE 35

The Great Lakes Basin, 1600–1653

CONRAD E. HEIDENREICH (Department of Geography, York University)

Primary sources

Biggar, Henry P., ed. *The Works of Samuel de Champlain.* 6 vols. Toronto: Champlain Society, 1922–36

PAC, NMC. Maps from the period 1600–60

Sagard, Gabriel (Théodat). *Histoire du Canada et voyages que les Frères mineurs Recollets y ont faicts pour la conversion des infidelles …* 4 vols. Paris: Tross, 1866

– *The Long Journey to the Country of the Hurons.* Ed. G.M. Wrong; transl. H.H. Langton. Toronto: Champlain Society, 1939

Thwaites, R.G., ed. *The Jesuit Relations and Allied Documents.* 73 vols. Cleveland: Burrows Bros., 1896–1901

Secondary sources

Heidenreich, Conrad E. *Huronia: A History and Geography of the Huron Indians, 1600–1650.* Toronto: McClelland and Stewart, 1971

Trigger, Bruce G. *The Children of Aataentsic: A History of the Huron People to 1660.* 2 vols. Montréal: McGill-Queen's University Press, 1976

PLATE 36

French Exploration

RICHARD I. RUGGLES (Department of Geography, Queen's University)

CONRAD E. HEIDENREICH (Department of Geography, York University)

Allouez, Claude, 1622–89 DCB 1: 57–8
Bellin, Jacques-Nicolas, 1703–72 Cartographer attached to French Marine Office
Bonnécamps, Joseph-Pierre de, 1707–90 DCB 4: 76–7
Brûlé, Étienne, 1592–1633 DCB 1: 130–3
Buache, Philippe, 1700–73 French geographer
Cavelier de La Salle, René-Robert, 1643–87 DCB 1: 172–84
Champlain, Samuel de, 1570–1635 DCB 1: 186–99
Chaussegros de Léry, Gaspard-Joseph, 1682–1756 DCB 3: 116–19
Coronelli, Vincenzo Maria, 1650–1718 Venetian cartographer
Delisle, Joseph-Nicolas, 1688–1768 French astronomer and cartographer working in St Petersburg, Russia
Denys de La Ronde, Pierre, 1631–1708 DCB 2: 178–9
Franquelin, Jean-Baptiste-Louis, b 1651, d after 1712 DCB 2: 228–30
Gaultier de Varennes et de La Vérendrye, Pierre, 1685–1749 DCB 3: 246–54
Hennepin, Louis, 1626–1705 DCB 2: 277–82
Jolliet, Louis, 1645–1700 DCB 1: 392–8
Laure, Pierre-Michel, 1688–1738 DCB 2: 357–8
Nicollet de Belleborne, Jean, 1598–1642 DCB 1: 516–18
Sanson, Nicolas, 1600–67 Founder of 17th-century French school of cartography

Primary sources

PAC. NMC. 17th- and 18th-century maps. As far as possible all surviving primary records of exploration were consulted.

Secondary sources

DCB, vols 1–4

Heidenreich, C.E. 'Mapping the Great Lakes: The Period of Exploration, 1603–1700.' *Cartographica* 17 (1980): 32–64

– 'Mapping the Great Lakes: The Period of Imperial Rivalries.' *Cartographica* 18 (1981): 74–109

PLATE 37

Re-Establishment of Trade, 1654–1666

CONRAD E. HEIDENREICH (Department of Geography, York University)

Congé A licence issued by the governor or intendant permitting a trader to send one canoe load of trade goods and three men into the interior
Coureurs de bois Men trading in the interior without a licence or any other form of permission
Entrepôt A major interior post with storage facilities and merchant residences where goods and furs were trans-shipped to other posts or Montréal
Livre (pesant) Unit of weight, about 1 pound (489.5 gms)
Pack of furs Furs bundled for canoe transportation, usually weighing 80–100 pounds (36–45 kg)
Société A small company, usually of short duration, composed of a number of partners

Prouville de Tracy, Alexandre de, 1596–1670 DCB 1: 554–7

Primary sources

Adams, A.T., ed. *The Explorations of Pierre Esprit Radisson.* Minneapolis: Ross and Haines, 1961
Alvord, C.W., and C.E. Carter, eds. *The Critical Period, 1763–1765.* Illinois State Historical Library Collections, 10, British series I. Springfield: The Library, 1915
– *The New Régime, 1765–1767.* Illinois State Historical Library Collections, 11, British series II. Springfield: The Library, 1916
ANQ. *Rapport de l'archiviste de la province de Québec.* 'Les Journaux de M. de Léry' (1926–7): 334–71. 'Correspondance entre M. de Vaudreuil et la Cour' (1938–9): 10–179; (1939–40): 355–463; (1942–3): 399–443; (1946–7): 371–460; (1947–8): 137–339. 'Journal de Louis Jolliet allant à la descouverte de Labrador, 1694' (1943–4): 149–206
Blair, E.H., ed and transl. *The Indian Tribes of the Upper Mississippi Valley and Region of the Great Lakes, as Described by Nicolas Perrot ... ; Bacqueville de la Potherie ...* 2 vols. Cleveland: Arthur H. Clark, 1911–12
Burpee, L.J., ed. 'York Factory to the Blackfeet Country – The Journal of Anthony Henday, 1754–55.' In *Transactions of the Royal Society of Canada.* 3rd series. 1, section II (1907): 307–64
– *Journals and Letters of Pierre Gaultier de Varennes de La Vérendrye and His Sons ...* Toronto: Champlain Society, 1927
Carver, J. *Travels through the Interior Parts of North America in the Years 1766, 1767 and 1768.* London: G. Robinson, 1778
Charlevoix, P.F.X. de. *Histoire et description générale de la Nouvelle France, avec le journal historique d'un voyage fait par ordre du roi dans l'Amérique septentrionnale.* 6 vols. Paris: Rolin Fils, 1744
[Dollier de Casson, François.] *A History of Montreal, 1640–1672, from the French of Dollier de Casson.* Ed and transl R. Flenley. Toronto, 1928
Doughty, A.G., and C. Martin, eds. *The Kelsey Papers.* Ottawa: PAC, 1929
Houck, L., ed. *The Spanish Régime in Missouri; A Collection of Papers and Documents Relating to Upper Louisiana Principally Within the Present Limits of Missouri During the Dominion of Spain, from the Archives of the Indies at Seville.* Chicago: R.R. Donnelly, 1909
Jameson, J.F., ed. *Narratives of New Netherlands, 1609–1664.* New York: Barnes and Noble, 1909
[Jérémie, Nicolas.] *Twenty Years of York Factory 1694–1714: Jérémie's Account of Hudson Strait and Bay.* Transl. R. Douglas and J.N. Wallace. Toronto: Thorburn and Abbott, 1926
Lamontagne, L., ed, R.A. Preston, transl. *Royal Fort Frontenac.* Toronto: Champlain Society, 1958
McIlwain, C.H. *An Abridgement of the Indian Affairs Contained in Four Folio Volumes, Transacted in the Colony of New York, from the Year 1678 to the Year 1751.* Ed P. Wraxhall. Harvard Historical Studies, XXI. Cambridge, Mass., 1915
'Memoir or Summary Journal of the Expedition of Jacques Repentigny Legardeur de Saint Pierre ... Charged with the Discovery of the Western Sea ... 1752.' PAC, *Report, 1886,* note C: clviii–clxix. Ottawa, 1887
Michigan Pioneer Collections. 40 vols. See esp vols 33–4: 'The Cadillac Papers,' 1903, 1904. Lansing, 1874–1929
O'Callaghan, E.G., and B. Fernow, eds. *Documents Relative to the Colonial History of the State of New York; Procured in Holland, England and France by John Romeyn Brodhead.* 15 vols. Albany: Wood, Parsons, 1853–87
Pease, T.C., and R.C. Werner, eds. *The French Foundations, 1680–1693.* Illinois State Historical Library Collections, 23, French Series, 1. Springfield: The Library, 1934
PAC. MG18, B12, 'Détail des noms et de la distance de chaque Nation, tant du Nord du lac Superieur, que des terres découvertes et établis dans l'Ouest, presenté à Monsieur Le Marquis de Beauharnois ... Par le Sr. de la Vérendrye ...' [ca 1740]. 6 pp
– NMC. An effort was made to consult all holdings dating from 1600 to 1763. For a summary of useful maps see Heidenreich, 1980, 1981, below.
Preston, R.A., ed. *Kingston before the War of 1812: A Collection of Documents.* Toronto: Champlain Society, 1959
Rich, E.E., and A.M. Johnson, eds. *James Isham's Observations on Hudsons Bay, 1743 and Notes and Observations on a Book Entitled 'A Voyage to Hudsons Bay in the Dobbs Galley,' 1749.* London: The Hudson's Bay Record Society, 1949
Rochemonteix, C. de, ed. *Relation par lettres de l'Amérique septentrionalle années 1709 et 1710.* Paris, 1904
Rowland, D., and A.G. Sanders, eds. *Mississippi Provincial Archives, 1701–1740, French Dominion.* 2 vols. Jackson, 1927–9
Thwaites, R.G., ed. *The Jesuit Relations and Allied Documents.* 73 vols. Cleveland: Burrows Bros, 1896–1901
– *Wisconsin State Historical Society Collections.* Vol 16: *The French Régime in Wisconsin, I: 1634–1727.* Vol 17: *The French Régime in Wisconsin, II: 1727–1748.* Vol 18: 'The French Régime in Wisconsin, 1743–1760.' Madison: The Society, 1902–8
– *A New Discovery of a Vast Country in America, by Father Louis Hennepin.* Repr from the second London issue of 1698. Chicago: A.C. McClung, 1903
– *Early Western Travels, 1748–1846.* 38 vols. Cleveland: Arthur H. Clark, 1904–7
– *New Voyages to North-America, by the Baron de Lahontan.* Repr from the English edition of 1703. 2 vols. Chicago: A.C. McClung, 1905
Tyrrell, J.B., ed. *Documents Relating to the Early History of Hudson Bay.* Toronto: Champlain Society, 1931

Secondary sources

Alvord, C.W. *The Illinois Country, 1673–1818.* Springfield: Illinois Centennial Commission, 1920
Bond, B.W. *The History of the State of Ohio.* Ed C. Witke. 2 vols. Columbus: Ohio State Archaeological and Historical Society, 1941–4
Caldwell, N.W. *The French in the Mississippi Valley, 1740–1750.* Philadelphia: Porcupine Press, 1974
Cooke, A., and C. Holland. *The Exploration of Northern Canada, 500 to 1920, A Chronology.* Toronto: Arctic History Press, 1978
Eccles, W.J. *Canada Under Louis XIV, 1663–1701.* Toronto: McClelland and Stewart, 1964
– *The Canadian Frontier, 1534–1760.* New York: Holt, Rinehart and Winston, 1969
Handbook of North American Indians. Vol 6: *Subarctic.* Ed J. Helm. Washington: Smithsonian Institution, 1981
Handbook of North American Indians. Vol 15: *Northeast.* Ed B.G. Trigger. Washington: Smithsonian Institution, 1978
Heidenreich, C.E. 'Mapping the Great Lakes: The Period of Exploration, 1603–1700.' *Cartographica* 17 (1980): 32–64
– 'Mapping the Great Lakes: the Period of Imperial Rivalries, 1700–1760.' *Cartographica* 18 (1981): 74–109
– 'Mapping the Location of Native Groups, 1600–1760.' *Mapping History* 2 (1981): 6–13
Hodge, F.W., ed. *Handbook of Indians North of Mexico.* 2 vols. Smithsonian Institution, Bureau of American Ethnology, Bulletin 30. Washington, 1907, 1910
Innis, H.A. *The Fur Trade in Canada.* Rev ed. Toronto: University of Toronto Press, 1956
Jennings, F. *The Ambiguous Iroquois Empire.* New York: Norton, 1984
Kellogg, Louise P. *The French Régime in Wisconsin and the Northwest.* Madison: State Historical Society of Wisconsin, 1925
Lanctot, G. *A History of Canada.* 3 vols. Toronto: Clarke Irwin, 1963
Morton, A.S. *A History of the Canadian West to 1870–71.* Toronto: University of Toronto Press, 1939
Norton, Thomas E. *The Fur Trade in Colonial New York, 1686–1776.* Madison: University of Wisconsin Press, 1974
Ray, A.J. *Indians in the Fur Trade, 1660–1870.* Toronto: University of Toronto Press, 1974
Severance, F.H. *An Old Frontier of New France: The Niagara Region and Adjacent Lakes under French Control.* 2 vols. New York: Dodd, Mead 1917
Stanley, G.F.G. *New France: The Last Phase, 1744–1760.* Toronto: McClelland and Stewart, 1968
Trudel, M. *The Beginnings of New France, 1524–1663.* Toronto: McClelland and Stewart, 1973

Native groups were mapped according to references in the primary sources (documents and maps). Spelling of names and linguistic affiliations are, as far as possible, according to entries in the *Handbook of North American Indians* (1978; 1981). In mapping native groups the assumption has been made that, if a group was in a certain location at an early date and was in the same location at a later date, it was also there in the intervening years, providing there is no evidence to the contrary. The same assumption was made in mapping posts, forts, and missions.

PLATE 38

Expansion of French Trade, 1667–1696

CONRAD E. HEIDENREICH (Department of Geography, York University)

See pl 37.

Brisay de Denonville, Jacques-René de, 1637–1710 DCB 2: 98–105
Cavelier de La Salle, René-Robert, 1643–87 DCB 1: 172–84
Greysolon Dulhut, Daniel, 1639–1710 DCB 2: 261–4
Perrot, Nicolas, 1644–1717 DCB 2: 516–20
Troyes, Pierre de, d 1688 DCB 1: 653–4

PLATE 39

Trade and Empire, 1697–1739

CONRAD E. HEIDENREICH (Department of Geography, York University)
FRANÇOISE NOËL (Department of History, Memorial University of Newfoundland)

See pl 37.

Gaultier de Varennes et de La Vérendrye, Pierre, 1685–1749 DCB 3: 246–54
La Porte de Louvigny, Louis de, 1662–1725 DCB 2: 345–7
Le Marchand de Lignery, Constant, 1663–1731 DCB 2: 389–90
Noyelles de Fleurimont, Nicolas-Joseph de, 1695–1761 DCB 3: 491–3
Renaud Dubuisson, Jacques-Charles, 1666–1739 DCB 2: 562–3

PLATE 40

France Secures the Interior, 1740–1755

CONRAD E. HEIDENREICH (Department of Geography, York University)
FRANÇOISE NOËL (Department of History, Memorial University of Newfoundland)

See pl 37.

Céloron de Blainville, Pierre-Joseph, 1693–1759 DCB 3: 99–101

PLATE 41

French Interior Settlements, 1750s

CONRAD E. HEIDENREICH (Department of Geography, York University)
FRANÇOISE NOËL (Department of History, Memorial University of Newfoundland)
GRATIEN ALLAIRE (Faculté Saint-Jean, University of Alberta)

Arpent As a linear measure, ca 192 ft (58.5 m); as an areal measure, ca 0.85 acres (0.34 ha)
Engagé A person employed for a specified term and on conditions fixed by notarial contract

Primary sources

Alvord, C.W., and C.E. Carter, eds. *The Critical Period, 1763–1765.* Illinois State Historical Library Collections, 10, British Series I. Springfield: The Library, 1915
– *The New Régime, 1765–1767.* Illinois State Historical Library Collections, 11, British Series II. Springfield: The Library, 1916
ANQ, Centre régional de Montréal. Minutes des actes des notaires. CN0601. *Contrats d'engagement* were written by notaries, a large number of them by Jean-Baptiste Adhémar, François Lepailleur, and Louis-Claude Danré de Blanzy.
– Centre régional de Montréal. Enregistrement de congés, ordonnances et arrêts (1721–6). (Registre de congés, 1728–30). Registres des audiences de la jurisdiction royale de Montréal, vols 8, 9, 12, 14, 15, and 23. Registre des insinuations, 1732. Congés and permissions (permits) had to be registered at the Jurisdiction royale of Montréal before the departure for the upper country.
Archives du ministère des Armées. Service historique de l'Armée, Vincennes, France. 'Plan Topographique du Détroit ... Dressé pour l'intelligence des Voyages du G^al. Collot ... 1796.' [Philippe-Joseph L'Étombe.] Copy in PAC, NMC-3096
Archives nationales, Paris, France. Section Outre-mer, Dépôt des fortifications des colonies, Amérique septentrionale, 548C, 'Plan du Fort du Détroit ... fait au détroit le 20 Août 1749, Léry fils'
– Section Outre-mer, Dépôt des fortifications des colonies, Amérique septentrionale, 547B, 'Carte de la Rivière du Détroit ... fait à Québec le 22 Octobre 1749, Léry fils'
– Section Outre-mer, Dépôt des fortifications des colonies, Louisiane, 32A, 'Plan du fort des francois Estably Chez les Scioux sur le Bord du fleuve du Mississipy en 1727'
Bibliothèque nationale, Paris, France. Service hydrographique de la Marine, Cartes et plans, 4040 C-25, 'Plan des différents villages françois dans le pays des Illynois ... 1778.' Copy in PAC, NMC-7508
'Congés de traite conservés aux Archives de la province de Québec.' *Rapport de l'archiviste de la province de Québec* (1922–3): 191–265
Hicks, F.C., ed. *Thomas Hutchins, A Topographical Description of Virginia, Pennsylvania, Maryland, and North Carolina. Reprinted from the Original Edition of 1778.* Cleveland, 1904
Hodder, F.H., ed. *The Present State of the European Settlements on the Mississippi with a Geographical Description of That River, Illustrated by Plans and Draughts by Captain Philip Pittman, London 1770.* Cleveland, 1906
Huntington Library, San Marino, California. Loudoun Papers, no. 426, 'Recensement général du pays des Ilinoice de 1752'
Lajeunesse, E.J., ed. *The Windsor Border Region, Canada's Southernmost Frontier.* Toronto: Champlain Society, 1960
Massicotte, E.Z. 'Congés et permis déposés ou enregistrés à Montréal sous le Régime française.' *Rapport de l'archiviste de la province de Québec* (1921–2): 189–255
– 'Répertoire des engagements pour l'Ouest conservés dans les Archives judiciaires de Montréal (1670–1778).' *Rapport de l'archiviste de la province de Québec* (1930–1): 353–453; (1931–2): 243–365; (1932–3), 245–77
Ministère de la Défense (Marine). Service historique de la Marine, Vincennes, France. Recueil 67, no. 71, 'Carte de la Rivière du Détroit depuis le Lac Erie jusques au Lac Ste Claire.' [Léry fils, 1752]
Thwaites, R.G., ed. *The Jesuit Relations and Allied Documents.* 73 vols. Vol 69: 143–9, 201–29. Cleveland: Burrows Bros, 1896–1901
– *Wisconsin State Historical Society, Collections.* Vol 17: 22–8. Madison: The Society, 1902–8

Secondary sources

Buckley, Thomas C., ed. *Rendezvous: Selected Papers of the Fourth North American Fur Trade Conference, 1981.* St Paul: North American Fur Trade Conference, 1984
Dechêne, Louise. *Habitants et marchands de Montréal au XVIIe siècle.* Paris: Plon, 1974
Eccles, W.J. *The Canadian Frontier, 1534–1760.* Rev ed. Albuquerque: University of New Mexico Press, 1983
Gérin-Lajoie, M. 'Fort Michilimackinac in 1749, Lotbinière's Plan and Description.' *Mackinac History* 2, leaflet no. 5 (1976): 2–12
Gipson, L.H. *Zones of International Friction: North America, South of the Great Lakes Region, 1748–1754.* New York: Knopf, 1939

For the table 'Fur Trade Employees Departing Montréal, 1700–1764': Computations for the years 1701–45 and 1755 are based on the notarial contracts; for the other years they are based on Massicotte's 'Répertoire des engagements,' which is not entirely accurate. The 189 engagements to Joseph Cadet, the *munitionnaire,* though listed by Massicotte, were excluded from the yearly totals for 1757, 1758, and 1759.

The number of men at posts during the summer and the winter were computed from the length of employment indicated in the *contrats d'engagement.* Engagés hired for the interior left Montréal in May-June of the first year of their contract and presumably returned in August of the last year of their contract, thus spending more than one summer in the upper country.

Thanks are due to Jean Lafleur, a student at Université du Québec à Montréal, who gathered the data on engagements for the year 1755.

PLATE 42

The Seven Years' War

W.J. ECCLES (Department of History, University of Toronto)
SUSAN L. LASKIN (Historical Atlas of Canada, Toronto)

Primary sources

FRANCE
Archives du ministère des Armées, Service historique de l'Armée, Vincennes. Archives historiques, Series A^1
Archives nationales, Paris. Fonds des Colonies. Series C^11A. Series F3 Collection Moreau de St-Méry

CANADA
Archives du séminaire de Québec. Fonds Viger-Verreau
Casgrain, H.-R., ed. *Collection des manuscrits du Maréchal de Lévis.* 12 vols. Montréal / Québec: Beauchemin / L.-J. Demers & Frère, 1889–95
Grenier, F. ed. *Papiers Contrecoeur et autres documents concernant le conflit anglo-français sur l'Ohio de 1745 à 1756.* Québec, 1952
O'Callaghan, E.B., and B. Fernow, eds. *Documents Relative to the Colonial History of the State of New-York; Procured ... by John Romeyn Brodhead.* 15 vols. Albany: Weed, Parsons, 1853–87
Pargellis, S.M., ed. *Military Affairs in North America 1748–1756: Selected Documents from the Cumberland Papers in Windsor Castle.* New York and London: Appleton-Century, 1936 (repr)
Rapport de l'archiviste de la province de Québec (1923–4). [Louis Antoine de Bougainville.] 'Journal de l'expédition d'Amérique commencée en l'année 1756.' 204–78. 'Mémoire sur l'état de la Nouvelle-France. 1757.' 42–70

Secondary sources

Anderson, Fred. *A People's Army. Massachusetts Soldiers and Society in the Seven Years' War.* Chapel Hill: University of North Carolina Press, 1984
Corbett, Sir Julian S. *England in the Seven Years' War. A Study in Combined Strategy.* 2 vols. London: Longmans, Green, 1907
Frégault, Guy. *La guerre de la conquête.* Montréal: Fides, 1955
Gipson, L.H. *The British Empire before the American Revolution.* 8 vols. New York: Knopf, 1939–54
Kennett, Lee. *The French Armies in the Seven Years' War.* Durham, NC: Duke University Press, 1967
Kopperman, Paul E. *Braddock at the Monongahela.* Pittsburgh: University of Pittsburgh Press, 1977
McLennan, J.S. *Louisbourg from Its Foundation to Its Fall.* London: Macmillan, 1918
McNeill, John Robert. *Atlantic Empires of France and Spain: Louisbourg and Havana, 1700–1763.* Chapel Hill: University of North Carolina Press, 1985
Stanley, G.F.G. *New France: The Last Phase, 1744–1760.* Toronto: McClelland and Stewart, 1968
Waddington, Richard. *Louis XV et le renversement des alliances. Préliminaires de la guerre de Sept Ans, 1754–1756.* Paris: Firmin-Didot, 1896
– *La guerre de Sept Ans. Histoire diplomatique et militaire.* 5 vols. Paris: Firmin-Didot, 1899–1914

Thanks are due to Donald Peter MacLeod; André Charbonneau, Yvon Desloges, Marc Lafrance, Louis R. Richer, ECHP, Québec; Franklin B. Wickwire, University of Massachusetts at Amherst; and Joan Winearls, Robarts Library, UT.

PLATE 43

The Battles for Quebec, 1759–1760

W.J. ECCLES (Department of History, University of Toronto)
SUSAN L. LASKIN (Historical Atlas of Canada, Toronto)

Primary sources

FRANCE

Archives nationales, Paris. Fonds des Colonies. Series C11A, vol 104. Series B, vol 112. Series F3, Collection Moreau de St-Méry, vols 15, 16

Archives du ministère des Armées, Service historique de l'Armée, Vincennes. Archives historiques, Series A1, vols 3540, 3574

CANADA

Archives du séminaire de Québec. Ms 18

Casgrain, H.-R., ed. *Collection des manuscrits du Maréchal de Lévis.* 12 vols. Montréal / Québec: Beauchemin / L.-J. Demers & Frère, 1889–95

Doughty, A.G., and G.W. Parmalee, eds. *The Siege of Quebec and the Battle of the Plains of Abraham.* 6 vols. Québec: Dussault, 1901

PAC. MG23, G II 1, vol 1, 'General Murray's Letters 1759–1760.' Series 2-7, 'Murray's Journal'

Pargellis, S.M., ed. *Military Affairs in North America, 1748–1765.* New York and London: Appleton-Century, 1936

Rapport de l'archiviste de la province de Québec. 1920–1, 1922–3, 1923–4, 1924–5, 1931–2, 1933–4, 1935–6, 1937–8, 1938–9, 1945–6

Secondary sources

Eccles, W.J. 'The French Forces in North America during the Seven Years' War.' DCB 3: xv–xxiii, Toronto: University of Toronto Press, 1974

Frégault, Guy. *La guerre de la conquête.* Montréal: Fides, 1955

Gipson, L.H. *The British Empire before the American Revolution.* 8 vols. New York: Knopf, 1939–54

Stacey, C.P. 'The British Forces in North America during the Seven Years' War.' DCB 3: xxiv–xxx. Toronto: University of Toronto Press, 1974

– *Quebec 1759: The Siege and the Battle.* Toronto: Macmillan, 1959

Stanley, G.F.G. *New France: The Last Phase, 1744–1760.* Toronto: McClelland and Stewart, 1968

Waddington, Richard. *La Guerre de Sept Ans. Histoire diplomatique et militaire.* 5 vols. Paris: Firmin-Didot, 1899–1914

Thanks are due to Donald Peter MacLeod; André Charbonneau, Yvon Desloges, Marc Lafrance, ECHP, Québec; Joan Winearls, Robarts Library, UT; Ed Dahl and staff, NMC.

PLATE 44

Indian War and American Invasion

W.J. ECCLES (Department of History, University of Toronto)
M.N. McCONNELL (Department of History, College of William and Mary, Williamsburg, Virginia)
SUSAN L.LASKIN (Historical Atlas of Canada, Toronto)

Primary sources

Cohen, Sheldon S., ed. *Canada Preserved: The Journal of Captain Thomas Ainslie.* Toronto: Copp Clark, 1968

'Documents relating to the War of 1775.' In PAC, *Report, 1904*

Literary and Historical Society of Quebec, Historical Documents, Quebec 1866, 1871, 1875, 1905, 1906. Journals and other documents relating to the American attempt on Quebec in 1775-6

Stanley, G.F.G., ed. *For Want of a Horse, Being a Journal of the Campaigns against the Americans in 1776 and 1777 conducted from Canada, by an Officer Who Served with Lt. Gen. Burgoyne.* Sackville, NB, 1961

Stevens, S.K., and D.H. Kent, eds. *The Papers of Col. Henry Bouquet.* 19 vols. Harrisburg: Pennsylvania Historical Commission, 1940–3

Sullivan, James, et al, eds. *The Papers of Sir William Johnson.* 14 vols. Albany: State University of New York, 1921–2

Secondary sources

Hatch, Robert McConnell. *Thrust for Canada: The American Attempt on Quebec in 1775–1776.* Boston: Houghton Mifflin, 1979

Lanctot, Gustave. *Canada and the American Revolution 1774–1783.* Toronto: Clarke, Irwin, 1967

Mackesy, Piers. *The War for America 1775–1783.* London: Longmans, 1964

Parkman, Francis. *The Conspiracy of Pontiac.* Boston: Little Brown, 1851

Peckham, Howard H. *Pontiac and the Indian Uprising.* Princeton: Princeton University Press, 1947

Smith, Justin H. *Our Struggle for the Fourteenth Colony.* 2 vols. Princeton: Princeton University Press, 1907

Sosin, Jack M. *Whitehall and the Wilderness.* Lincoln: University of Nebraska Press, 1961

Stanley, G.F.G. *Canada Invaded 1775–1776.* Toronto: Hakkert, 1973

Ward, Christopher. *The War of the Revolution.* 2 vols. New York: Macmillan, 1952

Thanks are due to Donald Peter MacLeod; Franklin B. Wickwire, University of Massachusetts at Amherst; Joan Winearls, Roberts Library, UT; Ed Dahl and staff, NMC.

PLATE 45

The French Origins of the Canadian Population, 1608–1759

HUBERT CHARBONNEAU (Département de démographie, Université de Montréal)
NORMAND ROBERT (Département de démographie, Université de Montréal)

Primary sources

Canada. Archives ordinolingues. Programme de recherche en démographie historique, Département de démographie, UMont. Registre de la population du Canada, 1621–1729

Secondary sources

Institut généalogique Drouin. *Dictionnaire national des Canadiens-français (1608–1760).* 2 vols. Montréal: Institut généalogique Drouin, 1979

Jetté, René, with the collaboration of the Programme de recherche en démographie historique. *Dictionnaire généalogique des familles du Québec – des origines à 1730.* Montréal: Les Presses de l'Université de Montréal, 1983

Tanguay, Cyprien. *Dictionnaire généalogique des familles canadiennes depuis la fondation de la colonie jusqu'à nos jours.* 7 vols. Montréal: Senécal, 1871–90

PLATE 46

Resettling the St Lawrence Valley

HUBERT CHARBONNEAU (Département de démographie, Université de Montréal)
R. COLE HARRIS (Department of Geography, University of British Columbia)

Sources

Agricultural capacity is based on the map series, Soil Capability for Agriculture (Ottawa: Surveys and Mapping Branch, Department of Energy, Mines, and Resources). Classes 1–3 are considered fair or better, classes 4–6 very limited.

The essential work on the establishment of parishes is André La Rose, *Les registres paroissiaux au Québec avant 1800: introduction a l'étude d'une institution ecclésiastique et civile,* Études et recherches archivistiques, no. 2 (Québec: Ministère des Affaires Culturelles, 1980). The graph is based on data assembled by the Programme de recherche en démographie historique, Département de démographie, UMont. Many of these data are identified in Hubert Charbonneau and Jacques Légaré, *Répertoire des actes de baptême, mariage, sépulture et des recensements du Québec ancien* (Montréal: Les Presses de l'Université de Montréal, 1980). The census of 1739, the last comprehensive census of Canada during the French regime, is in Archives nationales, Section Outre-mer, Series G1 (copy in PAC), and is summarized in the *Census of the Dominion of Canada, 1871,* vol 4. A series of maps of the changing distribution of population along the lower St Lawrence during the French regime is in R. Cole Harris, *The Seigneurial System in Early Canada* (Madison / Québec: University of Wisconsin Press / Les Presses de l'université Laval, 1966).

PLATE 47

Native Resettlement, 1635–1800

B.G. TRIGGER (Department of Anthropology, McGill University)

Primary sources

Census data for New France: Archives nationales, Paris, France. Section Outre-mer, G1, article 461

Map of Lac-des-Deux-Montagnes, 1743: Archives nationales, Section Outre-mer, Dépôt des fortifications des colonies, Amérique septentrionale, 490B

O'Callaghan, E.B., ed. *Documentary History of the State of New York.* 4 vols. Albany: Weed, Parsons, 1849–51

O'Callaghan, E.B., et al. *Documents Relative to the Colonial History of the State of New-York ...* 15 vols. Albany: Weed, Parsons, 1853–87

Thwaites, R.G., ed. *The Jesuit Relations and Allied Documents.* 73 vols. Cleveland: Burrows Bros, 1896–1901

Secondary sources

Day, Gordon F. *The Identity of the Saint Francis Indians.* Mercury Series, Canadian Ethnology Service, Paper No. 71. Ottawa: NMM 1981

Devine, E.J. *Historic Caughnawaga.* Montréal: Messanger Press, 1922

Gérin, Léon. 'La Seigneurie de Sillery et les Hurons de Lorette.' *Transactions of the Royal Society of Canada.* 2nd series. 6, section I (1900): 73–116

Handbook of North American Indians. Vol 15: *Northeast.* Ed B.G. Trigger. Washington: Smithsonian Institution, 1978. See especially articles on Eastern Abenaki, Western Abenaki, Indians of Southern New England and Long Island, Mohawk, Onondaga, Nipissing, Algonquin.
Michelson, Gunther. 'Iroquois Population Statistics.' *Man in the Northeast* 14 (1977): 3–17

The interpretation of the movements of the Indian groups from New England is based largely on Gordon Day's magisterial treatment, 1981. I also wish to thank Louise Dechêne for her advice concerning the interpretation of census data.

PLATE 48

Canadian North Atlantic Trade

THOMAS WIEN (Department of History, McGill University)
JAMES PRITCHARD (Department of History, Queen's University)

Hides Here defined as the skins, dressed or not, of deer, elk or wapati, and moose

Primary sources

BEAVER EXPORTS
Archives nationales, Paris, France. Fonds des Colonies, C11A; F2B, vol II – Section Outre-mer, G1, vol 466
British Library, London, Eng. Add Mss 21861
PAC. MG23 G1, vol 10, p 66
PRO. Shelburne Mss, vol 64, pp 161–4
Thwaites, R.G., ed. *The Jesuit Relations and Allied Documents.* 73 vols. Cleveland: Burrows Bros, 1886–1901

EUROPEAN SHIPPING
Archives départementales, France. Port records
British Library. Add Mss 21861 (PAC *Report,* 1882)
PRO. Customs 1611
Quebec Gazette

FUR IMPORTS
Archives de l'Université de Montréal, Montréal. P58, Collection Baby, fiches 1625ff
Archives municipales. Archives de la Chambre de Commerce, La Rochelle, nos 9385–9424
PRO. Customs 3 and 17

NORTH AMERICAN FUR EXPORTS
Archives de l'Université de Montréal. P58, Collection Baby, fiches 1625ff
PRO, Customs 17

PRICES, VALUES
ANQ, Québec. Collection J. Spears and collection Séminaire de Québec, C34, C36
Archives nationales. Fonds des Colonies, C11A, vol 121, fol 126
PAC. MG23 G III 28, Pierre Guy, livre no. 10; MG19 A2 series 3, vol 86, Lawrence Ermatinger
Quebec Gazette, account books

TRADE PATTERNS, SHIPPING
Archives nationales. Fonds des Colonies, F2B
PRO. Customs 16 / 1

VOYAGES
Archives nationales. Fonds des Colonies, F2B, vol II; C11C, vol 9, fol 81V; C8B, cart. 17
Archives départementales. Charente-Maritime, La Rochelle, B4202–4203

Secondary sources

Lunn, A.J.E. 'Economic Development in New France, 1713–1760.' PHD thesis, MCGU, 1942. Transl as *Développement économique de la Nouvelle-France 1713–1760.* Montréal: Les Presses de l'Université de Montréal, 1986
McCann, Paul. 'Québec's Balance of Payments, 1768, 1772.' MA thesis, UO, 1982
Mathieu, Jacques. *Le commerce entre la Nouvelle-France et les Antilles au XVIIIe siècle.* Montréal: Fides, 1981
Miquelon, Dale. *Dugard of Rouen.* Montréal: McGill-Queen's University Press, 1978
Moore, Christopher. 'The Other Louisbourg: Trade and Merchant Enterprise in Ile Royale 1713–58.' *Hist Soc* 12 (1979): 79–96
Ouellet, Fernand. *Histoire économique et sociale du Québec, 1760–1850.* Montréal: Fides, 1966
Pritchard, James. 'The Voyage of the *Fier.*' *Hist Soc* 6 (1973): 75–97
– 'The Pattern of French Colonial Shipping to Canada before 1760.' *Revue française d'histoire d'outre-mer* 63 (1976): 189–210

The Québec cargo of *La Revanche* was evaluated using 1733 prices. Calculations of the value of exports in 1771 do not include shipments of dressed deerskins and a few of the less important fancy furs. The values of North American fur exports and London fur imports were calculated on the basis of the lowest price paid in London for prime Canadian furs. In calculating exports of beaver we have assumed that one skin weighs 1.5 lbs. (1.39 livres or 0.681 kg).

We gratefully acknowledge the assistance of L. Dechêne, McGU, J. Gwyn, UO, and J. Mathieu, UL; of V. Chabot, PAC, and P. McCann and M. Treen Sears. The sketches of the ships were made from drawings provided by Musée de la Marine, Palais de Chaillot, Paris, and from Eric Rieth, 'Célébration des Goélettes,' *Cols bleus,* no. 1811 (28 July–4 August 1984).

PLATE 49

The Towns

MARC LAFRANCE (Environment Canada, National Historic Parks, Québec)
ANDRÉ CHARBONNEAU (Environment Canada, National Historic Parks, Québec)

Primary sources

MAPS OF QUÉBEC
1685. Robert de Villeneuve. Archives nationales, Paris, France. Section Outre-mer. Dépôt des fortifications des colonies, Amérique septentrionale, 394
1709. Attributed to Jacques Levasseur de Neré. Archives nationales, Section Outre-mer. Dépôt des fortifications des colonies, Amérique septentrionale, 375
1742. Gaspard-Joseph Chaussegros de Léry, fils. Archives nationales, Section Outre-mer. Dépôt des fortifications des colonies, Amérique septentrionale, 418
1759. Cartographer unknown. Copy attributed to Lt. Col. Symes, British Library, London, Eng. King's Maps, CXIX, 36

MAPS OF MONTRÉAL
1685. Attributed to Robert de Villeneuve. Archives nationales, Section Outre-mer. Dépôt des fortifications des colonies, Amérique septentrionale, 466c
1717. Joseph-Gaspard Chaussegros de Léry, père. Archives nationales, Section Outre-mer. Dépôt des fortifications des colonies, Amérique septentrionale, 472b
1752. Attributed to Louis Franquet. Archives du ministère des Armées, Paris, France. Bibliothèque du Génie, mss in fol., 210E
Reproductions of all these maps are in the NMC.

Secondary sources

Charbonneau, André, Yvon Desloges, and Marc Lafrance. *Québec, ville fortifiée du XVIIe au XIXe siècle.* Québec: Parcs Canada, Éditions du Pélican, 1982
Dechêne, Louise. 'La croissance de Montréal au XVIIIe siècle.' *Revue d'histoire de l'Amérique française* 27, no. 2 (1973)
Marsan, Jean-Claude. *Montréal en évolution.* 2nd ed. Montréal: Fides, 1974

PLATE 50

The Town of Québec, 18th Century

LOUISE DECHÊNE (Department of History, McGill University)

Primary sources and reference works

Recensement de la ville de Québec en 1716. Edited by Louis Beaudet. Québec, 1887
'Le recensement de Québec en 1744.' In *Rapport de l'archiviste de la province de Québec.* (1939–40): 1–154
'Les dénombrements de Québec faits en 1792, 1795, 1798 et 1805 par le curé Joseph-Octave Plessis.' In *Rapport de l'archiviste de la province de Québec* (1948–9): 3–250
DCB. Vols 1–4. Toronto: University of Toronto Press, 1966–80
Létourneau, H., and L. Labrèque. 'Inventaire de pièces détachées de la Prévôté de Québec (1668–1759).' In *Rapport de l'archiviste de la province de Québec* (1971): 55–473
PAC. NMC 11084, 'Plan of a Survey of the City and Fortifications of Quebec ... by William Hall, 1799'
Tanguay, Cyprien. *Dictionnaire généalogique des familles canadiennes ...* 7 vols. Senécal, 1871–90

Secondary sources

Dechêne, Louise. 'Quelques aspects de la ville de Québec au XVIIIe siècle d'après les dénombrements paroissiaux.' *Cahiers de géographie du Québec* 28, no. 75 (1984): 485–505
Gauvreau, Danielle. 'Reproduction humaine et reproduction sociale: la ville de Québec pendant le régime français.' PHD thesis, UMont, 1986
Lacelle, Claudette. *La propriété militaire dans la ville de Québec, 1760–1871.* Manuscript report no. 253. Ottawa: Parcs Canada 1978
Olivier-Lecamp, G., and J. Légaré. 'Quelques caractéristiques des ménages de la ville de Québec entre 1666 et 1716.' *Hist Soc* 12, no. 23 (1979): 66–78

Thanks are due to Mario Lalancette for assistance in collecting the data for pll 50 and 51.

PLATE 51

The Seigneuries

LOUISE DECHÊNE (Department of History, McGill University)

Seigneurie   A property conceded by the king, his viceroy, or a vassal company 'en toute propriété, fief (justice) et seigneurie,' and eventually existing in law and fact
Augmentation   A property added to an existing seigneurie, and intended to form with it 'une seule et même seigneurie'

Sources

Bouchette, Joseph. *A Topographical Description of the Province of Lower Canada ...* London: W. Faden, 1815
– *Topographical Map of the Province of Lower Canada Shewing Its Divisions into Districts, Counties, Seigniories & Townships, with All the Lands Reserved Both for the Crown and the Clergy ...* London: W. Faden, 1815
Cadastres abrégés des seigneuries de Montréal, Trois-Rivières, Québec et de la Couronne. 7 vols. Québec: S. Derbishire et G. Desbarats, 1863
DCB. Vols 1–5. Toronto: University of Toronto Press, 1966–83
'Liste des paroisses de la province de Québec ... ainsi que les seigneuries ...' (Hugh Finlay, 16 July 1791). 'List of New Subjects Proprietors of Fiefs and Seigneuries in the Province of Quebec' (Lymburner, 27 January 1790). Both lists are published in I. Caron, *La colonisation de la province de Québec: les débuts du régime anglais, 1760–1791,* appendixes VIII and IX. Québec, 1923
McLennan Library, McGill University. 'Plan of a Part of the Province of Lower Canada ... Compiled in the Surveyor General Office, in the Latter Part of the Year 1794 and the Early Part of the Year 1795, by Samuel Gale and Jean-Baptiste Duberger ...'
New Topographical Map of the Province of Lower Canada Compiled from All the Former as Well as the Latest Surveys Taken by Order of the Provincial Government ... , by William Vondenvelden, Lately Assistant Surveyor General and Louis Charland, Land Surveyor. London: Published by William Vondenvelden, no 20 Cannon Street, 1 Jan 1803
Roy, Pierre-Georges. *Inventaire des concessions en fief et seigneurie, fois et hommages et aveux et dénombrements conservés aux Archives de la province de Québec.* Publication des Archives de la province de Québec. 6 vols. Beauceville, 1927–9
Tanguay, Cyprien. *Dictionnaire généalogique des familles canadiennes ...* 7 vols. Montréal: Senécal, 1871–90
Trudel, Marcel. *Le terrier du Saint-Laurent en 1663.* Ottawa: Les Presses de l'Université d'Ottawa, 1973

PLATE 52

The Countryside

R. COLE HARRIS (Department of Geography, University of British Columbia)

Primary sources

Bibliothèque nationale, Paris, France. Service hydrographique de la Marine, Dépôt des Cartes et plans, portefeuille 127-7-4. Robert de Villeneuve. Carte des environs de Québec en la Nouvelle France, 1688. Copy NMC 2708
– Service hydrographique de la Marine, Dépôt des Cartes et plans, portefeuille 127. Gédéon Catalogne. Carte du gouvernement de Québec levée en l'année 1709. Copy NMC 16685
National Gallery of Canada, Ottawa. Thomas Davies. 'View from Château-Richer,' ca 1785

Secondary sources

Dechêne, Louise. *Habitants et marchands de Montréal au XVIIe siècle.* Paris: Plon, 1974
Deffontaines, Pierre. 'Le rang, type de peuplement rural au Canada français.' *Cahiers de géographie du Québec* 5 (1953)
Harris, R. Cole. *The Seigneurial System in Early Canada: A Geographical Study.* Madison / Québec: University of Wisconsin Press / Les Presses de l'université Laval, 1966

PLATE 53

The Agricultural Economy

R. COLE HARRIS (Department of Geography, University of British Columbia)

Primary sources

All the data for 1739 are from the census of that year, Archives nationales (Paris), Section Outre-mer, Series G[1], a summary of which is in the *Census of the Dominion of Canada,* vol 4 (1871). The distribution of villages in the early 1760s is established from the census of Canada taken by the British just after the conquest and published in the *Rapport de l'archiviste de la province de Québec* (1926–7, 1936–7, 1946–7). The distribution of villages at the beginning of the 19th century is based on Joseph Bouchette, *A Topographical Description of the Province of Lower Canada ...* (London: W. Faden, 1815). The bar graphs showing the number of cleared arpents per farm in different seigneuries are derived from seigneurial *aveux et dénombrements,* most of them filed by seigneurie in the Archives nationales du Québec. The map of the village of L'Assomption in 1781 is from Christian Roy, *Histoire de L'Assomption* (L'Assomption, 1967). The graph of wheat prices in Québec is taken from Jean Hamelin, *Économie et société en Nouvelle France* (Québec: Les Presses de l'Université Laval, 1960); and the graph of wheat prices in Montréal is taken from Louise Dechêne, *Habitants et marchands de Montréal au XVIIe siècle* (Paris: Plon, 1974). The bar graphs showing land use on typical farms are schematic representations.

Secondary sources

Courville, Serge. 'Esquisse du développement villageois au Québec: le cas de l'aire seigneuriale entre 1760 et 1854.' *Cahiers de géographie du Québec* 28, nos 73–4 (1984), 9–46
Dechêne, Louise. *Habitants et marchands de Montréal au XVIIe siècle.* Paris: Plon, 1974
Greer, Allan. *Peasant, Lord, and Merchant: Rural Society in Three Quebec Parishes, 1740–1840.* Toronto: University of Toronto Press, 1985
Harris, R. Cole. *The Seigneurial System in Early Canada: A Geographical Study.* Madison / Québec: University of Wisconsin Press / Les Presses de l'université Laval, 1966
Ouellet, Fernand. *Histoire économique et sociale du Québec, 1760–1850.* Montréal and Paris: Fides, 1966. Transl *Economic and Social History of Québec, 1760–1850.* Toronto: Gage, 1980

Thanks are due to Mario Lalancette, MCGU.

PLATE 54

Exploitation of the Gulf of St Lawrence

MARIO LALANCETTE (Department of History, McGill University)

Primary sources

Archives du Seminaire de Québec. Documents Faribault, no. 150, 'Recensement des paroisses du gouvernement de Québec, 1771–1772.' Includes for each parish a list of the type and number of fisheries
Great Britain. Privy Council. *In the Matter of the Boundary between the Dominion of Canada and the Colony of Newfoundland in the Labrador Peninsula.* 13 vols. Ottawa: King's Printer, 1927. See esp appendix: James White, 'Forts and Trading Posts in Labrador Peninsula and Adjoining Territories.'
J.C.B., *Voyage au Canada dans le nord de l'Amérique septentrionale fait depuis l'an 1751 à 1761.* Ed H. Casgrain. Québec: Léger-Brousseau, 1887
Canada, Province of. Legislative Assembly. *Journaux de l'Assemblée législative de la province du Canada.* 8 (1853), Appendix HHHH: 'Titres et brevets de ratification des concessions des seigneuries au Canada'
Pièces et documents relatifs à la tenure seigneuriale (au Bas-Canada). Québec, 1851–2
Rapport de l'archiviste de la province de Québec. 'État présent du Canada dressé sur nombre de mémoires et connaissances acquises sur les lieux par Nicolas Gaspard Boucault (1754).' (1920–1): 1–50
– 'François Martel de Berhouague, Brouague ou Brouage, commandant au Labrador.' (1922–3): 356–406
– 'Journal de Louis Jolliet allant à la découverte du Labrador, 1694.' (1943–4): 147–205
Roy, P.G. *Inventaire des concessions en fief et seigneurie, fois et hommages et aveux et dénombrements.* Publication des Archives de la province de Québec. 6 vols. Beauceville, 1927–9
– *Inventaire des pièces sur la côte de Labrador.* Publication des Archives de la province de Québec. 2 vols. Québec, 1940–2

Secondary sources

Bélanger, Jules, Marc Desjardins, Yves Frenette, with the collaboration of Pierre Dansereau. *Histoire de la Gaspésie.* Montréal: Boréal Express, 1981
Brière, Jean-François. 'Le trafic terre-neuvier malouin dans la première moitié du XVIIIe siècle, 1713–1755.' *Hist Soc* 11, no. 22 (1978): 356–74
Crevel, Jacques, and Maryvonne Crevel. *Honguédo ou l'histoire des premiers Gaspésiens.* Québec: Garneau, 1970
Crowhurst, R.P. 'The Labrador Question and the Society of Merchant Venturers, Bristol, 1763.' CHR 50, no. 4 (1969): 394–405
DCB. Vols 1–5. Toronto: University of Toronto Press, 1966–83
Emard, Michel. *Cahiers gaspésiens.* Nos 1–12. Pointe à Genièvre, 1980
Fauteux, Joseph-Noel. *Essai sur l'industrie au Canada sous le régime français.* 2 vols. Québec, 1927
Gosling, William G. *Labrador: Its Discovery, Exploration and Development.* London: A. Rivers, 1910
Innis, Harold A. *The Cod Fisheries: The History of an International Economy.* First publ 1940. Rev ed. Toronto: University of Toronto Press, 1954
La Morandière, Charles de. *Histoire de la pêche française de la morue dans l'Amérique septentrionale.* 3 vols. Paris: Maisonneuve et Larose, 1962–6

Lee, David. 'The French in Gaspé, 1534 to 1760.' *Canadian Historic Sites: Occasional Papers in Archaeology and History* no. 3 (1970): 25–41
– 'Gaspé 1760–1867.' *Canadian Historic Sites: Occasional Papers in Archaeology and History,* no. 23 (1980): 117–86
– *The Robins in Gaspé, 1766 to 1825.* Markham: Fitzhenry and Whiteside, 1984
Lunn, Elisabeth J. *Economic Development in New France.* Montréal: McGill-Queen's University Press, 1986
Moussette, Marcel. *La pêche sur le Saint-Laurent. Répertoire des méthodes et des engins de capture.* Montréal: Boréal Express, 1979
Ommer, Rosemary. 'From Outpost to Outport: The Jersey Merchant Triangle in the Nineteenth Century.' PHD thesis, McGU 1979
Proulx, Jean-Pierre. *La pêche à la baleine dans l'Atlantique Nord jusqu'au milieu du xixe siècle.* Parcs Canada, Études en archéologie, architecture et histoire. Ottawa, 1986
Prowse, Daniel W. *History of Newfoundland.* New York: Macmillan, 1985
Remiggi, Frank W., 'Nineteenth Century Settlement and Colonization on the Gaspé North Coast. An Historical-Geographical Interpretation.' PH D thesis, McGU, 1983
Revue d'histoire et de traditions populaires de la Gaspésie. See esp the articles by John LeGarignon, Arthur Legros, and Mario Mimeault.
Rothney, Gordon A. 'The Case of Bayne and Brymer: An Incident in the Early History of Labrador.' CHR 15, no. 3 (1934): 264–75
– 'L'annexion de la côte du Labrador à Terre-Neuve 1763.' *Revue d'histoire de l'Amérique française* 17, no. 2 (1963): 213–43
Samson, Roch, 'Gaspé 1760–1830: l'action du capital marchand chez les pêcheurs.' *Anthropologie et sociétés* 5, no. 1 (1981): 57–86
Thornton, Patricia A., 'The Demographic and Mercantile Bases of Initial Permanent Settlement in the Strait of Belle Isle.' In John J. Mannion. *The Peopling of Newfoundland.* 152–83. Institute of Social and Economic Research, Social and Economic Papers, no. 8. St John's: MUN, 1977
Townsend, C.W. *Captain Cartwright and His Labrador Journal.* Boston: Dana Este, 1911
Trudel, François. 'Les Inuits du Labrador méridional face à l'exploitation canadienne et française des pêcheries (1700–1760).' *Revue d'histoire de l'Amérique française* 31, no. 4 (1978): 481–500
Turgeon, Laurier. 'Le marché de la morue à Marseille au XVIIIe siècle.' *Hist Soc* 14 (1981): 295–322
Whiteley, William H. 'The Establishment of the Moravian Mission in Labrador and British Policy 1763–1783.' CHR 45, no. 1 (1964): 29–50
– 'Governor Palliser and the Newfoundland and Labrador fishery, 1764–1768.' CHR 50, no. 2 (1969): 141–63
– 'Newfoundland, Quebec and the Administration of the Coast of Labrador, 1774–1783.' *Acadiensis* 6, no. 1 (1976): 92–112
– 'Newfoundland, Quebec and the Labrador Merchants 1783–1809.' *The Newfoundland Quarterly* 73, no. 4 (1977): 17–26

PLATE 55

The House, 1660–1800

GEORGES-PIERRE LÉONIDOFF (Centre d'études sur la langue, les arts et les traditions, Université Laval)

Primary sources

The data on this plate and the next are based on a large, archival selection of notarized documents containing comprehensive, specific information about individual houses. For the period before 1760 the selection comprises 1 359 urban and 1 116 rural houses. For the full span of years from 1660–1800 it comprises 2 288 urban and 2 287 rural houses, a total of 4 575 different houses. The location of the houses, many details of their construction, and their size are known. This selection includes houses throughout the seigneurial territory from Lac des Deux-Montagnes to the Saguenay. Every care has been taken to make it as representative as possible.

These data permit a quantitative analysis of the materials, techniques of construction, and size of the early Canadian house. The maps and graphs on these two plates show the frequency with which different materials and techniques of construction were used and the average size of houses in three periods (1660–1727, 1728–60, and 1761–1800) and in nine different locations (the three towns and the two sides of the river in the governments of Québec, Trois-Rivières, and Montréal. The drawings illustrate common techniques of construction as well as the appearance and floor plans of several representative houses.

Secondary sources

Chapelot, Jean, and Robert Fossier. *Le village et la maison au Moyen-Age.* Paris: Hachette Littérature, 1980
Laframboise, Yves. *L'architecture traditionnelle au Québec: glossaire illustré de la maison aux 17e et 18e siècles.* Montréal: Les Éditions de l'Homme, 1975
Léonidoff, G.-P. 'Origine et évolution des principaux types d'architecture rurale au Québec et le cas de Charlevoix.' PHD thesis, UL, 1980
– L'habitat de bois en Nouvelle-France: son importance et ses techniques de construction.' *Bulletin d'histoire de la culture matérielle,* no. 14. Ottawa: NMM, 1982
Lessard, Michel, and Gilles Vilandré. *La maison traditionnelle au Québec.* Montréal: Éditions de l'Homme, 1974
Noppen, Luc, and Marc Grignon. *L'art de l'architecte: trois siècles de dessin d'architecture à Québec.* Québec: Musée du Québec / UL, 1983

PLATE 56

The Wooden House

GEORGES-PIERRE LÉONIDOFF (Centre d'études sur la langue, les arts, et les traditions, Université Laval)

Sources

See pl 55 and the following:
Phelps, Herman. *The Craft of Log Building.* Ottawa: Lee Valley, 1982
Séguin, Robert-Lionel. *La maison en Nouvelle France.* Ottawa: Musées nationaux du Canada, 1968
Weslager, C.A. *The Log Cabin in America from Pioneer Days to the Present.* New Brunswick, NJ: Rutgers University Press, 1969

PLATE 57

Rupert's Land

ARTHUR J. RAY (Department of History, University of British Columbia)
D. WAYNE MOODIE (Department of Geography, University of Manitoba)
CONRAD E. HEIDENREICH (Department of Geography, York University)

Primary sources

There are no hard data on the French trade in muskets. The patterns shown here are based on references scattered among the primary sources. Generally speaking the French did not trade muskets until the second half of the 17th century. Data on firearms traded by the Hudson's Bay Company are contained in account books of the respective posts.

PAM, HBC Archives, B, 3/d/1–78; 42/d/1–51; 135/d/1–37; 239/d/1–72

Secondary sources

Ewers, John C. *The Horse in Blackfoot Indian Culture.* Smithsonian Institution, American Ethnology, Bulletin no. 159. Washington: Government Printing Office, 1955
Ray, Arthur J. *Indians in the Fur Trade: Their Role as Hunters, Trappers and Middlemen in the Lands Southwest of Hudson Bay 1660–1870.* Toronto: University of Toronto Press, 1974
Ray, Arthur J., and D.B. Freeman. *Give Us Good Measure.* Toronto: University of Toronto Press, 1978
Rin, Denis. 'The Acquisition, Diffusion and Distribution of the European Horse among the Blackfoot Tribes in Western Canada.' MA thesis, UMan, 1975
Roe, Frank Gilbert. *The Indian and the Horse.* Norman: University of Oklahoma Press, 1955
Yerbury, J.C. *The Sub-Arctic Indians and the Fur Trade.* Vancouver: University of British Columbia Press, 1986

PLATE 58

Exploration from Hudson Bay

RICHARD I. RUGGLES (Department of Geography, Queen's University)

Bayly, Charles, fl ca 1630–80 DCB 1: 81–4
Chouart Des Groseilliers, Médard, 1618–96? DCB 1: 223–8
Coats, William, d 1752 DCB 3: 127–8
Cocking, Matthew, 1743–99 DCB 4: 156–8
Gillam, Zachariah, 1636–82 DCB 1: 336–8
Gorst, Thomas, fl ca 1668–87 DCB 1: 343
Grimington, Michael, d 1710 DCB 2: 264–7
Hearne, Samuel, 1745–92 DCB 4: 339–42
Henday, Anthony, fl 1750–62 DCB 3: 285–7
Kelsey, Henry, 1667–1724 DCB 2: 307–15
Middleton, Christopher, d 1770 DCB 3: 446–50
Mitchell, Thomas, fl 1743–51 DCB 3: 453–4
Nixon, John, 1623–92 DCB 1: 518–20
Norton, Moses, 1735–73 DCB 4: 583–5
Norton, Richard, 1701–41 DCB 3: 489–90
Radisson, Pierre-Esprit, 1640–1710 DCB 2: 535–40
Scroggs, John, fl 1718–24 DCB 2: 604
Smith, Joseph, d 1765 DCB 3: 594–5
Walker, Nehemiah, fl ca 1670–90 DCB 1: 666

The following were also Hudson's Bay Company traders: George Atkinson, Jr, Alex Brand, Thomas Buchan, John Clarke, James Clouston, John Isbister, Thomas Isbister, George Jackman, Christoper Norton, William Pink, James Robertson, William Robinson, William Stewart, William Tomison, Joseph Waggoner. Joseph Frobisher and Thomas Frobisher were Montréal traders.

Primary sources

The originals of the maps by Thornton, Coats, Norton, and Graham are in the HBC Archives, PAM. The map attributed to Dobbs, actually the work of Joseph La France, appeared in Arthur Dobbs, *An Account of the Countries Adjoining to Hudson's Bay in the North-West Part of America...* (London, 1744). The depictions of explorers' routes and of teritory explored are largely based on extensive research in the HBC Archives, particularly in the correspondance (A5, A6, A10, A11), in the post journals and letters between posts (B3/a and B3/b), and in the map collection. Much use has also been made of the map collection at the PAC.

Secondary sources

Cooke, Alan, and Clive Holland. *The Exploration of Northern Canada, 500–1920: A Chronology.* Toronto, Arctic History, 1978
Cummings, W.P., S.E. Hillier, D.B. Quinn, and G. Williams. *The Exploration of North America, 1630–1776.* Toronto: McClelland and Stewart, 1974
Rich, Edwin Ernest. *The History of the Hudson's Bay Company, 1670–1870.* 2 vols. London: HBC Record Society, 1958–9
Thomson, Don W. *Men and Meridians: The History of Surveying and Mapping in Canada.* Vol 1. Ottawa: Queen's Printer, 1966
Warkentin, John, and Richard I. Ruggles. *Historical Atlas of Manitoba, 1612–1969.* Winnipeg: Manitoba Historical Society, 1970

PLATE 59

Indian Maps

D. WAYNE MOODIE (Department of Geography, University of Manitoba)

Primary sources

INDIAN MAPS
PAM, HBC Archives. Ac ko mok ki 1801, G1/25; Cot aw ney yaz zah, 1810, E3/4, fol 14d.; Ki oo cus, 1802, E3/2, fol 105

Secondary sources

Beattie, Judith. 'Indian Maps in the Hudson's Bay Company Archives.' *Bulletin, Association of Canadian Map Libraries* 55 (June 1985): 19–31
Moodie, D.W. 'Indian Map-Making: Two Examples from the Fur Trade West.' *Bulletin, Association of Canadian Map Libraries* 55 (June 1985): 32–43
Moodie, D.W., and Barry Kaye. 'The Ac ko mok ki Map.' *The Beaver* 307, no. 4 (1977): 4–15
Pentland, David H. 'Cartographic Concepts of the Northern Algonquians.' *The Canadian Cartographer* 12, no. 2 (1975): 149–60

Thanks are due to the Hudson's Bay Company Archives, PAM, and to Victor Lytwyn, UMan.

PLATE 60

Bayside Trade, 1720–1780

ARTHUR J. RAY (Department of History, University of British Columbia)

Made beaver (MB) A unit of account used by the Hudson's Bay Company, equivalent to the value of one prime winter parchment or coat beaver skin

Primary sources

PAM, HBC Archives. Post account books, 1720–80

Secondary sources

Ray, Arthur J. *Indians in the Fur Trade.* Toronto: University of Toronto Press, 1974
Ray, Arthur J., and D.B. Freeman. *Give Us Good Measure.* Toronto: University of Toronto Press, 1978

PLATE 61

Competition and Consolidation, 1760–1825

D. WAYNE MOODIE (Department of Geography, University of Manitoba)
VICTOR P. LYTWYN (Department of geography, University of Manitoba)
BARRY KAYE (Department of Geography, University of Manitoba)
ARTHUR J. RAY (Department of History, University of British Columbia)

Primary sources

PAM, HBC Archives. Southern Department fur returns, B.135/h/1. Northern Department fur returns, B.239/h/1. Values of furs are based on A.63/5.

Published journals and accounts by Montréal and HBC traders were also consulted.

Secondary sources

Alwin, John A. 'Mode, Pattern and Pulse: Hudson's Bay Company Transport, 1670 to 1821.' PH D thesis, UMan, 1978
Davidson, G.C. *The Northwest Company.* New York: Russell and Russell, 1918; repr 1967
Historic Sites and Monuments Board of Canada, staff report. 'Thematic Study of the Fur Trade in the Canadian West, 1670–1870.' Agenda Paper 29. Ottawa, 1968
Morse, E.W. *Fur Trade Canoe Routes of Canada: Then and Now.* Ottawa: Queen's Printer, 1969
Morton, A.S. *A History of the Canadian West to 1870–71.* Toronto: University of Toronto Press, 1939; repr 1973
Rich, Edwin E. *Hudson's Bay Company, 1670–1870.* 3 vols. Toronto: McClelland and Stewart, 1960
Voorhis, Ernest. *Historic Forts and Trading Posts of the French Regime and of the English Fur Trading Companies.* Ottawa: Department of the Interior, Natural Resources Intelligence Service, 1930

Acknowledgment is due to the PAM, HBC Archives, and to Shirlee Smith, Keeper of the HBC Archives, for permission to consult and publish from the Company's records.

PLATE 62

Trading Posts, 1774–1821

D. WAYNE MOODIE (Department of Geography, University of Manitoba)
VICTOR P. LYTWYN (Department of Geography, University of Manitoba)
BARRY KAYE (Department of Geography, University of Manitoba)

Primary sources

PAM, HBC Archives. Miscellaneous letters, accounts, survey books, post journals, district reports, and manuscript maps
Published journals and accounts by Montréal traders

Secondary sources

Historic Sites and Monuments Board of Canada, staff report. 'Thematic Study of the Fur Trade in the Canadian West, 1670–1870.' Agenda Paper 29. Ottawa, 1968
Morton, A.S. *A History of the Canadian West to 1870–71.* Toronto: University of Toronto Press, 1939; repr 1973
Rich, E.E. *Hudson's Bay Company, 1670–1870.* 3 vols. Toronto: McClelland and Stewart, 1960
Voorhis, Ernest. *Historic Forts and Trading Posts of the French Regime and of the English Fur Trading Companies.* Ottawa: Department of the Interior, Natural Resources Intelligence Service, 1930

Thanks are due to Kevin Hayman for assembling maps at an early stage.

PLATE 63

Tranportation in the Petit Nord

VICTOR P. LYTWYN (Department of Geography, University of Manitoba)

Tracking Pulling a boat or canoe upstream by line (rope)

Secondary sources

Alwin, John A. 'Mode, Pattern and Pulse: Hudson's Bay Company Transport, 1670 to 1821.' PH D thesis, UMan, 1978

Bishop, Charles A. *The Northern Ojibwa and the Fur Trade: An Historical and Ecological Study.* Toronto: Holt, Rinehart and Winston, 1974

Innis, Harold A. *The Fur Trade in Canada.* First publ 1930. Rev ed. Toronto: University of Toronto Press, 1956

Katz, Irving F. 'Ezekiel Solomon: The First Jew in Michigan.' *Michigan History* 32 (1948): 247–56

Lytwyn, Victor P. 'Geographical Situation and the Early Fur Trade of the East Winnipeg Country.' *Regina Geographical Studies* 4 (1984): 33–40

Morse, Eric W. *Fur Trade Canoe Routes of Canada: Then and Now.* Toronto: University of Toronto Press, 1969

Morton, Arthur S. *A History of the Canadian West to 1870–71.* Toronto: University of Toronto Press, 1939; repr 1973

Ray, Arthur J. *Indians in the Fur Trade: Their Role as Trappers, Hunters, and Middlemen in the Lands Southwest of Hudson Bay, 1660–1870.* Toronto: University of Toronto Press, 1974

Rich, Edwin E. *Hudson's Bay Company, 1670–1870.* 3 vols. Toronto: McClelland and Stewart, 1960

Ross, Eric. *Beyond the River and the Bay.* Toronto: University of Toronto Press, 1970

Wallace, W. Stewart, ed. *Documents Relating to the North West Company.* Toronto: Champlain Society, 1934

Thanks are due to Shirlee Smith, Keeper of the HBC Archives, and to D. Wayne Moodie and Barry Kaye, UMan.

PLATE 64

Fur-Trade Settlements

D. WAYNE MOODIE (Department of Geography, University of Manitoba)
VICTOR P. LYTWYN (Department of Geography, University of Manitoba)

Richards, William, ca 1785–1811 Entered HBC service 1803, reputed to be the first native-born artist in the Hudson Bay region. DCB 5: 711–12

Names of HBC officers identified on map of HBC posts, 1789–90:
Churchill: William Jefferson
York Factory: Joseph Colen
Severn: John Ballenden, 1812–56 DCB 8: 59–60
Albany Fort: Edward Jarvis (author of map)
Moose Fort: John Thomas and George Donald
Eastmain: George Atkinson
Cumberland House: William Walker
Cat Lake: John Best and Simon Beaugrand
Asnaburgh: Robert Goodwin and Edward Clouston
Gloucester House: James Sutherland
Henley House: John Hodgson
Frederick House: John Mannall
New Brunswick House: William Bolland

Primary sources

Clements Library, University of Michigan, Ann Arbor, Michigan. Map of Hudson's Bay Company posts, 1789–90

PAM, HBC Archives. Paintings by William Richards

– Plans of Lesser Slave Lake House, York Factory, Naosquiscaw House, Red Lake House, Cumberland Houses, Edmonton Houses

Plan of Fort William, after original sketch by Lord Selkirk Published in G.B. Macgillivray. *Our Heritage.* Thunder Bay, 1970

Secondary sources

Anik, Norman. 'The Fur Trade in Eastern Canada until 1870.' National Historic Parks and Sites Branch, Parks Canada, Department of Indian and Northern Affairs. Manuscript Report 207. 2 vols. Ottawa, 1976

Berry, Virginia G. *A Boundless Horizon: Visual Records of Exploration and Settlement in Manitoba Region, 1624–1874.* Winnipeg: Winnipeg Art Gallery, 1983

Thanks are due to the HBC Archives and PAM.

PLATE 65

Peoples of the Boreal Forest and Parkland

D. WAYNE MOODIE (Department of Geography, University of Manitoba)
BARRY KAYE (Department of Geography, University of Manitoba)
VICTOR P. LYTWYN (Department of Geography, University of Manitoba)
ARTHUR J. RAY (Department of History, University of British Columbia)

Primary sources

Davidson, Gordon C. *The Northwest Company.* New York: Russell and Russell, 1918

Garry, Nicholas. 'Diary of Nicholas Garry.' *Transactions of the Royal Society of Canada.* Vol 6, section II (1900): 73–204

PAC, MG 19. List of North West Co. Men at Various Stations. Transcript

– Register of North West Company Servants by Department, 1811–21

PAM, HBC Archives. Account books, post journals, letters, lists of servants, and ledgers

Wallace, W. Stewart, ed. *Documents Relating to the Northwest Company.* Toronto: Champlain Society, 1934

Secondary sources

Ray, Arthur J. *Indians in the Fur Trade.* Toronto: University of Toronto Press, 1974

Yerbury, J.C. *The Sub-Arctic Indians and the Fur Trade.* Vancouver: University of British Columbia Press, 1986

Population estimates for native people are based on observations of explorers and fur traders. Although impressionistic, they give some idea of the relative numbers of different native groups.

PLATE 66

New Caledonia and Columbia

M.D. KINKADE (Department of Linguistics, University of British Columbia)
WAYNE SUTTLES (Department of Anthropology, University of Oregon)
ROBERT M. GALOIS (Vancouver)
SHEILA P. ROBINSON (Vancouver)

Primary sources

Cook, W. *Flood Tide of Empire: Spain and the Pacific Northwest, 1543–1819.* New Haven: Yale University Press, 1973

Gibson, J.R. 'The Survey of Kirill Khlebnikov.' *Pacific Northwest Quarterly* 63, no. 4 (1972): 1–13

– *Imperial Russia in Frontier America.* New York: Oxford University Press, 1976

Gough, B. *The Royal Navy and the Northwest Coast of North America, 1810–1914.* Vancouver: University of British Columbia Press, 1971

– *Distant Dominion: Britain and the Northwest Coast of North America, 1579–1809.* Vancouver: University of British Columbia Press, 1980

Howay, F.W. 'A List of Trading Vessels in the Maritime Fur Trade (1785–1825).' *Transactions of the Royal Society of Canada.* 3rd series. 24, section 2 (1930): 111–34; 25, section 2 (1931): 117–49; 26, section 2 (1932): 43–86; 27, section 2 (1933): 119–47; 28, section 2 (1934): 11–49

Pierce, R.A., ed. *Materials for the Study of Alaska History.* 24 vols. Kingston, Ont: Limestone Press, 1972–84

Vancouver, George. *A Voyage of Discovery to the North Pacific Ocean and round the World, 1791–1795.* Ed W.K. Lamb. 4 vols. London: Hakluyt Society, 1984

The primary source of data for the graph is Howay (1930–4). This has been supplemented, primarily, by sources on the Russian voyages (Pierce, 1972–84: Gibson, 1972, 1976). Cook (1973) provides a survey and a list of Spanish voyages; Gough (1972, 1976) does the same for British naval expeditions. A number of original ships' logs have survived, and many have been published, most recently Vancouver's journals (Lamb, 1984). These logs and unpublished manuscripts in the F.W. Howay and R.L. Reid Collection, Special Collections, UBC Library, have provided the data about trading locations and native names associated with the maritime fur trade.
Three basic sources list fur trade posts in the Cordillera:

Barry, J.N. 'Early Oregon Country Forts: A Chronological List.' *Oregon Historical Quarterly* 46, no. 2 (1945): 101–11

Ross, L.A. 'Early Nineteenth Century Euramerican Technology within the Columbia River Drainage System.' *Northwest Anthropological Research Notes* 9, no. 1 (1975): 32–50

Voorhis, E. *Historical Forts and Trading Posts of the French Regime and of the English Fur Trading Companies.* Ottawa: Department of the Interior, 1930

Documents on the land-based fur trade before 1821 are limited; therefore the surviving journals of fur traders are particularly important, especially those by Simon Fraser, Daniel Harmon, Alexander Ross, David Thompson, Alexander Henry, Ross Cox, and Gabriel Franchère. These are supplemented by a variety of primary material published in the *Oregon Historical Quarterly*, the *Pacific Northwest Quarterly* (formerly the *Washington Historical Quarterly*), and the *British Columbia Historical Quarterly*.

Secondary sources

FUR TRADES

Campbell, Marjory E. *The Northwest Company*. Toronto: Macmillan, 1957; repr Vancouver: Douglas and McIntyre, 1983

Fisher, Robin. *Contact and Conflict*. Vancouver: University of British Columbia Press, 1977

Gunther, Erna. *Indian Life on the Northwest Coast of North America as Seen by the Early Explorers and Fur Traders during the Last Decades of the Eighteenth Century*. Chicago: University of Chicago Press, 1972

Howay, F.W. 'An Outline Sketch of the Maritime Fur Trade.' Canadian Historical Association, *Report* (1932): 5–14

Merk, Frederick, ed. 'Introduction.' In *Fur Trade and Empire: George Simpson's Journal*. Cambridge, Mass.: Harvard University Press, 1931

LINGUISTICS

Barnett, Homer C. *The Coast Salish of British Columbia*. University of Oregon Monographs, Studies in Anthropology 4. Eugene, Oregon, 1955

Boas, Franz. 'Zur Ethnologie Britisch-Kolumbiens.' *Petermanns Geographische Mitteilungen* 5 (1887): 129–33

– *Kwakiutl Ethnography*. Ed Helen Codere. Chicago: University of Chicago Press, 1966

'Canada: Indian and Inuit Communities and Languages.' *The National Atlas of Canada*. 5th ed. Ottawa: Surveys and Mapping Branch, Energy, Mines and Resources, 1980

Drucker, Philip. *The Northern and Central Nootkan Tribes*. Bureau of American Ethnology, Bulletin 144. Washington: Government Printing Office, 1951

[Duff, Wilson]. 'British Columbia Native Indians: Distribution of Ethnic Groups – 1850.' *British Columbia Atlas of Resources*. Map No. 12. Victoria, 1956

Suttles, Wayne, and Cameron Suttles. *Native Languages of the Northwest Coast* [map]. Portland: Western Imprints, The Press of the Oregon Historical Society, 1985

Thompson, Laurence C., and M. Dale Kinkade. 'Linguistic Relations and Distributions.' In *Handbook of American Indians*. Vol 7: *The Northwest Coast*. Ed Wayne Suttles. Washington: Smithsonian Institution, forthcoming

Since it is not possible to list all villages known to have been occupied in the early 19th century, only better-known communities or groupings are listed, especially when there were slight speech differences. Spellings of languages, dialects, and communities are highly variable, and often not standardized; the most widely used and those felt to be most accurate in terms of native pronunciation have been selected for this map.

The following colleagues provided information on subdivisions, groupings, and spellings: T.M. Hess, University of Victoria; W.H. Jacobsen, Jr, University of Nevada; J.E.M. Kew and W.R. Ridington, UBC; M.E. Krauss and J. Leer, University of Alaska; A.H. Kuipers, University of Leiden (retired); J.C. Rath, Heiltsuk Cultural Education Centre, Bella Bella, BC; B.J. Rigsby, University of Queensland; S. Rose and J.P. van Eijk, Victoria, BC; and P.J. Wilson, Campbell River, BC.

PLATE 67

Exploration in the Far Northwest

RICHARD I. RUGGLES (Department of Geography, Queen's University)

RUSSIAN EXPLORERS

Vitus Joanassen Bering; Alexei Chirikov; Grigor Ivanovich Shelikov; Gerasim Grigorievich Ismailov; Master Bocharov; Joseph Billings, DCB 5: 79–81; Gavriil Andreevich Sarychev

SPANISH EXPLORERS

Juan Josef Pérez Hernández, DCB 4: 622–3; Juan Francisco de la Bodega y Quadra, DCB 4: 72–4; Francisco de Eliza y Reventa; Salvador Fidalgo; Cayetano Valdés y Flores Bazán; Dionisio Alcalá-Galiano, DCB 5: 11–12; Jacinto Caamano

BRITISH EXPLORERS

James Cook, DCB 4: 162–7; George Vancouver, DCB 4: 743–8

EXPLORERS OF THE INTERIOR

Peter Pond, DCB 5: 681–6; Alexander Mackenzie, DCB 5: 537–43; Philip Turnor, DCB 4: 740–2; Peter Fidler, DCB 6: 249–52; Malchom (Malcolm) Ross, DCB 4: 684–5; David Thompson, DCB 8: 878–84; Edward Jarvis, DCB 4: 389–90; John Kipling; George Sutherland, DCB 4: 726–7; James Sutherland, DCB 4: 727–8; James Hudson

EXPLORERS OF THE ARCTIC

John Ross, DCB 8: 770–4; William Edward Parry, DCB 8: 683–6; John Franklin; John Richardson, DCB 9: 658–61; George Back, DCB 10: 26–9

Primary sources

The Pond, Arrowsmith, and Taylor maps are from the collection at the PAC. The Hodgson map is from the collection in the HBC Archives, PAM. The original of the Thompson map is in the Ontario Archives; the version on this plate is based on a simplified drawing of the Thompson map published by the Champlain Society. For HBC sources see notes for pl 58.

Secondary sources

Cooke, Alan, and Clive Holland. *The Exploration of Northern Canada, 500–1920: A Chronology*. Toronto: Arctic History, 1978

Morton, A.S. *A History of the Canadian West to 1870–71*. Toronto: Nelson, 1939

Moulton, Gary E., ed. *Atlas of the Lewis and Clark Expedition*. Lincoln: University of Nebraska Press, 1983

Rich, Edwin Ernest. *The History of the Hudson's Bay Company, 1670–1870*. 2 vols. London: HBC Record Society, 1958–9

Ruggles, Richard I. 'The West of Canada in 1763: Imagination and Reality.' *The Canadian Geographer* 15, no. 4 (1971)

Schwartz, Seymour I., and Ralph E. Ehrenberg. *The Mapping of America*. New York: Abrams, 1980

Stuart-Stubbs, Basil, and Coolie Verner. *The Northpart of America*. Don Mills, Ont: Academic Press, 1979

Thomson, Don W. *Men and Meridians: The History of Surveying and Mapping in Canada*. Vol 1. Ottawa: Queen's Printer, 1966

Warkentin, John. *The Western Interior of Canada*. The Carleton Library, no. 15. Toronto: McClelland and Stewart, 1964

Warkentin, John, and Richard I. Ruggles. *Historical Atlas of Manitoba, 1612–1969*. Winnipeg: Manitoba Historical Society, 1970

PLATE 68

Eastern Canada in 1800

R. COLE HARRIS (Department of Geography, University of British Columbia)
DAVID WOOD (Department of Geography, Atkinson College, York University)

Sources

This plate summarizes data from other plates and adds some new information.

The data on settlement and the fisheries in Newfoundland are drawn from pll 25–7 and from the Newfoundland census of 1797 (PRO, CO 194/40). The data on settlement and trade in the Maritimes are derived from pl 32. The data on settlement and fisheries in the northern and western Gulf of St Lawrence are drawn from pl 54. The population of Lower Canada is based on the estimate on pl 46. The distribution of settlement and the extent of cleared land in Lower Canada are derived from Joseph Bouchette, *A Topographical Description of the Province of Lower Canada* ... (London: W. Faden, 1815). The distribution of English-speaking settlers in Québec is a considered estimate – as much as can be done until this matter is the subject of a specialized study. Fur routes are generalized and simplified, and are not intended to show exact locations. Nor does the plate attempt to show all trading posts (for more comprehensive distribution of posts in much of this territory see pl 62). Indian distributions are derived from pl 69, or from sources mentioned in the notes for that plate. The small native populations in the Canadian Shield cannot be usefully shown at the scale used on this plate and have been omitted.

The data on Upper Canada are not presented elsewhere in this volume. Estimates of the size and distribution of population are based on Lieutenant Governor Simcoe's correspondence (E.A. Cruikshank, ed, *The Correspondence of Lt Governor Simcoe*, 5 vols [Toronto: Ontario Historical Society, 1924]), the militia returns, and the civil secretary's papers in the PAC (RG 5 B26). The following have been helpful: county histories; Robert Gourlay's *Statistical Account of Upper Canada* ... (London: Simpkin and Marshall, 1822), abridged and with an introduction by S.R. Mealing (Toronto: McClelland and Stewart, 1974); and the dates of township survey given in W.G. Dean and G.J. Matthews, *Economic Atlas of Ontario* (Toronto: University of Toronto Press, 1969). Data on trade in Upper Canada have been derived in part from Douglas McCalla, 'The "Loyalist" Economy of Upper Canada, 1784–1806,' *Hist Soc* 16 (1983): 279–304.

This plate has depended upon the expertise and advice of Conrad E. Heidenreich, Mario Lalancette, Victor P. Lytwyn, John J. Mannion, D. Wayne Moodie, and Graeme Wynn.

PLATE 69

Native Canada, ca 1820

CONRAD E. HEIDENREICH (Department of Geography, York University)
ROBERT M. GALOIS (Vancouver)

Primary Sources

Great Britain, House of Commons. British North American Provinces. 'Copies of Extracts of Correspondence ... Respecting the Indians, 17 June, 1839.' In *British Parliamentary Papers.* Colonies, Canada, 12. Irish University Press, 1969

- House of Commons. Indian Department, Canada. 'Copies or Extracts of Recent Correspondence Respecting ... Indian Departments in Canada, 2 June, 1856.' In *British Parliamentary Papers.* Colonies, Canada, 21. Irish University Press, 1970
- Parliament. 'Aboriginal Tribes.' In *Imperial Blue Books on Affairs Relating to Canada* 5 (1834–6), paper 617: 1–229

Hind, H.Y. *Explorations of the Interior of the Labrador Peninsula, the Country of the Montagnais and Nasquapee Indians.* 2 vols. London: Longman, Green, 1863

Keating, W.H. *Narrative of an Expedition to the Sources of St. Peter's River ... Performed in the Year 1823.* Philadelphia: H.C. Carey and I. Lea, 1824

Mason, P.P., Ed. *Schoolcraft's Expedition to Lake Itasca.* East Lansing: Michigan State University, 1958

New Brunswick, *Journal of the House of Assembly.* 6th Session, 12th General Assembly, pp xcii–cxvii. Fredericton, 1842

PAC. RG10, vol 708, Census Records, 1810–36; vol 747, Census Records, 1840–52

- NMC. All maps by A. Arrowsmith and D. Thompson

PAM, HBC Archives. B/e: District Reports (Abitibi, B1/e/2, 1822–3 to York Factory, B239/e/3, 182) approximately covering the years 1818–25. B/2: various censuses compiled between 1815 and 1839. Maps: all maps drawn between 1815 and 1827

PANS. RG1, vol 431, Papers relating to Indians, 1832–6; vol. 432, Papers relating to Indians, 1842–3

Provincial Archives of British Columbia. Douglas papers, Second series, Microfilm 737A, pp 7–33; Transcript B/20/1853, pp 5–31. The originals are in the Bancroft Library, San Francisco.

Secondary sources

Boas, F. *The Central Eskimo.* Smithsonian Institution, Bureau of American Ethnology, 6th Annual Report. Washington, 1888

Brice-Bennett, C., ed. *Our Footprints Are Everywhere: Inuit Land Use and Occupancy in Labrador.* Nain: Labrador Inuit Association, 1977

Duff, W. *The Indian History of British Columbia.* Vol 1: *The Impact of the White Man.* Provincial Museum of Natural History and Anthropology, Memoir 5, 1964. Victoria, 1965

Freeman, M.M.R., ed. *Inuit Land Use and Occupancy Project.* 3 vols. Ottawa: Minister of Supply and Services, 1976

Handbook of North American Indians. Vol 6: *Subarctic.* Ed J. Helm. Washington: Smithsonian Institution, 1981

Handbook of North American Indians. Vol 15: *Northeast.* Ed B.G. Trigger. Washington: Smithsonian Institution, 1978

Hodge, F.W. ed. *Handbook of Indians North of Mexico.* 2 vols. Smithsonian Institution, Bureau of American Ethnology, Bulletin 30. Washington, 1907, 1910

Horr, D.A., ed. *Coast Salish and Western Washington Indians.* 5 vols. New York: Garland, 1974

- *Interior Salish and Eastern Washington Indians.* 5 vols. New York: Garland, 1974

Howley, J.P. *The Beothucks or Red Indians: The Aboriginal Inhabitants of Newfoundland.* Cambridge: Cambridge University Press, 1915

Krause, A. *The Tlingit Indians.* Transl E. Gunther. 1st ed. 1885. Seattle: University of Washington, 1956

Tanner, V. 'Outlines of the Geography, Life and Customs of Newfoundland-Labrador.' *Acta Geographica* 8, no. 1 (1944) 1–907

Much of the HBC census material is complete for men, women, and children. In cases where only men were counted, a total population was extrapolated using population ratios derived from nearby groups living in a similar environment with a similar economy. Where later censuses had to be used for native groups who were affected by epidemic diseases after 1821 (eg, Tlingit), the population totals were adjusted upward by one-third. Data for some of the Plains groups (eg, Blackfoot, Assiniboine) were originally given in numbers of tents. These were converted to population numbers on the basis of eight people per tent, as suggested by contemporary observers. It is impossible to determine how accurate the early censuses and estimates were.

Early 19th-century populations in the Cordillera are particularly difficult to establish. There were 11 HBC censuses of various areas, some overlapping, none surviving in original form. The copies that do survive, made in 1878 by one of H.H. Bancroft's researchers, usually do not indicate the date of the enumeration. Given these limitations it is no easy matter to resolve the contradictions arising between different, overlapping estimates. For example, there are five separate censuses of some or all of the Southern Kwakiutl but only one includes a date (summer 1838), and none indicates who was responsible for the compilation. Wilson Duff used this material and his own large knowledge of native British Columbia to prepare the population map in *The Indian History of British Columbia.* We have been over the same ground, correcting some mistakes on Duff's map while following its general patterns. A comprehensive analysis of these censuses and other estimates of early-contact native populations in the northern Cordillera remains to be done.

We gratefully acknowledge permission to consult the HBC Archives, PAM, as well as the help of the archivists, especially Shirlee A. Smith; and also the staff in Special Collections, the Library, UBC.

Colour separation: Herzig Somerville Limited

Composition: Cooper and Beatty Limited

Photomechanical services and colour proofs: Northway Map Technology Limited

Film assembly: Herzig Somerville Limited

Printer: Ashton-Potter Limited

Case Binder: Anstey Graphic Limited

LIVING IN
VIVRE A
SYDNEY

Photos | Fotos **Giorgio Possenti** Text | Texte **Antonella Boisi** Project | Projet | Projekt **Vega MG**

KÖLN LONDON MADRID NEW YORK PARIS TOKYO

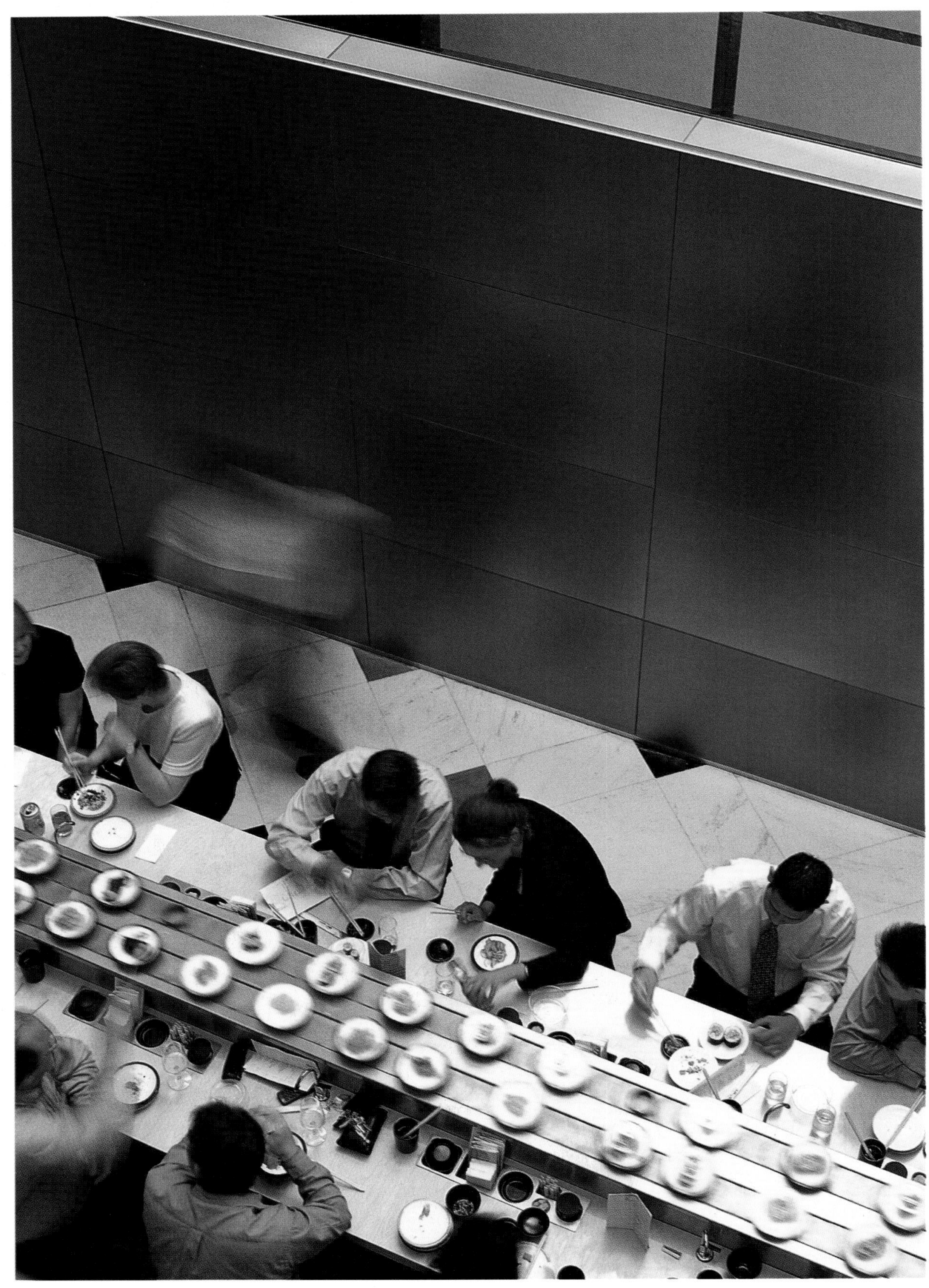

2. Sosumi sushi bar, Martin Place. **3.** Two cliffs reach out toward the ocean at the bay of Sydney, forming a sort of virtual gate to the city. – **2.** Le Sushi-bar Sosumi au Martin Place. **3.** Deux falaises délimitent l'intrusion de l'océan dans la baie de Sydney, formant une sorte de porte virtuelle de la ville. – **2.** Sushi-Bar Sosumi am Martin Place. **3.** Zwei Felsenriffe halten die in die Bucht von Sydney hereinbrechenden Wellen auf und bilden eine Art virtuelles Stadttor.

LONDON
TAVERN
1875
LONDON
TAVERN
LONDON TAVERN
HAPPY HOUR
LONDON Bars & Restaurant TAVERN

4. MLC Centre, Martin Place, design by Harry Seidler. **5.** London Tavern, Underwood Street, Paddington. – **4.** MLC Centre, Martin Place, un projet de Harry Seidler. **5.** La London Tavern, Underwood Street à Paddington. – **4.** MLC Centre, Martin Place, ein Projekt von Harry Seidler. **5.** London Tavern in der Underwood Street, Paddington.

6. In the streets of Sydney and inside the Poya Bar, Victoria Street, Darlinghurst. **7.** Exterior view of the Medusa Hotel, Darlinghurst Road. – **6.** Les rues de Sydney et l'intérieur du bar Poya au Victoria Street à Darlinghurst. **7.** La façade de l'hôtel au Darlinghurst Road. – **6.** Auf den Straßen von Sydney und in der Bar Poya in der Victoria Street, Darlinghurst. **7.** Die Fassade des Medusa Hotel in der Darlinghurst Road.

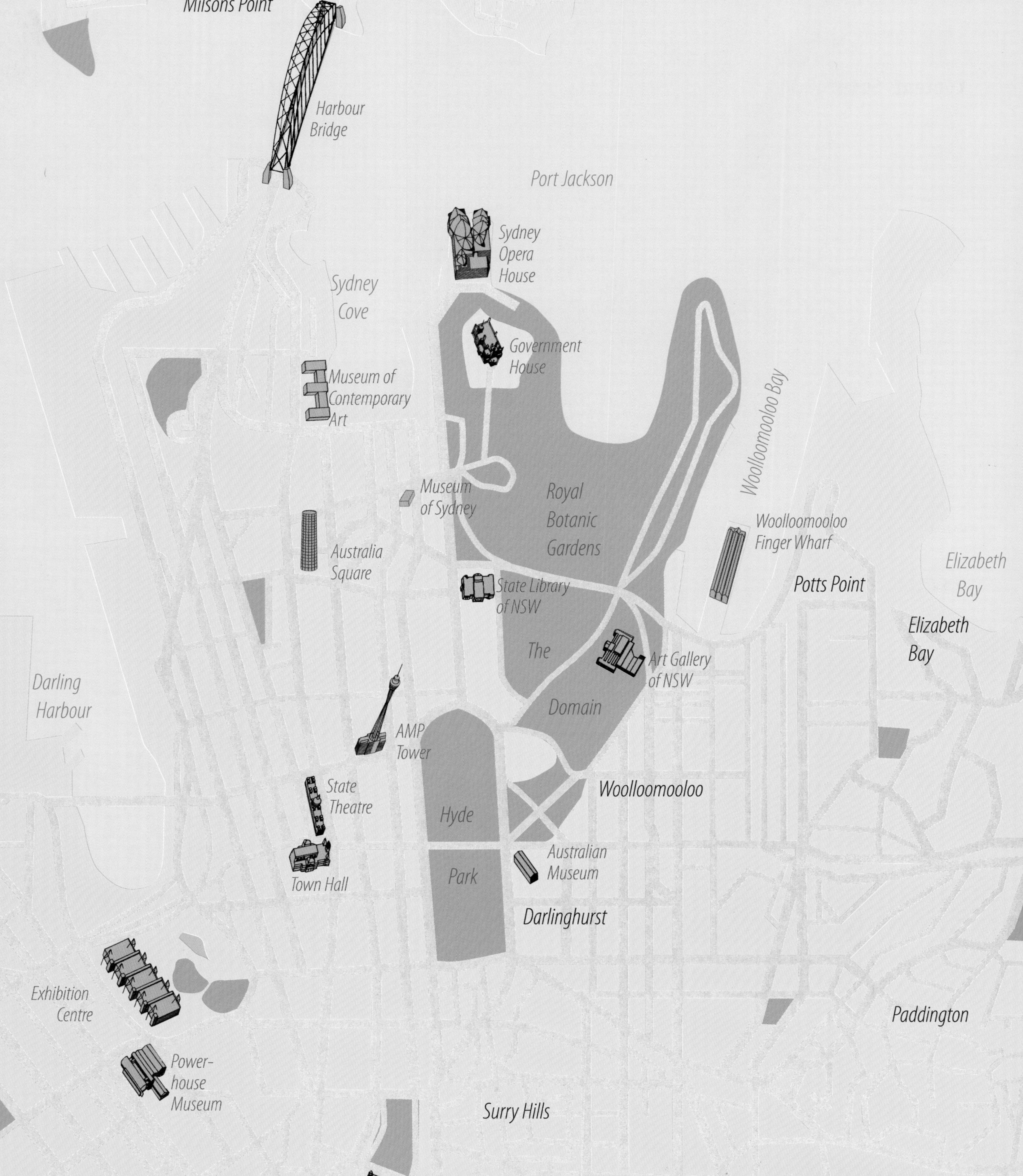
Milsons Point
Harbour Bridge
Port Jackson
Sydney Opera House
Sydney Cove
Government House
Museum of Contemporary Art
Woolloomooloo Bay
Museum of Sydney
Royal Botanic Gardens
Woolloomooloo Finger Wharf
Australia Square
Elizabeth Bay
Potts Point
State Library of NSW
Elizabeth Bay
The Domain
Art Gallery of NSW
Darling Harbour
AMP Tower
Woolloomooloo
State Theatre
Hyde Park
Australian Museum
Town Hall
Darlinghurst
Exhibition Centre
Paddington
Power-house Museum
Surry Hills
Central Station

Contents Sommaire Inhalt

Bay Watch House, Rose Bay

This house, built in the 30s on Rose Bay, one of the most beautiful seaside locations, offers a breathtaking view of Sydney Harbour, from the Opera House to the skyscrapers of the City and Harbour Bridge. It's no coincidence that the studio Jackson Clements Burrows has redesigned it for a young couple from Melbourne as an extension of the landscape, fostering a sense of continuity between the nature and the domestic environment. A suspended footbridge spans a tropical garden leading to the entrance. Inside, a large open space is set aside for the living areas, with a terrace facing the bay. On the lower level the bedroom zone features direct access to the swimming pool. The refined interior furnishings are by the design company Schamburg & Alvisse.

Perchée au-dessus de Rose Bay, une des plus belles baies de Sydney, cette maison des années 30 jouit d'une vue à couper le souffle sur le Harbour. Elle s'étend du célèbre opéra aux gratte-ciel de la City et à l'Harbour Bridge. Ce n'est pas pour rien que le cabinet d'architecture Jackson Clements Burrows l'a réaménagée pour un jeune couple de Melbourne comme une extension du paysage, privilégiant l'impression de continuité entre les milieux naturel et domestique. Un petit pont suspendu au-dessus d'un jardin tropical mène à la porte d'entrée qui s'ouvre sur un vaste espace ouvert consacré aux parties séjour et qui se prolonge sur la baie grâce à la terrasse. A l'étage inférieur, les chambres donnent directement sur la piscine. Le décor raffiné est l'œuvre de l'entreprise de design Schamburg & Alvisse.

Das Haus stammt aus den 30er Jahren und liegt in der Rose Bay, einer der schönsten Buchten von Sydney. Durch die erhöhte Lage bietet es eine atemberaubende Aussicht auf den Harbour, die vom Opera House bis zu den Hochhäusern der City und zur Harbour Bridge reicht. Es ist kein Zufall, dass das Architekturbüro Jackson Clements Burrows das für ein junges Melbourner Paar entworfene Wohnhaus so konzipiert hat, dass es wie in die Landschaft hineingewachsen scheint und die Räume wie eine Fortsetzung der umgebenden Natur wirken. Eine kleine Brücke über dem tropischen Garten führt zum Eingang, der in einen großzügigen, offen konzipierten Wohnbereich übergeht und sich bis zu der Terrasse mit Blick auf die Bucht fortsetzt. Die Schlafzimmer im unteren Stock besitzen einen direkten Zugang zum Pool. Die raffinierte Inneneinrichtung hat die Designfirma Schamburg & Alvisse entworfen.

10. Entrance to the house with the footbridge extending over the garden.
11. Tim Jackson, Jon Clements, Graham Burrows (from the left).

10. L'entrée de la maison avec le petit pont suspendu au-dessus du jardin.
11. Tim Jackson, Jon Clements, Graham Burrows (en partant de la gauche).

10. Der Hauseingang mit der kleinen Brücke, die sich über den Garten spannt. **11.** Tim Jackson, Jon Clements, Graham Burrows (von links).

12-13. The living room overlooking Rose Bay with the skyscrapers of the City in the background, in an evocative sunset view. **14.** A table in wood and steel, designed by Schamburg & Alvisse, and white *Bekko* chairs by the Melbourne-based company Basile & Evans furnish the dining area, which forms a single space with the kitchen. **15.** The made-to-measure kitchen with counters in black granite from Zimbabwe. The steel stools are by Space.

12-13. Le séjour ouvert sur Rose Bay, avec les gratte-ciel de la City en arrière-plan, se pare de teintes suggestives dans le coucher de soleil de Sydney. **14.** Une table en bois et acier, dessinée par Schamburg & Alvisse, et des chaises blanches *Bekko*, de Basile & Evans de Melbourne, meublent l'espace salle à manger uni à la cuisine. **15.** La cuisine design, réalisée avec des dalles de granit noir du Zimbabwe. Les tabourets en acier viennent de chez Space

12-13. Den Wohnbereich mit Blick auf Rose Bay und die Hochhäuser der City dahinter erfüllt bei Sonnenuntergang ein stimmungsvolles Lichtspiel. **14.** Das Esszimmer geht direkt in die Küche über und ist mit einem von Schamburg & Alvisse entworfenen Tisch aus Holz und Chromstahl sowie weißen Stühlen *Bekko* der Melbourner Firma Basile & Evans eingerichtet. **15.** Die Küche ist eine Maßanfertigung und besitzt Arbeitsflächen aus schwarzem Granit aus Simbabwe. Die Chromstahlhocker sind von Space.

16. The white sofa is by Schamburg & Alvisse, in the background a painting by Australian artist Peter Francis Lawrence. **17.** A zone of passage. On the wall, a painting by Peter Francis Lawrence. **18-19.** The lady of the house in a relaxing moment, wrapped in a blanket by Orson & Blake. The orange *RAR* rocker by Charles and Ray Eames lights up the white bedroom. **20.** Black granite for the counter in the bathroom.

16. Le canapé blanc est de Schamburg & Alvisse, à l'arrière-plan on voit un tableau de l'artiste australien Peter Francis Lawrence. **17.** Une aire de passage. Au mur, un tableau de Peter Francis Lawrence. **18-19.** La maîtresse de maison dans un moment de détente, drapée dans une couverture d'Orson & Blake. Le fauteuil orange *RAR* de Charles et Ray Eames forme une touche de couleur vive contre le blanc de la chambre à coucher. **20.** Pour la salle de bains, une dalle de granit noir.

16. Das weiße Sofa ist von Schamburg & Alvisse, im Hintergrund sieht man ein Gemälde des australischen Künstlers Peter Francis Lawrence. **17.** Ein Durchgangsraum. An der Wand hängt ein Gemälde von Peter Francis Lawrence. **18-19.** Die Hausbesitzerin relaxt in einer Decke von Orson & Blake. Der orange Armlehnstuhl *RAR* von Charles und Ray Eames bildet einen lebhaften Farbfleck im Weiß des Schlafzimmers. **20.** Schwarzer Granit wurde für die Ablagefläche im Badezimmer verwendet.

bod
HUSK

Jackson Clements Burrows Architects
One Harwood Place Melbourne 3000 Australia Ph +61 3 9654 6227 F +61 3 9654 6195 email: jacksonclementsburrows@jcba.com.au www.jcba.com.au

Timothy Jackson was born in San Francisco in 1964, **Jon Clements** in Melbourne in 1971, **Graham Burrows** in Johannesburg in 1972. **Studies, experiences, projects:** Tim graduated in 1987, Graham in 1995, both from the University of Melbourne; Jon graduated in 1995 from Deakin University. Before forming their practice, they all worked in the studio of Tim's father (Daryl Jackson Architects), participating in projects including: the Colonial Stadium, the Immigration Museum in Melbourne, the residence of the Australian ambassador in Berlin. Their own projects include showrooms for Bang & Olufsen and the Australian headquarters of Kookaï. **Favorites:** *Architects:* Alvar Aalto, Luis Barragán. *Building:* Casa Malaparte in Capri. *Designer:* Alvar Aalto. **In Sydney they recommend:** *Hotel:* Kirketon. *Restaurant:* Bill and Toni's. *Fashion boutique:* Luxe. *Museum:* Museum of Contemporary Art (MCA). *Bookstore:* Ariel.

Timothy Jackson est né en 1964 à San Francisco, **Jon Clements** en 1971 à Melbourne et **Graham Burrows** en 1972 à Johannesburg. **Etudes, expérience professionnelle, projets:** Tim et Graham ont obtenu leur diplôme d'architecture à l'université de Melbourne respectivement en 1987 et 1995; Jon a obtenu le sien en 1995 à la Deakin University. Avant de former leur entreprise, ils travaillaient tous dans le cabinet d'architecture du père de Tim (Daryl Jackson Architects) où ils ont collaboré, entre autres, aux projets suivants: le stade colonial et le Musée de l'immigration à Melbourne ainsi que la résidence de l'ambassadeur australien à Berlin. Parmi leurs propres réalisations on note plusieurs showrooms pour Bang & Olufsen ainsi que les sièges australiens de Kookaï. **Leurs favoris:** *Architectes:* Alvar Aalto, Luis Barragán. *Edifice:* la maison de Malaparte à Capri. *Designer:* Alvar Aalto. **A Sydney, ils recommandent:** *Hôtel:* Kirketon. *Restaurant:* Bill and Toni's. *Boutique de mode:* Luxe. *Musée:* Museum of Contemporary Art (MCA). *Librairie:* Ariel.

Timothy Jackson ist 1964 in San Francisco geboren, **Jon Clements** 1971 in Melbourne und **Graham Burrows** 1972 in Johannesburg. **Ausbildung, Erfahrungen, Projekte:** Tim und Graham schlossen ihr Studium 1987 bzw. 1995 an der University of Melbourne ab; Jon machte 1995 seinen Abschluss an der Deakin University. Vor der Gründung ihres gemeinsamen Büros arbeiteten sie alle im Architekturbüro von Tims Vater (Daryl Jackson Architects), wo sie u.a. an diesen Projekten teilnahmen: Colonial Stadium, Immigration Museum in Melbourne, das Privathaus des australischen Botschafters in Berlin. Zu den eigenen Projekten gehören Showrooms für Bang & Olufsen sowie die australischen Kookaï-Niederlassungen. **Sie bewundern:** *Architekten:* Alvar Aalto, Luis Barragán. *Gebäude:* Casa Malaparte auf Capri. *Designer:* Alvar Aalto. **Sie empfehlen in Sydney:** *Hotel:* Kirketon. *Restaurant:* Bill and Toni's. *Boutique:* Luxe. *Museum:* Museum of Contemporary Art (MCA). *Buchhandlung:* Ariel.

Bay Watch House, Rose Bay

Year of construction: 1999
Année de réalisation: 1999
Baujahr: 1999

Area: 393 m² (interior) + 426 m² (outdoor spaces)
Surface: 393 m² (intérieur) + 426m² (extérieur)
Nutzfläche: 393 m² (innen) + 426 m² (Außenbereich)

Cost: AUS $ 900,000
Coûts: AUS $ 900 000
Kosten: AUS $ 900 000

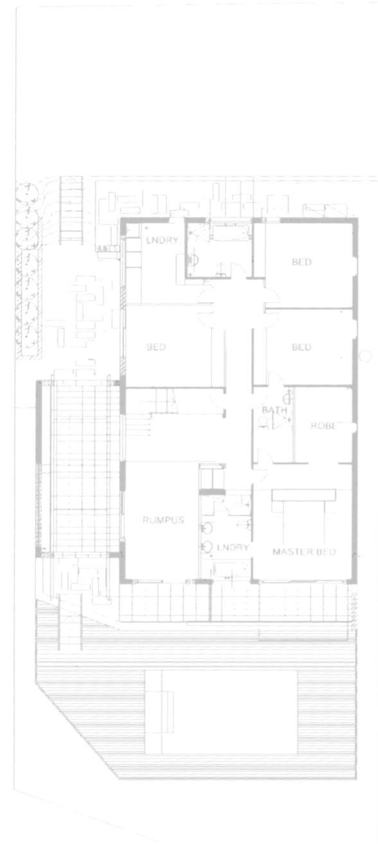

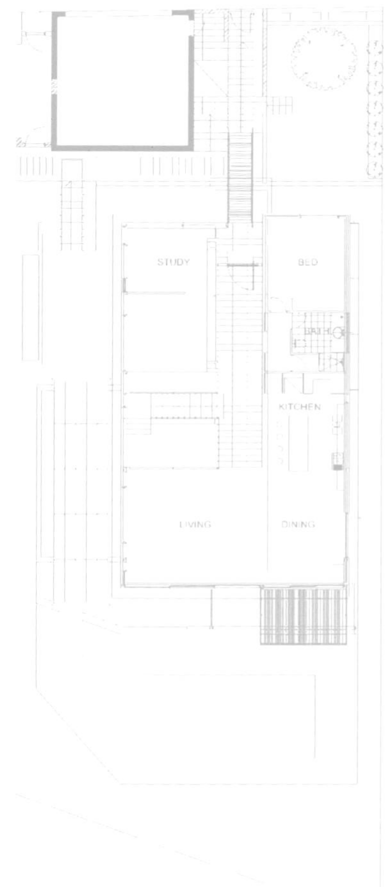

design Jackson Clements Burrows

Bay Watch House

English House, Coogee Beach

After a number of years of professional experience in Milan, Mitchell and Helen English returned to Sydney, and decided to live in a house near Coogee Beach, one of the city's long beaches, but also a small village inside the metropolis, far from the hectic pace of the City. The desire to spend time with their children, and the fact that they are both freelance professionals, led to the idea of creating a home that is also a showroom, atelier, and workshop, both private space and public showcase. Mitchell is an artist-potter, Helen a fashion stylist and designer: They share a passion for furniture and objects from the 50s, 60s, and 70s, and their home is a lively fusion of the forms, colors, and symbols of these decades; a personal design, free of rigid mental schemes and the pursuit of utopian perfection.

Après avoir travaillé plusieurs années à Milan, Mitchell et Helen English sont rentrés s'installer à Sydney, choisissant de vivre à l'abri des rythmes frénétiques de la City, à Coogee Beach, une des longues plages de la ville et également un petit village au sein de la métropole. Souhaitant rester auprès de leurs deux enfants et travaillant tous les deux en indépendants, ils se sont créé une maison qui leur sert également de salon d'exposition, d'atelier et de laboratoire, à la fois espace privé et vitrine publique. Mitchell est artiste céramiste, Helen styliste de mode et créatrice. Tous deux partagent une passion pour les meubles et les objets des années 50, 60 et 70 et leur maison est un mélange vivant des formes, couleurs et signes de ces décennies. C'est un projet personnel, libéré de l'étroitesse des idées reçues et de l'utopie de la perfection.

Nach einigen beruflichen Jahren in Mailand kehrten Mitchell und Helen English nach Sydney zurück und wählten für sich ein Haus in der Nähe von Coogee Beach, einem der langen Strände der Stadt, der trotzdem auch ein kleines Dorf innerhalb der Metropole ist, weit entfernt von der Hektik der City. Da sie viel Zeit mit ihren zwei Kindern verbringen wollten und beide freiberuflich tätig sind, haben sie für sich ein Wohnhaus gestaltet, das gleichzeitig Showroom, Studio und Werkstatt ist: Privatraum und Schaufenster in einem. Mitchell ist Keramikkünstler, Helen Modestylistin und Designerin. Beide haben eine Leidenschaft für Möbel und Objekte der 50er, 60er und 70er Jahre, und ihr Haus stellt eine lebendige Mischung der charakteristischen Formen, Farben und Merkmale dieser Dekaden dar. So entstand ein ganz persönliches Projekt, das frei ist von engmaschigen Schemata und utopischem Perfektionsdrang.

2

22. Coogee Beach seen from the English House. **23.** The owners, Mitchell and Helen English.

22. Coogee Beach vue depuis la maison English. **23.** Les propriétaires de la maison, Mitchell et Helen English.

22. Coogee Beach vom English House aus gesehen. **23.** Die Hausbesitzer Mitchell und Helen English.

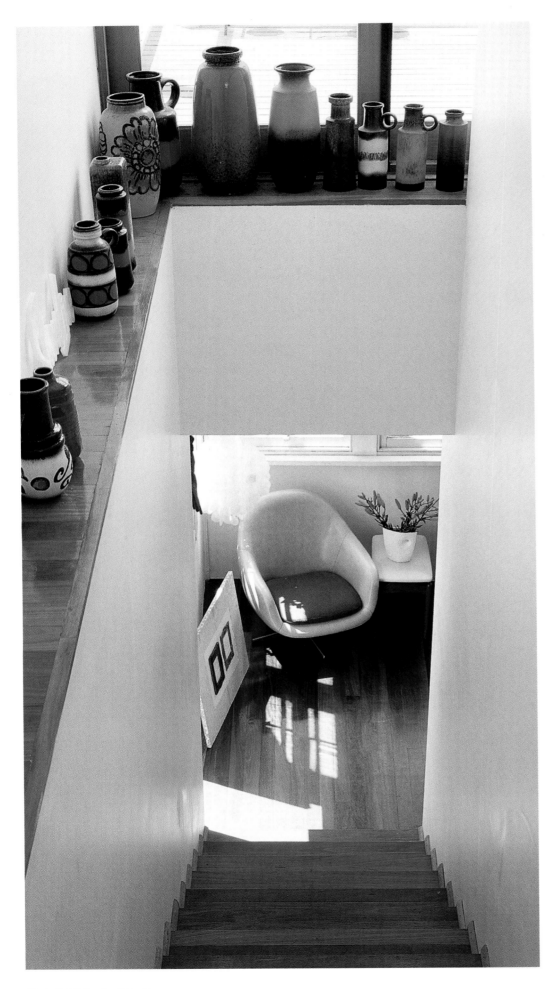

24. A collection of German ceramics redesigns the profile of the staircase, with a lamp by Verner Panton in the background, while in the living room a 50s cabinet, beside the lounge chair by Charles and Ray Eames from the same era, hosts a group of vases – the orange vase is by Dinosaur Designs. **25.** Sitting room with view of the dining area in fusion style: poltrona azzurra light blue 50s armchair, Anemone lamp, Chinese painting, 70s curtains.

24. Une collection de céramiques allemandes couronne la cage de l'escalier en bas duquel on entrevoit une lampe de Verner Panton. Dans le salon, à côté du fauteuil de Charles et Ray Eames, un meuble des années 50 sert de support à divers vases, dont un orange, de Dinosaur Designs. **25.** Le petit salon, derrière lequel on aperçoit l'espace salle à manger, est meublé dans un style éclectique: un fauteuil bleu des années 50, une lampe Anémone, un tableau chinois, des rideaux des années 70.

24. Eine Sammlung deutscher Keramiken verleiht der Treppe Profil. Unten sieht man eine Leuchte von Verner Panton. Im Wohnzimmer steht neben dem Lounge Chair von Charles und Ray Eames eine Kommode aus den 50er Jahren, auf der sich verschiedene Vasen befinden – die orange ist von Dinosaur Designs. **25.** Das kleine Wohnzimmer mit Blick auf den Essbereich im Hintergrund mischt verschiedene Stile: einen blauen Sessel aus den 50er Jahren, eine Anemonen-Leuchte, eine chinesische Zeichnung und Vorhänge aus den 70er Jahren.

AUSTRALIAN PAINTING TODAY
The Australians
THE LEXUS AND THE OLIVE TREE
100 Masterpieces from the Vitra Design
THE COMPLETE PIRELLI CALENDAR BOOK
Markus Lüpertz
MILLER
POP ART

26. In the bedroom, a 60s fabric is hung on the wall like a painting. **27.** Close-up of the hanging lamp by Verner Panton. Turkish food on the dining table in solid wood, 60s lighting fixture, plates by Combo Design, Sydney.

26. Dans la chambre à coucher, un tissu des années 60 suspendu au mur comme un tableau. **27.** Gros plan sur un lustre de Verner Panton. Sur la table, des mets turcs. Dans la salle à manger avec sa table en bois massif, des lampes des années 60 et des plats de Combo Design, Sydney.

26. Im Schlafzimmer hängt ein 60er-Jahre-Stoff wie ein Gemälde an der Wand. **27.** Eine Nahaufnahme der Leuchte von Verner Panton. Auf dem Tisch: türkische Gerichte. Auf dem Esstisch aus Massivholz steht Geschirr von Combo Design aus Sydney, darüber hängt eine Leuchte aus den 60er Jahren.

28. In the kitchen in white and blue wood, with a retro look, two ceramics collections: one from East Germany on the top shelf, the other from the creative workshop of the owner of the house.

28. Dans la cuisine en bois blanc et bleu à l'atmosphère rétro, deux collections de céramiques, l'une provenant d'Allemagne de l'Est sur l'étagère du haut, l'autre de l'atelier de créations du maître de maison.

28. In der weiß und blau gestrichenen Holzküche von nostalgischem Charme sind zwei Keramiksammlungen ausgestellt: auf dem obersten Regal eine Sammlung aus Ostdeutschland, die zweite stammt aus der kreativen Werkstatt des Hausbesitzers.

Mitchell & Helen English

8/2-16 Glenmore Road Paddington 2021 Sydney Australia Ph +61 2 9331 0075 F +61 2 9665 2063 email: english2english@ozemail.com.au www.english-plus.com

Mitchell English was born in Sydney in 1962. **Studies, experiences, projects:** Degree from the College of Fine Arts, Sydney. Masters in design from University of Western Sydney. 1993 exhibition "Fringedwellers" at Ute Grohebul Galerie in Karlsruhe, Germany. 1997 exhibition "Cars & Culture" at Powerhouse Museum, Sydney. 2000 he opens his first concept store in Sydney with his partner Helen. 2001 exhibition "Interior" at Object Gallery, Sydney. **Helen English** was born in Sydney in 1962. **Studies, experiences, projects:** 1984–1990 work experience in Milan in a number of design and fashion studios. 1993 her first fashion collection. 2000 participation in the Australian fashion week, Fox Studios, Sydney. 2000 opens her first concept store with her partner Mitchell. **Favorites:** *Architects-designers:* Lord Norman Foster, Robert Venturi, Sean Dean (young Sydney architect). *Furnishings:* Kafka (postwar Australian) and Shaker. **In Sydney they recommend:** *Hotel:* Regent's Court. *Restaurant:* Balzac. *Design and fashion shop:* English Shop. *Gallery:* Yuill/Crowley Gallery. *Museum:* Australian Museum. *Bookstore:* Berkelouw.

Mitchell English est né en 1962 à Sydney. **Etudes, expérience professionnelle, projets:** Diplômé de l'université des beaux-arts de Sydney. Master en design de l'University of Western Sydney. 1999, exposition «Fringedwellers» à la Ute Grohebul Galerie, Karlsruhe en Allemagne. 1997, exposition «Cars & Culture» au Powerhouse Museum, Sydney. 2000, ouverture de sa première boutique concept à Sydney avec sa compagne Helen. 2001, exposition «Interior», à l'Object Galerie, Sydney. **Helen English** est née en 1962 à Sydney. **Etudes, expérience professionnelle, projets:** De 1984 à 1990, fait son apprentissage à Milan dans divers bureaux de stylisme et de la mode. 1993, lance sa propre collection de mode. 2000, participe à la semaine de la mode australienne, Fox Studios, Sydney, et ouvre sa première boutique concept avec son compagnon Mitchell. **Leurs favoris:** *Architectes-designers:* Lord Norman Foster, Robert Venturi, Sean Dean, jeune architecte de Sydney. *Objets, mobilier:* Kafka (après-guerre australienne) et Shaker. **A Sydney, ils recommandent:** *Hôtel:* Regent's Court. *Restaurant:* Balzac. *Boutique de design et de mode:* English Shop. *Galerie d'art:* Yuill/Crowley Gallery. *Musée:* Australian Museum. *Librairie:* Berkelouw.

Mitchell English ist 1962 in Sydney geboren. **Ausbildung, Erfahrungen, Projekte:** Abschluss am College of Fine Arts in Sydney. Design-Master an der University of Western Sydney. 1993 Ausstellung »Fringedwellers« in der Galerie Ute Grohebul in Karlsruhe. 1997 Ausstellung »Cars & Culture« im Powerhouse Museum in Sydney. Im Jahr 2000 eröffnet er zusammen mit seiner Partnerin Helen seinen ersten Concept Store in Sydney. 2001 Ausstellung »Interior« in der Object Gallery in Sydney. **Helen English** ist 1962 in Sydney geboren. **Ausbildung, Erfahrungen, Projekte:** 1984–1990 Tätigkeit in verschiedenen Design- und Modestudios in Mailand. 1993 präsentiert sie ihre erste Modekollektion. Im Jahr 2000 nimmt sie an der australischen Modewoche in den Fox Studios, Sydney, teil und eröffnet mit Mitchell den ersten Concept Store. **Sie bewundern:** *Architekten/Designer:* Lord Norman Foster, Robert Venturi, Sean Dean (ein junger Architekt aus Sydney). *Möbeldesign:* Kafka (australischer Nachkriegsstil) und Shaker. **Sie empfehlen in Sydney:** *Hotel:* Regent's Court. *Restaurant:* Balzac. *Designgeschäft und Boutique:* English Shop. *Galerie:* Yuill/Crowley Gallery. *Museum:* Australian Museum. *Buchhandlung:* Berkelouw.

English House, Coogee Beach

Year of construction: 1997	**Area:** 420 m²	**Cost:** AUS $ 50,000
Année de réalisation: 1997	**Surface:** 420 m²	**Coûts:** AUS $ 50 000
Baujahr: 1997	**Nutzfläche:** 420 m²	**Kosten:** AUS $ 50 000

Seidler Penthouse, Milsons Point

This penthouse with openings like veritable tableaux of the natural scenery of Sydney Harbour is the home-studio of Harry Seidler, one of the historic figures of contemporary architecture in Australia. A designer of great conceptual and expressive rigor, he was influenced by Marcel Breuer, Oscar Niemeyer, and Pier Luigi Nervi, while developing his own autonomous architectural language. In steel and concrete, white stucco and granite, the residence – on the two upper levels of the building – is dominated by a large helicoidal staircase that underlines the open, decisive, sinuous geometry of the spaces. Their visual lightness is accentuated by the furnishings and colors, with a prevalance of whites, blacks, and grays, forming a backdrop for the colors of artworks by Roy Lichtenstein and Frank Stella.

Cette penthouse, percée de baies vitrées qui sont comme autant de tableaux vivants du Harbour de Sydney, est la maison-atelier d'Harry Seidler, un des pères historiques de l'architecture contemporaine en Australie. Son style, d'une rigueur conceptuelle et expressive extrême, intègre les leçons de Marcel Breuer, d'Oscar Niemeyer et de Pier Luigi Nervi, s'imposant avec toute la puissance d'une nouvelle élaboration linguistique qui lui est propre. Réalisé en acier, ciment, crépi blanc et granit, l'appartement, qui occupe deux étages, est dominé par un imposant escalier hélicoïdal qui souligne la géométrie ouverte, résolue et sinueuse des espaces. L'impression de légèreté est encore accentuée par la décoration et les couleurs: un jeu de blancs, de gris et de noirs qui contrastent avec les tons vifs des œuvres d'art de Roy Lichtenstein et de Frank Stella.

Die Fensteröffnungen dieses Penthouse rahmen den Blick auf Sydney Harbour und wirken dabei wie *tableaux vivants*. Es handelt sich hier um die Privatwohnung und das Büro von Harry Seidler, einem der Begründer der zeitgenössischen australischen Architektur. Die extreme Sachlichkeit in Konzept und Ausdruck spiegelt die architektonischen Erfahrungen von Marcel Breuer, Oscar Niemeyer und Pier Luigi Nervi und findet gleichzeitig zu einer kraftvollen eigenständigen Ausdrucksweise. Das Penthouse besteht aus einer Stahl- und Zementstruktur sowie aus weißem Putz und Granit und befindet sich in den oberen beiden Etagen des Gebäudes. Innen dominiert eine imposante Wendeltreppe, welche die entschiedene geschwungene Linienführung der offen gestalteten Räume betont. Die Einrichtung und das Farbenspiel in einer Kombination von Weiß-Schwarz-Grau heben die Leichtigkeit der Struktur hervor und kontrastieren mit den lebhaften Farben der Kunstwerke von Roy Lichtenstein und Frank Stella.

3

31. Australian architect Harry Seidler.

31. L'architecte australien Harry Seidler.

31. Der australische Architekt Harry Seidler.

32-33. The terrace, accessed from all the main spaces, offers an extraordinary view of the Harbour Bridge and the City, seen here in a nocturnal photo. **34-35.** The abundance of the architectural approach is summed up in the helicoidal staircase with its light, airy appearance, connecting the two levels of the residence. On the lower level the black Indian Tamin granite table designed by Harry Seidler is paired with chairs in black leather and steel by Marcel Breuer, which are also featured on the upper level in the living room, with a work by Roy Lichtenstein. The semicircular form of the table is designed to give all the guests a good view of the bay. **36.** A study-corner with a console in rosewood designed by Harry Seidler and a chair by Marcel Breuer. On the walls, a painting by the Aboriginal artist Thomas Rover and a projection clock. **37.** The bedroom seen from the living room through the transparent glazing that borders the space. The absolute white of the carpeting and the walls forms a backdrop for the black leather chaise longue by Le Corbusier.

32-33. Toutes les pièces principales donnent sur la terrasse d'où l'on jouit d'une vue extraordinaire sur le Harbour Bridge et la City, un spectacle fascinant que les lumières de la nuit rendent encore plus envoûtant. **34-35.** La générosité de l'architecture est synthétisée par l'escalier hélicoïdal qui s'élève avec légèreté entre les deux niveaux de l'appartement. A l'étage inférieur, la table en granit noir Indian Tamin, dessinée par Harry Seidler, accompagne des chaises en cuir noir et acier de Marcel Breuer que l'on retrouve dans le salon du niveau supérieur près d'une œuvre de Roy Lichtenstein. La table a été dessinée en demi lune pour permettre à tous les convives de profiter au mieux de la vue sur la baie. **36.** Un coin bureau réalisé avec une console en palissandre dessinée par Harry Seidler et un fauteuil de Marcel Breuer. Au mur, un tableau de l'artiste aborigène Thomas Rover et une horloge en projection. **37.** La chambre à coucher vue du salon à travers la cloison transparente qui délimite l'espace. Le blanc absolu des moquettes et des murs fait ressortir le cuir noir de la chaise longue de Le Corbusier.

32-33. Alle Haupträume gehen auf die Terrasse. Sie bietet eine herrliche Aussicht auf die Harbour Bridge und die City, die sich nachts in ein zauberhaftes Lichtermeer verwandelt. **34-35.** Die Großzügigkeit der Architektursprache findet ihr Sinnbild in der Wendeltreppe, die leicht im Raum schwebt und die beiden Ebenen der Wohnung miteinander verbindet. Unten wurde ein von Harry Seidler entworfener Tisch in schwarzem Indian-Tamin-Granit mit Armlehnstühlen von Marcel Breuer aus schwarzem Leder und Chromstahl kombiniert. Dieselben Stühle finden sich auch im Wohnzimmer der oberen Etage, zusammen mit einem Werk von Roy Lichtenstein. Der Tisch wurde als Halbkreis konzipiert, um jedem Gast die bestmögliche Aussicht auf die Bucht zu ermöglichen. **36.** Die Arbeitsecke mit einer Konsole aus Palisanderholz entwarf Harry Seidler und kombiniert sie mit einem Armlehnstuhl von Marcel Breuer. An der Wand ein Bild des Aboriginal Artist Thomas Rover sowie die Projektion einer Uhr. **37.** Blick aus dem Wohnzimmer durch die Glastrennwand in das Schlafzimmer. Das reine Weiß von Teppich und Wänden bildet den idealen Hintergrund für das schwarze Leder der Chaiselongue von Le Corbusier.

12
9
6

38. The bedroom open to the study is dominated by the presence of rosewood, selected by Seidler for all the custom-designed furnishings, in harmony with the guanaco leather bedspread. On the wall, a painting by Roy Lichtenstein.

38. La chambre à coucher, qui donne sur un petit cabinet de travail, est dominée par la présence du palissandre, choisi par Seidler pour tous les meubles qu'il a dessinés et qui s'harmonise avec le dessus-de-lit en peau de guanaco. Au mur, un tableau de Roy Lichtenstein.

38. Im Schlafzimmer, das zu dem kleinen Arbeitszimmer hin offen ist, dominiert Palisanderholz, das Harry Seidler für alle von ihm entworfenen Möbel ausgesucht hat und das gut harmoniert mit dem Überwurf aus Guanako-Fell. Das Gemälde an der Wand ist von Roy Lichtenstein.

Harry Seidler & Associates
2 Glen Street Milsons Point 2061 Sydney Australia Ph +61 2 9922 1388 F +61 2 9957 2947 email: hsa@seidler.net.au www.seidler.net.au

Born in Vienna in 1923. **Studies, experiences:** Studies in Vienna and England. 1944 degree in architecture, University of Manitoba, Canada. 1946 Masters at Harvard with Walter Gropius, design studies with Josef Albers. 1946–1948 assistant to Marcel Breuer in New York. Practice with Oscar Niemeyer in Rio de Janeiro. 1949 opens his own architecture studio in Sydney. **Constructed works include:** Rose Seidler House in Wahroonga (today a national monument), Australian Embassy in Paris; in Sydney: Australia Square, MLC Centre and apartment towers; in Melbourne: Grollo Tower. **Honors:** Honorary member of the American Institute of Architects, honorary member of the Royal Institute of British Architects (from which he received, in 1996, the Royal Gold Medal), member of the Royal Australian Institute of Architects (RAIA, 15 prizes), Companion of the Order of Australia AC (1987), Officer of the Most Excellent Order of the British Empire (1972). Harry Seidler has received many other prizes and honors.

Né en 1923 à Vienne. **Etudes, expérience professionnelle:** Etudes à Vienne et en Angleterre. 1944, diplôme d'architecture de l'University of Manitoba, Canada. 1946, Master à Harvard avec Walter Gropius, étudie le design sous la direction de Josef Albers. 1946–1948, assistant de Marcel Breuer à New York. Effectue un stage chez Oscar Niemeyer à Rio de Janeiro. 1949, ouvre son propre cabinet d'architecture à Sydney. **Parmi ses réalisations:** The Rose Seidler House à Wahroonga (qui est classé aujourd'hui monument national), l'ambassade d'Australie à Paris; à Sydney: l'Australia Square, le MLC Centre et des tours d'appartements; à Melbourne: Grollo Tower. **Récompenses:** Membre honoraire de l'American Institute of Architects; membre honoraire de la Royal Institute of British Architects qui, en 1996, lui a octroyé la médaille d'or royale; membre de la Royal Australian Institute of Architects (RAIA, 15 prix), Companion of the Order of Australia AC (1987), Officer of the Most Excellent Order of the British Empire (1972). Harry Seidler a reçu de nombreux autres prix et récompenses.

1923 in Wien geboren. **Ausbildung, Erfahrungen:** Studium in Wien und England. 1944 Abschluss des Architekturstudiums an der University of Manitoba in Kanada. 1946 Master in Harvard bei Walter Gropius. Design-Studium bei Josef Albers. 1946–1948 Assistent von Marcel Breuer in New York. Zusammenarbeit mit Oscar Niemeyer in Rio de Janeiro. 1949 eigenes Architekturbüro in Sydney. **Zu seinen realisierten Projekten zählen:** Rose Seidler House in Wahroonga (das heute unter Denkmalschutz steht), die Australische Botschaft in Paris; in Sydney: Australia Square, MLC Centre und Apartment-Türme; in Melbourne: Grollo Tower. **Ehrungen:** Ehrenmitglied des American Institute of Architects, Ehrenmitglied des Royal Institute of British Architects (das ihm 1996 die Royal Gold Medal verliehen hat), Mitglied des Royal Australian Institute of Architects (RAIA, 15 Preise), Companion of the Order of Australia AC (1987), Officer of the Most Excellent Order of the British Empire (1972). Harry Seidler hat zahlreiche weitere Preise und Auszeichnungen erhalten.

Seidler Penthouse, Milsons Point

Year of construction: 1988
Année de réalisation: 1988
Baujahr: 1988

Area: not available
Surface: non indiquée
Nutzfläche: ungenannt

Cost: not available
Coûts: non indiqués
Kosten: ungenannt

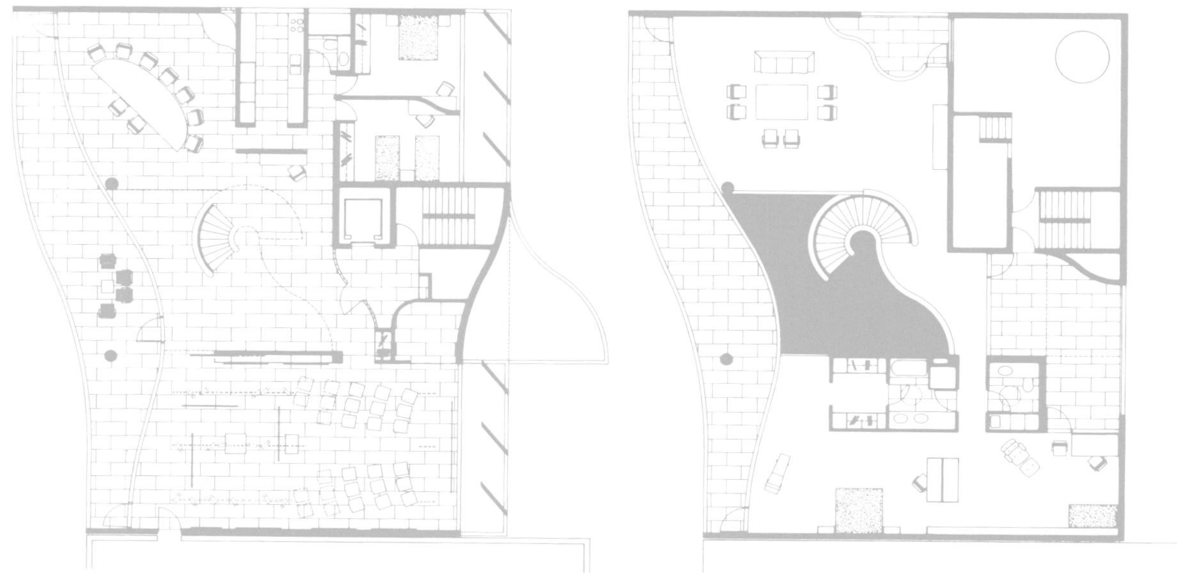

Gibbeson/Litynski House, Surry Hills

4

An anonymous 80s townhouse in the heart of the city, with a long, narrow layout on three levels, has been restructured by the studio Stanic Harding and is today a functional, rigorous home, with redesigned façade and exteriors, and new proportions for the interiors to optimize the available space. The composition features a perimeter staircase with a balustrade-backdrop in transparent glass, large surfaces in translucent glass or metal grillwork, deep vertical incisions in the walls, and skylight roofing. All well-defined, autonomous elements that allow the light to freely flow in the spaces, for a sense of openness, adding sculptural effects to an architecture dominated by marble, Corian, and wood, whose focal point is a pool-sculpture in the courtyard.

Ce qui était une maison de ville anonyme des années 80, en plein cœur de la métropole, toute en longueur et étroite sur trois niveaux, a cédé la place, une fois restructurée par le cabinet d'architecture Stanic Harding, à cette demeure fonctionnelle et rigoureuse. La façade et les parties extérieures ont été redessinées et les proportions des intérieurs ont été modifiées afin d'optimiser le peu d'espace disponible. La composition joue sur un escalier bordant un mur et ouvert de l'autre côté sur une cloison transparente, de vastes surfaces en verre translucide ou en grilles de métal, de profondes entailles verticales dans les murs et un toit percé d'une lucarne. Tous ces éléments bien définis et achevés permettent à la lumière de circuler librement dans les espaces, les faisant paraître plus grands et créant des effets plastiques dans une architecture dominée par le marbre, le Corian et le bois, qui trouve son point focal dans un bassin-sculpture dans la cour.

Ursprünglich ein unpersönliches Townhouse aus den 80er Jahren mitten im Stadtzentrum, wurde das langgestreckte schmale Gebäude mit drei Ebenen von dem Architekturbüro Stanic Harding zu einem funktionellen und sachlichen Wohnhaus umgebaut. Die Fassade und die Außenbereiche wurden neu gestaltet und die Innenräume neu proportioniert, um die beschränkten Raumverhältnisse optimal zu nutzen. An diesem Kompositionsspiel beteiligen sich eine Treppe mit einer Trennwand aus durchsichtigem Glas, großzügige Flächen aus durchscheinendem Glas und aus Metallgitter, tiefe vertikale Einschnitte in den Mauern sowie ein Dach mit Oberlicht. Diese überlegt eingesetzten Elemente erlauben dem Licht, frei in die Räume einzudringen, sie somit größer wirken zu lassen und der von den Materialien Marmor, Corian und Holz beherrschten Inneneinrichtung plastische Effekte zu verleihen. Zentraler Blickfang ist dabei das skulpturale Wasserbecken im Hof.

41. The architects: Andrew Stanic (left) and Andy Harding.

41. Les architectes: Andrew Stanic (à gauche) et Andy Harding.

41. Die Architekten: Andrew Stanic (links) und Andy Harding.

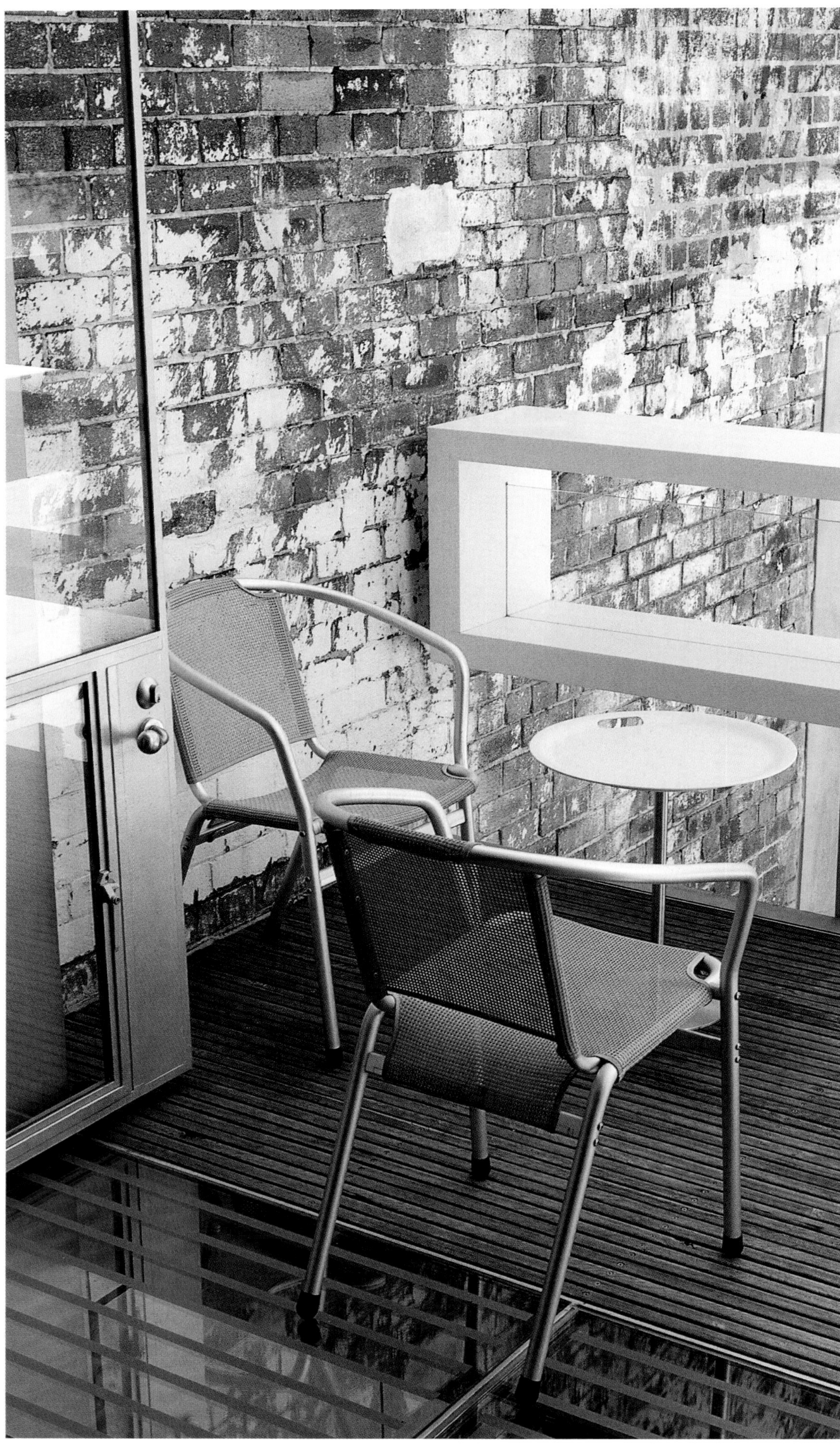

42. The terrace, a mixture of old and new elements, renovated brick-work, wood, steel, and glass. The white table is by Alessi. **43.** The garden with the pool-fountain designed by Stanic Harding, against the back-drop of a stone wall. Stones are also used for the channel crossing the concrete paving.

42. La petite terrasse, un mélange d'ancien et de neuf, de briques à la peinture écaillée, de bois, d'acier et de verre. Le guéridon blanc est d'Alessi. **43.** Le jardin, avec sa vasque fontaine dessinée par Stanic Harding, se détache sur un mur en galets. Des pierres également incrustées dans le sol tout autour du bassin.

42. Die kleine Terrasse, eine Mischung aus Alt und Neu, besteht aus Backsteinen mit Farbresten sowie aus Holz, Stahl und Glas. Das weiße Tischchen ist von Alessi. **43.** Der Garten mit dem von Stanic Harding entworfenen Wasserbecken zeichnet sich ab von der mit eingelassenen Steinen verzierten Mauer im Hintergrund. Auch in den Zementboden um das Becken wurden Steine eingelassen.

44. The linear staircase connecting the second and third levels is cantilevered on one side, and bordered by a divider in etched glass on the other. The living room on the second floor faces onto the terrace, and features two *Swan* armchairs by Arne Jacobsen and a white sofa by Stanic Harding. **45.** The custom kitchen features pure lines and soothing colors, in harmony with the dark wood floor.

44. L'escalier linéaire qui relie les deuxième et troisième niveaux est suspendu d'un côté et fermé de l'autre par la paroi en verre corrodé de la cuisine. Au deuxième étage, le salon qui donne sur la terrasse est aménagé avec deux fauteuils *Cygne* d'Arne Jacobson et un canapé blanc signé Stanic Harding. **45.** La cuisine design aux lignes sobres joue sur des tonalités reposantes qui s'harmonisent avec le parquet sombre.

44. Die Treppenrampe, welche die zweite mit der dritten Ebene verbindet, ist direkt an der Mauer aufgehängt und wird auf der anderen Seite, zur Küche hin, von einer geätzten Glastrennwand abgeschlossen. Das Wohnzimmer im zweiten Stock öffnet sich zur Terrasse hin und enthält zwei Sessel *Swan* von Arne Jacobsen sowie ein weißes Sofa von Stanic Harding. **45.** Die maßgearbeitete Küche von schlichter Ästhetik ist in entspannten Farbtönen gehalten, die mit dem dunklen Parkettboden harmonieren.

46. The bedroom on the third floor, designed by Stanic Harding, has a masculine tone, underlined by the colors: white and dark gray.

46. La chambre à coucher au troisième étage, dessinée par Stanic Harding, a un accent masculin que soulignent des couleurs appropriées: le blanc et le gris foncé.

46. Das von Stanic und Harding entworfene Schlafzimmer im dritten Stock besitzt einen maskulinen Charme, der noch unterstrichen wird von der Farbgebung: Weiß und Dunkelgrau.

Stanic Harding Architects

123 Commonwealth Street Surry Hills 2010 Sydney Australia Ph +61 2 9211 6710 F +61 2 9211 0366 email: architects@stanicharding.com.au

Andrew Stanic was born in Sydney in 1957. **Studies, experiences:** Degree in architecture, University of Technology, Sydney (UTS). Practice in the studio of George Freedman. **Andy Harding** was born in 1956 in Newcastle upon Tyne, England. **Studies, experiences:** Architecture degree from Strathclyde University, Glasgow. Practice in a number of different studios in Sydney. 1989 studio Stanic Harding Architects. **Awards:** RAIA 1996, 1997, 2000, 2001; "*Belle* Magazine Space Apartment of the Year" in 2001. **Favorites:** *Architects:* Le Corbusier, Peter Wilson. *Buildings:* Unité d'Habitation by Le Corbusier in Marseille, Maison de Verre in Paris by Pierre Chareau. *Designers:* Poul Kjaerholm, Charles and Ray Eames. **In Sydney they recommend:** *Hotel:* Regent's Court. *Restaurant:* Banc. *Fashion boutique:* Calibre. *Museum:* Casula Powerhouse Arts Centre.

Andrew Stanic est né en 1957 à Sydney. **Etudes, expérience professionnelle:** Diplôme d'architecture de l'University of Technology, Sydney (UTS). Apprentissage dans le cabinet de George Freedman. **Andy Harding** est né en 1956 à Newcastle upon Tyne en Angleterre. **Etudes, expérience professionnelle:** Diplôme d'architecture de la Strathclyde University de Glasgow. Apprentissage dans divers cabinets de Sydney. 1989, ouverture du cabinet Stanic Harding Architects. **Prix d'architecture:** RAIA: 1996, 1997, 2000, 2001; «*Belle* Magazine Space Apartment of the Year» en 2001. **Leurs favoris:** *Architectes:* Le Corbusier, Peter Wilson. *Edifices:* Unité d'habitation de Le Corbusier à Marseille, la Maison de verre de Pierre Chareau à Paris. *Designers:* Poul Kjaerholm, Charles et Ray Eames. **A Sydney, ils recommandent:** *Hôtel:* Regent's Court. *Restaurant:* Banc. *Boutique de mode:* Calibre. *Musée:* Casula Powerhouse Arts Centre.

Andrew Stanic ist 1957 in Sydney geboren. **Ausbildung, Erfahrungen:** Abgeschlossenes Architekturstudium an der University of Technology, Sydney (UTS). Tätigkeit im Architekturbüro von George Freedman. **Andy Harding** ist 1956 in Newcastle upon Tyne in England geboren. **Ausbildung, Erfahrungen:** Abgeschlossenes Architekturstudium an der Strathclyde University in Glasgow. Tätigkeit in verschiedenen Architekturbüros in Sydney. 1989 Gründung von Stanic Harding Architects. **Architekturpreise:** RAIA: 1996, 1997, 2000, 2001; »*Belle* Magazine Space Apartment of the Year« im Jahr 2001. **Sie bewundern:** *Architekten:* Le Corbusier, Peter Wilson. *Gebäude:* Unité d'Habitation von Le Corbusier in Marseille, Maison de Verre von Pierre Chareau in Paris. *Designer:* Poul Kjaerholm, Charles und Ray Eames. **Sie empfehlen in Sydney:** *Hotel:* Regent's Court. *Restaurant:* Banc. *Boutique:* Calibre. *Museum:* Casula Powerhouse Arts Centre.

Gibbeson/Litynski House, Surry Hills

Year of construction: 2000
Année de réalisation: 2000
Baujahr: 2000

Area: 410 m²
Surface: 410 m²
Nutzfläche: 410 m²

Cost: AUS $ 500,000
Coûts: AUS $ 500 000
Kosten: AUS $ 500 000

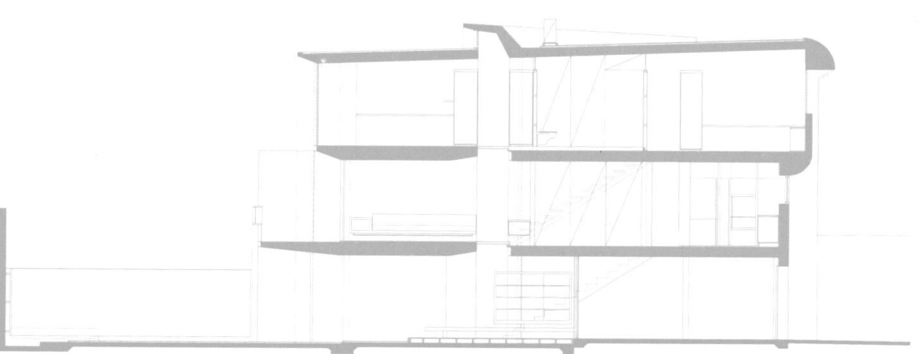

design Andrew Stanic & Andy Harding

Gibbeson/Litynski House

Sun House, Castlecrag

The revision of the layout of a house built on a problematic terraced lot involved the repositioning of the staircase to the south and a rationalization of the living areas. The house is accessed from the upper level by means of an external staircase leading to the entrance court facing north. The ample living room is connected to the court, while the bedrooms are located on the lower level. Large full-height windows, even in the corner solution, fill the rooms with light, while small openings in the walls add a sculptural dimension to the volume of the stairwell. In the evening the tonal lightness of the rooms, dominated by the white shades of the walls, casements, and furnishings and the wood utilized for the floors and fixed furnishings, is punctuated by the new colors in a creative interface with the lights of Sydney by night.

Pour redéfinir le plan de cette maison construite sur un terrain difficile en terrasses, il a fallu déplacer l'escalier au sud et rationaliser des aires de séjour. On y entre par le niveau supérieur, grâce à un escalier extérieur qui mène à une cour d'entrée orientée au nord. La vaste partie séjour donne sur cette cour tandis que les chambres à coucher sont situées à l'étage inférieur. De grandes baies vitrées allant du sol au plafond, même dans les angles, rendent les pièces très lumineuses, tandis que de petites fentes dans les murs apportent une dimension sculpturale aux volumes. Le soir venu, la pureté des pièces, dominées par la blancheur des murs, des cadres de portes et de fenêtres, des meubles, du parquet et des éléments fixes, se parsème de nouvelles couleurs dans un jeu créatif projeté par les lumières de la nuit de Sydney.

Bei der Umgestaltung dieses Hauses, das auf einem ungünstigem, terrassenartigen Grundstück steht, wurden die Wohnräume rationalisiert und gleichzeitig die Treppe nach Süden verlegt. Man betritt das Haus nun vom oberen Stock her über eine Außentreppe, die zu dem im Norden gelegenen Eingangshof führt. Der große Wohnbereich blickt auf diesen Hof, während sich die Schlafzimmer in der unteren Etage befinden. Glasflächen in voller Höhe und Breite schenken den Räumen helles Licht, während ihnen kleine Ritzen in den Mauern eine skulpturale Dimension verleihen. Die Räume werden beherrscht von weißen Wänden, Einfassungen und Möbeln sowie dem Holz der Böden und Einrichtungsgegenstände, doch in den Abendstunden erhalten sie neue Farbakzente im Zusammenspiel mit dem nächtlichen Lichtermeer von Sydney.

48. The glazed façade, oriented northward, that illuminates the living room. **49.** The architects: Andrew Stanic (left) and Andy Harding.

48. La façade vitrée, orientée au nord, inondant le séjour de lumière. **49.** Les architectes: Andrew Stanic (à gauche) et Andy Harding.

48. Die nach Norden ausgerichtete Glasfassade, die den Wohnraum mit Licht versieht. **49.** Andrew Stanic (links) und Andy Harding.

50. White walls, flooring in dark wood planks, and specular glazed walls: The living and dining area is a luminous space with modern black and white furnishings. On the terrace, Italian design: chairs designed by Carlo Colombo and table by Carlo Bartoli. **51.** For the custom kitchen, oriented toward the east, base cabinets in light wood and hanging units in white laminate. **52.** The bedroom is based on transparency and lightness, thanks to full-height windows with aluminum frames.

50. Murs blancs, parquet en lattes de bois sombre et des murs tapissés de miroirs: Le séjour/salle à manger est un espace lumineux aménagé avec des meubles modernes en blanc et noir. Sur la terrasse, du design italien: des chaises dessinées par Carlo Colombo et une petite table de Carlo Bartoli. **51.** Pour la cuisine design, orientée à l'est, une base de bois clair et des placards muraux en laminé blanc. **52.** Grâce aux baies vitrées qui vont du sol au plafond dans un cadre en aluminium, la chambre à coucher est toute en transparence et légèreté.

50. Weiße Mauern, ein Boden aus dunklen Holzlatten und Glaswände: Der Wohn- und Essbereich präsentiert sich als heller Raum mit modernen Möbeln in Weiß und Schwarz. Auf der Terrasse steht italienisches Design: Armlehnstühle von Carlo Colombo und ein Tischchen von Carlo Bartoli. **51.** Die maßgearbeitete, nach Osten ausgerichtete Küche ist mit Unterschränken aus hellem Holz und weißen Laminat-Hängeschränken eingerichtet. **52.** Das Schlafzimmer lebt von der Transparenz und Leichtigkeit der hohen Glasfenster, die von Aluminiumrahmen eingefasst werden.

Stanic Harding Architects
123 Commonwealth Street Surry Hills 2010 Sydney Australia Ph +61 2 9211 6710 F +61 2 9211 0366 email: architects@stanicharding.com.au

Andrew Stanic was born in Sydney in 1957. **Studies, experiences:** Degree in architecture, University of Technology, Sydney (UTS). Practice in the studio of George Freedman. **Andy Harding** was born in 1956 in Newcastle upon Tyne, England. **Studies, experiences:** Architecture degree from Strathclyde University, Glasgow. Practice in a number of different studios in Sydney. 1989 studio Stanic Harding Architects. **Awards:** RAIA 1996, 1997, 2000, 2001; "*Belle* Magazine Space Apartment of the Year" in 2001. **Favorites:** *Architects:* Le Corbusier, Peter Wilson. *Buildings:* Unité d'Habitation by Le Corbusier in Marseille, Maison de Verre in Paris by Pierre Chareau. *Designers:* Poul Kjaerholm, Charles and Ray Eames. **In Sydney they recommend:** *Hotel:* Regent's Court. *Restaurant:* Banc. *Fashion boutique:* Calibre. *Museum:* Casula Powerhouse Arts Centre.

Andrew Stanic est né en 1957 à Sydney. **Etudes, expérience professionnelle:** Diplôme d'architecture de l'University of Technology, Sydney (UTS). Apprentissage dans le cabinet de George Freedman. **Andy Harding** est né en 1956 à Newcastle upon Tyne en Angleterre. **Etudes, expérience professionnelle:** Diplôme d'architecture de la Strathclyde University de Glasgow. Apprentissage dans divers cabinets de Sydney. 1989, ouverture du cabinet Stanic Harding Architects. **Prix d'architecture:** RAIA: 1996, 1997, 2000, 2001; «*Belle* Magazine Space Apartment of the Year» en 2001. **Leurs favoris:** *Architectes:* Le Corbusier, Peter Wilson. *Edifices:* Unité d'habitation de Le Corbusier à Marseille, la Maison de verre de Pierre Chareau à Paris. *Designers:* Poul Kjaerholm, Charles et Ray Eames. **A Sydney, ils recommandent:** *Hôtel:* Regent's Court. *Restaurant:* Banc. *Boutique de mode:* Calibre. *Musée:* Casula Powerhouse Arts Centre.

Andrew Stanic ist 1957 in Sydney geboren. **Ausbildung, Erfahrungen:** Abgeschlossenes Architekturstudium an der University of Technology, Sydney (UTS). Tätigkeit im Architekturbüro von George Freedman. **Andy Harding** ist 1956 in Newcastle upon Tyne in England geboren. **Ausbildung, Erfahrungen:** Abgeschlossenes Architekturstudium an der Strathclyde University in Glasgow. Tätigkeit in verschiedenen Architekturbüros in Sydney. 1989 Gründung von Stanic Harding Architects. **Architekturpreise:** RAIA: 1996, 1997, 2000, 2001; »*Belle* Magazine Space Apartment of the Year« im Jahr 2001. **Sie bewundern:** *Architekten:* Le Corbusier, Peter Wilson. *Gebäude:* Unité d'Habitation von Le Corbusier in Marseille, Maison de Verre von Pierre Chareau in Paris. *Designer:* Poul Kjaerholm, Charles und Ray Eames. **Sie empfehlen in Sydney:** *Hotel:* Regent's Court. *Restaurant:* Banc. *Boutique:* Calibre. *Museum:* Casula Powerhouse Arts Centre.

Sun House, Castlecrag

Year of construction: 2000	**Area:** 438 m^2	**Cost:** AUS $ 540,000
Année de réalisation: 2000	**Surface:** 438 m^2	**Coûts:** AUS $ 540 000
Baujahr: 2000	**Nutzfläche:** 438 m^2	**Kosten:** AUS $ 540 000

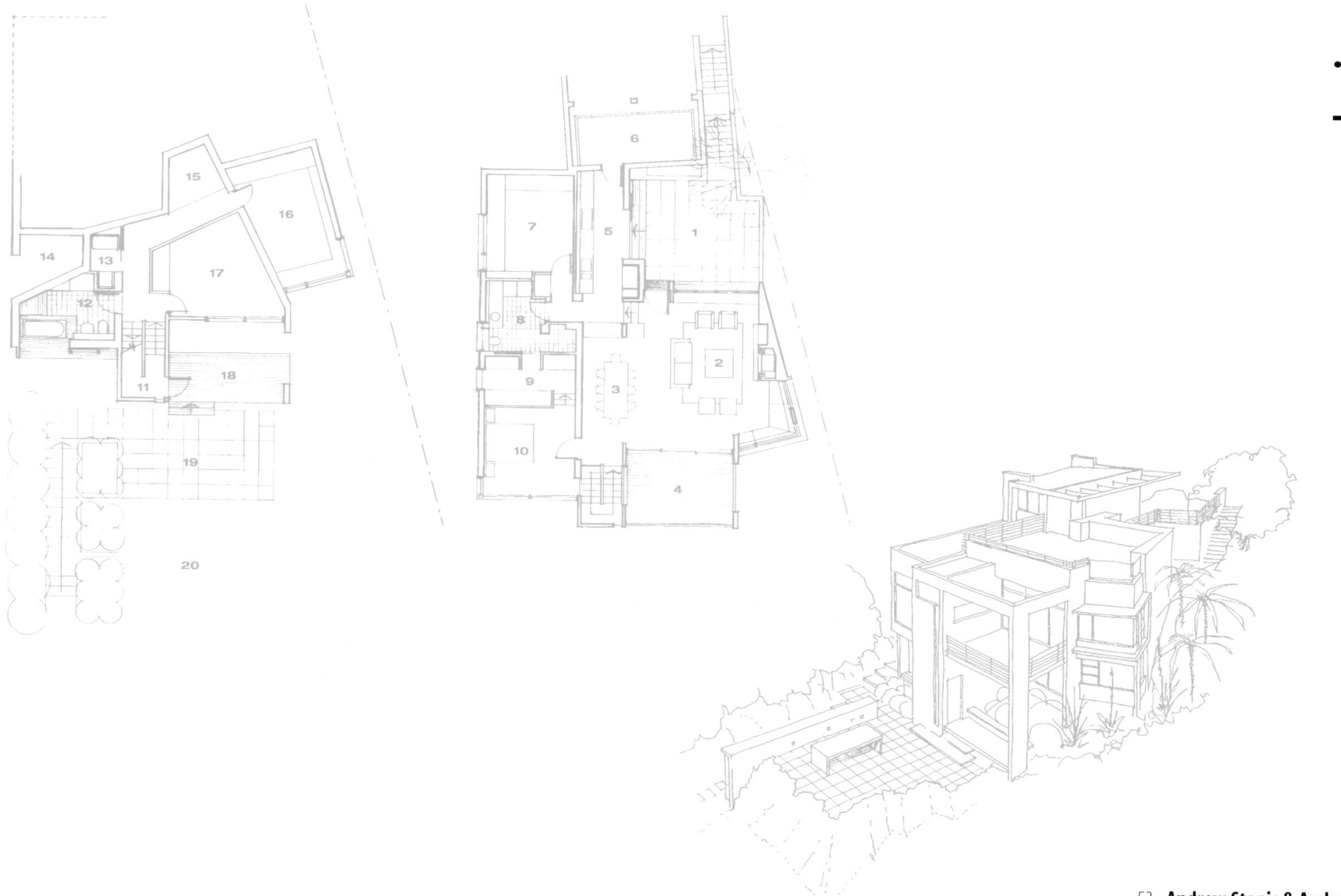
15
16
14
13
17
12
11
18
19
20
6
7
5
1
8
2
9
3
10
4

design Andrew Stanic & Andy Harding

Sun House

DO NOT
PARK ACROSS
ENTRANCE
13
PARKING

Marshall Residence, Darlinghurst

A former coach factory, built in 1903 in one of the lively suburbs around the city, filled with shops, restaurants, and bars alternating with rows of old terrace houses. The architect Sam Marshall has transformed this structure as his own home-studio, conserving the original wood floors and exposed brick walls, and then utilizing basic materials like sheet metal, wood, and glass to complete the restructuring. The ground floor is for the studio; the mezzanine contains the living areas in a large open space with exposed roofing in iron and wood; the loft hosts the bedroom area and bath. The furnishings have been made, for the most part, by Marshall himself, and enlivened with the colorful objects of Dinosaur Designs – the well-known Australian trademark of which Liane Rossler, Marshall's wife, is one of the three founding partners.

Cette ancienne fabrique de voitures à cheval datant de 1903 est située dans un des faubourgs animés qui bordent la City, bondé de boutiques, de restaurants et de bars alternant avec des rangées de vieilles maisons ouvrières. L'architecte Sam Marshall en a fait sa maison-atelier, conservant ses parquets d'origine et ses murs en briques nues, et utilisant des matériaux bruts tels que la tôle, le bois et le verre pour compléter sa restructuration. Le rez-de-chaussée a été consacré aux espaces de travail, la mezzanine aux différentes parties séjour réunies en un vaste loft chapeauté d'un toit ouvert en fer et bois, le grenier au coucher et à la salle de bains. La décoration a été réalisée en grande partie par Marshall lui-même et agrémentée d'objets colorés de Dinosaur Designs – la célèbre marque australienne dont Liane Rossler, son épouse, est l'un des associés fondateurs.

Dieses Haus befindet sich in einem der lebhaften Vororte, die sich um die City herum gruppieren und die voller Geschäfte, Restaurants und Bars sind. Ursprünglich war es eine Kutschenfabrik von 1903, heute wohnt und arbeitet hier der Architekt Sam Marshall, der das Gebäude selbst umgebaut hat. Dabei hat er die Originalböden aus Holzleisten und die nackten Backsteinmauern belassen sowie bei der Renovierung Materialien wie Blech, Holz und Glas in unbearbeitetem Zustand verwendet. Das Erdgeschoss ist den Arbeitsräumen vorbehalten, während der Wohnbereich im Zwischengeschoss liegt und als großer *open space* hinaufreicht bis zum Dachstuhl aus Eisen und Holz. Ein Hängeboden beherbergt Schlafbereich und Badezimmer. Die Einrichtung wurde hauptsächlich von Marshall selbst entworfen und wird ergänzt durch die farbenfrohen Objekte der bekannten australischen Designfirma Dinosaur Designs, die Marshalls Frau Liane Rossler mitbegründet hat.

6

55. Sam Marshall, architect and owner.

55. Sam Marshall, l'architecte et propriétaire.

55. Sam Marshall, der Architekt und Hausbesitzer.

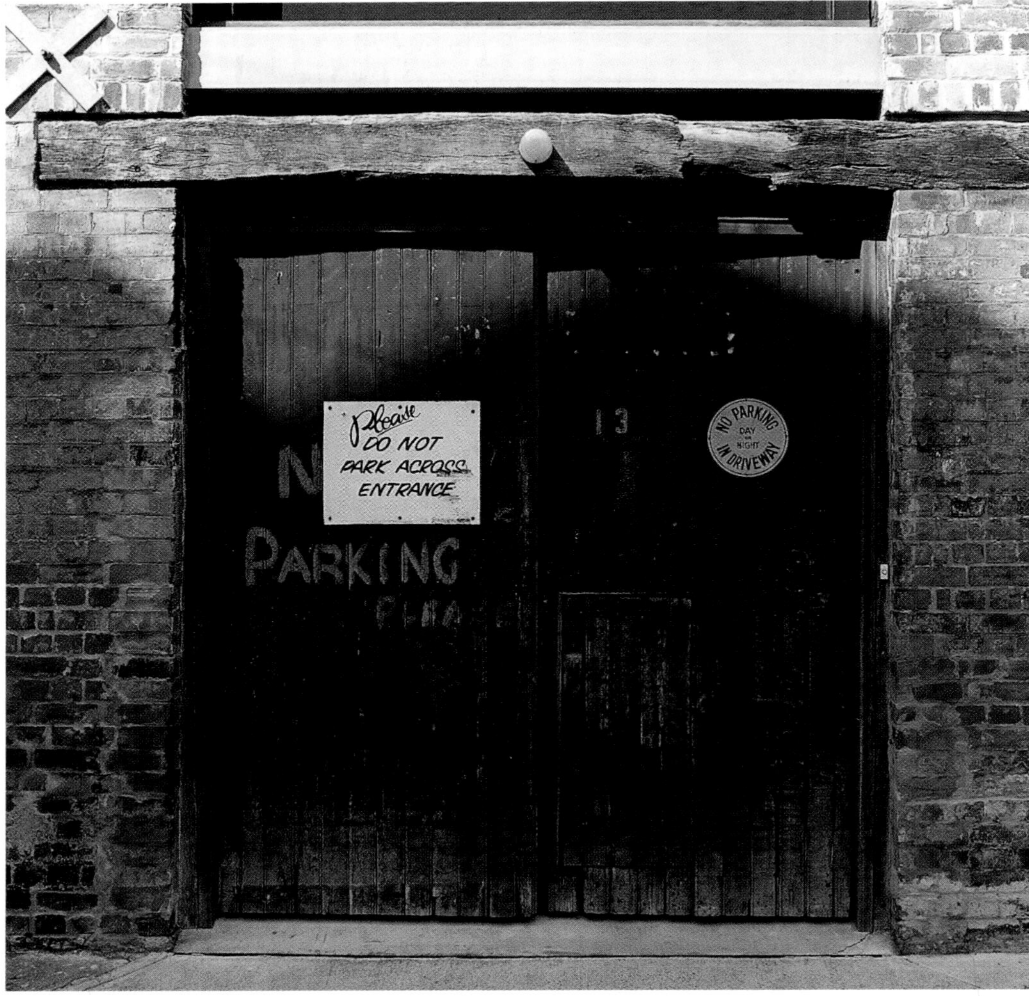
Please
DO NOT
PARK ACROSS
ENTRANCE
13
NO PARKING
DAY
NIGHT
IN DRIVEWAY
PARKING

56. The original entrance and the internal garden with the fish pond in white cement. **57.** The terrace accessed through a passage created in the roof.

56. Le portail d'origine et le jardin intérieur avec le bassin des poissons en ciment blanc. **57.** La petite terrasse à laquelle on accède par un passage ouvert dans le toit.

56. Das originale Eingangstor und der Innengarten mit dem Fischbassin aus Weißzement. **57.** Die kleine Terrasse erreicht man über einen in das Dach eingelassenen Gang.

58-59. The large two-story space containing the living areas. Its industrial look is emphasized by the wood plank flooring, the exposed bricks, and the structure of wooden beams, iron, and sheet metal of the loft. The staircase leads to the bedroom and bath zone on the upper level. Table and chairs by Charles and Ray Eames. Kitchen in white and black wood, designed by Sam Marshall.

58-59. Le vaste espace ouvert à double hauteur sous plafond qui rassemble les parties du séjour. Son atmosphère industrielle est soulignée par le sol en lattes de bois, les murs en briques nues et la structure en travées de bois, de fer et de tôle de la soupente. L'escalier permet d'accéder à la chambre à coucher et à la salle de bains au niveau supérieur. La table et les chaises sont de Charles et Ray Eames. La cuisine en bois blanc et noir a été dessinée par Sam Marshall.

58-59. In dem großen *open space* in doppelter Höhe sind die Wohnräume untergebracht. An die industrielle Vergangenheit erinnern die Holzleisten des Fußbodens, die Sichtbacksteine und die Balkenkonstruktion des Hängebodens in Holz, Eisen und Blech. Die Treppe führt zum Schlafbereich und zum Badezimmer. Tisch und Stühle sind von Charles und Ray Eames. Die Küchenzeile wurde nach einem Entwurf von Sam Marshall in weißem und schwarzem Holz gefertigt.

60. Details of the bedroom. Black and white vases in glass and resin by Dinosaur Designs on the partition that follows the form of the low cabinet in the kitchen. **61.** A sliding wooden door borders the stairwell leading from the entrance to the upper level of the open space. **62.** A corner of the living room. The furnishings are a mixture of recycled objects and custom-designed furniture, like the divan.

60. Détail de la chambre à coucher. Sur la corniche qui accompagne le développement linéaire des éléments bas de la cuisine, des vases en verre et résine blancs et noirs de chez Dinosaur Designs. **61.** Une porte coulissante sépare la cage d'escalier qui mène de l'entrée au niveau supérieur de l'espace ouvert. **62.** Un coin du salon. La décoration est un mélange de meubles de récupération et d'éléments créés spécialement tels que le canapé.

60. Detailansicht aus dem Schlafzimmer. Weiße und schwarze Glas- und Kunstharzvasen von Dinosaur Designs stehen auf einer Ablage, die das Pendant zu der niedrigen Küchenzeile darstellt. **61.** Eine Schiebetür aus Holz grenzt den Treppenraum ab, der vom Eingang bis in den oberen Teil des Wohnbereichs führt. **62.** Eine Ecke im Wohnzimmer. Die Einrichtung ist ein Mix aus Fundstücken und eigens entworfenen Objekten wie etwa das Sofa.

Sam Marshall
P.O. Box 780 Darlinghurst 1300 Sydney Australia Ph +61 2 9310 7555 F +61 2 9310 4144 email: sammarshall@ozemail.com.au

Studies, experiences: 1982 honours degree in architecture, University of New South Wales (UNSW), Sydney. Practice in 1984–1988 Marsh Freedman & Associates (associate in 1985). 1989 independent practice. **Awards:** RAIA: 1995, 1998, 2000; Dulux Award: 2001. **Favorites:** *Architect:* Peter Atkins. *Artist:* Donald Judd. *Building:* Sydney Opera House by Jørn Utzon. *Furnishing: Loop* chair by Willy Guhl. **In Sydney he recommends:** *Hotel:* Regent's Court. *Restaurant:* Sean's Panaroma. *Design shop:* Dinosaur Designs. *Fashion boutique:* Mooks. *Gallery:* Darren Knight Gallery. *Museum:* Museum of Sydney. *Bookstore:* Published Art.

Etudes, expérience professionnelle: 1982, diplôme d'architecture de l'université du New South Wales de Sydney (UNSW). 1984–1988, apprentissage auprès de Marsh Freedman & Associates (devient associé en 1985). 1989, travaille à son compte. **Prix d'architecture:** RAIA: 1995, 1998, 2000; Dulux Award: 2001. **Ses favoris:** *Architecte:* Peter Atkins. *Artiste:* Donald Judd. *Edifice:* Opéra de Sydney de Jørn Utzon. *Objets, meubles:* chaise *Loop* de Willy Guhl. **A Sydney, il recommande:** *Hôtel:* Regent's Court. *Restaurant:* Sean's Panaroma. *Boutique de design:* Dinosaur Designs. *Boutique de mode:* Mooks. *Galerie d'art:* Darren Knight Gallery. *Musée:* Museum of Sydney. *Librairie:* Published Art.

Ausbildung, Erfahrungen: 1982 Abschluss des Architekturstudiums an der University of New South Wales in Sydney (UNSW). Tätigkeit 1984–1988 bei Marsh Freedman & Associates (Teilhaber seit 1985). Seit 1989 eigenes Architekturbüro. **Architekturpreise:** RAIA: 1995, 1998, 2000; Dulux Award: 2001. **Er bewundert:** *Architekt:* Peter Atkins. *Künstler:* Donald Judd. *Gebäude:* Sydney Opera House von Jørn Utzon. *Möbeldesign:* Sitzschlaufe *Loop* von Willy Guhl. **Er empfiehlt in Sydney:** *Hotel:* Regent's Court. *Restaurant:* Sean's Panaroma. *Designgeschäft:* Dinosaur Designs. *Boutique:* Mooks. *Galerie:* Darren Knight Gallery. *Museum:* Museum of Sydney. *Buchhandlung:* Published Art.

Marshall Residence, Darlinghurst

Year of construction: 2000
Année de réalisation: 2000
Baujahr: 2000

Area: 230 m² (interiors) + 70 m² (outdoor spaces)
Surface: 230 m² (intérieur) + 70 m² (extérieur)
Nutzfläche: 230 m² (innen) + 70 m² (Außenbereich)

Cost: AUS $ 65,000
Coûts: AUS $ 65 000
Kosten: AUS $ 65 000

Marshall Residence
design Sam Marshall

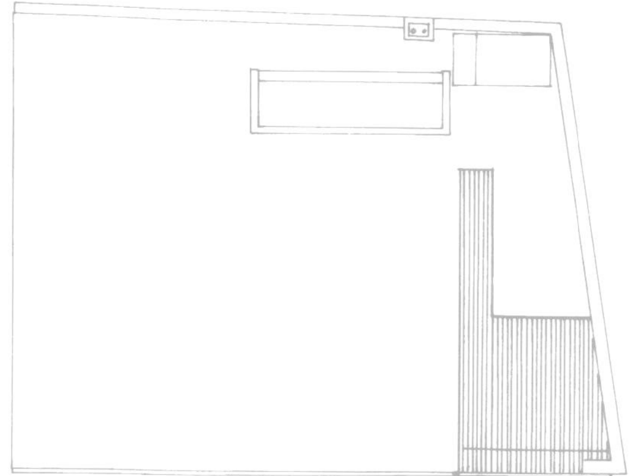

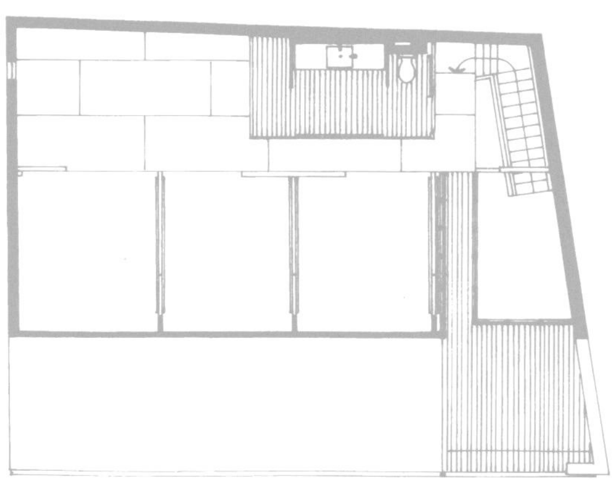

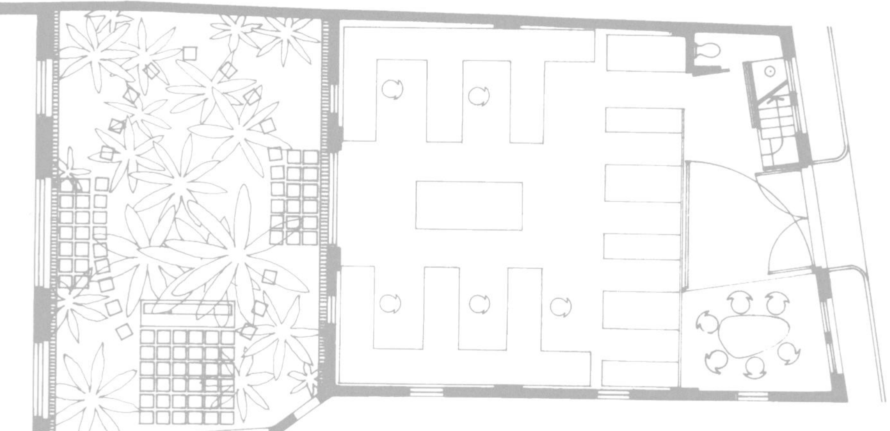

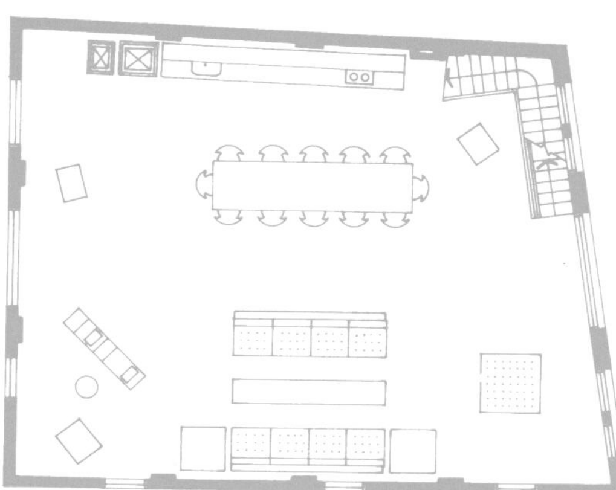

Xavier House, Mosman

Designed by Alex Popov for a couple with children in the lively Mosman residential zone, this white cement house with a fine view of Balmoral Bay has a U-shaped footprint. The two wings flank a swimming pool and a tropical garden oriented toward the northwest. The southeastern side of the house is closed, in discreet defense of privacy. Inside the U the walls are completely in glass to make the interiors luminous and fluid, qualities accentuated by the choice of white as the dominant color and the light stone of the flooring, creating a sense of continuity between indoors and outdoors, courtyard spaces and living areas, reinforced by the constantly changing light of the internal promenade connecting the spaces.

Conçue par l'architecte australien Alex Popov dans la zone résidentielle animée de Mosman pour un couple avec enfants, cette villa en ciment blanc avec une vue panoramique sur Balmoral Bay possède un plan en U qui étreint entre ses ailes une piscine et un jardin tropical orientés au nord-ouest. La façade sud-est, elle, tourne le dos à la rue, comme pour protéger son intimité. De grandes parois de verre délimitent son périmètre interne, apportant luminosité et fluidité aux intérieurs. Cette qualité est encore accentuée par le choix du blanc comme couleur dominante et par la pierre claire des sols, créant une impression de continuité entre l'intérieur et l'extérieur, entre la cour et le séjour, jouant avec les changements constants de la lumière dans la promenade intérieure qui relie les différents espaces.

Entworfen von dem australischen Architekten Alex Popov im lebhaften Wohnviertel Mosman für ein Ehepaar mit Kindern, besteht diese Villa aus Weißzement mit Panoramablick auf Balmoral Beach aus einer U-förmigen Anlage. Die beiden nach Nordwesten gerichteten Flügel umfassen ein Schwimmbecken und einen tropischen Garten, während sich die südöstliche Seite in diskreter Abschirmung der Privatsphäre den Blicken verschließt. Großflächige Glaswände begrenzen die Räume und verleihen ihnen einen lichtdurchfluteten und fließenden Aspekt, was noch durch die dominante Farbe Weiß sowie die hellen Steinplatten des Bodens verstärkt wird. So entsteht der Eindruck eines kontinuierlichen Übergangs zwischen innen und außen, zwischen Wohnraum und Hof, wozu auch die stetigen Veränderungen des Lichteinfalls in dem Innenumgang beitragen, der die einzelnen Räume miteinander verbindet.

7

64. The swimming pool faces the large windows of the living area across a zone for outdoor relaxation. **65.** Alex Popov, the architect.

64. La piscine, sur laquelle donnent les baies vitrées du séjour et bordée d'une aire de détente. **65.** Alex Popov, l'architecte.

64. Den Pool begleitet eine Relaxzone, auf welche die großen Glasfenster des Wohnbereichs blicken. **65.** Alex Popov, der Architekt.

66-67. Canadian maple and white cement, glass and steel are the main materials in the custom-designed kitchen, which communicates directly with the dining area, furnished with chairs *Series 7* by Arne Jacobsen.

66-67. L'érable canadien et le ciment blanc, le verre et l'acier dominent dans la cuisine dessinée par l'architecte. Elle communique directement avec la partie salle à manger, meublée avec des chaises *Série 7* d'Arne Jacobsen.

66-67. Kanadisches Ahornholz und Weißzement, Glas und Chromstahl beherrschen die von dem Architekten selbst entworfene Küche. Sie ist direkt verbunden mit dem Esszimmer, das mit *Series 7*-Stühlen von Arne Jacobsen eingerichtet ist.

68. Absolute white for the master bedroom with cupboards built into the walls.

68. Dans la chambre des maîtres règne un blanc absolu. Les placards sont encastrés dans les murs.

68. Reines Weiß beherrscht das Schlafzimmer der Hausbesitzer mit den in die Wand eingelassenen Schränken.

Alex Popov Architects
2 Glen Street Milsons Point 2061 Sydney Australia Ph +61 2 9955 5604 F +61 2 9955 9258 email: aparch@tig.com.au

1942 born in Shanghai. 1953 moved to Australia. **Studies, experiences:** 1966 degree in arts from UNSW Sydney. 1971 diploma Royal Academy of Fine Arts (Architecture) in Copenhagen. Practice in 1971–1983 with Jørgen Selchau, Henning Larsen, Jørn Utzon. Since 1983 independent practice in Sydney. 1993 Visiting Professor Royal Academy of Fine Arts in Copenhagen. **Awards:** Wilkinson Award, Robin Boyd Award, *Architecture Australia* Prize. **Favorites:** *Architects:* Louis Kahn, Jørn Utzon, Alvar Aalto. **In Sydney he recommends:** *Restaurant:* Dragonfly. *Design shop:* Anibou. *Book and coffee shop:* Bookocino.

Né en 1942 à Shanghai. Déménage en Australie en 1953. **Etudes, expérience professionnelle:** 1966, diplôme d'art de l'UNSW de Sydney. 1971, diplôme d'architecture de l'Académie Royale des Arts de Copenhague. 1971–1983, fait son apprentissage avec Jørgen Selchau, Henning Larsen et Jørn Utzon. Depuis 1983, travaille à son compte à Sydney. 1993, professeur invité à l'Académie Royale des Arts de Copenhague. **Prix d'architecture:** Wilkinson Award, Robin Boyd Award, *Architecture Australia* Prize. **Ses favoris:** *Architectes:* Louis Kahn, Jørn Utzon, Alvar Aalto. **A Sydney, il recommande:** *Restaurant:* Dragonfly. *Boutique de design:* Anibou. *Librairie et café:* Bookocino.

1942 in Shanghai geboren. 1953 Umzug nach Australien. **Ausbildung, Erfahrungen:** 1966 Abschluss des Kunststudiums an der UNSW, Sydney. 1971 Architektur-Diplom an der Kongelige Danske Kunstakademi in Kopenhagen. 1971–1983 Zusammenarbeit mit Jørgen Selchau, Henning Larsen und Jørn Utzon. Seit 1983 eigenes Architekturbüro in Sydney. 1993 Visiting Professor an der Kongelige Danske Kunstakademi in Kopenhagen. **Architekturpreise:** Wilkinson Award, Robin Boyd Award, *Architecture Australia* Prize. **Er bewundert:** *Architekten:* Louis Kahn, Jørn Utzon, Alvar Aalto. **Er empfiehlt in Sydney:** *Restaurant:* Dragonfly. *Designgeschäft:* Anibou. *Buchhandlung und Café:* Bookocino.

Xavier House, Mosman

Year of construction: 1999 **Area:** 310 m^2 **Cost:** not available
Année de réalisation: 1999 **Surface:** 310 m^2 **Coûts:** non indiqués
Baujahr: 1999 **Nutzfläche:** 310 m^2 **Kosten:** ungenannt

Xavier House

design Alex Popov

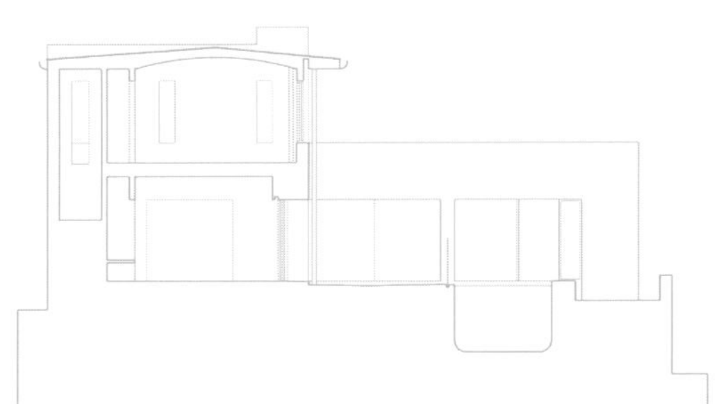

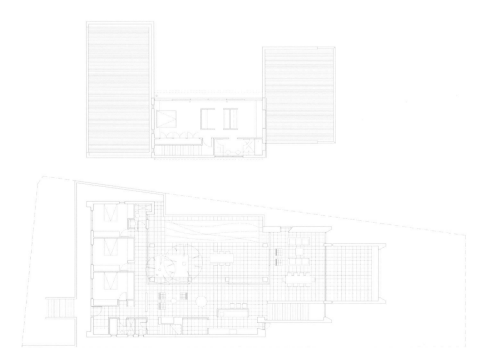

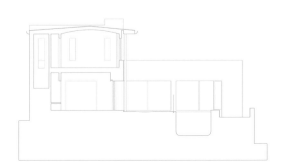

Adams House, Neutral Bay

Facing the luminous bay, the private home of the well-known architect Alex Popov and his partner Chris Adams is inserted in an urban context of low 50s buildings, on a long, sloping lot. The house is divided into two volumes, one for the owner and one for guests. Its figure is essential: a white volume with an overhanging copper roof and a measured sequence of terraces that contribute, with the large windows, to integrate outdoor and indoor spaces. The central patio functions as a filter between the living area and the studio. It features a pool, and is surrounded by glazings that regulate the internal micro-climate. The service functions of the house are positioned laterally.

Donnant sur Neutral Bay inondé de lumière, la maison privée du célèbre architecte Alex Popov et de sa partenaire Chris Adams s'intègre dans un contexte urbain marqué par des maisons basses des années 50. Composée de deux corps de bâtiment – un pour les maîtres de maison, l'autre pour les invités – elle est bâtie sur un terrain en longueur et en dénivelé. Sa silhouette est sobre: un volume blanc surmonté d'un toit en saillie et défini par une suite calibrée de terrasses qui alimentent, par l'intermédiaire de vastes baies vitrées, l'intégration des espaces extérieurs et intérieurs. Un patio central sert de sas entre la partie séjour et la partie travail. Il comporte un bassin entouré de baies vitrées qui régissent le microclimat, tandis que les parties de service de la maison sont situées sur les côtés.

Das Wohnhaus des bekannten Architekten Alex Popov und seiner Lebensgefährtin Chris Adams blickt auf die sonnige Bucht von Neutral Bay und integriert sich perfekt in das städtische Umfeld mit niedrigen Gebäuden aus den 50er Jahren. Es wurde auf einem langen und abfallenden Grundstück errichtet und besteht aus zwei Baukörpern: Der eine ist für den Hausbesitzer und der zweite für die Gäste bestimmt. Die Grundform ist auf das Wesentliche beschränkt: ein weisser Baukörper mit vorspringendem Dach sowie eine ausgeglichene Folge von Terrassen, die mittels großen Glasfenstern einen Übergang schaffen zwischen dem Hausinnern und der Umgebung. Diese Offenheit wird noch unterstrichen durch einen zentralen Patio mit Wasserbecken, der quasi als Filter zwischen dem Wohn- und dem Arbeitsbereich konzipiert ist. Die umgebenden Glasfenster regulieren das interne Mikroklima des Patios, während sich seitlich Badezimmer und Küche befinden.

8

70. The main volume seen from the garden. **71.** Alex Popov, the architect and owner of Adams House.

70. Le volume principal vu du jardin. **71.** Alex Popov, l'architecte et propriétaire de la maison Adams.

70. Blick vom Garten auf das Hauptgebäude. **71.** Alex Popov, der Architekt und Besitzer von Adams House.

72. The central patio with the reflecting pool is surrounded by windows that permit the outdoor space to become an integral part of the interior. The entrance, positioned in correspondence to the central patio that functions as a filter between the living area and the studio.

72. Le patio central avec son miroir d'eau est entouré de baies vitrées qui permettent à l'extérieur de devenir partie intégrante de l'intérieur. L'entrée donne directement sur ce patio central qui sert de filtre entre la partie séjour et le cabinet d'architecture.

72. Den zentralen Patio mit der spiegelnden Wasserfläche umgeben hohe Glasfenster, wodurch der Außenbereich optisch zum Bestandteil der Innenräume wird. Der Eingang öffnet sich direkt auf den Patio, der als Filterzone zwischen dem Wohn- und dem Arbeitsbereich dient.

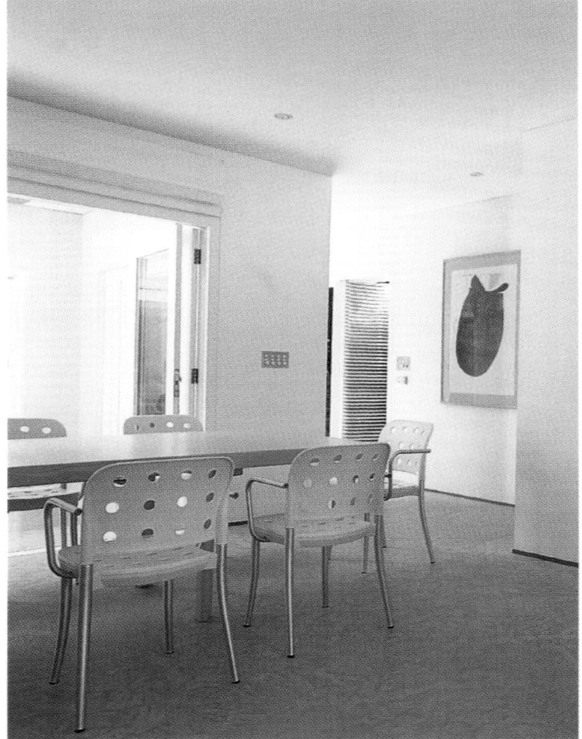

73. The custom kitchen. Around the counter, with top in Canadian wood and cement base, stools by Alvar Aalto. View of the dining area, with a table by Alvar Aalto and *Minni* chairs by Antonio Citterio. **74.** The living room, with the linear wooden staircase in the foreground, enclosed by two walls, leading to the bedroom area. The colors of the furnishings blend with the white of the walls and the warm tones of the sandstone flooring.

73. La cuisine design. Autour du comptoir, constitué d'une base en ciment surmontée d'un plateau en bois canadien, des tabourets en bois d'Alvar Aalto. Détail de la salle à manger avec une table d'Alvar Aalto et des chaises *Minni* d'Antonio Citterio. **74.** Le séjour avec, au premier plan, l'escalier en bois enfermé entre deux cloisons et conduisant aux chambres. Les couleurs des meubles s'harmonisent avec le blanc des murs et le ton chaud du sol en grès.

73. Die maßgearbeitete Küche. Neben dem Arbeitstisch mit Zementsockel und einer Platte aus kanadischem Holz stehen Holzhocker von Alvar Aalto. Blick in das Esszimmer mit einem Alvar-Aalto-Tisch und Stühlen *Minni* von Antonio Citterio. **74.** Im Wohnzimmer führt die zwischen zwei Wänden eingesetzte Holztreppe hoch zum Schlafbereich. Die Farben der Einrichtung harmonieren mit dem Weiß der Wände sowie mit dem warmen Farbton des Sandstein-Fußbodens.

Alex Popov Architects
2 Glen Street Milsons Point 2061 Sydney Australia Ph +61 2 9955 5604 F +61 2 9955 9258 email: aparch@tig.com.au

1942 born in Shanghai. 1953 moved to Australia. **Studies, experiences:** 1966 degree in arts from UNSW Sydney. 1971 diploma Royal Academy of Fine Arts (Architecture) in Copenhagen. Practice in 1971–1983 with Jørgen Selchau, Henning Larsen, Jørn Utzon. Since 1983 independent practice in Sydney. 1993 Visiting Professor Royal Academy of Fine Arts in Copenhagen. **Awards:** Wilkinson Award, Robin Boyd Award, *Architecture Australia* Prize. **Favorites:** *Architects:* Louis Kahn, Jørn Utzon, Alvar Aalto. **In Sydney he recommends:** *Restaurant:* Dragonfly. *Design shop:* Anibou. *Book and coffee shop:* Bookocino.

Né en 1942 à Shanghai. Déménage en Australie en 1953. **Etudes, expérience professionnelle:** 1966, diplôme d'art de l'UNSW de Sydney. 1971, diplôme d'architecture de l'Académie Royale des Arts de Copenhague. 1971–1983, fait son apprentissage avec Jørgen Selchau, Henning Larsen et Jørn Utzon. Depuis 1983, travaille à son compte à Sydney. 1993, professeur invité à l'Académie Royale des Arts de Copenhague. **Prix d'architecture:** Wilkinson Award, Robin Boyd Award, *Architecture Australia* Prize. **Ses favoris:** *Architectes:* Louis Kahn, Jørn Utzon, Alvar Aalto. **A Sydney, il recommande:** *Restaurant:* Dragonfly. *Boutique de design:* Anibou. *Librairie et café:* Bookocino.

1942 in Shanghai geboren. 1953 Umzug nach Australien. **Ausbildung, Erfahrungen:** 1966 Abschluss des Kunststudiums an der UNSW, Sydney. 1971 Architektur-Diplom an der Kongelige Danske Kunstakademi in Kopenhagen. 1971–1983 Zusammenarbeit mit Jørgen Selchau, Henning Larsen und Jørn Utzon. Seit 1983 eigenes Architekturbüro in Sydney. 1993 Visiting Professor an der Kongelige Danske Kunstakademi in Kopenhagen. **Architekturpreise:** Wilkinson Award, Robin Boyd Award, *Architecture Australia* Prize. **Er bewundert:** *Architekten:* Louis Kahn, Jørn Utzon, Alvar Aalto. **Er empfiehlt in Sydney:** *Restaurant:* Dragonfly. *Designgeschäft:* Anibou. *Buchhandlung und Café:* Bookocino.

Adams House, Neutral Bay

Year of construction: 1998
Année de réalisation: 1998
Baujahr: 1998

Area: 156 m^2
Surface: 156 m^2
Nutzfläche: 156 m^2

Cost: not available
Coûts: non indiqués
Kosten: ungenannt

design Alex Popov
Adams House

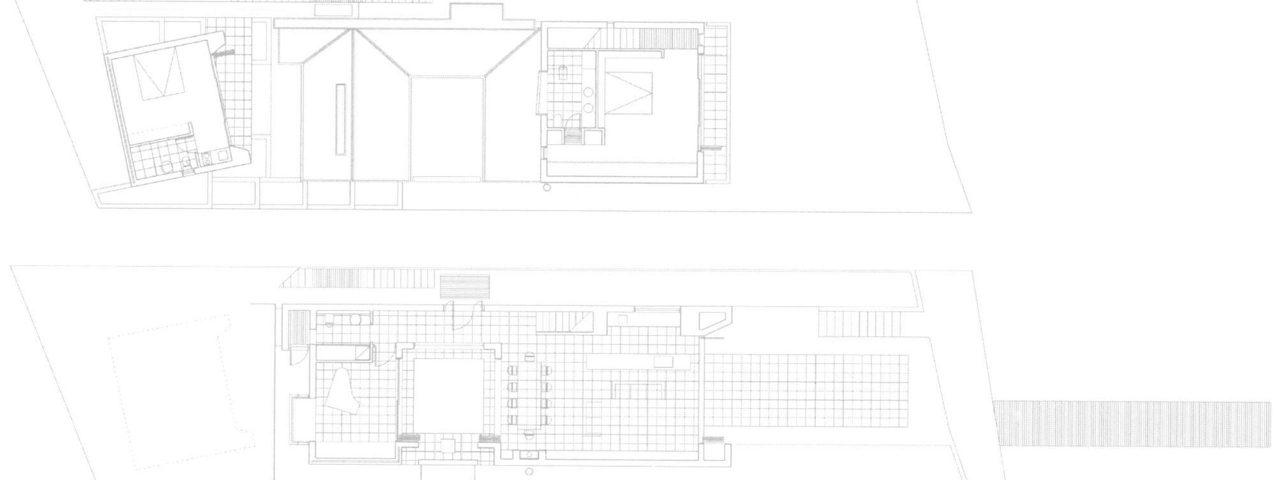

Markham/Qasabian Residence, Annandale

A minimal architecture that brings out the values of space and light, the pure image and colors of industrial materials: This is the home-studio of Christina Markham and Rita Qasabian, young Sydney-based architects. The intrinsic simplicity, inspired by the model of oriental homes, is immediately evident in the rock garden, with stones set into the ground to create Zen paths, underlining the sense of harmony communicated by a clear, terse spatial construction, in which walls and floors in exposed concrete create a direct reference to the poetics of Tadao Ando.

La maison-atelier de Christina Markham et Rita Qasabian, deux jeunes architectes de Sydney, témoigne d'une architecture minimaliste qui exalte les valeurs de l'espace, de la lumière, de l'esthétique pure et des couleurs des matériaux industriels. Sa simplicité intrinsèque, inspirée par le modèle des maisons orientales, se retrouve jusque dans le jardin en pierres, où des galets encastrés tracent des sentiers à la dimension zen qui se poursuivent à l'intérieur de la maison en en soulignant les dimensions harmonieuses. Dans cette construction spatiale limpide et sobre, les murs et les sols en ciment laissé brut créent une référence directe à la poésie de Tadao Ando.

Das Wohn- und Bürohaus der jungen Sydneyer Architektinnen Christina Markham und Rita Qasabian zeigt eine minimalistische Architektursprache, welche die Werte Raum, Licht sowie pure Ästhetik betont und mit den Farben von Industriematerialien hervorhebt. Die dem Gebäude innewohnende, von orientalischen Häusern beeinflusste Schlichtheit wird schon im Steingarten sichtbar, in dem Wege mit eingelassenen Kieselsteinen an Zen-Gärten erinnern. Diese Wege setzen sich auch im Hausinnern fort und unterstreichen die harmonischen Abmessungen der Räume, die klar und fließend konzipiert sind. Die Wände und Fußböden aus Zement wurden unverputzt belassen und stellen eine Anspielung auf die Poesie im Werk von Tadao Ando dar.

9

76. The house seen from the stone garden in Zen-style. The two glass walls illuminate the living and dining room. **77.** Rita Qasabian (left) and Christina Markham, the architects and owners.

76. La maison vue du jardin de graviers à la rigueur quasi zen. Les deux grandes baies vitrées illuminent l'espace ouvert du séjour-salle à manger. **77.** Rita Qasabian (à gauche) et Christina Markham, les architectes et propriétaires.

76. Das Haus vom Kieselsteingarten aus gesehen, der in seiner Strenge an Zen-Gärten erinnert. Die beiden großflächigen Glasfenster versehen den offen gestalteten Wohn- und Essbereich mit Licht. **77.** Rita Qasabian (links) und Christina Markham, die Architekten und Hausbesitzer.

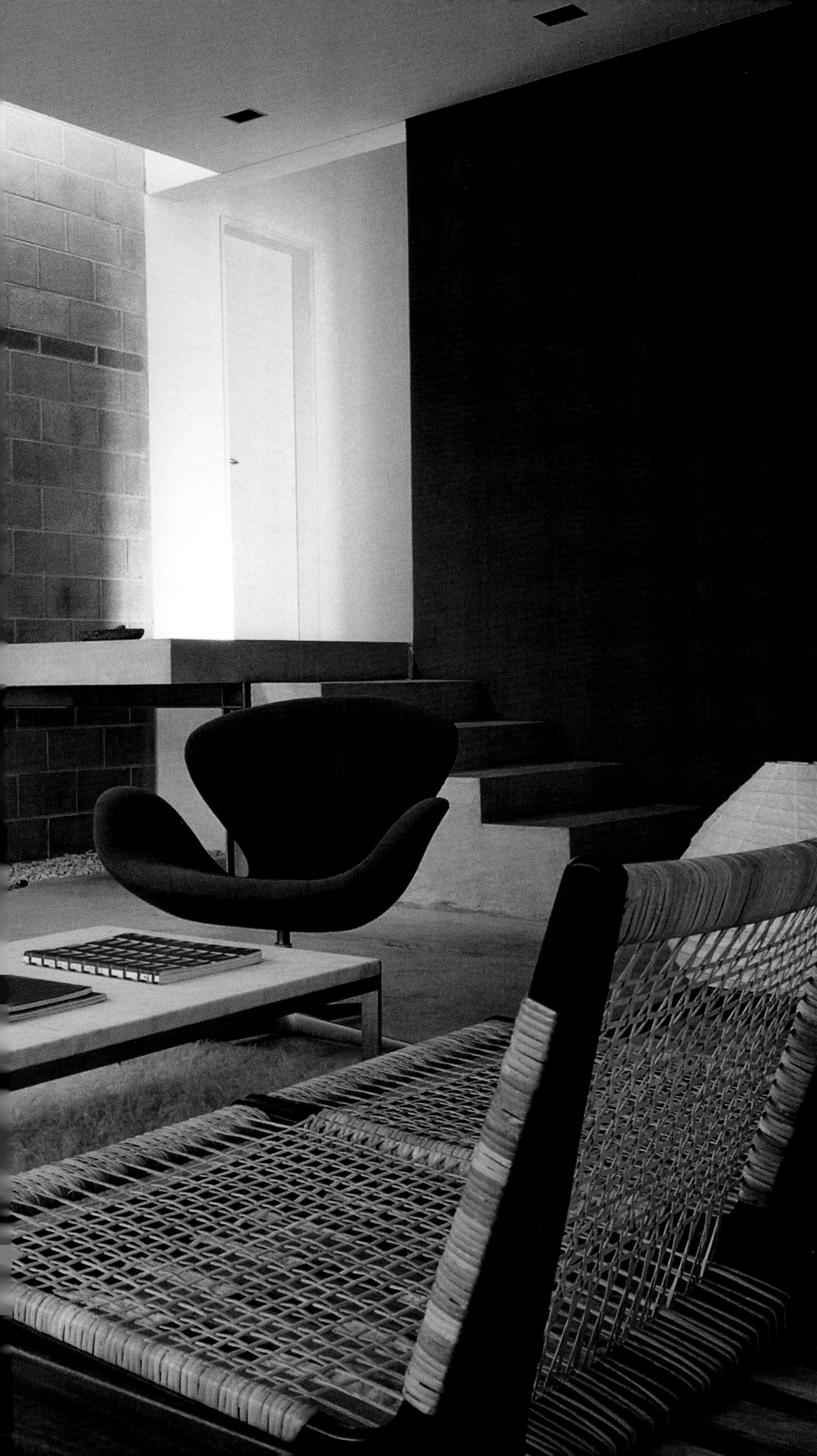

78-79. The living area, accessed from a short staircase in white concrete, is furnished with Nordic design classics: *Swan* armchair by Arne Jacobsen, chairs with woven cane seats and table by Poul Kjaerholm, small Danish sofa from the 50s. The suspended wooden cabinet conceals the sound system.

78-79. La partie séjour, à laquelle on accède par quelques marches en ciment blanc, est meublée avec des classiques du design scandinave: fauteuil *Swan* d'Arne Jacobsen, sièges cannées et table basse de Poul Kjaerholm, petit canapé danois des années 50. Le coffre en bois accroché au mur cache l'installation hi-fi.

78-79. Der Wohnbereich, den man über eine kurze Treppe in Weißzement erreicht, ist mit Klassikern des nordischen Designs eingerichtet: ein Sessel *Swan* von Arne Jacobsen, Rohrgeflecht-Stühle sowie ein Couchtisch von Poul Kjaerholm, dazu ein dänisches 50er-Jahre-Sofa. Die Holzschränke verbergen die Hi-Fi-Anlage.

80. The living area is an open space with a concrete block divider at the center that extends outdoors, flanked by a channel of stones set into the floor. **81.** On the coffee table by Poul Kjaerholm, a Japanese tea set. Gray or white cement, stones, iron beams: The materials underline the essential simplicity of the architecture.

80. Le séjour est un espace ouvert traversé en son centre par une cloison en parpaings qui se prolonge à l'extérieur. Elle est bordée d'une marge de galets incrustés dans le sol. **81.** Sur une table basse de Poul Kjaerholm, un service à thé japonais. Ciment gris ou blanc, pierre, cailloux, poutrelles en fer: Les matériaux utilisés soulignent la simplicité essentielle de l'architecture.

80. Der Wohnraum ist offen gestaltet und wird in der Mitte von einer Trennwand aus Zementbacksteinen unterteilt, die sich im Außenbereich fortsetzt. Sie wird begleitet von einer Furche mit eingelassenen Kieselsteinen. **81.** Auf dem Couchtisch von Poul Kjaerholm steht japanisches Teegeschirr. Grauer und weißer Zement, Stein, Kiesel, Eisenträger: Die gewählten Materialien unterstreichen die schlichte Architektur.

82. In the custom kitchen with stainless steel counter and glass shelving, a set of ceramic bowls and a service in steel by Arne Jacobsen. **83.** The studio facing the stone garden created in a corner of the entrance; table *Less* by Jean Nouvel and lamp *Tolomeo* by Michele De Lucchi and Giancarlo Fassina. Seating by Jørgen Rasmussen.

82. La cuisine design comporte un plan de travail en acier inoxydable surmonté d'une étagère en verre où se trouvent un ensemble de bols en céramique et un service en acier d'Arne Jacobsen. **83.** L'atelier donne sur un petit jardin de graviers récupéré sur un coin de l'entrée. Table *Less* de Jean Nouvel, lampe *Tolomeo* de Michele De Lucchi et Giancarlo Fassina et fauteuil de Jørgen Rasmussen.

82. In der maßgearbeiteten Küche mit einer Arbeitsfläche aus Edelstahl und Glasablagen stehen Keramikschalen und ein Chromstahl-Service von Arne Jacobsen. **83.** Das Büro blickt auf den Steingarten neben dem Eingang. Der Tisch *Less* ist von Jean Nouvel, die Leuchte *Tolomeo* von Micchele De Lucchi und Giancarlo Fassina, die Stühle sind von Jørgen Rasmussen.

NO
STOPPING

Moder

84. In the bedroom, tatami bed with futon, rice paper lamp by Isamu Noguchi, table by Poul Kjaerholm in the background, and artwork by Australian artist Lezlie Tilley. The black fiberglass chair is a famous piece designed by Charles and Ray Eames.

84. Dans la chambre à coucher, un tatami recouvert d'un futon, une lampe en papier de riz d'Isamu Noguchi, une table basse de Poul Kjaerholm à l'arrière-plan et une œuvre de l'artiste australienne Lezlie Tilley. Le fauteuil noir en fibres de verre est un classique de Charles et Ray Eames.

84. Im Schlafzimmer finden sich ein Bett mit Tatami und Futon, eine Reispapierleuchte von Isamu Noguchi, ein niedriges Tischchen von Poul Kjaerholm im Hintergrund sowie ein Werk der australischen Künstlerin Lezlie Tilley. Der schwarze Fiberglassessel ist ein berühmter Designklassiker von Charles und Ray Eames.

Christina Markham & Rita Qasabian **Studio Internationale**
Level 1 47 Queen Street Woollahra 2025 Sydney Australia Ph +61 2 9328 3348 F +61 2 9328 3347 email: si@studiointernationale.com

Christina Markham was born in 1965 in Sydney. **Studies, experiences:** 1989 degree in architecture, UTS, Sydney. 1995 Christina Markham Architectural studio. 1996 partnership with Rita Qasabian. 2000 founding of Studio Internationale. **Rita Qasabian** was born in 1965 in Sydney. **Studies, experiences, projects:** 1992–1996 studies in Fine Arts and Architecture at Sydney University. Markham/Qasabian Residence was "*Belle* Magazine House of the year" in 1997. **Favorites:** *Architects-designers:* Marcel Breuer, Peter Zumthor. *Building:* Notre-Dame-du-Haut at Ronchamp by Le Corbusier. *Furnishing:* Poul Kjaerholm. **In Sydney they recommend:** *Hotel:* W Hotel. *Restaurant:* Bistro Lulu. *Design shop:* De De Ce. *Fashion boutique:* Zambesi. *Gallery:* Gitte Weise Gallery. *Bookstore:* Published Art.

Christina Markham est née en 1965 à Sydney. **Etudes, expérience professionnelle:** 1989, diplôme d'architecture de l'UTS, Sydney. 1995, ouvre le Christina Markham Architectural Studio. 1996, s'associe avec Rita Qasabian. 2000, création de Studio Internationale. **Rita Qasabian** est née en 1965 à Sydney. **Etudes, expérience professionnelle, projets:** 1992–1996, études en beaux-arts et en architecture à la Sydney University. 1997, Markham/Qasabian Residence est «*Belle* Magazine House of the Year». **Leurs favoris:** *Architectes-designers:* Marcel Breuer, Peter Zumthor. *Edifice:* Notre-Dame-du-Haut à Ronchamp de Le Corbusier. *Objets, mobilier:* Poul Kjaerholm. **A Sydney, elles recommandent:** *Hôtel:* W Hotel. *Restaurant:* Bistro Lulu. *Boutique de design:* De De Ce. *Boutique de mode:* Zambesi. *Galerie d'art:* Gitte Weise Gallery. *Librairie:* Published Art.

Christina Markham ist 1965 in Sydney geboren. **Ausbildung, Erfahrungen:** 1989 Abschluss des Architekturstudiums an der UTS in Sydney. 1995 eröffnet sie das eigene Architekturbüro Christina Markham Architectural Studio. 1996 Partnerschaft mit Rita Qasabian. 2000 Eröffnung des Studio Internationale. **Rita Qasabian** ist 1965 in Sydney geboren. **Ausbildung, Erfahrungen, Projekte:** 1992–1996 Studium der angewandten Künste und der Architektur an der Sydney University. Die Markham/Qasabian Residence war 1997 »*Belle* Magazine House of the Year«. **Sie bewundern:** *Architekten/Designer:* Marcel Breuer, Peter Zumthor. *Gebäude:* Notre-Dame-du-Haut in Ronchamp von Le Corbusier. *Möbeldesign:* Poul Kjaerholm. **Sie empfehlen in Sydney:** *Hotel:* W Hotel. *Restaurant:* Bistro Lulu. *Designgeschäft:* De De Ce. *Boutique:* Zambesi. *Galerie:* Gitte Weise Gallery. *Buchhandlung:* Published Art.

Markham/Qasabian Residence, Annandale

Year of construction: 1992 + 1997 (final renovations)	**Area:** 162 m^2 (interiors) + 250 m^2 (outdoor spaces)	**Cost:** AUS $ 250,000
Année de réalisation: 1992 + 1997 (dernières renovations)	**Surface:** 162 m^2 (intérieur) + 250 m^2 (extérieur)	**Coûts:** AUS $ 250 000
Baujahr: 1992 + 1997 (letzte Umgestaltungen)	**Nutzfläche:** 162 m^2 (innen) + 250 m^2 (Außenbereich)	**Kosten:** AUS $ 250 000

design Christina Markham & Rita Qasabian

Markham/Qasabian Residence

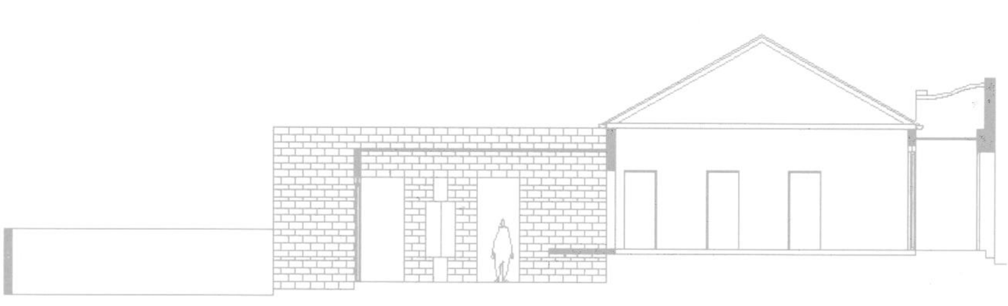

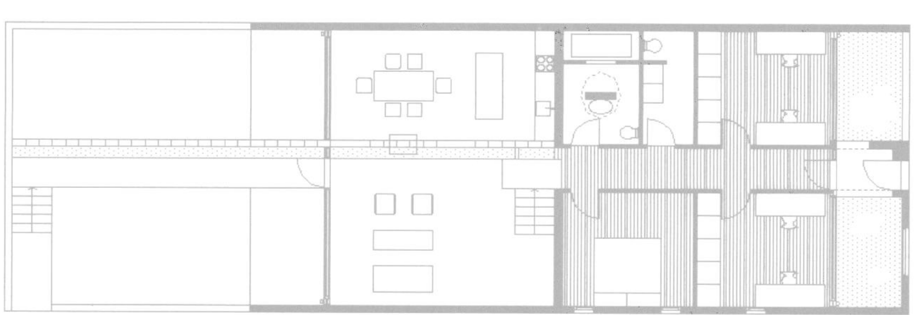

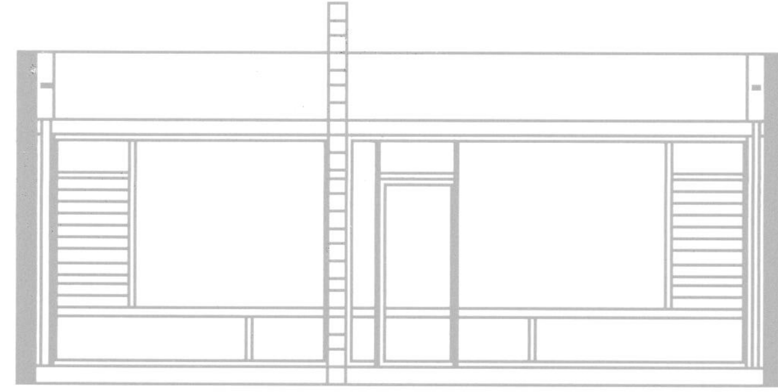

NO
STOPPING

10

Jones-Evans/Gregoriou House, Surry Hills

The home of Linda Gregoriou, an urban planner, and Dale Jones-Evans – architect and designer of this house – is in the Surry Hills zone, a suburban area of eccentric cottages, row houses, and workshops, which is becoming a vivacious neighborhood with many industrial spaces that have been converted as homes and studios, populated by architects, artists, and other creative personalities. This house is a former warehouse, on three levels, with dramatic cantilevered staircases, connecting, in ascending order, the bedroom area, living area, and studio, and based on the model of the art gallery with white, fluid, rarified spaces. The ideal setting for the paintings and sculptures of contemporary and Aboriginal art, the oriental objects and fabrics purchased by the owners in their travels.

La maison de Linda Gregoriou, urbaniste, et de Dale Jones-Evans, architecte et auteur de ce projet, se trouve dans le quartier de Surry Hills, qui, de banlieue aux pavillons excentriques, aux enfilades de maisons ouvrières et aux multiples petites usines, est en passe de devenir une zone branchée et pleine de vie. En effet, de nombreux entrepôts sont reconvertis en maisons et ateliers, notamment par des architectes, des artistes et des créateurs. Cette bâtisse est, elle aussi, un ancien dépôt restructuré sur trois niveaux, avec un spectaculaire escalier suspendu, qui relie, de bas en haut, les chambres, le séjour et l'aire de travail. L'espace blanc, fluide et épuré a été conçu comme une galerie d'art. C'est une scène idéale pour mettre en valeur les tableaux et les sculptures d'art contemporain ou aborigène, ainsi que les tissus et les objets orientaux achetés au fil des nombreux voyages des propriétaires.

Das Wohnhaus der Stadtplanerin Linda Gregoriou und des Architekten Dale Jones-Evans – der es selbst entworfen hat – befindet sich in Surry Hills, einem Vorort von Sydney, der sich mit seinen extravaganten Cottages, Reihenhäusern und Werkstätten zu einer lebhaften und dynamischen Zone entwickelt. Lagerhäuser werden umgebaut zu Wohnhäusern und Bürogebäuden, und das Viertel ist vor allem bei Architekten, Künstlern und Designern sehr beliebt. Auch dieses Gebäude war ursprünglich ein Lagerhaus, das umgebaut wurde und nun auf drei Etagen den Schlaf-, Wohn- und Arbeitsbereich durch effektvolle freitragende Treppen miteinander verbindet. Mit seinen weißen schlichten Räumen gleicht das Haus einer Kunstgalerie und bildet ein ideales Szenarium für die Gemälde und Skulpturen von zeitgenössischen Künstlern und Aboriginal Artists sowie für die Stoffe und orientalischen Objekten, die die Hausbesitzer auf ihren Reisen gesammelt haben.

87. Dale Jones-Evans and Linda Gregoriou.

87. Dale Jones-Evans et Linda Gregoriou.

87. Dale Jones-Evans und Linda Gregoriou.

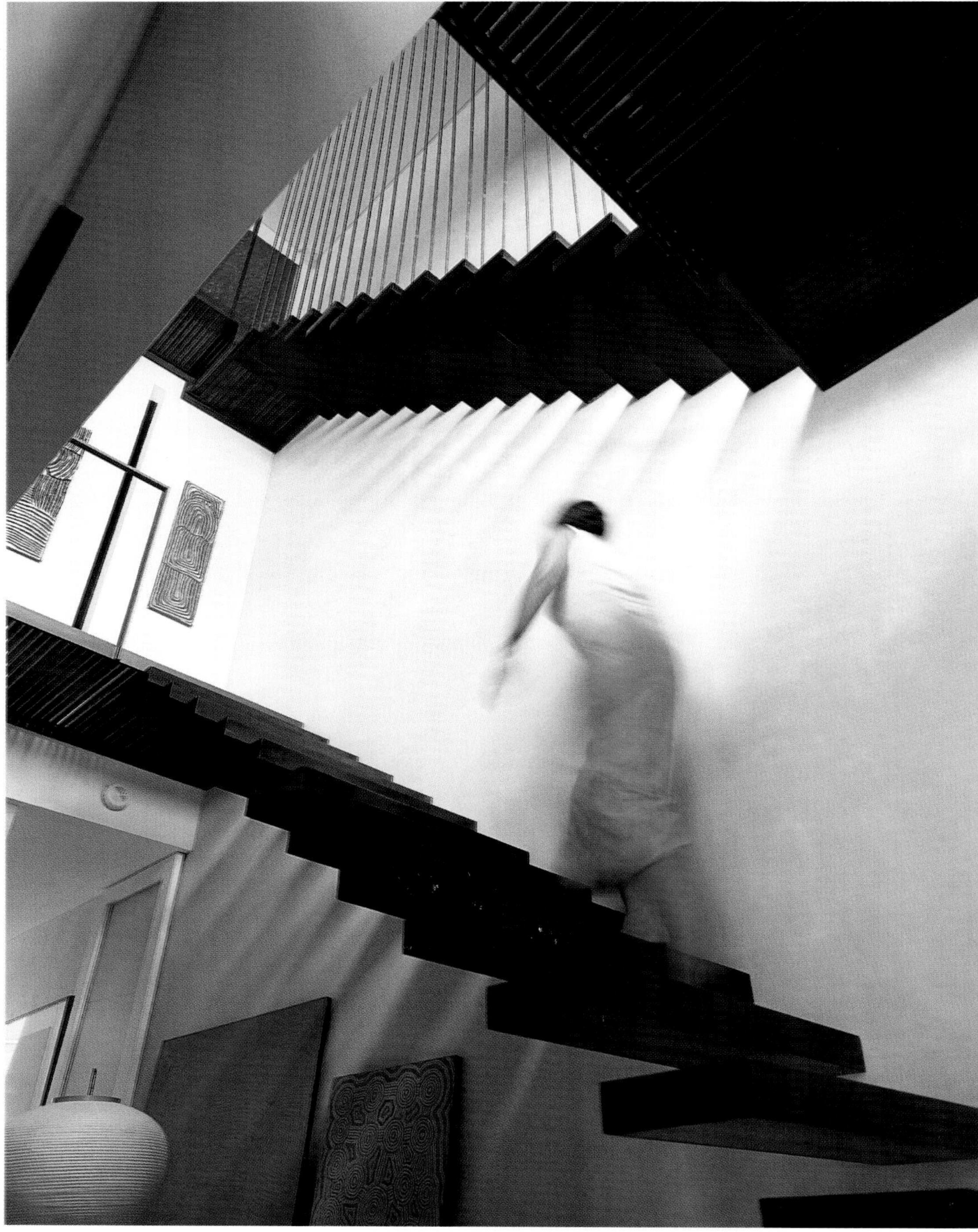

88. The staircase with cantilevered steps connecting the first and second levels. **89.** The living room, in refined tones of brown and green, is organized around the fireplace. *Charles* seating by Antonio Citterio and armchairs by Poul Kjaerholm. On the fireplace, a painting by Aboriginal artist Charlie Ward Tjakamarra, and to the right, a work by Peter Atkins. **90.** The bedroom. The silk fabrics on the bed are from Japan, purchased by the couple during their travels. On the wall, an artwork by Australian artist Janet Laurence.

88. L'escalier avec ses marches suspendues qui relient le premier et le deuxième niveau. **89.** Le séjour, dans des tons épurés marron et vert, est organisé autour de la cheminée. Sièges *Charles* d'Antonio Citterio et fauteuils de Poul Kjaerholm. Au-dessus de la cheminée, un tableau de l'artiste aborigène Charlie Ward Tjakamarra. A côté, une œuvre de Peter Atkins. **90.** La chambre. Les soieries qui recouvrent le lit ont été achetées par les propriétaires lors d'un voyage au Japon. Au mur, une œuvre de l'artiste australienne Janet Laurence.

88. Die freitragende Treppe verbindet den ersten mit dem zweiten Stock. **89.** Das Wohnzimmer in raffinierten Braun- und Grüntönen ist um den Kamin herum konzipiert und mit der Sitzgruppe *Charles* von Antonio Citterio und Sesseln von Poul Kjaerholm eingerichtet. Über dem Kamin hängt ein Gemälde des Aboriginal Artist Charlie Ward Tjakamarra, daneben ein Werk von Peter Atkins. **90.** Das Schlafzimmer. Der Seidenstoff der Bettwäsche stammt aus Japan und wurde auf einer der Reisen der Hausbesitzer erstanden. An der Wand hängt eine Arbeit der australischen Künstlerin Janet Laurence.

Jones-Evans/Gregoriou House

design Dale Jones-Evans

Dale Jones-Evans Architecture & Urban Design
Loft 1 50-54 Ann Street Surry Hills 2010 Sydney Australia Ph +61 2 9211 0626 F +61 2 9211 5998 email: dje@dje.com.au www.dje.com.au

Studies, experiences: Fine Arts degree (painting) and degree in architecture. 1983 independent practice. **Awards:** 1988 USA International Record Houses Award for Choong House; RAIA: 1985, 1987, 1991, 2001. **Favorites:** *Artists:* Aboriginal artists Emily Kngwarreye and Rover Thomas. *Furnishing:* Paper lamps by Isamu Noguchi. **In Sydney he recommends:** *Hotel:* Palisade. *Restaurant:* MG Garage. *Bookstore:* The Building Bookshop. *Fashion boutique:* Marcs.

Etudes, expérience professionnelle: Diplôme en beaux-arts (peinture) et d'architecture. 1983, travaille à son compte. **Prix d'architecture:** 1988, USA International Record Houses Award pour la maison Choong; RAIA: 1985, 1987, 1991, 2001. **Ses favoris:** *Artistes:* les artistes aborigènes Emily Kngwarreye et Rover Thomas. *Objets, mobilier:* Lampes en papier d'Isamu Noguchi. **A Sydney, il recommande:** *Hôtel:* Palisade. *Restaurant:* MG Garage. *Librerie:* The Building Bookshop. *Boutique de mode:* Marcs.

Ausbildung, Erfahrungen: Abschluss in bildender Kunst (Malerei) und in Architektur. Seit 1983 freiberuflich tätig. **Architekturpreise:** 1988 USA International Record Houses Award für Choong House; RAIA: 1985, 1987, 1991, 2001. **Er bewundert:** *Künstler:* Die Aboriginal Artists Emily Kngwarreye und Rover Thomas. *Objektdesign:* Papierleuchten von Isamu Noguchi. **Er empfiehlt in Sydney:** *Hotel:* Palisade. *Restaurant:* MG Garage. *Buchhandlung:* The Building Bookshop. *Boutique:* Marcs.

Jones-Evans/Gregoriou House, Surry Hills

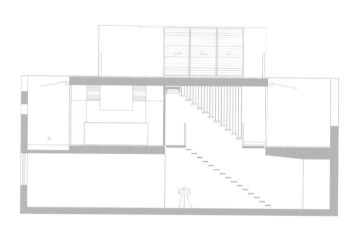

Year of construction: 1999
Année de réalisation: 1999
Baujahr: 1999

Area: 180 m² (interiors) + 250 m² (outdoor spaces)
Surface: 180 m² (intérieur) + 250 m² (extérieur)
Nutzfläche: 180 m² (innen) + 250 m² (Außenbereich)

Cost: not available
Coûts: non indiqués
Kosten: ungenannt

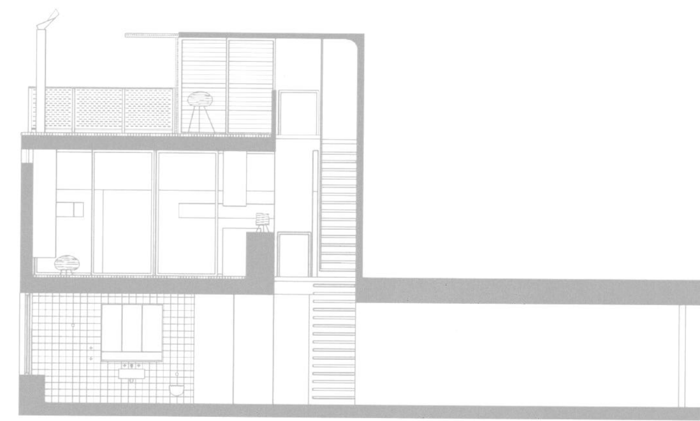

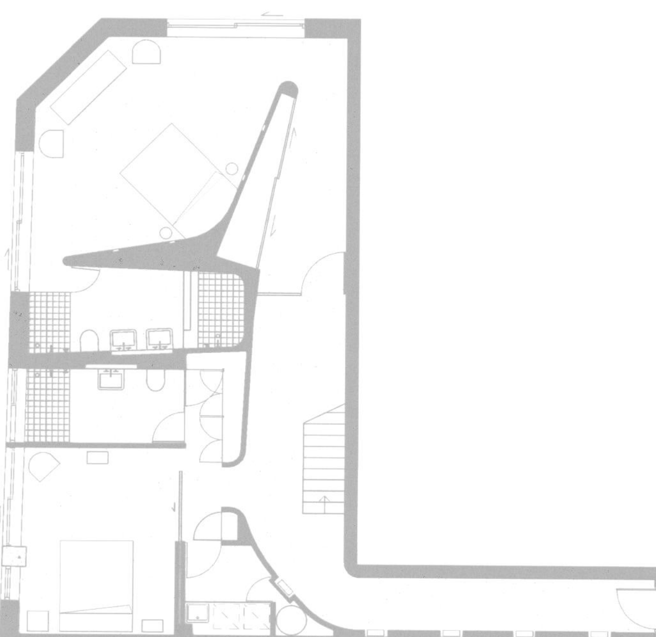

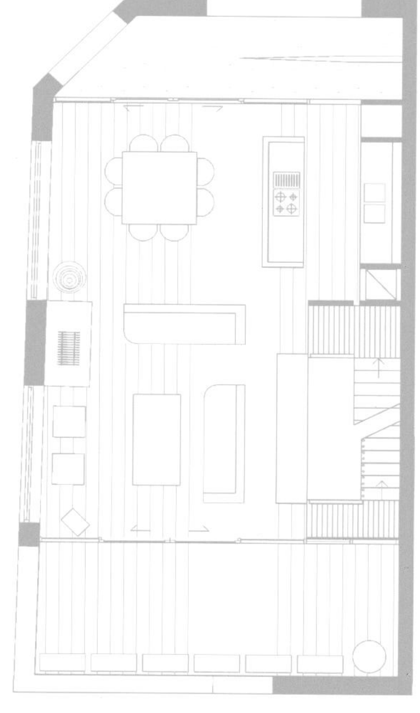

Archer House, Whale Beach

Nestled into the rocky coast, this vacation house is located to the north of Whale Beach, a residential zone known for its beach frequented by surfers. It has been restructured and expanded by the Tasmanian architect Craig Rosevear, utilizing concrete, iron, and glass, materials left in their "native" state to emphasize their tactile qualities. Linear design and large open spaces with windows open to the east, flooded with light, reflect this architect's passion for the work of Ludwig Mies van der Rohe. The house contains the bedroom area on the lower level, conceived as a concrete podium supporting a light glass pavilion, with visible iron beams and pilasters and a flat roof, containing the living areas in a spatial continuity underlined by the large full-height openings overlooking the ocean.

Nichée sur le récif, cette maison de vacances est située au nord de Whale Beach, une localité résidentielle célèbre pour sa plage fréquentée par les surfeurs. Elle a été restructurée et agrandie par l'architecte tasmanien Craig Rosevear, avec un recours généreux au ciment, au fer et au verre, matériaux laissés dans leur état brut afin de mettre en valeur leurs qualités tactiles. Le plan linéaire et les vastes espaces dégagés et vitrés, orientés à l'est et inondés de lumière, témoignent de sa passion pour l'œuvre de Ludwig Mies van der Rohe. Le niveau inférieur, qui abrite la partie coucher, est conçu comme une base en ciment sur lequel est posé un léger pavillon vitré, qui accueille la partie séjour, avec des travées et des poutrelles laissées visibles, surmontée d'un toit plat. L'impression de continuité spatiale est renforcée par de grandes ouvertures allant du sol au plafond, donnant sur l'océan.

Eingenistet auf einem Felsenriff, befindet sich dieses Ferienhaus nördlich der Wohnsiedlung Whale Beach, deren Strand bei Surfern sehr beliebt ist. Der tasmanische Architekt Craig Rosevear hat das Haus renoviert und erweitert und dabei großzügigen Gebrauch gemacht von den Baumaterialien Zement, Eisen und Glas, die alle unbearbeitet belassen wurden, um ihre taktilen Eigenschaften hervorzuheben. Der linear gestaltete Grundriss sowie die offen konzipierten lichtdurchfluteten Räume, die mit großen Fenstern versehen und nach Osten ausgerichtet sind, zeugen von seiner Bewunderung für Ludwig Mies van der Rohe. Das Untergeschoss mit dem Schlafbereich ist als Zementpodium konzipiert. Auf ihm ruht ein verglaster Pavillon mit unverkleideten Balken und Pfeilern aus Eisen sowie einem Flachdach. Der fließende Übergang zwischen dem Innern und der Umgebung wird noch betont durch die ganzflächigen Glasfenster, die auf den Ozean blicken.

11

93. The architect: Craig Rosevear.

93. L'architecte: Craig Rosevear.

93. Der Architekt: Craig Rosevear.

94. The living room with leather *Barcelona* chairs designed by Ludwig Mies van der Rohe in 1929. On the terrace, *PK25* chairs by Poul Kjaerholm with halyard seat and back. **95.** From the outside the construction displays only the open structural space of the first level, a scheme of iron beams and pilasters on a concrete base, and enclosed by glass walls facing the ocean.

94. Le séjour avec des fauteuils *Barcelona* en cuir de Ludwig Mies van der Rohe dessinés en 1929. Sur la terrasse, des chaises *PK25* de Poul Kjaerholm, avec siège et dossier en corde. **95.** De l'extérieur, on ne voit que la structure ouverte du premier niveau, un plan en travées et colonnes en fer sur une base de ciment, ceinte de parois de verre allant du sol au plafond, le tout tourné vers l'océan.

94. Das Wohnzimmer mit den Ledersesseln *Barcelona* von Ludwig Mies van der Rohe, die 1929 entworfen wurden. Auf der Terrasse stehen Easy Chairs *PK25* von Poul Kjaerholm mit Seilbespannung. **95.** Von außen erkennt man den *open space* der ersten Etage, eine Konstruktion aus Eisenbalken und -pfeilern auf einem Zementsockel, die eingefasst wird von ganzflächigen Glaswänden mit Blick auf den Ozean.

96-97. Through a glazed wall, symmetrical to the windows on the terrace, the living room opens onto a space for outdoor cooking, with fireplace and barbecue. The dining area features a eucalyptus table designed by Craig Rosevear and Stuart Houghton and *MR* chairs by Ludwig Mies van der Rohe.

96-97. Face à la paroi vitrée donnant sur la terrasse, un autre mur de verre s'ouvre sur une aire équipée d'une cheminée et d'un barbecue où l'on peut cuisiner en plein air. La salle à manger est meublée d'une table en eucalyptus dessinée par Craig Rosevear et Stuart Houghton, et de chaises *MR* de Ludwig Mies van der Rohe.

96-97. Als Gegenstück zu den Terrassenfenstern öffnet sich auf der anderen Seite des Wohnzimmers ebenfalls eine Glasfront in voller Höhe auf einen Hof mit Kamin und Barbecue, wo unter freiem Himmel gegrillt werden kann. Das Esszimmer ist mit einem von Craig Rosevear und Stuart Houghton entworfenen Eukalyptustisch sowie mit Freischwingern *MR* von Ludwig Mies van der Rohe eingerichtet.

98. The bedroom and bath establish a spatial and visual continuity, filtered by a sliding wooden door. The bed with structure in eucalyptus is custom-designed. A note of color in the total white: the painting "Tree" by John Coburn, who designed also tapestries for the Sydney Opera House. **99.** Protected by two glass balustrades, the staircase leading to the bedroom area on the lower level creates a central opening in the cement floor of the living room.

98. La chambre à coucher et la salle de bains forment une continuité spatiale et visuelle, filtrée par une haute porte coulissante en bois. Le lit en eucalyptus est réalisé sur mesure. «Tree», un tableau de John Coburn qui a dessiné aussi des tapisseries pour l'opéra de Sydney, apporte une tache de couleur dans le blanc dominant. **99.** Au centre du séjour, le sol en ciment s'ouvre sur un escalier protégé par deux balustrades en verre et qui descend vers les chambres au niveau inférieur.

98. Das Schlafzimmer und das Bad bilden optisch einen einzigen Raum, in dem nur eine raumhohe Holzschiebetür als Filter dient. Das Bett aus Eukalyptusholz ist maßgefertigt. Einen Farbtupfer stellt das Gemälde »Tree« von John Coburn dar, der auch Tapisserien für das Sydney Opera House designt hat. **99.** In den Zementfußboden des Wohnzimmers ist die Treppe eingeschnitten, die zum Schlafbereich im Untergeschoss führt und von zwei Glasgeländern gerahmt wird.

100. The black leather *Charles* divan and the *Tolomeo* lamps complete the furnishings of the living area. In the background, the terrace on the sea.

100. Un canapé *Charles* en cuir noir et des lampes *Toloméo* complètent la partie séjour. A l'arrière-plan on voit la terrasse sur la mer.

100. Das schwarze Ledersofa *Charles* und die Leuchten *Tolomeo* vervollständigen die Einrichtung des Wohnbereichs. Im Hintergrund sieht man die Terrasse über dem Meer.

Craig Rosevear
PO Box 322 Sandy Bay 7005 Tasmania Australia Ph/F +61 3 6224 8688 email: crarc@ozemail.com.au

Born in 1961 in Tasmania. **Studies, experiences:** 1989 degree in architecture at University of Tasmania (UTAS). 1994 scholarship to Domus Academy winter school at Royal Melbourne Institute of Technology (RMIT). 1987–1996 tutor in design and architecture, UTAS. **Awards:** RAIA: 1997, 1998, 2000; Wilkinson Award in 2001. **Favorites:** *Architect:* Ludwig Mies van der Rohe. *Building:* Notre-Dame-du-Haut at Ronchamp by Le Corbusier. *Designer:* Jasper Morrison. *Furnishing:* Rope chair *PK25* by Poul Kjaerholm.

1961, naissance en Tasmanie. **Etudes, expérience professionnelle:** 1989, diplôme d'architecture à l'University of Tasmania (UTAS). 1994, bourse à la Domus Academy Winter School au Royal Melbourne Institute of Technology (RMIT). 1987–1996, enseigne le design et l'architecture à l'UTAS. **Prix d'architecture:** RAIA: 1997, 1998, 2000; Wilkinson Award en 2001. **Ses favoris:** *Architecte:* Ludwig Mies van der Rohe. *Edifice:* Notre-Dame-du-Haut à Ronchamp de Le Corbusier. *Designer:* Jasper Morrison. *Objets, mobilier:* la chaise en corde *PK25* de Poul Kjaerholm.

1961 in Tasmanien geboren. **Ausbildung, Erfahrungen:** 1989 Abschluss des Architekturstudiums an der University of Tasmania (UTAS). 1994 Stipendium an der Domus Academy Winter School am Royal Melbourne Institute of Technology (RMIT). 1987–1996 Tutor für Design und Architektur an der UTAS. **Architekturpreise:** RAIA: 1997, 1998, 2000; Wilkinson Award 2001. **Er bewundert:** *Architekten:* Ludwig Mies van der Rohe. *Gebäude:* Notre-Dame-du-Haut in Ronchamp von Le Corbusier. *Designer:* Jasper Morrison. *Möbeldesign:* Rope Chair *PK25* von Poul Kjaerholm.

Archer House, Whale Beach

Year of construction: 2000
Année de réalisation: 2000
Baujahr: 2000

Area: 290 m² (interiors) + 120 m² (outdoor spaces)
Surface: 290 m² (intérieur) + 120 m² (extérieur)
Nutzfläche: 290 m² (innen) + 120 m² (Außenbereich)

Cost: not available
Coûts: non indiqués
Kosten: ungenannt

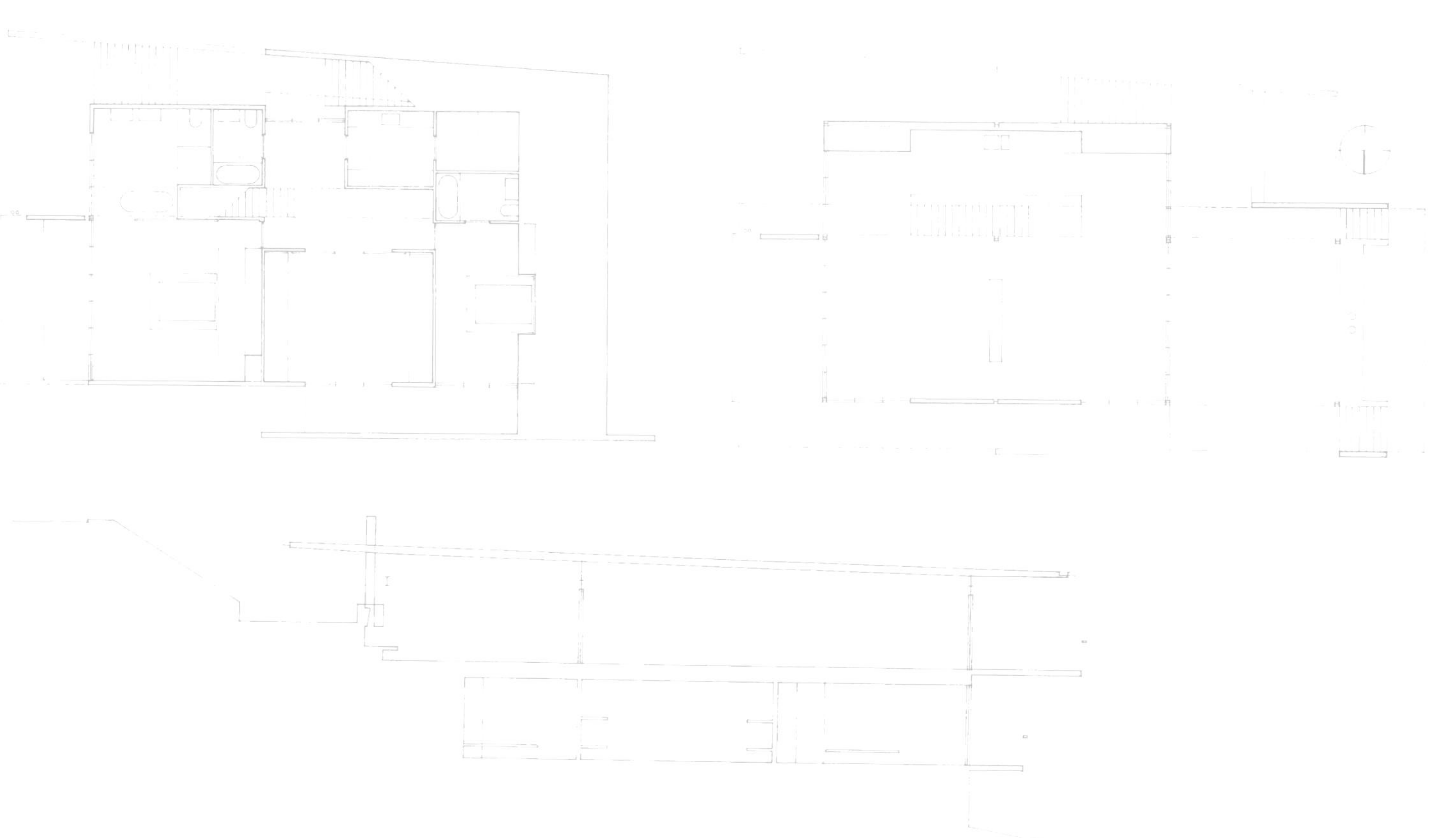

design Craig Rosevear

Archer House

Stone/Gale House, Chippendale

Chippendale is a suburb to the west of Sydney, populated by industrial buildings and warehouses alternated with old Victorian terrace houses. In a former bicycle factory, whose image is still vividly evident in the rough wood flooring, the exposed brick walls, and the large arched windows in the 30-meter northern façade, Hans Freymadl and Jonathan Richards have intervened with great sensitivity in a project of renovation and restructuring for residential use. The protagonists are a series of low transparent, opaque, or translucent diaphragms, which, parallel to the geometric axis of the entrance on the southern side, define the various spaces, underlining the open, essential, fluid dimension of the environment, enlivened by the colors of the collections of objects of the owners.

Chippendale est un faubourg situé à l'ouest de Sydney, historiquement siège d'industries et d'entrepôts, et connu pour ses enfilades de vieilles maisons ouvrières victoriennes. C'est là que, dans une ancienne usine de bicyclettes, Hans Freymadl et Jonathan Richards sont intervenus avec un projet de rénovation et de restructuration, en y créant un espace habitable faisant preuve d'une grande sensibilité. Conservant les parquets en bois brut, les murs en briques et les grandes fenêtres cintrées sur la façade nord longue de 30 mètres, ils ont construit une série de petits murets transparents, opaques ou translucides, qui, parallèles à l'axe géométrique de l'entrée du côté sud délimitent les différents espaces, soulignant la dimension ouverte, dépouillée et fluide du lieu, revigoré par les couleurs des différentes collections d'objets des maîtres de maison.

Chippendale ist ein Vorort im Westen Sydneys und traditionell ein Ort mit Industriebetrieben und Lagergebäuden, die sich abwechseln mit Reihen alter viktorianischer Terrace-Houses. Hier haben Hans Freymadl und Jonathan Richards eine ehemalige Fahrradfabrik mit großer Sensibilität renoviert und zu einem Wohnhaus umgebaut. Heute zeugen noch die unbearbeiteten Holzböden, die Mauern in Sichtbackstein und die großen Bogenfenster in der 30 Meter langen Nordfassade von der ehemaligen Nutzung. Die Grundidee des Projekts besteht in einer Reihe transparenter, opaker und durchscheinender niedriger Trennwände, welche die verschiedenen Räume parallel zur geometrischen Achse des Eingangs auf der Südseite unterteilen. Sie unterstreichen den offenen, geradlinigen und fließenden Charakter der Räume, die von der farbenfrohen Objektsammlung der Hausbesitzer belebt werden.

12

102. The living area, an open space with original plank flooring of Blackbutt wood. **103.** Jonathan Richards, one of the architects.

102. Le séjour, un espace ouvert avec les parquets d'origine en bois Blackbutt. **103.** Jonathan Richards, un des architectes.

102. Der *open space* des Wohnbereichs verfügt über die originalen Blackbutt-Holzdielen. **103.** Jonathan Richards, einer der Architekten.

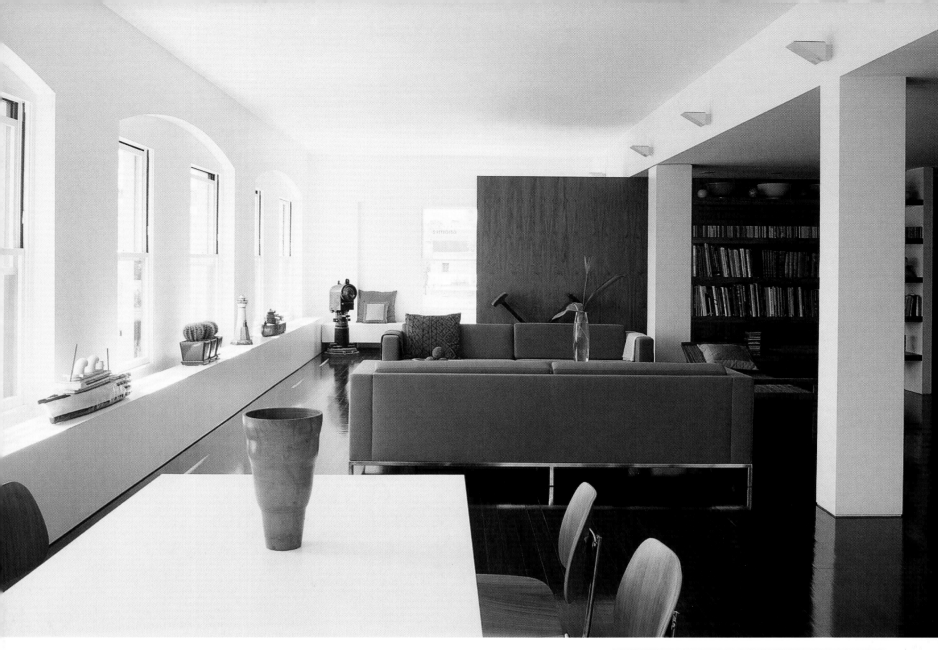

104. The living room with the brown divans and the custom-designed bookcase. The wooden partition separates the open space from the study. On the Balinese table, curios. **105.** The most ethnic zone of the living area with chaise longue and wooden vase from Bali, and cushions covered with Malaysian fabrics. In the background, an antique railroad lantern.

104. Le séjour avec des canapés marron et une bibliothèque en bois sur mesure. La paroi en bois sépare le séjour du petit bureau. Sur la table basse balinaise, des objets insolites. **105.** La partie plus ethnique du séjour avec une chaise longue et un pot en bois balinais. Les coussins sont revêtus de tissus malais. Au fond, une vieille lanterne de chemin de fer.

104. Im Wohnzimmer stehen braune Sofas und ein maßgearbeitetes Bücherregal aus Holz. Eine Holzwand trennt das Arbeitszimmer ab. Auf dem balinesischen Tischchen stehen eigenwillige Objekte. **105.** In der Ethno-Ecke des Wohnzimmers finden sich neben der Chaiselongue ein balinesischer Holztopf sowie Kissen mit Stoffbezügen aus Malaysia. Im Hintergrund sieht man eine alte Eisenbahnerlaterne.

Astridge/Galvin House, Surry Hills

13

For their own home in the Surry Hills district architects Abbie Galvin and David Astridge, partners in life and work, decided to work with light, a limited materic range based on steel, concrete, and glass left in their pure state, and with non-color, expressive tools that have led to a well-balanced transformation of a long, narrow industrial building, starting with the façade, which has been redesigned with a play of solid and empty, opaque and transparent portions. At ground level a large open space contains the kitchen, dining, and living areas, opening onto a small courtyard, while the upper level contains the bedrooms. The two levels are connected by a staircase-sculpture in steel reflecting the enthusiasm of the owners for the purist architecture of Louis Kahn and its organic relationship to furnishing.

Pour leur propre demeure dans le quartier de Surry Hills, les architectes Abbie Galvin et David Astridge, partenaires dans la vie comme dans le travail, ont choisi de travailler sur la lumière. Ils ont opté pour une palette réduite de matériaux bruts, se limitant à l'acier, le ciment et le verre, ainsi que pour la non couleur. Ces outils expressifs leur ont permis de reconvertir avec une belle sensibilité un ancien bâtiment industriel long et étroit, à commencer par la façade dont ils ont modifié les proportions en jouant sur les segments pleins ou vides, transparents ou opaques. Au rez-de-chaussée, un vaste espace ouvert réunit la cuisine, la salle à manger et le salon qui s'ouvrent sur une petite cour. L'étage supérieur est réservé aux chambres. Les deux niveaux sont reliés par un escalier sculptural en acier témoignant de la passion des propriétaires pour l'architecture puriste de Louis Kahn et sa traduction dans la décoration.

Bei dem Entwurf des eigenen Hauses im Wohnviertel Surry Hills haben sich die beiden Architekten Abbie Galvin und David Astridge, Partner im Privatleben und im Beruf, bewusst auf das Element Licht konzentriert. Sie arbeiteten mit einer beschränkten Palette von Materialien im Rohzustand, vor allem Stahl, Zement und Glas, verzichteten dabei auf den Einsatz von Farben und verwandelten das lange schmale ehemalige Industriegebäude vorsichtig in ein Wohnhaus. Auch die Fassade wurde neu proportioniert und lebt nun vom Spiel der Werte Fülle und Leere, Transparenz und Opazität. Im Erdgeschoss, einem *open space*, befinden sich Küche, Ess- und Wohnzimmer und blicken auf einen kleinen Hof, während oben der Schlafbereich liegt. Die beiden Ebenen sind durch eine skulpturale Treppe aus Chromstahl verbunden, welche die Bewunderung der Besitzer für die puristische Architektur von Louis Kahn und deren Umsetzung in der Einrichtung verrät.

111. Abbie Galvin and David Astridge.

111. Abbie Galvin et David Astridge.

111. Abbie Galvin und David Astridge.

112-113. The open space of the living-dining-kitchen area, whose continuity is underscored by the gray cement blocks of the walls and the white concrete flooring. Lounge chair by Charles and Ray Eames, *Tulip* table by Eero Saarinen, lamp-sculpture *Falkland* by Bruno Munari. The carpet is made of kangaroo skin.

112-113. L'espace ouvert réunit séjour, salle à manger et cuisine dans une continuité soulignée par les parpaings gris des murs et le ciment blanc du sol. Fauteuil de Charles et Ray Eames, table basse *Tulip* d'Eero Saarinen et lampe-sculpture *Falkland* de Bruno Munari de 1964. Le tapis est en peau de kangourou.

112-113. Der offene Raum, der den Wohn-, Ess- und Küchenbereich umfasst, wird in seinem Kontinuum betont durch die grauen Zementbacksteine der Wände und den weißen Zementfußboden. Den Lounge Chair entwarfen Charles und Ray Eames, das Tischchen *Tulip* ist von Eero Saarinen und die Leuchtenskulptur *Falkland* entwarf Bruno Munari 1964. Der Teppich ist aus Kängurufell gefertigt.

114. The dining area. The office table is combined with chairs by Charles and Ray Eames. The artwork is by renowned Australian photographer Bill Henson. **115.** The custom-designed kitchen with furnishings in dark gray lacquered wood and counter in black granite, which extends to become an integral part of the staircase-sculpture in steel. **116.** In the bedroom, Ikea stools based on a model by Alvar Aalto coexist with the lamp by Tom Dixon.

114. L'espace salle à manger. La table de bureau est entourée de chaises de Charles et Ray Eames. Le portrait est du photographe australien renommé Bill Henson. **115.** La cuisine design, avec des éléments en bois laqué gris foncé et un plan de travail en granit noir, fait partie intégrante de l'escalier-sculpture en acier. **116.** Dans la chambre à coucher, des tabourets Ikea d'après un modèle d'Alvar Aalto qui cohabitent avec une lampe de Tom Dixon.

114. Der Essbereich. Zum Schreibtisch gesellen sich Armlehnstühle von Charles und Ray Eames. Das Porträtfoto ist von dem renommierten australischen Fotografen Bill Henson. **115.** Die maßgefertigte Küche besteht aus lackierten dunkelgrauen Holzmöbeln und einer Arbeitsfläche aus schwarzem Granit. Der Raum bildet eine optische Einheit mit der skulpturalen Treppe aus Chromstahl. **116.** Im Schlafzimmer ein Hocker von Ikea nach einem Entwurf von Alvar Aalto sowie eine Leuchte von Tom Dixon.

Astridge/Galvin House

design David Astridge & Abbie Galvin

Astridge Galvin Architects
25 Griffin Street Surry Hills 2010 Sydney Australia Ph +61 2 9211 1825 F +61 2 9211 1825 email: Abbie_Galvin@bvn.com.au

Studies, experiences: Degree in architecture; practice with Mitchell Giurgola and Thorp, Engelen Moore, Bligh Voller Nield. **Favorites:** *Architects:* Louis Kahn, Le Corbusier, Ludwig Mies van der Rohe. **In Sydney they recommend:** *Fashion boutique:* Akira.

Etudes, expérience professionnelle: Diplôme d'architecture. Apprentissage auprès de Mitchell/Giurgola + Thorp, Engelen Moore, Bligh Voller Nield. **Leurs favoris:** *Architectes:* Louis Kahn, Le Corbusier, Ludwig Mies van der Rohe. **A Sydney, ils recommandent:** *Boutique de mode:* Akira.

Ausbildung, Erfahrungen: Abgeschlossenes Architektur-Studium. Tätigkeit im Büro von Mitchell/Giurgola + Thorp, Engelen Moore, Bligh Voller Nield. **Sie bewundern:** *Architekten:* Louis Kahn, Le Corbusier, Ludwig Mies van der Rohe. **Sie empfehlen in Sydney:** *Boutique:* Akira.

Astridge/Galvin House, Surry Hills

Year of construction: 1999
Année de réalisation: 1999
Baujahr: 1999

Area: 80 m^2 (interiors) + 65 m^2 (outdoor spaces) + 40 m^2 (roof)
Surface: 80 mq (intérieur) + 65 m^2 (extérieur) + 40 m^2 (toit)
Nutzfläche: 80 m^2 (innen) + 65 m^2 (Außenbereich) + 40 m^2 (Dach)

Cost: AUS $ 120,000
Coûts: AUS $ 120 000
Kosten: AUS $ 120 000

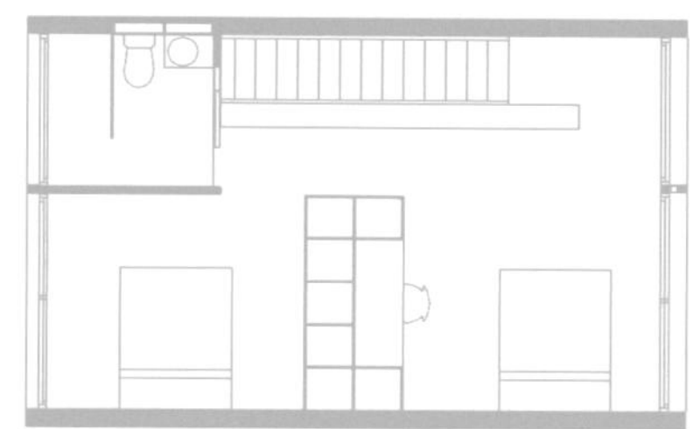

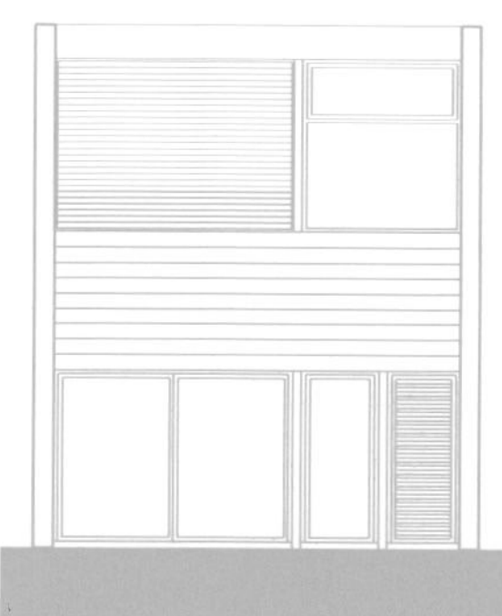

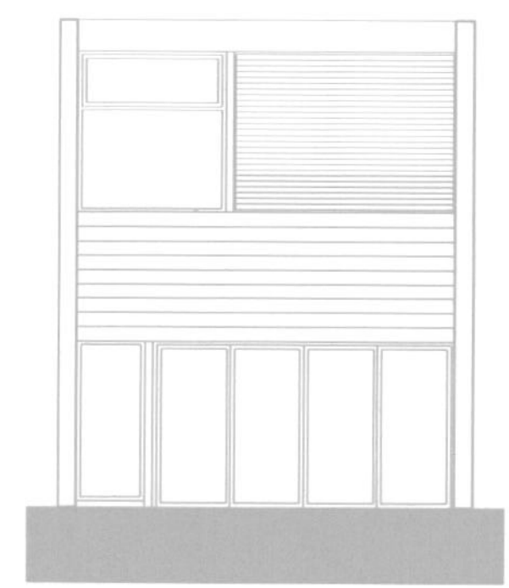

BISCUITS
CAKE
BREAD
1993
VIRGINIE
VIN DE PAYS D'OC
12X750 ML
WINE OF FRANCE
companion
The complete book of ingredients and recipes for the Australian kitchen

Crowley Apartment, Double Bay

Certain dwellings have the rare quality of being a mirror for the soul of their occupant. Homes that are personal projects, autobiographical narratives, of passions and memories, voyages and cherished dreams. This is the case of the home of the art dealer Kerry Crowley, director of the Yuill|Crowley Gallery in Sydney. A glamorous apartment, in the heart of the city, organized in small, intimate living spaces, filled with light filtered by light, colorful drapes. Rooms that are an erudite mixture of tradition and modernity, with free combinations of Australian rustic furnishings and design classics from the 40s and 50s, aboriginal crafts and artworks by young Australian talents like Stieg Persson and Robert MacPherson. A creative fusion of high culture and folk culture, valuable pieces and objets trouvés.

Certaines demeures ont la qualité rare refléter l'âme de ceux qui les habitent. Les maisons sont comme des projets personnels, des récits autobiographiques, racontant des passions et de souvenirs, des voyages et des rêves enfouis. C'est le cas de la maison de la galeriste Kerry Crowley, directrice de la Gallery Yuill|Crowley à Sydney, qui habite un appartement glamour, en plein cœur de la ville, composé de petits salons accueillants et intimes, baignés par une lumière feutrée, filtrée par de légers rideaux colorés. Les pièces sont un mélange savant de tradition et de modernité. Elles contiennent un assortiment de meubles rustiques australiens, de design des années 40 et 50, d'objets d'inspiration et de culture aborigènes et d'œuvres de jeunes artistes australiens tels que Stieg Persson et Robert MacPherson. Un mélange créatif de haute culture et de culture populaire, de pièces de valeur et d'objets trouvés.

Es gibt Wohnungen, die die seltene Gabe haben, die Seele ihrer Bewohner widerzuspiegeln. Häuser sind sehr persönliche Entwürfe und Lebensberichte, sie erzählen von Leidenschaften und Erinnerungen, von Reisen und Träumen. Dies gilt besonders für die Wohnung der Galeristin Kerry Crowley, Direktorin der Yuill|Crowley Gallery in Sydney, die in einem virtuos gestalteten Apartment mitten im Stadtzentrum lebt. Es besteht aus kleinen und gemütlichen Zimmern, in denen leichte farbige Vorhänge das hereinfallende Licht dämpfen. Die Einrichtung stellt einen kultivierten Mix aus Tradition und Moderne dar und ist ein freies Nebeneinander von australischen Country-Stücken und Designmöbeln der 40er und 50er Jahre, Objekten der Aboriginals sowie Werken junger australischer Künstler wie Stieg Persson und Robert MacPherson. So entsteht eine kreative Mischung von Kunst und Volkskunst, von wertvollen Objekten und Fundstücken.

14

119. The art dealer Kerry Crowley.

119. La galeriste Kerry Crowley.

119. Die Galeristin Kerry Crowley.

120. The dining room, separated from the living room by a glass door, is furnished with a table and chairs from the 40s. On the table, Mexican wooden candlesticks, Chinese cache-pots, a wooden plate from New Guinea; on the wall, a painting by Robert MacPherson. In the corner, a cabinet made with stacked soapboxes, for a 40s look. On the wooden stool, a sculpture by Robert MacPherson.

120. La salle à manger, séparée du séjour par une porte en verre, est meublée d'une table et de chaises des années 40. Sur la table, des chandeliers mexicains en bois, des cache-pots chinois, un plat en bois de Nouvelle-Guinée. Au mur, un tableau de Robert MacPherson. Dans le coin, un meuble réalisé avec une superposition de simples boîtes à savon des années 40. Sur l'escabeau en bois, une sculpture de Robert MacPherson.

120. Das Esszimmer ist durch eine Glastür vom Wohnzimmer abgetrennt und mit einem Tisch sowie Stühlen aus den 40er Jahren eingerichtet. Auf dem Tisch stehen mexikanische Kerzenständer aus Holz, chinesische Cachepots sowie ein Holzteller aus Neu-Guinea. An der Wand hängt ein Werk von Robert MacPherson und in der Ecke steht ein selbst gebautes Möbel, für das einfache Seifenkisten aus den 40er Jahren aufeinandergestellt wurden. Auf dem Holzhocker liegt eine Arbeit von Robert MacPherson.

121. The small, cosy living room with a fireplace with a white brick frame, furnished with a combination of upholstered furniture covered in white fabric reflecting the color of the carpeting, recovered wooden country objects, and colorful ethnic fabrics. On the American table made in 1910, wooden boxes, a collection of postcards, and two cups with feet from the 60s by Sandra Taylor.

121. Dans le séjour, petit et intime, avec sa cheminée en briques peintes en blanc, les canapés sont drapés de tissus blancs – qui reprennent la couleur de la moquette – et mariés avec des objets rustiques en bois ainsi que des étoffes ethniques colorées. Sur la table américaine de 1910, des boîtes en bois, une collection de cartes postales et deux coupes des années 60, montées sur des serres d'oiseaux et signées Sandra Taylor.

121. Klein und gemütlich ist das Wohnzimmer mit dem Kamin aus weißbemalten Backsteinen. Die Einrichtung spielt mit der Kontrastwirkung zwischen den weißen Polstern einerseits, die die Farbe des Teppichs aufnehmen, und den Country-Fundstücken sowie den farbenfrohen Ethno-Stoffen andererseits. Auf dem amerikanischen Tisch von 1910 stehen Holzschachteln, eine Postkartensammlung sowie zwei Becher mit Vogelfüßen von Sandra Taylor aus den 60er Jahren.

122. The music room, a small sitting room with light pink drapes, is dominated by a painting by Imants Tillers. In the corner, a wooden cabinet made in 1910 functions as a bookcase. The white and blue striped armchair is from the 50s.

122. Le salon de musique, une petite pièce aux voilages rouges, est dominé par un tableau d'Imants Tillers. Dans le coin, un meuble en bois datant de 1910 fait office de bibliothèque. Le fauteuil blanc à rayures bleues date des années 50.

122. Das Musikzimmer, ein kleiner Raum mit luftigen rosafarbenen Vorhängen, dominiert ein Gemälde von Imants Tillers. In der Ecke ein Holzmöbel aus dem Jahr 1910, das als Bücherregal dient. Der weiß-blau gestreifte Sessel ist aus den 50er Jahren.

Yuill|Crowley Gallery

Suite 1 8th Floor The Block 428 George Street 2000 Sydney Australia Ph +61 2 9223 1410 F +61 2 9232 1595 email: yuill_crowley@bigpond.com

Kerry Crowley has worked with contemporary artists for 30 years. In 1982 she co-founded Yuill|Crowley Gallery, one of Australia's most esteemed contemporary art galleries. **Favorites:** *Architects-designers:* Eileen Grey, Pierre Chareau. *Building:* MoMa, New York. *Furnishings:* Charles and Ray Eames. **In Sydney she recommends**: *Hotel:* Regent's Court. *Restaurant:* Odeon. *Design shop:* De De Ce. *Fashion boutique:* Belinda. *Museum:* Museum of Contemporary Art (MCA). *Bookstore:* Lesley McKay.

Kerry Crowley travaille avec des artistes contemporains depuis 30 ans. En 1982, elle a fondé avec un associé la Yuill|Crowley Gallery, l'une des galeries australiennes d'art contemporain les plus respectées. **Ses favoris:** *Architectes-designers:* Eileen Grey, Pierre Chareau. *Edifice:* MoMa, New York. *Objets, mobilier:* Charles et Ray Eames. **A Sydney, elle recommande**: *Hôtel:* Regent's Court. *Restaurant:* Odeon. *Boutique de design:* De De Ce. *Boutique de mode:* Belinda. *Musée:* Museum of Contemporary Art (MCA). *Librairie:* Lesley McKay.

Kerry Crowley arbeitet seit 30 Jahren mit zeitgenössischen Künstlern. Sie war 1982 Mitbegründerin der Yuill|Crowley Gallery, die eine der bedeutendsten australischen Galerien für zeitgenössische Kunst ist. **Sie bewundert**: *Architekten-Designer:* Eileen Grey, Pierre Chareau. *Gebäude:* MoMa, New York. *Einrichtung:* Charles und Ray Eames. **In Sydney empfiehlt sie:** *Hotel:* Regent's Court. *Restaurant:* Odeon. *Designgeschäft:* De De Ce. *Boutique:* Belinda. *Museum:* Museum of Contemporary Art (MCA). *Buchhandlung:* Lesley McKay.

design Kerry Crowley

Ormandy/Olsen House, Bronte Beach

The friendship of three young, creative talents was the start, 15 years ago, of the Dinosaur Designs venture, one of Australia's greatest successes in the world of designer objects and jewelry. Their latest conquests include the "Donna Karan Store" in New York and the "Eclectica" shop in Milan, where it is possible to find their objects in glass, ceramics, and colored resin. Two of the three founders, Stephen Ormandy and Louise Olsen, are also partners in life. Their house above Bronte Beach, one of the most famous for its giant waves appreciated by surfers, is a very personal mixture of colors, transparency, tactile and organic suggestions, in counterpoint with the purist architecture. The decor is based on furniture from the 60s and 70s, objects found during travels, and of course many products by Dinosaur Designs.

L'aventure de Dinosaur Designs est née il y a 15 ans de l'amitié de trois jeunes créatifs. Ce phénomène australien qui a rencontré un immense succès dans le monde des objets et bijoux de design compte parmi ses dernières conquêtes le «Donna Karan Store» à New York et la boutique «Eclectica» à Milan, qui présentent désormais ses objets en verre, céramique et résine colorée. Deux des trois fondateurs, Stephen Ormandy et Louise Olsen, ont prolongé leur association dans le privé. Leur maison au-dessus de Bronte Beach, une des plages les plus célèbres pour ses vagues gigantesques très prisées des surfeurs, est un mélange très personnel de couleurs, de transparences, de suggestions tactiles et organiques, contrastant avec les lignes puristes de l'architecture. Elle est aménagée avec des meubles et des objets des années 60 et 70, des souvenirs de voyage, et, naturellement, de nombreuses pièces de leur propre production.

Aus der Freundschaft von drei jungen kreativen Leuten entstand vor 15 Jahren das Abenteuer Dinosaur Designs, einer der größten australischen Erfolge im Bereich Objekt- und Schmuckdesign. Vor kurzem haben sie auch den »Donna Karan Store« in New York und »Eclectica« in Mailand erobert, wo man nun ihre Glas-, Keramik- und farbigen Kunstharzobjekte finden kann. Zwei der drei Gründer, Stephen Ormandy und Louise Olsen, haben im Privatleben ihre berufliche Verbindung fortgesetzt. Ihr Wohnhaus oberhalb von Bronte Beach, einem bekannten Strand und bei den Surfern sehr beliebt wegen der hohen Wellen, stellt eine sehr persönliche Kombination aus den Elementen Farbe und Transparenz sowie aus taktilen und organischen Eindrücken dar, die mit der puristischen Architektur kontrastieren. Die Einrichtungsgegenstände stammen aus den 60er und 70er Jahren und sind zum Teil Reiseerinnerungen, aber es gibt natürlich viele eigene Objekte.

125. Stephen Ormandy and Louise Olsen.

125. Stephen Ormandy et Louise Olsen.

125. Stephen Ormandy und Louise Olsen..

15

126. Corner of the living room with a 70s armchair. Vases by Dinosaur Designs, a lamp by Mitchell English, and, on the wall, an artwork by Australian artist Simeon Nelson. **127.** The reading corner, personalized with a surfboard beside the 1970s chair. A painting by John Olsen, Louise's father, forms a backdrop for vases by Dinosaur Designs.

126. Un angle du salon avec un fauteuil des années 70. Des vases de Dinosaur Designs, une lampe de Mitchell English et, sur le mur, un tableau-sculpture de l'artiste australien Simeon Nelson. **127.** Le coin bibliothèque a été personnalisé avec une planche de surf aux côtés d'un fauteuil des années 70. Un tableau de John Olsen, le père de Louise, au-dessus des vases de Dinosaur Designs.

126. Eine Ecke des Wohnzimmers mit einem Sessel aus den 70er Jahren. Die Vasen sind von Dinosaur Designs, die Leuchte von Mitchell English und an der Wand hängt eine Gemälde-Skulptur des australischen Künstlers Simeon Nelson. **127.** Die Bücherecke erhält einen persönlichen Akzent durch das Surfbrett neben dem Sessel aus den 70er Jahren. Ein Werk von John Olsen, dem Vater von Louise, hängt über Vasen von Dinosaur Designs.

Dualit

128. An original Dualit toaster from the 50s, Pavoni coffeemaker, cups, pitchers, and saucers in colored resin by Dinosaur Designs, vessels in glass and ceramic: Objects of different origins add texture to the clear lines of the spaces. In the kitchen and the dining room, with large windows and recycled wooden furnishings. In the corner, lamp by Verner Panton. **129.** The wooden kitchen, made to measure. In the foreground, a wood chair by Australian designer Grant Featherston. **130.** Free combinations are also found in the bedroom. Straw bags on a white 70s box used as a bedside table, with jewelry by Dinosaur Designs inside.

128. Un grille-pain original des années 50 de Dualit, une machine à café de Pavoni, des tasses, des cruches, des soucoupes en résine colorée de Dinosaur Designs, de la vaisselle en verre et en céramique: autant d'objets de provenances diverses et variées qui mettent en valeur les lignes claires des pièces. La cuisine et la salle à manger sont dominées par de grandes fenêtres et des meubles de récupération en bois. Dans l'angle, des luminaires de Verner Panton. **129.** La cuisine toute en bois, réalisée sur mesure. Au premier plan, un siège en bois du designer australien Grant Featherston. **130.** Même dans la chambre à coucher, les mélanges esthétiques sont de mise. Sur un cube blanc des années 70 reconverti en table de nuit, des paniers en paille. Dans le cube, des bijoux de Dinosaur Designs.

128. Ein Original-Toaster aus den 50er Jahren von Dualit, eine Kaffeemaschine von Pavoni, Tassen, Krüge, Unterteller aus farbigem Kunstharz von Dinosaur Designs, Tafelgeschirr aus Glas oder Keramik: Objekte verschiedenster Herkunft lockern die klaren Linien der Räume auf. Die Küche und das Esszimmer sind großzügig konzipierte Räume mit großen Glasfenstern. Die Holzmöbeln sind Fundstücke. In der Ecke hängt eine Leuchte von Verner Panton. **129.** Die Küche wurde in Holz maßgearbeitet. Im Vordergrund steht ein Holzstuhl des australischen Designers Grant Featherston. **130.** Auch die Schlafzimmereinrichtung wird beherrscht von einem freien Nebeneinander verschiedener Stile. Auf dem weißen Würfel aus den 70er Jahren, der als Nachttisch dient, stehen Strohtaschen und in der Aushöhlung liegt Schmuck von Dinosaur Designs.

Dinosaur Designs

585 Elizabeth Street Strawberry Hills 2010 Sydney Australia Ph +61 2 9698 3500 F +61 2 9698 3533 email: dinosaur@zip.com.au www.dinosaurdesigns.com.au

Louise Olsen and **Liane Rossler** were born in Sydney. **Stephen Ormandy** was born in Melbourne. **Studies, experiences, projects:** 1985 they established Dinosaur Designs. 1986 Post Graduate degree of Professional Art Studies at City Art Institute, Sydney. 1989 exhibited in "Australian Fashion The Contemporary Art" exhibition at Victoria & Albert Museum, London. 1992 exhibited at the Australian Pavilion, Expo. 1996 opened fourth retail outlet in Sydney. 1998 represented at Salone del mobile of Milan. 2000 commissioned to design installation for the Olympic Arts festival, Sydney. 2001 opened first international Dinosaur Designs store in Nolita, New York. **Favorites:** *Architects:* Penny Collins and Huw Turner, Glenn Murcutt, Sam Marshall. *Designers:* Harry Bertoia, Charles and Ray Eames. **In Sydney they recommend:** *Hotel:* Park Hyatt Sydney. *Fashion boutiques:* Akira Isogawa, Collette Dinnigan, Belinda. *Museum:* Art Gallery of New South Wales. *Bookstore:* Ariel.

Louise Olsen et **Liane Rossler** sont nées à Sydney, et **Stephen Ormandy** à Melbourne. **Etudes, expérience professionnelle, projets:** 1985, naissance de Dinosaur Designs. 1986, diplôme de troisième cycle en Art Professionnel au City Art Institute de Sydney. 1989, participation à l'exposition «Australian Fashion The Contemporary Art» au Victoria & Albert Museum, Londres. 1992, exposition au pavillon australien de l'Expo. 1996, ouverture de leur quatrième boutique à Sydney. 1998, participent au Salon du Meuble de Milan. 2000, installation de design à l'Olympic Arts Festival à Sydney. 2001, ouverture de la première boutique internationale Dinosaur Designs à Nolita, New York. **Leurs favoris:** *Architectes:* Penny Collins et Huw Turner, Glenn Murcutt, Sam Marshall. *Designers:* Harry Bertoia, Charles et Ray Eames. **A Sydney, ils recommandent:** *Hôtel:* Park Hyatt Sydney. *Boutiques de mode:* Akira Isogawa, Collette Dinnigan, Belinda. *Musée:* Art Gallery of New South Wales. *Librairie:* Ariel.

Louise Olsen und **Liane Rossler** sind in Sydney geboren, **Stephen Ormandy** in Melbourne. **Ausbildung, Erfahrungen, Projekte:** 1985 Gründung von Dinosaur Designs. 1986 Abschluss der Professional Art Studies am City Art Institute in Sydney. 1989 Teilnahme an der Ausstellung »Australian Fashion The Contemporary Art« im Victoria & Albert Museum in London. 1992 Ausstellung im australischen Pavillon auf der Expo. 1996 Eröffnung ihres vierten Store in Sydney. 1998 Teilnahme am Mailänder Salone del Mobile. 2000 Auftrag für eine Design-Installation des Olympic Arts Festival in Sydney. 2001 öffnete der erste internationale Dinosaur Designs Store in Nolita in New York. **Sie bewundern:** *Architekten:* Penny Collins und Huw Turner, Glenn Murcutt, Sam Marshall. *Designer:* Harry Bertoia, Charles und Ray Eames. **Sie empfehlen in Sydney:** *Hotel:* Park Hyatt Sydney. *Boutiquen:* Akira Isogawa, Collette Dinnigan, Belinda. *Museum:* Art Gallery of New South Wales. *Buchhandlung:* Ariel.

Ormandy/Olsen House, Bronte Beach

Year of construction: 1999	**Area:** 160 m^2	**Cost:** not available
Année de réalisation: 1999	**Surface:** 160 m^2	**Coûts:** non indiqués
Baujahr: 1999	**Nutzfläche:** 160 m^2	**Kosten:** ungenannt

design Stephen Ormandy & Louise Olsen

Reynolds House, Double Bay

With a large terrace overlooking Double Bay, this apartment restructured by Iain Halliday takes part in the allure of the landscape thanks to a play of mirror-finish and transparent glass walls to create effects of reflection and dilation, emphasized by the whiteness of the walls and ceilings. From the entrance one directly enters the living area, with a sliding glass door open to the landscape, duplicating the sliding mirror door that conceals the bedroom, with its black walls and a single window in frosted glass. This introverted character is contrasted in the other zones, especially in the living area, but also in the kitchen and a bath that open, without buffers, toward the glazing, like devices designed for a sense of visual well-being.

Pourvu d'une vaste terrasse donnant sur Double Bay, l'appartement restructuré par Iain Halliday jouit au mieux du paysage grâce à un jeu de parois en miroir et de baies vitrées qui créent des reflets sur le blanc des murs et des plafonds et agrandissent l'espace. L'entrée donne directement sur le séjour, dominé par une baie vitrée coulissante s'ouvrant sur la vue qui se reflète dans la paroi coulissante en miroir de la chambre à coucher. Celle-ci, avec ses murs badigeonnés en noir et une seule fenêtre en verre satiné, possède un caractère introverti aux antipodes des autres parties de l'appartement: notamment le séjour, mais également la cuisine et une salle de bains qui s'ouvrent directement sur la baie vitrée, comme entièrement absorbées par le bien-être environnant.

Eine große Terrasse mit Ausblick auf die Double Bay gehört zu der Wohnung, die der Architekt Iain Halliday umgebaut hat. Diese wird geradezu Teil der herrlichen Landschaft dank der Spiegel- und hohen Glaswände, die – unterstützt vom Weiß der Wände und der Decke – das Licht wirkungsvoll reflektieren und die Räume größer erscheinen lassen. Vom Eingang gelangt man direkt in das Wohnzimmer, das sich über eine Glasschiebetür zur Landschaft hin öffnet. Diese wiederum spiegelt sich in der verspiegelten Schiebewand, hinter der sich der Schlafbereich verbirgt. Schwarze Wände und ein einziges Fenster aus satiniertem Glas verleihen diesem einen introvertierten Charakter. Dieser Eindruck wird von den anderen Wohnbereichen wieder ausgeglichen, denn vor allem das Wohnzimmer, aber auch die Küche und das Badezimmer öffnen sich ohne jeden Sichtschutz in einer Glasfront und verschmelzen so mit der Umgebung.

16

132. View of the living area with the *Y's* Chair designed by Christophe Pillet. **133.** Iain Halliday, partner in the studio Burley Katon Halliday.

132. Détail du séjour avec la chaise *Y's* dessinée par Christophe Pillet. **133.** Iain Halliday, associé du cabinet Burley Katon Halliday.

132. Detailansicht des Wohnzimmers mit dem Stuhl *Y's* von Christophe Pillet. **133.** Iain Halliday, Teilhaber des Architekturbüros Burley Katon Halliday.

134-135. The rigorously white living room with the large sliding glass doors, overlooking the bay and limestone flooring, is punctuated by sculptural seating, including *La Chaise* by Charles and Ray Eames, a *Bird* armchair with hassock from Harry Bertoia, and the *Jack* luminous unit by Tom Dixon. To the left, the block divider faced in ebony concealing the kitchen. **136.** The bedroom, separated from the living room by a mirrored sliding door, is furnished with a white bed and a bedside unit, with the *Tizio* lamp by Richard Sapper. Reflected in the mirror, the dining room with custom table and chairs from Antonio Citterio.

134-135. Le séjour, rigoureusement blanc, avec sa grande baie vitrée coulissante donnant sur la baie et son sol en dalles de travertin. Ici et là, des sièges-sculptures, dont *La Chaise* de Charles et Ray Eames et un fauteuil *Bird* avec pouf de Harry Bertoia. Le luminaire *Jack* est de Tom Dixon. On entrevoit la cloison plaquée d'ébène derrière laquelle est cachée la cuisine. **136.** La chambre à coucher, séparée du séjour par une paroi coulissante en miroir, est meublée d'un lit blanc et d'une table de nuit sur laquelle est posée une lampe *Tizio* de Richard Sapper. Dans le miroir se reflète l'espace salle à manger, avec une table dessinée sur mesure et des sièges d'Antonio Citterio.

134-135. Das Wohnzimmer mit dem Kalkstein-Fußboden ist konsequent in schlichtem Weiß gehalten, eine große Glasschiebetür gibt den Blick frei auf die Bucht. Unter den skulptural wirkenden Sitzmöbeln befinden sich *La Chaise* von Charles und Ray Eames sowie ein *Bird*-Sessel mit Hocker von Harry Bertoia. Das Leuchtelement *Jack* ist von Tom Dixon. Hinter der mit Ebenholz verkleideten Trennwand verbirgt sich die Küche. **136.** Das Schlafzimmer wird vom Wohnzimmer abgetrennt durch eine verspiegelte Schiebetür und enthält ein weißes Bett sowie ein Nachttischchen, auf dem die Leuchte *Tizio* von Richard Sapper steht. Im Spiegel sieht man den Essbereich mit dem maßgefertigten Tisch und Stühlen von Antonio Citterio.

LIGHT ON YOGA

Burley Katon Halliday

6a Liverpool Street Paddington 2021 Sydney Australia Ph +61 2 9332 2233 F +61 2 9360 2048 email: bkh@bkh.com.au www.bkh.com.au

Iain Halliday was born in 1961 in Sydney. **Studies, experiences:** 1982 degree in Interior Design from Sydney College of Art. 1983/84 architectural studies at UTS. 1983/84 practice with Marsh Freedman & Associates. 1984–1986: Neil Burley & Partners. 1986 now partner and director of Burley Katon Halliday. **Favorites:** *Architect:* Ludwig Mies van der Rohe. *Building:* Fallingwater House by Frank Lloyd Wright in Bear Run, Pennsylvania. *Designers:* Jean-Michel Frank, Antonio Citterio, Philippe Starck. *Furnishing: Barcelona* chair by Ludwig Mies van der Rohe. **In Sydney he recommends:** *Hotel:* Kirketon. *Fashion boutique:* Louis Vuitton. *Gallery:* Roslyn Oxley 9 Gallery. *Museum:* The Art Gallery of New South Wales. *Bookstore:* Dome Books.

Iain Halliday est né en 1961 à Sydney. **Etudes, expérience professionnelle:** 1982, diplôme de décoration d'intérieur du Sydney College of Art. 1983/84, études d'architecture à l'UTS, Sydney. 1983/84, apprentissage chez Marsh Freedman & Associates. 1984–1986, Neil Burley & Partners. De 1986 à aujourd'hui, associé et directeur de Burley Katon Halliday. **Ses favoris:** *Architecte:* Ludwig Mies van der Rohe. *Edifice:* la maison Fallingwater de Frank Lloyd Wright à Bear Run, Pennsylvanie. *Designers:* Jean-Michel Frank, Antonio Citterio, Philippe Starck. *Objets, mobilier:* La chaise *Barcelona* de Ludwig Mies van der Rohe. **A Sydney, il recommande:** *Hôtel:* Kirketon. *Boutique de mode:* Louis Vuitton. *Galerie d'art:* Roslyn Oxley 9 Gallery. *Musée:* The Art Gallery of New South Wales. *Librairie:* Dome Books.

Iain Halliday ist 1961 in Sydney geboren. **Ausbildung, Erfahrungen:** 1982 Abschluss des Interior-Design-Studiums am Sydney College of Art. 1983/84 Architekturstudium an der UTS in Sydney. 1983/84: Zusammenarbeit mit Marsh Freedman & Associates. 1984–1986: Zusammenarbeit mit Neil Burley & Partners. Seit 1986 Teilhaber und Leiter des Architekturbüros Burley Katon Halliday. **Er bewundert:** *Architekt:* Ludwig Mies van der Rohe. *Gebäude:* Fallingwater House von Frank Lloyd Wright in Bear Run, Pennsylvania. *Designer:* Jean-Michel Frank, Antonio Citterio, Philippe Starck. *Möbeldesign:* Sessel *Barcelona* von Ludwig Mies van der Rohe. **Er empfiehlt in Sydney:** *Hotel:* Kirketon. *Boutique:* Louis Vuitton. *Galerie:* Roslyn Oxley 9 Gallery. *Museum:* The Art Gallery of New South Wales. *Buchhandlung:* Dome Books.

Reynolds House, Double Bay

Year of construction: 1998	Area: not available	Cost: AUS $ 450,000
Année de réalisation: 1998	Surface: non indiquée	Coûts: AUS $ 450 000
Baujahr: 1998	Nutzfläche: ungenannt	Kosten: AUS $ 450 000

design Iain Halliday

Reynolds House

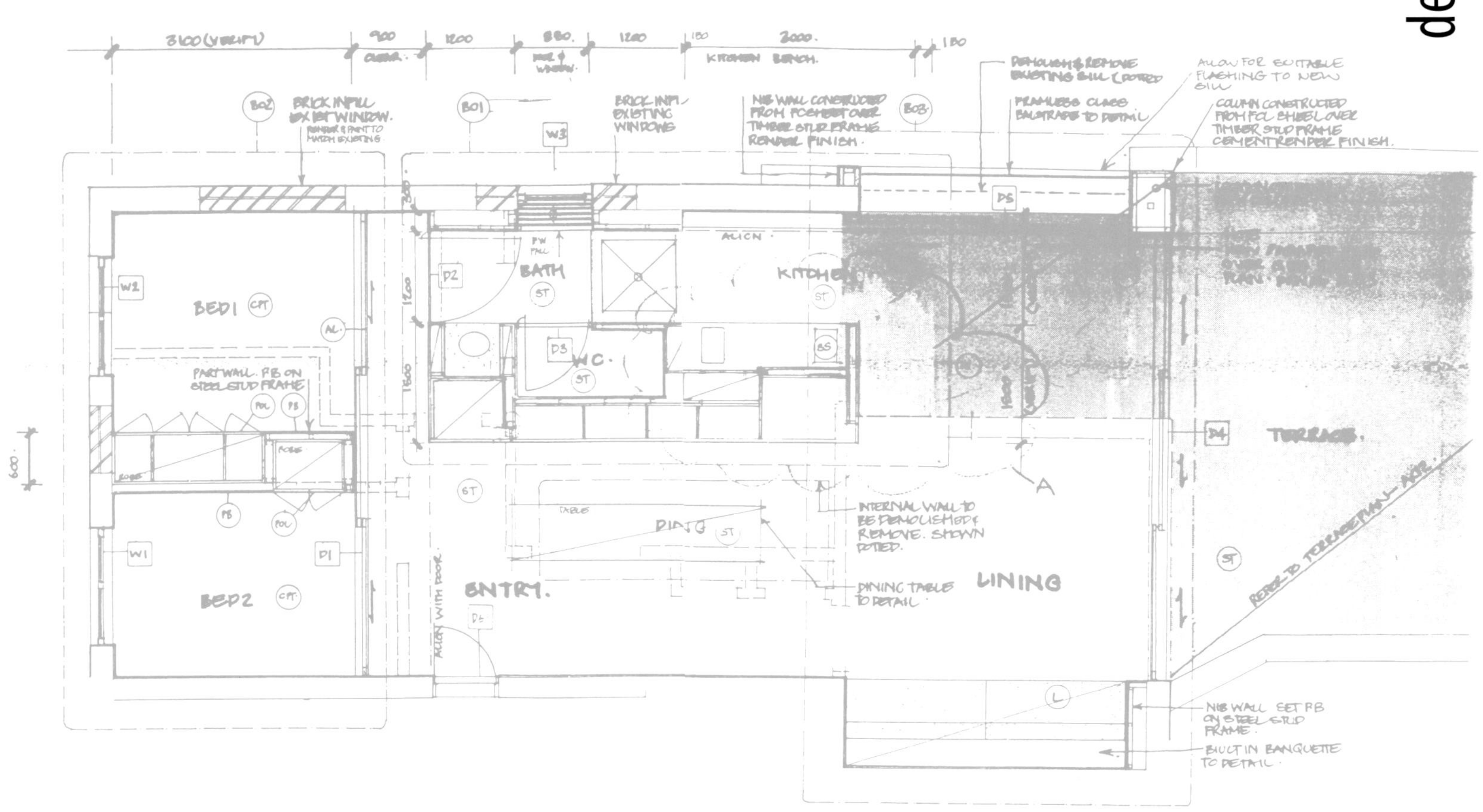
BED1
BED2
BATH
W.C.
ENTRY.
LIVING
TERRACE.

28 Billyard Avenue House, Elizabeth Bay

28 Billyard Avenue is a super-project by the Burley Katon Halliday studio, well-known for their modern, minimal style. This is an exclusive complex composed of six waterfront homes: apartments with terraces, gardens, swimming pool, and private dock on Elizabeth Bay. The residential unit shown here is on the second floor, and sums up the characteristics of the kind of luxury living in demand in Sydney: large, fluid spaces, ample glass surfaces with a large curved portion in the living area, sophisticated materials that are both durable and natural, like marble, stone, and wood, applied in contrasting juxtaposition with shiny steel and discreet touches of color. A neutral scenario where every choice is governed by the landscape and the natural light.

Le 28 Billyard Avenue est un immense projet réalisé par le cabinet Burley Katon Halliday, connu pour sa patte moderne et minimaliste. Ce luxueux immeuble en bord de mer est composé de six appartements avec terrasse, jardin, piscine et embarcadère privé dans la baie d'Elizabeth. Celui qui a été photographié ici est situé au second étage. Par son côté unique, il réunit tous les attributs d'une résidence de grand standing très recherchée à Sydney: des espaces généreux et fluides, de grandes baies vitrées avec une longue partie incurvée dans le séjour, des matériaux sophistiqués naturels et durables tel que le marbre, la pierre et le bois, qui contrastent avec l'éclat de l'acier et les petites touches de couleur ici et là. C'est un décor construit à partir d'une base neutre, où chaque choix a été influencé par le paysage environnant et la lumière extérieure.

28 Billyard Avenue ist ein virtuoses Projekt des Architekturbüros Burley Katon Halliday, dessen Markenzeichen eine moderne minimalistische Architektur ist. Es handelt hier um ein exklusives Gebäude aus sechs einzelnen *waterfront homes*: Apartments mit Terrasse, Garten, Pool sowie einem privaten Landungssteg an der Elizabeth Bay. Die abgebildete Wohnung befindet sich im zweiten Stock und fasst in einmaliger Weise die Kennzeichen der Luxuswohnungen zusammen, die in Sydney hoch im Kurs stehen: großzügig-fließende Räume, großflächige, gebogene Glaswände im Wohnbereich sowie ausgesuchte haltbare und natürliche Materialien wie Marmor, Stein und Holz, die mit glitzerndem Chromstahl und einigen kleinen Farbtupfern kontrastieren – ein neutrales Szenarium, in dem jedes Detail auf die äußere Umgebung und die Lichtverhältnisse Rücksicht nimmt.

17

138. 28 Billyard Avenue House with Elizabeth Bay in the background. **139.** David Katon, partner in the studio Burley Katon Halliday.

138. La maison 28 Billyard Avenue avec l'Elizabeth Bay en arrière-plan. **139.** David Katon, associé du cabinet Burley Katon Halliday.

138. 28 Billyard Avenue House mit der Elizabeth Bay im Hintergrund. **139.** David Katon, Mitinhaber des Architekturbüros Burley Katon Halliday.

1
2
3
4
5

140. The severe staircase in black granite, glass, and metal connecting the levels of the complex, which contains six residential units of different sizes. **141.** Another common area: the entrance with the mailboxes in shiny metal. **142-143.** View of the living area, defined by a large curved glass wall for a relationship of osmosis with the nature outside, also reflected in the light marble flooring. The custom-designed table in wood and steel is combined with the *Brno* chairs by Ludwig Mies van der Rohe.

140. L'escalier froid en granit noir, verre et métal qui relie les six appartements de différentes tailles que compte l'immeuble. **141.** Autre partie commune: l'entrée avec des boîtes aux lettres en métal brillant. **142-143.** Détail de la partie séjour. La vaste paroi vitrée incurvée recherche l'osmose avec la nature extérieure, qui se reflète jusque sur le sol en marbre clair. La table design en bois et acier est entourée de sièges *Brno* de Ludwig Mies van der Rohe.

140. Eine kühle Treppe aus schwarzem Granit, Glas und Metall verbindet die einzelnen Etagen des Gebäudes, das aus sechs Wohnungen von unterschiedlichem Zuschnitt besteht. **141.** Diese teilen sich den Eingang mit den glänzenden Metallbriefkästen. **142-143.** Eine Ecke des Wohnbereichs mit der geschwungenen Glasfront in voller Höhe, die die Grenze zwischen den Innenräumen und der umgebenden Natur aufhebt. Die Landschaft spiegelt sich in dem hellen Marmor-Fußboden. Um den maßgefertigten Tisch aus Holz und Chromstahl stehen die Sessel *Brno* von Ludwig Mies van der Rohe.

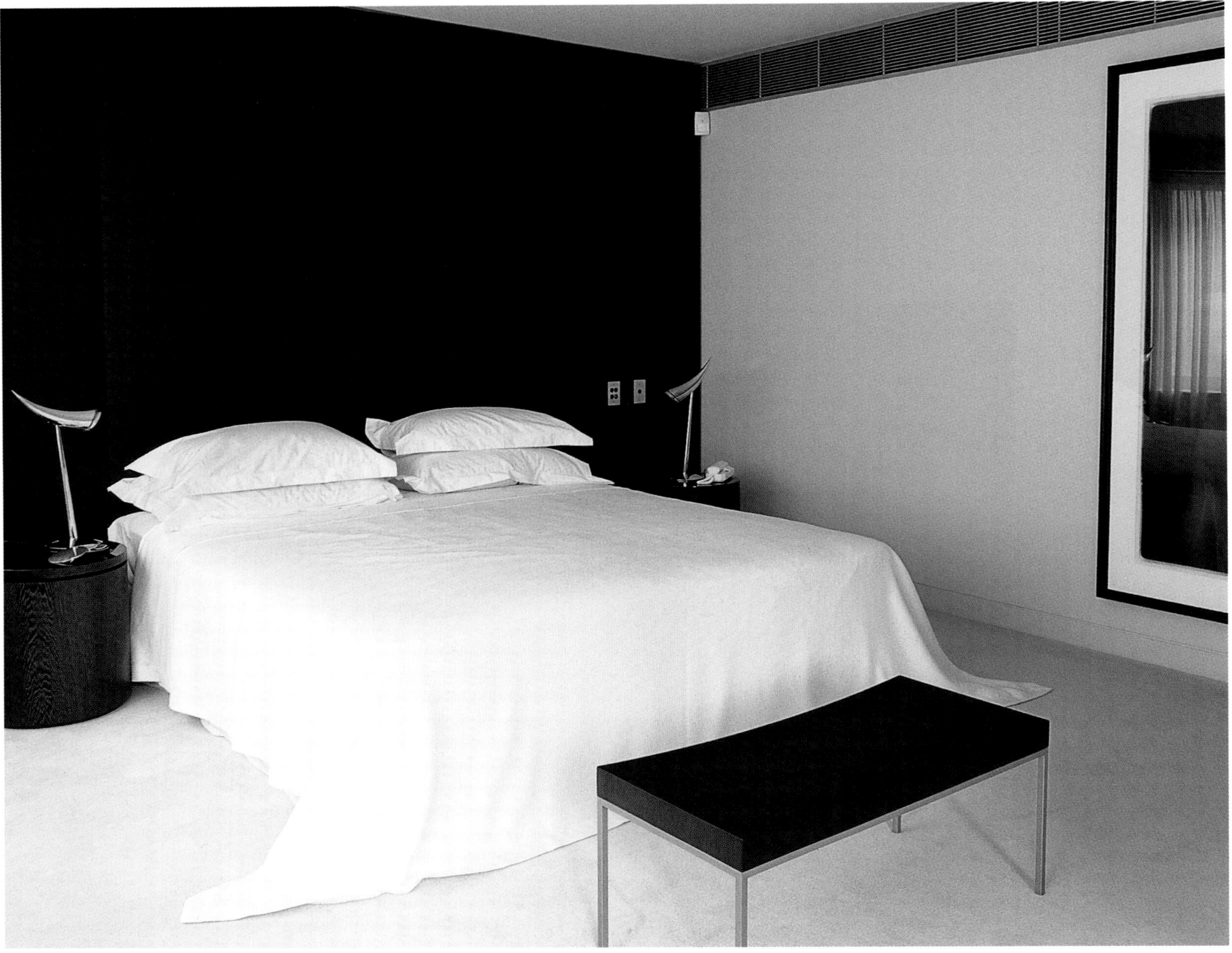

144. The essential design of the bedroom, with rigorously white carpeting and bed, creates a refined dynamic contrast with the dark tones of the furnishings and the silk panels on the headboard-partition. On the bedside units, *Ará* lamps designed by Philippe Starck in 1988.

144. Dans la chambre à coucher réduite à l'essentiel, la moquette et le lit d'un blanc rigoureux forment un contraste dynamique avec les teintes sombres du décor et des panneaux de soie qui tapissent le mur en tête de lit. Sur les tables de nuit, des lampes *Ará* dessinées par Philippe Starck en 1988.

144. Von grundlegender Schlichtheit ist das Schlafzimmer mit dem Teppich und dem Bett von konsequentem Weiß. Es bildet einen raffinierten dynamischen Kontrast zu den dunklen Farben der Einrichtung und der Seidenbahnen an der Kopfwand. Auf den Nachttisch stehen die Leuchten *Ará*, die Philippe Starck 1988 entwarf.

Burley Katon Halliday
6a Liverpool Street Paddington 2021 Sydney Australia Ph +61 2 9332 2233 F +61 2 9360 2048 email: bkh@bkh.com.au www.bkh.com.au

Works constructed by the studio Burley Katon Halliday include: Salt Restaurant, Paramount Restaurant, Darley Street Thai Restaurant, Kirketon Hotel, Powerhouse Museum (Decorative Art Galleries). **Favorites:** *Architect:* Ludwig Mies van der Rohe. *Buildings:* House Fallingwater in Bear Run, Pennsylvania, and Guggenheim Museum, New York, by Frank Lloyd Wright. *Designers:* Jean-Michel Frank, Antonio Citterio, Philippe Starck. *Furnishing: Barcelona* chair by Ludwig Mies van der Rohe. **In Sydney they recommend:** *Hotel:* Kirketon. *Restaurant:* Billy Kwong. *Fashion boutique:* Louis Vuitton. *Gallery:* Roslyn Oxley 9 Gallery. *Museum:* The Art Gallery of New South Wales. *Bookstore:* Dome Books.

Parmi les réalisations du cabinet Burley Katon Halliday: Le Salt Restaurant, le Paramount Restaurant, le Darley Street Thai Restaurant, l'hôtel Kirketon, les galeries des arts appliqués au Powerhouse Museum. **Leurs favoris:** *Architecte:* Ludwig Mies van der Rohe. *Edifices:* la maison Fallingwater à Bear Run, Pennsylvanie, et le Guggenheim Museum, New York, de Frank Lloyd Wright. *Designers:* Jean-Michel Frank, Antonio Citterio, Philippe Starck. *Objets, mobilier:* la chaise *Barcelona* de Ludwig Mies van der Rohe. **A Sydney, ils recommandent:** *Hôtel:* Kirketon. *Restaurant:* Billy Kwong. *Boutique de mode:* Louis Vuitton. *Galerie d'art:* Roslyn Oxley 9 Gallery. *Musée:* The Art Gallery of New South Wales. *Librairie:* Dome Books.

Einige Projekte des Architekturbüros Burley Katon Halliday: Salt Restaurant, Paramount Restaurant, Darley Street Thai Restaurant, Kirketon Hotel, Decorative Arts Galleries im Powerhouse Museum. **Sie bewundern:** *Architekt:* Ludwig Mies van der Rohe. *Gebäude:* Fallingwater House in Bear Run, Pennsylvania, und Guggenheim Museum, New York, von Frank Lloyd Wright. *Designer:* Jean-Michel Frank, Antonio Citterio, Philippe Starck. *Möbeldesign:* Sessel *Barcelona* von Ludwig Mies van der Rohe. **Sie empfehlen in Sydney:** *Hotel:* Kirketon. *Restaurant:* Billy Kwong. *Boutique:* Louis Vuitton. *Galerie:* Roslyn Oxley 9 Gallery. *Museum:* The Art Gallery of New South Wales. *Buchhandlung:* Dome Books.

28 Billyard Avenue House, Elizabeth Bay

Year of construction: 1998
Année de réalisation: 1998
Baujahr: 1998

Area: 275 m^2 (interiors) + 36 m^2 (outdoor spaces)
Superficie: 275 m^2 (intérieur) + 36 m^2 (extérieur)
Superficie: 275 m^2 (innen) + 36 m^2 (Außenbereich)

Cost: AUS $ 5 million
Coûts: AUS $ 5 million
Kosten: AUS $ 5 Millionen

design Burley Katon Halliday

28 Billyard Avenue House

Lift
Entry
Kitchen & Meals Area
Dining Area
Terrace
Master Bedroom
Bedroom 2
Bedroom 3
Bedroom 4
Living Area

Katon Residence, Elizabeth Bay

David Katon, partner in the studio Burley Katon Halliday, is one of Sydney's most successful interior designers. Known for his essential, glamorous style applied to restaurants, hotels, museums, and homes, for his own residence he has selected a small 50s apartment whose vestiges can be seen in the wooden window frames in the heart of the city, near Elizabeth Bay. Filled with a relaxing atmosphere, the space composed of a few rooms on a corridor is visually expanded thanks to the full-height mirrors attached to the walls. The effect is one of spatial multiplication of the living area, where the specular walls reflect objects, furnishing classics, and the bright light of the outdoors, amplified in its luminosity by the absolute white of the interiors.

David Katon, associé du cabinet Burley Katon Halliday, est l'un des décorateurs d'intérieur les plus prisés de Sydney. Célèbre pour l'empreinte dépouillée et glamour qu'il a laissée sur des restaurants, des hôtels, des musées et des demeures privées, il a choisi d'habiter dans un petit appartement des années 50, dont il reste les fenêtres en bois, en plein cœur de la ville, près d'Elizabeth Bay. Imprégné d'une atmosphère qui invite à la détente, l'espace composé de quelques pièces alignées le long d'un couloir a été agrandi par effet optique en tapissant certains murs de miroirs du sol au plafond. Le volume du séjour s'en trouve ainsi multiplié à l'infini, ses parois reflétant les objets et des meubles devenus des classiques du design ainsi qu'une vue étourdissante sur l'extérieur, le tout rendu encore plus absolu et lumineux par le blanc omniprésent.

David Katon, Mitinhaber des Architekturbüros Burley Katon Halliday, ist einer der gefragtesten Interior Designer von Sydney. Die von ihm gestalteten Restaurants, Hotels, Museen und Wohnhäuser sind unverwechselbar in ihrer Sachlichkeit und Eleganz. Für sich selbst hat er im Stadtzentrum nahe der Elizabeth Bay eine kleine Wohnung aus den 50er Jahren ausgesucht, die noch über die originalen Holzfenster verfügt. Die Atmosphäre lädt zum Entspannen ein, und die Wohnung besteht aus einigen Zimmern, die sich an einem Korridor entlang hintereinander aufreihen und durch die ausgewogene raumhohe Wandverkleidung mit Spiegelglas größer erscheinen. Besonders im Wohnzimmer wird dieser Kunstgriff effektvoll eingesetzt, denn an den Wänden spiegeln sich Objekte, Designklassiker und die atemberaubende Landschaft. Das vorherrschende Weiß der Räume unterstützt diese Wirkung noch.

18

146. The living area is visually opened by the floor-to-ceiling mirrors on the wall. **147.** David Katon, the interior designer and owner.

146. Le séjour est agrandi par l'effet visuel d'un mur tapissé de miroirs. **147.** David Katon, le décorateur d'intérieur et propriétaire.

146. Das Wohnzimmer wirkt durch die raumhohe Spiegelwand größer. **147.** David Katon, der Interior Designer und Besitzer.

Harry Seidler
New York Interiors
A HOUSE IS NOT A HOME
GA
ARCHITECTURE 2

148-149. The living-dining area with the original 50s windows in white wood is a lucid, luminous space, in which two mirror walls reflect objects, people, and design protagonists. Like the *Tulip* tables by Eero Saarinen, the *Jack* luminous unit by Tom Dixon, the *Bu Bu* stool by Philippe Starck. **150.** The studio: On the desk by Jean Nouvel an artwork in perspex by Mike Kitching adds a note of color. **151.** The custom-designed kitchen, enclosed in a block, features a steel tea set by Arne Jacobsen. The dining area is furnished with a table by Eero Saarinen, combined with the *Selene* chairs designed by Vico Magistretti in 1969.

148-149. Le séjour-salle à manger avec ses fenêtres des années 50 en bois blanc est un espace clair et lumineux. Les deux murs tapissés de miroirs reflètent les objets, les personnes et des classiques du design tels que les tables basses *Tulip* d'Eero Saarinen, le luminaire *Jack* de Tom Dixon, le tabouret *Bu Bu* de Philippe Starck. **150.** L'atelier. Sur le bureau de Jean Nouvel, un œuvre en Perspex de Mike Kitching apporte une touche de couleur. **151.** Dans la cuisine design enfermée dans un bloc, un service à thé d'Arne Jacobsen en acier. L'espace salle à manger est meublé d'une table d'Eero Saarinen, accompagnée de chaises *Selene* dessinées par Vico Magistretti en 1969.

148-149. Der Wohn- und Essbereich mit den originalen weißen Holzfenstern aus den 50er Jahren ist ein klarer und sonniger Raum. Die beiden Spiegelglaswände reflektieren Objekte, Personen und berühmte Designentwürfe: zum Beispiel die *Tulip*-Tischchen von Eero Saarinen, das Leuchtelement *Jack* von Tom Dixon und der Hocker *Bu Bu* von Philippe Starck. **150.** Das Arbeitszimmer. Ein Werk aus Perspex von Mike Kitching bildet einen Farbtupfer auf dem Schreibtisch von Jean Nouvel. **151.** Die maßgearbeitete Küche ist wie in eine Schachtel eingeschlossen. Das Teeservice aus Chromstahl gestaltete Arne Jacobsen. Der Essbereich ist eingerichtet mit einem Tisch von Eero Saarinen und den Stühlen *Selene*, die Vico Magistretti 1969 entwarf.

152. Calm, expansive atmospheres in black and white with a note of bright color for the TV zone leading to the bedroom. *Tulip* chairs by Eero Saarinen.

152. Le coin télévision, qui précède la chambre à coucher, baigne lui aussi dans une atmosphère d'espace et de détente avec ses tons noirs et blancs que vient égayer une touche de couleur vive. Les sièges *Tulip* du «Pedestal Group» sont d'Eero Saarinen.

152. Eine entspannte und ruhige Atmosphäre beherrscht die Fernsehecke, die zum Schlafzimmer führt. Ein Farbtupfer hellt das dominierende Schwarz und Weiß auf. Die *Tulip*-Stühle aus der »Pedestal Group« sind Entwürfe von Eero Saarinen.

Burley Katon Halliday
6a Liverpool Street Paddington 2021 Sydney Australia Ph +61 2 9332 2233 F +61 2 9360 2048 email: bkh@bkh.com.au www.bkh.com.au

David G. Katon was born in Sydney in 1948. **Studies, experiences:** 1966–1970 architectural studies at New South Wales Institute of Technology. Participation with NSW Government Architects on special projects including the addition to the Art Gallery of New South Wales. 1971–1981 practice with Frank Fox & Associates, Ian McKay & Partners, Jackson Teece Chesterman & Willis, Wills Denoon. From 1981 to present partner and director of Burley Katon Halliday. Tutor in Interior Design at UTS. **Favorites:** *Architect:* Ludwig Mies van der Rohe. *Building:* Guggenheim Museum, New York, by Frank Lloyd Wright. *Furnishing: Barcelona* chair by Ludwig Mies van der Rohe. **In Sydney he recommends:** *Hotel:* Kirketon. *Restaurant:* Billy Kwong. *Bookstore:* Dome Books.

David G. Katon est né à Sydney en 1948. **Etudes, expérience professionnelle:** 1966–1970, étudie l'architecture à la New South Wales Institute of Technology à Sydney. Avec le NSW Governement Architects, il participe à des projets spéciaux dont l'installation de la Art Gallery of New South Wales. 1971–1981, travaille chez Frank Fox & Associates, Ian McKay & Partners, Jackson Teece Chesterman & Willis, Wills Denoon. De 1981 à aujourd'hui, associé et directeur du cabinet Burley Katon Halliday. Enseigne la décoration d'intérieur à l'UTS. **Ses favoris:** *Architecte:* Ludwig Mies van der Rohe. *Edifice:* Guggenheim Museum à New York de Frank Lloyd Wright. *Objets, mobilier:* la chaise *Barcelona* de Ludwig Mies van der Rohe. **A Sydney, il recommande:** *Hôtel:* Kirketon. *Restaurant:* Billy Kwong. *Librairie:* Dome Books.

David G. Katon ist 1948 in Sydney geboren. **Ausbildung, Erfahrungen:** 1966–1970 Architekturstudium am New South Wales Institute of Technology in Sydney. Nimmt mit den NSW Government Architects teil an Spezialprojekten wie der Erweiterung der Art Gallery of New South Wales. 1971–1981 Zusammenarbeit mit Frank Fox & Associates, Ian McKay & Partners, Jackson Teece Chesterman & Willis sowie Wills Denoon. Seit 1981 Teilhaber und Leiter des Architekturbüros Burley Katon Halliday. Tutor für Interior Design an der UTS in Sydney. **Er bewundert:** *Architekt:* Ludwig Mies van der Rohe. *Gebäude:* Guggenheim Museum in New York von Frank Lloyd Wright. *Möbeldesign:* Sessel *Barcelona* von Ludwig Mies van der Rohe. **Er empfiehlt in Sydney:** *Hotel:* Kirketon. *Restaurant:* Billy Kwong. *Buchhandlung:* Dome Books.

Katon Residence, Elizabeth Bay

Year of construction: 1998	**Area:** not available	**Cost:** AUS $ 120,000
Année de réalisation: 1998	**Surface:** non indiquée	**Coûts:** AUS $ 120 000
Baujahr: 1998	**Nutzfläche:** ungenannt	**Kosten:** AUS $ 120 000

design David Katon

Katon Residence

1
2
3
4
5

Bingley/Pullin House, Chinamans Beach

Above Chinamans Beach the Balmoral area offers a breathtaking view of the bay and the greenery of a park protected by landscape heritage regulations. The flourishing natural setting interacts with the interiors of this home on four levels designed by Iain Halliday and furnished, in part, by the owner. The house is built on a structure from the 30s, and the interiors conserve a retro atmosphere. The entrance, on the second floor, leads through a gallery of artworks to the internal staircase, the guest zone, a studio, and a large living area. But the heart of the house is on the third floor: Here we see the opulence of an architecture that creates indoor-outdoor relations, joining the dining-kitchen-living area and terrace with the swimming pool in one environment.

Au-dessus de Chinamans Beach, dans le quartier de Balmoral, on jouit d'une vue sublime sur la baie et la végétation d'un parc protégé en tant que patrimoine paysager. L'exubérance de la nature a évidemment influencé la décoration de cette maison de quatre étages, conçue par Iain Halliday et décorée en partie par la propriétaire. La villa se dresse sur une structure des années 30 et ses intérieurs conservent eux aussi un parfum rétro. On entre directement par le premier étage, où une galerie d'œuvres d'art mène à l'escalier, à un bureau, aux quartiers des invités et à un premier salon spacieux. Toutefois, le vrai cœur de la maison se trouve au deuxième étage où l'architecture révèle toute sa générosité en mariant l'intérieur et l'extérieur, réunissant dans un même espace la salle à manger, la cuisine, le séjour, la terrasse et la piscine.

Im Wohnviertel Balmoral oberhalb von Chinamans Beach genießt man eine herrliche Aussicht auf die Bucht und einen grünen Park, der unter Landschaftsschutz steht. Natürlich sollten sich die Innenräume dieses vierstöckigen Wohnhauses, das von Iain Halliday gestaltet und von der Hausbesitzerin teilweise selbst eingerichtet wurde, an der verschwenderischen Natur inspirieren. Die Villa wurde auf der Basis eines bestehenden Gebäudes aus den 30er Jahren errichtet und auch die Innenräume besitzen noch einen gewissen nostalgischen Charme. Hinter dem Eingang im ersten Stock erstreckt sich eine Galerie mit Kunstwerken, von wo aus man über eine Innentreppe den Gästebereich, das Arbeitszimmer und ein erstes großes Wohnzimmer erreicht. Das Herzstück des Hauses liegt jedoch auf der zweiten Etage. Hier zeigt sich die Großzügigkeit der Architektursprache, die Innenräume und Umgebung miteinander in Beziehung setzt, denn Ess-, Küchen- und Wohnbereich bilden eine Einheit mit Terrasse und Pool.

19

155. Iain Halliday.

155. Iain Halliday.

155. Iain Halliday.

156-157. The terrace is equipped with an adjustable steel sunscreen. The table was designed by the owner, while the *Highframe* chairs are by Alberto Meda. The low chair and the chaise longue of 1996, also by Meda, are suitable for indoor and outdoor use. **158.** The bedroom, bath, and wardrobe, designed by Iain Halliday, feature stone for the floorings and the bathtub, and mirrors for the armoires. The blue partition separates the various functional zones.

156-157. La terrasse est équipée d'un auvent en acier réglable. La table a été dessinée par la propriétaire, les chaises *Highframe* sont d'Alberto Meda. La chaise basse et la chaise longue, également de Meda, dessinées en 1996, peuvent être utilisées aussi à l'extérieur. **158.** Dans la chambre à coucher, la salle de bains et le dressing, Iain Halliday a privilégié les revêtements en pierre pour les sols et la baignoire, et les panneaux en miroir pour les placards. La cloison teinte en bleu sépare les différents espaces fonctionnels.

156-157. Die Terrasse verfügt über eine regulierbare Sonnenschutzvorrichtung aus Stahl. Den Tisch hat die Hausbesitzerin selbst entworfen und die Stühle *Highframe* designte Alberto Meda. Der niedrige Armlehnstuhl und die Liege von 1996, ebenfalls von Meda, können auch im Außenbereich verwendet werden. **158.** Im Schlaf-, im Bade- und im Ankleidezimmer – alle von Iain Halliday gestaltet – wurden Fußböden und Badewanne mit Stein verkleidet sowie Spiegelpaneele für den Schrank verwendet. Eine blaue Wand trennt die einzelnen Bereiche.

Burley Katon Halliday
6a Liverpool Street Paddington 2021 Sydney Australia Ph +61 2 9332 2233 F +61 2 9360 2048 email: bkh@bkh.com.au www.bkh.com.au

Iain Halliday was born in 1961 in Sydney. **Studies, experiences:** 1982 degree in Interior Design from Sydney College of Art. 1983/84 architectural studies at UTS. 1983/84 practice with Marsh Freedman & Associates. 1984–1986: Neil Burley & Partners. 1986 now partner and director of Burley Katon Halliday. **Favorites:** *Architect:* Ludwig Mies van der Rohe. *Building:* Fallingwater House by Frank Lloyd Wright in Bear Run, Pennsylvania. *Designers:* Jean-Michel Frank, Antonio Citterio, Philippe Starck. *Furnishing: Barcelona* chair by Ludwig Mies van der Rohe. **In Sydney he recommends:** *Hotel:* Kirketon. *Fashion boutique:* Louis Vuitton. *Gallery:* Roslyn Oxley 9 Gallery. *Museum:* The Art Gallery of New South Wales. *Bookstore:* Dome Books.

Iain Halliday est né en 1961 à Sydney. **Etudes, expérience professionnelle:** 1982, diplôme de décoration d'intérieur du Sydney College of Art. 1983/84, études d'architecture à l'UTS, Sydney. 1983/84, apprentissage chez Marsh Freedman & Associates. 1984–1986, Neil Burley & Partners. De 1986 à aujourd'hui, associé et directeur de Burley Katon Halliday. **Ses favoris:** *Architecte:* Ludwig Mies van der Rohe. *Edifice:* la maison Fallingwater de Frank Lloyd Wright à Bear Run, Pennsylvanie. *Designers:* Jean-Michel Frank, Antonio Citterio, Philippe Starck. *Objets, mobilier:* La chaise *Barcelona* de Ludwig Mies van der Rohe. **A Sydney, il recommande:** *Hôtel:* Kirketon. *Boutique de mode:* Louis Vuitton. *Galerie d'art:* Roslyn Oxley 9 Gallery. *Musée:* The Art Gallery of New South Wales. *Librairie:* Dome Books.

Iain Halliday ist 1961 in Sydney geboren. **Ausbildung, Erfahrungen:** 1982 Abschluss des Interior-Design-Studiums am Sydney College of Art. 1983/84 Architekturstudium an der UTS in Sydney. 1983/84: Zusammenarbeit mit Marsh Freedman & Associates. 1984–1986: Zusammenarbeit mit Neil Burley & Partners. Seit 1986 Teilhaber und Leiter des Architekturbüros Burley Katon Halliday. **Er bewundert:** *Architekt:* Ludwig Mies van der Rohe. *Gebäude:* Fallingwater House von Frank Lloyd Wright in Bear Run, Pennsylvania. *Designer:* Jean-Michel Frank, Antonio Citterio, Philippe Starck. *Möbeldesign:* Sessel *Barcelona* von Ludwig Mies van der Rohe. **Er empfiehlt in Sydney:** *Hotel:* Kirketon. *Boutique:* Louis Vuitton. *Galerie:* Roslyn Oxley 9 Gallery. *Museum:* The Art Gallery of New South Wales. *Buchhandlung:* Dome Books.

Bingley/Pullin House, Chinamans Beach

Year of construction: 1998	**Area:** not available	**Cost:** AUS $ 500,000
Année de réalisation: 1998	**Surface:** non indiquée	**Coûts:** AUS $ 500 000
Baujahr: 1998	**Nutzfläche:** ungenannt	**Kosten:** AUS $ 500 000

Bolland House, Balmoral

Overlooking the bay of Balmoral Beach, in one of Sydney's most prestigious residential zones, this house, based on essential geometry and decisive colors – the original design was by the architect Alec Tzannes – is organized on two levels, flooded with light, which enters the stairwell through a skylight. The upper level contains the bedrooms and two baths, while the lower floor is a large open space containing the kitchen, the dining area, and the living room, facing the swimming pool through a sliding glass door. The pool, the new entrance, and the kitchen are all parts of the modifications designed by Iain Halliday of the firm Burley Katon Halliday, in a restructuring project whose most eloquent narrative element is the long entrance corridor with the stairs: a sort of nave, with a glass roof.

Faisant face à la baie de Balmoral Beach, dans un des quartiers résidentiels les plus prestigieux de Sydney, cette maison à la géométrie épurée et aux couleurs tranchées – l'architecte Alec Tzannes a conçu le projet original – se développe sur deux étages inondés par la lumière qui filtre par une cage d'escalier surmontée d'une verrière. Le niveau supérieur accueille les chambres à coucher et deux salles de bains tandis qu'au niveau inférieur, un vaste espace ouvert réunit la cuisine, l'espace salle à manger et le salon, le tout bordé d'une baie vitrée coulissante qui s'ouvre sur la piscine. Celle-ci, ainsi que la nouvelle entrée et la cuisine, fait partie des modifications apportées par le projet d'Iain Halliday du cabinet Burley Katon Halliday, dont la plus grande réussite est sans doute la création du long couloir de l'entrée qui se poursuit en escalier, sorte de nef coiffée d'un toit en verre.

Dieses Wohnhaus wurde mit Blick auf die Bucht von Balmoral Beach, einem der elegantesten Wohnviertel von Sydney, nach einem Originalentwurf des Architekten Alec Tzannes errichtet und zeichnet sich aus durch schnörkellose Geradlinigkeit und entschiedene Farbgebung. Das Licht fällt über ein Glasdach in das Treppenhaus ein und fließt weiter in die verschiedenen Räume der beiden Ebenen. Das Obergeschoss beherbergt den Schlafbereich und die beiden Badezimmer, während sich unten die Küche, der Ess- und der Wohnbereich zu einem einzigen großen offenen Raum verbinden, der sich über eine Glasschiebetür zum Pool hin öffnet. Dieser ist, zusammen mit dem neuen Eingang und der Küche, Teil der Änderungen, die Iain Halliday vom Architekturbüro Burley Katon Halliday am Originalentwurf vorgenommen hat. Das Element von größter gestalterischer Prägnanz ist der lange Eingangskorridor mit der Treppe: Er wirkt wie ein Kirchenschiff mit Glasdach.

20

160. The garden behind Bolland House. **161.** Iain Halliday.

160. Le jardin à l'arrière de la maison Bolland. **161.** Iain Halliday.

160. Garten an der Rückseite von Bolland House. **161.** Iain Halliday.

162. The entrance with the staircase with wooden steps becomes a long internal promenade bordered by two white walls. The effect is enhanced by the pitched skylight roofing. **163.** The decor of the open space combining the kitchen, dining area, and living room is a mixture of design classics – from the table by Eero Saarinen to the *Diamond* chairs by Harry Bertoia – and custom pieces by Iain Halliday: from the black leather day-bed to the kitchen with steel island. Striking chromatic contrast between the violet of the carpet and the black of the stained wood flooring.

162. L'entrée avec l'escalier en bois est une longue promenade intérieure délimitée par deux murs blancs. Son envolée est soulignée par la verrière voûtée qui le surplombe. **163.** L'espace ouvert qui rassemble la cuisine, la salle à manger et le séjour est meublée d'un mélange de classiques du design du début des annés 50 – de la table d'Eero Saarinen aux sièges *Diamond* d'Harry Bartoia – et de pièces créées spécialement par Iain Halliday: du lit de repos en cuir noir à la cuisine équipée d'un îlot en acier. Un contrast chromatique osé oppose le tapis violet et le parquet teinté en noir.

162. Der Eingang mit der Holztreppe ist als eine lange Innenpromenade konzipiert, die von zwei weißen Wände begrenzt und vom Satteldach des Oberlichts noch betont wird. **163.** Der offene Raum, der die Küche, das Ess- und das Wohnzimmer umfasst, ist eingerichtet mit einem Mix aus Designklassikern der frühen 50er Jahre – Tisch von Eero Saarinen und Stühle *Diamond* von Harry Bertoia – sowie eigens von Iain Halliday entworfenen Objekten: das Day-bed in schwarzem Leder und die Küche mit der Chromstahl-Insel. Der violette Teppich und das schwarz gestrichene Parkett bilden eine gewagte Farbkombination.

164. A purple carpet also in the bedroom with lamp by Philippe Starck.

164. Dans la chambre à coucher, avec une lampe de Philippe Starck, aussi une moquette mauve.

164. Auch in dem Schlafzimmer mit Leuchte von Philippe Starck liegt ein mauvefarbener Teppich.

SIR EDMUND HILLARY
VIEW FROM THE SUMMIT

Burley Katon Halliday
6a Liverpool Street Paddington 2021 Sydney Australia Ph +61 2 9332 2233 F +61 2 9360 2048 email: bkh@bkh.com.au www.bkh.com.au

Iain Halliday was born in 1961 in Sydney. **Studies, experiences:** 1982 degree in Interior Design from Sydney College of Art. 1983/84 architectural studies at UTS. 1983/84 practice with Marsh Freedman & Associates. 1984–1986: Neil Burley & Partners. 1986 now partner and director of Burley Katon Halliday. **Favorites:** *Architect:* Ludwig Mies van der Rohe. *Building:* Fallingwater House by Frank Lloyd Wright in Bear Run, Pennsylvania. *Designers:* Jean-Michel Frank, Antonio Citterio, Philippe Starck. *Furnishing: Barcelona* chair by Ludwig Mies van der Rohe. **In Sydney he recommends:** *Hotel:* Kirketon. *Fashion boutique:* Louis Vuitton. *Gallery:* Roslyn Oxley 9 Gallery. *Museum:* The Art Gallery of New South Wales. *Bookstore:* Dome Books.

Iain Halliday est né en 1961 à Sydney. **Etudes, expérience professionnelle:** 1982, diplôme de décoration d'intérieur du Sydney College of Art. 1983/84, études d'architecture à l'UTS, Sydney. 1983/84, apprentissage chez Marsh Freedman & Associates. 1984–1986, Neil Burley & Partners. De 1986 à aujourd'hui, associé et directeur de Burley Katon Halliday. **Ses favoris:** *Architecte:* Ludwig Mies van der Rohe. *Edifice:* la maison Fallingwater de Frank Lloyd Wright à Bear Run, Pennsylvanie. *Designers:* Jean-Michel Frank, Antonio Citterio, Philippe Starck. *Objets, mobilier:* La chaise *Barcelona* de Ludwig Mies van der Rohe. **A Sydney, il recommande:** *Hôtel:* Kirketon. *Boutique de mode:* Louis Vuitton. *Galerie d'art:* Roslyn Oxley 9 Gallery. *Musée:* The Art Gallery of New South Wales. *Librairie:* Dome Books.

Iain Halliday ist 1961 in Sydney geboren. **Ausbildung, Erfahrungen:** 1982 Abschluss des Interior-Design-Studiums am Sydney College of Art. 1983/84 Architekturstudium an der UTS in Sydney. 1983/84: Zusammenarbeit mit Marsh Freedman & Associates. 1984–1986: Zusammenarbeit mit Neil Burley & Partners. Seit 1986 Teilhaber und Leiter des Architekturbüros Burley Katon Halliday. **Er bewundert:** *Architekt:* Ludwig Mies van der Rohe. *Gebäude:* Fallingwater House von Frank Lloyd Wright in Bear Run, Pennsylvania. *Designer:* Jean-Michel Frank, Antonio Citterio, Philippe Starck. *Möbeldesign:* Sessel *Barcelona* von Ludwig Mies van der Rohe. **Er empfiehlt in Sydney:** *Hotel:* Kirketon. *Boutique:* Louis Vuitton. *Galerie:* Roslyn Oxley 9 Gallery. *Museum:* The Art Gallery of New South Wales. *Buchhandlung:* Dome Books.

Bolland House, Balmoral

Year of construction: 1998	**Area:** not available	**Cost:** AUS $ 500,000
Année de réalisation: 1998	**Surface:** non indiquée	**Coûts:** AUS $ 500 000
Baujahr: 1998	**Nutzfläche:** ungenannt	**Kosten:** AUS $ 500 000

Hipgrave/Waring House, East Redfern

Edward Waring lives and works in Sydney as a Location Manager for video and film productions, and lives in an open-plan house on three levels restructured by Peter Clark, characterized by a large glazed façade overlooking a small garden, where the studio is located. The house is also like a flexible set, to be reinvented on a daily basis, in keeping with a single leitmotiv: the pleasure of things. This focus on the joy of objects has also involved the work of Brian Keirnan for the recovery and restoration of furnishings from the 50s, 60s and 70s. The industrial character of the building is underlined by the materials utilized: aluminum, cement, Blackbutt wood, galvanized steel. The fluidity of the spatial construction is accentuated on all the levels by the new central service block, illuminated with louvres, around which the spaces are freely organized.

Edward Waring vit et travaille à Sydney où il est régisseur pour des productions vidéos et cinématographiques. Il habite dans un espace ouvert sur trois niveaux, restructuré par Peter Clark et caractérisé par une grande façade vitrée qui s'ouvre sur un petit jardin où est situé son bureau. Sa maison se présente comme un plateau de cinéma dont on peut chaque jour réinventer le décor selon un leitmotiv: le plaisir des belles choses qui, dans ce cas précis et grâce aux conseils de Brian Keirnan, incluent une intéressante sélection d'objets et de meubles des années 50, 60 et 70. Le côté industriel de l'édifice a été souligné par le choix des matériaux: aluminium, ciment, bois Blackbutt et acier galvanisé. La fluidité de la construction spatiale a été mise en relief à tous les étages par le nouveau bloc central des services, éclairé par des persiennes, autour duquel les espaces se déploient librement.

Edward Waring lebt und arbeitet in Sydney als Location Manager für Video- und Kinofilmproduktionen und wohnt in einem *open space* auf drei Ebenen, der von Peter Clark umgebaut wurde. Bemerkenswert ist die große Glasfassade, die auf einen kleinen Garten geht, wo sich das Büro befindet. Dieses Haus präsentiert sich quasi als Film-Set, das jeden Tag nach einem bestimmten Leitmotiv neu zusammengestellt werden kann: die Freude an der Einrichtung, die hier, auch dank der Beratung durch Brian Keirnan, Sammlerstücke der 50er, 60er und 70er Jahren mischt. Das Industrieflair des Gebäudes wird unterstrichen durch die verwendeten Materialien: Aluminium, Zement, Blackbutt-Holz, galvanisierter Stahl. Der neue zentrale Block mit den durch Lamellen erhellten Badezimmern, der sich durch die Stockwerke hindurchzieht und um den herum sich alle Räume anordnen, hebt das Konzept des Raumkontinuums hervor.

21

167. Mark Pearse, Peter Clark, Brian Keirnan (from the left).

167. Mark Pearse, Peter Clark, Brian Keirnan (en partant de la gauche).

167. Mark Pearse, Peter Clark und Brian Keirnan (von links).

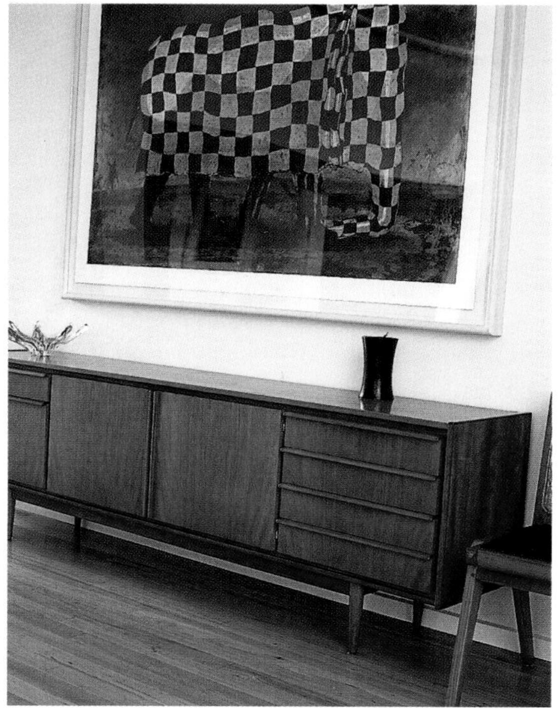

168-169. The open space combines the living, dining, and kitchen areas in a pleasant intermingling of colors, materials, and the lines of the furnishings from the 50s (like the wooden console), 60s, and 70s. The sofa and the table are new, designed by Brian Kiernan. The loft level contains a spacious bookcase, below the staircase leading to the bedroom zone. **170.** Recycled dentist's chairs for the custom-designed kitchen.

168-169. L'espace ouvert rassemble le séjour, la salle à manger et la cuisine dans un agréable assortiment de couleurs, de matériaux et de meubles des années 50 (tels que la console en bois), 60 et 70. En revanche, le canapé et la table dessinés par Brian Keirnan sont actuels. Sur la mezzanine, la bibliothèque. L'escalier mène aux chambres. **170.** Dans la cuisine design, des fauteuils de dentiste recyclés.

168-169. Ein offen konzipierter Raum verbindet den Wohn- und Essbereich mit der Küche in einem angenehmen Zusammenspiel von Farben, Materialien und Einrichtungsgegenständen aus den 50er (zum Beispiel die Holzkonsole), 60er und 70er Jahren. Zeitgenössisch sind hingegen das Sofa und der Tisch, die beide von Brian Kiernan entworfen wurden. Auf dem Hängeboden steht ein Bücherregal. Die Treppe führt zum Schlafbereich. **170.** In der maßgearbeiteten Küche stehen wiederverwendete Zahnarztstühle.

Clark Pearse Architects
Studio 16 94 Oxford Street Darlinghurst 2010 Sydney Australia Ph +61 2 9361 4657 F +61 2 9361 6327 email: clarkpearsearchitect@bigpond.com.au

Peter Clark was born in Bangkok in 1963. 1991 university graduation. **Mark Pearse** was born in Sydney in 1962. **Studies, experiences:** Degree in architecture, UTS, Sydney. Clark Pearse Architects established 1994. **Favorites:** *Architect:* Lord Norman Foster. *Building:* Casa Malaparte in Capri. **In Sydney they recommend:** *Hotel:* Kirketon. *Restaurant:* The Bathers Pavillion. *Design shop:* Space Interior Products. *Fashion boutique:* Marcs. *Gallery:* Kaliman Gallery. *Museum:* Museum of Contemporary Art (MCA). *Bookstore:* Ariel.

Peter Clark est né à Bangkok en 1963. 1991, diplôme universitaire. **Mark Pearse** à Sydney en 1962. **Etudes, expérience professionnelle:** Diplôme d'architecture de l'UTS, Sydney. 1994, ouverture du cabinet Clark Pearse Architects. **Leurs favoris:** *Architecte:* Lord Norman Foster. *Edifice:* La maison de Malaparte à Capri. **A Sydney, ils recommandent:** *Hôtel:* Kirketon. *Restaurant:* The Bathers Pavillion. *Boutique de design:* Space Interior Products. *Boutique de mode:* Marcs. *Galerie d'art:* Kaliman Gallery. *Musée:* le musée d'art contemporain (MCA). *Librairie:* Ariel.

Peter Clark ist 1963 in Bangkok geboren, 1991 Universitätsabschluss. **Mark Pearse** ist 1962 in Sydney geboren. **Ausbildung, Erfahrungen:** Abschluss des Architekturstudiums an der UTS in Sydney. 1994 Gründung des Architekturbüros Clark Pearse Architects. **Sie bewundern:** *Architekt:* Lord Norman Foster. *Gebäude:* Casa Malaparte auf Capri. **Sie empfehlen in Sydney:** *Hotel:* Kirketon. *Restaurant:* The Bathers Pavillion. *Designgeschäft:* Space Interior Products. *Boutique:* Marcs. *Galerie:* Kaliman Gallery. *Museum:* Museum of Contemporary Art (MCA). *Buchhandlung:* Ariel.

Hipgrave/Waring House, East Redfern

Year of construction: 1996 **Area:** 317 m^2 **Cost:** not available
Année de réalisation: 1996 **Surface:** 317 m^2 **Coûts:** non indiqués
Baujahr: 1996 **Nutzfläche:** 317 m^2 **Kosten:** ungenannt

design Peter Clark & Mark Pearse

Hipgrave/Waring House

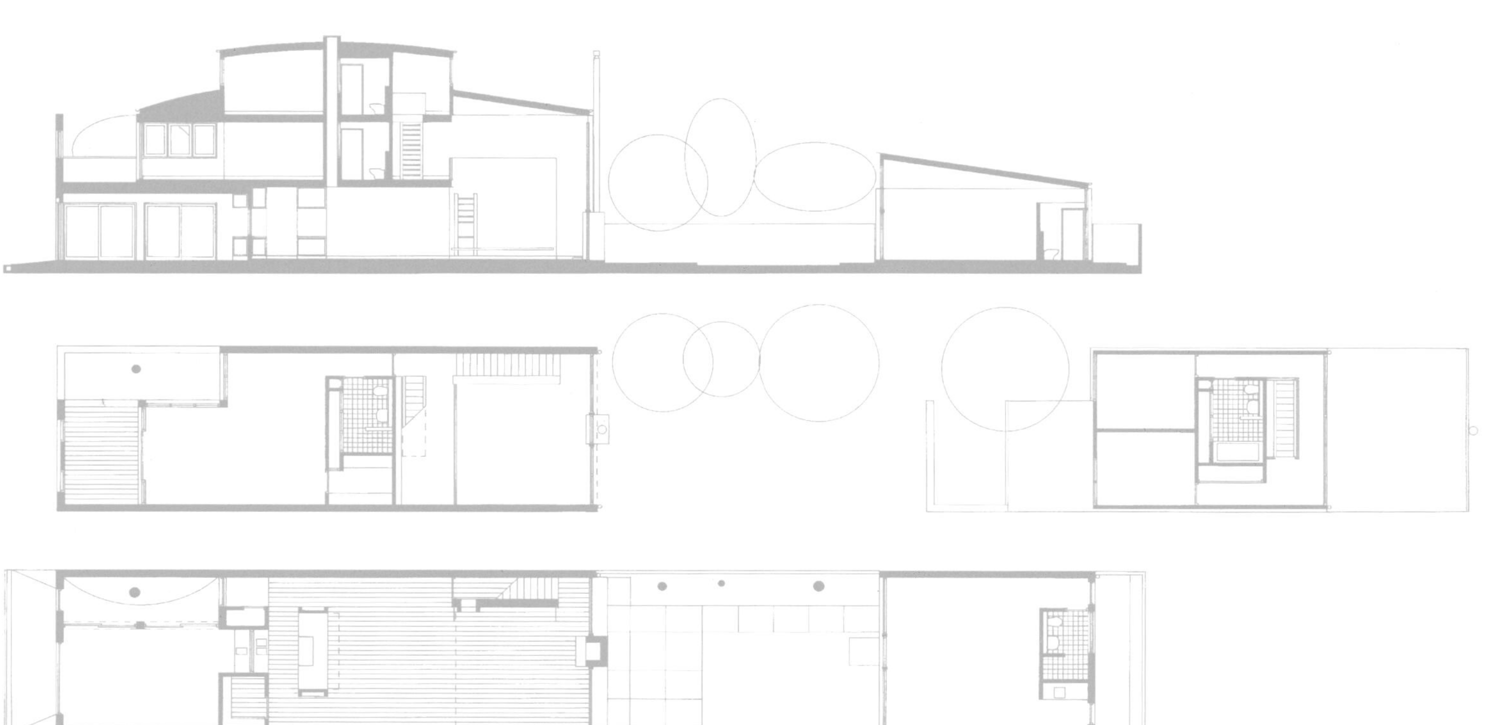

Kwok House, Hunters Hill

A house with a complex curved structure on multiple levels, open to the view of the sea on one side and closed off by a dense barrier of foliage on the other, following the contours of the hillside lot. The three terraces overlook a large reflecting pool at the garden level. The intense light of Sydney becomes the absolute protagonist of this home in the residential zone of Hunters Hill, entering through large lateral or zenithal openings, projecting a puzzle of shifting figures on the floors during the daytime. In the large open space of the main level the light flows uninterrupted over the low partitions that define the functional zones, vibrating on the surfaces of the resin flooring, the kitchen in glossy-iridescent blue laminate, and the bathroom in green mosaic.

Cette villa de plusieurs étages à la structure complexe en courbe s'ouvre, d'un côté, sur la mer, et de l'autre, sur un dense rideau d'arbres qui borde la colline. Trois terrasses donnent sur le jardin où s'étend un vaste miroir d'eau. Et puis, il y a la lumière de Sydney. Celle-ci occupe le premier rôle dans cette demeure du quartier de Hunters Hill, une des zones résidentielles de la ville. Elle se diffuse à travers de vastes ouvertures qui percent même le plafond, où des parties du toit en verrière projettent sur le sol un puzzle de silhouettes changeantes au fil des heures. On la retrouve au cœur de l'étage principal, un grand espace ouvert, où elle se déverse sans interruption entre les murets qui divisent les différentes aires, faisant vibrer la surface en résine des pavements, le laminé bleu iridescent de la cuisine et la mosaïque verte de la salle de bains.

Die Villa präsentiert sich als ein geschwungenes Gebäude, das sich auf mehreren Ebenen entwickelt und zu einer Seite hin den Blick auf das Meer freigibt, während die andere Seite durch eine dichte Baumreihe begrenzt wird, die sich am Hügel entlang zieht. Eine spiegelnde Wasserfläche beherrscht den Garten, auf den drei Terrassen blicken. Und dazu gibt es sehr viel Licht. Das charakteristische Licht von Sydney spielt eindeutig die Hauptrolle in diesem von Neil Durbach und Camilla Block entworfenen Haus in Hunters Hill, einem Wohnviertel der Metropole. Das Licht ergießt sich durch weite Öffnungen, auch im Dach, und zeichnet ein Figurenpuzzle auf den Boden, das sich im Lauf des Tages immer wieder ändert. Auch im Bereich der Hauptwohnfläche, einem weiträumigen offen gestalteten Raum, flutet das Licht frei zwischen den niedrigen Trennwänden, die die Wohnbereiche unterteilen, tanzt vibrierend auf den Oberflächen des Kunstharzbodens, der Laminatküche in glänzend-irisierendem Blau, sowie dem grünen Mosaik des Badezimmers.

22

173. Neil Durbach and Camilla Block, the architects.

173. Neil Durbach et Camilla Block, les architectes.

173. Neil Durbach und Camilla Block, die Architekten.

174-175. The entrance and the landing leading to the lower level. Large windows and zenithal openings in the roof allow the light to flood and envelope the interiors, visually dilated by the white of the walls and the resin flooring.

174-175. L'entrée et le dégagement qui communique avec l'étage inférieur. De grandes ouvertures, dans les murs mais également dans le toit, permettent à la lumière de se diffuser et de baigner les espaces intérieurs, magnifiant le blanc des murs et du sol en résine.

174-175. Der Eingang und der Durchgangsraum, der in den unteren Stock führt. Große Fenster und Dachöffnungen fangen das Licht ein, das sich in den Innenräumen ausbreitet und sie durchdringt, unterstützt vom Weiß der Wände und des Kunstharzbodens.

176-177. Nordic design classics for the living area: red armchair and chairs designed in the 30s by Alvar Aalto; *PK25* chairs from 1951 in wicker and chromium-plated steel by Poul Kjaerholm. The dining table is by Sydney-based firm Norman & Quaine, the coffee table by Jasper Morrison. On the white cabinet designed by Durbach Block, a porcelain vase by De De Ce.

176-177. Dans le séjour, des classiques du design scandinave: un fauteuil rouge et des chaises dessinés dans les années 30 par Alvar Aalto; des chauffeuses *PK25* cannées en acier brossé de Poul Kjaerholm datant de 1951. La table de la salle à manger est de Norman & Quaine à Sydney, la table basse de Jasper Morrison. Sur le petit meuble blanc, création de Durbach Block, un vase en porcelaine de De De Ce.

176-177. Im Wohnzimmer finden sich Klassiker des skandinavischen Designs: ein roter Sessel und Stühle aus den 30er Jahren von Alvar Aalto sowie die Poul-Kjaerholm-Stühle *PK25* von 1951 aus Rohrgeflecht und Chromstahl. Der Esstisch ist von Norman & Quaine aus Sydney, der niedrige Tisch von Jasper Morrison. Auf dem weißen, von Durbach Block entworfenen Möbelchen steht eine Porzellanvase von De De Ce.

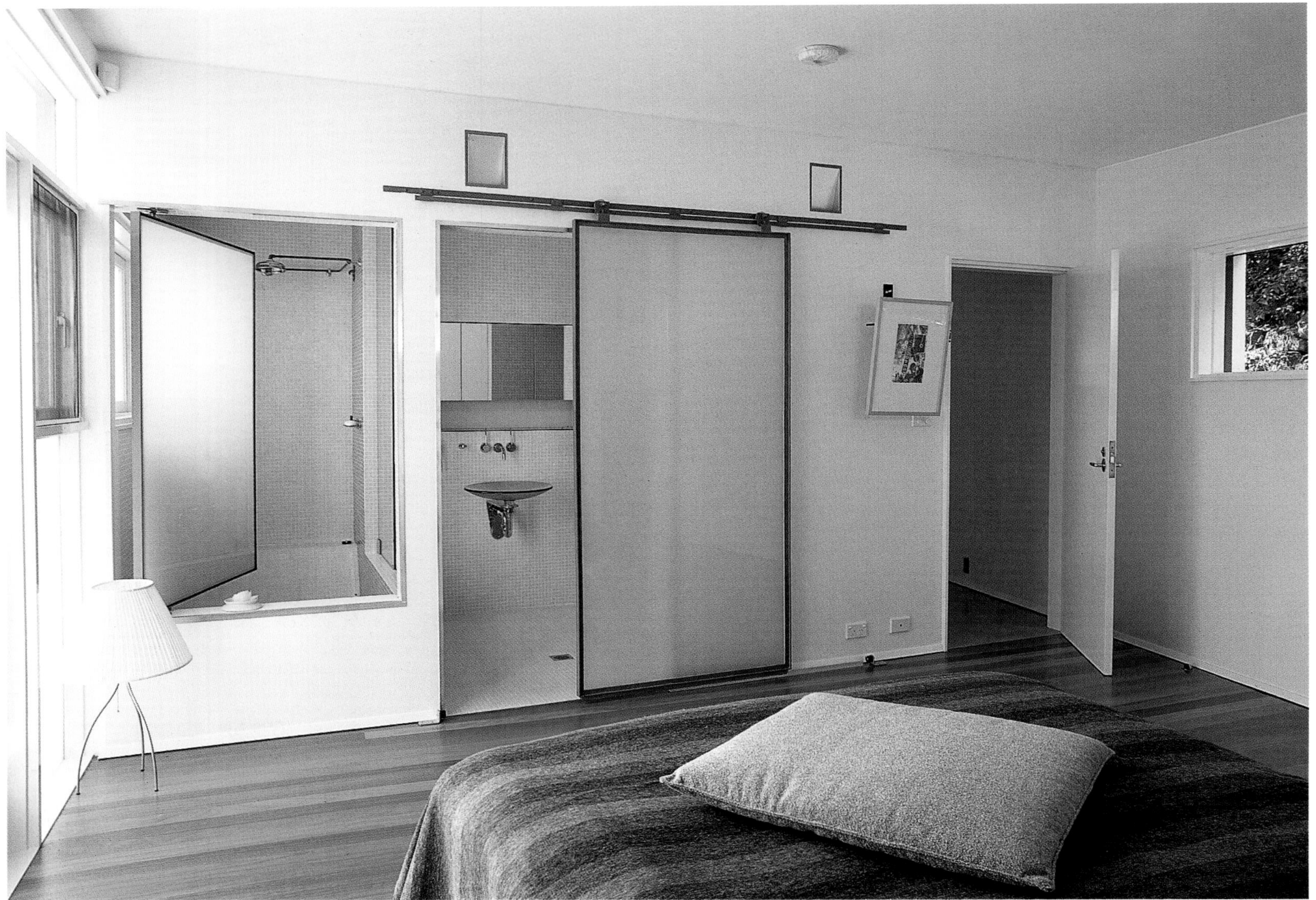

178. The bath opens onto the bedroom with a window revealing the shower stall, and a sliding door that frames the acid green glass wash-stand. All designed by Durbach Block.

178. La salle de bains s'ouvre sur la chambre à coucher; on aperçoit la douche par la fenêtre ouverte. Derrière la porte coulissante, un lavabo en cristal vert acide. Tout a été dessiné par Durbach Block.

178. Badezimmer und Schlafzimmer sind als ein einziger Raum konzipiert. Ein Fenster gibt den Blick auf die Dusche frei und hinter der Schiebetür sieht man das Waschbecken aus eisgrünem Kristallglas. Alles wurde nach Entwürfen von Durbach Block angefertigt.

Durbach Block Architects
Level 3 441 Kent Street Sydney 2000 Australia Ph +61 2 9261 3941 F +61 2 9261 2207 email: neild@ozemail.com.au

Neil Durbach was born in 1954 in Cape Town. **Studies, experiences:** 1978 degree in architecture, University of Cape Town. 1979–1989 practice in different studios in San Francisco and Sydney. 1992 studio Durbach Block Architects. 1985–1995 tutor Architectural Design, University of Sydney. **Camilla Block** was born in 1966 in Johannesburg in South Africa. **Studies, experiences:** 1991 degree in architecture, University of Sydney. 1987–1992 practice in different studios. 1992 studio Durbach Block Architects. 1993–1996 tutor Architectural Design, University of Sydney. **Awards:** RAIA: 1997, 1998. 1999/2000 The Droga Penthouse project featured in a traveling exhibition in Europe. **Favorites:** *Architect:* Rem Koolhaas. **In Sydney they recommend:** *Hotel:* Ravesis Bondi Beach. *Restaurant:* Bistro Moncur. *Design shop:* De De Ce. *Fashion boutique:* Marcs. *Museum:* New South Wales Art Gallery.

Neil Durbach est né en 1954 à Cape Town. **Etudes, expérience professionnelle:** 1978, diplôme d'architecture, University of Cape Town. 1979–1989, travaille dans divers cabinets entre San Francisco et Sydney. 1992, ouverture du cabinet Durbach Block Architects. 1985–1995, enseigne le design architectural, University of Sydney. **Camilla Block** est née en 1966 à Johannesburg. **Etudes, expérience professionnelle:** 1991, diplôme d'architecture, University of Sydney. 1987–1992, travaille dans divers cabinets d'architecture. 1992, cabinet Durbach Block Architects. 1993–1996, enseigne le design architectural, University of Sydney. **Prix d'architecture:** RAIA: 1997, 1998. 1999/2000 le Droga Penthouse Projet fait l'objet d'une exposition itinérante en Europe. **Leurs favoris:** *Architecte:* Rem Koolhaas. **A Sydney, ils recommandent:** *Hôtel:* Ravesis Bondi Beach. *Restaurant:* Bistro Moncur. *Boutique de design:* De De Ce. *Boutique de mode:* Marcs. *Musée:* New South Wales Art Gallery.

Neil Durbach ist 1954 in Cape Town geboren. **Ausbildung, Erfahrungen:** 1978 Abschluss des Architekturstudiums an der University of Cape Town. 1979–1989 Tätigkeit in verschiedenen Architekturbüros in San Francisco und Sydney. 1992 Gründung des Architekturbüros Durbach Block Architects. 1985–1995 Tutor für Architectural Design an der University of Sydney. **Camilla Block** ist 1966 in Johannesburg geboren. **Ausbildung, Erfahrungen:** 1991 Abschluss des Architekturstudiums an der University of Sydney. 1987–1992 Tätigkeit in verschiedenen Architekturbüros. 1992 Gründung des Architekturbüros Durbach Block Architects. 1993–1996 Tutor für Architectural Design an der University of Sydney. **Architekturpreise:** RAIA: 1997, 1998. 1999/2000 The Droga Penthouse in Sydney, das an einer Wanderausstellung durch Europa teilnahm. **Sie bewundern:** *Architekt:* Rem Koolhaas. **Sie empfehlen in Sydney:** *Hotel:* Ravesis Bondi Beach. *Restaurant:* Bistro Moncur. *Design:* De De Ce. *Boutique:* Marcs. *Museum:* The Art Gallery of New South Wales.

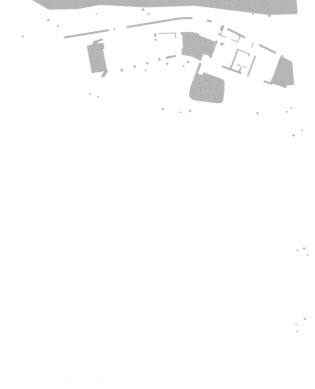

Kwok House, Hunters Hill

Year of construction: 1998
Année de réalisation: 1998
Baujahr: 1998

Area: 245 m^2
Surface: 245 m^2
Nutzfläche: 245 m^2

Cost: AUS $ 950,000
Coûts: AUS $ 950 000
Kosten: AUS $ 950 000

design Neil Durbach & Camilla Block

Kwok House

Tree House, Darling Point

Above Rushcutters Bay, the home of the proprietor of the Weiss clothing line is surrounded by a flourishing, discreet garden, forming a setting for the the swimming pool. This is the environment that sums up the relaxing tone of the house, a safe haven in a life of frequent travel. The interior is conceived as an extension of the outdoor spaces, with large windows and open two-story areas that amplify the light, filtered by wooden Venetian blinds during the brightest hours of the day. A ribbon staircase between two walls in front of the kitchen connects the ground floor living spaces with the bedroom zone above, dominated by the presence of wood. An interesting detail: The door-window of the bedroom leads directly to the walkway to the swimming pool.

Située au-dessus de Rushcutters Bay, la maison du propriétaire de la ligne de vêtements Weiss a la chance d'être entourée d'un jardin rigoureux et discret où se détache la silhouette de la piscine. Celle-ci exprime l'atmosphère de détente de la maison, recherchée par le propriétaire pour compenser ses nombreux déplacements professionnels. L'intérieur a été conçu comme un prolongement de l'extérieur, avec de grandes fenêtres et des espaces ouverts bénéficiant d'une double hauteur sous plafond afin d'amplifier la lumière, filtrée par des stores vénitiens en bois pendant les heures où le soleil est le plus ardent. Devant la cuisine, un escalier droit enfermé entre deux cloisons relie la partie jour, au rez-de-chaussée, à la partie nuit, à l'étage. Partout, le bois domine. Détail insolite: depuis la porte-fenêtre de la chambre à coucher, on accède à une passerelle qui mène à la piscine.

Oberhalb der Rushcutters Bay steht das Wohnhaus des Inhabers der Bekleidungsmarke Weiss, das ein üppiger und diskreter Garten mit Pool umgibt. Damit ist das Wesentliche schon ausgedrückt, nämlich die Relax-dimension des Hauses, die einen Ausgleich zu den häufigen Geschäftsreisen des Hausbesitzers bieten soll. Die Innenräume sind als Verlängerung der Außenbereiche konzipiert und leben von großflächigen Fenstern und offenen Räumen, die in der Höhe zwei Etagen umfassen. Das hereinfallende Licht durchströmt sie und wird mittags und in den frühen Nachmittagsstunden von Holzjalousien gefiltert. Eine Treppe gegenüber der Küche wird von zwei Wänden eingefasst und verbindet den Wohnbereich im Erdgeschoss mit den Schlafräumen im ersten Stock, wo Holz das dominierende Material ist. Bemerkenswert ist das Türfenster des Schlafzimmers, das über einen Laufgang direkt zum Pool führt.

23

180. Tree House seen from the garden. **181.** Neil Durbach of the studio Durbach Block.

180. La maison Tree vue du jardin. **181.** Neil Durbach du cabinet Durbach Block.

180. Tree House vom Garten aus gesehen. **181.** Neil Durbach vom Architekturbüro Durbach Block.

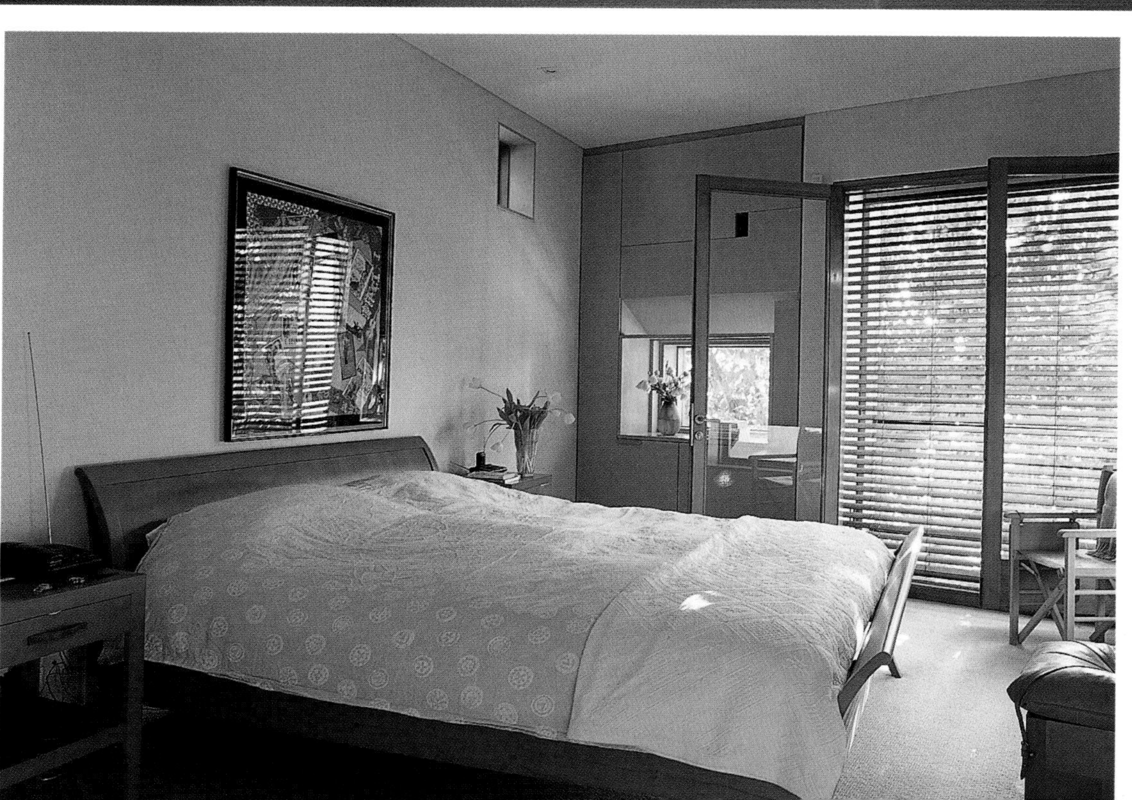

182. The staircase connecting the two levels is inserted between a wall and the structure facing the kitchen. **183.** The living room opens upward to the view of the balcony. It is furnished with an elephant leather divan, a lamp by Philippe Starck, a custom table and green and white chairs, combined with Indonesian crafts. **184.** The kitchen with furnishings in briar-effect laminate. The bedroom is protected by a Venetian blind.

182. L'escalier qui relie les deux niveaux est coincé entre une paroi et la structure qui fait face à la cuisine. **183.** Le séjour, qui s'ouvre vers le haut par le jeu des coursives, est meublé avec un canapé en peau d'éléphant, une lampe de Philippe Starck, une table design et des chaises blanches et vertes. Des objets artisanaux indonésiens complètent le décor. **184.** La cuisine, avec des éléments en laminé travaillé façon bois de racine. Dans la chambre, des stores vénitiens filtrent la lumière.

182. Die Treppe, die die beiden Ebenen miteinander verbindet, wird auf der einen Seite von einer Wand und auf der anderen Seite von der dem Kochbereich gegenüberliegenden Wandstruktur eingefasst. **183.** Das Wohnzimmer ist nach oben hin offen und gibt den Blick frei auf die Galerie. Es ist eingerichtet mit einem Sofa aus Elefantenhaut, einer Leuchte von Philippe Starck, einem maßgefertigten Tisch und grünweißen Stühlen. Dazu kommen einige indonesische kunsthandwerkliche Objekte. **184.** Die Laminatküche mit Wurzelholz-Effekt. Das Schlafzimmer wird von Jalousien abgeschirmt.

Durbach Block Architects
Level 3 441 Kent Street Sydney 2000 Australia Ph +61 2 9261 3941 F +61 2 9261 2207 email: neild@ozemail.com.au

Neil Durbach was born in 1954 in Cape Town. **Studies, experiences:** 1978 degree in architecture, University of Cape Town. 1979–1989 practice in different studios in San Francisco and Sydney. 1992 studio Durbach Block Architects. 1985–1995 tutor Architectural Design, University of Sydney. **Camilla Block** was born in 1966 in Johannesburg in South Africa. **Studies, experiences:** 1991 degree in architecture, University of Sydney. 1987–1992 practice in different studios. 1992 studio Durbach Block Architects. 1993–1996 tutor Architectural Design, University of Sydney. **Awards:** RAIA: 1997, 1998. 1999/2000 The Droga Penthouse project featured in a traveling exhibition in Europe. **Favorites:** *Architect:* Rem Koolhaas. **In Sydney they recommend:** *Hotel:* Ravesis Bondi Beach. *Restaurant:* Bistro Moncur. *Design shop:* De De Ce. *Fashion boutique:* Marcs. *Museum:* New South Wales Art Gallery.

Neil Durbach est né en 1954 à Cape Town. **Etudes, expérience professionnelle:** 1978, diplôme d'architecture, University of Cape Town. 1979–1989, travaille dans divers cabinets entre San Francisco et Sydney. 1992, ouverture du cabinet Durbach Block Architects. 1985–1995, enseigne le design architectural, University of Sydney. **Camilla Block** est née en 1966 à Johannesburg. **Etudes, expérience professionnelle:** 1991, diplôme d'architecture, University of Sydney. 1987–1992, travaille dans divers cabinets d'architecture. 1992, cabinet Durbach Block Architects. 1993–1996, enseigne le design architectural, University of Sydney. **Prix d'architecture:** RAIA: 1997, 1998, 1999/2000 le Droga Penthouse Projet fait l'objet d'une exposition itinérante en Europe. **Leurs favoris:** *Architecte:* Rem Koolhaas. **A Sydney, ils recommandent:** *Hôtel:* Ravesis Bondi Beach. *Restaurant:* Bistro Moncur. *Boutique de design:* De De Ce. *Boutique de mode:* Marcs. *Musée:* New South Wales Art Gallery.

Neil Durbach ist 1954 in Cape Town geboren. **Ausbildung, Erfahrungen:** 1978 Abschluss in Architektur an der University of Cape Town. 1979–1989 Tätigkeit in verschiedenen Architekturbüros in San Francisco und Sydney. 1992 Gründung des Architekturbüros Durbach Block Architects. 1985–1995 Tutor für Architectural Design an der University of Sydney. **Camilla Block** ist 1966 in Johannesburg geboren. **Ausbildung, Erfahrungen:** 1991 Abschluss in Architektur an der University of Sydney. 1987–1992 Tätigkeit in verschiedenen Architekturbüros. 1992 Gründung des Architekturbüros Durbach Block Architects. 1993–1996 Tutor für Architectural Design an der University of Sydney. **Architekturpreise:** RAIA: 1997, 1998. 1999/2000 The Droga Penthouse in Sydney, das an einer Wanderausstellung durch Europa teilnahm. **Sie bewundern:** *Architekt:* Rem Koolhaas. **Sie empfehlen in Sydney:** *Hotel:* Ravesis Bondi Beach. *Restaurant:* Bistro Moncur. *Design:* De De Ce. *Boutique:* Marcs. *Museum:* The Art Gallery of New South Wales.

Tree House, Darling Point

Year of construction: 1994 **Area:** 140 m^2 **Cost:** AUS $ 400,000
Année de réalisation: 1994 **Surface:** 140 m^2 **Coûts:** AUS $ 400 000
Baujahr: 1994 **Nutzfläche:** 140 m^2 **Kosten:** AUS $ 400 000

design Neil Durbach & Camilla Block

Tree House

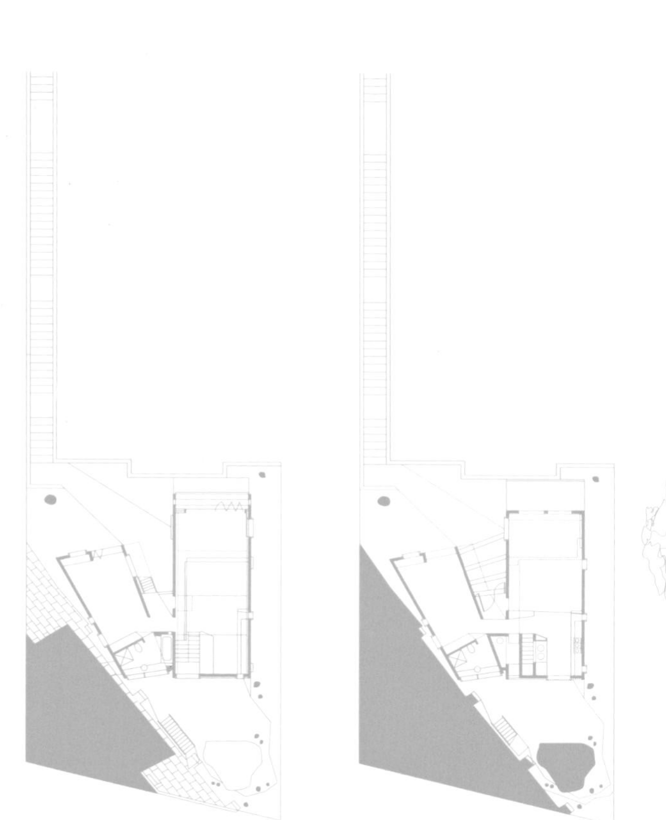

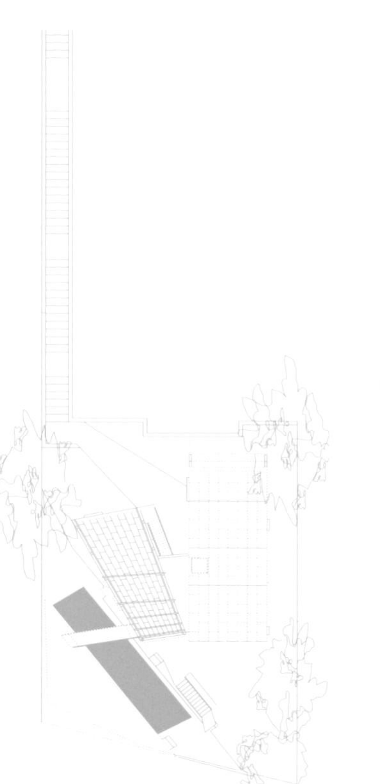

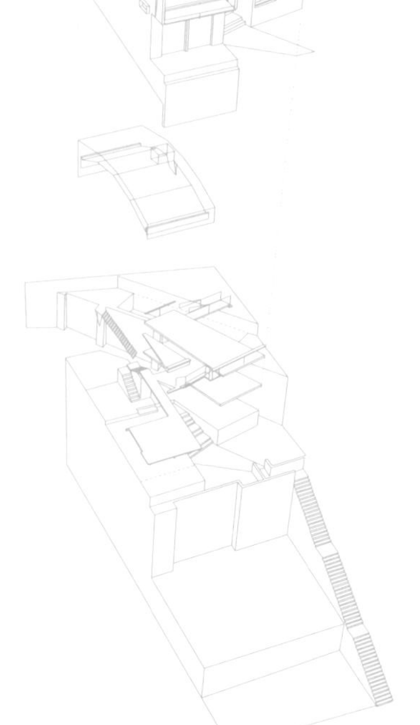

Levisohn House, Greenwich

Seen from the outside, with its sloping roof, façades in dark brick and cement, and wooden balconies, this home looks more like a mountain chalet than a classic Sydney suburban house. But this is just a first impression. Once inside, the characteristics of the local style return: bright white walls to reflect light, windows facing the garden to the north and the city to the south, positioned to offer the finest views and to allow the light to penetrate the depths of the spaces. The form of the flat roof is transformed in the image of a swimming pool alongside the garden that ascends to the hill behind the house. The reason for the pitched roofing becomes evident, with its glazed portions that remind us of origami: it follows the path of the sun, compensating for the orientation of an L-shaped layout completed by the garden to the north, faced by the living area, while the bedrooms are located on the level below.

Vue de l'extérieur avec son toit pentu, sa façade en briques sombres et ciment et ses balcons en lattes de bois, cette maison située dans un faubourg de Sydney rappelle un chalet de montagne. Mais cette impression ne dure qu'un instant. Une fois passée la porte, on retrouve les classiques de l'architecture locale tel que le blanc étourdissant des murs qui réfléchissent la lumière; les baies vitrées donnant sur le jardin au nord et sur la ville au sud, étudiées pour jouir au maximum de la vue et permettre au soleil de pénétrer au plus profond des pièces; la surface lisse de la piscine qui s'étire derrière la maison à fleur d'un jardin qui s'étend jusqu'au pied d'une colline. Le toit, lui, tout en pans inclinés et avec des parties vitrées, évoque la silhouette d'un origami: il suit le trajet du soleil et contrebalance l'orientation d'un plan en L, qui se prolonge au nord par le jardin sur lequel donne le séjour, tandis que l'étage inférieur accueille les chambres à coucher.

Von außen gleicht dieses Haus mit Satteldach, Fassade aus dunklem Backstein und Zement sowie Balkonen aus Holzdauben eher einem Chalet in den Bergen als einem Wohnhaus in einem Vorort von Sydney. Aber dieser Eindruck trügt. Sobald man die Türschwelle überschritten hat, fallen sofort die charakteristischen Kennzeichen der lokalen Architektursprache ins Auge: das blendende Weiß der Mauern, die das Licht reflektieren, hohe Glasfenster, die den Blick freigeben auf den Garten im Norden und auf die Stadt im Süden und die so angelegt wurden, dass sie die bestmögliche Aussicht bieten und dem Licht erlauben, tief in die Räume einzufließen, und schließlich der Pool an der Rückseite des Hauses mit einem Garten, der sich bis zum angrenzenden Hügel erstreckt. Das unregelmäßige, verglaste Satteldach erinnert an ein Origami und folgt in seiner Ausrichtung dem Lauf der Sonne, um die Nachteile der L-förmigen Anlage auszugleichen, bei welcher der Garten und der Wohnbereich nach Norden ausgerichtet sind. Im Untergeschoss befindet sich der Schlafbereich.

24

188-189. The living, dining, and kitchen areas form a single space, underlined by the uniformity of the wooden flooring. Alongside the dining area with the table and *DCM* chairs in plywood and steel designed by Charles and Ray Eames in 1946 stands the kitchen, designed by Durbach Block.

188-189. Le séjour, la salle à manger et la cuisine occupent un même espace. Le parquet uniforme renforce l'impression d'unité. Près de la salle à manger meublée d'une table et de chaises *DCM* en contreplaqué et acier dessinées par Charles et Ray Eames en 1946, la cuisine, entièrement conçue par le cabinet Durbach Block.

188-189. Wohn- und Esszimmer sowie Küche bilden einen einzigen Raum, was noch durch den gemeinsamen Parkett-Fußboden unterstrichen wird. Neben dem Essbereich mit Tisch und *DCM*-Stühlen aus Schichtholz und Chromstahl, die 1946 von Charles und Ray Eames entworfen wurden, befindet sich die nach einem Entwurf von Durbach Block gebaute Küche.

190. The rear of the house with the swimming pool and the garden. The colored cots invite relaxation. In the background, the small structure of the guests' building.

190. L'arrière de la maison avec la piscine et le jardin. Les chaises longues invitent à la détente. Au fond, le petit corps de bâtiment réservé aux invités.

190. Die Rückseite des Hauses mit dem Pool und dem Garten. Hier laden die farbigen Liegestühle zum Entspannen ein. Im Hintergrund sieht man das für Gäste bestimmte kleine Gebäude.

Durbach Block Architects
Level 3 441 Kent Street Sydney 2000 Australia Ph +61 2 9261 3941 F +61 2 9261 2207 email: neild@ozemail.com.au

Neil Durbach was born in 1954 in Cape Town. **Studies, experiences:** 1978 degree in architecture, University of Cape Town. 1979–1989 practice in different studios in San Francisco and Sydney. 1992 studio Durbach Block Architects. 1985–1995 tutor Architectural Design, University of Sydney. **Camilla Block** was born in 1966 in Johannesburg in South Africa. **Studies, experiences:** 1991 degree in architecture, University of Sydney. 1987–1992 practice in different studios. 1992 studio Durbach Block Architects. 1993–1996 tutor Architectural Design, University of Sydney. **Awards:** RAIA: 1997, 1998. 1999/2000 The Droga Penthouse project featured in a traveling exhibition in Europe. **Favorites:** *Architect:* Rem Koolhaas. **In Sydney they recommend:** *Hotel:* Ravesis Bondi Beach. *Restaurant:* Bistro Moncur. *Design shop:* De De Ce. *Fashion boutique:* Marcs. *Museum:* New South Wales Art Gallery.

Neil Durbach est né en 1954 à Cape Town. **Etudes, expérience professionnelle:** 1978, diplôme d'architecture, University of Cape Town. 1979–1989, travaille dans divers cabinets entre San Francisco et Sydney. 1992, ouverture du cabinet Durbach Block Architects. 1985–1995, enseigne le design architectural, University of Sydney. **Camilla Block** est née en 1966 à Johannesburg. **Etudes, expérience professionnelle:** 1991, diplôme d'architecture, University of Sydney. 1987–1992, travaille dans divers cabinets d'architecture. 1992, cabinet Durbach Block Architects. 1993–1996, enseigne le design architectural, University of Sydney. **Prix d'architecture:** RAIA: 1997, 1998. 1999/2000 le Droga Penthouse Projet fait l'objet d'une exposition itinérante en Europe. **Leurs favoris:** *Architecte:* Rem Koolhaas. **A Sydney, ils recommandent:** *Hôtel:* Ravesis Bondi Beach. *Restaurant:* Bistro Moncur. *Boutique de design:* De De Ce. *Boutique de mode:* Marcs. *Musée:* New South Wales Art Gallery.

Neil Durbach ist 1954 in Cape Town geboren. **Ausbildung, Erfahrungen:** 1978 Abschluss in Architektur an der University of Cape Town. 1979–1989 Tätigkeit in verschiedenen Architekturbüros in San Francisco und Sydney. 1992 Gründung des Architekturbüros Durbach Block Architects. 1985–1995 Tutor für Architectural Design an der University of Sydney. **Camilla Block** ist 1966 in Johannesburg geboren. **Ausbildung, Erfahrungen:** 1991 Abschluss in Architektur an der University of Sydney. 1987–1992 Tätigkeit in verschiedenen Architekturbüros. 1992 Gründung des Architekturbüros Durbach Block Architects. 1993–1996 Tutor für Architectural Design an der University of Sydney. **Architekturpreise:** RAIA: 1997, 1998. 1999/2000 The Droga Penthouse in Sydney, das an einer Wanderausstellung durch Europa teilnahm. **Sie bewundern:** *Architekt:* Rem Koolhaas. **Sie empfehlen in Sydney:** *Hotel:* Ravesis Bondi Beach. *Restaurant:* Bistro Moncur. *Design:* De De Ce. *Boutique:* Marcs. *Museum:* The Art Gallery of New South Wales.

Levisohn House, Greenwich

Year of construction: 2000
Année de réalisation: 2000
Baujahr: 2000

Area: 220 m²
Surface: 220 m²
Nutzfläche: 220 m²

Cost: AUS $ 1.1 million
Coûts: AUS $ 1,1 million
Kosten: AUS $ 1,1 Millionen

design Neil Durbach & Camilla Block

Levisohn House

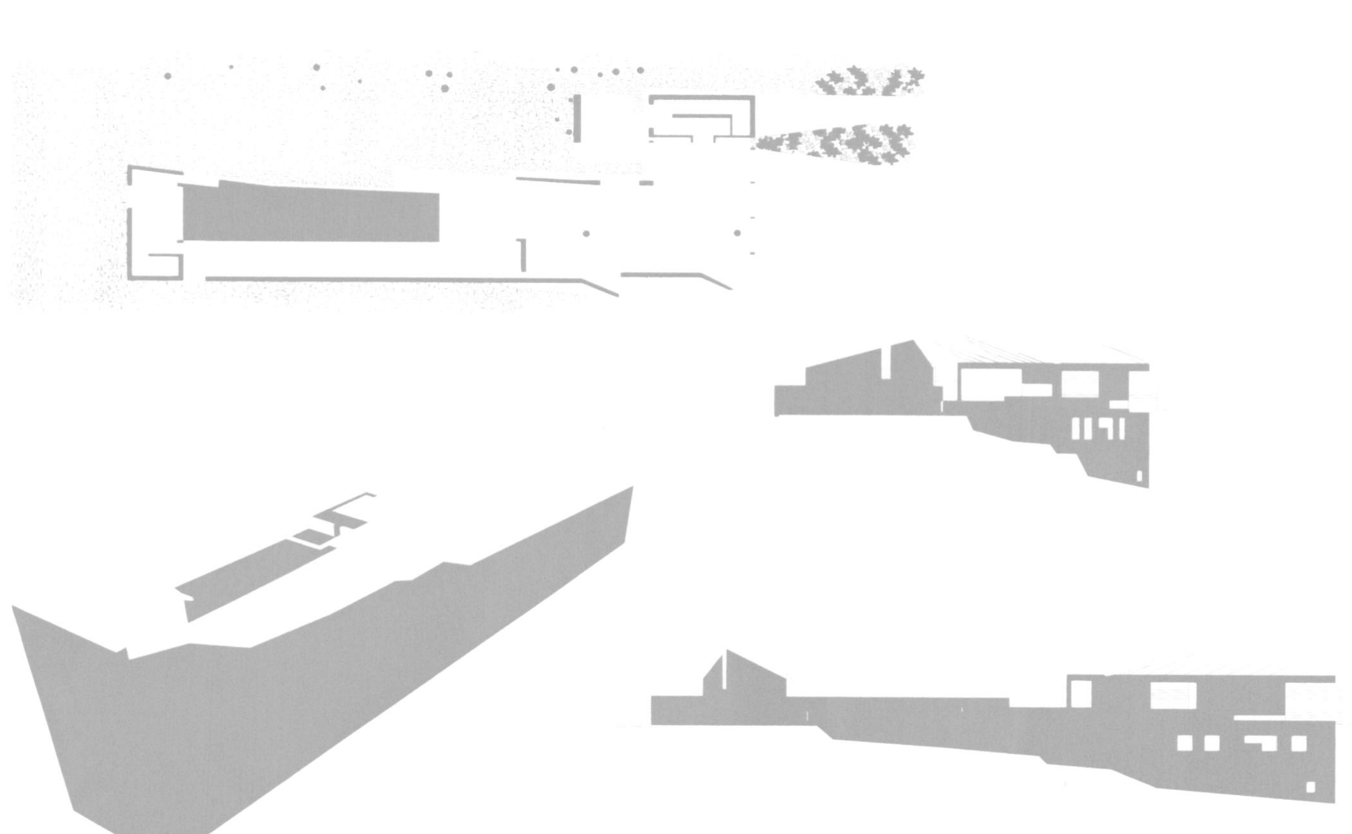

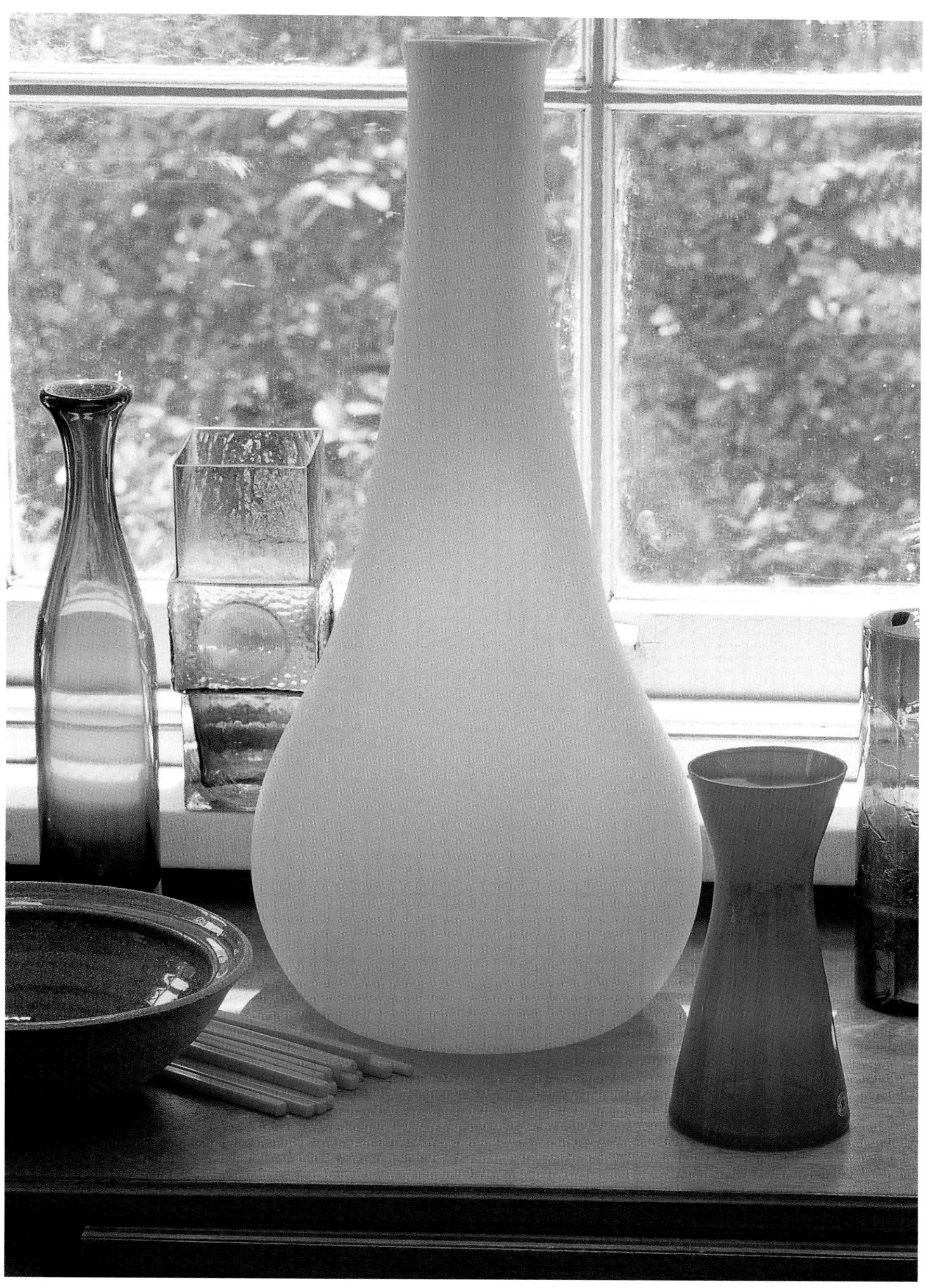

192. Living with light and color: glass and ceramic vases by Dinosaur Designs in the home of Stephen Ormandy and Louise Olsen. **193.** Detail view of Scandinavian and Italian vases in the home of Mitchell and Helen English. – **192.** Vivre dans la lumière et la couleur: des vases en verre et en céramique de Dinosaur Designs dans la maison de Stephen Ormandy et Louise Olsen. **193.** Détail avec des vases scandinaves et italiens dans la maison de Mitchell et Helen English. – **192.** Leben mit Licht und Farbe: Glas- und Keramikvasen von Dinosaur Designs im Haus von Stephen Ormandy und Louise Olsen. **193.** Detailansicht mit skandinavischen und italienischen Vasen in dem Haus von Mitchell und Helen English.

194. The beautiful dining area of the Archer House. **195.** The terrace of 28 Billyard Avenue House seems to float above sunny Elizabeth Bay. **196-197.** The spacious penthouse of Harry Seidler. **199.** Detail view of the Archer House. – **194.** La très belle salle à manger de la maison Archer. **195.** La terrasse de la maison 28 Billyard Avenue semble planer au-dessus de la Elizabeth Bay ensoleillée. **196-197.** La penthouse généreuse de Harry Seidler. **199.** Détail de la maison Archer. – **194.** Der wunderschöne Essbereich des Archer House. **195.** Die Terrasse des 28 Billyard Avenue House scheint über der sonnigen Elizabeth Bay zu schweben. **196-197.** Das großzügige Penthouse von Harry Seidler. **199.** Detailansicht aus Archer House.

Picture Credits:
Map p. 8: Erik Heckens, Cologne
p. 23: Paul Vermeesch/Atomic
p. 41: Paul Gosney
p. 49: Andy Harding
p. 55: Liane Rossler
pp. 65, 71: Kraig Carlstrom
p. 93: Ronny Berg
p. 119: Ginny Green
p. 167: Alex Hennings, Look: Production, Casting and Artists Management Pty Ltd
pp. 173, 181, 187: Bernhard Nickel

Hohenzollernring 53, D-50672 Köln
www.taschen.com

Design and layout by Alfaroli-Brambilla, Milan
Texts edited by Ursula Fethke, Cologne
Production by Horst Neuzner, Cologne
English translation by Steve Piccolo, Milan
French translation by Philippe Safavi, Paris
German translation by Bettina Müller Renzoni, Pisa

Printed in France
ISBN 3-8228-1384-2
ISBN 3-8228-1876-3 (edition with French cover)